Handbook of
U.S. Labor Statistics

Employment, Earnings, Prices, Productivity, and Other Labor Data

Ninth Edition, 2006

Handbook of
U.S. Labor Statistics

Employment, Earnings, Prices, Productivity, and Other Labor Data

Ninth Edition, 2006

EDITOR
Eva E. Jacobs

ASSOCIATE EDITOR
Mary Meghan Ryan

ISBN: 1-59888-005-5

ISSN: 1526-2553

Printed by Automated Graphic Systems, Inc., White Plains, MD, on acid-free paper that meets the American National Standards Institute Z39-48 standard.

2006 2005   4 3 2 1

BERNAN PRESS
4611-F Assembly Drive
Lanham, MD 20706
800-274-4447
email: info@bernan.com
www.bernanpress.com

CONTENTS

LIST OF TABLES

LIST OF CHARTS

ABOUT THE EDITORS

Eva E. Jacobs, editor of *Handbook of U.S. Labor Statistics* since the first edition, served as Chief of the Division of Consumer Expenditure Surveys at the U.S. Bureau of Labor Statistics (BLS) for over 20 years. As manager of this division, Ms. Jacobs was responsible for the ongoing Consumer Expenditure Survey, which tracked the expenditure patterns of U.S. households over time. Ms. Jacobs also held positions in the Productivity Division and the Economic Growth Division. More recently, she acted as advisor on cost of living projects for both government and private consultants. Currently, Ms. Jacobs serves as chair of a panel advising the Safe Harbor Working Group on issues related to cost of living adjustments for federal employees in Alaska, Hawaii, Guam, Puerto Rico, and the Virgin Islands. Ms. Jacobs was the 1998 recipient of the Julius Shiskin Award, given by the National Association of Business Economists and the Washington Statistical Society for distinguished contributions to economic statistics.

Mary Meghan Ryan is a data analyst with Bernan Press. She received her bachelor's degree in economics from the University of Maryland and is a former economist with the American Economics Group. Additionally, Ms. Ryan has worked as a research assistant for FRANDATA. Ms. Ryan is also an associate editor of the eighth edition of *Business Statistics of the United States* and the first edition of *Vital Statistics of the United States*, both published by Bernan Press.

PREFACE

A changing economy brings different problems to the economic forefront. During the period of recession and slow growth from 2000-2003, attention was focused on employment, unemployment, and the weakening manufacturing sector. Prior to the recession and during the recovery period, it was the possibility of inflation and the movement of the Producer and Consumer Price Indexes that were the subject of scrutiny. More recently, the sharp rise in oil prices and the possible ramifications through the entire economy have demanded the attention of policy makers and analysts.

Other problems are persistent and continue to be debated. One is the increasing cost of medical care faced by government, industry, and individuals. How much have prescription drugs and medical services increased in price? What are the factors driving these costs? How do these costs affect medical benefits provided by employers to employees and retirees?

At the same time, various non-cyclical changes are taking place that raise questions and require analysis and policy decisions. What has been the impact of immigration on the structure of the labor force? Which industries are expected to provide employment growth in the future? How will technology change the occupational and educational requirements of industry? How have the demographic changes in population affected the pattern of pension plans offered by employers? How have the consumption patterns of various groups in the population changed?

Answering questions such as these for the future requires information about the present and the past. The U.S. Bureau of Labor Statistics (BLS) provides a treasure trove of historical information about the labor market, prices, and productivity. Bernan Press is pleased to present a compilation of such BLS data this ninth edition of its award-winning *Handbook of U.S. Labor Statistics*. The current publication maintains and updates the content of the previous editions and adds additional data and new features.

FEATURES OF THIS PUBLICATION

- Approximately 200 tables present authoritative data on workers, industries, wages, prices, productivity, and international comparisons.

- Each *Handbook* begins with articles that introduce new surveys or present current research that applies the data within to users' areas of interest. Three articles in this *Handbook* illustrate the uses of the data related to public policy issues:

  The first article, "Employment from the BLS Household and Payroll Surveys: Summary of Recent Trends," is an examination of the differences in the trends of employment as estimated from the Current Population Survey, which surveys households, and the Current Employment Survey, which derives data from establishments. The difference in trends between the surveys over certain periods has disturbed users for some time. The article concludes that an inexplicable difference remains in place, even after making numerous adjustments to account for dissimilarities in methodology and definitions.

The second article, "The Relationship Between Labor Costs and Inflation: A Cyclical Viewpoint," examines how well various BLS measures of labor cost inflation have anticipated cyclical ups and downs in consumer price inflation. The author concludes that the comparisons suggest that labor cost inflation is not a consistent predictor of cyclical upswings and downswings in general consumer price inflation.

The third article, "How BLS Measures Price Change for Motor Fuels in the Consumer Price Index," is particularly topical in view of the recent rapid increases in the price of gasoline.

Previous editions of the *Handbook* have described the new American Time Use Survey (sixth edition) and introduced the new classification systems for occupations (SOC, third edition) and industries (NAICS, sixth edition).

- An introduction to each part highlights salient data in the numerous tables.

- One or more charts in each part that call attention to noteworthy trends. A summary of important economic trends can be found at the beginning of the *Handbook*.

- Each major section is preceded by a concise description of the data sources, concepts, definitions, and methodology from which the tables are derived.

- The introductory notes also contain references to more comprehensive reports that provide more data and more detailed descriptions of estimation methods and reliability measures.

NEW TABLES IN THIS EDITION

Contingent workers. These tables were discontinued in the eighth edition of this *Handbook* because the survey had not been conducted since 2001. The survey was resumed as a supplement to the Current Population Survey in 2004 and the new data are now included in five new tables.

Foreign-born workers. Previous editions of this *Handbook* showed employment by citizenship. The five new tables show the labor force status of foreign-born workers and their characteristics. This is more comprehensive than citizenship, as it includes both illegal residents and foreign-born workers who are not citizens but are legal residents.

Flexible schedules. Five new tables show the number of workers on various kinds of flexible schedules and shift arrangements and their characteristics. These are the first data on this subject since 2001.

Consumer Expenditures Survey. More tables were added and modifications were made to this survey in order to conform to new classifications of race and ethnicity and to permit publishing more information with additional classes. For example, a new column showing information for Asians is included in the race table.

American Time Use Survey. A second year of experience with this survey has led to the inclusion of three new tables with more data about time spent at work.

Other additional information. More tables by industry and occupation now use the new industry and occupation classifications. All data are updated to what was available at the time of preparation. The notes and definitions and sources of additional information are also updated.

SOURCES OF ADDITIONAL INFORMATION

For the most part, BLS data are derived from surveys conducted by the federal government or through federal-state cooperative arrangements. The comparability of data over time can be affected by changes in the surveys, which are needed to keep pace with the current structure of economic institutions or to take advantage of improved survey techniques. Revisions of current data are also periodically made as a result of the availability of new information. In addition, some tables in this *Handbook* were dropped due to the data being from a one-time survey that is now outdated, such as the data on training (1995), or the survey being entirely restructured. Introductory notes to each part summarize specific factors that may affect the data. In the tables, the ellipsis character ("...") has been used to indicate data that are not available.

More extensive methodological information, including sampling and estimation procedures for all BLS programs, is contained in the *BLS Handbook of Methods*, BLS Bulletin 2490, April 1997. That publication is being updated as each chapter is completed. The completed chapters are available on the BLS Web site. Other sources of current data and analytical are on the *Monthly Labor Review* and a daily Internet publication, *The Editor's Desk* (TED). The Web site for the BLS home page is <http://www.bls.gov>. Other relevant publications are noted at the end of each individual part.

ACKNOWLEDGEMENTS

Preparation of this book was very much a team activity. Mary Meghan Ryan capably researched the data and compiled the tables. Deirdre Gaquin prepared the special tabulations of data from the Current Population Survey. Jo A. Wilson, assisted by Rebecca Zayas, prepared the graphics and layout. Shana Hertz copyedited this edition. I extend my sincere gratitude to these individuals for their skills, professionalism, and cooperative effort—all of which made this publication possible.

Particular thanks go to the BLS staff members too numerous to mention by name who patiently answered questions and provided material.

OTHER PUBLICATIONS BY BERNAN PRESS

The *Handbook of U.S. Labor Statistics* is one of a number of publications in Bernan Press' award-winning U.S. DataBook Series. Other titles in the U.S. DataBook Series include *Business Statistics of the United States: Patterns of Economic Change*; *Vital Statistics of the United States: Births, Life Expectancy, Deaths, and Selected Health Data*; *The Almanac of American Education*; and *United States Foreign Trade Highlights*. Each of these titles provides the public with statistical information from official government sources.

Other publications published by Bernan Press include *The Encyclopedia of the Library of Congress: For Congress, the Nation & the World* and *Datapedia of the United States: American History in Numbers*.

If you have any questions or suggestions on how we may make future editions even more useful, please contact us by email at bpress@bernan.com or write us at Bernan Press, 4611-F Assembly Dr., Lanham, MD 20706. Visit our Web site at <http://www.bernanpress.com>.

ARTICLE 1
EMPLOYMENT FROM THE BLS HOUSEHOLD AND PAYROLL SURVEYS: SUMMARY OF RECENT TRENDS

This article is adapted from one that appeared on the Bureau of Labor Statistics (BLS) Website on June 3, 2005. The original article is considerably longer and more detailed. The original article also refers the reader to additional articles describing the extensive research BLS has done on this subject. The complete article can be found at <http://www.bls.gov/web/ces_cps_trends.pdf>.

OVERVIEW

The BLS has two monthly surveys that measure employment levels and trends: the Current Population Survey (CPS), also known as the household survey, and the Current Employment Statistics (CES) survey, also known as the payroll or establishment survey. (Data from the CPS appear in Part 1 of this *Handbook* and data from the CES appear in Part 2.)

Estimates from both surveys are published in the "Employment Situation" news release each month. The household and payroll surveys use different definitions of employment and distinct survey and estimation methods. This article is designed to help data users better understand the differences in the surveys' employment measures and the divergences that sometimes occur in their trends. The following information includes summary comparison of household and payroll survey concepts, definitions, and methodologies; employment trends as measured by the payroll and household surveys; and possible causes of differences in employment trends.

TABLE 1. SUMMARY COMPARISON OF THE HOUSEHOLD AND PAYROLL SURVEYS

Comparison by	Household Survey	Payroll Survey
Universe	Civilian noninstitutional population age 16 and over	Nonfarm wage and salary jobs
Type of survey	Monthly sample survey of approximately 60,000 households	Monthly sample survey of about 160,000 businesses and government agencies covering approximately 400,000 establishments
Major outputs	Labor force, employment, unemployment, and associated rates with significant demographic detail	Employment, hours, and earnings with significant industry and geographic detail
Reference period	Calendar week that includes the 12th of the month	Employer pay period that includes the 12th of the month (could be weekly, biweekly, monthly, or other)
Employment concept	Estimate of employed persons (multiple jobholders are counted only once)	Estimate of jobs (multiple jobholders counted for each nonfarm payroll job)
Employment definition differences	Includes the unincorporated self-employed, unpaid family members, agriculture and related workers, private household workers, and workers absent without pay	Excludes all of the groups listed at left, except for the logging component of agriculture and related industries
Size of over-the-month change in employment required for a statistically significant movement	±436,000[1]	±108,000
Benchmark adjustments to survey results	No direct benchmark for employment—adjustments to underlying population base revised annually to intercensal estimates, and every 10 years to the decennial census	Employment benchmarked annually to employment counts derived primarily from unemployment insurance (UI) tax records

[1]This figure is updated periodically to incorporate more current data. The latest update (March 2005) also included a correction in the program used to calculate it.

EMPLOYMENT TRENDS AS MEASURED BY THE HOUSEHOLD AND PAYROLL SURVEYS

The household survey employment level normally exceeds that of the payroll survey. When the household survey is adjusted to more closely match the payroll survey definition, trend discrepancies between the two surveys are more discernible. In particular, there is a multi-year period from the late 1990s through the onset of the 2001 recession in which payroll employment was growing significantly faster than household survey employment. More recently, the two series converged.

Table 2 shows recent employment trends in the payroll and household surveys. This table uses an adjusted household employment that is more comparable with the payroll survey. Even with this adjustment, the difference in employment change as measured by the two surveys is significant.

TABLE 2. RECENT TRENDS IN PAYROLL EMPLOYMENT AND HOUSEHOLD SURVEY EMPLOYMENT ADJUSTED TO AN EMPLOYMENT CONCEPT MORE SIMILAR TO THAT OF THE PAYROLL SURVEY (NUMBERS IN THOUSANDS)

	April 2005–May 2005	May 2004–May 2005	March 2001 (peak)–May 2005	November 2001 (trough)– May 2005
Payroll survey: Total nonfarm employment, seasonally adjusted[2]	78	1,974	836	2,468
Household survey: Total employment, smoothed for population control revisions, adjusted to be more like the payroll survey, and seasonally adjusted	210	2,279	3,381	4,626
Difference	132	305	2,545	2,158

[2]Payroll employment for May 2005 is preliminary and subject to revision.

POSSIBLE CAUSES OF DIFFERENCES IN EMPLOYMENT TRENDS

The following summarizes some issues with the surveys that are important to consider when comparing changes in employment from the two sources.

Sampling error – The payroll survey has a much larger sample size than the household survey. Household survey employment is therefore subject to larger sampling error—about four times that of the payroll survey on a monthly basis. (Table 1)

Payroll survey benchmark – The payroll survey estimates are benchmarked once a year against a full universe count of employment derived from unemployment insurance (UI) tax records that nearly all employers are required to file. Payroll employment thus continues to track closely with the universe of nonfarm payroll employment.

With regard to the benchmark source data, BLS has reviewed information from publicly available UI management reports concerning the timeliness of new business enrollments into the UI system.

New business births in the payroll survey – The payroll survey sample does not include new firms immediately. They are incorporated with a lag.

Job changing - Employment estimates from the payroll survey are a count of jobs. This is different than the household survey, which provides a count of employed persons.

If a person changes jobs within a payroll survey reference period, which is defined as the pay period including the 12th of the month, both jobs will be counted by the payroll survey estimates. If the rate of job-to-job movement changes substantially over time, it could impact trends produced from the payroll survey.

Population controls in the household survey – Population controls determine the weights used in the household survey to adjust the sample results to the overall level of the U.S. population. There are limitations to the population control estimates primarily due to the difficulties associated with estimating the net international migration component.

Worker classification in the household survey – Adjusting for the measurable differences in the surveys' employment definitions resolves only a portion of the discrepancy. The adjustment process is imperfect because precise data are not available in many cases. This type of reporting issue limits BLS' ability to fully reconcile the two employment measures. (Table 2)

"Off-the-books" employment – Workers who are paid "off-the-books" are not reported in the payroll survey. The household survey may include some of these workers, but BLS cannot determine the extent to which they might affect the results for household survey employment.

SUMMARY

BLS has estimated the measurable definitional differences between the household and payroll surveys and found they provide a partial explanation for the employment trend differences. There are a number of definitional differences between the surveys that cannot be readily measured or quantified. These differences may contribute to divergences in the surveys' trends, but their effects are either unknown or can only be conjectured. In addition, although BLS has devoted considerable attention to this issue, there may be other contributing factors that have not been identified.

BLS is continuing to investigate possible causes of the recent divergences in employment growth between the payroll and household surveys. BLS also has implemented improvements to address past limitations. The redesign of the payroll survey, for example, has led to the use of a probability sample, the increased updating of the survey sample frame, and the development of a more effective means for estimating business births and deaths.

Both the payroll and household surveys are needed for a complete picture of the labor market. The payroll survey provides a highly reliable gauge of monthly change in non-farm wage and salary employment. This survey has a large probability sample and is benchmarked annually to a universe count of jobs derived from the unemployment insurance tax system. The payroll survey offers detailed levels of industry and geographic information. The household survey provides a broader picture of employment including agriculture and the self-employed. This survey also provides detailed information on the demographic composition of the employed and the unemployed.

ARTICLE 2
THE RELATIONSHIP BETWEEN LABOR COSTS AND INFLATION: A CYCLICAL VIEWPOINT

This article, authored by Anirvan Banerji[1], was abstracted from the May 2005 edition of "Compensation and Working Conditions" and is available online on at the BLS Bureau of Labor Statistics (BLS) Web site at <http://www.bls.gov/opub/cwc/cm20050517ar01p1.htm>.

This study examines how well various BLS measures of labor cost inflation have anticipated cyclical ups and downs in consumer price inflation.

CONVENTIONAL WISDOM

It is commonly believed that labor costs are a key predictor of inflation, because they represent roughly two-thirds of the total costs to private U.S. businesses.[2] This view implies a cost-push model of inflation, which is based on the idea that the primary determinant of higher prices is higher costs. An alternative view is that firms will charge whatever the market will bear, regardless of their actual costs. If the market's acceptance of higher prices is the dominant determinant of inflation, the cost-push model would have less validity.

One way to test the cost-push model's validity is to examine the historical record to see how well traditional measures of labor cost inflation have anticipated the cyclical ups and downs in of general inflation. This article compares various BLS measures of labor costs with the Consumer Price Index (CPI)—a standard measure of inflation—for the 1982–2004 period. The record turns out to be mixed on this issue.

INFLATION CYCLES

Inflation has always had an important cyclical aspect. The late Geoffrey H. Moore, who served as the Commissioner of Labor Statistics from 1969 to 1973, and later founded the Economic Cycle Research Institute (ECRI), held the view that market-oriented economies exhibit inflation cycles, made up of alternating periods of rising and falling inflation. ECRI maintains a historical chronology of U.S. inflation cycles, which are determined using the kinds of rules that are used to date business cycles, such as those used in the Bry-Boschan "peak-trough" procedure for determining cyclical turning points.[3] The Bry-Boschan procedure is an objective algorithmic formulation of the National Bureau of Economic Research (NBER) rules for identifying cyclical turns, and it remains the standard for turning-point determination procedures.

While inflation is cyclical, inflation downturns do not always follow slowdowns in economic growth. A quarter of the time, inflation starts easing *before* a slowdown in growth.[4] In addition, there are episodes—such as the stagflation of the late 1970s and the noninflationary growth of the late 1990s—when there appears to be no is no apparent connection between economic growth and inflation. Thus, inflation cycles are distinct from cycles in economic growth—one of the reasons why it is important

to specifically assess the ability of economic indicators to predict turns in the inflation cycle.

Labor cost inflation, as measured by the growth rates of various measures of labor costs, is also cyclical in nature. While there is obviously some rough correspondence between labor cost inflation and consumer price inflation, the question is whether, empirically, cyclical turns in the former systematically anticipate cyclical turns in the latter. If so, labor cost inflation would be an important predictor of consumer price inflation, thus validating the cost-push model of inflation.

The critical test for any predictor of inflation is whether it can systematically anticipate the cyclical peaks and troughs in the inflation cycle. In other words, is it a leading indicator of inflation? In this article, the cyclical analysis is conducted in three steps. First, the cyclical turning points of each time series are determined using the Bry-Boschan procedure. Second, the data are charted against inflation cycles. Finally, the lead and lag characteristics are established.

This article also examines three popular measures of labor cost inflation to see how well they predict peaks and troughs in consumer price inflation. Specifically, it compares the growth rates of the Employment Cost Index (ECI), Average Hourly Earnings (AHE), and Unit Labor Costs (ULC) with the growth rate of the Consumer Price Index–All Urban Consumers (CPI-U). Where there is any ambiguity about the best choice of the peaks and troughs in the inflation cycle based on the growth rate of the CPI-U, evidence from alternative coincident measures of inflation is also considered, such as the personal consumption deflator or the GDP implicit price deflator. This procedure is analogous to that used by the National Bureau of Economic Research (NBER) for business cycle dating, which is based on the consensus of multiple coincident indicators of economic activity.

Over the 1982–2004 period, there were five periods of inflation cycle downturns, with four peaks and five troughs in the growth rate of the CPI-U that can be included in this study. The reason for only four peaks is because the initial peak in the CPI-U growth rate occurs occured at the very beginning of the study period. Of the three comparisons, only the ULC comparison includes four peaks and five troughs. The ECI and AHE growth rate series only include three peaks and four troughs in the analysis. In the case of the ECI, the first trough in the CPI-U growth rate is left out of the analysis because the ECI series does not start until the second quarter of 1981.[5] In addition, there is one CPI-U peak that the ECI missed. In the case of the AHE growth rate series, there simply is no corresponding trough and peak for the first trough and peak in price inflation.

GROWTH RATE METHODOLOGY

The six-month smoothed annualized rate (SMSAR) of growth is used throughout this analysis, because it has key advantages over the more common year-over-year growth rate (YOYGR) measure. The main advantages of the YOYGR method are that it is relatively simple and straightforward, and that it automatically performs a kind of seasonal adjustment on any time series to which it is applied. However, sophisticated seasonal adjustment procedures have been available for many decades, so there is no need for indirect seasonal adjustment using the YOYGR. More importantly, the YOYGR measure is subject to the vagaries of the base effect, in which whatever happened a year earlier can substantially affect the growth rate, either positively or negatively.[6]

In cyclical terms, the SMSAR method has the additional advantage that it compares the latest data point to a 1-year moving average centered 6.5 months before the current month, or 2.5 quarters before the current quarter. In other words, it is focused on the percent change over a 6.5-month span or over a 2.5-quarter span. This is in contrast to the YOYGR, which focuses on the percent change over a 1-year time span. Therefore, when there is a cyclical turn in an indicator, its SMSAR tends to turn up or down more quickly than the YOYGR does, without adding more statistical noise or volatility. It is therefore particularly suitable for cyclical analysis. [7]

THE EMPLOYMENT COST INDEX

The BLS Employment Cost Index (ECI) measures changes in the cost of labor compensation (absent the influence of employment shifts among occupations and industries), including wages, benefits, and payroll taxes. The ECI covers managers as well as production or nonsupervisory workers. A potential drawback of the ECI is that it is a quarterly series, unlike the Average Hourly Earnings (AHE) series used in this article. It generally is released almost a month after the end of the relevant quarter.

A cyclical analysis shows that the growth rate of the ECI has a median lead of 5 months at inflation cycle peaks, and a median lag of 11 months at inflation cycle troughs. In fact, downturns in ECI growth anticipate two-thirds of the downturns in consumer price inflation, but upturns in ECI growth actually lag 100 percent of the upturns in CPI inflation. This is because ECI growth peaked before CPI-U growth in 2 of 3 cases, but ECI growth reached a trough after CPI-U growth in 4 of 4 cases. Therefore, ECI growth is a leading indicator of inflation peaks but a lagging indi-

cator of inflation troughs. Analysts thus cannot rule out an upcoming cyclical upturn in the inflation rate just because the ECI growth rate has not yet turned up.

AVERAGE HOURLY EARNINGS

The BLS Average Hourly Earnings (AHE) series (from the Current Employment Statistics (CES) program) is a popular indicator of labor costs, because it is published monthly and is generally released on the first Friday of each month as part of the employment report. Thus, the figures are usually available less than a week after the end of the relevant month. On the other hand, AHE is a narrower gauge of labor costs than is the ECI, because it measures wage rates including overtime and does not include benefit costs and payroll taxes. In addition, unlike the ECI, only the earnings of production or nonsupervisory workers are included in the AHE series—it does not include managers' earnings.

A cyclical analysis shows that the growth rate of the AHE series has a median lead of 3 months at inflation cycle peaks, but a median lag of 3.5 months at inflation cycle troughs. In fact, downturns in AHE growth anticipate some two-thirds of the downturns in consumer price inflation, but upturns in AHE growth actually lag upturns in CPI inflation growth three-quarters of the time. This is because AHE growth peaked before CPI-U growth in 2 of 3 cases, while AHE growth reached a trough after CPI-U growth in 3 of 4 cases. Therefore, AHE growth is a leading indicator of inflation peaks but a lagging indicator of inflation troughs. As with the ECI, an upcoming cyclical upturn in the rate of inflation cannot be ruled out just because the AHE growth rate has not turned up.

UNIT LABOR COSTS

Many economists prefer to examine growth in the BLS Unit Labor Costs (ULC) series as a predictor of inflation because this series, a product of the productivity and costs program, measures the cost of labor per unit of production (rather than per hour), allows analysts to determine how much the labor cost of an employer increases with each additional unit produced. The ULC measure takes into account variations in productivity growth in determining how much employer costs are rising. Like the ECI, the ULC series is published quarterly, and it generally is released about 5 weeks after the end of the relevant quarter.[8]

A cyclical analysis shows that ULC growth has a median lead of 5 months at inflation cycle peaks, but a median lag of 2 months at inflation cycle troughs. In fact, downturns in ULC growth anticipate about half of the downturns in consumer price inflation, but upturns in ULC growth actually lag upturns in CPI inflation 80 percent of the time. This is because ULC growth peaked before CPI-U growth in one-half of cases, but ULC growth reached a trough after CPI-U growth in 4 of 5 cases. Therefore, ULC growth often is a leading indicator of inflation peaks, but it is a lagging indicator of inflation troughs. Regardless of its conceptual advantages, then, the ULC series, like the ECI and AHE series, cannot be relied upon as an accurate predictor of cyclical upturns in inflation.

CYCLICAL ASYMMETRY OF LEADS

No matter what standard econometric models might suggest, the empirical cyclical evidence indicates that labor cost inflation is not a consistent predictor of cyclical upturns in inflation. In fact, a fair amount of asymmetry exists in the cyclical behavior of the growth rates of the ECI, AHE, and ULC when compared with inflation cycles. All three series lead consumer price inflation at peaks, and lag it at troughs.

Specifically, the three labor cost measures lead about half to two-thirds of the cyclical downturns in general inflation, and their median lead varies between 3 and 5 months. In other words, labor cost inflation is a somewhat inconsistent leading indicator of downturns in the general rate of inflation. Moreover, the three measures lag between 75 percent and 100 percent of the cyclical upturns in general inflation, and their median lag varies between 2 and 11 months. Therefore, labor cost inflation is a fairly consistent lagging indicator of upturns in general inflation.

These comparisons suggest that labor cost inflation is not a consistent predictor of cyclical upswings and downswings in general consumer price inflation. As a result, analysts should use caution when interpreting cyclical swings in labor costs growth rates–as recent history shows, price inflation may enter a cyclical upturn before labor cost inflation does.

ENDNOTES

[1]Anirvan Banerji is the Director of Research with the Economic Cycle Research Institute.

[2]According to data from the BLS multifactor productivity (MFP) program, for example, the labor share in costs for the private business sector (excluding government enterprises) averaged 67 percent over the 20-year period from 1982 to 2001. For more information on this series, see "Private Business and Private Nonfarm Business MFP Tables," on the Multifactor Productivity Trends page of the BLS Web site at <http://www.bls.gov/web/prod3.supp.toc.htm>.

[3]Gerhard Bry and Charlotte Boschan, *Cyclical Analysis of Time Series: Selected Procedures and Computer Programs* (New York, National Bureau of Economic Research, 1971).

[4]Dimitra Visviki, "Growth and Inflation: Insights into a Troubled Relationship," presented at the Eastern Economic Association Annual Conference, New York City, March 4-6, 2005.

[5]The growth rate methodology used in this study requires a year of data prior to the year being considered; hence, because 1982 is the first full year for which ECI data are available, the ECI portion of the analysis begins in 1983.

[6] This is why analysts so frequently talk about favorable and unfavorable comparisons when interpreting the YOYGR, because idiosyncrasies in the data from a year earlier can distort the YOYGR measure of growth. This is a moot issue with the SMSAR, which is based on a comparison of the latest month's data to the average over the previous year, which smooths out the idiosyncratic month-to-month fluctuations.

[7]For more information on the SMSAR method's advantages in cyclical analysis, see Anirvan Banerji, "The Three Ps: Simple Tools for Monitoring Economic Cycles," *Business Economics*, October 1999, pp. 72-76.

[8]Although both the Employment Cost Index (ECI) and the Unit Labor Costs (ULC) series are published quarterly, the ULC series generally is published 5 to 7 days later than the ECI.

HOW BLS MEASURES PRICE CHANGE FOR MOTOR FUELS IN THE CONSUMER PRICE INDEX

This article is relevant to current analyses of the volatile oil price situation and appeared in July 2005 on the Bureau of Labor Statistics (BLS) Web site at <www.bls.gov/cpi/cpigasfac.htm>. Data on CPI indexes for motor fuel appear in Part 7 of this Handbook.

INTRODUCTION

The motor fuel index, a component of the private transportation index, is included in the transportation group of the Consumer Price Index (CPI). Together with the index for household fuels, it makes up the special energy index. The motor fuel index is published on a monthly basis for all areas that provide data for the CPI.

RELATIVE IMPORTANCE

The individual items, which make up the motor fuel index, together with their relative importance values within the U.S. city average of the CPI for All Urban Consumers (CPI-U), as of December 2004 are as follows:

TABLE 1: RELATIVE IMPORTANCE OF SELECTED TRANSPORTATION COMPONENTS OF THE CPI FOR ALL URBAN CONSUMERS (CPI-U): U.S. CITY AVERAGE, DECEMBER 2004

Item	Relative importance
Motor fuel	3.969
Gasoline	3.934
Other motor fuels	0.035

The gasoline (all types) index, which carries the majority in the weight of the motor fuel index, is composed of three types of grades of gasoline:

- Unleaded regular gasoline—gasoline with an octane rating greater than or equal to 85 and less than 88;
- Midgrade gasoline—gasoline with an octane rating greater than or equal to 88 and less than or equal to 90;
- Premium gasoline—gasoline with an octane rating greater than 90.

High altitude areas of the country may have gasoline octane ratings that are different than the ranges given above. The other motor fuels index is composed of automotive diesel fuel and alternative automotive fuels.

SELECTION AND IDENTIFYING CHARACTERISTICS TO BE PRICED

Information from the Telephone Point-of-Purchase Survey (TPOPS) is used to select the outlets surveyed for the motor fuel index. Prices are collected for every grade of gasoline available at each selected outlet. The prices collected are classified as a per-gallon pricing unit. Prices include both excise and sales taxes. The monthly price change in the motor fuel index is determined by the price changes reported for selected items in the selected outlets. The current CPI outlet sample for all grades of gasoline is approximately 630 outlets.

CPI field staff must first determine the type of motor fuel priced by observing the motor fuel pump at the outlet. The following are characteristics that need to be identified:

- Type of service – self-service or full service
- Payment type – cash, credit card, debit card, etc.
- Brand name – the specific name of gasoline company
- Pricing unit – usually per gallon
- Octane rating – as specified on pump (usually between 85 and 93)

NOTES ON SUBSTITUTION AND QUALITY ADJUSTMENTS

Since motor fuels are generally always available, there are very few item substitutions due to lack of item availability. Additionally, octane level changes, within a specified range, and outlet or brand name changes are situations where there would be no need for item substitutions. A scenario that would precipitate the need for an item substitution would be a change in the level of service (full service versus self-service) available at the outlet.

There are no explicit quality adjustments made for changes in fuel or service quality. Adjustments are not made for switches in gasoline content due to mandated air quality requirements.[1]

TABLE 2: DISTRIBUTION OF OBSERVATIONS

Item	Number of Observations
Gasoline (all types)	1892
Other motor fuels	238

OTHER SOURCES OF INFORMATION ON MOTOR FUEL PRICE CHANGES

Although the CPI for motor fuel is reported monthly, there are numerous government agencies and independent associations that report motor fuel data using different time periods. In addition, sampling techniques and sampling methodology differ for the various groups reporting data. Three of the better-known agencies reporting motor gasoline prices are:

Energy Information Administration (EIA)—a division of the U.S. Department of Energy which publishes retail gasoline prices weekly for all three grades of gasoline from a sample of approximately 800 retail gasoline outlets. The prices collected represent self-service, except in areas having only full service. The sampling methodology used by EIA is as follows: "The sample for the Motor Gasoline Price Survey was drawn from a frame of approximately 115,000 retail gasoline outlets. The gasoline outlet frame was constructed by combining information purchased from a private commercial source with information contained on existing EIA petroleum product frames and surveys. Outlet names and zip codes were obtained from the private commercial data source. Additional information was obtained directly from companies selling retail gasoline to supplement information on the frame. The individual frame outlets were mapped to counties using their zip codes. The outlets were then assigned to the published geographic areas as defined by the Environmental Protection Agency (EPA) program area, or for conventional gasoline areas, as defined by the Census Bureau's Standard Metropolitan Statistical Areas (SMSA) by using their county assignment." [2]

American Automobile Association (AAA)—an independent agency which publishes updated retail gasoline price data daily. Price data are derived from credit card transactions at over 60,000 gasoline stations throughout the country.

Lundberg Survey—an independent market research company offering local and national coverage of fuel prices and fuel taxes. Retail prices of gasoline and diesel fuel are gathered twice monthly in 68 markets, in all 50 states and Washington, D.C. Data are also gathered on special request in other areas and frequencies.

Although these other sources may appear to show different fuel price movements than the CPI, these apparent differences are due to timing. For example, the EIA data are released each week and correspond to prices on a particular day. The CPI motor fuels index corresponds to average prices over a calendar month. BLS research has consistently shown that when timing differences are taken into account, the CPI and EIA are extremely similar in their movements.

ENDNOTES

[1]CPI Detailed Report, "Treatment of Mandated Pollution Control Measures in the CPI," (September 1998).

[2]Energy Information Association, "Sampling Methodology," available at <http://www.eia.doe.gov/oil_gas/petroleum/data_publications/wrgp/sampling_methodology.html> (visited June 25, 2005).

SUMMARY OF SELECTED ECONOMIC INDICATORS

These charts, which appear in the relevant parts of this book, show the significant changes that took place during the recovery from the recession of 2000. They are also important indicators of factors that will affect the economy in the future. While employment has recovered, manufacturing employment is still declining—though at a much slower rate than the previous three years. The costs of providing employee benefits continue to have important implications for total compensation costs, as real wages stagnate and the labor force ages. Finally, there are problems created by the rapid rise of fuel prices.

Percent Distribution of Employed Civilians by Age, 1994 and 2004

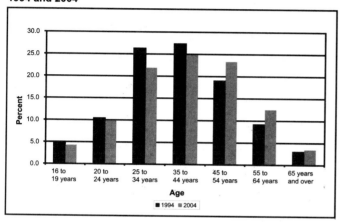

Percent Change in Nonfarm Payroll Employment, 1994–2004

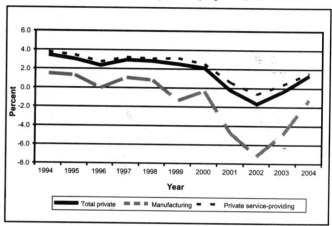

Average Weekly Earnings of Production or Nonsupervisory Workers on Total Private Nonfarm Payrolls, in Current and Constant Dollars, 1994–2004

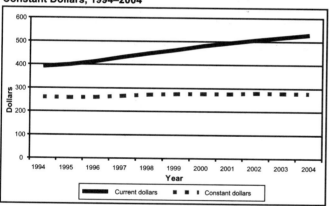

Indexes of Productivity, Business, 1994–2004

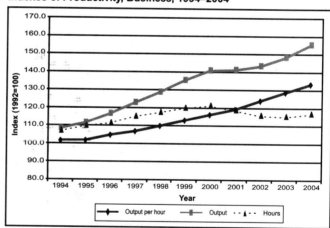

Private Industry Wages, Salaries and Benefits, Percent Change, 1994–2004

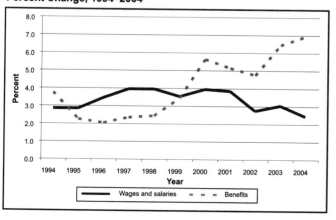

Producer and Consumer Price Indexes, Energy Commodities, 1994–2004

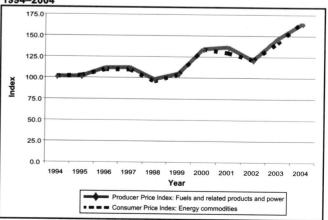

PART ONE

POPULATION, LABOR FORCE, AND EMPLOYMENT STATUS

POPULATION, LABOR FORCE, AND EMPLOYMENT STATUS

HIGHLIGHTS

This part presents detailed historical information collected in the Current Population Survey (CPS), a survey of households that collects data on the employment status of the population. Basic data on labor force, employment, and unemployment are shown for various characteristics of the population such as age, sex, race, and marital status.

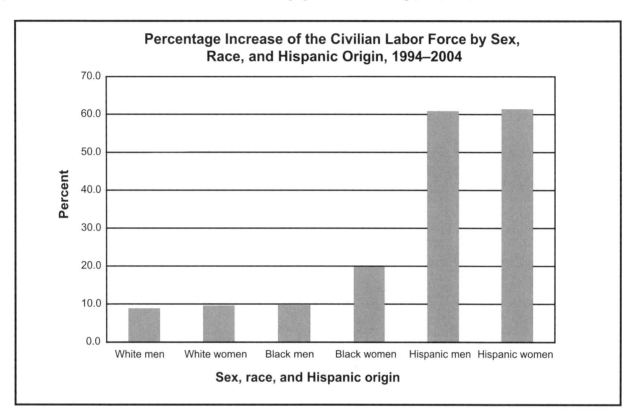

The rapid rise of Hispanics in the labor force continued in 2004. Although the total labor force increased only 0.6 percent from 2003 to 2004, the number of Hispanics in the labor force increased 2.4 percent. (Hispanics may be White or Black.) (Table 1-3)

OTHER HIGHLIGHTS:

- The share of both White men and White women in the labor force declined between 1994 and 2004. The percentage of Black men in the labor force also declined during this period, but at a slower rate. However, the share of Black women in the labor force increased from 5.7 percent to 6.0 percent over the same period. (Table 1-3)

- In 1994, there were approximately 324,000 more Black women than Black men in the labor force. By 2004, nearly 1.1 million more Black women than Black men were in the labor force. (Table 1-3)

- The labor force participation rate declined for both men and women in 2004. Women's participation has dropped every year since 2000. For men, it has been gradually declining since the 1970s. Education is one reason for the decline; as people stay in school longer, they delay their entry into the labor force. Among women, the increasing number of entrants into the labor force typically compensated for that. However, even that trend seems to have slowed recently. (Table 1-8)

- A decline in the labor force participation rate can also be associated with a downturn in the economy and with discouraged workers leaving the labor force. However, the recovery of 2004 has not yet been reflected in increased labor force participation. The total participation rate declined to 66 percent in 2004, down from 67.1 percent in 2000. (Table 1-1)

- In 2004, the Midwest had the highest labor force participation rate (68.4 percent, which was 2.4 points above the national average). The West followed with a 66.6 percent participation rate, the Northeast was next at 64.9 percent, and the South was last with a 64.7 percent labor force participation rate. (Table 1-5)

3

NOTES AND DEFINITIONS

CURRENT POPULATION SURVEY OF HOUSEHOLDS

Collection and Coverage

The Bureau of Labor Statistics (BLS) uses data from the Current Population Survey (CPS) to compile statistics on the employment status of the population and related data. The Census Bureau—using a scientifically selected sample of the civilian noninstitutional population—conducts the CPS, a monthly survey of households, for the BLS.

The CPS sample has been increased from 50,000 to 60,000 households. The new sample was introduced beginning September 2, 2000. However, in order to evaluate the impact of the change, the estimates of the national labor force from the additional sample were not introduced at that time. Since the estimates from the two samples were virtually the same, BLS began incorporating the additional sample into official national estimates in July 2001.

Respondents are interviewed to obtain information about the employment status of each household member 16 years of age and over. The inquiry relates to the household member's status during the calendar week, Sunday through Saturday, that includes the 12th day of the month. This is known as the "reference week." Actual field interviewing is conducted during the following week, referred to as the "survey week."

Part of the sample is changed each month. The rotation plan provides for three-fourths of the sample to be common from one month to the next, and one-half to be common with the same month a year earlier.

Concepts and Definitions

The concepts and definitions underlying labor force data have been modified—but not substantially altered—since the inception of the survey in 1940. Current definitions of some of the major concepts used in the CPS are given below.

The civilian noninstitutional population includes persons 16 years of age and older residing in the 50 states and the District of Columbia who are not inmates of institutions (such as penal and mental facilities and homes for the aged), and who are not on active duty in the armed forces.

Employed persons are all persons who, during the reference week, (1) did any work at all (at least one hour) as paid employees; worked in their own business, profession, or on their own farm; or who worked 15 hours or more as unpaid workers in an enterprise operated by a member of the family; and (2) all those who were not working but who had jobs or businesses from which they were temporarily absent due to vacation, illness, bad weather, child care problems, maternity or paternity leave, labor-management disputes, job training, or other family or personal reasons, despite whether they were paid for the time off or were seeking other jobs.

Each employed person is counted only once, even if he or she holds more than one job. For purposes of occupation and industry classification, multiple jobholders are counted as being in the job at which they worked the greatest number of hours during the reference week.

Included in the total are employed citizens of foreign countries who are temporarily in the United States but not living on the premises of an embassy. Excluded are persons whose only activity consisted of work around their own house (painting, repairing, or own home housework) or volunteer work for religious, charitable, and other organizations.

Unemployed persons are all persons who had no employment during the reference week, but who were available for work (except for temporary illness), and who had made specific efforts to find employment some time during the four-week period ending with the reference week. Persons who were waiting to be recalled to a job from which they had been laid off need not have been looking for work to be classified as unemployed.

Duration of unemployment represents the length of time (through the current reference week) that persons classified as unemployed had been looking for work. For persons on layoff, duration of unemployment represents the number of full weeks they had been on layoff. Mean duration is the arithmetic average computed from single weeks of unemployment; median duration is the midpoint of a distribution of weeks of unemployment.

Reasons for unemployment are divided into four major groups: (1) Job losers, defined as (a) persons on temporary layoff, who have been given a date to return to work or who expect to return within six months (persons on layoff need not be looking for work to be classified as unemployed); (b) permanent job losers, whose employment ended involuntarily and who began looking for work; and (c) persons who completed a temporary job, and who began looking for work after the job ended; (2) Job leavers, defined as persons who quit or otherwise terminated their employment voluntarily and immediately began looking for work; (3) Reentrants, defined as persons who previously worked but were out of the labor force prior to beginning their job search; and (4) New entrants, defined as persons who had never worked but were searching for work.

The civilian labor force comprises all civilians classified as employed or unemployed.

The unemployment rate is the number of unemployed as a percent of the civilian labor force.

The participation rate represents the proportion of the civilian noninstitutional population currently in the labor force.

The employment to population ratio represents the proportion of the population that is employed.

Persons not in the labor force are all persons in the civilian noninstitutional population who are neither employed nor unemployed. Information is collected about their desire for and availability to take a job at the time of the CPS interview, job search activity in the prior year, and reason for not looking for work in the four-week period ending with the reference week. Persons not in the labor force who want and are available for a job and who have looked for work sometime in the past 12 months (or since the end of their last job if they held one within the past 12 months), but who are not currently looking, are designated as "marginally attached to the labor force." The marginally attached are divided into those not currently looking because they believe their search would be futile—so-called discouraged workers—and those not currently looking for other reasons such as family responsibilities, ill health, or lack of transportation.

Discouraged workers are defined as persons not in the labor force who want and are available for a job and who have looked for work sometime in the past 12 months (or since the end of their last job if they held one within the past 12 months), but are not currently looking, because they believe there are no jobs available or there are none for which they would qualify. The reasons for not currently looking for work are that the individual believes that no work is available in his or her line of work or area; he or she could not find any work; he or she lacks necessary schooling, training, skills, or experience; employers would think he or she is too young or too old; or he or she would encounter hiring discrimination.

Usual full- or part-time status refers to hours usually worked per week. Full-time workers are those who usually work 35 hours or more. This group includes some individuals who worked less than 35 hours during the reference week for either economic or noneconomic reasons. Part-time workers are those who usually work less than 35 hours per week (at all jobs), regardless of the number of hours worked during the reference week. These concepts are used to differentiate a person's normal schedule from their specific activity during the reference week. Unemployed persons who are looking for full-time work or are on layoff from full-time jobs are counted as part of the full-time labor force; unemployed persons who are seeking or who are on layoff from part-time jobs are counted as part of the part-time labor force. Unemployment rates for full- and part-time workers are

calculated using the concepts of the full- and part-time labor force.

Occupation, industry, and class of worker for the employed is determined by the job held in the reference week. Persons with two or more jobs are classified as being in the job at which they worked the greatest number of hours. The unemployed are classified according to their last job. Beginning in 2003, the occupational and industrial classifications of CPS data are based on the 2002 Census Bureau occupational and industrial classification systems, which are derived from the 2000 Standard Occupational Classification (SOC) system and the 2002 North American Industry Classification System (NAICS). (See the following section on historical comparability for a discussion of previous classification systems used in the CPS.) The class-of-worker breakdown assigns workers to the following categories: private and government wage and salary workers, self-employed workers, and unpaid family workers. Wage and salary workers receive wages, salaries, commissions, tips, or pay in kind from a private employer or from a government unit. Self-employed persons are those who work for profit or fees in their own business, profession, trade, or farm. Only the unincorporated self-employed are included in the self-employed category in the class-of-worker typology. Self-employed persons who respond that their businesses are incorporated are included among wage and salary workers, because they are technically paid employees of a corporation. Unpaid family workers are persons working without pay for 15 hours a week or more on a farm or in a business operated by a member of the household to whom they are related by birth or marriage.

Multiple jobholders are employed persons who, during the reference week, had two or more jobs as a wage and salary worker, were self-employed and also held a wage and salary job, or worked as an unpaid family worker and also held a wage and salary job. A person employed only in private households (cleaner, gardener, babysitter, etc.) who worked for two or more employers during the reference week is not counted as a multiple jobholder, since working for several employers is considered an inherent characteristic of private household work. Also excluded are self-employed persons with multiple businesses and persons with multiple jobs as unpaid family workers.

At work part-time for economic reasons, sometimes referred to as involuntary part-time, describes individuals who gave an economic reason for working 1 to 34 hours during the reference week. Economic reasons include slack work or unfavorable business conditions, inability to find full-time work, and seasonal declines in demand. Those who usually work part-time must also indicate that they want and are available to work full-time to be classified as part-time for economic reasons.

At work part-time for noneconomic reasons refers to persons who usually work part-time and were at work 1 to 34 hours during the reference week for a noneconomic reason. Noneconomic reasons include illness or other medical limitations; child care problems or other family or personal obligations; school or training; retirement or Social Security limits on earnings; and being in a job where full-time work is less than 35 hours. The group also includes those who gave an economic reason for usually working 1 to 34 hours but said they do not want to work full-time or were unavailable for such work.

White, Black, and Asian are terms used to describe the race of persons. Persons in these categories are those who selected that race only. Persons in the remaining race categories—American Indian or Alaskan Native, Native Hawaiian or Other Pacific Islander, and persons who selected more than one race category—are included in the estimates of total employment and unemployment but are not shown separately because the number of survey respondents is too small to develop estimates of sufficient quality for monthly publication. In the enumeration process, the household respondent determines race.

Hispanic origin refers to persons who identified themselves in the enumeration process as being Spanish, Hispanic, or Latino. Persons whose ethnicity is identified as Hispanic or Latino may be of any race.

Single, never married; married, spouse present; and *other marital status* are the terms used to define the marital status of individuals at the time of interview. Married, spouse present, applies to husband and wife if both were living in the same household, even though one may be temporarily absent on business, vacation, on a visit, in a hospital, etc. Other marital status applies to persons who are married, spouse absent; widowed; or divorced. Married, spouse absent, relates to persons who are separated due to marital problems, as well as husbands and wives who are living apart because one or the other was employed elsewhere, on duty with the armed forces, or any other reasons.

A household consists of all persons—related family members and all unrelated persons—who occupy a housing unit and have no other usual address. A house, an apartment, a group of rooms, or a single room is regarded as a housing unit when occupied or intended for occupancy as separate living quarters. A householder is the person (or one of the persons) in whose name the housing unit is owned or rented. The term is not applied to either husbands or wives in married-couple families but only to persons in families maintained by either men or women without a spouse.

Family is defined as a group of two or more persons residing together who are related by birth, marriage, or adoption. All such persons are considered as members of one family. Families are classified as either married-couple families or families maintained by women or men without spouses. A family maintained by a woman or a man is one

in which the householder is single; widowed; divorced; or married, spouse absent.

The annual CPS data on the employment characteristics of families and family members begin with data for 1995. These data are not strictly comparable with family data derived from the March CPS. The annual data are derived by averaging the data for each month of the year, whereas the March data refer to that particular month. The annual average data provide a larger sample size, while the March family data provide a longer historical series.

Additional Concepts and Definitions: CPS Supplements

In addition to the above concepts and definitions, the definitions below apply to the special labor force data collected annually in the March supplement to the monthly CPS and to the data on tenure usually collected in the February supplement.

Persons with work experience are civilians who worked at any time during the preceding calendar year at full- or part-time jobs for pay or profit (including paid vacations and sick leave) or who worked without pay on a farm or in a business that was family operated. From 1989 forward, these supplementary tables also include members of the armed forces within the United States.

Tenure refers to length of time a worker has been continuously employed by his or her current employer. The data were collected through a supplement to the CPS. All employed persons were asked how long he or she has been working continuously for their present employer and, if the length of time was one or two years, the exact number of months. The follow-up question was asked for the first time in the 1998 February supplement. Prior to 1983, the question was asked differently. Data prior to 1983 thus are not strictly comparable to data for subsequent years.

Year-round full-time workers are workers who worked primarily at full-time jobs for 50 weeks or more during the preceding calendar year. Part-year workers worked either full- or part-time for 1 to 49 weeks.

Spell of unemployment is a continuous period of unemployment of at least one week's duration. A spell is terminated by either employment or withdrawal from the labor force.

Extent of unemployment refers to the number and proportion of the labor force that were unemployed at some time during the year. The number of weeks unemployed is the total number of weeks accumulated during the entire year.

Children refer to "own" children of the husband, wife, or person maintaining the family, including sons and daughters, stepchildren, and adopted children. Excluded are other related children, such as grandchildren, nieces, nephews, cousins, and unrelated children.

Earnings are all money income of $1 or more from wages and salaries and net money income of $1 or more from farm and nonfarm self-employment.

Educational attainment refers to years of school completed in regular schools, which include graded public, private, and parochial elementary and high schools, whether day or night school; and also colleges, universities, and professional schools.

Minimum wages refers to the prevailing federal minimum wage, which was $5.15 per hour in 2004. Data are for wage and salary workers who are paid hourly rates. They refer to a person's earnings at their sole or principal job.

Absences are defined as instances when persons who usually work 35 or more hours a week worked less than that during the reference period for reasons of illness or family obligations. Excluded are situations in which work was missed for vacation, holidays, or other non-illness or family reasons. The estimates are based on one-fourth of the sample only.

Historical Comparability

While current survey concepts and methods are very similar to those introduced at the inception of the survey in 1940, a number of changes have been made over the years to improve the accuracy and usefulness of the data. Only the latest changes are described here.

Major changes to the CPS were introduced in 1994, such as a complete redesign of the questionnaire and the use of computer-assisted interviewing for the entire survey. In addition, there were revisions to some of the labor force concepts and definitions, including the implementation of changes recommended in 1979 by the National Commission on Employment and Unemployment Statistics (NCEUS, also known as the Levitan Commission). Some of the major changes to the survey were:

1) The introduction of a redesigned and automated questionnaire. The CPS questionnaire was totally redesigned in order to obtain more accurate, comprehensive, and relevant information, and to take advantage of state-of-the-art computer interviewing techniques.

2) The addition of two criteria to make the definition of discouraged workers more objective. Beginning in 1994, persons classified as discouraged must have looked for a job within the past year (or since their last job, if they worked during the year), and must have been available for work during the reference week (a direct question on availability was added in 1994). These changes were made because the NCEUS and others felt that the previous def-

inition of discouraged workers was too subjective, relying mainly on an individual's stated desire for a job and not on prior testing of the labor market.

3) Similarly, the identification of persons employed part-time for economic reasons (working less than 35 hours in the reference week because of poor business conditions or because of an inability to find full-time work) was tightened by adding two new criteria for persons who usually work part-time: they must want and be available for full-time work. (Persons who usually work full-time but worked part-time for economic reasons during the reference week are assumed to meet these criteria.)

4) Specific questions were added about the expectation of recall for persons who indicate that they are on layoff. To be classified as "on temporary layoff," persons must expect to be recalled to their jobs.

5) Persons volunteering that they were waiting to start a new job within 30 days must have looked for work in the four weeks prior to the survey in order to be classified as unemployed.

Comparability of Labor Force Levels

In addition to the refinements in concepts, definitions, and methodology made over the years, other changes—made to improve the accuracy of the estimates—have also affected the comparability of the labor force data. The most important of these is the adjustment of the population totals as a result of new information from the decennial censuses. It is also crucial to correct for estimating errors during the intercensal years. Those changes affecting the most recent decade are described below.

Beginning in January 1997, updated information on the demographic characteristics of immigrants and emigrants was introduced. This raised the overall population by about 470,000, the labor force by 320,000, and employment by 290,000, with similar upward adjustments for Hispanics. Unemployment and other percentage rates were not affected.

Beginning in January 1998, new estimating procedures were introduced, which reduced the labor force by about 229,000 and employment by 256,000. However, these new procedures raised unemployment by 27,000. New information about immigration and emigration was also incorporated, which increased the Hispanic population by about 57,000. Unemployment rates were not significantly affected.

Beginning in January 1999, new information on immigration raised the population by about 310,000, with differing impacts on different demographic groups. The population of men was lowered by about 185,000, but the population of women was raised by 490,000. The Hispanic population was lowered by about 165,000, while the rest of the population was raised by about 470,000. Hispanic labor force and employment estimates were each reduced by over 200,000. The impact on unemployment rates and other percentages was small.

Beginning in January 2003, several other changes were introduced into the CPS. These changes included:

1) Population controls that reflected the results of Census 2000 were introduced into the monthly CPS estimation process. These new population size controls substantially increased the size of the civilian noninstitutional population and the civilian labor force. Data from January 2000 through December 2002 were revised to reflect the higher population estimates from Census 2000 and the higher rates of population growth since the census. The entire amount of this adjustment was added to the labor force data in January 2003, resulting in increases of 941,000 to the civilian noninstitutional population and 615,000 to the civilian labor force. The unemployment rate and other ratios were not substantially affected by either of these population control adjustments.

2) Questions on race and Hispanic origin were modified to comply with the new standards for maintaining, collecting, and presenting federal data on race and ethnicity for federal statistical agencies. The questions were reworded to indicate that individuals could select more than once race category and to convey more clearly that individuals should report their own perception of what race is. These changes had no impact on the overall civilian noninstitutional population and civilian labor force. However, they did reduce the population and labor force levels of Whites, Blacks, and Asians, beginning in January 2003.

Changes in the Occupational and Industrial Classification System

Beginning in January 1983, the occupational and industrial classification systems used in the 1980 census were introduced into the CPS. The 1980 census occupational classification system was so radically different in concepts and nomenclature from the 1970 system that comparisons of historical data are not possible without major adjustments.

The industrial classification system used in the 1980 census was based on the 1972 Standard Industrial Classification (SIC) system, as modified in 1977. The adoption of the new industrial system had much less of an adverse effect on historical comparability than did the new occupational system.

Beginning in January 1992, the occupational and industrial classification systems used in the 1990 census were introduced into the CPS. There were a few breaks in comparability between the 1980 and 1990 census-based systems, particularly within the "technical, sales, and administrative support" categories. The most notable changes in industry classification were the shift of several industries from "business services" to "professional services" and the splitting of some industries into smaller, more detailed categories.

Beginning in January 2003, the 2002 Census Bureau occupational and industrial classification system were introduced into the CPS and re-estimated for 2000 and 2001. These systems were derived from the 2000 SOC and the 2002 NAICS, which were described in the third and sixth editions of this *Handbook,* respectively. The composition of detailed occupational and industrial classification in the new systems was substantially changes from the previous systems in use as was the structure for aggregating them into broad groups. Consequently, the use of the new data classification systems created breaks in existing data series at all levels of aggregation beginning with the year 2000.

Sources of Additional Information

A complete description of sampling and estimation procedures and further information on the impact of historical changes in the survey can be found in *Employment and Earnings*, February 2003 and February 2004, and the updated Chapter 1 of the BLS *Handbook of Methods,* April 17, 2003, available on line at the BLS Web site. Technical papers, which describe revisions and adjustments, are also available on the BLS Web site.

Table 1-1. Employment Status of the Civilian Noninstitutional Population, 1947–2004

(Thousands of people, percent.)

Year	Civilian noninstitutional population	Civilian labor force								Not in labor force
		Total	Participation rate	Employed				Unemployed		
				Total	Percent of population	Agriculture	Nonagricultural industries	Number	Unemployment rate	
1947	101 827	59 350	58.3	57 038	56.0	7 890	49 148	2 311	3.9	42 477
1948	103 068	60 621	58.8	58 343	56.6	7 629	50 714	2 276	3.8	42 447
1949	103 994	61 286	58.9	57 651	55.4	7 658	49 993	3 637	5.9	42 708
1950	104 995	62 208	59.2	58 918	56.1	7 160	51 758	3 288	5.3	42 787
1951	104 621	62 017	59.2	59 961	57.3	6 726	53 235	2 055	3.3	42 604
1952	105 231	62 138	59.0	60 250	57.3	6 500	53 749	1 883	3.0	43 093
1953 [1]	107 056	63 015	58.9	61 179	57.1	6 260	54 919	1 834	2.9	44 041
1954	108 321	63 643	58.8	60 109	55.5	6 205	53 904	3 532	5.5	44 678
1955	109 683	65 023	59.3	62 170	56.7	6 450	55 722	2 852	4.4	44 660
1956	110 954	66 552	60.0	63 799	57.5	6 283	57 514	2 750	4.1	44 402
1957	112 265	66 929	59.6	64 071	57.1	5 947	58 123	2 859	4.3	45 336
1958	113 727	67 639	59.5	63 036	55.4	5 586	57 450	4 602	6.8	46 088
1959	115 329	68 369	59.3	64 630	56.0	5 565	59 065	3 740	5.5	46 960
1960 [1]	117 245	69 628	59.4	65 778	56.1	5 458	60 318	3 852	5.5	47 617
1961	118 771	70 459	59.3	65 746	55.4	5 200	60 546	4 714	6.7	48 312
1962 [1]	120 153	70 614	58.8	66 702	55.5	4 944	61 759	3 911	5.5	49 539
1963	122 416	71 833	58.7	67 762	55.4	4 687	63 076	4 070	5.7	50 583
1964	124 485	73 091	58.7	69 305	55.7	4 523	64 782	3 786	5.2	51 394
1965	126 513	74 455	58.9	71 088	56.2	4 361	66 726	3 366	4.5	52 058
1966	128 058	75 770	59.2	72 895	56.9	3 979	68 915	2 875	3.8	52 288
1967	129 874	77 347	59.6	74 372	57.3	3 844	70 527	2 975	3.8	52 527
1968	132 028	78 737	59.6	75 920	57.5	3 817	72 103	2 817	3.6	53 291
1969	134 335	80 734	60.1	77 902	58.0	3 606	74 296	2 832	3.5	53 602
1970	137 085	82 771	60.4	78 678	57.4	3 463	75 215	4 093	4.9	54 315
1971	140 216	84 382	60.2	79 367	56.6	3 394	75 972	5 016	5.9	55 834
1972 [1]	144 126	87 034	60.4	82 153	57.0	3 484	78 669	4 882	5.6	57 091
1973 [1]	147 096	89 429	60.8	85 064	57.8	3 470	81 594	4 365	4.9	57 667
1974	150 120	91 949	61.3	86 794	57.8	3 515	83 279	5 156	5.6	58 171
1975	153 153	93 774	61.2	85 846	56.1	3 408	82 438	7 929	8.5	59 377
1976	156 150	96 158	61.6	88 752	56.8	3 331	85 421	7 406	7.7	59 991
1977	159 033	99 008	62.3	92 017	57.9	3 283	88 734	6 991	7.1	60 025
1978 [1]	161 910	102 250	63.2	96 048	59.3	3 387	92 661	6 202	6.1	59 659
1979	164 863	104 962	63.7	98 824	59.9	3 347	95 477	6 137	5.8	59 900
1980	167 745	106 940	63.8	99 302	59.2	3 364	95 938	7 637	7.1	60 806
1981	170 130	108 670	63.9	100 397	59.0	3 368	97 030	8 273	7.6	61 460
1982	172 271	110 204	64.0	99 526	57.8	3 401	96 125	10 678	9.7	62 067
1983	174 215	111 550	64.0	100 834	57.9	3 383	97 450	10 717	9.6	62 665
1984	176 383	113 544	64.4	105 005	59.5	3 321	101 685	8 539	7.5	62 839
1985	178 206	115 461	64.8	107 150	60.1	3 179	103 971	8 312	7.2	62 744
1986 [1]	180 587	117 834	65.3	109 597	60.7	3 163	106 434	8 237	7.0	62 752
1987	182 753	119 865	65.6	112 440	61.5	3 208	109 232	7 425	6.2	62 888
1988	184 613	121 669	65.9	114 968	62.3	3 169	111 800	6 701	5.5	62 944
1989	186 393	123 869	66.5	117 342	63.0	3 199	114 142	6 528	5.3	62 523
1990 [1]	189 164	125 840	66.5	118 793	62.8	3 223	115 570	7 047	5.6	63 324
1991	190 925	126 346	66.2	117 718	61.7	3 269	114 449	8 628	6.8	64 578
1992	192 805	128 105	66.4	118 492	61.5	3 247	115 245	9 613	7.5	64 700
1993	194 838	129 200	66.3	120 259	61.7	3 115	117 144	8 940	6.9	65 638
1994 [1]	196 814	131 056	66.6	123 060	62.5	3 409	119 651	7 996	6.1	65 758
1995	198 584	132 304	66.6	124 900	62.9	3 440	121 460	7 404	5.6	66 280
1996	200 591	133 943	66.8	126 708	63.2	3 443	123 264	7 236	5.4	66 647
1997 [1]	203 133	136 297	67.1	129 558	63.8	3 399	126 159	6 739	4.9	66 836
1998 [1]	205 220	137 673	67.1	131 463	64.1	3 378	128 085	6 210	4.5	67 547
1999 [1]	207 753	139 368	67.1	133 488	64.3	3 281	130 207	5 880	4.2	68 385
2000 [1]	212 577	142 583	67.1	136 891	64.4	2 464	134 427	5 692	4.0	69 994
2001	215 092	143 734	66.8	136 933	63.7	2 299	134 635	6 801	4.7	71 359
2002	217 570	144 863	66.6	136 485	62.7	2 311	134 174	8 378	5.8	72 707
2003 [1]	221 168	146 510	66.2	137 736	62.3	2 275	135 461	8 774	6.0	74 658
2004 [1]	223 357	147 401	66.0	139 252	62.3	2 232	137 020	8 149	5.5	75 956

[1]Not strictly comparable with data for prior years. See "Notes and Definitions" for information on historical comparability.

Table 1-2. Employment Status of the Civilian Noninstitutional Population by Sex, 1970–2004

(Thousands of people, percent.)

Year	Civilian noninstitutional population	Civilian labor force		Employed				Unemployed		Not in labor force
		Total	Participation rate	Total	Percent of population	Agriculture	Non-agricultural industries	Number	Unemployment rate	
Men										
1970	64 304	51 228	79.7	48 990	76.2	2 862	46 128	2 238	4.4	13 076
1971	65 942	52 180	79.1	49 390	74.9	2 795	46 595	2 789	5.3	13 762
1972 [1]	67 835	53 555	78.9	50 896	75.0	2 849	48 047	2 659	5.0	14 280
1973 [1]	69 292	54 624	78.8	52 349	75.5	2 847	49 502	2 275	4.2	14 667
1974	70 808	55 739	78.7	53 024	74.9	2 919	50 105	2 714	4.9	15 069
1975	72 291	56 299	77.9	51 857	71.7	2 824	49 032	4 442	7.9	15 993
1976	73 759	57 174	77.5	53 138	72.0	2 744	50 394	4 036	7.1	16 585
1977	75 193	58 396	77.7	54 728	72.8	2 671	52 057	3 667	6.3	16 797
1978 [1]	76 576	59 620	77.9	56 479	73.8	2 718	53 761	3 142	5.3	16 956
1979	78 020	60 726	77.8	57 607	73.8	2 686	54 921	3 120	5.1	17 293
1980	79 398	61 453	77.4	57 186	72.0	2 709	54 477	4 267	6.9	17 945
1981	80 511	61 974	77.0	57 397	71.3	2 700	54 697	4 577	7.4	18 537
1982	81 523	62 450	76.6	56 271	69.0	2 736	53 534	6 179	9.9	19 073
1983	82 531	63 047	76.4	56 787	68.8	2 704	54 083	6 260	9.9	19 484
1984	83 605	63 835	76.4	59 091	70.7	2 668	56 423	4 744	7.4	19 771
1985	84 469	64 411	76.3	59 891	70.9	2 535	57 356	4 521	7.0	20 058
1986 [1]	85 798	65 422	76.3	60 892	71.0	2 511	58 381	4 530	6.9	20 376
1987	86 899	66 207	76.2	62 107	71.5	2 543	59 564	4 101	6.2	20 692
1988	87 857	66 927	76.2	63 273	72.0	2 493	60 780	3 655	5.5	20 930
1989	88 762	67 840	76.4	64 315	72.5	2 513	61 802	3 525	5.2	20 923
1990 [1]	90 377	69 011	76.4	65 104	72.0	2 546	62 559	3 906	5.7	21 367
1991	91 278	69 168	75.8	64 223	70.4	2 589	61 634	4 946	7.2	22 110
1992	92 270	69 964	75.8	64 440	69.8	2 575	61 866	5 523	7.9	22 306
1993	93 332	70 404	75.4	65 349	70.0	2 478	62 871	5 055	7.2	22 927
1994 [1]	94 354	70 817	75.1	66 450	70.4	2 554	63 896	4 367	6.2	23 538
1995	95 178	71 360	75.0	67 377	70.8	2 559	64 818	3 983	5.6	23 818
1996	96 206	72 086	74.9	68 207	70.9	2 573	65 634	3 880	5.4	24 119
1997 [1]	97 715	73 261	75.0	69 685	71.3	2 552	67 133	3 577	4.9	24 454
1998 [1]	98 758	73 959	74.9	70 693	71.6	2 553	68 140	3 266	4.4	24 799
1999 [1]	99 722	74 512	74.7	71 446	71.6	2 432	69 014	3 066	4.1	25 210
2000 [1]	101 964	76 280	74.8	73 305	71.9	1 861	71 444	2 975	3.9	25 684
2001	103 282	76 886	74.4	73 196	70.9	1 708	71 488	3 690	4.8	26 396
2002	104 585	77 500	74.1	72 903	69.7	1 724	71 179	4 597	5.9	27 085
2003 [1]	106 435	78 238	73.5	73 332	68.9	1 695	71 636	4 906	6.3	28 197
2004 [1]	107 710	78 980	73.3	74 524	69.2	1 687	72 838	4 456	5.6	28 730
Women										
1970	72 782	31 543	43.3	29 688	40.8	601	29 087	1 855	5.9	41 239
1971	74 274	32 202	43.4	29 976	40.4	599	29 377	2 227	6.9	42 072
1972 [1]	76 290	33 479	43.9	31 257	41.0	635	30 622	2 222	6.6	42 811
1973 [1]	77 804	34 804	44.7	32 715	42.0	622	32 093	2 089	6.0	43 000
1974	79 312	36 211	45.7	33 769	42.6	596	33 173	2 441	6.7	43 101
1975	80 860	37 475	46.3	33 989	42.0	584	33 404	3 486	9.3	43 386
1976	82 390	38 983	47.3	35 615	43.2	588	35 027	3 369	8.6	43 406
1977	83 840	40 613	48.4	37 289	44.5	612	36 677	3 324	8.2	43 227
1978 [1]	85 334	42 631	50.0	39 569	46.4	669	38 900	3 061	7.2	42 703
1979	86 843	44 235	50.9	41 217	47.5	661	40 556	3 018	6.8	42 608
1980	88 348	45 487	51.5	42 117	47.7	656	41 461	3 370	7.4	42 861
1981	89 618	46 696	52.1	43 000	48.0	667	42 333	3 696	7.9	42 922
1982	90 748	47 755	52.6	43 256	47.7	665	42 591	4 499	9.4	42 993
1983	91 684	48 503	52.9	44 047	48.0	680	43 367	4 457	9.2	43 181
1984	92 778	49 709	53.6	45 915	49.5	653	45 262	3 794	7.6	43 068
1985	93 736	51 050	54.5	47 259	50.4	644	46 615	3 791	7.4	42 686
1986 [1]	94 789	52 413	55.3	48 706	51.4	652	48 054	3 707	7.1	42 376
1987	95 853	53 658	56.0	50 334	52.5	666	49 668	3 324	6.2	42 195
1988	96 756	54 742	56.6	51 696	53.4	676	51 020	3 046	5.6	42 014
1989	97 630	56 030	57.4	53 027	54.3	687	52 341	3 003	5.4	41 601
1990 [1]	98 787	56 829	57.5	53 689	54.3	678	53 011	3 140	5.5	41 957
1991	99 646	57 178	57.4	53 496	53.7	680	52 815	3 683	6.4	42 468
1992	100 535	58 141	57.8	54 052	53.8	672	53 380	4 090	7.0	42 394
1993	101 506	58 795	57.9	54 910	54.1	637	54 273	3 885	6.6	42 711
1994 [1]	102 460	60 239	58.8	56 610	55.3	855	55 755	3 629	6.0	42 221
1995	103 406	60 944	58.9	57 523	55.6	881	56 642	3 421	5.6	42 462
1996	104 385	61 857	59.3	58 501	56.0	871	57 630	3 356	5.4	42 528
1997 [1]	105 418	63 036	59.8	59 873	56.8	847	59 026	3 162	5.0	42 382
1998 [1]	106 462	63 714	59.8	60 771	57.1	825	59 945	2 944	4.6	42 748
1999 [1]	108 031	64 855	60.0	62 042	57.4	849	61 193	2 814	4.3	43 175
2000 [1]	110 613	66 303	59.9	63 586	57.5	602	62 983	2 717	4.1	44 310
2001	111 811	66 848	59.8	63 737	57.0	591	63 147	3 111	4.7	44 962
2002	112 985	67 363	59.6	63 582	56.3	587	62 995	3 781	5.6	45 621
2003 [1]	114 733	68 272	59.5	64 404	56.1	580	63 824	3 868	5.7	46 461
2004 [1]	115 647	68 421	59.2	64 728	56.0	546	64 182	3 694	5.4	47 225

[1]Not strictly comparable with data for prior years. See "Notes and Definitions" for information on historical comparability.

Table 1-3. Employment Status of the Civilian Noninstitutional Population by Sex, Race, Hispanic Origin, and Age, 1985–2004

(Thousands of people.)

Employment status, sex, and age	1985	1986	1987	1988	1989	1990	1991	1992	1993	1994
Total Civilian Noninstitutional Population										
Civilian noninstitutional population	178 206	180 587	182 753	184 613	186 393	189 164	190 925	192 805	194 838	196 814
Civilian labor force	115 461	117 834	119 865	121 669	123 869	125 840	126 346	128 105	129 200	131 056
Employed	107 150	109 597	112 440	114 968	117 342	118 793	117 718	118 492	120 259	123 060
Agriculture	3 179	3 163	3 208	3 169	3 199	3 223	3 269	3 247	3 115	3 409
Nonagricultural industries	103 971	106 434	109 232	111 800	114 142	115 570	114 449	115 245	117 144	119 651
Unemployed	8 312	8 237	7 425	6 701	6 528	7 047	8 628	9 613	8 940	7 996
Not in labor force	62 744	62 752	62 888	62 944	62 523	63 324	64 578	64 700	65 638	65 758
Men, 16 Years and Older										
Civilian noninstitutional population	84 469	85 798	86 899	87 857	88 762	90 377	91 278	92 270	93 332	94 355
Civilian labor force	64 411	65 422	66 207	66 927	67 840	69 011	69 168	69 964	70 404	70 817
Employed	59 891	60 892	62 107	63 273	64 315	65 104	64 223	64 440	65 349	66 450
Agriculture	2 535	2 511	2 543	2 493	2 513	2 546	2 589	2 575	2 478	2 554
Nonagricultural industries	57 356	58 381	59 564	60 780	61 802	62 559	61 634	61 866	62 871	63 896
Unemployed	4 521	4 530	4 101	3 655	3 525	3 906	4 946	5 523	5 055	4 367
Not in labor force	20 058	20 376	20 692	20 930	20 923	21 367	22 110	22 306	22 927	23 538
Men, 20 Years and Older										
Civilian noninstitutional population	77 195	78 523	79 565	80 553	81 619	83 030	84 144	85 247	86 256	87 151
Civilian labor force	60 277	61 320	62 095	62 768	63 704	64 916	65 374	66 213	66 642	66 921
Employed	56 562	57 569	58 726	59 781	60 837	61 678	61 178	61 496	62 355	63 294
Agriculture	2 278	2 292	2 329	2 271	2 307	2 329	2 383	2 385	2 293	2 351
Nonagricultural industries	54 284	55 277	56 397	57 510	58 530	59 349	58 795	59 111	60 063	60 943
Unemployed	3 715	3 751	3 369	2 987	2 867	3 239	4 195	4 717	4 287	3 627
Not in labor force	16 918	17 203	17 470	17 785	17 915	18 114	18 770	19 034	19 613	20 230
Women, 16 Years and Older										
Civilian noninstitutional population	93 736	94 789	95 853	96 756	97 630	98 787	99 646	100 535	101 506	102 460
Civilian labor force	51 050	52 413	53 658	54 742	56 030	56 829	57 178	58 141	58 795	60 239
Employed	47 259	48 706	50 334	51 696	53 027	53 689	53 496	54 052	54 910	56 610
Agriculture	644	652	666	676	687	678	680	672	637	855
Nonagricultural industries	46 615	48 054	49 668	51 020	52 341	53 011	52 815	53 380	54 273	55 755
Unemployed	3 791	3 707	3 324	3 046	3 003	3 140	3 683	4 090	3 885	3 629
Not in labor force	42 686	42 376	42 195	42 014	41 601	41 957	42 468	42 394	42 711	42 221
Women, 20 Years and Older										
Civilian noninstitutional population	86 506	87 567	88 583	89 532	90 550	91 614	92 708	93 718	94 647	95 467
Civilian labor force	47 283	48 589	49 783	50 870	52 212	53 131	53 708	54 796	55 388	56 655
Employed	44 154	45 556	47 074	48 383	49 745	50 535	50 634	51 328	52 099	53 606
Agriculture	596	614	622	625	642	631	639	625	598	809
Nonagricultural industries	43 558	44 943	46 453	47 757	49 103	49 904	49 995	50 702	51 501	52 796
Unemployed	3 129	3 032	2 709	2 487	2 467	2 596	3 074	3 469	3 288	3 049
Not in labor force	39 222	38 979	38 800	38 662	38 339	38 483	39 000	38 922	39 260	38 813
Both Sexes, 16 to 19 Years										
Civilian noninstitutional population	14 506	14 496	14 606	14 527	14 223	14 520	14 073	13 840	13 935	14 196
Civilian labor force	7 901	7 926	7 988	8 031	7 954	7 792	7 265	7 096	7 170	7 481
Employed	6 434	6 472	6 640	6 805	6 759	6 581	5 906	5 669	5 805	6 161
Agriculture	305	258	258	273	250	264	247	237	224	249
Nonagricultural industries	6 129	6 215	6 382	6 532	6 510	6 317	5 659	5 432	5 580	5 912
Unemployed	1 468	1 454	1 347	1 226	1 194	1 212	1 359	1 427	1 365	1 320
Not in labor force	6 604	6 570	6 618	6 497	6 270	6 727	6 808	6 745	6 765	6 715

Table 1-3. Employment Status of the Civilian Noninstitutional Population by Sex, Race, Hispanic Origin, and Age, 1985–2004—*Continued*

(Thousands of people.)

Employment status, sex, and age	1995	1996	1997	1998	1999	2000	2001	2002	2003	2004
Total Civilian Noninstitutional Population										
Civilian noninstitutional population	198 584	200 591	203 133	205 220	207 753	212 577	215 092	217 570	221 168	223 357
Civilian labor force	132 304	133 943	136 297	137 673	139 368	142 583	143 734	144 863	146 510	147 401
Employed	124 900	126 708	129 558	131 463	133 488	136 891	136 933	136 485	137 736	139 252
Agriculture	3 440	3 443	3 399	3 378	3 281	2 464	2 299	2 311	2 275	2 232
Nonagricultural industries	121 460	123 264	126 159	128 085	130 207	134 427	134 635	134 174	135 461	137 020
Unemployed	7 404	7 236	6 739	6 210	5 880	5 692	6 801	8 378	8 774	8 149
Not in labor force	66 280	66 647	66 837	67 547	68 385	69 994	71 359	72 707	74 658	75 956
Men, 16 Years and Older										
Civilian noninstitutional population	95 178	96 206	97 715	98 758	99 722	101 964	103 282	104 585	106 435	107 710
Civilian labor force	71 360	72 087	73 261	73 959	74 512	76 280	76 886	77 500	78 238	78 980
Employed	67 377	68 207	69 685	70 693	71 446	73 305	73 196	72 903	73 332	74 524
Agriculture	2 559	2 573	2 552	2 553	2 432	1 861	1 708	1 724	1 695	1 688
Nonagricultural industries	64 818	65 634	67 133	68 140	69 014	71 444	71 488	71 179	71 636	72 836
Unemployed	3 983	3 880	3 577	3 266	3 066	2 975	3 690	4 597	4 906	4 456
Not in labor force	23 818	24 119	24 454	24 799	25 210	25 684	26 396	27 085	28 197	28 730
Men, 20 Years and Older										
Civilian noninstitutional population	87 811	88 606	89 879	90 790	91 555	93 875	95 181	96 439	98 272	99 476
Civilian labor force	67 324	68 044	69 166	69 715	70 194	72 010	72 816	73 630	74 623	75 364
Employed	64 085	64 897	66 284	67 135	67 761	69 634	69 776	69 734	70 415	71 572
Agriculture	2 335	2 356	2 356	2 350	2 244	1 756	1 613	1 629	1 614	1 596
Nonagricultural industries	61 750	62 541	63 927	64 785	65 517	67 878	68 163	68 104	68 801	69 976
Unemployed	3 239	3 146	2 882	2 580	2 433	2 376	3 040	3 896	4 209	3 791
Not in labor force	20 487	20 563	20 713	21 075	21 362	21 864	22 365	22 809	23 649	24 113
Women, 16 Years and Older										
Civilian noninstitutional population	103 406	104 385	105 418	106 462	108 031	110 613	111 811	112 985	114 733	115 647
Civilian labor force	60 944	61 857	63 036	63 714	64 855	66 303	66 848	67 363	68 272	68 421
Employed	57 523	58 501	59 873	60 771	62 042	63 586	63 737	63 582	64 404	64 728
Agriculture	881	871	847	825	849	602	591	587	580	547
Nonagricultural industries	56 642	57 630	59 026	59 945	61 193	62 983	63 147	62 995	63 824	64 181
Unemployed	3 421	3 356	3 162	2 944	2 814	2 717	3 111	3 781	3 868	3 694
Not in labor force	42 462	42 528	42 382	42 748	43 175	44 310	44 962	45 621	46 461	47 225
Women, 20 Years and Older										
Civilian noninstitutional population	96 262	97 050	97 889	98 786	100 158	102 790	103 983	105 136	106 800	107 658
Civilian labor force	57 215	58 094	59 198	59 702	60 840	62 301	63 016	63 648	64 716	64 923
Employed	54 396	55 311	56 613	57 278	58 555	60 067	60 417	60 420	61 402	61 773
Agriculture	830	827	798	768	803	567	558	557	550	515
Nonagricultural industries	53 566	54 484	55 815	56 510	57 752	59 500	59 860	59 863	60 852	61 258
Unemployed	2 819	2 783	2 585	2 424	2 285	2 235	2 599	3 228	3 314	3 150
Not in labor force	39 047	38 956	38 691	39 084	39 318	40 488	40 967	41 488	42 083	42 735
Both Sexes, 16 to 19 Years										
Civilian noninstitutional population	14 511	14 934	15 365	15 644	16 040	15 912	15 929	15 994	16 096	16 222
Civilian labor force	7 765	7 806	7 932	8 256	8 333	8 271	7 902	7 585	7 170	7 114
Employed	6 419	6 500	6 661	7 051	7 172	7 189	6 740	6 332	5 919	5 907
Agriculture	275	261	244	261	234	141	128	124	111	121
Nonagricultural industries	6 144	6 239	6 417	6 790	6 938	7 049	6 611	6 207	5 808	786
Unemployed	1 346	1 306	1 271	1 205	1 162	1 081	1 162	1 253	1 251	
Not in labor force	6 746	7 128	7 433	7 388	7 706	7 642	8 027	8 409	8 926	9 1

Table 1-3. Employment Status of the Civilian Noninstitutional Population by Sex, Race, Hispanic Origin, and Age, 1985–2004—*Continued*

(Thousands of people.)

Employment status, sex, and age	1985	1986	1987	1988	1989	1990	1991	1992	1993	1994
Total, White[1]										
Civilian noninstitutional population	153 679	155 432	156 958	158 194	159 338	160 625	161 759	162 972	164 289	165 555
Civilian labor force	99 926	101 801	103 290	104 756	106 355	107 447	107 743	108 837	109 700	111 082
Employed	93 736	95 660	97 789	99 812	101 584	102 261	101 182	101 669	103 045	105 190
Agriculture	2 936	2 958	2 986	2 965	2 996	2 998	3 026	3 018	2 895	3 162
Nonagricultural industries	90 799	92 703	94 803	96 846	98 588	99 263	98 157	98 650	100 150	102 027
Unemployed	6 191	6 140	5 501	4 944	4 770	5 186	6 560	7 169	6 655	5 892
Not in labor force	53 753	53 631	53 669	53 349	52 983	53 178	54 061	54 135	54 589	54 473
White Men, 16 Years and Older[1]										
Civilian noninstitutional population	73 373	74 390	75 189	75 855	76 468	77 369	77 977	78 651	79 371	80 059
Civilian labor force	56 472	57 217	57 779	58 317	58 988	59 638	59 656	60 168	60 484	60 727
Employed	53 046	53 785	54 647	55 550	56 352	56 703	55 797	55 959	56 656	57 452
Agriculture	2 325	2 340	2 354	2 318	2 345	2 353	2 384	2 378	2 286	2 347
Nonagricultural industries	50 720	51 444	52 293	53 232	54 007	54 350	53 413	53 580	54 370	55 104
Unemployed	3 426	3 433	3 132	2 766	2 636	2 935	3 859	4 209	3 828	3 275
Not in labor force	16 901	17 173	17 410	17 538	17 480	17 731	18 321	18 484	18 887	19 332
White Men, 20 Years and Older[1]										
Civilian noninstitutional population	67 386	68 413	69 175	69 887	70 654	71 457	72 274	73 040	73 721	74 311
Civilian labor force	52 895	53 675	54 232	54 734	55 441	56 116	56 387	56 976	57 284	57 411
Employed	50 061	50 818	51 649	52 466	53 292	53 685	53 103	53 357	54 021	54 676
Agriculture	2 085	2 131	2 150	2 104	2 149	2 148	2 192	2 197	2 114	2 151
Nonagricultural industries	47 976	48 687	49 499	50 362	51 143	51 537	50 912	51 160	51 907	52 525
Unemployed	2 834	2 857	2 584	2 268	2 149	2 431	3 284	3 620	3 263	2 735
Not in labor force	14 490	14 738	14 942	15 153	15 213	15 340	15 887	16 064	16 436	16 900
White Women, 16 Years and Older[1]										
Civilian noninstitutional population	80 306	81 042	81 769	82 340	82 871	83 256	83 781	84 321	84 918	85 496
Civilian labor force	43 455	44 584	45 510	46 439	47 367	47 809	48 087	48 669	49 216	50 356
Employed	40 690	41 876	43 142	44 262	45 232	45 558	45 385	45 710	46 390	47 738
Agriculture	611	617	632	648	651	645	641	640	609	815
Nonagricultural industries	40 079	41 259	42 509	43 614	44 581	44 913	44 744	45 070	45 780	46 923
Unemployed	2 765	2 708	2 369	2 177	2 135	2 251	2 701	2 959	2 827	2 617
Not in labor force	36 852	36 458	36 258	35 901	35 504	35 447	35 695	35 651	35 702	35 141
White Women, 20 Years and Older[1]										
Civilian noninstitutional population	74 394	75 140	75 845	76 470	77 154	77 539	78 285	78 928	79 490	79 980
Civilian labor force	40 190	41 264	42 164	43 081	44 105	44 648	45 111	45 839	46 311	47 314
Employed	37 907	39 050	40 242	41 316	42 346	42 796	42 862	43 327	43 910	45 116
Agriculture	566	580	590	599	608	598	601	594	572	772
Nonagricultural industries	37 341	38 471	39 652	40 717	41 738	42 198	42 261	42 733	43 339	44 344
Unemployed	2 283	2 213	1 922	1 766	1 758	1 852	2 248	2 512	2 400	2 197
Not in labor force	34 204	33 876	33 681	33 389	33 050	32 891	33 174	33 089	33 179	32 666
White, Both Sexes, 16 to 19 Years[1]										
Civilian noninstitutional population	11 900	11 879	11 939	11 838	11 530	11 630	11 200	11 004	11 078	11 264
Civilian labor force	6 841	6 862	6 893	6 940	6 809	6 683	6 245	6 022	6 105	6 357
Employ	5 768	5 792	5 898	6 030	5 946	5 779	5 216	4 985	5 113	5 398
Ac ure	285	247	246	263	239	252	233	228	209	239
agricultural industries	5 483	5 545	5 652	5 767	5 707	5 528	4 984	4 757	4 904	5 158
employed	1 074	1 070	995	910	863	903	1 029	1 037	992	960
t in labor force	5 058	5 017	5 045	4 897	4 721	4 947	4 955	4 982	4 973	4 907

[1]Beginning in 2003, persons who selected this race group only; persons who selected more than one race group are not included. Prior to 2003, persons who reported more than one race group were included in the group they identified as the main race.

Table 1-3. Employment Status of the Civilian Noninstitutional Population by Sex, Race, Hispanic Origin, and Age, 1985–2004—*Continued*

(Thousands of people.)

Employment status, sex, and age	1995	1996	1997	1998	1999	2000	2001	2002	2003	2004
Total, White[1]										
Civilian noninstitutional population	166 914	168 317	169 993	171 478	173 085	176 220	178 111	179 783	181 292	182 643
Civilian labor force	111 950	113 108	114 693	115 415	116 509	118 545	119 399	120 150	120 546	121 086
Employed	106 490	107 808	109 856	110 931	112 235	114 424	114 430	114 013	114 235	115 239
Agriculture	3 194	3 276	3 208	3 160	3 083	2 320	2 174	2 171	2 148	2 103
Nonagricultural industries	103 296	104 532	106 648	107 770	109 152	112 104	112 256	111 841	112 087	113 136
Unemployed	5 459	5 300	4 836	4 484	4 273	4 121	4 969	6 137	6 311	5 847
Not in labor force	54 965	55 209	55 301	56 064	56 577	57 675	58 713	59 633	60 746	61 558
White Men, 16 Years and Older[1]										
Civilian noninstitutional population	80 733	81 489	82 577	83 352	83 930	85 370	86 452	87 361	88 249	89 044
Civilian labor force	61 146	61 783	62 639	63 034	63 413	64 466	64 966	65 308	65 509	65 994
Employed	58 146	58 888	59 998	60 604	61 139	62 289	62 212	61 849	61 866	62 712
Agriculture	2 347	2 436	2 389	2 376	2 273	1 743	1 606	1 611	1 597	1 583
Nonagricultural industries	55 800	56 452	57 608	58 228	58 866	60 546	60 606	60 238	60 269	61 129
Unemployed	2 999	2 896	2 641	2 431	2 274	2 177	2 754	3 459	3 643	3 282
Not in labor force	19 587	19 706	19 938	20 317	20 517	20 905	21 486	22 053	22 740	23 050
White Men, 20 Years and Older[1]										
Civilian noninstitutional population	74 879	75 454	76 320	76 966	77 432	78 966	80 029	80 922	81 860	82 615
Civilian labor force	57 719	58 340	59 126	59 421	59 747	60 850	61 519	62 067	62 473	62 944
Employed	55 254	55 977	56 986	57 500	57 934	59 119	59 245	59 124	59 348	60 159
Agriculture	2 132	2 224	2 201	2 182	2 094	1 640	1 512	1 519	1 517	1 495
Nonagricultural industries	53 122	53 753	54 785	55 319	55 839	57 479	57 733	57 605	57 831	58 664
Unemployed	2 465	2 363	2 140	1 920	1 813	1 731	2 275	2 943	3 125	2 785
Not in labor force	17 161	17 114	17 194	17 545	17 685	18 116	18 510	18 855	19 386	19 671
White Women, 16 Years and Older[1]										
Civilian noninstitutional population	86 181	86 828	87 417	88 126	89 156	90 850	91 660	92 422	93 043	93 599
Civilian labor force	50 804	51 325	52 054	52 380	53 096	54 079	54 433	54 842	55 037	55 092
Employed	48 344	48 920	49 859	50 327	51 096	52 136	52 218	52 164	52 369	52 527
Agriculture	847	840	819	784	810	578	568	560	551	520
Nonagricultural industries	47 497	48 080	49 040	49 543	50 286	51 558	51 650	51 604	51 818	52 007
Unemployed	2 460	2 404	2 195	2 053	1 999	1 944	2 215	2 678	2 668	2 565
Not in labor force	35 377	35 503	35 363	35 746	36 060	36 770	37 227	37 581	38 006	38 508
White Women, 20 Years and Older[1]										
Civilian noninstitutional population	80 567	81 041	81 492	82 073	82 953	84 718	85 526	86 266	86 905	87 430
Civilian labor force	47 686	48 162	48 847	49 029	49 714	50 740	51 218	51 717	52 099	52 212
Employed	45 643	46 164	47 063	47 342	48 098	49 145	49 369	49 448	49 823	50 040
Agriculture	799	798	771	729	765	546	537	532	522	488
Nonagricultural industries	44 844	45 366	46 292	46 612	47 333	48 599	48 831	48 916	49 301	49 552
Unemployed	2 042	1 998	1 784	1 688	1 616	1 595	1 849	2 269	2 276	2 172
Not in labor force	32 881	32 879	32 645	33 044	33 239	33 978	34 308	34 548	34 806	35 218
White, Both Sexes, 16 to 19 Years[1]										
Civilian noninstitutional population	11 468	11 822	12 181	12 439	12 700	12 535	12 556	12 596	12 527	12 599
Civilian labor force	6 545	6 607	6 720	6 965	7 048	6 955	6 661	6 366	5 973	5 929
Employed	5 593	5 667	5 807	6 089	6 204	6 160	5 817	5 441	5 064	5 039
Agriculture	262	254	236	250	224	135	125	121	109	116
Nonagricultural industries	5 331	5 413	5 571	5 839	5 980	6 025	5 692	5 320	4 955	4 923
Unemployed	952	939	912	876	844	795	845	925	909	890
Not in labor force	4 923	5 215	5 462	5 475	5 652	5 581	5 894	6 230	6 554	6 669

[1]Beginning in 2003, persons who selected this race group only; persons who selected more than one race group are not included. Prior to 2003, persons who reported more than one race group were included in the group they identified as the main race.

Table 1-3. Employment Status of the Civilian Noninstitutional Population by Sex, Race, Hispanic Origin, and Age, 1985–2004—*Continued*

(Thousands of people.)

Employment status, sex, and age	1985	1986	1987	1988	1989	1990	1991	1992	1993	1994
Total, Black[1]										
Civilian noninstitutional population	19 664	19 989	20 352	20 692	21 021	21 477	21 799	22 147	22 521	22 879
Civilian labor force	12 364	12 654	12 993	13 205	13 497	13 740	13 797	14 162	14 225	14 502
Employed	10 501	10 814	11 309	11 658	11 953	12 175	12 074	12 151	12 382	12 835
Agriculture	189	155	164	153	150	142	160	153	143	136
Nonagricultural industries	10 312	10 659	11 145	11 505	11 803	12 034	11 914	11 997	12 239	12 699
Unemployed	1 864	1 840	1 684	1 547	1 544	1 565	1 723	2 011	1 844	1 666
Not in labor force	7 299	7 335	7 359	7 487	7 524	7 737	8 002	7 985	8 296	8 377
Black Men, 16 Years and Older[1]										
Civilian noninstitutional population	8 790	8 956	9 128	9 289	9 439	9 573	9 725	9 896	10 083	10 258
Civilian labor force	6 220	6 373	6 486	6 596	6 701	6 802	6 851	6 997	7 019	7 089
Employed	5 270	5 428	5 661	5 824	5 928	5 995	5 961	5 930	6 047	6 241
Agriculture	167	133	142	133	127	124	139	138	128	118
Nonagricultural industries	5 103	5 295	5 519	5 691	5 802	5 872	5 822	5 791	5 919	6 122
Unemployed	951	946	826	771	773	806	890	1 067	971	848
Not in labor force	2 570	2 583	2 642	2 694	2 738	2 772	2 874	2 899	3 064	3 169
Black Men, 20 Years and Older[1]										
Civilian noninstitutional population	7 731	7 907	8 063	8 063	8 215	8 364	8 479	8 652	8 840	9 171
Civilian labor force	5 749	5 915	6 023	6 023	6 127	6 221	6 357	6 451	6 568	6 646
Employed	4 992	5 150	5 357	5 357	5 509	5 602	5 692	5 706	5 681	5 964
Agriculture	154	125	135	135	129	119	117	131	131	115
Nonagricultural industries	4 837	5 025	5 222	5 222	5 381	5 483	5 576	5 575	5 550	5 849
Unemployed	757	765	666	666	617	619	664	745	886	682
Not in labor force	1 982	1 991	2 040	2 040	2 089	2 143	2 122	2 202	801	2 525
Black Women, 16 Years and Older[1]										
Civilian noninstitutional population	10 873	11 033	11 224	11 402	11 582	11 904	12 074	12 251	12 438	12 621
Civilian labor force	6 144	6 281	6 507	6 609	6 796	6 938	6 946	7 166	7 206	7 413
Employed	5 231	5 386	5 648	5 834	6 025	6 180	6 113	6 221	6 334	6 595
Agriculture	22	22	22	20	24	18	21	15	15	18
Nonagricultural industries	5 209	5 364	5 626	5 814	6 001	6 162	6 092	6 206	6 320	6 577
Unemployed	913	894	858	776	772	758	833	944	872	818
Not in labor force	4 729	4 752	4 717	4 793	4 786	4 965	5 129	5 086	5 231	5 208
Black Women, 20 Years and Older[1]										
Civilian noninstitutional population	9 773	9 945	10 126	10 298	10 482	10 760	10 959	11 152	11 332	11 496
Civilian labor force	5 727	5 855	6 071	6 190	6 352	6 517	6 652	6 778	6 824	7 004
Employed	4 977	5 128	5 365	5 548	5 727	5 884	5 874	5 978	6 095	6 320
Agriculture	19	22	20	18	23	18	20	15	14	17
Nonagricultural industries	4 959	5 106	5 345	5 530	5 703	5 867	5 853	5 963	6 081	6 303
Unemployed	750	728	706	642	625	633	698	800	729	685
Not in labor force	4 046	4 090	4 054	4 108	4 130	4 243	4 388	4 374	4 508	4 492
Black, Both Sexes, 16 to 19 Years[1]										
Civilian noninstitutional population	2 160	2 137	2 163	2 179	2 176	2 238	2 187	2 155	2 181	2 211
Civilian labor force	889	883	899	889	925	866	774	816	807	852
Employed	532	536	587	601	625	598	494	492	494	552
Agriculture	16	8	9	7	8	7	8	7	9	1
Nonagricultural industries	516	529	578	594	617	591	486	485	485	547
Unemployed	357	347	312	288	300	268	280	324	313	300
Not in labor force	1 271	1 254	1 264	1 291	1 251	1 372	1 413	1 339	1 374	1 360

[1]Beginning in 2003, persons who selected this race group only; persons who selected more than one race group are not included. Prior to 2003, persons who reported more than one race group were included in the group they identified as the main race.

Table 1-3. Employment Status of the Civilian Noninstitutional Population by Sex, Race, Hispanic Origin, and Age, 1985–2004—*Continued*

(Thousands of people.)

Employment status, sex, and age	1995	1996	1997	1998	1999	2000	2001	2002	2003	2004
Total, Black[1]										
Civilian noninstitutional population	23 246	23 604	24 003	24 373	24 855	24 902	25 138	25 578	25 686	26 065
Civilian labor force	14 817	15 134	15 529	15 982	16 365	16 397	16 421	16 565	16 526	16 638
Employed	13 279	13 542	13 969	14 556	15 056	15 156	15 006	14 872	14 739	14 909
Agriculture	101	98	117	138	117	77	62	69	63	50
Nonagricultural industries	13 178	13 444	13 852	14 417	14 939	15 079	14 944	14 804	14 676	14 859
Unemployed	1 538	1 592	1 560	1 426	1 309	1 241	1 416	1 693	1 787	1 729
Not in labor force	8 429	8 470	8 474	8 391	8 490	8 505	8 717	9 013	9 161	9 428
Black Men, 16 Years and Older[1]										
Civilian noninstitutional population	10 411	10 575	10 763	10 927	11 143	11 129	11 172	11 391	11 454	11 656
Civilian labor force	7 183	7 264	7 354	7 542	7 652	7 702	7 647	7 794	7 711	7 773
Employed	6 422	6 456	6 607	6 871	7 027	7 082	6 938	6 959	6 820	6 912
Agriculture	93	86	103	118	99	67	56	63	52	43
Nonagricultural industries	6 329	6 371	6 504	6 752	6 952	7 015	6 882	6 896	6 768	6 869
Unemployed	762	808	747	671	671	620	709	835	891	860
Not in labor force	3 228	3 311	3 409	3 386	3 386	3 427	3 525	3 597	3 743	3 884
Black Men, 20 Years and Older[1]										
Civilian noninstitutional population	9 280	9 414	9 575	9 727	9 926	9 952	9 993	10 196	10 278	10 461
Civilian labor force	6 730	6 806	6 910	7 053	7 182	7 240	7 200	7 347	7 346	7 414
Employed	6 137	6 167	6 325	6 530	6 702	6 741	6 627	6 652	6 586	6 681
Agriculture	89	83	101	112	96	67	55	62	51	43
Nonagricultural industries	6 048	6 084	6 224	6 418	6 606	6 675	55	6 591	6 535	6 638
Unemployed	593	639	585	524	480	499	573	695	760	733
Not in labor force	2 550	2 608	2 665	2 673	2 743	2 711	2 792	2 848	2 932	3 047
Black Women, 16 Years and Older[1]										
Civilian noninstitutional population	12 835	13 029	13 241	13 446	13 711	13 772	13 966	14 187	14 232	14 409
Civilian labor force	7 634	7 869	8 175	8 441	8 713	8 695	8 774	8 772	8 815	8 865
Employed	6 857	7 086	7 362	7 685	8 029	8 073	8 068	7 914	7 919	7 997
Agriculture	8	13	14	20	18	10	6	6	11	7 990
Nonagricultural industries	6 849	7 073	7 348	7 665	8 011	8 064	8 062	7 907	7 908	7
Unemployed	777	784	813	756	684	621	706	858	895	868
Not in labor force	5 201	5 159	5 066	5 005	4 999	5 078	5 192	5 415	5 418	5 544
Black Women, 20 Years and Older[1]										
Civilian noninstitutional population	11 682	11 833	12 016	12 023	12 451	12 561	12 758	12 966	13 026	13 182
Civilian labor force	7 175	7 405	7 686	7 912	8 224	8 215	8 323	8 348	8 409	8 462
Employed	6 556	6 762	7 013	7 290	7 663	7 703	7 741	7 610	7 636	7 707
Agriculture	7	12	13	19	17	9	6	5	10	7 701
Nonagricultural industries	6 548	6 749	7 000	7 272	7 646	7 694	7 735	7 604	7 626	6
Unemployed	620	643	673	622	561	512	582	738	772	755
Not in labor force	4 507	4 428	4 330	4 291	4 226	4 346	4 434	4 618	4 618	4 720
Black, Both Sexes, 16 to 19 Years[1]										
Civilian noninstitutional population	2 284	2 356	2 412	2 443	2 479	2 389	2 388	2 416	2 382	2 423
Civilian labor force	911	923	933	1 017	959	941	898	870	771	762
Employed	586	613	631	736	691	711	637	611	516	520
Agriculture	5	3	3	8	4	1	1	2	1	0
Nonagricultural industries	581	611	611	728	687	710	637	609	515	520
Unemployed	325	310	310	281	268	230	260	260	255	241
Not in labor force	1 372	1 434	1 434	1 427	1 520	1 448	1 490	1 546	1 611	1 661

[1]Beginning in 2003, persons who selected this race group only; persons who selected more than one race group are not included. Prior to 2003, persons who reported more than one race group were included in the group they identified as the main race.

Table 1-3. Employment Status of the Civilian Noninstitutional Population by Sex, Race, Hispanic Origin, and Age, 1985–2004—*Continued*

(Thousands of people.)

Employment status, sex, and age	1985	1986	1987	1988	1989	1990	1991	1992	1993	1994
Total, Hispanic										
Civilian noninstitutional population	11 915	12 344	12 867	13 325	13 791	15 904	16 425	16 961	17 532	18 117
Civilian labor force	7 698	8 076	8 541	8 982	9 323	10 720	10 920	11 338	11 610	11 975
Employed	6 888	7 219	7 790	8 250	8 573	9 845	9 828	10 027	10 361	10 788
Agriculture	302	329	398	407	440	517	512	524	523	560
Nonagricultural industries	6 586	6 890	7 391	7 843	8 133	9 328	9 315	9 503	9 838	10 227
Unemployed	811	857	751	732	750	876	1 092	1 311	1 248	1 187
Not in labor force	4 217	4 268	4 327	4 342	4 468	5 184	5 506	5 623	5 922	6 142
Hispanic Men, 16 Years and Older										
Civilian noninstitutional population	5 885	6 106	6 371	6 604	6 825	8 041	8 296	8 553	8 824	9 104
Civilian labor force	4 729	4 948	5 163	5 409	5 595	6 546	6 664	6 900	7 076	7 210
Employed	4 245	4 428	4 713	4 972	5 172	6 021	5 979	6 093	6 328	6 530
Agriculture	264	287	351	356	393	449	453	468	469	494
Nonagricultural industries	3 981	4 140	4 361	4 616	4 779	5 572	5 526	5 625	5 860	6 036
Unemployed	483	520	451	437	423	524	685	807	747	680
Not in labor force	1 157	1 158	1 208	1 195	1 230	1 495	1 632	1 654	1 749	1 894
Hispanic Men, 20 Years and Older										
Civilian noninstitutional population	5 232	5 451	5 700	5 921	6 114	7 126	7 392	7 655	7 930	8 178
Civilian labor force	4 395	4 612	4 818	5 031	5 195	6 034	6 198	6 432	6 621	6 747
Employed	3 994	4 174	4 444	4 680	4 853	5 609	5 623	5 757	5 992	6 189
Agriculture	239	263	327	327	366	415	419	437	441	466
Nonagricultural industries	3 754	3 911	4 118	4 353	4 487	5 195	5 204	5 320	5 551	5 722
Unemployed	401	438	374	351	342	425	575	675	629	558
Not in labor force	837	839	882	890	919	1 092	1 194	1 223	1 309	1 431
Hispanic Women, 16 Years and Older										
Civilian noninstitutional population	6 029	6 238	6 496	6 721	6 965	7 863	8 130	8 408	8 708	9 014
Civilian labor force	2 970	3 128	3 377	3 573	3 728	4 174	4 256	4 439	4 534	4 765
Employed	2 642	2 791	3 077	3 278	3 401	3 823	3 848	3 934	4 033	4 258
Agriculture	38	42	47	51	48	68	59	57	55	66
Nonagricultural industries	2 604	2 749	3 030	3 227	3 353	3 755	3 789	3 877	3 978	4 191
Unemployed	327	337	300	296	327	351	407	504	501	508
Not in labor force	3 059	3 110	3 119	3 147	3 237	3 689	3 874	3 969	4 174	4 248
Hispanic Women, 20 Years and Older										
Civilian noninstitutional population	5 385	5 591	5 835	6 050	6 278	7 041	7 301	7 569	7 846	8 122
Civilian labor force	2 893	3 112	3 281	3 448	3 857	3 941	4 110	4 218	4 421	4 520
Employed	2 456	2 615	2 872	3 047	3 172	3 567	3 603	3 693	3 800	3 989
Agriculture	31	39	45	49	44	62	53	51	49	61
Nonagricultural industries	2 424	2 576	2 827	2 998	3 128	3 505	3 549	3 642	3 751	3 928
Unemployed	269	278	241	234	276	289	339	418	418	431
Not in labor force	2 660	2 698	2 723	2 769	2 830	3 184	3 360	3 459	3 628	3 701
Hispanic Both Sexes, 16 to 19 Years										
Civilian noninstitutional population	1 298	1 302	1 332	1 354	1 399	1 737	1 732	1 737	1 756	1 818
Civilian labor force	579	571	610	671	680	829	781	796	771	807
Employed	438	430	474	523	548	668	602	577	570	609
Agriculture	31	27	27	32	31	40	41	36	33	32
Nonagricultural industries	407	403	447	492	517	628	562	541	537	577
Unemployed	141	141	136	148	132	161	179	219	201	198
Not in labor force	719	730	722	683	719	907	951	941	985	1 010

Table 1-3. Employment Status of the Civilian Noninstitutional Population by Sex, Race, Hispanic Origin, and Age, 1985–2004—*Continued*

(Thousands of people.)

Employment status, sex, and age	1995	1996	1997	1998	1999	2000	2001	2002	2003	2004
Total, Hispanic										
Civilian noninstitutional population	18 629	19 213	20 321	21 070	21 650	23 938	24 942	25 963	27 551	28 109
Civilian labor force	12 267	12 774	13 796	14 317	14 665	16 689	17 328	17 943	18 813	19 272
Employed	11 127	11 642	12 726	13 291	13 720	15 735	16 190	16 590	17 372	17 930
Agriculture	604	609	660	742	734	536	423	448	446	441
Nonagricultural industries	10 524	11 033	12 067	12 549	12 986	15 199	15 767	16 141	16 927	17 489
Unemployed	1 140	1 132	1 069	1 026	945	954	1 138	1 353	1 441	1 342
Not in labor force	6 362	6 439	6 526	6 753	6 985	7 249	7 614	8 020	8 738	8 837
Hispanic Men, 16 Years and Older										
Civilian noninstitutional population	9 329	9 604	10 368	10 734	10 713	12 174	12 695	13 221	14 098	14 417
Civilian labor force	7 376	7 646	8 309	8 571	8 546	9 923	10 279	10 609	11 288	11 587
Employed	6 725	7 039	7 728	8 018	8 067	9 428	9 668	9 845	10 479	10 832
Agriculture	527	537	571	651	642	449	345	361	350	356
Nonagricultural industries	6 198	6 502	7 157	7 367	7 425	8 979	9 323	9 484	10 129	10 476
Unemployed	651	607	582	552	480	494	611	764	809	755
Not in labor force	1 952	1 957	2 059	2 164	2 167	2 252	2 416	2 613	2 810	2 831
Hispanic Men, 20 Years and Older										
Civilian noninstitutional population	8 375	8 611	9 250	9 573	9 523	10 841	11 386	11 928	12 797	13 082
Civilian labor force	6 898	7 150	7 779	8 005	7 950	9 247	9 595	9 977	10 756	11 020
Employed	6 367	6 655	7 307	7 570	7 576	8 859	9 100	9 341	10 063	10 385
Agriculture	501	510	544	621	602	423	328	345	336	335
Nonagricultural industries	5 866	6 145	6 763	6 949	6 974	8 435	8 773	8 996	9 727	10 050
Unemployed	530	495	471	436	374	388	495	636	693	635
Not in labor force	1 477	1 461	1 471	1 568	1 573	1 595	1 791	1 951	2 041	2 061
Hispanic Women, 16 Years and Older										
Civilian noninstitutional population	9 300	9 610	9 953	10 335	10 937	11 764	12 247	12 742	13 452	13 692
Civilian labor force	4 891	5 128	5 486	5 746	6 119	6 767	7 049	7 334	7 525	7 685
Employed	4 403	4 602	4 999	5 273	5 653	6 307	6 522	6 744	6 894	7 098
Agriculture	76	72	89	91	92	87	77	87	96	85
Nonagricultural industries	4 326	4 531	4 910	5 182	5 561	6 220	6 445	6 657	6 798	7 013
Unemployed	488	525	488	473	466	460	527	590	631	587
Not in labor force	4 409	4 482	4 466	4 589	4 819	4 997	5 198	5 408	5 928	6 007
Hispanic Women, 20 Years and Older										
Civilian noninstitutional population	8 382	8 654	8 950	9 292	9 821	10 574	11 049	11 528	12 211	12 420
Civilian labor force	4 779	5 106	5 304	5 666	6 275	6 557	6 863	7 096	7 096	7 257
Employed	4 116	4 341	4 705	4 928	5 290	5 903	6 121	6 367	6 541	6 752
Agriculture	72	69	83	85	88	81	73	84	91	78
Nonagricultural industries	4 044	4 272	4 622	4 843	5 202	5 822	6 048	6 283	6 450	6 674
Unemployed	404	438	401	376	376	371	436	496	555	504
Not in labor force	3 863	3 875	3 845	3 988	4 155	4 299	4 492	4 666	5 114	5 163
Hispanic Both Sexes, 16 to 19 Years										
Civilian noninstitutional population	1 872	1 948	2 121	2 204	2 307	2 523	2 508	2 507	2 543	2 608
Civilian labor force	850	845	911	1 007	1 049	1 168	1 176	1 103	960	995
Employed	645	646	714	793	854	973	969	882	768	792
Agriculture	31	29	33	36	45	31	22	19	19	25
Nonagricultural industries	614	617	682	757	809	942	947	863	749	767
Unemployed	205	199	197	214	196	194	208	221	192	203
Not in labor force	1 022	1 103	1 210	1 197	1 257	1 355	1 331	1 404	1 583	1 612

Note: Persons of Hispanic origin may be of any race.

Table 1-4. Employment Status of the Civilian Noninstitutional Population by Marital Status, Sex, and Race, 1985–2004

(Thousands of people.)

Year	Men				Women			
	Civilian noninstitutional population	Civilian labor force			Civilian noninstitutional population	Civilian labor force		
		Total	Employed	Unemployed		Total	Employed	Unemployed
Total: Single								
1985	23 328	17 208	15 022	2 186	19 768	13 163	11 758	1 404
1986	23 662	17 553	15 407	2 146	20 113	13 512	12 071	1 442
1987	23 947	17 772	15 794	1 978	20 596	13 885	12 561	1 323
1988	24 572	18 345	16 521	1 824	20 961	14 194	12 979	1 215
1989	24 831	18 738	16 936	1 801	21 141	14 377	13 175	1 202
1990	25 870	19 357	17 405	1 952	21 901	14 612	13 336	1 276
1991	26 197	19 411	17 011	2 400	22 173	14 681	13 198	1 482
1992	26 436	19 709	17 098	2 611	22 475	14 872	13 263	1 609
1993	26 570	19 706	17 261	2 445	22 713	15 031	13 484	1 547
1994	26 786	19 786	17 604	2 181	23 000	15 333	13 847	1 486
1995	26 918	19 841	17 833	2 007	23 151	15 467	14 053	1 413
1996	27 387	20 071	18 055	2 016	23 623	15 842	14 403	1 439
1997	28 311	20 689	18 783	1 906	24 285	16 492	15 037	1 455
1998	28 693	21 037	19 240	1 798	24 941	17 087	15 755	1 332
1999	29 104	21 351	19 686	1 665	25 576	17 575	16 267	1 308
2000	29 887	22 002	20 339	1 663	25 920	17 849	16 628	1 221
2001	30 646	22 285	20 298	1 988	26 462	18 021	16 635	1 386
2002	31 072	22 289	19 983	2 306	26 999	18 203	16 583	1 621
2003	31 691	22 297	19 841	2 457	27 802	18 397	16 723	1 674
2004	32 422	22 776	20 395	2 381	28 228	18 616	16 995	1 621
Total: Married, Spouse Present								
1985	52 128	41 014	39 248	1 767	51 832	27 894	26 336	1 558
1986	52 769	41 477	39 658	1 819	52 158	28 623	27 144	1 479
1987	53 223	41 889	40 265	1 625	52 532	29 381	28 107	1 273
1988	53 246	41 832	40 472	1 360	52 775	29 921	28 756	1 166
1989	53 530	42 036	40 760	1 276	52 885	30 548	29 404	1 145
1990	53 793	42 275	40 829	1 446	52 917	30 901	29 714	1 188
1991	54 158	42 303	40 429	1 875	53 169	31 112	29 698	1 415
1992	54 509	42 491	40 341	2 150	53 501	31 700	30 100	1 600
1993	55 178	42 834	40 935	1 899	53 838	31 980	30 499	1 482
1994	55 560	43 005	41 414	1 592	54 155	32 888	31 536	1 352
1995	56 100	43 472	42 048	1 424	54 716	33 359	32 063	1 296
1996	56 363	43 739	42 417	1 322	54 970	33 618	32 406	1 211
1997	56 396	43 808	42 642	1 167	54 915	33 802	32 755	1 047
1998	56 670	43 957	42 923	1 034	55 331	33 857	32 872	985
1999	57 089	44 244	43 254	990	56 178	34 372	33 450	921
2000	58 167	44 987	44 078	908	57 557	35 146	34 209	937
2001	58 448	45 233	44 007	1 226	57 610	35 236	34 153	1 083
2002	59 102	45 766	44 116	1 650	58 165	35 477	34 153	1 323
2003	60 063	46 404	44 653	1 751	59 069	36 046	34 695	1 352
2004	60 412	46 550	45 084	1 466	59 278	35 845	34 600	1 244
Total: Divorced, Widowed, or Separated								
1985	9 013	6 190	5 621	568	22 136	9 993	9 165	828
1986	9 367	6 392	5 827	565	22 518	10 277	9 491	787
1987	9 729	6 546	6 048	498	22 726	10 393	9 665	727
1988	10 039	6 751	6 280	471	23 020	10 627	9 962	665
1989	10 401	7 066	6 618	448	23 604	11 104	10 448	656
1990	10 714	7 378	6 871	508	23 968	11 315	10 639	676
1991	10 924	7 454	6 783	671	24 304	11 385	10 600	786
1992	11 325	7 763	7 001	762	24 559	11 570	10 689	881
1993	11 584	7 864	7 153	711	24 955	11 784	10 927	856
1994	12 008	2 076	7 432	594	25 304	12 018	11 227	791
1995	12 160	2 018	7 496	551	25 539	12 118	11 407	712
1996	12 456	2 103	7 735	541	25 791	12 397	11 691	706
1997	13 009	2 316	8 260	504	26 218	12 742	12 082	660
1998	13 394	2 332	8 530	435	26 190	12 771	12 143	628
1999	13 528	2 290	8 507	411	26 276	12 909	12 324	585
2000	13 910	9 291	8 888	403	27 135	13 308	12 748	559
2001	14 188	9 367	8 892	476	27 738	13 592	12 949	642
2002	14 411	9 445	8 804	641	27 821	13 683	12 846	837
2003	14 680	9 537	8 838	699	27 862	13 828	12 986	842
2004	14 875	9 654	9 045	608	28 141	13 961	13 133	828

Table 1-4. Employment Status of the Civilian Noninstitutional Population by Marital Status, Sex, and Race, 1985–2004—*Continued*

(Thousands of people.)

Year	Men				Women			
	Civilian noninstitutional population	Civilian labor force			Civilian noninstitutional population	Civilian labor force		
		Total	Employed	Unemployed		Total	Employed	Unemployed
White: Single[1]								
1985	19 100	14 426	12 875	1 550	15 472	10 705	9 828	877
1986	19 316	14 672	13 162	1 510	15 686	10 965	10 060	906
1987	19 526	14 850	13 449	1 401	15 990	11 196	10 382	815
1988	19 966	15 279	13 982	1 297	16 218	11 428	10 674	754
1989	20 076	15 511	14 249	1 263	16 289	11 474	10 741	734
1990	20 746	15 993	14 617	1 376	16 555	11 522	10 729	794
1991	20 899	15 989	14 233	1 756	16 569	11 497	10 557	939
1992	21 025	16 129	14 285	1 844	16 684	11 502	10 526	976
1993	20 974	16 033	14 303	1 730	16 768	11 613	10 633	980
1994	21 071	16 074	14 539	1 535	16 936	11 805	10 885	920
1995	21 132	16 080	14 674	1 406	17 046	11 830	10 967	864
1996	21 454	16 285	14 891	1 394	17 282	11 977	11 099	878
1997	22 236	16 810	15 507	1 303	17 728	12 322	11 443	879
1998	22 513	17 007	15 746	1 261	18 247	12 742	11 945	797
1999	22 788	17 272	16 116	1 157	18 635	13 029	12 206	823
2000	23 266	17 659	16 504	1 154	18 808	13 215	12 449	766
2001	23 979	17 970	16 561	1 409	19 253	13 368	12 491	877
2002	24 289	17 924	16 289	1 635	19 625	13 556	12 550	1 006
2003	24 419	17 755	16 031	1 723	19 924	13 462	12 461	1 001
2004	24 929	18 090	16 435	1 655	20 210	13 597	12 628	969
White: Married, Spouse Present[1]								
1985	46 925	36 934	35 472	1 462	46 728	24 777	23 468	1 308
1986	47 399	37 230	35 727	1 503	46 892	25 368	24 141	1 226
1987	47 690	37 486	36 127	1 359	47 180	26 014	24 969	1 045
1988	47 685	37 429	36 304	1 125	47 364	26 499	25 540	959
1989	47 883	37 589	36 545	1 044	47 382	27 030	26 083	947
1990	47 841	37 515	36 338	1 177	47 240	27 271	26 285	986
1991	48 137	37 507	35 923	1 585	47 456	27 479	26 290	1 189
1992	48 416	37 671	35 886	1 785	47 705	27 951	26 623	1 329
1993	48 937	37 953	36 396	1 557	47 944	28 221	26 993	1 228
1994	49 169	38 008	36 719	1 288	48 120	29 017	27 888	1 129
1995	49 597	38 376	37 211	1 165	48 497	29 360	28 290	1 070
1996	49 800	38 616	37 522	1 094	48 684	29 517	28 496	1 020
1997	49 719	38 593	37 636	957	48 542	29 664	28 809	855
1998	49 901	38 629	37 793	836	48 722	29 534	28 727	808
1999	50 091	38 765	37 968	797	49 296	29 806	29 056	749
2000	50 775	39 169	38 451	717	50 194	30 344	29 582	762
2001	50 850	39 246	38 265	981	50 077	30 336	29 472	864
2002	51 284	39 580	38 261	1 319	50 489	30 511	29 463	1 048
2003	51 859	39 908	38 529	1 379	50 957	30 805	29 740	1 065
2004	51 992	39 935	38 774	1 161	50 939	30 544	29 549	996
White: Divorced, Widowed, or Separated[1]								
1985	7 348	5 112	4 698	414	18 106	7 973	7 393	580
1986	7 675	5 315	4 896	420	18 463	8 251	7 675	576
1987	7 974	5 443	5 070	373	18 599	8 300	7 791	509
1988	8 204	5 608	5 265	344	18 758	8 512	8 047	464
1989	8 509	5 887	5 558	329	19 200	8 863	8 409	454
1990	8 782	6 131	5 748	382	19 461	9 016	8 544	471
1991	8 941	6 159	5 641	518	19 757	9 111	8 538	573
1992	9 210	6 368	5 788	580	19 931	9 216	8 561	654
1993	9 459	6 498	5 957	541	20 206	9 382	8 764	618
1994	9 819	6 644	6 193	451	20 439	9 533	8 965	569
1995	10 005	6 689	6 261	428	20 638	9 613	9 087	526
1996	10 234	6 883	6 474	408	20 862	9 831	9 325	506
1997	10 622	7 236	6 855	382	21 147	10 068	9 607	461
1998	10 937	7 398	7 064	334	21 157	10 104	9 656	449
1999	11 050	7 375	7 056	320	21 225	10 261	9 834	427
2000	11 329	7 638	7 333	305	21 847	10 521	10 105	416
2001	11 623	7 750	7 386	364	22 330	10 729	10 255	474
2002	11 789	7 804	7 299	505	22 308	10 775	10 151	624
2003	11 971	7 846	7 305	541	22 162	10 769	10 168	602
2004	12 124	7 969	7 503	466	22 450	10 950	10 350	600

[1]Beginning in 2003, persons who selected this race group only; persons who selected more than one race group are not included. Prior to 2003, persons who reported more than one race group were included in the group they identified as the main race.

Table 1-4. Employment Status of the Civilian Noninstitutional Population by Marital Status, Sex, and Race, 1985–2004—*Continued*

(Thousands of people.)

Year	Men				Women			
	Civilian noninstitutional population	Civilian labor force			Civilian noninstitutional population	Civilian labor force		
		Total	Employed	Unemployed		Total	Employed	Unemployed
Black and Other Races: Single[1]								
1985	4 228	2 782	2 147	635	4 297	2 458	1 930	528
1986	4 345	2 881	2 245	636	4 427	2 547	2 011	536
1987	4 421	2 922	2 345	577	4 606	2 688	2 179	509
1988	4 606	3 066	2 539	527	4 743	2 766	2 304	461
1989	4 755	3 227	2 687	538	4 852	2 903	2 434	468
1990	5 124	3 364	2 788	576	5 346	3 090	2 607	482
1991	5 298	3 422	2 778	644	5 604	3 184	2 641	543
1992	5 411	3 580	2 813	767	5 791	3 370	2 737	633
1993	5 596	3 673	2 958	715	5 945	3 418	2 851	567
1994	5 715	3 712	3 065	646	6 064	3 528	2 962	566
1995	5 786	3 761	3 159	601	6 105	3 637	3 086	549
1996	5 933	3 786	3 164	622	6 341	3 865	3 304	561
1997	6 075	3 879	3 276	603	6 557	4 170	3 594	576
1998	6 180	4 030	3 494	537	6 694	4 345	3 810	535
1999	6 316	4 079	3 570	508	6 941	4 546	4 061	485
2000	6 621	4 343	3 835	509	7 112	4 634	4 179	455
2001	6 667	4 315	3 737	579	7 209	4 653	4 144	509
2002	6 783	4 365	3 694	671	7 374	4 647	4 033	615
2003	7 272	4 542	3 810	734	7 878	4 935	4 262	673
2004	7 493	4 686	3 960	726	8 018	5 019	4 367	652
Black and Other Races: Married, Spouse Present[1]								
1985	5 203	4 080	3 775	305	5 104	3 118	2 868	250
1986	5 370	4 247	3 931	316	5 266	3 255	3 003	253
1987	5 534	4 403	4 137	266	5 352	3 367	3 138	228
1988	5 560	4 403	4 168	234	5 411	3 422	3 215	207
1989	5 647	4 447	4 215	232	5 503	3 518	3 321	198
1990	5 952	4 760	4 491	269	5 677	3 630	3 429	202
1991	6 021	4 796	4 506	290	5 713	3 633	3 408	226
1992	6 093	4 820	4 455	365	5 796	3 749	3 477	271
1993	6 241	4 881	4 539	342	5 894	3 759	3 506	254
1994	6 391	4 997	4 695	304	6 035	3 871	3 648	223
1995	6 503	5 096	4 837	259	6 219	3 999	3 773	226
1996	6 563	5 123	4 895	228	6 286	4 101	3 910	191
1997	6 677	5 215	5 006	210	6 373	4 138	3 946	192
1998	6 769	5 328	5 130	198	6 609	4 323	4 145	177
1999	6 998	5 479	5 286	193	6 882	4 566	4 394	172
2000	7 392	5 818	5 627	191	7 363	4 802	4 627	175
2001	7 598	5 987	5 742	245	7 533	4 900	4 681	219
2002	7 818	6 186	5 855	331	7 676	4 966	4 690	275
2003	8 204	6 496	6 124	372	8 112	5 241	4 955	287
2004	8 420	6 615	6 310	305	8 339	5 301	5 051	248
Black and Other Races: Divorced, Widowed or Separated[1]								
1985	1 665	1 078	923	155	4 030	2 020	1 772	248
1986	1 692	1 076	931	146	4 055	2 026	1 816	210
1987	1 755	1 103	977	125	4 127	2 093	1 875	218
1988	1 836	1 142	1 015	127	4 262	2 115	1 914	201
1989	1 892	1 179	1 060	119	4 404	2 241	2 039	202
1990	1 932	1 247	1 123	126	4 507	2 299	2 095	205
1991	1 983	1 295	1 142	153	4 547	2 274	2 062	213
1992	2 115	1 395	1 213	182	4 628	2 354	2 128	227
1993	2 125	1 366	1 196	170	4 749	2 402	2 163	238
1994	2 189	1 382	1 239	143	4 865	2 485	2 262	222
1995	2 155	1 358	1 235	123	4 901	2 505	2 320	186
1996	2 222	1 394	1 261	133	4 929	2 566	2 366	200
1997	2 387	1 528	1 405	122	5 071	2 674	2 475	199
1998	2 457	1 567	1 466	101	5 033	2 667	2 487	179
1999	2 478	1 543	1 451	91	5 051	2 648	2 490	158
2000	2 581	1 653	1 555	98	5 288	2 787	2 643	143
2001	2 565	1 617	1 506	112	5 408	2 863	2 694	168
2002	2 622	1 641	1 505	136	5 513	2 908	2 695	213
2003	2 709	1 691	1 533	158	5 700	3 059	2 818	240
2004	2 751	1 685	1 542	142	5 691	3 011	2 783	228

Note: See "Notes and Definitions" for information on historical comparability.

[1]Beginning in 2003, persons who selected this race group only; persons who selected more than one race group are not included. Prior to 2003, persons who reported more than one race group were included in the group they identified as the main race.

Table 1-5. Employment Status of the Civilian Noninstitutional Population by Region, Division, and State, 2003–2004

(Thousands of people, percent.)

Region, division, and state	2003						2004					
	Civilian noninstitutional population	Civilian labor force					Civilian noninstitutional population	Civilian labor force				
		Total	Participation rate	Employed	Unemployed	Unemploy-ment rate		Total	Participation rate	Employed	Unemployed	Unemploy-ment rate
UNITED STATES [1]	221 168	146 510	66.2	137 736	8 774	6.0	223 357	147 401	66.0	139 252	8 149	5.5
Northeast	42 237	27 408	64.9	25 796	1 612	5.9	42 429	27 546	64.9	26 081	1 466	5.3
New England	11 091	7 551	68.1	7 140	410	5.4	11 155	7 529	67.5	7 166	363	4.8
Connecticut	2 680	1 805	67.4	1 706	99	5.5	2 700	1 797	66.6	1 710	88	4.9
Maine	1 042	694	66.6	660	35	5.0	1 055	699	66.3	667	32	4.6
Massachusetts	5 027	3 414	67.9	3 216	198	5.8	5 036	3 393	67.4	3 219	174	5.1
New Hampshire	1 005	717	71.3	685	32	4.5	1 018	723	71.0	696	27	3.8
Rhode Island	844	569	67.4	538	31	5.4	848	562	66.3	533	29	5.2
Vermont	494	352	71.3	336	16	4.5	499	353	70.7	340	13	3.7
Middle Atlantic	31 146	19 857	63.8	18 656	1 202	6.1	31 274	20 018	64.0	18 915	1 103	5.5
New Jersey	6 618	4 371	66.0	4 115	256	5.9	6 666	4 388	65.8	4 176	212	4.8
New York	14 875	9 300	62.5	8 705	595	6.4	14 906	9 355	62.8	8 812	543	5.8
Pennsylvania	9 653	6 186	64.1	5 835	351	5.7	9 702	6 275	64.7	5 927	348	5.5
Midwest	49 984	34 284	68.6	32 263	2 020	5.9	50 378	34 440	68.4	32 472	1 968	5.7
East North Central	34 981	23 522	67.2	22 033	1 489	6.3	35 222	23 601	67.0	22 167	1 434	6.1
Illinois	9 576	6 361	66.4	5 934	427	6.7	9 641	6 396	66.3	6 000	396	6.2
Indiana	4 687	3 169	67.6	3 001	168	5.3	4 725	3 170	67.1	3 005	165	5.2
Michigan	7 703	5 054	65.6	4 695	358	7.1	7 748	5 079	65.6	4 719	360	7.1
Ohio	8 781	5 869	66.8	5 506	363	6.2	8 828	5 885	66.7	5 523	362	6.1
Wisconsin	4 233	3 069	72.5	2 897	172	5.6	4 280	3 071	71.8	2 919	152	4.9
West North Central	15 003	10 762	71.7	10 231	531	4.9	15 156	10 838	71.5	10 305	533	4.9
Iowa	2 287	1 620	70.8	1 548	72	4.4	2 307	1 624	70.4	1 545	78	4.8
Kansas	2 053	1 447	70.5	1 366	81	5.6	2 069	1 464	70.8	1 384	80	5.5
Minnesota	3 898	2 929	75.1	2 786	143	4.9	3 943	2 952	74.9	2 814	138	4.7
Missouri	4 378	3 014	68.8	2 846	168	5.6	4 424	3 031	68.5	2 859	172	5.7
Nebraska	1 318	976	74.1	937	39	4.0	1 331	985	74.0	948	37	3.8
North Dakota	492	351	71.3	339	13	3.6	497	354	71.2	342	12	3.4
South Dakota	578	424	73.4	409	15	3.5	586	428	73.0	413	15	3.5
South	78 713	51 235	65.1	48 300	2 935	5.7	80 003	51 767	64.7	49 037	2 730	5.3
South Atlantic	41 316	26 939	65.2	25 526	1 414	5.2	42 053	27 297	64.9	25 975	1 322	4.8
Delaware	630	420	66.7	404	17	4.0	643	423	65.8	406	17	4.1
District of Columbia	448	298	66.5	277	21	7.2	443	299	67.5	274	24	8.2
Florida	13 197	8 195	62.1	7 764	431	5.3	13 521	8 396	62.1	7 997	399	4.8
Georgia	6 416	4 341	67.7	4 135	206	4.7	6 534	4 390	67.2	4 188	202	4.6
Maryland	4 178	2 880	68.9	2 751	128	4.5	4 223	2 883	68.3	2 761	122	4.2
North Carolina	6 340	4 230	66.7	3 957	273	6.5	6 439	4 256	66.1	4 021	236	5.5
South Carolina	3 147	2 013	64.0	1 878	135	6.7	3 193	2 046	64.1	1 907	140	6.8
Virginia	5 516	3 767	68.3	3 612	155	4.1	5 605	3 815	68.1	3 674	140	3.7
West Virginia	1 445	796	55.1	748	48	6.0	1 452	788	54.3	747	42	5.3
East South Central	13 267	8 337	62.8	7 845	492	5.9	13 411	8 361	62.3	7 899	461	5.5
Alabama	3 451	2 133	61.8	2 009	124	5.8	3 484	2 149	61.7	2 029	119	5.6
Kentucky	3 163	1 979	62.6	1 856	123	6.2	3 194	1 974	61.8	1 870	104	5.3
Mississippi	2 146	1 322	61.6	1 237	85	6.4	2 169	1 330	61.3	1 248	82	6.2
Tennessee	4 507	2 903	64.4	2 742	161	5.5	4 564	2 908	63.7	2 752	156	5.4
West South Central	24 129	15 959	66.1	14 929	1 030	6.5	24 539	16 110	65.7	15 163	946	5.9
Arkansas	2 076	1 279	61.6	1 205	75	5.9	2 102	1 306	62.1	1 232	74	5.7
Louisiana	3 349	2 042	61.0	1 915	128	6.3	3 377	2 058	60.9	1 940	117	5.7
Oklahoma	2 647	1 710	64.6	1 614	95	5.6	2 671	1 710	64.0	1 628	83	4.8
Texas	16 057	10 927	68.1	10 196	731	6.7	16 388	11 035	67.3	10 363	672	6.1
West	49 706	33 228	66.8	31 048	2 181	6.6	50 546	33 648	66.6	31 663	1 985	5.9
Mountain	14 441	9 859	68.3	9 302	557	5.6	14 790	10 057	68.0	9 549	509	5.1
Arizona	4 137	2 707	65.4	2 553	154	5.7	4 266	2 774	65.0	2 637	137	5.0
Colorado	3 427	2 480	72.4	2 325	155	6.2	3 468	2 522	72.7	2 383	139	5.5
Idaho	1 014	691	68.1	654	37	5.3	1 039	703	67.7	670	33	4.7
Montana	717	473	66.0	452	21	4.4	730	483	66.2	462	21	4.4
Nevada	1 686	1 149	68.1	1 090	59	5.1	1 759	1 178	67.0	1 126	51	4.3
New Mexico	1 407	893	63.5	841	53	5.9	1 436	912	63.5	860	52	5.7
Utah	1 664	1 188	71.4	1 121	67	5.7	1 697	1 203	70.9	1 140	63	5.2
Wyoming	389	277	71.2	265	12	4.4	395	282	71.4	271	11	3.9
Pacific	35 266	23 370	66.3	21 746	1 624	6.9	35 755	23 591	66.0	22 114	1 476	6.3
Alaska	457	331	72.4	305	26	7.7	465	333	71.6	308	25	7.5
California	26 412	17 414	65.9	16 223	1 190	6.8	26 768	17 552	65.6	16 460	1 092	6.2
Hawaii	932	612	65.7	589	24	3.9	946	616	65.1	596	20	3.3
Oregon	2 768	1 852	66.9	1 702	151	8.1	2 800	1 856	66.3	1 719	138	7.4
Washington	4 696	3 160	67.3	2 927	233	7.4	4 777	3 234	67.7	3 032	201	6.2
Puerto Rico [2]	2 918	1 364	46.7	1 200	163	12.0	2 938	1 371	46.7	1 226	145	10.6

Note: Data refer to place of residence. Region and division data are derived from summing the component states. Sub-national data except for Puerto Rico incorporate updated Census 2000-based population controls.

[1]Due to separate processing and weighing procedures, totals for the United States differ from the results obtained by aggregating data for regions, divisions, or states.
[2]Data from Puerto Rico are derived from a monthly household survey similar to the Current Population Survey (CPS).

Table 1-6. Civilian Noninstitutional Population by Sex, Race, Age, and Hispanic Origin, 1948–2004

(Thousands of people.)

Year, sex, race, and Hispanic origin	16 years and over	16 to 19 years			20 years and over						
		Total	16 to 17 years	18 to 19 years	Total	20 to 24 years	25 to 34 years	35 to 44 years	45 to 54 years	55 to 64 years	65 years and over
Total											
1948	103 068	8 449	4 265	4 185	94 618	11 530	22 610	20 097	16 771	12 885	10 720
1949	103 994	8 215	4 139	4 079	95 778	11 312	22 822	20 401	17 002	13 201	11 035
1950	104 995	8 143	4 076	4 068	96 851	11 080	23 013	20 681	17 240	13 469	11 363
1951	104 621	7 865	4 096	3 771	96 755	10 167	22 843	20 863	17 464	13 692	11 724
1952	105 231	7 922	4 234	3 689	97 305	9 389	23 044	21 137	17 716	13 889	12 126
1953	107 056	8 014	4 241	3 773	99 041	8 960	23 266	21 922	17 991	13 830	13 075
1954	108 321	8 224	4 336	3 889	100 095	8 885	23 304	22 135	18 305	14 085	13 375
1955	109 683	8 364	4 440	3 925	101 318	9 036	23 249	22 348	18 643	14 309	13 728
1956	110 954	8 434	4 482	3 953	102 518	9 271	23 072	22 567	19 012	14 516	14 075
1957	112 265	8 612	4 587	4 026	103 653	9 486	22 849	22 786	19 424	14 727	14 376
1958	113 727	8 986	4 872	4 114	104 737	9 733	22 563	23 025	19 832	14 923	14 657
1959	115 329	9 618	5 337	4 282	105 711	9 975	22 201	23 207	20 203	15 134	14 985
1960	117 245	10 187	5 573	4 615	107 056	10 273	21 998	23 437	20 601	15 409	15 336
1961	118 771	10 513	5 462	5 052	108 255	10 583	21 829	23 585	20 893	15 675	15 685
1962	120 153	10 652	5 503	5 150	109 500	10 852	21 503	23 797	20 916	15 874	16 554
1963	122 416	11 370	6 301	5 070	111 045	11 464	21 400	23 948	21 144	16 138	16 945
1964	124 485	12 111	6 974	5 139	112 372	12 017	21 367	23 940	21 452	16 442	17 150
1965	126 513	12 930	6 936	5 995	113 582	12 442	21 417	23 832	21 728	16 727	17 432
1966	128 058	13 592	6 914	6 679	114 463	12 638	21 543	23 579	21 977	17 007	17 715
1967	129 874	13 480	7 003	6 480	116 391	13 421	22 057	23 313	22 256	17 310	18 029
1968	132 028	13 698	7 200	6 499	118 328	13 891	22 912	23 036	22 534	17 614	18 338
1969	134 335	14 095	7 422	6 673	120 238	14 488	23 645	22 709	22 806	17 930	18 657
1970	137 085	14 519	7 643	6 876	122 566	15 323	24 435	22 489	23 059	18 250	19 007
1971	140 216	15 022	7 849	7 173	125 193	16 345	25 337	22 274	23 244	18 581	19 406
1972	144 126	15 510	8 076	7 435	128 614	17 143	26 740	22 358	23 338	19 007	20 023
1973	147 096	15 840	8 227	7 613	131 253	17 692	28 172	22 287	23 431	19 281	20 389
1974	150 120	16 180	8 373	7 809	133 938	17 994	29 439	22 461	23 578	19 517	20 945
1975	153 153	16 418	8 419	7 999	136 733	18 595	30 710	22 526	23 535	19 844	21 525
1976	156 150	16 614	8 442	8 171	139 536	19 109	31 953	22 796	23 409	20 185	22 083
1977	159 033	16 688	8 482	8 206	142 345	19 582	33 117	23 296	23 197	20 557	22 597
1978	161 910	16 695	8 484	8 211	145 216	20 007	34 091	24 099	22 977	20 875	23 166
1979	164 863	16 657	8 389	8 268	148 205	20 353	35 261	24 861	22 752	21 210	23 767
1980	167 745	16 543	8 279	8 264	151 202	20 635	36 558	25 578	22 563	21 520	24 350
1981	170 130	16 214	8 068	8 145	153 916	20 820	37 777	26 291	22 422	21 756	24 850
1982	172 271	15 763	7 714	8 049	156 508	20 845	38 492	27 611	22 264	21 909	25 387
1983	174 215	15 274	7 385	7 889	158 941	20 799	39 147	28 932	22 167	22 003	25 892
1984	176 383	14 735	7 196	7 538	161 648	20 688	39 999	30 251	22 226	22 052	26 433
1985	178 206	14 506	7 232	7 274	163 700	20 097	40 670	31 379	22 418	22 140	26 997
1986	180 587	14 496	7 386	7 110	166 091	19 569	41 731	32 550	22 732	22 011	27 497
1987	182 753	14 606	7 501	7 104	168 147	18 970	42 297	33 755	23 183	21 835	28 108
1988	184 613	14 527	7 284	7 243	170 085	18 434	42 611	34 784	24 004	21 641	28 612
1989	186 393	14 223	6 886	7 338	172 169	18 025	42 845	35 977	24 744	21 406	29 173
1990	189 164	14 520	6 893	7 626	174 644	18 902	42 976	37 719	25 081	20 719	29 247
1991	190 925	14 073	6 901	7 173	176 852	18 963	42 688	39 116	25 709	20 675	29 700
1992	192 805	13 840	6 907	6 933	178 965	18 846	42 278	39 852	27 206	20 604	30 179
1993	194 838	13 935	7 010	6 925	180 903	18 642	41 771	40 733	28 549	20 574	30 634
1994	196 814	14 196	7 245	6 951	182 619	18 353	41 306	41 534	29 778	20 635	31 012
1995	198 584	14 511	7 407	7 104	184 073	17 864	40 798	42 254	30 974	20 735	31 448
1996	200 591	14 934	7 678	7 256	185 656	17 409	40 252	43 086	32 167	20 990	31 751
1997	203 133	15 365	7 861	7 504	187 769	17 442	39 559	43 883	33 391	21 505	31 989
1998	205 220	15 644	7 895	7 749	189 576	17 593	38 778	44 299	34 373	22 296	32 237
1999	207 753	16 040	8 060	7 979	191 713	17 968	37 976	44 635	35 587	23 064	32 484
2000	212 577	15 912	7 978	7 934	196 664	18 311	38 703	44 312	37 642	24 230	33 466
2001	215 092	15 929	8 020	7 909	199 164	18 877	38 505	44 195	38 904	25 011	33 672
2002	217 570	15 994	8 099	7 895	201 576	19 348	38 472	43 894	39 711	26 343	33 808
2003	221 168	16 096	8 561	7 535	205 072	19 801	39 021	43 746	40 522	27 728	34 253
2004	223 357	16 222	8 574	7 648	207 134	20 197	38 939	43 226	41 245	28 919	34 609

Table 1-6. Civilian Noninstitutional Population by Sex, Race, Age, and Hispanic Origin, 1948–2004
—Continued

(Thousands of people.)

Year, sex, race, and Hispanic origin	16 years and over	16 to 19 years			20 years and over						
		Total	16 to 17 years	18 to 19 years	Total	20 to 24 years	25 to 34 years	35 to 44 years	45 to 54 years	55 to 64 years	65 years and over
Men											
1948	49 996	4 078	2 128	1 951	45 918	5 527	10 767	9 798	8 290	6 441	5 093
1949	50 321	3 946	2 062	1 884	46 378	5 405	10 871	9 926	8 379	6 568	5 226
1950	50 725	3 962	2 043	1 920	46 763	5 270	10 963	10 034	8 472	6 664	5 357
1951	49 727	3 725	2 039	1 687	46 001	4 451	10 709	10 049	8 551	6 737	5 503
1952	49 700	3 767	2 121	1 647	45 932	3 788	10 855	10 164	8 655	6 798	5 670
1953	50 750	3 823	2 122	1 701	46 927	3 482	11 020	10 632	8 878	6 798	6 119
1954	51 395	3 953	2 174	1 780	47 441	3 509	11 067	10 718	9 018	6 885	6 241
1955	52 109	4 022	2 225	1 798	48 086	3 708	11 068	10 804	9 164	6 960	6 380
1956	52 723	4 020	2 238	1 783	48 704	3 970	10 983	10 889	9 322	7 032	6 505
1957	53 315	4 083	2 284	1 800	49 231	4 166	10 889	10 965	9 499	7 109	6 602
1958	54 033	4 293	2 435	1 858	49 740	4 339	10 787	11 076	9 675	7 179	6 683
1959	54 793	4 652	2 681	1 971	50 140	4 488	10 625	11 149	9 832	7 259	6 785
1960	55 662	4 963	2 805	2 159	50 698	4 679	10 514	11 230	10 000	7 373	6 901
1961	56 286	5 112	2 742	2 371	51 173	4 844	10 440	11 286	10 112	7 483	7 006
1962	56 831	5 150	2 764	2 386	51 681	4 925	10 207	11 389	10 162	7 610	7 386
1963	57 921	5 496	3 162	2 334	52 425	5 240	10 165	11 476	10 274	7 740	7 526
1964	58 847	5 866	3 503	2 364	52 981	5 520	10 144	11 466	10 402	7 873	7 574
1965	59 782	6 318	3 488	2 831	53 463	5 701	10 182	11 427	10 512	7 990	7 649
1966	60 262	6 658	3 478	3 180	53 603	5 663	10 224	11 294	10 598	8 099	7 723
1967	60 905	6 537	3 528	3 010	54 367	5 977	10 495	11 161	10 705	8 218	7 809
1968	61 847	6 683	3 634	3 049	55 165	6 127	10 944	11 040	10 819	8 336	7 897
1969	62 898	6 928	3 741	3 187	55 969	6 379	11 309	10 890	10 935	8 464	7 990
1970	64 304	7 145	3 848	3 299	57 157	6 861	11 750	10 810	11 052	8 590	8 093
1971	65 942	7 430	3 954	3 477	58 511	7 511	12 227	10 721	11 129	8 711	8 208
1972	67 835	7 705	4 081	3 624	60 130	8 061	12 911	10 762	11 167	8 895	8 330
1973	69 292	7 855	4 152	3 703	61 436	8 429	13 641	10 746	11 202	8 990	8 426
1974	70 808	8 012	4 231	3 781	62 796	8 600	14 262	10 834	11 315	9 140	8 641
1975	72 291	8 134	4 252	3 882	64 158	8 950	14 899	10 874	11 298	9 286	8 852
1976	73 759	8 244	4 266	3 978	65 515	9 237	15 528	11 010	11 243	9 444	9 053
1977	75 193	8 288	4 290	4 000	66 904	9 477	16 108	11 260	11 144	9 616	9 297
1978	76 576	8 309	4 295	4 014	68 268	9 693	16 598	11 665	11 045	9 758	9 509
1979	78 020	8 310	4 251	4 060	69 709	9 873	17 193	12 046	10 944	9 907	9 746
1980	79 398	8 260	4 195	4 064	71 138	10 023	17 833	12 400	10 861	10 042	9 979
1981	80 511	8 092	4 087	4 005	72 419	10 116	18 427	12 758	10 797	10 151	10 170
1982	81 523	7 879	3 911	3 968	73 644	10 136	18 787	13 410	10 726	10 215	10 371
1983	82 531	7 659	3 750	3 908	74 872	10 140	19 143	14 067	10 689	10 261	10 573
1984	83 605	7 386	3 655	3 731	76 219	10 108	19 596	14 719	10 724	10 285	10 788
1985	84 469	7 275	3 689	3 586	77 195	9 746	19 864	15 265	10 844	10 392	11 084
1986	85 798	7 275	3 768	3 507	78 523	9 498	20 498	15 858	10 986	10 336	11 347
1987	86 899	7 335	3 824	3 510	79 565	9 195	20 781	16 475	11 215	10 267	11 632
1988	87 857	7 304	3 715	3 588	80 553	8 931	20 937	17 008	11 625	10 193	11 859
1989	88 762	7 143	3 524	3 619	81 619	8 743	21 080	17 590	11 981	10 092	12 134
1990	90 377	7 347	3 534	3 813	83 030	9 320	21 117	18 529	12 238	9 778	12 049
1991	91 278	7 134	3 548	3 586	84 144	9 367	20 977	19 213	12 554	9 780	12 254
1992	92 270	7 023	3 542	3 481	85 247	9 326	20 792	19 585	13 271	9 776	12 496
1993	93 332	7 076	3 595	3 481	86 256	9 216	20 569	20 037	13 944	9 773	12 717
1994	94 355	7 203	3 718	3 486	87 151	9 074	20 361	20 443	14 545	9 810	12 918
1995	95 178	7 367	3 794	3 573	87 811	8 835	20 079	20 800	15 111	9 856	13 130
1996	96 206	7 600	3 955	3 645	88 606	8 611	19 775	21 222	15 674	9 997	13 327
1997	97 715	7 836	4 053	3 783	89 879	8 706	19 478	21 669	16 276	10 282	13 469
1998	98 758	7 968	4 059	3 909	90 790	8 804	19 094	21 857	16 773	10 649	13 613
1999	99 722	8 167	4 143	4 024	91 555	8 899	18 565	21 969	17 335	11 008	13 779
2000	101 964	8 089	4 096	3 993	93 875	9 101	19 106	21 683	18 365	11 583	14 037
2001	103 282	8 101	4 102	3 999	95 181	9 368	19 056	21 643	18 987	11 972	14 155
2002	104 585	8 146	4 140	4 006	96 439	9 627	19 037	21 523	19 379	12 641	14 233
2003	106 435	8 163	4 365	3 797	98 272	9 878	19 347	21 463	19 784	13 305	14 496
2004	107 710	8 234	4 318	3 916	99 476	10 125	19 358	21 255	20 160	13 894	14 684

Table 1-6. Civilian Noninstitutional Population by Sex, Race, Age, and Hispanic Origin, 1948–2004 —*Continued*

(Thousands of people.)

Year, sex, race, and Hispanic origin	16 years and over	16 to 19 years			20 years and over						
		Total	16 to 17 years	18 to 19 years	Total	20 to 24 years	25 to 34 years	35 to 44 years	45 to 54 years	55 to 64 years	65 years and over
Women											
1948	53 071	4 371	2 137	2 234	48 700	6 003	11 843	10 299	8 481	6 444	5 627
1949	53 670	4 269	2 077	2 195	49 400	5 907	11 951	10 475	8 623	6 633	5 809
1950	54 270	4 181	2 033	2 148	50 088	5 810	12 050	10 647	8 768	6 805	6 006
1951	54 895	4 140	2 057	2 084	50 754	5 716	12 134	10 814	8 913	6 955	6 221
1952	55 529	4 155	2 113	2 042	51 373	5 601	12 189	10 973	9 061	7 091	6 456
1953	56 305	4 191	2 119	2 072	52 114	5 478	12 246	11 290	9 113	7 032	6 956
1954	56 925	4 271	2 162	2 109	52 654	5 376	12 237	11 417	9 287	7 200	7 134
1955	57 574	4 342	2 215	2 127	53 232	5 328	12 181	11 544	9 479	7 349	7 348
1956	58 228	4 414	2 244	2 170	53 814	5 301	12 089	11 678	9 690	7 484	7 570
1957	58 951	4 529	2 303	2 226	54 421	5 320	11 960	11 821	9 925	7 618	7 774
1958	59 690	4 693	2 437	2 256	54 997	5 394	11 776	11 949	10 157	7 744	7 974
1959	60 534	4 966	2 656	2 311	55 570	5 487	11 576	12 058	10 371	7 875	8 200
1960	61 582	5 224	2 768	2 456	56 358	5 594	11 484	12 207	10 601	8 036	8 435
1961	62 484	5 401	2 720	2 681	57 082	5 739	11 389	12 299	10 781	8 192	8 679
1962	63 321	5 502	2 739	2 764	57 819	5 927	11 296	12 408	10 754	8 264	9 168
1963	64 494	5 874	3 139	2 736	58 620	6 224	11 235	12 472	10 870	8 398	9 419
1964	65 637	6 245	3 471	2 775	59 391	6 497	11 223	12 474	11 050	8 569	9 576
1965	66 731	6 612	3 448	3 164	60 119	6 741	11 235	12 405	11 216	8 737	9 783
1966	67 795	6 934	3 436	3 499	60 860	6 975	11 319	12 285	11 379	8 908	9 992
1967	68 968	6 943	3 475	3 470	62 026	7 445	11 562	12 152	11 551	9 092	10 220
1968	70 179	7 015	3 566	3 450	63 164	7 764	11 968	11 996	11 715	9 278	10 441
1969	71 436	7 167	3 681	3 486	64 269	8 109	12 336	11 819	11 871	9 466	10 667
1970	72 782	7 373	3 796	3 578	65 408	8 462	12 684	11 679	12 008	9 659	10 914
1971	74 274	7 591	3 895	3 697	66 682	8 834	13 110	11 553	12 115	9 870	11 198
1972	76 290	7 805	3 994	3 811	68 484	9 082	13 829	11 597	12 171	10 113	11 693
1973	77 804	7 985	4 076	3 909	69 819	9 263	14 531	11 541	12 229	10 290	11 963
1974	79 312	8 168	4 142	4 028	71 144	9 393	15 177	11 627	12 263	10 377	12 304
1975	80 860	8 285	4 168	4 117	72 576	9 645	15 811	11 652	12 237	10 558	12 673
1976	82 390	8 370	4 176	4 194	74 020	9 872	16 425	11 786	12 166	10 742	13 030
1977	83 840	8 400	4 193	4 206	75 441	10 103	17 008	12 036	12 053	10 940	13 300
1978	85 334	8 386	4 189	4 197	76 948	10 315	17 493	12 435	11 932	11 118	13 658
1979	86 843	8 347	4 139	4 208	78 496	10 480	18 070	12 815	11 808	11 303	14 021
1980	88 348	8 283	4 083	4 200	80 065	10 612	18 725	13 177	11 701	11 478	14 372
1981	89 618	8 121	3 981	4 140	81 497	10 705	19 350	13 533	11 625	11 605	14 680
1982	90 748	7 884	3 804	4 081	82 864	10 709	19 705	14 201	11 538	11 694	15 017
1983	91 684	7 616	3 635	3 981	84 069	10 660	20 004	14 865	11 478	11 742	15 319
1984	92 778	7 349	3 542	3 807	85 429	10 580	20 403	15 532	11 501	11 768	15 645
1985	93 736	7 231	3 543	3 688	86 506	10 351	20 805	16 114	11 574	11 748	15 913
1986	94 789	7 221	3 618	3 603	87 567	10 072	21 233	16 692	11 746	11 675	16 150
1987	95 853	7 271	3 677	3 594	88 583	9 776	21 516	17 279	11 968	11 567	16 476
1988	96 756	7 224	3 569	3 655	89 532	9 503	21 674	17 776	12 378	11 448	16 753
1989	97 630	7 080	3 361	3 719	90 550	9 282	21 765	18 387	12 763	11 314	17 039
1990	98 787	7 173	3 359	3 813	91 614	9 582	21 859	19 190	12 843	10 941	17 198
1991	99 646	6 939	3 353	3 586	92 708	9 597	21 711	19 903	13 155	10 895	17 446
1992	100 535	6 818	3 366	3 452	93 718	9 520	21 486	20 267	13 935	10 828	17 682
1993	101 506	6 859	3 415	3 444	94 647	9 426	21 202	20 696	14 605	10 801	17 917
1994	102 460	6 993	3 528	3 465	95 467	9 279	20 945	21 091	15 233	10 825	18 094
1995	103 406	7 144	3 613	3 531	96 262	9 029	20 719	21 454	15 862	10 879	18 318
1996	104 385	7 335	3 723	3 612	97 050	8 798	20 477	21 865	16 493	10 993	18 424
1997	105 418	7 528	3 808	3 721	97 889	8 736	20 081	22 214	17 115	11 224	18 520
1998	106 462	7 676	3 835	3 840	98 786	8 790	19 683	22 442	17 600	11 646	18 625
1999	108 031	7 873	3 917	3 955	100 158	9 069	19 411	22 666	18 251	12 056	18 705
2000	110 613	7 823	3 882	3 941	102 790	9 211	19 597	22 628	19 276	12 647	19 430
2001	111 811	7 828	3 917	3 910	103 983	9 509	19 449	22 552	19 917	13 039	19 517
2002	112 985	7 848	3 959	3 889	105 136	9 721	19 435	22 371	20 332	13 703	19 575
2003	114 733	7 934	4 195	3 738	106 800	9 924	19 674	22 283	20 738	14 423	19 758
2004	115 647	7 989	4 257	3 732	107 658	10 072	19 581	21 970	21 085	15 025	19 925

Table 1-6. Civilian Noninstitutional Population by Sex, Race, Age, and Hispanic Origin, 1948–2004
—Continued

(Thousands of people.)

Year, sex, race, and Hispanic origin	16 years and over	16 to 19 years			20 years and over						
		Total	16 to 17 years	18 to 19 years	Total	20 to 24 years	25 to 34 years	35 to 44 years	45 to 54 years	55 to 64 years	65 years and over
White[1]											
1954	97 705	7 180	3 786	3 394	90 524	7 794	20 818	19 915	16 569	12 993	12 438
1955	98 880	7 292	3 874	3 419	91 586	7 912	20 742	20 110	16 869	13 169	12 785
1956	99 976	7 346	3 908	3 438	92 629	8 106	20 564	20 314	17 198	13 341	13 105
1957	101 119	7 505	4 007	3 498	93 612	8 293	20 342	20 514	17 562	13 518	13 383
1958	102 392	7 843	4 271	3 573	94 547	8 498	20 063	20 734	17 924	13 681	13 645
1959	103 803	8 430	4 707	3 725	95 370	8 697	19 715	20 893	18 257	13 858	13 951
1960	105 282	8 924	4 909	4 016	96 355	8 927	19 470	21 049	18 578	14 070	14 260
1961	106 604	9 211	4 785	4 427	97 390	9 203	19 289	21 169	18 845	14 304	14 581
1962	107 715	9 343	4 818	4 526	98 371	9 484	18 974	21 293	18 872	14 450	15 297
1963	109 705	9 978	5 549	4 430	99 725	10 069	18 867	21 398	19 082	14 681	15 629
1964	111 534	10 616	6 137	4 481	100 916	10 568	18 838	21 375	19 360	14 957	15 816
1965	113 284	11 319	6 049	5 271	101 963	10 935	18 882	21 258	19 604	15 215	16 070
1966	114 566	11 862	5 993	5 870	102 702	11 094	18 989	21 005	19 822	15 469	16 322
1967	116 100	11 682	6 051	5 632	104 417	11 797	19 464	20 745	20 067	15 745	16 602
1968	117 948	11 840	6 225	5 616	106 107	12 184	20 245	20 474	20 310	16 018	16 875
1969	119 913	12 179	6 418	5 761	107 733	12 677	20 892	20 156	20 546	16 305	17 156
1970	122 174	12 521	6 591	5 931	109 652	13 359	21 546	19 929	20 760	16 591	17 469
1971	124 758	12 937	6 750	6 189	111 821	14 208	22 295	19 694	20 907	16 884	17 833
1972	127 906	13 301	6 910	6 392	114 603	14 897	23 555	19 673	20 950	17 250	18 278
1973	130 097	13 533	7 021	6 512	116 563	15 264	24 685	19 532	20 991	17 484	18 607
1974	132 417	13 784	7 114	6 671	118 632	15 502	25 711	19 628	21 061	17 645	19 085
1975	134 790	13 941	7 132	6 808	120 849	15 980	26 746	19 641	20 981	17 918	19 587
1976	137 106	14 055	7 125	6 930	123 050	16 368	27 757	19 827	20 816	18 220	20 064
1977	139 380	14 095	7 150	6 944	125 285	16 728	28 703	20 231	20 575	18 540	20 508
1978	141 612	14 060	7 132	6 928	127 552	17 038	29 453	20 932	20 322	18 799	21 007
1979	143 894	13 994	7 029	6 964	129 900	17 284	30 371	21 579	20 058	19 071	21 538
1980	146 122	13 854	6 912	6 943	132 268	17 484	31 407	22 174	19 837	19 316	22 050
1981	147 908	13 516	6 704	6 813	134 392	17 609	32 367	22 778	19 666	19 485	22 487
1982	149 441	13 076	6 383	6 693	136 366	17 579	32 863	23 910	19 478	19 591	22 945
1983	150 805	12 623	6 089	6 534	138 183	17 492	33 286	25 027	19 349	19 625	23 403
1984	152 347	12 147	5 918	6 228	140 200	17 304	33 889	26 124	19 348	19 629	23 906
1985	153 679	11 900	5 922	5 978	141 780	16 853	34 450	27 100	19 405	19 620	24 352
1986	155 432	11 879	6 036	5 843	143 553	16 353	35 293	28 062	19 587	19 477	24 780
1987	156 958	11 939	6 110	5 829	145 020	15 808	35 667	29 036	19 965	19 242	25 301
1988	158 194	11 838	5 893	5 945	146 357	15 276	35 876	29 818	20 652	18 996	25 739
1989	159 338	11 530	5 506	6 023	147 809	14 879	35 951	30 774	21 287	18 743	26 175
1990	160 625	11 630	5 464	6 166	148 996	15 538	35 661	31 739	21 535	18 204	26 319
1991	161 759	11 200	5 451	5 749	150 558	15 516	35 342	32 854	22 052	18 074	26 721
1992	162 972	11 004	5 478	5 526	151 968	15 354	34 885	33 305	23 364	17 951	27 108
1993	164 289	11 078	5 562	5 516	153 210	15 087	34 365	33 919	24 456	17 892	27 493
1994	165 555	11 264	5 710	5 554	154 291	14 708	33 865	34 582	25 435	17 924	27 776
1995	166 914	11 468	5 822	5 646	155 446	14 313	33 355	35 222	26 418	17 986	28 153
1996	168 317	11 822	6 026	5 796	156 495	13 907	32 852	35 810	27 403	18 136	28 387
1997	169 993	12 181	6 213	5 968	157 812	13 983	32 091	36 325	28 388	18 511	28 514
1998	171 478	12 439	6 264	6 176	159 039	14 138	31 286	36 610	29 132	19 231	28 642
1999	173 085	12 700	6 342	6 358	160 385	14 394	30 516	36 755	30 048	19 855	28 818
2000	176 220	12 535	6 264	6 271	163 685	14 552	30 948	36 261	31 550	20 757	29 617
2001	178 111	12 556	6 291	6 265	165 556	15 001	30 770	36 113	32 475	21 434	29 762
2002	179 783	12 596	6 346	6 250	167 187	15 360	30 676	35 750	33 012	22 540	29 849
2003	181 292	12 527	6 629	5 898	168 765	15 536	30 789	35 352	33 466	23 589	30 033
2004	182 643	12 599	6 561	6 038	170 045	15 817	30 585	34 845	34 005	24 549	30 245

[1]Beginning in 2003, persons who selected this race group only; persons who selected more than one race group are not included. Prior to 2003, persons who reported more than one race group were included in the group they identified as the main race.

Table 1-6. Civilian Noninstitutional Population by Sex, Race, Age, and Hispanic Origin, 1948–2004
—Continued

(Thousands of people.)

Year, sex, race, and Hispanic origin	16 years and over	16 to 19 years			20 years and over						
		Total	16 to 17 years	18 to 19 years	Total	20 to 24 years	25 to 34 years	35 to 44 years	45 to 54 years	55 to 64 years	65 years and over
Black[1]											
1972	14 526	2 018	1 061	956	12 508	2 027	2 809	2 329	2 139	1 601	1 605
1973	14 917	2 095	1 095	1 000	12 823	2 132	2 957	2 333	2 156	1 616	1 628
1974	15 329	2 137	1 122	1 014	13 192	2 137	3 103	2 382	2 202	1 679	1 689
1975	15 751	2 191	1 146	1 046	13 560	2 228	3 258	2 395	2 211	1 717	1 755
1976	16 196	2 264	1 165	1 098	13 932	2 303	3 412	2 435	2 220	1 736	1 826
1977	16 605	2 273	1 175	1 097	14 332	2 400	3 566	2 493	2 225	1 765	1 883
1978	16 970	2 270	1 169	1 101	14 701	2 483	3 717	2 547	2 226	1 794	1 932
1979	17 397	2 276	1 167	1 109	15 121	2 556	3 899	2 615	2 240	1 831	1 980
1980	17 824	2 289	1 171	1 119	15 535	2 606	4 095	2 687	2 249	1 870	2 030
1981	18 219	2 288	1 161	1 127	15 931	2 642	4 290	2 758	2 260	1 913	2 069
1982	18 584	2 252	1 119	1 134	16 332	2 697	4 438	2 887	2 263	1 935	2 113
1983	18 925	2 225	1 092	1 133	16 700	2 734	4 607	2 999	2 260	1 964	2 135
1984	19 348	2 161	1 056	1 105	17 187	2 783	4 789	3 167	2 288	1 977	2 183
1985	19 664	2 160	1 083	1 077	17 504	2 649	4 873	3 290	2 372	2 060	2 259
1986	19 989	2 137	1 090	1 048	17 852	2 625	5 026	3 410	2 413	2 079	2 298
1987	20 352	2 163	1 123	1 040	18 189	2 578	5 139	3 563	2 460	2 097	2 352
1988	20 692	2 179	1 130	1 049	18 513	2 527	5 234	3 716	2 524	2 110	2 402
1989	21 021	2 176	1 116	1 060	18 846	2 479	5 308	3 900	2 587	2 118	2 454
1990	21 477	2 238	1 101	1 138	19 239	2 554	5 407	4 328	2 618	1 970	2 362
1991	21 799	2 187	1 085	1 102	19 612	2 585	5 419	4 538	2 682	1 985	2 403
1992	22 147	2 155	1 086	1 069	19 992	2 615	5 404	4 722	2 809	1 996	2 446
1993	22 521	2 181	1 113	1 069	20 339	2 600	5 409	4 886	2 941	2 016	2 487
1994	22 879	2 211	1 168	1 044	20 668	2 616	5 362	5 038	3 084	2 045	2 524
1995	23 246	2 284	1 198	1 086	20 962	2 554	5 337	5 178	3 244	2 079	2 571
1996	23 604	2 356	1 238	1 118	21 248	2 519	5 311	5 290	3 408	2 110	2 609
1997	24 003	2 412	1 255	1 158	21 591	2 515	5 279	5 410	3 571	2 164	2 653
1998	24 373	2 443	1 241	1 202	21 930	2 546	5 221	5 510	3 735	2 224	2 695
1999	24 855	2 479	1 250	1 229	22 376	2 615	5 197	5 609	3 919	2 295	2 741
2000	24 902	2 389	1 205	1 183	22 513	2 611	5 089	5 488	4 168	2 407	2 750
2001	25 138	2 388	1 212	1 176	22 750	2 686	5 003	5 467	4 343	2 478	2 775
2002	25 578	2 416	1 235	1 181	23 162	2 779	5 015	5 460	4 513	2 571	2 823
2003	25 686	2 382	1 309	1 074	23 304	2 773	4 978	5 387	4 628	2 692	2 846
2004	26 065	2 423	1 350	1 072	23 643	2 821	5 020	5 335	4 739	2 827	2 899
Hispanic											
1973	6 104	867	. . .	. . .	5 238	. . .	. . .	. . .	. . .	. . .	. . .
1974	6 564	926	. . .	. . .	5 645	. . .	. . .	. . .	. . .	. . .	. . .
1975	6 862	962	. . .	. . .	5 900	. . .	. . .	. . .	. . .	. . .	. . .
1976	6 910	953	494	480	6 075	1 053	1 775	1 261	936	570	479
1977	7 362	1 024	513	508	6 376	1 163	1 869	1 283	989	587	485
1978	7 912	1 076	561	515	6 836	1 265	2 004	1 378	1 033	627	529
1979	8 207	1 095	544	551	7 113	1 296	2 117	1 458	1 015	659	566
1980	9 598	1 281	638	643	8 317	1 564	2 508	1 575	1 190	782	698
1981	10 120	1 301	641	660	8 819	1 650	2 698	1 680	1 231	832	728
1982	10 580	1 307	639	668	9 273	1 724	2 871	1 779	1 264	880	755
1983	11 029	1 304	635	670	9 725	1 790	3 045	1 883	1 298	928	781
1984	11 478	1 300	633	667	10 178	1 839	3 224	1 996	1 336	973	810
1985	11 915	1 298	638	661	10 617	1 864	3 401	2 117	1 377	1 015	843
1986	12 344	1 302	658	644	11 042	1 899	3 510	2 239	1 496	1 023	875
1987	12 867	1 332	651	681	11 536	1 910	3 714	2 464	1 492	1 061	895
1988	13 325	1 354	662	692	11 970	1 948	3 807	2 565	1 571	1 159	920
1989	13 791	1 399	672	727	12 392	1 950	3 953	2 658	1 649	1 182	1 001
1990	15 904	1 737	821	915	14 167	2 428	4 589	3 001	1 817	1 247	1 084
1991	16 425	1 732	819	913	14 693	2 481	4 674	3 243	1 879	1 283	1 134
1992	16 961	1 737	836	901	15 224	2 444	4 806	3 458	1 980	1 321	1 216
1993	17 532	1 756	855	901	15 776	2 487	4 887	3 632	2 094	1 324	1 353
1994	18 117	1 818	902	916	16 300	2 518	5 000	3 756	2 223	1 401	1 401
1995	18 629	1 872	903	969	16 757	2 528	5 050	3 965	2 294	1 483	1 437
1996	19 213	1 948	962	986	17 265	2 524	5 181	4 227	2 275	1 546	1 512
1997	20 321	2 121	1 088	1 033	18 200	2 623	5 405	4 453	2 581	1 580	1 558
1998	21 070	2 204	1 070	1 135	18 865	2 731	5 447	4 636	2 775	1 615	1 662
1999	21 650	2 307	1 113	1 194	19 344	2 700	5 512	4 833	2 868	1 713	1 718
2000	23 938	2 523	1 214	1 309	21 415	3 255	6 466	5 189	3 061	1 736	1 708
2001	24 942	2 508	1 173	1 334	22 435	3 417	6 726	5 346	3 339	1 816	1 792
2002	25 963	2 507	1 216	1 291	23 456	3 508	7 010	5 606	3 494	1 953	1 885
2003	27 551	2 543	1 346	1 197	25 008	3 533	7 506	6 003	3 845	2 093	2 027
2004	28 109	2 608	1 337	1 270	25 502	3 666	7 470	6 055	3 987	2 208	2 115

[1]Beginning in 2003, persons who selected this race group only; persons who selected more than one race group are not included. Prior to 2003, persons who reported more than one race group were included in the group they identified as the main race.
. . . = Not available.

Table 1-6. Civilian Noninstitutional Population by Sex, Race, Age, and Hispanic Origin, 1948–2004
—Continued

(Thousands of people.)

Year, sex, race, and Hispanic origin	16 years and over	16 to 19 years			20 years and over						
		Total	16 to 17 years	18 to 19 years	Total	20 to 24 years	25 to 34 years	35 to 44 years	45 to 54 years	55 to 64 years	65 years and over
White Men[1]											
1954	46 462	3 455	1 902	1 553	43 007	3 074	9 948	9 688	8 172	6 341	5 787
1955	47 076	3 507	1 945	1 563	43 569	3 241	9 936	9 768	8 303	6 398	5 923
1956	47 602	3 500	1 955	1 546	44 102	3 464	9 851	9 848	8 446	6 455	6 038
1957	48 119	3 556	2 000	1 557	44 563	3 638	9 758	9 917	8 605	6 518	6 127
1958	48 745	3 747	2 140	1 607	44 998	3 783	9 656	10 018	8 765	6 574	6 203
1959	49 408	4 079	2 370	1 710	45 329	3 903	9 499	10 081	8 909	6 639	6 298
1960	50 065	4 349	2 476	1 874	45 716	4 054	9 373	10 131	9 042	6 721	6 395
1961	50 608	4 479	2 407	2 073	46 129	4 204	9 290	10 178	9 148	6 819	6 490
1962	51 054	4 520	2 426	2 094	46 534	4 306	9 080	10 239	9 191	6 917	6 801
1963	52 031	4 827	2 792	2 036	47 204	4 610	9 039	10 309	9 297	7 031	6 919
1964	52 869	5 148	3 090	2 059	47 721	4 862	9 024	10 301	9 417	7 153	6 963
1965	53 681	5 541	3 050	2 492	48 140	5 017	9 056	10 262	9 516	7 261	7 028
1966	54 061	5 820	3 023	2 798	48 241	4 974	9 085	10 136	9 592	7 362	7 092
1967	54 608	5 671	3 058	2 613	48 937	5 257	9 339	10 013	9 688	7 474	7 167
1968	55 434	5 787	3 153	2 635	49 647	5 376	9 752	9 902	9 790	7 585	7 242
1969	56 348	6 005	3 246	2 759	50 343	5 589	10 074	9 760	9 895	7 705	7 320
1970	57 516	6 179	3 329	2 851	51 336	5 988	10 441	9 678	9 999	7 822	7 409
1971	58 900	6 420	3 412	3 008	52 481	6 546	10 841	9 578	10 066	7 933	7 517
1972	60 473	6 627	3 503	3 125	53 845	7 042	11 495	9 568	10 078	8 089	7 573
1973	61 577	6 737	3 555	3 182	54 842	7 312	12 075	9 514	10 099	8 178	7 664
1974	62 791	6 851	3 604	3 247	55 942	7 476	12 599	9 564	10 165	8 288	7 849
1975	63 981	6 929	3 609	3 320	57 052	7 766	13 131	9 578	10 134	8 413	8 031
1976	65 132	6 993	3 609	3 384	58 138	7 987	13 655	9 674	10 063	8 556	8 203
1977	66 301	7 024	3 625	3 399	59 278	8 175	14 139	9 880	9 957	8 708	8 420
1978	67 401	7 022	3 619	3 404	60 378	8 335	14 528	10 236	9 845	8 826	8 608
1979	68 547	7 007	3 568	3 439	61 540	8 470	15 008	10 563	9 730	8 949	8 820
1980	69 634	6 941	3 508	3 433	62 694	8 581	15 529	10 863	9 636	9 059	9 027
1981	70 480	6 764	3 401	3 363	63 715	8 644	16 005	11 171	9 560	9 139	9 195
1982	71 211	6 556	3 249	3 307	64 655	8 621	16 260	11 756	9 463	9 188	9 367
1983	71 922	6 340	3 098	3 242	65 581	8 597	16 499	12 314	9 408	9 208	9 556
1984	72 723	6 113	3 019	3 094	66 610	8 522	16 816	12 853	9 434	9 217	9 768
1985	73 373	5 987	3 026	2 961	67 386	8 246	17 042	13 337	9 488	9 262	10 010
1986	74 390	5 977	3 084	2 894	68 413	8 002	17 564	13 840	9 578	9 201	10 229
1987	75 189	6 015	3 125	2 890	69 175	7 729	17 754	14 338	9 771	9 101	10 481
1988	75 855	5 968	3 015	2 953	69 887	7 473	17 867	14 743	10 114	9 001	10 688
1989	76 468	5 813	2 817	2 996	70 654	7 279	17 908	15 237	10 434	8 900	10 897
1990	77 369	5 913	2 809	3 103	71 457	7 764	17 766	15 770	10 598	8 680	10 879
1991	77 977	5 704	2 805	2 899	72 274	7 748	17 615	16 340	10 856	8 640	11 074
1992	78 651	5 611	2 819	2 792	73 040	7 676	17 403	16 579	11 513	8 602	11 268
1993	79 371	5 650	2 862	2 788	73 721	7 545	17 158	16 900	12 058	8 590	11 470
1994	80 059	5 748	2 938	2 810	74 311	7 357	16 915	17 247	12 545	8 618	11 629
1995	80 733	5 854	2 995	2 859	74 879	7 163	16 653	17 567	13 028	8 653	11 815
1996	81 489	6 035	3 099	2 936	75 454	6 971	16 395	17 868	13 518	8 734	11 968
1997	82 577	6 257	3 209	3 048	76 320	7 087	16 043	18 163	14 030	8 929	12 067
1998	83 352	6 386	3 233	3 153	76 966	7 170	15 644	18 310	14 400	9 286	12 155
1999	83 930	6 498	3 266	3 232	77 432	7 244	15 150	18 340	14 834	9 581	12 283
2000	85 370	6 404	3 224	3 181	78 966	7 329	15 528	18 003	15 578	10 028	12 501
2001	86 452	6 422	3 229	3 194	80 029	7 564	15 486	17 960	16 047	10 369	12 604
2002	87 361	6 439	3 251	3 189	80 922	7 750	15 470	17 792	16 317	10 918	12 676
2003	88 249	6 390	3 378	3 012	81 860	7 856	15 569	17 620	16 555	11 442	12 818
2004	89 044	6 429	3 301	3 129	82 615	8 024	15 486	17 404	16 834	11 922	12 946

[1]Beginning in 2003, persons who selected this race group only; persons who selected more than one race group are not included. Prior to 2003, persons who reported more than one race group were included in the group they identified as the main race.

Table 1-6. Civilian Noninstitutional Population by Sex, Race, Age, and Hispanic Origin, 1948–2004
—Continued

(Thousands of people.)

Year, sex, race, and Hispanic origin	16 years and over	16 to 19 years			20 years and over						
		Total	16 to 17 years	18 to 19 years	Total	20 to 24 years	25 to 34 years	35 to 44 years	45 to 54 years	55 to 64 years	65 years and over
White Women[1]											
1954	51 242	3 725	1 884	1 841	47 517	4 720	10 870	10 227	8 397	6 652	6 651
1955	51 802	3 785	1 929	1 856	48 017	4 671	10 806	10 342	8 566	6 771	6 862
1956	52 373	3 846	1 953	1 892	48 527	4 642	10 713	10 466	8 752	6 886	7 067
1957	52 998	3 949	2 007	1 941	49 049	4 655	10 584	10 597	8 957	7 000	7 256
1958	53 645	4 096	2 131	1 966	49 549	4 715	10 407	10 716	9 159	7 107	7 442
1959	54 392	4 351	2 337	2 015	50 041	4 794	10 216	10 812	9 348	7 219	7 653
1960	55 214	4 575	2 433	2 142	50 639	4 873	10 097	10 918	9 536	7 349	7 865
1961	55 993	4 732	2 378	2 354	51 261	4 999	9 999	10 991	9 697	7 485	8 091
1962	56 660	4 823	2 392	2 432	51 837	5 178	9 894	11 054	9 681	7 533	8 496
1963	57 672	5 151	2 757	2 394	52 521	5 459	9 828	11 089	9 785	7 650	8 710
1964	58 663	5 468	3 047	2 422	53 195	5 706	9 814	11 074	9 943	7 804	8 853
1965	59 601	5 778	2 999	2 779	53 823	5 918	9 826	10 996	10 088	7 954	9 042
1966	60 503	6 042	2 970	3 072	54 461	6 120	9 904	10 869	10 230	8 107	9 230
1967	61 491	6 011	2 993	3 019	55 480	6 540	10 125	10 732	10 379	8 271	9 435
1968	62 512	6 053	3 072	2 981	56 460	6 809	10 493	10 572	10 520	8 433	9 633
1969	63 563	6 174	3 172	3 002	57 390	7 089	10 818	10 396	10 651	8 600	9 836
1970	64 656	6 342	3 262	3 080	58 315	7 370	11 105	10 251	10 761	8 769	10 060
1971	65 857	6 518	3 338	3 180	59 340	7 662	11 454	10 117	10 841	8 951	10 315
1972	67 431	6 673	3 407	3 267	60 758	7 855	12 060	10 105	10 872	9 161	10 705
1973	68 517	6 796	3 466	3 331	61 721	7 951	12 610	10 018	10 891	9 306	10 943
1974	69 623	6 933	3 510	3 424	62 690	8 026	13 112	10 064	10 896	9 356	11 236
1975	70 810	7 011	3 523	3 488	63 798	8 214	13 615	10 063	10 847	9 505	11 556
1976	71 974	7 062	3 516	3 546	64 912	8 381	14 102	10 153	10 752	9 664	11 860
1977	73 077	7 071	3 525	3 545	66 007	8 553	14 564	10 351	10 618	9 832	12 088
1978	74 213	7 038	3 513	3 524	67 174	8 704	14 926	10 696	10 476	9 974	12 399
1979	75 347	6 987	3 460	3 527	68 360	8 815	15 363	11 017	10 327	10 122	12 717
1980	76 489	6 914	3 403	3 511	69 575	8 904	15 878	11 313	10 201	10 256	13 022
1981	77 428	6 752	3 303	3 449	70 677	8 965	16 362	11 606	10 106	10 346	13 292
1982	78 230	6 519	3 134	3 385	71 711	8 959	16 603	12 154	10 015	10 402	13 579
1983	78 884	6 282	2 991	3 292	72 601	8 895	16 788	12 714	9 941	10 418	13 847
1984	79 624	6 034	2 899	3 135	73 590	8 782	17 073	13 271	9 914	10 412	14 138
1985	80 306	5 912	2 895	3 017	74 394	8 607	17 409	13 762	9 917	10 358	14 342
1986	81 042	5 902	2 953	2 949	75 140	8 351	17 728	14 223	10 009	10 277	14 551
1987	81 769	5 924	2 985	2 939	75 845	8 079	17 913	14 698	10 194	10 141	14 820
1988	82 340	5 869	2 878	2 991	76 470	7 804	18 009	15 074	10 537	9 994	15 052
1989	82 871	5 716	2 690	3 027	77 154	7 600	18 043	15 537	10 853	9 843	15 278
1990	83 256	5 717	2 654	3 063	77 539	7 774	17 895	15 969	10 937	9 524	15 440
1991	83 781	5 497	2 646	2 850	78 285	7 768	17 726	16 514	11 196	9 435	15 647
1992	84 321	5 393	2 659	2 734	78 928	7 678	17 482	16 727	11 851	9 350	15 841
1993	84 918	5 428	2 700	2 728	79 490	7 542	17 206	17 019	12 398	9 302	16 023
1994	85 496	5 516	2 772	2 744	79 980	7 351	16 950	17 335	12 890	9 306	16 148
1995	86 181	5 614	2 827	2 787	80 567	7 150	16 702	17 654	13 390	9 333	16 337
1996	86 828	5 787	2 927	2 860	81 041	6 936	16 457	17 943	13 884	9 402	16 419
1997	87 417	5 924	3 004	2 920	81 492	6 896	16 047	18 162	14 357	9 582	16 447
1998	88 126	6 053	3 031	3 023	82 073	6 969	15 642	18 300	14 732	9 944	16 486
1999	89 156	6 202	3 076	3 127	82 953	7 150	15 366	18 415	15 214	10 274	16 536
2000	90 850	6 131	3 041	3 090	84 718	7 223	15 420	18 258	15 972	10 729	17 116
2001	91 660	6 134	3 062	3 071	85 526	7 438	15 284	18 153	16 428	11 065	17 158
2002	92 422	6 157	3 096	3 061	86 266	7 611	15 207	17 958	16 695	11 622	17 173
2003	93 043	6 137	3 251	2 886	86 905	7 680	15 220	17 731	16 911	12 147	17 216
2004	93 599	6 169	3 260	2 909	87 430	7 794	15 099	17 441	17 170	12 627	17 299

[1]Beginning in 2003, persons who selected this race group only; persons who selected more than one race group are not included. Prior to 2003, persons who reported more than one race group were included in the group they identified as the main race.

Table 1-6. Civilian Noninstitutional Population by Sex, Race, Age, and Hispanic Origin, 1948–2004 —Continued

(Thousands of people.)

Year, sex, race, and Hispanic origin	16 years and over	16 to 19 years			20 years and over						
		Total	16 to 17 years	18 to 19 years	Total	20 to 24 years	25 to 34 years	35 to 44 years	45 to 54 years	55 to 64 years	65 years and over
Black Men[1]											
1972	6 538	978	525	453	5 559	921	1 251	1 026	963	720	679
1973	6 704	1 007	539	468	5 697	979	1 327	1 027	962	718	684
1974	6 875	1 027	554	471	5 848	956	1 381	1 055	997	753	707
1975	7 060	1 051	565	486	6 009	1 002	1 452	1 060	997	769	730
1976	7 265	1 099	579	518	6 167	1 036	1 521	1 077	999	774	756
1977	7 431	1 102	586	516	6 329	1 080	1 589	1 102	998	786	774
1978	7 577	1 093	579	514	6 484	1 120	1 657	1 128	995	794	789
1979	7 761	1 100	581	519	6 661	1 151	1 738	1 159	998	809	804
1980	7 944	1 110	583	526	6 834	1 171	1 828	1 191	999	825	822
1981	8 117	1 110	577	534	7 007	1 189	1 914	1 224	1 003	844	835
1982	8 283	1 097	556	542	7 186	1 225	1 983	1 282	1 003	848	846
1983	8 447	1 087	542	545	7 360	1 254	2 068	1 333	1 000	857	847
1984	8 654	1 055	524	531	7 599	1 292	2 164	1 411	1 012	858	861
1985	8 790	1 059	543	517	7 731	1 202	2 180	1 462	1 060	924	902
1986	8 956	1 049	548	503	7 907	1 195	2 264	1 517	1 072	934	924
1987	9 128	1 065	566	499	8 063	1 173	2 320	1 587	1 092	944	947
1988	9 289	1 074	569	505	8 215	1 151	2 367	1 656	1 121	951	970
1989	9 439	1 075	575	501	8 364	1 128	2 403	1 741	1 145	956	989
1990	9 573	1 094	555	540	8 479	1 144	2 412	1 968	1 183	855	917
1991	9 725	1 072	546	526	8 652	1 168	2 417	2 060	1 211	864	933
1992	9 896	1 056	544	512	8 840	1 194	2 409	2 150	1 268	868	951
1993	10 083	1 075	559	516	9 008	1 181	2 425	2 228	1 330	874	969
1994	10 258	1 087	586	501	9 171	1 207	2 399	2 300	1 392	889	985
1995	10 411	1 131	601	530	9 280	1 161	2 388	2 362	1 462	901	1 006
1996	10 575	1 161	623	538	9 414	1 154	2 373	2 413	1 534	914	1 025
1997	10 763	1 188	634	553	9 575	1 153	2 363	2 471	1 607	936	1 045
1998	10 927	1 201	623	578	9 727	1 166	2 335	2 520	1 682	956	1 068
1999	11 143	1 218	628	589	9 926	1 197	2 321	2 566	1 765	986	1 091
2000	11 129	1 178	605	572	9 952	1 195	2 277	2 471	1 889	1 067	1 053
2001	11 172	1 179	606	573	9 993	1 224	2 212	2 440	1 960	1 096	1 060
2002	11 391	1 195	615	580	10 196	1 281	2 223	2 437	2 042	1 137	1 075
2003	11 454	1 176	661	515	10 278	1 291	2 210	2 401	2 094	1 189	1 093
2004	11 656	1 195	680	516	10 461	1 326	2 242	2 382	2 150	1 250	1 111
Black Women[1]											
1972	7 988	1 040	536	503	6 948	1 106	1 558	1 302	1 176	881	925
1973	8 214	1 088	556	532	7 126	1 153	1 631	1 306	1 194	898	944
1974	8 454	1 110	567	542	7 344	1 181	1 723	1 327	1 206	926	981
1975	8 691	1 141	581	560	7 550	1 226	1 806	1 334	1 213	948	1 025
1976	8 931	1 165	585	580	7 765	1 266	1 890	1 357	1 220	962	1 070
1977	9 174	1 171	590	581	8 003	1 320	1 978	1 390	1 228	979	1 108
1978	9 394	1 177	589	588	8 217	1 363	2 061	1 419	1 231	999	1 143
1979	9 636	1 176	586	589	8 460	1 405	2 160	1 455	1 242	1 022	1 176
1980	9 880	1 180	587	593	8 700	1 435	2 267	1 496	1 250	1 045	1 208
1981	10 102	1 178	584	593	8 924	1 453	2 376	1 534	1 257	1 069	1 234
1982	10 300	1 155	563	592	9 146	1 472	2 455	1 605	1 260	1 087	1 267
1983	10 477	1 138	550	588	9 340	1 480	2 539	1 666	1 260	1 107	1 288
1984	10 694	1 106	532	574	9 588	1 491	2 625	1 756	1 276	1 119	1 322
1985	10 873	1 101	540	560	9 773	1 447	2 693	1 828	1 312	1 136	1 357
1986	11 033	1 088	542	545	9 945	1 430	2 762	1 893	1 341	1 145	1 374
1987	11 224	1 098	557	541	10 126	1 405	2 819	1 976	1 368	1 153	1 405
1988	11 402	1 105	561	544	10 298	1 376	2 867	2 060	1 403	1 159	1 432
1989	11 582	1 100	541	559	10 482	1 351	2 905	2 159	1 441	1 162	1 464
1990	11 904	1 144	546	598	10 760	1 410	2 995	2 360	1 435	1 114	1 446
1991	12 074	1 115	539	576	10 959	1 417	3 003	2 478	1 471	1 121	1 470
1992	12 251	1 099	542	557	11 152	1 421	2 995	2 573	1 542	1 127	1 495
1993	12 438	1 106	554	552	11 332	1 419	2 983	2 659	1 611	1 142	1 518
1994	12 621	1 125	582	543	11 496	1 410	2 963	2 738	1 692	1 156	1 538
1995	12 835	1 153	597	556	11 682	1 392	2 948	2 816	1 782	1 178	1 565
1996	13 029	1 195	615	580	11 833	1 364	2 938	2 877	1 874	1 196	1 584
1997	13 241	1 225	620	604	12 016	1 362	2 916	2 939	1 964	1 228	1 608
1998	13 446	1 243	618	624	12 203	1 380	2 886	2 991	2 053	1 268	1 626
1999	13 711	1 261	621	640	12 451	1 418	2 876	3 043	2 153	1 310	1 650
2000	13 772	1 211	600	611	12 561	1 416	2 812	3 017	2 279	1 340	1 697
2001	13 966	1 209	606	603	12 758	1 462	2 790	3 026	2 383	1 382	1 714
2002	14 187	1 221	620	601	12 966	1 498	2 792	3 023	2 471	1 434	1 747
2003	14 232	1 206	648	558	13 026	1 482	2 768	2 986	2 534	1 504	1 753
2004	14 409	1 227	670	557	13 182	1 495	2 778	2 954	2 590	1 577	1 789

[1]Beginning in 2003, persons who selected this race group only; persons who selected more than one race group are not included. Prior to 2003, persons who reported more than one race group were included in the group they identified as the main race.

Table 1-6. Civilian Noninstitutional Population by Sex, Race, Age, and Hispanic Origin, 1948–2004
—Continued

(Thousands of people.)

Year, sex, race, and Hispanic origin	16 years and over	16 to 19 years			20 years and over						
		Total	16 to 17 years	18 to 19 years	Total	20 to 24 years	25 to 34 years	35 to 44 years	45 to 54 years	55 to 64 years	65 years and over
Hispanic Men											
1973	2 891	...	...	...	2 472	...	...	...	...	...	...
1974	3 130	...	...	...	2 680	...	...	...	...	...	...
1975	3 219	...	...	...	2 741	...	...	...	...	...	...
1976	3 241	...	...	...	2 764	...	...	...	...	...	...
1977	3 483	...	...	...	2 982	...	...	...	...	...	...
1978	3 750	...	...	...	3 228	...	...	...	...	...	...
1979	3 917	...	...	...	3 362	...	...	...	...	...	...
1980	4 689	...	...	...	4 036	...	...	...	...	...	...
1981	4 968	...	...	...	4 306	...	...	...	...	...	...
1982	5 203	...	...	...	4 539	...	...	...	...	...	...
1983	5 432	...	...	...	4 771	...	...	...	...	...	...
1984	5 661	...	...	...	5 005	...	...	...	...	...	...
1985	5 885	...	...	...	5 232	...	...	...	...	...	...
1986	6 106	...	...	...	5 451	...	...	...	...	...	...
1987	6 371	...	...	...	5 700	...	...	...	...	...	...
1988	6 604	...	...	...	5 921	...	...	...	...	...	...
1989	6 825	...	...	...	6 114	...	...	...	...	...	...
1990	8 041	...	...	...	7 126	...	...	...	...	...	...
1991	8 296	...	...	...	7 392	...	...	...	...	...	...
1992	8 553	...	...	...	7 655	...	...	...	...	...	...
1993	8 824	...	...	...	7 930	...	...	...	...	...	...
1994	9 104	926	472	454	8 178	1 346	2 627	1 871	1 076	644	614
1995	9 329	954	481	473	8 375	1 337	2 657	1 966	1 127	668	619
1996	9 604	992	485	507	8 611	1 321	2 692	2 144	1 111	712	630
1997	10 368	1 119	585	534	9 250	1 439	2 872	2 275	1 266	747	651
1998	10 734	1 161	586	575	9 573	1 462	2 907	2 377	1 342	771	714
1999	10 713	1 190	571	619	9 523	1 398	2 805	2 407	1 397	767	749
2000	12 174	1 333	640	693	10 841	1 784	3 380	2 626	1 527	799	725
2001	12 695	1 310	619	690	11 386	1 846	3 529	2 765	1 650	848	749
2002	13 221	1 293	615	678	11 928	1 890	3 727	2 875	1 716	902	817
2003	14 098	1 301	674	627	12 797	1 905	4 033	3 098	1 910	989	862
2004	14 417	1 336	664	672	13 082	1 981	4 024	3 147	1 990	1 046	894
Hispanic Women											
1973	3 213	...	...	...	2 766	...	...	...	...	...	...
1974	3 434	...	...	...	2 959	...	...	...	...	...	...
1975	3 644	...	...	...	3 161	...	...	...	...	...	...
1976	3 669	...	...	...	3 263	...	...	...	...	...	...
1977	3 879	...	...	...	3 377	...	...	...	...	...	...
1978	4 159	...	...	...	3 608	...	...	...	...	...	...
1979	4 291	...	...	...	3 751	...	...	...	...	...	...
1980	4 909	...	...	...	4 281	...	...	...	...	...	...
1981	5 151	...	...	...	4 513	...	...	...	...	...	...
1982	5 377	...	...	...	4 734	...	...	...	...	...	...
1983	5 597	...	...	...	4 954	...	...	...	...	...	...
1984	5 816	...	...	...	5 173	...	...	...	...	...	...
1985	6 029	...	...	...	5 385	...	...	...	...	...	...
1986	6 238	...	...	...	5 591	...	...	...	...	...	...
1987	6 496	...	...	...	5 835	...	...	...	...	...	...
1988	6 721	...	...	...	6 050	...	...	...	...	...	...
1989	6 965	...	...	...	6 278	...	...	...	...	...	...
1990	7 863	...	...	...	7 041	...	...	...	...	...	...
1991	8 130	...	...	...	7 301	...	...	...	...	...	...
1992	8 408	...	...	...	7 569	...	...	...	...	...	...
1993	8 708	...	...	...	7 846	...	...	...	...	...	...
1994	9 014	892	430	462	8 122	1 173	2 373	1 885	1 147	757	787
1995	9 300	918	422	496	8 382	1 191	2 393	1 999	1 167	815	818
1996	9 610	956	477	479	8 654	1 203	2 489	2 082	1 164	834	882
1997	9 953	1 003	503	500	8 950	1 184	2 533	2 178	1 315	833	907
1998	10 335	1 044	483	560	9 292	1 269	2 539	2 259	1 433	844	948
1999	10 937	1 116	542	575	9 821	1 302	2 707	2 425	1 470	947	969
2000	11 764	1 190	574	616	10 574	1 471	3 086	2 564	1 534	937	982
2001	12 247	1 198	554	644	11 049	1 571	3 198	2 581	1 689	968	1 043
2002	12 742	1 214	601	613	11 528	1 617	3 283	2 732	1 777	1 051	1 068
2003	13 452	1 242	672	570	12 211	1 628	3 473	2 905	1 935	1 105	1 166
2004	13 692	1 272	674	598	12 420	1 685	3 447	2 908	1 997	1 162	1 221

Note: Persons of Hispanic origin may be of any race.

. . . = Not available.

Table 1-7. Civilian Labor Force by Sex, Race, Age, and Hispanic Origin, 1948–2004

(Thousands of people.)

Year, sex, race, and Hispanic origin	16 years and over	16 to 19 years			20 years and over						
		Total	16 to 17 years	18 to 19 years	Total	20 to 24 years	25 to 34 years	35 to 44 years	45 to 54 years	55 to 64 years	65 years and over
Total											
1948	60 621	4 435	1 780	2 654	56 187	7 392	14 258	13 397	10 914	7 329	2 897
1949	61 286	4 288	1 704	2 583	57 000	7 340	14 415	13 711	11 107	7 426	3 010
1950	62 208	4 216	1 659	2 557	57 994	7 307	14 619	13 954	11 444	7 633	3 036
1951	62 017	4 103	1 743	2 360	57 914	6 594	14 668	14 100	11 739	7 796	3 020
1952	62 138	4 064	1 806	2 257	58 075	5 840	14 904	14 383	11 961	7 980	3 005
1953	63 015	4 027	1 727	2 299	58 989	5 481	14 898	15 099	12 249	8 024	3 236
1954	63 643	3 976	1 643	2 300	59 666	5 475	14 983	15 221	12 524	8 269	3 192
1955	65 023	4 092	1 711	2 382	60 931	5 666	15 058	15 400	12 992	8 513	3 305
1956	66 552	4 296	1 878	2 418	62 257	5 940	14 961	15 694	13 407	8 830	3 423
1957	66 929	4 275	1 843	2 433	62 653	6 071	14 826	15 847	13 768	8 853	3 290
1958	67 639	4 260	1 818	2 442	63 377	6 272	14 668	16 028	14 179	9 031	3 199
1959	68 369	4 492	1 971	2 522	63 876	6 413	14 435	16 127	14 518	9 227	3 158
1960	69 628	4 841	2 095	2 747	64 788	6 702	14 382	16 269	14 852	9 385	3 195
1961	70 459	4 936	1 984	2 951	65 524	6 950	14 319	16 402	15 071	9 636	3 146
1962	70 614	4 916	1 919	2 997	65 699	7 082	14 023	16 589	15 096	9 757	3 154
1963	71 833	5 139	2 171	2 966	66 695	7 473	14 050	16 788	15 338	10 006	3 041
1964	73 091	5 388	2 449	2 940	67 702	7 963	14 056	16 771	15 637	10 182	3 090
1965	74 455	5 910	2 486	3 425	68 543	8 259	14 233	16 840	15 756	10 350	3 108
1966	75 770	6 558	2 664	3 893	69 219	8 410	14 458	16 738	15 984	10 575	3 053
1967	77 347	6 521	2 734	3 786	70 825	9 010	15 055	16 703	16 172	10 792	3 097
1968	78 737	6 619	2 817	3 803	72 118	9 305	15 708	16 591	16 397	10 964	3 153
1969	80 734	6 970	3 009	3 959	73 763	9 879	16 336	16 458	16 730	11 135	3 227
1970	82 771	7 249	3 135	4 115	75 521	10 597	17 036	16 437	16 949	11 283	3 222
1971	84 382	7 470	3 192	4 278	76 913	11 331	17 714	16 305	17 024	11 390	3 149
1972	87 034	8 054	3 420	4 636	78 980	12 130	18 960	16 398	16 967	11 412	3 114
1973	89 429	8 507	3 665	4 839	80 924	12 846	20 376	16 492	16 983	11 256	2 974
1974	91 949	8 871	3 810	5 059	83 080	13 314	21 654	16 763	17 131	11 284	2 934
1975	93 775	8 870	3 740	5 131	84 904	13 750	22 864	16 903	17 084	11 346	2 956
1976	96 158	9 056	3 767	5 288	87 103	14 284	24 203	17 317	16 982	11 422	2 895
1977	99 009	9 351	3 919	5 431	89 658	14 825	25 500	17 943	16 878	11 577	2 934
1978	102 251	9 652	4 127	5 526	92 598	15 370	26 703	18 821	16 891	11 744	3 070
1979	104 962	9 638	4 079	5 559	95 325	15 769	27 938	19 685	16 897	11 931	3 104
1980	106 940	9 378	3 883	5 496	97 561	15 922	29 227	20 463	16 910	11 985	3 054
1981	108 670	8 988	3 647	5 340	99 682	16 099	30 392	21 211	16 970	11 969	3 042
1982	110 204	8 526	3 336	5 189	101 679	16 082	31 186	22 431	16 889	12 062	3 030
1983	111 550	8 171	3 073	5 098	103 379	16 052	31 834	23 611	16 851	11 992	3 040
1984	113 544	7 943	3 050	4 894	105 601	16 046	32 723	24 933	17 006	11 961	2 933
1985	115 461	7 901	3 154	4 747	107 560	15 718	33 550	26 073	17 322	11 991	2 907
1986	117 834	7 926	3 287	4 639	109 908	15 441	34 591	27 232	17 739	11 894	3 010
1987	119 865	7 988	3 384	4 604	111 878	14 977	35 233	28 460	18 210	11 877	3 119
1988	121 669	8 031	3 286	4 745	113 638	14 505	35 503	29 435	19 104	11 808	3 284
1989	123 869	7 954	3 125	4 828	115 916	14 180	35 896	30 601	19 916	11 877	3 446
1990	125 840	7 792	2 937	4 856	118 047	14 700	35 929	32 145	20 248	11 575	3 451
1991	126 346	7 265	2 789	4 476	119 082	14 548	35 507	33 312	20 828	11 473	3 413
1992	128 105	7 096	2 769	4 327	121 009	14 521	35 369	33 899	22 160	11 587	3 473
1993	129 200	7 170	2 831	4 338	122 030	14 354	34 780	34 562	23 296	11 599	3 439
1994	131 056	7 481	3 134	4 347	123 576	14 131	34 353	35 226	24 318	11 713	3 834
1995	132 304	7 765	3 225	4 540	124 539	13 688	34 198	35 751	25 223	11 860	3 819
1996	133 943	7 806	3 263	4 543	126 137	13 377	33 833	36 556	26 397	12 146	3 828
1997	136 297	7 932	3 237	4 695	128 365	13 532	33 380	37 326	27 574	12 665	3 887
1998	137 673	8 256	3 335	4 921	129 417	13 638	32 813	37 536	28 368	13 215	3 847
1999	139 368	8 333	3 337	4 996	131 034	13 933	32 143	37 882	29 388	13 682	4 005
2000	142 583	8 271	3 261	5 010	134 312	14 250	32 755	37 567	31 071	14 356	4 312
2001	143 734	7 902	3 088	4 814	135 832	14 557	32 361	37 404	32 025	15 104	4 382
2002	144 863	7 585	2 870	4 715	137 278	14 781	32 196	36 926	32 597	16 309	4 469
2003	146 510	7 170	2 857	4 313	139 340	14 928	32 343	36 695	33 270	17 312	4 792
2004	147 401	7 114	2 747	4 367	140 287	15 154	32 207	36 158	33 758	18 013	4 998

Table 1-7. Civilian Labor Force by Sex, Race, Age, and Hispanic Origin, 1948–2004—*Continued*

(Thousands of people.)

Year, sex, race, and Hispanic origin	16 years and over	16 to 19 years			20 years and over						
		Total	16 to 17 years	18 to 19 years	Total	20 to 24 years	25 to 34 years	35 to 44 years	45 to 54 years	55 to 64 years	65 years and over
Men											
1948	43 286	2 600	1 109	1 490	40 687	4 673	10 327	9 596	7 943	5 764	2 384
1949	43 498	2 477	1 056	1 420	41 022	4 682	10 418	9 722	8 008	5 748	2 454
1950	43 819	2 504	1 048	1 456	41 316	4 632	10 527	9 793	8 117	5 794	2 453
1951	43 001	2 347	1 081	1 266	40 655	3 935	10 375	9 799	8 205	5 873	2 469
1952	42 869	2 312	1 101	1 210	40 558	3 338	10 585	9 945	8 326	5 949	2 416
1953	43 633	2 320	1 070	1 249	41 315	3 053	10 736	10 437	8 570	5 975	2 543
1954	43 965	2 295	1 023	1 272	41 669	3 051	10 771	10 513	8 702	6 105	2 526
1955	44 475	2 369	1 070	1 299	42 106	3 221	10 806	10 595	8 838	6 122	2 526
1956	45 091	2 433	1 142	1 291	42 658	3 485	10 685	10 663	9 002	6 220	2 602
1957	45 197	2 415	1 127	1 289	42 780	3 629	10 571	10 731	9 153	6 222	2 477
1958	45 521	2 428	1 133	1 295	43 092	3 771	10 475	10 843	9 320	6 304	2 378
1959	45 886	2 596	1 206	1 390	43 289	3 940	10 346	10 899	9 438	6 345	2 322
1960	46 388	2 787	1 290	1 496	43 603	4 123	10 251	10 967	9 574	6 399	2 287
1961	46 653	2 794	1 210	1 583	43 860	4 253	10 176	11 012	9 668	6 530	2 220
1962	46 600	2 770	1 178	1 592	43 831	4 279	9 920	11 115	9 715	6 560	2 241
1963	47 129	2 907	1 321	1 586	44 222	4 514	9 876	11 187	9 836	6 675	2 135
1964	47 679	3 074	1 499	1 575	44 604	4 754	9 876	11 156	9 956	6 741	2 124
1965	48 255	3 397	1 532	1 866	44 857	4 894	9 903	11 120	10 045	6 763	2 132
1966	48 471	3 685	1 609	2 075	44 788	4 820	9 948	10 983	10 100	6 847	2 089
1967	48 987	3 634	1 658	1 976	45 354	5 043	10 207	10 859	10 189	6 937	2 118
1968	49 533	3 681	1 687	1 995	45 852	5 070	10 610	10 725	10 267	7 025	2 154
1969	50 221	3 870	1 770	2 100	46 351	5 282	10 941	10 556	10 344	7 058	2 170
1970	51 228	4 008	1 810	2 199	47 220	5 717	11 327	10 469	10 417	7 126	2 165
1971	52 180	4 172	1 856	2 315	48 009	6 233	11 731	10 347	10 451	7 155	2 090
1972	53 555	4 476	1 955	2 522	49 079	6 766	12 350	10 372	10 412	7 155	2 026
1973	54 624	4 693	2 073	2 618	49 932	7 183	13 056	10 338	10 416	7 028	1 913
1974	55 739	4 861	2 138	2 721	50 879	7 387	13 665	10 401	10 431	7 063	1 932
1975	56 299	4 805	2 065	2 740	51 494	7 565	14 192	10 398	10 401	7 023	1 914
1976	57 174	4 886	2 069	2 817	52 288	7 866	14 784	10 500	10 293	7 020	1 826
1977	58 396	5 048	2 155	2 893	53 348	8 109	15 353	10 771	10 158	7 100	1 857
1978	59 620	5 149	2 227	2 923	54 471	8 327	15 814	11 159	10 083	7 151	1 936
1979	60 726	5 111	2 192	2 919	55 615	8 535	16 387	11 531	10 008	7 212	1 943
1980	61 453	4 999	2 102	2 897	56 455	8 607	16 971	11 836	9 905	7 242	1 893
1981	61 974	4 777	1 957	2 820	57 197	8 648	17 479	12 166	9 868	7 170	1 866
1982	62 450	4 470	1 776	2 694	57 980	8 604	17 793	12 781	9 784	7 174	1 845
1983	63 047	4 303	1 621	2 682	58 744	8 601	18 038	13 398	9 746	7 119	1 842
1984	63 835	4 134	1 591	2 542	59 701	8 594	18 488	14 037	9 776	7 050	1 755
1985	64 411	4 134	1 663	2 471	60 277	8 283	18 808	14 506	9 870	7 060	1 750
1986	65 422	4 102	1 707	2 395	61 320	8 148	19 383	15 029	9 994	6 954	1 811
1987	66 207	4 112	1 745	2 367	62 095	7 837	19 656	15 587	10 176	6 940	1 899
1988	66 927	4 159	1 714	2 445	62 768	7 594	19 742	16 074	10 566	6 831	1 960
1989	67 840	4 136	1 630	2 505	63 704	7 458	19 905	16 622	10 919	6 783	2 017
1990	69 011	4 094	1 537	2 557	64 916	7 866	19 872	17 481	11 103	6 627	1 967
1991	69 168	3 795	1 452	2 343	65 374	7 820	19 641	18 077	11 362	6 550	1 924
1992	69 964	3 751	1 453	2 297	66 213	7 770	19 495	18 347	12 040	6 551	2 010
1993	70 404	3 762	1 497	2 265	66 642	7 671	19 214	18 713	12 562	6 502	1 980
1994	70 817	3 896	1 630	2 266	66 921	7 540	18 854	18 966	12 962	6 423	2 176
1995	71 360	4 036	1 668	2 368	67 324	7 338	18 670	19 189	13 421	6 504	2 201
1996	72 087	4 043	1 665	2 378	68 044	7 104	18 430	19 602	13 967	6 693	2 247
1997	73 261	4 095	1 676	2 419	69 166	7 184	18 110	20 058	14 564	6 952	2 298
1998	73 959	4 244	1 728	2 516	69 715	7 221	17 796	20 242	14 963	7 253	2 240
1999	74 512	4 318	1 732	2 587	70 194	7 291	17 318	20 382	15 394	7 477	2 333
2000	76 280	4 269	1 676	2 594	72 010	7 521	17 844	20 093	16 269	7 795	2 488
2001	76 886	4 070	1 568	2 501	72 816	7 640	17 671	20 018	16 804	8 171	2 511
2002	77 500	3 870	1 431	2 439	73 630	7 769	17 596	19 828	17 143	8 751	2 542
2003	78 238	3 614	1 405	2 209	74 623	7 906	17 767	19 762	17 352	9 144	2 692
2004	78 980	3 616	1 329	2 288	75 364	8 057	17 798	19 539	17 635	9 547	2 787

Table 1-7. Civilian Labor Force by Sex, Race, Age, and Hispanic Origin, 1948–2004—*Continued*

(Thousands of people.)

Year, sex, race, and Hispanic origin	16 years and over	16 to 19 years			20 years and over						
		Total	16 to 17 years	18 to 19 years	Total	20 to 24 years	25 to 34 years	35 to 44 years	45 to 54 years	55 to 64 years	65 years and over
Women											
1948	17 335	1 835	671	1 164	15 500	2 719	3 931	3 801	2 971	1 565	513
1949	17 788	1 811	648	1 163	15 978	2 658	3 997	3 989	3 099	1 678	556
1950	18 389	1 712	611	1 101	16 678	2 675	4 092	4 161	3 327	1 839	583
1951	19 016	1 756	662	1 094	17 259	2 659	4 293	4 301	3 534	1 923	551
1952	19 269	1 752	705	1 047	17 517	2 502	4 319	4 438	3 635	2 031	589
1953	19 382	1 707	657	1 050	17 674	2 428	4 162	4 662	3 679	2 049	693
1954	19 678	1 681	620	1 028	17 997	2 424	4 212	4 708	3 822	2 164	666
1955	20 548	1 723	641	1 083	18 825	2 445	4 252	4 805	4 154	2 391	779
1956	21 461	1 863	736	1 127	19 599	2 455	4 276	5 031	4 405	2 610	821
1957	21 732	1 860	716	1 144	19 873	2 442	4 255	5 116	4 615	2 631	813
1958	22 118	1 832	685	1 147	20 285	2 501	4 193	5 185	4 859	2 727	821
1959	22 483	1 896	765	1 132	20 587	2 473	4 089	5 228	5 080	2 882	836
1960	23 240	2 054	805	1 251	21 185	2 579	4 131	5 302	5 278	2 986	908
1961	23 806	2 142	774	1 368	21 664	2 697	4 143	5 390	5 403	3 106	926
1962	24 014	2 146	741	1 405	21 868	2 803	4 103	5 474	5 381	3 197	913
1963	24 704	2 232	850	1 380	22 473	2 959	4 174	5 601	5 502	3 331	906
1964	25 412	2 314	950	1 365	23 098	3 209	4 180	5 615	5 681	3 441	966
1965	26 200	2 513	954	1 559	23 686	3 365	4 330	5 720	5 711	3 587	976
1966	27 299	2 873	1 055	1 818	24 431	3 590	4 510	5 755	5 884	3 728	964
1967	28 360	2 887	1 076	1 810	25 475	3 966	4 848	5 844	5 983	3 855	979
1968	29 204	2 938	1 130	1 808	26 266	4 235	5 098	5 866	6 130	3 939	999
1969	30 513	3 100	1 239	1 859	27 413	4 597	5 395	5 902	6 386	4 077	1 057
1970	31 543	3 241	1 325	1 916	28 301	4 880	5 708	5 968	6 532	4 157	1 056
1971	32 202	3 298	1 336	1 963	28 904	5 098	5 983	5 957	6 573	4 234	1 059
1972	33 479	3 578	1 464	2 114	29 901	5 364	6 610	6 027	6 555	4 257	1 089
1973	34 804	3 814	1 592	2 221	30 991	5 663	7 320	6 154	6 567	4 228	1 061
1974	36 211	4 010	1 672	2 338	32 201	5 926	7 989	6 362	6 699	4 221	1 002
1975	37 475	4 065	1 674	2 391	33 410	6 185	8 673	6 505	6 683	4 323	1 042
1976	38 983	4 170	1 698	2 470	34 814	6 418	9 419	6 817	6 689	4 402	1 069
1977	40 613	4 303	1 765	2 538	36 310	6 717	10 149	7 171	6 720	4 477	1 078
1978	42 631	4 503	1 900	2 603	38 128	7 043	10 888	7 662	6 807	4 593	1 134
1979	44 235	4 527	1 887	2 639	39 708	7 234	11 551	8 154	6 889	4 719	1 161
1980	45 487	4 381	1 781	2 599	41 106	7 315	12 257	8 627	7 004	4 742	1 161
1981	46 696	4 211	1 691	2 520	42 485	7 451	12 912	9 045	7 101	4 799	1 176
1982	47 755	4 056	1 561	2 495	43 699	7 477	13 393	9 651	7 105	4 888	1 185
1983	48 503	3 868	1 452	2 416	44 636	7 451	13 796	10 213	7 105	4 873	1 198
1984	49 709	3 810	1 458	2 351	45 900	7 451	14 234	10 896	7 230	4 911	1 177
1985	51 050	3 767	1 491	2 276	47 283	7 434	14 742	11 567	7 452	4 932	1 156
1986	52 413	3 824	1 580	2 244	48 589	7 293	15 208	12 204	7 746	4 940	1 199
1987	53 658	3 875	1 638	2 237	49 783	7 140	15 577	12 873	8 034	4 937	1 221
1988	54 742	3 872	1 572	2 300	50 870	6 910	15 761	13 361	8 537	4 977	1 324
1989	56 030	3 818	1 495	2 323	52 212	6 721	15 990	13 980	8 997	5 095	1 429
1990	56 829	3 698	1 400	2 298	53 131	6 834	16 058	14 663	9 145	4 948	1 483
1991	57 178	3 470	1 337	2 133	53 708	6 728	15 867	15 235	9 465	4 924	1 489
1992	58 141	3 345	1 316	2 030	54 796	6 750	15 875	15 552	10 120	5 035	1 464
1993	58 795	3 408	1 335	2 073	55 388	6 683	15 566	15 849	10 733	5 097	1 459
1994	60 239	3 585	1 504	2 081	56 655	6 592	15 499	16 259	11 357	5 289	1 658
1995	60 944	3 729	1 557	2 172	57 215	6 349	15 528	16 562	11 801	5 356	1 618
1996	61 857	3 763	1 599	2 164	58 094	6 273	15 403	16 954	12 430	5 452	1 581
1997	63 036	3 837	1 561	2 277	59 198	6 348	15 271	17 268	13 010	5 713	1 590
1998	63 714	4 012	1 607	2 405	59 702	6 418	15 017	17 294	13 405	5 962	1 607
1999	64 855	4 015	1 606	2 410	60 840	6 643	14 826	17 501	13 994	6 204	1 673
2000	66 303	4 002	1 585	2 416	62 301	6 730	14 912	17 473	14 802	6 561	1 823
2001	66 848	3 832	1 520	2 313	63 016	6 917	14 690	17 386	15 221	6 932	1 870
2002	67 363	3 715	1 439	2 277	63 648	7 012	14 600	17 098	15 454	7 559	1 926
2003	68 272	3 556	1 452	2 104	64 716	7 021	14 576	16 933	15 919	8 168	2 099
2004	68 421	3 498	1 418	2 080	64 923	7 097	14 409	16 619	16 123	8 466	2 211

Table 1-7. Civilian Labor Force by Sex, Race, Age, and Hispanic Origin, 1948–2004—*Continued*

(Thousands of people.)

Year, sex, race, and Hispanic origin	16 years and over	16 to 19 years			20 years and over						
		Total	16 to 17 years	18 to 19 years	Total	20 to 24 years	25 to 34 years	35 to 44 years	45 to 54 years	55 to 64 years	65 years and over
White[1]											
1954	56 816	3 501	1 448	2 054	53 315	4 752	13 226	13 540	11 258	7 591	2 946
1955	58 085	3 598	1 511	2 087	54 487	4 941	13 267	13 729	11 680	7 810	3 062
1956	59 428	3 771	1 656	2 113	55 657	5 194	13 154	14 000	12 061	8 080	3 166
1957	59 754	3 775	1 637	2 135	55 979	5 283	13 044	14 117	12 382	8 091	3 049
1958	60 293	3 757	1 615	2 144	56 536	5 449	12 884	14 257	12 727	8 254	2 964
1959	60 952	4 000	1 775	2 225	56 952	5 544	12 670	14 355	13 048	8 411	2 925
1960	61 915	4 275	1 871	2 405	57 640	5 787	12 594	14 450	13 322	8 522	2 964
1961	62 656	4 362	1 767	2 594	58 294	6 026	12 503	14 557	13 517	8 773	2 917
1962	62 750	4 354	1 709	2 645	58 396	6 164	12 218	14 695	13 551	8 856	2 912
1963	63 830	4 559	1 950	2 608	59 271	6 537	12 229	14 859	13 789	9 067	2 790
1964	64 921	4 784	2 211	2 572	60 137	6 952	12 235	14 852	14 043	9 239	2 817
1965	66 137	5 267	2 221	3 044	60 870	7 189	12 391	14 900	14 162	9 392	2 839
1966	67 276	5 827	2 367	3 460	61 449	7 324	12 591	14 785	14 370	9 583	2 793
1967	68 699	5 749	2 432	3 318	62 950	7 886	13 123	14 765	14 545	9 817	2 821
1968	69 976	5 839	2 519	3 320	64 137	8 109	13 740	14 683	14 756	9 968	2 884
1969	71 778	6 168	2 698	3 470	65 611	8 614	14 289	14 564	15 057	10 132	2 954
1970	73 556	6 442	2 824	3 617	67 113	9 238	14 896	14 525	15 269	10 255	2 930
1971	74 963	6 681	2 894	3 787	68 282	9 889	15 445	14 374	15 343	10 351	2 880
1972	77 275	7 193	3 096	4 098	70 082	10 605	16 584	14 399	15 283	10 402	2 809
1973	79 151	7 579	3 320	4 260	71 572	11 182	17 764	14 440	15 256	10 240	2 687
1974	81 281	7 899	3 441	4 459	73 381	11 600	18 862	14 644	15 375	10 241	2 656
1975	82 831	7 899	3 375	4 525	74 932	12 019	19 897	14 753	15 308	10 287	2 668
1976	84 767	8 088	3 410	4 679	76 678	12 444	20 990	15 088	15 187	10 371	2 599
1977	87 141	8 352	3 562	4 790	78 789	12 892	22 099	15 604	15 053	10 495	2 647
1978	89 634	8 555	3 715	4 839	81 079	13 309	23 067	16 353	15 004	10 602	2 745
1979	91 923	8 548	3 668	4 881	83 375	13 632	24 101	17 123	14 965	10 767	2 787
1980	93 600	8 312	3 485	4 827	85 286	13 769	25 181	17 811	14 956	10 812	2 759
1981	95 052	7 962	3 274	4 688	87 089	13 926	26 208	18 445	14 993	10 764	2 753
1982	96 143	7 518	3 001	4 518	88 625	13 866	26 814	19 491	14 879	10 832	2 742
1983	97 021	7 186	2 765	4 421	89 835	13 816	27 237	20 488	14 798	10 732	2 766
1984	98 492	6 952	2 720	4 232	91 540	13 733	27 958	21 588	14 899	10 701	2 660
1985	99 926	6 841	2 777	4 065	93 085	13 469	28 640	22 591	15 101	10 679	2 605
1986	101 801	6 862	2 895	3 967	94 939	13 176	29 497	23 571	15 379	10 583	2 732
1987	103 290	6 893	2 963	3 931	96 396	12 764	29 956	24 581	15 792	10 497	2 806
1988	104 756	6 940	2 861	4 079	97 815	12 311	30 167	25 358	16 573	10 462	2 943
1989	106 355	6 809	2 685	4 124	99 546	11 940	30 388	26 312	17 278	10 533	3 094
1990	107 447	6 683	2 543	4 140	100 764	12 397	30 174	27 265	17 515	10 290	3 123
1991	107 743	6 245	2 432	3 813	101 498	12 248	29 794	28 213	18 028	10 129	3 086
1992	108 837	6 022	2 388	3 633	102 815	12 187	29 518	28 580	19 200	10 196	3 135
1993	109 700	6 105	2 458	3 647	103 595	11 987	29 027	29 056	20 181	10 215	3 129
1994	111 082	6 357	2 681	3 677	104 725	11 688	28 580	29 626	21 026	10 319	3 486
1995	111 950	6 545	2 749	3 796	105 404	11 266	28 325	30 112	21 804	10 432	3 466
1996	113 108	6 607	2 780	3 826	106 502	11 003	27 901	30 683	22 781	10 648	3 485
1997	114 693	6 720	2 779	3 941	107 973	11 127	27 362	31 171	23 709	11 086	3 517
1998	115 415	6 965	2 860	4 105	108 450	11 244	26 707	31 221	24 282	11 548	3 448
1999	116 509	7 048	2 849	4 199	109 461	11 436	25 978	31 391	25 102	11 960	3 595
2000	118 545	6 955	2 768	4 186	111 590	11 626	26 336	30 968	26 353	12 463	3 846
2001	119 399	6 661	2 626	4 035	112 737	11 883	26 010	30 778	27 062	13 121	3 883
2002	120 150	6 366	2 445	3 921	113 784	12 073	25 908	30 286	27 405	14 148	3 965
2003	120 546	5 973	2 414	3 560	114 572	12 064	25 752	29 788	27 786	14 944	4 238
2004	121 086	5 929	2 309	3 620	115 156	12 192	25 548	29 305	28 181	15 522	4 408

[1]Beginning in 2003, persons who selected this race group only; persons who selected more than one race group are not included. Prior to 2003, persons who reported more than one race group were included in the group they identified as the main race.

Table 1-7. Civilian Labor Force by Sex, Race, Age, and Hispanic Origin, 1948–2004—*Continued*

(Thousands of people.)

Year, sex, race, and Hispanic origin	16 years and over	16 to 19 years			20 years and over						
		Total	16 to 17 years	18 to 19 years	Total	20 to 24 years	25 to 34 years	35 to 44 years	45 to 54 years	55 to 64 years	65 years and over
Black[1]											
1972	8 707	788	293	496	7 919	1 393	2 107	1 735	1 496	909	281
1973	8 976	833	307	525	8 143	1 489	2 242	1 741	1 513	901	258
1974	9 167	851	317	534	8 317	1 492	2 358	1 777	1 517	917	253
1975	9 263	838	312	524	8 426	1 477	2 466	1 775	1 519	929	258
1976	9 561	837	304	532	8 724	1 544	2 646	1 824	1 518	925	268
1977	9 932	861	304	557	9 072	1 641	2 798	1 894	1 530	943	267
1978	10 432	930	341	589	9 501	1 739	2 961	1 975	1 560	978	289
1979	10 678	912	340	572	9 766	1 793	3 094	2 039	1 584	974	281
1980	10 865	891	326	565	9 975	1 802	3 259	2 081	1 596	978	257
1981	11 086	862	308	554	10 224	1 828	3 365	2 164	1 608	1 009	249
1982	11 331	824	268	556	10 507	1 849	3 492	2 303	1 610	1 012	243
1983	11 647	809	248	561	10 838	1 871	3 675	2 406	1 630	1 032	224
1984	12 033	827	268	558	11 206	1 926	3 800	2 565	1 671	1 020	224
1985	12 364	889	311	578	11 476	1 854	3 888	2 681	1 742	1 059	252
1986	12 654	883	322	562	11 770	1 881	4 028	2 793	1 793	1 051	224
1987	12 993	899	336	563	12 094	1 818	4 147	2 942	1 838	1 098	251
1988	13 205	889	344	545	12 316	1 782	4 226	3 069	1 894	1 069	276
1989	13 497	925	353	572	12 573	1 789	4 295	3 227	1 954	1 023	285
1990	13 740	866	306	560	12 874	1 758	4 307	3 566	2 003	977	262
1991	13 797	774	266	508	13 023	1 750	4 254	3 719	2 042	1 001	256
1992	14 162	816	285	532	13 346	1 763	4 309	3 843	2 142	1 029	259
1993	14 225	807	283	524	13 418	1 764	4 232	3 960	2 212	1 013	237
1994	14 502	852	351	501	13 650	1 800	4 199	4 068	2 308	1 007	267
1995	14 817	911	366	545	13 906	1 754	4 267	4 165	2 404	1 046	271
1996	15 134	923	366	556	14 211	1 738	4 305	4 287	2 553	1 073	255
1997	15 529	933	352	580	14 596	1 783	4 329	4 401	2 724	1 093	265
1998	15 982	1 017	370	646	14 966	1 797	4 332	4 531	2 863	1 163	278
1999	16 365	959	352	607	15 406	1 866	4 430	4 653	2 992	1 180	285
2000	16 397	941	356	585	15 456	1 873	4 281	4 515	3 203	1 264	320
2001	16 421	898	332	565	15 524	1 878	4 180	4 483	3 298	1 335	350
2002	16 565	870	297	574	15 695	1 908	4 134	4 458	3 435	1 407	353
2003	16 526	771	289	482	15 755	1 892	4 060	4 465	3 506	1 466	366
2004	16 638	762	272	489	15 876	1 926	4 076	4 380	3 578	1 538	380
Hispanic											
1973	3 673	407	. . .	. . .	. . .	. . .	. . .	. . .	. . .	. . .	. . .
1974	4 012	442	. . .	. . .	. . .	. . .	. . .	. . .	. . .	. . .	. . .
1975	4 171	444	. . .	. . .	. . .	. . .	. . .	. . .	. . .	. . .	. . .
1976	4 205	447	176	285	3 820	729	1 248	875	625	294	48
1977	4 536	493	184	305	4 059	813	1 325	916	656	293	55
1978	4 979	533	221	312	4 446	901	1 446	1 008	701	323	67
1979	5 219	551	207	343	4 668	960	1 532	1 062	704	339	72
1980	6 146	645	241	404	5 502	1 136	1 843	1 163	860	414	85
1981	6 492	603	215	388	5 888	1 231	2 015	1 239	886	430	87
1982	6 734	585	192	393	6 148	1 251	2 163	1 313	891	444	85
1983	7 033	590	189	401	6 442	1 282	2 267	1 380	931	495	86
1984	7 451	618	209	409	6 833	1 325	2 436	1 509	954	524	84
1985	7 698	579	199	379	7 119	1 358	2 571	1 595	985	527	82
1986	8 076	571	203	368	7 505	1 414	2 685	1 713	1 097	511	84
1987	8 541	610	206	404	7 931	1 425	2 890	1 904	1 086	545	81
1988	8 982	671	234	437	8 311	1 486	2 957	1 996	1 147	621	103
1989	9 323	680	224	456	8 643	1 483	3 118	2 092	1 205	625	120
1990	10 720	829	276	554	9 891	1 839	3 590	2 386	1 320	647	110
1991	10 920	781	249	532	10 139	1 835	3 596	2 539	1 376	681	111
1992	11 338	796	263	533	10 542	1 815	3 740	2 735	1 442	687	122
1993	11 610	771	246	525	10 839	1 811	3 800	2 865	1 534	684	145
1994	11 975	807	285	522	11 168	1 863	3 865	2 965	1 626	698	151
1995	12 267	850	291	559	11 417	1 818	3 943	3 113	1 671	720	152
1996	12 774	845	284	561	11 929	1 845	4 054	3 361	1 697	806	166
1997	13 796	911	315	596	12 884	2 004	4 298	3 601	1 945	850	186
1998	14 317	1 007	320	688	13 310	2 077	4 372	3 707	2 090	894	169
1999	14 665	1 049	333	717	13 616	2 052	4 330	3 929	2 178	927	199
2000	16 689	1 168	368	800	15 521	2 546	5 197	4 241	2 387	940	209
2001	17 328	1 176	352	824	16 152	2 616	5 380	4 377	2 583	1 000	195
2002	17 943	1 103	335	769	16 840	2 678	5 645	4 545	2 657	1 091	224
2003	18 813	960	322	638	17 853	2 672	5 960	4 867	2 894	1 201	259
2004	19 272	995	297	698	18 277	2 732	5 931	4 931	3 093	1 284	306

[1]Beginning in 2003, persons who selected this race group only; persons who selected more than one race group are not included. Prior to 2003, persons who reported more than one race group were included in the group they identified as the main race.
. . . = Not available.

Table 1-7. Civilian Labor Force by Sex, Race, Age, and Hispanic Origin, 1948–2004—*Continued*

(Thousands of people.)

Year, sex, race, and Hispanic origin	16 years and over	16 to 19 years			20 years and over						
		Total	16 to 17 years	18 to 19 years	Total	20 to 24 years	25 to 34 years	35 to 44 years	45 to 54 years	55 to 64 years	65 years and over
White Men[1]											
1954	39 759	1 989	896	1 095	37 770	2 654	9 695	9 516	7 913	5 653	2 339
1955	40 197	2 056	935	1 121	38 141	2 803	9 721	9 597	8 025	5 654	2 343
1956	40 734	2 114	1 002	1 110	38 620	3 036	9 595	9 661	8 175	5 736	2 417
1957	40 826	2 108	992	1 114	38 718	3 152	9 483	9 719	8 317	5 735	2 307
1958	41 080	2 116	1 001	1 116	38 964	3 278	9 386	9 822	8 465	5 800	2 213
1959	41 397	2 279	1 077	1 202	39 118	3 409	9 261	9 876	8 581	5 833	2 158
1960	41 743	2 433	1 140	1 293	39 310	3 559	9 153	9 919	8 689	5 861	2 129
1961	41 986	2 439	1 067	1 372	39 547	3 681	9 072	9 961	8 776	5 988	2 068
1962	41 931	2 432	1 041	1 391	39 499	3 726	8 846	10 029	8 820	5 995	2 082
1963	42 404	2 563	1 183	1 380	39 841	3 955	8 805	10 079	8 944	6 090	1 967
1964	42 894	2 716	1 345	1 371	40 178	4 166	8 800	10 055	9 053	6 161	1 942
1965	43 400	2 999	1 359	1 639	40 401	4 279	8 824	10 023	9 130	6 188	1 959
1966	43 572	3 253	1 423	1 830	40 319	4 200	8 859	9 892	9 189	6 250	1 928
1967	44 041	3 191	1 464	1 727	40 851	4 416	9 102	9 785	9 260	6 348	1 944
1968	44 553	3 236	1 504	1 732	41 318	4 432	9 477	9 662	9 340	6 427	1 981
1969	45 185	3 413	1 583	1 830	41 772	4 615	9 773	9 509	9 413	6 467	1 996
1970	46 035	3 551	1 629	1 922	42 483	4 988	10 099	9 414	9 487	6 517	1 978
1971	46 904	3 719	1 681	2 039	43 185	5 448	10 444	9 294	9 528	6 550	1 922
1972	48 118	3 980	1 758	2 223	44 138	5 937	11 039	9 278	9 473	6 562	1 846
1973	48 920	4 174	1 875	2 300	44 747	6 274	11 621	9 212	9 445	6 452	1 740
1974	49 843	4 312	1 922	2 391	45 532	6 470	12 135	9 246	9 455	6 464	1 759
1975	50 324	4 290	1 871	2 418	46 034	6 642	12 579	9 231	9 415	6 425	1 742
1976	51 033	4 357	1 869	2 489	46 675	6 890	13 092	9 289	9 310	6 437	1 657
1977	52 033	4 496	1 949	2 548	47 537	7 097	13 575	9 509	9 175	6 492	1 688
1978	52 955	4 565	2 002	2 563	48 390	7 274	13 939	9 858	9 068	6 508	1 744
1979	53 856	4 537	1 974	2 563	49 320	7 421	14 415	10 183	8 968	6 571	1 761
1980	54 473	4 424	1 881	2 543	50 049	7 479	14 893	10 455	8 877	6 618	1 727
1981	54 895	4 224	1 751	2 473	50 671	7 521	15 340	10 740	8 836	6 530	1 704
1982	55 133	3 933	1 602	2 331	51 200	7 438	15 549	11 289	8 727	6 520	1 677
1983	55 480	3 764	1 452	2 312	51 716	7 406	15 707	11 817	8 649	6 446	1 691
1984	56 062	3 609	1 420	2 189	52 453	7 370	16 037	12 348	8 683	6 410	1 606
1985	56 472	3 576	1 467	2 109	52 895	7 122	16 306	12 767	8 730	6 376	1 595
1986	57 217	3 542	1 502	2 040	53 675	6 986	16 769	13 207	8 791	6 260	1 663
1987	57 779	3 547	1 524	2 023	54 232	6 717	16 963	13 674	8 945	6 200	1 733
1988	58 317	3 583	1 487	2 095	54 734	6 468	17 018	14 068	9 285	6 108	1 787
1989	58 988	3 546	1 401	2 146	55 441	6 316	17 077	14 516	9 615	6 082	1 835
1990	59 638	3 522	1 333	2 189	56 116	6 688	16 920	15 026	9 713	5 957	1 811
1991	59 656	3 269	1 266	2 003	56 387	6 619	16 709	15 523	9 926	5 847	1 763
1992	60 168	3 192	1 260	1 932	56 976	6 542	16 512	15 701	10 570	5 821	1 830
1993	60 484	3 200	1 292	1 908	57 284	6 449	16 244	15 971	11 010	5 784	1 825
1994	60 727	3 315	1 403	1 912	57 411	6 294	15 879	16 188	11 327	5 726	1 998
1995	61 146	3 427	1 429	1 998	57 719	6 096	15 669	16 414	11 730	5 809	2 000
1996	61 783	3 444	1 421	2 023	58 340	5 922	15 475	16 728	12 217	5 943	2 054
1997	62 639	3 513	1 440	2 073	59 126	6 029	15 120	17 019	12 710	6 154	2 094
1998	63 034	3 614	1 487	2 127	59 421	6 063	14 770	17 157	13 003	6 415	2 013
1999	63 413	3 666	1 478	2 188	59 747	6 151	14 292	17 201	13 368	6 618	2 117
2000	64 466	3 615	1 422	2 193	60 850	6 244	14 666	16 880	13 977	6 840	2 243
2001	64 966	3 446	1 334	2 112	61 519	6 363	14 536	16 809	14 400	7 169	2 241
2002	65 308	3 241	1 215	2 026	62 067	6 444	14 499	16 583	14 615	7 665	2 261
2003	65 509	3 036	1 193	1 843	62 473	6 479	14 529	16 398	14 708	7 973	2 386
2004	65 994	3 050	1 127	1 923	62 944	6 586	14 429	16 192	14 934	8 326	2 478

[1]Beginning in 2003, persons who selected this race group only; persons who selected more than one race group are not included. Prior to 2003, persons who reported more than one race group were included in the group they identified as the main race.

Table 1-7. Civilian Labor Force by Sex, Race, Age, and Hispanic Origin, 1948–2004—*Continued*

(Thousands of people.)

Year, sex, race, and Hispanic origin	16 years and over	16 to 19 years			20 years and over						
		Total	16 to 17 years	18 to 19 years	Total	20 to 24 years	25 to 34 years	35 to 44 years	45 to 54 years	55 to 64 years	65 years and over
White Women[1]											
1954	17 057	1 512	552	959	15 545	2 098	3 531	4 024	3 345	1 938	607
1955	17 888	1 542	576	966	16 346	2 138	3 546	4 132	3 655	2 156	719
1956	18 694	1 657	654	1 003	17 037	2 158	3 559	4 339	3 886	2 344	749
1957	18 928	1 667	645	1 021	17 261	2 131	3 561	4 398	4 065	2 356	742
1958	19 213	1 641	614	1 028	17 572	2 171	3 498	4 435	4 262	2 454	751
1959	19 555	1 721	698	1 023	17 834	2 135	3 409	4 479	4 467	2 578	767
1960	20 172	1 842	731	1 112	18 330	2 228	3 441	4 531	4 633	2 661	835
1961	20 670	1 923	700	1 222	18 747	2 345	3 431	4 596	4 741	2 785	849
1962	20 819	1 922	668	1 254	18 897	2 438	3 372	4 666	4 731	2 861	830
1963	21 426	1 996	767	1 228	19 430	2 582	3 424	4 780	4 845	2 977	823
1964	22 027	2 068	866	1 201	19 959	2 786	3 435	4 797	4 990	3 078	875
1965	22 737	2 268	862	1 405	20 469	2 910	3 567	4 877	5 032	3 204	880
1966	23 704	2 574	944	1 630	21 130	3 124	3 732	4 893	5 181	3 333	865
1967	24 658	2 558	968	1 591	22 100	3 471	4 021	4 980	5 285	3 469	877
1968	25 423	2 603	1 015	1 588	22 821	3 677	4 263	5 021	5 416	3 541	903
1969	26 593	2 755	1 115	1 640	23 839	3 999	4 516	5 055	5 644	3 665	958
1970	27 521	2 891	1 195	1 695	24 630	4 250	4 797	5 111	5 781	3 738	952
1971	28 060	2 962	1 213	1 748	25 097	4 441	5 001	5 080	5 816	3 801	958
1972	29 157	3 213	1 338	1 875	25 945	4 668	5 544	5 121	5 810	3 839	963
1973	30 231	3 405	1 445	1 960	26 825	4 908	6 143	5 228	5 811	3 788	947
1974	31 437	3 588	1 520	2 068	27 850	5 131	6 727	5 399	5 920	3 777	897
1975	32 508	3 610	1 504	2 107	28 898	5 378	7 318	5 522	5 892	3 862	926
1976	33 735	3 731	1 541	2 189	30 004	5 554	7 898	5 799	5 877	3 935	940
1977	35 108	3 856	1 614	2 243	31 253	5 795	8 523	6 095	5 877	4 003	959
1978	36 679	3 990	1 713	2 276	32 689	6 035	9 128	6 495	5 936	4 094	1 001
1979	38 067	4 011	1 694	2 318	34 056	6 211	9 687	6 940	5 997	4 196	1 024
1980	39 127	3 888	1 605	2 284	35 239	6 290	10 289	7 356	6 079	4 194	1 032
1981	40 157	3 739	1 523	2 216	36 418	6 406	10 868	7 704	6 157	4 235	1 049
1982	41 010	3 585	1 399	2 186	37 425	6 428	11 264	8 202	6 152	4 313	1 065
1983	41 541	3 422	1 314	2 109	38 119	6 410	11 530	8 670	6 149	4 285	1 074
1984	42 431	3 343	1 300	2 043	39 087	6 363	11 922	9 240	6 217	4 292	1 054
1985	43 455	3 265	1 310	1 955	40 190	6 348	12 334	9 824	6 371	4 303	1 010
1986	44 584	3 320	1 393	1 927	41 264	6 191	12 729	10 364	6 588	4 323	1 069
1987	45 510	3 347	1 439	1 908	42 164	6 047	12 993	10 907	6 847	4 297	1 073
1988	46 439	3 358	1 374	1 984	43 081	5 844	13 149	11 291	7 288	4 354	1 156
1989	47 367	3 262	1 284	1 978	44 105	5 625	13 311	11 796	7 663	4 451	1 259
1990	47 809	3 161	1 210	1 951	44 648	5 709	13 254	12 239	7 802	4 333	1 312
1991	48 087	2 976	1 166	1 810	45 111	5 629	13 085	12 689	8 101	4 282	1 324
1992	48 669	2 830	1 128	1 702	45 839	5 645	13 006	12 879	8 630	4 375	1 305
1993	49 216	2 905	1 167	1 739	46 311	5 539	12 783	13 085	9 171	4 430	1 304
1994	50 356	3 042	1 278	1 764	47 314	5 394	12 702	13 439	9 699	4 593	1 487
1995	50 804	3 118	1 320	1 798	47 686	5 170	12 656	13 697	10 074	4 622	1 466
1996	51 325	3 163	1 360	1 803	48 162	5 081	12 426	13 955	10 563	4 706	1 431
1997	52 054	3 207	1 339	1 867	48 847	5 099	12 242	14 153	10 999	4 932	1 422
1998	52 380	3 351	1 373	1 977	49 029	5 180	11 937	14 064	11 279	5 133	1 435
1999	53 096	3 382	1 371	2 010	49 714	5 285	11 685	14 190	11 734	5 342	1 478
2000	54 079	3 339	1 346	1 993	50 740	5 381	11 669	14 088	12 376	5 623	1 602
2001	54 433	3 215	1 292	1 923	51 218	5 519	11 474	13 969	12 662	5 952	1 642
2002	54 842	3 125	1 229	1 895	51 717	5 628	11 409	13 703	12 790	6 482	1 704
2003	55 037	2 937	1 221	1 716	52 099	5 584	11 223	13 390	13 078	6 970	1 852
2004	55 092	2 879	1 182	1 697	52 212	5 606	11 119	13 114	13 247	7 197	1 930

[1]Beginning in 2003, persons who selected this race group only; persons who selected more than one race group are not included. Prior to 2003, persons who reported more than one race group were included in the group they identified as the main race.

Table 1-7. Civilian Labor Force by Sex, Race, Age, and Hispanic Origin, 1948–2004—*Continued*

(Thousands of people.)

Year, sex, race, and Hispanic origin	16 years and over	16 to 19 years			20 years and over						
		Total	16 to 17 years	18 to 19 years	Total	20 to 24 years	25 to 34 years	35 to 44 years	45 to 54 years	55 to 64 years	65 years and over
Black Men[1]											
1972	4 816	453	180	272	4 364	761	1 158	935	824	522	165
1973	4 924	460	175	286	4 464	819	1 217	935	842	499	153
1974	5 020	480	189	291	4 540	798	1 279	953	838	519	152
1975	5 016	447	168	279	4 569	790	1 328	948	833	520	150
1976	5 101	454	168	285	4 648	820	1 383	969	824	504	149
1977	5 263	476	178	299	4 787	856	1 441	1 003	818	515	154
1978	5 435	491	186	306	4 943	883	1 504	1 022	829	540	166
1979	5 559	480	179	301	5 079	928	1 577	1 049	844	524	156
1980	5 612	479	181	298	5 134	935	1 659	1 061	830	509	138
1981	5 685	462	169	293	5 223	940	1 702	1 093	829	524	134
1982	5 804	436	137	300	5 368	964	1 769	1 152	824	525	135
1983	5 966	433	134	300	5 533	997	1 840	1 196	845	536	119
1984	6 126	440	141	299	5 686	1 022	1 924	1 270	847	505	118
1985	6 220	471	162	310	5 749	950	1 937	1 313	879	544	125
1986	6 373	458	164	294	5 915	957	2 029	1 359	901	552	116
1987	6 486	463	179	284	6 023	914	2 074	1 406	915	586	130
1988	6 596	469	186	283	6 127	913	2 114	1 459	936	565	139
1989	6 701	480	190	291	6 221	904	2 157	1 544	945	530	141
1990	6 802	445	161	284	6 357	879	2 142	1 733	988	496	119
1991	6 851	400	140	260	6 451	896	2 111	1 806	1 010	507	122
1992	6 997	429	149	280	6 568	900	2 121	1 859	1 037	521	130
1993	7 019	425	154	270	6 594	875	2 118	1 918	1 065	506	112
1994	7 089	443	176	266	6 646	891	2 068	1 975	1 102	484	125
1995	7 183	453	184	269	6 730	866	2 089	1 987	1 148	490	150
1996	7 264	458	182	276	6 806	848	2 077	2 036	1 204	509	132
1997	7 354	444	178	266	6 910	832	2 052	2 096	1 287	508	134
1998	7 542	488	181	307	7 053	837	2 034	2 142	1 343	548	150
1999	7 652	470	180	291	7 182	835	2 069	2 206	1 387	547	138
2000	7 702	462	181	281	7 240	875	1 999	2 105	1 497	612	151
2001	7 647	447	166	281	7 200	853	1 915	2 073	1 537	645	177
2002	7 794	446	149	297	7 347	906	1 909	2 064	1 623	664	181
2003	7 711	365	138	228	7 346	918	1 872	2 058	1 627	685	186
2004	7 773	359	128	231	7 414	927	1 931	2 000	1 654	714	188
Black Women[1]											
1972	3 890	335	113	224	3 555	632	949	800	672	387	116
1973	4 052	373	133	240	3 678	670	1 026	806	670	402	105
1974	4 148	371	128	243	3 777	694	1 079	824	679	398	100
1975	4 247	391	144	245	3 857	687	1 138	827	686	409	108
1976	4 460	384	136	247	4 076	723	1 264	855	694	421	119
1977	4 670	385	127	258	4 286	785	1 357	891	712	429	113
1978	4 997	439	155	283	4 558	856	1 456	953	731	439	124
1979	5 119	432	161	271	4 687	865	1 517	990	740	451	124
1980	5 253	412	144	267	4 841	867	1 600	1 020	767	469	119
1981	5 401	400	139	261	5 001	888	1 663	1 071	779	485	115
1982	5 527	387	131	256	5 140	885	1 723	1 151	786	487	108
1983	5 681	375	114	261	5 306	874	1 835	1 210	785	496	105
1984	5 907	387	127	260	5 520	904	1 876	1 294	823	515	106
1985	6 144	417	149	268	5 727	904	1 951	1 368	862	515	127
1986	6 281	425	157	268	5 855	924	1 999	1 434	892	499	107
1987	6 507	435	157	278	6 071	904	2 073	1 537	924	512	121
1988	6 609	419	158	262	6 190	869	2 112	1 610	958	504	137
1989	6 796	445	163	281	6 352	885	2 138	1 683	1 009	493	144
1990	6 938	421	145	276	6 517	879	2 165	1 833	1 015	481	143
1991	6 946	374	126	248	6 572	854	2 143	1 913	1 032	494	135
1992	7 166	387	135	252	6 778	863	2 188	1 985	1 105	508	129
1993	7 206	383	129	254	6 824	889	2 115	2 042	1 147	506	125
1994	7 413	409	174	235	7 004	909	2 131	2 093	1 206	523	142
1995	7 634	458	182	276	7 175	887	2 177	2 178	1 256	556	121
1996	7 869	464	184	280	7 405	890	2 228	2 251	1 349	565	122
1997	8 175	489	175	314	7 686	951	2 277	2 305	1 437	585	131
1998	8 441	528	189	339	7 912	960	2 298	2 390	1 520	615	128
1999	8 713	489	172	316	8 224	1 031	2 360	2 447	1 606	633	147
2000	8 695	479	175	305	8 215	998	2 282	2 409	1 706	652	168
2001	8 774	451	166	284	8 323	1 025	2 265	2 410	1 762	690	173
2002	8 772	424	148	276	8 348	1 002	2 225	2 394	1 812	743	171
2003	8 815	406	151	255	8 409	973	2 188	2 407	1 879	781	180
2004	8 865	403	144	259	8 462	999	2 144	2 380	1 924	824	192

[1]Beginning in 2003, persons who selected this race group only; persons who selected more than one race group are not included. Prior to 2003, persons who reported more than one race group were included in the group they identified as the main race.

Table 1-7. Civilian Labor Force by Sex, Race, Age, and Hispanic Origin, 1948–2004—*Continued*

(Thousands of people.)

Year, sex, race, and Hispanic origin	16 years and over	16 to 19 years			20 years and over						
		Total	16 to 17 years	18 to 19 years	Total	20 to 24 years	25 to 34 years	35 to 44 years	45 to 54 years	55 to 64 years	65 years and over
Hispanic Men											
1973	2 356	. . .	. . .	. . .	2 124	. . .	. . .	. . .	. . .	. . .	. . .
1974	2 556	. . .	. . .	. . .	2 306	. . .	. . .	. . .	. . .	. . .	. . .
1975	2 597	. . .	. . .	. . .	2 343	. . .	. . .	. . .	. . .	. . .	. . .
1976	2 580	260	104	155	2 326	433	771	541	398	189	34
1977	2 817	285	105	179	2 530	485	828	567	416	197	42
1978	3 041	299	129	171	2 742	546	882	620	425	217	52
1979	3 184	315	121	194	2 869	562	941	648	445	216	56
1980	3 818	392	147	245	3 426	697	1 161	713	522	270	62
1981	4 005	359	130	229	3 647	747	1 269	756	535	278	61
1982	4 148	333	111	221	3 815	759	1 361	808	539	290	58
1983	4 362	348	109	239	4 014	789	1 447	852	557	311	58
1984	4 563	345	113	232	4 218	822	1 540	910	570	325	51
1985	4 729	334	116	218	4 395	835	1 629	957	591	331	53
1986	4 948	336	114	222	4 612	888	1 669	1 015	661	323	56
1987	5 163	345	112	233	4 818	865	1 801	1 121	652	325	55
1988	5 409	378	123	255	5 031	897	1 834	1 189	686	355	69
1989	5 595	400	129	271	5 195	909	1 899	1 221	719	375	71
1990	6 546	512	165	346	6 034	1 182	2 230	1 403	775	380	65
1991	6 664	466	141	325	6 198	1 202	2 260	1 487	780	401	67
1992	6 900	468	154	314	6 432	1 141	2 366	1 593	844	414	74
1993	7 076	455	145	310	6 621	1 147	2 417	1 675	900	394	88
1994	7 210	463	163	300	6 747	1 184	2 430	1 713	922	410	89
1995	7 376	479	168	311	6 898	1 153	2 469	1 795	965	417	98
1996	7 646	496	156	340	7 150	1 132	2 510	1 966	967	469	105
1997	8 309	531	177	354	7 779	1 267	2 684	2 091	1 112	511	113
1998	8 571	565	188	377	8 005	1 288	2 733	2 173	1 164	541	106
1999	8 546	596	181	415	7 950	1 231	2 633	2 219	1 205	526	136
2000	9 923	676	204	471	9 247	1 590	3 181	2 451	1 337	555	134
2001	10 279	684	200	484	9 595	1 602	3 294	2 562	1 430	582	125
2002	10 609	632	183	449	9 977	1 627	3 484	2 647	1 478	607	134
2003	11 288	532	164	368	10 756	1 642	3 776	2 877	1 630	680	150
2004	11 587	567	156	410	11 020	1 671	3 765	2 934	1 736	728	186
Hispanic Women											
1973	1 317	. . .	. . .	. . .	1 142	. . .	. . .	. . .	. . .	. . .	. . .
1974	1 456	. . .	. . .	. . .	1 264	. . .	. . .	. . .	. . .	. . .	. . .
1975	1 574	. . .	. . .	. . .	1 384	. . .	. . .	. . .	. . .	. . .	. . .
1976	1 625	201	71	130	1 454	295	479	334	227	105	13
1977	1 720	204	80	125	1 523	327	497	349	240	96	13
1978	1 938	233	93	142	1 704	354	564	388	275	106	16
1979	2 035	235	86	149	1 800	397	590	413	258	124	15
1980	2 328	252	93	159	2 076	439	682	450	337	144	22
1981	2 486	244	85	159	2 242	484	745	483	351	152	27
1982	2 586	252	81	172	2 333	492	802	504	352	155	28
1983	2 671	242	80	162	2 429	493	820	529	374	184	29
1984	2 888	273	96	177	2 615	503	896	599	384	199	34
1985	2 970	245	84	161	2 725	524	943	639	394	196	29
1986	3 128	236	89	147	2 893	526	1 016	698	436	189	28
1987	3 377	265	94	171	3 112	559	1 090	783	434	220	27
1988	3 573	293	111	182	3 281	589	1 123	806	461	267	34
1989	3 728	280	95	185	3 448	574	1 219	871	486	251	49
1990	4 174	318	110	207	3 857	657	1 360	983	545	268	45
1991	4 256	315	107	207	3 941	633	1 336	1 052	596	279	44
1992	4 439	328	110	219	4 110	674	1 374	1 142	599	273	48
1993	4 534	316	101	215	4 218	664	1 383	1 190	633	290	57
1994	4 765	345	122	222	4 421	679	1 435	1 252	704	288	62
1995	4 891	371	123	249	4 520	666	1 473	1 318	706	303	54
1996	5 128	349	128	221	4 779	713	1 544	1 395	729	338	61
1997	5 486	381	138	242	5 106	737	1 614	1 510	833	338	73
1998	5 746	442	132	310	5 304	789	1 639	1 533	927	353	62
1999	6 119	453	151	302	5 666	821	1 698	1 710	973	401	63
2000	6 767	492	164	328	6 275	956	2 016	1 791	1 051	386	75
2001	7 049	492	152	340	6 557	1 014	2 086	1 815	1 153	418	70
2002	7 334	471	152	320	6 863	1 051	2 161	1 897	1 179	484	90
2003	7 525	428	158	271	7 096	1 030	2 183	1 990	1 264	520	109
2004	7 685	429	141	288	7 257	1 060	2 166	1 998	1 357	556	119

Note: Persons of Hispanic origin may be of any race.

. . . = Not available.

Table 1-8. Civilian Labor Force Participation Rates by Sex, Race, Age, and Hispanic Origin, 1948–2004

(Percent.)

Year, sex, race, and Hispanic origin	16 years and over	16 to 19 years	20 years and over						
			Total	20 to 24 years	25 to 34 years	35 to 44 years	45 to 54 years	55 to 64 years	65 years and over
Total									
1948	58.8	52.5	59.4	64.1	63.1	66.7	65.1	56.9	27.0
1949	58.9	52.2	59.5	64.9	63.2	67.2	65.3	56.2	27.3
1950	59.2	51.8	59.9	65.9	63.5	67.5	66.4	56.7	26.7
1951	59.2	52.2	59.8	64.8	64.2	67.6	67.2	56.9	25.8
1952	59.0	51.3	59.7	62.2	64.7	68.0	67.5	57.5	24.8
1953	58.9	50.2	59.6	61.2	64.0	68.9	68.1	58.0	24.8
1954	58.8	48.3	59.6	61.6	64.3	68.8	68.4	58.7	23.9
1955	59.3	48.9	60.1	62.7	64.8	68.9	69.7	59.5	24.1
1956	60.0	50.9	60.7	64.1	64.8	69.5	70.5	60.8	24.3
1957	59.6	49.6	60.4	64.0	64.9	69.5	70.9	60.1	22.9
1958	59.5	47.4	60.5	64.4	65.0	69.6	71.5	60.5	21.8
1959	59.3	46.7	60.4	64.3	65.0	69.5	71.9	61.0	21.1
1960	59.4	47.5	60.5	65.2	65.4	69.4	72.2	60.9	20.8
1961	59.3	46.9	60.5	65.7	65.6	69.5	72.1	61.5	20.1
1962	58.8	46.1	60.0	65.3	65.2	69.7	72.2	61.5	19.1
1963	58.7	45.2	60.1	65.1	65.6	70.1	72.5	62.0	17.9
1964	58.7	44.5	60.2	66.3	65.8	70.0	72.9	61.9	18.0
1965	58.9	45.7	60.3	66.4	66.4	70.7	72.5	61.9	17.8
1966	59.2	48.2	60.5	66.5	67.1	71.0	72.7	62.2	17.2
1967	59.6	48.4	60.9	67.1	68.2	71.6	72.7	62.3	17.2
1968	59.6	48.3	60.9	67.0	68.6	72.0	72.8	62.2	17.2
1969	60.1	49.4	61.3	68.2	69.1	72.5	73.4	62.1	17.3
1970	60.4	49.9	61.6	69.2	69.7	73.1	73.5	61.8	17.0
1971	60.2	49.7	61.4	69.3	69.9	73.2	73.2	61.3	16.2
1972	60.4	51.9	61.4	70.8	70.9	73.3	72.7	60.0	15.6
1973	60.8	53.7	61.7	72.6	72.3	74.0	72.5	58.4	14.6
1974	61.3	54.8	62.0	74.0	73.6	74.6	72.7	57.8	14.0
1975	61.2	54.0	62.1	73.9	74.4	75.0	72.6	57.2	13.7
1976	61.6	54.5	62.4	74.7	75.7	76.0	72.5	56.6	13.1
1977	62.3	56.0	63.0	75.7	77.0	77.0	72.8	56.3	13.0
1978	63.2	57.8	63.8	76.8	78.3	78.1	73.5	56.3	13.3
1979	63.7	57.9	64.3	77.5	79.2	79.2	74.3	56.2	13.1
1980	63.8	56.7	64.5	77.2	79.9	80.0	74.9	55.7	12.5
1981	63.9	55.4	64.8	77.3	80.5	80.7	75.7	55.0	12.2
1982	64.0	54.1	65.0	77.1	81.0	81.2	75.9	55.1	11.9
1983	64.0	53.5	65.0	77.2	81.3	81.6	76.0	54.5	11.7
1984	64.4	53.9	65.3	77.6	81.8	82.4	76.5	54.2	11.1
1985	64.8	54.5	65.7	78.2	82.5	83.1	77.3	54.2	10.8
1986	65.3	54.7	66.2	78.9	82.9	83.7	78.0	54.0	10.9
1987	65.6	54.7	66.5	78.9	83.3	84.3	78.6	54.4	11.1
1988	65.9	55.3	66.8	78.7	83.3	84.6	79.6	54.6	11.5
1989	66.5	55.9	67.3	78.7	83.8	85.1	80.5	55.5	11.8
1990	66.5	53.7	67.6	77.8	83.6	85.2	80.7	55.9	11.8
1991	66.2	51.6	67.3	76.7	83.2	85.2	81.0	55.5	11.5
1992	66.4	51.3	67.6	77.0	83.7	85.1	81.5	56.2	11.5
1993	66.3	51.5	67.5	77.0	83.3	84.9	81.6	56.4	11.2
1994	66.6	52.7	67.7	77.0	83.2	84.8	81.7	56.8	12.4
1995	66.6	53.5	67.7	76.6	83.8	84.6	81.4	57.2	12.1
1996	66.8	52.3	67.9	76.8	84.1	84.8	82.1	57.9	12.1
1997	67.1	51.6	68.4	77.6	84.4	85.1	82.6	58.9	12.2
1998	67.1	52.8	68.3	77.5	84.6	84.7	82.5	59.3	11.9
1999	67.1	52.0	68.3	77.5	84.6	84.9	82.6	59.3	12.3
2000	67.1	52.0	68.3	77.8	84.6	84.8	82.5	59.2	12.9
2001	66.8	49.6	68.2	77.1	84.0	84.6	82.3	60.4	13.0
2002	66.6	47.4	68.1	76.4	83.7	84.1	82.1	61.9	13.2
2003	66.2	44.5	67.9	75.4	82.9	83.9	82.1	62.4	14.0
2004	66.0	43.9	67.7	75.0	82.7	83.6	81.8	62.3	14.4

Table 1-8. Civilian Labor Force Participation Rates by Sex, Race, Age, and Hispanic Origin, 1948–2004
    —Continued

(Percent.)

Year, sex, race, and Hispanic origin	16 years and over	16 to 19 years	20 years and over						
			Total	20 to 24 years	25 to 34 years	35 to 44 years	45 to 54 years	55 to 64 years	65 years and over
Men									
1948	86.6	63.7	88.6	84.6	95.9	97.9	95.8	89.5	46.8
1949	86.4	62.8	88.5	86.6	95.8	97.9	95.6	87.5	47.0
1950	86.4	63.2	88.4	87.9	96.0	97.6	95.8	86.9	45.8
1951	86.3	63.0	88.2	88.4	96.9	97.5	95.9	87.2	44.9
1952	86.3	61.3	88.3	88.1	97.5	97.8	96.2	87.5	42.6
1953	86.0	60.7	88.0	87.7	97.4	98.2	96.5	87.9	41.6
1954	85.5	58.0	87.8	86.9	97.3	98.1	96.5	88.7	40.5
1955	85.4	58.9	87.6	86.9	97.6	98.1	96.4	87.9	39.6
1956	85.5	60.5	87.6	87.8	97.3	97.9	96.6	88.5	40.0
1957	84.8	59.1	86.9	87.1	97.1	97.9	96.3	87.5	37.5
1958	84.2	56.6	86.6	86.9	97.1	97.9	96.3	87.8	35.6
1959	83.7	55.8	86.3	87.8	97.4	97.8	96.0	87.4	34.2
1960	83.3	56.1	86.0	88.1	97.5	97.7	95.7	86.8	33.1
1961	82.9	54.6	85.7	87.8	97.5	97.6	95.6	87.3	31.7
1962	82.0	53.8	84.8	86.9	97.2	97.6	95.6	86.2	30.3
1963	81.4	52.9	84.4	86.1	97.1	97.5	95.7	86.2	28.4
1964	81.0	52.4	84.2	86.1	97.3	97.3	95.7	85.6	28.0
1965	80.7	53.8	83.9	85.8	97.2	97.3	95.6	84.6	27.9
1966	80.4	55.3	83.6	85.1	97.3	97.2	95.3	84.5	27.1
1967	80.4	55.6	83.4	84.4	97.2	97.3	95.2	84.4	27.1
1968	80.1	55.1	83.1	82.8	96.9	97.1	94.9	84.3	27.3
1969	79.8	55.9	82.8	82.8	96.7	96.9	94.6	83.4	27.2
1970	79.7	56.1	82.6	83.3	96.4	96.9	94.3	83.0	26.8
1971	79.1	56.1	82.1	83.0	95.9	96.5	93.9	82.1	25.5
1972	78.9	58.1	81.6	83.9	95.7	96.4	93.2	80.4	24.3
1973	78.8	59.7	81.3	85.2	95.7	96.2	93.0	78.2	22.7
1974	78.7	60.7	81.0	85.9	95.8	96.0	92.2	77.3	22.4
1975	77.9	59.1	80.3	84.5	95.2	95.6	92.1	75.6	21.6
1976	77.5	59.3	79.8	85.2	95.2	95.4	91.6	74.3	20.2
1977	77.7	60.9	79.7	85.6	95.3	95.7	91.1	73.8	20.0
1978	77.9	62.0	79.8	85.9	95.3	95.7	91.3	73.3	20.4
1979	77.8	61.5	79.8	86.4	95.3	95.7	91.4	72.8	19.9
1980	77.4	60.5	79.4	85.9	95.2	95.5	91.2	72.1	19.0
1981	77.0	59.0	79.0	85.5	94.9	95.4	91.4	70.6	18.4
1982	76.6	56.7	78.7	84.9	94.7	95.3	91.2	70.2	17.8
1983	76.4	56.2	78.5	84.8	94.2	95.2	91.2	69.4	17.4
1984	76.4	56.0	78.3	85.0	94.4	95.4	91.2	68.5	16.3
1985	76.3	56.8	78.1	85.0	94.7	95.0	91.0	67.9	15.8
1986	76.3	56.4	78.1	85.8	94.6	94.8	91.0	67.3	16.0
1987	76.2	56.1	78.0	85.2	94.6	94.6	90.7	67.6	16.3
1988	76.2	56.9	77.9	85.0	94.3	94.5	90.9	67.0	16.5
1989	76.4	57.9	78.1	85.3	94.4	94.5	91.1	67.2	16.6
1990	76.4	55.7	78.2	84.4	94.1	94.3	90.7	67.8	16.3
1991	75.8	53.2	77.7	83.5	93.6	94.1	90.5	67.0	15.7
1992	75.8	53.4	77.7	83.3	93.8	93.7	90.7	67.0	16.1
1993	75.4	53.2	77.3	83.2	93.4	93.4	90.1	66.5	15.6
1994	75.1	54.1	76.8	83.1	92.6	92.8	89.1	65.5	16.8
1995	75.0	54.8	76.7	83.1	93.0	92.3	88.8	66.0	16.8
1996	74.9	53.2	76.8	82.5	93.2	92.4	89.1	67.0	16.9
1997	75.0	52.3	77.0	82.5	93.0	92.6	89.5	67.6	17.1
1998	74.9	53.3	76.8	82.0	93.2	92.6	89.2	68.1	16.5
1999	74.7	52.9	76.7	81.9	93.3	92.8	88.8	67.9	16.9
2000	74.8	52.8	76.7	82.6	93.4	92.7	88.6	67.3	17.7
2001	74.4	50.2	76.5	81.6	92.7	92.5	88.5	68.3	17.7
2002	74.1	47.5	76.3	80.7	92.4	92.1	88.5	69.2	17.9
2003	73.5	44.3	75.9	80.0	91.8	92.1	87.7	68.7	18.6
2004	73.3	43.9	75.8	79.6	91.9	91.9	87.5	68.7	19.0

Table 1-8. Civilian Labor Force Participation Rates by Sex, Race, Age, and Hispanic Origin, 1948–2004
—Continued

(Percent.)

Year, sex, race, and Hispanic origin	16 years and over	16 to 19 years	20 years and over						
			Total	20 to 24 years	25 to 34 years	35 to 44 years	45 to 54 years	55 to 64 years	65 years and over
Women									
1948	32.7	42.0	31.8	45.3	33.2	36.9	35.0	24.3	9.1
1949	33.1	42.4	32.3	45.0	33.4	38.1	35.9	25.3	9.6
1950	33.9	41.0	33.3	46.0	34.0	39.1	37.9	27.0	9.7
1951	34.6	42.4	34.0	46.5	35.4	39.8	39.7	27.6	8.9
1952	34.7	42.2	34.1	44.7	35.4	40.4	40.1	28.7	9.1
1953	34.4	40.7	33.9	44.3	34.0	41.3	40.4	29.1	10.0
1954	34.6	39.4	34.2	45.1	34.4	41.2	41.2	30.0	9.3
1955	35.7	39.7	35.4	45.9	34.9	41.6	43.8	32.5	10.6
1956	36.9	42.2	36.4	46.3	35.4	43.1	45.5	34.9	10.8
1957	36.9	41.1	36.5	45.9	35.6	43.3	46.5	34.5	10.5
1958	37.1	39.0	36.9	46.3	35.6	43.4	47.8	35.2	10.3
1959	37.1	38.2	37.1	45.1	35.3	43.4	49.0	36.6	10.2
1960	37.7	39.3	37.6	46.1	36.0	43.4	49.9	37.2	10.8
1961	38.1	39.7	38.0	47.0	36.4	43.8	50.1	37.9	10.7
1962	37.9	39.0	37.8	47.3	36.3	44.1	50.0	38.7	10.0
1963	38.3	38.0	38.3	47.5	37.2	44.9	50.6	39.7	9.6
1964	38.7	37.0	38.9	49.4	37.2	45.0	51.4	40.2	10.1
1965	39.3	38.0	39.4	49.9	38.5	46.1	50.9	41.1	10.0
1966	40.3	41.4	40.1	51.5	39.8	46.8	51.7	41.8	9.6
1967	41.1	41.6	41.1	53.3	41.9	48.1	51.8	42.4	9.6
1968	41.6	41.9	41.6	54.5	42.6	48.9	52.3	42.4	9.6
1969	42.7	43.2	42.7	56.7	43.7	49.9	53.8	43.1	9.9
1970	43.3	44.0	43.3	57.7	45.0	51.1	54.4	43.0	9.7
1971	43.4	43.4	43.3	57.7	45.6	51.6	54.3	42.9	9.5
1972	43.9	45.8	43.7	59.1	47.8	52.0	53.9	42.1	9.3
1973	44.7	47.8	44.4	61.1	50.4	53.3	53.7	41.1	8.9
1974	45.7	49.1	45.3	63.1	52.6	54.7	54.6	40.7	8.1
1975	46.3	49.1	46.0	64.1	54.9	55.8	54.6	40.9	8.2
1976	47.3	49.8	47.0	65.0	57.3	57.8	55.0	41.0	8.2
1977	48.4	51.2	48.1	66.5	59.7	59.6	55.8	40.9	8.1
1978	50.0	53.7	49.6	68.3	62.2	61.6	57.1	41.3	8.3
1979	50.9	54.2	50.6	69.0	63.9	63.6	58.3	41.7	8.3
1980	51.5	52.9	51.3	68.9	65.5	65.5	59.9	41.3	8.1
1981	52.1	51.8	52.1	69.6	66.7	66.8	61.1	41.4	8.0
1982	52.6	51.4	52.7	69.8	68.0	68.0	61.6	41.8	7.9
1983	52.9	50.8	53.1	69.9	69.0	68.7	61.9	41.5	7.8
1984	53.6	51.8	53.7	70.4	69.8	70.1	62.9	41.7	7.5
1985	54.5	52.1	54.7	71.8	70.9	71.8	64.4	42.0	7.3
1986	55.3	53.0	55.5	72.4	71.6	73.1	65.9	42.3	7.4
1987	56.0	53.3	56.2	73.0	72.4	74.5	67.1	42.7	7.4
1988	56.6	53.6	56.8	72.7	72.7	75.2	69.0	43.5	7.9
1989	57.4	53.9	57.7	72.4	73.5	76.0	70.5	45.0	8.4
1990	57.5	51.6	58.0	71.3	73.5	76.4	71.2	45.2	8.6
1991	57.4	50.0	57.9	70.1	73.1	76.5	72.0	45.2	8.5
1992	57.8	49.1	58.5	70.9	73.9	76.7	72.6	46.5	8.3
1993	57.9	49.7	58.5	70.9	73.4	76.6	73.5	47.2	8.1
1994	58.8	51.3	59.3	71.0	74.0	77.1	74.6	48.9	9.2
1995	58.9	52.2	59.4	70.3	74.9	77.2	74.4	49.2	8.8
1996	59.3	51.3	59.9	71.3	75.2	77.5	75.4	49.6	8.6
1997	59.8	51.0	60.5	72.7	76.0	77.7	76.0	50.9	8.6
1998	59.8	52.3	60.4	73.0	76.3	77.1	76.2	51.2	8.6
1999	60.0	51.0	60.7	73.2	76.4	77.2	76.7	51.5	8.9
2000	59.9	51.2	60.6	73.1	76.1	77.2	76.8	51.9	9.4
2001	59.8	49.0	60.6	72.7	75.5	77.1	76.4	53.2	9.6
2002	59.6	47.3	60.5	72.1	75.1	76.4	76.0	55.2	9.8
2003	59.5	44.8	60.6	70.8	74.1	76.0	76.8	56.6	10.6
2004	59.2	43.8	60.3	70.5	73.6	75.6	76.5	56.3	11.1

Table 1-8. Civilian Labor Force Participation Rates by Sex, Race, Age, and Hispanic Origin, 1948–2004
—*Continued*

(Percent.)

Year, sex, race, and Hispanic origin	16 years and over	16 to 19 years	20 years and over						
			Total	20 to 24 years	25 to 34 years	35 to 44 years	45 to 54 years	55 to 64 years	65 years and over
White[1]									
1954	58.2	48.8	58.9	61.0	63.5	68.0	67.9	58.4	23.7
1955	58.7	49.3	59.5	62.4	64.0	68.3	69.2	59.3	23.9
1956	59.4	51.3	60.1	64.1	64.0	68.9	70.1	60.6	24.2
1957	59.1	50.3	59.8	63.7	64.1	68.8	70.5	59.9	22.8
1958	58.9	47.9	59.8	64.1	64.2	68.8	71.0	60.3	21.7
1959	58.7	47.4	59.7	63.7	64.3	68.7	71.5	60.7	21.0
1960	58.8	47.9	59.8	64.8	64.7	68.6	71.7	60.6	20.8
1961	58.8	47.4	59.9	65.5	64.8	68.8	71.7	61.3	20.0
1962	58.3	46.6	59.4	65.0	64.4	69.0	71.8	61.3	19.0
1963	58.2	45.7	59.4	64.9	64.8	69.4	72.3	61.8	17.9
1964	58.2	45.1	59.6	65.8	64.9	69.5	72.5	61.8	17.8
1965	58.4	46.5	59.7	65.7	65.6	70.1	72.2	61.7	17.7
1966	58.7	49.1	59.8	66.0	66.3	70.4	72.5	61.9	17.1
1967	59.2	49.2	60.3	66.8	67.4	71.2	72.5	62.3	17.0
1968	59.3	49.3	60.4	66.6	67.9	71.7	72.7	62.2	17.1
1969	59.9	50.6	60.9	67.9	68.4	72.3	73.3	62.1	17.2
1970	60.2	51.4	61.2	69.2	69.1	72.9	73.5	61.8	16.8
1971	60.1	51.6	61.1	69.6	69.3	73.0	73.4	61.3	16.1
1972	60.4	54.1	61.2	71.2	70.4	73.2	72.9	60.3	15.4
1973	60.8	56.0	61.4	73.3	72.0	73.9	72.7	58.6	14.4
1974	61.4	57.3	61.9	74.8	73.4	74.6	73.0	58.0	13.9
1975	61.5	56.7	62.0	75.2	74.4	75.1	73.0	57.4	13.6
1976	61.8	57.5	62.3	76.0	75.6	76.1	73.0	56.9	13.0
1977	62.5	59.3	62.9	77.1	77.0	77.1	73.2	56.6	12.9
1978	63.3	60.8	63.6	78.1	78.3	78.1	73.8	56.4	13.1
1979	63.9	61.1	64.2	78.9	79.4	79.3	74.6	56.5	12.9
1980	64.1	60.0	64.5	78.7	80.2	80.3	75.4	56.0	12.5
1981	64.3	58.9	64.8	79.1	81.0	81.0	76.2	55.2	12.2
1982	64.3	57.5	65.0	78.9	81.6	81.5	76.4	55.3	12.0
1983	64.3	56.9	65.0	79.0	81.8	81.9	76.5	54.7	11.8
1984	64.6	57.2	65.3	79.4	82.5	82.6	77.0	54.5	11.1
1985	65.0	57.5	65.7	79.9	83.1	83.4	77.8	54.4	10.7
1986	65.5	57.8	66.1	80.6	83.6	84.0	78.5	54.3	11.0
1987	65.8	57.7	66.5	80.7	84.0	84.7	79.1	54.6	11.1
1988	66.2	58.6	66.8	80.6	84.1	85.0	80.3	55.1	11.4
1989	66.7	59.1	67.3	80.2	84.5	85.5	81.2	56.2	11.8
1990	66.9	57.5	67.6	79.8	84.6	85.9	81.3	56.5	11.9
1991	66.6	55.8	67.4	78.9	84.3	85.9	81.8	56.0	11.6
1992	66.8	54.7	67.7	79.4	84.6	85.8	82.2	56.8	11.6
1993	66.8	55.1	67.6	79.5	84.5	85.7	82.5	57.1	11.4
1994	67.1	56.4	67.9	79.5	84.4	85.7	82.7	57.6	12.5
1995	67.1	57.1	67.8	78.7	84.9	85.5	82.5	58.0	12.3
1996	67.2	55.9	68.1	79.1	84.9	85.7	83.1	58.7	12.3
1997	67.5	55.2	68.4	79.6	85.3	85.8	83.5	59.9	12.3
1998	67.3	56.0	68.2	79.5	85.4	85.3	83.4	60.1	12.0
1999	67.3	55.5	68.2	79.5	85.1	85.4	83.5	60.2	12.5
2000	67.3	55.5	68.2	79.9	85.1	85.4	83.5	60.0	13.0
2001	67.0	53.1	68.1	79.2	84.5	85.2	83.3	61.2	13.0
2002	66.8	50.5	68.1	78.6	84.5	84.7	83.0	62.8	13.3
2003	66.5	47.7	67.9	77.7	83.6	84.3	83.0	63.3	14.1
2004	66.3	47.1	67.7	77.1	83.5	84.1	82.9	63.2	14.6

[1]Beginning in 2003, persons who selected this race group only; persons who selected more than one race group are not included. Prior to 2003, persons who reported more than one race group were included in the group they identified as the main race.

Table 1-8. Civilian Labor Force Participation Rates by Sex, Race, Age, and Hispanic Origin, 1948–2004
—Continued

(Percent.)

Year, sex, race, and Hispanic origin	16 years and over	16 to 19 years	20 years and over						
			Total	20 to 24 years	25 to 34 years	35 to 44 years	45 to 54 years	55 to 64 years	65 years and over
Black[1]									
1972	59.9	39.1	63.3	68.6	74.9	74.4	70.0	56.9	17.5
1973	60.2	39.8	63.4	69.7	75.7	74.5	70.3	55.9	16.0
1974	59.8	39.8	63.0	69.8	75.8	74.6	69.1	54.7	15.1
1975	58.8	38.2	62.0	66.1	75.6	74.1	69.0	54.3	14.9
1976	59.0	37.0	62.5	66.8	77.4	74.9	68.6	53.4	14.9
1977	59.8	37.9	63.2	68.2	78.3	75.9	69.0	53.7	14.5
1978	61.5	41.0	64.5	69.9	79.6	77.4	70.4	54.8	15.3
1979	61.4	40.1	64.5	70.0	79.2	77.9	71.1	53.5	14.5
1980	61.0	38.9	64.1	69.0	79.5	77.4	71.4	52.6	13.0
1981	60.8	37.7	64.2	69.2	78.5	78.4	71.2	52.8	12.0
1982	61.0	36.6	64.3	68.6	78.7	79.8	71.1	52.3	11.5
1983	61.5	36.4	64.9	68.4	79.8	80.2	72.1	52.5	10.5
1984	62.2	38.3	65.2	69.2	79.3	81.0	73.0	51.6	10.3
1985	62.9	41.2	65.6	70.0	79.8	81.5	73.4	51.4	11.2
1986	63.3	41.3	65.9	71.7	80.1	81.9	74.3	50.6	9.7
1987	63.8	41.6	66.5	70.5	80.7	82.6	74.7	52.4	10.7
1988	63.8	40.8	66.5	70.5	80.8	82.6	75.0	50.6	11.5
1989	64.2	42.5	66.7	72.2	80.9	82.7	75.5	48.3	11.6
1990	64.0	38.7	66.9	68.8	79.7	82.4	76.5	49.6	11.1
1991	63.3	35.4	66.4	67.7	78.5	82.0	76.2	50.4	10.7
1992	63.9	37.9	66.8	67.4	79.7	81.4	76.2	51.6	10.6
1993	63.2	37.0	66.0	67.8	78.3	81.0	75.2	50.2	9.5
1994	63.4	38.5	66.0	68.8	78.3	80.8	74.8	49.3	10.6
1995	63.7	39.9	66.3	68.7	80.0	80.4	74.1	50.3	10.5
1996	64.1	39.2	66.9	69.0	81.1	81.0	74.9	50.9	9.8
1997	64.7	38.7	67.6	70.9	82.0	81.4	76.3	50.5	10.0
1998	65.6	41.6	68.2	70.6	83.0	82.2	76.7	52.3	10.3
1999	65.8	38.7	68.9	71.4	85.2	83.0	76.4	51.4	10.4
2000	65.8	39.4	68.7	71.8	84.1	82.3	76.9	52.5	11.6
2001	65.3	37.6	68.2	69.9	83.6	82.0	75.9	53.9	12.6
2002	64.8	36.0	67.8	68.6	82.4	81.6	76.1	54.7	12.5
2003	64.3	32.4	67.6	68.2	81.6	82.9	75.8	54.4	12.9
2004	63.8	31.4	67.2	68.3	81.2	82.1	75.5	54.4	13.1
Hispanic									
1973	60.2	46.9	. . .	. . .	. . .	. . .	. . .	. . .	. . .
1974	61.1	47.7	. . .	. . .	. . .	. . .	. . .	. . .	. . .
1975	60.8	46.2	. . .	. . .	. . .	. . .	. . .	. . .	. . .
1976	60.8	46.9	62.9	. . .	. . .	. . .	. . .	. . .	. . .
1977	61.6	48.2	63.7	. . .	. . .	. . .	. . .	. . .	. . .
1978	62.9	49.6	65.0	. . .	. . .	. . .	. . .	. . .	. . .
1979	63.6	50.3	65.6	. . .	. . .	. . .	. . .	. . .	. . .
1980	64.0	50.3	66.2	. . .	. . .	. . .	. . .	. . .	. . .
1981	64.1	46.4	66.8	. . .	. . .	. . .	. . .	. . .	. . .
1982	63.6	44.8	66.3	. . .	. . .	. . .	. . .	. . .	. . .
1983	63.8	45.3	66.2	. . .	. . .	. . .	. . .	. . .	. . .
1984	64.9	47.5	67.1	. . .	. . .	. . .	. . .	. . .	. . .
1985	64.6	44.6	67.1	. . .	. . .	. . .	. . .	. . .	. . .
1986	65.4	43.9	68.0	. . .	. . .	. . .	. . .	. . .	. . .
1987	66.4	45.8	68.8	. . .	. . .	. . .	. . .	. . .	. . .
1988	67.4	49.6	69.4	. . .	. . .	. . .	. . .	. . .	. . .
1989	67.6	48.6	69.7	. . .	. . .	. . .	. . .	. . .	. . .
1990	67.4	47.8	69.8	. . .	. . .	. . .	. . .	. . .	. . .
1991	66.5	45.1	69.0	. . .	. . .	. . .	. . .	. . .	. . .
1992	66.8	45.8	69.2	. . .	. . .	. . .	. . .	. . .	. . .
1993	66.2	43.9	68.7	. . .	. . .	. . .	. . .	. . .	. . .
1994	66.1	44.4	68.5	74.0	77.3	78.9	73.1	49.8	10.7
1995	65.8	45.4	68.1	71.9	78.1	78.5	72.8	48.6	10.5
1996	66.5	43.4	69.1	73.1	78.2	79.5	74.6	52.2	11.0
1997	67.9	43.0	70.8	76.4	79.5	80.9	75.4	53.8	11.9
1998	67.9	45.7	70.6	76.1	80.3	80.0	75.3	55.4	10.1
1999	67.7	45.5	70.4	76.0	78.6	81.3	75.9	54.1	11.6
2000	69.7	46.3	72.5	78.2	80.4	81.7	78.0	54.2	12.3
2001	69.5	46.9	72.0	76.6	80.0	81.9	77.4	55.1	10.9
2002	69.1	44.0	71.8	76.3	80.5	81.1	76.1	55.8	11.9
2003	68.3	37.7	71.4	75.6	79.4	81.1	75.3	57.4	12.8
2004	68.6	38.2	71.7	74.5	79.4	81.4	77.6	58.1	14.5

[1]Beginning in 2003, persons who selected this race group only; persons who selected more than one race group are not included. Prior to 2003, persons who reported more than one race group were included in the group they identified as the main race.
. . . = Not available.

Table 1-8. Civilian Labor Force Participation Rates by Sex, Race, Age, and Hispanic Origin, 1948–2004
—*Continued*

(Percent.)

Year, sex, race, and Hispanic origin	16 years and over	16 to 19 years	20 years and over						
			Total	20 to 24 years	25 to 34 years	35 to 44 years	45 to 54 years	55 to 64 years	65 years and over
White Men[1]									
1954	85.6	57.6	87.8	86.3	97.5	98.2	96.8	89.1	40.4
1955	85.4	58.6	87.5	86.5	97.8	98.2	96.7	88.4	39.6
1956	85.6	60.4	87.6	87.6	97.4	98.1	96.8	88.9	40.0
1957	84.8	59.2	86.9	86.6	97.2	98.0	96.7	88.0	37.7
1958	84.3	56.5	86.6	86.7	97.2	98.0	96.6	88.2	35.7
1959	83.8	55.9	86.3	87.3	97.5	98.0	96.3	87.9	34.3
1960	83.4	55.9	86.0	87.8	97.7	97.9	96.1	87.2	33.3
1961	83.0	54.5	85.7	87.6	97.7	97.9	95.9	87.8	31.9
1962	82.1	53.8	84.9	86.5	97.4	97.9	96.0	86.7	30.6
1963	81.5	53.1	84.4	85.8	97.4	97.8	96.2	86.6	28.4
1964	81.1	52.7	84.2	85.7	97.5	97.6	96.1	86.1	27.9
1965	80.8	54.1	83.9	85.3	97.4	97.7	95.9	85.2	27.9
1966	80.6	55.9	83.6	84.4	97.5	97.6	95.8	84.9	27.2
1967	80.6	56.3	83.5	84.0	97.5	97.7	95.6	84.9	27.1
1968	80.4	55.9	83.2	82.4	97.2	97.6	95.4	84.7	27.4
1969	80.2	56.8	83.0	82.6	97.0	97.4	95.1	83.9	27.3
1970	80.0	57.5	82.8	83.3	96.7	97.3	94.9	83.3	26.7
1971	79.6	57.9	82.3	83.2	96.3	97.0	94.7	82.6	25.6
1972	79.6	60.1	82.0	84.3	96.0	97.0	94.0	81.1	24.4
1973	79.4	62.0	81.6	85.8	96.2	96.8	93.5	78.9	22.7
1974	79.4	62.9	81.4	86.6	96.3	96.7	93.0	78.0	22.4
1975	78.7	61.9	80.7	85.5	95.8	96.4	92.9	76.4	21.7
1976	78.4	62.3	80.3	86.3	95.9	96.0	92.5	75.2	20.2
1977	78.5	64.0	80.2	86.8	96.0	96.2	92.1	74.6	20.0
1978	78.6	65.0	80.1	87.3	95.9	96.3	92.1	73.7	20.3
1979	78.6	64.8	80.1	87.6	96.0	96.4	92.2	73.4	20.0
1980	78.2	63.7	79.8	87.2	95.9	96.2	92.1	73.1	19.1
1981	77.9	62.4	79.5	87.0	95.8	96.1	92.4	71.5	18.5
1982	77.4	60.0	79.2	86.3	95.6	96.0	92.2	71.0	17.9
1983	77.1	59.4	78.9	86.1	95.2	96.0	91.9	70.0	17.7
1984	77.1	59.0	78.7	86.5	95.4	96.1	92.0	69.5	16.4
1985	77.0	59.7	78.5	86.4	95.7	95.7	92.0	68.8	15.9
1986	76.9	59.3	78.5	87.3	95.5	95.4	91.8	68.0	16.3
1987	76.8	59.0	78.4	86.9	95.5	95.4	91.6	68.1	16.5
1988	76.9	60.0	78.3	86.6	95.2	95.4	91.8	67.9	16.7
1989	77.1	61.0	78.5	86.8	95.4	95.3	92.2	68.3	16.8
1990	77.1	59.6	78.5	86.2	95.2	95.3	91.7	68.6	16.6
1991	76.5	57.3	78.0	85.4	94.9	95.0	91.4	67.7	15.9
1992	76.5	56.9	78.0	85.2	94.9	94.7	91.8	67.7	16.2
1993	76.2	56.6	77.7	85.5	94.7	94.5	91.3	67.3	15.9
1994	75.9	57.7	77.3	85.5	93.9	93.9	90.3	66.4	17.2
1995	75.7	58.5	77.1	85.1	94.1	93.4	90.0	67.1	16.9
1996	75.8	57.1	77.3	85.0	94.4	93.6	90.4	68.0	17.2
1997	75.9	56.1	77.5	85.1	94.2	93.7	90.6	68.9	17.4
1998	75.6	56.6	77.2	84.6	94.4	93.7	90.3	69.1	16.6
1999	75.6	56.4	77.2	84.9	94.3	93.8	90.1	69.1	17.2
2000	75.5	56.5	77.1	85.2	94.5	93.8	89.7	68.2	17.9
2001	75.1	53.7	76.9	84.1	93.9	93.6	89.7	69.1	17.8
2002	74.8	50.3	76.7	83.2	93.7	93.2	89.6	70.2	17.8
2003	74.2	47.5	76.3	82.5	93.3	93.1	88.8	69.7	18.6
2004	74.1	47.4	76.2	82.1	93.2	93.0	88.7	69.8	19.1

[1]Beginning in 2003, persons who selected this race group only; persons who selected more than one race group are not included. Prior to 2003, persons who reported more than one race group were included in the group they identified as the main race.

Table 1-8. Civilian Labor Force Participation Rates by Sex, Race, Age, and Hispanic Origin, 1948–2004
—Continued

(Percent.)

Year, sex, race, and Hispanic origin	16 years and over	16 to 19 years	20 years and over						
			Total	20 to 24 years	25 to 34 years	35 to 44 years	45 to 54 years	55 to 64 years	65 years and over
White Women[1]									
1954	33.3	40.6	32.7	44.4	32.5	39.3	39.8	29.1	9.1
1955	34.5	40.7	34.0	45.8	32.8	40.0	42.7	31.8	10.5
1956	35.7	43.1	35.1	46.5	33.2	41.5	44.4	34.0	10.6
1957	35.7	42.2	35.2	45.8	33.6	41.5	45.4	33.7	10.2
1958	35.8	40.1	35.5	46.0	33.6	41.4	46.5	34.5	10.1
1959	36.0	39.6	35.6	44.5	33.4	41.4	47.8	35.7	10.0
1960	36.5	40.3	36.2	45.7	34.1	41.5	48.6	36.2	10.6
1961	36.9	40.6	36.6	46.9	34.3	41.8	48.9	37.2	10.5
1962	36.7	39.8	36.5	47.1	34.1	42.2	48.9	38.0	9.8
1963	37.2	38.7	37.0	47.3	34.8	43.1	49.5	38.9	9.4
1964	37.5	37.8	37.5	48.8	35.0	43.3	50.2	39.4	9.9
1965	38.1	39.2	38.0	49.2	36.3	44.4	49.9	40.3	9.7
1966	39.2	42.6	38.8	51.0	37.7	45.0	50.6	41.1	9.4
1967	40.1	42.5	39.8	53.1	39.7	46.4	50.9	41.9	9.3
1968	40.7	43.0	40.4	54.0	40.6	47.5	51.5	42.0	9.4
1969	41.8	44.6	41.5	56.4	41.7	48.6	53.0	42.6	9.7
1970	42.6	45.6	42.2	57.7	43.2	49.9	53.7	42.6	9.5
1971	42.6	45.4	42.3	58.0	43.7	50.2	53.6	42.5	9.3
1972	43.2	48.1	42.7	59.4	46.0	50.7	53.4	41.9	9.0
1973	44.1	50.1	43.5	61.7	48.7	52.2	53.4	40.7	8.7
1974	45.2	51.7	44.4	63.9	51.3	53.6	54.3	40.4	8.0
1975	45.9	51.5	45.3	65.5	53.8	54.9	54.3	40.6	8.0
1976	46.9	52.8	46.2	66.3	56.0	57.1	54.7	40.7	7.9
1977	48.0	54.5	47.3	67.8	58.5	58.9	55.3	40.7	7.9
1978	49.4	56.7	48.7	69.3	61.2	60.7	56.7	41.1	8.1
1979	50.5	57.4	49.8	70.5	63.1	63.0	58.1	41.5	8.1
1980	51.2	56.2	50.6	70.6	64.8	65.0	59.6	40.9	7.9
1981	51.9	55.4	51.5	71.5	66.4	66.4	60.9	40.9	7.9
1982	52.4	55.0	52.2	71.8	67.8	67.5	61.4	41.5	7.8
1983	52.7	54.5	52.5	72.1	68.7	68.2	61.9	41.1	7.8
1984	53.3	55.4	53.1	72.5	69.8	69.6	62.7	41.2	7.5
1985	54.1	55.2	54.0	73.8	70.9	71.4	64.2	41.5	7.0
1986	55.0	56.3	54.9	74.1	71.8	72.9	65.8	42.1	7.3
1987	55.7	56.5	55.6	74.8	72.5	74.2	67.2	42.4	7.2
1988	56.4	57.2	56.3	74.9	73.0	74.9	69.2	43.6	7.7
1989	57.2	57.1	57.2	74.0	73.8	75.9	70.6	45.2	8.2
1990	57.4	55.3	57.6	73.4	74.1	76.6	71.3	45.5	8.5
1991	57.4	54.1	57.6	72.5	73.8	76.8	72.4	45.4	8.5
1992	57.7	52.5	58.1	73.5	74.4	77.0	72.8	46.8	8.2
1993	58.0	53.5	58.3	73.4	74.3	76.9	74.0	47.6	8.1
1994	58.9	55.1	59.2	73.4	74.9	77.5	75.2	49.4	9.2
1995	59.0	55.5	59.2	72.3	75.8	77.6	75.2	49.5	9.0
1996	59.1	54.7	59.4	73.3	75.5	77.8	76.1	50.1	8.7
1997	59.5	54.1	59.9	73.9	76.3	77.9	76.6	51.5	8.6
1998	59.4	55.4	59.7	74.3	76.3	76.9	76.6	51.6	8.7
1999	59.6	54.5	59.9	73.9	76.0	77.1	77.1	52.0	8.9
2000	59.5	54.5	59.9	74.5	75.7	77.2	77.5	52.4	9.4
2001	59.4	52.4	59.9	74.2	75.1	77.0	77.1	53.8	9.6
2002	59.3	50.8	60.0	74.0	75.0	76.3	76.6	55.8	9.9
2003	59.2	47.9	59.9	72.7	73.7	75.5	77.3	57.4	10.8
2004	58.9	46.7	59.7	71.9	73.6	75.2	77.1	57.0	11.2

[1]Beginning in 2003, persons who selected this race group only; persons who selected more than one race group are not included. Prior to 2003, persons who reported more than one race group were included in the group they identified as the main race.

Table 1-8. Civilian Labor Force Participation Rates by Sex, Race, Age, and Hispanic Origin, 1948–2004
—*Continued*

(Percent.)

Year, sex, race, and Hispanic origin	16 years and over	16 to 19 years	20 years and over						
			Total	20 to 24 years	25 to 34 years	35 to 44 years	45 to 54 years	55 to 64 years	65 years and over
Black Men[1]									
1972	73.6	46.3	78.5	82.7	92.7	91.1	85.4	72.5	24.2
1973	73.4	45.7	78.4	83.7	91.8	91.0	87.4	69.5	22.3
1974	72.9	46.7	77.6	83.6	92.8	90.4	84.0	68.9	21.6
1975	70.9	42.6	76.0	78.7	91.6	89.4	83.5	67.7	20.7
1976	70.0	41.3	75.4	79.0	90.9	89.9	82.4	65.1	19.8
1977	70.6	43.2	75.6	79.2	90.7	91.0	82.0	65.5	20.0
1978	71.5	44.9	76.2	78.8	90.9	90.5	83.2	67.9	21.1
1979	71.3	43.6	76.3	80.7	90.8	90.4	84.5	64.8	19.5
1980	70.3	43.2	75.1	79.9	90.9	89.1	83.0	61.9	16.9
1981	70.0	41.6	74.5	79.2	88.9	89.3	82.7	62.1	16.0
1982	70.1	39.8	74.7	78.7	89.2	89.8	82.2	61.9	15.9
1983	70.6	39.9	75.2	79.4	89.0	89.7	84.5	62.6	14.0
1984	70.8	41.7	74.8	79.1	88.9	90.0	83.7	58.9	13.7
1985	70.8	44.6	74.4	79.0	88.8	89.8	83.0	58.9	13.9
1986	71.2	43.7	74.8	80.1	89.6	89.6	84.1	59.1	12.6
1987	71.1	43.6	74.7	77.8	89.4	88.6	83.7	62.1	13.7
1988	71.0	43.8	74.6	79.3	89.3	88.2	83.5	59.4	14.3
1989	71.0	44.6	74.4	80.2	89.7	88.7	82.5	55.5	14.3
1990	71.0	40.7	75.0	76.8	88.8	88.1	83.5	58.0	13.0
1991	70.4	37.3	74.6	76.7	87.3	87.7	83.4	58.7	13.0
1992	70.7	40.6	74.3	75.4	88.0	86.5	81.8	60.0	13.7
1993	69.6	39.5	73.2	74.1	87.3	86.1	80.0	57.9	11.6
1994	69.1	40.8	72.5	73.9	86.2	85.9	79.1	54.5	12.7
1995	69.0	40.1	72.5	74.6	87.5	84.1	78.5	54.4	14.9
1996	68.7	39.5	72.3	73.4	87.5	84.4	78.5	55.6	12.9
1997	68.3	37.4	72.2	72.1	86.8	84.8	80.1	54.3	12.9
1998	69.0	40.7	72.5	71.8	87.1	85.0	79.9	57.3	14.0
1999	68.7	38.6	72.4	69.8	89.2	86.0	78.5	55.5	12.7
2000	69.2	39.2	72.8	73.3	87.8	85.2	79.2	57.4	14.4
2001	68.4	37.9	72.1	69.7	86.6	84.9	78.4	58.9	16.7
2002	68.4	37.3	72.1	70.7	85.9	84.7	79.5	58.4	16.9
2003	67.3	31.1	71.5	71.1	84.7	85.7	77.7	57.6	17.0
2004	66.7	30.0	70.9	69.9	86.1	84.0	76.9	57.1	17.0
Black Women[1]									
1972	48.7	32.2	51.2	57.0	60.8	61.4	57.2	44.0	12.6
1973	49.3	34.2	51.6	58.0	62.7	61.7	56.1	44.7	11.4
1974	49.0	33.4	51.4	58.8	62.4	62.2	56.4	42.8	10.4
1975	48.8	34.2	51.1	55.9	62.8	62.0	56.6	43.1	10.7
1976	49.8	32.9	52.5	56.9	66.7	63.0	56.8	43.7	11.3
1977	50.8	32.9	53.6	59.3	68.5	64.1	57.9	43.7	10.5
1978	53.1	37.3	55.5	62.7	70.6	67.2	59.4	43.8	11.1
1979	53.1	36.8	55.4	61.5	70.1	68.0	59.6	44.0	10.9
1980	53.1	34.9	55.6	60.2	70.5	68.1	61.4	44.8	10.2
1981	53.5	34.0	56.0	61.1	70.0	69.8	62.0	45.4	9.3
1982	53.7	33.5	56.2	60.1	70.2	71.7	62.4	44.8	8.5
1983	54.2	33.0	56.8	59.1	72.3	72.6	62.3	44.8	8.2
1984	55.2	35.0	57.6	60.7	71.5	73.7	64.5	46.1	8.0
1985	56.5	37.9	58.6	62.5	72.4	74.8	65.7	45.3	9.4
1986	56.9	39.1	58.9	64.6	72.4	75.8	66.5	43.6	7.8
1987	58.0	39.6	60.0	64.4	73.5	77.8	67.5	44.4	8.6
1988	58.0	37.9	60.1	63.2	73.7	78.1	68.3	43.4	9.6
1989	58.7	40.4	60.6	65.5	73.6	78.0	70.0	42.4	9.8
1990	58.3	36.8	60.6	62.4	72.3	77.7	70.7	43.2	9.9
1991	57.5	33.5	60.0	60.3	71.4	77.2	70.2	44.1	9.2
1992	58.5	35.2	60.8	60.8	73.1	77.1	71.7	45.1	8.6
1993	57.9	34.6	60.2	62.6	70.9	76.8	71.2	44.4	8.3
1994	58.7	36.3	60.9	64.5	71.9	76.4	71.3	45.3	9.2
1995	59.5	39.8	61.4	63.7	73.9	77.3	70.5	47.2	7.7
1996	60.4	38.9	62.6	65.2	75.9	78.2	72.0	47.2	7.7
1997	61.7	39.9	64.0	69.9	78.1	78.4	73.2	47.6	8.2
1998	62.8	42.5	64.8	69.6	79.6	79.9	74.0	48.5	7.9
1999	63.5	38.8	66.1	72.7	82.1	80.4	74.6	48.4	8.9
2000	63.1	39.6	65.4	70.5	81.1	79.9	74.9	48.6	9.9
2001	62.8	37.3	65.2	70.1	81.2	79.6	73.9	49.9	10.1
2002	61.8	34.7	64.4	66.9	79.7	79.2	73.3	51.8	9.8
2003	61.9	33.7	64.6	65.7	79.1	80.6	74.2	51.9	10.3
2004	61.5	32.8	64.2	66.8	77.2	80.6	74.3	52.3	10.7

[1]Beginning in 2003, persons who selected this race group only; persons who selected more than one race group are not included. Prior to 2003, persons who reported more than one race group were included in the group they identified as the main race.

Table 1-8. Civilian Labor Force Participation Rates by Sex, Race, Age, and Hispanic Origin, 1948–2004
—Continued

(Percent.)

Year, sex, race, and Hispanic origin	16 years and over	16 to 19 years	20 years and over						
			Total	20 to 24 years	25 to 34 years	35 to 44 years	45 to 54 years	55 to 64 years	65 years and over
Hispanic Men									
1973	81.5	...	85.9	...	...	...	...	...	...
1974	81.7	...	86.0	...	...	...	...	...	...
1975	80.7	...	85.5	...	...	...	...	...	...
1976	79.6	...	84.2	...	...	...	...	...	...
1977	80.9	...	84.8	...	...	...	...	...	...
1978	81.1	...	84.9	...	...	...	...	...	...
1979	81.3	...	85.3	...	...	...	...	...	...
1980	81.4	...	84.9	...	...	...	...	...	...
1981	80.6	...	84.7	...	...	...	...	...	...
1982	79.7	...	84.0	...	...	...	...	...	...
1983	80.3	...	84.1	...	...	...	...	...	...
1984	80.6	...	84.3	...	...	...	...	...	...
1985	80.3	...	84.0	...	...	...	...	...	...
1986	81.0	...	84.6	...	...	...	...	...	...
1987	81.0	...	84.5	...	...	...	...	...	...
1988	81.9	...	85.0	...	...	...	...	...	...
1989	82.0	...	85.0	...	...	...	...	...	...
1990	81.4	...	84.7	...	...	...	...	...	...
1991	80.3	...	83.8	...	...	...	...	...	...
1992	80.7	...	84.0	...	...	...	...	...	...
1993	80.2	...	83.5	...	...	...	...	...	...
1994	79.2	50.0	82.5	88.0	92.5	91.5	85.7	63.6	14.4
1995	79.1	50.2	82.4	86.2	92.9	91.3	85.6	62.4	15.8
1996	79.6	50.0	83.0	85.7	93.2	91.7	87.0	65.9	16.7
1997	80.1	47.4	84.1	88.1	93.5	91.9	87.8	68.4	17.3
1998	79.8	48.7	83.6	88.1	94.0	91.4	86.7	70.2	14.9
1999	79.8	50.1	83.5	88.1	93.9	92.2	86.2	68.6	18.2
2000	81.5	50.7	85.3	89.1	94.1	93.3	87.6	69.4	18.5
2001	81.0	52.2	84.3	86.8	93.4	92.7	86.7	68.6	16.8
2002	80.2	48.8	83.6	86.1	93.5	92.1	86.1	67.3	16.3
2003	80.1	40.9	84.1	86.2	93.6	92.9	85.4	68.8	17.4
2004	80.4	42.4	84.2	84.4	93.6	93.2	87.2	69.6	20.8
Hispanic Women									
1973	41.0	...	41.3	...	...	...	...	...	...
1974	42.4	...	42.7	...	...	...	...	...	...
1975	43.2	...	43.8	...	...	...	...	...	...
1976	44.3	...	44.6	...	...	...	...	...	...
1977	44.3	...	45.1	...	...	...	...	...	...
1978	46.6	...	47.2	...	...	...	...	...	...
1979	47.4	...	48.0	...	...	...	...	...	...
1980	47.4	...	48.5	...	...	...	...	...	...
1981	48.3	...	49.7	...	...	...	...	...	...
1982	48.1	...	49.3	...	...	...	...	...	...
1983	47.7	...	49.0	...	...	...	...	...	...
1984	49.6	...	50.5	...	...	...	...	...	...
1985	49.3	...	50.6	...	...	...	...	...	...
1986	50.1	...	51.7	...	...	...	...	...	...
1987	52.0	...	53.3	...	...	...	...	...	...
1988	53.2	...	54.2	...	...	...	...	...	...
1989	53.5	...	54.9	...	...	...	...	...	...
1990	53.1	...	54.8	...	...	...	...	...	...
1991	52.4	...	54.0	...	...	...	...	...	...
1992	52.8	...	54.3	...	...	...	...	...	...
1993	52.1	...	53.8	...	...	...	...	...	...
1994	52.9	38.7	54.4	57.9	60.5	66.4	61.4	38.1	7.9
1995	52.6	40.4	53.9	55.9	61.6	65.9	60.5	37.2	6.6
1996	53.4	36.5	55.2	59.2	62.0	67.0	62.7	40.5	6.9
1997	55.1	38.0	57.0	62.3	63.7	69.3	63.3	40.6	8.1
1998	55.6	42.4	57.1	62.2	64.5	67.9	64.7	41.9	6.6
1999	55.9	40.6	57.7	63.0	62.7	70.5	66.2	42.4	6.5
2000	57.5	41.4	59.3	65.0	65.3	69.9	68.5	41.2	7.7
2001	57.6	41.1	59.3	64.6	65.2	70.3	68.3	43.2	6.7
2002	57.6	38.8	59.5	65.0	65.8	69.5	66.3	46.1	8.5
2003	55.9	34.5	58.1	63.3	62.9	68.5	65.3	47.1	9.4
2004	56.1	33.7	58.4	62.9	62.9	68.7	67.9	47.8	9.8

Note: Persons of Hispanic origin may be of any race.

. . . = Not available.

Table 1-9. Employed and Unemployed Full- and Part-Time Workers by Age, Sex, and Race, 1994–2004

(Thousands of people.)

Year, age, sex, and race	Employed [1]								Unemployed	
	Full-time workers				Part-time workers				Looking for full-time work	Looking for part-time work
	Total	At work		Not at work	Total	At work [2]		Not at work		
		35 hours or more	1 to 34 hours for economic or noneconomic reasons			Part-time for economic reasons	Part-time for noneconomic reasons			
Total, 16 Years and Over										
1994	99 772	85 686	9 980	4 106	23 288	3 453	18 321	1 513	6 513	1 483
1995	101 679	87 736	9 924	4 020	23 220	3 215	18 443	1 562	5 909	1 495
1996	103 537	89 020	10 381	4 137	23 170	3 080	18 459	1 631	5 803	1 433
1997	106 334	92 399	9 922	4 013	23 224	2 826	18 856	1 542	5 395	1 344
1998	108 202	91 880	12 260	4 062	23 261	2 497	19 239	1 524	4 916	1 293
1999	110 302	96 276	10 079	3 947	23 186	2 216	19 509	1 461	4 669	1 211
2000	113 846	100 533	9 125	4 188	23 044	2 003	19 548	1 493	4 538	1 154
2001	113 573	99 047	10 464	4 061	23 361	2 297	19 494	1 570	5 546	1 254
2002	112 700	99 042	9 746	3 912	23 785	2 755	19 549	1 481	7 063	1 314
2003	113 324	99 539	9 841	3 944	24 412	3 184	19 702	1 525	7 361	1 413
2004	114 518	100 496	10 053	3 969	24 734	3 113	20 109	1 513	6 762	1 388
Total, 20 Years and Over										
1994	97 890	84 126	9 711	4 052	19 010	3 094	14 580	1 337	5 865	811
1995	99 651	86 043	9 643	3 965	18 830	2 853	14 613	1 365	5 253	806
1996	101 496	87 344	10 070	4 083	18 712	2 733	14 556	1 423	5 157	773
1997	104 168	90 613	9 601	3 954	18 729	2 500	14 872	1 357	4 748	719
1998	105 882	89 966	11 915	4 001	18 530	2 197	15 007	1 326	4 332	672
1999	107 917	94 270	9 754	3 893	18 399	1 939	15 187	1 273	4 094	624
2000	111 353	98 439	8 787	4 127	18 348	1 747	15 297	1 304	3 978	632
2001	111 323	97 161	10 156	4 006	18 870	2 013	15 486	1 371	4 956	682
2002	110 679	97 342	9 474	3 862	19 475	2 448	15 704	1 322	6 395	730
2003	111 578	98 087	9 587	3 904	20 239	2 875	16 001	1 363	6 705	818
2004	112 747	99 034	9 789	3 924	20 598	2 817	16 436	1 345	6 178	764
Men, 16 Years and Over										
1994	58 832	51 615	5 144	2 073	7 617	1 524	5 691	403	3 745	622
1995	59 936	52 833	5 120	1 984	7 441	1 401	5 626	414	3 374	609
1996	60 762	53 425	5 290	2 047	7 445	1 322	5 692	431	3 276	604
1997	62 258	55 216	5 040	2 001	7 427	1 187	5 821	418	3 012	564
1998	63 189	55 080	6 136	1 973	7 504	1 063	6 026	416	2 707	559
1999	63 930	57 034	4 971	1 924	7 516	946	6 178	392	2 548	518
2000	65 930	59 345	4 555	2 030	7 375	856	6 105	414	2 486	488
2001	65 623	58 386	5 241	1 996	7 573	1 021	6 129	424	3 144	546
2002	65 205	58 318	4 971	1 916	7 697	1 246	6 050	401	4 029	568
2003	65 379	58 428	5 023	1 927	7 953	1 473	6 056	423	4 291	615
2004	66 444	59 363	5 148	1 933	8 080	1 405	6 258	417	3 843	613
Men, 20 Years and Over										
1994	57 707	50 678	4 989	2 040	5 587	1 351	3 908	329	3 359	269
1995	58 707	51 793	4 960	1 955	5 377	1 228	3 828	322	2 988	251
1996	59 543	52 411	5 117	2 015	5 354	1 155	3 859	341	2 899	248
1997	60 974	54 148	4 857	1 969	5 310	1 023	3 944	343	2 644	239
1998	61 837	53 947	5 950	1 940	5 297	925	4 050	322	2 366	214
1999	62 514	55 827	4 790	1 897	5 247	809	4 127	311	2 222	211
2000	64 464	58 095	4 370	2 000	5 170	733	4 109	328	2 162	214
2001	64 311	57 273	5 072	1 966	5 465	881	4 253	331	2 801	239
2002	64 006	57 302	4 815	1 889	5 728	1 093	4 299	336	3 642	254
2003	64 364	57 580	4 879	1 905	6 051	1 314	4 388	348	3 906	302
2004	65 377	58 471	5 000	1 906	6 196	1 251	4 600	345	3 511	281
Women, 16 Years and Over										
1994	40 940	34 071	4 836	2 033	15 670	1 929	12 631	1 111	2 768	861
1995	41 743	34 903	4 805	2 036	15 779	1 814	12 817	1 148	2 535	886
1996	42 776	35 594	5 091	2 090	15 725	1 758	12 767	1 200	2 527	829
1997	44 076	37 183	4 882	2 011	15 797	1 638	13 035	1 124	2 383	779
1998	45 014	36 800	6 124	2 090	15 757	1 435	13 214	1 108	2 210	734
1999	46 372	39 242	5 108	2 022	15 670	1 270	13 330	1 069	2 121	693
2000	47 916	41 188	4 570	2 158	15 670	1 147	13 443	1 080	2 052	666
2001	47 950	40 661	5 223	2 065	15 788	1 276	13 365	1 146	2 402	709
2002	47 494	40 723	4 775	1 996	16 088	1 509	13 498	1 080	3 034	747
2003	47 946	41 111	4 818	2 017	16 459	1 711	13 646	1 102	3 070	798
2004	48 073	41 133	4 905	2 036	16 654	1 708	13 851	1 096	2 919	775

[1]Employed persons are classified as full- or part-time workers based on their usual weekly hours at all jobs, regardless of the number of hours they are at work during the reference week. Persons absent from work also are classified according to their usual status.
[2]Includes some persons at work 35 hours or more classified by their reason for working part-time.

Table 1-9. Employed and Unemployed Full- and Part-Time Workers by Age, Sex, and Race, 1994–2004—*Continued*

(Thousands of people.)

Year, age, sex, and race	Employed [1]								Unemployed	
	Full-time workers				Part-time workers				Looking for full-time work	Looking for part-time work
	Total	At work		Not at work	Total	At work [2]		Not at work		
		35 hours or more	1 to 34 hours for economic or noneconomic reasons			Part-time for economic reasons	Part-time for noneconomic reasons			
Women, 20 Years and Over										
1994	40 183	33 449	4 722	2 012	13 423	1 743	10 672	1 008	2 506	543
1995	40 943	34 250	4 683	2 010	13 453	1 623	10 785	1 043	2 265	554
1996	41 953	34 933	4 953	2 068	13 357	1 579	10 697	1 082	2 258	525
1997	43 194	36 465	4 744	1 985	13 419	1 477	10 927	1 015	2 105	480
1998	44 045	36 019	5 965	2 061	13 233	1 272	10 957	1 004	1 966	458
1999	45 403	38 443	4 964	1 996	13 152	1 131	11 059	962	1 872	413
2000	46 889	40 344	4 417	2 128	13 178	1 013	11 188	976	1 816	419
2001	47 012	39 889	5 083	2 040	13 405	1 132	11 233	1 040	2 155	444
2002	46 673	40 040	4 660	1 973	13 747	1 355	11 406	986	2 752	476
2003	47 215	40 507	4 708	2 000	14 188	1 560	11 613	1 015	2 799	515
2004	47 371	40 563	4 790	2 017	14 402	1 567	11 836	1 000	2 667	483
White Men, 16 Years and Over [3]										
1994	50 964	44 750	4 431	1 783	6 487	1 192	4 946	350	2 800	475
1995	51 768	45 634	4 406	1 728	6 378	1 100	4 921	357	2 525	475
1996	52 527	46 208	4 547	1 772	6 361	1 046	4 941	374	2 426	470
1997	53 640	47 563	4 358	1 719	6 358	909	5 084	365	2 202	440
1998	54 206	47 239	5 257	1 709	6 398	829	5 209	360	1 999	432
1999	54 756	48 834	4 274	1 647	6 383	730	5 314	339	1 883	391
2000	56 068	50 434	3 896	1 738	6 221	656	5 213	351	1 798	379
2001	55 830	49 625	4 504	1 701	6 381	793	5 225	364	2 323	431
2002	55 369	49 459	4 267	1 644	6 480	980	5 150	350	3 017	443
2003	55 216	49 323	4 266	1 628	6 650	1 146	5 148	357	3 164	479
2004	55 926	49 891	4 396	1 638	6 786	1 092	5 331	363	2 805	477
White Men, 20 Years and Over [3]										
1994	49 959	43 912	4 291	1 756	4 717	1 048	3 382	287	2 533	203
1995	50 691	44 726	4 263	1 702	4 563	958	3 330	275	2 260	204
1996	51 442	45 300	4 397	1 745	4 534	907	3 330	297	2 167	197
1997	52 498	46 609	4 199	1 691	4 488	771	3 419	298	1 946	194
1998	53 017	46 240	5 095	1 682	4 483	716	3 487	280	1 756	164
1999	53 513	47 764	4 124	1 626	4 420	618	3 534	268	1 651	162
2000	54 778	49 335	3 733	1 710	4 341	558	3 505	278	1 566	165
2001	54 666	48 636	4 354	1 676	4 579	677	3 616	285	2 080	195
2002	54 333	48 581	4 133	1 619	4 790	857	3 640	293	2 743	200
2003	54 339	48 585	4 145	1 609	5 010	1 016	3 703	291	2 893	231
2004	55 005	49 124	4 267	1 614	5 154	961	3 895	299	2 567	217
White Women, 16 Years and Over [3]										
1994	33 906	28 170	4 031	1 705	13 832	1 517	11 316	1 000	1 935	682
1995	34 422	28 685	4 039	1 697	13 922	1 431	11 448	1 043	1 755	705
1996	35 057	29 124	4 196	1 737	13 863	1 388	11 398	1 077	1 749	656
1997	35 965	30 286	4 036	1 643	13 894	1 260	11 623	1 011	1 587	608
1998	36 553	29 792	5 039	1 722	13 774	1 089	11 695	990	1 481	572
1999	37 417	31 577	4 157	1 684	13 679	947	11 768	964	1 469	530
2000	38 438	32 942	3 729	1 767	13 698	867	11 870	961	1 422	521
2001	38 445	32 491	4 252	1 702	13 773	971	11 787	1 015	1 664	551
2002	38 152	32 623	3 896	1 633	14 011	1 152	11 903	956	2 084	595
2003	38 249	32 659	3 939	1 652	14 120	1 304	11 860	956	2 038	629
2004	38 240	32 555	4 018	1 667	14 287	1 280	12 038	969	1 968	597
White Women, 20 Years and Over [3]										
1994	33 250	27 628	3 936	1 686	11 866	1 359	9 596	912	1 754	443
1995	33 728	28 116	3 938	1 674	11 916	1 277	9 690	949	1 579	463
1996	34 350	28 553	4 078	1 719	11 814	1 243	9 598	973	1 570	427
1997	35 216	29 677	3 919	1 620	11 847	1 136	9 788	923	1 396	388
1998	35 738	29 130	4 910	1 698	11 604	953	9 749	902	1 318	370
1999	36 602	30 905	4 036	1 662	11 496	839	9 789	867	1 297	319
2000	37 585	32 242	3 600	1 743	11 560	754	9 935	872	1 256	339
2001	37 658	31 839	4 139	1 680	11 711	853	9 933	924	1 492	357
2002	37 467	32 049	3 803	1 615	11 981	1 029	10 079	873	1 888	381
2003	37 640	32 158	3 845	1 637	12 183	1 180	10 124	879	1 866	411
2004	37 663	32 085	3 927	1 652	12 377	1 166	10 326	885	1 795	377

[1]Employed persons are classified as full- or part-time workers based on their usual weekly hours at all jobs, regardless of the number of hours they are at work during the reference week. Persons absent from work also are classified according to their usual status.
[2]Includes some persons at work 35 hours or more classified by their reason for working part-time.
[3]Beginning in 2003, persons who selected this race group only; persons who selected more than one race group are not included. Prior to 2003, persons who reported more than one race group were included in the group they identified as the main race.

Table 1-9. Employed and Unemployed Full- and Part-Time Workers by Age, Sex, and Race, 1994–2004—Continued

(Thousands of people.)

Year, age, sex, and race	Employed[1]								Unemployed	
	Full-time workers				Part-time workers				Looking for full-time work	Looking for part-time work
	Total	At work		Not at work	Total	At work[2]		Not at work		
		35 hours or more	1 to 34 hours for economic or noneconomic reasons			Part-time for economic reasons	Part-time for noneconomic reasons			
Black Men, 16 Years and Over[3]										
1994	5 452	4 723	520	209	788	247	504	38	738	111
1995	5 685	4 995	513	177	737	216	479	43	660	101
1996	5 723	4 971	547	206	733	199	494	40	705	103
1997	5 894	5 193	490	211	713	203	474	36	648	98
1998	6 148	5 322	637	189	723	168	520	34	572	99
1999	6 263	5 574	494	196	764	163	568	33	528	97
2000	6 350	5 704	445	202	732	144	548	41	542	78
2001	6 178	5 509	468	200	761	165	557	39	626	83
2002	6 194	5 541	480	173	765	188	546	30	749	86
2003	6 055	5 414	453	188	765	221	505	39	804	87
2004	6 177	5 538	460	179	736	205	499	32	763	98
Black Men, 20 Years and Over[3]										
1994	5 369	4 655	509	205	595	223	343	29	634	47
1995	5 582	4 906	502	175	554	193	326	36	558	35
1996	5 622	4 892	528	201	545	177	338	30	602	37
1997	5 790	5 111	471	208	535	179	326	30	549	35
1998	6 023	5 218	620	185	507	147	334	25	487	37
1999	6 140	5 477	471	192	561	142	392	27	446	35
2000	6 222	5 594	429	199	520	125	363	32	468	31
2001	6 069	5 417	455	197	558	145	382	31	542	31
2002	6 073	5 437	465	171	579	166	387	26	660	35
2003	5 980	5 355	439	185	607	201	372	34	717	43
2004	6 089	5 463	449	177	592	189	376	27	689	44
Black Women, 16 Years and Over[3]										
1994	5 289	4 408	627	253	1 306	319	906	79	678	140
1995	5 542	4 679	594	268	1 315	290	952	74	637	140
1996	5 776	4 785	710	280	1 310	289	933	88	652	132
1997	6 026	5 085	652	289	1 336	305	952	79	677	136
1998	6 281	5 166	828	288	1 404	278	1 045	81	624	131
1999	6 641	5 651	734	256	1 388	257	1 059	72	554	130
2000	6 780	5 862	632	287	1 293	211	1 005	77	515	106
2001	6 761	5 777	715	270	1 307	223	998	85	584	122
2002	6 588	5 685	640	263	1 326	259	991	76	744	114
2003	6 552	5 709	595	247	1 367	274	1 017	76	774	121
2004	6 597	5 740	611	246	1 399	306	1 022	71	744	124
Black Women, 20 Years and Over[3]										
1994	5 211	4 346	612	251	1 108	300	740	69	608	76
1995	5 469	4 623	580	266	1 087	263	757	66	553	66
1996	5 684	4 714	693	277	1 078	263	737	79	570	73
1997	5 921	5 001	634	286	1 092	273	755	64	603	70
1998	6 159	5 073	803	283	1 131	256	807	68	555	66
1999	6 519	5 549	717	252	1 145	230	850	65	486	75
2000	6 651	5 753	615	283	1 052	197	788	67	456	56
2001	6 647	5 684	695	268	1 094	203	816	75	521	61
2002	6 492	5 605	626	261	1 117	234	816	68	671	67
2003	6 468	5 639	583	246	1 168	257	842	69	698	75
2004	6 512	5 674	595	243	1 195	287	844	64	679	76

Note: Beginning in January 2004, data reflect revised population controls used in the household survey. See "Notes and Definitions" for information on historical comparability.

[1]Employed persons are classified as full- or part-time workers based on their usual weekly hours at all jobs, regardless of the number of hours they are at work during the reference week. Persons absent from work also are classified according to their usual status.
[2]Includes some persons at work 35 hours or more classified by their reason for working part-time.
[3]Beginning in 2003, persons who selected this race group only; persons who selected more than one race group are not included. Prior to 2003, persons who reported more than one race group were included in the group they identified as the main race.

Table 1-10. Persons Not in the Labor Force by Desire and Availability for Work, Age, and Sex, 1999–2004

(Thousands of people.)

Category	Total		Age						Sex			
			16 to 24 years		25 to 54 years		55 and over		Men		Women	
	1999	2000	1999	2000	1999	2000	1999	2000	1999	2000	1999	2000
TOTAL, NOT IN THE LABOR FORCE	68 385	69 994	11 740	11 702	18 785	19 263	37 861	39 029	25 210	25 684	43 175	44 310
Do Not Want a Job Now [1]	63 818	65 581	9 938	10 083	16 814	17 286	37 066	38 212	23 307	23 818	40 511	41 762
Want a Job [1]	4 568	4 413	1 802	1 619	1 971	1 977	795	817	1 903	1 866	2 665	2 547
Did not search for work in the previous year	2 723	2 705	981	899	1 144	1 164	599	642	1 083	1 076	1 640	1 628
Searched for work in the previous year [2]	1 844	1 708	822	720	827	813	196	175	820	789	1 024	919
Not available to work now	644	552	345	276	258	242	41	34	249	216	395	335
Available to work now	1 201	1 157	477	444	569	571	155	142	571	573	629	584
Reason not currently looking:												
Discouragement over job prospects [3]	273	266	86	79	146	148	41	40	161	164	113	102
Reasons other than discouragement	927	891	391	365	423	423	114	102	411	409	517	482
Family responsibilities	132	120	29	26	92	84	11	10	29	23	103	96
In school or training	214	184	176	157	34	27	4	1	110	97	104	88
Ill health or disability	97	96	13	15	57	58	26	22	39	49	58	47
Other [4]	485	491	173	167	239	254	73	69	234	240	251	251

Category	Total		Age						Sex			
			16 to 24 years		25 to 54 years		55 and over		Men		Women	
	2001	2002	2001	2002	2001	2002	2001	2002	2001	2002	2001	2002
TOTAL, NOT IN THE LABOR FORCE	71 359	72 707	12 347	12 976	19 814	20 358	39 198	39 373	26 396	27 085	44 962	45 621
Do Not Want a Job Now [1]	66 769	68 029	10 616	11 254	17 797	18 286	38 355	38 489	24 403	24 994	42 366	43 035
Want a Job [1]	4 590	4 677	1 730	1 722	2 017	2 071	842	884	1 993	2 091	2 597	2 586
Did not search for work in the previous year	2 731	2 673	939	910	1 150	1 112	642	651	1 134	1 135	1 597	1 538
Searched for work in the previous year [2]	1 859	2 004	791	812	867	960	201	233	859	956	1 000	1 048
Not available to work now	593	565	300	272	256	252	37	41	228	227	365	338
Available to work now	1 266	1 439	492	540	611	708	163	191	631	729	634	710
Reason not currently looking:												
Discouragement over job prospects [3]	321	369	104	110	170	209	47	51	192	226	129	143
Reasons other than discouragement	945	1 070	388	430	441	499	116	141	440	503	505	567
Family responsibilities	133	150	32	31	89	99	13	20	29	34	105	116
In school or training	203	238	172	195	30	41	1	2	111	126	92	112
Ill health or disability	96	107	16	16	56	61	25	30	45	50	51	56
Other [4]	513	575	168	188	266	299	77	88	255	292	257	283

Category	Total		Age						Sex			
			16 to 24 years		25 to 54 years		55 and over		Men		Women	
	2003	2004	2003	2004	2003	2004	2003	2004	2003	2004	2003	2004
TOTAL, NOT IN THE LABOR FORCE	74 658	75 956	13 800	14 151	20 980	21 288	39 878	40 517	28 197	28 730	46 461	47 225
Do Not Want a Job Now [1]	69 932	71 103	12 079	12 422	18 857	19 136	38 996	39 545	26 073	26 565	43 859	44 538
Want a Job [1]	4 726	4 852	1 721	1 729	2 124	2 152	882	971	2 124	2 165	2 603	2 687
Did not search for work in the previous year	2 631	2 715	882	886	1 129	1 145	620	684	1 127	1 126	1 503	1 590
Searched for work in the previous year [2]	2 096	2 137	838	843	995	1 006	262	288	996	1 040	1 099	1 097
Not available to work now	564	563	274	279	248	242	43	42	231	230	333	333
Available to work now	1 531	1 574	565	565	747	764	220	245	765	809	766	765
Reason not currently looking:												
Discouragement over job prospects [3]	457	466	134	142	248	240	75	84	266	288	190	178
Reasons other than discouragement	1 075	1 108	431	423	499	524	145	161	499	521	576	587
Family responsibilities	153	157	37	28	94	104	22	24	35	38	118	119
In school or training	239	244	194	199	42	43	3	2	125	131	114	112
Ill health or disability	113	123	15	18	72	71	26	35	51	56	62	67
Other [4]	570	584	184	178	292	306	94	100	288	296	282	288

Note: Beginning in January 2004, data reflect revised population controls used in the household survey. See "Notes and Definitions" for information on historical comparability.

[1] Includes some persons who are not asked if they want a job.
[2] Persons who had a job in the prior 12 months must have searched since the end of that job.
[3] Includes believes no work available, could not find work, lacks necessary schooling or training, employer thinks too young or old, and other types of discrimination.
[4] Includes those who did not actively look for work in the prior four weeks for such reasons as child care and transportation problems, as well as a small number for which reason for nonparticipation was not ascertained.

EMPLOYMENT

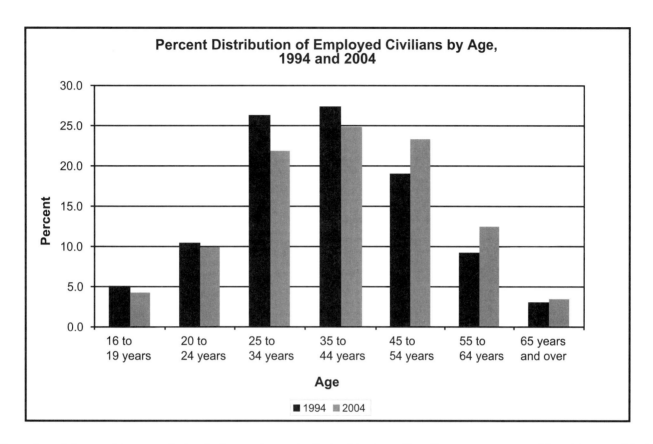

The aging of the working population is shown dramatically in this chart. For all age groups up to 35 to 44 years old, the proportion of employed civilians is lower in 2004 than it was in 1994. At the same time, the percentage of employed civilians aged 45 and over is considerably higher for 2004 than for 1994. Even the proportion of employed civilians aged 65 and over rose in 2004. (Table 1-11)

OTHER HIGHLIGHTS:

- The number of employed men age 25 to 44 years old actually declined between 1994 and 2004. Conversely, the number of employed men age 45 and over increased by over 8 million—a gain of almost 40 percent. For women, the change is even more striking. The number of employed women age 45 and over increased nearly 47 percent from 1994 to 2004. (Table 1-11)

- The Hispanic working population is younger than average. 13.8 percent of total Hispanic employment is made up of 20 to 24 years olds, compared to less than 10 percent for the total population. Among 25 to 34 year olds, the difference is even greater: 31 percent, compared to the national average of 21.8 percent. In contrast, only 6.7 percent of Hispanic employment is made up of 55 to 64 year olds (compared to 12.4 percent of the total population). (Table 1-11)

- In management, professional, and related occupations, about half of those employed in 2004 were men and half were women. Within this group, 58 percent of those in management, business, and financial operations were men and 56 percent of those in professional and related occupations, which included teachers, were women. (Table 1-13)

- While total employment only increased 1.1 percent from 2003 to 2004, employment in construction increased 6.2 percent. Among the major industries, employment in manufacturing continued to decline but still accounted for nearly 12 percent of the total. Employment increased in most other industries by a small amount, although it declined by nearly 6.1 percent in the information industry. (Table 1-15)

Table 1-11. Employed Civilians by Age, Sex, Race, and Hispanic Origin, 1948–2004

(Thousands of people.)

Year, sex, race, and Hispanic origin	16 years and over	16 to 19 years			20 years and over						
		Total	16 to 17 years	18 to 19 years	Total	20 to 24 years	25 to 34 years	35 to 44 years	45 to 54 years	55 to 64 years	65 years and over
Total											
1948	58 343	4 026	1 600	2 426	54 318	6 937	13 801	13 050	10 624	7 103	2 804
1949	57 651	3 712	1 466	2 246	53 940	6 660	13 639	13 108	10 636	7 042	2 864
1950	58 918	3 703	1 433	2 270	55 218	6 746	13 917	13 424	10 966	7 265	2 899
1951	59 961	3 767	1 575	2 192	56 196	6 321	14 233	13 746	11 421	7 558	2 917
1952	60 250	3 719	1 626	2 092	56 536	5 572	14 515	14 058	11 687	7 785	2 919
1953	61 179	3 720	1 577	2 142	57 460	5 225	14 519	14 774	11 969	7 806	3 166
1954	60 109	3 475	1 422	2 053	56 634	4 971	14 190	14 541	11 976	7 895	3 060
1955	62 170	3 642	1 500	2 143	58 528	5 270	14 481	14 879	12 556	8 158	3 185
1956	63 799	3 818	1 647	2 171	59 983	5 545	14 407	15 218	12 978	8 519	3 314
1957	64 071	3 778	1 613	2 167	60 291	5 641	14 253	15 348	13 320	8 553	3 179
1958	63 036	3 582	1 519	2 063	59 454	5 571	13 675	15 157	13 448	8 559	3 045
1959	64 630	3 838	1 670	2 168	60 791	5 870	13 709	15 454	13 915	8 822	3 023
1960	65 778	4 129	1 770	2 360	61 648	6 119	13 630	15 598	14 238	8 989	3 073
1961	65 746	4 108	1 621	2 486	61 638	6 227	13 429	15 552	14 320	9 120	2 987
1962	66 702	4 195	1 607	2 588	62 508	6 446	13 311	15 901	14 491	9 346	3 013
1963	67 762	4 255	1 751	2 504	63 508	6 815	13 318	16 114	14 749	9 596	2 915
1964	69 305	4 516	2 013	2 503	64 789	7 303	13 449	16 166	15 094	9 804	2 973
1965	71 088	5 036	2 075	2 962	66 052	7 702	13 704	16 294	15 320	10 028	3 005
1966	72 895	5 721	2 269	3 452	67 178	7 964	14 017	16 312	15 615	10 310	2 961
1967	74 372	5 682	2 334	3 348	68 690	8 499	14 575	16 281	15 789	10 536	3 011
1968	75 920	5 781	2 403	3 377	70 141	8 762	15 265	16 220	16 083	10 745	3 065
1969	77 902	6 117	2 573	3 543	71 785	9 319	15 883	16 100	16 410	10 919	3 155
1970	78 678	6 144	2 598	3 546	72 534	9 731	16 318	15 922	16 473	10 974	3 118
1971	79 367	6 208	2 596	3 613	73 158	10 201	16 781	15 675	16 451	11 009	3 040
1972	82 153	6 746	2 787	3 959	75 407	10 999	18 082	15 822	16 457	11 044	3 003
1973	85 064	7 271	3 032	4 239	77 793	11 839	19 509	16 041	16 553	10 966	2 886
1974	86 794	7 448	3 111	4 338	79 347	12 101	20 610	16 203	16 633	10 964	2 835
1975	85 846	7 104	2 941	4 162	78 744	11 885	21 087	15 953	16 190	10 827	2 801
1976	88 752	7 336	2 972	4 363	81 416	12 570	22 493	16 468	16 224	10 912	2 747
1977	92 017	7 688	3 138	4 550	84 329	13 196	23 850	17 157	16 212	11 126	2 787
1978	96 048	8 070	3 330	4 739	87 979	13 887	25 281	18 128	16 338	11 400	2 946
1979	98 824	8 083	3 340	4 743	90 741	14 327	26 492	18 981	16 357	11 585	2 999
1980	99 303	7 710	3 106	4 605	91 593	14 087	27 204	19 523	16 234	11 586	2 960
1981	100 397	7 225	2 866	4 359	93 172	14 122	28 180	20 145	16 255	11 525	2 945
1982	99 526	6 549	2 505	4 044	92 978	13 690	28 149	20 879	15 923	11 414	2 923
1983	100 834	6 342	2 320	4 022	94 491	13 722	28 756	21 960	15 812	11 315	2 927
1984	105 005	6 444	2 404	4 040	98 562	14 207	30 348	23 598	16 178	11 395	2 835
1985	107 150	6 434	2 492	3 941	100 716	13 980	31 208	24 732	16 509	11 474	2 813
1986	109 597	6 472	2 622	3 850	103 125	13 790	32 201	25 861	16 949	11 405	2 919
1987	112 440	6 640	2 736	3 905	105 800	13 524	33 105	27 179	17 487	11 465	3 041
1988	114 968	6 805	2 713	4 092	108 164	13 244	33 574	28 269	18 447	11 433	3 197
1989	117 342	6 759	2 588	4 172	110 582	12 962	34 045	29 443	19 279	11 499	3 355
1990	118 793	6 581	2 410	4 171	112 213	13 401	33 935	30 817	19 525	11 189	3 346
1991	117 718	5 906	2 202	3 704	111 812	12 975	33 061	31 593	19 882	11 001	3 300
1992	118 492	5 669	2 128	3 540	112 824	12 872	32 667	31 923	21 022	10 998	3 341
1993	120 259	5 805	2 226	3 579	114 455	12 840	32 385	32 666	22 175	11 058	3 331
1994	123 060	6 161	2 510	3 651	116 899	12 758	32 286	33 599	23 348	11 228	3 681
1995	124 900	6 419	2 573	3 846	118 481	12 443	32 356	34 202	24 378	11 435	3 666
1996	126 708	6 500	2 646	3 853	120 208	12 138	32 077	35 051	25 514	11 739	3 690
1997	129 558	6 661	2 648	4 012	122 897	12 380	31 809	35 908	26 744	12 296	3 761
1998	131 463	7 051	2 762	4 289	124 413	12 557	31 394	36 278	27 587	12 872	3 725
1999	133 488	7 172	2 793	4 379	126 316	12 891	30 865	36 728	28 635	13 315	3 882
2000	136 891	7 189	2 759	4 431	129 701	13 229	31 549	36 433	30 310	14 002	4 179
2001	136 933	6 740	2 558	4 182	130 194	13 348	30 863	36 049	31 036	14 645	4 253
2002	136 485	6 332	2 330	4 002	130 154	13 351	30 306	35 235	31 281	15 674	4 306
2003	137 736	5 919	2 312	3 607	131 817	13 433	30 383	34 881	31 914	16 598	4 608
2004	139 252	5 907	2 193	3 714	133 345	13 723	30 423	34 580	32 469	17 331	4 819

Table 1-11. Employed Civilians by Age, Sex, Race, and Hispanic Origin, 1948–2004—*Continued*

(Thousands of people.)

Year, sex, race, and Hispanic origin	16 years and over	16 to 19 years			20 years and over						
		Total	16 to 17 years	18 to 19 years	Total	20 to 24 years	25 to 34 years	35 to 44 years	45 to 54 years	55 to 64 years	65 years and over
Men											
1948	41 725	2 344	996	1 348	39 382	4 349	10 038	9 363	7 742	5 587	2 303
1949	40 925	2 124	911	1 213	38 803	4 197	9 879	9 308	7 661	5 438	2 329
1950	41 578	2 186	909	1 277	39 394	4 255	10 060	9 445	7 790	5 508	2 336
1951	41 780	2 156	979	1 177	39 626	3 780	10 134	9 607	8 012	5 711	2 382
1952	41 682	2 107	985	1 121	39 578	3 183	10 352	9 753	8 144	5 804	2 343
1953	42 430	2 136	976	1 159	40 296	2 901	10 500	10 229	8 374	5 808	2 483
1954	41 619	1 985	881	1 104	39 634	2 724	10 254	10 082	8 330	5 830	2 414
1955	42 621	2 095	936	1 159	40 526	2 973	10 453	10 267	8 553	5 857	2 424
1956	43 379	2 164	1 008	1 156	41 216	3 245	10 337	10 385	8 732	6 004	2 512
1957	43 357	2 115	987	1 130	41 239	3 346	10 222	10 427	8 851	6 002	2 394
1958	42 423	2 012	948	1 064	40 411	3 293	9 790	10 291	8 828	5 955	2 254
1959	43 466	2 198	1 015	1 183	41 267	3 597	9 862	10 492	9 048	6 058	2 210
1960	43 904	2 361	1 090	1 271	41 543	3 754	9 759	10 552	9 182	6 105	2 191
1961	43 656	2 315	989	1 325	41 342	3 795	9 591	10 505	9 195	6 155	2 098
1962	44 177	2 362	990	1 372	41 815	3 898	9 475	10 711	9 333	6 260	2 138
1963	44 657	2 406	1 073	1 334	42 251	4 118	9 431	10 801	9 478	6 385	2 038
1964	45 474	2 587	1 242	1 345	42 886	4 370	9 531	10 832	9 637	6 478	2 039
1965	46 340	2 918	1 285	1 634	43 422	4 583	9 611	10 837	9 792	6 542	2 057
1966	46 919	3 253	1 389	1 863	43 668	4 599	9 709	10 764	9 904	6 668	2 024
1967	47 479	3 186	1 417	1 769	44 294	4 809	9 988	10 674	9 990	6 774	2 058
1968	48 114	3 255	1 453	1 802	44 859	4 812	10 405	10 554	10 102	6 893	2 093
1969	48 818	3 430	1 526	1 904	45 388	5 012	10 736	10 401	10 187	6 931	2 122
1970	48 990	3 409	1 504	1 905	45 581	5 237	10 936	10 216	10 170	6 928	2 094
1971	49 390	3 478	1 510	1 968	45 912	5 593	11 218	10 028	10 139	6 916	2 019
1972	50 896	3 765	1 598	2 167	47 130	6 138	11 884	10 088	10 139	6 929	1 953
1973	52 349	4 039	1 721	2 318	48 310	6 655	12 617	10 126	10 197	6 857	1 856
1974	53 024	4 103	1 744	2 359	48 922	6 739	13 119	10 135	10 181	6 880	1 869
1975	51 857	3 839	1 621	2 219	48 018	6 484	13 205	9 891	9 902	6 722	1 811
1976	53 138	3 947	1 626	2 321	49 190	6 915	13 869	10 069	9 881	6 724	1 732
1977	54 728	4 174	1 733	2 441	50 555	7 232	14 483	10 399	9 832	6 848	1 761
1978	56 479	4 336	1 800	2 535	52 143	7 559	15 124	10 845	9 806	6 954	1 855
1979	57 607	4 300	1 799	2 501	53 308	7 791	15 688	11 202	9 735	7 015	1 876
1980	57 186	4 085	1 672	2 412	53 101	7 532	15 832	11 355	9 548	6 999	1 835
1981	57 397	3 815	1 526	2 289	53 582	7 504	16 266	11 613	9 478	6 909	1 812
1982	56 271	3 379	1 307	2 072	52 891	7 197	16 002	11 902	9 234	6 781	1 776
1983	56 787	3 300	1 213	2 087	53 487	7 232	16 216	12 450	9 133	6 686	1 770
1984	59 091	3 322	1 244	2 078	55 769	7 571	17 166	13 309	9 326	6 694	1 703
1985	59 891	3 328	1 300	2 029	56 562	7 339	17 564	13 800	9 411	6 753	1 695
1986	60 892	3 323	1 352	1 971	57 569	7 250	18 092	14 266	9 554	6 654	1 753
1987	62 107	3 381	1 393	1 988	58 726	7 058	18 487	14 898	9 750	6 682	1 850
1988	63 273	3 492	1 403	2 089	59 781	6 918	18 702	15 457	10 201	6 591	1 911
1989	64 315	3 477	1 327	2 150	60 837	6 799	18 952	16 002	10 569	6 548	1 968
1990	65 104	3 427	1 254	2 173	61 678	7 151	18 779	16 771	10 690	6 378	1 909
1991	64 223	3 044	1 135	1 909	61 178	6 909	18 265	17 086	10 813	6 245	1 860
1992	64 440	2 944	1 096	1 848	61 496	6 819	17 966	17 230	11 365	6 173	1 943
1993	65 349	2 994	1 155	1 839	62 355	6 805	17 877	17 665	11 927	6 166	1 916
1994	66 450	3 156	1 288	1 868	63 294	6 771	17 741	18 111	12 439	6 142	2 089
1995	67 377	3 292	1 316	1 977	64 085	6 665	17 709	18 374	12 958	6 272	2 108
1996	68 207	3 310	1 318	1 992	64 897	6 429	17 527	18 816	13 483	6 470	2 172
1997	69 685	3 401	1 355	2 045	66 284	6 548	17 338	19 327	14 107	6 735	2 229
1998	70 693	3 558	1 398	2 161	67 135	6 638	17 097	19 634	14 544	7 052	2 171
1999	71 446	3 685	1 437	2 249	67 761	6 729	16 694	19 811	14 991	7 274	2 263
2000	73 305	3 671	1 394	2 276	69 634	6 974	17 241	19 537	15 871	7 606	2 406
2001	73 196	3 420	1 268	2 151	69 776	6 952	16 915	19 305	16 268	7 900	2 437
2002	72 903	3 169	1 130	2 040	69 734	6 978	16 573	18 932	16 419	8 378	2 455
2003	73 332	2 917	1 115	1 802	70 415	7 065	16 670	18 774	16 588	8 733	2 585
2004	74 524	2 952	1 037	1 915	71 572	7 246	16 818	18 700	16 951	9 174	2 683

Table 1-11. Employed Civilians by Age, Sex, Race, and Hispanic Origin, 1948–2004—*Continued*

(Thousands of people.)

Year, sex, race, and Hispanic origin	16 years and over	16 to 19 years			20 years and over						
		Total	16 to 17 years	18 to 19 years	Total	20 to 24 years	25 to 34 years	35 to 44 years	45 to 54 years	55 to 64 years	65 years and over
Women											
1948	16 617	1 682	604	1 078	14 936	2 588	3 763	3 687	2 882	1 516	501
1949	16 723	1 588	555	1 033	15 137	2 463	3 760	3 800	2 975	1 604	535
1950	17 340	1 517	524	993	15 824	2 491	3 857	3 979	3 176	1 757	563
1951	18 181	1 611	596	1 015	16 570	2 541	4 099	4 139	3 409	1 847	535
1952	18 568	1 612	641	971	16 958	2 389	4 163	4 305	3 543	1 981	576
1953	18 749	1 584	601	983	17 164	2 324	4 019	4 545	3 595	1 998	683
1954	18 490	1 490	541	949	17 000	2 247	3 936	4 459	3 646	2 065	646
1955	19 551	1 547	564	984	18 002	2 297	4 028	4 612	4 003	2 301	761
1956	20 419	1 654	639	1 015	18 767	2 300	4 070	4 833	4 246	2 515	802
1957	20 714	1 663	626	1 037	19 052	2 295	4 031	4 921	4 469	2 551	785
1958	20 613	1 570	571	999	19 043	2 278	3 885	4 866	4 620	2 604	791
1959	21 164	1 640	655	985	19 524	2 273	3 847	4 962	4 867	2 764	813
1960	21 874	1 768	680	1 089	20 105	2 365	3 871	5 046	5 056	2 884	882
1961	22 090	1 793	632	1 161	20 296	2 432	3 838	5 047	5 125	2 965	889
1962	22 525	1 833	617	1 216	20 693	2 548	3 836	5 190	5 158	3 086	875
1963	23 105	1 849	678	1 170	21 257	2 697	3 887	5 313	5 271	3 211	877
1964	23 831	1 929	771	1 158	21 903	2 933	3 918	5 334	5 457	3 326	934
1965	24 748	2 118	790	1 328	22 630	3 119	4 093	5 457	5 528	3 486	948
1966	25 976	2 468	880	1 589	23 510	3 365	4 308	5 548	5 711	3 642	937
1967	26 893	2 496	917	1 579	24 397	3 690	4 587	5 607	5 799	3 762	953
1968	27 807	2 526	950	1 575	25 281	3 950	4 860	5 666	5 981	3 852	972
1969	29 084	2 687	1 047	1 639	26 397	4 307	5 147	5 699	6 223	3 988	1 033
1970	29 688	2 735	1 094	1 641	26 952	4 494	5 382	5 706	6 303	4 046	1 023
1971	29 976	2 730	1 086	1 645	27 246	4 609	5 563	5 647	6 313	4 093	1 021
1972	31 257	2 980	1 188	1 792	28 276	4 861	6 197	5 734	6 318	4 115	1 051
1973	32 715	3 231	1 310	1 920	29 484	5 184	6 893	5 915	6 356	4 109	1 029
1974	33 769	3 345	1 367	1 978	30 424	5 363	7 492	6 068	6 451	4 084	966
1975	33 989	3 263	1 320	1 943	30 726	5 401	7 882	6 061	6 288	4 105	989
1976	35 615	3 389	1 346	2 043	32 226	5 655	8 624	6 400	6 343	4 188	1 017
1977	37 289	3 514	1 403	2 110	33 775	5 965	9 367	6 758	6 380	4 279	1 027
1978	39 569	3 734	1 530	2 204	35 836	6 328	10 157	7 282	6 532	4 446	1 091
1979	41 217	3 783	1 541	2 242	37 434	6 538	10 802	7 779	6 622	4 569	1 124
1980	42 117	3 625	1 433	2 192	38 492	6 555	11 370	8 168	6 686	4 587	1 125
1981	43 000	3 411	1 340	2 070	39 590	6 618	11 914	8 532	6 777	4 616	1 133
1982	43 256	3 170	1 198	1 972	40 086	6 492	12 147	8 977	6 689	4 634	1 147
1983	44 047	3 043	1 107	1 935	41 004	6 490	12 540	9 510	6 678	4 629	1 157
1984	45 915	3 122	1 161	1 962	42 793	6 636	13 182	10 289	6 852	4 700	1 133
1985	47 259	3 105	1 193	1 913	44 154	6 640	13 644	10 933	7 097	4 721	1 118
1986	48 706	3 149	1 270	1 879	45 556	6 540	14 109	11 595	7 395	4 751	1 165
1987	50 334	3 260	1 343	1 917	47 074	6 466	14 617	12 281	7 737	4 783	1 191
1988	51 696	3 313	1 310	2 003	48 383	6 326	14 872	12 811	8 246	4 841	1 286
1989	53 027	3 282	1 261	2 021	49 745	6 163	15 093	13 440	8 711	4 950	1 388
1990	53 689	3 154	1 156	1 998	50 535	6 250	15 155	14 046	8 835	4 811	1 437
1991	53 496	2 862	1 067	1 794	50 634	6 066	14 796	14 507	9 069	4 756	1 440
1992	54 052	2 724	1 032	1 692	51 328	6 053	14 701	14 693	9 657	4 825	1 398
1993	54 910	2 811	1 071	1 740	52 099	6 035	14 508	15 002	10 248	4 892	1 414
1994	56 610	3 005	1 222	1 783	53 606	5 987	14 545	15 488	10 908	5 085	1 592
1995	57 523	3 127	1 258	1 869	54 396	5 779	14 647	15 828	11 421	5 163	1 558
1996	58 501	3 190	1 328	1 862	55 311	5 709	14 549	16 235	12 031	5 269	1 518
1997	59 873	3 260	1 293	1 967	56 613	5 831	14 471	16 581	12 637	5 561	1 532
1998	60 771	3 493	1 364	2 128	57 278	5 919	14 298	16 644	13 043	5 820	1 554
1999	62 042	3 487	1 357	2 130	58 555	6 163	14 171	16 917	13 644	6 041	1 619
2000	63 586	3 519	1 364	2 154	60 067	6 255	14 308	16 897	14 438	6 396	1 773
2001	63 737	3 320	1 289	2 031	60 417	6 396	13 948	16 744	14 768	6 745	1 815
2002	63 582	3 162	1 200	1 962	60 420	6 374	13 733	16 303	14 863	7 296	1 851
2003	64 404	3 002	1 197	1 805	61 402	6 367	13 714	16 106	15 326	7 866	2 023
2004	64 728	2 955	1 156	1 799	61 773	6 477	13 605	15 880	15 518	8 157	2 135

Table 1-11. Employed Civilians by Age, Sex, Race, and Hispanic Origin, 1948–2004—*Continued*

(Thousands of people.)

Year, sex, race, and Hispanic origin	16 years and over	16 to 19 years			20 years and over						
		Total	16 to 17 years	18 to 19 years	Total	20 to 24 years	25 to 34 years	35 to 44 years	45 to 54 years	55 to 64 years	65 years and over
White[1]											
1954	53 957	3 078	1 257	1 822	50 879	4 358	12 616	13 000	10 811	7 262	2 831
1955	55 833	3 225	1 330	1 896	52 608	4 637	12 855	13 327	11 322	7 510	2 957
1956	57 269	3 389	1 465	1 922	53 880	4 897	12 748	13 637	11 706	7 822	3 068
1957	57 465	3 374	1 442	1 931	54 091	4 952	12 619	13 716	12 009	7 829	2 951
1958	56 613	3 216	1 370	1 847	53 397	4 908	12 128	13 571	12 113	7 849	2 828
1959	58 006	3 475	1 520	1 955	54 531	5 138	12 144	13 830	12 552	8 063	2 805
1960	58 850	3 700	1 598	2 103	55 150	5 331	12 021	13 930	12 820	8 192	2 855
1961	58 913	3 693	1 472	2 220	55 220	5 460	11 835	13 905	12 906	8 335	2 778
1962	59 698	3 774	1 447	2 327	55 924	5 676	11 703	14 173	13 066	8 511	2 795
1963	60 622	3 851	1 600	2 250	56 771	6 036	11 689	14 341	13 304	8 718	2 683
1964	61 922	4 076	1 846	2 230	57 846	6 444	11 794	14 380	13 596	8 916	2 717
1965	63 446	4 562	1 892	2 670	58 884	6 752	11 992	14 473	13 804	9 116	2 748
1966	65 021	5 176	2 052	3 124	59 845	6 986	12 268	14 449	14 072	9 356	2 713
1967	66 361	5 114	2 121	2 993	61 247	7 493	12 763	14 429	14 224	9 596	2 746
1968	67 750	5 195	2 193	3 002	62 555	7 687	13 410	14 386	14 487	9 781	2 804
1969	69 518	5 508	2 347	3 161	64 010	8 182	13 935	14 270	14 788	9 947	2 888
1970	70 217	5 571	2 386	3 185	64 645	8 559	14 326	14 092	14 854	9 979	2 835
1971	70 878	5 670	2 404	3 266	65 208	9 000	14 713	13 858	14 843	10 014	2 780
1972	73 370	6 173	2 581	3 592	67 197	9 718	15 904	13 940	14 845	10 077	2 714
1973	75 708	6 623	2 806	3 816	69 086	10 424	17 099	14 083	14 886	9 983	2 610
1974	77 184	6 796	2 881	3 916	70 388	10 676	18 040	14 196	14 948	9 958	2 568
1975	76 411	6 487	2 721	3 770	69 924	10 546	18 485	13 979	14 555	9 827	2 533
1976	78 853	6 724	2 762	3 962	72 129	11 119	19 662	14 407	14 549	9 923	2 470
1977	81 700	7 068	2 926	4 142	74 632	11 696	20 844	14 984	14 483	10 107	2 518
1978	84 936	7 367	3 085	4 282	77 569	12 251	22 008	15 809	14 550	10 311	2 642
1979	87 259	7 356	3 079	4 278	79 904	12 594	23 033	16 578	14 522	10 477	2 699
1980	87 715	7 021	2 861	4 161	80 694	12 405	23 653	17 071	14 405	10 475	2 684
1981	88 709	6 588	2 645	3 943	82 121	12 477	24 551	17 617	14 414	10 386	2 676
1982	87 903	5 984	2 317	3 667	81 918	12 097	24 531	18 268	14 083	10 283	2 656
1983	88 893	5 799	2 156	3 643	83 094	12 138	24 955	19 194	13 961	10 169	2 678
1984	92 120	5 836	2 209	3 627	86 284	12 451	26 235	20 552	14 239	10 227	2 580
1985	93 736	5 768	2 270	3 498	87 968	12 235	26 945	21 552	14 459	10 247	2 530
1986	95 660	5 792	2 386	3 406	89 869	12 027	27 746	22 515	14 750	10 176	2 654
1987	97 789	5 898	2 468	3 431	91 890	11 748	28 429	23 596	15 216	10 164	2 738
1988	99 812	6 030	2 424	3 606	93 782	11 438	28 796	24 468	16 054	10 153	2 874
1989	101 584	5 946	2 278	3 668	95 638	11 084	29 091	25 442	16 775	10 223	3 024
1990	102 261	5 779	2 141	3 638	96 481	11 498	28 773	26 282	16 933	9 960	3 035
1991	101 182	5 216	1 971	3 246	95 966	11 116	27 989	26 883	17 269	9 719	2 990
1992	101 669	4 985	1 904	3 081	96 684	11 031	27 552	27 097	18 285	9 701	3 019
1993	103 045	5 113	1 990	3 123	97 932	10 931	27 274	27 645	19 273	9 772	3 037
1994	105 190	5 398	2 210	3 188	99 792	10 736	27 101	28 442	20 247	9 912	3 354
1995	106 490	5 593	2 273	3 320	100 897	10 400	27 014	28 951	21 127	10 070	3 335
1996	107 808	5 667	2 325	3 343	102 141	10 149	26 678	29 566	22 071	10 313	3 364
1997	109 856	5 807	2 341	3 466	104 049	10 362	26 294	30 137	23 061	10 785	3 411
1998	110 931	6 089	2 436	3 653	104 842	10 512	25 729	30 320	23 662	11 272	3 347
1999	112 235	6 204	2 435	3 769	106 032	10 716	25 113	30 548	24 507	11 657	3 491
2000	114 424	6 160	2 383	3 777	108 264	10 944	25 500	30 151	25 762	12 169	3 738
2001	114 430	5 817	2 224	3 593	108 613	11 054	24 948	29 793	26 301	12 743	3 774
2002	114 013	5 441	2 037	3 404	108 572	11 096	24 568	29 049	26 401	13 630	3 828
2003	114 235	5 064	1 999	3 065	109 171	11 052	24 399	28 501	26 762	14 375	4 083
2004	115 239	5 039	1 895	3 145	110 199	11 233	24 337	28 176	27 228	14 965	4 260

[1]Beginning in 2003, persons who selected this race group only; persons who selected more than one race group are not included. Prior to 2003, persons who reported more than one race group were included in the group they identified as the main race.

Table 1-11. Employed Civilians by Age, Sex, Race, and Hispanic Origin, 1948–2004—*Continued*

(Thousands of people.)

Year, sex, race, and Hispanic origin	16 years and over	16 to 19 years			20 years and over						
		Total	16 to 17 years	18 to 19 years	Total	20 to 24 years	25 to 34 years	35 to 44 years	45 to 54 years	55 to 64 years	65 years and over
Black[1]											
1972	7 802	509	180	329	7 292	1 166	1 924	1 629	1 434	872	269
1973	8 128	570	194	378	7 559	1 258	2 062	1 659	1 460	872	249
1974	8 203	554	190	364	7 649	1 231	2 157	1 682	1 452	884	243
1975	7 894	507	183	325	7 386	1 115	2 145	1 617	1 393	874	241
1976	8 227	508	170	338	7 719	1 193	2 309	1 679	1 416	870	252
1977	8 540	508	169	339	8 031	1 244	2 443	1 754	1 448	892	251
1978	9 102	571	191	380	8 531	1 359	2 641	1 848	1 479	932	273
1979	9 359	579	204	376	8 780	1 424	2 759	1 902	1 502	927	266
1980	9 313	547	192	356	8 765	1 376	2 827	1 910	1 487	925	239
1981	9 355	505	170	335	8 849	1 346	2 872	1 957	1 489	954	231
1982	9 189	428	138	290	8 761	1 283	2 830	2 025	1 469	928	225
1983	9 375	416	123	294	8 959	1 280	2 976	2 107	1 456	937	204
1984	10 119	474	146	328	9 645	1 423	3 223	2 311	1 533	945	209
1985	10 501	532	175	356	9 969	1 399	3 325	2 427	1 598	985	235
1986	10 814	536	183	353	10 278	1 429	3 464	2 524	1 666	982	214
1987	11 309	587	203	385	10 722	1 421	3 614	2 695	1 714	1 036	241
1988	11 658	601	223	378	11 057	1 433	3 725	2 839	1 783	1 018	261
1989	11 953	625	237	388	11 328	1 467	3 801	2 981	1 844	970	265
1990	12 175	598	194	404	11 577	1 409	3 803	3 287	1 897	933	248
1991	12 074	494	161	334	11 580	1 373	3 714	3 401	1 892	957	243
1992	12 151	492	157	335	11 659	1 343	3 699	3 441	1 964	965	246
1993	12 382	494	171	323	11 888	1 377	3 700	3 584	2 059	941	226
1994	12 835	552	224	328	12 284	1 449	3 732	3 722	2 178	953	251
1995	13 279	586	223	363	12 693	1 443	3 844	3 861	2 288	1 004	253
1996	13 542	613	233	380	12 929	1 411	3 851	3 974	2 426	1 025	241
1997	13 969	631	229	401	13 339	1 456	3 903	4 094	2 588	1 048	249
1998	14 556	736	246	490	13 820	1 496	3 967	4 238	2 739	1 118	262
1999	15 056	691	243	448	14 365	1 594	4 091	4 404	2 872	1 134	271
2000	15 156	711	260	451	14 444	1 593	3 993	4 261	3 073	1 226	300
2001	15 006	637	230	408	14 368	1 571	3 840	4 200	3 139	1 283	335
2002	14 872	611	193	417	14 262	1 543	3 726	4 109	3 220	1 332	332
2003	14 739	516	196	320	14 222	1 516	3 618	4 080	3 289	1 373	346
2004	14 909	520	169	351	14 389	1 572	3 635	4 039	3 332	1 452	359
Hispanic											
1973	3 396	325	...	...	...	...	...	...	...	...	...
1974	3 687	355	...	...	...	...	...	...	...	...	...
1975	3 663	322	...	...	...	...	...	...	...	...	...
1976	3 720	341	124	230	3 436	614	1 135	803	573	269	42
1977	4 079	381	135	245	3 715	715	1 212	860	608	269	50
1978	4 527	423	159	264	4 104	803	1 330	942	661	307	62
1979	4 785	445	152	292	4 340	860	1 430	996	666	319	69
1980	5 527	500	174	325	5 028	998	1 675	1 074	811	389	80
1981	5 813	459	155	304	5 354	1 060	1 837	1 147	829	399	82
1982	5 805	410	119	291	5 394	1 030	1 896	1 173	816	399	80
1983	6 072	423	125	297	5 649	1 068	1 997	1 224	837	441	81
1984	6 651	468	148	320	6 182	1 160	2 201	1 385	883	474	79
1985	6 888	438	144	294	6 449	1 187	2 316	1 473	913	486	75
1986	7 219	430	146	284	6 789	1 231	2 427	1 570	1 011	474	76
1987	7 790	474	149	325	7 316	1 273	2 668	1 775	1 010	512	76
1988	8 250	523	171	353	7 727	1 341	2 749	1 876	1 078	585	97
1989	8 573	548	165	383	8 025	1 325	2 900	1 968	1 129	589	114
1990	9 845	668	208	460	9 177	1 672	3 327	2 229	1 235	611	103
1991	9 828	602	169	433	9 225	1 622	3 264	2 333	1 266	637	103
1992	10 027	577	169	408	9 450	1 575	3 350	2 468	1 316	628	112
1993	10 361	570	160	410	9 792	1 574	3 446	2 605	1 402	630	135
1994	10 788	609	195	415	10 178	1 643	3 517	2 737	1 495	647	139
1995	11 127	645	194	450	10 483	1 609	3 618	2 889	1 565	666	135
1996	11 642	646	199	447	10 996	1 628	3 758	3 115	1 595	748	152
1997	12 726	714	228	487	12 012	1 798	4 029	3 371	1 846	794	173
1998	13 291	793	230	563	12 498	1 883	4 113	3 504	1 994	846	158
1999	13 720	854	254	600	12 866	1 881	4 097	3 738	2 074	886	190
2000	15 735	973	285	688	14 762	2 356	4 950	4 052	2 308	898	197
2001	16 190	969	268	701	15 221	2 404	5 065	4 149	2 472	944	187
2002	16 590	882	254	628	15 708	2 413	5 272	4 273	2 511	1 029	209
2003	17 372	768	242	525	16 604	2 399	5 541	4 573	2 711	1 132	249
2004	17 930	792	211	581	17 138	2 477	5 560	4 671	2 932	1 210	288

[1]Beginning in 2003, persons who selected this race group only; persons who selected more than one race group are not included. Prior to 2003, persons who reported more than one race group were included in the group they identified as the main race.
... = Not available.

Table 1-11. Employed Civilians by Age, Sex, Race, and Hispanic Origin, 1948–2004—*Continued*

(Thousands of people.)

Year, sex, race, and Hispanic origin	16 years and over	16 to 19 years			20 years and over						
		Total	16 to 17 years	18 to 19 years	Total	20 to 24 years	25 to 34 years	35 to 44 years	45 to 54 years	55 to 64 years	65 years and over
White Men[1]											
1954	37 846	1 723	771	953	36 123	2 394	9 287	9 175	7 614	5 412	2 241
1955	38 719	1 824	821	1 004	36 895	2 607	9 461	9 351	7 792	5 431	2 254
1956	39 368	1 893	890	1 002	37 475	2 850	9 330	9 449	7 950	5 559	2 336
1957	39 349	1 865	874	990	37 484	2 930	9 226	9 480	8 067	5 542	2 234
1958	38 591	1 783	852	932	36 808	2 896	8 861	9 386	8 061	5 501	2 103
1959	39 494	1 961	915	1 046	37 533	3 153	8 911	9 560	8 261	5 588	2 060
1960	39 755	2 092	973	1 119	37 663	3 264	8 777	9 589	8 372	5 618	2 043
1961	39 588	2 055	891	1 164	37 533	3 311	8 630	9 566	8 394	5 670	1 961
1962	40 016	2 098	883	1 215	37 918	3 426	8 514	9 718	8 512	5 749	1 998
1963	40 428	2 156	972	1 184	38 272	3 646	8 463	9 782	8 650	5 844	1 887
1964	41 115	2 316	1 128	1 188	38 799	3 856	8 538	9 800	8 787	5 945	1 872
1965	41 844	2 612	1 159	1 453	39 232	4 025	8 598	9 795	8 924	5 998	1 892
1966	42 331	2 913	1 245	1 668	39 418	4 028	8 674	9 719	9 029	6 096	1 871
1967	42 833	2 849	1 278	1 571	39 985	4 231	8 931	9 632	9 093	6 208	1 892
1968	43 411	2 908	1 319	1 589	40 503	4 226	9 315	9 522	9 198	6 316	1 926
1969	44 048	3 070	1 385	1 685	40 978	4 401	9 608	9 379	9 279	6 359	1 953
1970	44 178	3 066	1 374	1 692	41 112	4 601	9 784	9 202	9 271	6 340	1 914
1971	44 595	3 157	1 393	1 764	41 438	4 935	10 026	9 026	9 256	6 339	1 856
1972	45 944	3 416	1 470	1 947	42 528	5 431	10 664	9 047	9 236	6 363	1 786
1973	47 085	3 660	1 590	2 071	43 424	5 863	11 268	9 046	9 257	6 299	1 689
1974	47 674	3 728	1 611	2 117	43 946	5 965	11 701	9 027	9 242	6 304	1 706
1975	46 697	3 505	1 502	2 002	43 192	5 770	11 783	8 818	9 005	6 160	1 656
1976	47 775	3 604	1 501	2 103	44 171	6 140	12 362	8 944	8 968	6 176	1 579
1977	49 150	3 824	1 607	2 217	45 326	6 437	12 893	9 212	8 898	6 279	1 605
1978	50 544	3 950	1 664	2 286	46 594	6 717	13 413	9 608	8 840	6 339	1 677
1979	51 452	3 904	1 654	2 250	47 546	6 868	13 888	9 930	8 748	6 406	1 707
1980	51 127	3 708	1 534	2 174	47 419	6 652	14 009	10 077	8 586	6 412	1 684
1981	51 315	3 469	1 402	2 066	47 846	6 652	14 398	10 307	8 518	6 309	1 662
1982	50 287	3 079	1 214	1 865	47 209	6 372	14 164	10 593	8 267	6 188	1 624
1983	50 621	3 003	1 124	1 879	47 618	6 386	14 297	11 062	8 152	6 084	1 637
1984	52 462	3 001	1 140	1 861	49 461	6 647	15 045	11 776	8 320	6 108	1 564
1985	53 046	2 985	1 185	1 800	50 061	6 428	15 374	12 214	8 374	6 118	1 552
1986	53 785	2 966	1 225	1 741	50 818	6 340	15 790	12 620	8 442	6 012	1 612
1987	54 647	2 999	1 252	1 747	51 649	6 150	16 084	13 138	8 596	5 991	1 690
1988	55 550	3 084	1 248	1 836	52 466	5 987	16 241	13 590	8 992	5 909	1 748
1989	56 352	3 060	1 171	1 889	53 292	5 839	16 383	14 046	9 335	5 891	1 797
1990	56 703	3 018	1 119	1 899	53 685	6 179	16 124	14 496	9 383	5 744	1 760
1991	55 797	2 694	1 017	1 677	53 103	5 942	15 644	14 743	9 488	5 578	1 707
1992	55 959	2 602	990	1 612	53 357	5 855	15 357	14 842	10 027	5 503	1 772
1993	56 656	2 634	1 031	1 603	54 021	5 830	15 230	15 178	10 497	5 514	1 772
1994	57 452	2 776	1 144	1 632	54 676	5 738	15 052	15 562	10 910	5 490	1 925
1995	58 146	2 892	1 169	1 723	55 254	5 613	14 958	15 793	11 359	5 609	1 921
1996	58 888	2 911	1 161	1 750	55 977	5 444	14 820	16 136	11 834	5 755	1 987
1997	59 998	3 011	1 206	1 806	56 986	5 590	14 567	16 470	12 352	5 972	2 037
1998	60 604	3 103	1 233	1 870	57 500	5 659	14 259	16 715	12 661	6 251	1 955
1999	61 139	3 205	1 254	1 951	57 934	5 753	13 851	16 781	13 046	6 447	2 056
2000	62 289	3 169	1 205	1 965	59 119	5 876	14 238	16 477	13 675	6 678	2 175
2001	62 212	2 967	1 102	1 865	59 245	5 870	13 989	16 280	13 987	6 941	2 178
2002	61 849	2 725	987	1 738	59 124	5 882	13 727	15 910	14 060	7 360	2 184
2003	61 866	2 518	972	1 546	59 348	5 890	13 731	15 675	14 117	7 640	2 295
2004	62 712	2 553	903	1 650	60 159	6 026	13 735	15 572	14 418	8 018	2 390

[1]Beginning in 2003, persons who selected this race group only; persons who selected more than one race group are not included. Prior to 2003, persons who reported more than one race group were included in the group they identified as the main race.

Table 1-11. Employed Civilians by Age, Sex, Race, and Hispanic Origin, 1948–2004—*Continued*

(Thousands of people.)

Year, sex, race, and Hispanic origin	16 years and over	16 to 19 years			20 years and over						
		Total	16 to 17 years	18 to 19 years	Total	20 to 24 years	25 to 34 years	35 to 44 years	45 to 54 years	55 to 64 years	65 years and over
White Women[1]											
1954	16 111	1 355	486	869	14 756	1 964	3 329	3 825	3 197	1 850	590
1955	17 114	1 401	509	892	15 713	2 030	3 394	3 976	3 530	2 079	703
1956	17 901	1 496	575	920	16 405	2 047	3 418	4 188	3 756	2 263	732
1957	18 116	1 509	568	941	16 607	2 022	3 393	4 236	3 942	2 287	717
1958	18 022	1 433	518	915	16 589	2 012	3 267	4 185	4 052	2 348	725
1959	18 512	1 514	605	909	16 998	1 985	3 233	4 270	4 291	2 475	745
1960	19 095	1 608	625	984	17 487	2 067	3 244	4 341	4 448	2 574	812
1961	19 325	1 638	581	1 056	17 687	2 149	3 205	4 339	4 512	2 665	817
1962	19 682	1 676	564	1 112	18 006	2 250	3 189	4 455	4 554	2 762	797
1963	20 194	1 695	628	1 066	18 499	2 390	3 226	4 559	4 654	2 874	796
1964	20 807	1 760	718	1 042	19 047	2 588	3 256	4 580	4 809	2 971	845
1965	21 602	1 950	733	1 217	19 652	2 727	3 394	4 678	4 880	3 118	856
1966	22 690	2 263	807	1 456	20 427	2 958	3 594	4 730	5 043	3 260	842
1967	23 528	2 265	843	1 422	21 263	3 262	3 832	4 797	5 131	3 388	854
1968	24 339	2 287	874	1 413	22 052	3 461	4 095	4 864	5 289	3 465	878
1969	25 470	2 438	962	1 476	23 032	3 781	4 327	4 891	5 509	3 588	935
1970	26 039	2 505	1 012	1 493	23 534	3 959	4 542	4 890	5 582	3 640	921
1971	26 283	2 513	1 011	1 502	23 770	4 065	4 687	4 831	5 588	3 675	924
1972	27 426	2 755	1 111	1 645	24 669	4 286	5 240	4 893	5 608	3 714	928
1973	28 623	2 962	1 217	1 746	25 661	4 562	5 831	5 036	5 628	3 684	920
1974	29 511	3 069	1 269	1 799	26 442	4 711	6 340	5 169	5 706	3 654	862
1975	29 714	2 983	1 215	1 767	26 731	4 775	6 701	5 161	5 550	3 667	877
1976	31 078	3 120	1 260	1 860	27 958	4 978	7 300	5 462	5 580	3 746	891
1977	32 550	3 244	1 319	1 923	29 306	5 259	7 950	5 772	5 585	3 829	912
1978	34 392	3 416	1 420	1 996	30 975	5 535	8 595	6 201	5 710	3 972	964
1979	35 807	3 451	1 423	2 027	32 357	5 726	9 145	6 648	5 773	4 071	993
1980	36 587	3 314	1 327	1 986	33 275	5 753	9 644	6 994	5 818	4 064	1 001
1981	37 394	3 119	1 242	1 877	34 275	5 826	10 153	7 311	5 896	4 077	1 013
1982	37 615	2 905	1 103	1 802	34 710	5 724	10 367	7 675	5 816	4 095	1 032
1983	38 272	2 796	1 032	1 764	35 476	5 751	10 659	8 132	5 809	4 084	1 041
1984	39 659	2 835	1 069	1 766	36 823	5 804	11 190	8 776	5 920	4 118	1 015
1985	40 690	2 783	1 085	1 698	37 907	5 807	11 571	9 338	6 084	4 128	978
1986	41 876	2 825	1 160	1 665	39 050	5 687	11 956	9 895	6 307	4 164	1 042
1987	43 142	2 900	1 216	1 684	40 242	5 598	12 345	10 459	6 620	4 172	1 047
1988	44 262	2 946	1 176	1 770	41 316	5 450	12 555	10 878	7 062	4 244	1 126
1989	45 232	2 886	1 107	1 779	42 346	5 245	12 708	11 395	7 440	4 332	1 227
1990	45 558	2 762	1 023	1 739	42 796	5 319	12 649	11 785	7 551	4 217	1 275
1991	45 385	2 523	954	1 569	42 862	5 174	12 344	12 139	7 781	4 141	1 283
1992	45 710	2 383	915	1 468	43 327	5 176	12 195	12 254	8 258	4 198	1 246
1993	46 390	2 479	959	1 520	43 910	5 101	12 044	12 467	8 776	4 258	1 265
1994	47 738	2 622	1 066	1 556	45 116	4 997	12 049	12 880	9 338	4 423	1 429
1995	48 344	2 701	1 104	1 597	45 643	4 787	12 056	13 157	9 768	4 461	1 415
1996	48 920	2 756	1 164	1 592	46 164	4 705	11 858	13 430	10 237	4 558	1 376
1997	49 859	2 796	1 136	1 660	47 063	4 773	11 727	13 667	10 709	4 813	1 374
1998	50 327	2 986	1 203	1 783	47 342	4 853	11 470	13 604	11 001	5 021	1 392
1999	51 096	2 999	1 181	1 817	48 098	4 963	11 262	13 767	11 461	5 211	1 435
2000	52 136	2 991	1 178	1 813	49 145	5 068	11 262	13 674	12 087	5 490	1 564
2001	52 218	2 850	1 122	1 727	49 369	5 184	10 959	13 513	12 314	5 802	1 597
2002	52 164	2 716	1 050	1 665	49 448	5 214	10 842	13 138	12 341	6 269	1 644
2003	52 369	2 546	1 027	1 519	49 823	5 161	10 668	12 826	12 645	6 735	1 788
2004	52 527	2 486	991	1 495	50 040	5 207	10 602	12 604	12 810	6 947	1 870

[1]Beginning in 2003, persons who selected this race group only; persons who selected more than one race group are not included. Prior to 2003, persons who reported more than one race group were included in the group they identified as the main race.

Table 1-11. Employed Civilians by Age, Sex, Race, and Hispanic Origin, 1948–2004—*Continued*

(Thousands of people.)

Year, sex, race, and Hispanic origin	16 years and over	16 to 19 years			20 years and over						
		Total	16 to 17 years	18 to 19 years	Total	20 to 24 years	25 to 34 years	35 to 44 years	45 to 54 years	55 to 64 years	65 years and over
Black Men[1]											
1972	4 368	309	114	195	4 058	648	1 074	890	793	499	156
1973	4 527	330	112	220	4 197	711	1 142	898	816	483	148
1974	4 527	322	114	209	4 204	668	1 176	912	803	500	145
1975	4 275	276	98	179	3 998	595	1 159	865	755	487	137
1976	4 404	283	100	184	4 120	635	1 217	897	763	472	137
1977	4 565	291	105	186	4 273	659	1 271	940	777	484	143
1978	4 796	312	106	206	4 483	697	1 357	969	788	516	155
1979	4 923	316	111	205	4 606	754	1 425	983	801	498	147
1980	4 798	299	109	191	4 498	713	1 438	975	770	478	126
1981	4 794	273	95	178	4 520	693	1 457	991	764	492	123
1982	4 637	223	65	158	4 414	660	1 414	997	750	471	122
1983	4 753	222	64	158	4 531	684	1 483	1 034	749	477	105
1984	5 124	252	79	173	4 871	750	1 635	1 138	780	460	108
1985	5 270	278	92	186	4 992	726	1 669	1 187	795	501	114
1986	5 428	278	96	182	5 150	732	1 756	1 211	831	507	112
1987	5 661	304	109	195	5 357	728	1 821	1 283	853	547	124
1988	5 824	316	122	193	5 509	736	1 881	1 348	878	536	131
1989	5 928	327	124	202	5 602	742	1 931	1 415	886	498	131
1990	5 995	303	99	204	5 692	702	1 895	1 586	926	469	114
1991	5 961	255	85	170	5 706	695	1 859	1 634	923	481	114
1992	5 930	249	78	170	5 681	679	1 819	1 650	930	478	124
1993	6 047	254	88	166	5 793	674	1 858	1 717	978	461	106
1994	6 241	276	107	169	5 964	718	1 850	1 795	1 030	455	115
1995	6 422	285	111	174	6 137	714	1 895	1 836	1 085	468	138
1996	6 456	289	109	180	6 167	685	1 867	1 878	1 129	482	126
1997	6 607	282	108	174	6 325	668	1 874	1 955	1 215	487	127
1998	6 871	341	120	221	6 530	686	1 886	2 008	1 284	524	142
1999	7 027	325	120	205	6 702	700	1 926	2 092	1 327	525	131
2000	7 082	341	129	211	6 741	730	1 865	1 984	1 425	596	142
2001	6 938	311	115	196	6 627	703	1 757	1 931	1 452	614	170
2002	6 959	306	95	212	6 652	725	1 729	1 899	1 503	624	172
2003	6 820	234	89	145	6 586	726	1 660	1 868	1 518	638	176
2004	6 912	231	76	155	6 681	739	1 720	1 840	1 534	668	180
Black Women[1]											
1972	3 433	200	65	134	3 233	519	850	739	641	373	113
1973	3 601	239	81	158	3 362	546	920	761	644	389	101
1974	3 677	232	77	155	3 445	562	981	770	649	383	98
1975	3 618	231	85	146	3 388	520	985	752	638	387	104
1976	3 823	224	70	154	3 599	558	1 092	782	653	398	115
1977	3 975	217	64	153	3 758	585	1 172	814	671	408	109
1978	4 307	260	85	175	4 047	662	1 283	879	691	416	118
1979	4 436	263	92	171	4 174	670	1 333	919	702	428	119
1980	4 515	248	82	165	4 267	663	1 389	936	717	448	113
1981	4 561	232	75	157	4 329	653	1 415	966	725	462	108
1982	4 552	205	73	132	4 347	623	1 416	1 028	719	457	103
1983	4 622	194	59	136	4 428	596	1 493	1 073	707	460	99
1984	4 995	222	67	155	4 773	673	1 588	1 173	753	485	101
1985	5 231	254	83	171	4 977	673	1 656	1 240	804	484	121
1986	5 386	259	87	171	5 128	696	1 708	1 313	835	475	102
1987	5 648	283	93	190	5 365	693	1 793	1 412	860	489	117
1988	5 834	285	101	184	5 548	697	1 844	1 491	905	482	129
1989	6 025	298	113	185	5 727	725	1 870	1 566	959	472	134
1990	6 180	296	96	200	5 884	707	1 907	1 701	971	464	135
1991	6 113	239	76	164	5 874	677	1 855	1 768	969	476	129
1992	6 221	243	79	164	5 978	664	1 880	1 791	1 034	487	123
1993	6 334	239	82	157	6 095	703	1 842	1 867	1 081	480	121
1994	6 595	275	117	158	6 320	731	1 882	1 926	1 147	497	136
1995	6 857	301	112	189	6 556	729	1 949	2 025	1 202	536	114
1996	7 086	324	124	200	6 762	726	1 984	2 096	1 297	543	115
1997	7 362	349	122	227	7 013	789	2 029	2 139	1 373	561	122
1998	7 685	395	126	268	7 290	810	2 081	2 230	1 455	594	120
1999	8 029	366	123	243	7 663	893	2 165	2 312	1 545	609	139
2000	8 073	370	131	240	7 703	862	2 128	2 277	1 647	630	158
2001	8 068	327	115	212	7 741	868	2 084	2 269	1 686	668	165
2002	7 914	304	99	205	7 610	819	1 997	2 209	1 717	708	160
2003	7 919	283	107	175	7 636	790	1 959	2 211	1 770	735	171
2004	7 997	289	93	196	7 707	833	1 914	2 199	1 798	784	179

[1]Beginning in 2003, persons who selected this race group only; persons who selected more than one race group are not included. Prior to 2003, persons who reported more than one race group were included in the group they identified as the main race.

Table 1-11. Employed Civilians by Age, Sex, Race, and Hispanic Origin, 1948–2004—*Continued*

(Thousands of people.)

Year, sex, race, and Hispanic origin	16 years and over	16 to 19 years			20 years and over						
		Total	16 to 17 years	18 to 19 years	Total	20 to 24 years	25 to 34 years	35 to 44 years	45 to 54 years	55 to 64 years	65 years and over
Hispanic Men											
1973	2 198	...	...	...	2 010	...	...	...	...	...	...
1974	2 369	...	...	...	2 165	...	...	...	...	...	...
1975	2 301	...	...	...	2 117	...	...	...	...	...	...
1976	2 303	199	74	125	2 109	364	708	504	369	173	...
1977	2 564	225	78	147	2 335	427	763	540	394	184	...
1978	2 808	241	93	147	2 568	494	824	590	405	207	...
1979	2 962	260	93	168	2 701	511	891	615	427	205	...
1980	3 448	306	109	198	3 142	611	1 065	662	491	254	...
1981	3 597	272	90	182	3 325	642	1 157	707	504	259	...
1982	3 583	229	66	162	3 354	621	1 192	729	498	261	...
1983	3 771	248	71	177	3 523	655	1 280	760	499	275	...
1984	4 083	258	78	180	3 825	718	1 398	841	530	292	...
1985	4 245	251	82	169	3 994	727	1 473	888	550	308	...
1986	4 428	254	82	172	4 174	773	1 510	929	614	297	...
1987	4 713	268	81	188	4 444	777	1 664	1 044	606	303	...
1988	4 972	292	87	205	4 680	815	1 706	1 120	645	331	...
1989	5 172	319	94	225	4 853	821	1 787	1 152	676	350	...
1990	6 021	412	126	286	5 609	1 083	2 076	1 312	722	355	...
1991	5 979	356	94	263	5 623	1 063	2 050	1 360	719	369	...
1992	6 093	336	97	238	5 757	985	2 127	1 437	768	372	...
1993	6 328	337	95	242	5 992	1 003	2 200	1 527	822	360	...
1994	6 530	341	109	233	6 189	1 056	2 227	1 600	847	379	79
1995	6 725	358	110	248	6 367	1 030	2 284	1 675	908	384	85
1996	7 039	384	107	277	6 655	1 015	2 345	1 842	918	438	96
1997	7 728	420	130	290	7 307	1 142	2 547	1 978	1 059	477	105
1998	8 018	449	133	315	7 570	1 173	2 592	2 077	1 115	512	101
1999	8 067	491	139	352	7 576	1 135	2 524	2 135	1 151	502	130
2000	9 428	570	159	411	8 859	1 486	3 063	2 358	1 295	532	126
2001	9 668	568	149	419	9 100	1 473	3 142	2 446	1 375	545	119
2002	9 845	504	141	363	9 341	1 476	3 271	2 503	1 396	569	125
2003	10 479	415	121	294	10 063	1 485	3 537	2 724	1 533	639	144
2004	10 832	446	108	338	10 385	1 514	3 557	2 801	1 654	687	174
Hispanic Women											
1973	1 198	...	...	...	1 060	...	...	...	...	...	...
1974	1 319	...	...	...	1 166	...	...	...	...	...	...
1975	1 362	...	...	...	1 224	...	...	...	...	...	...
1976	1 417	155	50	106	1 288	249	427	300	204	96	...
1977	1 516	155	57	98	1 370	288	449	320	214	86	...
1978	1 719	182	65	117	1 537	308	506	352	256	99	...
1979	1 824	185	60	125	1 638	349	539	381	241	115	...
1980	2 079	193	65	128	1 886	387	610	412	320	136	...
1981	2 216	187	65	122	2 029	418	680	440	326	139	...
1982	2 222	181	52	129	2 040	409	704	444	318	139	...
1983	2 301	175	54	120	2 127	413	717	464	338	166	...
1984	2 568	211	71	140	2 357	442	804	544	354	181	...
1985	2 642	187	62	125	2 456	460	843	585	362	178	...
1986	2 791	176	64	112	2 615	458	917	641	397	177	...
1987	3 077	206	69	137	2 872	496	1 004	732	405	209	...
1988	3 278	231	84	147	3 047	526	1 042	756	434	254	...
1989	3 401	229	71	158	3 172	504	1 114	816	453	239	...
1990	3 823	256	82	174	3 567	588	1 251	917	513	256	...
1991	3 848	246	76	170	3 603	559	1 214	972	548	268	...
1992	3 934	242	72	170	3 693	591	1 223	1 031	548	256	...
1993	4 033	233	65	168	3 800	571	1 246	1 077	581	269	...
1994	4 258	268	86	182	3 989	587	1 290	1 137	648	268	59
1995	4 403	287	85	202	4 116	579	1 334	1 213	657	282	50
1996	4 602	261	92	169	4 341	612	1 412	1 273	677	310	56
1997	4 999	294	98	196	4 705	656	1 482	1 393	787	318	69
1998	5 273	345	97	247	4 928	710	1 521	1 428	879	334	57
1999	5 653	363	115	248	5 290	746	1 574	1 603	923	384	60
2000	6 307	404	127	277	5 903	870	1 887	1 695	1 013	366	72
2001	6 522	401	119	282	6 121	931	1 923	1 703	1 097	398	67
2002	6 744	378	113	265	6 367	937	2 001	1 770	1 114	460	84
2003	6 894	353	121	231	6 541	914	2 004	1 849	1 178	493	105
2004	7 098	346	103	243	6 752	964	2 003	1 870	1 279	523	114

Note: Persons of Hispanic origin may be of any race.

. . . = Not available.

Table 1-12. Civilian Employment to Population Ratios by Sex, Race, Hispanic Origin, and Age, 1948–2004

(Percent.)

Year, race, and Hispanic origin	Total			Men			Women		
	16 years and over	16 to 19 years	20 years and over	16 years and over	16 to 19 years	20 years and over	16 years and over	16 to 19 years	20 years and over
Total									
1948	56.6	47.7	57.4	83.5	57.5	85.8	31.3	38.5	30.7
1949	55.4	45.2	56.3	81.3	53.8	83.7	31.2	37.2	30.6
1950	56.1	45.5	57.0	82.0	55.2	84.2	32.0	36.3	31.6
1951	57.3	47.9	58.1	84.0	57.9	86.1	33.1	38.9	32.6
1952	57.3	46.9	58.1	83.9	55.9	86.2	33.4	38.8	33.0
1953	57.1	46.4	58.0	83.6	55.9	85.9	33.3	37.8	32.9
1954	55.5	42.3	56.6	81.0	50.2	83.5	32.5	34.9	32.3
1955	56.7	43.5	57.8	81.8	52.1	84.3	34.0	35.6	33.8
1956	57.5	45.3	58.5	82.3	53.8	84.6	35.1	37.5	34.9
1957	57.1	43.9	58.2	81.3	51.8	83.8	35.1	36.7	35.0
1958	55.4	39.9	56.8	78.5	46.9	81.2	34.5	33.5	34.6
1959	56.0	39.9	57.5	79.3	47.2	82.3	35.0	33.0	35.1
1960	56.1	40.5	57.6	78.9	47.6	81.9	35.5	33.8	35.7
1961	55.4	39.1	56.9	77.6	45.3	80.8	35.4	33.2	35.6
1962	55.5	39.4	57.1	77.7	45.9	80.9	35.6	33.3	35.8
1963	55.4	37.4	57.2	77.1	43.8	80.6	35.8	31.5	36.3
1964	55.7	37.3	57.7	77.3	44.1	80.9	36.3	30.9	36.9
1965	56.2	38.9	58.2	77.5	46.2	81.2	37.1	32.0	37.6
1966	56.9	42.1	58.7	77.9	48.9	81.5	38.3	35.6	38.6
1967	57.3	42.2	59.0	78.0	48.7	81.5	39.0	35.9	39.3
1968	57.5	42.2	59.3	77.8	48.7	81.3	39.6	36.0	40.0
1969	58.0	43.4	59.7	77.6	49.5	81.1	40.7	37.5	41.1
1970	57.4	42.3	59.2	76.2	47.7	79.7	40.8	37.1	41.2
1971	56.6	41.3	58.4	74.9	46.8	78.5	40.4	36.0	40.9
1972	57.0	43.5	58.6	75.0	48.9	78.4	41.0	38.2	41.3
1973	57.8	45.9	59.3	75.5	51.4	78.6	42.0	40.5	42.2
1974	57.8	46.0	59.2	74.9	51.2	77.9	42.6	41.0	42.8
1975	56.1	43.3	57.6	71.7	47.2	74.8	42.0	39.4	42.3
1976	56.8	44.2	58.3	72.0	47.9	75.1	43.2	40.5	43.5
1977	57.9	46.1	59.2	72.8	50.4	75.6	44.5	41.8	44.8
1978	59.3	48.3	60.6	73.8	52.2	76.4	46.4	44.5	46.6
1979	59.9	48.5	61.2	73.8	51.7	76.5	47.5	45.3	47.7
1980	59.2	46.6	60.6	72.0	49.5	74.6	47.7	43.8	48.1
1981	59.0	44.6	60.5	71.3	47.1	74.0	48.0	42.0	48.6
1982	57.8	41.5	59.4	69.0	42.9	71.8	47.7	40.2	48.4
1983	57.9	41.5	59.5	68.8	43.1	71.4	48.0	40.0	48.8
1984	59.5	43.7	61.0	70.7	45.0	73.2	49.5	42.5	50.1
1985	60.1	44.4	61.5	70.9	45.7	73.3	50.4	42.9	51.0
1986	60.7	44.6	62.1	71.0	45.7	73.3	51.4	43.6	52.0
1987	61.5	45.5	62.9	71.5	46.1	73.8	52.5	44.8	53.1
1988	62.3	46.8	63.6	72.0	47.8	74.2	53.4	45.9	54.0
1989	63.0	47.5	64.2	72.5	48.7	74.5	54.3	46.4	54.9
1990	62.8	45.3	64.3	72.0	46.6	74.3	54.3	44.0	55.2
1991	61.7	42.0	63.2	70.4	42.7	72.7	53.7	41.2	54.6
1992	61.5	41.0	63.0	69.8	41.9	72.1	53.8	40.0	54.8
1993	61.7	41.7	63.3	70.0	42.3	72.3	54.1	41.0	55.0
1994	62.5	43.4	64.0	70.4	43.8	72.6	55.3	43.0	56.2
1995	62.9	44.2	64.4	70.8	44.7	73.0	55.6	43.8	56.5
1996	63.2	43.5	64.7	70.9	43.6	73.2	56.0	43.5	57.0
1997	63.8	43.4	65.5	71.3	43.4	73.7	56.8	43.3	57.8
1998	64.1	45.1	65.6	71.6	44.7	73.9	57.1	45.5	58.0
1999	64.3	44.7	65.9	71.6	45.1	74.0	57.4	44.3	58.5
2000	64.4	45.2	66.0	71.9	45.4	74.2	57.5	45.0	58.4
2001	63.7	42.3	65.4	70.9	42.2	73.3	57.0	42.4	58.1
2002	62.7	39.6	64.6	69.7	38.9	72.3	56.3	40.3	57.5
2003	62.3	36.8	64.3	68.9	35.7	71.7	56.1	37.8	57.5
2004	62.3	36.4	64.4	69.2	35.9	71.9	56.0	37.0	57.4

Table 1-12. Civilian Employment to Population Ratios by Sex, Race, Hispanic Origin, and Age, 1948–2004—*Continued*

(Percent.)

Year, race, and Hispanic origin	Total			Men			Women		
	16 years and over	16 to 19 years	20 years and over	16 years and over	16 to 19 years	20 years and over	16 years and over	16 to 19 years	20 years and over
White[1]									
1954	55.2	42.9	56.2	81.5	49.9	84.0	31.4	36.4	31.1
1955	56.5	44.2	57.4	82.2	52.0	84.7	33.0	37.0	32.7
1956	57.3	46.1	58.2	82.7	54.1	85.0	34.2	38.9	33.8
1957	56.8	45.0	57.8	81.8	52.4	84.1	34.2	38.2	33.9
1958	55.3	41.0	56.5	79.2	47.6	81.8	33.6	35.0	33.5
1959	55.9	41.2	57.2	79.9	48.1	82.8	34.0	34.8	34.0
1960	55.9	41.5	57.2	79.4	48.1	82.4	34.6	35.1	34.5
1961	55.3	40.1	56.7	78.2	45.9	81.4	34.5	34.6	34.5
1962	55.4	40.4	56.9	78.4	46.4	81.5	34.7	34.8	34.7
1963	55.3	38.6	56.9	77.7	44.7	81.1	35.0	32.9	35.2
1964	55.5	38.4	57.3	77.8	45.0	81.3	35.5	32.2	35.8
1965	56.0	40.3	57.8	77.9	47.1	81.5	36.2	33.7	36.5
1966	56.8	43.6	58.3	78.3	50.1	81.7	37.5	37.5	37.5
1967	57.2	43.8	58.7	78.4	50.2	81.7	38.3	37.7	38.3
1968	57.4	43.9	59.0	78.3	50.3	81.6	38.9	37.8	39.1
1969	58.0	45.2	59.4	78.2	51.1	81.4	40.1	39.5	40.1
1970	57.5	44.5	59.0	76.8	49.6	80.1	40.3	39.5	40.4
1971	56.8	43.8	58.3	75.7	49.2	79.0	39.9	38.6	40.1
1972	57.4	46.4	58.6	76.0	51.5	79.0	40.7	41.3	40.6
1973	58.2	48.9	59.3	76.5	54.3	79.2	41.8	43.6	41.6
1974	58.3	49.3	59.3	75.9	54.4	78.6	42.4	44.3	42.2
1975	56.7	46.5	57.9	73.0	50.6	75.7	42.0	42.5	41.9
1976	57.5	47.8	58.6	73.4	51.5	76.0	43.2	44.2	43.1
1977	58.6	50.1	59.6	74.1	54.4	76.5	44.5	45.9	44.4
1978	60.0	52.4	60.8	75.0	56.3	77.2	46.3	48.5	46.1
1979	60.6	52.6	61.5	75.1	55.7	77.3	47.5	49.4	47.3
1980	60.0	50.7	61.0	73.4	53.4	75.6	47.8	47.9	47.8
1981	60.0	48.7	61.1	72.8	51.3	75.1	48.3	46.2	48.5
1982	58.8	45.8	60.1	70.6	47.0	73.0	48.1	44.6	48.4
1983	58.9	45.9	60.1	70.4	47.4	72.6	48.5	44.5	48.9
1984	60.5	48.0	61.5	72.1	49.1	74.3	49.8	47.0	50.0
1985	61.0	48.5	62.0	72.3	49.9	74.3	50.7	47.1	51.0
1986	61.5	48.8	62.6	72.3	49.6	74.3	51.7	47.9	52.0
1987	62.3	49.4	63.4	72.7	49.9	74.7	52.8	49.0	53.1
1988	63.1	50.9	64.1	73.2	51.7	75.1	53.8	50.2	54.0
1989	63.8	51.6	64.7	73.7	52.6	75.4	54.6	50.5	54.9
1990	63.7	49.7	64.8	73.3	51.0	75.1	54.7	48.3	55.2
1991	62.6	46.6	63.7	71.6	47.2	73.5	54.2	45.9	54.8
1992	62.4	45.3	63.6	71.1	46.4	73.1	54.2	44.2	54.9
1993	62.7	46.2	63.9	71.4	46.6	73.3	54.6	45.7	55.2
1994	63.5	47.9	64.7	71.8	48.3	73.6	55.8	47.5	56.4
1995	63.8	48.8	64.9	72.0	49.4	73.8	56.1	48.1	56.7
1996	64.1	47.9	65.3	72.3	48.2	74.2	56.3	47.6	57.0
1997	64.6	47.7	65.9	72.7	48.1	74.7	57.0	47.2	57.8
1998	64.7	48.9	65.9	72.7	48.6	74.7	57.1	49.3	57.7
1999	64.8	48.8	66.1	72.8	49.3	74.8	57.3	48.3	58.0
2000	64.9	49.1	66.1	73.0	49.5	74.9	57.4	48.8	58.0
2001	64.2	46.3	65.6	72.0	46.2	74.0	57.0	46.5	57.7
2002	63.4	43.2	64.9	70.8	42.3	73.1	56.4	44.1	57.3
2003	63.0	40.4	64.7	70.1	39.4	72.5	56.3	41.5	57.3
2004	63.1	40.0	64.8	70.4	39.7	72.8	56.1	40.3	57.2

[1]Beginning in 2003, persons who selected this race group only; persons who selected more than one race group are not included. Prior to 2003, persons who reported more than one race group were included in the group they identified as the main race.

Table 1-12. Civilian Employment to Population Ratios by Sex, Race, Hispanic Origin, and Age, 1948–2004—*Continued*

(Percent.)

Year, race, and Hispanic origin	Total			Men			Women		
	16 years and over	16 to 19 years	20 years and over	16 years and over	16 to 19 years	20 years and over	16 years and over	16 to 19 years	20 years and over
Black[1]									
1972	53.7	25.2	58.3	66.8	31.6	73.0	43.0	19.2	46.5
1973	54.5	27.2	58.9	67.5	32.8	73.7	43.8	22.0	47.2
1974	53.5	25.9	58.0	65.8	31.4	71.9	43.5	20.9	46.9
1975	50.1	23.1	54.5	60.6	26.3	66.5	41.6	20.2	44.9
1976	50.8	22.4	55.4	60.6	25.8	66.8	42.8	19.2	46.4
1977	51.4	22.3	56.0	61.4	26.4	67.5	43.3	18.5	47.0
1978	53.6	25.2	58.0	63.3	28.5	69.1	45.8	22.1	49.3
1979	53.8	25.4	58.1	63.4	28.7	69.1	46.0	22.4	49.3
1980	52.3	23.9	56.4	60.4	27.0	65.8	45.7	21.0	49.1
1981	51.3	22.1	55.5	59.1	24.6	64.5	45.1	19.7	48.5
1982	49.4	19.0	53.6	56.0	20.3	61.4	44.2	17.7	47.5
1983	49.5	18.7	53.6	56.3	20.4	61.6	44.1	17.0	47.4
1984	52.3	21.9	56.1	59.2	23.9	64.1	46.7	20.1	49.8
1985	53.4	24.6	57.0	60.0	26.3	64.6	48.1	23.1	50.9
1986	54.1	25.1	57.6	60.6	26.5	65.1	48.8	23.8	51.6
1987	55.6	27.1	58.9	62.0	28.5	66.4	50.3	25.8	53.0
1988	56.3	27.6	59.7	62.7	29.4	67.1	51.2	25.8	53.9
1989	56.9	28.7	60.1	62.8	30.4	67.0	52.0	27.1	54.6
1990	56.7	26.7	60.2	62.6	27.7	67.1	51.9	25.8	54.7
1991	55.4	22.6	59.0	61.3	23.8	65.9	50.6	21.5	53.6
1992	54.9	22.8	58.3	59.9	23.6	64.3	50.8	22.1	53.6
1993	55.0	22.6	58.4	60.0	23.6	64.3	50.9	21.6	53.8
1994	56.1	24.9	59.4	60.8	25.4	65.0	52.3	24.5	55.0
1995	57.1	25.7	60.5	61.7	25.2	66.1	53.4	26.1	56.1
1996	57.4	26.0	60.8	61.1	24.9	65.5	54.4	27.1	57.1
1997	58.2	26.1	61.8	61.4	23.7	66.1	55.6	28.5	58.4
1998	59.7	30.1	63.0	62.9	28.4	67.1	57.2	31.8	59.7
1999	60.6	27.9	64.2	63.1	26.7	67.5	58.6	29.0	61.5
2000	60.9	29.8	64.2	63.6	28.9	67.7	58.6	30.6	61.3
2001	59.7	26.7	63.2	62.1	26.4	66.3	57.8	27.0	60.7
2002	58.1	25.3	61.6	61.1	25.6	65.2	55.8	24.9	58.7
2003	57.4	21.7	61.0	59.5	19.9	64.1	55.6	23.4	58.6
2004	57.2	21.5	60.9	59.3	19.3	63.9	55.5	23.6	58.5
Hispanic									
1973	55.6	. . .	. . .	. . .	. . .	. . .	. . .	. . .	. . .
1974	56.2	. . .	. . .	. . .	. . .	. . .	. . .	. . .	. . .
1975	53.4	. . .	. . .	. . .	. . .	. . .	. . .	. . .	. . .
1976	53.8	. . .	56.6	. . .	. . .	. . .	. . .	. . .	. . .
1977	55.4	. . .	58.3	. . .	. . .	. . .	. . .	. . .	. . .
1978	57.2	. . .	60.0	. . .	. . .	. . .	. . .	. . .	. . .
1979	58.3	. . .	61.0	. . .	. . .	. . .	. . .	. . .	. . .
1980	57.6	. . .	60.5	. . .	. . .	. . .	. . .	. . .	. . .
1981	57.4	. . .	60.7	. . .	. . .	. . .	. . .	. . .	. . .
1982	54.9	. . .	58.2	. . .	. . .	. . .	. . .	. . .	. . .
1983	55.1	. . .	58.1	. . .	. . .	. . .	. . .	. . .	. . .
1984	57.9	. . .	60.7	. . .	. . .	. . .	. . .	. . .	. . .
1985	57.8	. . .	60.7	. . .	. . .	. . .	. . .	. . .	. . .
1986	58.5	. . .	61.5	. . .	. . .	. . .	. . .	. . .	. . .
1987	60.5	. . .	63.4	. . .	. . .	. . .	. . .	. . .	. . .
1988	61.9	. . .	64.6	. . .	. . .	. . .	. . .	. . .	. . .
1989	62.2	. . .	64.8	. . .	. . .	. . .	. . .	. . .	. . .
1990	61.9	. . .	64.8	. . .	. . .	. . .	. . .	. . .	. . .
1991	59.8	. . .	62.8	. . .	. . .	. . .	. . .	. . .	. . .
1992	59.1	. . .	62.1	. . .	. . .	. . .	. . .	. . .	. . .
1993	59.1	. . .	62.1	. . .	. . .	. . .	. . .	. . .	. . .
1994	59.5	33.5	62.4	71.7	36.8	. . .	47.2	30.1	. . .
1995	59.7	34.4	62.6	72.1	37.5	. . .	47.3	31.3	. . .
1996	60.6	33.1	63.7	73.3	38.8	. . .	47.9	27.3	. . .
1997	62.6	33.7	66.0	74.5	37.6	. . .	50.2	29.3	. . .
1998	63.1	36.0	66.2	74.7	38.6	. . .	51.0	33.0	. . .
1999	63.4	37.0	66.5	75.3	41.2	. . .	51.7	32.5	. . .
2000	65.7	38.6	. . .	77.4	42.8	81.7	53.6	33.9	55.8
2001	64.9	38.6	67.8	76.2	43.3	79.9	53.3	33.5	55.4
2002	63.9	35.2	67.0	74.5	39.0	78.3	52.9	31.1	55.2
2003	63.1	30.2	66.4	74.3	31.9	78.6	51.2	28.4	53.6
2004	63.8	30.4	67.2	75.1	33.4	79.4	51.8	27.2	54.4

Note: Persons of Hispanic origin may be of any race.

[1]Beginning in 2003, persons who selected this race group only; persons who selected more than one race group are not included. Prior to 2003, persons who reported more than one race group were included in the group they identified as the main race.
. . . = Not available.

Table 1-13. Employed Civilians by Occupation, Sex, Race, and Hispanic Origin, New Series, 2002–2004

(Thousands of people.)

Occupation	Total	Men	Women	White[1]	Black[1]	Hispanic
2002						
Total	136 485	72 903	63 582	114 013	14 872	16 590
Management, professional, and related occupations	47 180	23 612	23 568	40 318	3 818	2 822
Management, business, and financial operations occupations	19 823	11 619	8 204	17 435	1 364	1 142
Professional and related occupations	27 358	11 993	15 364	22 883	2 454	1 679
Life, physical, and social science occupations	1 287	741	545	1 079	67	27
Community and social services occupations	2 151	836	1 315	1 675	662	175
Service occupations	21 766	9 504	12 261	16 962	3 519	3 979
Healthcare support occupations	2 694	260	2 434	1 836	712	324
Protective service occupations	2 696	2 139	557	2 082	522	276
Food preparation and serving related occupations	6 968	3 077	3 891	5 647	823	1 342
Building and grounds cleaning and maintenance occupations	5 050	3 094	1 956	4 000	819	1 492
Personal care and service occupations	4 358	934	3 424	3 397	643	545
Sales and office occupations	35 408	12 821	22 587	29 745	3 872	3 632
Office and administrative support occupations	19 580	4 690	14 890	16 123	2 515	2 058
Natural resources, construction, and maintenance occupations	13 562	12 874	688	12 071	1 009	2 747
Farming, fishing, and forestry occupations	1 040	788	252	928	58	430
Construction and extraction occupations	7 898	7 674	224	7 076	573	1 754
Installation, maintenance, and repair occupations	4 623	4 412	212	4 067	377	563
Production, transportation, and material moving occupations	18 569	14 091	4 478	14 918	2 654	3 410
Transportation and material moving occupations	8 488	7 228	1 260	6 797	1 348	1 400
2003						
Total	137 736	73 332	64 404	114 235	14 739	17 372
Management, professional, and related occupations	47 929	23 735	24 194	40 558	3 923	2 925
Management, business, and financial operations occupations	19 934	11 534	8 400	17 377	1 368	1 176
Professional and related occupations	27 995	12 201	15 794	23 181	2 555	1 749
Life, physical, and social science occupations	1 375	783	592	1 113	86	81
Community and social services occupations	2 184	862	1 323	1 663	408	184
Service occupations	22 086	9 460	12 626	17 132	3 408	4 175
Healthcare support occupations	2 926	311	2 616	1 996	738	365
Protective service occupations	2 727	2 164	563	2 098	511	276
Food preparation and serving related occupations	7 254	3 151	4 104	5 797	842	1 441
Building and grounds cleaning and maintenance occupations	4 947	2 920	2 027	3 920	740	1 542
Personal care and service occupations	4 232	915	3 316	3 321	578	550
Sales and office occupations	35 496	12 851	22 645	29 555	3 881	3 820
Office and administrative support occupations	19 536	4 714	14 823	15 968	2 465	2 167
Natural resources, construction, and maintenance occupations	14 205	13 541	665	12 600	1 022	3 023
Farming, fishing, and forestry occupations	1 050	819	231	954	49	423
Construction and extraction occupations	8 114	7 891	223	7 242	578	1 926
Installation, maintenance, and repair occupations	5 041	4 830	211	4 404	395	674
Production, transportation, and material moving occupations	18 020	13 745	4 274	14 391	2 504	3 430
Transportation and material moving occupations	8 320	7 049	1 270	6 625	1 301	8 320
2004						
Total	139 252	74 524	64 728	115 239	14 909	17 930
Management, professional, and related occupations	48 532	24 136	24 396	41 027	3 949	3 101
Management, business, and financial operations occupations	20 235	11 718	8 517	17 590	1 408	1 290
Professional and related occupations	28 297	12 418	15 879	23 438	2 541	1 811
Life, physical, and social science occupations	1 365	777	588	1 143	76	69
Community and social services occupations	2 170	845	1 325	1 650	415	203
Service occupations	22 720	9 826	12 894	17 544	3 543	4 336
Healthcare support occupations	2 921	311	2 609	1 991	758	384
Protective service occupations	2 847	2 230	616	2 197	510	315
Food preparation and serving related occupations	7 279	3 196	4 084	5 854	835	1 405
Building and grounds cleaning and maintenance occupations	5 185	3 085	2 100	4 094	773	1 661
Personal care and service occupations	4 488	1 004	3 484	3 407	667	571
Sales and office occupations	35 464	12 805	22 660	29 399	3 918	3 818
Office and administrative support occupations	19 481	4 700	14 781	15 842	2 487	2 164
Natural resources, construction, and maintenance occupations	14 582	13 930	652	12 928	1 012	3 229
Farming, fishing, and forestry occupations	991	786	204	885	53	387
Construction and extraction occupations	8 522	8 306	216	7 642	572	2 127
Installation, maintenance, and repair occupations	5 069	4 838	231	4 401	387	715
Production, transportation, and material moving occupations	17 954	13 827	4 126	14 340	2 488	3 446
Transportation and material moving occupations	8 491	7 240	1 251	6 746	1 364	1 552

Note: Persons of Hispanic origin may be of any race.

[1] Beginning in 2003, persons who selected this race group only; persons who selected more than one race group are not included. Prior to 2003, persons who reported more than one race group were included in the group they identified as the main race.

Table 1-14. Employed Civilians by Occupation, Sex, Race, and Hispanic Origin, Old Series, 1984–1999

(Thousands of people.)

Occupation	1984						1985					
	Total	Men	Women	White	Black	Hispanic	Total	Men	Women	White	Black	Hispanic
Total	118 793	65 104	53 689	102 261	12 175	9 845	117 718	64 223	53 496	101 182	12 074	9 828
Managerial and professional specialty	30 602	16 601	14 001	27 416	1 945	1 208	30 934	16 623	14 311	27 706	1 972	1 259
Executive, administrative, and managerial	14 802	8 872	5 931	13 432	869	630	14 904	8 858	6 046	13 513	875	653
Professional specialty	15 800	7 729	8 071	13 984	1 076	578	16 030	7 765	8 265	14 193	1 097	606
Technical, sales, and administrative support	36 913	13 054	23 859	32 136	3 465	2 366	36 318	12 852	23 466	31 524	3 443	2 413
Technicians and related support	3 866	1 973	1 893	3 298	357	182	3 814	1 937	1 877	3 257	344	196
Sales occupations	14 285	7 247	7 038	12 871	937	848	14 052	7 180	6 872	12 590	955	867
Administrative support, including clerical	18 762	3 834	14 928	15 967	2 170	1 336	18 452	3 735	14 717	15 677	2 145	1 349
Service occupations	16 012	6 470	9 543	12 565	2 757	1 984	16 254	6 610	9 644	12 739	2 783	2 005
Private household	792	29	763	571	191	168	799	33	766	608	162	179
Protective service	2 000	1 708	293	1 618	334	131	2 083	1 765	318	1 682	351	144
Service, except private household and protective	13 220	4 732	8 488	10 376	2 233	1 685	13 372	4 812	8 560	10 449	2 270	1 682
Precision production, craft, and repair	13 745	12 580	1 166	12 255	1 083	1 301	13 250	12 112	1 138	11 824	1 039	1 269
Operators, fabricators, and laborers	18 071	13 494	4 577	14 732	2 715	2 436	17 456	13 075	4 380	14 205	2 613	2 311
Machine operators, assemblers, and inspectors	8 200	4 931	3 269	6 668	1 184	1 249	7 820	4 693	3 127	6 284	1 159	1 142
Transportation and material moving occupations	4 886	4 449	436	4 010	757	466	4 913	4 476	437	4 022	774	462
Handlers, equipment cleaners, helpers, and laborers	4 985	4 114	871	4 054	775	721	4 723	3 906	816	3 899	680	707
Farming, forestry, and fishing	3 450	2 907	544	3 157	209	550	3 506	2 951	556	3 184	224	570

Occupation	1986						1987					
	Total	Men	Women	White	Black	Hispanic	Total	Men	Women	White	Black	Hispanic
Total	118 492	64 440	54 052	101 669	12 151	10 027	120 259	65 349	54 910	103 045	12 382	10 361
Managerial and professional specialty	31 085	16 387	14 698	27 719	2 044	1 322	32 231	16 811	15 419	28 647	2 181	1 437
Executive, administrative, and managerial	14 722	8 612	6 110	13 327	872	683	15 338	8 897	6 441	13 783	977	762
Professional specialty	16 363	7 775	8 588	14 393	1 172	639	16 893	7 915	8 978	14 863	1 204	675
Technical, sales, and administrative support	37 048	13 379	23 669	32 167	3 423	2 492	37 058	13 417	23 641	32 096	3 501	2 578
Technicians and related support	4 277	2 185	2 092	3 620	418	216	4 039	2 000	2 039	3 433	395	223
Sales occupations	14 014	7 286	6 728	12 576	891	882	14 342	7 418	6 924	12 824	974	940
Administrative support, including clerical	18 757	3 908	14 849	15 971	2 114	1 395	18 677	3 999	14 679	15 839	2 132	1 415
Service occupations	16 377	6 676	9 701	12 778	2 843	2 037	16 821	6 867	9 953	13 145	2 901	2 069
Private household	891	37	854	695	162	187	928	45	883	735	154	214
Protective service	2 114	1 760	354	1 669	383	168	2 165	1 792	373	1 729	380	160
Service, except private household and protective	13 373	4 879	8 493	10 414	2 298	1 682	13 727	5 030	8 697	10 681	2 367	1 695
Precision production, craft, and repair	13 225	12 087	1 137	11 798	1 016	1 345	13 429	12 279	1 150	11 990	1 006	1 372
Operators, fabricators, and laborers	17 247	12 954	4 294	14 018	2 599	2 243	17 341	13 109	4 232	14 090	2 580	2 310
Machine operators, assemblers, and inspectors	7 658	4 623	3 035	6 141	1 153	1 130	7 553	4 642	2 911	6 066	1 117	1 140
Transportation and material moving occupations	4 908	4 482	426	4 069	730	460	5 036	4 570	465	4 195	706	481
Handlers, equipment cleaners, helpers, and laborers	4 682	3 850	832	3 808	716	653	4 753	3 897	856	3 829	757	689
Farming, forestry, and fishing	3 510	2 957	553	3 188	226	588	3 379	2 864	515	3 078	212	596

Occupation	1988						1989					
	Total	Men	Women	White	Black	Hispanic	Total	Men	Women	White	Black	Hispanic
Total	123 060	66 450	56 610	105 190	12 835	10 788	124 900	67 377	57 523	106 490	13 279	11 127
Managerial and professional specialty	33 847	17 583	16 264	30 045	2 405	1 517	35 318	18 378	16 940	31 323	2 651	1 548
Executive, administrative, and managerial	16 312	9 298	7 014	14 605	1 103	807	17 186	9 840	7 346	15 398	1 233	821
Professional specialty	17 536	8 285	9 250	15 439	1 302	709	18 132	8 539	9 593	15 924	1 418	727
Technical, sales, and administrative support	37 306	13 322	23 984	32 232	3 637	2 639	37 417	13 310	24 107	32 184	3 808	2 719
Technicians and related support	3 869	1 856	2 013	3 301	376	205	3 909	1 900	2 009	3 361	378	240
Sales occupations	14 817	7 543	7 273	13 235	1 056	1 010	15 119	7 634	7 485	13 366	1 183	1 048
Administrative support, including clerical	18 620	3 923	14 697	15 696	2 205	1 424	18 389	3 776	14 613	15 457	2 248	1 431
Service occupations	16 912	6 840	10 072	13 207	2 890	2 131	16 930	6 774	10 155	13 208	2 880	2 195
Private household	817	30	787	643	136	223	821	37	784	638	137	204
Protective service	2 249	1 873	376	1 778	407	167	2 237	1 881	356	1 772	406	166
Service, except private household and protective	13 847	4 938	8 909	10 787	2 346	1 741	13 872	4 857	9 015	10 799	2 337	1 825
Precision production, craft, and repair	13 489	12 241	1 248	11 974	1 040	1 407	13 524	12 323	1 201	11 949	1 073	1 430
Operators, fabricators, and laborers	17 876	13 535	4 341	14 416	2 677	2 474	18 068	13 675	4 393	14 496	2 712	2 577
Machine operators, assemblers, and inspectors	7 754	4 800	2 954	6 166	1 167	1 151	7 907	4 958	2 949	6 221	1 218	1 250
Transportation and material moving occupations	5 136	4 654	483	4 227	749	511	5 171	4 682	490	4 254	760	512
Handlers, equipment cleaners, helpers, and laborers	4 986	4 081	904	4 023	760	811	4 990	4 035	955	4 022	734	816
Farming, forestry, and fishing	3 629	2 928	701	3 315	187	620	3 642	2 916	726	3 330	154	658

Table 1-14. Employed Civilians by Occupation, Sex, Race, and Hispanic Origin, Old Series, 1984–1999
—Continued

(Thousands of people.)

Occupation	1990						1991					
	Total	Men	Women	White	Black	Hispanic	Total	Men	Women	White	Black	Hispanic
Total	118 793	65 104	53 689	102 261	12 175	9 845	117 718	64 223	53 496	101 182	12 074	9 828
Managerial and professional specialty	30 602	16 601	14 001	27 416	1 945	1 208	30 934	16 623	14 311	27 706	1 972	1 259
Executive, administrative, and managerial	14 802	8 872	5 931	13 432	869	630	14 904	8 858	6 046	13 513	875	653
Professional specialty	15 800	7 729	8 071	13 984	1 076	578	16 030	7 765	8 265	14 193	1 097	606
Technical, sales, and administrative support	36 913	13 054	23 859	32 136	3 465	2 366	36 318	12 852	23 466	31 524	3 443	2 413
Technicians and related support	3 866	1 973	1 893	3 298	357	182	3 814	1 937	1 877	3 257	344	196
Sales occupations	14 285	7 247	7 038	12 871	937	848	14 052	7 180	6 872	12 590	955	867
Administrative support, including clerical	18 762	3 834	14 928	15 967	2 170	1 336	18 452	3 735	14 717	15 677	2 145	1 349
Service occupations	16 012	6 470	9 543	12 565	2 757	1 984	16 254	6 610	9 644	12 739	2 783	2 005
Private household	792	29	763	571	191	168	799	33	766	608	162	179
Protective service	2 000	1 708	293	1 618	334	131	2 083	1 765	318	1 682	351	144
Service, except private household and protective	13 220	4 732	8 488	10 376	2 233	1 685	13 372	4 812	8 560	10 449	2 270	1 682
Precision production, craft, and repair	13 745	12 580	1 166	12 255	1 083	1 301	13 250	12 112	1 138	11 824	1 039	1 269
Operators, fabricators, and laborers	18 071	13 494	4 577	14 732	2 715	2 436	17 456	13 075	4 380	14 205	2 613	2 311
Machine operators, assemblers, and inspectors	8 200	4 931	3 269	6 668	1 184	1 249	7 820	4 693	3 127	6 284	1 159	1 142
Transportation and material moving occupations	4 886	4 449	436	4 010	757	466	4 913	4 476	437	4 022	774	462
Handlers, equipment cleaners, helpers, and laborers	4 985	4 114	871	4 054	775	721	4 723	3 906	816	3 899	680	707
Farming, forestry, and fishing	3 450	2 907	544	3 157	209	550	3 506	2 951	556	3 184	224	570

Occupation	1992						1993					
	Total	Men	Women	White	Black	Hispanic	Total	Men	Women	White	Black	Hispanic
Total	118 492	64 440	54 052	101 669	12 151	10 027	120 259	65 349	54 910	103 045	12 382	10 361
Managerial and professional specialty	31 085	16 387	14 698	27 719	2 044	1 322	32 231	16 811	15 419	28 647	2 181	1 437
Executive, administrative, and managerial	14 722	8 612	6 110	13 327	872	683	15 338	8 897	6 441	13 783	977	762
Professional specialty	16 363	7 775	8 588	14 393	1 172	639	16 893	7 915	8 978	14 863	1 204	675
Technical, sales, and administrative support	37 048	13 379	23 669	32 167	3 423	2 492	37 058	13 417	23 641	32 096	3 501	2 578
Technicians and related support	4 277	2 185	2 092	3 620	418	216	4 039	2 000	2 039	3 433	395	223
Sales occupations	14 014	7 286	6 728	12 576	891	882	14 342	7 418	6 924	12 824	974	940
Administrative support, including clerical	18 757	3 908	14 849	15 971	2 114	1 395	18 677	3 999	14 679	15 839	2 132	1 415
Service occupations	16 377	6 676	9 701	12 778	2 843	2 037	16 821	6 867	9 953	13 145	2 901	2 069
Private household	891	37	854	695	162	187	928	45	883	735	154	214
Protective service	2 114	1 760	354	1 669	383	168	2 165	1 792	373	1 729	380	160
Service, except private household and protective	13 373	4 879	8 493	10 414	2 298	1 682	13 727	5 030	8 697	10 681	2 367	1 695
Precision production, craft, and repair	13 225	12 087	1 137	11 798	1 016	1 345	13 429	12 279	1 150	11 990	1 006	1 372
Operators, fabricators, and laborers	17 247	12 954	4 294	14 018	2 599	2 243	17 341	13 109	4 232	14 090	2 580	2 310
Machine operators, assemblers, and inspectors	7 658	4 623	3 035	6 141	1 153	1 130	7 553	4 642	2 911	6 066	1 117	1 140
Transportation and material moving occupations	4 908	4 482	426	4 069	730	460	5 036	4 570	465	4 195	706	481
Handlers, equipment cleaners, helpers, and laborers	4 682	3 850	832	3 808	716	653	4 753	3 897	856	3 829	757	689
Farming, forestry, and fishing	3 510	2 957	553	3 188	226	588	3 379	2 864	515	3 078	212	596

Occupation	1994						1995					
	Total	Men	Women	White	Black	Hispanic	Total	Men	Women	White	Black	Hispanic
Total	123 060	66 450	56 610	105 190	12 835	10 788	124 900	67 377	57 523	106 490	13 279	11 127
Managerial and professional specialty	33 847	17 583	16 264	30 045	2 405	1 517	35 318	18 378	16 940	31 323	2 651	1 548
Executive, administrative, and managerial	16 312	9 298	7 014	14 605	1 103	807	17 186	9 840	7 346	15 398	1 233	821
Professional specialty	17 536	8 285	9 250	15 439	1 302	709	18 132	8 539	9 593	15 924	1 418	727
Technical, sales, and administrative support	37 306	13 322	23 984	32 232	3 637	2 639	37 417	13 310	24 107	32 184	3 808	2 719
Technicians and related support	3 869	1 856	2 013	3 301	376	205	3 909	1 900	2 009	3 361	378	240
Sales occupations	14 817	7 543	7 273	13 235	1 056	1 010	15 119	7 634	7 485	13 366	1 183	1 048
Administrative support, including clerical	18 620	3 923	14 697	15 696	2 205	1 424	18 389	3 776	14 613	15 457	2 248	1 431
Service occupations	16 912	6 840	10 072	13 207	2 890	2 131	16 930	6 774	10 155	13 208	2 880	2 195
Private household	817	30	787	643	136	223	821	37	784	638	137	204
Protective service	2 249	1 873	376	1 778	407	167	2 237	1 881	356	1 772	406	166
Service, except private household and protective	13 847	4 938	8 909	10 787	2 346	1 741	13 872	4 857	9 015	10 799	2 337	1 825
Precision production, craft, and repair	13 489	12 241	1 248	11 974	1 040	1 407	13 524	12 323	1 201	11 949	1 073	1 430
Operators, fabricators, and laborers	17 876	13 535	4 341	14 416	2 677	2 474	18 068	13 675	4 393	14 496	2 712	2 577
Machine operators, assemblers, and inspectors	7 754	4 800	2 954	6 166	1 167	1 151	7 907	4 958	2 949	6 221	1 218	1 250
Transportation and material moving occupations	5 136	4 654	483	4 227	749	511	5 171	4 682	490	4 254	760	512
Handlers, equipment cleaners, helpers, and laborers	4 986	4 081	904	4 023	760	811	4 990	4 035	955	4 022	734	816
Farming, forestry, and fishing	3 629	2 928	701	3 315	187	620	3 642	2 916	726	3 330	154	658

Table 1-14. Employed Civilians by Occupation, Sex, Race, and Hispanic Origin, Old Series, 1984–1999
—Continued

(Thousands of people.)

Occupation	1996						1997					
	Total	Men	Women	White	Black	Hispanic	Total	Men	Women	White	Black	Hispanic
Total	126 708	68 207	58 501	107 808	13 542	11 642	129 558	69 685	59 873	109 856	13 969	12 726
Managerial and professional specialty	36 497	18 744	17 754	32 116	2 706	1 654	37 686	19 249	18 437	33 089	2 764	1 867
Executive, administrative, and managerial	17 746	9 979	7 767	15 807	1 218	854	18 440	10 271	8 170	16 420	1 267	1 001
Professional specialty	18 752	8 764	9 987	16 309	1 488	799	19 245	8 978	10 267	16 669	1 497	866
Technical, sales, and administrative support	37 683	13 489	24 194	32 177	3 877	2 849	38 309	13 760	24 549	32 624	4 032	3 026
Technicians and related support	3 926	1 865	2 061	3 334	368	248	4 214	2 028	2 186	3 571	410	256
Sales occupations	15 404	7 782	7 622	13 519	1 218	1 085	15 734	7 840	7 894	13 730	1 271	1 198
Administrative support, including clerical	18 353	3 842	14 511	15 323	2 291	1 516	18 361	3 892	14 469	15 323	2 352	1 572
Service occupations	17 177	6 967	10 210	13 447	2 962	2 349	17 537	7 122	10 416	13 604	3 092	2 560
Private household	804	41	764	637	139	211	795	37	758	642	129	212
Protective service	2 187	1 811	375	1 748	389	175	2 300	1 890	411	1 800	430	202
Service, except private household and protective	14 186	5 115	9 071	11 062	2 435	1 963	14 442	5 195	9 247	11 162	2 533	2 146
Precision production, craft, and repair	13 587	12 368	1 219	12 020	1 069	1 498	14 124	12 868	1 256	12 472	1 144	1 714
Operators, fabricators, and laborers	18 197	13 750	4 447	14 697	2 789	2 607	18 399	13 858	4 540	14 813	2 781	2 839
Machine operators, assemblers, and inspectors	7 874	4 902	2 972	6 270	1 193	1 295	7 962	4 962	3 000	6 322	1 178	1 426
Transportation and material moving occupations	5 302	4 799	504	4 412	772	548	5 389	4 872	518	4 435	819	592
Handlers, equipment cleaners, helpers, and laborers	5 021	4 049	971	4 016	824	764	5 048	4 025	1 023	4 057	784	821
Farming, forestry, and fishing	3 566	2 889	677	3 350	139	685	3 503	2 828	675	3 254	156	721

Occupation	1998						1999					
	Total	Men	Women	White	Black	Hispanic	Total	Men	Women	White	Black	Hispanic
Total	131 463	70 693	60 771	110 931	14 556	13 291	133 488	71 446	62 042	112 235	15 056	13 720
Managerial and professional specialty	38 937	19 867	19 070	34 063	2 947	1 933	40 467	20 446	20 021	35 125	3 233	2 040
Executive, administrative, and managerial	19 054	10 585	8 469	16 903	1 368	1 028	19 584	10 744	8 840	17 235	1 484	1 097
Professional specialty	19 883	9 282	10 602	17 160	1 579	905	20 883	9 702	11 181	17 890	1 749	943
Technical, sales, and administrative support	38 521	13 792	24 728	32 490	4 264	3 186	38 921	14 079	24 842	32 779	4 356	3 286
Technicians and related support	4 261	1 976	2 285	3 557	441	283	4 355	2 094	2 261	3 622	467	279
Sales occupations	15 850	7 875	7 975	13 704	1 415	1 245	16 118	8 049	8 069	13 956	1 405	1 267
Administrative support, including clerical	18 410	3 941	14 469	15 229	2 408	1 657	18 448	3 936	14 512	15 201	2 484	1 740
Service occupations	17 836	7 222	10 614	13 807	3 148	2 670	17 915	7 093	10 822	13 725	3 275	2 716
Private household	847	46	801	704	116	262	831	40	791	670	126	244
Protective service	2 417	1 986	431	1 892	463	204	2 440	1 980	460	1 886	484	200
Service, except private household and protective	14 572	5 190	9 382	11 211	2 569	2 204	14 644	5 074	9 570	11 168	2 666	2 271
Precision production, craft, and repair	14 411	13 208	1 203	12 729	1 158	1 793	14 593	13 286	1 307	12 908	1 174	1 871
Operators, fabricators, and laborers	18 256	13 769	4 487	14 609	2 866	2 917	18 167	13 793	4 374	14 535	2 847	3 014
Machine operators, assemblers, and inspectors	7 791	4 882	2 909	6 146	1 200	1 340	7 386	4 637	2 749	5 824	1 143	1 364
Transportation and material moving occupations	5 363	4 818	545	4 351	872	640	5 516	4 968	548	4 488	879	659
Handlers, equipment cleaners, helpers, and laborers	5 102	4 069	1 033	4 112	795	938	5 265	4 188	1 077	4 223	825	992
Farming, forestry, and fishing	3 502	2 835	668	3 233	172	792	3 426	2 749	676	3 165	172	793

Note: Detail for the above race and Hispanic-origin groups will not sum to totals because data for the "Other" races group are not presented and Hispanics are included in both the White and Black population groups. See "Notes and Definitions" for information on historical comparability.

Table 1-15. Employed Civilians by Industry and Occupation, New Series, 2002–2004

(Thousands of people.)

Industry	Total employed	Management, professional, and related occupations	Life, physical, and social science occupations	Service occupations	Sales and office occupations	Natural resources, construction, and maintenance occupations	Production, transportation, and material moving occupations
2002							
Total	136 485	47 180	1 287	21 766	35 408	13 562	18 569
Agriculture, forestry, fishing, and hunting	2 311	1 173	24	69	108	864	96
Mining	502	127	15	9	47	202	117
Construction	9 981	1 673	8	82	764	6 940	522
Manufacturing	17 233	4 626	272	280	2 447	1 250	8 630
Durable goods	10 833	3 116	71	136	1 452	854	5 274
Nondurable goods	6 400	1 510	201	144	995	395	3 356
Wholesale trade	4 144	668	20	53	2 286	242	895
Retail trade	15 663	1 634	14	589	10 892	815	1 733
Transportation and warehousing	5 971	636	4	281	1 601	374	3 078
Utilities	1 273	387	30	34	269	297	287
Information	3 691	1 778	11	87	1 270	380	175
Finance and insurance	6 749	3 051	20	63	3 560	29	46
Real estate and rental and leasing	2 816	850	6	345	1 346	141	133
Professional and technical services	8 408	6 344	288	110	1 659	127	170
Management, administrative, and waste services	5 607	1 118	22	2 285	1 325	228	651
Educational services	11 724	8 695	161	1 281	1 261	158	329
Healthcare and social assistance	15 900	8 297	184	4 725	2 486	99	294
Arts, entertainment, and recreation	2 639	836	11	1 233	410	91	68
Accommodation and food services	8 902	1 347	3	6 060	1 079	54	362
Other services	6 665	1 452	15	2 269	1 141	1 008	794
Public administration	6 307	2 489	181	1 912	1 455	263	189
2003							
Total	137 736	47 929	1 375	22 086	35 496	14 205	18 020
Agriculture, forestry, fishing, and hunting	2 275	1 088	29	80	112	901	94
Mining	525	133	18	6	57	203	127
Construction	10 138	1 590	6	60	693	7 277	519
Manufacturing	16 902	4 733	287	252	2 340	1 150	8 428
Durable goods	10 520	3 207	58	128	1 370	756	5 060
Nondurable goods	6 382	1 526	229	123	970	394	3 368
Wholesale trade	4 486	782	20	47	2 477	239	941
Retail trade	16 220	1 679	15	569	11 273	888	1 811
Transportation and warehousing	5 758	630	6	268	1 614	401	2 845
Utilities	1 193	376	28	21	252	293	251
Information	3 687	1 852	12	91	1 188	380	176
Finance and insurance	6 834	3 142	26	67	3 561	36	29
Real estate and rental and leasing	2 914	881	6	304	1 421	194	114
Professional and technical services	8 243	6 237	320	122	1 627	130	128
Management, administrative, and waste services	5 636	1 131	25	2 321	1 286	262	637
Educational services	11 826	8 808	170	1 274	1 236	187	322
Healthcare and social assistance	16 434	8 665	201	4 785	2 565	127	291
Arts, entertainment, and recreation	2 587	891	9	1 193	361	92	50
Accommodation and food services	9 021	1 267	2	6 393	988	57	315
Other services	6 815	1 482	14	2 321	1 064	1 144	804
Public administration	6 243	2 563	182	1 912	1 384	245	138
2004							
Total	139 252	48 532	1 365	22 720	35 464	14 582	17 954
Agriculture, forestry, fishing, and hunting	2 232	1 092	28	95	106	837	103
Mining	539	118	13	5	51	232	133
Construction	10 768	1 696	5	70	732	7 743	527
Manufacturing	16 484	4 719	265	225	2 185	1 151	8 203
Durable goods	10 329	3 202	53	113	1 247	771	4 996
Nondurable goods	6 155	1 517	212	113	938	380	3 207
Wholesale trade	4 600	754	12	60	2 553	292	940
Retail trade	16 269	1 759	16	571	11 295	815	1 830
Transportation and warehousing	5 844	593	3	277	1 636	383	2 955
Utilities	1 168	373	35	22	266	276	231
Information	3 463	1 766	19	93	1 102	341	161
Finance and insurance	6 940	3 311	17	69	3 495	34	30
Real estate and rental and leasing	3 029	931	2	280	1 502	201	115
Professional and technical services	8 386	6 333	326	108	1 651	139	156
Management, administrative, and water services	5 722	1 050	26	2 503	1 249	278	642
Educational services	12 058	9 036	170	1 298	1 201	184	338
Healthcare and social assistance	16 661	8 756	211	4 860	2 634	127	285
Arts, entertainment, and recreation	2 690	898	15	1 266	372	86	67
Accommodation and food services	9 131	1 286	4	6 487	1 000	70	289
Other services	6 903	1 467	16	2 408	1 082	1 134	812
Public administration	6 365	2 594	181	2 021	1 354	259	138

Table 1-16. Employed Civilians by Industry and Occupation, Old Series, 1990–1999

(Thousands of people.)

Industry	Total employed	Managerial and professional specialty		Technical, sales, and administrative support			Service occupations		Precision production, craft, and repair	Operators, fabricators, and laborers			Farming, forestry, and fishing
		Executive, adminis-trative, and man-agerial	Profes-sional specialty	Techni-cians and related support	Sales	Adminis-trative support, including clerical	Private household	Other services, including protective		Machine operators, assem-blers, and inspectors	Transpor-tation and material moving	Handlers, equip-ment cleaners, helpers, and laborers	
1990													
Agriculture	3 223	95	85	30	23	108	. . .	17	42	13	49	21	2 740
Mining	724	110	63	32	9	72	. . .	9	243	26	123	36	2
Construction	7 764	1 034	133	64	75	426	. . .	35	4 445	114	524	890	23
Manufacturing	21 346	2 530	1 794	765	779	2 363	. . .	374	3 964	6 696	805	1 173	102
Durable goods	12 630	1 521	1 225	533	326	1 363	. . .	197	2 721	3 685	416	552	91
Nondurable goods	8 717	1 010	569	232	453	1 000	. . .	178	1 243	3 011	389	621	11
Transportation and public utilities	8 168	915	459	306	340	2 166	. . .	293	1 259	122	1 812	481	14
Wholesale trade	4 669	528	88	50	1 862	788	. . .	39	323	138	464	380	10
Retail trade	19 953	1 557	379	89	8 295	1 633	. . .	4 584	1 181	197	512	1 498	27
Finance, insurance, and real estate	8 051	2 087	225	155	1 904	3 097	. . .	296	155	19	17	25	71
Services	39 267	4 745	11 786	2 125	971	6 561	792	8 194	1 898	831	521	436	408
Services, except private households	38 231	4 742	11 773	2 121	969	6 552	. . .	8 098	1 881	829	514	417	336
Professional services	25 351	2 642	10 425	1 719	162	4 763	. . .	4 545	400	228	276	101	91
Public administration	5 627	1 199	788	251	26	1 549	. . .	1 380	235	43	60	44	53
1991													
Agriculture	3 269	91	78	31	22	102	. . .	18	41	12	54	16	2 803
Mining	732	112	65	37	8	81	. . .	12	244	24	115	34	1
Construction	7 140	969	137	53	71	386	. . .	29	4 077	100	497	797	24
Manufacturing	20 580	2 499	1 777	749	729	2 283	. . .	355	3 837	6 402	780	1 076	92
Durable goods	12 015	1 489	1 178	512	292	1 260	. . .	185	2 630	3 459	404	525	80
Nondurable goods	8 565	1 010	599	237	437	1 023	. . .	170	1 207	2 943	376	551	13
Transportation and public utilities	8 234	973	474	301	331	2 170	. . .	262	1 285	125	1 833	465	16
Wholesale trade	4 660	537	77	37	1 868	776	. . .	36	319	135	490	374	11
Retail trade	19 758	1 591	372	103	8 181	1 589	. . .	4 605	1 142	173	530	1 450	23
Finance, insurance, and real estate	7 806	2 027	216	133	1 849	3 022	. . .	270	167	18	14	20	69
Services	39 884	4 873	12 035	2 148	967	6 534	799	8 455	1 884	792	537	444	416
Services, except private households	38 868	4 871	12 029	2 144	966	6 522	. . .	8 375	1 870	791	531	422	346
Professional services	25 853	2 706	10 629	1 742	162	4 788	. . .	4 749	393	211	295	87	92
Public administration	5 655	1 231	798	223	27	1 508	. . .	1 414	253	41	62	46	51
1992													
Agriculture	3 247	91	74	44	21	118	. . .	17	45	10	44	19	2 764
Mining	666	100	58	31	7	79	. . .	12	214	28	106	31	1
Construction	7 063	892	147	67	73	410	. . .	34	4 073	99	480	762	28
Manufacturing	20 124	2 401	1 640	758	768	2 268	. . .	330	3 808	6 244	749	1 074	84
Durable goods	11 561	1 405	1 069	525	306	1 251	. . .	158	2 569	3 344	374	485	75
Nondurable goods	8 563	996	571	234	462	1 017	. . .	172	1 239	2 901	375	589	8
Transportation and public utilities	8 284	946	461	375	250	2 281	. . .	274	1 227	114	1 874	464	18
Wholesale trade	4 783	556	85	46	1 883	820	. . .	42	302	118	490	405	38
Retail trade	19 938	1 603	374	146	8 229	1 591	. . .	4 717	1 117	180	530	1 428	25
Finance, insurance, and real estate	7 780	1 966	224	162	1 851	2 991	. . .	290	171	19	13	22	73
Services	40 967	4 937	12 473	2 379	908	6 728	891	9 259	2 022	810	563	440	449
Services, except private households	39 821	4 933	12 463	2 373	906	6 714	. . .	8 368	2 007	807	555	421	372
Professional services	27 713	3 150	11 168	2 040	175	5 032	. . .	5 017	411	208	314	102	95
Public administration	5 640	1 231	829	268	25	1 472	. . .	1 404	246	37	59	38	31
1993													
Agriculture	3 115	99	87	39	14	114	. . .	15	45	8	53	20	2 621
Mining	672	102	75	24	4	73	. . .	8	233	25	103	25	. . .
Construction	7 276	928	137	46	74	390	. . .	35	4 292	79	517	753	25
Manufacturing	19 711	2 432	1 688	693	739	2 161	. . .	312	3 744	6 124	710	1 012	95
Durable goods	11 385	1 415	1 085	463	282	1 181	. . .	161	2 553	3 352	361	446	87
Nondurable goods	8 326	1 017	603	231	457	981	. . .	151	1 191	2 772	349	566	9
Transportation and public utilities	8 526	975	500	329	241	2 318	. . .	266	1 271	131	2 000	479	18
Wholesale trade	4 622	533	85	49	1 819	771	. . .	40	296	115	492	378	44
Retail trade	20 521	1 652	351	129	8 543	1 571	. . .	4 873	1 095	179	543	1 563	23
Finance, insurance, and real estate	7 975	2 089	244	161	1 918	2 967	. . .	290	183	21	13	19	70
Services	42 059	5 234	12 864	2 300	963	6 841	928	8 579	2 047	831	551	467	453
Services, except private households	40 924	5 231	12 857	2 298	961	6 830	. . .	8 497	2 035	831	547	446	392
Professional services	28 365	3 299	11 476	1 969	176	5 111	. . .	5 163	419	223	314	108	105
Public administration	5 782	1 294	862	270	26	1 469	. . .	1 475	224	39	54	39	31

. . . = Not available.

Table 1-16. Employed Civilians by Industry and Occupation, Old Series, 1990–1999—*Continued*

(Thousands of people.)

Industry	Total employed	Managerial and professional specialty		Technical, sales, and administrative support			Service occupations		Precision production, craft, and repair	Operators, fabricators, and laborers			Farming, forestry, and fishing
		Executive, administrative, and managerial	Professional specialty	Technicians and related support	Sales	Administrative support, including clerical	Private household	Other services, including protective		Machine operators, assemblers, and inspectors	Transportation and material moving	Handlers, equipment cleaners, helpers, and laborers	
1994													
Agriculture	3 409	97	88	38	14	145	. . .	18	42	5	45	19	2 897
Mining	669	110	76	22	10	67	. . .	9	222	21	109	21	1
Construction	7 493	1 055	138	60	59	429	. . .	34	4 263	86	529	818	22
Manufacturing	20 157	2 588	1 814	611	745	2 093	. . .	290	3 803	6 298	744	1 082	89
Durable goods	11 792	1 555	1 170	412	310	1 146	. . .	152	2 622	3 415	416	514	80
Nondurable goods	8 365	1 033	644	200	435	946	. . .	138	1 181	2 883	328	569	9
Transportation and public utilities	8 692	1 065	486	329	248	2 337	. . .	246	1 270	120	2 049	528	15
Wholesale trade	4 713	531	89	37	1 880	775	. . .	34	296	150	464	398	60
Retail trade	20 986	1 704	402	119	8 772	1 555	. . .	4 948	1 145	197	548	1 569	27
Finance, insurance, and real estate	8 141	2 198	272	160	2 029	2 915	. . .	282	167	18	17	18	66
Services	42 986	5 649	13 319	2 274	1 032	6 864	817	8 654	2 071	825	567	493	421
Services, except private households	42 009	5 645	13 311	2 272	1 031	6 855	. . .	8 584	2 063	825	564	480	380
Professional services	29 030	3 559	11 888	1 968	193	5 083	. . .	5 134	470	222	314	94	105
Public administration	5 814	1 315	853	221	28	1 440	. . .	1 579	211	32	64	39	30
1995													
Agriculture	3 440	105	92	45	15	145	. . .	16	35	17	45	19	2 907
Mining	627	100	60	22	4	53	. . .	5	228	28	101	25	2
Construction	7 668	1 117	145	43	63	431	. . .	33	4 362	85	513	858	18
Manufacturing	20 493	2 804	1 787	615	756	2 108	. . .	294	3 837	6 386	728	1 067	111
Durable goods	12 015	1 683	1 160	404	311	1 117	. . .	156	2 660	3 498	390	535	100
Nondurable goods	8 478	1 121	627	211	445	991	. . .	138	1 177	2 888	338	532	11
Transportation and public utilities	8 709	1 124	510	310	259	2 337	. . .	247	1 223	121	2 079	487	12
Wholesale trade	4 986	554	108	48	1 979	792	. . .	37	308	187	488	423	62
Retail trade	21 086	1 740	425	141	8 949	1 501	. . .	4 844	1 111	214	578	1 548	34
Finance, insurance, and real estate	7 983	2 258	268	148	1 985	2 757	. . .	269	183	14	14	19	68
Services	43 953	6 029	13 755	2 307	1 086	6 848	821	8 788	2 008	824	572	510	405
Services, except private households	42 982	6 023	13 746	2 305	1 086	6 838	. . .	8 719	2 002	822	569	497	374
Professional services	29 661	3 721	12 233	1 974	199	5 114	. . .	5 284	465	178	312	87	94
Public administration	5 957	1 356	981	230	24	1 417	. . .	1 577	229	32	52	35	25
1996													
Agriculture	3 443	108	88	40	19	174	. . .	28	41	11	34	13	2 888
Mining	569	90	44	21	10	47	. . .	7	208	21	105	17	1
Construction	7 943	1 221	165	45	65	452	. . .	32	4 442	96	513	890	21
Manufacturing	20 518	2 840	1 882	631	766	2 033	. . .	264	3 814	6 350	767	1 069	101
Durable goods	12 202	1 690	1 204	425	337	1 131	. . .	144	2 677	3 561	425	518	90
Nondurable goods	8 316	1 150	678	206	429	903	. . .	120	1 137	2 789	342	551	11
Transportation and public utilities	8 817	1 159	529	332	288	2 319	. . .	251	1 185	132	2 126	489	7
Wholesale trade	4 956	563	100	52	2 005	749	. . .	48	320	142	515	400	62
Retail trade	21 541	1 818	410	123	9 055	1 577	. . .	4 983	1 137	204	614	1 583	39
Finance, insurance, and real estate	8 076	2 274	271	162	2 052	2 744	. . .	298	165	15	13	28	54
Services	45 043	6 347	14 312	2 312	1 120	6 905	804	8 876	2 055	875	573	496	367
Services, except private households	44 107	6 343	14 302	2 310	1 119	6 900	. . .	8 821	2 048	875	572	484	335
Professional services	30 085	3 853	12 592	1 941	204	5 090	. . .	5 340	417	190	301	88	69
Public administration	5 802	1 325	951	208	25	1 353	. . .	1 585	221	28	43	37	25

. . . = Not available.

Table 1-16. Employed Civilians by Industry and Occupation, Old Series, 1990–1999—*Continued*

(Thousands of people.)

Industry	Total employed	Managerial and professional specialty		Technical, sales, and administrative support			Service occupations		Precision production, craft, and repair	Operators, fabricators, and laborers			Farming, forestry, and fishing
		Executive, adminis-trative, and man-agerial	Profes-sional specialty	Techni-cians and related support	Sales	Adminis-trative support, including clerical	Private household	Other services, including protective		Machine operators, assem-blers, and inspectors	Transpor-tation and material moving	Handlers, equip-ment cleaners, helpers, and laborers	
1997													
Agriculture	3 399	124	83	48	19	160	. . .	24	34	10	51	26	2 821
Mining	634	92	51	25	10	66	. . .	4	236	24	101	24	1
Construction	8 302	1 274	158	45	72	425	. . .	35	4 731	97	558	884	22
Manufacturing	20 835	2 882	1 938	689	785	2 029	. . .	268	3 887	6 471	762	1 027	96
Durable goods	12 437	1 699	1 261	441	316	1 133	. . .	145	2 753	3 685	406	512	87
Nondurable goods	8 399	1 183	677	249	469	896	. . .	123	1 134	2 786	356	515	9
Transportation and public utilities	9 182	1 230	562	342	283	2 297	. . .	301	1 257	133	2 230	531	16
Wholesale trade	4 907	589	110	47	1 928	740	. . .	56	326	133	520	393	66
Retail trade	21 869	1 893	427	155	9 303	1 480	. . .	5 048	1 173	202	572	1 580	36
Finance, insurance, and real estate	8 297	2 428	308	151	2 092	2 749	. . .	307	175	12	11	28	38
Services	46 393	6 642	14 677	2 490	1 210	7 113	795	9 055	2 115	854	537	521	384
Services, except private households	45 472	6 638	14 671	2 485	1 210	7 107	. . .	8 988	2 109	853	537	514	359
Professional services	30 935	4 057	12 846	2 110	225	5 177	. . .	5 432	420	207	279	89	93
Public administration	5 738	1 287	932	221	32	1 303	. . .	1 644	191	27	46	33	23
1998													
Agriculture	3 378	110	105	51	23	136	. . .	21	39	20	42	19	2 814
Mining	620	101	63	19	11	53	. . .	8	208	31	105	18	1
Construction	8 518	1 380	144	47	56	415	. . .	28	4 889	94	535	910	21
Manufacturing	20 733	3 008	2 007	646	764	1 982	. . .	291	3 956	6 219	765	1 019	76
Durable goods	12 566	1 796	1 351	430	318	1 127	. . .	150	2 807	3 594	415	509	71
Nondurable goods	8 168	1 212	656	217	446	856	. . .	141	1 150	2 625	350	510	5
Transportation and public utilities	9 307	1 307	561	324	273	2 349	. . .	296	1 285	135	2 243	522	13
Wholesale trade	5 090	622	131	43	2 054	756	. . .	57	346	137	493	380	71
Retail trade	22 113	1 916	459	188	9 306	1 438	. . .	5 125	1 177	230	575	1 670	30
Finance, insurance, and real estate	8 605	2 489	356	166	2 143	2 860	. . .	323	177	12	13	17	49
Services	47 212	6 793	15 090	2 541	1 197	7 118	847	9 117	2 154	887	551	516	399
Services, except private households	46 244	6 787	15 084	2 540	1 196	7 109	. . .	9 061	2 151	887	548	509	374
Professional services	31 392	4 164	13 122	2 132	213	5 132	. . .	5 485	473	195	294	99	85
Public administration	5 887	1 329	968	234	25	1 302	. . .	1 722	182	27	40	30	27
1999													
Agriculture	3 281	118	97	53	15	149	. . .	15	36	10	48	18	2 722
Mining	565	83	69	19	7	35	. . .	6	198	24	102	21	1
Construction	8 987	1 379	159	60	67	406	. . .	33	5 224	108	543	984	22
Manufacturing	20 070	2 955	1 981	645	736	1 883	. . .	242	3 883	5 896	726	1 035	88
Durable goods	12 283	1 799	1 286	440	351	1 067	. . .	125	2 715	3 504	394	520	82
Nondurable goods	7 787	1 156	694	205	385	816	. . .	117	1 168	2 391	332	515	7
Transportation and public utilities	9 554	1 340	557	359	275	2 386	. . .	304	1 335	123	2 318	546	14
Wholesale trade	5 189	630	158	50	2 047	819	. . .	52	324	118	523	406	62
Retail trade	22 383	1 967	461	207	9 489	1 495	. . .	5 122	1 108	229	625	1 643	38
Finance, insurance, and real estate	8 815	2 664	380	200	2 224	2 780	. . .	294	177	10	12	23	50
Services	48 687	7 061	16 031	2 533	1 230	7 242	831	9 275	2 119	847	575	547	395
Services, except private households	47 747	7 056	16 026	2 530	1 230	7 234	. . .	9 219	2 116	847	573	535	382
Professional services	32 370	4 307	13 796	2 074	210	5 333	. . .	5 536	463	167	301	91	90
Public administration	5 958	1 386	992	229	28	1 253	. . .	1 741	189	22	42	42	34

Note: See "Notes and Definitions" for information on historical comparability.

. . . = Not available.

Table 1-17. Employed Civilians in Agriculture and Nonagricultural Industries by Class of Worker and Sex, 1980–2004

(Thousands of people.)

Year and sex	Total employed	Agriculture				Nonagricultural industries						
		Total	Wage and salary workers	Self-employed workers	Unpaid family workers	Total	Wage and salary workers				Self-employed workers	Unpaid family workers
							Total	Government	Private household	Other private		
Total												
1980	99 302	3 364	1 425	1 642	297	95 938	88 525	15 912	1 192	71 421	7 000	413
1981	100 398	3 368	1 464	1 638	266	97 030	89 543	15 689	1 208	72 646	7 097	390
1982	99 526	3 401	1 505	1 636	261	96 125	88 462	15 516	1 207	71 739	7 262	401
1983	100 833	3 383	1 579	1 565	240	97 450	89 500	15 537	1 244	72 719	7 575	376
1984	105 006	3 321	1 555	1 553	213	101 685	93 565	15 770	1 238	76 557	7 785	335
1985	107 150	3 179	1 535	1 458	185	103 971	95 871	16 031	1 249	78 591	7 811	289
1986	109 597	3 163	1 547	1 447	169	106 434	98 299	16 342	1 235	80 722	7 881	255
1987	112 440	3 208	1 632	1 423	153	109 232	100 771	16 800	1 208	82 763	8 201	260
1988	114 969	3 169	1 621	1 398	150	111 800	103 021	17 114	1 153	84 754	8 519	260
1989	117 341	3 199	1 665	1 403	131	114 142	105 259	17 469	1 101	86 689	8 605	279
1990	118 793	3 223	1 740	1 378	105	115 570	106 598	17 769	1 027	87 802	8 719	253
1991	117 718	3 269	1 729	1 423	118	114 449	105 373	17 934	1 010	86 429	8 851	226
1992	118 492	3 247	1 750	1 385	112	115 245	106 437	18 136	1 135	87 166	8 575	233
1993	120 259	3 115	1 689	1 320	106	117 144	107 966	18 579	1 126	88 261	8 959	218
1994	123 060	3 409	1 715	1 645	49	119 651	110 517	18 293	966	91 258	9 003	131
1995	124 900	3 440	1 814	1 580	45	121 460	112 448	18 362	963	93 123	8 902	110
1996	126 707	3 443	1 869	1 518	56	123 264	114 171	18 217	928	95 026	8 971	122
1997	129 558	3 399	1 890	1 457	51	126 159	116 983	18 131	915	97 937	9 056	120
1998	131 463	3 378	2 000	1 341	38	128 085	119 019	18 383	962	99 674	8 962	103
1999	133 488	3 281	1 944	1 297	40	130 207	121 323	18 903	933	101 487	8 790	95
2000	136 891	2 464	1 421	1 010	33	134 427	125 114	19 248	718	105 148	9 205	108
2001	136 933	2 299	1 283	988	28	134 635	125 407	19 335	694	105 378	9 121	107
2002	136 485	2 311	1 282	1 003	26	134 174	125 156	19 636	757	104 764	8 923	95
2003	137 736	2 275	1 299	951	25	135 461	126 015	19 634	764	105 616	9 344	101
2004	139 252	2 232	1 242	964	27	137 020	127 463	19 983	779	106 701	9 467	90
Men												
1980	57 186	2 709	1 149	1 458	101	54 477	49 517	7 822	149	41 546	4 904	56
1981	57 397	2 700	1 168	1 442	91	54 697	49 745	7 676	192	41 877	4 905	47
1982	56 270	2 736	1 208	1 433	95	53 534	48 529	7 598	188	40 743	4 954	52
1983	56 787	2 704	1 265	1 355	84	54 083	48 896	7 623	208	41 065	5 136	51
1984	59 091	2 668	1 254	1 350	65	56 423	51 151	7 720	178	43 253	5 219	52
1985	59 891	2 535	1 230	1 244	60	57 356	52 111	7 757	170	44 184	5 207	38
1986	60 892	2 511	1 230	1 227	54	58 381	53 075	7 805	180	45 090	5 271	35
1987	62 107	2 543	1 290	1 194	58	59 564	54 102	8 013	180	45 909	5 423	39
1988	63 273	2 493	1 268	1 174	50	60 780	55 177	8 074	157	46 946	5 564	39
1989	64 315	2 513	1 302	1 167	44	61 802	56 202	8 116	156	47 930	5 562	38
1990	65 105	2 546	1 355	1 151	39	62 559	56 913	8 245	149	48 519	5 597	48
1991	64 223	2 589	1 359	1 185	45	61 634	55 899	8 300	143	47 456	5 700	35
1992	64 441	2 575	1 371	1 164	40	61 866	56 212	8 348	156	47 708	5 613	41
1993	65 349	2 478	1 323	1 117	39	62 871	56 926	8 435	146	48 345	5 894	50
1994	66 450	2 554	1 330	1 197	27	63 896	58 300	8 327	99	49 874	5 560	37
1995	67 377	2 559	1 395	1 138	26	64 818	59 332	8 267	96	50 969	5 461	25
1996	68 207	2 573	1 418	1 124	31	65 634	60 133	8 110	99	51 924	5 465	36
1997	69 685	2 552	1 439	1 084	29	67 133	61 595	8 015	81	53 499	5 506	31
1998	70 693	2 553	1 526	1 005	23	68 140	62 630	8 178	86	54 366	5 480	29
1999	71 446	2 432	1 450	962	20	69 014	63 624	8 278	74	55 272	5 366	25
2000	73 305	1 861	1 116	725	20	71 444	65 838	8 309	71	57 458	5 573	33
2001	73 196	1 708	990	703	15	71 488	65 930	8 342	63	57 524	5 527	31
2002	72 903	1 724	979	731	14	71 179	65 726	8 437	76	57 212	5 425	29
2003	73 332	1 695	991	694	11	71 636	65 871	8 368	59	57 444	5 736	30
2004	74 525	1 687	970	702	15	72 838	66 951	8 616	60	58 275	5 860	27
Women												
1980	42 117	656	275	184	197	41 461	39 007	8 090	1 044	29 873	2 097	357
1981	43 000	667	296	196	176	42 333	39 798	8 013	1 016	30 769	2 192	343
1982	43 256	665	296	203	166	42 591	39 934	7 918	1 019	30 997	2 309	348
1983	44 047	680	314	210	156	43 367	40 603	7 913	1 036	31 654	2 439	325
1984	45 915	653	301	203	148	45 262	42 413	8 050	1 061	33 302	2 566	283
1985	47 259	644	305	214	125	46 615	43 761	8 274	1 078	34 409	2 603	251
1986	48 706	652	317	220	115	48 054	45 225	8 537	1 055	35 633	2 610	219
1987	50 334	666	342	229	95	49 668	46 669	8 788	1 029	36 852	2 778	221
1988	51 696	676	353	224	99	51 020	47 844	9 039	996	37 809	2 955	220
1989	53 028	687	363	236	87	52 341	49 057	9 353	945	38 759	3 043	240
1990	53 689	678	385	227	66	53 011	49 685	9 524	879	39 282	3 122	205
1991	53 495	680	369	237	73	52 815	49 474	9 635	867	38 972	3 150	191
1992	54 052	672	379	221	73	53 380	50 225	9 788	979	39 458	2 963	192
1993	54 910	637	367	204	67	54 273	51 040	10 144	980	39 916	3 065	168
1994	56 610	855	384	448	23	55 755	52 217	9 965	867	41 385	3 443	95
1995	57 523	881	419	442	20	56 642	53 115	10 095	867	42 153	3 440	86
1996	58 501	871	452	394	25	57 630	54 037	10 107	830	43 100	3 506	87
1997	59 873	847	451	373	23	59 026	55 388	10 116	834	44 438	3 550	89
1998	60 770	825	474	336	15	59 945	56 389	10 205	876	45 308	3 482	74
1999	62 042	849	494	335	20	61 193	57 699	10 625	859	46 215	3 424	70
2000	63 586	602	305	285	12	62 983	59 277	10 939	647	47 690	3 631	76
2001	63 737	591	293	284	13	63 147	59 477	10 993	630	47 853	3 594	75
2002	63 582	587	303	272	12	62 995	59 431	11 199	680	47 552	3 499	66
2003	64 404	580	309	257	14	63 824	60 144	11 267	705	48 172	3 609	72
2004	64 728	546	271	262	12	64 182	60 512	11 367	719	48 426	3 607	63

Note: See "Notes and Definitions" for information on historical comparabilty.

Table 1-18. Number of Employed Persons 25 Years and Over by Educational Attainment, Race, Hispanic Origin, and Sex, 1994–2004

(Thousands of people.)

Year, race, Hispanic origin, and sex	Total	Less than a high school diploma	High school graduates, no college	Some college, no degree	Associate degree	College graduates Total	College graduates Bachelor's degree only
Total							
1994	104 141	11 053	35 135	19 861	8 834	29 257	19 225
1995	106 037	10 945	34 999	20 436	9 245	30 412	19 924
1996	108 070	11 317	36 300	20 590	9 404	31 459	20 742
1997	110 518	11 546	36 163	20 678	9 643	32 488	21 524
1998	111 855	11 673	35 976	20 626	9 850	33 730	22 260
1999	113 425	11 294	36 017	21 129	10 079	34 905	22 973
2000	116 473	11 692	36 452	21 601	10 707	36 020	23 706
2001	116 846	11 669	36 078	21 459	11 127	36 514	23 907
2002	116 802	11 535	35 779	20 928	11 166	37 395	24 570
2003	118 385	11 537	35 857	21 107	11 313	38 570	25 188
2004	119 622	11 408	35 944	21 284	11 693	39 293	25 484
White[1]							
1994	89 057	8 879	30 004	16 893	7 622	25 658	16 719
1995	90 498	8 690	29 776	17 265	7 970	26 796	17 434
1996	91 992	9 258	30 042	17 249	8 072	27 371	17 978
1997	93 687	9 414	30 552	17 302	8 271	28 148	18 801
1998	94 330	9 510	30 249	17 101	8 426	29 044	19 107
1999	95 316	9 235	30 211	17 388	8 556	29 925	19 668
2000	97 320	9 544	30 438	17 770	9 075	30 493	20 078
2001	97 560	9 550	30 126	17 671	9 393	30 821	20 136
2002	97 476	9 394	29 836	17 209	9 440	31 597	20 670
2003	98 120	9 437	29 645	17 227	9 476	32 335	21 103
2004	98 967	9 335	29 571	17 445	9 817	32 799	21 299
Black[1]							
1994	10 834	1 543	4 016	2 340	902	2 034	1 483
1995	11 249	1 482	4 142	2 517	960	2 149	1 538
1996	11 518	1 534	4 192	2 640	969	2 183	1 539
1997	11 882	1 578	4 409	2 681	984	2 230	1 591
1998	12 324	1 579	4 504	2 776	1 020	2 446	1 741
1999	12 771	1 488	4 631	2 924	1 108	2 621	1 814
2000	12 852	1 499	4 571	2 910	1 160	2 713	1 866
2001	12 797	1 492	4 492	2 871	1 216	2 727	1 921
2002	12 719	1 498	4 453	2 843	1 210	2 715	1 955
2003	12 706	1 376	4 465	2 780	1 199	2 887	2 056
2004	12 817	1 326	4 606	2 717	1 195	2 973	2 097
Hispanic							
1994	8 535	3 078	2 503	1 353	530	1 071	740
1995	8 873	3 204	2 624	1 427	534	1 084	759
1996	9 368	3 450	2 746	1 453	568	1 151	813
1997	10 214	3 738	2 945	1 603	611	1 316	926
1998	10 615	3 889	3 018	1 622	660	1 427	1 007
1999	10 985	3 926	3 213	1 696	660	1 491	1 034
2000	12 406	4 468	3 658	1 828	756	1 696	1 198
2001	12 817	4 601	3 796	1 916	781	1 723	1 223
2002	13 294	4 744	3 921	1 900	823	1 906	1 370
2003	14 205	5 073	4 169	2 037	889	2 039	1 468
2004	14 661	5 135	4 330	2 137	931	2 127	1 538
Men							
1994	56 523	6 851	18 418	10 402	4 184	16 668	10 672
1995	57 420	6 691	18 426	10 653	4 394	17 255	10 983
1996	58 468	7 058	18 639	10 759	4 416	17 596	11 266
1997	59 736	7 210	19 124	10 876	4 517	18 010	11 587
1998	60 497	7 238	19 188	10 684	4 731	18 656	12 028
1999	61 032	6 921	19 125	10 941	4 838	19 208	12 343
2000	62 661	7 199	19 388	11 260	5 013	19 800	12 742
2001	62 824	7 188	19 274	11 076	5 226	20 060	12 872
2002	62 756	7 220	19 154	10 811	5 221	20 350	13 076
2003	63 349	7 290	19 200	10 858	5 231	20 770	13 354
2004	64 326	7 276	19 535	10 896	5 426	21 192	13 575
Women							
1994	47 618	4 202	16 717	9 459	4 650	12 589	8 553
1995	48 617	4 254	16 573	9 783	4 851	13 157	8 941
1996	49 602	4 259	16 661	9 831	4 988	13 863	9 475
1997	50 782	4 336	17 039	9 802	5 126	14 478	9 937
1998	51 359	4 435	16 788	9 943	5 119	15 074	10 231
1999	52 392	4 372	16 893	10 189	5 242	15 697	10 630
2000	53 812	4 493	17 064	10 341	5 694	16 220	10 964
2001	54 021	4 480	16 804	10 383	5 901	16 453	11 035
2002	54 046	4 315	16 624	10 117	5 945	17 045	11 493
2003	55 035	4 248	16 657	10 249	6 081	17 800	11 834
2004	55 296	4 132	16 409	10 387	6 267	18 101	11 908

[1]Beginning in 2003, persons who selected this race group only; persons who selected more than one race group are not included. Prior to 2003, persons who reported more than one race group were included in the group they identified as the main race.

Table 1-18. Number of Employed Persons 25 Years and Over by Educational Attainment, Race, Hispanic Origin, and Sex, 1994–2004—*Continued*

(Thousands of people.)

Year, race, Hispanic origin, and sex	Total	Less than a high school diploma	High school graduates, no college	Some college, no degree	Associate degree	College graduates	
						Total	Bachelor's degree only
White Men[1]							
1994	48 938	5 633	15 833	8 990	3 667	14 814	9 435
1995	49 641	5 444	15 760	9 155	3 856	15 426	9 780
1996	50 533	5 920	15 995	9 197	3 861	15 559	9 965
1997	51 397	6 049	16 330	9 245	3 941	15 832	10 191
1998	51 842	6 123	16 308	9 009	4 118	16 284	10 490
1999	52 180	5 883	16 193	9 182	4 160	16 763	10 806
2000	53 243	6 085	16 373	9 435	4 320	17 030	11 029
2001	53 375	6 080	16 292	9 344	4 501	17 158	11 060
2002	53 242	6 072	16 148	9 102	4 497	17 423	11 217
2003	53 458	6 192	16 068	9 042	4 431	17 725	11 461
2004	54 133	6 188	16 297	9 125	4 613	17 910	11 555
White Women[1]							
1994	40 119	3 246	14 171	7 902	3 955	10 844	7 285
1995	40 857	3 246	14 016	8 110	4 115	11 370	7 655
1996	41 459	3 337	14 046	8 052	4 211	11 812	8 012
1997	42 290	3 365	14 222	8 058	4 330	12 316	8 410
1998	42 488	3 387	13 941	8 092	4 308	12 760	8 618
1999	43 135	3 352	14 018	8 207	4 396	13 162	8 862
2000	44 077	3 459	14 065	8 335	4 755	13 463	9 049
2001	44 184	3 469	13 834	8 327	4 891	13 663	9 075
2002	44 234	3 322	13 688	8 107	4 944	14 173	9 453
2003	44 662	3 245	13 576	8 185	5 045	14 610	9 643
2004	44 834	3 146	13 275	8 320	5 203	14 888	9 744
Black Men[1]							
1994	5 246	844	2 001	1 057	373	970	712
1995	5 423	778	2 101	1 142	393	1 010	717
1996	5 483	861	2 104	1 177	382	960	666
1997	5 658	868	2 181	1 241	385	983	710
1998	5 844	811	2 248	1 267	413	1 104	802
1999	6 001	741	2 339	1 313	469	1 140	789
2000	6 011	755	2 253	1 326	466	1 210	828
2001	5 924	762	2 232	1 258	486	1 186	834
2002	5 928	785	2 212	1 264	482	1 185	855
2003	5 860	693	2 190	1 256	492	1 230	890
2004	5 942	676	2 287	1 172	503	1 305	931
Black Women[1]							
1994	5 589	699	2 015	1 283	529	1 064	771
1995	5 826	704	2 042	1 375	566	1 139	822
1996	6 035	673	2 088	1 463	587	1 224	873
1997	6 225	710	2 229	1 439	600	1 247	882
1998	6 480	768	2 256	1 509	607	1 341	939
1999	6 770	746	2 292	1 612	639	1 481	1 025
2000	6 841	743	2 318	1 583	694	1 503	1 038
2001	6 873	730	2 260	1 612	729	1 541	1 087
2002	6 791	713	2 241	1 579	729	1 530	1 101
2003	6 846	683	2 275	1 524	707	1 657	1 166
2004	6 874	650	2 319	1 545	691	1 668	1 166
Hispanic Men							
1994	5 133	2 059	1 416	761	287	610	413
1995	5 337	2 125	1 501	818	279	615	408
1996	5 640	2 320	1 588	790	271	671	456
1997	6 165	2 502	1 714	899	302	747	502
1998	6 397	2 594	1 764	913	336	790	547
1999	6 441	2 554	1 839	917	334	797	540
2000	7 373	2 937	2 128	995	397	916	634
2001	7 628	3 041	2 174	1 082	386	945	669
2002	7 865	3 141	2 244	1 029	415	1 035	732
2003	8 578	3 424	2 461	1 105	451	1 137	806
2004	8 872	3 508	2 583	1 158	468	1 155	837
Hispanic Women							
1994	3 402	1 019	1 087	592	242	461	327
1995	3 536	1 079	1 123	609	255	470	351
1996	3 729	1 131	1 159	663	297	480	357
1997	4 049	1 236	1 231	704	309	569	425
1998	4 219	1 295	1 254	708	325	637	459
1999	4 544	1 372	1 373	778	327	694	494
2000	5 033	1 531	1 529	833	359	780	564
2001	5 190	1 560	1 622	834	395	778	553
2002	5 429	1 604	1 676	871	408	871	638
2003	5 627	1 649	1 708	932	438	901	661
2004	5 789	1 628	1 746	980	463	972	701

Note: Persons of Hispanic origin may be of any race.

[1]Beginning in 2003, persons who selected this race group only; persons who selected more than one race group are not included. Prior to 2003, persons who reported more than one race group were included in the group they identified as the main race.

Table 1-19. Multiple Jobholders and Multiple Jobholding Rates by Selected Characteristics, May of Selected Years, 1970–2005

(Thousands of people, percent, not seasonally adjusted.)

Year	Total employed	Multiple jobholders				Multiple jobholding rate [1]				
		Total	Men	Women		Total	Men	Women	White	Black [2]
				Number	Percent of all multiple jobholders					
1970	78 358	4 048	3 412	636	15.7	5.2	7.0	2.2	5.3	4.4
1971	78 708	4 035	3 270	765	19.0	5.1	6.7	2.6	5.3	3.8
1972	81 224	3 770	3 035	735	19.5	4.6	6.0	2.4	4.8	3.7
1973	83 758	4 262	3 393	869	20.4	5.1	6.6	2.7	5.1	4.7
1974	85 786	3 889	3 022	867	22.3	4.5	5.8	2.6	4.6	3.8
1975	84 146	3 918	2 962	956	24.4	4.7	5.8	2.9	4.8	3.7
1976	87 278	3 948	3 037	911	23.1	4.5	5.8	2.6	4.7	2.8
1977	90 482	4 558	3 317	1 241	27.2	5.0	6.2	3.4	5.3	2.6
1978	93 904	4 493	3 212	1 281	28.5	4.8	5.8	3.3	5.0	3.1
1979	96 327	4 724	3 317	1 407	29.8	4.9	5.9	3.5	5.1	3.0
1980	96 809	4 759	3 210	1 549	32.5	4.9	5.8	3.8	5.1	3.2
1985	106 878	5 730	3 537	2 192	38.3	5.4	5.9	4.7	5.7	3.2
1989	117 084	7 225	4 115	3 109	43.0	6.2	6.4	5.9	6.5	4.3
1991	116 626	7 183	4 054	3 129	43.6	6.2	6.4	5.9	6.4	4.9
1994	122 946	7 316	3 973	3 343	45.7	6.0	6.0	5.9	6.1	4.9
1995	124 554	7 952	4 225	3 727	46.9	6.4	6.3	6.5	6.6	5.2
1996	126 391	7 846	4 352	3 494	44.5	6.2	6.4	6.0	6.4	5.1
1997	129 565	8 197	4 398	3 800	46.4	6.3	6.3	6.4	6.5	5.7
1998	131 476	8 126	4 438	3 688	45.4	6.2	6.3	6.1	6.3	5.5
1999	133 411	7 895	4 117	3 778	47.9	5.9	5.8	6.1	6.0	5.5
2000	136 685	7 751	4 084	3 667	47.3	5.7	5.6	5.8	5.9	4.9
2001	137 121	7 540	3 914	3 626	48.1	5.5	5.3	5.7	5.6	5.3
2002	136 559	7 247	3 736	3 511	48.4	5.3	5.1	5.6	5.5	4.7
2003	137 567	7 338	3 841	3 498	47.7	5.3	5.3	5.4	5.5	4.3
2004	138 867	7 258	3 653	3 605	49.7	5.2	4.9	5.6	5.3	5.1
2005	141 591	7 348	3 741	3 607	49.1	5.2	4.9	5.5	5.4	4.4

Note: Data prior to 1985 reflect 1970 census-based population controls; for 1985–1991, 1980 census-based controls; for 1994–1997, 1990 census-based controls adjusted for the estimated undercount. Beginning in 1994, data reflect the introduction of a major redesign of the Current Population Survey (CPS). Beginning in 1997, data reflect revised population controls. Beginning in 1998, data reflect new composite estimation procedures and revised population controls. Beginning in 1999, 2000, and 2004 data reflect revised population controls. These changes affect comparability with data for prior periods. Comprehensive surveys of multiple jobholders were not conducted in 1981–1984, 1986–1988, 1990, and 1992–1993.

[1]Multiple jobholders as a percent of all employed persons in specified group.
[2]Data for years prior to 1977 refer to the Black-and-Other population group.

Table 1-20. Multiple Jobholders by Sex, Age, Marital Status, Race, Hispanic Origin, and Job Status, 2001–2004

(Thousands of people, percent.)

Characteristic	Both sexes Number 2001	2002	Rate[1] 2001	2002	Men Number 2001	2002	Rate[1] 2001	2002	Women Number 2001	2002	Rate[1] 2001	2002
Age												
Total, 16 years and over[2]	7 357	7 291	5.4	5.3	3 834	3 734	5.2	5.1	3 523	3 557	5.5	5.6
16 to 19 years	303	286	4.5	4.5	124	114	3.6	3.6	179	171	5.4	5.4
20 to 24 years	736	740	5.5	5.5	331	335	4.8	4.8	404	405	6.3	6.4
25 to 34 years	1 644	1 551	5.3	5.1	895	833	5.3	5.0	750	718	5.4	5.2
35 to 44 years	2 046	2 016	5.7	5.7	1 099	1 055	5.7	5.6	947	961	5.7	5.9
45 to 54 years	1 762	1 808	5.7	5.8	901	927	5.5	5.6	862	881	5.8	5.9
55 to 64 years	716	752	4.9	4.8	391	394	4.9	4.7	326	358	4.8	4.9
65 years and over	150	139	3.5	3.2	95	76	3.9	3.1	55	63	3.0	3.4
Marital Status												
Single	1 981	1 980	5.4	5.4	950	920	4.7	4.6	1 031	1 060	6.2	6.4
Married, spouse present	4 073	3 998	5.2	5.1	2 408	2 362	5.5	5.4	1 665	1 636	4.9	4.8
Widowed, divorced, or separated	1 304	1 313	6.0	6.1	477	452	5.4	5.1	827	861	6.4	6.7
Race and Hispanic Origin												
White[3]	6 300	6 270	5.5	5.5	3 298	3 233	5.3	5.2	3 002	3 037	5.7	5.8
Black[3]	747	709	5.0	4.8	380	343	5.5	4.9	367	366	4.5	4.6
Hispanic origin	551	579	3.4	3.5	328	347	3.4	3.5	223	232	3.4	3.4
Full-or Part-time Status												
Primary job full-time, secondary job part-time	4 019	3 937	...	...	2 327	2 235	...	...	1 692	1 701	...	...
Primary and secondary jobs both part-time	1 578	1 590	...	...	510	493	...	...	1 068	1 097	...	...
Primary and secondary jobs both full-time	283	276	...	...	184	186	...	...	100	90	...	...
Hours vary on primary or secondary job	1 437	1 449	...	...	793	801	...	...	644	647	...	...

Characteristic	Both sexes Number 2003	2004	Rate[1] 2003	2004	Men Number 2003	2004	Rate[1] 2003	2004	Women Number 2003	2004	Rate[1] 2003	2004
Age												
Total, 16 years and over[2]	7 315	7 473	5.3	5.4	3 716	3 835	5.1	5.1	3 599	3 638	5.6	5.6
16 to 19 years	280	274	4.7	4.6	107	107	3.7	3.6	173	167	5.7	5.7
20 to 24 years	778	795	5.8	5.8	350	377	5.0	5.2	428	419	6.7	6.5
25 to 34 years	1 513	1 608	5.0	5.3	817	853	4.9	5.1	696	755	5.1	5.6
35 to 44 years	1 918	1 898	5.5	5.5	998	1 012	5.3	5.4	920	886	5.7	5.6
45 to 54 years	1 835	1 855	5.8	5.7	927	935	5.6	5.5	908	920	5.9	5.9
55 to 64 years	837	869	5.0	5.0	430	451	4.9	4.9	407	417	5.2	5.1
65 years and over	154	173	3.3	3.6	87	100	3.4	3.7	67	74	3.3	3.4
Marital Status												
Single	1 978	2 044	5.4	5.5	907	964	4.6	4.7	1 070	1 080	6.4	6.4
Married, spouse present	4 067	4 125	5.1	5.2	2 398	2 408	5.4	5.3	1 669	1 718	4.8	5.0
Widowed, divorced, or separated	1 270	1 303	5.8	5.9	410	463	4.6	5.1	860	840	6.6	6.4
Race and Hispanic Origin												
White[3]	6 273	6 357	5.5	5.5	3 190	3 266	5.2	5.2	3 083	3 091	5.9	5.9
Black[3]	645	705	4.4	4.7	328	360	4.8	5.2	317	345	4.0	4.3
Hispanic origin	554	612	3.2	3.4	325	363	3.1	3.4	229	248	3.3	3.5
Full-or Part-time Status												
Primary job full-time, secondary job part-time	3 825	3 908	...	...	2 164	2 210	...	...	1 661	1 697	...	...
Primary and secondary jobs both part-time	1 651	1 678	...	...	510	540	...	...	1 141	1 138	...	...
Primary and secondary jobs both full-time	273	286	...	...	187	187	...	...	86	100	...	...
Hours vary on primary or secondary job	1 523	1 564	...	...	831	879	...	...	692	685	...	...

Note: Estimates for the above race groups (White or Black) do not sum to totals because data are not presented for all races. In addition, persons whose ethnicity is identified as Hispanic or Latino may be of any race and, therefore, are classified by ethnicity as well as by race. Beginning in January 2003, data reflect revised population controls used in the household survey.

[1]Multiple jobholders as a percent of all employed persons in specified group.
[2]Includes a small number of persons who work part-time on their primary job and full-time on their secondary job(s), not shown separately.
[3]Beginning in 2003, persons who selected this race group only; persons who selected more than one race group are not included. Prior to 2003, persons who reported more than one race group were included in the group they identified as the main race.
... = Not available.

Table 1-21. Multiple Jobholders by Industry of Principal Secondary Job and Sex, 2002–2004, Annual Averages

(Thousands of people.)

Industry of secondary job	Total	Men	Women
2002			
Nonagricultural Industries, Wage and Salary Workers	5 066	2 333	2 733
Mining	4	2	2
Construction	240	197	43
Manufacturing	174	110	64
Durable goods	100	71	29
Nondurable goods	74	40	35
Wholesale and retail trade	1 106	473	633
Wholesale trade	104	63	40
Retail trade	1 003	410	593
Transportation and warehousing	177	121	56
Utilities	10	7	3
Information	184	117	67
Financial activities	342	197	145
Professional and business services	874	513	361
Education and health services	1 425	500	925
Leisure and hospitality	1 071	499	572
Other services	545	253	292
Other services, except private households	473	249	225
Other servces, private households	71	4	67
Public administration	191	129	63
2003			
Nonagricultural Industries, Wage and Salary Workers	5 134	2 402	2 732
Mining	3	2	1
Construction	141	90	51
Manufacturing	147	94	53
Durable goods	80	55	25
Nondurable goods	67	39	28
Wholesale and retail trade	875	382	493
Wholesale trade	76	57	19
Retail trade	799	325	474
Transportation and warehousing	173	122	51
Utilities	13	10	4
Information	144	92	52
Financial activities	251	142	109
Professional and business services	483	270	213
Education and health services	1 296	437	859
Leisure and hospitality	966	444	521
Other services	439	181	258
Other services, except private households	364	175	189
Other servces, private households	75	6	68
Public administration	217	146	71
2004			
Nonagricultural Industries, Wage and Salary Workers	5 149	2 444	2 705
Mining	9	6	4
Construction	246	196	49
Manufacturing	169	102	67
Durable goods	92	60	32
Nondurable goods	77	42	35
Wholesale and retail trade	1 137	488	648
Wholesale trade	89	48	40
Retail trade	1 048	440	608
Transportation and warehousing	172	127	45
Utilities	13	10	3
Information	197	123	74
Financial activities	371	224	147
Professional and business services	850	483	366
Education and health services	1 455	511	945
Leisure and hospitality	1 114	560	554
Other services	533	235	298
Other services, except private households	455	228	226
Other servces, private households	79	7	71
Public administration	196	133	63

Table 1-22. Employment and Unemployment in Families by Race and Hispanic Origin, 1995–2004, Annual Averages

(Thousands of people, percent.)

Characteristic	1995	1996	1997	1998	1999	2000	2001	2002	2003	2004
TOTAL										
Total Families	68 552	69 203	69 714	70 218	71 250	71 680	73 306	74 169	75 301	75 872
With employed member(s)	55 633	56 342	57 289	57 986	59 185	59 626	60 707	61 121	61 761	62 424
As percent of total families	81.2	81.4	82.2	82.6	83.1	83.2	82.8	82.4	82.0	82.3
Some usually work full time [1]	51 473	52 249	53 226	53 945	55 123	55 683	56 519	56 742	57 229	57 813
With no employed member	12 919	12 860	12 425	12 232	12 065	12 054	12 600	13 048	13 540	13 447
As percent of total families	18.8	18.6	17.8	17.4	16.9	16.8	17.2	17.6	18.0	17.7
With unemployed member(s)	5 404	5 270	4 913	4 503	4 260	4 110	4 847	5 809	6 079	5 593
As percent of total families	7.9	7.6	7.0	6.4	6.0	5.7	6.6	7.8	8.1	7.4
Some member(s) employed	3 795	3 678	3 445	3 177	3 091	2 973	3 494	4 126	4 285	3 915
As percent of families with unemployed member(s)	70.2	69.8	70.1	70.6	72.6	72.3	72.1	71.0	70.5	70.0
Some usually work full time [1]	3 334	3 265	3 070	2 830	2 771	2 675	3 122	3 668	3 790	3 494
As percent of families with unemployed member(s)	61.7	62.0	62.5	62.8	65.0	65.1	64.4	63.1	62.3	62.5
WHITE [2]										
Total Families	57 650	58 315	58 514	58 930	59 661	59 918	60 921	61 494	61 995	62 250
With employed member(s)	47 216	47 882	48 378	48 850	49 632	49 877	50 505	50 785	51 002	51 350
As percent of total families	81.9	82.1	82.7	82.9	83.2	83.2	83.0	82.6	82.3	82.5
Some usually work full time [1]	43 804	44 522	45 069	45 567	46 333	46 639	47 060	47 193	47 356	47 620
With no employed member	10 433	10 434	10 135	10 080	10 029	10 042	10 416	10 709	10 993	10 900
As percent of total families	18.1	17.9	17.3	17.1	16.8	16.8	17.0	17.4	17.7	17.5
With unemployed member(s)	4 002	3 896	3 566	3 299	3 134	3 010	3 553	4 275	4 411	4 078
As percent of total families	6.9	6.7	6.1	5.6	5.3	5.0	5.8	7.0	7.1	6.6
Some member(s) employed	2 934	2 875	2 632	2 463	2 374	2 276	2 661	3 164	3 245	3 000
As percent of families with unemployed member(s)	73.3	73.8	73.8	74.7	75.8	75.6	74.9	74.0	73.6	73.6
Some usually work full time [1]	2 579	2 557	2 353	2 204	2 132	2 052	2 379	2 808	2 873	2 677
As percent of families with unemployed member(s)	64.4	65.6	66.0	66.8	68.0	68.2	67.0	65.7	65.1	65.7
BLACK [2]										
Total Families	8 015	8 149	8 308	8 317	8 498	8 600	8 674	8 845	8 869	8 860
With employed member(s)	5 991	6 137	6 409	6 554	6 847	6 964	6 933	6 987	6 906	6 920
As percent of total families	74.7	75.3	77.1	78.8	80.6	81.0	80.0	79.0	77.9	78.1
Some usually work full time [1]	5 419	5 563	5 810	5 953	6 249	6 401	6 373	6 390	6 270	6 292
With no employed member	2 024	2 012	1 899	1 763	1 652	1 636	1 742	1 858	1 963	1 940
As percent of total families	25.3	24.7	22.9	21.2	19.4	19.0	20.1	21.0	22.1	21.9
With unemployed member(s)	1 080	1 121	1 104	984	905	881	990	1 162	1 213	1 127
As percent of total families	13.5	13.8	13.3	11.8	10.6	10.2	11.4	13.1	13.7	12.7
Some member(s) employed	631	627	631	555	551	535	596	689	695	625
As percent of families with unemployed member(s)	58.4	55.9	57.2	56.4	60.9	60.8	60.2	59.3	57.3	55.5
Some usually work full time [1]	556	553	553	485	486	476	533	611	612	556
As percent of families with unemployed member(s)	51.5	49.3	50.1	49.3	53.7	54.1	53.8	52.6	50.5	49.3
HISPANIC										
Total Families	6 233	6 465	6 779	7 025	7 403	7 581	8 140	8 650	9 185	9 305
With employed member(s)	5 086	5 312	5 701	5 947	6 405	6 633	7 100	7 485	7 907	8 071
As percent of total families	81.6	82.2	84.1	84.7	86.5	87.5	87.2	86.5	86.1	86.7
Some usually work full time [1]	4 673	4 917	5 285	5 545	6 017	6 255	6 692	6 989	7 383	7 566
With no employed member	1 147	1 153	1 078	1 078	998	947	1 040	1 165	1 277	1 235
As percent of total families	18.4	17.8	15.9	15.3	13.5	12.5	12.8	13.5	13.9	13.3
With unemployed member(s)	841	841	789	744	715	679	809	965	1 020	950
As percent of total families	13.5	13.0	11.6	10.6	9.7	9.0	9.9	11.2	11.1	10.2
Some member(s) employed	568	563	532	522	518	493	592	686	715	664
As percent of families with unemployed member(s)	67.5	66.9	67.4	70.2	72.4	72.7	73.2	71.1	70.1	69.9
Some usually work full time [1]	490	497	473	467	467	446	537	615	640	594
As percent of families with unemployed member(s)	58.3	59.1	59.9	62.8	65.3	65.8	66.4	63.7	62.7	62.5

Note: The race or ethnicity of the family is determined by that of the householder. Estimates for the above race groups (White or Black) do not sum to totals because data are not presented for all races. In addition, persons whose ethnicity is identified as Hispanic or Latino may be of any race and, therefore, are classified by ethnicity as well as by race. Detail may not sum to totals due to rounding. Data for 2003 reflect revised population controls used in the Current Population Survey (CPS).

[1] Usually work 35 hours or more a week at all jobs.
[2] Beginning in 2003, families where the householder selected this race group only; families where the householder selected more than one race group are excluded. Prior to 2003, families where the householder selected more than one race group were included in the group that the householder identified as their main race.

Table 1-23. Families by Presence and Relationship of Employed Members and Family Type, 1999–2004, Annual Averages

(Thousands of people, percent.)

Characteristic	Number						Percent distribution					
	1999	2000	2001	2002	2003	2004	1999	2000	2001	2002	2003	2004
MARRIED-COUPLE FAMILIES												
Total	54 468	54 704	55 749	56 280	57 074	57 188	100.0	100.0	100.0	100.0	100.0	100.0
Member(s) employed, total	45 800	45 967	46 680	46 976	47 535	47 767	84.1	84.0	83.7	83.5	83.3	83.5
Husband only	10 533	10 500	10 833	11 174	11 403	11 712	19.3	19.2	19.4	19.9	20.0	20.5
Wife only	2 980	2 946	3 257	3 613	3 863	3 843	5.5	5.4	5.8	6.4	6.8	6.7
Husband and wife	28 882	29 128	29 241	28 873	29 077	28 991	53.0	53.2	52.5	51.3	50.9	50.7
Other employment combinations	3 404	3 394	3 350	3 317	3 193	3 222	6.2	6.2	6.0	5.9	5.6	5.6
No member(s) employed	8 668	8 737	9 068	9 303	9 539	9 420	15.9	16.0	16.3	16.5	16.7	16.5
FAMILIES MAINTAINED BY WOMEN [1]												
Total	12 625	12 775	13 037	13 215	13 450	13 614	100.0	100.0	100.0	100.0	100.0	100.0
Member(s) employed, total	9 797	10 026	10 131	10 169	10 187	10 358	77.6	78.5	77.7	77.0	75.7	76.1
Householder only	5 566	5 581	5 667	5 944	5 987	6 021	44.1	43.7	43.5	45.0	44.5	44.2
Householder and other member(s)	2 663	2 806	2 778	2 559	2 539	2 701	21.1	22.0	21.3	19.4	18.9	19.8
Other member(s), not householder	1 568	1 639	1 686	1 666	1 660	1 636	12.4	12.8	12.9	12.6	12.3	12.0
No member(s) employed	2 827	2 749	2 906	3 047	3 263	3 255	22.4	21.5	22.3	23.1	24.3	23.9
FAMILIES MAINTAINED BY MEN [1]												
Total	4 158	4 200	4 521	4 674	4 777	5 071	100.0	100.0	100.0	100.0	100.0	100.0
Member(s) employed, total	3 588	3 632	3 895	3 976	4 039	4 299	86.3	86.5	86.2	85.1	84.6	84.8
Householder only	1 718	1 761	1 875	1 939	1 954	2 060	41.3	41.9	41.5	41.5	40.9	40.6
Householder and other member(s)	1 353	1 358	1 450	1 440	1 427	1 557	32.5	32.3	32.1	30.8	29.9	30.7
Other member(s), not householder	517	514	570	598	658	682	12.4	12.2	12.6	12.8	13.8	13.5
No member(s) employed	569	567	625	698	739	772	13.7	13.5	13.8	14.9	15.5	15.2

Note: Detail may not sum to totals due to rounding. Data for 2003 reflect revised population controls used in the Current Population Survey (CPS).

[1]No spouse present.

Table 1-24. Unemployment in Families by Presence and Relationship of Employed Members and Family Type, 1999–2004, Annual Averages

(Thousands of people, percent.)

Characteristic	Number						Percent distribution					
	1999	2000	2001	2002	2003	2004	1999	2000	2001	2002	2003	2004
MARRIED-COUPLE FAMILIES												
With Unemployed Member(s),Total	2 705	2 584	3 081	3 772	3 857	3 521	100.0	100.0	100.0	100.0	100.0	100.0
No member employed	440	411	531	676	713	615	16.3	15.9	17.2	17.9	18.5	17.5
Some member(s) employed	2 265	2 174	2 550	3 096	3 144	2 906	83.7	84.1	82.8	82.1	81.5	82.5
Husband unemployed	924	836	1 160	1 523	1 600	1 333	34.2	32.3	37.7	40.4	41.5	37.9
Wife employed	589	531	736	993	1 023	850	21.8	20.5	23.9	26.3	26.5	24.2
Wife unemployed	790	789	918	1 117	1 129	1 041	29.2	30.5	29.8	29.6	29.3	29.6
Husband employed	696	694	809	969	991	913	25.8	26.8	26.3	25.7	25.7	25.9
Other family member unemployed	991	959	1 003	1 133	1 129	1 147	36.6	37.1	32.6	30.0	29.3	32.6
FAMILIES MAINTAINED BY WOMEN [1]												
With Unemployed Member(s), Total	1 222	1 194	1 324	1 504	1 612	1 521	100.0	100.0	100.0	100.0	100.0	100.0
No member employed	613	587	643	787	842	829	50.2	49.1	48.6	52.3	52.2	54.5
Some member(s) employed	609	607	681	717	770	692	49.8	50.9	51.4	47.7	47.8	45.5
Householder unemployed	560	522	593	737	791	758	45.8	43.7	44.8	49.0	49.1	49.8
Other member(s) employed	110	102	129	147	162	146	9.0	8.5	9.7	9.8	10.0	9.6
Other member(s) unemployed	662	672	731	767	821	764	54.2	56.3	55.2	51.0	50.9	50.2
FAMILIES MAINTAINED BY MEN [1]												
With Unemployed Member(s), Total	333	331	442	533	610	551	100.0	100.0	100.0	100.0	100.0	100.0
No member employed	115	139	178	220	239	234	34.6	42.0	40.3	41.3	39.2	42.5
Some member(s) employed	218	192	264	313	371	316	65.4	58.0	59.7	58.7	60.8	57.5
Householder unemployed	154	173	234	303	340	296	46.4	52.2	52.9	56.8	55.7	53.7
Other member(s) employed	71	67	96	129	158	117	21.4	20.4	21.7	24.2	25.9	21.3
Other member(s) unemployed	178	158	208	230	270	255	53.6	47.8	47.1	43.2	44.3	46.3

Note: Detail may not sum to totals due to rounding. Data for 2003 reflect revised population controls used in the Current Population Survey (CPS).

[1]No spouse present.

Table 1-25. Employment Status of the Population by Sex, Marital Status, and Presence and Age of Own Children Under 18, 1999–2004, Annual Averages

(Thousands of people, percent.)

Characteristic	1999			2000			2001		
	Total	Men	Women	Total	Men	Women	Total	Men	Women
With Own Children Under 18 Years, Total									
Civilian noninstitutional population	63 158	27 573	35 585	63 267	27 673	35 595	64 100	28 076	36 024
Civilian labor force	51 778	26 092	25 686	51 944	26 202	25 742	52 489	26 551	25 938
Participation rate	82.0	94.6	72.2	82.1	94.7	72.3	81.9	94.6	72.0
Employed	50 010	25 472	24 538	50 259	25 622	24 637	50 455	25 750	24 704
Employment-population ratio	79.2	92.4	69.0	79.4	92.6	69.2	78.7	91.7	68.6
Full-time workers [1]	43 033	24 712	18 321	43 365	24 922	18 443	43 424	24 964	18 460
Part-time workers [2]	6 977	761	6 216	6 894	699	6 195	7 031	787	6 244
Unemployed	1 768	620	1 149	1 685	581	1 104	2 034	801	1 233
Unemployment rate	3.4	2.4	4.5	3.2	2.2	4.3	3.9	3.0	4.8
Married, Spouse Present									
Civilian noninstitutional population	51 302	25 462	25 840	51 415	25 540	25 874	51 981	25 796	26 185
Civilian labor force	42 260	24 222	18 038	42 361	24 290	18 072	42 712	24 512	18 201
Participation rate	82.4	95.1	69.8	82.4	95.1	69.8	82.2	95.0	69.5
Employed	41 193	23 688	17 505	41 357	23 816	17 541	41 431	23 849	17 581
Employment-population ratio	80.3	93.0	67.7	80.4	93.2	67.8	79.7	92.5	67.1
Full-time workers [1]	35 568	23 024	12 544	35 793	23 212	12 581	35 772	23 169	12 603
Part-time workers [2]	5 625	664	4 961	5 564	604	4 960	5 659	680	4 979
Unemployed	1 067	534	533	1 004	474	531	1 282	662	619
Unemployment rate	2.5	2.2	3.0	2.4	2.0	2.9	3.0	2.7	3.4
Other Marital Status [3]									
Civilian noninstitutional population	11 856	2 110	9 746	11 853	2 132	9 720	12 119	2 280	9 839
Civilian labor force	9 518	1 870	7 648	9 583	1 913	7 670	9 777	2 039	7 737
Participation rate	80.3	88.6	78.5	80.8	89.7	78.9	80.7	89.4	78.6
Employed	8 817	1 784	7 032	8 902	1 806	7 096	9 024	1 902	7 123
Employment-population ratio	74.4	84.6	72.2	75.1	84.7	73.0	74.5	83.4	72.4
Full-time workers [1]	7 465	1 687	5 777	7 572	1 710	5 862	7 652	1 795	5 857
Part-time workers [2]	1 352	97	1 255	1 330	96	1 234	1 372	107	1 265
Unemployed	702	86	616	681	107	574	752	138	614
Unemployment rate	7.4	4.6	8.1	7.1	5.6	7.5	7.7	6.8	7.9
With Own Children 6 to 17 Years, None Younger									
Civilian noninstitutional population	34 662	15 090	19 572	34 737	15 165	19 572	35 523	15 486	20 038
Civilian labor force	29 403	14 092	15 311	29 576	14 178	15 398	30 182	14 489	15 693
Participation rate	84.8	93.4	78.2	85.1	93.5	78.7	85.0	93.6	78.3
Employed	28 528	13 782	14 747	28 744	13 877	14 868	29 174	14 096	15 078
Employment-population ratio	82.3	91.3	75.3	82.7	91.5	76.0	82.1	91.0	75.2
Full-time workers [1]	24 807	13 385	11 422	25 042	13 513	11 529	25 382	13 689	11 693
Part-time workers [2]	3 722	397	3 325	3 703	364	3 339	3 792	407	3 385
Unemployed	875	310	564	832	302	530	1 008	393	615
Unemployment rate	3.0	2.2	3.7	2.8	2.1	3.4	3.3	2.7	3.9
With Own Children Under 6 Years									
Civilian noninstitutional population	28 496	12 482	16 014	28 530	12 508	16 022	28 577	12 590	15 986
Civilian labor force	22 375	12 000	10 375	22 368	12 024	10 344	22 307	12 062	10 245
Participation rate	78.5	96.1	64.8	78.4	96.1	64.6	78.1	95.8	64.1
Employed	21 482	11 691	9 791	21 515	11 745	9 770	21 280	11 654	9 626
Employment-population ratio	75.4	93.7	61.1	75.4	93.9	61.0	74.5	92.6	60.2
Full-time workers [1]	18 227	11 327	6 900	18 323	11 410	6 914	18 041	11 274	6 767
Part-time workers [2]	3 255	364	2 891	3 191	335	2 856	3 239	380	2 859
Unemployed	894	310	584	853	279	574	1 026	408	619
Unemployment rate	4.0	2.6	5.6	3.8	2.3	5.6	4.6	3.4	6.0
With No Children Under 18 Years									
Civilian noninstitutional population	143 160	70 714	72 446	145 199	71 825	73 374	149 643	73 857	75 786
Civilian labor force	86 424	47 255	39 169	88 014	48 140	39 874	90 171	49 249	40 922
Participation rate	60.4	66.8	54.1	60.6	67.0	54.3	60.3	66.7	54.0
Employed	82 333	44 828	37 504	84 058	45 781	38 278	85 421	46 371	39 050
Employment-population ratio	57.5	63.4	51.8	57.9	63.7	52.2	57.1	62.8	51.5
Full-time workers [1]	66 136	38 086	28 051	68 046	39 136	28 910	69 074	39 596	29 478
Part-time workers [2]	16 196	6 743	9 454	16 012	6 645	9 367	16 347	6 776	9 572
Unemployed	4 091	2 426	1 665	3 956	2 359	1 596	4 750	2 878	1 872
Unemployment rate	4.7	5.1	4.3	4.5	4.9	4.0	5.3	5.8	4.6

[1]Usually work 35 hours or more a week at all jobs.
[2]Usually work less than 35 hours a week at all jobs.
[3]Includes never-married, divorced, separated, and widowed persons.

Table 1-25. Employment Status of the Population by Sex, Marital Status, and Presence and Age of Own Children Under 18, 1999–2004, Annual Averages—*Continued*

(Thousands of people, percent.)

Characteristic	2002			2003			2004		
	Total	Men	Women	Total	Men	Women	Total	Men	Women
With Own Children Under 18 Years, Total									
Civilian noninstitutional population	64 399	28 137	36 263	64 932	28 402	36 530	64 758	28 272	36 486
Civilian labor force	52 566	26 529	26 036	52 727	26 739	25 988	52 288	26 607	25 681
Participation rate	81.6	94.3	71.8	81.2	94.1	71.1	80.7	94.1	70.4
Employed	50 022	25 474	24 549	50 103	25 638	24 466	49 957	25 696	24 261
Employment-population ratio	77.7	90.5	67.7	77.2	90.3	67.0	77.1	90.9	66.5
Full-time workers [1]	42 884	24 644	18 240	42 880	24 762	18 118	42 758	24 794	17 964
Part-time workers [2]	7 138	829	6 308	7 223	876	6 347	7 200	902	6 298
Unemployed	2 543	1 056	1 488	2 624	1 101	1 523	2 331	911	1 420
Unemployment rate	4.8	4.0	5.7	5.0	4.1	5.9	4.5	3.4	5.5
Married, Spouse Present									
Civilian noninstitutional population	51 947	25 781	26 166	52 476	26 049	26 427	52 109	25 852	26 258
Civilian labor force	42 492	24 425	18 067	42 776	24 638	18 138	42 247	24 449	17 798
Participation rate	81.8	94.7	69.0	81.5	94.6	68.6	81.1	94.6	67.8
Employed	40 867	23 533	17 334	41 128	23 712	17 416	40 847	23 703	17 144
Employment-population ratio	78.7	91.3	66.2	78.4	91.0	65.9	78.4	91.7	65.3
Full-time workers [1]	35 180	22 825	12 356	35 315	22 954	12 360	35 141	22 935	12 206
Part-time workers [2]	5 687	708	4 979	5 813	757	5 056	5 706	768	4 938
Unemployed	1 625	893	733	1 648	926	722	1 400	747	653
Unemployment rate	3.8	3.7	4.1	3.9	3.8	4.0	3.3	3.1	3.7
Other Marital Status [3]									
Civilian noninstitutional population	12 452	2 355	10 096	12 455	2 354	10 102	12 649	2 420	10 229
Civilian labor force	10 073	2 103	7 970	9 950	2 100	7 850	10 042	2 158	7 883
Participation rate	80.9	89.3	78.9	79.9	89.2	77.7	79.4	89.2	77.1
Employed	9 155	1 941	7 215	8 975	1 926	7 050	9 110	1 993	7 117
Employment-population ratio	73.5	82.4	71.5	72.1	81.8	69.8	72.0	82.4	69.6
Full-time workers [1]	7 704	1 820	5 885	7 566	1 807	5 759	7 617	1 859	5 757
Part-time workers [2]	1 451	122	1 329	1 411	118	1 291	1 494	134	1 360
Unemployed	918	163	755	976	175	800	931	165	766
Unemployment rate	9.1	7.8	9.5	9.8	8.3	10.2	9.3	7.6	9.7
With Own Children 6 to 17 Years, None Younger									
Civilian noninstitutional population	35 829	15 580	20 250	35 943	15 653	20 290	35 874	15 597	20 277
Civilian labor force	30 371	14 541	15 830	30 362	14 572	15 790	30 182	14 516	15 666
Participation rate	84.8	93.3	78.2	84.5	93.1	77.8	84.1	93.1	77.3
Employed	29 122	14 023	15 099	29 040	14 008	15 032	29 013	14 056	14 957
Employment-population ratio	81.3	90.0	74.6	80.8	89.5	74.1	80.9	90.1	73.8
Full-time workers [1]	25 225	13 586	11 638	25 116	13 558	11 557	25 069	13 597	11 473
Part-time workers [2]	3 898	437	3 461	3 925	450	3 475	3 944	459	3 485
Unemployed	1 249	518	731	1 322	564	758	1 170	460	709
Unemployment rate	4.1	3.6	4.6	4.4	3.9	4.8	3.9	3.2	4.5
With Own Children Under 6 Years									
Civilian noninstitutional population	28 570	12 557	16 013	28 988	12 749	16 240	28 884	12 675	16 210
Civilian labor force	22 194	11 988	10 206	22 365	12 167	10 198	22 106	12 091	10 014
Participation rate	77.7	95.5	63.7	77.2	95.4	62.8	76.5	95.4	61.8
Employed	20 900	11 450	9 450	21 063	11 630	9 433	20 944	11 640	9 304
Employment-population ratio	73.2	91.2	59.0	72.7	91.2	58.1	72.5	91.8	57.4
Full-time workers [1]	17 660	11 058	6 602	17 764	11 203	6 561	17 689	11 197	6 491
Part-time workers [2]	3 240	392	2 848	3 299	426	2 872	3 256	443	2 813
Unemployed	1 294	538	757	1 302	538	765	1 162	451	710
Unemployment rate	5.8	4.5	7.4	5.8	4.4	7.5	5.3	3.7	7.1
With No Children Under 18 Years									
Civilian noninstitutional population	151 715	74 993	76 722	154 714	76 510	78 204	156 900	77 739	79 160
Civilian labor force	90 971	49 644	41 327	92 319	50 036	42 284	93 511	50 771	42 740
Participation rate	60.0	66.2	53.9	59.7	65.4	54.1	59.6	65.3	54.0
Employed	85 187	46 154	39 034	86 233	46 294	39 939	87 748	47 282	40 467
Employment-population ratio	56.1	61.5	50.9	55.7	60.5	51.1	55.9	60.8	51.1
Full-time workers [1]	68 574	39 319	29 254	69 073	39 245	29 827	70 244	40 134	30 110
Part-time workers [2]	16 614	6 834	9 779	17 160	7 049	10 111	17 505	7 148	10 357
Unemployed	5 784	3 491	2 293	6 087	3 741	2 345	5 763	3 489	2 274
Unemployment rate	6.4	7.0	5.5	6.6	7.5	5.5	6.2	6.9	5.3

Note: Own children include sons, daughters, stepchildren, and adopted children. Not included are nieces, nephews, grandchildren, and other related and unrelated children. Detail may not sum to totals due to rounding. Data for 2003 reflect revised population controls used in the Current Population Survey (CPS).

[1] Usually work 35 hours or more a week at all jobs.
[2] Usually work less than 35 hours a week at all jobs.
[3] Includes never-married, divorced, separated, and widowed persons.

UNEMPLOYMENT

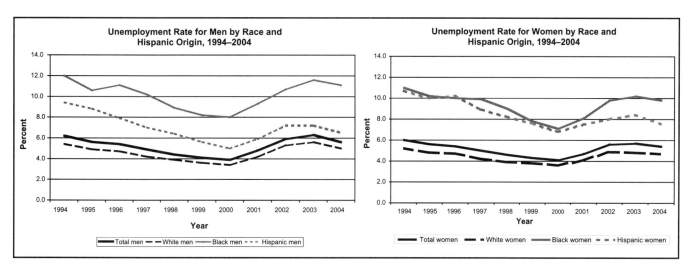

As the economy continued to recover, the unemployment rate fell for all groups in 2004. Overall, it dropped 0.5 percentage points to 5.5 percent between 2003 and 2004. The decline for White women was very small during this period, (4.8 percent to 4.7 percent). While the unemployment rate dropped much more significantly for Black men and Black women, it remained more than double that of White men and White women. (Table 1-29)

OTHER HIGHLIGHTS:

- From 2003 to 2004, the number of unemployed persons dropped 7.1 percent to 8.1 million. In contrast, the number of unemployed increased by over 3 million, or 54 percent, from 2000 to 2003. (Table 1-30)

- The differences in the unemployment rate between the various age groups continued to be substantial. Among all 16 to 19 year olds, the unemployment rate was 17.0 percent—more than three times the overall unemployment rate. The unemployment rate was even higher for 16 to 19 year old males (18.4 percent). Women typically had lower unemployment rates than men in all age groups. (Table 1-29)

- The average duration of unemployment increased from 19.2 to 19.6 weeks. However, the median length of unemployment dropped from 10.1 to 9.8 weeks. Those unemployed for 27 weeks or more still accounted for more than 20 percent of the total unemployed. (Table 1-36)

- In 2004, most states experienced a lower unemployment rate than in 2003. Even states with relatively high unemployment rates, such as Washington, showed declines. In Washington, the unemployment rate dropped from 7.4 percent to 6.2 percent; in Oregon, it fell from 8.1 percent to 7.4 percent; and in Alaska, it declined from 7.7 percent to 7.5 percent. A few states, such as Michigan and South Dakota, saw no change in their unemployment rates from 2003 to 2004. In Delaware and South Carolina, the unemployment rate increased slightly. (Table 1-5)

Table 1-26. Employment Status of Mothers with Own Children Under 3 Years Old by Age of Youngest Child, and Marital Status, 2000–2004, Annual Averages

(Thousands of people, percent.)

Year and characteristic	Civilian noninsti-tutional population	Civilian labor force		Employed				Unemployed	
		Total	Percent of population	Total	Percent of population	Full-time workers [1]	Part-time workers [2]	Number	Percent of labor force
2000									
Total Mothers with Own Children Under 3 Years	9 356	5 653	60.4	5 311	56.8	3 614	1 697	342	6.0
2 years	2 803	1 807	64.5	1 712	61.1	1 193	519	95	5.3
1 year	3 300	2 069	62.7	1 939	58.8	1 310	629	130	6.3
Under 1 year	3 253	1 777	54.6	1 660	51.0	1 112	548	117	6.6
Married, Spouse Present with Own Children Under 3 Years	7 056	4 090	58.0	3 940	55.8	2 613	1 327	150	3.7
2 years	2 096	1 276	60.9	1 233	58.9	823	411	42	3.3
1 year	2 499	1 503	60.1	1 448	57.9	953	495	55	3.6
Under 1 year	2 461	1 312	53.3	1 259	51.1	837	421	53	4.1
Other Marital Status with Own Children Under 3 Years [3]	2 300	1 563	67.9	1 371	59.6	1 002	370	191	12.2
2 years	707	531	75.1	478	67.6	370	108	53	9.9
1 year	801	566	70.7	491	61.3	357	134	75	13.2
Under 1 year	792	465	58.8	402	50.7	275	127	64	13.7
2001									
Total Mothers with Own Children Under 3 Years	9 352	5 613	60.0	5 227	55.9	3 591	1 636	387	6.9
2 years	2 844	1 868	65.7	1 751	61.6	1 218	533	117	6.3
1 year	3 405	2 050	60.2	1 911	56.1	1 308	603	140	6.8
Under 1 year	3 103	1 695	54.6	1 565	50.4	1 065	500	130	7.7
Married, Spouse Present with Own Children Under 3 Years	7 079	4 058	57.3	3 884	54.9	2 601	1 282	175	4.3
2 years	2 120	1 310	61.8	1 258	59.3	839	419	53	4.0
1 year	2 589	1 479	57.1	1 416	54.7	940	475	63	4.3
Under 1 year	2 370	1 269	53.5	1 210	51.1	822	388	59	4.6
Other Marital Status with Own Children Under 3 Years [3]	2 269	1 555	68.5	1 343	59.2	989	352	212	13.6
2 years	723	558	77.2	493	68.2	379	114	65	11.6
1 year	814	571	70.1	495	60.8	367	127	76	13.3
Under 1 year	732	426	58.2	355	48.5	243	111	71	16.7
2002									
Total Mothers with Own Children Under 3 Years	9 350	5 632	60.2	5 181	55.4	3 513	1 667	451	8.0
2 years	2 949	1 895	64.3	1 758	59.6	1 234	524	137	7.2
1 year	3 310	2 003	60.5	1 852	56.0	1 241	610	151	7.5
Under 1 year	3 091	1 734	56.1	1 571	50.8	1 038	533	163	9.4
Married, Spouse Present with Own Children Under 3 Years	7 073	4 071	57.6	3 869	54.7	2 572	1 297	203	5.0
2 years	2 201	1 333	60.6	1 274	57.9	870	404	59	4.4
1 year	2 509	1 446	57.6	1 379	55.0	902	477	67	4.6
Under 1 year	2 363	1 292	54.7	1 216	51.5	800	416	77	6.0
Other Marital Status with Own Children Under 3 Years [3]	2 278	1 562	68.6	1 313	57.6	941	372	248	15.9
2 years	748	562	75.1	484	64.7	364	120	77	13.7
1 year	802	557	69.5	473	59.0	340	134	84	15.1
Under 1 year	728	443	60.9	356	48.9	237	118	87	19.6
2003									
Total Mothers with Own Children Under 3 Years	9 450	5 563	58.9	5 115	54.1	3 430	1 685	446	8.0
2 years	2 987	1 896	63.5	1 752	58.7	1 205	547	143	7.5
1 year	3 353	1 997	59.6	1 842	54.9	1 223	619	154	7.7
Under 1 year	3 110	1 670	53.7	1 521	48.9	1 002	519	149	8.9
Married, Spouse Present with Own Children Under 3 Years	7 165	4 068	56.8	3 872	54.0	2 529	1 342	197	4.8
2 years	2 243	1 350	60.2	1 281	57.1	853	428	69	5.1
1 year	2 541	1 458	57.4	1 395	54.9	906	488	64	4.4
Under 1 year	2 381	1 260	52.9	1 196	50.2	770	426	64	5.1
Other Marital Status with Own Children Under 3 Years [3]	2 287	1 495	65.4	1 244	54.4	902	341	250	16.7
2 years	744	546	73.4	471	63.3	352	118	75	13.7
1 year	813	539	66.3	448	55.1	317	131	91	16.9
Under 1 year	730	410	56.2	325	44.5	233	92	84	20.5
2004									
Total Mothers with Own Children Under 3 Years	9 345	5 377	57.5	4 964	53.1	3 360	1 604	414	7.7
2 years	2 813	1 746	62.1	1 630	57.9	1 152	477	116	6.6
1 year	3 273	1 906	58.2	1 759	53.7	1 172	587	147	7.7
Under 1 year	3 259	1 725	52.9	1 575	48.3	1 035	540	151	8.7
Married, Spouse Present with Own Children Under 3 Years	7 071	3 910	55.3	3 740	52.9	2 513	1 227	170	4.4
2 years	2 111	1 246	59.0	1 200	56.8	839	361	46	3.7
1 year	2 519	1 401	55.6	1 337	53.1	877	459	65	4.6
Under 1 year	2 441	1 262	51.7	1 203	49.3	797	406	59	4.7
Other Marital Status with Own Children Under 3 Years [3]	2 274	1 467	64.5	1 224	53.8	847	377	243	16.6
2 years	702	499	71.1	430	61.2	314	116	70	13.9
1 year	754	505	66.9	422	56.0	295	127	82	16.3
Under 1 year	818	463	56.6	372	45.4	238	134	91	19.7

Note: Own children include sons, daughters, stepchildren, and adopted children. Not included are nieces, nephews, grandchildren, and other related and unrelated children. Detail may not sum to totals due to rounding. Data for 2003 reflect revised population controls used in the Current Population Survey (CPS).

[1] Usually work 35 hours or more a week at all jobs.
[2] Usually work less than 35 hours a week at all jobs.
[3] Includes never-married, divorced, separated, and widowed persons.

Table 1-27. Unemployment Rate According to Selected Characteristics, 1948–2004

(Unemployment as a percent of civilian labor force.)

Year	All civilian workers	Both sexes 16 to 19 years	Men 20 years and over	Women 20 years and over	White	Black	Asian	Hispanic	Married men, spouse present	Married women, spouse present	Women who maintain families
1948	3.8	9.2	3.2	3.6	...	...	...	...	...	...	...
1949	5.9	13.4	5.4	5.3	...	...	...	...	...	...	...
1950	5.3	12.2	4.7	5.1	...	...	...	...	...	...	...
1951	3.3	8.2	2.5	4.0	...	...	...	...	...	...	...
1952	3.0	8.5	2.4	3.2	...	...	...	...	...	...	...
1953	2.9	7.6	2.5	2.9	...	...	...	...	...	...	...
1954	5.5	12.6	4.9	5.5	5.0	...	...	...	...	...	...
1955	4.4	11.0	3.8	4.4	3.9	...	...	...	2.6	3.7	...
1956	4.1	11.1	3.4	4.2	3.6	...	...	...	2.3	3.6	...
1957	4.3	11.6	3.6	4.1	3.8	...	...	...	2.8	4.3	...
1958	6.8	15.9	6.2	6.1	6.1	...	...	...	5.1	6.5	...
1959	5.5	14.6	4.7	5.2	4.8	...	...	...	3.6	5.2	...
1960	5.5	14.7	4.7	5.1	5.0	...	...	...	3.7	5.2	...
1961	6.7	16.8	5.7	6.3	6.0	...	...	...	4.6	6.4	...
1962	5.5	14.7	4.6	5.4	4.9	...	...	...	3.6	5.4	...
1963	5.7	17.2	4.5	5.4	5.0	...	...	...	3.4	5.4	...
1964	5.2	16.2	3.9	5.2	4.6	...	...	...	2.8	5.1	...
1965	4.5	14.8	3.2	4.5	4.1	...	...	...	2.4	4.5	...
1966	3.8	12.8	2.5	3.8	3.4	...	...	...	1.9	3.7	...
1967	3.8	12.9	2.3	4.2	3.4	...	...	...	1.8	4.5	4.9
1968	3.6	12.7	2.2	3.8	3.2	...	...	...	1.6	3.9	4.4
1969	3.5	12.2	2.1	3.7	3.1	...	...	...	1.5	3.9	4.4
1970	4.9	15.3	3.5	4.8	4.5	...	...	...	2.6	4.9	5.4
1971	5.9	16.9	4.4	5.7	5.4	...	...	...	3.2	5.7	7.3
1972	5.6	16.2	4.0	5.4	5.1	10.4	...	...	2.8	5.4	7.2
1973	4.9	14.5	3.3	4.9	4.3	9.4	...	7.5	2.3	4.7	7.1
1974	5.6	16.0	3.8	5.5	5.0	10.5	...	8.1	2.7	5.3	7.0
1975	8.5	19.9	6.8	8.0	7.8	14.8	...	12.2	5.1	7.9	10.0
1976	7.7	19.0	5.9	7.4	7.0	14.0	...	11.5	4.2	7.1	10.1
1977	7.1	17.8	5.2	7.0	6.2	14.0	...	10.1	3.6	6.5	9.4
1978	6.1	16.4	4.3	6.0	5.2	12.8	...	9.1	2.8	5.5	8.5
1979	5.8	16.1	4.2	5.7	5.1	12.3	...	8.3	2.8	5.1	8.3
1980	7.1	17.8	5.9	6.4	6.3	14.3	...	10.1	4.2	5.8	9.2
1981	7.6	19.6	6.3	6.8	6.7	15.6	...	10.4	4.3	6.0	10.4
1982	9.7	23.2	8.8	8.3	8.6	18.9	...	13.8	6.5	7.4	11.7
1983	9.6	22.4	8.9	8.1	8.4	19.5	...	13.7	6.5	7.0	12.2
1984	7.5	18.9	6.6	6.8	6.5	15.9	...	10.7	4.6	5.7	10.3
1985	7.2	18.6	6.2	6.6	6.2	15.1	...	10.5	4.3	5.6	10.4
1986	7.0	18.3	6.1	6.2	6.0	14.5	...	10.6	4.4	5.2	9.8
1987	6.2	16.9	5.4	5.4	5.3	13.0	...	8.8	3.9	4.3	9.2
1988	5.5	15.3	4.8	4.9	4.7	11.7	...	8.2	3.3	3.9	8.1
1989	5.3	15.0	4.5	4.7	4.5	11.4	...	8.0	3.0	3.7	8.1
1990	5.6	15.5	5.0	4.9	4.8	11.4	...	8.2	3.4	3.8	8.3
1991	6.8	18.7	6.4	5.7	6.1	12.5	...	10.0	4.4	4.5	9.3
1992	7.5	20.1	7.1	6.3	6.6	14.2	...	11.6	5.1	5.0	10.0
1993	6.9	19.0	6.4	5.9	6.1	13.0	...	10.8	4.4	4.6	9.7
1994	6.1	17.6	5.4	5.4	5.3	11.5	...	9.9	3.7	4.1	8.9
1995	5.6	17.3	4.8	4.9	4.9	10.4	...	9.3	3.3	3.9	8.0
1996	5.4	16.7	4.6	4.8	4.7	10.5	...	8.9	3.0	3.6	8.2
1997	4.9	16.0	4.2	4.4	4.2	10.0	...	7.7	2.7	3.1	8.1
1998	4.5	14.6	3.7	4.1	3.9	8.9	...	7.2	2.4	2.9	7.2
1999	4.2	13.9	3.5	3.8	3.7	8.0	...	6.4	2.2	2.7	6.4
2000	4.0	13.1	3.3	3.6	3.5	7.6	3.6	5.7	2.0	2.7	5.9
2001	4.7	14.7	4.2	4.1	4.2	8.6	4.5	6.6	2.7	3.1	6.6
2002	5.8	16.5	5.3	5.1	5.1	10.2	5.9	7.5	3.6	3.7	8.0
2003	6.0	17.5	5.6	5.1	5.2	10.8	6.0	7.7	3.8	3.7	8.5
2004	5.5	17.0	5.0	4.9	4.8	10.4	4.4	7.0	3.1	3.5	8.0

Note: Persons of Hispanic origin may be of any race. See "Notes and Definitions" for information on historical comparability.

. . . = Not available.

Table 1-28. Unemployed Persons by Sex, Race, Age, and Hispanic Origin, 1948–2004

(Thousands of people.)

Year, sex, race, and Hispanic origin	16 years and over	16 to 19 years			20 years and over						
		Total	16 to 17 years	18 to 19 years	Total	20 to 24 years	25 to 34 years	35 to 44 years	45 to 54 years	55 to 64 years	65 years and over
Total											
1948	2 276	409	180	228	1 869	455	457	347	290	226	93
1949	3 637	576	238	337	3 060	680	776	603	471	384	146
1950	3 288	513	226	287	2 776	561	702	530	478	368	137
1951	2 055	336	168	168	1 718	273	435	354	318	238	103
1952	1 883	345	180	165	1 539	268	389	325	274	195	86
1953	1 834	307	150	157	1 529	256	379	325	280	218	70
1954	3 532	501	221	247	3 032	504	793	680	548	374	132
1955	2 852	450	211	239	2 403	396	577	521	436	355	120
1956	2 750	478	231	247	2 274	395	554	476	429	311	109
1957	2 859	497	230	266	2 362	430	573	499	448	300	111
1958	4 602	678	299	379	3 923	701	993	871	731	472	154
1959	3 740	654	301	354	3 085	543	726	673	603	405	135
1960	3 852	712	325	387	3 140	583	752	671	614	396	122
1961	4 714	828	363	465	3 886	723	890	850	751	516	159
1962	3 911	721	312	409	3 191	636	712	688	605	411	141
1963	4 070	884	420	462	3 187	658	732	674	589	410	126
1964	3 786	872	436	437	2 913	660	607	605	543	378	117
1965	3 366	874	411	463	2 491	557	529	546	436	322	103
1966	2 875	837	395	441	2 041	446	441	426	369	265	92
1967	2 975	839	400	438	2 140	511	480	422	383	256	86
1968	2 817	838	414	426	1 978	543	443	371	314	219	88
1969	2 832	853	436	416	1 978	560	453	358	320	216	72
1970	4 093	1 106	537	569	2 987	866	718	515	476	309	104
1971	5 016	1 262	596	665	3 755	1 130	933	630	573	381	109
1972	4 882	1 308	633	676	3 573	1 132	878	576	510	368	111
1973	4 365	1 235	634	600	3 130	1 008	866	451	430	290	88
1974	5 156	1 422	699	722	3 733	1 212	1 044	559	498	321	99
1975	7 929	1 767	799	968	6 161	1 865	1 776	951	893	520	155
1976	7 406	1 719	796	924	5 687	1 714	1 710	849	758	510	147
1977	6 991	1 663	781	881	5 330	1 629	1 650	785	666	450	147
1978	6 202	1 583	796	787	4 620	1 483	1 422	694	552	345	123
1979	6 137	1 555	739	816	4 583	1 442	1 446	705	540	346	104
1980	7 637	1 669	778	890	5 969	1 835	2 024	940	676	399	94
1981	8 273	1 763	781	981	6 510	1 976	2 211	1 065	715	444	98
1982	10 678	1 977	831	1 145	8 701	2 392	3 037	1 552	966	647	107
1983	10 717	1 829	753	1 076	8 888	2 330	3 078	1 650	1 039	677	114
1984	8 539	1 499	646	854	7 039	1 838	2 374	1 335	828	566	97
1985	8 312	1 468	662	806	6 844	1 738	2 341	1 340	813	518	93
1986	8 237	1 454	665	789	6 783	1 651	2 390	1 371	790	489	91
1987	7 425	1 347	648	700	6 077	1 453	2 129	1 281	723	412	78
1988	6 701	1 226	573	653	5 475	1 261	1 929	1 166	657	375	87
1989	6 528	1 194	537	657	5 333	1 218	1 851	1 159	637	379	91
1990	7 047	1 212	527	685	5 835	1 299	1 995	1 328	723	386	105
1991	8 628	1 359	587	772	7 269	1 573	2 447	1 719	946	473	113
1992	9 613	1 427	641	787	8 186	1 649	2 702	1 976	1 138	589	132
1993	8 940	1 365	606	759	7 575	1 514	2 395	1 896	1 121	541	108
1994	7 996	1 320	624	696	6 676	1 373	2 067	1 627	971	485	153
1995	7 404	1 346	652	695	6 058	1 244	1 841	1 549	844	425	153
1996	7 236	1 306	617	689	5 929	1 239	1 757	1 505	883	406	139
1997	6 739	1 271	589	683	5 467	1 152	1 571	1 418	830	369	127
1998	6 210	1 205	573	632	5 005	1 081	1 419	1 258	782	343	122
1999	5 880	1 162	544	618	4 718	1 042	1 278	1 154	753	367	124
2000	5 692	1 081	502	579	4 611	1 022	1 207	1 133	762	355	132
2001	6 801	1 162	531	632	5 638	1 209	1 498	1 355	989	458	129
2002	8 378	1 253	540	714	7 124	1 430	1 890	1 691	1 315	635	163
2003	8 774	1 251	545	706	7 523	1 495	1 960	1 815	1 356	713	183
2004	8 149	1 208	554	653	6 942	1 431	1 784	1 578	1 288	682	179

Table 1-28. Unemployed Persons by Sex, Race, Age, and Hispanic Origin, 1948–2004—*Continued*

(Thousands of people.)

Year, sex, race, and Hispanic origin	16 years and over	16 to 19 years			20 years and over						
		Total	16 to 17 years	18 to 19 years	Total	20 to 24 years	25 to 34 years	35 to 44 years	45 to 54 years	55 to 64 years	65 years and over
Men											
1948	1 559	256	113	142	1 305	324	289	233	201	177	81
1949	2 572	353	145	207	2 219	485	539	414	347	310	125
1950	2 239	318	139	179	1 922	377	467	348	327	286	117
1951	1 221	191	102	89	1 029	155	241	192	193	162	87
1952	1 185	205	116	89	980	155	233	192	182	145	73
1953	1 202	184	94	90	1 019	152	236	208	196	167	60
1954	2 344	310	142	168	2 035	327	517	431	372	275	112
1955	1 854	274	134	140	1 580	248	353	328	285	265	102
1956	1 711	269	134	135	1 442	240	348	278	270	216	90
1957	1 841	300	140	159	1 541	283	349	304	302	220	83
1958	3 098	416	185	231	2 681	478	685	552	492	349	124
1959	2 420	398	191	207	2 022	343	484	407	390	287	112
1960	2 486	426	200	225	2 060	369	492	415	392	294	96
1961	2 997	479	221	258	2 518	458	585	507	473	375	122
1962	2 423	408	188	220	2 016	381	445	404	382	300	103
1963	2 472	501	248	252	1 971	396	445	386	358	290	97
1964	2 205	487	257	230	1 718	384	345	324	319	263	85
1965	1 914	479	247	232	1 435	311	292	283	253	221	75
1966	1 551	432	220	212	1 120	221	239	219	196	179	65
1967	1 508	448	241	207	1 060	235	219	185	199	163	60
1968	1 419	426	234	193	993	258	205	171	165	132	61
1969	1 403	440	244	196	963	270	205	155	157	127	48
1970	2 238	599	306	294	1 638	479	391	253	247	198	71
1971	2 789	693	346	347	2 097	640	513	320	313	239	71
1972	2 659	711	357	355	1 948	628	466	284	272	227	73
1973	2 275	653	352	300	1 624	528	439	211	219	171	57
1974	2 714	757	394	362	1 957	649	546	266	250	183	63
1975	4 442	966	445	521	3 476	1 081	986	507	499	302	103
1976	4 036	939	443	496	3 098	951	914	431	411	296	94
1977	3 667	874	421	453	2 794	877	869	373	326	252	97
1978	3 142	813	426	388	2 328	768	691	314	277	198	81
1979	3 120	811	393	418	2 308	744	699	329	272	196	67
1980	4 267	913	429	485	3 353	1 076	1 137	482	357	243	58
1981	4 577	962	431	531	3 615	1 144	1 213	552	390	261	55
1982	6 179	1 090	469	621	5 089	1 407	1 791	879	550	393	69
1983	6 260	1 003	408	595	5 257	1 369	1 822	947	613	433	73
1984	4 744	812	348	464	3 932	1 023	1 322	728	450	356	53
1985	4 521	806	363	443	3 715	944	1 244	706	459	307	55
1986	4 530	779	355	424	3 751	899	1 291	763	440	301	58
1987	4 101	732	353	379	3 369	779	1 169	689	426	258	49
1988	3 655	667	311	356	2 987	676	1 040	617	366	240	49
1989	3 525	658	303	355	2 867	660	953	619	351	234	49
1990	3 906	667	283	384	3 239	715	1 092	711	413	249	59
1991	4 946	751	317	433	4 195	911	1 375	990	550	305	64
1992	5 523	806	357	449	4 717	951	1 529	1 118	675	378	67
1993	5 055	768	342	426	4 287	865	1 338	1 049	636	336	64
1994	4 367	740	342	398	3 627	768	1 113	855	522	281	88
1995	3 983	744	352	391	3 239	673	961	815	464	233	94
1996	3 880	733	347	387	3 146	675	903	786	484	223	76
1997	3 577	694	321	373	2 882	636	772	732	457	217	69
1998	3 266	686	330	355	2 580	583	699	609	420	201	69
1999	3 066	633	295	338	2 433	562	624	571	403	203	70
2000	2 975	599	281	317	2 376	547	602	557	398	189	83
2001	3 690	650	300	350	3 040	688	756	714	536	272	74
2002	4 597	700	301	399	3 896	792	1 023	897	725	373	87
2003	4 906	697	291	407	4 209	841	1 097	988	764	412	107
2004	4 456	664	292	372	3 791	811	980	839	684	373	104

Table 1-28. Unemployed Persons by Sex, Race, Age, and Hispanic Origin, 1948–2004—*Continued*

(Thousands of people.)

Year, sex, race, and Hispanic origin	16 years and over	16 to 19 years			20 years and over						
		Total	16 to 17 years	18 to 19 years	Total	20 to 24 years	25 to 34 years	35 to 44 years	45 to 54 years	55 to 64 years	65 years and over
Women											
1948	717	153	67	86	564	131	168	114	89	49	12
1949	1 065	223	93	130	841	195	237	189	124	74	21
1950	1 049	195	87	108	854	184	235	182	151	82	20
1951	834	145	66	79	689	118	194	162	125	76	16
1952	698	140	64	76	559	113	156	133	92	50	13
1953	632	123	56	67	510	104	143	117	84	51	10
1954	1 188	191	79	79	997	177	276	249	176	99	20
1955	998	176	77	99	823	148	224	193	151	90	18
1956	1 039	209	97	112	832	155	206	198	159	95	19
1957	1 018	197	90	107	821	147	224	195	146	80	28
1958	1 504	262	114	148	1 242	223	308	319	239	123	30
1959	1 320	256	110	147	1 063	200	242	266	213	118	23
1960	1 366	286	125	162	1 080	214	260	256	222	102	26
1961	1 717	349	142	207	1 368	265	305	343	278	141	37
1962	1 488	313	124	189	1 175	255	267	284	223	111	38
1963	1 598	383	172	210	1 216	262	287	288	231	120	29
1964	1 581	385	179	207	1 195	276	262	281	224	115	32
1965	1 452	395	164	231	1 056	246	237	263	183	101	28
1966	1 324	405	175	229	921	225	202	207	173	86	27
1967	1 468	391	159	231	1 078	277	261	237	184	93	26
1968	1 397	412	180	233	985	285	238	200	149	87	27
1969	1 429	413	192	220	1 015	290	248	203	163	89	24
1970	1 855	506	231	275	1 349	387	327	262	229	111	33
1971	2 227	568	250	318	1 658	489	420	310	260	142	38
1972	2 222	598	276	322	1 625	503	413	293	237	141	38
1973	2 089	583	282	301	1 507	480	427	240	212	119	31
1974	2 441	665	305	360	1 777	564	497	294	248	137	36
1975	3 486	802	355	447	2 684	783	791	444	395	219	52
1976	3 369	780	352	429	2 588	763	795	417	346	214	53
1977	3 324	789	361	428	2 535	752	782	412	340	198	50
1978	3 061	769	370	399	2 292	714	731	381	275	148	43
1979	3 018	743	346	396	2 276	697	748	375	268	150	38
1980	3 370	755	349	407	2 615	760	886	459	318	155	36
1981	3 696	800	350	450	2 895	833	998	513	325	184	43
1982	4 499	886	362	524	3 613	985	1 246	673	416	254	38
1983	4 457	825	344	481	3 632	961	1 255	703	427	244	41
1984	3 794	687	298	390	3 107	815	1 052	607	378	211	45
1985	3 791	661	298	363	3 129	794	1 098	634	355	211	39
1986	3 707	675	310	365	3 032	752	1 099	609	350	189	33
1987	3 324	616	295	321	2 709	674	960	592	298	155	30
1988	3 046	558	262	297	2 487	585	889	550	291	136	38
1989	3 003	536	234	302	2 467	558	897	540	286	144	41
1990	3 140	544	243	301	2 596	584	902	617	310	137	46
1991	3 683	608	270	338	3 074	662	1 071	728	396	168	49
1992	4 090	621	283	338	3 469	698	1 173	858	463	210	66
1993	3 885	597	264	333	3 288	648	1 058	847	485	205	45
1994	3 629	580	282	298	3 049	605	954	772	449	204	66
1995	3 421	602	299	303	2 819	571	880	735	381	193	60
1996	3 356	573	270	303	2 783	564	854	720	399	183	63
1997	3 162	577	268	310	2 585	516	800	686	373	152	58
1998	2 944	519	242	277	2 424	498	720	650	362	141	53
1999	2 814	529	249	280	2 285	480	654	584	350	163	54
2000	2 717	483	221	262	2 235	475	604	577	364	165	50
2001	3 111	512	230	282	2 599	521	742	641	453	187	55
2002	3 781	553	238	315	3 228	638	866	795	591	263	76
2003	3 868	554	255	299	3 314	654	863	827	592	302	76
2004	3 694	543	262	281	3 150	619	804	739	605	309	75

Table 1-28. Unemployed Persons by Sex, Race, Age, and Hispanic Origin, 1948–2004—*Continued*

(Thousands of people.)

Year, sex, race, and Hispanic origin	16 years and over	16 to 19 years			20 years and over						
		Total	16 to 17 years	18 to 19 years	Total	20 to 24 years	25 to 34 years	35 to 44 years	45 to 54 years	55 to 64 years	65 years and over
White[1]											
1954	2 859	423	191	232	2 436	394	610	540	447	329	115
1955	2 252	373	181	191	1 879	304	412	402	358	300	105
1956	2 159	382	191	191	1 777	297	406	363	355	258	98
1957	2 289	401	195	204	1 888	331	425	401	373	262	98
1958	3 680	541	245	297	3 139	541	756	686	614	405	136
1959	2 946	525	255	270	2 421	406	526	525	496	348	120
1960	3 065	575	273	302	2 490	456	573	520	502	330	109
1961	3 743	669	295	374	3 074	566	668	652	611	438	139
1962	3 052	580	262	318	2 472	488	515	522	485	345	117
1963	3 208	708	350	358	2 500	501	540	518	485	349	107
1964	2 999	708	365	342	2 291	508	441	472	447	323	100
1965	2 691	705	329	374	1 986	437	399	427	358	276	91
1966	2 255	651	315	336	1 604	338	323	336	298	227	80
1967	2 338	635	311	325	1 703	393	360	336	321	221	75
1968	2 226	644	326	318	1 582	422	330	297	269	187	80
1969	2 260	660	351	309	1 601	432	354	294	269	185	66
1970	3 339	871	438	432	2 468	679	570	433	415	275	95
1971	4 085	1 011	491	521	3 074	887	732	517	500	338	100
1972	3 906	1 021	515	506	2 885	887	679	459	439	324	95
1973	3 442	955	513	443	2 486	758	664	358	371	257	77
1974	4 097	1 104	561	544	2 993	925	821	448	427	283	88
1975	6 421	1 413	657	755	5 007	1 474	1 413	774	753	460	136
1976	5 914	1 364	649	715	4 550	1 326	1 329	682	637	448	128
1977	5 441	1 284	636	648	4 157	1 195	1 255	621	569	388	129
1978	4 698	1 189	631	558	3 509	1 059	1 059	543	453	290	104
1979	4 664	1 193	589	603	3 472	1 038	1 068	545	443	290	87
1980	5 884	1 291	625	666	4 593	1 364	1 528	740	550	335	74
1981	6 343	1 374	629	745	4 968	1 449	1 658	827	578	379	77
1982	8 241	1 534	683	851	6 707	1 770	2 283	1 223	796	549	86
1983	8 128	1 387	609	778	6 741	1 678	2 282	1 294	837	563	88
1984	6 372	1 116	510	605	5 256	1 282	1 723	1 036	660	475	81
1985	6 191	1 074	507	567	5 117	1 235	1 695	1 039	642	432	75
1986	6 140	1 070	509	561	5 070	1 149	1 751	1 056	629	407	78
1987	5 501	995	495	500	4 506	1 017	1 527	984	576	333	68
1988	4 944	910	437	473	4 033	874	1 371	890	520	309	69
1989	4 770	863	407	456	3 908	856	1 297	871	503	311	70
1990	5 186	903	401	502	4 283	899	1 401	983	582	330	88
1991	6 560	1 029	461	568	5 532	1 132	1 805	1 330	759	410	96
1992	7 169	1 037	484	553	6 132	1 156	1 967	1 483	915	495	116
1993	6 655	992	468	523	5 663	1 057	1 754	1 411	907	442	92
1994	5 892	960	471	489	4 933	952	1 479	1 184	779	407	132
1995	5 459	952	476	476	4 507	866	1 311	1 161	676	362	131
1996	5 300	939	456	484	4 361	854	1 223	1 117	709	336	122
1997	4 836	912	438	475	3 924	765	1 068	1 035	648	302	106
1998	4 484	876	424	451	3 608	731	978	901	620	276	101
1999	4 273	844	414	430	3 429	720	865	843	595	303	104
2000	4 121	795	386	409	3 326	682	835	817	591	294	107
2001	4 969	845	402	443	4 124	829	1 062	985	761	378	109
2002	6 137	925	407	518	5 212	977	1 340	1 237	1 004	518	137
2003	6 311	909	414	495	5 401	1 012	1 354	1 287	1 025	569	155
2004	5 847	890	414	476	4 957	959	1 211	1 130	953	557	148

[1]Beginning in 2003, persons who selected this race group only; persons who selected more than one race group are not included. Prior to 2003, persons who reported more than one race group were included in the group they identified as the main race.

Table 1-28. Unemployed Persons by Sex, Race, Age, and Hispanic Origin, 1948–2004—*Continued*

(Thousands of people.)

Year, sex, race, and Hispanic origin	16 years and over	16 to 19 years			20 years and over						
		Total	16 to 17 years	18 to 19 years	Total	20 to 24 years	25 to 34 years	35 to 44 years	45 to 54 years	55 to 64 years	65 years and over
Black[1]											
1972	906	279	113	167	627	226	183	106	62	37	12
1973	846	262	114	148	584	231	181	82	53	29	9
1974	965	297	127	170	666	261	201	95	65	33	10
1975	1 369	330	130	200	1 040	362	321	157	126	54	17
1976	1 334	330	134	195	1 005	350	338	145	101	54	16
1977	1 393	354	135	218	1 040	397	355	140	81	51	16
1978	1 330	360	150	210	972	379	320	127	82	47	17
1979	1 319	333	137	197	986	369	335	137	82	48	15
1980	1 553	343	134	210	1 209	426	433	171	109	53	18
1981	1 731	357	138	219	1 374	483	493	207	119	55	17
1982	2 142	396	130	266	1 747	565	662	278	141	84	17
1983	2 272	392	125	267	1 879	591	700	299	174	95	21
1984	1 914	353	122	230	1 561	504	577	253	138	75	15
1985	1 864	357	135	221	1 507	455	562	254	143	74	18
1986	1 840	347	138	209	1 493	453	564	269	127	69	10
1987	1 684	312	134	178	1 373	397	533	247	124	62	10
1988	1 547	288	121	167	1 259	349	502	230	111	51	15
1989	1 544	300	116	184	1 245	322	494	246	109	53	20
1990	1 565	268	112	156	1 297	349	505	278	106	44	14
1991	1 723	280	105	175	1 443	378	539	318	151	44	13
1992	2 011	324	127	197	1 687	421	610	402	178	64	13
1993	1 844	313	112	201	1 530	387	532	376	153	72	11
1994	1 666	300	127	173	1 366	351	468	346	130	55	16
1995	1 538	325	143	182	1 213	311	423	303	116	42	18
1996	1 592	310	133	177	1 282	327	454	313	127	48	13
1997	1 560	302	123	179	1 258	327	426	307	136	45	16
1998	1 426	281	124	156	1 146	301	366	294	125	45	16
1999	1 309	268	109	159	1 041	273	339	249	121	46	14
2000	1 241	230	96	134	1 011	281	289	254	131	38	20
2001	1 416	260	102	158	1 155	307	340	283	159	52	15
2002	1 693	260	103	156	1 433	365	407	349	215	76	21
2003	1 787	255	93	162	1 532	375	442	385	217	93	20
2004	1 729	241	103	138	1 487	353	441	341	245	86	21
Hispanic											
1973	277	80	...	...	...	...	...	...	...	...	...
1974	325	88	...	...	...	...	...	...	...	...	...
1975	508	123	...	...	...	...	...	...	...	...	...
1976	485	106	51	55	385	116	113	72	53	26	6
1977	456	113	50	60	344	98	114	56	48	24	5
1978	452	110	63	47	342	98	116	65	41	16	5
1979	434	106	54	51	329	100	102	65	37	20	4
1980	620	145	66	79	474	138	168	90	49	24	5
1981	678	144	60	84	533	171	178	92	57	31	5
1982	929	175	73	102	754	221	267	140	75	45	6
1983	961	167	64	104	793	214	270	156	93	54	5
1984	800	149	60	88	651	164	235	124	71	51	5
1985	811	141	55	85	670	171	256	123	73	41	7
1986	857	141	57	84	716	183	258	143	85	38	9
1987	751	136	57	79	615	152	222	128	75	33	5
1988	732	148	63	84	585	145	209	120	69	36	6
1989	750	132	59	73	618	158	218	124	76	36	6
1990	876	161	68	94	714	167	263	156	85	36	7
1991	1 092	179	79	99	913	214	332	206	110	44	8
1992	1 311	219	94	124	1 093	240	390	267	126	59	10
1993	1 248	201	86	115	1 047	237	354	261	132	54	10
1994	1 187	198	90	108	989	220	348	227	132	51	12
1995	1 140	205	96	109	934	209	325	224	106	54	16
1996	1 132	199	85	114	933	217	296	246	101	59	14
1997	1 069	197	87	110	872	206	269	229	99	56	13
1998	1 026	214	89	125	812	194	260	203	96	48	11
1999	945	196	79	117	750	171	233	190	104	42	10
2000	954	194	83	112	759	190	247	189	79	42	12
2001	1 138	208	84	123	931	212	315	228	111	56	9
2002	1 353	221	81	140	1 132	265	373	271	146	62	15
2003	1 441	192	79	113	1 249	273	419	294	183	69	10
2004	1 342	203	86	117	1 139	255	371	261	161	74	18

[1]Beginning in 2003, persons who selected this race group only; persons who selected more than one race group are not included. Prior to 2003, persons who reported more than one race group were included in the group they identified as the main race.
. . . = Not available.

Table 1-28. Unemployed Persons by Sex, Race, Age, and Hispanic Origin, 1948–2004—*Continued*

(Thousands of people.)

Year, sex, race, and Hispanic origin	16 years and over	16 to 19 years			20 years and over						
		Total	16 to 17 years	18 to 19 years	Total	20 to 24 years	25 to 34 years	35 to 44 years	45 to 54 years	55 to 64 years	65 years and over
White Men[1]											
1954	1 913	266	125	142	1 647	260	408	341	299	241	98
1955	1 478	232	114	117	1 246	196	260	246	233	223	89
1956	1 366	221	112	108	1 145	186	265	212	225	177	81
1957	1 477	243	118	124	1 234	222	257	239	250	193	73
1958	2 489	333	149	184	2 156	382	525	436	404	299	110
1959	1 903	318	162	156	1 585	256	350	316	320	245	98
1960	1 988	341	167	174	1 647	295	376	330	317	243	86
1961	2 398	384	176	208	2 014	370	442	395	382	318	107
1962	1 915	334	158	176	1 581	300	332	311	308	246	84
1963	1 976	407	211	196	1 569	309	342	297	294	246	80
1964	1 779	400	217	183	1 379	310	262	255	266	216	70
1965	1 556	387	200	186	1 169	254	226	228	206	190	67
1966	1 241	340	178	162	901	172	185	173	160	154	57
1967	1 208	342	186	156	866	185	171	153	167	140	52
1968	1 142	328	185	143	814	206	162	140	142	111	55
1969	1 137	343	198	145	794	214	165	130	134	108	43
1970	1 857	485	255	230	1 372	388	316	212	216	177	64
1971	2 309	562	288	275	1 747	513	418	268	272	211	66
1972	2 173	564	288	276	1 610	506	375	231	237	199	60
1973	1 836	513	284	229	1 323	411	353	166	188	153	51
1974	2 169	584	311	274	1 585	505	434	218	213	161	53
1975	3 627	785	369	416	2 841	871	796	412	411	265	86
1976	3 258	754	368	385	2 504	750	730	346	341	259	78
1977	2 883	672	342	330	2 211	660	682	297	276	213	82
1978	2 411	615	338	277	1 797	558	525	250	227	169	68
1979	2 405	633	319	313	1 773	553	526	253	220	165	56
1980	3 345	716	347	369	2 629	827	884	378	291	206	44
1981	3 580	755	349	406	2 825	869	943	433	317	221	42
1982	4 846	854	387	467	3 991	1 066	1 385	696	460	331	53
1983	4 859	761	328	433	4 098	1 019	1 410	755	497	362	54
1984	3 600	608	280	328	2 992	722	991	572	363	302	42
1985	3 426	592	282	310	2 834	694	931	553	356	257	43
1986	3 433	576	276	299	2 857	645	978	586	349	248	51
1987	3 132	548	272	276	2 584	568	879	536	350	209	43
1988	2 766	499	239	260	2 268	480	777	477	293	200	40
1989	2 636	487	230	257	2 149	476	694	470	280	191	38
1990	2 935	504	214	290	2 431	510	796	530	330	214	51
1991	3 859	575	249	327	3 284	677	1 064	780	438	269	55
1992	4 209	590	270	319	3 620	686	1 155	858	543	318	58
1993	3 828	565	261	305	3 263	619	1 015	793	512	270	53
1994	3 275	540	259	280	2 735	555	827	626	417	236	74
1995	2 999	535	260	275	2 465	483	711	621	371	200	79
1996	2 896	532	260	273	2 363	478	655	592	383	188	67
1997	2 641	502	234	268	2 140	439	553	549	358	182	58
1998	2 431	510	254	257	1 920	405	512	441	342	164	58
1999	2 274	461	223	237	1 813	398	441	419	322	172	61
2000	2 177	446	217	229	1 731	368	428	403	302	162	68
2001	2 754	479	232	247	2 275	494	547	529	413	229	64
2002	3 459	516	228	288	2 943	562	772	672	554	305	77
2003	3 643	518	221	298	3 125	589	798	723	591	333	91
2004	3 282	497	224	274	2 785	560	694	620	516	307	88

[1]Beginning in 2003, persons who selected this race group only; persons who selected more than one race group are not included. Prior to 2003, persons who reported more than one race group were included in the group they identified as the main race.

Table 1-28. Unemployed Persons by Sex, Race, Age, and Hispanic Origin, 1948–2004—*Continued*

(Thousands of people.)

Year, sex, race, and Hispanic origin	16 years and over	16 to 19 years			20 years and over						
		Total	16 to 17 years	18 to 19 years	Total	20 to 24 years	25 to 34 years	35 to 44 years	45 to 54 years	55 to 64 years	65 years and over
White Women[1]											
1954	946	157	66	90	789	134	202	199	148	88	17
1955	774	141	67	74	633	108	152	156	125	77	16
1956	793	161	79	83	632	111	141	151	130	81	17
1957	812	158	77	80	654	109	168	162	123	69	25
1958	1 191	208	96	113	983	159	231	250	210	106	26
1959	1 043	207	93	114	836	150	176	209	176	103	22
1960	1 077	234	106	128	843	161	197	190	185	87	23
1961	1 345	285	119	166	1 060	196	226	257	229	120	32
1962	1 137	246	104	142	891	188	183	211	177	99	33
1963	1 232	301	139	162	931	192	198	221	191	103	27
1964	1 220	308	148	159	912	198	179	217	181	107	30
1965	1 135	318	129	188	817	183	173	199	152	86	24
1966	1 014	311	137	174	703	166	138	163	138	73	23
1967	1 130	293	125	169	837	209	189	183	154	81	23
1968	1 084	316	141	175	768	216	168	157	127	76	25
1969	1 123	317	153	164	806	218	189	164	135	77	23
1970	1 482	386	183	202	1 096	291	254	221	199	98	31
1971	1 777	449	203	246	1 328	376	314	249	228	126	34
1972	1 733	457	227	230	1 275	381	304	227	202	125	35
1973	1 606	442	228	214	1 164	347	311	192	183	104	26
1974	1 927	519	250	270	1 408	420	387	230	214	122	35
1975	2 794	628	288	340	2 166	602	617	362	342	195	49
1976	2 656	611	280	330	2 045	577	598	336	296	188	49
1977	2 558	612	294	318	1 946	536	573	323	293	175	47
1978	2 287	574	292	281	1 713	500	533	294	226	122	37
1979	2 260	560	270	290	1 699	485	542	293	223	125	32
1980	2 540	576	278	298	1 964	537	645	362	259	129	31
1981	2 762	620	281	339	2 143	580	715	394	261	158	36
1982	3 395	680	296	384	2 715	704	898	527	337	217	33
1983	3 270	626	282	345	2 643	659	872	539	340	201	33
1984	2 772	508	231	277	2 264	559	731	464	297	173	39
1985	2 765	482	225	257	2 283	541	763	486	286	175	32
1986	2 708	495	233	262	2 213	504	773	470	281	159	27
1987	2 369	447	223	224	1 922	449	648	448	227	124	25
1988	2 177	412	198	214	1 766	393	594	413	227	110	30
1989	2 135	376	177	199	1 758	380	603	401	223	120	32
1990	2 251	399	187	212	1 852	389	605	453	251	116	37
1991	2 701	453	212	241	2 248	455	741	550	320	141	41
1992	2 959	447	214	233	2 512	469	811	625	372	177	58
1993	2 827	426	208	219	2 400	438	739	618	395	172	39
1994	2 617	420	211	208	2 197	397	652	558	361	170	58
1995	2 460	418	216	201	2 042	384	600	540	306	162	52
1996	2 404	407	196	211	1 998	376	568	525	326	148	55
1997	2 195	411	204	207	1 784	326	515	486	290	119	49
1998	2 053	365	171	195	1 688	327	467	460	279	112	43
1999	1 999	383	190	193	1 616	322	423	423	273	131	43
2000	1 944	349	168	180	1 595	314	407	414	289	133	39
2001	2 215	366	170	196	1 849	335	515	456	348	150	45
2002	2 678	409	179	230	2 269	415	567	565	449	213	60
2003	2 668	391	194	197	2 276	423	555	564	434	235	64
2004	2 565	393	191	202	2 172	399	516	510	437	250	60

[1]Beginning in 2003, persons who selected this race group only; persons who selected more than one race group are not included. Prior to 2003, persons who reported more than one race group were included in the group they identified as the main race.

Table 1-28. Unemployed Persons by Age, Sex, Race, and Hispanic Origin, 1948–2004—*Continued*

(Thousands of people.)

Year, sex, race, and Hispanic origin	16 years and over	16 to 19 years			20 years and over						
		Total	16 to 17 years	18 to 19 years	Total	20 to 24 years	25 to 34 years	35 to 44 years	45 to 54 years	55 to 64 years	65 years and over
Black Men[1]											
1972	448	143	66	77	305	113	84	45	31	23	9
1973	395	128	62	66	267	108	75	37	27	16	5
1974	494	159	75	82	336	129	103	41	35	19	8
1975	741	170	71	100	571	195	169	83	78	33	13
1976	698	170	69	103	528	185	166	73	60	32	13
1977	698	187	73	114	512	197	170	63	40	31	12
1978	641	180	80	101	462	185	148	53	40	24	11
1979	636	164	68	97	473	174	152	66	44	27	10
1980	815	179	72	108	636	222	222	88	60	32	12
1981	891	188	73	115	703	248	245	102	65	32	10
1982	1 167	213	72	141	954	304	355	154	74	54	12
1983	1 213	211	70	142	1 002	313	358	162	96	59	14
1984	1 003	188	62	126	815	272	289	132	67	45	9
1985	951	193	69	124	757	224	268	127	85	43	11
1986	946	180	68	112	765	225	273	148	70	44	5
1987	826	160	70	90	666	186	253	122	61	39	6
1988	771	154	64	90	617	177	233	111	58	30	8
1989	773	153	65	88	619	162	226	129	59	33	10
1990	806	142	62	80	664	177	247	146	62	27	6
1991	890	145	54	91	745	201	252	172	87	25	7
1992	1 067	180	71	109	886	221	301	208	107	42	6
1993	971	170	66	104	801	201	260	201	87	46	7
1994	848	167	69	97	682	173	218	180	72	29	10
1995	762	168	73	95	593	153	195	150	63	21	11
1996	808	169	73	96	639	163	210	158	75	26	7
1997	747	162	70	92	585	165	178	141	72	22	7
1998	671	147	61	86	524	151	148	133	60	24	8
1999	626	145	60	85	480	135	143	114	60	22	7
2000	620	121	52	70	499	145	134	121	72	17	9
2001	709	136	51	85	573	150	159	142	84	31	7
2002	835	140	54	85	695	181	180	165	120	40	9
2003	891	132	49	83	760	192	212	189	109	47	10
2004	860	128	52	75	733	188	211	160	120	46	8
Black Women[1]											
1972	458	136	47	90	322	113	99	61	31	14	3
1973	451	134	51	82	317	123	105	45	26	13	4
1974	470	139	51	87	331	132	98	55	30	14	2
1975	629	160	60	100	469	167	153	75	48	22	4
1976	637	160	66	93	477	165	172	73	41	23	3
1977	695	167	63	104	528	200	185	77	41	21	4
1978	690	179	70	110	510	194	173	74	41	23	6
1979	683	169	69	100	513	195	183	71	38	21	5
1980	738	164	62	102	574	204	211	83	49	21	6
1981	840	169	65	104	671	235	248	105	54	23	7
1982	975	182	58	124	793	261	307	123	67	29	5
1983	1 059	181	56	125	878	278	342	137	77	36	7
1984	911	165	60	104	747	231	288	121	71	30	5
1985	913	164	66	98	750	231	295	127	58	31	7
1986	894	167	70	97	728	228	291	121	57	25	5
1987	858	152	64	88	706	211	280	125	63	23	4
1988	776	134	57	78	642	172	269	118	53	22	7
1989	772	147	51	96	625	160	267	118	50	21	9
1990	758	126	49	76	633	172	258	132	44	17	8
1991	833	135	51	84	698	177	288	145	64	19	6
1992	944	144	56	88	800	200	308	194	71	22	6
1993	872	143	46	97	729	186	272	175	66	26	5
1994	818	133	57	76	685	178	249	166	59	26	6
1995	777	157	. . .	87	620	158	228	153	53	20	. . .
1996	784	141	60	80	643	164	244	155	52	21	7
1997	813	140	53	87	673	163	248	166	64	24	9
1998	756	134	63	71	622	150	218	160	65	21	8
1999	684	123	49	74	561	138	196	135	61	25	7
2000	621	109	44	65	512	136	154	132	59	22	10
2001	706	124	52	72	582	157	181	141	75	21	8
2002	858	120	49	71	738	183	228	185	95	35	12
2003	895	123	44	79	772	183	230	195	109	46	10
2004	868	114	51	63	755	166	230	180	126	40	13

[1]Beginning in 2003, persons who selected this race group only; persons who selected more than one race group are not included. Prior to 2003, persons who reported more than one race group were included in the group they identified as the main race.
. . . = Not available.

Table 1-28. Unemployed Persons by Sex, Race, Age, and Hispanic Origin, 1948–2004—*Continued*

(Thousands of people.)

Year, sex, race, and Hispanic origin	16 years and over	16 to 19 years			20 years and over						
		Total	16 to 17 years	18 to 19 years	Total	20 to 24 years	25 to 34 years	35 to 44 years	45 to 54 years	55 to 64 years	65 years and over
Hispanic Men											
1973	158	...	...	...	114	...	...	...	...	...	...
1974	187	...	...	...	139	...	...	...	...	...	...
1975	296	...	...	...	225	...	...	...	...	...	...
1976	278	60	30	31	217	69	63	38	29	16	...
1977	253	60	27	33	195	57	65	28	22	15	...
1978	234	59	35	24	175	51	59	30	20	10	...
1979	223	55	29	27	168	52	50	33	19	11	...
1980	370	86	39	47	284	85	96	51	31	16	...
1981	408	87	40	47	321	105	113	49	31	19	...
1982	565	104	45	59	461	138	169	80	40	29	...
1983	591	100	38	62	491	134	168	92	57	36	...
1984	480	87	36	51	393	103	142	69	41	33	...
1985	483	82	34	49	401	108	156	69	40	23	...
1986	520	82	33	50	438	115	159	86	46	26	...
1987	451	77	32	45	374	88	137	77	46	22	...
1988	437	86	36	50	351	83	128	70	42	24	...
1989	423	81	36	45	342	88	113	69	43	25	...
1990	524	100	40	60	425	99	154	91	53	25	...
1991	685	110	47	62	575	139	210	126	62	33	...
1992	807	132	56	75	675	156	239	156	75	42	...
1993	747	118	50	68	629	144	217	148	79	33	...
1994	680	121	54	67	558	128	203	113	75	30	9
1995	651	121	59	63	530	123	185	120	57	33	13
1996	607	112	49	63	495	117	165	124	49	31	9
1997	582	110	47	63	471	125	137	113	54	35	8
1998	552	117	54	62	436	115	142	97	49	29	5
1999	480	106	42	63	374	96	109	83	54	24	7
2000	494	106	46	60	388	105	118	93	42	23	8
2001	611	117	52	65	495	129	152	116	55	36	6
2002	764	127	42	86	636	151	213	144	82	38	8
2003	809	116	42	74	693	157	239	153	98	41	5
2004	755	120	48	72	635	158	207	133	82	41	13
Hispanic Women											
1973	119	...	...	...	83	...	...	...	...	...	...
1974	137	...	...	...	98	...	...	...	...	...	...
1975	212	...	...	...	160	...	...	...	...	...	...
1976	207	45	22	24	166	47	52	33	22	10	...
1977	204	50	23	27	153	40	49	28	25	11	...
1978	219	51	28	23	168	46	58	36	20	8	...
1979	211	50	26	24	160	48	52	32	18	10	...
1980	249	59	28	31	190	53	72	39	18	8	...
1981	269	57	20	37	212	65	65	43	25	13	...
1982	364	71	28	43	293	83	98	60	35	16	...
1983	369	68	26	42	302	80	102	65	36	18	...
1984	320	62	25	37	258	61	93	55	30	17	...
1985	327	58	22	37	269	63	100	54	32	18	...
1986	337	59	25	35	278	68	99	57	39	12	...
1987	300	59	25	34	241	64	85	51	29	11	...
1988	296	62	27	34	234	63	81	50	27	12	...
1989	327	51	23	28	276	70	105	55	33	11	...
1990	351	62	28	34	289	68	109	65	32	11	...
1991	407	69	32	37	339	74	122	80	48	12	...
1992	504	87	38	49	418	84	151	111	51	17	...
1993	501	83	36	47	418	93	136	113	53	21	...
1994	508	77	36	40	431	92	145	115	57	21	2
1995	488	84	38	46	404	86	140	104	50	21	3
1996	525	88	36	52	438	100	131	122	52	27	5
1997	488	87	40	46	401	81	132	117	46	21	4
1998	473	98	35	63	376	80	118	106	48	19	5
1999	466	90	36	54	376	75	124	107	50	17	3
2000	460	88	37	51	371	86	129	96	38	19	4
2001	527	91	33	58	436	83	163	112	56	20	3
2002	590	94	39	54	496	113	160	127	65	24	7
2003	631	76	37	39	555	116	180	141	86	28	5
2004	587	83	38	45	504	97	164	128	78	32	5

Note: Persons of Hispanic origin may be of any race.

. . . = Not available.

Table 1-29. Unemployment Rates of Civilian Workers by Age, Sex, Race, and Hispanic Origin, 1948–2004

(Percent of labor force.)

Year, sex, race, and Hispanic origin	16 years and over	16 to 19 years			20 years and over						
		Total	16 to 17 years	18 to 19 years	Total	20 to 24 years	25 to 34 years	35 to 44 years	45 to 54 years	55 to 64 years	65 years and over
Total											
1948	3.8	9.2	10.1	8.6	3.3	6.2	3.2	2.6	2.7	3.1	3.2
1949	5.9	13.4	14.0	13.0	5.4	9.3	5.4	4.4	4.2	5.2	4.9
1950	5.3	12.2	13.6	11.2	4.8	7.7	4.8	3.8	4.2	4.8	4.5
1951	3.3	8.2	9.6	7.1	3.0	4.1	3.0	2.5	2.7	3.1	3.4
1952	3.0	8.5	10.0	7.3	2.7	4.6	2.6	2.3	2.3	2.4	2.9
1953	2.9	7.6	8.7	6.8	2.6	4.7	2.5	2.2	2.3	2.7	2.2
1954	5.5	12.6	13.5	10.7	5.1	9.2	5.3	4.5	4.4	4.5	4.1
1955	4.4	11.0	12.3	10.0	3.9	7.0	3.8	3.4	3.4	4.2	3.6
1956	4.1	11.1	12.3	10.2	3.7	6.6	3.7	3.0	3.2	3.5	3.2
1957	4.3	11.6	12.5	10.9	3.8	7.1	3.9	3.1	3.3	3.4	3.4
1958	6.8	15.9	16.4	15.5	6.2	11.2	6.8	5.4	5.2	5.2	4.8
1959	5.5	14.6	15.3	14.0	4.8	8.5	5.0	4.2	4.2	4.4	4.3
1960	5.5	14.7	15.5	14.1	4.8	8.7	5.2	4.1	4.1	4.2	3.8
1961	6.7	16.8	18.3	15.8	5.9	10.4	6.2	5.2	5.0	5.4	5.1
1962	5.5	14.7	16.3	13.6	4.9	9.0	5.1	4.1	4.0	4.2	4.5
1963	5.7	17.2	19.3	15.6	4.8	8.8	5.2	4.0	3.8	4.1	4.1
1964	5.2	16.2	17.8	14.9	4.3	8.3	4.3	3.6	3.5	3.7	3.8
1965	4.5	14.8	16.5	13.5	3.6	6.7	3.7	3.2	2.8	3.1	3.3
1966	3.8	12.8	14.8	11.3	2.9	5.3	3.1	2.5	2.3	2.5	3.0
1967	3.8	12.9	14.6	11.6	3.0	5.7	3.2	2.5	2.4	2.4	2.8
1968	3.6	12.7	14.7	11.2	2.7	5.8	2.8	2.2	1.9	2.0	2.8
1969	3.5	12.2	14.5	10.5	2.7	5.7	2.8	2.2	1.9	1.9	2.2
1970	4.9	15.3	17.1	13.8	4.0	8.2	4.2	3.1	2.8	2.7	3.2
1971	5.9	16.9	18.7	15.5	4.9	10.0	5.3	3.9	3.4	3.3	3.5
1972	5.6	16.2	18.5	14.6	4.5	9.3	4.6	3.5	3.0	3.2	3.6
1973	4.9	14.5	17.3	12.4	3.9	7.8	4.2	2.7	2.5	2.6	3.0
1974	5.6	16.0	18.3	14.3	4.5	9.1	4.8	3.3	2.9	2.8	3.4
1975	8.5	19.9	21.4	18.9	7.3	13.6	7.8	5.6	5.2	4.6	5.2
1976	7.7	19.0	21.1	17.5	6.5	12.0	7.1	4.9	4.5	4.5	5.1
1977	7.1	17.8	19.9	16.2	5.9	11.0	6.5	4.4	3.9	3.9	5.0
1978	6.1	16.4	19.3	14.2	5.0	9.6	5.3	3.7	3.3	2.9	4.0
1979	5.8	16.1	18.1	14.7	4.8	9.1	5.2	3.6	3.2	2.9	3.4
1980	7.1	17.8	20.0	16.2	6.1	11.5	6.9	4.6	4.0	3.3	3.1
1981	7.6	19.6	21.4	18.4	6.5	12.3	7.3	5.0	4.2	3.7	3.2
1982	9.7	23.2	24.9	22.1	8.6	14.9	9.7	6.9	5.7	5.4	3.5
1983	9.6	22.4	24.5	21.1	8.6	14.5	9.7	7.0	6.2	5.6	3.7
1984	7.5	18.9	21.2	17.4	6.7	11.5	7.3	5.4	4.9	4.7	3.3
1985	7.2	18.6	21.0	17.0	6.4	11.1	7.0	5.1	4.7	4.3	3.2
1986	7.0	18.3	20.2	17.0	6.2	10.7	6.9	5.0	4.5	4.1	3.0
1987	6.2	16.9	19.1	15.2	5.4	9.7	6.0	4.5	4.0	3.5	2.5
1988	5.5	15.3	17.4	13.8	4.8	8.7	5.4	4.0	3.4	3.2	2.7
1989	5.3	15.0	17.2	13.6	4.6	8.6	5.2	3.8	3.2	3.2	2.6
1990	5.6	15.5	17.9	14.1	4.9	8.8	5.6	4.1	3.6	3.3	3.0
1991	6.8	18.7	21.0	17.2	6.1	10.8	6.9	5.2	4.5	4.1	3.3
1992	7.5	20.1	23.1	18.2	6.8	11.4	7.6	5.8	5.1	5.1	3.8
1993	6.9	19.0	21.4	17.5	6.2	10.5	6.9	5.5	4.8	4.7	3.2
1994	6.1	17.6	19.9	16.0	5.4	9.7	6.0	4.6	4.0	4.1	4.0
1995	5.6	17.3	20.2	15.3	4.9	9.1	5.4	4.3	3.3	3.6	4.0
1996	5.4	16.7	18.9	15.2	4.7	9.3	5.2	4.1	3.3	3.3	3.6
1997	4.9	16.0	18.2	14.5	4.3	8.5	4.7	3.8	3.0	2.9	3.3
1998	4.5	14.6	17.2	12.8	3.9	7.9	4.3	3.4	2.8	2.6	3.2
1999	4.2	13.9	16.3	12.4	3.6	7.5	4.0	3.0	2.6	2.7	3.1
2000	4.0	13.1	15.4	11.6	3.4	7.2	3.7	3.0	2.5	2.5	3.1
2001	4.7	14.7	17.2	13.1	4.2	8.3	4.6	3.6	3.1	3.0	2.9
2002	5.8	16.5	18.8	15.1	5.2	9.7	5.9	4.6	4.0	3.9	3.6
2003	6.0	17.5	19.1	16.4	5.4	10.0	6.1	4.9	4.1	4.1	3.8
2004	5.5	17.0	20.2	15.0	4.9	9.4	5.5	4.4	3.8	3.8	3.6

**Table 1-29. Unemployment Rates of Civilian Workers by Age, Sex, Race, and Hispanic Origin, 1948–2004
—Continued**

(Percent of labor force.)

Year, sex, race, and Hispanic origin	16 years and over	16 to 19 years			20 years and over						
		Total	16 to 17 years	18 to 19 years	Total	20 to 24 years	25 to 34 years	35 to 44 years	45 to 54 years	55 to 64 years	65 years and over
Men											
1948	3.6	9.8	10.2	9.5	3.2	6.9	2.8	2.4	2.5	3.1	3.4
1949	5.9	14.3	13.7	14.6	5.4	10.4	5.2	4.3	4.3	5.4	5.1
1950	5.1	12.7	13.3	12.3	4.7	8.1	4.4	3.6	4.0	4.9	4.8
1951	2.8	8.1	9.4	7.0	2.5	3.9	2.3	2.0	2.4	2.8	3.5
1952	2.8	8.9	10.5	7.4	2.4	4.6	2.2	1.9	2.2	2.4	3.0
1953	2.8	7.9	8.8	7.2	2.5	5.0	2.2	2.0	2.3	2.8	2.4
1954	5.3	13.5	13.9	13.2	4.9	10.7	4.8	4.1	4.3	4.5	4.4
1955	4.2	11.6	12.5	10.8	3.8	7.7	3.3	3.1	3.2	4.3	4.0
1956	3.8	11.1	11.7	10.5	3.4	6.9	3.3	2.6	3.0	3.5	3.5
1957	4.1	12.4	12.4	12.3	3.6	7.8	3.3	2.8	3.3	3.5	3.4
1958	6.8	17.1	16.3	17.8	6.2	12.7	6.5	5.1	5.3	5.5	5.2
1959	5.2	15.3	15.8	14.9	4.7	8.7	4.7	3.7	4.1	4.5	4.8
1960	5.4	15.3	15.5	15.0	4.7	8.9	4.8	3.8	4.1	4.6	4.2
1961	6.4	17.1	18.3	16.3	5.7	10.8	5.7	4.6	4.9	5.7	5.5
1962	5.2	14.7	16.0	13.8	4.6	8.9	4.5	3.6	3.9	4.6	4.6
1963	5.2	17.2	18.8	15.9	4.5	8.8	4.5	3.5	3.6	4.3	4.5
1964	4.6	15.8	17.1	14.6	3.9	8.1	3.5	2.9	3.2	3.9	4.0
1965	4.0	14.1	16.1	12.4	3.2	6.4	2.9	2.5	2.5	3.3	3.5
1966	3.2	11.7	13.7	10.2	2.5	4.6	2.4	2.0	1.9	2.6	3.1
1967	3.1	12.3	14.5	10.5	2.3	4.7	2.1	1.7	2.0	2.3	2.8
1968	2.9	11.6	13.9	9.7	2.2	5.1	1.9	1.6	1.6	1.9	2.8
1969	2.8	11.4	13.8	9.3	2.1	5.1	1.9	1.5	1.5	1.8	2.2
1970	4.4	15.0	16.9	13.4	3.5	8.4	3.5	2.4	2.4	2.8	3.3
1971	5.3	16.6	18.7	15.0	4.4	10.3	4.4	3.1	3.0	3.3	3.4
1972	5.0	15.9	18.3	14.1	4.0	9.3	3.8	2.7	2.6	3.2	3.6
1973	4.2	13.9	17.0	11.4	3.3	7.3	3.4	2.0	2.1	2.4	3.0
1974	4.9	15.6	18.4	13.3	3.8	8.8	4.0	2.6	2.4	2.6	3.3
1975	7.9	20.1	21.6	19.0	6.8	14.3	6.9	4.9	4.8	4.3	5.4
1976	7.1	19.2	21.4	17.6	5.9	12.1	6.2	4.1	4.0	4.2	5.1
1977	6.3	17.3	19.5	15.6	5.2	10.8	5.7	3.5	3.2	3.6	5.2
1978	5.3	15.8	19.1	13.3	4.3	9.2	4.4	2.8	2.7	2.8	4.2
1979	5.1	15.9	17.9	14.3	4.2	8.7	4.3	2.9	2.7	2.7	3.4
1980	6.9	18.3	20.4	16.7	5.9	12.5	6.7	4.1	3.6	3.4	3.1
1981	7.4	20.1	22.0	18.8	6.3	13.2	6.9	4.5	4.0	3.6	2.9
1982	9.9	24.4	26.4	23.1	8.8	16.4	10.1	6.9	5.6	5.5	3.7
1983	9.9	23.3	25.2	22.2	8.9	15.9	10.1	7.1	6.3	6.1	3.9
1984	7.4	19.6	21.9	18.3	6.6	11.9	7.2	5.2	4.6	5.0	3.0
1985	7.0	19.5	21.9	17.9	6.2	11.4	6.6	4.9	4.6	4.3	3.1
1986	6.9	19.0	20.8	17.7	6.1	11.0	6.7	5.1	4.4	4.3	3.2
1987	6.2	17.8	20.2	16.0	5.4	9.9	5.9	4.4	4.2	3.7	2.6
1988	5.5	16.0	18.2	14.6	4.8	8.9	5.3	3.8	3.5	3.5	2.5
1989	5.2	15.9	18.6	14.2	4.5	8.8	4.8	3.7	3.2	3.5	2.4
1990	5.7	16.3	18.4	15.0	5.0	9.1	5.5	4.1	3.7	3.8	3.0
1991	7.2	19.8	21.8	18.5	6.4	11.6	7.0	5.5	4.8	4.6	3.3
1992	7.9	21.5	24.6	19.5	7.1	12.2	7.8	6.1	5.6	5.8	3.3
1993	7.2	20.4	22.9	18.8	6.4	11.3	7.0	5.6	5.1	5.2	3.2
1994	6.2	19.0	21.0	17.6	5.4	10.2	5.9	4.5	4.0	4.4	4.0
1995	5.6	18.4	21.1	16.5	4.8	9.2	5.1	4.2	3.5	3.6	4.3
1996	5.4	18.1	20.8	16.3	4.6	9.5	4.9	4.0	3.5	3.3	3.4
1997	4.9	16.9	19.1	15.4	4.2	8.9	4.3	3.6	3.1	3.1	3.0
1998	4.4	16.2	19.1	14.1	3.7	8.1	3.9	3.0	2.8	2.8	3.1
1999	4.1	14.7	17.0	13.1	3.5	7.7	3.6	2.8	2.6	2.7	3.0
2000	3.9	14.0	16.8	12.2	3.3	7.3	3.4	2.8	2.4	2.4	3.3
2001	4.8	16.0	19.1	14.0	4.2	9.0	4.3	3.6	3.2	3.3	3.0
2002	5.9	18.1	21.1	16.4	5.3	10.2	5.8	4.5	4.2	4.3	3.4
2003	6.3	19.3	20.7	18.4	5.6	10.6	6.2	5.0	4.4	4.5	4.0
2004	5.6	18.4	22.0	16.3	5.0	10.1	5.5	4.3	3.9	3.9	3.7

Table 1-29. Unemployment Rates of Civilian Workers by Age, Sex, Race, and Hispanic Origin, 1948–2004
    —*Continued*

(Percent of labor force.)

Year, sex, race, and Hispanic origin	16 years and over	16 to 19 years			20 years and over						
		Total	16 to 17 years	18 to 19 years	Total	20 to 24 years	25 to 34 years	35 to 44 years	45 to 54 years	55 to 64 years	65 years and over
Women											
1948	4.1	8.3	10.0	7.4	3.6	4.8	4.3	3.0	3.0	3.1	2.3
1949	6.0	12.3	14.4	11.2	5.3	7.3	5.9	4.7	4.0	4.4	3.8
1950	5.7	11.4	14.2	9.8	5.1	6.9	5.7	4.4	4.5	4.5	3.4
1951	4.4	8.3	10.0	7.2	4.0	4.4	4.5	3.8	3.5	4.0	2.9
1952	3.6	8.0	9.1	7.3	3.2	4.5	3.6	3.0	2.5	2.5	2.2
1953	3.3	7.2	8.5	6.4	2.9	4.3	3.4	2.5	2.3	2.5	1.4
1954	6.0	11.4	12.7	7.7	5.5	7.3	6.6	5.3	4.6	4.6	3.0
1955	4.9	10.2	12.0	9.1	4.4	6.1	5.3	4.0	3.6	3.8	2.3
1956	4.8	11.2	13.2	9.9	4.2	6.3	4.8	3.9	3.6	3.6	2.3
1957	4.7	10.6	12.6	9.4	4.1	6.0	5.3	3.8	3.2	3.0	3.4
1958	6.8	14.3	16.6	12.9	6.1	8.9	7.3	6.2	4.9	4.5	3.7
1959	5.9	13.5	14.4	13.0	5.2	8.1	5.9	5.1	4.2	4.1	2.8
1960	5.9	13.9	15.5	12.9	5.1	8.3	6.3	4.8	4.2	3.4	2.9
1961	7.2	16.3	18.3	15.1	6.3	9.8	7.4	6.4	5.1	4.5	4.0
1962	6.2	14.6	16.7	13.5	5.4	9.1	6.5	5.2	4.1	3.5	4.2
1963	6.5	17.2	20.2	15.2	5.4	8.9	6.9	5.1	4.2	3.6	3.2
1964	6.2	16.6	18.8	15.2	5.2	8.6	6.3	5.0	3.9	3.3	3.3
1965	5.5	15.7	17.2	14.8	4.5	7.3	5.5	4.6	3.2	2.8	2.9
1966	4.8	14.1	16.6	12.6	3.8	6.3	4.5	3.6	2.9	2.3	2.8
1967	5.2	13.5	14.8	12.8	4.2	7.0	5.4	4.1	3.1	2.4	2.7
1968	4.8	14.0	15.9	12.9	3.8	6.7	4.7	3.4	2.4	2.2	2.7
1969	4.7	13.3	15.5	11.8	3.7	6.3	4.6	3.4	2.6	2.2	2.3
1970	5.9	15.6	17.4	14.4	4.8	7.9	5.7	4.4	3.5	2.7	3.1
1971	6.9	17.2	18.7	16.2	5.7	9.6	7.0	5.2	4.0	3.3	3.6
1972	6.6	16.7	18.8	15.2	5.4	9.4	6.2	4.9	3.6	3.3	3.5
1973	6.0	15.3	17.7	13.5	4.9	8.5	5.8	3.9	3.2	2.8	2.9
1974	6.7	16.6	18.2	15.4	5.5	9.5	6.2	4.6	3.7	3.2	3.6
1975	9.3	19.7	21.2	18.7	8.0	12.7	9.1	6.8	5.9	5.1	5.0
1976	8.6	18.7	20.8	17.4	7.4	11.9	8.4	6.1	5.2	4.9	5.0
1977	8.2	18.3	20.5	16.9	7.0	11.2	7.7	5.7	5.1	4.4	4.7
1978	7.2	17.1	19.5	15.3	6.0	10.1	6.7	5.0	4.0	3.2	3.8
1979	6.8	16.4	18.3	15.0	5.7	9.6	6.5	4.6	3.9	3.2	3.3
1980	7.4	17.2	19.6	15.6	6.4	10.4	7.2	5.3	4.5	3.3	3.1
1981	7.9	19.0	20.7	17.9	6.8	11.2	7.7	5.7	4.6	3.8	3.6
1982	9.4	21.9	23.2	21.0	8.3	13.2	9.3	7.0	5.9	5.2	3.2
1983	9.2	21.3	23.7	19.9	8.1	12.9	9.1	6.9	6.0	5.0	3.4
1984	7.6	18.0	20.4	16.6	6.8	10.9	7.4	5.6	5.2	4.3	3.8
1985	7.4	17.6	20.0	16.0	6.6	10.7	7.4	5.5	4.8	4.3	3.3
1986	7.1	17.6	19.6	16.3	6.2	10.3	7.2	5.0	4.5	3.8	2.8
1987	6.2	15.9	18.0	14.3	5.4	9.4	6.2	4.6	3.7	3.1	2.4
1988	5.6	14.4	16.6	12.9	4.9	8.5	5.6	4.1	3.4	2.7	2.9
1989	5.4	14.0	15.7	13.0	4.7	8.3	5.6	3.9	3.2	2.8	2.9
1990	5.5	14.7	17.4	13.1	4.9	8.5	5.6	4.2	3.4	2.8	3.1
1991	6.4	17.5	20.2	15.9	5.7	9.8	6.8	4.8	4.2	3.4	3.3
1992	7.0	18.6	21.5	16.6	6.3	10.3	7.4	5.5	4.6	4.2	4.5
1993	6.6	17.5	19.8	16.1	5.9	9.7	6.8	5.3	4.5	4.0	3.1
1994	6.0	16.2	18.7	14.3	5.4	9.2	6.2	4.7	4.0	3.9	4.0
1995	5.6	16.1	19.2	14.0	4.9	9.0	5.7	4.4	3.2	3.6	3.7
1996	5.4	15.2	16.9	14.0	4.8	9.0	5.5	4.2	3.2	3.4	4.0
1997	5.0	15.0	17.2	13.6	4.4	8.1	5.2	4.0	2.9	2.7	3.6
1998	4.6	12.9	15.1	11.5	4.1	7.8	4.8	3.8	2.7	2.4	3.3
1999	4.3	13.2	15.5	11.6	3.8	7.2	4.4	3.3	2.5	2.6	3.2
2000	4.1	12.1	13.9	10.8	3.6	7.1	4.1	3.3	2.5	2.5	2.7
2001	4.7	13.4	15.2	12.2	4.1	7.5	5.1	3.7	3.0	2.7	2.9
2002	5.6	14.9	16.6	13.8	5.1	9.1	5.9	4.6	3.8	3.5	3.9
2003	5.7	15.6	17.5	14.2	5.1	9.3	5.9	4.9	3.7	3.7	3.6
2004	5.4	15.5	18.5	13.5	4.9	8.7	5.6	4.4	3.7	3.6	3.4

**Table 1-29. Unemployment Rates of Civilian Workers by Age, Sex, Race, and Hispanic Origin, 1948–2004
—Continued**

(Percent of labor force.)

Year, sex, race, and Hispanic origin	16 years and over	16 to 19 years			20 years and over						
		Total	16 to 17 years	18 to 19 years	Total	20 to 24 years	25 to 34 years	35 to 44 years	45 to 54 years	55 to 64 years	65 years and over
White[1]											
1954	5.0	12.1	13.2	11.3	4.6	8.3	4.6	4.0	4.0	4.3	3.9
1955	3.9	10.4	12.0	9.2	3.4	6.2	3.1	2.9	3.1	3.8	3.4
1956	3.6	10.1	11.5	9.0	3.2	5.7	3.1	2.6	2.9	3.2	3.1
1957	3.8	10.6	11.9	9.6	3.4	6.3	3.3	2.8	3.0	3.2	3.2
1958	6.1	14.4	15.2	13.9	5.6	9.9	5.9	4.8	4.8	4.9	4.6
1959	4.8	13.1	14.4	12.1	4.3	7.3	4.2	3.7	3.8	4.1	4.1
1960	5.0	13.5	14.6	12.6	4.3	7.9	4.5	3.6	3.8	3.9	3.7
1961	6.0	15.3	16.7	14.4	5.3	9.4	5.3	4.5	4.5	5.0	4.8
1962	4.9	13.3	15.3	12.0	4.2	7.9	4.2	3.6	3.6	3.9	4.0
1963	5.0	15.5	17.9	13.7	4.2	7.7	4.4	3.5	3.5	3.8	3.8
1964	4.6	14.8	16.5	13.3	3.8	7.3	3.6	3.2	3.2	3.5	3.5
1965	4.1	13.4	14.8	12.3	3.3	6.1	3.2	2.9	2.5	2.9	3.2
1966	3.4	11.2	13.3	9.7	2.6	4.6	2.6	2.3	2.1	2.4	2.9
1967	3.4	11.0	12.8	9.8	2.7	5.0	2.7	2.3	2.2	2.3	2.7
1968	3.2	11.0	12.9	9.6	2.5	5.2	2.4	2.0	1.8	1.9	2.8
1969	3.1	10.7	13.0	8.9	2.4	5.0	2.5	2.0	1.8	1.8	2.2
1970	4.5	13.5	15.5	11.9	3.7	7.3	3.8	3.0	2.7	2.7	3.2
1971	5.4	15.1	17.0	13.8	4.5	9.0	4.7	3.6	3.3	3.3	3.5
1972	5.1	14.2	16.6	12.3	4.1	8.4	4.1	3.2	2.9	3.1	3.4
1973	4.3	12.6	15.4	10.4	3.5	6.8	3.7	2.5	2.4	2.5	2.9
1974	5.0	14.0	16.3	12.2	4.1	8.0	4.4	3.1	2.8	2.8	3.3
1975	7.8	17.9	19.5	16.7	6.7	12.3	7.1	5.2	4.9	4.5	5.1
1976	7.0	16.9	19.0	15.3	5.9	10.7	6.3	4.5	4.2	4.3	4.9
1977	6.2	15.4	17.9	13.5	5.3	9.3	5.7	4.0	3.8	3.7	4.9
1978	5.2	13.9	17.0	11.5	4.3	8.0	4.6	3.3	3.0	2.7	3.8
1979	5.1	14.0	16.1	12.4	4.2	7.6	4.4	3.2	3.0	2.7	3.1
1980	6.3	15.5	17.9	13.8	5.4	9.9	6.1	4.2	3.7	3.1	2.7
1981	6.7	17.3	19.2	15.9	5.7	10.4	6.3	4.5	3.9	3.5	2.8
1982	8.6	20.4	22.8	18.8	7.6	12.8	8.5	6.3	5.4	5.1	3.1
1983	8.4	19.3	22.0	17.6	7.5	12.1	8.4	6.3	5.7	5.2	3.2
1984	6.5	16.0	18.8	14.3	5.7	9.3	6.2	4.8	4.4	4.4	3.0
1985	6.2	15.7	18.3	13.9	5.5	9.2	5.9	4.6	4.3	4.0	2.9
1986	6.0	15.6	17.6	14.1	5.3	8.7	5.9	4.5	4.1	3.8	2.9
1987	5.3	14.4	16.7	12.7	4.7	8.0	5.1	4.0	3.7	3.2	2.4
1988	4.7	13.1	15.3	11.6	4.1	7.1	4.5	3.5	3.1	3.0	2.4
1989	4.5	12.7	15.2	11.1	3.9	7.2	4.3	3.3	2.9	3.0	2.3
1990	4.8	13.5	15.8	12.1	4.3	7.3	4.6	3.6	3.3	3.2	2.8
1991	6.1	16.5	19.0	14.9	5.5	9.2	6.1	4.7	4.2	4.0	3.1
1992	6.6	17.2	20.3	15.2	6.0	9.5	6.7	5.2	4.8	4.9	3.7
1993	6.1	16.2	19.0	14.4	5.5	8.8	6.0	4.9	4.5	4.3	3.0
1994	5.3	15.1	17.6	13.3	4.7	8.1	5.2	4.0	3.7	3.9	3.8
1995	4.9	14.5	17.3	12.5	4.3	7.7	4.6	3.9	3.1	3.5	3.8
1996	4.7	14.2	16.4	12.6	4.1	7.8	4.4	3.6	3.1	3.2	3.5
1997	4.2	13.6	15.8	12.0	3.6	6.9	3.9	3.3	2.7	2.7	3.0
1998	3.9	12.6	14.8	11.0	3.3	6.5	3.7	2.9	2.6	2.4	2.9
1999	3.7	12.0	14.5	10.2	3.1	6.3	3.3	2.7	2.4	2.5	2.9
2000	3.5	11.4	13.9	9.8	3.0	5.9	3.2	2.6	2.2	2.4	2.8
2001	4.2	12.7	15.3	11.0	3.7	7.0	4.1	3.2	2.8	2.9	2.8
2002	5.1	14.5	16.7	13.2	4.6	8.1	5.2	4.1	3.7	3.7	3.5
2003	5.2	15.2	17.2	13.9	4.7	8.4	5.3	4.3	3.7	3.8	3.7
2004	4.8	15.0	17.9	13.1	4.3	7.9	4.7	3.9	3.4	3.6	3.3

[1]Beginning in 2003, persons who selected this race group only; persons who selected more than one race group are not included. Prior to 2003, persons who reported more than one race group were included in the group they identified as the main race.

Table 1-29. Unemployment Rates of Civilian Workers by Age, Sex, Race, and Hispanic Origin, 1948–2004
—Continued

(Percent of labor force.)

Year, sex, race, and Hispanic origin	16 years and over	16 to 19 years			20 years and over						
		Total	16 to 17 years	18 to 19 years	Total	20 to 24 years	25 to 34 years	35 to 44 years	45 to 54 years	55 to 64 years	65 years and over
Black[1]											
1972	10.4	35.4	38.7	33.6	7.9	16.3	8.7	6.1	4.2	4.1	4.3
1973	9.4	31.5	37.0	28.1	7.2	15.5	8.1	4.7	3.5	3.2	3.5
1974	10.5	35.0	40.0	31.8	8.0	17.5	8.5	5.4	4.3	3.6	3.9
1975	14.8	39.5	41.6	38.1	12.3	24.5	13.0	8.9	8.3	5.9	6.6
1976	14.0	39.3	44.2	36.7	11.5	22.7	12.8	8.0	6.7	5.9	5.9
1977	14.0	41.1	44.5	39.2	11.5	24.2	12.7	7.4	5.3	5.5	5.9
1978	12.8	38.7	43.9	35.7	10.2	21.8	10.8	6.4	5.2	4.8	5.8
1979	12.3	36.5	40.2	34.4	10.1	20.6	10.8	6.7	5.2	4.9	5.3
1980	14.3	38.5	41.1	37.1	12.1	23.6	13.3	8.2	6.8	5.4	6.9
1981	15.6	41.4	44.8	39.5	13.4	26.4	14.7	9.5	7.4	5.5	7.0
1982	18.9	48.0	48.6	47.8	16.6	30.6	19.0	12.1	8.7	8.3	7.1
1983	19.5	48.5	50.5	47.6	17.3	31.6	19.0	12.4	10.7	9.2	9.2
1984	15.9	42.7	45.7	41.2	13.9	26.1	15.2	9.9	8.2	7.4	6.5
1985	15.1	40.2	43.6	38.3	13.1	24.5	14.5	9.5	8.2	7.0	7.0
1986	14.5	39.3	43.0	37.2	12.7	24.1	14.0	9.6	7.1	6.6	4.5
1987	13.0	34.7	39.7	31.6	11.3	21.8	12.8	8.4	6.8	5.6	3.9
1988	11.7	32.4	35.1	30.7	10.2	19.6	11.9	7.5	5.9	4.8	5.5
1989	11.4	32.4	32.9	32.2	9.9	18.0	11.5	7.6	5.6	5.2	6.9
1990	11.4	30.9	36.5	27.8	10.1	19.9	11.7	7.8	5.3	4.6	5.3
1991	12.5	36.1	39.5	34.4	11.1	21.6	12.7	8.5	7.4	4.4	5.2
1992	14.2	39.7	44.7	37.1	12.6	23.8	14.2	10.5	8.3	6.2	4.9
1993	13.0	38.8	39.7	38.4	11.4	21.9	12.6	9.5	6.9	7.1	4.7
1994	11.5	35.2	36.1	34.6	10.0	19.5	11.1	8.5	5.6	5.4	6.2
1995	10.4	35.7	39.1	33.4	8.7	17.7	9.9	7.3	4.8	4.0	6.7
1996	10.5	33.6	36.3	31.7	9.0	18.8	10.5	7.3	5.0	4.4	5.3
1997	10.0	32.4	35.0	30.8	8.6	18.3	9.9	7.0	5.0	4.2	6.1
1998	8.9	27.6	33.6	24.2	7.7	16.8	8.4	6.5	4.4	3.9	5.6
1999	8.0	27.9	31.0	26.2	6.8	14.6	7.6	5.3	4.0	3.9	5.0
2000	7.6	24.5	26.9	22.9	6.5	15.0	6.7	5.6	4.1	3.0	6.1
2001	8.6	29.0	30.8	27.9	7.4	16.3	8.1	6.3	4.8	3.9	4.3
2002	10.2	29.8	34.9	27.2	9.1	19.1	9.9	7.8	6.3	5.4	5.9
2003	10.8	33.0	32.2	33.5	9.7	19.8	10.9	8.6	6.2	6.3	5.4
2004	10.4	31.7	37.8	28.3	9.4	18.4	10.8	7.8	6.9	5.6	5.5
Hispanic											
1973	7.5	19.7	23.4	17.3	6.0	8.5	5.7	5.6	4.7	5.5	3.9
1974	8.1	19.8	23.5	17.2	6.6	9.8	6.3	5.9	4.6	6.1	6.3
1975	12.2	27.7	30.0	26.5	10.3	16.7	9.9	8.6	8.1	7.7	9.9
1976	11.5	23.8	29.2	19.2	10.1	15.9	9.1	8.2	8.4	8.8	12.6
1977	10.1	22.9	27.0	19.6	8.5	12.0	8.6	6.1	7.3	8.2	9.2
1978	9.1	20.7	28.3	15.1	7.7	10.9	8.0	6.5	5.8	5.0	7.5
1979	8.3	19.2	26.0	14.9	7.0	10.4	6.7	6.2	5.2	6.0	5.7
1980	10.1	22.5	27.6	19.5	8.6	12.1	9.1	7.7	5.7	5.9	6.0
1981	10.4	23.9	28.0	21.7	9.1	13.9	8.8	7.4	6.4	7.3	5.4
1982	13.8	29.9	38.1	25.9	12.3	17.7	12.3	10.7	8.4	10.1	6.5
1983	13.7	28.4	33.8	25.8	12.3	16.7	11.9	11.3	10.0	10.9	5.8
1984	10.7	24.1	28.9	21.6	9.5	12.4	9.7	8.2	7.5	9.7	6.1
1985	10.5	24.3	27.8	22.5	9.4	12.6	9.9	7.7	7.4	7.8	8.1
1986	10.6	24.7	28.1	22.9	9.5	12.9	9.6	8.4	7.8	7.3	10.1
1987	8.8	22.3	27.7	19.5	7.8	10.6	7.7	6.7	6.9	6.0	6.5
1988	8.2	22.0	27.1	19.3	7.0	9.8	7.1	6.0	6.0	5.8	5.6
1989	8.0	19.4	26.4	16.0	7.2	10.7	7.0	5.9	6.3	5.8	5.3
1990	8.2	19.5	24.5	16.9	7.2	9.1	7.3	6.6	6.4	5.6	6.0
1991	10.0	22.9	31.9	18.7	9.0	11.6	9.2	8.1	8.0	6.5	7.0
1992	11.6	27.5	35.7	23.4	10.4	13.2	10.4	9.8	8.8	8.6	8.1
1993	10.8	26.1	35.1	21.8	9.7	13.1	9.3	9.1	8.6	8.0	6.6
1994	9.9	24.5	31.7	20.6	8.9	11.8	9.0	7.7	8.1	7.3	7.9
1995	9.3	24.1	33.1	19.5	8.2	11.5	8.2	7.2	6.4	7.5	10.6
1996	8.9	23.6	30.0	20.3	7.8	11.8	7.3	7.3	6.0	7.3	8.2
1997	7.7	21.6	27.7	18.4	6.8	10.3	6.3	6.4	5.1	6.5	6.8
1998	7.2	21.3	28.0	18.1	6.1	9.4	5.9	5.5	4.6	5.3	6.4
1999	6.4	18.6	23.7	16.3	5.5	8.3	5.4	4.8	4.8	4.5	5.0
2000	5.7	16.6	22.5	13.9	4.9	7.5	4.8	4.5	3.3	4.5	5.7
2001	6.6	17.7	24.0	15.0	5.8	8.1	5.9	5.2	4.3	5.6	4.5
2002	7.5	20.1	24.2	18.2	6.7	9.9	6.6	6.0	5.5	5.7	6.8
2003	7.7	20.0	24.6	17.7	7.0	10.2	7.0	6.0	6.3	5.7	3.9
2004	7.0	20.4	29.0	16.8	6.2	9.3	6.3	5.3	5.2	5.8	6.0

[1]Beginning in 2003, persons who selected this race group only; persons who selected more than one race group are not included. Prior to 2003, persons who reported more than one race group were included in the group they identified as the main race.

Table 1-29. Unemployment Rates of Civilian Workers by Age, Sex, Race, and Hispanic Origin, 1948–2004
—Continued

(Percent of labor force.)

Year, sex, race, and Hispanic origin	16 years and over	16 to 19 years			20 years and over						
		Total	16 to 17 years	18 to 19 years	Total	20 to 24 years	25 to 34 years	35 to 44 years	45 to 54 years	55 to 64 years	65 years and over
White Men[1]											
1954	4.8	13.4	14.0	13.0	4.4	9.8	4.2	3.6	3.8	4.3	4.2
1955	3.7	11.3	12.2	10.4	3.3	7.0	2.7	2.6	2.9	3.9	3.8
1956	3.4	10.5	11.2	9.7	3.0	6.1	2.8	2.2	2.8	3.1	3.4
1957	3.6	11.5	11.9	11.1	3.2	7.0	2.7	2.5	3.0	3.4	3.2
1958	6.1	15.7	14.9	16.5	5.5	11.7	5.6	4.4	4.8	5.2	5.0
1959	4.6	14.0	15.0	13.0	4.1	7.5	3.8	3.2	3.7	4.2	4.5
1960	4.8	14.0	14.6	13.5	4.2	8.3	4.1	3.3	3.6	4.1	4.0
1961	5.7	15.7	16.5	15.2	5.1	10.1	4.9	4.0	4.4	5.3	5.2
1962	4.6	13.7	15.2	12.7	4.0	8.1	3.8	3.1	3.5	4.1	4.0
1963	4.7	15.9	17.8	14.2	3.9	7.8	3.9	2.9	3.3	4.0	4.1
1964	4.1	14.7	16.1	13.3	3.4	7.4	3.0	2.5	2.9	3.5	3.6
1965	3.6	12.9	14.7	11.3	2.9	5.9	2.6	2.3	2.3	3.1	3.4
1966	2.8	10.5	12.5	8.9	2.2	4.1	2.1	1.7	1.7	2.5	3.0
1967	2.7	10.7	12.7	9.0	2.1	4.2	1.9	1.6	1.8	2.2	2.7
1968	2.6	10.1	12.3	8.3	2.0	4.6	1.7	1.4	1.5	1.7	2.8
1969	2.5	10.0	12.5	7.9	1.9	4.6	1.7	1.4	1.4	1.7	2.2
1970	4.0	13.7	15.7	12.0	3.2	7.8	3.1	2.3	2.3	2.7	3.2
1971	4.9	15.1	17.1	13.5	4.0	9.4	4.0	2.9	2.9	3.2	3.4
1972	4.5	14.2	16.4	12.4	3.6	8.5	3.4	2.5	2.5	3.0	3.3
1973	3.8	12.3	15.2	10.0	3.0	6.6	3.0	1.8	2.0	2.4	2.9
1974	4.4	13.5	16.2	11.5	3.5	7.8	3.6	2.4	2.2	2.5	3.0
1975	7.2	18.3	19.7	17.2	6.2	13.1	6.3	4.5	4.4	4.1	5.0
1976	6.4	17.3	19.7	15.5	5.4	10.9	5.6	3.7	3.7	4.0	4.7
1977	5.5	15.0	17.6	13.0	4.7	9.3	5.0	3.1	3.0	3.3	4.9
1978	4.6	13.5	16.9	10.8	3.7	7.7	3.8	2.5	2.5	2.6	3.9
1979	4.5	13.9	16.1	12.2	3.6	7.5	3.7	2.5	2.5	2.5	3.2
1980	6.1	16.2	18.5	14.5	5.3	11.1	5.9	3.6	3.3	3.1	2.5
1981	6.5	17.9	19.9	16.4	5.6	11.6	6.1	4.0	3.6	3.4	2.4
1982	8.8	21.7	24.2	20.0	7.8	14.3	8.9	6.2	5.3	5.1	3.2
1983	8.8	20.2	22.6	18.7	7.9	13.8	9.0	6.4	5.7	5.6	3.2
1984	6.4	16.8	19.7	15.0	5.7	9.8	6.2	4.6	4.2	4.7	2.6
1985	6.1	16.5	19.2	14.7	5.4	9.7	5.7	4.3	4.1	4.0	2.7
1986	6.0	16.3	18.4	14.7	5.3	9.2	5.8	4.4	4.0	4.0	3.0
1987	5.4	15.5	17.9	13.7	4.8	8.4	5.2	3.9	3.9	3.4	2.5
1988	4.7	13.9	16.1	12.4	4.1	7.4	4.6	3.4	3.2	3.3	2.2
1989	4.5	13.7	16.4	12.0	3.9	7.5	4.1	3.2	2.9	3.1	2.1
1990	4.9	14.3	16.1	13.2	4.3	7.6	4.7	3.5	3.4	3.6	2.8
1991	6.5	17.6	19.7	16.3	5.8	10.2	6.4	5.0	4.4	4.6	3.1
1992	7.0	18.5	21.5	16.5	6.4	10.5	7.0	5.5	5.1	5.5	3.2
1993	6.3	17.7	20.2	16.0	5.7	9.6	6.2	5.0	4.7	4.7	2.9
1994	5.4	16.3	18.5	14.7	4.8	8.8	5.2	3.9	3.7	4.1	3.7
1995	4.9	15.6	18.2	13.8	4.3	7.9	4.5	3.8	3.2	3.4	4.0
1996	4.7	15.5	18.3	13.5	4.1	8.1	4.2	3.5	3.1	3.2	3.2
1997	4.2	14.3	16.3	12.9	3.6	7.3	3.7	3.2	2.8	3.0	2.7
1998	3.9	14.1	17.1	12.1	3.2	6.7	3.5	2.6	2.6	2.6	2.9
1999	3.6	12.6	15.1	10.8	3.0	6.5	3.1	2.4	2.4	2.6	2.9
2000	3.4	12.3	15.3	10.4	2.8	5.9	2.9	2.4	2.2	2.4	3.0
2001	4.2	13.9	17.4	11.7	3.7	7.8	3.8	3.1	2.9	3.2	2.8
2002	5.3	15.9	18.8	14.2	4.7	8.7	5.3	4.1	3.8	4.0	3.4
2003	5.6	17.1	18.5	16.1	5.0	9.1	5.5	4.4	4.0	4.2	3.8
2004	5.0	16.3	19.8	14.2	4.4	8.5	4.8	3.8	3.5	3.7	3.5

[1]Beginning in 2003, persons who selected this race group only; persons who selected more than one race group are not included. Prior to 2003, persons who reported more than one race group were included in the group they identified as the main race.

Table 1-29. Unemployment Rates of Civilian Workers by Age, Sex, Race, and Hispanic Origin, 1948–2004
—Continued

(Percent of labor force.)

Year, sex, race, and Hispanic origin	16 years and over	16 to 19 years			20 years and over						
		Total	16 to 17 years	18 to 19 years	Total	20 to 24 years	25 to 34 years	35 to 44 years	45 to 54 years	55 to 64 years	65 years and over
White Women[1]											
1954	5.5	10.4	12.0	9.4	5.1	6.4	5.7	4.9	4.4	4.5	2.8
1955	4.3	9.1	11.6	7.7	3.9	5.1	4.3	3.8	3.4	3.6	2.2
1956	4.2	9.7	12.1	8.3	3.7	5.1	4.0	3.5	3.3	3.5	2.3
1957	4.3	9.5	11.9	7.8	3.8	5.1	4.7	3.7	3.0	2.9	3.4
1958	6.2	12.7	15.6	11.0	5.6	7.3	6.6	5.6	4.9	4.3	3.5
1959	5.3	12.0	13.3	11.1	4.7	7.0	5.2	4.7	3.9	4.0	2.9
1960	5.3	12.7	14.5	11.5	4.6	7.2	5.7	4.2	4.0	3.3	2.8
1961	6.5	14.8	17.0	13.6	5.7	8.4	6.6	5.6	4.8	4.3	3.8
1962	5.5	12.8	15.6	11.3	4.7	7.7	5.4	4.5	3.7	3.5	4.0
1963	5.8	15.1	18.1	13.2	4.8	7.4	5.8	4.6	3.9	3.5	3.3
1964	5.5	14.9	17.1	13.2	4.6	7.1	5.2	4.5	3.6	3.5	3.4
1965	5.0	14.0	15.0	13.4	4.0	6.3	4.9	4.1	3.0	2.7	2.7
1966	4.3	12.1	14.5	10.7	3.3	5.3	3.7	3.3	2.7	2.2	2.7
1967	4.6	11.5	12.9	10.6	3.8	6.0	4.7	3.7	2.9	2.3	2.6
1968	4.3	12.1	13.9	11.0	3.4	5.9	3.9	3.1	2.3	2.1	2.8
1969	4.2	11.5	13.7	10.0	3.4	5.5	4.2	3.2	2.4	2.1	2.4
1970	5.4	13.4	15.3	11.9	4.4	6.9	5.3	4.3	3.4	2.6	3.3
1971	6.3	15.1	16.7	14.1	5.3	8.5	6.3	4.9	3.9	3.3	3.6
1972	5.9	14.2	17.0	12.3	4.9	8.2	5.5	4.4	3.5	3.3	3.7
1973	5.3	13.0	15.8	10.9	4.3	7.1	5.1	3.7	3.2	2.7	2.8
1974	6.1	14.5	16.4	13.0	5.1	8.2	5.8	4.3	3.6	3.2	3.9
1975	8.6	17.4	19.2	16.1	7.5	11.2	8.4	6.5	5.8	5.0	5.3
1976	7.9	16.4	18.2	15.1	6.8	10.4	7.6	5.8	5.0	4.8	5.3
1977	7.3	15.9	18.2	14.2	6.2	9.3	6.7	5.3	5.0	4.4	4.9
1978	6.2	14.4	17.1	12.4	5.2	8.3	5.8	4.5	3.8	3.0	3.7
1979	5.9	14.0	15.9	12.5	5.0	7.8	5.6	4.2	3.7	3.0	3.1
1980	6.5	14.8	17.3	13.1	5.6	8.5	6.3	4.9	4.3	3.1	3.0
1981	6.9	16.6	18.4	15.3	5.9	9.1	6.6	5.1	4.2	3.7	3.4
1982	8.3	19.0	21.2	17.6	7.3	10.9	8.0	6.4	5.5	5.0	3.1
1983	7.9	18.3	21.4	16.4	6.9	10.3	7.6	6.2	5.5	4.7	3.1
1984	6.5	15.2	17.8	13.6	5.8	8.8	6.1	5.0	4.8	4.0	3.7
1985	6.4	14.8	17.2	13.1	5.7	8.5	6.2	4.9	4.5	4.1	3.1
1986	6.1	14.9	16.7	13.6	5.4	8.1	6.1	4.5	4.3	3.7	2.6
1987	5.2	13.4	15.5	11.7	4.6	7.4	5.0	4.1	3.3	2.9	2.4
1988	4.7	12.3	14.4	10.8	4.1	6.7	4.5	3.7	3.1	2.5	2.6
1989	4.5	11.5	13.8	10.1	4.0	6.8	4.5	3.4	2.9	2.7	2.5
1990	4.7	12.6	15.5	10.9	4.1	6.8	4.6	3.7	3.2	2.7	2.8
1991	5.6	15.2	18.2	13.3	5.0	8.1	5.7	4.3	4.0	3.3	3.1
1992	6.1	15.8	18.9	13.7	5.5	8.3	6.2	4.9	4.3	4.0	4.5
1993	5.7	14.7	17.8	12.6	5.2	7.9	5.8	4.7	4.3	3.9	3.0
1994	5.2	13.8	16.6	11.8	4.6	7.4	5.1	4.2	3.7	3.7	3.9
1995	4.8	13.4	16.4	11.2	4.3	7.4	4.7	3.9	3.0	3.5	3.5
1996	4.7	12.9	14.4	11.7	4.1	7.4	4.6	3.8	3.1	3.1	3.8
1997	4.2	12.8	15.2	11.1	3.7	6.4	4.2	3.4	2.6	2.4	3.4
1998	3.9	10.9	12.4	9.8	3.4	6.3	3.9	3.3	2.5	2.2	3.0
1999	3.8	11.3	13.9	9.6	3.3	6.1	3.6	3.0	2.3	2.5	2.9
2000	3.6	10.4	12.5	9.0	3.1	5.8	3.5	2.9	2.3	2.4	2.4
2001	4.1	11.4	13.1	10.2	3.6	6.1	4.5	3.3	2.7	2.5	2.7
2002	4.9	13.1	14.6	12.1	4.4	7.4	5.0	4.1	3.5	3.3	3.5
2003	4.8	13.3	15.9	11.5	4.4	7.6	4.9	4.2	3.3	3.4	3.5
2004	4.7	13.6	16.1	11.9	4.2	7.1	4.6	3.9	3.3	3.5	3.1

[1]Beginning in 2003, persons who selected this race group only; persons who selected more than one race group are not included. Prior to 2003, persons who reported more than one race group were included in the group they identified as the main race.

Table 1-29. Unemployment Rates of Civilian Workers by Age, Sex, Race, and Hispanic Origin, 1948–2004
    —*Continued*

(Percent of labor force.)

Year, sex, race, and Hispanic origin	16 years and over	16 to 19 years			20 years and over						
		Total	16 to 17 years	18 to 19 years	Total	20 to 24 years	25 to 34 years	35 to 44 years	45 to 54 years	55 to 64 years	65 years and over
Black Men[1]											
1972	9.3	31.7	36.7	28.4	7.0	14.9	7.2	4.8	3.8	4.4	5.4
1973	8.0	27.8	35.7	23.0	6.0	13.2	6.2	3.9	3.2	3.2	3.3
1974	9.8	33.1	39.9	28.3	7.4	16.2	8.1	4.3	4.2	3.6	5.3
1975	14.8	38.1	41.9	35.9	12.5	24.7	12.7	8.7	9.3	6.3	8.7
1976	13.7	37.5	40.8	36.0	11.4	22.6	12.0	7.5	7.3	6.3	8.7
1977	13.3	39.2	41.0	38.2	10.7	23.0	11.8	6.2	4.9	6.0	7.8
1978	11.8	36.7	43.0	32.9	9.3	21.0	9.8	5.1	4.9	4.4	6.6
1979	11.4	34.2	37.9	32.2	9.3	18.7	9.6	6.3	5.2	5.1	6.4
1980	14.5	37.5	39.7	36.2	12.4	23.7	13.4	8.2	7.2	6.2	8.7
1981	15.7	40.7	43.2	39.2	13.5	26.4	14.4	9.3	7.8	6.1	7.5
1982	20.1	48.9	52.7	47.1	17.8	31.5	20.1	13.4	9.0	10.3	9.3
1983	20.3	48.8	52.2	47.3	18.1	31.4	19.4	13.5	11.4	11.0	11.8
1984	16.4	42.7	44.0	42.2	14.3	26.6	15.0	10.4	7.9	8.9	7.9
1985	15.3	41.0	42.9	40.0	13.2	23.5	13.8	9.6	9.7	7.9	8.9
1986	14.8	39.3	41.4	38.2	12.9	23.5	13.5	10.9	7.8	8.0	4.3
1987	12.7	34.4	39.0	31.6	11.1	20.3	12.2	8.7	6.7	6.6	4.3
1988	11.7	32.7	34.4	31.7	10.1	19.4	11.0	7.6	6.2	5.2	5.6
1989	11.5	31.9	34.4	30.3	10.0	17.9	10.5	8.4	6.2	6.2	7.4
1990	11.9	31.9	38.8	28.0	10.4	20.1	11.5	8.4	6.3	5.4	4.6
1991	13.0	36.3	39.0	34.8	11.5	22.4	11.9	9.5	8.6	5.0	6.1
1992	15.2	42.0	47.5	39.1	13.5	24.6	14.2	11.2	10.3	8.1	4.9
1993	13.8	40.1	42.7	38.6	12.1	23.0	12.3	10.5	8.1	9.0	5.8
1994	12.0	37.6	39.3	36.5	10.3	19.4	10.6	9.1	6.5	6.0	8.2
1995	10.6	37.1	39.7	35.4	8.8	17.6	9.3	7.6	5.5	4.4	7.6
1996	11.1	36.9	39.9	34.9	9.4	19.2	10.1	7.8	6.3	5.2	5.0
1997	10.2	36.5	39.5	34.4	8.5	19.8	8.7	6.7	5.6	4.2	5.5
1998	8.9	30.1	33.9	27.9	7.4	18.0	7.3	6.2	4.4	4.5	5.2
1999	8.2	30.9	33.3	29.4	6.7	16.2	6.9	5.2	4.3	3.9	5.0
2000	8.0	26.2	28.5	24.7	6.9	16.6	6.7	5.8	4.8	2.7	6.3
2001	9.3	30.4	30.5	30.4	8.0	17.6	8.3	6.9	5.5	4.8	4.0
2002	10.7	31.3	36.6	28.7	9.5	20.0	9.4	8.0	7.4	6.1	5.0
2003	11.6	36.0	35.6	36.3	10.3	20.9	11.3	9.2	6.7	6.8	5.6
2004	11.1	35.6	40.8	32.7	9.9	20.3	10.9	8.0	7.2	6.4	4.2
Black Women[1]											
1972	11.8	40.5	42.0	40.1	9.0	17.9	10.5	7.6	4.6	3.7	2.6
1973	11.1	36.1	38.6	34.2	8.6	18.4	10.3	5.6	3.9	3.3	3.7
1974	11.3	37.4	40.2	36.0	8.8	19.0	9.0	6.6	4.4	3.6	1.9
1975	14.8	41.0	41.2	40.6	12.2	24.3	13.4	9.0	7.0	5.3	3.6
1976	14.3	41.6	48.4	37.6	11.7	22.8	13.6	8.5	5.9	5.4	2.4
1977	14.9	43.4	49.5	40.4	12.3	25.5	13.6	8.7	5.8	4.8	3.4
1978	13.8	40.8	45.0	38.7	11.2	22.7	11.9	7.8	5.6	5.2	4.7
1979	13.3	39.1	42.7	36.9	10.9	22.6	12.1	7.2	5.2	4.7	3.9
1980	14.0	39.8	42.9	38.2	11.9	23.5	13.2	8.2	6.4	4.5	4.9
1981	15.6	42.2	46.5	39.8	13.4	26.4	14.9	9.8	6.9	4.7	6.0
1982	17.6	47.1	44.2	48.6	15.4	29.6	17.8	10.7	8.5	6.1	4.5
1983	18.6	48.2	48.6	48.0	16.5	31.8	18.6	11.4	9.9	7.3	6.3
1984	15.4	42.6	47.5	40.2	13.5	25.6	15.4	9.4	8.6	5.9	4.9
1985	14.9	39.2	44.3	36.4	13.1	25.6	15.1	9.3	6.8	6.0	5.2
1986	14.2	39.2	44.6	36.1	12.4	24.7	14.6	8.5	6.4	5.0	4.9
1987	13.2	34.9	40.5	31.7	11.6	23.3	13.5	8.1	6.9	4.5	3.4
1988	11.7	32.0	35.9	29.6	10.4	19.8	12.7	7.4	5.6	4.3	5.4
1989	11.4	33.0	31.1	34.0	9.8	18.1	12.5	7.0	5.0	4.2	6.4
1990	10.9	29.9	34.1	27.6	9.7	19.6	11.9	7.2	4.3	3.6	5.9
1991	12.0	36.0	40.1	33.9	10.6	20.7	13.4	7.6	6.2	3.8	4.4
1992	13.2	37.2	41.7	34.8	11.8	23.1	14.1	9.8	6.4	4.2	5.0
1993	12.1	37.4	36.1	38.1	10.7	20.9	12.9	8.6	5.8	5.1	3.6
1994	11.0	32.6	32.9	32.5	9.8	19.6	11.7	8.0	4.9	4.9	4.4
1995	10.2	34.3	38.5	31.5	8.6	17.8	10.5	7.0	4.2	3.6	. . .
1996	10.0	30.3	32.8	28.6	8.7	18.4	11.0	6.9	3.8	3.8	5.6
1997	9.9	28.7	30.3	27.8	8.8	17.1	10.9	7.2	4.4	4.1	6.6
1998	9.0	25.3	33.2	20.9	7.9	15.7	9.5	6.7	4.3	3.4	6.1
1999	7.8	25.1	28.5	23.3	6.8	13.4	8.3	5.5	3.8	3.9	5.0
2000	7.1	22.8	25.3	21.3	6.2	13.6	6.8	5.5	3.4	3.3	6.0
2001	8.1	27.5	31.2	25.4	7.0	15.3	8.0	5.8	4.3	3.1	4.6
2002	9.8	28.3	33.2	25.6	8.8	18.3	10.2	7.7	5.3	4.7	6.9
2003	10.2	30.3	29.1	31.1	9.2	18.8	10.5	8.1	5.8	5.9	5.3
2004	9.8	28.2	35.2	24.3	8.9	16.6	10.7	7.6	6.5	4.8	6.8

[1]Beginning in 2003, persons who selected this race group only; persons who selected more than one race group are not included. Prior to 2003, persons who reported more than one race group were included in the group they identified as the main race.
. . . = Not available.

Table 1-29. Unemployment Rates of Civilian Workers by Age, Sex, Race, and Hispanic Origin, 1948–2004
—Continued

(Percent of labor force.)

Year, sex, race, and Hispanic origin	16 years and over	16 to 19 years			20 years and over						
		Total	16 to 17 years	18 to 19 years	Total	20 to 24 years	25 to 34 years	35 to 44 years	45 to 54 years	55 to 64 years	65 years and over
Hispanic Men											
1973	6.7	19.0	20.9	17.7	5.4	8.2	5.0	4.2	4.5	5.4	. . .
1974	7.3	19.0	22.0	17.1	6.0	9.9	5.5	5.0	4.3	5.4	. . .
1975	11.4	27.6	29.3	26.5	9.6	16.3	9.6	7.9	7.0	6.8	. . .
1976	10.8	23.3	28.7	19.7	9.4	16.0	8.1	7.0	7.4	8.7	. . .
1977	9.0	20.9	25.9	18.2	7.7	11.7	7.9	4.9	5.4	7.4	. . .
1978	7.7	19.7	27.5	13.9	6.4	9.4	6.6	4.8	4.8	4.4	. . .
1979	7.0	17.5	23.5	13.8	5.8	9.2	5.3	5.1	4.4	5.0	. . .
1980	9.7	21.9	26.2	19.3	8.3	12.2	8.3	7.1	6.0	5.9	. . .
1981	10.2	24.3	30.9	20.3	8.8	14.1	8.9	6.5	5.9	6.7	. . .
1982	13.6	31.3	40.2	26.8	12.1	18.2	12.4	9.9	7.5	10.0	. . .
1983	13.6	28.7	34.7	25.9	12.2	17.0	11.6	10.8	10.3	11.7	. . .
1984	10.5	25.2	31.5	22.2	9.3	12.5	9.2	7.6	7.2	10.2	. . .
1985	10.2	24.7	29.1	22.4	9.1	12.9	9.6	7.2	6.8	7.0	. . .
1986	10.5	24.5	28.5	22.4	9.5	13.0	9.5	8.5	7.0	8.0	. . .
1987	8.7	22.2	28.2	19.3	7.8	10.2	7.6	6.9	7.1	6.7	. . .
1988	8.1	22.7	29.5	19.5	7.0	9.2	7.0	5.9	6.1	6.7	. . .
1989	7.6	20.2	27.6	16.8	6.6	9.7	5.9	5.7	6.0	6.6	. . .
1990	8.0	19.5	24.0	17.4	7.0	8.4	6.9	6.5	6.8	6.5	. . .
1991	10.3	23.5	33.6	19.2	9.3	11.6	9.3	8.5	7.9	8.1	. . .
1992	11.7	28.2	36.6	24.0	10.5	13.7	10.1	9.8	8.9	10.2	. . .
1993	10.6	25.9	34.5	21.9	9.5	12.6	9.0	8.8	8.8	8.5	. . .
1994	9.4	26.3	33.3	22.5	8.3	10.8	8.4	6.6	8.1	7.4	10.5
1995	8.8	25.3	34.8	20.2	7.7	10.6	7.5	6.7	5.9	7.9	12.9
1996	7.9	22.5	31.5	18.4	6.9	10.3	6.6	6.3	5.1	6.7	8.3
1997	7.0	20.8	26.5	17.9	6.1	9.8	5.1	5.4	4.8	6.8	7.2
1998	6.4	20.6	29.0	16.4	5.4	8.9	5.2	4.5	4.2	5.3	5.0
1999	5.6	17.8	23.4	15.3	4.7	7.8	4.1	3.8	4.5	4.6	5.0
2000	5.0	15.7	22.3	12.8	4.2	6.6	3.7	3.8	3.1	4.1	6.2
2001	5.9	17.1	25.8	13.4	5.2	8.1	4.6	4.5	3.8	6.3	4.8
2002	7.2	20.2	22.9	19.1	6.4	9.3	6.1	5.4	5.5	6.2	6.3
2003	7.2	21.9	25.9	20.1	6.4	9.6	6.3	5.3	6.0	6.0	3.6
2004	6.5	21.2	30.7	17.6	5.8	9.4	5.5	4.5	4.7	5.7	6.9
Hispanic Women											
1973	9.0	20.7	26.8	16.7	7.3	9.0	6.9	8.3	5.1	5.6	. . .
1974	9.4	20.8	25.3	17.4	7.7	9.7	7.7	7.5	5.3	7.5	. . .
1975	13.5	27.9	31.0	26.4	11.5	17.2	10.5	9.9	10.0	9.3	. . .
1976	12.7	22.2	30.3	18.7	11.4	15.8	10.8	10.0	9.8	9.0	. . .
1977	11.9	24.4	28.5	21.9	10.1	12.1	9.8	8.2	10.6	11.0	. . .
1978	11.3	21.8	29.9	16.6	9.8	13.0	10.3	9.2	7.4	7.2	. . .
1979	10.3	21.2	30.0	15.8	8.9	12.1	8.9	7.7	7.1	7.9	. . .
1980	10.7	23.4	29.7	19.8	9.2	12.0	10.6	8.6	5.3	5.8	. . .
1981	10.8	23.4	23.5	23.4	9.5	13.5	8.7	8.9	7.2	8.4	. . .
1982	14.1	28.2	35.1	25.0	12.5	16.8	12.2	11.9	9.9	10.4	. . .
1983	13.8	28.0	32.5	25.7	12.4	16.2	12.5	12.2	9.7	9.6	. . .
1984	11.1	22.8	26.1	21.0	9.9	12.2	10.3	9.1	7.9	8.8	. . .
1985	11.0	23.8	26.2	22.6	9.9	12.1	10.6	8.5	8.1	9.2	. . .
1986	10.8	25.1	27.6	23.6	9.6	12.9	9.8	8.2	8.9	6.2	. . .
1987	8.9	22.4	27.1	19.9	7.7	11.4	7.8	6.5	6.7	5.0	. . .
1988	8.3	21.0	24.5	18.9	7.1	10.7	7.2	6.2	5.9	4.6	. . .
1989	8.8	18.2	24.7	14.9	8.0	12.2	8.6	6.3	6.7	4.5	. . .
1990	8.4	19.4	25.4	16.2	7.5	10.4	8.0	6.7	6.0	4.3	. . .
1991	9.6	21.9	29.6	17.9	8.6	11.7	9.1	7.6	8.1	4.1	. . .
1992	11.4	26.4	34.5	22.4	10.2	12.4	11.0	9.7	8.5	6.2	. . .
1993	11.0	26.3	36.0	21.7	9.9	14.0	9.9	9.5	8.3	7.2	. . .
1994	10.7	22.2	29.7	18.1	9.8	13.5	10.1	9.2	8.0	7.1	3.6
1995	10.0	22.6	30.7	18.7	8.9	13.0	9.5	7.9	7.0	6.8	6.4
1996	10.2	25.1	28.2	23.3	9.2	14.1	8.5	8.7	7.2	8.1	8.0
1997	8.9	22.7	29.2	19.1	7.9	11.0	8.2	7.7	5.5	6.1	6.0
1998	8.2	22.1	26.4	20.2	7.1	10.1	7.2	6.9	5.1	5.4	8.8
1999	7.6	19.8	24.0	17.7	6.6	9.1	7.3	6.3	5.1	4.3	4.8
2000	6.8	18.0	22.7	15.6	5.9	9.0	6.4	5.4	3.6	5.0	4.8
2001	7.5	18.5	21.6	17.1	6.6	8.2	7.8	6.2	4.8	4.8	4.0
2002	8.0	19.9	25.8	17.0	7.2	10.8	7.4	6.7	5.5	5.0	7.5
2003	8.4	17.7	23.2	14.4	7.8	11.3	8.2	7.1	6.8	5.3	4.4
2004	7.6	19.3	27.0	15.5	7.0	9.1	7.6	6.4	5.8	5.8	4.6

Note: Persons of Hispanic origin may be of any race.

. . . = Not available.

Table 1-30. Unemployed Persons and Unemployment Rates by Occupation, New Series, 2000–2004

(Thousands of people, percent of civilian labor force.)

Occupation	2000	2001	2002	2003	2004
Total Unemployed Persons, 16 Years and Over [1]	5 692	6 801	8 378	8 774	8 149
Management, professional, and related occupations	827	1 102	1 482	1 556	1 346
Management, business, and financial operations occupations	320	455	622	627	544
Professional and related occupations	507	647	859	929	801
Service occupations	1 132	1 311	1 544	1 681	1 617
Sales and office occupations	1 446	1 652	2 110	2 070	1 937
Sales and related occupations	673	779	998	995	912
Office and administrative support occupations	773	873	1 112	1 076	1 025
Natural resources, construction, and maintenance occupations	758	943	1 155	1 244	1 140
Farming, fishing, and forestry occupations	133	163	142	136	132
Construction and extraction occupations	507	626	788	814	786
Installation, maintenance, and repair occupations	119	154	225	295	222
Production, transportation, and material moving occupations	1 081	1 318	1 530	1 555	1 393
Production occupations	575	759	848	807	714
Transportation and material moving occupations	505	559	682	748	679
Total Unemployment Rate, 16 Years and Over [1]	4.0	4.7	5.8	6.0	5.5
Management, professional, and related occupations	1.8	2.3	3.0	3.1	2.7
Management, business, and financial operations occupations	1.6	2.2	3.0	3.1	2.6
Professional and related occupations	1.9	2.3	3.0	3.2	2.8
Service occupations	5.2	5.8	6.6	7.1	6.6
Sales and office occupations	3.8	4.4	5.6	5.5	5.2
Sales and related occupations	4.1	4.7	5.9	5.9	5.4
Office and administrative support occupations	3.6	4.2	5.4	5.2	5.0
Natural resources, construction, and maintenance occupations	5.3	6.4	7.8	8.1	7.3
Farming, fishing, and forestry occupations	10.2	13.4	12.0	11.4	11.8
Construction and extraction occupations	6.2	7.3	9.1	9.1	8.4
Installation, maintenance, and repair occupations	2.4	3.2	4.6	5.5	4.2
Production, transportation, and material moving occupations	5.1	6.4	7.6	7.9	7.2
Production occupations	4.8	6.6	7.8	7.7	7.0
Transportation and material moving occupations	5.6	6.2	7.4	8.2	7.4

[1]Includes people with no work experience and those whose last job was in the armed forces.

Table 1-31. Unemployed Persons and Unemployment Rates by Occupation, Old Series, 1988–1999

(Thousands of people, percent of civilian labor force.)

Occupation	1988	1989	1990	1991	1992	1993	1994	1995	1996	1997	1998	1999
Unemployed Persons, Total, 16 Years and Over [1]	6 701	6 528	7 047	8 628	9 613	8 940	7 996	7 404	7 236	6 739	6 210	5 880
Managerial and professional specialty	577	614	666	889	1 009	984	907	880	869	761	722	770
Executive, administrative, and managerial	311	348	350	494	576	527	454	420	431	359	343	376
Professional specialty	266	265	316	395	433	457	453	460	438	403	380	394
Technical, sales, and administrative support	1 479	1 470	1 641	1 977	2 308	2 111	1 962	1 744	1 766	1 646	1 550	1 477
Technicians and related support	95	90	116	133	176	165	127	113	114	104	96	101
Sales occupations	652	643	720	857	985	927	907	795	843	814	745	714
Administrative support, including clerical	732	738	804	988	1 147	1 020	928	836	810	728	710	662
Service occupations	1 136	1 088	1 139	1 330	1 461	1 401	1 471	1 378	1 334	1 255	1 216	1 081
Private household	54	55	47	56	66	65	91	99	79	73	74	67
Protective service	81	74	74	101	108	108	96	86	84	89	85	72
Service, except private household and protective	1 000	960	1 018	1 172	1 287	1 228	1 285	1 193	1 170	1 093	1 057	943
Precision production, craft, and repair	773	762	861	1 149	1 294	1 155	910	860	795	719	630	607
Mechanics and repairers	166	161	175	246	281	258	201	182	174	167	149	136
Construction trades	405	428	483	655	730	631	518	501	456	406	338	330
Other precision production, craft, and repair	202	173	202	248	284	266	191	177	165	145	143	142
Operators, fabricators, and laborers	1 620	1 578	1 714	2 062	2 151	1 926	1 761	1 618	1 570	1 490	1 304	1 207
Machine operators, assemblers, and inspectors	673	678	727	903	922	816	672	629	654	551	494	440
Transportation and material moving occupations	317	306	329	398	428	404	364	329	292	306	279	235
Handlers, equipment cleaners, helpers, and laborers	630	594	657	761	802	706	725	660	625	633	531	532
Construction laborers	192	152	177	204	200	172	172	179	158	167	136	140
Other handlers, equipment cleaners, helpers, and laborers	439	442	481	556	601	534	552	481	467	467	395	392
Farming, forestry, and fishing	260	234	237	299	320	310	333	311	293	267	244	249
Unemployment Rate, Total, 16 Years and Over [1]	5.5	5.3	5.6	6.8	7.5	6.9	6.1	5.6	5.4	4.9	4.5	4.2
Managerial and professional specialty	1.9	2.0	2.1	2.8	3.1	3.0	2.6	2.4	2.3	2.0	1.8	1.9
Executive, administrative, and managerial	2.1	2.3	2.3	3.2	3.8	3.3	2.7	2.4	2.4	1.9	1.8	1.9
Professional specialty	1.7	1.7	2.0	2.4	2.6	2.6	2.5	2.5	2.3	2.1	1.9	1.9
Technical, sales, and administrative support	4.0	3.9	4.3	5.2	5.9	5.4	5.0	4.5	4.5	4.1	3.9	3.7
Technicians and related support	2.6	2.4	2.9	3.4	4.0	3.9	3.2	2.8	2.8	2.4	2.2	2.3
Sales occupations	4.5	4.4	4.8	5.7	6.6	6.1	5.8	5.0	5.2	4.9	4.5	4.2
Administrative support, including clerical	3.9	3.9	4.1	5.1	5.8	5.2	4.7	4.3	4.2	3.8	3.7	3.5
Service occupations	6.9	6.5	6.6	7.6	8.2	7.7	8.0	7.5	7.2	6.7	6.4	5.7
Private household	5.7	5.9	5.6	6.5	6.9	6.5	10.0	10.7	9.0	8.4	8.0	7.4
Protective service	4.0	3.6	3.6	4.6	4.9	4.7	4.1	3.7	3.7	3.7	3.4	2.9
Service, except private household and protective	7.4	7.0	7.1	8.1	8.8	8.2	8.5	7.9	7.6	7.0	6.8	6.0
Precision production, craft, and repair	5.4	5.2	5.9	8.0	8.9	7.9	6.3	6.0	5.5	4.8	4.2	4.0
Mechanics and repairers	3.6	3.4	3.8	5.2	5.9	5.5	4.3	4.0	3.7	3.5	3.0	2.7
Construction trades	7.4	7.7	8.5	11.9	13.1	11.1	9.4	9.0	8.2	7.0	5.7	5.4
Other precision production, craft, and repair	4.7	4.0	4.7	5.9	6.7	6.3	4.5	4.2	4.0	3.4	3.4	3.5
Operators, fabricators, and laborers	8.3	8.0	8.7	10.6	11.1	10.0	9.0	8.2	7.9	7.5	6.7	6.2
Machine operators, assemblers, and inspectors	7.7	7.6	8.1	10.4	10.7	9.7	8.0	7.4	7.7	6.5	6.0	5.6
Transportation and material moving occupations	6.2	5.9	6.3	7.5	8.0	7.4	6.6	6.0	5.2	5.4	4.9	4.1
Handlers, equipment cleaners, helpers, and laborers	11.5	10.8	11.6	13.9	14.6	12.9	12.7	11.7	11.1	11.1	9.4	9.2
Construction laborers	19.4	16.8	18.1	22.1	22.9	20.3	18.9	18.7	16.3	17.1	14.2	13.2
Other handlers, equipment cleaners, helpers, and laborers	9.7	9.7	10.3	12.2	13.0	11.6	11.5	10.3	10.0	9.9	8.4	8.3
Farming, forestry, and fishing	7.0	6.4	6.4	7.9	8.3	8.4	8.4	7.9	7.6	7.1	6.5	6.8

[1]Includes a small number of persons whose last job was in the armed forces.

Table 1-32. Unemployed Persons by Industry and Class of Worker, New Series, 2000–2004

(Thousands of people.)

Industry and class of worker	2000	2001	2002	2003	2004
Total, 16 Years and Over	5 692	6 801	8 378	8 774	8 149
Nonagricultural private wage and salary workers	4 483	5 540	6 926	7 131	6 484
Mining	21	23	33	37	21
Construction	513	609	800	810	769
Manufacturing	691	992	1 205	1 166	966
Durable goods	400	630	789	762	590
Nondurable goods	290	362	416	404	375
Wholesale trade and retail trade	837	945	1 202	1 237	1 197
Transportation and utilities	193	236	274	283	236
Information	124	190	253	246	189
Financial activities	208	252	320	319	332
Professional and business services	573	768	1 009	1 042	861
Education and health services	383	463	570	640	617
Leisure and hospitality	720	833	961	1 006	972
Other services	219	229	301	347	324
Agriculture and related private wage and salary workers	134	153	139	140	129
Government workers	422	430	512	568	548
Self-employed and unpaid family members	219	218	265	294	303

Note: See "Notes and Definitions" for information on historical comparability.

Table 1-33. Unemployed Persons by Industry and Class of Worker, Old Series, 1948–1999

(Thousands of people.)

Year			Experienced wage and salary workers									
	Total [1]	Agriculture	Wage and salary workers in private nonagricultural industries, except private households									
			Total	Mining	Construc-tion	Manufacturing			Transpor-tation and public utilities	Wholesale and retail trade	Finance, insurance, and real estate	Services, except private house-holds
						Total	Durable goods	Nondura-ble goods				
1948	2 046	96	1 756	28	232	678	339	339	149	415	30	224
1949	3 310	132	2 871	73	380	1 242	652	590	252	578	36	310
1950	2 990	162	2 512	61	348	981	466	515	189	580	40	313
1951	1 857	71	1 578	36	218	637	271	366	95	373	27	192
1952	1 707	73	1 453	35	218	573	266	307	95	326	33	173
1953	1 671	81	1 419	45	227	536	253	283	90	315	34	172
1954	3 230	133	2 827	106	386	1 232	720	512	231	549	46	277
1955	2 568	124	2 188	69	337	821	436	385	163	464	49	285
1956	2 443	126	2 081	50	313	832	448	384	127	459	39	261
1957	2 542	118	2 181	41	349	901	502	399	139	461	42	248
1958	4 096	180	3 584	72	523	1 605	1 036	569	246	705	68	365
1959	3 252	158	2 782	59	466	1 055	611	444	178	617	63	344
1960	3 337	159	2 847	59	463	1 103	626	477	193	637	63	329
1961	4 061	173	3 516	67	544	1 376	835	541	218	783	91	437
1962	3 342	127	2 889	46	466	1 045	575	470	166	678	82	406
1963	3 415	158	2 916	41	456	1 061	573	488	170	689	75	424
1964	3 134	158	2 643	37	390	941	498	443	143	649	75	408
1965	2 732	114	2 320	29	364	775	382	393	118	585	70	379
1966	2 331	89	1 957	20	286	651	325	326	88	528	62	322
1967	2 489	96	2 098	19	257	775	418	357	100	521	80	346
1968	2 356	86	1 971	16	247	691	368	323	87	513	74	343
1969	2 372	76	1 997	15	225	705	382	323	99	530	73	350
1970	3 526	94	3 070	16	380	1 195	719	475	150	732	102	495
1971	4 300	100	3 731	23	428	1 401	841	559	178	948	128	625
1972	4 122	103	3 537	19	450	1 154	653	501	168	994	138	613
1973	3 646	95	3 091	19	407	939	500	439	143	896	117	570
1974	4 391	110	3 769	20	486	1 257	703	554	162	1 058	139	648
1975	6 970	151	6 110	31	807	2 333	1 431	902	278	1 493	217	952
1976	6 387	180	5 421	37	694	1 700	987	714	246	1 527	200	1 017
1977	5 915	171	4 987	33	593	1 474	805	669	242	1 473	186	986
1978	5 220	142	4 359	37	530	1 244	661	583	201	1 295	161	891
1979	5 217	148	4 391	45	541	1 306	702	603	206	1 250	165	879
1980	6 634	175	5 710	65	740	1 991	1 254	736	280	1 443	188	1 004
1981	7 129	201	6 089	70	809	1 915	1 139	777	304	1 609	199	1 182
1982	9 275	260	8 128	154	1 031	2 771	1 788	983	397	2 066	276	1 433
1983	9 276	300	7 985	182	1 005	2 454	1 562	892	424	2 109	272	1 539
1984	7 236	243	6 145	103	817	1 654	955	699	330	1 710	232	1 299
1985	7 074	233	6 088	96	778	1 694	1 004	690	316	1 679	228	1 297
1986	7 019	222	6 097	134	809	1 559	910	650	313	1 706	239	1 336
1987	6 313	191	5 434	87	724	1 305	749	556	277	1 582	225	1 234
1988	5 718	192	4 943	62	669	1 161	653	508	246	1 433	221	1 151
1989	5 616	176	4 866	42	634	1 140	634	506	251	1 412	230	1 157
1990	6 104	190	5 354	36	718	1 289	762	527	252	1 551	221	1 287
1991	7 512	231	6 593	60	946	1 572	950	621	353	1 851	290	1 522
1992	8 361	251	7 344	56	1 020	1 663	979	685	373	2 097	332	1 802
1993	7 708	224	6 751	52	874	1 487	842	645	352	1 964	303	1 719
1994	7 092	218	6 113	37	724	1 154	630	524	340	1 899	271	1 688
1995	6 533	225	5 636	34	737	1 030	534	496	314	1 682	240	1 599
1996	6 389	213	5 532	30	666	1 013	563	450	291	1 679	201	1 653
1997	5 900	190	5 131	24	623	885	445	440	260	1 645	229	1 465
1998	5 477	180	4 781	20	532	816	426	390	254	1 493	197	1 470
1999	5 202	189	4 511	33	520	739	434	305	235	1 422	191	1 371

Note: See "Notes and Definitions" for information on historical comparability.

[1]Includes private household members, not shown separately.

Table 1-34. Unemployment Rates [1] by Industry and Class of Worker, New Series, 2000–2004

(Percent of civilian labor force.)

Industry and class of worker	2000	2001	2002	2003	2004
Total, 16 Years and Over	4.0	4.7	5.8	6.0	5.5
Nonagricultural private wage and salary workers	4.1	5.0	6.2	6.3	5.7
Mining	4.4	4.2	6.3	6.7	3.9
Construction	6.2	7.1	9.2	9.3	8.4
Manufacturing	3.5	5.2	6.7	6.6	5.7
Durable goods	3.2	5.2	6.9	6.9	5.5
Nondurable goods	4.0	5.2	6.2	6.1	5.9
Wholesale trade and retail trade	4.3	4.9	6.1	6.0	5.8
Transportation and utilities	3.4	4.3	4.9	5.3	4.4
Information	3.2	4.9	6.9	6.8	5.7
Financial activities	2.4	2.9	3.5	3.5	3.6
Professional and business services	4.8	6.1	7.9	8.2	6.8
Education and health services	2.5	2.8	3.4	3.6	3.4
Leisure and hospitality	6.6	7.5	8.4	8.7	8.3
Other services	3.9	4.0	5.1	5.7	5.3
Agriculture and related private wage and salary workers	9.0	11.2	10.1	10.2	9.9
Government workers	2.1	2.2	2.5	2.8	2.7
Self-employed and unpaid family members	2.1	2.1	2.6	2.7	2.8

Note: See "Notes and Definitions" for information on historical comparability.

[1]Includes people with no work experience and those whose last job was in the armed forces.

Table 1-35. Unemployment Rates by Industry and Class of Worker, Old Series, 1948–1999

(Percent of civilian labor force.)

Year	Total [1]	Agriculture	Experienced wage and salary workers										
			Wage and salary workers in private nonagricultural industries, except private households										
			Total	Mining	Construc-tion	Manufacturing			Transpor-tation and public utilities	Wholesale and retail trade	Finance, insurance, and real estate	Services, except private house-holds
						Total	Durable goods	Nondura-ble goods				
1948	4.3	5.5	4.5	3.1	8.7	4.2	4.0	4.4	3.5	4.7	1.8	5.0
1949	6.8	7.1	7.3	8.9	14.0	8.0	8.1	7.8	5.9	6.2	2.1	6.5
1950	6.0	9.0	6.2	6.9	12.2	6.2	5.7	6.7	4.6	6.0	2.2	6.2
1951	3.7	4.4	3.9	4.0	7.2	3.9	3.1	4.7	2.3	3.9	1.5	4.0
1952	3.4	4.8	3.6	3.8	6.7	3.5	3.0	4.1	2.3	3.5	1.8	3.4
1953	3.2	5.6	3.4	4.6	7.2	3.1	2.6	3.8	2.2	3.4	1.8	3.3
1954	6.2	9.0	6.7	14.4	12.9	7.1	7.3	6.9	5.6	5.7	2.3	5.2
1955	4.8	7.2	5.1	9.1	10.9	4.7	4.4	5.2	4.0	4.7	2.4	5.1
1956	4.4	7.4	4.7	6.8	10.0	4.7	4.4	5.2	3.0	4.5	1.8	4.4
1957	4.6	6.9	4.9	5.9	10.9	5.1	4.9	5.3	3.3	4.5	1.8	4.0
1958	7.3	10.3	8.0	11.0	15.3	9.3	10.6	7.7	6.1	6.8	2.9	5.6
1959	5.7	9.1	6.2	9.7	13.4	6.1	6.2	6.0	4.4	5.8	2.5	5.1
1960	5.7	8.3	6.2	9.7	13.5	6.2	6.4	6.1	4.6	5.9	2.4	4.8
1961	6.8	9.6	7.5	11.1	15.7	7.8	8.5	6.8	5.3	7.3	3.3	6.0
1962	5.6	7.5	6.2	7.8	13.5	5.8	5.7	6.0	4.1	6.3	3.0	5.4
1963	5.6	9.2	6.1	7.2	13.3	5.7	5.5	6.0	4.2	6.2	2.7	5.6
1964	5.0	9.7	5.4	6.7	11.2	5.0	4.7	5.4	3.5	5.7	2.6	5.2
1965	4.3	7.6	4.6	5.4	10.1	4.0	3.5	4.7	2.9	5.0	2.3	4.6
1966	3.5	6.6	3.8	3.7	8.0	3.2	2.8	3.8	2.1	4.4	2.1	3.8
1967	3.6	6.9	3.9	3.4	7.4	3.7	3.4	4.1	2.4	4.2	2.5	3.9
1968	3.4	6.3	3.6	3.1	6.9	3.3	3.0	3.7	2.0	4.0	2.2	3.7
1969	3.3	6.1	3.5	2.9	6.0	3.3	3.0	3.7	2.2	4.1	2.1	3.5
1970	4.8	7.5	5.3	3.1	9.7	5.6	5.7	5.4	3.2	5.3	2.8	4.7
1971	5.7	7.9	6.3	4.0	10.4	6.8	7.0	6.5	3.8	6.4	3.3	5.8
1972	5.3	7.7	5.8	3.2	10.3	5.6	5.5	5.8	3.5	6.4	3.4	5.4
1973	4.5	7.0	4.9	2.9	8.9	4.4	3.9	5.0	3.0	5.7	2.7	4.8
1974	5.3	7.5	5.8	3.0	10.7	5.8	5.4	6.3	3.3	6.5	3.1	5.2
1975	8.2	10.4	9.2	4.1	18.0	10.9	11.3	10.4	5.6	8.7	4.9	7.2
1976	7.3	11.8	8.0	4.6	15.5	7.9	7.7	8.2	5.0	8.6	4.3	7.3
1977	6.6	11.2	7.1	3.8	12.7	6.7	6.2	7.4	4.7	8.0	3.8	6.8
1978	5.6	8.9	6.0	4.2	10.6	5.5	5.0	6.3	3.7	6.9	3.1	5.8
1979	5.5	9.3	5.8	4.9	10.3	5.6	5.0	6.5	3.7	6.5	3.0	5.5
1980	6.9	11.0	7.4	6.4	14.1	8.5	8.9	7.9	4.9	7.4	3.4	6.0
1981	7.3	12.1	7.7	6.0	15.6	8.3	8.2	8.4	5.2	8.1	3.5	6.7
1982	9.3	14.7	10.2	13.4	20.0	12.3	13.3	10.8	6.8	10.0	4.7	7.7
1983	9.2	16.0	9.9	17.0	18.4	11.2	12.1	10.0	7.4	10.0	4.5	7.9
1984	7.1	13.5	7.4	10.0	14.3	7.5	7.2	7.8	5.5	8.0	3.7	6.5
1985	6.8	13.2	7.2	9.5	13.1	7.7	7.6	7.8	5.1	7.6	3.5	6.2
1986	6.6	12.5	7.0	13.5	13.1	7.1	6.9	7.4	5.1	7.6	3.5	6.1
1987	5.8	10.5	6.2	10.0	11.6	6.0	5.8	6.3	4.5	6.9	3.1	5.4
1988	5.2	10.6	5.5	7.9	10.6	5.3	5.0	5.7	3.9	6.2	3.0	4.8
1989	5.0	9.6	5.3	5.8	10.0	5.1	4.8	5.5	3.9	6.0	3.1	4.7
1990	5.3	9.8	5.7	4.8	11.1	5.8	5.8	5.8	3.9	6.4	3.0	5.0
1991	6.6	11.8	7.1	7.8	15.5	7.3	7.5	6.9	5.3	7.6	4.0	5.8
1992	7.2	12.5	7.8	8.0	16.8	7.8	8.0	7.6	5.5	8.4	4.6	6.5
1993	6.6	11.7	7.1	7.4	14.4	7.2	7.1	7.4	5.1	7.8	4.1	6.1
1994	5.9	11.3	6.3	5.4	11.8	5.6	5.2	6.0	4.8	7.4	3.6	5.7
1995	5.4	11.1	5.7	5.2	11.5	4.9	4.4	5.7	4.5	6.5	3.3	5.2
1996	5.2	10.2	5.5	5.1	10.1	4.8	4.5	5.2	4.1	6.4	2.7	5.2
1997	4.7	9.1	5.0	3.8	9.0	4.2	3.5	5.1	3.5	6.2	3.0	4.5
1998	4.3	8.3	4.6	3.2	7.5	3.9	3.4	4.7	3.4	5.5	2.5	4.4
1999	4.0	8.9	4.3	5.7	7.0	3.6	3.5	3.9	3.0	5.2	2.3	4.0

Note: See "Notes and Definitions" for information on historical comparability.

[1] Includes private household members, not shown separately.

Table 1-36. Unemployed Persons by Duration of Unemployment, 1948–2004

(Thousands of people.)

Year	Total unemployed	Less than 5 weeks	5 to 14 weeks	15 weeks and over			Average duration, in weeks	Median duration, in weeks
				Total	15 to 26 weeks	27 weeks and over		
1948	2 276	1 300	669	309	193	116	8.6	...
1949	3 637	1 756	1 194	684	428	256	10.0	...
1950	3 288	1 450	1 055	782	425	357	12.1	...
1951	2 055	1 177	574	303	166	137	9.7	...
1952	1 883	1 135	516	232	148	84	8.4	...
1953	1 834	1 142	482	210	132	78	8.0	...
1954	3 532	1 605	1 116	812	495	317	11.8	...
1955	2 852	1 335	815	702	366	336	13.0	...
1956	2 750	1 412	805	533	301	232	11.3	...
1957	2 859	1 408	891	560	321	239	10.5	...
1958	4 602	1 753	1 396	1 452	785	667	13.9	...
1959	3 740	1 585	1 114	1 040	469	571	14.4	...
1960	3 852	1 719	1 176	957	503	454	12.8	...
1961	4 714	1 806	1 376	1 532	728	804	15.6	...
1962	3 911	1 663	1 134	1 119	534	585	14.7	...
1963	4 070	1 751	1 231	1 088	535	553	14.0	...
1964	3 786	1 697	1 117	973	491	482	13.3	...
1965	3 366	1 628	983	755	404	351	11.8	...
1966	2 875	1 573	779	526	287	239	10.4	...
1967	2 975	1 634	893	448	271	177	8.7	2.3
1968	2 817	1 594	810	412	256	156	8.4	4.5
1969	2 832	1 629	827	375	242	133	7.8	4.4
1970	4 093	2 139	1 290	663	428	235	8.6	4.9
1971	5 016	2 245	1 585	1 187	668	519	11.3	6.3
1972	4 882	2 242	1 472	1 167	601	566	12.0	6.2
1973	4 365	2 224	1 314	826	483	343	10.0	5.2
1974	5 156	2 604	1 597	955	574	381	9.8	5.2
1975	7 929	2 940	2 484	2 505	1 303	1 203	14.2	8.4
1976	7 406	2 844	2 196	2 366	1 018	1 348	15.8	8.2
1977	6 991	2 919	2 132	1 942	913	1 028	14.3	7.0
1978	6 202	2 865	1 923	1 414	766	648	11.9	5.9
1979	6 137	2 950	1 946	1 241	706	535	10.8	5.4
1980	7 637	3 295	2 470	1 871	1 052	820	11.9	6.5
1981	8 273	3 449	2 539	2 285	1 122	1 162	13.7	6.9
1982	10 678	3 883	3 311	3 485	1 708	1 776	15.6	8.7
1983	10 717	3 570	2 937	4 210	1 652	2 559	20.0	10.1
1984	8 539	3 350	2 451	2 737	1 104	1 634	18.2	7.9
1985	8 312	3 498	2 509	2 305	1 025	1 280	15.6	6.8
1986	8 237	3 448	2 557	2 232	1 045	1 187	15.0	6.9
1987	7 425	3 246	2 196	1 983	943	1 040	14.5	6.5
1988	6 701	3 084	2 007	1 610	801	809	13.5	5.9
1989	6 528	3 174	1 978	1 375	730	646	11.9	4.8
1990	7 047	3 265	2 257	1 525	822	703	12.0	5.3
1991	8 628	3 480	2 791	2 357	1 246	1 111	13.7	6.8
1992	9 613	3 376	2 830	3 408	1 453	1 954	17.7	8.7
1993	8 940	3 262	2 584	3 094	1 297	1 798	18.0	8.3
1994	7 996	2 728	2 408	2 860	1 237	1 623	18.8	9.2
1995	7 404	2 700	2 342	2 363	1 085	1 278	16.6	8.3
1996	7 236	2 633	2 287	2 316	1 053	1 262	16.7	8.3
1997	6 739	2 538	2 138	2 062	995	1 067	15.8	8.0
1998	6 210	2 622	1 950	1 637	763	875	14.5	6.7
1999	5 880	2 568	1 832	1 480	755	725	13.4	6.4
2000	5 692	2 558	1 815	1 318	669	649	12.6	5.9
2001	6 801	2 853	2 196	1 752	951	801	13.1	6.8
2002	8 378	2 893	2 580	2 904	1 369	1 535	16.6	9.1
2003	8 774	2 785	2 612	3 378	1 442	1 936	19.2	10.1
2004	8 149	2 696	2 382	3 072	1 293	1 779	19.6	9.8

Note: Beginning in January 2004, data reflect revised population controls used in the household survey. See "Notes and Definitions" for information on historical comparability.

. . . = Not available.

Table 1-37. Long-Term Unemployment by Industry and Occupation, New Series, 2000–2004

(Thousands of people.)

Industry and occupation	2000	2001	2002	2003	2004
UNEMPLOYED 15 WEEKS AND OVER					
Total	1 318	1 752	2 904	3 378	3 072
Wage and Salary Workers by Industry					
Agriculture and related industries	32	44	39	44	38
Mining	7	7	11	17	8
Construction	107	130	236	262	248
Manufacturing	184	303	528	575	467
Durable goods	99	183	348	389	293
Nondurable goods	86	120	180	186	174
Wholesale and retail trade	186	241	423	472	455
Transportation and utilities	57	71	124	132	114
Information	33	52	119	128	87
Financial activities	58	75	131	144	139
Professional and business services	143	217	377	440	345
Education and health services	124	149	232	300	304
Leisure and hospitality	146	196	279	328	321
Other services	54	58	95	132	126
Public administration	41	36	51	59	72
Experienced Workers by Occupation					
Management, professional, and related occupations	213	313	603	692	571
Service occupations	246	323	447	564	565
Sales and office occupations	331	419	759	810	750
Natural resources, construction, and maintenance occupations	161	212	346	424	386
Production, transportation, and material moving occupations	273	360	575	654	561
UNEMPLOYED 27 WEEKS AND OVER					
Total	649	801	1 535	1 936	1 779
Wage and Salary Workers by Industry					
Agriculture and related industries	13	16	18	21	18
Mining	4	3	5	10	6
Construction	44	60	111	132	133
Manufacturing	100	132	291	366	302
Durable goods	50	75	191	255	196
Nondurable goods	50	57	100	111	106
Wholesale and retail trade	80	114	226	261	261
Transportation and utilities	27	33	67	74	63
Information	18	21	62	80	58
Financial activities	32	34	131	88	79
Professional and business services	67	90	377	262	193
Education and health services	63	71	232	167	168
Leisure and hospitality	69	90	279	166	169
Other services	26	31	95	71	76
Public administration	23	18	51	33	44
Experienced Workers by Occupation					
Management, professional, and related occupations	101	135	340	429	356
Service occupations	128	156	225	295	307
Sales and office occupations	151	185	397	459	419
Natural resources, construction, and maintenance occupations	74	96	164	229	221
Production, transportation, and material moving occupations	140	162	313	388	336

Note: Beginning in January 2004, data reflect revised population controls used in the household survey. See "Notes and Definitions" for information on historical comparability.

Table 1-38. Long-Term Unemployment by Industry and Occupation, Old Series, 1988–1999

(Thousands of people.)

Industry and occupation	1988	1989	1990	1991	1992	1993	1994	1995	1996	1997	1998	1999
UNEMPLOYED 15 WEEKS AND OVER												
Total	1 610	1 375	1 525	2 357	3 408	3 094	2 860	2 363	2316	2 062	1 637	1480
Wage and Salary Workers by Industry [1]												
Agriculture	39	32	31	47	57	56	72	58	65	50	44	41
Mining	28	15	11	23	25	27	21	13	11	9	3	. . .
Construction	169	153	162	285	402	330	238	233	208	171	134	127
Manufacturing	361	299	353	525	725	655	482	371	374	309	230	221
Durable goods	228	177	221	334	457	394	283	198	207	155	115	137
Nondurable goods	133	123	132	192	268	262	199	172	168	154	115	84
Transportation and public utilities	86	74	75	130	190	171	171	135	118	103	80	74
Wholesale and retail trade	295	268	303	448	699	630	628	493	486	456	359	318
Finance and services	405	350	403	615	921	840	825	711	729	645	533	460
Public administration	55	42	36	66	71	85	79	57	63	50	44	45
Experienced Workers by Occupation												
Managerial and professional specialty	164	156	184	310	473	429	371	320	316	258	211	214
Technical, sales, and administrative support	338	281	352	543	858	773	699	553	558	487	393	347
Service	232	209	215	308	427	404	470	407	396	376	320	271
Precision production, craft, and repair	215	193	211	363	533	460	335	287	262	222	161	147
Operators, fabricators, and laborers	462	376	413	618	810	722	640	517	516	457	341	322
Farming, forestry, and fishing	63	48	43	62	75	82	113	81	91	75	63	57
UNEMPLOYED 27 WEEKS AND OVER												
Total	809	646	703	1 111	1 954	1 798	1 623	1 278	1 262	1 067	875	725
Wage and Salary Workers by Industry [1]												
Agriculture	16	13	13	17	26	26	36	27	29	25	20	17
Mining	17	8	5	13	19	16	14	9	7	4	2	. . .
Construction	78	66	69	125	219	188	125	125	105	78	66	55
Manufacturing	194	146	168	255	455	392	282	203	207	167	113	108
Durable goods	128	85	102	160	294	237	170	108	116	84	58	67
Nondurable goods	66	62	65	95	162	155	113	95	90	83	56	41
Transportation and public utilities	46	39	34	67	120	102	107	77	62	53	49	38
Wholesale and retail trade	154	120	139	203	378	368	350	259	251	218	191	151
Finance and services	191	160	179	293	527	492	452	380	409	333	282	228
Public administration	28	22	20	32	45	53	50	32	37	30	27	24
Experienced Workers by Occupation												
Managerial and professional specialty	73	73	86	153	290	266	214	181	177	143	112	107
Technical, sales, and administrative support	162	119	152	247	498	460	389	289	295	232	206	157
Service	125	97	104	146	231	234	268	228	220	209	177	148
Precision production, craft, and repair	108	98	95	169	308	270	184	156	144	108	84	66
Operators, fabricators, and laborers	247	183	197	302	480	416	373	276	280	234	177	156
Farming, forestry, and fishing	29	22	17	25	33	39	57	41	42	39	27	26

Note: See "Notes and Definitions" for information on historical comparability.

[1]Includes wage and salary workers only.
. . . = Not available.

Table 1-39. Unemployed Persons and Unemployment Rates by Sex, Age, and Reason for Unemployment, 1970–2004

(Thousands of people, percent.)

| Year and sex | Number of unemployed | | | | | Unemployed as a percent of the total civilian labor force | | | |
| | Total | Job losers | Job leavers | Entrants | | Job losers | Job leavers | Entrants | |
				Reentrants	New entrants			Reentrants	New entrants
Total									
1970	4 093	1 811	550	1 228	504	2.2	0.7	1.5	0.6
1971	5 016	2 323	590	1 472	630	2.8	0.7	1.7	0.7
1972	4 882	2 108	641	1 456	677	2.4	0.7	1.7	0.8
1973	4 365	1 694	683	1 340	649	1.9	0.8	1.5	0.7
1974	5 156	2 242	768	1 463	681	2.4	0.8	1.6	0.7
1975	7 929	4 386	827	1 892	823	4.7	0.9	2.0	0.9
1976	7 406	3 679	903	1 928	895	3.8	0.9	2.0	0.9
1977	6 991	3 166	909	1 963	953	3.2	0.9	2.0	1.0
1978	6 202	2 585	874	1 857	885	2.5	0.9	1.8	0.9
1979	6 137	2 635	880	1 806	817	2.5	0.8	1.7	0.8
1980	7 637	3 947	891	1 927	872	3.7	0.8	1.8	0.8
1981	8 273	4 267	923	2 102	981	3.9	0.8	1.9	0.9
1982	10 678	6 268	840	2 384	1 185	5.7	0.8	2.2	1.1
1983	10 717	6 258	830	2 412	1 216	5.6	0.7	2.2	1.1
1984	8 539	4 421	823	2 184	1 110	3.9	0.7	1.9	1.0
1985	8 312	4 139	877	2 256	1 039	3.6	0.8	2.0	0.9
1986	8 237	4 033	1 015	2 160	1 029	3.4	0.9	1.8	0.9
1987	7 425	3 566	965	1 974	920	3.0	0.8	1.6	0.8
1988	6 701	3 092	983	1 809	816	2.5	0.8	1.5	0.7
1989	6 528	2 983	1 024	1 843	677	2.4	0.8	1.5	0.5
1990	7 047	3 387	1 041	1 930	688	2.7	0.8	1.5	0.5
1991	8 628	4 694	1 004	2 139	792	3.7	0.8	1.7	0.6
1992	9 613	5 389	1 002	2 285	937	4.2	0.8	1.8	0.7
1993	8 940	4 848	976	2 198	919	3.8	0.8	1.7	0.7
1994	7 996	3 815	791	2 786	604	2.9	0.6	2.1	0.5
1995	7 404	3 476	824	2 525	579	2.6	0.6	1.9	0.4
1996	7 236	3 370	774	2 512	580	2.5	0.6	1.9	0.4
1997	6 739	3 037	795	2 338	569	2.2	0.6	1.7	0.4
1998	6 210	2 822	734	2 132	520	2.1	0.5	1.5	0.4
1999	5 880	2 622	783	2 005	469	1.9	0.6	1.4	0.3
2000	5 692	2 517	780	1 961	434	1.8	0.5	1.4	0.3
2001	6 801	3 476	835	2 031	459	2.4	0.6	1.4	0.3
2002	8 378	4 607	866	2 368	536	3.2	0.6	1.6	0.4
2003	8 774	4 838	818	2 477	641	3.3	0.6	1.7	0.4
2004	8 149	4 197	858	2 408	686	2.8	0.6	1.6	0.5
Men, 20 Years and Over									
1970	1 638	1 066	209	318	44	2.2	0.4	0.7	0.1
1971	2 097	1 391	239	411	57	2.9	0.5	0.9	0.1
1972	1 948	1 219	248	420	60	2.5	0.5	0.9	0.1
1973	1 624	959	258	350	56	1.9	0.5	0.7	0.1
1974	1 957	1 276	276	356	48	2.5	0.5	0.7	0.1
1975	3 476	2 598	298	506	76	5.0	0.6	1.0	0.1
1976	3 098	2 167	323	521	86	4.1	0.6	1.0	0.2
1977	2 794	1 816	335	540	103	3.4	0.6	1.0	0.2
1978	2 328	1 433	337	471	86	2.6	0.6	0.9	0.2
1979	2 308	1 464	325	446	73	2.6	0.6	0.8	0.1
1980	3 353	2 389	359	516	90	4.2	0.6	0.9	0.2
1981	3 615	2 565	356	592	102	4.5	0.6	1.0	0.2
1982	5 089	3 965	327	678	119	6.8	0.6	1.2	0.2
1983	5 257	4 088	336	695	138	6.9	0.6	1.2	0.2
1984	3 932	2 800	324	663	146	4.7	0.5	1.1	0.2
1985	3 715	2 568	352	671	124	4.3	0.6	1.1	0.2
1986	3 751	2 568	444	611	128	4.1	0.7	1.0	0.2
1987	3 369	2 289	413	558	108	3.7	0.7	0.9	0.2
1988	2 987	1 939	416	534	98	3.1	0.7	0.9	0.2
1989	2 867	1 843	394	541	88	2.9	0.6	0.8	0.1
1990	3 239	2 100	431	626	82	3.2	0.7	1.0	0.1
1991	4 195	2 982	411	698	105	4.6	0.6	1.1	0.2
1992	4 717	3 420	421	765	111	5.2	0.6	1.2	0.2
1993	4 287	2 996	429	747	114	4.5	0.6	1.1	0.2
1994	3 627	2 296	367	898	65	3.4	0.5	1.3	0.1
1995	3 239	2 051	356	775	57	3.0	0.5	1.2	0.1
1996	3 146	2 043	322	731	51	3.0	0.5	1.1	0.1
1997	2 882	1 795	358	675	55	2.6	0.5	1.0	0.1
1998	2 580	1 588	318	611	63	2.3	0.5	0.9	0.1
1999	2 433	1 459	336	592	46	2.1	0.5	0.8	0.1
2000	2 376	1 416	328	577	55	2.0	0.5	0.8	0.1
2001	3 040	1 999	372	612	56	2.7	0.5	0.8	0.1
2002	3 896	2 702	386	743	65	3.7	0.5	1.0	0.1
2003	4 209	2 899	376	846	88	3.9	0.5	1.1	0.1
2004	3 791	2 503	398	791	99	3.3	0.5	1.0	0.1

Table 1-39. Unemployed Persons and Unemployment Rates by Sex, Age, and Reason for Unemployment, 1970–2004—*Continued*

(Thousands of people, percent.)

Year and sex	Number of unemployed					Unemployed as a percent of the total civilian labor force			
	Total	Job losers	Job leavers	Entrants		Job losers	Job leavers	Entrants	
				Reentrants	New entrants			Reentrants	New entrants
Women, 20 Years and Over									
1970	1 349	546	214	531	58	1.9	0.8	1.9	0.2
1971	1 658	700	235	651	72	2.5	0.8	2.3	0.2
1972	1 625	641	264	641	80	2.2	0.9	2.1	0.3
1973	1 507	522	280	625	80	1.6	0.9	2.0	0.3
1974	1 777	685	319	673	100	2.1	1.0	2.1	0.3
1975	2 684	1 339	375	858	114	4.0	1.1	2.6	0.3
1976	2 588	1 124	427	912	126	3.2	1.2	2.6	0.4
1977	2 535	1 031	419	945	140	2.8	1.2	2.6	0.4
1978	2 292	852	371	930	138	2.2	1.0	2.4	0.4
1979	2 276	851	370	908	145	2.1	0.9	2.3	0.4
1980	2 615	1 170	376	930	139	2.8	0.9	2.3	0.3
1981	2 895	1 317	404	1 023	151	3.1	1.0	2.4	0.4
1982	3 613	1 844	379	1 197	192	4.2	0.9	2.7	0.4
1983	3 632	1 801	384	1 235	212	4.0	0.9	2.8	0.5
1984	3 107	1 350	386	1 151	220	2.9	0.8	2.5	0.5
1985	3 129	1 296	412	1 195	227	2.7	0.9	2.5	0.5
1986	3 032	1 225	426	1 175	206	2.5	0.9	2.4	0.4
1987	2 709	1 067	406	1 041	194	2.2	0.8	2.1	0.4
1988	2 487	946	408	965	168	1.9	0.8	1.9	0.3
1989	2 467	942	430	958	137	1.8	0.8	1.8	0.3
1990	2 596	1 054	429	966	146	2.0	0.8	1.8	0.3
1991	3 074	1 423	413	1 075	163	2.6	0.8	2.0	0.3
1992	3 469	1 710	433	1 142	183	3.1	0.8	2.1	0.3
1993	3 288	1 619	395	1 098	176	2.9	0.7	2.0	0.3
1994	3 049	1 334	339	1 253	122	2.4	0.6	2.2	0.2
1995	2 819	1 211	366	1 135	107	2.1	0.6	2.0	0.2
1996	2 783	1 145	361	1 156	120	2.0	0.6	2.0	0.2
1997	2 585	1 069	333	1 057	126	1.8	0.6	1.8	0.2
1998	2 424	1 053	330	944	97	1.8	0.6	1.6	0.2
1999	2 285	990	333	866	96	1.6	0.5	1.4	0.2
2000	2 235	943	343	868	80	1.5	0.6	1.4	0.1
2001	2 599	1 291	365	850	92	2.0	0.6	1.3	0.1
2002	3 228	1 708	389	1 028	102	2.7	0.6	1.6	0.2
2003	3 314	1 751	357	1 076	130	2.7	0.6	1.7	0.2
2004	3 150	1 529	384	1 107	131	2.4	0.6	1.7	0.2
Both Sexes, 16 to 19 Years									
1970	1 106	200	126	378	401	2.8	1.7	5.2	5.5
1971	1 262	233	117	410	501	3.1	1.6	5.5	6.7
1972	1 308	248	129	395	536	3.1	1.6	4.9	6.6
1973	1 235	212	146	364	513	2.4	1.7	4.3	6.0
1974	1 422	280	173	436	533	3.1	2.0	4.9	6.0
1975	1 767	450	155	529	634	5.1	1.7	6.0	7.1
1976	1 719	387	153	496	683	4.3	1.7	5.5	7.5
1977	1 663	318	156	477	711	3.4	1.7	5.1	7.6
1978	1 583	300	167	455	660	3.1	1.7	4.7	6.8
1979	1 555	319	184	452	599	3.3	1.9	4.7	6.2
1980	1 669	388	156	481	643	4.1	1.7	5.1	6.9
1981	1 763	385	162	487	728	4.3	1.8	5.4	8.1
1982	1 977	460	134	509	874	5.4	1.6	6.0	10.2
1983	1 829	370	110	482	867	4.6	1.3	5.9	10.6
1984	1 499	271	114	370	745	3.4	1.4	4.7	9.4
1985	1 468	275	113	390	689	3.5	1.4	4.9	8.7
1986	1 454	240	145	374	695	3.0	1.8	4.7	8.8
1987	1 347	210	146	375	617	2.7	1.8	4.7	7.7
1988	1 226	207	159	310	550	2.6	2.0	3.9	6.8
1989	1 194	198	200	345	452	2.5	2.5	4.3	5.7
1990	1 212	233	181	338	460	3.0	2.3	4.3	5.9
1991	1 359	289	180	365	524	4.0	2.5	5.0	7.2
1992	1 427	259	149	377	643	3.6	2.1	5.3	9.1
1993	1 365	233	151	353	628	3.3	2.1	4.9	8.8
1994	1 320	185	84	634	416	2.5	1.1	8.5	5.6
1995	1 346	214	102	615	415	2.8	1.3	7.9	5.3
1996	1 306	182	91	625	409	2.3	1.2	8.0	5.2
1997	1 271	174	104	606	388	2.2	1.3	7.6	4.9
1998	1 205	181	86	577	361	2.2	1.0	7.0	4.4
1999	1 162	173	114	547	328	2.1	1.4	6.6	3.9
2000	1 081	157	109	516	299	1.9	1.3	6.2	3.6
2001	1 162	185	98	568	311	2.3	1.2	7.2	3.9
2002	1 253	197	91	597	368	2.6	1.2	7.9	4.9
2003	1 251	188	85	554	424	2.6	1.2	7.7	5.9
2004	1 208	165	76	510	456	2.3	1.1	7.2	6.4

Note: See "Notes and Definitions" for information on historical comparability.

Table 1-40. Percentage of the Population with Work Experience During the Year by Sex and Age, 1987–2004

(Percent.)

Year	Total	16 to 17 years	18 to 19 years	20 to 24 years	25 to 34 years	35 to 44 years	45 to 54 years	55 to 59 years	60 to 64 years	65 to 69 years	70 years and over
Total											
1987	69.7	51.8	76.6	85.5	85.7	86.1	81.6	69.4	51.3	26.2	10.2
1988	70.2	50.6	75.5	85.7	86.0	86.8	82.2	70.5	52.2	27.9	10.3
1989	70.5	51.9	75.4	84.9	86.6	86.9	82.8	70.4	52.5	28.4	10.0
1990	70.2	48.6	74.2	84.1	86.2	87.0	82.8	70.9	53.4	28.3	10.2
1991	69.5	43.4	70.8	83.4	85.9	86.6	83.0	70.3	52.9	27.2	9.8
1992	69.1	43.8	69.9	82.7	85.2	85.9	82.8	70.8	53.5	25.5	9.8
1993	69.2	42.1	70.4	82.0	85.0	85.3	82.8	71.6	51.6	27.5	10.7
1994	69.6	44.1	71.5	82.5	85.5	85.6	83.8	72.2	52.8	27.5	10.0
1995	69.6	44.4	71.2	82.0	85.6	85.9	83.4	72.2	53.3	28.0	10.2
1996	69.9	43.3	70.5	83.1	86.1	85.7	84.3	73.3	54.3	27.8	10.4
1997	70.1	43.6	70.5	83.0	87.1	85.9	84.4	73.8	53.8	28.5	10.0
1998	70.1	42.1	69.9	82.9	86.7	86.3	84.2	73.7	54.5	29.2	10.6
1999	70.7	43.7	71.2	82.7	87.3	86.9	85.0	72.3	55.8	30.5	11.6
2000	70.5	42.2	69.6	82.6	87.1	87.0	84.6	72.9	55.1	30.8	11.4
2001	69.4	37.7	66.7	80.8	86.1	85.8	83.7	73.5	56.7	30.6	10.5
2002	68.5	34.5	62.8	78.5	84.4	85.0	83.7	74.7	56.8	33.1	10.4
2003	67.8	32.0	61.7	77.5	83.7	84.0	82.9	73.9	56.5	33.2	11.4
2004	67.7	32.6	59.8	76.9	83.3	84.2	82.6	73.9	57.0	32.7	12.2
Men											
1987	78.9	52.4	77.4	90.4	94.3	94.1	91.9	83.3	63.2	34.2	15.4
1988	79.1	51.8	78.9	90.7	94.3	94.6	91.6	82.1	63.1	35.6	15.6
1989	79.4	53.2	77.7	89.9	94.7	94.7	91.9	82.0	64.2	35.4	15.1
1990	78.9	50.3	76.7	88.7	94.4	94.7	91.3	82.0	65.8	35.8	14.0
1991	77.9	45.4	72.2	87.9	93.5	93.6	91.3	81.5	63.6	35.0	14.4
1992	77.4	46.6	73.7	87.1	93.3	92.8	89.9	80.9	63.2	32.4	14.3
1993	76.8	43.9	71.4	86.6	92.5	92.0	89.3	79.8	59.1	34.3	15.3
1994	77.2	44.4	74.7	87.2	92.9	92.0	90.0	81.3	61.4	33.9	14.8
1995	77.0	43.7	73.6	86.4	92.6	92.2	89.7	81.5	62.1	34.5	14.9
1996	77.2	44.1	71.8	86.7	93.4	92.1	90.4	81.8	62.5	33.6	15.2
1997	77.1	43.4	70.3	86.6	94.1	92.3	90.7	81.4	62.9	33.8	13.9
1998	76.9	40.4	71.6	86.4	93.5	92.7	90.1	81.7	63.5	35.5	14.7
1999	77.3	44.7	72.3	85.5	93.9	93.2	89.9	79.2	65.1	37.4	16.5
2000	77.1	42.1	70.2	85.1	93.4	93.6	89.8	80.6	64.4	38.4	16.0
2001	76.3	37.4	67.7	84.8	93.2	92.2	89.1	80.4	64.3	37.8	14.5
2002	75.2	34.7	62.8	82.1	91.6	91.8	88.9	80.7	64.3	39.3	14.6
2003	74.3	32.8	61.7	80.2	90.8	90.9	87.7	80.9	63.1	37.3	15.8
2004	74.2	32.1	58.9	80.2	91.0	91.1	87.9	80.1	64.5	37.1	16.7
Women											
1987	61.3	51.1	75.8	81.0	77.3	78.5	71.9	56.7	41.0	19.6	6.8
1988	62.1	49.3	72.2	81.0	78.1	79.4	73.5	60.0	42.5	21.4	6.8
1989	62.3	50.6	73.1	80.2	78.6	79.3	74.2	59.9	42.4	22.5	6.7
1990	62.2	46.8	71.7	79.6	78.0	79.6	74.9	60.4	42.5	22.1	7.7
1991	61.8	41.4	69.4	79.0	78.3	79.9	75.3	59.9	43.6	20.6	6.7
1992	61.5	40.9	66.1	78.4	77.2	79.1	76.1	61.5	44.4	20.0	6.7
1993	62.1	40.3	69.4	77.5	77.6	78.7	76.5	63.9	44.7	22.1	7.7
1994	62.5	43.7	68.4	77.8	78.1	79.4	78.0	63.9	45.0	22.2	6.8
1995	62.8	45.2	68.7	77.7	78.8	79.8	77.6	63.2	45.6	22.4	7.1
1996	63.2	42.5	69.2	79.5	78.9	79.5	78.4	65.4	46.9	23.0	7.1
1997	63.6	43.9	70.7	79.5	80.1	79.6	78.4	66.7	45.6	24.0	7.3
1998	63.7	44.1	68.2	79.4	80.1	80.0	78.6	66.3	46.2	23.8	7.8
1999	64.5	42.6	70.1	79.9	80.9	80.7	80.3	66.2	47.3	24.4	8.2
2000	64.3	42.3	69.0	80.2	80.9	80.5	79.5	65.7	47.0	23.9	8.2
2001	63.1	38.1	65.7	76.9	79.2	79.5	78.6	67.1	49.8	24.2	7.9
2002	62.3	34.3	62.8	74.9	77.2	78.4	78.7	69.1	50.0	27.8	7.4
2003	61.7	31.2	61.6	74.6	76.6	77.2	78.4	67.3	50.7	29.6	8.3
2004	61.5	33.1	60.7	73.7	75.6	77.4	77.5	68.2	50.3	28.7	9.0

Note: See "Notes and Definitions" for information on historical comparability.

Table 1-41. Persons with Work Experience During the Year by Industry and Class of Worker of Job Held the Longest, 2002–2004

(Thousands of people.)

Industry and class of worker	2002	2003	2004
TOTAL	151 546	151 553	153 024
Agriculture	2 490	2 521	2 492
Wage and salary workers	1 583	1 605	1 549
Self-employed workers	875	894	918
Unpaid family workers	33	22	25
Nonagricultural Industries	149 055	149 032	150 532
Wage and salary workers	139 909	139 747	140 885
Mining	594	576	630
Construction	9 488	9 423	10 076
Manufacturing	17 660	17 349	17 196
Durable goods	11 013	10 622	10 814
Nondurable goods	6 647	6 727	6 382
Wholesale and retail trade	21 615	21 650	22 091
Wholesale trade	4 402	4 691	4 470
Retail trade	17 213	16 959	17 621
Transportation and utilities	7 039	6 934	7 040
Transportation and warehousing	5 745	5 736	5 827
Utilities	1 294	1 198	1 213
Information	3 989	3 755	3 359
Financial activities	9 591	9 822	9 956
Finance and insurance	6 986	7 135	7 192
Real estate and rental and leasing	2 605	2 687	2 764
Professional and business services	13 883	13 485	13 277
Professional, scientific, and technical	7 989	7 855	7 793
Management, administration, and waste management	5 894	5 629	5 484
Education and health services	29 343	29 571	29 814
Educational services	12 765	13 026	13 169
Health care and social assistance	16 578	16 544	16 645
Leisure and hospitality	13 260	13 110	13 345
Arts, entertainment, and recreation	2 852	2 789	2 888
Accommodation and food services	10 408	10 321	10 457
Other services and private household	6 416	6 529	6 473
Private households	873	897	907
Public administration	6 290	6 734	6 897
Self-employed workers	9 023	9 169	9 520
Unpaid family workers	124	116	128

Note: See "Notes and Definitions" for information on historical comparability.

Table 1-42. Number of Persons with Work Experience During the Year by Sex and Extent of Employment, 1987–2004

(Thousands of people.)

Year and sex	Total	Full-time				Part-time			
		Total	50 to 52 weeks	27 to 49 weeks	1 to 26 weeks	Total	50 to 52 weeks	27 to 49 weeks	1 to 26 weeks
Total									
1987	128 315	100 288	77 015	13 361	9 912	28 027	10 973	6 594	10 460
1988	130 451	102 131	79 627	12 875	9 629	28 320	11 384	6 624	10 312
1989	132 817	104 876	81 117	14 271	9 488	27 941	11 275	6 987	9 679
1990	133 535	105 323	80 932	14 758	9 633	28 212	11 507	7 012	9 693
1991	133 410	104 472	80 385	14 491	9 596	28 938	11 946	7 003	9 989
1992	133 912	104 813	81 523	13 587	9 703	29 099	12 326	6 841	9 932
1993	136 354	106 299	83 384	13 054	9 861	30 055	12 818	6 777	10 460
1994	138 468	108 141	85 764	13 051	9 326	30 327	12 936	6 956	10 435
1995	139 724	110 063	88 173	12 970	8 920	29 661	12 725	6 831	10 105
1996	142 201	112 313	90 252	12 997	9 064	29 888	13 382	6 643	9 863
1997	143 968	113 879	92 631	12 508	8 740	30 089	13 810	6 565	9 714
1998	145 566	116 412	95 772	12 156	8 484	29 155	13 538	6 480	9 137
1999	148 295	119 096	97 941	12 294	8 861	29 199	13 680	6 317	9 202
2000	149 361	120 591	100 349	12 071	8 171	28 770	13 865	6 161	8 744
2001	151 042	121 921	100 357	13 172	8 392	29 121	14 038	6 139	8 944
2002	151 546	121 726	100 659	12 544	8 523	29 819	14 635	6 184	9 000
2003	151 553	121 158	100 700	11 972	8 486	30 395	15 333	6 027	9 035
2004	153 024	122 404	102 427	11 862	8 115	30 621	15 552	6 077	8 992
Men									
1987	69 144	59 736	47 040	7 503	5 193	9 408	3 260	2 191	3 957
1988	70 021	60 504	48 299	7 329	4 876	9 517	3 468	2 199	3 850
1989	71 640	62 108	49 693	7 642	4 773	9 532	3 619	2 254	3 659
1990	71 953	62 319	49 175	8 188	4 956	9 634	3 650	2 322	3 662
1991	71 700	61 636	47 895	8 324	5 417	10 064	3 820	2 342	3 902
1992	72 007	61 722	48 300	7 965	5 457	10 285	3 864	2 354	4 067
1993	72 872	62 513	49 832	7 317	5 364	10 359	4 005	2 144	4 210
1994	73 958	63 634	51 582	7 094	4 958	10 324	3 948	2 358	4 018
1995	74 381	64 145	52 671	6 973	4 501	10 236	4 034	2 257	3 945
1996	75 760	65 356	53 795	6 891	4 670	10 404	4 321	2 136	3 947
1997	76 408	66 089	54 918	6 638	4 533	10 319	4 246	2 274	3 799
1998	76 918	67 250	56 953	6 208	4 089	9 669	4 197	2 090	3 382
1999	78 145	68 347	57 520	6 401	4 426	9 797	4 297	2 062	3 438
2000	78 804	68 925	58 756	6 094	4 075	9 879	4 485	1 957	3 437
2001	79 971	70 074	58 715	7 087	4 272	9 897	4 306	1 989	3 602
2002	80 282	70 132	58 765	6 804	4 563	10 151	4 519	2 042	3 590
2003	80 317	69 766	58 778	6 479	4 509	10 551	5 042	1 872	3 637
2004	81 261	70 780	60 096	6 428	4 256	10 482	4 987	1 992	3 503
Women									
1987	59 171	40 552	29 975	5 858	4 719	18 619	7 713	4 403	6 503
1988	60 430	41 627	31 328	5 546	4 753	18 803	7 916	4 425	6 462
1989	61 178	42 768	31 424	6 629	4 715	18 410	7 656	4 733	6 021
1990	61 582	43 004	31 757	6 570	4 677	18 578	7 857	4 690	6 031
1991	61 712	42 837	32 491	6 167	4 179	18 875	8 126	4 662	6 087
1992	61 904	43 090	33 223	5 621	4 246	18 814	8 462	4 487	5 865
1993	63 481	43 785	33 552	5 736	4 497	19 696	8 813	4 633	6 250
1994	64 511	44 508	34 182	5 957	4 369	20 003	8 988	4 598	6 417
1995	65 342	45 917	35 502	5 997	4 418	19 425	8 691	4 574	6 160
1996	66 439	46 955	36 457	6 105	4 393	19 484	9 061	4 507	5 916
1997	67 559	47 790	37 713	5 870	4 207	19 769	9 564	4 291	5 914
1998	68 648	49 162	38 819	5 948	4 395	19 486	9 341	4 390	5 755
1999	70 150	50 748	40 421	5 892	4 435	19 402	9 383	4 255	5 764
2000	70 556	51 665	41 593	5 977	4 095	18 891	9 380	4 204	5 307
2001	71 071	51 848	41 642	6 085	4 120	19 223	9 731	4 150	5 342
2002	71 263	51 593	41 893	5 741	3 959	19 671	10 117	4 143	5 411
2003	71 236	51 391	41 921	5 493	3 977	19 844	10 291	4 155	5 398
2004	71 763	51 624	42 331	5 434	3 859	20 139	10 565	4 085	5 489

Note: See "Notes and Definitions" for information on historical comparability.

Table 1-43. Percentage Distribution of the Population with Work Experience During the Year by Sex and Extent of Employment, 1987–2004

(Percent of total people with work experience.)

Year and sex	Total	Full-time				Part-time			
		Total	50 to 52 weeks	27 to 49 weeks	1 to 26 weeks	Total	50 to 52 weeks	27 to 49 weeks	1 to 26 weeks
Total									
1987	100.0	78.1	60.0	10.4	7.7	21.9	8.6	5.1	8.2
1988	100.0	78.3	61.0	9.9	7.4	21.7	8.7	5.1	7.9
1989	100.0	78.9	61.1	10.7	7.1	21.1	8.5	5.3	7.3
1990	100.0	78.9	60.6	11.1	7.2	21.2	8.6	5.3	7.3
1991	100.0	78.4	60.3	10.9	7.2	21.7	9.0	5.2	7.5
1992	100.0	78.2	60.9	10.1	7.2	21.7	9.2	5.1	7.4
1993	100.0	78.0	61.2	9.6	7.2	22.1	9.4	5.0	7.7
1994	100.0	78.0	61.9	9.4	6.7	21.8	9.3	5.0	7.5
1995	100.0	78.8	63.1	9.3	6.4	21.2	9.1	4.9	7.2
1996	100.0	79.0	63.5	9.1	6.4	21.0	9.4	4.7	6.9
1997	100.0	79.1	64.3	8.7	6.1	20.9	9.6	4.6	6.7
1998	100.0	80.0	65.8	8.4	5.8	20.1	9.3	4.5	6.3
1999	100.0	80.3	66.0	8.3	6.0	19.7	9.2	4.3	6.2
2000	100.0	80.8	67.2	8.1	5.5	19.3	9.3	4.1	5.9
2001	100.0	80.7	66.4	8.7	5.6	19.3	9.3	4.1	5.9
2002	100.0	80.3	66.4	8.3	5.6	19.7	9.7	4.1	5.9
2003	100.0	79.9	66.4	7.9	5.6	20.1	10.1	4.0	6.0
2004	100.0	80.0	66.9	7.8	5.3	20.1	10.2	4.0	5.9
Men									
1987	100.0	86.4	68.0	10.9	7.5	13.6	4.7	3.2	5.7
1988	100.0	86.5	69.0	10.5	7.0	13.6	5.0	3.1	5.5
1989	100.0	86.8	69.4	10.7	6.7	13.3	5.1	3.1	5.1
1990	100.0	86.6	68.3	11.4	6.9	13.4	5.1	3.2	5.1
1991	100.0	86.0	66.8	11.6	7.6	14.0	5.3	3.3	5.4
1992	100.0	85.8	67.1	11.1	7.6	14.3	5.4	3.3	5.6
1993	100.0	85.8	68.4	10.0	7.4	14.2	5.5	2.9	5.8
1994	100.0	86.0	69.7	9.6	6.7	13.9	5.3	3.2	5.4
1995	100.0	86.3	70.8	9.4	6.1	13.7	5.4	3.0	5.3
1996	100.0	86.3	71.0	9.1	6.2	13.7	5.7	2.8	5.2
1997	100.0	86.5	71.9	8.7	5.9	13.6	5.6	3.0	5.0
1998	100.0	87.4	74.0	8.1	5.3	12.6	5.5	2.7	4.4
1999	100.0	87.5	73.6	8.2	5.7	12.5	5.5	2.6	4.4
2000	100.0	87.5	74.6	7.7	5.2	12.6	5.7	2.5	4.4
2001	100.0	87.6	73.4	8.9	5.3	12.4	5.4	2.5	4.5
2002	100.0	87.4	73.2	8.5	5.7	12.6	5.6	2.5	4.5
2003	100.0	86.9	73.2	8.1	5.6	13.1	6.3	2.3	4.5
2004	100.0	87.1	74.0	7.9	5.2	12.9	6.1	2.5	4.3
Women									
1987	100.0	68.6	50.7	9.9	8.0	31.4	13.0	7.4	11.0
1988	100.0	68.9	51.8	9.2	7.9	31.1	13.1	7.3	10.7
1989	100.0	69.9	51.4	10.8	7.7	30.0	12.5	7.7	9.8
1990	100.0	69.9	51.6	10.7	7.6	30.2	12.8	7.6	9.8
1991	100.0	69.4	52.6	10.0	6.8	30.7	13.2	7.6	9.9
1992	100.0	69.7	53.7	9.1	6.9	30.4	13.7	7.2	9.5
1993	100.0	69.0	52.9	9.0	7.1	31.0	13.9	7.3	9.8
1994	100.0	69.0	53.0	9.2	6.8	30.9	13.9	7.1	9.9
1995	100.0	70.3	54.3	9.2	6.8	29.7	13.3	7.0	9.4
1996	100.0	70.7	54.9	9.2	6.6	29.3	13.6	6.8	8.9
1997	100.0	70.7	55.8	8.7	6.2	29.4	14.2	6.4	8.8
1998	100.0	71.6	56.5	8.7	6.4	28.4	13.6	6.4	8.4
1999	100.0	72.3	57.6	8.4	6.3	27.7	13.4	6.1	8.2
2000	100.0	73.2	58.9	8.5	5.8	26.8	13.3	6.0	7.5
2001	100.0	73.0	58.6	8.6	5.8	27.0	13.7	5.8	7.5
2002	100.0	72.5	58.8	8.1	5.6	27.6	14.2	5.8	7.6
2003	100.0	72.1	58.8	7.7	5.6	27.8	14.4	5.8	7.6
2004	100.0	72.0	59.0	7.6	5.4	28.0	14.7	5.7	7.6

Note: See "Notes and Definitions" for information on historical comparability.

Table 1-44. Extent of Unemployment During the Year by Sex, 1994–2004

(Thousands of people, percent.)

Sex and extent of unemployment	1994	1995	1996	1997	1998	1999	2000	2001	2002	2003	2004
TOTAL											
Total Who Worked or Looked for Work	141 325	142 413	144 528	146 096	147 295	149 798	150 786	153 056	154 205	154 315	155 576
Percent with unemployment	13.4	12.7	11.6	10.7	9.5	8.7	8.1	10.4	10.9	10.7	9.7
Total with Unemployment	18 966	18 067	16 789	15 637	14 044	13 068	12 269	15 843	16 824	16 462	15 074
Did not work but looked for work	2 857	2 690	2 329	2 129	1 729	1 503	1 425	2 014	2 660	2 762	2 551
Worked during the year	16 109	15 377	14 460	13 508	12 316	11 566	10 845	13 829	14 164	13 699	12 522
Year-round workers with 1 or 2 weeks of unemployment	746	715	589	611	630	562	573	602	584	534	465
Part-year workers with unemployment	15 363	14 662	13 871	12 897	11 686	11 004	10 272	13 227	13 580	13 165	12 057
1 to 4 weeks	2 788	2 812	2 550	2 582	2 323	2 361	2 233	2 368	2 002	1 839	1 985
5 to 10 weeks	2 983	2 725	2 671	2 601	2 495	2 218	2 014	2 557	2 373	2 264	2 100
11 to 14 weeks	2 265	2 147	2 020	1 822	1 701	1 594	1 505	2 038	1 970	1 749	1 773
15 to 26 weeks	4 158	4 013	3 662	3 378	3 019	2 803	2 641	3 683	3 848	3 778	3 448
27 weeks or more	3 169	2 965	2 968	2 514	2 148	2 028	1 879	2 582	3 387	3 535	2 751
With 2 or more spells of unemployment	4 783	4 468	4 237	4 044	3 628	3 225	3 079	3 421	3 226	3 093	2 896
2 spells	2 207	1 963	1 982	1 853	1 650	1 449	1 397	1 643	1 556	1 585	1 344
3 or more spells	2 576	2 505	2 255	2 191	1 978	1 776	1 682	1 779	1 670	1 508	1 552
MEN											
Total Who Worked or Looked for Work	75 244	75 698	76 786	77 385	77 704	78 905	79 546	80 975	81 651	81 804	82 478
Percent with unemployment	14.1	13.2	11.9	11.1	9.4	9.0	8.6	11.0	11.8	11.4	10.0
Total with Unemployment	10 582	9 996	9 157	8 604	7 284	7 091	6 806	8 928	9 621	9 339	8 256
Did not work but looked for work	1 286	1 317	1 026	978	787	760	742	1 004	1 369	1 487	1 217
Worked during the year	9 296	8 679	8 130	7 626	6 497	6 332	6 064	7 924	8 252	7 854	7 039
Year-round workers with 1 or 2 weeks of unemployment	527	462	395	382	386	373	379	421	365	359	289
Part-year workers with unemployment	8 769	8 217	7 735	7 244	6 111	5 959	5 685	7 502	7 887	7 495	6 750
1 to 4 weeks	1 365	1 398	1 272	1 275	1 085	1 166	1 070	1 247	1 075	958	1 028
5 to 10 weeks	1 666	1 434	1 478	1 474	1 363	1 168	1 135	1 446	1 342	1 314	1 170
11 to 14 weeks	1 370	1 253	1 258	1 068	980	937	880	1 207	1 186	1 039	1 021
15 to 26 weeks	2 449	2 439	2 076	1 949	1 585	1 655	1 595	2 191	2 282	2 178	2 065
27 weeks or more	1 919	1 693	1 651	1 478	1 098	1 033	1 005	1 412	2 002	2 006	1 466
With 2 or more spells of unemployment	2 940	2 793	2 554	2 437	2 014	1 845	1 809	2 100	1 920	1 882	1 828
2 spells	1 266	1 110	1 109	1 078	880	787	804	1 002	914	946	808
3 or more spells	1 674	1 683	1 445	1 359	1 134	1 058	1 005	1 099	1 006	936	1 020
WOMEN											
Total Who Worked or Looked for Work	66 081	66 716	67 742	68 710	69 591	70 893	71 240	72 081	72 554	72 511	73 097
Percent with unemployment	12.7	12.1	11.3	10.2	9.7	8.4	7.7	9.6	9.9	9.8	9.3
Total with Unemployment	8 383	8 070	7 632	7 033	6 760	5 976	5 463	6 915	7 203	7 123	6 818
Did not work but looked for work	1 570	1 373	1 303	1 151	942	743	683	1 010	1 291	1 275	1 334
Worked during the year	6 813	6 696	6 330	5 882	5 816	5 234	4 779	5 905	5 913	5 848	5 484
Year-round workers with 1 or 2 weeks of unemployment	219	253	194	229	243	189	193	180	220	176	177
Part-year workers with unemployment	6 594	6 443	6 136	5 653	5 573	5 045	4 586	5 725	5 693	5 672	5 307
1 to 4 weeks	1 422	1 413	1 279	1 307	1 237	1 194	1 164	1 121	927	882	957
5 to 10 weeks	1 317	1 291	1 192	1 127	1 131	1 050	878	1 111	1 031	950	929
11 to 14 weeks	896	893	762	754	721	657	625	831	784	710	752
15 to 26 weeks	1 708	1 574	1 586	1 429	1 434	1 148	1 045	1 492	1 566	1 600	1 384
27 weeks or more	1 251	1 272	1 317	1 036	1 050	996	874	1 170	1 385	1 530	1 285
With 2 or more spells of unemployment	1 843	1 675	1 682	1 607	1 614	1 379	1 270	1 321	1 306	1 211	1 069
2 spells	941	853	872	775	770	662	593	641	642	639	537
3 or more spells	902	822	810	832	844	717	677	680	664	572	532

Note: See "Notes and Definitions" for information on historical comparability.

Table 1-45. Percentage Distribution of Persons with Unemployment During the Year by Sex and Extent of Unemployment, 1994–2004

(Percent.)

Sex and extent of unemployment	1994	1995	1996	1997	1998	1999	2000	2001	2002	2003	2004
TOTAL											
Total with Unemployment Who Worked During the Year	100.0	100.0	100.0	100.0	100.0	100.0	100.0	100.0	100.0	100.0	100.0
Year-round workers with 1 or 2 weeks of unemployment	4.6	4.6	4.1	4.5	5.1	4.9	5.3	4.4	4.1	3.9	3.7
Part-year workers with unemployment	95.4	95.4	96.0	95.5	95.0	95.1	94.8	95.6	95.9	96.1	96.3
1 to 4 weeks	17.3	18.3	17.6	19.1	18.9	20.4	20.6	17.1	14.1	13.4	15.9
5 to 10 weeks	18.5	17.7	18.5	19.3	20.3	19.2	18.6	18.5	16.8	16.5	16.8
11 to 14 weeks	14.1	14.0	14.0	13.5	13.8	13.8	13.9	14.7	13.9	12.8	14.2
15 to 26 weeks	25.8	26.1	25.3	25.0	24.5	24.2	24.4	26.6	27.2	27.6	27.5
27 weeks or more	19.7	19.3	20.6	18.6	17.5	17.5	17.3	18.7	23.9	25.8	22.0
With 2 or more spells of unemployment	29.7	29.1	29.3	29.9	29.5	27.9	28.4	24.8	22.8	22.6	23.1
2 spells	13.7	12.8	13.7	13.7	13.4	12.5	12.9	11.9	11.0	11.6	10.7
3 or more spells	16.0	16.3	15.6	16.2	16.1	15.4	15.5	12.9	11.8	11.0	12.4
MEN											
Total with Unemployment Who Worked During the Year	100.0	100.0	100.0	100.0	100.0	100.0	100.0	100.0	100.0	100.0	100.0
Year-round workers with 1 or 2 weeks of unemployment	5.7	5.3	4.9	5.0	5.9	5.9	6.3	5.3	4.4	4.6	4.1
Part-year workers with unemployment	94.3	94.7	95.1	95.1	94.1	94.0	93.6	94.7	95.6	95.4	95.9
1 to 4 weeks	14.7	16.1	15.6	16.7	16.7	18.4	17.6	15.7	13.0	12.2	14.6
5 to 10 weeks	17.9	16.5	18.2	19.3	21.0	18.4	18.7	18.2	16.3	16.7	16.6
11 to 14 weeks	14.7	14.4	15.5	14.0	15.1	14.8	14.5	15.2	14.4	13.2	14.5
15 to 26 weeks	26.4	28.1	25.5	25.6	24.4	26.1	26.3	27.6	27.7	27.7	29.3
27 weeks or more	20.6	19.5	20.3	19.4	16.9	16.3	16.5	17.8	24.3	25.5	20.8
With 2 or more spells of unemployment	31.6	32.2	31.4	31.9	31.0	29.1	29.9	26.5	23.3	24.0	26.0
2 spells	13.6	12.8	13.6	14.1	13.5	12.4	13.3	12.6	11.1	12.1	11.5
3 or more spells	18.0	19.4	17.8	17.8	17.5	16.7	16.6	13.9	12.2	11.9	14.5
WOMEN											
Total With Unemployment Who Worked During the Year	99.9	100.0	100.0	100.0	100.0	100.0	100.0	100.0	100.0	100.0	100.0
Year-round workers with 1 or 2 weeks of unemployment	3.2	3.8	3.1	3.9	4.2	3.6	4.0	3.1	3.7	3.0	3.2
Part-year workers with unemployment	96.7	96.2	96.9	96.1	95.8	96.4	96.0	96.9	96.3	97.0	96.8
1 to 4 weeks	20.9	21.1	20.2	22.2	21.3	22.8	24.3	19.0	15.7	15.1	17.4
5 to 10 weeks	19.3	19.3	18.8	19.2	19.4	20.1	18.4	18.8	17.4	16.2	16.9
11 to 14 weeks	13.1	13.3	12.0	12.8	12.4	12.6	13.1	14.1	13.3	12.1	13.7
15 to 26 weeks	25.1	23.5	25.1	24.3	24.7	21.9	21.9	25.3	26.5	27.4	25.2
27 weeks or more	18.3	19.0	20.8	17.6	18.0	19.0	18.3	19.8	23.4	26.2	23.5
With 2 or more spells of unemployment	27.0	25.0	26.6	27.3	27.7	26.3	26.6	22.4	22.1	20.7	19.5
2 spells	13.8	12.7	13.8	13.2	13.2	12.6	12.4	10.9	10.9	10.9	9.8
3 or more spells	13.2	12.3	12.8	14.1	14.5	13.7	14.2	11.5	11.2	9.8	9.7

Note: See "Notes and Definitions" for information on historical comparability.

Table 1-46. Number and Median Annual Earnings of Year-Round Full-Time Wage and Salary Workers by Age, Sex, and Race, 1990–2004

(Thousands of people, dollars.)

Age, sex and race	1990	1991	1992	1993	1994	1995	1996	1997	1998	1999	2000	2001	2002	2003	2004
NUMBER															
Total, 16 Years and Over	74 728	74 449	75 517	77 427	79 875	83 407	85 611	86 905	89 748	91 722	94 359	94 531	94 526	94 731	96 098
16 to 24 years	6 978	6 571	6 224	6 685	6 684	6 892	6 809	7 063	7 618	7 631	8 384	7 989	7 903	7 631	7 702
25 to 44 years	45 086	44 811	45 022	45 951	47 150	48 695	49 225	49 513	50 264	50 532	51 159	49 939	49 120	48 343	48 421
25 to 34 years	23 201	22 541	22 469	22 637	23 193	23 310	23 071	23 186	23 048	22 952	23 044	22 744	22 657	22 512	22 405
35 to 44 years	21 885	22 270	22 553	23 314	23 957	25 385	26 154	26 327	27 216	27 580	28 115	27 195	26 463	25 831	26 016
45 to 54 years	14 070	14 718	15 652	16 424	17 366	18 436	19 714	20 109	21 274	22 375	23 307	23 855	23 999	24 507	25 074
55 to 64 years	7 458	7 219	7 590	7 208	7 500	8 122	8 455	8 901	9 273	9 594	9 870	10 948	11 584	12 207	12 812
65 years and over	1 137	1 130	1 029	1 159	1 174	1 263	1 408	1 318	1 318	1 590	1 639	1 800	1 921	2 042	2 090
Men, 16 Years and Over	44 574	43 523	43 894	45 494	47 255	49 334	50 407	50 772	52 509	53 132	54 477	54 630	54 420	54 575	55 610
16 to 24 years	3 982	3 596	3 457	3 853	3 918	4 094	3 942	4 021	4 479	4 347	4 602	4 605	4 570	4 421	4 493
25 to 44 years	27 069	26 353	26 335	27 161	28 000	28 940	29 282	29 453	29 763	29 738	30 080	29 271	28 855	28 499	28 763
25 to 34 years	13 941	13 303	13 146	13 400	13 749	13 844	13 817	13 735	13 612	13 471	13 497	13 386	13 400	13 288	13 430
35 to 44 years	13 128	13 050	13 189	13 761	14 251	15 096	15 465	15 718	16 151	16 267	16 583	15 885	15 455	15 211	15 333
45 to 54 years	8 168	8 479	8 908	9 522	10 120	10 589	11 372	11 388	12 030	12 546	13 045	13 363	13 330	13 616	13 975
55 to 64 years	4 650	4 403	4 588	4 238	4 460	4 884	4 908	5 133	5 438	5 498	5 693	6 253	6 502	6 872	7 165
65 years and over	705	694	606	719	757	827	903	775	801	1 003	1 057	1 138	1 163	1 165	1 213
Women, 16 Years and Over	30 155	30 925	31 622	31 933	32 619	34 073	35 203	36 133	37 239	38 591	39 887	39 901	40 106	40 156	40 488
16 to 24 years	2 995	2 976	2 767	2 832	2 767	2 798	2 867	3 041	3 140	3 285	3 782	3 384	3 333	3 210	3 209
25 to 44 years	18 017	18 458	18 688	18 790	19 150	19 755	19 942	20 060	20 503	20 794	21 081	20 668	20 264	19 844	19 656
25 to 34 years	9 260	9 238	9 323	9 237	9 444	9 467	9 254	9 451	9 437	9 481	9 548	9 358	9 257	9 224	8 974
35 to 44 years	8 757	9 220	9 365	9 553	9 706	10 288	10 688	10 609	11 066	11 313	11 533	11 310	11 007	10 620	10 682
45 to 54 years	5 902	6 239	6 744	6 902	7 246	7 847	8 343	8 721	9 244	9 829	10 263	10 493	10 669	10 891	11 099
55 to 64 years	2 808	2 816	3 002	2 970	3 040	3 238	3 547	3 767	3 836	4 096	4 178	4 695	5 082	5 335	5 647
65 years and over	433	436	423	439	417	436	505	543	517	586	583	662	758	877	877
White, 16 Years and Over	64 128	63 926	64 706	65 656	67 370	70 430	72 068	72 650	75 046	76 203	77 790	78 306	77 632	77 545	78 236
Men	38 915	38 018	38 267	39 347	40 589	42 608	43 554	43 429	44 901	45 211	46 105	46 373	45 823	45 816	46 317
Women	25 213	25 908	26 439	26 309	26 782	27 822	28 514	29 221	30 145	30 992	31 685	31 933	31 809	31 729	31 919
Black, 16 Years and Over	8 027	7 941	7 995	8 478	9 074	9 446	9 706	10 248	10 532	11 145	11 899	11 001	10 966	10 979	11 301
Men	4 162	4 001	4 011	4 259	4 598	4 686	4 682	5 026	5 202	5 411	5 636	5 281	5 150	5 196	5 470
Women	3 865	3 940	3 984	4 219	4 476	4 759	5 024	5 222	5 329	5 734	6 264	5 720	5 816	5 783	5 832
MEDIAN ANNUAL EARNINGS															
Total, 16 Years and Over	24 000	25 000	25 871	26 000	26 620	27 000	28 000	30 000	30 000	31 000	32 000	34 000	35 000	35 000	35 672
16 to 24 years	14 400	14 100	15 000	15 000	15 000	15 500	15 500	16 000	18 000	18 000	19 000	20 000	20 000	20 000	20 000
25 to 34 years	22 000	23 000	24 000	24 000	24 480	25 000	25 300	27 000	28 500	30 000	30 000	31 000	31 800	32 000	33 000
35 to 44 years	27 970	28 000	29 483	30 000	30 000	30 000	31 000	32 000	33 000	34 992	35 000	36 000	37 000	39 000	40 000
45 to 54 years	28 000	29 000	30 000	30 500	32 343	32 000	33 000	35 000	35 000	36 000	38 000	39 500	40 000	40 000	40 000
55 to 64 years	26 000	27 000	27 430	28 000	30 000	30 000	30 000	32 000	34 000	35 000	35 000	36 400	39 145	40 000	40 000
65 years and over	23 841	22 000	24 000	24 000	24 377	29 600	26 496	28 200	26 000	30 000	32 000	32 000	33 000	32 000	35 000
Men, 16 Years and Over	28 000	29 120	30 000	30 000	30 000	31 000	32 000	34 000	35 000	36 000	37 600	38 500	40 000	40 000	40 000
16 to 24 years	15 000	15 000	15 000	15 000	15 000	16 000	17 000	17 000	18 720	19 000	20 000	20 000	20 000	20 800	20 800
25 to 34 years	25 000	25 000	26 000	25 000	26 000	27 000	28 000	29 852	30 000	32 000	33 500	34 000	34 740	35 000	35 000
35 to 44 years	32 000	33 000	34 000	35 000	35 000	35 000	36 000	37 000	38 000	40 000	40 000	42 000	43 000	43 900	45 000
45 to 54 years	35 000	36 000	37 000	38 000	40 000	40 000	40 000	41 000	42 000	44 616	45 000	45 000	47 000	48 000	48 000
55 to 64 years	31 875	33 000	33 000	34 000	36 000	36 000	36 000	39 000	40 000	40 853	44 000	45 000	47 000	50 000	50 000
65 years and over	29 000	28 000	30 000	28 000	30 000	36 000	33 000	36 400	35 000	36 000	35 999	35 000	37 861	42 000	40 000
Women, 16 Years and Over	20 000	20 000	21 500	22 000	22 150	23 000	24 000	25 000	25 000	26 000	27 500	29 000	30 000	30 000	30 001
16 to 24 years	13 392	13 800	14 000	14 872	14 560	15 000	15 000	15 000	17 000	17 000	18 000	19 000	19 000	20 000	20 000
25 to 34 years	19 500	20 000	21 000	21 000	22 000	22 000	23 000	24 000	25 000	26 000	27 000	28 080	29 500	30 000	30 000
35 to 44 years	22 000	22 510	23 397	24 000	25 000	25 000	25 000	26 000	27 200	28 000	29 000	30 000	30 400	32 000	32 800
45 to 54 years	21 000	22 000	24 000	24 000	25 000	25 000	26 000	27 040	28 132	30 000	30 000	32 000	32 000	33 466	34 771
55 to 64 years	19 000	20 000	22 000	21 500	22 000	22 500	24 000	24 800	25 775	27 000	28 000	30 000	31 410	32 000	33 000
65 years and over	18 586	17 000	18 500	20 000	19 000	23 290	20 800	24 000	22 000	20 800	24 000	25 000	28 000	26 000	27 000
White, 16 Years and Over	25 000	25 000	26 200	27 000	28 000	28 000	29 000	30 000	31 000	32 000	34 000	35 000	35 000	36 000	37 000
Men	29 000	30 000	31 000	30 700	32 000	32 000	33 000	35 000	36 000	37 200	39 000	40 000	40 000	40 000	42 000
Women	20 000	20 500	22 000	22 000	23 000	23 000	24 000	25 000	26 000	27 000	28 000	30 000	30 000	31 000	31 800
Black, 16 Years and Over	19 350	20 000	21 000	20 800	21 000	22 000	23 784	24 000	25 000	25 760	26 000	28 500	29 000	30 000	30 000
Men	20 800	22 000	22 312	23 000	23 500	24 500	26 000	26 000	27 000	30 000	30 000	30 000	30 000	30 000	30 000
Women	18 000	18 500	20 000	19 843	20 000	20 000	21 000	22 000	23 000	24 000	25 000	26 000	26 000	27 000	28 000

Note: Detail for the above race groups will not sum to totals because data for the "Other" races group are not presented. See "Notes and Definitions" for information on historical comparability.

Table 1-47. Number and Median Annual Earnings of Year-Round Full-Time Wage and Salary Workers by Sex and Occupation of Job Held the Longest, 2002–2004

(Thousands of people, dollars.)

Occupation	2002	2003	2004
Total, Number of Workers			
Management, business, and financial operations occupations	15 707	15 552	15 575
Management occupations	11 350	11 102	11 125
Business and financial operations occupations	4 357	4 450	4 451
Professional and related occupations	19 149	19 607	19 592
Computer and mathematical occupations	2 644	2 598	2 680
Architecture and engineering occupations	2 257	2 273	2 349
Life, physical, and social science occupations	1 094	1 010	999
Community and social services occupations	1 694	1 698	1 632
Legal occupations	1 006	1 149	1 087
Education, training, and library occupations	4 606	4 918	4 742
Arts, design, entertainment, sports, and media occupations	1 453	1 374	1 416
Healthcare practitioner and technical occupations	4 395	4 586	4 688
Service occupations	12 011	11 990	12 457
Healthcare support occupations	1 767	1 703	1 781
Protective service occupations	2 042	2 385	2 406
Food preparation and serving related occupations	3 592	3 223	3 383
Building and grounds cleaning and maintenance occupations	2 843	2 942	3 116
Personal care and service occupations	1 767	1 735	1 771
Sales and office occupations	23 791	23 766	23 619
Sales and related occupations	9 929	9 804	9 951
Office and administrative support occupations	13 862	13 962	13 668
Natural resources, construction, and maintenance occupations	9 823	9 709	10 574
Farming, fishing, and forestry occupations	573	562	629
Construction and extraction occupations	5 256	5 070	5 711
Installation, maintenance, and repair occupations	3 994	4 077	4 234
Production, transportation, and material moving occupations	13 386	13 391	13 648
Production occupations	7 736	7 670	7 787
Transportation and material moving occupations	5 650	5 721	5 861
Armed forces	658	717	632
Total, Median Annual Earnings			
Management, business, and financial operations occupations	50 000	52 000	55 000
Management occupations	55 000	58 000	60 000
Business and financial operations occupations	44 000	45 000	45 000
Professional and related occupations	46 000	46 000	48 000
Computer and mathematical occupations	60 000	60 000	62 000
Architecture and engineering occupations	59 400	62 000	60 000
Life, physical, and social science occupations	50 000	50 000	50 000
Community and social services occupations	34 000	34 349	36 000
Legal occupations	61 860	75 000	70 000
Education, training, and library occupations	38 000	39 000	40 000
Arts, design, entertainment, sports, and media occupations	43 500	40 000	40 000
Healthcare practitioner and technical occupations	46 000	48 000	50 000
Service occupations	22 000	22 000	22 000
Healthcare support occupations	22 100	22 000	22 000
Protective service occupations	38 000	42 000	42 000
Food preparation and serving related occupations	18 000	18 000	18 000
Building and grounds cleaning and maintenance occupations	20 000	20 000	20 000
Personal care and service occupations	21 840	20 678	22 537
Sales and office occupations	30 000	30 000	30 000
Sales and related occupations	35 000	35 000	35 000
Office and administrative support occupations	28 000	29 000	30 000
Natural resources, construction, and maintenance occupations	33 000	34 000	35 000
Farming, fishing, and forestry occupations	20 000	20 000	20 000
Construction and extraction occupations	31 200	32 000	33 000
Installation, maintenance, and repair occupations	36 000	38 000	38 300
Production, transportation, and material moving occupations	28 704	30 000	30 000
Production occupations	28 000	30 000	30 000
Transportation and material moving occupations	29 000	30 000	30 000
Armed forces	36 000	36 000	40 000

Table 1-47. Number and Median Annual Earnings of Year-Round Full-Time Wage and Salary Workers by Sex and Occupation of Job Held the Longest, 2002–2004—Continued

(Thousands of people, dollars.)

Occupation	2002	2003	2004
Men, Number of Workers			
Management, business, and financial operations occupations	9 178	8 961	8 849
Management occupations	7 145	6 991	6 911
Business and financial operations occupations	2 033	1 970	1 938
Professional and related occupations	9 299	9 535	9 497
Computer and mathematical occupations	1 953	1 913	1 972
Architecture and engineering occupations	1 984	2 004	2 049
Life, physical, and social science occupations	667	668	626
Community and social services occupations	726	730	705
Legal occupations	490	610	537
Education, training, and library occupations	1 407	1 476	1 386
Arts, design, entertainment, sports, and media occupations	847	811	848
Healthcare practitioner and technical occupations	1 225	1 323	1 374
Service occupations	5 988	6 204	6 314
Healthcare supporting occupations	181	178	208
Protective service occupations	1 689	1 967	1 906
Food preparation and serving related occupations	1 836	1 638	1 716
Building and grounds cleaning and maintenance occupations	1 788	1 914	2 002
Personal care and service occupations	494	508	482
Sales and office occupations	9 453	9 398	9 380
Sales and related occupations	5 933	5 891	5 892
Office and administrative support occupations	3 520	3 507	3 488
Natural resources, construction, and maintenance occupations	9 434	9 348	10 178
Farming, fishing, and forestry occupations	463	470	536
Construction and extraction occupations	5 156	4 972	5 576
Installation, maintenance, and repair occupations	3 815	3 905	4 065
Production, transportation, and material moving occupations	10 472	10 492	10 812
Production occupations	5 517	5 513	5 637
Transportation and material moving occupations	4 955	4 979	5 176
Armed forces	600	636	580
Men, Median Annual Earnings			
Management, business, and financial operations occupations	60 000	60 200	65 000
Management occupations	65 000	65 000	70 000
Business and financial operations occupations	52 000	51 000	55 000
Professional and related occupations	55 000	58 000	58 000
Computer and mathematical occupations	60 000	65 000	65 000
Architecture and engineering occupations	60 000	64 558	61 785
Life, physical, and social science occupations	52 000	50 801	55 000
Community and social services occupations	35 000	35 000	38 000
Legal occupations	100 000	100 000	101 000
Education, training, and library occupations	45 600	48 000	47 000
Arts, design, entertainment, sports, and media occupations	46 000	45 000	45 000
Healthcare practitioner and technical occupations	72 000	65 500	70 000
Service occupations	25 000	26 000	25 000
Healthcare support occupations	24 000	22 537	20 400
Protective service occupations	40 000	44 000	44 000
Food preparation and serving related occupations	20 000	18 720	18 720
Building and grounds cleaning and maintenance occupations	24 500	22 156	24 000
Personal care and service occupations	30 000	28 559	26 000
Sales and office occupations	38 000	39 000	40 000
Sales and related occupations	41 600	41 000	44 000
Office and administrative support occupations	32 000	32 000	34 000
Natural resources, construction, and maintenance occupations	33 592	34 283	35 000
Farming, fishing, and forestry occupations	22 000	22 000	22 000
Construction and extraction occupations	31 304	32 000	33 000
Installation, maintenance, and repair occupations	36 000	38 000	38 870
Production, transportation, and material moving occupations	30 000	32 000	33 000
Production occupations	30 360	32 000	34 000
Transportation and material moving occupations	30 000	30 000	32 000
Armed forces	36 000	36 000	40 000

Table 1-47. Number and Median Annual Earnings of Year-Round Full-Time Wage and Salary Workers by Sex and Occupation of Job Held the Longest, 2002–2004—*Continued*

(Thousands of people, dollars.)

Occupation	2002	2003	2004
Women, Number of Workers			
Management, business and financial operations occupations	6 529	6 591	6 726
Management occupations	4 205	4 111	4 214
Business and financial operations occupations	2 324	2 479	2 512
Professional and related occupations	9 851	10 071	10 095
Computer and mathematical occupations	691	685	708
Architecture and engineering occupations	273	269	300
Life, physical, and social science occupations	428	342	373
Community and social services occupations	968	968	927
Legal occupations	516	539	550
Education, training, and library occupations	3 199	3 441	3 356
Arts, design, entertainment, sports, and media occupations	606	563	568
Healthcare practitioner and technical occupations	3 170	3 263	3 314
Service occupations	6 026	5 786	6 144
Healthcare support occupations	1 586	1 525	1 573
Protective service occupations	354	419	500
Food preparation and serving related occupations	1 757	1 585	1 668
Building and grounds cleaning and maintenance occupations	1 055	1 029	1 115
Personal care and service occupations	1 274	1 228	1 289
Sales and office occupations	14 338	14 368	14 239
Sales and related occupations	3 996	3 913	4 060
Office and administrative support occupations	10 342	10 455	10 180
Natural resources, construction, and maintenance occupations	391	361	396
Farming, fishing, and forestry occupations	111	92	93
Construction and extraction occupations	100	97	135
Installation, maintenance, and repair occupations	180	172	169
Production, transportation, and material moving occupations	2 914	2 899	2 835
Production occupations	2 219	2 157	2 150
Transportation and material moving occupations	695	742	685
Armed forces	58	81	52
Women, Median Annual Earnings			
Management, business, and financial operations occupations	41 000	43 000	43 000
Management occupations	44 000	47 000	46 000
Business and financial operations occupations	38 500	40 000	40 000
Professional and related occupations	40 000	40 000	40 000
Computer and mathematical occupations	51 627	52 000	57 000
Architecture and engineering occupations	50 000	48 000	47 500
Life, physical, and social science occupations	44 000	45 000	45 995
Community and social services occupations	33 000	33 000	35 000
Legal occupations	45 000	45 000	46 000
Education, training, and library occupations	35 000	35 000	37 000
Arts, design, entertainment, sports, and media occupations	40 000	35 000	36 000
Healthcare practitioner and technical occupations	41 000	43 000	45 000
Service occupations	20 000	20 000	20 000
Healthcare support occupations	22 000	22 000	22 000
Protective service occupations	30 900	32 000	32 000
Food preparation and serving related occupations	16 160	17 000	16 000
Building and grounds cleaning and maintenance occupations	16 491	16 000	16 866
Personal care and service occupations	20 000	20 000	21 000
Sales and office occupations	26 989	28 000	28 000
Sales and related occupations	25 000	26 000	26 000
Office and administrative support occupations	27 000	28 000	28 000
Natural resources, construction, and maintenance	26 000	28 000	30 000
Farming, fishing, and forestry occupations	17 000	16 000	15 700
Construction and extraction occupations	26 000	29 500	40 000
Installation, maintenance, and repair occupations	34 000	37 000	33 000
Production, transportation, and material moving occupations	22 000	22 100	23 000
Production occupations	21 632	22 000	23 000
Transportation and material moving occupations	22 000	22 710	23 000
Armed forces	40 000	32 000	35 100

Note: See "Notes and Definitions" for information on historical comparability.

Table 1-48. Wage and Salary Workers Paid Hourly Rates with Earnings at or Below the Prevailing Federal Minimum Wage by Selected Characteristics, 2003–2004

(Thousands of people, percent.)

Characteristic	Workers paid hourly rates				
	Total	Below prevailing federal minimum wage	At prevailing federal minimum wage	Total at or below prevailing federal minimum wage	
				Number	Percent of hourly-paid workers
2003					
Sex and Age					
Total, 16 years and over	72 946	1 555	545	2 100	2.9
16 to 24 years	15 871	776	330	1 105	7.0
25 years and over	57 075	780	215	995	1.7
Men, 16 years and over	35 853	493	213	706	2.0
16 to 24 years	8 031	237	154	392	4.9
25 years and over	27 823	256	58	315	1.1
Women, 16 years and over	37 093	1 062	332	1 394	3.8
16 to 24 years	7 841	538	175	713	9.1
25 years and over	29 252	524	157	681	2.3
Race, Hispanic Origin, and Sex					
White, 16 years and over [1]	59 109	1 325	421	1 746	3.0
Men	29 441	390	163	553	1.9
Women	29 668	935	257	1 193	4.0
Black, 16 years and over [1]	9 419	145	105	249	2.6
Men	4 246	71	41	112	2.6
Women	5 173	74	64	138	2.7
Hispanic origin, 16 years and over	11 462	214	94	308	2.7
Men	6 775	89	39	128	1.9
Women	4 687	125	55	180	3.8
Full-and Part-Time Status and Sex [2]					
Full-time workers	54 887	639	156	796	1.4
Men	30 141	243	60	303	1.0
Women	24 745	396	97	493	2.0
Part-time workers	17 932	910	388	1 299	7.2
Men	5 651	249	153	402	7.1
Women	12 282	661	235	896	7.3
2004					
Sex and Age					
Total, 16 years and over	73 939	1 483	520	2 003	2.7
16 to 24 years	16 174	750	272	1 021	6.3
25 years and over	57 765	733	249	982	1.7
Men, 16 years and over	36 806	470	210	680	1.8
16 to 24 years	8 305	239	127	366	4.4
25 years and over	28 500	231	83	314	1.1
Women, 16 years and over	37 133	1 013	310	1 323	3.6
16 to 24 years	7 869	510	145	655	8.3
25 years and over	29 265	502	166	668	2.3
Race, Hispanic Origin, and Sex					
White, 16 years and over [1]	59 877	1 286	395	1 681	2.8
Men	30 255	393	161	555	1.8
Women	29 621	892	234	1 126	3.8
Black, 16 years and over [1]	9 417	128	99	228	2.4
Men	4 243	49	40	89	2.1
Women	5 174	79	59	138	2.7
Hispanic origin, 16 years and over	12 073	168	82	250	2.1
Men	7 183	66	32	99	1.4
Women	4 890	102	49	151	3.1
Full-and Part-Time Status and Sex [2]					
Full-time workers	55 739	583	177	760	1.4
Men	30 951	223	77	300	1.0
Women	24 788	360	100	460	1.9
Part-time workers	18 046	897	343	1 240	6.9
Men	5 770	246	132	378	6.6
Women	12 276	651	210	861	7.0

Note: The prevailing federal minimum wage was $5.15 per hour in 2004. Data are for wage and salary workers, excluding the incorporated self-employed. They refer to a person's earnings for their sole or principal job, and pertain only to workers who are paid hourly rates. Salaried workers and other non-hourly workers are not included. The presence of workers with hourly earnings below the minimum wage does not necessarily indicate violations of the Fair Labor Standards Act, as there are exceptions to the minimum wage provisions of the law. In addition, some survey respondents might have rounded hourly earnings to the nearest dollar, and, as a result, reported hourly earnings below the minimum wage even though they earned the minimum wage or higher. Beginning in January 2003, data reflect revised population controls used in the household survey. Persons of Hispanic origin may be of any race.

[1] Beginning in 2003, persons who selected this race group only; persons who selected more than one race group are not included. Prior to 2003, persons who reported more than one race group were included in the group they identified as the main race.
[2] The distinction between full- and part-time workers is based on the hours usually worked. These data will not sum to totals because full- or part-time status on the principal job is not identifiable for a small number of multiple jobholders.

Table 1-49. Absences from Work of Employed Full-Time Wage and Salary Workers by Age and Sex, 2002–2004

(Thousands of people, percent.)

Age and sex	Total employed	Absence rate [1]			Lost worktime rate [2]		
		Total	Illness or injury	Other reasons	Total	Illness or injury	Other reasons
2002							
Total, 16 Years and Over	100 228	3.5	2.5	1.0	1.9	1.3	0.6
16 to 19 years	1 902	2.9	2.1	0.9	1.3	0.8	0.4
20 to 24 years	9 267	3.5	2.3	1.2	1.8	1.1	0.7
25 years and over	89 060	3.6	2.5	1.0	1.9	1.4	0.5
25 to 54 years	76 585	3.5	2.4	1.1	1.9	1.3	0.6
55 years and over	12 475	3.8	3.1	0.7	2.1	1.8	0.3
Men, 16 Years and Over	56 458	2.6	2.0	0.6	1.4	1.1	0.3
16 to 19 years	1 139	2.2	1.7	0.5	0.9	0.7	0.2
20 to 24 years	5 210	2.3	1.8	0.5	1.1	0.9	0.2
25 years and over	50 109	2.6	2.0	0.6	1.4	1.1	0.3
25 to 54 years	43 220	2.5	1.9	0.6	1.3	1.0	0.3
55 years and over	6 889	3.2	2.7	0.5	1.9	1.7	0.2
Women, 16 Years and Over	43 771	4.8	3.2	1.6	2.6	1.7	0.9
16 to 19 years	763	4.1	2.7	1.5	1.8	1.1	0.8
20 to 24 years	4 057	4.9	2.9	2.1	2.6	1.3	1.4
25 years and over	38 951	4.8	3.3	1.5	2.6	1.7	0.9
25 to 54 years	33 365	4.8	3.2	1.6	2.6	1.6	1.0
55 years and over	5 586	4.5	3.7	0.9	2.4	2.0	0.4
2003							
Total, 16 Years and Over	100 198	3.3	2.4	1.0	1.8	1.3	0.5
16 to 19 years	1 633	2.8	2.0	0.8	1.4	0.9	0.5
20 to 24 years	9 183	3.1	2.0	1.1	1.5	0.9	0.6
25 years and over	89 382	3.4	2.4	0.9	1.8	1.3	0.5
25 to 54 years	76 216	3.3	2.3	1.0	1.8	1.2	0.5
55 years and over	13 166	3.6	2.9	0.6	2.1	1.8	0.3
Men, 16 Years and Over	56 159	2.5	1.9	0.6	1.3	1.1	0.3
16 to 19 years	956	2.2	1.6	0.6	1.1	0.8	0.3
20 to 24 years	5 201	2.1	1.5	0.5	1.0	0.7	0.3
25 years and over	50 001	2.5	1.9	0.6	1.4	1.1	0.3
25 to 54 years	42 863	2.4	1.8	0.6	1.3	1.0	0.3
55 years and over	7 138	2.9	2.4	0.5	1.7	1.5	0.2
Women, 16 Years and Over	44 039	4.4	3.0	1.4	2.4	1.6	0.8
16 to 19 years	677	3.7	2.6	1.1	1.7	1.0	0.7
20 to 24 years	3 981	4.5	2.7	1.8	2.2	1.1	1.1
25 years and over	39 381	4.4	3.0	1.4	2.4	1.6	0.8
25 to 54 years	33 353	4.4	2.9	1.5	2.4	1.5	0.9
55 years and over	6 028	4.3	3.5	0.8	2.5	2.1	0.4
2004							
Total, 16 Years and Over	101 011	3.2	2.3	0.9	1.7	1.2	0.5
16 to 19 years	1 663	3.2	2.4	0.8	1.7	1.2	0.5
20 to 24 years	9 191	3.1	2.0	1.1	1.6	0.9	0.6
25 years and over	90 157	3.2	2.3	0.9	1.8	1.3	0.5
25 to 54 years	76 458	3.1	2.2	1.0	1.7	1.2	0.5
55 years and over	13 699	3.5	2.9	0.7	2.1	1.8	0.3
Men, 16 Years and Over	56 922	2.3	1.8	0.5	1.2	1.0	0.2
16 to 19 years	1 015	2.9	2.4	0.5	1.7	1.4	0.3
20 to 24 years	5 242	2.2	1.6	0.5	1.1	0.8	0.2
25 years and over	50 665	2.3	1.8	0.5	1.3	1.0	0.2
25 to 54 years	43 177	2.2	1.7	0.5	1.2	0.9	0.2
55 years and over	7 489	3.0	2.4	0.5	1.9	1.6	0.2
Women, 16 Years and Over	44 088	4.4	2.9	1.4	2.4	1.5	0.9
16 to 19 years	648	3.7	2.3	1.3	1.8	0.9	0.9
20 to 24 years	3 949	4.4	2.6	1.8	2.3	1.1	1.2
25 years and over	39 492	4.4	3.0	1.4	2.4	1.6	0.8
25 to 54 years	33 282	4.4	2.9	1.5	2.4	1.5	0.9
55 years and over	6 210	4.2	3.4	0.9	2.4	2.0	0.4

Note: Beginning in January 2003, data reflect revised population controls used in the household survey.

[1]Absences are defined as instances when persons who usually work 35 or more hours a week worked less than 35 hours during the reference week for reasons including: own illness, injury, or medical problems; child care problems; other family or personal obligations; civic or military duty; and maternity or paternity leave. Excluded are situations in which work was missed due to vacation or personal days, holiday, labor dispute, and other reasons. For multiple jobholders, absence data refer only to work missed at their main jobs. The absence rate is the ratio of workers with absences to total full-time wage and salary employment. The estimates of full-time wage and salary employment shown in this table do not match those in other tables because the estimates in this table are based on the full Current Population Survey (CPS) sample. Those in the other tables are based on a quarter of the sample only.
[2]Hours absent as a percentage of the hours usually worked.

Table 1-50. Median Years of Tenure with Current Employer for Employed Wage and Salary Workers by Age and Sex, Selected Years, 1983–2004

(Number.)

Age and sex	January 1983	January 1987	January 1991	January 1996	February 1998	February 2000	January 2002	January 2004
Total								
16 years and over	3.5	3.4	3.6	3.8	3.6	3.5	3.7	4.0
16 to 17 years	0.7	0.6	0.7	0.7	0.6	0.6	0.7	0.7
18 to 19 years	0.8	0.7	0.8	0.7	0.7	0.7	0.8	0.8
20 to 24 years	1.5	1.3	1.3	1.2	1.1	1.1	1.2	1.3
25 years and over	5.0	5.0	4.8	5.0	4.7	4.7	4.7	4.9
25 to 34 years	3.0	2.9	2.9	2.8	2.7	2.6	2.7	2.9
35 to 44 years	5.2	5.5	5.4	5.3	5.0	4.8	4.6	4.9
45 to 54 years	9.5	8.8	8.9	8.3	8.1	8.2	7.6	7.7
55 to 64 years	12.2	11.6	11.1	10.2	10.1	10.0	9.9	9.6
65 years and over	9.6	9.5	8.1	8.4	7.8	9.4	8.6	9.0
Men								
16 years and over	4.1	4.0	4.1	4.0	3.8	3.8	3.9	4.1
16 to 17 years	0.7	0.6	0.7	0.6	0.6	0.6	0.8	0.7
18 to 19 years	0.8	0.7	0.8	0.7	0.7	0.7	0.8	0.8
20 to 24 years	1.5	1.3	1.4	1.2	1.2	1.2	1.4	1.3
25 years and over	5.9	5.7	5.4	5.3	4.9	4.9	4.9	5.1
25 to 34 years	3.2	3.1	3.1	3.0	2.8	2.7	2.8	3.0
35 to 44 years	7.3	7.0	6.5	6.1	5.5	5.3	5.0	5.2
45 to 54 years	12.8	11.8	11.2	10.1	9.4	9.5	9.1	9.6
55 to 64 years	15.3	14.5	13.4	10.5	11.2	10.2	10.2	9.8
65 years and over	8.3	8.3	7.0	8.3	7.1	9.0	8.1	8.2
Women								
16 years and over	3.1	3.0	3.2	3.5	3.4	3.3	3.4	3.8
16 to 17 years	0.7	0.6	0.7	0.7	0.7	0.6	0.7	0.6
18 to 19 years	0.8	0.7	0.8	0.7	0.7	0.7	0.7	0.8
20 to 24 years	1.5	1.3	1.3	1.2	1.1	1.0	1.1	1.3
25 years and over	4.2	4.3	4.3	4.7	4.4	4.4	4.4	4.7
25 to 34 years	2.8	2.6	2.7	2.7	2.5	2.5	2.5	2.8
35 to 44 years	4.1	4.4	4.5	4.8	4.5	4.3	4.2	4.5
45 to 54 years	6.3	6.8	6.7	7.0	7.2	7.3	6.5	6.4
55 to 64 years	9.8	9.7	9.9	10.0	9.6	9.9	9.6	9.2
65 years and over	10.1	9.9	9.5	8.4	8.7	9.7	9.5	9.6

Note: Data beginning 2000 reflect the introduction of Census 2000 population controls in January 2003 and are not strictly comparable with data for prior years. In addition, data for 2004 reflect the introduction of revised population controls in January 2003 and January 2004. Data for 1996 and 1998 are based on population controls from the 1990 census. Data for the period 1983–1991 are based on population controls from the 1980 census. Also, beginning in 1996, the figures incorporate the effects of the redesign of the Current Population Survey (CPS) introduced in January 1994. Data exclude the incorporated and unincorporated self-employed.

Table 1-51. Median Years of Tenure with Current Employer for Employed Wage and Salary Workers by Industry, Selected Years, 2000–2004

(Number.)

Industry	February 2000	January 2002	January 2004
TOTAL, 16 YEARS AND OVER	3.5	3.7	4.0
Private sector	3.2	3.3	3.5
Agriculture and related industries	3.7	4.2	3.7
Nonagricultural industries	3.2	3.3	3.5
Mining	4.8	4.5	5.2
Construction	2.7	3.0	3.0
Manufacturing	4.9	5.4	5.8
Durable goods manufacturing	4.8	5.5	6.0
Nonmetallic mineral products	5.5	5.3	4.8
Primary metals and fabricated metal products	5.0	6.3	6.4
Machinery manufacturing	5.3	6.8	6.4
Computers and electronic products	3.9	4.7	5.2
Electrical equipment and appliances	5.0	5.5	9.8
Transportation equipment	6.4	7.0	7.7
Wood products	3.7	4.3	5.0
Furniture and fixtures	4.4	4.7	4.7
Miscellaneous manufacturing	3.7	4.5	4.6
Nondurable goods manufacturing	5.0	5.3	5.5
Food manufacturing	4.6	5.0	4.9
Beverage and tobacco products	5.5	4.6	8.0
Textiles, apparel, and leather	4.7	5.0	5.0
Paper and printing	5.1	6.2	6.9
Petroleum and coal products	9.5	9.8	11.4
Chemicals	6.0	5.7	5.3
Plastics and rubber products	4.6	5.3	5.7
Wholesale and retail trade	2.7	2.8	3.1
Wholesale trade	3.9	3.9	4.3
Retail trade	2.5	2.6	2.8
Transportation and utilities	4.7	4.9	5.3
Transportation and warehousing	4.0	4.3	4.7
Utilities	11.5	13.4	13.3
Information [1]	3.4	3.3	4.3
Publishing, except Internet	4.2	4.8	4.7
Motion picture and sound recording industries	1.6	2.3	2.2
Broadcasting, except Internet	3.6	3.1	4.0
Telecommunications	4.3	3.4	4.6
Financial activities	3.5	3.6	3.9
Finance and insurance	3.6	3.9	4.1
Finance	3.3	3.6	4.0
Insurance	4.4	4.5	4.4
Real estate and rental and leasing	3.1	3.0	3.3
Real estate	3.1	3.2	3.5
Rental and leasing services	3.0	2.2	2.9
Professional and business services	2.4	2.7	3.2
Professional and technical services	2.6	3.1	3.6
Management, administrative, and waste services [1]	2.0	2.1	2.6
Administrative and support services	1.8	1.9	2.4
Waste management and remediation services	3.6	4.3	3.4
Education and health services	3.4	3.5	3.6
Educational services	3.2	3.6	3.8
Health care and social assistance	3.5	3.5	3.6
Hospitals	5.1	4.9	4.7
Health services, except hospitals	3.2	3.1	3.3
Social assistance	2.4	2.5	2.8
Leisure and hospitality	1.7	1.8	2.0
Arts, entertainment, and recreation	2.6	2.3	2.8
Accommodation and food services	1.5	1.6	1.9
Accommodation	2.8	2.7	3.1
Food services and drinking places	1.4	1.4	1.6
Other services	3.1	3.3	3.3
Other services, except private households	3.2	3.3	3.5
Repair and maintenance	3.0	3.0	3.2
Personal and laundry services	2.7	2.8	3.4
Membership associations and organizations	4.0	4.1	3.9
Other services, private households	3.0	2.7	2.3
Public sector	7.1	6.7	6.9
Federal government	11.5	11.3	10.4
State government	5.5	5.4	6.4
Local government	6.7	6.2	6.4

Note: Data reflect the introduction of Census 2000 population controls in January 2003 and are not strictly comparable with data for prior years. In addition, data for 2004 reflect the introduction of additional revised population controls in January 2003 and January 2004. Industries reflect the introduction of the 2002 Census industry classification system derived from the 2002 North American Industry Classification System (NAICS) into the Current Population Survey (CPS). Data refer to the sole or principal job of full- and part-time workers. Excluded are all self-employed workers, regardless of whether or not their businesses are incorporated.

[1]Includes other industries, not shown separately.

Table 1-52. Employment Status of the Population by Sex and Marital Status, March 1990–2005

(Thousands of people, percent.)

Marital status and year	Men Population	Men Labor force Total Number	Men Labor force Total Percent of population	Men Employed	Men Unemployed Number	Men Unemployed Percent of labor force	Women Population	Women Labor force Total Number	Women Labor force Total Percent of population	Women Employed	Women Unemployed Number	Women Unemployed Percent of labor force
Single												
1990	25 757	18 829	73.1	16 893	1 936	10.3	21 088	14 003	66.4	12 856	1 147	8.2
1991	26 220	19 014	72.5	16 418	2 596	13.7	21 688	14 125	65.1	12 887	1 238	8.8
1992	26 529	19 229	72.5	16 401	2 828	14.7	21 738	14 072	64.7	12 793	1 279	9.1
1993	26 951	19 625	72.8	16 858	2 767	14.1	21 848	14 091	64.5	12 711	1 380	9.8
1994	28 350	20 365	71.8	17 826	2 539	12.5	22 885	14 903	65.1	13 419	1 484	10.0
1995	28 318	20 449	72.2	18 286	2 163	10.6	22 853	14 974	65.5	13 673	1 301	8.7
1996	28 695	20 561	71.7	18 097	2 464	12.0	23 632	15 417	65.2	14 084	1 333	8.6
1997	29 294	20 942	71.5	18 683	2 259	10.8	24 215	16 178	66.8	14 747	1 431	8.8
1998	29 558	21 255	71.9	19 124	2 131	10.0	24 808	16 885	68.1	15 626	1 259	7.5
1999	29 883	21 329	71.4	19 465	1 864	8.7	25 674	17 486	68.1	16 185	1 301	7.4
2000	30 232	21 641	71.6	19 823	1 818	8.4	25 863	17 749	68.6	16 446	1 303	7.3
2001	30 968	22 232	71.8	20 239	1 993	9.0	26 180	17 900	68.4	16 631	1 269	7.1
2002	32 220	22 761	70.6	20 066	2 695	11.8	26 942	18 079	67.1	16 499	1 580	8.7
2003	32 852	22 821	69.5	20 194	2 627	11.5	27 527	17 901	65.0	16 219	1 682	9.4
2004	33 786	23 212	68.7	20 434	2 778	12.0	28 033	18 089	64.5	16 506	1 583	8.8
2005	34 069	23 335	68.5	20 831	2 504	10.7	28 508	18 554	65.1	16 902	1 652	8.9
Married, Spouse Present												
1990	52 464	41 020	78.2	39 562	1 458	3.6	53 207	30 967	58.2	29 870	1 097	3.5
1991	52 460	40 883	77.9	38 843	2 040	5.0	53 176	31 103	58.5	29 668	1 435	4.6
1992	52 780	40 930	77.5	38 650	2 280	5.6	53 464	31 686	59.3	30 130	1 556	4.9
1993	53 488	41 255	77.1	39 069	2 186	5.3	54 146	32 158	59.4	30 757	1 401	4.4
1994	53 436	40 993	76.7	39 085	1 908	4.7	54 198	32 863	60.6	31 397	1 466	4.5
1995	54 166	41 806	77.2	40 262	1 544	3.7	54 902	33 563	61.1	32 267	1 296	3.9
1996	53 996	41 837	77.5	40 356	1 481	3.5	54 640	33 382	61.1	32 258	1 124	3.4
1997	53 981	41 967	77.7	40 628	1 339	3.2	54 611	33 907	62.1	32 836	1 071	3.2
1998	54 685	42 288	77.3	41 039	1 249	3.0	55 241	34 136	61.8	33 028	1 108	3.2
1999	55 256	42 557	77.0	41 476	1 081	2.5	55 801	34 349	61.6	33 403	946	2.8
2000	55 897	43 254	77.4	42 261	993	2.3	56 432	34 959	61.9	33 998	961	2.7
2001	56 152	43 463	77.4	42 245	1 218	2.8	56 740	35 234	62.1	34 273	961	2.7
2002	57 325	44 271	77.2	42 508	1 763	4.0	57 883	35 624	61.5	34 295	1 329	3.7
2003	57 940	44 700	77.1	42 797	1 903	4.3	58 545	36 185	61.8	34 806	1 379	3.8
2004	58 395	44 860	76.8	43 247	1 613	3.6	59 008	35 918	60.9	34 582	1 336	3.7
2005	58 854	45 263	76.9	43 763	1 500	3.3	59 449	35 809	60.2	34 738	1 071	3.0
Widowed, Divorced, or Separated												
1990	11 152	7 513	67.4	6 959	554	7.4	23 857	11 168	46.8	10 530	638	5.7
1991	11 588	7 804	67.3	6 985	819	10.5	24 105	11 145	46.2	10 386	759	6.8
1992	11 927	8 049	67.5	7 140	909	11.3	24 582	11 486	46.7	10 610	876	7.6
1993	11 861	7 956	67.1	7 055	901	11.3	24 661	11 308	45.9	10 528	780	6.9
1994	12 239	8 156	66.6	7 382	774	9.5	25 098	11 879	47.3	10 995	884	7.4
1995	12 410	8 315	67.0	7 632	683	8.2	25 373	12 001	47.3	11 308	693	5.8
1996	13 176	8 697	66.0	7 976	721	8.3	25 786	12 430	48.2	11 742	688	5.5
1997	14 113	9 420	66.7	8 715	705	7.5	26 301	12 814	48.7	12 071	743	5.8
1998	14 166	9 482	66.9	8 954	528	5.6	26 092	12 880	49.4	12 235	645	5.0
1999	14 225	9 449	66.4	8 971	478	5.1	26 199	12 951	49.4	12 307	644	5.0
2000	14 289	9 623	67.3	9 152	471	4.9	26 354	13 228	50.2	12 657	571	4.3
2001	14 392	9 421	65.5	8 927	494	5.2	26 747	13 454	50.3	12 887	567	4.2
2002	14 617	9 650	66.0	8 931	719	7.5	27 802	13 716	49.3	12 855	861	6.3
2003	15 180	9 855	64.9	9 020	835	8.5	28 240	14 154	50.1	13 240	914	6.5
2004	15 059	9 789	65.0	9 059	730	7.5	28 228	14 194	50.3	13 324	870	6.1
2005	15 779	10 256	65.0	9 569	687	6.7	28 576	14 233	49.8	13 472	761	5.3

Table 1-52. Employment Status of the Population by Sex and Marital Status, March 1990–2005—*Continued*

(Thousands of people, percent.)

Marital status and year	Men						Women					
	Population	Labor force					Population	Labor force				
		Total		Employed	Unemployed			Total		Employed	Unemployed	
		Number	Percent of population		Number	Percent of labor force		Number	Percent of population		Number	Percent of labor force
Widowed												
1990	2 331	519	22.3	490	29	5.6	11 477	2 243	19.5	2 149	94	4.2
1991	2 385	486	20.4	448	38	7.8	11 288	2 150	19.0	2 044	106	4.9
1992	2 529	566	22.4	501	65	11.5	11 325	2 131	18.8	2 029	102	4.8
1993	2 468	596	24.1	535	61	10.2	11 214	1 961	17.5	1 856	105	5.4
1994	2 220	474	21.4	440	34	7.2	11 073	1 945	17.6	1 825	120	6.2
1995	2 282	496	21.7	469	27	5.4	11 080	1 941	17.5	1 844	97	5.0
1996	2 476	487	19.7	466	21	4.3	11 070	1 916	17.3	1 820	96	5.0
1997	2 686	559	20.8	529	30	5.4	11 058	2 018	18.2	1 926	92	4.6
1998	2 567	563	21.9	551	12	2.1	11 027	2 157	19.6	2 071	86	4.0
1999	2 540	562	22.1	532	30	5.3	10 943	2 039	18.6	1 942	97	4.8
2000	2 601	583	22.4	547	36	6.2	11 061	2 011	18.2	1 911	100	5.0
2001	2 638	568	21.5	546	22	3.9	11 182	2 137	19.1	2 045	92	4.3
2002	2 635	629	23.9	581	48	7.6	11 411	2 001	17.5	1 887	114	5.7
2003	2 694	628	23.3	588	40	6.4	11 295	2 087	18.5	1 991	96	4.6
2004	2 651	581	21.9	558	23	4.0	11 159	2 157	19.3	2 048	109	5.1
2005	2 729	618	22.6	590	28	4.5	11 125	2 111	19.0	2 005	106	5.0
Divorced												
1990	6 256	5 004	80.0	4 639	365	7.3	8 845	6 678	75.5	6 333	345	5.2
1991	6 586	5 262	79.9	4 722	540	10.3	9 152	6 779	74.1	6 365	414	6.1
1992	6 743	5 418	80.3	4 823	595	11.0	9 569	7 076	73.9	6 578	498	7.0
1993	6 770	5 330	78.7	4 736	594	11.1	9 879	7 183	72.7	6 736	447	6.2
1994	7 222	5 548	76.8	5 028	520	9.4	10 113	7 473	73.9	6 962	511	6.8
1995	7 343	5 739	78.2	5 266	473	8.2	10 262	7 559	73.7	7 206	353	4.7
1996	7 734	5 954	77.0	5 468	486	8.2	10 508	7 829	74.5	7 468	361	4.6
1997	8 191	6 298	76.9	5 851	447	7.1	11 102	8 092	72.9	7 666	426	5.3
1998	8 307	6 378	76.8	6 045	333	5.2	11 065	8 038	72.6	7 687	351	4.4
1999	8 529	6 481	76.0	6 151	330	5.1	11 130	8 171	73.4	7 841	330	4.0
2000	8 532	6 583	77.2	6 279	304	4.6	11 061	8 505	76.9	8 217	288	3.4
2001	8 580	6 403	74.6	6 074	329	5.1	11 719	8 662	73.9	8 335	327	3.8
2002	8 643	6 519	75.4	6 053	466	7.1	12 227	8 902	72.8	8 416	486	5.5
2003	8 938	6 621	74.1	6 052	569	8.6	12 653	9 191	72.6	8 673	518	5.6
2004	8 942	6 622	74.1	6 104	518	7.8	12 817	9 246	72.1	8 706	540	5.8
2005	9 196	6 754	73.4	6 281	473	7.0	12 950	9 253	71.5	8 836	417	4.5
Separated												
1990	2 565	1 990	77.6	1 830	160	8.0	3 535	2 247	63.6	2 048	199	8.9
1991	2 616	2 057	78.6	1 816	241	11.7	3 665	2 216	60.5	1 977	239	10.8
1992	2 655	2 065	77.8	1 816	249	12.1	3 688	2 279	61.8	2 003	276	12.1
1993	2 623	2 030	77.4	1 784	246	12.1	3 568	2 165	60.7	1 937	228	10.5
1994	2 797	2 134	76.3	1 914	220	10.3	3 911	2 461	62.9	2 208	253	10.3
1995	2 784	2 081	74.7	1 898	183	8.8	4 031	2 501	62.0	2 258	243	9.7
1996	2 966	2 255	76.0	2 041	214	9.5	4 209	2 684	63.8	2 453	231	8.6
1997	3 236	2 563	79.2	2 335	228	8.9	4 141	2 705	65.3	2 480	225	8.3
1998	3 293	2 542	77.2	2 358	184	7.2	4 000	2 683	67.1	2 476	207	7.7
1999	3 156	2 405	76.2	2 287	118	4.9	4 126	2 740	66.4	2 523	217	7.9
2000	3 157	2 456	77.8	2 326	130	5.3	4 012	2 711	67.6	2 528	183	6.8
2001	3 174	2 450	77.2	2 307	143	5.8	3 846	2 654	69.0	2 507	147	5.5
2002	3 339	2 502	74.9	2 297	205	8.2	4 164	2 812	67.5	2 551	261	9.3
2003	3 548	2 606	73.4	2 380	226	8.7	4 293	2 877	67.0	2 576	301	10.5
2004	3 466	2 586	74.6	2 397	189	7.3	4 251	2 791	65.7	2 569	222	8.0
2005	3 855	2 884	74.8	2 698	186	6.4	4 501	2 870	63.8	2 632	238	8.3

Note: See "Notes and Definitions" for information on historical comparability.

Table 1-53. Employment Status of All Women and Single Women by Presence and Age of Children, March 1990–2005

(Thousands of people, percent.)

Age of children and year	All women							Single women						
	Civilian labor force	Civilian labor force as percent of population	Employed			Unemployed		Civilian labor force	Civilian labor force as percent of population	Employed			Unemployed	
			Number	Percent full-time	Percent part-time	Number	Percent of labor force			Number	Percent full-time	Percent part-time	Number	Percent of labor force
Women with No Children Under 18 Years														
1990	33 942	52.3	32 391	74.4	25.6	1 551	4.6	12 478	68.1	11 611	65.9	34.1	866	6.9
1991	34 047	52.0	32 167	74.0	26.0	1 880	5.5	12 472	67.0	11 529	66.2	33.8	943	7.6
1992	34 487	52.3	32 481	74.3	25.7	2 006	5.8	12 355	66.9	11 374	66.6	33.4	982	7.9
1993	34 495	52.1	32 476	74.6	25.4	2 020	5.9	12 223	66.4	11 201	66.1	33.9	1 022	8.4
1994	35 454	53.1	33 343	72.7	27.3	2 110	6.0	12 737	66.8	11 674	64.5	35.5	1 063	8.3
1995	35 843	52.9	34 054	72.9	27.1	1 789	5.0	12 870	67.1	11 919	64.5	35.5	951	7.4
1996	36 509	53.0	34 698	73.3	26.7	1 811	5.0	13 172	66.1	12 255	64.6	35.4	918	7.0
1997	37 295	53.6	35 572	73.7	26.3	1 723	4.6	13 405	66.5	12 442	64.0	36.0	964	7.2
1998	38 253	54.1	36 680	74.1	25.9	1 573	4.1	13 888	67.2	13 082	64.8	35.2	806	5.8
1999	39 316	54.3	37 589	74.6	25.4	1 727	4.4	14 435	67.1	13 491	65.6	34.4	944	6.5
2000	40 142	54.8	38 408	75.4	24.6	1 733	4.3	14 677	67.6	13 713	66.6	33.4	964	6.6
2001	40 836	54.9	39 219	75.7	24.3	1 617	4.0	14 877	67.4	13 993	67.3	32.7	884	5.9
2002	41 278	54.0	39 038	75.1	24.9	2 241	5.4	14 855	65.6	13 682	65.9	34.1	1 173	7.9
2003	42 039	54.1	39 667	74.8	25.2	2 372	5.6	14 678	63.5	13 430	65.1	34.9	1 249	8.5
2004	42 289	53.8	40 000	74.6	25.4	2 289	5.4	14 828	63.0	13 670	65.5	34.5	1 157	7.8
2005	42 039	54.1	39 667	74.8	25.2	2 372	5.6	14 678	63.5	13 430	65.1	34.9	1 249	8.5
Women with Children Under 18 Years														
1990	22 196	66.7	20 865	73.0	27.0	1 331	6.0	1 525	55.2	1 244	79.1	20.9	280	18.4
1991	22 327	66.6	20 774	73.0	27.0	1 552	7.0	1 654	53.6	1 358	76.4	23.6	296	17.9
1992	22 756	67.2	21 052	73.8	26.2	1 704	7.5	1 716	52.5	1 420	75.9	24.1	297	17.3
1993	23 063	66.9	21 521	73.9	26.1	1 541	6.7	1 869	54.4	1 510	74.8	25.2	359	19.2
1994	24 191	68.4	22 467	70.8	29.2	1 724	7.1	2 166	56.9	1 745	73.9	26.1	421	19.4
1995	24 695	69.7	23 195	71.7	28.3	1 500	6.1	2 104	57.5	1 754	73.6	26.4	350	16.6
1996	24 720	70.2	23 386	72.6	27.4	1 334	5.4	2 245	60.5	1 829	73.5	26.5	416	18.5
1997	25 604	72.1	24 082	74.1	25.9	1 522	5.9	2 772	68.1	2 305	76.6	23.4	467	16.8
1998	25 647	72.3	24 209	74.0	26.0	1 438	5.6	2 997	72.5	2 544	75.6	24.4	453	15.1
1999	25 469	72.1	24 305	74.1	25.9	1 165	4.6	3 051	73.4	2 694	75.8	24.2	357	11.7
2000	25 795	72.9	24 693	74.6	25.4	1 102	4.3	3 073	73.9	2 734	79.7	20.3	339	11.0
2001	25 751	73.1	24 572	75.6	24.4	1 179	4.6	3 022	73.8	2 638	81.8	18.2	385	12.7
2002	26 140	72.2	24 612	74.8	25.2	1 529	5.8	3 224	75.3	2 818	79.1	20.9	406	12.6
2003	26 202	71.7	24 598	74.3	25.7	1 603	6.1	3 222	73.1	2 789	79.5	20.5	433	13.4
2004	25 913	70.7	24 413	74.2	25.8	1 501	5.8	3 262	72.6	2 836	76.8	23.2	426	13.1
2005	26 202	71.7	24 598	74.3	25.7	1 603	6.1	3 222	73.1	2 789	79.5	20.5	433	13.4
Women with Children Under 6 Years														
1990	9 397	58.2	8 732	69.6	30.4	664	7.1	929	48.7	736	75.0	25.0	194	20.9
1991	9 636	58.4	8 758	69.5	30.5	878	9.1	1 050	48.8	819	72.2	27.8	231	22.0
1992	9 573	58.0	8 662	70.2	29.8	911	9.5	1 029	45.8	829	73.2	26.8	200	19.4
1993	9 621	57.9	8 764	70.1	29.9	857	8.9	1 125	47.4	869	70.0	30.0	257	22.8
1994	10 328	60.3	9 394	67.1	32.9	935	9.1	1 379	52.2	1 062	70.0	30.0	317	23.0
1995	10 395	62.3	9 587	67.5	32.5	809	7.8	1 328	53.0	1 069	68.6	31.4	259	19.5
1996	10 293	62.3	9 592	68.4	31.6	701	6.8	1 378	55.1	1 099	67.3	32.7	279	20.2
1997	10 610	65.0	9 800	70.5	29.5	810	7.6	1 755	65.1	1 424	71.6	28.4	330	18.8
1998	10 619	65.2	9 839	69.8	30.2	780	7.3	1 755	67.3	1 448	71.7	28.3	307	17.5
1999	10 322	64.4	9 674	69.0	31.0	648	6.3	1 811	68.1	1 565	71.0	29.0	246	13.6
2000	10 316	65.3	9 763	70.5	29.5	553	5.4	1 835	70.5	1 603	75.3	24.7	232	12.6
2001	10 200	64.9	9 618	71.2	28.8	582	5.7	1 783	69.7	1 542	79.1	20.9	242	13.6
2002	10 193	64.1	9 441	70.4	29.6	752	7.4	1 819	71.0	1 568	74.5	25.5	251	13.8
2003	10 209	62.9	9 433	70.0	30.0	776	7.6	1 893	70.2	1 614	75.2	24.8	279	14.7
2004	10 131	62.2	9 407	69.4	30.6	724	7.1	1 885	68.4	1 605	70.1	29.9	279	14.8
2005	10 209	62.9	9 433	70.0	30.0	776	7.6	1 893	70.2	1 614	75.2	24.8	279	14.7

Note: See "Notes and Definitions" for information on historical comparability.

Table 1-54. Employment Status of Ever-Married Women and Married Women, Spouse Present, by Presence and Age of Children, March 1990–2005

(Thousands of people, percent.)

Age of children and year	Ever-married women [1]						Married women, spouse present					
	Civilian labor force	Civilian labor force as percent of population	Employed		Unemployed		Civilian labor force	Civilian labor force as percent of population	Employed		Unemployed	
			Number	Percent full-time	Percent part-time	Number	Percent of labor force			Number	Percent full-time	Percent part-time	Number	Percent of labor force

Age of children and year	Civilian labor force	Civilian labor force as percent of population	Number	Percent full-time	Percent part-time	Number	Percent of labor force	Civilian labor force	Civilian labor force as percent of population	Number	Percent full-time	Percent part-time	Number	Percent of labor force
Women with No Children Under 18 Years														
1990	21 464	46.1	20 779	79.1	20.9	685	3.2	14 467	51.1	14 068	77.3	22.7	399	2.8
1991	21 575	46.1	20 637	78.4	21.6	937	4.3	14 529	51.2	13 976	77.6	22.4	552	3.8
1992	22 132	46.6	21 108	78.5	21.5	1 024	4.6	14 851	51.9	14 247	77.8	22.2	604	4.1
1993	22 273	46.6	21 275	79.0	21.0	998	4.5	15 211	52.4	14 630	77.6	22.4	581	3.8
1994	22 716	47.6	21 669	77.1	22.9	1 047	4.6	15 234	53.2	14 641	75.6	24.4	593	3.9
1995	22 973	47.3	22 134	77.4	22.6	839	3.7	15 594	53.2	15 072	76.3	23.7	522	3.3
1996	23 337	47.7	22 444	78.1	21.9	893	3.8	15 628	53.4	15 123	76.8	23.2	506	3.2
1997	23 890	48.3	23 130	78.9	21.1	760	3.2	15 750	54.2	15 315	77.7	22.3	435	2.8
1998	24 366	48.7	23 598	79.3	20.7	767	3.1	16 007	54.1	15 581	78.3	21.7	426	2.7
1999	24 881	48.9	24 098	79.7	20.3	783	3.1	16 484	54.4	16 061	78.2	21.8	423	2.6
2000	25 465	49.4	24 695	80.3	19.7	769	3.0	16 786	54.7	16 357	79.1	20.9	429	2.6
2001	25 959	49.6	25 226	80.4	19.6	733	2.8	16 909	54.8	16 528	78.7	21.3	381	2.3
2002	26 423	49.1	25 356	80.0	20.0	1 068	4.0	17 353	54.8	16 780	78.4	21.6	573	3.3
2003	27 361	50.1	26 238	79.7	20.3	1 123	4.1	17 901	55.7	17 273	78.6	21.4	628	3.5
2004	27 461	49.8	26 329	79.3	20.7	1 131	4.1	17 965	55.0	17 367	78.6	21.4	598	3.3
2005	27 361	50.1	26 238	79.7	20.3	1 123	4.1	17 901	55.7	17 273	78.6	21.4	628	3.5
Women with Children Under 18 Years														
1990	20 671	67.8	19 621	72.6	27.4	1 051	5.1	16 500	66.3	15 803	69.8	30.2	698	4.2
1991	20 673	67.9	19 416	72.8	27.2	1 257	6.1	16 575	66.8	15 692	70.1	29.9	883	5.3
1992	21 040	68.8	19 633	73.6	26.4	1 407	6.7	16 835	67.8	15 884	71.3	28.7	952	5.7
1993	21 194	68.3	20 011	73.9	26.1	1 183	5.6	16 947	67.5	16 127	71.4	28.6	820	4.8
1994	22 025	69.8	20 722	70.5	29.5	1 303	5.9	17 628	69.0	16 755	68.0	32.0	873	5.0
1995	22 591	71.1	21 441	71.5	28.5	1 150	5.1	17 969	70.2	17 195	68.8	31.2	774	4.3
1996	22 475	71.4	21 556	72.5	27.5	919	4.1	17 754	70.0	17 136	69.6	30.4	618	3.5
1997	22 831	72.6	21 777	73.9	26.1	1 054	4.6	18 157	71.1	17 521	71.6	28.4	636	3.5
1998	22 650	72.3	21 665	73.8	26.2	985	4.3	18 129	70.6	17 447	71.5	28.5	682	3.8
1999	22 419	71.9	21 611	73.9	26.1	808	3.6	17 865	70.1	17 342	71.5	28.5	523	2.9
2000	22 722	72.7	21 960	74.0	26.0	763	3.4	18 174	70.6	17 641	71.7	28.3	533	2.9
2001	22 729	73.0	21 934	74.9	25.1	795	3.5	18 325	70.8	17 745	72.6	27.4	580	3.2
2002	22 917	71.8	21 794	74.3	25.7	1 122	4.9	18 271	69.6	17 515	71.7	28.3	756	4.1
2003	22 979	71.5	21 809	73.7	26.3	1 170	5.1	18 284	69.2	17 533	71.0	29.0	751	4.1
2004	22 651	70.5	21 576	73.8	26.2	1 075	4.7	17 953	68.2	17 215	71.3	28.7	738	4.1
2005	22 979	71.5	21 809	73.7	26.3	1 170	5.1	18 284	69.2	17 533	71.0	29.0	751	4.1
Women with Children Under 6 Years														
1990	8 467	59.5	7 996	69.1	30.9	471	5.6	7 247	58.9	6 901	67.4	32.6	346	4.8
1991	8 585	59.9	7 938	69.2	30.8	647	7.5	7 434	59.9	6 933	67.5	32.5	501	6.7
1992	8 544	60.0	7 832	69.9	30.1	711	8.3	7 333	59.9	6 819	68.5	31.5	514	7.0
1993	8 496	59.6	7 895	70.2	29.8	600	7.1	7 289	59.6	6 840	68.8	31.2	450	6.2
1994	8 949	61.8	8 332	66.7	33.3	617	6.9	7 723	61.7	7 291	65.4	34.6	432	5.6
1995	9 067	63.9	8 517	67.4	32.6	550	6.1	7 759	63.5	7 349	66.1	33.9	409	5.3
1996	8 915	63.6	8 493	68.6	31.4	422	4.7	7 590	62.7	7 297	66.5	33.5	293	3.9
1997	8 856	64.9	8 376	70.3	29.7	480	5.4	7 582	63.6	7 252	69.1	30.9	330	4.4
1998	8 864	64.8	8 391	69.5	30.5	473	5.3	7 655	63.7	7 309	68.1	31.9	346	4.5
1999	8 511	63.7	8 109	68.6	31.4	402	4.7	7 246	61.8	6 979	67.1	32.9	267	3.7
2000	8 481	64.3	8 159	69.5	30.5	321	3.8	7 341	62.8	7 087	68.1	31.9	254	3.5
2001	8 417	64.0	8 077	69.7	30.3	340	4.0	7 319	62.5	7 062	68.5	31.5	257	3.5
2002	8 373	62.8	7 873	69.6	30.4	501	6.0	7 166	60.8	6 804	67.7	32.3	363	5.1
2003	8 315	61.4	7 818	68.9	31.1	497	6.0	7 175	59.8	6 826	67.1	32.9	349	4.9
2004	8 246	61.0	7 801	69.3	30.7	445	5.4	7 107	59.3	6 774	68.1	31.9	332	4.7
2005	8 315	61.4	7 818	68.9	31.1	497	6.0	7 175	59.8	6 826	67.1	32.9	349	4.9

[1]Ever-married women are women who are, or have been married.

Table 1-55. Employment Status of Women Who Maintain Families by Marital Status and Presence and Age of Children, March 1990–2005

(Thousands of people, percent.)

Family status, age of children, and year	Civilian noninstitutional population	Civilian labor force			Unemployed		Not in the labor force
		Number	Percent of the population	Employed	Number	Percent of the labor force	
Women Who Maintain Families, Total							
1990	11 309	7 088	62.7	6 471	617	8.7	4 221
1991	11 765	7 329	62.3	6 657	672	9.2	4 436
1992	12 214	7 517	61.5	6 798	719	9.6	4 697
1993	12 489	7 777	62.3	7 093	684	8.8	4 712
1994	12 963	8 214	63.4	7 413	801	9.8	4 750
1995	12 762	8 192	64.2	7 527	665	8.1	4 570
1996	12 993	8 460	65.1	7 832	628	7.4	4 532
1997	13 258	8 998	67.9	8 192	806	9.0	4 260
1998	13 102	8 976	68.5	8 309	667	7.4	4 127
1999	13 191	9 213	69.8	8 596	617	6.7	3 978
2000	13 145	9 226	70.2	8 592	634	6.9	3 918
2001	12 930	9 034	69.9	8 453	581	6.4	3 897
2002	13 489	9 523	70.6	8 755	768	8.1	3 966
2003	14 000	9 759	69.7	8 898	861	8.8	4 241
2004	14 165	9 869	69.7	9 054	815	8.3	4 297
2005	14 391	9 941	69.1	9 140	801	8.1	4 450
Women with No Children Under 18 Years							
1990	4 290	2 227	51.9	2 132	95	4.3	2 062
1991	4 447	2 364	53.2	2 231	133	5.6	2 083
1992	4 651	2 427	52.2	2 307	120	4.9	2 223
1993	4 708	2 466	52.4	2 339	127	5.2	2 242
1994	4 758	2 609	54.8	2 489	120	4.6	2 149
1995	4 610	2 471	53.6	2 394	77	3.1	2 139
1996	4 847	2 552	52.7	2 462	90	3.5	2 295
1997	4 909	2 663	54.2	2 571	92	3.5	2 246
1998	4 952	2 649	53.5	2 578	71	2.7	2 303
1999	4 942	2 667	54.0	2 556	111	4.2	2 275
2000	5 097	2 707	53.1	2 546	161	5.9	2 390
2001	5 185	2 772	53.5	2 668	104	3.8	2 413
2002	5 119	2 764	54.0	2 628	136	4.9	2 355
2003	5 457	2 934	53.8	2 728	206	7.0	2 522
2004	5 551	3 052	55.0	2 855	197	6.5	2 499
2005	5 692	3 095	54.4	2 961	134	4.3	2 597
Women with Children Under 18 Years							
1990	7 018	4 860	69.3	4 338	522	10.7	2 159
1991	7 318	4 965	67.8	4 426	539	10.9	2 353
1992	7 564	5 090	67.3	4 491	599	11.8	2 473
1993	7 781	5 311	68.3	4 755	556	10.5	2 470
1994	8 205	5 604	68.3	4 924	680	12.1	2 601
1995	8 152	5 720	70.2	5 132	588	10.3	2 431
1996	8 146	5 908	72.5	5 370	538	9.1	2 237
1997	8 348	6 335	75.9	5 621	714	11.3	2 014
1998	8 151	6 327	77.6	5 731	596	9.4	1 823
1999	8 248	6 546	79.4	6 040	506	7.7	1 702
2000	8 048	6 520	81.0	6 046	474	7.3	1 528
2001	7 746	6 261	80.8	5 785	476	7.6	1 484
2002	8 370	6 759	80.8	6 127	632	9.4	1 611
2003	8 543	6 825	79.9	6 170	655	9.6	1 718
2004	8 614	6 817	79.1	6 199	618	9.1	1 798
2005	8 699	6 846	78.7	6 179	667	9.7	1 853
Single Women with No Children Under 18 Years							
1990	642	450	70.1	425	25	5.6	192
1991	682	469	68.8	441	28	6.0	214
1992	745	505	67.8	475	30	5.9	241
1993	752	531	70.6	494	37	7.0	221
1994	704	490	69.6	451	39	8.0	213
1995	779	534	68.5	508	26	4.9	245
1996	895	588	65.7	572	16	2.7	308
1997	860	585	68.0	563	22	3.8	275
1998	893	637	71.3	613	24	3.8	256
1999	969	674	69.6	638	36	5.3	295
2000	1 004	720	71.7	642	78	10.8	284
2001	1 096	787	71.8	756	31	3.9	309
2002	1 154	796	69.0	747	49	6.2	358
2003	1 254	814	64.9	713	101	12.4	440
2004	1 381	977	70.7	887	90	9.2	404
2005	1 388	926	66.7	855	71	7.7	463

Table 1-55. Employment Status of Women Who Maintain Families by Marital Status and Presence and Age of Children, March 1990–2005—*Continued*

(Thousands of people, percent.)

Family status, age of children, and year	Civilian noninstitutional population	Civilian labor force					Not in the labor force
		Number	Percent of the population	Employed	Unemployed		
					Number	Percent of the labor force	
Single Women with Children Under 18 Years							
1990	1 953	1 095	56.1	874	221	20.2	858
1991	2 208	1 187	53.8	985	202	17.0	1 021
1992	2 376	1 256	52.9	1 067	189	15.0	1 120
1993	2 445	1 414	57.8	1 161	253	17.9	1 031
1994	2 790	1 625	58.2	1 328	297	18.3	1 165
1995	2 613	1 510	57.8	1 261	249	16.5	1 102
1996	2 639	1 633	61.9	1 346	287	17.6	1 006
1997	3 012	2 087	69.3	1 749	338	16.2	925
1998	3 083	2 280	74.0	1 960	320	14.0	803
1999	3 163	2 415	76.4	2 146	269	11.1	748
2000	3 167	2 413	76.2	2 151	262	10.9	754
2001	3 097	2 351	75.9	2 055	296	12.6	745
2002	3 315	2 566	77.4	2 241	325	12.7	749
2003	3 421	2 584	75.5	2 272	312	12.1	837
2004	3 414	2 568	75.2	2 233	335	13.0	846
2005	3 591	2 708	75.4	2 325	383	14.1	882
Widowed, Divorced, or Separated Women with No Children Under 18 Years							
1990	3 648	1 778	48.7	1 708	70	3.9	1 870
1991	3 765	1 896	50.4	1 791	105	5.5	1 869
1992	3 905	1 923	49.2	1 832	91	4.7	1 982
1993	3 956	1 935	48.9	1 845	90	4.7	2 021
1994	4 054	2 118	52.2	2 037	81	3.8	1 936
1995	3 831	1 938	50.6	1 887	51	2.6	1 894
1996	3 952	1 964	49.7	1 890	74	3.8	1 988
1997	4 049	2 077	51.3	2 008	69	3.3	1 971
1998	4 058	2 011	49.6	1 965	46	2.3	2 047
1999	3 974	1 993	50.2	1 918	75	3.8	1 980
2000	4 093	1 987	48.5	1 904	83	4.2	2 106
2001	4 088	1 985	48.6	1 912	73	3.7	2 104
2002	3 964	1 968	49.6	1 882	86	4.4	1 997
2003	4 203	2 121	50.5	2 016	105	5.0	2 082
2004	4 170	2 075	49.8	1 968	107	5.2	2 095
2005	4 304	2 170	50.4	2 106	64	2.9	2 135
Widowed, Divorced, or Separated Women with Children Under 18							
1990	5 065	3 765	74.3	3 464	301	8.0	1 301
1991	5 109	3 778	73.9	3 441	337	8.9	1 331
1992	5 187	3 834	73.9	3 424	410	10.7	1 353
1993	5 336	3 897	73.0	3 594	303	7.8	1 439
1994	5 415	3 979	73.5	3 596	383	9.6	1 436
1995	5 539	4 210	76.0	3 871	339	8.1	1 329
1996	5 507	4 275	77.6	4 024	251	5.9	1 231
1997	5 337	4 248	79.6	3 872	376	8.9	1 089
1998	5 068	4 047	79.9	3 771	276	6.8	1 020
1999	5 086	4 131	81.2	3 894	237	5.7	955
2000	4 881	4 107	84.1	3 895	212	5.2	774
2001	4 649	3 910	84.1	3 730	180	4.6	739
2002	5 056	4 193	82.9	3 886	307	7.3	862
2003	5 122	4 241	82.8	3 898	343	8.1	881
2004	5 201	4 249	81.7	3 966	283	6.7	952
2005	5 108	4 137	81.0	3 854	283	6.8	971

Note: See "Notes and Definitions" for information on historical comparability.

Table 1-56. Number and Age of Children in Families by Type of Family and Labor Force Status of Mother, March 1990–2005

(Thousands of children.)

Age of children and year	Total children	Mother in labor force	Mother not in labor force	Married-couple families			Families maintained by women			Families maintained by men
				Total	Mother in labor force	Mother not in labor force	Total	Mother in labor force	Mother not in labor force	
Children Under 18 Years										
1990	59 596	36 712	21 110	45 898	29 077	16 820	11 925	7 635	4 290	1 774
1991	60 330	36 968	21 526	45 912	29 056	16 856	12 582	7 912	4 670	1 836
1992	61 262	38 081	21 176	45 966	29 882	16 084	13 291	8 199	5 093	2 005
1993	62 020	38 542	21 444	46 499	30 054	16 445	13 487	8 488	4 999	2 034
1994	63 407	40 186	21 188	47 247	31 279	15 968	14 127	8 907	5 220	2 033
1995	63 989	41 365	20 421	47 675	32 190	15 486	14 111	9 176	4 935	2 202
1996	64 506	41 573	20 449	47 484	31 764	15 720	14 538	9 809	4 729	2 484
1997	64 710	42 747	19 223	47 529	32 263	15 265	14 441	10 483	3 958	2 740
1998	65 043	43 156	19 069	47 909	32 533	15 376	14 317	10 623	3 694	2 818
1999	65 191	43 419	19 074	47 945	32 193	15 752	14 547	11 226	3 322	2 699
2000	65 601	44 188	18 674	48 902	33 149	15 753	13 960	11 039	2 921	2 739
2001	65 777	44 051	18 864	49 352	33 436	15 916	13 563	10 615	2 948	2 862
2002	65 978	43 821	19 243	48 836	32 673	16 163	14 228	11 149	3 079	2 914
2003	66 521	43 769	19 782	49 004	32 411	16 593	14 547	11 359	3 189	2 970
2004	66 386	43 144	20 229	48 656	31 892	16 764	14 717	11 252	3 465	3 014
2005	66 526	43 239	20 179	48 688	31 886	16 802	14 729	11 352	3 377	3 108
Children from 6 to 17 Years										
1990	39 095	25 805	12 079	29 726	20 067	9 659	8 157	5 737	2 420	1 211
1991	39 470	25 806	12 392	29 598	19 907	9 691	8 599	5 899	2 701	1 272
1992	40 064	26 666	12 067	29 673	20 586	9 087	9 060	6 079	2 980	1 331
1993	40 622	27 046	12 291	30 233	20 796	9 437	9 104	6 249	2 854	1 285
1994	41 795	28 179	12 287	30 895	21 663	9 233	9 570	6 516	3 054	1 329
1995	42 423	28 931	12 000	31 298	22 239	9 059	9 633	6 692	2 941	1 492
1996	42 964	29 381	11 897	31 231	22 092	9 139	10 047	7 289	2 758	1 685
1997	43 488	30 308	11 400	31 509	22 602	8 906	10 199	7 705	2 493	1 781
1998	43 771	30 579	11 367	31 707	22 706	9 001	10 238	7 873	2 365	1 826
1999	44 110	30 885	11 370	31 975	22 706	9 269	10 281	8 179	2 101	1 855
2000	44 562	31 531	11 198	32 732	23 393	9 339	9 997	8 138	1 859	1 833
2001	44 458	31 411	11 153	32 957	23 599	9 358	9 608	7 813	1 795	1 894
2002	44 865	31 437	11 510	32 799	23 296	9 504	10 148	8 142	2 006	1 918
2003	45 273	31 559	11 635	32 782	23 160	9 622	10 412	8 399	2 013	2 080
2004	45 066	31 040	11 968	32 506	22 736	9 769	10 502	8 304	2 199	2 058
2005	45 027	30 930	11 995	32 412	22 565	9 847	10 514	8 366	2 148	2 102
Children Under 6 Years										
1990	20 502	10 907	9 031	16 171	9 010	7 161	3 767	1 897	1 870	563
1991	20 860	11 162	9 134	16 313	9 148	7 165	3 983	2 013	1 969	563
1992	21 198	11 415	9 109	16 293	9 296	6 997	4 232	2 119	2 112	674
1993	21 398	11 496	9 153	16 266	9 258	7 008	4 383	2 239	2 145	749
1994	21 612	12 007	8 901	16 352	9 617	6 735	4 556	2 391	2 166	704
1995	21 566	12 435	8 421	16 377	9 951	6 427	4 478	2 484	1 995	710
1996	21 542	12 192	8 552	16 253	9 672	6 581	4 491	2 520	1 971	799
1997	21 222	12 439	7 823	16 020	9 661	6 359	4 243	2 778	1 464	959
1998	21 272	12 577	7 703	16 201	9 827	6 375	4 079	2 751	1 328	992
1999	21 081	12 533	7 704	15 971	9 487	6 484	4 267	3 046	1 220	844
2000	21 039	12 657	7 476	16 170	9 757	6 413	3 963	2 901	1 062	906
2001	21 318	12 640	7 711	16 395	9 837	6 558	3 956	2 802	1 153	968
2002	21 113	12 384	7 733	16 037	9 377	6 660	4 080	3 007	1 073	996
2003	21 248	12 210	8 147	16 222	9 251	6 971	4 136	2 960	1 176	890
2004	21 321	12 104	8 261	16 151	9 156	6 995	4 214	2 948	1 266	956
2005	21 498	12 308	8 184	16 276	9 321	6 955	4 216	2 987	1 229	1 006

Note: See "Notes and Definitions" for information on historical comparability.

Table 1-57. Number of Families and Median Family Income by Type of Family and Earner Status of Members, 1992–2004

(Thousands of families, dollars.)

Number of families and median family income	1992	1993	1994	1995	1996	1997	1998	1999	2000	2001	2002	2003	2004
NUMBER OF FAMILIES													
Married-Couple Families, Total	53 254	53 248	53 929	53 621	53 654	54 362	54 829	55 352	55 650	56 798	57 362	57 767	58 180
No earners	7 250	7 281	7 225	7 276	7 145	7 286	7 257	7 160	7 297	7 662	7 803	8 043	7 998
One earner	12 053	11 806	11 715	11 708	11 493	11 700	12 246	12 290	12 450	12 852	13 503	14 061	14 385
Husband	9 182	8 715	8 673	8 792	8 611	8 770	9 173	9 062	9 319	9 573	10 121	10 478	10 853
Wife	2 145	2 405	2 364	2 251	2 207	2 298	2 411	2 585	2 545	2 689	2 821	3 027	2 993
Other family member	726	686	678	666	674	632	662	643	586	590	560	557	539
Two earners	26 344	26 742	27 263	27 180	27 260	27 712	27 593	28 010	28 329	28 779	28 891	28 693	28 806
Husband and wife	24 255	24 543	25 123	25 274	25 274	25 731	25 696	26 134	26 447	26 829	26 966	26 860	26 758
Husband and other family member	1 447	1 582	1 565	1 393	1 483	1 406	1 306	1 325	1 277	1 424	1 391	1 322	1 462
Husband not an earner	642	617	574	513	502	575	590	552	605	526	534	511	586
Three earners or more	7 606	7 419	7 727	7 456	7 756	7 664	7 733	7 892	7 575	7 504	7 165	6 970	6 991
Husband and wife	6 882	6 723	6 987	6 770	7 126	7 023	7 102	7 220	6 917	6 859	6 565	6 349	6 459
Husband, not wife	550	535	543	531	479	478	456	528	537	530	455	467	381
Husband not an earner	175	162	196	155	150	163	176	144	120	115	145	154	152
Families Maintained by Women, Total	12 504	12 982	12 771	13 007	13 277	13 115	13 206	13 164	12 950	13 517	14 033	14 196	14 404
No earners	2 968	3 100	2 848	2 664	2 574	2 332	2 143	1 883	1 786	2 076	2 228	2 451	2 610
One earner	6 184	6 407	6 407	6 815	7 027	7 091	7 351	7 441	7 462	7 693	8 153	8 012	8 074
Householder	5 042	5 278	5 415	5 590	5 817	5 841	6 167	6 127	6 132	6 436	6 832	6 725	6 788
Other family member	1 142	1 129	1 091	1 225	1 211	1 251	1 183	1 314	1 331	1 257	1 321	1 286	1 285
Two earners or more	3 352	3 476	3 417	3 527	3 675	3 692	3 712	3 840	3 702	3 748	3 652	3 733	3 720
Householder and other family member(s)	2 998	3 139	3 126	3 225	3 431	3 398	3 399	3 508	3 376	3 442	3 290	3 364	3 399
Householder not an earner	354	337	291	302	245	294	313	332	325	306	362	369	321
Families Maintained by Men, Total	3 094	2 992	3 287	3 557	3 924	3 982	4 041	4 086	4 316	4 499	4 747	4 778	4 953
No earners	345	329	383	357	359	344	381	376	380	461	466	530	492
One earner	1 544	1 593	1 705	1 800	1 972	2 104	2 027	2 044	2 223	2 319	2 434	2 466	2 573
Householder	1 305	1 352	1 428	1 548	1 667	1 791	1 725	1 721	1 879	1 911	2 026	2 053	2 152
Other family member	239	241	277	253	305	313	302	323	344	408	408	413	421
Two earners or more	1 204	1 070	1 198	1 400	1 593	1 534	1 634	1 666	1 713	1 719	1 847	1 782	1 888
Householder and other family member(s)	1 117	1 002	1 128	1 302	1 469	1 427	1 532	1 522	1 585	1 629	1 709	1 625	1 736
Householder not an earner	88	67	71	98	124	107	102	143	128	90	138	157	152
MEDIAN FAMILY INCOME													
Married-Couple Families, Total	42 000	43 000	44 893	47 000	49 614	51 475	54 043	56 792	59 200	60 100	61 000	62 388	63 627
No earners	20 023	19 983	20 604	21 888	22 622	23 782	24 525	25 262	25 356	25 900	25 954	26 312	26 798
One earner	32 500	32 084	33 393	35 100	36 468	39 140	40 519	41 261	44 424	44 400	45 000	46 546	47 749
Husband	34 714	34 401	35 000	36 052	38 150	40 300	42 000	44 200	47 010	47 500	48 004	48 948	50 000
Wife	27 343	27 502	28 661	32 098	30 301	34 050	35 625	35 546	36 458	36 140	39 072	41 180	41 000
Other family member	33 622	30 254	32 578	37 784	39 644	40 317	42 414	41 120	45 492	44 270	40 927	45 936	46 324
Two earners	47 737	49 650	51 190	53 500	56 000	58 020	61 300	64 007	67 500	69 543	71 282	73 309	75 100
Husband and wife	48 050	49 980	51 500	53 626	56 392	58 564	61 900	64 950	68 132	70 000	72 150	74 500	76 000
Husband and other family member	45 694	48 862	48 517	52 530	49 610	53 854	57 680	53 541	56 503	65 240	62 848	60 100	66 120
Husband not an earner	40 124	38 800	42 800	47 121	46 490	47 979	50 955	52 466	53 430	58 725	54 840	58 000	63 050
Three earners or more	61 640	63 535	66 172	68 996	70 400	75 593	78 973	81 940	83 990	86 090	88 632	93 000	94 212
Husband and wife	62 674	64 099	66 674	69 371	71 148	76 105	79 907	83 000	84 634	87 000	89 962	94 353	95 524
Husband, not wife	57 015	60 712	63 633	60 360	61 824	68 890	71 001	69 561	70 050	76 230	82 180	77 316	87 000
Husband not an earner	47 551	54 805	54 655	61 196	55 495	62 684	63 205	69 275	68 050	80 661	68 400	91 771	73 137
Families Maintained by Women, Total	16 431	16 800	17 600	19 306	19 416	20 470	21 875	23 100	25 000	25 064	26 000	26 000	26 400
No earners	5 964	6 492	6 805	7 440	7 092	7 476	7 737	8 010	8 988	8 160	8 808	8 344	8 400
One earner	16 468	16 745	17 226	18 824	18 500	19 000	20 000	20 092	22 306	23 008	24 597	24 752	25 040
Householder	15 905	15 700	16 603	17 890	18 000	18 000	18 800	19 000	21 400	22 001	23 760	23 832	24 801
Other family member	19 709	20 800	21 300	23 166	21 000	22 870	25 981	26 800	27 524	28 476	29 524	28 857	29 700
Two earners or more	32 705	33 300	33 820	35 000	36 400	39 275	40 000	41 144	43 035	45 244	46 580	47 576	48 549
Householder and other family member(s)	33 280	33 165	33 357	34 674	36 400	39 000	39 713	40 855	43 000	44 842	46 000	46 701	47 974
Householder not an earner	30 460	35 394	37 531	39 444	38 249	47 471	43 725	48 004	45 600	51 000	51 248	57 267	56 799
Families Maintained by Men, Total	27 400	25 856	27 486	30 000	31 500	32 984	35 000	37 000	37 040	36 000	37 440	37 914	40 000
No earners	9 416	10 900	11 293	12 240	12 030	14 252	15 468	13 752	14 946	12 840	15 200	15 408	14 167
One earner	23 020	22 300	24 011	25 337	26 100	26 897	29 125	31 038	30 160	30 800	30 139	32 097	35 000
Householder	23 000	22 079	24 000	25 069	25 874	27 000	29 125	30 483	30 816	30 500	30 014	31 355	35 000
Other family member	24 359	26 916	26 253	27 291	28 584	25 486	28 241	34 756	29 118	31 052	32 000	35 525	35 438
Two earners or more	39 000	38 000	41 439	43 100	44 275	49 900	51 288	51 040	55 010	55 024	55 000	57 840	57 600
Householder and other family member(s)	39 300	38 363	41 534	43 000	43 065	50 000	50 954	50 960	55 400	54 850	55 220	57 400	57 058
Householder not an earner	36 445	33 700	37 386	55 133	47 001	44 786	68 257	57 407	51 945	61 824	49 852	64 658	65 400

Note: See "Notes and Definitions" for information on historical comparability.

Table 1-58. Employment Status of the Foreign Born and Native Born Populations by Selected Characteristics, 2003–2004

(Thousands of people, percent.)

Characteristic	Civilian noninstitutional population	Civilian labor force				
		Total	Participation rate	Employed	Unemployed	
					Number	Rate
2003						
TOTAL						
Total, 16 years and over	221 168	146 510	66.2	137 736	8 774	6.0
Men	106 435	78 238	73.5	73 332	4 906	6.3
Women	114 733	68 272	59.5	64 404	3 868	5.7
FOREIGN BORN						
Total, 16 years and over	31 331	21 117	67.4	19 731	1 385	6.6
Men	15 669	12 634	80.6	11 850	784	6.2
Women	15 662	8 482	54.2	7 881	601	7.1
Age						
16 to 24 years	4 135	2 456	59.4	2 203	252	10.3
25 to 34 years	7 784	5 925	76.1	5 551	375	6.3
35 to 44 years	7 450	6 026	80.9	5 673	353	5.9
45 to 54 years	5 245	4 200	80.1	3 935	264	6.3
55 to 64 years	3 195	2 016	63.1	1 903	113	5.6
65 years and over	3 521	494	14.0	465	28	5.8
Race and Hispanic Ethnicity						
White non-Hispanic or Latino	7 128	4 267	59.9	4 048	219	5.1
Black non-Hispanic or Latino	2 391	1 782	74.5	1 631	152	8.5
Asian non-Hispanic or Latino	6 867	4 613	67.2	4 324	289	6.3
Hispanic or Latino ethnicity	14 627	10 226	69.9	9 513	713	7.0
Educational Attainment						
Total, 25 years and over	27 196	18 661	68.6	17 528	1 133	6.1
Less than a high school diploma	8 823	5 376	60.9	4 949	427	7.9
High school graduates, no college [1]	6 778	4 596	67.8	4 335	261	5.7
Some college or associate degree	4 147	2 991	72.1	2 811	180	6.0
Bachelor's degree or higher [2]	7 447	5 698	76.5	5 433	265	4.7
NATIVE BORN						
Total, 16 years and over	189 837	125 393	66.1	118 005	7 389	5.9
Men	90 766	65 603	72.3	61 481	4 122	6.3
Women	99 072	59 790	60.4	56 523	3 267	5.5
Age						
16 to 24 years	31 762	19 642	61.8	17 148	2 494	12.7
25 to 34 years	31 237	26 418	84.6	24 832	1 585	6.0
35 to 44 years	36 296	30 669	84.5	29 207	1 462	4.8
45 to 54 years	35 277	29 071	82.4	27 979	1 092	3.8
55 to 64 years	24 533	15 296	62.3	14 696	600	3.9
65 years and over	30 733	4 298	14.0	4 143	155	3.6
Race and Hispanic Ethnicity						
White non-Hispanic or Latino	148 569	98 833	66.5	94 057	4 776	4.8
Black non-Hispanic or Latino	22 484	14 215	63.2	12 644	1 571	11.1
Asian non-Hispanic or Latino	2 228	1 414	63.5	1 342	73	5.1
Hispanic or Latino ethnicity	12 924	8 587	66.4	7 859	727	8.5
Educational Attainment						
Total, 25 years and over	158 075	105 751	66.9	100 857	4 894	4.6
Less than a high school diploma	19 333	7 271	37.6	6 588	682	9.4
High school graduates, no college [1]	52 701	33 330	63.2	31 522	1 808	5.4
Some college or associate degree	42 594	31 058	72.9	29 609	1 449	4.7
Bachelor's degree or higher [2]	43 447	34 093	78.5	33 138	955	2.8

[1]Includes persons with a high school diploma or equivalent.
[2]Includes persons with bachelor's, master's, professional, and doctoral degrees.

Table 1-58. Employment Status of the Foreign Born and Native Born Populations by Selected Characteristics, 2003–2004 —*Continued*

(Thousands of people, percent.)

Characteristic	Civilian noninstitutional population	Civilian labor force				
		Total	Participation rate	Employed	Unemployed	
					Number	Rate
2004						
TOTAL						
Total, 16 years and over	223 357	147 401	66.0	139 252	8 149	5.5
Men	107 710	78 980	73.3	74 524	4 456	5.6
Women	115 647	68 421	59.2	64 728	3 694	5.4
FOREIGN BORN						
Total, 16 years and over	31 763	21 433	67.5	20 255	1 178	5.5
Men	15 913	12 905	81.1	12 263	642	5.0
Women	15 849	8 528	53.8	7 992	536	6.3
Age						
16 to 24 years	4 191	2 497	59.6	2 278	219	8.8
25 to 34 years	7 821	5 988	76.6	5 670	318	5.3
35 to 44 years	7 481	6 085	81.3	5 787	298	4.9
45 to 54 years	5 342	4 305	80.6	4 096	210	4.9
55 to 64 years	3 294	2 050	62.2	1 945	105	5.1
65 years and over	3 634	507	14.0	479	28	5.5
Race and Hispanic Ethnicity						
White non-Hispanic or Latino	7 141	4 282	60.0	4 088	194	4.5
Black non-Hispanic or Latino	2 360	1 731	73.4	1 595	136	7.9
Asian non-Hispanic or Latino	7 062	4 738	67.1	4 530	208	4.4
Hispanic or Latino ethnicity	14 878	10 439	70.2	9 808	631	6.0
Educational Attainment						
Total, 25 years and over	27 572	18 936	68.7	17 977	959	5.1
Less than a high school diploma	8 796	5 351	60.8	4 974	377	7.0
High school graduates, no college [1]	6 929	4 707	67.9	4 493	214	4.5
Some college or associate degree	4 259	3 104	72.9	2 944	161	5.2
Bachelor's degree and higher [2]	7 587	5 773	76.1	5 566	207	3.6
NATIVE BORN						
Total 16 years and over	191 594	125 968	65.7	118 997	6 971	5.5
Men	91 797	66 075	72.0	62 261	3 813	5.8
Women	99 797	59 893	60.0	56 736	3 158	5.3
Age						
16 to 24 years	32 228	19 771	61.3	17 352	2 419	12.2
25 to 34 years	31 118	26 219	84.3	24 753	1 466	5.6
35 to 44 years	35 745	30 072	84.1	28 793	1 280	4.3
45 to 54 years	35 904	29 452	82.0	28 374	1 079	3.7
55 to 64 years	25 625	15 963	62.3	15 386	577	3.6
65 years and over	30 975	4 490	14.5	4 339	151	3.4
Race and Hispanic Ethnicity						
White non-Hispanic or Latino	149 414	98 920	66.2	94 480	4 440	4.5
Black non-Hispanic or Latino	22 876	14 355	62.8	12 817	1 537	10.7
Asian non-Hispanic or Latino	2 358	1 455	61.7	1 391	64	4.4
Hispanic or Latino ethnicity	13 231	8 833	66.8	8 122	711	8.0
Educational Attainment						
Total, 25 years and over	159 366	106 197	66.6	101 645	4 552	4.3
Less than a high school diploma	18 873	7 118	37.7	6 434	684	9.6
High school graduates, no college [1]	52 930	33 128	62.6	31 451	1 676	5.1
Some college or associate degree	43 297	31 334	72.4	30 033	1 301	4.2
Bachelor's degree or higher [2]	44 266	34 617	78.2	33 727	891	2.6

Note: Due to the introduction of revised population controls in January 2004, estimated levels for 2004 are not strictly comparable with those for 2003. Data for race/ethnicity groups do not sum to total because data are not presented for all races. Persons of Hispanic origin may be of any race.

[1]Includes persons with a high school diploma or equivalent.
[2]Includes persons with bachelor's, master's, professional, and doctoral degrees.

Table 1-59. Employment Status of the Foreign Born and Native Born Populations 16 Years and Over by Presence and Age of Youngest Child and Sex, 2003–2004 Averages

(Thousands of people, percent.)

Characteristic	2003			2004		
	Total	Men	Women	Total	Men	Women
FOREIGN BORN						
With Own Children Under 18 Years						
Civilian noninstitutional population	12 520	5 985	6 534	12 740	6 060	6 680
Civilian labor force	9 488	5 593	3 895	9 614	5 710	3 904
Participation rate	75.8	93.4	59.6	75.5	94.2	58.4
Employed	8 896	5 284	3 611.0	9 125	5 474	3 652
Employment-population ratio	71.1	88.3	55.3	71.6	90.3	54.7
Unemployed	592	309	283.0	489	236	253
Unemployment rate	6.2	5.5	7.3	5.1	4.1	6.5
With Own Children 6 to 17 Years, None Younger						
Civilian noninstitutional population	6 253	2 893	3 360	6 268	2 907	3 361
Civilian labor force	4 975	2 663	2 313	5 024	2 715	2 309
Participation rate	79.6	92.0	68.8	80.1	93.4	68.7
Employed	4 688	2 516	2 172	4 785	2 605	2 180
Employment-population ratio	75.0	87.0	64.7	76.3	89.6	64.9
Unemployed	287	147	140	238	110	129
Unemployment rate	5.8	5.5	6.1	4.7	4.0	5.6
With Own Children Under 6 Years						
Civilian noninstitutional population	6 267	3 092	3 174	6 472	3 153	3 319
Civilian labor force	4 513	2 930	1 582	4 590	2 995	1 595
Participation rate	72.0	94.8	49.8	70.9	95.0	48.1
Employed	4 208	2 769	1 439	4 340	2 869	1 471
Employment-population ratio	67.1	89.5	45.3	67.1	91.0	44.3
Unemployed	305	162	143	250	126	124
Unemployment rate	6.8	5.5	9.0	5.5	4.2	7.8
With Own Children Under 3 Years						
Civilian noninstitutional population	3 740	1 878	1 862	3 789	1 865	1 924
Civilian labor force	2 618	1 786	832	2 596	1 778	819
Participation rate	70.0	95.1	44.7	68.5	95.3	42.6
Employed	2 450	1 693	757	2 457	1 705	751
Employment-population ratio	65.5	90.2	40.6	64.8	91.4	39.1
Unemployed	168	93	75	139	72	67
Unemployment rate	6.4	5.2	9.0	5.4	4.1	8.2
With No Own Children Under 18 Years						
Civilian noninstitutional population	18 811	9 684	9 127	19 023	9 853	9 170
Civilian labor force	11 629	7 041	4 588	11 819	7 195	4 624
Participation rate	61.8	72.7	50.3	62.1	73.0	50.4
Employed	10 836	6 566	4 270	11 130	6 789	4 340
Employment-population ratio	57.6	67.8	46.8	58.5	68.9	47.3
Unemployed	793	475	318	690	406	283
Unemployment rate	6.8	6.8	6.9	5.8	5.6	6.1

Table 1-59. Employment Status of the Foreign Born and Native Born Populations 16 Years and Over by Presence and Age of Youngest Child and Sex, 2003–2004 Averages—*Continued*

(Thousands of people, percent.)

Characteristic	2003			2004		
	Total	Men	Women	Total	Men	Women
NATIVE BORN						
With Own Children Under 18 Years						
Civilian noninstitutional population	53 492	23 593	29 899	53 136	23 424	29 712
Civilian labor force	44 271	22 261	22 010	43 757	22 053	21 703
Participation rate	82.8	94.4	73.6	82.3	94.1	73.0
Employed	42 196	21 421	20 774	41 882	21 342	20 540
Employment-population ratio	78.9	90.8	69.5	78.8	91.1	69.1
Unemployed	2 075	839	1 236	1 875	711	1 163
Unemployment rate	4.7	3.8	5.6	4.3	3.2	5.4
With Own Children 6 to 17 Years, None Younger						
Civilian noninstitutional population	30 167	13 334	16 833	30 101	13 279	16 821
Civilian labor force	25 839	12 444	13 394	25 642	12 358	13 284
Participation rate	85.7	93.3	79.6	85.2	93.1	79.0
Employed	24 784	12 004	12 780	24 700	11 993	12 707
Employment-population ratio	82.2	90.0	75.9	82.1	90.3	75.5
Unemployed	1 054	440	614	942	365	577
Unemployment rate	4.1	3.5	4.6	3.7	3.0	4.3
With Own Children Under 6 Years						
Civilian noninstitutional population	23 324	10 259	13 065	23 036	10 145	12 891
Civilian labor force	18 432	9 816	8 616	18 115	9 696	8 419
Participation rate	79.0	95.7	65.9	78.6	95.6	65.3
Employed	17 411	9 417	7 994	17 182	9 349	7 833
Employment-population ratio	74.6	91.8	61.2	74.6	92.2	60.8
Unemployed	1 021	399	621	933	347	586
Unemployment rate	5.5	4.1	7.2	5.1	3.6	7.0
With Own Children Under 3 Years						
Civilian noninstitutional population	13 625	6 037	7 588	13 363	5 941	7 422
Civilian labor force	10 518	5 787	4 731	10 252	5 693	4 559
Participation rate	77.2	95.9	62.3	76.7	95.8	61.4
Employed	9 900	5 541	4 359	9 696	5 483	4 212
Employment-population ratio	72.7	91.8	57.4	72.6	92.3	56.8
Unemployed	617	245	372	556	210	346
Unemployment rate	5.9	4.2	7.9	5.4	3.7	7.6
With No Own Children Under 18 Years						
Civilian noninstitutional population	136 346	67 173	69 173	138 458	68 373	70 085
Civilian labor force	81 123	43 343	37 780	82 212	44 021	38 190
Participation rate	59.5	64.5	54.6	59.4	64.4	54.5
Employed	75 809	40 060	35 749	77 115	40 919	36 196
Employment-population ratio	55.6	59.6	51.7	55.7	59.8	51.6
Unemployed	5 314	3 283	2 031	5 096	3 102	1 994
Unemployment rate	6.6	7.6	5.4	6.2	7.0	5.2

Note: Due to the introduction of revised population controls in January 2004, estimated levels for 2004 are not strictly comparable with those for 2003.

Table 1-60. Employment Status of the Foreign Born and Native Born Population 25 Years and Over, by Educational Attainment, Race, and Hispanic or Latino Ethnicity, 2003–2004 Averages

(Thousands of people, percent.)

Characteristic	2003				2004			
	Less than a high school diploma	High school graduates, no college [1]	Some college or associate degree	Bachelor's degree and higher [2]	Less than a high school diploma	High school graduates, no college [1]	Some college or associate degree	Bachelor's degree and higher [2]
FOREIGN BORN								
White non-Hispanic or Latino								
Civilian noninstitutional population	910	1 857	1 238	2 506	899	1 833	1 281	2 474
Civilian labor force	291	1 029	772	1 825	298	981	811	1 814
Participation rate	32.0	55.4	62.4	72.8	33.2	53.5	63.3	73.3
Employed	274	978	730	1 749	279	948	768	1 747
Employment-population ratio	30.1	52.6	59.0	69.8	31.1	51.7	60.0	70.6
Unemployed	17	51	42	76	19	33	43	67
Unemployment rate	6.0	5.0	5.5	4.2	6.4	3.4	5.3	3.7
Black non-Hispanic or Latino								
Civilian noninstitutional population	366	629	477	564	371	650	451	569
Civilian labor force	223	494	393	490	220	495	364	487
Participation rate	60.9	78.5	82.2	86.9	59.4	76.1	80.7	85.6
Employed	195	458	361	458	198	463	332	463
Employment-population ratio	53.3	72.9	75.7	81.2	53.4	71.1	73.7	81.3
Unemployed	28	35	31	32	22	32	31	25
Unemployment rate	12.5	7.1	7.9	6.6	10.1	6.5	8.6	5.0
Asian non-Hispanic or Latino								
Civilian noninstitutional population	867	1 304	932	3 033	874	1 291	986	3 163
Civilian labor force	405	863	675	2 321	390	862	727	2 394
Participation rate	46.7	66.2	72.4	76.5	44.6	66.8	73.8	75.7
Employed	366	811	628	2 211	366	819	688	2 321
Employment-population ratio	42.2	62.2	67.3	72.9	41.9	63.4	69.8	73.4
Unemployed	39	51	47	110	24	43	40	72
Unemployment rate	9.7	6.0	7.0	4.7	6.1	5.0	5.4	3.0
Hispanic or Latino Ethnicity								
Civilian noninstitutional population	6 645	2 916	1 428	1 247	6 618	3 088	1 474	1 280
Civilian labor force	4 436	2 160	1 093	983	4 422	2 315	1 147	997
Participation rate	66.8	74.1	76.6	78.9	66.8	75.0	77.9	77.9
Employed	4 095	2 040	1 036	940	4 111	2 209	1 102	957
Employment-population ratio	61.6	70.0	72.6	75.4	62.1	71.5	74.8	74.8
Unemployed	341	120	58	44	311	105	46	40
Unemployment rate	7.7	5.6	5.3	4.4	7.0	4.6	4.0	4.0
NATIVE BORN								
White non-Hispanic or Latino								
Civilian noninstitutional population	13 010	42 044	33 809	37 843	12 622	42 042	34 302	38 440
Civilian labor force	4 713	26 005	24 276	29 493	4 546	25 719	24 536	29 797
Participation rate	36.2	61.9	71.8	77.9	36.0	61.2	71.5	77.5
Employed	4 348	24 811	23 312	28 708	4 193	24 615	23 681	29 079
Employment-population ratio	33.0	59.0	69.0	76.0	33.0	59.0	69.0	75.6
Unemployed	365	1 194	965	786	353	1 103	854	718
Unemployment rate	7.7	4.6	4.0	2.7	7.8	4.3	3.5	2.4
Black non-Hispanic or Latino								
Civilian noninstitutional population	3 448	6 410	5 001	3 022	3 391	6 600	5 068	3 097
Civilian labor force	1 267	4 292	3 820	2 458	1 228	4 400	3 768	2 554
Participation rate	36.8	67.0	76.4	81.3	36.2	66.7	74.4	82.5
Employed	1 088	3 878	3 521	2 364	1 025	4 004	3 483	2 451
Employment-population ratio	31.6	60.5	70.4	78.2	30.2	60.7	68.7	79.1
Unemployed	179	414	298	95	203	396	285	104
Unemployment rate	14.1	9.6	7.8	3.9	16.5	9.0	7.6	4.1
Asian non-Hispanic or Latino								
Civilian noninstitutional population	132	294	358	755	142	320	381	807
Civilian labor force	50	174	251	611	55	174	259	640
Participation rate	38.0	59.0	70.2	81.0	38.4	54.6	68.0	79.2
Employed	46	167	243	593	52	170	252	624
Employment-population ratio	35.0	57.0	68.0	79.0	37.0	53.0	65.9	77.3
Unemployed	4	7	8	18	2	4	8	16
Unemployment rate	8.8	3.8	3.1	3.0	4.2	2.4	3.0	2.5
Hispanic or Latino Ethnicity								
Civilian noninstitutional population	2 324	3 078	2 487	1 350	2 297	3 084	2 590	1 406
Civilian labor force	1 088	2 270	2 008	1 142	1 131	2 251	2 075	1 207
Participation rate	46.8	73.7	80.7	84.6	49.2	73.0	80.1	85.9
Employed	977	2 129	1 890	1 099	1 024	2 120	1 966	1 170
Employment-population ratio	42.1	69.1	76.0	81.4	44.6	68.8	75.9	83.3
Unemployed	110	141	118	43	106	131	109	37
Unemployment rate	10.2	6.2	5.9	3.8	9.4	5.8	5.2	3.1

Note: Data for race/ethnicity groups do not sum to totals because data are not presented for all races. Persons of Hispanic origin may be of any race. Due to the introduction of revised population controls in January 2004, estimated levels for 2004 are not strictly comparable with those for 2003.

[1]Includes persons with a high school diploma or equivalent.
[2]Includes persons with bachelor's, master's, professional, and doctoral degrees.

Table 1-61. Employed Foreign Born and Native Born Persons 16 Years and Over by Occupation and Sex, 2003–2004 Averages

(Thousands of people, percent.)

Characteristic	2003			2004		
	Total	Men	Women	Total	Men	Women
TOTAL EMPLOYED	20 255	12 263	7 992	118 997	62 261	56 736
Percent	100.0	100.0	100.0	100.0	100.0	100.0
Management, professional, and related occupations	26.5	24.4	29.8	36.3	34.0	38.8
Management, business, and financial operations occupations	9.8	9.8	9.8	15.3	16.9	13.6
Management occupations	7.1	7.9	5.9	11.0	13.2	8.6
Business and financial operations occupations	2.7	1.9	3.9	4.3	3.7	5.0
Professional and related occupations	16.7	14.6	20.0	20.9	17.1	25.2
Computer and mathematical occupations	3.0	3.8	1.9	2.1	2.9	1.2
Architecture and engineering occupations	2.1	2.9	0.8	2.0	3.3	0.6
Life, physical, and social science occupations	1.1	1.0	1.2	1.0	1.0	0.9
Community and social services occupations	0.9	0.7	1.4	1.7	1.2	2.1
Legal occupations	0.5	0.3	0.8	1.2	1.2	1.2
Education, training, and library occupations	3.2	2.0	5.1	6.1	3.0	9.5
Arts, design, entertainment, sports, and media occupations	1.5	1.3	1.8	2.0	2.0	2.0
Healthcare practitioner and technical occupations	4.4	2.6	7.1	4.9	2.4	7.7
Service occupations	22.8	18.3	29.8	15.2	12.2	18.5
Healthcare support occupations	2.3	0.5	5.1	2.1	0.4	3.9
Protective service occupations	1.0	1.3	0.4	2.2	3.3	1.0
Food preparation and serving related occupations	7.5	7.5	7.5	4.8	3.7	6.1
Building and grounds cleaning and maintenance occupations	8.4	7.5	9.8	2.9	3.5	2.3
Personal care and service occupations	3.6	1.4	6.9	3.2	1.3	5.2
Sales and office occupations	18.4	13.3	26.3	26.7	18.0	36.2
Sales and related occupations	9.2	8.1	11.0	11.9	11.4	12.3
Office and administrative support occupations	9.2	5.2	15.4	14.8	6.5	23.9
Natural resources, construction, and maintenance occupations	14.7	23.3	1.6	9.7	17.8	0.9
Farming, fishing, and forestry occupations	1.8	2.4	0.9	0.5	0.8	0.2
Construction and extraction occupations	9.7	15.8	0.3	5.5	10.2	0.3
Installation, maintenance, and repair occupations	3.2	5.1	0.4	3.7	6.8	0.4
Production, transportation, and material moving occupations	17.5	20.7	12.5	12.1	18.1	5.5
Production occupations	10.6	11.3	9.6	6.1	8.4	3.7
Transportation and material moving occupations	6.8	9.4	2.8	6.0	9.8	1.8

Note: Due to the introduction of revised population controls in January 2004, estimated levels for 2004 are not strictly comparable with those for 2003.

Table 1-62. Median Usual Weekly Earnings of Full-Time Wage and Salary Workers for the Foreign Born and Native Born by Selected Characteristics, 2003–2004 Averages

(Thousands of people, dollars.)

Characteristic	Foreign born		Native born		Earnings of foreign born as a percent of native born [1]
	Number	Median weekly earnings	Number	Median weekly earnings	
2003					
Total, 16 Years and Over	15 227	489	85 076	643	76.0
Men	9 666	503	46 560	732	68.7
Women	5 560	459	38 516	567	80.8
Age					
16 to 24 years	1 512	345	9 278	393	87.7
25 to 34 years	4 642	466	20 134	615	75.8
35 to 44 years	4 493	522	22 602	716	72.8
45 to 54 years	2 984	567	21 461	742	76.4
55 to 64 years	1 355	600	10 084	725	82.8
65 years and over	241	500	1 516	518	96.6
Race and Hispanic or Latino Ethnicity					
White non-Hispanic or Latino	2 863	681	66 371	683	99.7
Black non-Hispanic or Latino	1 266	515	10 258	515	99.8
Asian non-Hispanic or Latino	3 250	689	991	732	94.0
Hispanic or Latino ethnicity	7 690	398	5 944	523	76.1
Educational Attainment					
Total, 25 years and over	13 715	511	75 798	688	74.2
Less than a high school diploma	4 034	369	4 559	430	86.0
High school graduates, no college [2]	3 359	467	23 724	569	82.1
Some college	2 135	576	22 475	647	89.0
Bachelor's degree and higher [3]	4 186	909	25 040	971	93.6
2004					
Total, 16 Years and Over	15 580	502	85 644	664	75.6
Men	9 902	518	47 099	749	69.1
Women	5 678	473	38 545	585	81.0
Age					
16 to 24 years	1 551	341	9 325	397	85.8
25 to 34 years	4 631	491	20 126	624	78.7
35 to 44 years	4 538	540	22 323	741	72.9
45 to 54 years	3 187	565	21 799	764	73.9
55 to 64 years	1 409	607	10 523	740	82.0
65 years and over	264	552	1 548	562	98.2
Race and Hispanic or Latino Ethnicity					
White non-Hispanic or Latino	2 852	731	66 563	702	104.1
Black non-Hispanic or Latino	1 268	533	10 374	529	100.8
Asian non-Hispanic or Latino	3 383	699	1 009	738	94.8
Hispanic or Latino ethnicity	7 899	402	6 163	539	74.5
Educational Attainment					
Total, 25 years and over	14 029	524	76 319	710	73.7
Less than a high school diploma	4 094	373	4 439	433	86.2
High school graduates, no college [2]	3 486	478	23 655	586	81.5
Some college	2 216	595	22 630	668	89.0
Bachelor's degree and higher [3]	4 234	943	25 595	994	94.9

Note: Due to the introduction of revised population controls in January 2004, estimated levels for 2004 are not strictly comparable with those for 2003. Data for race/ethnicity groups do not sum to totals because data are not presented for all races. Persons of Hispanic origin may be of any race.

[1]These figures are computed using unrounded medians and may differ slightly from percents computed using the rounded medians displayed in this table.
[2]Includes persons with a high school diploma or equivalent.
[3]Includes persons with bachelor's, master's, professional, and doctoral degrees.

Table 1-63. Percentage Distribution of the Civilian Labor Force 25 to 64 Years of Age by Educational Attainment, Sex, and Race, March 1990–2005

(Number, percent.)

Sex, race, and year	Civilian labor force (thousands)	Percent distribution				
		Total	Less than a high school diploma	4 years of high school only	1 to 3 years of college	4 or more years of college
Total						
1990	99 175	100.0	13.4	39.5	20.7	26.4
1991	100 480	100.0	13.0	39.4	21.1	26.5
1992	102 387	100.0	12.2	36.2	25.2	26.4
1993	103 504	100.0	11.5	35.2	26.3	27.0
1994	104 868	100.0	11.0	34.0	27.7	27.3
1995	106 519	100.0	10.8	33.1	27.8	28.3
1996	108 037	100.0	10.9	32.9	27.7	28.5
1997	110 514	100.0	10.9	33.0	27.4	28.6
1998	111 857	100.0	10.7	32.8	27.4	29.1
1999	112 542	100.0	10.3	32.3	27.4	30.0
2000	114 052	100.0	9.8	31.8	27.9	30.4
2001	115 073	100.0	9.8	31.4	28.1	30.7
2002	117 738	100.0	10.1	30.6	27.7	31.6
2003	119 261	100.0	10.1	30.1	27.8	31.9
2004	119 392	100.0	9.7	30.1	27.8	32.4
2005	120 461	100.0	9.8	30.1	27.8	32.3
Men						
1990	54 476	100.0	15.1	37.2	19.7	28.0
1991	55 165	100.0	14.7	37.5	20.2	27.6
1992	55 917	100.0	13.9	34.7	23.8	27.5
1993	56 544	100.0	13.2	33.9	24.7	28.1
1994	56 633	100.0	12.7	32.9	25.8	28.6
1995	57 454	100.0	12.2	32.3	25.7	29.7
1996	58 121	100.0	12.7	32.2	26.0	29.1
1997	59 268	100.0	12.8	32.2	25.8	29.2
1998	59 905	100.0	12.3	32.3	25.8	29.6
1999	60 030	100.0	11.7	32.0	25.8	30.5
2000	60 510	100.0	11.1	31.8	26.1	30.9
2001	61 091	100.0	11.0	31.6	26.3	31.1
2002	62 794	100.0	11.8	30.6	25.9	31.7
2003	63 466	100.0	12.0	30.1	25.8	32.1
2004	63 699	100.0	11.5	30.5	25.8	32.2
2005	64 562	100.0	11.6	31.4	25.4	31.6
Women						
1990	44 699	100.0	11.3	42.4	21.9	24.5
1991	45 315	100.0	10.9	41.6	22.2	25.2
1992	46 469	100.0	10.2	37.9	26.9	25.0
1993	46 961	100.0	9.3	36.7	28.2	25.8
1994	48 235	100.0	9.1	35.3	29.8	25.8
1995	49 065	100.0	9.1	34.1	30.2	26.6
1996	49 916	100.0	8.8	33.7	29.7	27.8
1997	51 246	100.0	8.7	34.0	29.3	28.0
1998	51 953	100.0	8.8	33.3	29.3	28.6
1999	52 512	100.0	8.7	32.7	29.2	29.5
2000	53 541	100.0	8.4	31.8	30.0	29.8
2001	53 982	100.0	8.5	31.1	30.1	30.2
2002	54 944	100.0	8.2	30.6	29.7	31.5
2003	55 795	100.0	8.0	30.1	30.1	31.8
2004	55 693	100.0	7.7	29.6	30.2	32.5
2005	55 899	100.0	7.8	28.6	30.5	33.1

Table 1-63. Percentage Distribution of the Civilian Labor Force 25 to 64 Years of Age by Educational Attainment, Sex, and Race, March 1990–2005—*Continued*

(Number, percent.)

Sex, race, and year	Civilian labor force (thousands)	Percent distribution				
		Total	Less than a high school diploma	4 years of high school only	1 to 3 years of college	4 or more years of college
White[1]						
1990	85 238	100.0	12.6	39.6	20.6	27.1
1991	86 344	100.0	12.2	39.3	21.1	27.4
1992	87 656	100.0	11.3	36.1	25.5	27.1
1993	88 457	100.0	10.7	35.0	26.4	27.9
1994	89 009	100.0	10.5	33.7	27.7	28.1
1995	90 192	100.0	10.0	32.8	27.8	29.3
1996	91 506	100.0	10.4	32.8	27.5	29.3
1997	93 179	100.0	10.4	32.8	27.3	29.5
1998	93 527	100.0	10.2	32.7	27.4	29.8
1999	94 216	100.0	9.8	32.2	27.2	30.8
2000	95 073	100.0	9.5	31.8	27.7	31.0
2001	95 562	100.0	9.5	31.0	28.0	31.4
2002	97 699	100.0	9.8	30.6	27.6	32.0
2003	98 241	100.0	9.9	30.0	27.7	32.4
2004	98 030	100.0	9.5	29.8	27.8	32.9
2005	98 581	100.0	9.7	29.8	27.8	32.7
Black[1]						
1990	10 537	100.0	19.9	42.5	22.1	15.5
1991	10 650	100.0	19.5	42.9	22.1	15.4
1992	10 936	100.0	19.2	40.3	24.9	15.6
1993	11 051	100.0	16.8	39.5	27.6	16.1
1994	11 368	100.0	14.5	39.3	29.2	17.0
1995	11 695	100.0	14.1	38.6	29.6	17.7
1996	11 891	100.0	14.2	37.2	31.2	17.4
1997	12 253	100.0	14.3	37.8	31.3	16.6
1998	12 893	100.0	14.3	37.3	30.1	18.2
1999	12 945	100.0	13.0	37.2	30.4	19.5
2000	13 383	100.0	11.8	36.1	31.5	20.7
2001	13 617	100.0	12.0	37.1	31.1	19.8
2002	13 319	100.0	12.4	34.5	32.0	21.0
2003	13 315	100.0	11.3	35.6	31.5	21.6
2004	13 372	100.0	11.0	36.6	30.5	21.9
2005	13 635	100.0	11.2	37.3	29.9	21.6

[1]Beginning in 2003, persons who selected this race group only; persons who selected more than one race group are not included. Prior to 2003, persons who reported more than one race group were included in the group they identified as the main race.

Table 1-64. Labor Force Participation Rates of Persons 25 to 64 Years of Age by Educational Attainment, Sex, and Race, March 1990–2005

(Civilian labor force as a percent of the civilian noninstitutional population.)

Sex, race, and year	Participation rates				
	Total	Less than a high school diploma	4 years of high school only	1 to 3 years of college	4 or more years of college
Total					
1990	78.6	60.7	78.2	83.3	88.4
1991	78.6	60.7	78.1	83.2	88.4
1992	79.0	60.3	78.3	83.5	88.4
1993	78.9	59.6	77.7	82.9	88.3
1994	78.9	58.3	77.8	83.2	88.2
1995	79.3	59.8	77.3	83.2	88.7
1996	79.4	60.2	77.9	83.7	87.8
1997	80.1	61.7	78.5	83.7	88.5
1998	80.2	63.0	78.4	83.5	88.0
1999	80.0	62.7	78.1	83.0	87.6
2000	80.3	62.7	78.4	83.2	87.8
2001	80.2	63.5	78.4	83.0	87.0
2002	79.7	63.5	77.7	82.1	86.7
2003	79.4	64.1	76.9	81.9	86.2
2004	78.8	63.2	76.1	81.2	85.9
2005	78.5	62.9	75.7	81.1	85.7
Men					
1990	88.8	75.1	89.9	91.5	94.5
1991	88.6	75.1	89.3	92.0	94.2
1992	88.6	75.1	89.0	91.8	93.7
1993	88.1	74.9	88.1	90.6	93.7
1994	87.0	71.5	86.8	90.3	93.2
1995	87.4	72.0	86.9	90.1	93.8
1996	87.5	74.3	86.9	90.0	92.9
1997	87.7	75.2	86.4	90.6	93.5
1998	87.8	75.3	86.7	90.0	93.4
1999	87.5	74.4	86.6	89.4	93.0
2000	87.5	74.9	86.2	88.9	93.3
2001	87.4	75.4	85.8	89.1	92.9
2002	87.0	75.5	85.3	88.8	92.4
2003	86.4	76.1	84.3	87.5	92.2
2004	85.9	75.2	83.8	87.0	91.9
2005	86.0	75.7	83.7	87.5	91.7
Women					
1990	68.9	46.2	68.7	75.9	81.1
1991	69.1	46.2	68.6	75.2	81.8
1992	70.0	45.6	69.1	76.2	82.2
1993	70.0	44.2	68.8	76.1	82.2
1994	71.1	44.7	70.0	77.0	82.5
1995	71.5	47.2	68.9	77.3	82.8
1996	71.8	45.7	69.8	78.1	82.3
1997	72.8	47.1	71.4	77.6	83.2
1998	73.0	49.8	70.9	77.8	82.3
1999	72.8	50.5	70.4	77.4	81.9
2000	73.5	50.4	71.2	78.3	82.0
2001	73.4	51.7	71.3	77.7	80.9
2002	72.7	50.4	70.4	76.4	81.0
2003	72.6	50.5	69.8	77.1	80.1
2004	72.0	49.7	68.6	76.2	80.0
2005	71.4	48.7	67.4	75.8	79.8

Table 1-64. Labor Force Participation Rates of Persons 25 to 64 Years of Age by Educational Attainment, Sex, and Race, March 1990–2005—*Continued*

(Civilian labor force as a percent of the civilian noninstitutional population.)

Sex, race, and year	Participation rates				
	Total	Less than a high school diploma	4 years of high school only	1 to 3 years of college	4 or more years of college
White[1]					
1990	79.2	62.5	78.4	83.3	88.3
1991	79.4	62.5	78.3	83.1	88.6
1992	79.8	61.5	78.7	83.8	88.7
1993	79.7	61.1	78.2	83.1	88.8
1994	79.8	60.3	78.3	83.5	88.5
1995	80.1	61.6	77.9	83.4	88.8
1996	80.4	62.5	78.6	83.9	88.2
1997	81.0	63.8	79.2	83.9	89.0
1998	80.6	63.8	78.6	83.5	88.3
1999	80.6	64.2	78.5	83.3	87.9
2000	80.8	64.2	78.7	83.1	87.9
2001	80.7	64.5	78.7	83.1	87.2
2002	80.3	65.0	78.2	82.4	87.0
2003	80.1	65.7	77.5	82.3	86.5
2004	79.5	64.6	76.7	81.6	86.2
2005	79.2	63.8	76.4	81.5	86.1
Black[1]					
1990	74.6	54.5	78.2	84.2	92.0
1991	73.9	53.9	77.1	84.1	90.2
1992	74.4	55.4	76.9	83.4	89.1
1993	73.8	53.4	74.7	83.0	89.6
1994	73.5	49.4	75.2	82.4	89.5
1995	74.2	51.0	74.5	82.8	90.9
1996	73.7	50.1	74.3	83.0	87.9
1997	74.9	52.9	75.0	83.8	89.0
1998	77.7	59.3	77.0	85.0	88.8
1999	76.5	55.1	76.5	82.9	88.6
2000	77.9	55.5	77.0	84.2	90.3
2001	78.1	58.7	76.8	83.0	90.5
2002	76.4	56.6	75.0	81.7	88.9
2003	75.8	55.4	73.9	81.2	88.2
2004	75.0	55.2	73.4	79.0	87.9
2005	75.2	58.2	72.6	79.5	87.2

[1]Beginning in 2003, persons who selected this race group only; persons who selected more than one race group are not included. Prior to 2003, persons who reported more than one race group were included in the group they identified as the main race.

Table 1-65. Unemployment Rates of Persons 25 to 64 Years of Age by Educational Attainment and Sex, March 1990–2005

(Unemployment as a percent of the civilian labor force.)

Sex, race, and year	Unemployment rates				
	Total	Less than a high school diploma	4 years of high school only	1 to 3 years of college	4 or more years of college
Total					
1990	4.5	9.6	4.9	3.7	1.9
1991	6.1	12.3	6.7	5.0	2.9
1992	6.7	13.5	7.7	5.9	2.9
1993	6.4	13.0	7.3	5.5	3.2
1994	5.8	12.6	6.7	5.0	2.9
1995	4.8	10.0	5.2	4.5	2.5
1996	4.8	10.9	5.5	4.1	2.2
1997	4.4	10.4	5.1	3.8	2.0
1998	4.0	8.5	4.8	3.6	1.8
1999	3.5	7.7	4.0	3.1	1.9
2000	3.3	7.9	3.8	3.0	1.5
2001	3.5	8.1	4.2	2.9	2.0
2002	5.0	10.2	6.1	4.5	2.8
2003	5.3	9.9	6.4	5.2	3.0
2004	5.1	10.5	5.9	4.9	2.9
2005	4.4	9.0	5.5	4.1	2.3
Men					
1990	4.8	9.6	5.3	3.9	2.1
1991	6.8	13.4	7.7	5.2	3.2
1992	7.5	14.8	8.8	6.4	3.2
1993	7.3	14.1	8.7	6.3	3.4
1994	6.2	12.8	7.2	5.3	2.9
1995	5.1	10.9	5.7	4.4	2.6
1996	5.3	11.0	6.4	4.5	2.3
1997	4.7	9.9	5.6	4.0	2.1
1998	4.1	8.0	5.1	3.7	1.7
1999	3.5	7.0	4.1	3.2	1.9
2000	3.3	7.1	3.9	3.1	1.6
2001	3.7	7.5	4.6	3.2	1.9
2002	5.5	9.9	6.7	4.9	3.0
2003	5.8	9.5	6.9	6.0	3.2
2004	5.4	9.4	6.6	5.4	3.0
2005	4.7	7.9	6.0	4.3	2.5
Women					
1990	4.2	9.5	4.6	3.5	1.7
1991	5.2	10.7	5.5	4.8	2.5
1992	5.7	11.4	6.5	5.3	2.5
1993	5.2	11.2	5.8	4.6	2.9
1994	5.4	12.4	6.2	4.7	2.9
1995	4.4	8.6	4.6	4.5	2.4
1996	4.1	10.7	4.4	3.8	2.1
1997	4.1	11.3	4.5	3.6	2.0
1998	3.9	9.3	4.4	3.5	1.9
1999	3.5	8.8	3.9	3.0	1.9
2000	3.2	9.1	3.6	2.9	1.4
2001	3.3	8.9	3.8	2.6	2.0
2002	4.6	10.6	5.4	4.1	2.6
2003	4.8	10.6	5.9	4.4	2.8
2004	4.7	12.2	5.2	4.3	2.9
2005	4.2	10.9	4.8	4.0	2.2

Table 1-66. Workers Age 25 to 64 by Educational Attainment, Occupation of Longest Job Held, and Sex, 2003–2004

(Thousands of people with work experience during the year.)

Sex and occupation	Total	Less than a high school diploma	4 years of high school only	1 to 3 years of college	4 or more years of college
2003					
Total	122 312	11 727	36 703	34 356	39 526
Management, business, and financial operations occupations	19 051	399	3 508	5 076	10 068
Management occupations	13 645	352	2 686	3 647	6 961
Business and financial operations occupations	5 406	48	822	1 429	3 107
Professional and related occupations	26 431	186	2 336	5 907	18 002
Computer and mathematical occupations	2 995	24	233	784	1 953
Architecture and engineering occupations	2 449	5	254	602	1 588
Life, physical, and social science occupations	1 240	0	98	144	998
Community and social services occupations	1 999	24	167	343	1 465
Legal occupations	1 466	9	87	228	1 142
Education, training, and library occupations	7 587	64	661	933	5 929
Arts, design, entertainment, sports, and media occupations	2 384	36	325	683	1 340
Healthcare practitioner and technical occupations	6 311	23	510	2 191	3 587
Service occupations	17 269	3 319	6 862	5 020	2 068
Healthcare supporting occupations	2 418	308	939	936	235
Protective service occupations	2 542	96	693	1 126	628
Food preparation and serving related occupations	4 442	1 021	1 933	1 051	437
Building and grounds cleaning and maintenance occupations	4 368	1 465	1 908	729	265
Personal care and service occupations	3 499	429	1 390	1 177	503
Sales and office occupations	29 555	1 502	10 357	10 678	7 019
Sales and related occupations	12 624	767	3 890	3 949	4 018
Office and administrative support occupations	16 931	735	6 467	6 728	3 001
Natural resources, construction, and maintenance occupations	12 938	2 917	5 701	3 437	884
Farming, fishing, and forestry occupations	897	462	281	105	49
Construction and extraction occupations	7 527	1 878	3 413	1 771	465
Installation, maintenance, and repair occupations	4 514	577	2 006	1 560	370
Production, transportation, and material moving occupations	16 438	3 400	7 828	3 957	1 253
Production occupations	9 025	1 909	4 218	2 211	686
Transportation and material moving occupations	7 413	1 491	3 610	1 746	566
Armed forces	630	4	111	282	233
Men	64 929	7 330	19 785	16 945	20 867
Management, business, and financial operations occupations	10 742	253	1 898	2 626	5 964
Management occupations	8 421	233	1 686	2 128	4 373
Business and financial operations occupations	2 321	20	212	499	1 591
Professional and related occupations	11 273	62	793	2 099	8 319
Computer and mathematical occupations	2 128	19	140	546	1 422
Architecture and engineering occupations	2 131	4	208	529	1 391
Life, physical, and social science occupations	741	. . .	63	88	590
Community and social services occupations	777	14	63	119	581
Legal occupations	750	1	8	31	710
Education, training, and library occupations	1 924	4	78	150	1 692
Arts, design, entertainment, sports, and media occupations	1 234	16	161	364	693
Healthcare practitioner and technical occupations	1 588	3	72	273	1 240
Service occupations	7 214	1 404	2 568	2 146	1 096
Healthcare supporting occupations	218	23	69	84	43
Protective service occupations	2 020	64	512	914	529
Food preparation and serving related occupations	1 795	479	689	420	207
Building and grounds cleaning and maintenance occupations	2 500	764	1 058	500	179
Personal care and service occupations	681	74	240	227	139
Sales and office occupations	10 553	567	3 024	3 467	3 495
Sales and related occupations	6 789	284	1 782	2 128	2 595
Office and administrative support occupations	3 764	282	1 242	1 339	900
Natural resources, construction, and maintenance occupations	12 259	2 730	5 446	3 279	803
Farming, fishing, and forestry occupations	656	321	206	87	41
Construction and extraction occupations	7 313	1 849	3 323	1 700	440
Installation, maintenance, and repair occupations	4 290	559	1 916	1 492	322
Production, transportation, and material moving occupations	12 329	2 310	5 957	3 074	988
Production occupations	6 209	1 126	2 961	1 617	506
Transportation and material moving occupations	6 120	1 184	2 996	1 458	482
Armed forces	559	4	99	254	202
Women	57 384	4 397	16 918	17 411	18 658
Management, business, and financial operations occupations	8 310	146	1 610	2 450	4 103
Management occupations	5 225	118	1 000	1 519	2 587
Business and financial operations occupations	3 085	28	611	930	1 516
Professional and related occupations	15 158	125	1 543	3 808	9 683
Computer and mathematical occupations	867	5	93	238	531
Architecture and engineering occupations	318	1	47	73	197
Life, physical, and social science occupations	500	0	36	56	408
Community and social services occupations	1 222	11	104	224	884
Legal occupations	716	8	79	197	432
Education, training, and library occupations	5 663	60	583	783	4 238
Arts, design, entertainment, sports, and media occupations	1 150	20	164	319	647
Healthcare practitioner and technical occupations	4 722	19	438	1 919	2 346
Service occupations	10 054	1 915	4 294	2 874	972
Healthcare supporting occupations	2 200	285	870	852	192
Protective service occupations	522	32	180	212	98
Food preparation and serving related occupations	2 647	542	1 244	630	230
Building and grounds cleaning and maintenance occupations	1 867	701	850	229	87
Personal care and service occupations	2 818	355	1 150	950	364
Sales and office occupations	19 002	935	7 333	7 211	3 523
Sales and related occupations	5 835	482	2 108	1 822	1 423
Office and administrative support occupations	13 168	453	5 225	5 389	2 100
Natural resources, construction, and maintenance occupations	680	187	255	157	80
Farming, fishing, and forestry occupations	241	140	75	18	7
Construction and extraction occupations	214	29	90	70	25
Installation, maintenance, and repair occupations	225	18	90	69	48
Production, transportation, and material moving occupations	4 109	1 089	1 872	883	265
Production occupations	2 815	783	1 258	594	180
Transportation and material moving occupations	1 293	307	614	289	84
Armed forces	71	. . .	11	28	32

. . . = Not available.

Table 1-66. Workers Age 25 to 64 by Educational Attainment, Occupation of Longest Job Held, and Sex, 2003–2004—*Continued*

(Thousands of people with work experience during the year.)

Sex and occupation	Total	Less than a high school diploma	4 years of high school only	1 to 3 years of college	4 or more years of college
2004					
Total	123 578	12 018	37 168	34 480	39 913
Management, business, and financial operations occupations	18 667	396	3 308	4 890	10 073
Management occupations	13 311	347	2 586	3 444	6 934
Business and financial operations occupations	5 356	50	722	1 446	3 139
Professional and related occupations	26 599	203	2 290	6 031	18 075
Computer and mathematical occupations	3 137	13	230	840	2 053
Architecture and engineering occupations	2 470	6	263	604	1 597
Life, physical, and social science occupations	1 249	2	99	118	1 031
Community and social services occupations	1 918	23	188	358	1 348
Legal occupations	1 427	5	87	251	1 083
Education, training, and library occupations	7 740	61	652	993	6 034
Arts, design, entertainment, sports, and media occupations	2 392	45	321	633	1 393
Healthcare practitioner and technical occupations	6 267	47	450	2 234	3 537
Service occupations	18 016	3 437	7 238	5 163	2 179
Healthcare supporting occupations	2 526	314	997	997	219
Protective service occupations	2 564	92	717	1 098	658
Food preparation and serving related occupations	4 672	1 096	2 078	1 071	426
Building and grounds cleaning and maintenance occupations	4 708	1 541	2 068	804	295
Personal care and service occupations	3 547	395	1 379	1 193	581
Sales and office occupations	29 571	1 490	10 335	10 658	7 087
Sales and related occupations	12 839	825	3 991	3 983	4 040
Office and administrative support occupations	16 732	665	6 344	6 675	3 047
Natural resources, construction, and maintenance occupations	13 718	3 139	5 938	3 623	1 018
Farming, fishing, and forestry occupations	947	474	297	108	68
Construction and extraction occupations	8 076	2 095	3 585	1 883	514
Installation, maintenance, and repair occupations	4 694	571	2 056	1 632	436
Production, transportation, and material moving occupations	16 436	3 345	7 930	3 890	1 271
Production occupations	9 062	1 890	4 298	2 167	706
Transportation and material moving occupations	7 374	1 455	3 632	1 723	565
Armed forces	571	8	129	225	210
Men	65 840	7 582	20 572	16 845	20 841
Management, business, and financial operations occupations	10 428	273	1 798	2 446	5 910
Management occupations	8 208	249	1 596	2 011	4 352
Business and financial operations occupations	2 219	24	203	435	1 558
Professional and related occupations	11 365	75	867	2 116	8 306
Computer and mathematical occupations	2 272	10	161	603	1 498
Architecture and engineering occupations	2 135	5	230	521	1 380
Life, physical, and social science occupations	724	. . .	67	70	586
Community and social services occupations	773	10	68	126	569
Legal occupations	701	. . .	10	23	668
Education, training, and library occupations	1 916	4	85	159	1 669
Arts, design, entertainment, sports, and media occupations	1 249	34	161	346	707
Healthcare practitioner and technical occupations	1 594	11	86	268	1 228
Service occupations	7 540	1 402	2 873	2 144	1 121
Healthcare supporting occupations	274	28	93	119	35
Protective service occupations	1 983	56	550	851	526
Food preparation and serving related occupations	1 890	490	749	430	221
Building and grounds cleaning and maintenance occupations	2 703	784	1 212	524	183
Personal care and service occupations	688	45	269	219	157
Sales and office occupations	10 605	520	3 210	3 437	3 439
Sales and related occupations	6 826	304	1 873	2 068	2 582
Office and administrative support occupations	3 779	216	1 337	1 369	857
Natural resources, construction, and maintenance occupations	13 015	2 960	5 700	3 432	923
Farming, fishing, and forestry occupations	704	346	228	77	53
Construction and extraction occupations	7 826	2 056	3 493	1 798	479
Installation, maintenance, and repair occupations	4 484	558	1 979	1 557	391
Production, transportation, and material moving occupations	12 363	2 344	6 006	3 059	954
Production occupations	6 231	1 157	3 011	1 588	474
Transportation and material moving occupations	6 132	1 187	2 995	1 470	480
Armed forces	524	8	118	211	188
Women	57 740	4 436	16 594	17 636	19 070
Management, business, and financial operations occupations	8 240	123	1 509	2 445	4 162
Management occupations	5 103	97	990	1 433	2 582
Business and financial operations occupations	3 137	26	519	1 011	1 581
Professional and related occupations	15 234	127	1 423	3 915	9 769
Computer and mathematical occupations	864	3	70	237	555
Architecture and engineering occupations	335	2	33	84	217
Life, physical, and social science occupations	525	2	32	47	445
Community and social services occupations	1 144	12	120	233	779
Legal occupations	726	5	78	228	415
Education, training, and library occupations	5 824	57	567	834	4 365
Arts, design, entertainment, sports, and media occupations	1 143	11	159	287	686
Healthcare practitioner and technical occupations	4 673	36	364	1 966	2 308
Service occupations	10 477	2 034	4 365	3 019	1 058
Healthcare supporting occupations	2 251	286	904	877	184
Protective service occupations	580	36	166	247	132
Food preparation and serving related occupations	2 782	606	1 329	641	206
Building and grounds cleaning and maintenance occupations	2 004	757	856	280	112
Personal care and service occupations	2 859	350	1 110	975	424
Sales and office occupations	18 965	971	7 125	7 221	3 648
Sales and related occupations	6 012	521	2 117	1 915	1 459
Office and administrative support occupations	12 953	449	5 008	5 306	2 190
Natural resources, construction, and maintenance occupations	703	180	238	191	94
Farming, fishing, and forestry occupations	243	128	69	31	14
Construction and extraction occupations	250	38	92	85	35
Installation, maintenance, and repair occupations	210	14	77	75	45
Production, transportation, and material moving occupations	4 073	1 001	1 923	831	317
Production occupations	2 831	733	1 287	579	232
Transportation and material moving occupations	1 242	268	636	252	85
Armed forces	48	. . .	11	14	22

. . . = Not available.

Table 1-67. Percent Distribution of Workers Age 25 to 64 by Educational Attainment, Occupation of Longest Job Held, and Sex, 2003–2004

(Percent of total workers in occupation.)

Sex and occupation	Total	Less than a high school diploma	4 years of high school only	1 to 3 years of college	4 or more years of college
2003					
Total	100.0	9.6	30.0	28.1	32.3
Management, business, and financial operations occupations	100.0	2.1	18.4	26.6	52.8
Management occupations	100.0	2.6	19.7	26.7	51.0
Business and financial operations occupations	100.0	0.9	15.2	26.4	57.5
Professional and related occupations	100.0	0.7	8.8	22.3	68.1
Computer and mathematical occupations	100.0	0.8	7.8	26.2	65.2
Architecture and engineering occupations	100.0	0.2	10.4	24.6	64.8
Life, physical, and social science occupations	100.0	0.0	7.9	11.6	80.4
Community and social services occupations	100.0	1.2	8.4	17.2	73.3
Legal occupations	100.0	0.6	5.9	15.5	77.9
Education, training, and library occupations	100.0	0.8	8.7	12.3	78.2
Arts, design, entertainment, sports, and media occupations	100.0	1.5	13.6	28.6	56.2
Healthcare practitioner and technical occupations	100.0	0.4	8.1	34.7	56.8
Service occupations	100.0	19.2	39.7	29.1	12.0
Healthcare supporting occupations	100.0	12.7	38.8	38.7	9.7
Protective service occupations	100.0	3.8	27.2	44.3	24.7
Food preparation and serving related occupations	100.0	23.0	43.5	23.7	9.8
Building and grounds cleaning and maintenance occupations	100.0	33.5	43.7	16.7	6.1
Personal care and service occupations	100.0	12.3	39.7	33.6	14.4
Sales and office occupations	100.0	5.1	35.0	36.1	23.7
Sales and related occupations	100.0	6.1	30.8	31.3	31.8
Office and administrative support occupations	100.0	4.3	38.2	39.7	17.7
Natural resources, construction, and maintenance occupations	100.0	22.5	44.1	26.6	6.8
Farming, fishing, and forestry occupations	100.0	51.5	31.4	11.8	5.4
Construction and extraction occupations	100.0	25.0	45.3	23.5	6.2
Installation, maintenance, and repair occupations	100.0	12.8	44.4	34.6	8.2
Production, transportation, and material moving occupations	100.0	20.7	47.6	24.1	7.6
Production occupations	100.0	21.2	46.7	24.5	7.6
Transportation and material moving occupations	100.0	20.1	48.7	23.6	7.6
Armed forces	100.0	0.7	17.5	44.7	37.1
Men					
Management, business, and financial operations occupations	100.0	2.4	17.7	24.4	55.5
Management occupations	100.0	2.8	20.0	25.3	51.9
Business and financial operations occupations	100.0	0.8	9.1	21.5	68.6
Professional and related occupations	100.0	0.5	7.0	18.6	73.8
Computer and mathematical occupations	100.0	0.9	6.6	25.7	66.8
Architecture and engineering occupations	100.0	0.2	9.7	24.8	65.3
Life, physical, and social science occupations	100.0	. . .	8.5	11.9	79.7
Community and social services occupations	100.0	1.7	8.1	15.3	74.8
Legal occupations	100.0	0.1	1.1	4.1	94.6
Education, training, and library occupations	100.0	0.2	4.1	7.8	87.9
Arts, design, entertainment, sports, and media occupations	100.0	1.3	13.0	29.5	56.2
Healthcare practitioner and technical occupations	100.0	0.2	4.6	17.2	78.1
Service occupations	100.0	19.5	35.6	29.7	15.2
Healthcare supporting occupations	100.0	10.4	31.5	38.5	19.5
Protective service occupations	100.0	3.2	25.4	45.2	26.2
Food preparation and serving related occupations	100.0	26.7	38.4	23.4	11.5
Building and grounds cleaning and maintenance occupations	100.0	30.5	42.3	20.0	7.1
Personal care and service occupations	100.0	10.8	35.3	33.4	20.4
Sales and office occupations	100.0	5.4	28.7	32.9	33.1
Sales and related occupations	100.0	4.2	26.3	31.3	38.2
Office and administrative support occupations	100.0	7.5	33.0	35.6	23.9
Natural resources, construction, and maintenance occupations	100.0	22.3	44.4	26.8	6.6
Farming, fishing, and forestry occupations	100.0	48.9	31.4	13.3	6.3
Construction and extraction occupations	100.0	25.3	45.4	23.3	6.0
Installation, maintenance, and repair occupations	100.0	13.0	44.7	34.8	7.5
Production, transportation, and material moving occupations	100.0	18.7	48.3	24.9	8.0
Production occupations	100.0	18.1	47.7	26.0	8.1
Transportation and material moving occupations	100.0	19.4	49.0	23.8	7.9
Armed forces	100.0	0.7	17.8	45.4	36.1
Women					
Management, business, and financial operations occupations	100.0	1.8	19.4	29.5	49.4
Management occupations	100.0	2.3	19.1	29.1	49.5
Business and financial operations occupations	100.0	0.9	19.8	30.2	49.1
Professional and related occupations	100.0	0.8	10.2	25.1	63.9
Computer and mathematical occupations	100.0	0.6	10.7	27.4	61.3
Architecture and engineering occupations	100.0	0.3	14.7	23.0	61.9
Life, physical, and social science occupations	100.0	0.1	7.2	11.2	81.6
Community and social services occupations	100.0	0.9	8.5	18.3	72.3
Legal occupations	100.0	1.2	11.0	27.5	60.4
Education, training, and library occupations	100.0	1.1	10.3	13.8	74.8
Arts, design, entertainment, sports, and media occupations	100.0	1.7	14.3	27.8	56.3
Healthcare practitioner and technical occupations	100.0	0.4	9.3	40.6	49.7
Service occupations	100.0	19.0	42.7	28.6	9.7
Healthcare supporting occupations	100.0	12.9	39.6	38.7	8.8
Protective service occupations	100.0	6.1	34.5	40.6	18.8
Food preparation and serving related occupations	100.0	20.5	47.0	23.8	8.7
Building and grounds cleaning and maintenance occupations	100.0	37.6	45.5	12.3	4.7
Personal care and service occupations	100.0	12.6	40.8	33.7	12.9
Sales and office occupations	100.0	4.9	38.6	37.9	18.5
Sales and related occupations	100.0	8.3	36.1	31.2	24.4
Office and administrative support occupations	100.0	3.4	39.7	40.9	16.0
Natural resources, construction, and maintenance occupations	100.0	27.6	37.5	23.1	11.8
Farming, fishing, and forestry occupations	100.0	58.3	31.2	7.5	3.0
Construction and extraction occupations	100.0	13.6	41.9	32.9	11.7
Installation, maintenance, and repair occupations	100.0	8.0	40.0	30.6	21.4
Production, transportation, and material moving occupations	100.0	26.5	45.6	21.5	6.4
Production occupations	100.0	27.8	44.7	21.1	6.4
Transportation and material moving occupations	100.0	23.7	47.5	22.3	6.5
Armed forces	100.0	. . .	16.0	39.4	44.6

. . . = Not available.

Table 1-67. Percent Distribution of Workers Age 25 to 64 by Educational Attainment, Occupation of Longest Job Held, and Sex, 2003–2004—*Continued*

(Percent of total workers in occupation.)

Sex and occupation	Total	Less than a high school diploma	4 years of high school only	1 to 3 years of college	4 or more years of college
2004					
Total	100.0	9.7	30.1	27.9	32.3
Management, business, and financial operations occupations	100.0	2.1	17.7	26.2	54.0
Management occupations	100.0	2.6	19.4	25.9	52.1
Business and financial operations occupations	100.0	0.9	13.5	27.0	58.6
Professional and related occupations	100.0	0.8	8.6	22.7	68.0
Computer and mathematical occupations	100.0	0.4	7.3	26.8	65.5
Architecture and engineering occupations	100.0	0.3	10.6	24.5	64.6
Life, physical, and social science occupations	100.0	0.1	7.9	9.4	82.5
Community and social services occupations	100.0	1.2	9.8	18.7	70.3
Legal occupations	100.0	0.4	6.1	17.6	75.9
Education, training, and library occupations	100.0	0.8	8.4	12.8	78.0
Arts, design, entertainment, sports, and media occupations	100.0	1.9	13.4	26.5	58.2
Healthcare practitioner and technical occupations	100.0	0.7	7.2	35.6	56.4
Service occupations	100.0	19.1	40.2	28.7	12.1
Healthcare supporting occupations	100.0	12.4	39.5	39.5	8.7
Protective service occupations	100.0	3.6	27.9	42.8	25.7
Food preparation and serving related occupations	100.0	23.5	44.5	22.9	9.1
Building and grounds cleaning and maintenance occupations	100.0	32.7	43.9	17.1	6.3
Personal care and service occupations	100.0	11.1	38.9	33.6	16.4
Sales and office occupations	100.0	5.0	35.0	36.0	24.0
Sales and related occupations	100.0	6.4	31.1	31.0	31.5
Office and administrative support occupations	100.0	4.0	37.9	39.9	18.2
Natural resources, construction, and maintenance occupations	100.0	22.9	43.3	26.4	7.4
Farming, fishing, and forestry occupations	100.0	50.0	31.4	11.4	7.1
Construction and extraction occupations	100.0	25.9	44.4	23.3	6.4
Installation, maintenance, and repair occupations	100.0	12.2	43.8	34.8	9.3
Production, transportation, and material moving occupations	100.0	20.4	48.2	23.7	7.7
Production occupations	100.0	20.9	47.4	23.9	7.8
Transportation and material moving occupations	100.0	19.7	49.3	23.4	7.7
Armed forces	100.0	1.4	22.6	39.3	36.7
Men					
Management, business, and financial operations occupations	100.0	2.6	17.2	23.5	56.7
Management occupations	100.0	3.0	19.4	24.5	53.0
Business and financial operations occupations	100.0	1.1	9.1	19.6	70.2
Professional and related occupations	100.0	0.7	7.6	18.6	73.1
Computer and mathematical occupations	100.0	0.5	7.1	26.5	65.9
Architecture and engineering occupations	100.0	0.2	10.8	24.4	64.6
Life, physical, and social science occupations	100.0	. . .	9.3	9.7	81.0
Community and social services occupations	100.0	1.4	8.8	16.3	73.6
Legal occupations	100.0	. . .	1.4	3.3	95.3
Education, training, and library occupations	100.0	0.2	4.4	8.3	87.1
Arts, design, entertainment, sports, and media occupations	100.0	2.8	12.9	27.7	56.6
Healthcare practitioner and technical occupations	100.0	0.7	5.4	16.8	77.1
Service occupations	100.0	18.6	38.1	28.4	14.9
Healthcare supporting occupations	100.0	10.2	33.8	43.4	12.6
Protective service occupations	100.0	2.8	27.7	42.9	26.5
Food preparation and serving related occupations	100.0	25.9	39.6	22.8	11.7
Building and grounds cleaning and maintenance occupations	100.0	29.0	44.8	19.4	6.8
Personal care and service occupations	100.0	6.5	39.0	31.8	22.7
Sales and office occupations	100.0	4.9	30.3	32.4	32.4
Sales and related occupations	100.0	4.4	27.4	30.3	37.8
Office and administrative support occupations	100.0	5.7	35.4	36.2	22.7
Natural resources, construction, and maintenance occupations	100.0	22.7	43.8	26.4	7.1
Farming, fishing, and forestry occupations	100.0	49.1	32.4	10.9	7.6
Construction and extraction occupations	100.0	26.3	44.6	23.0	6.1
Installation, maintenance, and repair occupations	100.0	12.4	44.1	34.7	8.7
Production, transportation, and material moving occupations	100.0	19.0	48.6	24.7	7.7
Production occupations	100.0	18.6	48.3	25.5	7.6
Transportation and material moving occupations	100.0	19.3	48.8	24.0	7.8
Armed forces	100.0	1.5	22.5	40.2	35.8
Women					
Management, business, and financial operations occupations	100.0	1.5	18.3	29.7	50.5
Management occupations	100.0	1.9	19.4	28.1	50.6
Business and financial operations occupations	100.0	0.8	16.5	32.2	50.4
Professional and related occupations	100.0	0.8	9.3	25.7	64.1
Computer and mathematical occupations	100.0	0.4	8.1	27.4	64.2
Architecture and engineering occupations	100.0	0.4	9.8	25.0	64.7
Life, physical, and social science occupations	100.0	0.3	6.1	9.0	84.6
Community and social services occupations	100.0	1.1	10.5	20.3	68.1
Legal occupations	100.0	0.7	10.7	31.5	57.1
Education, training, and library occupations	100.0	1.0	9.7	14.3	75.0
Arts, design, entertainment, sports, and media occupations	100.0	1.0	13.9	25.1	60.0
Healthcare practitioner and technical occupations	100.0	0.8	7.8	42.1	49.4
Service occupations	100.0	19.4	41.7	28.8	10.1
Healthcare supporting occupations	100.0	12.7	40.2	39.0	8.2
Protective service occupations	100.0	6.2	28.7	42.5	22.7
Food preparation and serving related occupations	100.0	21.8	47.8	23.0	7.4
Building and grounds cleaning and maintenance occupations	100.0	37.8	42.7	14.0	5.6
Personal care and service occupations	100.0	12.2	38.8	34.1	14.8
Sales and office occupations	100.0	5.1	37.6	38.1	19.2
Sales and related occupations	100.0	8.7	35.2	31.9	24.3
Office and administrative support occupations	100.0	3.5	38.7	41.0	16.9
Natural resources, construction, and maintenance occupations	100.0	25.6	33.9	27.2	13.4
Farming, fishing, and forestry occupations	100.0	52.7	28.5	12.9	5.9
Construction and extraction occupations	100.0	15.4	36.7	33.9	14.0
Installation, maintenance, and repair occupations	100.0	6.4	36.6	35.6	21.3
Production, transportation, and material moving occupations	100.0	24.6	47.2	20.4	7.8
Production occupations	100.0	25.9	45.5	20.4	8.2
Transportation and material moving occupations	100.0	21.6	51.3	20.3	6.8
Armed forces	100.0	. . .	23.9	29.6	46.5

. . . = Not available.

Table 1-68. Median Annual Earnings by Educational Attainment and Sex, Year-Round Full-Time Wage and Salary Workers, Age 25 to 64, 2000–2004

(Thousands of workers, dollars.)

Year and sex	Total	Less than a high school diploma	4 years of high school only	1 to 3 years of college	4 or more years of college
2000					
Total					
Number of workers	84 337	7 354	26 144	24 064	26 775
Median annual earnings	35 000	20 000	28 600	34 000	50 000
Men					
Number of workers	48 816	4 738	15 057	13 242	15 780
Median annual earnings	40 000	22 500	33 000	40 000	60 000
Women					
Number of workers	35 521	2 616	11 087	10 822	10 995
Median annual earnings	29 000	16 000	24 000	28 000	40 000
2001					
Total					
Number of workers	84 743	7 623	25 522	23 719	27 879
Median annual earnings	35 000	20 800	29 000	35 000	50 000
Men					
Number of workers	48 887	5 049	14 655	12 968	16 215
Median annual earnings	40 000	24 000	33 800	40 000	60 000
Women					
Number of workers	35 856	2 574	10 867	10 751	11 664
Median annual earnings	30 000	17 000	24 000	30 000	42 000
2002					
Total					
Number of workers	84 702	7 578	25 078	23 604	28 443
Median annual earnings	36 000	21 000	30 000	35 100	52 000
Men					
Number of workers	48 687	5 102	14 306	12 677	16 602
Median annual earnings	41 000	23 400	34 000	41 500	61 000
Women					
Number of workers	36 015	2 476	10 772	10 927	11 841
Median annual earnings	30 000	18 000	25 000	30 000	43 500
2003					
Total					
Number of workers	85 058	7 245	25 352	23 702	28 759
Median annual earnings	37 752	21 000	30 000	36 000	53 000
Men					
Number of workers	48 988	4 879	14 657	12 766	16 686
Median annual earnings	42 000	24 000	35 000	42 000	62 000
Women					
Number of workers	36 070	2 366	10 695	10 936	12 073
Median annual earnings	32 000	18 000	25 111	31 000	45 000
2004					
Total					
Number of workers	86 306	7 648	25 786	23 897	28 976
Median annual earnings	38 000	21 840	30 000	37 000	55 000
Men					
Number of workers	49 904	5 178	15 263	12 822	16 642
Median annual earnings	42 900	24 000	35 000	43 000	65 000
Women					
Number of workers	36 402	2 470	10 523	11 074	12 334
Median annual earnings	32 000	18 000	25 280	31 200	45 000

NOTES AND DEFINITIONS

CONTINGENT WORKERS

Note: This is the first release of contingent worker data since 2001. Data for that year appear in the 7th edition of this *Handbook.*

Collection and Coverage

The data on contingent workers were collected through a supplement to the February 2005 Current Population Survey (CPS), a monthly survey of about 60,000 households that provides data on employment and unemployment for the nation. The U.S. Census Bureau conducts the CPS for the Bureau of Labor Statistics (BLS). The purpose of this supplement was to obtain information from workers on whether they held contingent jobs (jobs which are expected to last only a limited period of time). Information was also collected on several alternative employment arrangements, namely working on call and as independent contractors, as well as working through temporary help agencies or contract firms.

Several major changes introduced into the CPS in 2003 affect the data that are presented in this release. These include the introduction of Census 2000 population controls, the use of new questions about race and Hispanic or Latino ethnicity, the presentation of data for Asians, and the introduction of new industry and occupational classification systems. All employed persons, except unpaid family workers, were included in the supplement. For persons holding more than one job, the questions referred to the characteristics of their main job—the job at which they worked the most hours. Similar surveys were conducted in February of 1995, 1997, 1999, and 2001.

Concepts and Definitions

Contingent workers are defined as those who do not have an explicit or implicit contract for long-term employment. Several pieces of information are collected in the supplement from which the existence of a contingent employment arrangement can be discerned. These include: whether the job is temporary or not expected to continue, how long the worker expects to be able to hold the job, and how long the worker has held the job. For workers who have a job with an intermediary (namely a temporary help agency or a contract company), information is collected about their employment at the place they are assigned to work by the intermediary as well as about their employment with the intermediary itself.

The key factor used to determine whether a worker's job fits the conceptual definition of contingent is whether the job is temporary or not expected to continue. The first questions of the supplement include: (1) some people are in temporary jobs that last only for a limited time or until the completion of a project. Is your job temporary? (2) Provided the economy does not change and your job performance is adequate, can you continue to work for your current employer as long as you wish? Respondents who answer "yes" to the first question or "no" to the second are then asked a series of questions to distinguish persons in temporary jobs from those who, for personal reasons, are temporarily holding jobs that offer the opportunity of ongoing employment. For example, students holding part-time jobs in fast-food restaurants while in school might view those jobs as temporary if they intend to leave them at the end of the school year. Other workers, however, would fill the jobs themselves once the students leave.

To assess the impact of altering some of the defining factors on the estimated size of the contingent workforce, three measures of contingent employment were developed, as follows:

1) Estimate one, which is the narrowest, measures contingent workers as wage and salary workers who indicate that they expect to work in their current job for one year or less and who have worked for their current employer for one year or less. Self-employed workers, both incorporated and unincorporated, and independent contractors are excluded from the count of contingent workers under estimate one; individuals who work for temporary help agencies or contract companies are considered contingent under estimate one only if they expect their employment arrangement with the temporary help or contract company to last for one year or less and they have worked for that company for one year or less.

2) Estimate two expands the measure of the contingent work force by including the self-employed—both the incorporated and the unincorporated—and independent contractors who expect to be, and have been, in such employment arrangements for one year or less. (The questions asked of the self-employed are different from those asked of wage and salary workers.) In addition, temporary help and contract company workers are classified as contingent under estimate two if they have worked and expect to work with the customers to whom they have been assigned for one year or less.

3) Estimate three expands the count of contingency by removing the one-year requirement on both expected duration of the job and current tenure for wage and salary workers. Thus, the estimate effectively includes all the wage and salary workers who do not expect their employment to last, except for those who, for personal reasons, expect to leave jobs that they would otherwise be able to keep. A worker who has held a job for five years could be considered contingent if he or she now views the job as temporary. These conditions on expected and current tenure are not relaxed for the self-employed and inde-

pendent contractors because they are asked a different set of questions than wage and salary workers.

Sources of Additional Information

A complete description of the survey and additional tables are available from BLS new release USDL 05-1433.

Table 1-69. Employed Contingent and Noncontingent Workers by Selected Characteristics, February 2005

(Numbers in thousands.)

Characteristic	Total employed	Contingent Workers			Noncontingent workers
		Estimate 1	Estimate 2	Estimate 3	
Age and Sex					
Total, 16 years and over	138 952	2 504	3 177	5 705	133 247
16 to 19 years	5 510	308	338	476	5 035
20 to 24 years	13 114	606	688	1 077	12 036
25 to 34 years	30 103	693	874	1 447	28 656
35 to 44 years	34 481	415	580	1 044	33 437
45 to 54 years	32 947	263	387	875	32 072
55 to 64 years	17 980	143	198	536	17 445
65 years and over	4 817	76	111	250	4 567
Men, 16 years and over	73 946	1 325	1 648	2 914	71 032
16 to 19 years	2 579	145	157	229	2 351
20 to 24 years	6 928	358	394	597	6 331
25 to 34 years	16 624	395	512	829	15 794
35 to 44 years	18 523	245	303	540	17 983
45 to 54 years	17 193	95	140	368	16 825
55 to 64 years	9 485	70	107	261	9 224
65 years and over	2 615	17	35	92	2 523
Women, 16 years and over	65 006	1 180	1 529	2 790	62 216
16 to 19 years	2 931	163	182	247	2 684
20 to 24 years	6 186	249	294	481	5 705
25 to 34 years	13 480	298	362	618	12 862
35 to 44 years	15 958	171	277	504	15 454
45 to 54 years	15 754	168	247	508	15 247
55 to 64 years	8 495	73	91	275	8 220
65 years and over	2 202	58	76	158	2 044
Race and Hispanic or Latino Ethnicity					
White	115 043	2 007	2 534	4 521	110 522
Black	14 688	296	387	660	14 028
Asian	6 083	121	161	350	5 733
Hispanic or Latino ethnicity	18 062	603	704	1 185	16 876
Full- or Part-time Status					
Full-time workers	113 798	1 367	1 812	3 410	110 387
Part-time workers	25 154	1 137	1 364	2 294	22 860

Note: Noncontingent workers are those who do not fall into any estimate of "contingent" workers. Estimates for the above race groups (White, Black, and Asian) do not sum to totals because data are not presented for all races. In addition, persons whose ethnicity is Hispanic or Latino may be of any race and, therefore, are classified by ethnicity as well as by race. Detail for other characteristics may not sum to totals due to rounding.

Table 1-70. Employed Contingent and Noncontingent Workers by Occupation and Industry, February 2005

(Numbers in thousands, percent.)

Characteristic	Contingent Workers			Noncontingent workers
	Estimate 1	Estimate 2	Estimate 3	
OCCUPATION				
Total, 16 Years and Over	2 504	3 177	5 705	133 247
Percent	100.0	100.0	100.0	100.0
Management, professional, and related occupations	28.4	30.7	35.9	35.2
Management, business, and financial operations occupations	5.5	8.0	8.7	14.6
Professional and related occupations	22.8	22.6	27.2	20.6
Service occupations	17.3	17.6	15.7	15.6
Sales and office occupations	24.3	22.5	20.6	26.0
Sales and related occupations	4.9	6.0	5.7	12.1
Office and administrative support occupations	19.4	16.5	14.8	13.9
Natural resources, construction, and maintenance occupations	16.5	16.7	16.1	10.2
Farming, fishing, and forestry occupations	2.4	2.0	2.1	0.5
Construction and extraction occupations	11.4	12.3	11.1	5.8
Installation, maintenance, and repair occupations	2.7	2.4	2.9	3.8
Production, transportation, and material moving occupations	13.6	12.5	11.7	13.1
Production occupations	4.5	4.0	5.2	6.8
Transportation and material moving occupations	9.1	8.5	6.5	6.2
INDUSTRY				
Total, 16 Years and Over	2 504	3 177	5 705	133 247
Percent	100.0	100.0	100.0	100.0
Agriculture and related industries	2.5	2.3	1.7	1.3
Mining	0.7	0.6	0.4	0.4
Construction	13.0	14.0	12.3	7.2
Manufacturing	6.7	6.0	6.4	11.9
Wholesale trade	3.2	2.9	2.2	3.2
Retail trade	6.4	6.7	6.4	12.4
Transportation and utilities	5.0	4.7	3.7	5.3
Information	1.6	1.3	2.1	2.3
Financial activities	1.4	2.6	3.1	7.7
Professional and business services	18.2	20.7	18.2	9.7
Education and health services	23.5	21.8	27.1	20.8
Leisure and hospitality	10.1	8.9	7.4	8.1
Other services	5.0	5.3	4.9	4.7
Public administration	2.8	2.3	4.0	4.9

Note: Noncontingent workers are those who do not fall into any estimate of "contingent" workers. Detail may not sum to totals due to rounding.

Table 1-71. Employed Workers with Alternative and Traditional Work Arrangements by Selected Characteristics, February 2005

(Numbers in thousands.)

| Characteristic | Total employed | Workers with alternative arrangements | | | | Workers with traditional arrangements |
		Independent contractors	On-call workers	Temporary help agency workers	Workers provided by contract firms	
Age and Sex						
Total, 16 years and over	138 952	10 342	2 454	1 217	813	123 843
16 to 19 years	5 510	89	133	33	7	5 194
20 to 24 years	13 114	356	355	202	87	12 055
25 to 34 years	30 103	1 520	535	362	205	27 427
35 to 44 years	34 481	2 754	571	253	196	30 646
45 to 54 years	32 947	2 799	417	200	186	29 324
55 to 64 years	17 980	1 943	267	135	114	15 496
65 years and over	4 817	881	175	33	18	3 701
Men, 16 years and over	73 946	6 696	1 241	574	561	64 673
16 to 19 years	2 579	32	82	24	7	2 389
20 to 24 years	6 928	194	200	107	61	6 331
25 to 34 years	16 624	1 006	299	185	138	14 950
35 to 44 years	18 523	1 824	252	120	140	16 130
45 to 54 years	17 193	1 764	209	71	143	15 003
55 to 64 years	9 485	1 287	108	52	70	7 954
65 years and over	2 615	589	91	16	3	1 917
Women, 16 years and over	65 006	3 647	1 212	643	252	59 170
16 to 19 years	2 931	57	52	9	0	2 805
20 to 24 years	6 186	162	155	95	27	5 724
25 to 34 years	13 480	514	236	177	67	12 477
35 to 44 years	15 958	930	319	133	57	14 516
45 to 54 years	15 754	1 035	208	129	43	14 322
55 to 64 years	8 495	656	158	83	44	7 542
65 years and over	2 202	292	84	17	15	1 785
Race and Hispanic or Latino Ethnicity						
White	115 043	9 169	2 097	840	637	102 052
Black	14 688	583	212	276	121	13 471
Asian	6 083	370	64	63	43	5 538
Hispanic or Latino ethnicity	18 062	951	385	255	133	16 202
Full- or Part-time Status						
Full-time workers	113 798	7 732	1 370	979	695	102 889
Part-time workers	25 154	2 611	1 084	238	119	20 954

Note: Workers with traditional arrangements are those who do not fall into any of the "alternative arrangements" categories. Detail may not add to totals because the total employed includes day laborers (an alternative arrangement, not shown separately) and a small number of workers who were both "on call" and "provided by contract firms." Estimates for the above race groups (White, Black, and Asian) do not sum to totals because data are not presented for all races. In addition, persons whose ethnicity is Hispanic or Latino may be of any race and, therefore, are classified by ethnicity as well as by race. Detail for other characteristics may not sum to totals due to rounding.

Table 1-72. Employed Contingent and Noncontingent Workers and Those with Alternative and Traditional Work Arrangements by Health Insurance Coverage and Eligibility for Employer Provided Pension Plans, February 2005

(Numbers in thousands, percent.)

Characteristic	Total employed	Percent with health insurance coverage		Percent eligible for employer-provided pension plan [1]	
		Total	Provided by employer [2]	Total	Included in employer provided pension plan
Contingent Workers					
Estimate 1	2 504	51.8	9.4	9.2	4.6
Estimate 2	3 177	52.5	7.9	8.3	4.1
Estimate 3	5 705	59.1	18.1	18.6	12.4
Noncontingent Workers	133 247	79.4	52.1	49.6	44.7
With Alternative Arrangements					
Independent contractors	10 342	69.3	X	2.6	1.9
On-call workers	2 454	66.9	25.7	33.2	27.8
Temporary help agency workers	1 217	39.7	8.3	8.9	3.8
Workers provided by contract firms	813	80.2	48.9	42.6	33.5
With Traditional Arrangements	123 843	80.0	56.0	52.9	47.7

Note: Noncontingent workers are those who do not fall into any estimate of "contingent" workers. Workers with traditional arrangements are those who do not fall into any of the "alternative arrangements" categories.

[1]Excludes the self-employed (incorporated and unincorporated); includes independent contractors who were self-employed.
[2]Excludes the self-employed (incorporated and unincorporated) and independent contractors.
X = Not applicable.

Table 1-73. Median Usual Weekly Earnings of Full and Part-Time Contingent Wage and Salary Workers and Those with Alternative Work Arrangements by Sex, Race, and Hispanic or Latino Ethnicity, February 2005

(Dollars.)

Characteristic	Contingent workers			Workers with alternative arrangements			
	Estimate 1	Estimate 2	Estimate 3	Independent contractors	On-call workers	Temporary help agency workers	Workere provided by contract firms
Full-Time Workers							
Total, 16 years and over	405	411	488	716	519	414	756
Men	427	440	505	794	586	405	860
Women	376	383	423	462	394	424	595
White	413	421	498	731	561	418	772
Black	344	375	387	474	303	375	(1)
Asian	(1)	(1)	619	889	(1)	(1)	(1)
Hispanic or Latino ethnicity	335	331	370	603	417	311	513
Part-Time Workers							
Total, 16 years and over	152	152	161	253	173	224	204
Men	165	169	183	330	206	253	(1)
Women	142	138	149	216	159	202	(1)
White	154	154	163	252	177	247	(1)
Black	133	133	145	196	(1)	(1)	(1)
Asian	(1)	(1)	190	(1)	(1)	(1)	0
Hispanic or Latino ethnicity	152	153	175	207	249	(1)	(1)

Note: Earnings data for contingent workers exclude the incorporated self-employed and independent contractors. Data for independent contractors include the incorporated and unincorporated self-employed. These groups, however, are excluded from the data for workers with other arrangements. Full- or part-time status is determined by hours usually worked at the sole or primary job.

[1] Data not shown where base is less than 100,000.

NOTES AND DEFINITIONS

FLEXIBLE WORKERS

Collection and Coverage

These data and other information on work schedules were obtained from a supplement to the May 2004 Current Population Survey (CPS). This was the first time since 2001 that the supplemental survey was conducted. Respondents to the May 2004 supplement answered questions about flexible and shift schedules, the reasons for working particular shifts, the beginning and ending hours of work, formal flextime programs, home-based work, and other related topics. The data cover the incidence and nature of flexible and shift schedules and pertain to wage and salary workers who usually worked 35 hours or more per week at their principal job. The data exclude all self-employed persons, regardless of whether or not their businesses were incorporated.

Sources of Additional Information

For further information, see USDL news release 05-1198.

Table 1-74. Flexible Schedules: Full-Time Wage and Salary Workers by Selected Characteristics, May 2004

(Thousands of people, percent.)

Characteristic	Total [1]	With flexible schedules		Total [1]	With flexible schedules		Total [1]	With flexible schedules	
		Number	Percent of total		Number	Percent of total		Number	Percent of total
Age									
Total 16 years and over	99 778	27 411	27.5	56 412	15 853	28.1	43 366	11 558	26.7
16 to 19 years	1 427	336	23.6	903	185	20.5	524	151	28.9
20 years and over	98 351	27 075	27.5	55 509	15 668	28.2	42 842	11 406	26.6
20 to 24 years	9 004	2 058	22.9	5 147	1 065	20.7	3 856	993	25.8
25 to 34 years	24 640	6 902	28.0	14 358	4 051	28.2	10 283	2 851	27.7
35 to 44 years	26 766	7 807	29.2	15 424	4 605	29.9	11 342	3 202	28.2
45 to 54 years	24 855	6 651	26.8	13 440	3 769	28.0	11 415	2 882	25.2
55 to 64 years	11 745	3 181	27.1	6 383	1 865	29.2	5 361	1 316	24.5
65 years and over	1 341	475	35.4	757	314	41.4	585	161	27.6
Race and Hispanic or Latino Ethnicity									
White	80 498	23 121	28.7	46 222	13 582	29.4	34 276	9 539	27.8
Black	12 578	2 476	19.7	6 447	1 193	18.5	6 131	1 283	20.9
Asian	4 136	1 132	27.4	2 300	720	31.3	1 836	412	22.4
Hispanic or Latino ethnicity	14 110	2 596	18.4	8 621	1 430	16.6	5 489	1 166	21.2
Marital Status									
Married, spouse present	57 630	16 270	28.2	34 926	10 382	29.7	22 704	5 888	25.9
Not married	42 148	11 141	26.4	21 486	5 471	25.5	20 662	5 670	27.4
Never married	25 144	6 693	26.6	14 469	3 605	24.9	10 676	3 088	28.9
Other marital status	17 004	4 448	26.2	7 018	1 866	26.6	9 986	2 582	25.9
Presence and Age of Children									
Without own children under 18 years	61 761	16 759	27.1	34 680	9 410	27.1	27 081	7 349	27.1
With own children under 18 years	38 018	10 652	28.0	21 733	6 443	29.6	16 285	4 209	25.8
With youngest child 6 to 17 years	21 739	5 960	27.4	11 477	3 341	29.1	10 262	2 619	25.5
With youngest child under 6 years	16 279	4 692	28.8	10 256	3 102	30.2	6 023	1 590	26.4

Note: Data relate to the sole or principal job of full-time wage and salary workers and exclude all self-employed persons, regardless of whether or not their businesses were incorporated. Detail for the above race and Hispanic-origin groups will not sum to totals because data for the "other races" group are not presented. Hispanics are included in both the White and Black population groups. Own children include sons, daughters, stepchildren, and adopted children. Not included are nieces, nephews, grandchildren, and other related and unrelated children.

[1] Includes persons who did not provide information on flexible schedules.

Table 1-75. Flexible Schedules: Full-Time Wage and Salary Workers by Sex, Occupation, and Industry, May 2004

(Thousands of people, percent.)

Occupation and industry	Both sexes			Men			Women		
	Total [1]	With flexible schedules		Total [1]	With flexible schedules		Total [1]	With flexible schedules	
		Number	Percent of total		Number	Percent of total		Number	Percent of total
Occupation									
Total, 16 years and over	99 778	27 411	27.5	56 412	15 853	28.1	43 366	11 558	26.7
Management, professional, and related occupations	36 200	13 325	36.8	17 911	7 832	43.7	18 289	5 492	30.0
Management, business, and financial operations occupations	14 496	6 483	44.7	7 969	3 741	46.9	6 527	2 742	42.0
Management occupations	10 036	4 598	45.8	6 000	2 862	47.7	4 035	1 736	43.0
Business and financial operations occupations	4 461	1 885	42.3	1 969	879	44.7	2 492	1 006	40.4
Professional and related occupations	21 704	6 842	31.5	9 942	4 091	41.1	11 762	2 751	23.4
Computer and mathematical occupations	2 683	1 405	52.4	2 023	1 085	53.6	660	320	48.5
Architecture and engineering occupations	2 478	1 080	43.6	2 147	917	42.7	330	163	49.3
Life, physical, and social science occupations	1 016	483	47.5	640	285	44.6	376	198	52.6
Community and social services occupations	1 866	860	46.1	786	430	54.7	1 080	430	39.8
Legal occupations	1 118	497	44.5	536	312	58.2	582	185	31.8
Education, training, and library occupations	6 414	843	13.1	1 779	374	21.0	4 635	469	10.1
Arts, design, entertainment, sports, and media occupations	1 502	613	40.8	915	396	43.3	587	217	37.0
Healthcare practitioner and technical occupations	4 626	1 060	22.9	1 115	291	26.1	3 511	769	21.9
Service occupations	13 423	2 849	21.2	6 858	1 339	19.5	6 566	1 510	23.0
Healthcare support occupations	1 908	315	16.5	199	37	18.7	1 708	278	16.3
Protective service occupations	2 224	419	18.8	1 807	312	17.2	417	107	25.7
Food preparation and serving related occupations	3 881	972	25.0	2 086	524	25.1	1 795	448	25.0
Building and grounds cleaning and maintenance occupations	3 481	531	15.2	2 260	318	14.1	1 221	213	17.4
Personal care and service occupations	1 929	612	31.7	505	148	29.2	1 424	465	32.6
Sales and office occupations	24 359	7 196	29.5	9 561	3 069	32.1	14 798	4 127	27.9
Sales and related occupations	9 634	3 669	38.1	5 683	2 305	40.6	3 952	1 364	34.5
Office and administrative support occupations	14 724	3 527	24.0	3 878	764	19.7	10 847	2 763	25.5
Natural resources, construction, and maintenance occupations	10 848	1 908	17.6	10 403	1 820	17.5	445	88	19.8
Farming, fishing, and forestry occupations	744	172	23.1	591	132	22.4	152	39	25.7
Construction and extraction occupations	5 825	942	16.2	5 750	925	16.1	74	17	(2)
Installation, maintenance, and repair occupations	4 280	795	18.6	4 061	762	18.8	218	32	14.7
Production, transportation, and material moving occupations	14 948	2 133	14.3	11 679	1 793	15.3	3 268	340	10.4
Production occupations	8 281	1 030	12.4	5 928	806	13.6	2 353	224	9.5
Transportation and material moving occupations	6 666	1 102	16.5	5 751	986	17.1	915	116	12.7
Industry									
Private sector	82 870	23 978	28.9	48 724	14 119	29.0	34 145	9 859	28.9
Agriculture and related industries	888	233	26.3	702	180	25.6	186	53	28.7
Nonagricultural industries	81 982	23 745	29.0	48 023	13 939	29.0	33 959	9 806	28.9
Mining	446	102	22.9	416	84	20.2	30	18	(2)
Construction	6 617	1 341	20.3	6 059	1 153	19.0	558	188	33.7
Manufacturing	15 125	3 631	24.0	10 659	2 638	24.7	4 466	993	22.2
Durable goods	9 249	2 351	25.4	6 881	1 794	26.1	2 368	558	23.6
Nondurable goods	5 875	1 280	21.8	3 777	844	22.3	2 098	436	20.8
Wholesale and retail trade	14 008	4 100	29.3	8 717	2 544	29.2	5 291	1 557	29.4
Wholesale trade	3 771	1 209	32.1	2 698	910	33.7	1 072	300	27.9
Retail trade	10 237	2 891	28.2	6 019	1 634	27.1	4 219	1 257	29.8
Transportation and utilities	4 226	1 086	25.7	3 454	906	26.2	771	179	23.2
Transportation and warehousing	3 482	912	26.2	2 858	767	26.8	624	145	23.3
Utilities	744	173	23.3	596	139	23.4	147	34	23.0
Information [3]	2 716	948	34.9	1 674	600	35.8	1 041	348	33.4
Publishing, except Internet	648	274	42.3	364	165	45.4	284	109	38.4
Motion picture and sound recording industries	211	74	35.3	162	62	38.5	49	12	(2)
Broadcasting, except Internet	512	116	22.7	319	79	24.7	193	37	19.4
Telecommunications	1 180	419	35.5	732	254	34.7	448	164	36.7

[1] Includes persons who did not provide information on flexible schedules.
[2] Percent not shown where base is less than 75,000.
[3] Includes other industries not shown separately.

Table 1-75. Flexible Schedules: Full-Time Wage and Salary Workers by Sex, Occupation, and Industry, May 2004—*Continued*

(Thousands of people, percent.)

Occupation and industry	Both sexes			Men			Women		
	Total [1]	With flexible schedules		Total [1]	With flexible schedules		Total [1]	With flexible schedules	
		Number	Percent of total		Number	Percent of total		Number	Percent of total
Financial activities	7 341	2 767	37.7	3 117	1 323	42.4	4 224	1 444	34.2
Finance and insurance	5 537	2 056	37.1	2 100	943	44.9	3 437	1 113	32.4
Finance	3 633	1 218	33.5	1 443	584	40.5	2 190	633	28.9
Insurance	1 904	838	44.0	657	359	54.6	1 247	480	38.5
Real estate and rental and leasing	1 805	711	39.4	1 017	380	37.3	787	332	42.1
Professional and business services	8 997	3 381	37.6	5 342	2 072	38.8	3 655	1 309	35.8
Professional and technical services	5 476	2 570	46.9	3 113	1 596	51.3	2 364	974	41.2
Management, administrative, and waste services	3 521	811	23.0	2 229	477	21.4	1 292	335	25.9
Education and health services	12 485	3 202	25.6	2 969	862	29.0	9 517	2 339	24.6
Educational services	2 260	541	23.9	812	246	30.3	1 448	295	20.4
Health care and social assistance	10 226	2 661	26.0	2 157	616	28.6	8 069	2 045	25.3
Leisure and hospitality	6 111	1 686	27.6	3 458	956	27.6	2 653	730	27.5
Arts, entertainment, and recreation	1 134	312	27.5	630	165	26.2	504	147	29.2
Accommodation and food services	4 977	1 374	27.6	2 828	791	28.0	2 149	583	27.1
Accommodation	1 123	252	22.4	546	147	26.9	577	105	18.2
Food services and drinking places	3 854	1 122	29.1	2 282	644	28.2	1 572	478	30.4
Other services	3 911	1 502	38.4	2 158	801	37.1	1 753	701	40.0
Other services, except private households	3 584	1 370	38.2	2 140	792	37.0	1 444	577	40.0
Other services, private households	327	132	40.4	18	9	(2)	309	123	39.9
Public sector	16 909	3 433	20.3	7 688	1 734	22.6	9 221	1 699	18.4
Federal government	2 786	803	28.8	1 617	453	28.0	1 169	351	30.0
State government	4 724	1 340	28.4	2 089	640	30.7	2 635	700	26.6
Local government	9 399	1 289	13.7	3 982	641	16.1	5 417	648	12.0

Note: Data relate to the sole or principal job of full-time wage and salary workers and exclude all self-employed persons, regardless of whether or not their businesses were incorporated.

[1] Includes persons who did not provide information on flexible schedules.
[2] Percent not shown where base is less than 75,000.

Table 1-76. Flexible Schedules: Full-Time Wage and Salary Workers by Formal Flextime Program Status, Occupation, and Industry, May 2004

(Thousands of people, percent.)

Occupation and industry	Total [1]	With flexible schedules	With a formal flextime program		
			Number	Percent of total employed	Percent of workers with flexible schedules
Occupation					
Total, 16 years and over	99 778	27 411	10 642	10.7	38.8
Management, professional, and related occupations	36 200	13 325	5 137	14.2	38.6
Management, business, and financial operations occupations	14 496	6 483	2 293	15.8	35.4
Management occupations	10 036	4 598	1 436	14.3	31.2
Business and financial operations occupations	4 461	1 885	857	19.2	45.5
Professional and related occupations	21 704	6 842	2 844	13.1	41.6
Computer and mathematical occupations	2 683	1 405	729	27.1	51.8
Architecture and engineering occupations	2 478	1 080	509	20.5	47.1
Life, physical, and social science occupations	1 016	483	203	19.9	42.0
Community and social services occupations	1 866	860	325	17.4	37.8
Legal occupations	1 118	497	140	12.6	28.2
Education, training, and library occupations	6 414	843	278	4.3	33.0
Arts, design, entertainment, sports, and media occupations	1 502	613	272	18.1	44.4
Healthcare practitioner and technical occupations	4 626	1 060	389	8.4	36.6
Service occupations	13 423	2 849	1 188	8.9	41.7
Healthcare support occupations	1 908	315	139	7.3	44.3
Protective service occupations	2 224	419	192	8.6	45.8
Food preparation and serving related occupations	3 881	972	423	10.9	43.5
Building and grounds cleaning and maintenance occupations	3 481	531	178	5.1	33.5
Personal care and service occupations	1 929	612	256	13.3	41.8
Sales and office occupations	24 359	7 196	2 734	11.2	38.0
Sales and related occupations	9 634	3 669	1 175	12.2	32.0
Office and administrative support occupations	14 724	3 527	1 559	10.6	44.2
Natural resources, construction, and maintenance occupations	10 848	1 908	697	6.4	36.5
Farming, fishing, and forestry occupations	744	172	47	6.3	27.1
Construction and extraction occupations	5 825	942	416	7.1	44.2
Installation, maintenance, and repair occupations	4 280	795	234	5.5	29.5
Production, transportation, and material moving occupations	14 948	2 133	885	5.9	41.5
Production occupations	8 281	1 030	490	5.9	47.6
Transportation and material moving occupations	6 666	1 102	395	5.9	35.8
Industry					
Private sector	82 870	23 978	8 816	10.6	36.8
Agriculture and related industries	888	233	53	6.0	22.9
Nonagricultural industries	81 982	23 745	8 762	10.7	36.9
Mining	446	102	47	10.5	46.1
Construction	6 617	1 341	493	7.5	36.8
Manufacturing	15 125	3 631	1 618	10.7	44.6
Durable goods	9 249	2 351	1 061	11.5	45.1
Nondurable goods	5 875	1 280	557	9.5	43.5
Wholesale and retail trade	14 008	4 100	1 302	9.3	31.8
Wholesale trade	3 771	1 209	300	8.0	24.8
Retail trade	10 237	2 891	1 002	9.8	34.6
Transportation and utilities	4 226	1 086	432	10.2	39.8
Transportation and warehousing	3 482	912	335	9.6	36.7
Utilities	744	173	97	13.0	55.9
Information [2]	2 716	948	371	13.7	39.2
Publishing, except Internet	648	274	102	15.8	37.3
Motion picture and sound recording industries	211	74	33	15.9	(3)
Broadcasting, except Internet	512	116	43	8.4	37.2
Telecommunications	1 180	419	170	14.4	40.5

[1]Includes persons who did not provide information on flexible schedules.
[2]Includes other industries not shown separately.
[3]Percent not shown where base is less than 75,000.

Table 1-76. Flexible Schedules: Full-Time Wage and Salary Workers by Formal Flextime Program Status, Occupation, and Industry, May 2004—*Continued*

(Thousands of people, percent.)

Occupation and industry	Total [1]	With flexible schedules	With a formal flextime program		
			Number	Percent of total employed	Percent of workers with flexible schedules
Financial activities	7 341	2 767	1 066	14.5	38.5
Finance and insurance	5 537	2 056	868	15.7	42.2
Finance	3 633	1 218	425	11.7	34.9
Insurance	1 904	838	443	23.3	52.9
Real estate and rental and leasing	1 805	711	198	11.0	27.9
Professional and business services	8 997	3 381	1 294	14.4	38.3
Professional and technical services	5 476	2 570	991	18.1	38.6
Management, administrative, and waste services	3 521	811	303	8.6	37.3
Education and health services	12 485	3 202	1 118	9.0	34.9
Educational services	2 260	541	156	6.9	28.8
Health care and social assistance	10 226	2 661	962	9.4	36.2
Leisure and hospitality	6 111	1 686	598	9.8	35.4
Arts, entertainment, and recreation	1 134	312	84	7.4	27.1
Accommodation and food services	4 977	1 374	513	10.3	37.4
Accommodation	1 123	252	105	9.3	41.5
Food services and drinking places	3 854	1 122	408	10.6	36.4
Other services	3 911	1 502	422	10.8	28.1
Other services, except private households	3 584	1 370	404	11.3	29.5
Other services, private households	327	132	18	5.5	13.6
Public sector	16 909	3 433	1 826	10.8	53.2
Federal government	2 786	803	561	20.1	69.9
State government	4 724	1 340	665	14.1	49.6
Local government	9 399	1 289	600	6.4	46.5

Note: Data relate to the sole or principal job of full-time wage and salary workers and exclude all self-employed persons, regardless of whether or not their businesses were incorporated.

[1] Includes persons who did not provide information on flexible schedules.

Table 1-77. Shift Usually Worked: Full-Time Wage and Salary Workers by Selected Characteristics, May 2004

(Thousands of people, percent.)

Occupation and industry	Total [1]	Regular daytime schedule	Shift Workers						
			Total	Evening shift	Night shift	Rotating shift	Split shift	Employer-arranged irregular schedule	Other shift
Age and Sex									
Total, 16 years and over	99 778	84.6	14.8	4.7	3.2	2.5	0.5	3.1	0.7
16 to 19 years	1 427	64.9	34.6	14.5	4.4	6.1	1.0	8.3	0.2
20 years and over	98 351	84.9	14.6	4.6	3.2	2.5	0.5	3.0	0.7
20 to 24 years	9 004	76.8	22.3	8.8	3.7	3.3	0.9	4.6	0.9
25 to 34 years	24 640	84.1	15.2	5.0	3.4	2.7	0.5	2.8	0.8
35 to 44 years	26 766	85.4	14.1	4.1	3.2	2.5	0.4	3.1	0.7
45 to 54 years	24 855	86.8	12.8	3.6	3.2	2.3	0.5	2.5	0.7
55 to 64 years	11 745	87.1	12.5	3.8	2.6	2.0	0.4	3.0	0.7
65 years and over	1 341	88.8	10.3	3.5	1.8	1.4	0.5	2.9	0.2
Men	56 412	82.7	16.7	5.2	3.6	2.8	0.5	3.6	0.9
Women	43 366	87.0	12.4	4.1	2.8	2.2	0.5	2.4	0.4
Race and Hispanic or Latino Etnicity									
White	80 498	85.8	13.7	4.1	3.0	2.3	0.5	3.1	0.7
Black	12 578	78.0	20.8	7.9	4.5	4.1	0.4	3.0	0.7
Asian	4 136	83.6	15.7	5.4	4.1	1.6	1.2	2.6	0.8
Hispanic or Latino ethnicity	14 110	83.1	16.0	5.8	3.9	2.1	0.6	2.6	0.9
Marital Status and Presence and Age of Children									
Men									
Married, spouse present	34 926	84.8	14.9	3.9	3.3	2.9	0.5	3.4	0.9
Not married	21 486	79.5	19.7	7.4	3.9	2.6	0.7	4.0	1.0
Never married	14 469	78.6	20.6	8.1	3.8	2.6	0.8	4.2	1.0
Other marital status	7 018	81.4	17.8	5.9	4.2	2.8	0.4	3.6	1.0
Without own children under 18 years	34 680	81.8	17.6	6.0	3.6	2.7	0.6	3.8	0.9
With own children under 18 years	21 733	84.3	15.3	4.0	3.6	3.0	0.5	3.2	1.0
With youngest child 6 to 17 years	11 477	85.1	14.6	3.9	3.2	3.1	0.2	3.4	0.8
With youngest child under 6 years	10 256	83.5	16.1	4.2	3.9	2.9	0.8	3.0	1.2
Women									
Married, spouse present	22 704	90.4	9.2	2.8	2.4	1.4	0.3	1.9	0.3
Not married	20 662	83.2	16.0	5.6	3.2	3.0	0.6	2.9	0.6
Never married	10 676	81.2	17.9	6.3	3.0	3.6	0.8	3.6	0.6
Other marital status	9 986	85.5	13.9	4.8	3.5	2.3	0.4	2.1	0.6
Without own children under 18 years	27 081	86.4	13.0	4.1	2.7	2.5	0.6	2.7	0.4
With own children under 18 years	16 285	87.9	11.5	4.3	2.9	1.7	0.3	1.9	0.4
With youngest child 6 to 17 years	10 262	89.1	10.5	3.4	3.0	1.6	0.2	1.8	0.5
With youngest child under 6 years	6 023	86.0	13.2	5.8	2.7	1.8	0.4	2.1	0.4

Note: Data relate to the sole or principal job of full-time wage and salary workers and exclude all self-employed persons, regardless of whether or not their businesses were incorporated. Detail for the above race and Hispanic-origin groups will not sum to totals because data for the "other races" group are not presented and Hispanics are included in both the White and Black population groups. Own children include sons, daughters, stepchildren, and adopted children. Not included are nieces, nephews, grandchildren, and other related and unrelated children.

[1]Includes persons who did not provide information on shift usually worked.

Table 1-78. Shift Usually Worked: Full-Time Wage and Salary Workers by Occupation and Industry, May 2004

(Thousands of people, percent.)

Occupation and industry	Total [1]	Regular daytime schedule	Shift workers						
			Total	Evening shift	Night shift	Rotating shift	Split shift	Employer-arranged irregular schedule	Other shift
Occupation									
Total, 16 years and over	99 778	84.6	14.8	4.7	3.2	2.5	0.5	3.1	0.7
Management, professional, and related occupations	36 200	91.9	7.6	1.7	1.6	1.3	0.3	2.2	0.5
Management, business, and financial operations occupations	14 496	94.6	5.0	1.1	0.5	0.9	0.2	2.0	0.3
Management occupations	10 036	93.6	6.1	1.4	0.5	1.1	0.3	2.4	0.4
Business and financial operations occupations	4 461	96.8	2.7	0.5	0.6	0.4	0.1	0.9	0.2
Professional and related occupations	21 704	90.1	9.4	2.1	2.4	1.6	0.3	2.3	0.7
Computer and mathematical occupations	2 683	95.2	4.1	1.1	1.3	0.8	0.3	0.4	0.4
Architecture and engineering occupations	2 478	95.7	3.9	0.9	1.2	0.7	0.1	0.7	0.4
Life, physical, and social science occupations	1 016	93.9	5.8	1.1	1.4	2.0	0.0	1.2	0.1
Community and social services occupations	1 866	87.0	12.7	1.9	1.3	2.2	0.3	4.9	2.0
Legal occupations	1 118	97.4	1.8	0.0	0.0	0.0	0.2	1.4	0.2
Education, training, and library occupations	6 414	97.3	2.3	0.6	0.1	0.2	0.4	0.9	0.2
Arts, design, entertainment, sports, and media occupations	1 502	84.7	14.7	3.1	1.6	2.2	0.4	6.0	1.2
Healthcare practitioner and technical occupations	4 626	74.5	24.6	5.8	8.3	4.4	0.5	4.4	1.1
Service occupations	13 423	66.5	32.6	12.5	6.2	5.2	1.4	5.5	1.7
Healthcare support occupations	1 908	70.4	28.0	12.5	7.1	3.8	0.7	3.1	0.7
Protective service occupations	2 224	48.3	50.6	14.4	12.9	11.9	0.6	6.2	4.3
Food preparation and serving related occupations	3 881	58.7	40.4	17.6	3.4	5.8	3.3	8.9	1.1
Building and grounds cleaning and maintenance occupations	3 481	82.1	17.5	8.3	5.4	1.5	0.5	1.1	0.7
Personal care and service occupations	1 929	70.9	28.1	7.3	4.6	4.5	1.0	8.1	2.7
Sales and office occupations	24 359	87.3	12.0	3.5	2.6	2.3	0.3	2.8	0.3
Sales and related occupations	9 634	83.8	15.2	3.5	1.9	3.8	0.6	5.0	0.4
Office and administrative support occupations	14 724	89.6	9.9	3.6	3.0	1.4	0.2	1.4	0.3
Natural resources, construction, and maintenance occupations	10 848	92.0	7.5	2.1	1.9	1.3	0.1	1.5	0.5
Farming, fishing, and forestry occupations	744	89.8	9.8	0.6	2.4	1.4	1.0	2.4	2.0
Construction and extraction occupations	5 825	95.1	4.4	0.8	0.8	1.2	0.1	1.3	0.3
Installation, maintenance, and repair occupations	4 280	88.2	11.4	4.3	3.4	1.5	0.0	1.7	0.5
Production, transportation, and material moving occupations	14 948	73.3	26.2	9.1	6.5	4.2	0.8	4.6	1.1
Production occupations	8 281	75.0	24.4	10.1	7.1	4.7	0.3	1.4	0.8
Transportation and material moving occupations	6 666	71.2	28.5	7.8	5.7	3.7	1.4	8.4	1.5
Industry									
Private sector	82 870	84.0	15.4	5.0	3.3	2.6	0.5	3.3	0.7
Agriculture and related industries	888	90.1	9.9	1.4	2.3	1.1	1.0	3.2	1.0
Nonagricultural industries	81 982	83.9	15.5	5.1	3.3	2.6	0.5	3.3	0.7
Mining	446	68.0	31.9	3.6	4.9	15.1	0.2	6.1	2.1
Construction	6 617	96.6	2.9	0.5	0.5	0.3	0.0	1.3	0.2
Manufacturing	15 125	81.5	18.1	7.2	5.2	3.3	0.3	1.2	0.8
Durable goods	9 249	85.3	14.4	6.7	4.2	1.9	0.2	0.7	0.7
Nondurable goods	5 875	75.6	23.8	8.1	6.8	5.4	0.5	1.9	1.1
Wholesale and retail trade	14 008	82.9	16.3	4.4	3.2	3.6	0.4	4.1	0.5
Wholesale trade	3 771	91.5	8.0	2.7	1.8	0.7	0.1	2.3	0.2
Retail trade	10 237	79.8	19.4	5.0	3.7	4.6	0.5	4.8	0.6
Transportation and utilities	4 226	71.4	27.9	5.0	4.8	4.0	1.7	11.0	1.3
Transportation and warehousing	3 482	67.5	31.8	5.6	5.6	3.9	1.9	13.1	1.4
Utilities	744	89.5	9.5	1.9	0.8	4.4	0.9	1.1	0.5

[1] Includes persons who did not provide information on shift usually worked.

Table 1-78. Shift Usually Worked: Full-Time Wage and Salary Workers by Occupation and Industry, May 2004—*Continued*

(Thousands of people, percent.)

Occupation and industry	Total [1]	Regular daytime schedule	Shift workers						
			Total	Evening shift	Night shift	Rotating shift	Split shift	Employer-arranged irregular schedule	Other shift
Information [2]	2 716	87.3	11.7	4.2	2.4	1.7	0.1	2.6	0.6
Publishing, except Internet	648	87.6	10.3	2.3	3.6	0.8	0.3	2.0	1.3
Motion picture and sound recording industries	211	85.0	15.0	5.5	2.2	1.8	0.0	5.5	0.0
Broadcasting, except Internet	512	84.4	15.0	6.4	0.1	2.9	0.3	3.3	1.3
Telecommunications	1 180	88.8	10.5	3.6	2.7	1.9	0.0	2.3	0.0
Financial activities	7 341	94.0	5.4	2.0	0.6	0.6	0.1	1.8	0.3
Finance and insurance	5 537	96.7	2.8	1.2	0.4	0.5	0.1	0.5	0.1
Finance	3 633	96.8	2.6	1.2	0.5	0.5	0.0	0.3	0.1
Insurance	1 904	96.5	3.1	1.2	0.3	0.4	0.2	0.8	0.2
Real estate and rental and leasing	1 805	85.6	13.4	4.3	1.4	1.0	0.2	5.9	0.7
Professional and business services	8 997	92.0	7.8	2.7	2.4	0.7	0.1	1.4	0.5
Professional and technical services	5 476	96.5	3.2	0.6	0.5	0.4	0.1	1.3	0.4
Management, administrative, and waste services	3 521	84.9	15.0	6.1	5.3	1.1	0.2	1.5	0.8
Education and health services	12 485	83.2	16.0	5.5	4.5	2.4	0.5	2.3	0.7
Educational services	2 260	93.9	5.6	3.0	0.4	0.3	0.5	1.3	0.2
Health care and social assistance	10 226	80.9	18.3	6.0	5.4	2.9	0.5	2.6	0.8
Leisure and hospitality	6 111	60.8	38.3	15.2	4.8	5.2	2.4	9.4	1.2
Arts, entertainment, and recreation	1 134	67.7	31.9	10.2	7.9	1.6	0.7	9.2	2.1
Accommodation and food services	4 977	59.3	39.8	16.4	4.1	6.0	2.9	9.5	1.0
Accommodation	1 123	70.2	29.4	11.1	6.6	4.2	0.7	5.9	0.9
Food services and drinking places	3 854	56.1	42.8	17.9	3.3	6.6	3.5	10.5	1.0
Other services	3 911	88.9	10.6	1.5	1.0	1.9	0.3	4.8	1.0
Other services, except private households	3 584	89.3	10.3	1.4	1.0	1.9	0.3	4.9	0.8
Other services, private households	327	85.0	14.1	3.3	0.6	2.7	0.6	4.0	3.0
Public sector	16 909	87.6	11.9	3.4	2.9	2.4	0.4	1.9	0.9
Federal government	2 786	84.8	14.7	4.4	4.9	1.2	0.2	3.1	0.7
State government	4 724	87.9	11.5	3.8	3.3	1.9	0.4	1.4	0.7
Local government	9 399	88.3	11.3	2.9	2.0	3.0	0.4	1.8	1.1

Note: Data relate to the sole or principal job of full-time wage and salary workers and exclude all self-employed persons, regardless of whether or not their businesses were incorporated.

[1] Includes persons who did not provide information on shift usually worked.
[2] Includes other industries not shown separately.

PART TWO

EMPLOYMENT, HOURS, AND EARNINGS

EMPLOYMENT AND HOURS

HIGHLIGHTS

The employment, hours, and earnings data by industry and state in this section are derived from the Current Employment Statistics (CES) Survey, which covers 300,000 nonfarm establishments. The employment numbers differ from those presented by the household survey in Part 1 because of the differences in methodology, concepts, definitions, and coverage. As the CES data are obtained from payroll records, they are consistent for industry classifications. The data on hours and earnings are also likely to be more accurate.

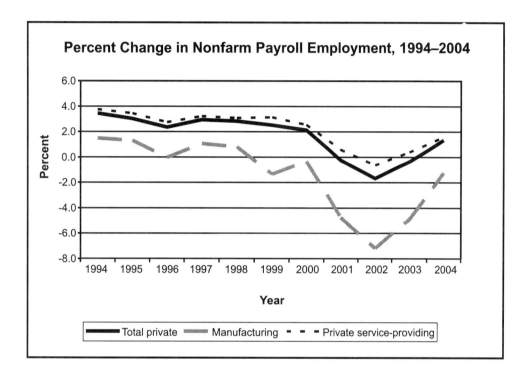

Percent Change in Nonfarm Payroll Employment, 1994–2004

Total employment continued to climb, rising by more than 1.4 million from 2003 to 2004. The service-providing sector accounted for the majority of new jobs. All major service-providing industries, except utilities and information, showed increases in employment. Manufacturing employment continued to drop off in 2004; however, it did so at a much slower rate than that of previous years. (Table 2-1)

OTHER HIGHLIGHTS:

- Although total government employment rose in 2004, federal and state employment actually decreased. Local government accounted for the entire increase, rising by 85,000 jobs. (Table 2-1)

- Employment in the construction industry expanded faster than employment in any other sector (3.4 percent). Construction accounted for over 6 percent of total private employment in 2004 and its additional 229,000 jobs represented 16 percent of the total increase in private employment. (Table 2-1)

- The number of women employed rose only slightly in 2004. Educational and health services, local government, and retail trade continued to be popular fields among females. (Table 2-3)

- While employment dropped in manufacturing in 2004, average weekly overtime of production workers increased from 4.2 hours to 4.6 hours—the highest increase in a decade. (Table 2-15)

- Nevada was the state with the fastest growing employment rate (5.9 percent) from 2003 to 2004. Arizona and Florida followed with rates of 3.4 percent and 3.3 percent, respectively. Larger states generally experienced smaller increases: employment in Texas went up 1.2 percent, California rose 1.0 percent, and New York saw an increase of only 0.5 percent. (Table 2-29)

NOTES AND DEFINITIONS

Collection and Coverage

BLS cooperates with state employment security agencies in the Current Employment Statistics (CES), or establishment survey, to collect data each month on employment, hours, and earnings from a sample of nonfarm establishments (including government). The sample includes about 160,000 businesses and government agencies, covering approximately 400,000 individual worksites drawn from a sampling frame of over 8 million unemployment insurance tax accounts. The active CES sample includes approximately one-third of all nonfarm payroll workers. From these data, a large number of employment, hours, and earnings series with considerable industry and geographic detail are prepared and published each month. The first article describes the differences between the CES and the Current Population Survey (CPS) in great detail.

The most frequently used data collection method is touchtone data entry (TDE). Under the TDE system, the respondent uses a touchtone telephone to call a toll-free number and activate an interview session. The next most frequently used data collection mode is computer-assisted telephone interviewing (CATI).

Establishment survey data are adjusted annually to accord with comprehensive counts of employment in March of the preceding year, called "benchmarks." The adjustments are published with the release of May data each year. The benchmarks are derived mainly from employment reports from all employers subject to unemployment insurance. Each year's benchmarking results in recalculation of employment data for the current and two previous years. The related series on production and nonsupervisory workers, hours, and earnings are recalculated to be consistent with the employment benchmarks.

Concepts and Definitions

Industry classification

In 2003, the basis for industry classification changed from the 1987 Standard Industrial Classification System (SIC) to the 2002 North American Industry Classification System (NAICS). SIC-based data will no longer be produced or published by BLS. It will still be available, but it will no longer be updated.

The foundation of industrial classification within NAICS has changed how establishments are classified into industries and how businesses, as they exist today, are recognized.

Establishments reporting on Form BLS 790 are classified into industries on the basis of their primary activity. Those that use comparable capital equipment, labor, and raw material inputs are classified together. This information is collected on a supplement to the quarterly unemployment insurance tax reports filed by employers. For an establishment engaging in more than one activity, the entire employment of the establishment is included under the industry indicated by the principal activity.

Industry employment

Employment data refer to persons on establishment payrolls who received pay for any part of the pay period that includes the 12th day of the month. The data exclude proprietors, the self-employed, unpaid volunteer or family workers, farm workers, and domestic workers. Salaried officers of corporations are included. Government employment covers only civilian employees; military personnel are excluded. Employees of the Central Intelligence Agency, the National Security Agency, the National Imagery and Mapping Agency, and the Defense Intelligence Agency are also excluded.

Persons on establishment payrolls who are on paid sick leave (for cases in which pay is received directly from the firm), paid holiday, paid vacation, or who work during a part of the pay period even though they are unemployed or on strike for the rest of the period are counted as employed. Not counted as employed are persons who are on layoff, on leave without pay, on strike for the entire period, or who were hired but had not yet reported during the period.

Beginning with the June 2003 publication of May data, the CES national federal government employment series is estimated from a sample of federal establishments and benchmarked annually to counts from unemployment insurance tax records. It reflects employee counts as of the pay period including the 12th of the month, consistent with other CES industry series. Previously, the national series was an end-of-month count produced by the Office of Personnel Management.

The exclusion from the payroll survey of farm employment, self-employment, and domestic service employment accounts in part for the differences in employment figures between the household and payroll surveys. The payroll survey also excludes persons on leave without pay (who are counted as employed in the household survey). Persons who worked in more than one establishment during the reporting period are counted each time their names appear on payrolls, whereas such persons are only counted once in the household survey.

Industry hours and earnings. Average hours and earnings data are derived from reports of payrolls and hours for production and related workers in manufacturing and natural resources and mining, construction workers in con-

struction, and nonsupervisory employees in private service-providing industries.

Production and related workers. This category includes working supervisors and all nonsupervisory workers (including group leaders and trainees) engaged in fabricating, processing, assembling, inspecting, receiving, storing, handling, packing, warehousing, shipping, trucking, hauling, maintenance, repair, janitorial, guard services, product development, auxiliary production for plant's own use (such as power plant), record keeping, and other services closely associated with the above production operations.

Construction workers. This group includes the following employees in the construction division: working supervisors, qualified craft workers, mechanics, apprentices, helpers, and laborers engaged in new work, alterations, demolition, repair, maintenance, and the like, whether working at the site of construction or at jobs in shops or yards at jobs (such as precutting and pre-assembling) ordinarily performed by members of the construction trades.

Nonsupervisory workers. These are employees (not above the working-supervisor level) such as office and clerical workers, repairers, salespersons, operators, drivers, physicians, lawyers, accountants, nurses, social workers, research aides, teachers, drafters, photographers, beauticians, musicians, restaurant workers, custodial workers, attendants, line installers and repairers, laborers, janitors, guards, and other employees at similar occupational levels whose services are closely associated with those of the employees listed.

Payroll. This refers to the payroll for full- and part-time production, construction, or nonsupervisory workers who received pay for any part of the pay period that includes the 12th day of the month. The payroll is reported before deductions of any kind, such as those for old age and unemployment insurance, group insurance, withholding tax, bonds, or union dues. Also included is pay for overtime, holidays, and vacation, and for sick leave paid directly by the firm. Bonuses (unless earned and paid regularly each pay period); other pay not earned in the pay period reported (such as retroactive pay); tips; and the value of free rent, fuel, meals, or other payment in kind are excluded. Employee benefits (such as health and other types of insurance, contributions to retirement, and so forth, as paid by the employer) also are excluded.

Hours. These are the hours paid for during the pay period that includes the 12th day of the month for production, construction, or nonsupervisory workers. Included are hours paid for holidays, vacations, and sick leave, when pay is received directly from the firm.

Overtime hours. These are hours worked by production or related workers for which overtime premiums were paid, because the hours were in excess of the number of hours of either the straight-time workday or the workweek during the pay period including the 12th of the month. Weekend and holiday hours are included only if overtime premiums were paid. Hours for which only shift differential, hazard, incentive, or other similar types of premiums were paid are excluded.

Average weekly hours. The workweek information relates to the average hours for which pay was received and is different from standard or scheduled hours. Such factors as unpaid absenteeism, labor turnover, part-time work, and stoppages cause average weekly hours to be lower than scheduled hours of work for an establishment. Group averages further reflect changes in the workweek of component industries.

Indexes of aggregate weekly hours and payrolls. The indexes of aggregate weekly hours are calculated by dividing the current month's aggregate by the average of the 12 monthly figures for 1982. For basic industries, the hours aggregates are the product of average weekly hours and production worker or nonsupervisory worker employment. At all higher levels of industry aggregation, hours aggregates are the sum of the component aggregates.

The indexes of aggregate weekly payrolls are calculated by dividing the current month's aggregate by the average of the 12 monthly figures for 1982. For basic industries, the payroll aggregates are the product of average hourly earnings and aggregate weekly hours. At all higher levels of industry aggregation, payroll aggregates are the sum of the component aggregates.

Average overtime hours. Overtime hours represent that portion of average weekly hours that exceeded regular hours and for which overtime premiums were paid. If an employee were to work on a paid holiday at regular rates, receiving as total compensation his or her holiday pay plus straight-time pay for hours worked that day, no overtime hours would be reported.

Since overtime hours are premium hours by definition, weekly hours and overtime hours do not necessarily move in the same direction from month to month. Factors such as work stoppages, absenteeism, and labor turnover may not have the same influence on overtime hours as on average hours. Diverse trends at the industry group level may also be caused by a marked change in hours for a component industry in which little or no overtime was worked in both the previous and current months.

Average hourly earnings. Average hourly earnings are on a "gross" basis. They reflect not only changes in basic hourly and incentive wage rates, but also such variable factors as premium pay for overtime and late-shift work and changes in output of workers paid on an incentive plan. They also reflect shifts in the number of employees between relatively high-paid and low-paid work and changes in workers' earnings in individual establishments. Averages for groups and divisions further reflect changes in average hourly earnings for individual industries.

Averages of hourly earnings differ from wage rates. Earnings are the actual return to the worker for a stated period; rates are the amount stipulated for a given unit of work or time. The earnings series do not measure the level of total labor costs on the part of the employer because the following are excluded: irregular bonuses, retroactive items, payroll taxes paid by employers, and earnings for those employees not covered under production worker, construction worker, or nonsupervisory employee definitions.

Average hourly earnings, excluding overtime-premium pay, are computed by dividing the total production worker payroll for the industry group by the sum of total production worker hours and one-half of total overtime hours. No adjustments are made for other premium payment provisions, such as holiday pay, late-shift premiums, and overtime rates other than time and one-half.

Average weekly earnings. These estimates are derived by multiplying average weekly hours estimates by average hourly earnings estimates. Therefore, weekly earnings are affected not only by changes in average hourly earnings but also by changes in the length of the workweek. Monthly variations in factors such as the proportion of part-time workers, stoppages for varying reasons, labor turnover during the survey period, and absenteeism for which employees are not paid may cause the average workweek to fluctuate.

Long-term trends of average weekly earnings can be affected by structural changes in the makeup of the work-force. For example, persistent long-term increases in the proportion of part-time workers in retail trade and many of the services industries have reduced average work-weeks in these industries and have affected the average weekly earnings series.

These earnings are in constant dollars and are calculated from the earnings averages for the current month using a deflator derived from the Consumer Price Index for Urban Wage Earnings and Clerical Workers (CPI-W). The reference year for these series is 1982.

Future Plans

BLS is planning several changes to the Current Employment Statistics (CES) survey to improve its relevance to the needs of data users, as well as its value as an input to other key economic statistics. The planned improvements to the CES are new data on the hours and regular earnings of all employees, and new data on total earnings—both regular and irregular pay—for all employees. The CES series that BLS will discontinue to accommodate the above improvements are women workers series—discontinued as of August 5, 2005—and production or nonsupervisory worker hours and earnings series.

Sources of Additional Information

For further information on sampling and estimation methods see Bureau of Labor Statistics, *Employment and Earnings*, June 2003 and subsequent issues of that monthly publication, BLS news releases, and publications on the BLS Web site.

Table 2-1. Employees on Nonfarm Payrolls by Super Sector and Selected Component Groups, NAICS Basis, 1994–2004

(Thousands of people.)

Industry	1994	1995	1996	1997	1998	1999	2000	2001	2002	2003	2004
TOTAL	114 291	117 298	119 708	122 776	125 930	128 993	131 785	131 826	130 341	129 999	131 480
Total Private	95 016	97 866	100 169	103 113	106 021	108 686	110 996	110 707	108 828	108 416	109 862
Goods–Producing	22 774	23 156	23 410	23 886	24 354	24 465	24 649	23 873	22 557	21 816	21 884
Natural Resources and Mining	659	641	637	654	645	598	599	606	583	572	591
Mining	576.5	558.1	556.4	571.3	564.7	517.4	520.2	532.5	512.2	502.7	523.2
Oil and gas extraction	162.4	151.7	146.9	144.1	140.8	131.2	124.9	123.7	121.9	120.2	123.1
Mining, except oil and gas	255.2	252.4	249.4	249.5	243.1	234.5	224.8	218.7	210.6	202.7	207.1
Construction	5 095	5 274	5 536	5 813	6 149	6 545	6 787	6 826	6 716	6 735	6 964
Construction of buildings	1 300.8	1 325.4	1 380.2	1 435.4	1 508.8	1 586.3	1 632.5	1 588.9	1 574.8	1 575.8	1 632.2
Heavy and civil engineering	761.7	774.7	800.1	824.9	865.3	908.7	937.0	953.0	930.6	903.1	902.5
Specialty trade contractors	3 032.5	3 174.1	3 355.1	3 552.6	3 775.1	4 049.6	4 217.0	4 283.9	4 210.4	4 255.7	4 429.7
Manufacturing	17 021	17 241	17 237	17 419	17 560	17 322	17 263	16 441	15 259	14 510	14 329
Durable goods	10 131.0	10 372.0	10 485.0	10 704.0	10 910.0	10 830.0	10 876.0	10 335.0	9 483.0	8 963.0	8 923.0
Wood products	560.6	573.7	582.8	595.4	609.2	620.3	613.0	574.1	554.9	537.6	548.4
Nonmetallic mineral products	505.3	513.1	517.3	525.7	535.3	540.8	554.2	544.5	516.0	494.2	504.8
Primary metals	630.4	641.7	639.3	638.8	641.5	625.0	621.8	570.9	509.4	477.4	465.9
Fabricated metal products	1 565.3	1 623.4	1 647.5	1 695.8	1 739.5	1 728.4	1 752.6	1 676.4	1 548.5	1 478.9	1 497.5
Machinery	1 379.2	1 440.2	1 466.8	1 493.7	1 511.9	1 466.1	1 454.7	1 368.3	1 229.5	1 149.4	1 141.5
Computer and electronic products	1 651.1	1 688.4	1 746.6	1 803.3	1 830.9	1 780.5	1 820.0	1 748.8	1 507.2	1 355.2	1 326.2
Electrical equipment and appliances	588.5	592.8	591.0	586.3	591.6	588.0	590.9	556.9	496.5	459.6	446.8
Transportation equipment	1 936.1	1 977.2	1 973.7	2 026.2	2 077.0	2 087.3	2 055.8	1 937.9	1 828.9	1 774.1	1 763.5
Furniture and related products	600.2	606.7	603.8	615.1	641.2	664.8	679.7	642.4	604.1	572.9	572.7
Miscellaneous manufacturing	713.8	714.5	715.6	723.1	731.7	729.0	733.0	714.5	688.3	663.3	655.5
Nondurable goods	6 890.0	6 869.0	6 752.0	6 716.0	6 650.0	6 492.0	6 388.0	6 107.0	5 775.0	5 547.0	5 406.0
Food manufacturing	1 539.2	1 560.0	1 562.0	1 557.9	1 554.9	1 549.8	1 553.1	1 551.2	1 525.7	1 517.5	1 497.4
Beverage and tobacco products	204.6	202.6	204.4	206.3	208.9	208.3	207.0	209.0	207.4	199.6	194.3
Textile mills	477.6	468.5	443.2	436.2	424.5	397.1	378.2	332.9	290.9	261.3	238.5
Textile product mills	218.6	219.0	216.2	217.0	217.1	217.3	216.3	205.7	194.6	179.3	177.7
Apparel	856.3	814.1	743.1	700.2	639.0	555.6	496.8	426.5	359.7	312.3	284.8
Paper and paper products	639.4	639.5	631.4	630.6	624.9	615.6	604.7	577.6	546.6	516.2	499.1
Printing and related support activities	802.2	817.3	815.8	821.1	827.9	814.6	806.8	768.4	706.6	680.5	665.0
Petroleum and coal products	144.0	140.4	137.3	136.0	134.5	127.8	123.2	121.1	118.1	114.3	112.8
Chemicals	1 004.7	987.9	984.5	986.8	992.6	982.5	980.4	959.0	927.5	906.1	887.0
Plastics and rubber products	889.4	915.1	920.1	934.1	942.8	948.3	952.2	897.4	848.0	815.4	806.6
Private Service–Providing	72 242	74 710	76 759	79 227	81 667	84 221	86 346	86 834	86 271	86 599	87 978
Trade, Transportation, and Utilities	23 128	23 834	24 239	24 700	25 186	25 771	26 225	25 983	25 497	25 287	25 510
Wholesale Trade	5 247	5 433	5 522	5 664	5 795	5 892	5 933	5 773	5 652	5 608	5 655
Durable goods	2 786.0	2 908.8	2 977.8	3 071.9	3 162.4	3 219.6	3 250.7	3 130.4	3 007.9	2 940.6	2 949.1
Nondurable goods	1 927.0	1 969.3	1 977.5	2 007.9	2 032.7	2 061.1	2 064.8	2 031.3	2 015.0	2 004.6	2 007.1
Electronic markets, agents, and brokers	534.4	555.0	566.7	584.1	600.1	611.8	617.7	611.1	629.4	662.2	698.8
Retail Trade	13 491	13 897	14 142	14 389	14 609	14 970	15 280	15 239	15 025	14 917	15 035
Motor vehicle and parts dealers	1 564.7	1 627.1	1 685.6	1 723.4	1 740.9	1 796.6	1 846.9	1 854.6	1 879.4	1 882.9	1 901.2
Furniture and home furnishing stores	441.6	461.2	474.2	484.7	499.1	524.4	543.5	541.2	538.7	547.3	560.2
Electronic and appliance stores	417.0	448.7	470.2	494.0	510.2	542.2	564.4	554.5	525.3	512.2	514.4
Building material and garden supply stores	946.2	981.8	1 007.2	1 043.1	1 062.3	1 101.0	1 142.1	1 151.8	1 176.5	1 185.0	1 226.0
Food and beverage stores	2 825.0	2 879.8	2 927.8	2 956.9	2 965.7	2 984.5	2 993.0	2 950.5	2 881.6	2 838.4	2 826.3
Health and personal care stores	797.0	811.9	826.4	853.3	876.0	898.2	927.6	951.5	938.8	938.1	941.7
Gasoline stations	902.3	922.3	946.4	956.2	961.3	943.5	935.7	925.3	895.9	882.0	877.1
Clothing and clothing accessories stores	1 261.7	1 246.3	1 220.6	1 235.9	1 268.6	1 306.6	1 321.6	1 321.1	1 312.5	1 304.5	1 361.8
Sporting goods, hobby, and music stores	577.6	605.8	614.0	626.2	635.4	664.3	685.7	679.2	661.3	646.5	639.2
General merchandise stores	2 541.0	2 635.4	2 657.3	2 657.6	2 686.5	2 751.8	2 819.8	2 842.2	2 812.0	2 822.4	2 843.5
Miscellaneous store retailers	795.7	841.1	874.3	913.2	950.3	985.5	1 007.1	993.3	959.5	930.7	918.6
Nonstore retailers	421.2	435.4	438.5	444.5	453.0	471.6	492.4	473.5	443.7	427.3	424.8
Transportation and Warehousing	3 701	3 838	3 935	4 026	4 168	4 300	4 410	4 372	4 224	4 185	4 250
Air transportation	511.2	510.9	525.7	542.0	562.7	586.3	614.4	615.3	563.5	528.3	514.8
Rail transportation	234.6	232.5	225.2	221.0	225.0	228.8	231.7	226.7	217.8	217.7	224.1
Water transportation	52.3	50.8	51.0	50.7	50.5	51.7	56.0	54.0	52.6	54.5	57.2
Truck transportation	1 206.2	1 249.1	1 282.4	1 308.2	1 354.4	1 391.5	1 405.8	1 386.8	1 339.3	1 325.6	1 350.7
Transit and ground passenger transportation	316.6	327.9	339.1	349.6	362.7	371.0	372.1	374.8	380.8	382.2	385.5
Pipeline transportation	57.0	53.6	51.4	49.7	48.1	46.9	46.0	45.4	41.7	40.2	38.8
Scenic and sightseeing transportation	21.3	22.0	23.2	24.5	25.4	26.1	27.5	29.1	25.6	26.6	26.7
Support activities for transportation	404.7	430.4	445.8	473.4	496.8	518.1	537.4	539.2	524.7	520.3	535.6
Couriers and messengers	466.2	516.8	539.9	546.0	568.2	585.9	605.0	587.0	560.9	561.7	560.5
Warehousing and storage	431.0	443.8	451.8	461.5	474.2	494.1	514.4	513.8	516.7	528.3	556.0

Table 2-1. Employees on Nonfarm Payrolls by Super Sector and Selected Component Groups, NAICS Basis, 1994–2004—*Continued*

(Thousands of people.)

Industry	1994	1995	1996	1997	1998	1999	2000	2001	2002	2003	2004
Utilities	689	666	640	621	613	608	601	599	596	577	570
Information	2 738	2 843	2 940	3 084	3 218	3 419	3 631	3 629	3 395	3 188	3 138
Publishing industries, except the Internet	891.0	910.7	927.2	955.5	982.3	1 004.8	1 035.0	1 020.7	964.1	924.8	909.8
Motion picture and sound recording industry	278.4	311.1	334.7	353.0	369.5	384.4	382.6	376.8	387.9	376.2	389.0
Broadcasting, except the Internet	290.1	298.1	309.1	313.0	321.2	329.4	343.5	344.6	334.1	324.3	326.6
Internet publishing and broadcasting	16.9	18.6	21.0	23.5	27.1	37.1	50.5	45.5	33.7	29.2	31.3
Telecommunications	961.1	975.7	997.0	1 059.5	1 107.8	1 179.7	1 262.6	1 302.1	1 186.5	1 082.3	1 042.5
ISPs, search portals, and data processing	268.0	291.2	311.6	338.8	369.1	439.3	510.1	493.6	441.0	402.4	388.1
Other information services	32.8	38.2	39.4	40.1	41.4	43.8	46.2	46.1	47.3	48.7	50.9
Financial Activities	6 867	6 827	6 969	7 178	7 462	7 648	7 687	7 807	7 847	7 977	8 052
Finance and insurance	5 135.2	5 071.7	5 154.2	5 305.1	5 532.0	5 668.4	5 680.4	5 773.1	5 817.3	5 922.6	5 965.6
Monetary authorities–central bank	23.4	23.0	22.8	22.8	21.7	22.6	22.8	23.0	23.4	22.6	21.6
Credit intermediation	2 375.7	2 314.4	2 368.2	2 433.6	2 531.9	2 591.0	2 547.8	2 597.7	2 686.0	2 792.4	2 832.3
Securities, commodities	553.4	562.2	589.6	636.1	692.2	737.3	804.5	830.5	789.4	757.7	766.8
Insurance carriers and related activities	2 118.8	2 108.2	2 108.0	2 143.6	2 209.4	2 236.1	2 220.6	2 233.7	2 233.2	2 266.0	2 260.3
Funds, trust, and other financial vehicles	63.9	63.9	65.6	69.8	76.9	81.5	84.8	88.3	85.4	83.9	84.7
Real estate and rental and leasing	1 731.5	1 755.4	1 814.3	1 872.8	1 930.3	1 979.0	2 006.8	2 034.5	2 029.6	2 053.9	2 086.2
Real estate	1 183.2	1 178.9	1 205.8	1 240.7	1 274.2	1 299.0	1 312.2	1 339.5	1 352.9	1 383.6	1 417.0
Rental and leasing services	529.9	557.4	587.7	609.5	630.8	653.1	666.8	666.3	649.1	643.1	643.9
Lessors of nonfinancial intangible assets	18.4	19.0	20.8	22.6	25.3	26.8	27.8	28.7	27.6	27.3	25.4
Professional and Business Services	12 174	12 844	13 462	14 335	15 147	15 957	16 666	16 476	15 976	15 987	16 414
Professional and technical services	4 843.6	5 101.3	5 337.1	5 655.5	6 021.0	6 375.4	6 733.9	6 902.2	6 675.6	6 629.5	6 762.0
Management of companies and enterprises	1 665.9	1 685.8	1 702.7	1 729.7	1 756.1	1 773.8	1 796.0	1 779.0	1 705.4	1 687.2	1 718.0
Administrative and waste services	5 664.1	6 056.8	6 422.1	6 949.9	7 369.3	7 807.4	8 136.0	7 794.9	7 595.2	7 669.8	7 934.0
Administrative and support services	5 403.4	5 783.4	6 140.0	6 659.4	7 069.9	7 496.9	7 823.1	7 477.6	7 276.8	7 347.7	7 608.7
Waste management and remediation services	260.7	273.3	282.0	290.5	299.3	310.5	312.9	317.3	318.3	322.1	325.3
Education and Health Services	12 807	13 289	13 683	14 087	14 446	14 798	15 109	15 645	16 199	16 588	16 954
Educational services	1 894.9	2 010.2	2 077.6	2 155.0	2 232.9	2 320.4	2 390.4	2 510.6	2 642.8	2 695.1	2 766.4
Health care and social assistance	10 911.7	11 278.4	11 604.9	11 932.2	12 213.5	12 477.1	12 718.0	13 134.0	13 555.7	13 892.6	14 187.3
Ambulatory health care services	3 578.8	3 767.5	3 939.9	4 093.0	4 161.2	4 226.6	4 320.3	4 461.5	4 633.2	4 786.4	4 946.4
Hospitals	3 724.0	3 733.7	3 772.8	3 821.6	3 892.4	3 935.5	3 954.3	4 050.9	4 159.6	4 244.6	4 293.6
Nursing and residential health facilities	2 227.0	2 307.7	2 379.9	2 443.4	2 487.3	2 528.8	2 583.2	2 675.8	2 743.3	2 786.2	2 814.8
Social assistance	1 381.9	1 469.5	1 512.3	1 574.2	1 672.6	1 786.2	1 860.2	1 945.9	2 019.7	2 075.4	2 132.5
Leisure and Hospitality	10 100	10 501	10 777	11 018	11 232	11 543	11 862	12 036	11 986	12 173	12 479
Arts, entertainment, and recreation	1 375.6	1 459.4	1 522.1	1 599.9	1 645.2	1 709.1	1 787.9	1 824.4	1 782.6	1 812.9	1 833.0
Performing arts and spectator sports	296.1	307.7	328.6	349.6	350.0	361.1	381.8	382.3	363.7	371.7	364.8
Museums, historical sites	81.8	83.9	88.9	93.8	97.4	103.1	110.4	115.0	114.0	114.7	117.1
Amusements, gambling, and recreation	997.7	1 067.8	1 104.5	1 156.5	1 197.9	1 244.9	1 295.7	1 327.1	1 305.0	1 326.5	1 351.1
Accommodation and food service	8 724.1	9 041.6	9 254.3	9 417.9	9 586.2	9 833.7	10 073.5	10 211.3	10 203.2	10 359.8	10 646.0
Accommodations	1 615.3	1 652.5	1 698.9	1 729.5	1 773.5	1 831.7	1 884.4	1 852.2	1 778.6	1 775.4	1 795.9
Food services and drinking places	7 108.7	7 389.1	7 555.4	7 688.5	7 812.7	8 002.0	8 189.1	8 359.1	8 424.6	8 584.4	8 850.1
Other services	4 428.0	4 572.0	4 690.0	4 825.0	4 976.0	5 087.0	5 168.0	5 258.0	5 372.0	5 401.0	5 431.0
Repair and maintenance	1 023.5	1 078.9	1 135.5	1 169.3	1 189.2	1 222.0	1 241.5	1 256.5	1 246.9	1 233.6	1 227.6
Personal and laundry services	1 120.3	1 143.9	1 165.7	1 180.4	1 205.6	1 220.3	1 242.9	1 255.0	1 257.2	1 263.5	1 274.1
Membership associations and organizations	2 284.5	2 348.9	2 389.1	2 474.9	2 581.3	2 644.4	2 683.3	2 746.4	2 867.8	2 903.6	2 929.1
Government	19 275	19 432	19 539	19 664	19 909	20 307	20 790	21 118	21 513	21 583	21 618
Federal	3 018.0	2 949.0	2 877.0	2 806.0	2 772.0	2 769.0	2 865.0	2 764.0	2 766.0	2 761.0	2 728.0
Federal, except Postal Service	2 197.2	2 098.8	2 009.8	1 940.2	1 891.3	1 879.5	1 984.8	1 891.0	1 923.8	1 952.4	1 943.4
State	4 576.0	4 635.0	4 606.0	4 582.0	4 612.0	4 709.0	4 786.0	4 905.0	5 029.0	5 002.0	4 985.0
State, excluding education	2 693.6	2 715.5	2 695.1	2 677.9	2 690.2	2 725.6	2 755.9	2 791.8	2 786.3	2 747.6	2 736.2
Local	11 682.0	11 849.0	12 056.0	12 276.0	12 525.0	12 829.0	13 139.0	13 449.0	13 718.0	13 820.0	13 905.0
Local, excluding education	5 352.2	5 396.0	5 464.1	5 516.9	5 603.9	5 708.6	5 844.6	5 970.0	6 063.2	6 110.2	6 143.0

Table 2-2. Employees on Nonfarm Payrolls by Major Industry Groups, SIC Basis, 1948–1989

(Thousands of people.)

Industry	1948	1949	1950	1951	1952	1953	1954	1955	1956	1957	1958	1959	1960	1961
TOTAL	44 866	43 754	45 197	47 819	48 793	50 202	48 990	50 641	52 369	52 855	51 322	53 270	54 189	53 999
Total Private	39 216	37 897	39 170	41 430	42 185	43 556	42 238	43 727	45 091	45 239	43 483	45 186	45 836	45 404
Goods-Producing	18 774	17 565	18 506	19 959	20 198	21 074	19 751	20 513	21 104	20 967	19 513	20 411	20 434	19 857
Mining	994	930	901	929	898	866	791	792	822	828	751	732	712	672
Construction	2 198	2 194	2 364	2 637	2 668	2 659	2 646	2 839	3 039	2 962	2 817	3 004	2 926	2 859
Manufacturing	15 582	14 441	15 241	16 393	16 632	17 549	16 314	16 882	17 243	17 176	15 945	16 675	16 796	16 326
Service–Producing	26 092	26 189	26 691	27 860	28 595	29 128	29 239	30 128	31 264	31 889	31 811	32 857	33 755	34 142
Transportation and public utilities	4 189	4 001	4 034	4 226	4 248	4 290	4 084	4 141	4 244	4 241	3 976	4 011	4 004	3 903
Wholesale trade	2 612	2 610	2 643	2 735	2 821	2 862	2 875	2 934	3 027	3 037	2 989	3 092	3 153	3 142
Retail trade	6 659	6 654	6 743	7 007	7 184	7 385	7 360	7 601	7 831	7 848	7 761	8 035	8 238	8 195
Finance, insurance, and real estate	1 800	1 828	1 888	1 956	2 035	2 111	2 200	2 298	2 389	2 438	2 481	2 549	2 628	2 688
Services	5 181	5 239	5 356	5 547	5 699	5 835	5 969	6 240	6 497	6 708	6 765	7 087	7 378	7 619
Government	5 650	5 856	6 026	6 389	6 609	6 645	6 751	6 914	7 278	7 616	7 839	8 083	8 353	8 594
Federal	1 863	1 908	1 928	2 302	2 420	2 305	2 188	2 187	2 209	2 217	2 191	2 233	2 270	2 279
State	. . .	. . .	. . .	. . .	. . .	. . .	. . .	1 168	1 250	1 328	1 415	1 484	1 536	1 607
Local	. . .	. . .	. . .	. . .	. . .	. . .	. . .	3 558	3 819	4 071	4 232	4 366	4 547	4 708

Industry	1962	1963	1964	1965	1966	1967	1968	1969	1970	1971	1972	1973	1974	1975
TOTAL	55 549	56 653	58 283	60 763	63 901	65 803	67 897	70 384	70 880	71 211	73 675	76 790	78 265	76 945
Total Private	46 660	47 429	48 686	50 689	53 116	54 413	56 058	58 189	58 325	58 331	60 341	63 058	64 095	62 259
Goods-Producing	20 451	20 640	21 005	21 926	23 158	23 308	23 737	24 361	23 578	22 935	23 668	24 893	24 794	22 600
Mining	650	635	634	632	627	613	606	619	623	609	628	642	697	752
Construction	2 948	3 010	3 097	3 232	3 317	3 248	3 350	3 575	3 588	3 704	3 889	4 097	4 020	3 525
Manufacturing	16 853	16 995	17 274	18 062	19 214	19 447	19 781	20 167	19 367	18 623	19 151	20 154	20 077	18 323
Service–Producing	35 098	36 013	37 278	38 839	40 743	42 495	44 158	46 023	47 302	48 276	50 007	51 897	53 471	54 345
Transportation and public utilities	3 906	3 903	3 951	4 036	4 158	4 268	4 318	4 442	4 515	4 476	4 541	4 656	4 725	4 542
Wholesale trade	3 207	3 258	3 347	3 477	3 608	3 700	3 791	3 919	4 006	4 014	4 127	4 291	4 447	4 430
Retail trade	8 359	8 520	8 812	9 239	9 637	9 906	10 308	10 785	11 034	11 338	11 822	12 315	12 539	12 630
Finance, insurance, and real estate	2 754	2 830	2 911	2 977	3 058	3 185	3 337	3 512	3 645	3 772	3 908	4 046	4 148	4 165
Services	7 982	8 277	8 660	9 036	9 498	10 045	10 567	11 169	11 548	11 797	12 276	12 857	13 441	13 892
Government	8 890	9 225	9 596	10 074	10 784	11 391	11 839	12 195	12 554	12 881	13 334	13 732	14 170	14 686
Federal	2 340	2 358	2 348	2 378	2 564	2 719	2 737	2 758	2 731	2 696	2 684	2 663	2 724	2 748
State	1 668	1 747	1 856	1 996	2 141	2 302	2 442	2 533	2 664	2 747	2 859	2 923	3 039	3 179
Local	4 881	5 121	5 392	5 700	6 080	6 371	6 660	6 904	7 158	7 437	7 790	8 146	8 407	8 758

Industry	1976	1977	1978	1979	1980	1981	1982	1983	1984	1985	1986	1987	1988	1989
TOTAL	79 382	82 471	86 697	89 823	90 406	91 152	89 544	90 152	94 408	97 387	99 344	101 958	105 209	107 884
Total Private	64 511	67 344	71 026	73 876	74 166	75 121	73 707	74 282	78 384	80 992	82 651	84 948	87 823	90 105
Goods-Producing	23 352	24 346	25 585	26 461	25 658	25 497	23 812	23 330	24 718	24 842	24 533	24 674	25 125	25 254
Mining	779	813	851	958	1 027	1 139	1 128	952	966	927	777	717	713	692
Construction	3 576	3 851	4 229	4 463	4 346	4 188	3 904	3 946	4 380	4 668	4 810	4 958	5 098	5 171
Manufacturing	18 997	19 682	20 505	21 040	20 285	20 170	18 780	18 432	19 372	19 248	18 947	18 999	19 314	19 391
Service–Producing	56 030	58 125	61 113	63 363	64 748	65 655	65 732	66 821	69 690	72 544	74 811	77 284	80 084	82 630
Transportation and public utilities	4 582	4 713	4 923	5 136	5 146	5 165	5 081	4 952	5 156	5 233	5 247	5 362	5 512	5 614
Wholesale trade	4 562	4 723	4 985	5 221	5 292	5 375	5 295	5 283	5 568	5 727	5 761	5 848	6 030	6 187
Retail trade	13 193	13 792	14 556	14 972	15 018	15 171	15 158	15 587	16 512	17 315	17 880	18 422	19 023	19 475
Finance, insurance, and real estate	4 271	4 467	4 724	4 975	5 160	5 298	5 340	5 466	5 684	5 948	6 273	6 533	6 630	6 668
Services	14 551	15 302	16 252	17 112	17 890	18 615	19 021	19 664	20 746	21 927	22 957	24 110	25 504	26 907
Government	14 871	15 127	15 672	15 947	16 241	16 031	15 837	15 869	16 024	16 394	16 693	17 010	17 386	17 779
Federal	2 733	2 727	2 753	2 773	2 866	2 772	2 739	2 774	2 807	2 875	2 899	2 943	2 971	2 988
State	3 273	3 377	3 474	3 541	3 610	3 640	3 640	3 662	3 734	3 832	3 893	3 967	4 076	4 182
Local	8 865	9 023	9 446	9 633	9 765	9 619	9 458	9 434	9 482	9 687	9 901	10 100	10 339	10 609

Note: Data include Alaska and Hawaii beginning in 1959.

. . . = Not available.

Table 2-3. Women Employees on Nonfarm Payrolls by Super Sector and Selected Component Groups, NAICS Basis, 1990–2004

(Thousands of people.)

Industry	1990	1991	1992	1993	1994	1995	1996	1997	1998	1999	2000	2001	2002	2003	2004
TOTAL NONFARM	51 586	51 681	52 132	53 175	54 759	56 213	57 406	58 914	60 309	61 810	63 222	63 683	63 360	63 237	63 762
Total Private	41 731	41 696	41 970	42 849	44 228	45 514	46 573	47 923	49 144	50 358	51 452	51 669	51 033	50 901	51 426
Goods-Producing	6 470	6 243	6 119	6 090	6 168	6 225	6 214	6 294	6 353	6 299	6 297	5 961	5 486	5 192	5 121
Natural resources and mining	112	114	109	105	102	98	96	99	100	96	92	90	85	80	80
Construction	656	628	599	609	636	666	700	730	769	818	846	832	827	822	839
Manufacturing	5 702	5 501	5 410	5 377	5 430	5 462	5 417	5 466	5 484	5 386	5 359	5 039	4 574	4 290	4 202
Private Service-Providing	35 262	35 453	35 851	36 759	38 061	39 289	40 360	41 629	42 791	44 059	45 155	45 708	45 547	45 709	46 305
Trade, transportation, and utilities	9 363	9 243	9 176	9 259	9 564	9 870	10 043	10 230	10 413	10 658	10 859	10 768	10 466	10 321	10 350
Wholesale trade	1 611	1 587	1 565	1 554	1 607	1 668	1 701	1 746	1 778	1 809	1 826	1 770	1 718	1 700	1 711
Retail trade	6 696	6 588	6 534	6 599	6 813	7 020	7 142	7 272	7 380	7 542	7 680	7 635	7 449	7 339	7 374
Transportation and warehousing	879	891	901	932	974	1 018	1 042	1 060	1 103	1 154	1 202	1 212	1 149	1 134	1 117
Utilities	177	177	176	174	169	163	157	153	152	152	151	151	150	147	148
Information	1 324	1 319	1 295	1 304	1 334	1 380	1 433	1 481	1 514	1 600	1 697	1 684	1 554	1 428	1 375
Financial activities	4 055	4 036	4 022	4 114	4 196	4 164	4 241	4 359	4 515	4 605	4 638	4 726	4 755	4 830	4 841
Professional and business services	5 105	5 026	5 160	5 399	5 682	5 979	6 273	6 705	7 030	7 370	7 680	7 591	7 314	7 248	7 369
Educational and health services	8 422	8 840	9 141	9 454	9 822	10 181	10 474	10 779	11 042	11 323	11 586	12 037	12 474	12 786	13 073
Leisure and hospitality	4 829	4 806	4 876	4 994	5 192	5 382	5 520	5 640	5 760	5 933	6 082	6 224	6 215	6 319	6 510
Other services	2 164	2 184	2 181	2 236	2 269	2 333	2 376	2 435	2 517	2 570	2 614	2 677	2 769	2 779	2 788
Government	9 855	9 985	10 162	10 326	10 531	10 698	10 832	10 991	11 164	11 452	11 771	12 015	12 327	12 337	12 336
Federal	1 378	1 329	1 335	1 321	1 306	1 285	1 261	1 240	1 184	1 174	1 231	1 148	1 155	1 173	1 167
State	2 137	2 173	2 197	2 238	2 281	2 326	2 316	2 324	2 354	2 412	2 464	2 534	2 621	2 599	2 564
Local	6 340	6 483	6 630	6 767	6 943	7 088	7 255	7 426	7 627	7 866	8 076	8 333	8 551	8 565	8 605

Table 2-4. Women Employees on Nonfarm Payrolls by Major Industry, SIC Basis, 1959–1989

(Thousands of people.)

Year	Total	Mining	Construc-tion	Manufacturing			Transpor-tation and public utilities	Whole-sale trade	Retail trade	Finance, insur-ance, and real estate	Services	Government			
				Total	Durable goods	Nondur-able goods						Total	Federal	State	Local
1959	...	...	...	4 358	1 692	2 667	...	...	...	...	...	...	...	...	...
1960	...	36	...	4 371	1 702	2 670	...	717	3 579	...	...	...	...	...	...
1961	...	35	...	4 292	1 662	2 630	...	703	3 564	...	...	...	...	...	...
1962	...	35	...	4 474	1 770	2 705	...	712	3 643	...	...	...	...	...	...
1963	...	35	...	4 482	1 767	2 715	...	720	3 708	...	...	...	...	...	...
1964	19 662	34	152	4 537	1 777	2 760	723	741	3 878	1 464	4 415	3 718	530	708	2 480
1965	20 660	34	152	4 768	1 911	2 857	748	768	4 113	1 496	4 611	3 970	542	768	2 660
1966	22 168	34	156	5 213	2 204	3 009	786	809	4 315	1 549	4 931	4 375	610	841	2 924
1967	23 272	35	158	5 353	2 300	3 053	835	832	4 465	1 624	5 267	4 703	674	931	3 099
1968	24 395	36	164	5 490	2 361	3 129	860	857	4 669	1 709	5 632	4 979	710	1 013	3 256
1969	25 595	37	174	5 667	2 469	3 197	911	904	4 937	1 819	5 994	5 153	723	1 087	3 343
1970	26 132	37	186	5 448	2 307	3 141	957	924	5 083	1 907	6 224	5 365	723	1 126	3 517
1971	26 466	37	199	5 229	2 152	3 078	955	917	5 211	1 978	6 438	5 502	715	1 118	3 669
1972	27 541	40	219	5 470	2 280	3 190	953	939	5 410	2 032	6 718	5 759	747	1 162	3 849
1973	28 988	43	241	5 865	2 567	3 298	987	996	5 686	2 138	7 023	6 010	780	1 216	4 014
1974	30 124	49	262	5 849	2 618	3 230	1 018	1 050	5 928	2 245	7 454	6 270	798	1 287	4 185
1975	30 178	55	256	5 257	2 271	2 985	996	1 053	5 998	2 287	7 822	6 454	805	1 373	4 276
1976	31 570	60	281	5 607	2 444	3 163	1 010	1 100	6 301	2 371	8 256	6 586	808	1 448	4 329
1977	33 252	65	304	5 880	2 645	3 235	1 051	1 153	6 611	2 511	8 771	6 907	856	1 510	4 540
1978	35 349	76	331	6 237	2 894	3 343	1 133	1 243	7 036	2 708	9 368	7 216	866	1 537	4 813
1979	37 096	91	355	6 466	3 085	3 380	1 237	1 328	7 369	2 882	9 919	7 450	860	1 572	5 018
1980	38 186	105	372	6 317	3 003	3 314	1 292	1 371	7 480	3 039	10 452	7 759	908	1 632	5 219
1981	39 035	129	380	6 341	3 029	3 312	1 340	1 404	7 585	3 158	10 969	7 730	878	1 659	5 193
1982	39 041	134	377	5 990	2 822	3 168	1 339	1 424	7 653	3 198	11 330	7 595	883	1 637	5 075
1983	39 826	117	388	5 964	2 788	3 176	1 313	1 463	7 912	3 277	11 755	7 637	939	1 584	5 114
1984	42 022	118	427	6 295	3 031	3 265	1 386	1 557	8 519	3 430	12 413	7 878	975	1 678	5 224
1985	43 851	120	463	6 230	3 022	3 208	1 448	1 632	9 037	3 634	13 129	8 159	1 009	1 776	5 374
1986	45 476	106	495	6 181	2 974	3 207	1 480	1 684	9 404	3 886	13 819	8 420	1 031	1 848	5 541
1987	47 188	95	523	6 242	2 987	3 255	1 532	1 736	9 764	4 076	14 549	8 672	1 048	1 919	5 705
1988	49 053	96	539	6 352	3 032	3 320	1 619	1 815	10 113	4 134	15 454	8 931	1 060	2 000	5 870
1989	50 690	94	547	6 399	3 048	3 351	1 643	1 891	10 384	4 188	16 296	9 248	1 105	2 070	6 073

Note: Data include Alaska and Hawaii beginning in 1959.

. . . = Not available.

Table 2-5. Production or Nonsupervisory Workers on Private Nonfarm Payrolls by Super Sector, NAICS Basis, 1990–2004

(Thousands of people.)

Industry	1990	1991	1992	1993	1994	1995	1996	1997	1998	1999	2000	2001	2002	2003	2004
TOTAL PRIVATE	73 684	72 520	72 786	74 591	77 382	79 845	81 773	84 158	86 316	88 430	90 336	89 983	88 393	87 658	88 976
Goods–Producing	17 322	16 352	16 043	16 236	16 795	17 137	17 318	17 698	18 008	18 067	18 169	17 466	16 400	15 732	15 823
Natural resources and mining	538	515	478	462	461	458	461	479	473	438	446	457	436	420	440
Construction	4 115	3 674	3 546	3 704	3 973	4 113	4 325	4 546	4 807	5 105	5 295	5 332	5 196	5 123	5 300
Manufacturing	12 669	12 164	12 020	12 070	12 361	12 566	12 532	12 673	12 729	12 524	12 428	11 677	10 768	10 190	10 083
Private Service–Providing	56 362	56 168	56 743	58 355	60 587	62 708	64 455	66 460	68 308	70 363	72 167	72 517	71 993	71 926	73 152
Trade, transportation, and utilities	19 032	18 640	18 506	18 752	19 392	19 984	20 325	20 698	21 059	21 576	21 965	21 709	21 337	21 078	21 298
Wholesale trade	4 198	4 122	4 071	4 072	4 196	4 361	4 423	4 523	4 605	4 673	4 686	4 555	4 474	4 396	4 438
Retail trade	11 308	11 008	10 931	11 104	11 502	11 841	12 057	12 274	12 440	12 772	13 040	12 952	12 774	12 655	12 766
Transportation and warehousing	2 941	2 928	2 934	3 019	3 153	3 260	3 339	3 407	3 522	3 642	3 753	3 718	3 611	3 563	3 638
Utilities	585	582	570	557	541	522	506	494	492	489	485	483	478	464	455
Information	1 866	1 871	1 871	1 896	1 928	2 007	2 096	2 181	2 217	2 351	2 502	2 530	2 398	2 347	2 389
Financial activities	4 973	4 911	4 908	5 057	5 183	5 165	5 279	5 415	5 605	5 728	5 737	5 810	5 872	5 967	6 001
Professional and business services	8 889	8 748	8 971	9 451	10 078	10 645	11 161	11 896	12 566	13 184	13 790	13 588	13 049	12 910	13 306
Educational and health services	9 748	10 212	10 555	10 908	11 338	11 765	12 123	12 478	12 791	13 089	13 362	13 846	14 311	14 532	14 771
Leisure and hospitality	8 299	8 247	8 406	8 667	8 979	9 330	9 565	9 780	9 947	10 216	10 516	10 662	10 576	10 666	10 945
Other services	3 555	3 539	3 526	3 623	3 689	3 812	3 907	4 013	4 124	4 219	4 296	4 373	4 449	4 426	4 442

Table 2-6. Production or Nonsupervisory Workers on Private Nonfarm Payrolls by Major Industry, SIC Basis, 1947–1989

(Thousands of people.)

| Year | Total private | Mining | Construction | Manufacturing | | | Transportation and public utilities | Wholesale trade | Retail trade | Finance, insurance, and real estate | Services |
				Total	Durable goods	Nondurable goods					
1947	33 747	871	1 786	12 990	7 064	5 926	. . .	2 248	6 000	1 436	. . .
1948	34 489	906	1 954	12 910	6 962	5 950	. . .	2 361	6 275	1 496	. . .
1949	33 159	839	1 949	11 790	6 158	5 633	. . .	2 354	6 248	1 517	. . .
1950	34 349	816	2 101	12 523	6 741	5 781	. . .	2 382	6 368	1 565	. . .
1951	36 225	840	2 343	13 368	7 514	5 854	. . .	2 456	6 642	1 622	. . .
1952	36 643	801	2 360	13 359	7 583	5 777	. . .	2 533	6 807	1 683	. . .
1953	37 694	765	2 341	14 055	8 186	5 869	. . .	2 554	6 964	1 742	. . .
1954	36 276	686	2 316	12 817	7 226	5 591	. . .	2 536	6 928	1 807	. . .
1955	37 500	680	2 477	13 288	7 580	5 708	. . .	2 574	7 109	1 889	. . .
1956	38 495	702	2 653	13 436	7 701	5 735	. . .	2 645	7 296	1 961	. . .
1957	38 384	695	2 577	13 189	7 581	5 607	. . .	2 639	7 292	1 998	. . .
1958	36 608	611	2 420	11 997	6 611	5 387	. . .	2 572	7 174	2 029	. . .
1959	38 080	590	2 577	12 603	7 065	5 538	. . .	2 661	7 434	2 086	. . .
1960	38 516	570	2 497	12 586	7 060	5 526	. . .	2 705	7 618	2 145	. . .
1961	37 989	532	2 426	12 083	6 650	5 433	. . .	2 684	7 558	2 189	. . .
1962	38 979	512	2 500	12 488	6 967	5 521	. . .	2 726	7 682	2 237	. . .
1963	39 553	498	2 562	12 555	7 059	5 495	. . .	2 758	7 811	2 291	. . .
1964	40 560	497	2 637	12 781	7 245	5 537	3 490	2 832	8 037	2 346	7 939
1965	42 278	494	2 749	13 434	7 746	5 688	3 561	2 932	8 426	2 388	8 295
1966	44 249	487	2 818	14 296	8 400	5 895	3 638	3 033	8 787	2 441	8 749
1967	45 137	469	2 741	14 308	8 396	5 912	3 718	3 095	9 026	2 533	9 246
1968	46 473	461	2 822	14 514	8 489	6 024	3 757	3 164	9 378	2 651	9 727
1969	48 208	472	3 012	14 767	8 683	6 084	3 863	3 271	9 822	2 797	10 205
1970	48 156	473	2 990	14 044	8 088	5 956	3 914	3 340	10 034	2 879	10 481
1971	48 148	455	3 071	13 544	7 697	5 847	3 872	3 327	10 288	2 936	10 655
1972	49 939	475	3 257	14 045	8 025	6 022	3 943	3 418	10 717	3 024	11 059
1973	52 201	486	3 405	14 838	8 699	6 138	4 034	3 560	11 152	3 121	11 606
1974	52 809	530	3 294	14 638	8 634	6 004	4 079	3 683	11 316	3 169	12 100
1975	50 991	571	2 808	13 043	7 532	5 510	3 894	3 650	11 373	3 173	12 479
1976	52 897	592	2 814	13 638	7 888	5 750	3 918	3 759	11 890	3 243	13 043
1977	55 179	618	3 021	14 135	8 280	5 855	4 008	3 892	12 424	3 397	13 683
1978	58 156	638	3 354	14 734	8 777	5 956	4 142	4 109	13 110	3 593	14 476
1979	60 367	719	3 565	15 068	9 082	5 986	4 299	4 290	13 458	3 776	15 193
1980	60 331	762	3 421	14 214	8 416	5 798	4 293	4 328	13 484	3 907	15 921
1981	60 923	841	3 261	14 020	8 270	5 751	4 283	4 375	13 582	3 999	16 562
1982	59 468	821	2 998	12 742	7 290	5 451	4 190	4 261	13 594	3 996	16 867
1983	60 028	673	3 031	12 528	7 095	5 433	4 072	4 239	13 989	4 066	17 429
1984	63 339	686	3 404	13 280	7 715	5 565	4 258	4 466	14 736	4 226	18 284
1985	65 475	658	3 655	13 084	7 618	5 466	4 335	4 607	15 421	4 410	19 305
1986	66 866	545	3 770	12 864	7 399	5 465	4 339	4 623	15 925	4 637	20 163
1987	68 771	511	3 870	12 952	7 409	5 543	4 446	4 685	16 378	4 797	21 132
1988	71 099	512	3 980	13 193	7 582	5 611	4 555	4 858	16 869	4 811	22 323
1989	73 017	493	4 035	13 230	7 594	5 636	4 655	4 981	17 262	4 829	23 532

Note: Data include Alaska and Hawaii beginning in 1959.

. . . = Not available.

Table 2-7. Production Workers on Durable Goods Manufacturing Payrolls by Industry, NAICS Basis, 1990–2004

(Thousands of people.)

Industry	1990	1991	1992	1993	1994	1995	1996	1997	1998	1999	2000	2001	2002	2003	2004
Total Durable Goods	7 396	7 000	6 852	6 879	7 132	7 351	7 425	7 597	7 720	7 650	7 658	7 163	6 529	6 152	6 137
Wood products	449.9	413	417.0	436.8	468.7	477.5	484.9	496.6	507.9	514.4	505.6	468.3	448.7	433.0	443.2
Nonmetallic mineral products	413.2	384	378.4	380.7	392.3	399.7	404.8	412.5	420.6	426.0	439.5	427.1	398.8	374.7	387.4
Primary metals	525.1	497	478.7	473.3	487.4	500.3	500.3	501.6	505.3	491.9	490.0	446.9	396.2	370.3	363.0
Fabricated metal products	1 190.1	1 132	1 101.0	1 116.9	1 172.0	1 223.0	1 241.6	1 285.3	1 319.6	1 304.9	1 325.8	1 253.5	1 147.0	1 092.5	1 109.2
Machinery	937.6	884	856.3	874.1	921.1	968.5	983.2	1 005.5	1 014.7	977.0	959.9	889.1	785.4	730.9	727.7
Computer and electronic products	980.2	926	876.3	856.4	863.9	890.3	915.2	951.1	964.7	932.9	949.3	875.8	744.1	672.7	657.4
Electrical equipment and appliances	465.2	436	425.0	421.8	434.7	438.4	433.9	427.7	431.8	433.2	433.1	402.2	351.9	319.5	308.5
Transportation equipment	1 472.5	1 406	1 387.7	1 366.1	1 414.6	1 471.1	1 480.0	1 520.8	1 529.2	1 525.4	1 496.7	1 397.7	1 309.3	1 268.5	1 262.5
Furniture and related products	475.2	440	442.8	454.2	475.7	480.0	477.9	489.7	512.1	532.4	544.3	509.0	474.8	444.2	443.3
Miscellaneous manufacturing	487.2	484	489.1	498.2	502.1	502.2	503.3	506.6	514.3	512.2	513.2	493.1	472.5	445.3	435.1

Table 2-8. Production Workers on Durable Goods Manufacturing Payrolls by Industry, Selected Years, SIC Basis, 1939–1989

(Thousands of people.)

Year	Total	Lumber and wood products	Furniture and fixtures	Stone, clay, and glass products	Primary metal industries		Fabricated metal products	Industrial machinery and equipment	Electronic and other electrical equipment	Transportation equipment		Instruments and related products	Miscellaneous manufacturing
					Total	Blast furnaces and basic steel products				Total	Motor vehicles and equipment		
1939	3 926	...	...	297.0	...	452.6	...	...	...	539.5	388.3	...	...
1940	4 506	...	...	310.7	...	519.6	...	...	...	710.7	448.6	...	...
1945	7 571	...	...	334.4	...	527.3	...	...	...	2 057.4	519.7	...	...
1950	6 741	777.2	301.8	447.6	1 030.5	586.8	861.5	938.6	...	1 016.4	677.1	...	343.7
1955	7 580	706.3	292.6	469.1	1 069.4	604.5	974.5	1 082.1	...	1 418.1	718.3	...	330.4
1956	7 701	696.0	300.6	479.9	1 084.6	595.4	977.0	1 170.9	...	1 366.2	619.5	...	333.1
1957	7 581	622.0	298.2	466.5	1 071.4	600.1	989.1	1 155.6	...	1 394.5	601.7	...	315.3
1958	6 611	581.8	284.4	433.5	890.8	486.6	892.2	956.3	...	1 128.8	452.5	...	299.5
1959	7 065	628.5	305.7	469.7	914.2	470.9	939.5	1 038.9	...	1 183.8	537.5	...	312.9
1960	7 060	595.8	303.5	465.5	956.9	528.4	943.4	1 047.4	...	1 134.6	563.3	...	314.3
1961	6 650	551.4	289.5	444.4	880.8	478.4	896.5	987.3	...	1 029.2	479.1	...	303.5
1962	6 967	562.7	304.5	452.3	901.5	476.3	944.8	1 049.4	...	1 096.5	534.0	...	313.2
1963	7 059	565.8	308.7	458.1	911.7	479.1	965.4	1 070.9	...	1 142.9	573.6	...	310.4
1964	7 245	574.8	320.9	467.4	967.1	515.6	992.2	1 131.8	...	1 144.7	579.2	...	317.9
1965	7 746	579.3	340.3	477.8	1 022.7	538.4	1 059.5	1 227.4	...	1 259.2	658.9	...	335.5
1966	8 400	587.4	364.4	489.9	1 055.5	530.9	1 158.9	1 358.1	...	1 385.3	670.3	...	346.1
1967	8 396	570.6	357.6	473.5	1 015.7	509.5	1 204.8	1 383.2	...	1 390.9	626.9	...	338.3
1968	8 489	581.0	371.5	482.0	1 002.6	506.2	1 243.5	1 357.5	...	1 449.9	680.8	...	340.4
1969	8 683	594.3	382.9	498.5	1 042.2	513.6	1 283.6	1 397.1	...	1 443.3	708.0	...	344.6
1970	8 088	563.5	362.4	484.9	999.7	499.7	1 188.3	1 335.8	...	1 222.7	605.3	...	328.7
1971	7 697	588.4	364.5	485.5	923.3	454.6	1 128.0	1 195.1	...	1 196.1	655.4	...	317.6
1972	8 025	636.7	400.4	515.5	932.9	452.6	1 189.1	1 258.4	...	1 225.7	676.0	...	339.9
1973	8 699	664.9	420.0	545.8	1 010.5	484.8	1 276.7	1 415.9	...	1 324.1	754.9	...	356.4
1974	8 634	618.1	401.9	539.1	1 029.5	487.3	1 255.9	1 494.3	...	1 256.3	687.5	...	353.8
1975	7 532	525.6	337.3	472.7	886.6	428.1	1 089.6	1 350.2	...	1 141.7	602.4	...	310.6
1976	7 888	585.4	364.0	486.2	904.4	430.5	1 138.2	1 352.0	...	1 222.5	682.4	...	328.7
1977	8 280	625.8	381.8	504.6	922.1	432.6	1 197.5	1 434.7	...	1 277.0	734.7	...	334.2
1978	8 777	656.5	406.3	524.9	954.3	441.7	1 269.3	1 540.0	...	1 369.5	781.7	...	344.5
1979	9 082	663.7	405.9	529.1	986.4	451.3	1 298.3	1 648.2	...	1 408.5	764.4	...	338.8
1980	8 416	587.2	375.8	486.0	877.6	395.7	1 194.3	1 614.4	...	1 220.3	575.4	...	313.1
1981	8 270	562.5	373.8	464.8	861.9	391.6	1 170.6	1 592.4	...	1 206.8	586.0	...	302.1
1982	7 290	496.7	341.8	412.7	683.4	293.9	1 027.5	1 367.1	...	1 067.7	511.9	...	276.4
1983	7 095	555.3	356.1	411.6	619.8	256.3	993.6	1 206.9	...	1 084.8	568.3	...	266.7
1984	7 715	598.2	389.9	431.0	651.4	256.8	1 078.4	1 342.3	...	1 202.5	663.9	...	277.5
1985	7 618	592.2	393.6	426.7	611.4	231.5	1 082.9	1 319.8	...	1 243.6	684.5	...	264.0
1986	7 399	605.0	397.4	426.2	565.3	208.7	1 051.0	1 233.7	...	1 258.0	670.2	...	261.6
1987	7 409	627.8	412.0	428.7	562.2	202.8	1 037.6	1 203.4	...	1 278.2	673.1	...	269.4
1988	7 582	638.9	420.2	442.7	589.0	215.4	1 061.5	1 256.1	1 112.3	1 272.8	667.4	508.0	280.3
1989	7 594	625.7	417.7	443.6	588.9	215.2	1 070.4	1 281.5	1 101.7	1 277.7	663.8	509.4	277.6

Note: Data include Alaska and Hawaii beginning in 1959.

. . . = Not available.

Table 2-9. Production Workers on Nondurable Goods Manufacturing Payrolls by Industry, NAICS Basis, 1990–2004

(Thousands of people.)

Industry	1990	1991	1992	1993	1994	1995	1996	1997	1998	1999	2000	2001	2002	2003	2004
Total Nondurable Goods	5 273	5 164	5 168	5 192	5 229	5 215	5 107	5 076	5 009	4 873	4 770	4 514	4 239	4 038	3 945
Food manufacturing	1 165.0	1 174.2	1 182.0	1 195.3	1 200.4	1 221.0	1 227.7	1 227.7	1 227.6	1 228.7	1 227.9	1 221.3	1 202.3	1 192.5	1 180.9
Beverage and tobacco products	117.2	116.9	116.2	117.6	118.2	117.3	120.1	121.4	122.5	120.1	116.9	115.6	119.5	106.4	106.4
Textile mills	417.9	407.2	406.0	403.9	403.3	393.2	371.7	367.1	357.2	333.7	315.2	275.8	242.2	216.9	195.2
Textile product mills	170.1	160.9	163.0	167.2	176.0	176.3	173.4	174.7	173.9	173.4	171.8	163.9	153.7	141.3	142.4
Apparel	830.0	805.1	809.8	788.0	763.1	719.3	650.2	611.5	549.9	471.8	415.4	351.2	294.3	248.6	224.7
Leather and allied products	116.6	107.5	104.4	101.4	97.2	88.5	78.5	73.6	67.0	59.9	55.4	46.8	40.0	34.9	33.6
Paper and paper products	493.2	488.4	489.9	490.9	492.8	493.8	487.5	488.7	484.1	474.0	467.5	446.3	421.4	392.7	376.5
Printing and related support	597.6	581.7	573.6	579.7	591.4	599.1	594.0	597.0	598.4	585.1	575.7	544.4	492.6	471.2	461.1
Petroleum and coal products	97.5	97.4	96.8	93.0	90.9	88.8	87.2	87.8	87.1	84.6	83.1	80.9	78.0	74.4	77.4
Chemicals	620.3	599.7	586.2	590.1	595.6	598.4	595.1	593.3	600.6	595.2	587.7	562.2	531.9	524.9	520.0
Plastics and rubber products	647.7	624.8	639.8	664.7	699.6	719.8	721.3	732.7	740.4	747.0	753.6	705.3	662.7	634.3	627.2

Table 2-10. Production Workers on Nondurable Goods Manufacturing Payrolls by Industry, Selected Years, SIC Basis, 1939–1989

(Thousands of people.)

Industry	Total	Food and kindred products	Tobacco products	Textile mill products	Apparel and other textile products	Paper and allied products	Printing and publishing	Chemicals and allied products	Petroleum and coal products	Rubber and miscellaneous plastics products	Leather and leather products
1939	4 392	989.0	...	1 108.0	814.0	264.6	320.0	252.0	100.0	149.0	349.0
1940	4 434	1 003.0	...	1 090.0	819.0	276.8	321.0	274.0	105.0	161.0	337.0
1945	5 438	1 380.0	...	1 074.0	973.0	342.8	381.0	518.0	148.0	255.0	325.0
1950	5 781	1 331.0	95.0	1 169.0	1 080.0	413.0	494.0	461.0	165.0	279.0	355.0
1955	5 708	1 291.7	94.4	961.6	1 086.4	450.6	539.0	518.1	163.2	316.3	344.0
1956	5 735	1 302.1	90.1	944.3	1 088.1	461.5	559.6	525.7	161.2	319.5	340.9
1957	5 607	1 263.2	85.3	893.3	1 072.0	460.3	563.7	519.7	156.6	318.1	331.0
1958	5 387	1 222.0	84.1	832.5	1 039.5	451.2	563.2	493.7	146.9	290.2	318.2
1959	5 538	1 222.1	83.9	857.4	1 091.4	468.7	575.1	505.6	139.9	317.7	332.9
1960	5 526	1 211.8	83.3	835.1	1 098.2	476.5	588.9	509.9	137.9	320.5	320.9
1961	5 433	1 191.1	79.6	805.0	1 079.6	474.9	591.7	505.0	129.9	314.7	316.4
1962	5 521	1 178.4	78.7	812.1	1 122.9	482.8	594.5	519.3	125.5	343.3	318.9
1963	5 495	1 167.1	76.6	793.4	1 138.0	483.2	590.3	525.3	119.9	349.8	307.8
1964	5 537	1 157.3	78.4	798.2	1 158.3	485.6	602.1	529.4	114.2	364.1	305.5
1965	5 688	1 159.1	74.8	826.7	1 205.6	494.4	620.6	546.1	112.9	394.3	310.0
1966	5 895	1 180.0	71.8	858.8	1 245.7	514.9	646.4	574.3	114.7	427.1	318.5
1967	5 912	1 187.3	73.9	850.2	1 237.2	522.9	661.6	592.3	114.7	425.3	303.7
1968	6 024	1 191.6	71.9	880.7	1 240.1	532.7	667.0	609.9	118.0	463.2	306.3
1969	6 084	1 201.8	69.6	884.0	1 237.9	547.0	681.7	621.9	112.2	491.3	294.4
1970	5 956	1 206.9	69.0	855.0	1 196.4	539.6	679.0	604.0	118.2	472.7	273.4
1971	5 847	1 203.2	63.4	837.2	1 177.5	518.4	658.0	587.8	124.1	478.5	257.1
1972	6 022	1 191.8	62.2	866.6	1 208.0	528.1	665.7	592.8	125.1	524.8	256.4
1973	6 138	1 166.8	64.8	886.2	1 249.7	539.6	672.9	610.5	123.9	579.1	245.0
1974	6 004	1 163.6	63.8	842.2	1 174.9	540.8	660.4	623.0	126.1	576.5	232.3
1975	5 510	1 120.3	62.4	752.4	1 066.6	476.6	624.0	579.6	123.0	492.7	212.6
1976	5 750	1 145.1	63.6	800.4	1 134.3	505.0	624.7	600.1	127.8	521.6	227.0
1977	5 855	1 161.0	57.0	792.3	1 129.4	514.8	646.5	616.0	131.3	587.7	218.4
1978	5 956	1 173.9	56.2	783.1	1 144.6	521.3	671.9	627.6	135.5	622.1	220.4
1979	5 986	1 190.8	55.5	770.9	1 116.8	532.1	697.2	633.3	137.1	643.0	209.1
1980	5 798	1 174.6	53.6	736.9	1 079.4	519.3	698.9	625.8	124.7	588.2	196.6
1981	5 751	1 149.5	54.7	712.5	1 059.5	515.0	699.3	628.3	133.9	596.8	201.1
1982	5 451	1 125.5	53.4	642.1	981.2	490.7	699.1	598.6	119.9	557.8	182.9
1983	5 433	1 113.5	52.0	639.2	983.5	491.2	711.5	578.6	118.0	574.2	171.1
1984	5 565	1 118.9	48.6	645.6	1 002.1	508.1	757.7	582.8	111.3	632.2	158.0
1985	5 466	1 117.0	48.0	606.3	943.9	508.4	787.9	577.4	108.5	631.7	136.6
1986	5 465	1 129.4	44.1	608.1	926.0	507.2	815.7	567.6	105.9	638.5	122.7
1987	5 543	1 145.1	41.5	629.5	921.7	512.3	839.4	574.6	106.8	652.6	119.7
1988	5 611	1 154.8	40.7	631.8	912.4	516.3	863.6	596.0	104.3	673.5	117.8
1989	5 636	1 176.2	37.0	621.9	906.8	520.5	863.2	603.1	101.8	691.5	114.1

Note: Data include Alaska and Hawaii beginning in 1959.

. . . = Not available.

Table 2-11. Average Weekly Hours of Production or Nonsupervisory Workers on Private Nonfarm Payrolls by Super Sector, NAICS Basis, 1990–2004

(Number.)

Industry	1990	1991	1992	1993	1994	1995	1996	1997	1998	1999	2000	2001	2002	2003	2004
TOTAL PRIVATE	34.3	34.1	34.2	34.3	34.5	34.3	34.3	34.5	34.5	34.3	34.3	34.0	33.9	33.7	33.7
Goods–Producing	40.1	40.1	40.2	40.6	41.1	40.8	40.8	41.1	40.8	40.8	40.7	39.9	39.9	39.8	40.0
Natural resources and mining	45.0	45.3	44.6	44.9	45.3	45.3	46.0	46.2	44.9	44.2	44.4	44.6	43.2	43.6	44.5
Construction	38.3	38.1	38.0	38.4	38.8	38.8	38.9	38.9	38.8	39.0	39.2	38.7	38.4	38.4	38.3
Manufacturing	40.5	40.4	40.7	41.1	41.7	41.3	41.3	41.7	41.4	41.4	41.3	40.3	40.5	40.4	40.8
Private Service–Providing	32.5	32.4	32.5	32.5	32.7	32.6	32.6	32.8	32.8	32.7	32.7	32.5	32.5	32.4	32.3
Trade, transportation, and utilities	33.7	33.7	33.8	34.1	34.3	34.1	34.1	34.3	34.2	33.9	33.8	33.5	33.6	33.6	33.5
Wholesale trade	38.4	38.4	38.6	38.5	38.8	38.6	38.6	38.8	38.6	38.6	38.8	38.4	38.0	37.9	37.8
Retail trade	30.6	30.4	30.7	30.7	30.9	30.8	30.7	30.9	30.9	30.8	30.7	30.7	30.9	30.9	30.7
Transportation and warehousing	37.7	37.4	37.4	38.9	39.5	38.9	39.1	39.4	38.7	37.6	37.4	36.7	36.8	36.8	37.2
Utilities	41.5	41.5	41.7	42.1	42.3	42.3	42.0	42.0	42.0	42.0	42.0	41.4	40.9	41.1	40.9
Information	35.8	35.6	35.8	36.0	36.0	36.0	36.4	36.3	36.6	36.7	36.8	36.9	36.5	36.2	36.3
Financial activities	35.5	35.5	35.6	35.5	35.5	35.5	35.5	35.7	36.0	35.8	35.9	35.8	35.6	35.5	35.5
Professional and business services	34.2	34.0	34.0	34.0	34.1	34.0	34.1	34.3	34.3	34.4	34.5	34.2	34.2	34.1	34.2
Educational and health services	31.9	31.9	32.0	32.0	32.0	32.0	31.9	32.2	32.2	32.1	32.2	32.3	32.4	32.3	32.4
Leisure and hospitality	26.0	25.6	25.7	25.9	26.0	25.9	25.9	26.0	26.2	26.1	26.1	25.8	25.8	25.6	25.7
Other services	32.8	32.7	32.6	32.6	32.7	32.6	32.5	32.7	32.6	32.5	32.5	32.3	32.0	31.4	31.0

Table 2-12. Average Weekly Hours of Production or Nonsupervisory Workers on Private Nonfarm Payrolls by Major Industry, SIC Basis, 1947–1989

(Number.)

Year	Total private	Mining	Construction	Manufacturing			Transportation and public utilities	Wholesale trade	Retail trade	Finance, insurance, and real estate	Services
				Total	Durable goods	Nondurable goods					
1947	40.3	40.8	38.2	40.4	40.5	40.2	. . .	41.1	40.3	37.9	. . .
1948	40.0	39.4	38.1	40.0	40.4	39.6	. . .	41.0	40.2	37.9	. . .
1949	39.4	36.3	37.7	39.1	39.4	38.9	. . .	40.8	40.4	37.8	. . .
1950	39.8	37.9	37.4	40.5	41.1	39.7	. . .	40.7	40.4	37.7	. . .
1951	39.9	38.4	38.1	40.6	41.5	39.6	. . .	40.8	40.4	37.7	. . .
1952	39.9	38.6	38.9	40.7	41.4	39.7	. . .	40.7	39.8	37.8	. . .
1953	39.6	38.8	37.9	40.5	41.2	39.6	. . .	40.6	39.1	37.7	. . .
1954	39.1	38.6	37.2	39.6	40.1	39.0	. . .	40.5	39.2	37.6	. . .
1955	39.6	40.7	37.1	40.7	41.3	39.9	. . .	40.7	39.0	37.6	. . .
1956	39.3	40.8	37.5	40.4	41.0	39.6	. . .	40.5	38.6	36.9	. . .
1957	38.8	40.1	37.0	39.8	40.3	39.2	. . .	40.3	38.1	36.7	. . .
1958	38.5	38.9	36.8	39.2	39.5	38.8	. . .	40.2	38.1	37.1	. . .
1959	39.0	40.5	37.0	40.3	40.7	39.7	. . .	40.6	38.2	37.3	. . .
1960	38.6	40.4	36.7	39.7	40.1	39.2	. . .	40.5	38.0	37.2	. . .
1961	38.6	40.5	36.9	39.8	40.2	39.3	. . .	40.5	37.6	36.9	. . .
1962	38.7	41.0	37.0	40.4	40.9	39.7	. . .	40.6	37.4	37.3	. . .
1963	38.8	41.6	37.3	40.5	41.1	39.6	. . .	40.6	37.3	37.5	. . .
1964	38.7	41.9	37.2	40.7	41.5	39.7	41.1	40.7	37.0	37.3	36.1
1965	38.8	42.3	37.4	41.2	42.0	40.1	41.3	40.8	36.6	37.2	35.9
1966	38.6	42.7	37.6	41.4	42.1	40.2	41.2	40.7	35.9	37.3	35.5
1967	38.0	42.6	37.7	40.6	41.2	39.7	40.5	40.3	35.3	37.1	35.1
1968	37.8	42.6	37.3	40.7	41.4	39.8	40.6	40.1	34.7	37.0	34.7
1969	37.7	43.0	37.9	40.6	41.3	39.7	40.7	40.2	34.2	37.1	34.7
1970	37.1	42.7	37.3	39.8	40.3	39.1	40.5	39.9	33.8	36.7	34.4
1971	36.9	42.4	37.2	39.9	40.3	39.3	40.1	39.4	33.7	36.6	33.9
1972	37.0	42.6	36.5	40.5	41.2	39.7	40.4	39.4	33.4	36.6	33.9
1973	36.9	42.4	36.8	40.7	41.4	39.6	40.5	39.2	33.1	36.6	33.8
1974	36.5	41.9	36.6	40.0	40.6	39.1	40.2	38.8	32.7	36.5	33.6
1975	36.1	41.9	36.4	39.5	39.9	38.8	39.7	38.6	32.4	36.5	33.5
1976	36.1	42.4	36.8	40.1	40.6	39.4	39.8	38.7	32.1	36.4	33.3
1977	36.0	43.4	36.5	40.3	41.0	39.4	39.9	38.8	31.6	36.4	33.0
1978	35.8	43.4	36.8	40.4	41.1	39.4	40.0	38.8	31.0	36.4	32.8
1979	35.7	43.0	37.0	40.2	40.8	39.3	39.9	38.8	30.6	36.2	32.7
1980	35.3	43.3	37.0	39.7	40.1	39.0	39.6	38.4	30.2	36.2	32.6
1981	35.2	43.7	36.9	39.8	40.2	39.2	39.4	38.5	30.1	36.3	32.6
1982	34.8	42.7	36.7	38.9	39.3	38.4	39.0	38.3	29.9	36.2	32.6
1983	35.0	42.5	37.1	40.1	40.7	39.4	39.0	38.5	29.8	36.2	32.7
1984	35.2	43.3	37.8	40.7	41.4	39.7	39.4	38.5	29.8	36.5	32.6
1985	34.9	43.4	37.7	40.5	41.2	39.6	39.5	38.4	29.4	36.4	32.5
1986	34.8	42.2	37.4	40.7	41.3	39.9	39.2	38.3	29.2	36.4	32.5
1987	34.8	42.4	37.8	41.0	41.5	40.2	39.2	38.1	29.2	36.3	32.5
1988	34.7	42.3	37.9	41.1	41.8	40.2	38.2	38.1	29.1	35.9	32.6
1989	34.6	43.0	37.9	41.0	41.6	40.2	38.3	38.0	28.9	35.8	32.6

Note: Data include Alaska and Hawaii beginning in 1959.

. . . = Not available.

Table 2-13. Average Weekly Hours of Production Workers on Manufacturing Payrolls by Industry, NAICS Basis, 1990–2004

(Number.)

Industry	1990	1991	1992	1993	1994	1995	1996	1997	1998	1999	2000	2001	2002	2003	2004
DURABLE GOODS															
Total	41.1	40.9	41.3	41.9	42.6	42.1	42.1	42.6	42.1	41.9	41.8	40.6	40.8	40.8	41.3
Wood products	40.4	40.2	40.9	41.2	41.7	41.0	41.2	41.4	41.4	41.3	41.0	40.2	39.9	40.4	40.6
Nonmetallic mineral products	40.9	40.5	41.0	41.5	42.2	41.8	42.0	41.9	42.2	42.1	41.6	41.6	42.0	42.2	42.3
Primary metals	42.0	41.5	42.4	43.1	44.1	43.4	43.6	44.3	43.5	43.8	44.2	42.4	42.4	42.3	43.1
Fabricated metal products	41.0	40.8	41.2	41.6	42.3	41.9	41.9	42.3	41.9	41.7	41.9	40.6	40.6	40.7	41.1
Machinery	42.1	41.9	42.4	43.2	43.9	43.5	43.3	44.0	43.1	42.3	42.3	40.9	40.5	40.8	41.9
Computer and electronic products	41.3	40.9	41.4	41.8	42.2	42.2	41.9	42.5	41.8	41.5	41.4	39.8	39.7	40.4	40.4
Electrical equipment and appliances	41.2	41.5	41.8	42.4	43.0	41.9	42.1	42.1	41.8	41.8	41.6	39.8	40.1	40.6	40.7
Transportation equipment	42.0	41.9	41.9	43.0	44.3	43.7	43.8	44.2	43.2	43.6	43.3	41.9	42.5	41.9	42.5
Furniture and related products	38.0	37.8	38.7	39.0	39.3	38.5	38.3	39.1	39.4	39.3	39.2	38.3	39.2	38.9	39.5
Miscellaneous manufacturing	39.0	39.1	39.3	39.2	39.4	39.2	39.1	39.7	39.2	39.3	39.0	38.8	38.6	38.4	38.5
NONDURABLE GOODS															
Total	39.6	39.7	40.0	40.1	40.5	40.1	40.1	40.5	40.5	40.4	40.3	39.9	40.1	39.8	40.0
Food manufacturing	39.3	39.2	39.2	39.3	39.8	39.6	39.5	39.8	40.1	40.2	40.1	39.6	39.6	39.3	39.3
Beverage and tobacco products	38.9	38.8	38.7	38.3	39.3	39.3	39.7	40.0	40.3	41.0	42.0	40.9	39.4	39.1	39.2
Textile mills	40.2	40.7	41.3	41.6	41.9	40.9	40.8	41.6	41.0	41.0	41.4	40.0	40.6	39.1	40.1
Textile product mills	39.0	39.1	39.2	39.8	39.9	39.1	39.2	39.6	39.5	39.4	39.0	38.6	39.2	39.6	38.9
Apparel	34.8	35.4	35.6	35.5	35.7	35.3	35.2	35.5	35.5	35.4	35.7	36.0	36.7	35.6	36.0
Leather and allied products	37.4	37.6	37.9	38.4	38.2	37.7	37.8	38.2	37.4	37.2	37.5	36.4	37.5	39.3	38.4
Paper and paper products	43.6	43.6	43.8	43.8	44.2	43.4	43.5	43.9	43.6	43.6	42.8	42.1	41.9	41.5	42.1
Printing and related support	38.7	38.6	39.0	39.2	39.6	39.1	39.1	39.5	39.3	39.1	39.2	38.7	38.4	38.2	38.4
Petroleum and coal products	44.4	43.9	43.6	44.0	44.3	43.7	43.7	43.1	43.6	42.6	42.7	43.8	43.0	44.5	44.9
Chemicals	42.8	43.1	43.3	43.2	43.4	43.3	43.3	43.4	43.2	42.7	42.2	41.9	42.3	42.4	42.8
Plastics and rubber products	40.6	40.5	41.2	41.4	41.8	41.1	41.0	41.4	41.3	41.3	40.8	40.0	40.6	40.4	40.4

Table 2-14. Average Weekly Hours of Production Workers on Manufacturing Payrolls by Industry, SIC Basis, 1947–1989

(Number.)

Year	Durable goods												
	Total	Lumber and wood products	Furniture and fixtures	Stone, clay, and glass products	Primary metal industries		Fabricated metal products	Industrial machinery and equipment	Electronic and other electrical equipment	Transportation equipment		Instruments and related products	Miscellaneous manufacturing
					Total	Blast furnaces and basic steel products				Total	Motor vehicles and equipment		
1947	40.5	40.3	41.5	41.0	39.9	39.0	40.9	41.5	. . .	39.7	39.8	. . .	40.5
1948	40.4	40.0	41.0	40.7	40.2	39.5	40.7	41.3	. . .	39.4	39.2	. . .	40.6
1949	39.4	39.2	40.0	39.7	38.4	38.2	39.7	39.6	. . .	39.6	39.7	. . .	39.6
1950	41.1	39.5	41.8	41.1	40.9	39.9	41.5	41.9	. . .	41.4	42.1	. . .	40.8
1951	41.5	39.3	41.1	41.4	41.6	40.9	41.8	43.5	. . .	41.2	40.4	. . .	40.5
1952	41.4	39.7	41.4	41.1	40.8	40.0	41.7	43.0	. . .	41.8	41.4	. . .	40.7
1953	41.2	39.3	40.9	40.8	41.0	40.5	41.8	42.4	. . .	41.6	42.0	. . .	40.5
1954	40.1	39.1	40.0	40.5	38.8	37.8	40.8	40.7	. . .	40.9	41.5	. . .	39.6
1955	41.3	39.5	41.4	41.4	41.3	40.5	41.7	41.9	. . .	42.3	43.6	. . .	40.3
1956	41.0	38.9	40.7	41.1	41.0	40.5	41.3	42.3	. . .	41.4	41.2	. . .	40.0
1957	40.3	38.4	39.9	40.4	39.6	39.1	40.9	41.1	. . .	40.8	40.9	. . .	39.7
1958	39.5	38.6	39.3	40.0	38.3	37.5	39.9	39.8	. . .	40.0	39.7	. . .	39.2
1959	40.7	39.7	40.7	41.2	40.5	40.1	40.9	41.5	. . .	40.7	41.1	. . .	39.9
1960	40.1	39.1	40.0	40.6	39.0	38.2	40.5	41.0	. . .	40.7	41.0	. . .	39.3
1961	40.2	39.5	40.0	40.7	39.5	38.9	40.5	40.9	. . .	40.5	40.1	. . .	39.5
1962	40.9	39.8	40.7	41.0	40.2	39.2	41.1	41.7	. . .	42.0	42.7	. . .	39.7
1963	41.1	40.2	40.9	41.4	41.0	40.2	41.3	41.8	. . .	42.0	42.8	. . .	39.6
1964	41.5	40.4	41.2	41.7	41.7	41.2	41.7	42.4	. . .	42.1	43.0	. . .	39.6
1965	42.0	40.9	41.5	42.0	42.1	41.2	42.1	43.1	. . .	42.9	44.2	. . .	39.9
1966	42.1	40.8	41.5	42.0	42.1	41.0	42.4	43.8	. . .	42.6	42.8	. . .	40.0
1967	41.2	40.3	40.4	41.6	41.1	40.2	41.5	42.5	. . .	41.4	40.8	. . .	39.4
1968	41.4	40.6	40.6	41.8	41.6	41.0	41.7	42.0	. . .	42.2	43.1	. . .	39.4
1969	41.3	40.2	40.4	41.9	41.8	41.3	41.6	42.5	. . .	41.5	41.7	. . .	39.0
1970	40.3	39.6	39.2	41.2	40.4	40.0	40.7	41.1	. . .	40.3	40.3	. . .	38.7
1971	40.3	39.8	39.8	41.6	40.1	39.6	40.4	40.6	. . .	40.7	41.2	. . .	38.9
1972	41.2	40.4	40.2	42.0	41.4	40.6	41.2	42.1	. . .	41.7	43.0	. . .	39.5
1973	41.4	40.0	40.0	41.9	42.3	41.7	41.6	42.8	. . .	42.1	43.5	. . .	39.0
1974	40.6	39.2	39.1	41.3	41.6	41.3	40.8	42.1	. . .	40.5	40.6	. . .	38.7
1975	39.9	38.8	38.0	40.4	40.0	39.5	40.1	40.8	. . .	40.4	40.3	. . .	38.5
1976	40.6	39.9	38.8	41.1	40.8	40.3	40.8	41.2	. . .	41.7	42.9	. . .	38.8
1977	41.0	39.9	39.0	41.3	41.3	40.5	41.0	41.5	. . .	42.5	44.0	. . .	38.8
1978	41.1	39.8	39.3	41.6	41.8	41.5	41.0	42.0	. . .	42.2	43.3	. . .	38.8
1979	40.8	39.5	38.7	41.5	41.4	41.2	40.7	41.7	. . .	41.1	41.1	. . .	38.8
1980	40.1	38.6	38.1	40.8	40.1	39.4	40.4	41.0	. . .	40.6	40.0	. . .	38.7
1981	40.2	38.7	38.4	40.6	40.5	40.4	40.3	40.9	. . .	40.9	40.9	. . .	38.8
1982	39.3	38.1	37.2	40.1	38.6	37.9	39.2	39.7	. . .	40.5	40.5	. . .	38.4
1983	40.7	40.1	39.4	41.5	40.5	39.5	40.6	40.5	. . .	42.1	43.3	. . .	39.1
1984	41.4	39.9	39.7	42.0	41.7	40.7	41.4	41.9	. . .	42.7	43.8	. . .	39.4
1985	41.2	39.9	39.4	41.9	41.5	41.1	41.3	41.5	. . .	42.6	43.5	. . .	39.4
1986	41.3	40.4	39.8	42.2	41.9	41.7	41.3	41.6	. . .	42.3	42.6	. . .	39.6
1987	41.5	40.6	40.0	42.3	43.1	43.4	41.6	42.2	. . .	42.2	42.2	. . .	39.4
1988	41.8	40.1	39.4	42.3	43.5	44.0	41.9	42.7	41.0	42.7	43.5	41.4	39.2
1989	41.6	40.1	39.5	42.3	43.0	43.4	41.6	42.4	40.8	42.4	43.1	41.1	39.4

. . . = Not available.

Table 2-14. Average Weekly Hours of Production Workers on Manufacturing Payrolls by Industry, SIC Basis, 1947–1989—*Continued*

(Number.)

Year	Nondurable goods										
	Total	Food and kindred products	Tobacco products	Textile mill products	Apparel and other textile products	Paper and allied products	Printing and publishing	Chemicals and allied products	Petroleum and coal products	Rubber and miscellaneous plastics products	Leather and leather products
1947	40.2	43.2	38.9	39.6	36.0	43.1	40.2	41.2	40.6	40.0	38.6
1948	39.6	42.4	38.3	39.2	35.8	42.8	39.4	41.2	40.6	39.3	37.2
1949	38.9	41.9	37.3	37.7	35.4	41.7	38.8	40.7	40.3	38.5	36.6
1950	39.7	41.9	38.1	39.6	36.0	43.3	38.9	41.2	40.8	41.0	37.6
1951	39.6	42.1	38.5	38.8	35.6	43.1	38.9	41.3	40.8	40.8	36.9
1952	39.7	41.9	38.4	39.1	36.3	42.8	38.9	40.9	40.5	40.9	38.4
1953	39.6	41.5	38.1	39.1	36.1	43.0	39.0	41.0	40.7	40.4	37.7
1954	39.0	41.3	37.6	38.3	35.3	42.3	38.5	40.8	40.7	39.8	36.9
1955	39.9	41.5	38.7	40.1	36.3	43.1	38.9	41.1	40.9	41.7	37.9
1956	39.6	41.3	38.8	39.7	36.0	42.8	38.9	41.1	41.0	40.4	37.6
1957	39.2	40.8	38.4	38.9	35.7	42.3	38.6	40.9	40.8	40.6	37.4
1958	38.8	40.8	39.1	38.6	35.1	41.9	38.0	40.7	40.9	39.3	36.7
1959	39.7	41.0	39.1	40.4	36.3	42.8	38.5	41.4	41.2	41.3	37.9
1960	39.2	40.8	38.2	39.5	35.5	42.1	38.4	41.3	41.1	40.0	36.9
1961	39.3	40.9	39.0	39.9	35.4	42.5	38.2	41.4	41.2	40.4	37.4
1962	39.7	41.0	38.6	40.6	36.2	42.6	38.3	41.6	41.6	41.0	37.6
1963	39.6	41.0	38.7	40.6	36.1	42.7	38.3	41.6	41.7	40.9	37.5
1964	39.7	41.0	38.8	41.0	35.9	42.8	38.5	41.6	41.8	41.3	37.9
1965	40.1	41.1	37.9	41.7	36.4	43.1	38.6	41.9	42.2	42.0	38.2
1966	40.2	41.2	38.9	41.9	36.4	43.4	38.8	42.0	42.4	42.0	38.6
1967	39.7	40.9	38.6	40.9	36.0	42.8	38.4	41.6	42.7	41.4	38.2
1968	39.8	40.8	37.9	41.2	36.1	42.9	38.3	41.8	42.5	41.5	38.3
1969	39.7	40.8	37.4	40.8	35.9	43.0	38.3	41.8	42.6	41.2	37.2
1970	39.1	40.5	37.8	39.9	35.3	41.9	37.7	41.6	42.8	40.3	37.2
1971	39.3	40.3	37.8	40.6	35.6	42.1	37.5	41.6	42.8	40.4	37.7
1972	39.7	40.5	37.6	41.3	36.0	42.8	37.7	41.7	42.7	41.2	38.3
1973	39.6	40.4	38.6	40.9	35.9	42.9	37.7	41.8	42.4	41.2	37.8
1974	39.1	40.4	38.3	39.5	35.2	42.2	37.5	41.5	42.1	40.6	36.9
1975	38.8	40.3	38.2	39.3	35.2	41.6	36.9	41.0	41.2	39.9	37.1
1976	39.4	40.5	37.5	40.1	35.8	42.5	37.5	41.6	42.1	40.7	37.4
1977	39.4	40.0	37.8	40.4	35.6	42.9	37.7	41.7	42.7	41.1	36.9
1978	39.4	39.7	38.1	40.4	35.6	42.9	37.6	41.9	43.6	40.9	37.1
1979	39.3	39.9	38.0	40.4	35.3	42.6	37.5	41.9	43.8	40.6	36.5
1980	39.0	39.7	38.1	40.1	35.4	42.2	37.1	41.5	41.8	40.0	36.7
1981	39.2	39.7	38.8	39.6	35.7	42.5	37.3	41.6	43.2	40.3	36.7
1982	38.4	39.4	37.8	37.5	34.7	41.8	37.1	40.9	43.9	39.6	35.6
1983	39.4	39.5	37.4	40.4	36.2	42.6	37.6	41.6	43.9	41.2	36.8
1984	39.7	39.8	38.9	39.9	36.4	43.1	37.9	41.9	43.7	41.7	36.8
1985	39.6	40.0	37.2	39.7	36.4	43.1	37.8	41.9	43.0	41.1	37.2
1986	39.9	40.0	37.4	41.1	36.7	43.2	38.0	41.9	43.8	41.4	36.9
1987	40.2	40.2	39.0	41.8	37.0	43.4	38.0	42.3	44.0	41.6	38.2
1988	40.2	40.3	39.8	41.0	37.0	43.3	38.0	42.2	44.4	41.7	37.5
1989	40.2	40.7	38.6	40.9	36.9	43.3	37.9	42.4	44.3	41.4	37.9

Note: Data include Alaska and Hawaii beginning in 1959.

Table 2-15. Average Weekly Overtime Hours of Production Workers on Manufacturing Payrolls by Industry, NAICS Basis, 1990–2004

(Number.)

Industry	1990	1991	1992	1993	1994	1995	1996	1997	1998	1999	2000	2001	2002	2003	2004
TOTAL MANUFACTURING	3.8	3.8	4.0	4.4	5.0	4.7	4.8	5.1	4.8	4.8	4.7	4.0	4.2	4.2	4.6
Total Durable Goods	3.9	3.7	3.9	4.5	5.3	5.0	5.0	5.4	5.0	5.0	4.8	3.9	4.2	4.3	4.7
Wood products	3.3	3.1	3.6	3.9	4.3	3.9	4.0	4.0	4.0	4.2	4.1	3.7	3.9	4.1	4.4
Nonmetallic mineral products	5.0	4.7	5.0	5.4	5.9	5.7	6.1	6.0	6.4	6.1	6.1	5.5	5.9	5.8	6.1
Primary metals	4.6	4.2	4.7	5.2	6.2	5.7	5.8	6.3	5.9	6.3	6.5	5.5	5.6	5.5	6.5
Fabricated metal products	3.9	3.7	3.9	4.4	5.1	4.8	4.8	5.3	4.9	4.8	4.9	4.1	4.1	4.1	4.5
Machinery	4.0	3.8	4.1	4.8	5.6	5.3	5.2	5.8	5.1	5.0	5.1	3.9	4.0	4.2	4.8
Computer and electronic products	3.8	3.8	3.9	4.3	4.8	4.9	4.7	5.2	4.8	4.6	4.6	3.2	3.4	3.8	3.6
Electrical equipment and appliances	3.0	3.0	3.2	3.7	4.2	3.5	3.7	3.9	3.6	3.6	3.7	3.0	3.1	3.4	4.0
Transportation equipment	4.5	4.3	4.3	5.5	7.0	6.5	6.7	7.2	6.4	6.1	5.5	4.5	5.1	5.0	5.5
Furniture and related products	2.3	2.2	2.7	2.9	3.3	2.8	2.9	3.3	3.6	3.9	3.5	2.7	3.4	3.5	3.6
Miscellaneous manufacturing	3.0	3.1	3.1	3.2	3.5	3.4	3.4	3.7	3.4	3.7	3.1	2.8	2.9	2.7	3.2
Total Nondurable Goods	3.8	3.9	4.1	4.2	4.5	4.3	4.4	4.6	4.5	4.6	4.4	4.1	4.2	4.1	4.4
Food manufacturing	4.1	4.1	4.2	4.2	4.5	4.4	4.4	4.6	4.8	5.0	4.8	4.6	4.6	4.4	4.7
Beverage and tobacco products	3.8	3.9	3.8	4.0	4.9	4.8	5.0	4.8	5.0	5.3	5.8	4.9	4.8	4.0	4.3
Textile mills	4.2	4.7	5.1	5.3	5.5	5.0	5.0	5.5	5.2	5.0	4.8	3.8	4.2	4.0	4.4
Textile product mills	3.0	3.1	3.2	3.8	3.9	3.4	3.8	4.1	4.1	4.1	3.5	2.7	3.3	3.2	3.0
Apparel	2.0	2.3	2.4	2.2	2.4	2.2	2.3	2.4	2.2	2.4	2.1	1.8	2.3	2.0	2.1
Leather and allied products	4.0	4.6	4.9	5.3	4.9	4.0	4.0	4.7	4.7	4.1	4.6	2.2	2.9	2.7	2.2
Paper and paper products	4.9	5.1	5.5	5.6	5.9	5.5	5.7	6.0	5.8	5.9	5.7	4.9	5.1	5.1	5.4
Printing and related support	3.6	3.4	3.7	3.9	4.3	3.8	3.8	4.2	3.9	3.6	3.7	3.4	3.4	3.2	3.4
Petroleum and coal products	6.2	6.3	6.3	6.2	6.6	6.3	6.4	6.4	6.8	6.6	6.5	7.9	7.0	8.3	8.2
Chemicals	4.9	5.1	5.3	5.3	5.6	5.6	5.7	5.8	5.6	5.2	5.0	4.6	4.7	4.5	4.9
Plastics and rubber products	3.4	3.4	3.9	4.2	4.5	3.9	4.0	4.3	4.2	4.2	3.9	3.6	3.9	3.9	4.2

Table 2-16. Average Weekly Overtime Hours of Production Workers on Manufacturing Payrolls by Industry, SIC Basis, 1956–1989

(Number.)

Year	Total manufac-turing	Durable goods												Miscella-neous manufac-turing
		Total	Lumber and wood products	Furniture and fixtures	Stone, clay, and glass products	Total	Blast furnaces and basic steel products	Fabricated metal products	Industrial machinery and equipment	Electronic and other electrical equipment	Total	Motor vehicles and equipment	Instru-ments and related products	
1956	2.8	3.0	2.6	2.3	3.3	2.8	...	3.1	3.9	...	3.1	...	...	2.8
1957	2.3	2.4	2.2	1.9	2.8	2.0	...	2.8	2.8	...	2.5	...	...	2.4
1958	2.0	1.9	2.3	2.0	2.8	1.4	0.9	2.1	1.8	...	2.1	2.3	...	1.9
1959	2.7	2.7	3.2	2.8	3.6	2.6	2.2	2.8	2.9	...	2.6	3.1	...	2.4
1960	2.5	2.4	2.9	2.5	3.1	1.8	1.3	2.6	2.7	...	2.7	3.2	...	2.1
1961	2.4	2.4	2.9	2.4	3.2	1.9	1.3	2.4	2.5	...	2.5	2.6	...	2.2
1962	2.8	2.8	3.2	2.9	3.4	2.2	1.4	2.9	3.1	...	3.5	4.1	...	2.3
1963	2.8	3.0	3.3	3.0	3.7	2.7	1.9	3.0	3.2	...	3.6	4.4	...	2.2
1964	3.1	3.3	3.4	3.2	3.9	3.2	2.4	3.4	3.9	...	3.9	5.0	...	2.4
1965	3.6	3.9	3.8	3.6	4.2	3.8	2.8	4.0	4.6	...	4.8	6.2	...	2.7
1966	3.9	4.3	4.0	3.8	4.5	4.0	2.7	4.5	5.5	...	4.7	4.9	...	3.0
1967	3.4	3.5	3.6	3.0	4.2	3.2	2.1	3.8	4.4	...	3.7	3.4	...	2.6
1968	3.6	3.8	3.9	3.4	4.5	3.8	2.9	4.1	4.0	...	4.6	5.8	...	2.5
1969	3.6	3.8	3.8	3.3	4.8	4.1	3.2	4.2	4.5	...	3.8	4.2	...	2.6
1970	3.0	3.0	3.3	2.3	4.2	3.0	2.3	3.3	3.2	...	2.9	3.2	...	2.2
1971	2.9	2.9	3.6	2.6	4.5	3.0	2.3	2.8	2.6	...	3.1	3.6	...	2.2
1972	3.5	3.6	4.0	3.1	4.8	3.6	2.6	3.5	3.8	...	4.3	5.3	...	2.7
1973	3.8	4.1	3.9	3.1	5.0	4.5	3.5	4.1	4.8	...	4.9	6.1	...	2.6
1974	3.3	3.4	3.3	2.4	4.4	3.9	3.1	3.5	4.2	...	3.4	3.5	...	2.2
1975	2.6	2.6	2.9	1.8	3.7	2.6	1.9	2.6	2.9	...	2.8	2.6	...	1.9
1976	3.1	3.2	3.5	2.0	4.1	3.3	2.5	3.2	3.3	...	4.2	5.4	...	2.2
1977	3.5	3.7	3.7	2.4	4.6	3.7	2.8	3.6	4.0	...	5.0	6.4	...	2.2
1978	3.6	3.8	3.7	2.7	4.8	4.2	3.5	3.8	4.3	...	5.0	6.1	...	2.4
1979	3.3	3.5	3.5	2.2	4.5	3.9	3.4	3.4	4.0	...	4.2	4.4	...	2.2
1980	2.8	2.8	2.8	1.7	3.8	2.8	2.2	2.8	3.4	...	3.2	2.6	...	1.9
1981	2.8	2.8	2.6	1.8	3.8	3.0	2.7	2.7	3.2	...	3.2	3.0	...	1.9
1982	2.3	2.2	2.3	1.5	3.5	2.0	1.5	2.0	2.2	...	2.7	2.5	...	1.6
1983	3.0	3.0	3.1	2.3	4.1	3.0	2.3	2.9	2.7	...	3.9	4.8	...	2.0
1984	3.4	3.6	3.2	2.5	4.8	3.9	3.1	3.6	3.7	...	4.7	5.6	...	2.2
1985	3.3	3.5	3.2	2.4	4.8	3.8	3.2	3.5	3.4	...	4.8	5.4	...	2.2
1986	3.4	3.5	3.5	2.6	4.9	4.1	3.8	3.5	3.4	...	4.3	4.4	...	2.4
1987	3.7	3.8	3.8	2.8	5.1	4.9	5.0	3.8	4.0	...	4.2	4.3	...	2.6
1988	3.9	4.1	3.6	2.7	5.2	5.5	5.8	4.1	4.4	3.4	4.7	5.2	3.0	2.5
1989	3.8	3.9	3.5	2.7	5.1	5.2	5.5	3.9	4.3	3.2	4.6	4.7	2.8	2.5

. . . = Not available.

Table 2-16. Average Weekly Overtime Hours of Production Workers on Manufacturing Payrolls by Industry, SIC Basis, 1956–1989—*Continued*

(Number.)

Year	Nondurable goods										
	Total	Food and kindred products	Tobacco products	Textile mill products	Apparel and other textile products	Paper and allied products	Printing and publishing	Chemicals and allied products	Petroleum and coal products	Rubber and miscellaneous plastics products	Leather and leather products
1956	2.4	3.1	1.3	2.6	1.0	4.5	3.1	2.1	2.2	2.2	1.4
1957	2.3	2.9	1.4	2.2	1.0	4.2	2.9	2.0	2.0	2.2	1.3
1958	2.2	3.1	1.3	2.1	1.0	3.9	2.5	1.9	1.8	2.0	1.1
1959	2.7	3.3	1.2	3.1	1.3	4.5	2.8	2.5	2.0	3.5	1.4
1960	2.5	3.3	1.0	2.6	1.2	4.1	2.9	2.3	2.0	2.4	1.2
1961	2.5	3.3	1.1	2.7	1.1	4.2	2.7	2.3	2.0	2.7	1.4
1962	2.7	3.4	1.0	3.2	1.3	4.4	2.8	2.5	2.3	3.1	1.4
1963	2.7	3.4	1.1	3.2	1.3	4.5	2.7	2.5	2.3	3.0	1.4
1964	2.9	3.6	1.6	3.6	1.3	4.7	2.9	2.7	2.5	3.5	1.7
1965	3.2	3.8	1.1	4.2	1.4	5.0	3.1	3.0	2.8	4.1	1.8
1966	3.4	4.0	1.4	4.4	1.5	5.5	3.5	3.3	3.2	4.4	2.1
1967	3.1	4.0	1.8	3.7	1.3	5.0	3.2	3.0	3.5	4.0	1.9
1968	3.3	4.1	1.8	4.1	1.4	5.3	3.1	3.3	3.6	4.2	2.1
1969	3.4	4.2	1.4	3.9	1.3	5.5	3.4	3.4	3.9	4.2	1.8
1970	3.0	4.0	1.7	3.3	1.1	4.6	2.8	3.1	3.8	3.4	1.7
1971	3.0	3.8	1.7	3.8	1.2	4.6	2.6	3.1	3.7	3.3	1.9
1972	3.3	4.0	1.6	4.5	1.5	4.9	2.9	3.2	3.8	4.0	2.3
1973	3.4	4.1	2.4	4.4	1.5	5.2	3.0	3.5	3.9	4.3	2.1
1974	3.0	4.1	2.1	3.3	1.2	4.6	2.7	3.3	3.9	3.5	1.8
1975	2.7	3.9	2.0	3.1	1.2	4.0	2.2	2.7	3.0	2.9	1.9
1976	3.0	4.1	1.3	3.4	1.3	4.8	2.5	3.2	3.5	3.6	1.9
1977	3.2	4.1	1.9	3.5	1.3	4.8	2.8	3.4	4.0	3.7	1.8
1978	3.2	4.0	2.1	3.6	1.3	5.1	3.0	3.5	4.3	3.7	1.8
1979	3.1	4.0	1.3	3.5	1.0	4.8	2.8	3.5	4.3	3.1	1.4
1980	2.8	3.8	1.7	3.2	1.0	4.3	2.5	3.1	3.7	2.7	1.5
1981	2.8	3.7	2.0	3.0	1.1	4.5	2.4	3.3	3.8	3.1	1.4
1982	2.5	3.6	1.4	2.2	1.0	4.1	2.3	2.8	3.9	2.7	1.2
1983	3.0	3.6	1.2	3.5	1.3	4.6	2.6	3.1	4.0	3.5	1.4
1984	3.1	3.8	1.4	3.2	1.4	4.9	2.8	3.4	4.2	3.9	1.4
1985	3.1	3.8	1.1	3.2	1.4	4.7	2.7	3.3	4.2	3.6	1.5
1986	3.3	3.9	1.4	4.0	1.6	4.8	2.9	3.6	4.5	3.8	1.5
1987	3.6	4.1	2.8	4.4	1.8	5.2	3.1	4.0	5.0	4.1	2.2
1988	3.6	4.2	2.6	4.0	1.8	5.0	3.1	4.1	5.5	4.1	2.0
1989	3.6	4.4	2.1	4.0	1.9	4.5	3.0	4.2	5.8	3.8	2.0

Note: Data include Alaska and Hawaii beginning in 1959.

Table 2-17. Indexes of Aggregate Weekly Hours of Production or Nonsupervisory Workers on Private Nonfarm Payrolls by Super Sector, NAICS Basis, 1990–2004

(2002 = 100.)

Industry	1990	1991	1992	1993	1994	1995	1996	1997	1998	1999	2000	2001	2002	2003	2004
TOTAL PRIVATE	84.4	82.6	83.1	85.5	89.2	91.6	93.8	97.1	99.4	101.5	103.6	102.1	100.0	98.7	100.3
Goods–Producing	106.1	100.1	98.7	100.8	105.6	106.8	108.1	111.2	112.3	112.6	113.1	106.6	100.0	95.8	96.8
Natural resources and mining	128.6	123.8	113.3	110.3	111.0	110.2	112.7	117.6	112.8	102.9	105.1	108.3	100.0	97.4	104.1
Construction	78.8	70.1	67.5	71.3	77.3	79.9	84.3	88.6	93.4	99.7	104.0	103.2	100.0	98.4	101.5
Manufacturing	117.7	112.8	112.4	113.9	118.3	119.0	118.8	121.4	121.0	118.9	117.7	108.1	100.0	94.5	94.4
Private Service–Providing	78.3	77.8	78.8	81.2	84.6	87.3	89.7	93.1	95.8	98.4	101.0	100.8	100.0	99.5	101.2
Trade, transportation, and utilities	89.5	87.4	87.3	89.0	92.7	95.1	96.6	98.8	100.3	101.9	103.5	101.5	100.0	98.6	99.4
Wholesale trade	94.9	93.3	92.4	92.4	95.8	99.2	100.7	103.4	104.8	106.2	107.1	102.9	100.0	98.0	98.7
Retail trade	87.5	84.8	85.1	86.3	89.8	92.3	93.7	95.9	97.2	99.5	101.3	100.5	100.0	98.9	99.3
Transportation and warehousing	83.5	82.4	82.7	88.4	93.8	95.6	98.3	101.0	102.7	103.2	105.6	102.8	100.0	98.8	101.9
Utilities	124.3	123.5	121.6	119.9	117.1	112.9	108.6	106.1	105.8	105.0	104.2	102.4	100.0	97.4	95.3
Information	76.2	76.1	76.5	78.0	79.2	82.5	86.9	90.4	92.6	98.5	104.9	106.6	100.0	97.0	99.0
Financial activities	84.5	83.3	83.5	85.9	88.0	87.8	89.8	92.6	96.5	98.0	98.5	99.5	100.0	101.5	102.1
Professional and business services ...	68.1	66.7	68.4	71.9	77.0	81.2	85.2	91.5	96.7	101.7	106.6	104.0	100.0	98.7	101.9
Educational and health services	67.2	70.2	72.9	75.4	78.3	81.2	83.4	86.7	88.9	90.6	92.8	96.6	100.0	101.4	103.3
Leisure and hospitality	78.9	77.3	79.3	82.2	85.6	88.5	90.8	93.4	95.5	97.9	100.6	100.7	100.0	100.1	102.9
Other services	81.8	81.2	80.6	82.8	84.5	87.1	89.1	91.9	94.3	96.3	97.8	99.1	100.0	97.5	96.5

Table 2-18. Indexes of Aggregate Weekly Hours of Production or Nonsupervisory Workers on Private Nonfarm Payrolls by Industry, SIC Basis, 1947–1989

(1982 = 100.)

Year	Total private	Goods–producing						Service–producing					
		Total	Mining	Construc-tion	Manufacturing			Total	Transpor-tation and public utilities	Wholesale trade	Retail trade	Finance, insurance, and real estate	Services
					Total	Durable goods	Nondur-able goods						
1947	. . .	98.0	101.4	62.0	105.8	99.2	114.9	. . .	. . .	56.8	. . .	. . .	. . .
1948	. . .	97.8	101.9	67.6	104.2	97.4	113.8	. . .	. . .	59.5	. . .	. . .	. . .
1949	. . .	88.2	86.8	66.7	93.0	84.0	105.6	. . .	. . .	59.0	. . .	. . .	. . .
1950	. . .	96.1	88.3	71.3	102.2	96.0	110.8	. . .	. . .	59.7	. . .	. . .	. . .
1951	. . .	103.7	91.9	81.0	109.6	108.0	111.7	. . .	. . .	61.7	. . .	. . .	. . .
1952	. . .	103.9	88.2	83.3	109.6	108.9	110.6	. . .	. . .	63.3	. . .	. . .	. . .
1953	. . .	107.3	84.8	80.5	114.8	116.9	112.0	. . .	. . .	63.7	. . .	. . .	. . .
1954	. . .	96.8	75.5	78.2	102.4	100.5	105.3	. . .	. . .	63.1	. . .	. . .	. . .
1955	. . .	103.0	78.9	83.4	109.0	108.5	109.8	. . .	. . .	64.4	. . .	. . .	. . .
1956	. . .	104.7	81.5	90.2	109.5	109.5	109.5	. . .	. . .	65.9	. . .	. . .	. . .
1957	. . .	101.1	79.6	86.6	105.9	105.8	106.0	. . .	. . .	65.4	. . .	. . .	. . .
1958	. . .	90.9	67.9	80.8	94.8	90.4	100.9	. . .	. . .	63.6	. . .	. . .	. . .
1959	. . .	97.8	68.1	86.7	102.3	99.6	106.1	. . .	. . .	66.4	. . .	. . .	. . .
1960	. . .	95.8	65.7	83.2	100.7	98.1	104.4	. . .	. . .	67.3	. . .	. . .	. . .
1961	. . .	92.4	61.5	81.4	97.0	92.8	103.0	. . .	. . .	66.8	. . .	. . .	. . .
1962	. . .	96.3	59.8	83.9	101.6	98.8	105.6	. . .	. . .	68.1	. . .	. . .	. . .
1963	. . .	97.4	59.1	86.8	102.4	100.6	105.0	. . .	. . .	68.8	. . .	. . .	. . .
1964	75.8	99.7	59.4	89.1	104.9	104.1	106.1	65.1	87.7	70.6	73.2	60.4	51.9
1965	79.1	105.6	59.6	93.4	111.5	112.7	109.9	67.3	89.9	73.3	75.9	61.4	54.0
1966	82.5	112.0	59.3	96.3	119.2	122.7	114.4	69.3	91.7	75.7	77.6	62.8	56.4
1967	82.9	109.8	57.0	93.8	117.1	119.8	113.3	70.8	92.1	76.5	78.3	64.8	58.9
1968	84.9	111.7	56.0	95.6	119.2	121.7	115.7	72.8	93.4	77.7	80.1	67.8	61.3
1969	87.7	114.5	57.9	103.6	121.0	124.2	116.5	75.7	96.3	80.6	82.6	71.6	64.2
1970	86.3	107.8	57.6	101.3	112.8	113.0	112.4	76.7	96.9	81.7	83.4	73.0	65.3
1971	85.8	105.0	54.9	103.6	108.8	107.4	110.8	77.2	95.1	80.4	85.3	74.3	65.6
1972	89.2	110.5	57.8	107.9	114.8	115.4	114.1	79.6	97.3	82.5	88.2	76.5	68.0
1973	93.2	116.9	58.8	113.7	121.7	125.8	116.0	82.5	99.9	85.6	90.9	78.9	71.3
1974	93.2	113.7	63.4	109.5	118.1	122.4	112.1	84.0	100.4	87.6	91.0	79.8	73.9
1975	88.8	99.9	68.3	92.7	103.8	104.9	102.1	83.9	94.6	86.4	90.6	79.9	76.0
1976	92.3	105.4	71.5	94.0	110.3	111.9	108.1	86.4	95.5	89.1	93.9	81.5	78.8
1977	96.0	110.3	76.5	100.2	115.0	118.4	110.2	89.5	97.9	92.5	96.5	85.4	82.0
1978	100.7	116.5	79.0	112.2	120.1	125.9	112.0	93.6	101.3	97.7	100.0	90.3	86.3
1979	104.0	119.9	88.2	119.9	122.1	129.1	112.3	96.9	104.9	102.0	101.5	94.4	90.2
1980	102.8	112.9	94.1	115.1	113.8	117.8	108.1	98.3	104.1	101.9	100.1	97.8	94.3
1981	104.1	111.6	104.8	109.3	112.5	116.1	107.6	100.8	103.3	103.3	100.6	105.5	98.2
1982	100.0	100.0	100.0	100.0	100.0	100.0	100.0	100.0	100.0	100.0	100.0	100.0	100.0
1983	101.5	100.5	81.5	102.2	101.4	100.7	102.4	102.0	97.3	99.9	102.7	101.6	103.6
1984	107.7	109.0	84.9	116.8	109.0	111.5	105.5	107.1	102.8	105.3	108.2	106.4	108.2
1985	110.5	108.7	81.4	125.3	106.9	109.5	103.4	111.3	104.6	108.4	111.7	110.9	114.0
1986	112.3	107.3	65.7	128.2	105.7	106.8	104.2	114.6	104.0	108.5	114.3	116.7	119.2
1987	115.6	109.0	61.8	132.7	107.0	107.4	106.6	118.5	106.5	109.4	117.9	120.1	124.9
1988	119.3	111.4	61.7	136.9	109.3	110.5	107.7	122.8	108.2	113.3	121.0	119.2	132.2
1989	122.1	111.7	60.5	138.9	109.3	110.1	108.2	126.8	111.1	116.1	122.9	119.5	139.3

Note: Data include Alaska and Hawaii beginning in 1959.

. . . = Not available.

Table 2-19. Indexes of Aggregate Weekly Hours of Production Workers on Manufacturing Payrolls by Industry, NAICS Basis, 1990–2004

(2002 = 100.)

Industry	1990	1991	1992	1993	1994	1995	1996	1997	1998	1999	2000	2001	2002	2003	2004
DURABLE GOODS															
Total	114.2	107.6	106.4	108.2	114.2	116.3	117.5	121.6	122.0	120.6	120.4	109.3	100.0	94.3	95.1
Wood products	101.5	92.6	95.2	100.5	109.1	109.3	111.6	114.8	117.5	118.6	115.8	105.0	100.0	97.8	100.6
Nonmetallic mineral products	100.8	92.8	92.6	94.2	98.8	99.7	101.5	103.2	105.8	106.9	109.1	106.1	100.0	94.3	97.9
Primary metals	131.5	122.9	120.8	121.4	128.0	129.3	129.9	132.3	131.1	128.4	128.9	113.0	100.0	93.4	93.2
Fabricated metal products	104.7	99.1	97.3	99.7	106.3	109.9	111.6	116.6	118.6	116.7	119.1	109.3	100.0	95.3	97.8
Machinery	123.9	116.3	113.9	118.6	127.0	132.3	133.8	139.0	137.4	129.9	127.6	114.1	100.0	93.6	95.9
Computer and electronic products	137.2	128.1	122.9	121.1	123.5	127.1	129.9	136.8	136.7	131.1	133.0	117.9	100.0	92.1	90.0
Electrical equipment and appliances	136.0	128.0	125.9	126.8	132.5	130.3	129.4	127.7	127.8	128.3	127.8	113.4	100.0	92.0	89.1
Transportation equipment	111.1	105.8	104.4	105.5	112.6	115.4	116.4	120.7	118.7	119.5	116.4	105.3	100.0	95.4	96.3
Furniture and related products	97.2	89.5	92.1	95.3	100.5	99.3	98.3	102.9	108.5	112.6	114.8	104.8	100.0	93.0	94.1
Miscellaneous manufacturing	104.0	103.8	105.2	106.9	108.2	107.7	107.7	110.0	110.3	110.3	109.5	104.8	100.0	93.6	91.8
NONDURABLE GOODS															
Total	123.0	120.8	121.7	122.6	124.7	123.1	120.5	120.9	119.4	116.1	113.3	106.0	100.0	94.7	93.0
Food manufacturing	96.2	96.6	97.3	98.7	100.5	101.6	101.8	102.6	103.4	103.8	103.5	101.5	100.0	98.4	97.4
Beverage and tobacco products	96.9	96.4	95.4	95.6	98.7	97.9	101.4	103.1	104.9	104.7	104.2	100.3	100.0	88.4	88.7
Textile mills	170.4	168.4	170.3	170.8	171.6	163.5	154.1	155.2	148.9	139.1	132.4	112.2	100.0	86.3	79.5
Textile product mills	110.3	104.5	106.0	110.6	116.6	114.4	112.8	114.8	114.1	113.5	111.1	105.0	100.0	92.9	92.0
Apparel	267.4	264.2	267.5	259.4	252.6	235.4	211.9	201.4	181.2	154.7	137.4	117.1	100.0	81.9	75.0
Leather and allied products	290.0	268.9	263.5	259.1	246.9	221.8	197.5	187.1	166.6	148.3	138.4	113.3	100.0	91.3	85.9
Paper and paper products	121.8	120.6	121.7	121.9	123.5	121.4	120.1	121.5	119.5	117.1	113.4	106.6	100.0	92.4	89.9
Printing and related support	122.3	118.7	118.4	120.3	123.8	123.9	122.8	124.6	124.3	120.9	119.4	111.5	100.0	95.3	93.7
Petroleum and coal products	128.9	127.5	126.0	122.0	120.0	115.5	113.5	112.7	113.4	107.6	105.8	105.6	100.0	98.7	103.6
Chemicals	118.2	115.0	112.9	113.4	115.1	115.4	114.7	114.6	115.4	113.1	110.4	104.7	100.0	98.9	98.9
Plastics and rubber products	97.7	94.2	98.1	102.4	108.8	109.9	110.1	112.7	113.8	114.6	114.3	105.0	100.0	95.2	94.3

Table 2-20. Indexes of Aggregate Weekly Hours of Production Workers on Manufacturing Payrolls by Industry, SIC Basis, 1947–1989

(1982 = 100.)

Year	Durable goods												
	Total	Lumber and wood products	Furniture and fixtures	Stone, clay, and glass products	Primary metal industries		Fabricated metal products	Industrial machinery and equipment	Electronic and other electrical equipment	Transportation equipment		Instruments and related products	Miscellaneous manufacturing industries
					Total	Blast furnaces and basic steel products				Total	Motor vehicles and equipment		
1947	99.2	173.6	92.0	110.4	161.7	201.2	89.1	83.9	. . .	94.3	120.4	. . .	140.1
1948	97.4	167.0	93.3	111.7	163.5	210.8	87.0	82.4	. . .	92.6	119.5	. . .	139.1
1949	84.0	146.9	82.0	100.4	135.0	180.8	74.9	66.3	. . .	88.3	117.7	. . .	121.9
1950	96.0	162.4	99.2	111.1	159.7	210.1	88.8	72.5	. . .	97.4	137.5	. . .	131.8
1951	108.0	167.4	94.5	120.2	177.4	227.4	98.4	91.4	. . .	115.6	132.9	. . .	132.1
1952	108.9	158.2	94.7	112.7	160.7	194.4	97.7	93.1	. . .	130.8	123.8	. . .	127.3
1953	116.9	152.8	96.7	115.3	174.6	225.7	107.8	93.6	. . .	151.5	149.9	. . .	136.0
1954	100.5	139.1	86.3	107.6	143.5	185.5	94.1	79.5	. . .	127.4	120.5	. . .	121.6
1955	108.5	147.5	95.1	117.5	167.3	219.8	100.9	83.7	. . .	138.7	151.2	. . .	125.2
1956	109.5	143.1	96.1	119.2	168.7	216.3	100.2	91.4	. . .	130.8	123.1	. . .	125.4
1957	105.8	126.3	93.5	113.9	161.0	210.7	100.6	87.5	. . .	131.7	118.7	. . .	117.6
1958	90.4	118.9	87.9	104.8	129.1	163.7	88.5	70.2	. . .	104.4	86.8	. . .	110.5
1959	99.6	132.0	97.7	117.0	140.2	169.3	95.6	79.4	. . .	111.4	106.5	. . .	117.6
1960	98.1	123.1	95.4	114.1	141.4	181.1	95.0	79.2	. . .	106.8	111.4	. . .	116.4
1961	92.8	115.2	90.9	109.3	132.0	166.9	90.2	74.5	. . .	96.4	92.8	. . .	113.0
1962	98.8	118.5	97.5	112.0	137.4	167.5	96.5	80.7	. . .	106.6	110.0	. . .	117.1
1963	100.6	120.2	99.2	114.6	141.7	172.7	99.2	82.5	. . .	111.2	118.5	. . .	115.7
1964	104.1	122.8	103.8	117.9	153.0	190.6	102.8	88.5	. . .	111.5	120.3	. . .	118.3
1965	112.7	125.3	111.1	121.2	163.2	199.1	110.8	97.6	. . .	125.0	140.5	. . .	126.0
1966	122.7	126.9	118.8	124.4	168.4	195.2	122.1	109.6	. . .	136.7	138.4	. . .	130.3
1967	119.8	121.5	113.5	119.1	158.1	184.0	124.2	108.5	. . .	133.2	123.4	. . .	125.6
1968	121.7	124.8	118.6	121.9	158.1	186.1	128.8	105.2	. . .	141.7	141.6	. . .	126.1
1969	124.2	126.5	121.5	126.4	165.1	190.5	132.6	109.4	. . .	138.5	142.4	. . .	126.5
1970	113.0	117.9	111.6	120.9	152.9	179.5	120.3	101.2	. . .	114.1	117.7	. . .	119.8
1971	107.4	123.8	114.0	122.2	140.5	161.5	113.2	89.5	. . .	112.6	130.3	. . .	116.2
1972	115.4	136.1	126.6	131.1	146.3	165.1	121.9	97.8	. . .	118.4	140.5	. . .	126.2
1973	125.8	140.6	132.0	138.4	161.8	181.5	131.8	111.8	. . .	129.1	158.5	. . .	130.9
1974	122.4	128.2	123.4	134.5	162.4	180.7	127.4	116.1	. . .	117.9	134.9	. . .	128.8
1975	104.9	107.8	100.7	115.6	134.3	151.8	108.4	101.6	. . .	106.8	117.3	. . .	112.5
1976	111.9	123.5	111.0	120.8	140.0	155.6	115.3	102.6	. . .	117.9	141.2	. . .	120.1
1977	118.4	132.0	117.2	125.9	144.2	157.2	121.9	109.8	. . .	125.6	156.0	. . .	122.2
1978	125.9	138.3	125.6	132.1	151.3	164.6	129.3	119.4	. . .	133.6	163.3	. . .	125.9
1979	129.1	138.6	123.5	132.8	154.8	167.0	131.4	126.9	. . .	134.1	151.8	. . .	123.8
1980	117.8	119.9	112.4	119.8	133.4	139.8	119.8	122.1	. . .	114.6	111.0	. . .	113.9
1981	116.1	115.1	112.7	114.1	132.5	141.9	117.1	120.2	. . .	114.2	115.7	. . .	110.5
1982	100.0	100.0	100.0	100.0	100.0	100.0	100.0	100.0	. . .	100.0	100.0	. . .	100.0
1983	100.7	117.7	110.3	103.2	95.2	90.8	100.3	90.1	. . .	105.7	118.9	. . .	98.1
1984	111.5	126.3	121.6	109.5	102.9	93.7	111.0	103.8	. . .	118.9	140.2	. . .	102.9
1985	109.5	124.9	121.9	108.1	96.1	85.3	111.2	101.0	. . .	122.7	143.6	. . .	97.8
1986	106.8	129.2	124.2	108.7	89.8	78.2	107.8	94.7	. . .	123.3	137.7	. . .	97.5
1987	107.4	134.9	129.5	109.7	91.8	79.0	107.1	93.8	. . .	124.3	137.2	. . .	99.9
1988	110.5	135.6	130.1	113.3	97.2	85.1	110.5	98.8	113.1	125.8	140.0	89.9	103.5
1989	110.1	132.6	129.6	113.5	96.0	83.9	110.6	100.3	111.5	125.3	138.0	89.6	103.0

Note: Data include Alaska and Hawaii beginning in 1959.

. . . = Not available.

Table 2-20. Indexes of Aggregate Weekly Hours of Production Workers on Manufacturing Payrolls by Industry, SIC Basis, 1947–1989—Continued

(1982 = 100.)

Year	Nondurable goods										
	Total	Food and kindred products	Tobacco products	Textile mill products	Apparel and other textile products	Paper and allied products	Printing and publishing	Chemicals and allied products	Petroleum and coal products	Rubber and miscellaneous plastics products	Leather and leather products
1947	114.9	136.0	212.3	200.9	110.6	84.8	75.6	82.2	131.0	52.6	221.8
1948	113.8	131.3	202.2	203.3	112.7	84.6	75.0	81.6	135.3	50.0	211.2
1949	105.6	126.6	186.4	172.6	109.4	78.6	73.1	74.7	129.7	43.8	195.8
1950	110.8	125.7	178.9	192.5	114.0	87.1	74.2	77.6	127.7	51.7	205.0
1951	111.7	127.1	182.8	184.8	113.0	90.9	75.8	84.7	133.9	55.2	193.1
1952	110.6	125.7	184.8	174.5	115.8	87.5	76.6	84.6	130.0	55.0	203.0
1953	112.0	124.5	180.5	172.9	118.2	92.3	78.5	87.6	134.0	57.8	202.2
1954	105.3	120.7	177.2	151.7	109.1	90.4	78.0	83.9	129.1	51.1	188.4
1955	109.8	120.8	180.7	160.3	115.9	94.6	81.0	87.0	127.0	59.8	200.0
1956	109.5	121.2	173.0	155.6	114.9	96.3	84.0	88.2	125.6	58.5	196.9
1957	106.0	116.3	162.2	144.3	112.4	94.9	83.9	86.7	121.6	58.4	190.4
1958	100.9	112.3	162.7	133.7	107.2	92.1	82.6	82.1	114.3	51.6	179.3
1959	106.1	112.8	162.2	144.1	116.3	97.7	85.4	85.6	109.5	59.4	193.6
1960	104.4	111.5	157.6	137.1	114.3	97.9	87.4	86.0	107.7	58.0	181.9
1961	103.0	109.8	153.7	133.4	112.1	98.4	87.3	85.3	101.9	57.5	181.6
1962	105.6	108.8	150.4	137.0	119.4	100.2	87.9	88.1	99.2	63.7	184.4
1963	105.0	107.8	146.5	133.8	120.7	100.7	87.2	89.2	94.9	64.8	177.2
1964	106.1	107.0	150.8	136.1	122.1	101.3	89.4	89.9	90.9	68.2	177.7
1965	109.9	107.4	140.3	143.4	128.7	104.0	92.4	93.5	90.6	75.0	182.0
1966	114.4	109.5	138.2	149.5	133.2	109.0	96.8	98.6	92.4	81.3	188.8
1967	113.3	109.4	141.0	144.4	130.8	109.1	97.9	100.6	93.0	79.7	178.0
1968	115.7	109.5	134.8	150.6	131.3	111.4	98.5	104.1	95.4	87.0	180.0
1969	116.5	110.5	128.8	150.0	130.5	114.6	100.9	106.2	90.9	91.6	168.1
1970	112.4	110.2	129.2	141.8	123.9	110.2	98.9	102.5	96.2	86.3	156.4
1971	110.8	109.3	118.7	141.3	122.9	106.4	95.3	99.8	100.9	87.5	148.7
1972	114.1	108.7	115.9	148.9	127.8	110.3	96.5	100.9	101.5	97.8	150.7
1973	116.0	106.3	124.0	150.7	131.7	112.7	97.4	104.2	99.9	107.9	142.3
1974	112.1	106.0	120.9	138.5	121.3	111.2	95.5	105.7	100.9	105.8	131.8
1975	102.1	101.8	118.1	122.9	110.2	96.8	88.9	97.1	96.3	89.0	121.3
1976	108.1	104.4	118.2	133.3	119.3	104.7	90.3	102.0	102.3	96.1	130.6
1977	110.2	104.6	106.8	132.9	117.9	107.6	94.1	105.0	106.6	109.2	123.9
1978	112.0	105.1	106.1	131.6	119.5	109.0	97.5	107.4	112.2	115.3	125.5
1979	112.3	107.0	104.4	129.3	115.6	110.5	101.0	108.3	114.0	118.2	117.1
1980	108.1	105.1	101.2	122.7	112.2	106.9	100.1	106.0	99.1	106.7	110.7
1981	107.6	102.8	105.1	117.3	111.0	106.8	100.6	106.8	110.0	109.0	113.6
1982	100.0	100.0	100.0	100.0	100.0	100.0	100.0	100.0	100.0	100.0	100.0
1983	102.4	99.1	96.3	107.4	104.5	102.1	103.3	98.3	98.4	107.2	96.8
1984	105.5	100.3	93.5	107.0	107.2	106.8	110.9	99.8	92.5	119.6	89.3
1985	103.4	100.6	88.4	100.1	100.7	106.8	114.9	98.9	88.7	117.6	78.1
1986	104.2	101.7	81.6	103.8	99.7	106.9	119.6	97.3	88.1	119.6	69.5
1987	106.6	103.7	80.1	109.4	100.1	108.5	123.2	99.3	89.4	123.1	70.3
1988	107.7	105.0	80.1	107.7	99.0	108.9	126.7	102.9	88.1	127.3	67.9
1989	108.2	107.8	70.6	105.6	98.3	109.9	126.2	104.5	85.7	129.6	66.4

Note: Data include Alaska and Hawaii beginning in 1959.

EARNINGS

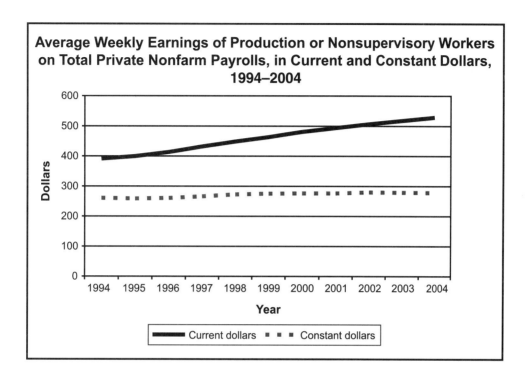

Average Weekly Earnings of Production or Nonsupervisory Workers on Total Private Nonfarm Payrolls, in Current and Constant Dollars, 1994–2004

While average weekly earnings of production and non-supervisory workers rose 2.2 percent in 2004, real earnings actually declined slightly as consumer prices rose 2.7 percent. Real earnings have been virtually flat since 1999. (Table 2-25)

OTHER HIGHLIGHTS:

• Real earnings remained flat or declined in almost all major industry sectors in 2004. This was true for construction, which showed a significant increase in employment. Natural resources and mining was the only major industry in which real earnings increased by more than 2 percent; however, this industry has seen a 1.5 percent decrease in its overall real earnings since 1999. Educational and health services have experienced the largest increase, 7.4 percent, over the past 5 years. (Table 2-25)

• Although Michigan and Washington state had among the highest average hourly earnings for manufacturing production workers in 2004, they suffered from higher than average unemployment. (Table 2-36)

• Average weekly earnings for production and nonsupervisory workers ranged from $228.63 in leisure and hospitality to $1048.52 in utilities. The average for all private industries was $528.56, with workers in goods-producing industries earning nearly 40 percent more than those in service-providing industries. (Table 2-25)

Table 2-21. Average Hourly Earnings of Production or Nonsupervisory Workers on Private Nonfarm Payrolls by Super Sector, NAICS Basis, 1990–2004

(Dollars.)

Industry	1990	1991	1992	1993	1994	1995	1996	1997	1998	1999	2000	2001	2002	2003	2004
TOTAL PRIVATE	10.19	10.50	10.76	11.03	11.32	11.64	12.03	12.49	13.00	13.47	14.00	14.53	14.95	15.35	15.67
Goods–Producing	11.46	11.76	11.99	12.28	12.63	12.96	13.38	13.82	14.23	14.71	15.27	15.78	16.33	16.80	17.19
Natural resources and mining	13.40	13.82	14.09	14.12	14.41	14.78	15.10	15.57	16.20	16.33	16.55	17.00	17.19	17.56	18.08
Construction	13.42	13.65	13.81	14.04	14.38	14.73	15.11	15.67	16.23	16.80	17.48	18.00	18.52	18.95	19.23
Manufacturing	10.78	11.13	11.40	11.70	12.04	12.34	12.75	13.14	13.45	13.85	14.32	14.76	15.29	15.74	16.14
Private Service–Providing	9.71	10.05	10.33	10.60	10.87	11.19	11.57	12.05	12.59	13.07	13.60	14.16	14.56	14.96	15.26
Trade, transportation, and utilities	9.83	10.08	10.30	10.55	10.80	11.10	11.46	11.90	12.39	12.82	13.31	13.70	14.02	14.34	14.59
Wholesale trade	11.58	11.95	12.21	12.57	12.93	13.34	13.80	14.41	15.07	15.62	16.28	16.77	16.98	17.36	17.66
Retail trade	7.71	7.89	8.12	8.36	8.61	8.85	9.21	9.59	10.05	10.45	10.86	11.29	11.67	11.90	12.08
Transportation and warehousing	12.50	12.61	12.77	12.71	12.84	13.18	13.45	13.78	14.12	14.55	15.05	15.33	15.76	16.25	16.53
Utilities	16.14	16.70	17.17	17.95	18.66	19.19	19.78	20.59	21.48	22.03	22.75	23.58	23.96	24.77	25.62
Information	13.40	13.90	14.29	14.86	15.32	15.68	16.30	17.14	17.67	18.40	19.07	19.80	20.20	21.01	21.42
Financial activities	9.99	10.42	10.86	11.36	11.82	12.28	12.71	13.22	13.93	14.47	14.98	15.59	16.17	17.14	17.53
Professional and business services	11.14	11.50	11.78	11.96	12.15	12.53	13.00	13.57	14.27	14.85	15.52	16.33	16.81	17.21	17.46
Educational and health services	10.00	10.49	10.87	11.21	11.50	11.80	12.17	12.56	13.00	13.44	13.95	14.64	15.21	15.64	16.16
Leisure and hospitality	5.88	6.06	6.20	6.32	6.46	6.62	6.82	7.13	7.48	7.76	8.11	8.35	8.58	8.76	8.91
Other services	9.08	9.39	9.66	9.90	10.18	10.51	10.85	11.29	11.79	12.26	12.73	13.27	13.72	13.84	13.98

Table 2-22. Average Hourly Earnings of Production or Nonsupervisory Workers on Private Nonfarm Payrolls by Industry, SIC Basis, 1947–1989

(Dollars.)

| Year | Total private | Mining | Construction | Manufacturing | | | Transport-ation and public utilities | Wholesale trade | Retail trade | Finance, insurance, and real estate | Services |
				Total	Durable goods	Nondurable goods					
1947	1.13	1.47	1.54	1.22	1.28	1.15	. . .	1.22	0.84	1.14	. . .
1948	1.23	1.66	1.71	1.33	1.39	1.25	. . .	1.31	0.90	1.20	. . .
1949	1.28	1.72	1.79	1.38	1.45	1.30	. . .	1.36	0.95	1.26	. . .
1950	1.34	1.77	1.86	1.44	1.45	1.30	. . .	1.36	0.98	1.26	. . .
1951	1.45	1.93	2.02	1.56	1.65	1.45	. . .	1.52	1.06	1.45	. . .
1952	1.52	2.01	2.13	1.64	1.74	1.51	. . .	1.61	1.09	1.51	. . .
1953	1.61	2.14	2.28	1.74	1.85	1.58	. . .	1.69	1.16	1.58	. . .
1954	1.65	2.14	2.38	1.78	1.89	1.62	. . .	1.76	1.20	1.65	. . .
1955	1.71	2.20	2.45	1.85	1.98	1.68	. . .	1.83	1.25	1.70	. . .
1956	1.80	2.33	2.57	1.95	2.08	1.77	. . .	1.93	1.30	1.78	. . .
1957	1.89	2.45	2.71	2.04	2.18	1.85	. . .	2.02	1.37	1.84	. . .
1958	1.95	2.47	2.82	2.10	2.25	1.92	. . .	2.09	1.42	1.89	. . .
1959	2.02	2.56	2.93	2.19	2.35	1.98	. . .	2.18	1.47	1.95	. . .
1960	2.09	2.60	3.07	2.26	2.42	2.05	. . .	2.24	1.52	2.02	. . .
1961	2.14	2.64	3.20	2.32	2.48	2.11	. . .	2.31	1.56	2.09	. . .
1962	2.22	2.70	3.31	2.39	2.55	2.17	. . .	2.37	1.63	2.17	. . .
1963	2.28	2.75	3.41	2.45	2.63	2.22	. . .	2.45	1.68	2.25	. . .
1964	2.36	2.81	3.55	2.53	2.70	2.29	2.89	2.52	1.75	2.30	1.94
1965	2.46	2.92	3.70	2.61	2.78	2.36	3.03	2.60	1.82	2.39	2.05
1966	2.56	3.05	3.89	2.71	2.89	2.45	3.11	2.73	1.91	2.47	2.17
1967	2.68	3.19	4.11	2.82	2.99	2.57	3.23	2.87	2.01	2.58	2.29
1968	2.85	3.35	4.41	3.01	3.18	2.74	3.42	3.04	2.16	2.75	2.42
1969	3.04	3.60	4.79	3.19	3.38	2.91	3.63	3.23	2.30	2.93	2.61
1970	3.23	3.85	5.24	3.35	3.55	3.08	3.85	3.43	2.44	3.07	2.81
1971	3.45	4.06	5.69	3.57	3.79	3.27	4.21	3.64	2.60	3.22	3.04
1972	3.70	4.44	6.06	3.82	4.07	3.48	4.65	3.85	2.75	3.36	3.27
1973	3.94	4.75	6.41	4.09	4.35	3.70	5.02	4.07	2.91	3.53	3.47
1974	4.24	5.23	6.81	4.42	4.70	4.01	5.41	4.38	3.14	3.77	3.75
1975	4.53	5.95	7.31	4.83	5.15	4.37	5.88	4.72	3.36	4.06	4.02
1976	4.86	6.46	7.71	5.22	5.57	4.71	6.45	5.02	3.57	4.27	4.31
1977	5.25	6.94	8.10	5.68	6.06	5.11	6.99	5.39	3.85	4.54	4.65
1978	5.69	7.67	8.66	6.17	6.58	5.54	7.57	5.88	4.20	4.89	4.99
1979	6.16	8.49	9.27	6.70	7.12	6.01	8.16	6.39	4.53	5.27	5.36
1980	6.66	9.17	9.94	7.27	7.75	6.56	8.87	6.95	4.88	5.79	5.85
1981	7.25	10.04	10.82	7.99	8.53	7.19	9.70	7.55	5.25	6.31	6.41
1982	7.68	10.77	11.63	8.49	9.03	7.75	10.32	8.08	5.48	6.78	6.92
1983	8.02	11.28	11.94	8.83	9.38	8.09	10.79	8.54	5.74	7.29	7.31
1984	8.32	11.63	12.13	9.19	9.73	8.39	11.12	8.88	5.85	7.63	7.59
1985	8.57	11.98	12.32	9.54	10.09	8.72	11.40	9.15	5.94	7.94	7.90
1986	8.76	12.46	12.48	9.73	10.28	8.95	11.70	9.34	6.03	8.36	8.18
1987	8.98	12.54	12.71	9.91	10.43	9.19	12.03	9.59	6.12	8.73	8.49
1988	9.28	12.80	13.08	10.19	10.71	9.45	12.24	9.98	6.31	9.06	8.88
1989	9.66	13.26	13.54	10.48	11.01	9.75	12.57	10.39	6.53	9.53	9.38

Note: Data include Alaska and Hawaii beginning in 1959.

. . . = Not available.

Table 2-23. Average Hourly Earnings of Production Workers on Manufacturing Payrolls by Industry, NAICS Basis, 1990–2004

(Dollars.)

Industry	1990	1991	1992	1993	1994	1995	1996	1997	1998	1999	2000	2001	2002	2003	2004
DURABLE GOODS															
Total	11.40	11.81	12.09	12.41	12.78	13.05	13.45	13.83	14.07	14.46	14.93	15.38	16.02	16.45	16.82
Wood products	8.82	9.03	9.24	9.41	9.66	9.92	10.24	10.53	10.85	11.18	11.63	11.99	12.33	12.71	13.03
Nonmetallic mineral products	11.11	11.34	11.57	11.83	12.11	12.39	12.80	13.17	13.59	13.97	14.53	14.86	15.40	15.76	16.25
Primary metals	12.97	13.37	13.72	14.08	14.47	14.75	15.12	15.40	15.66	16.00	16.64	17.06	17.68	18.13	18.57
Fabricated metal products	10.64	10.97	11.16	11.40	11.64	11.91	12.26	12.64	12.97	13.34	13.77	14.19	14.68	15.01	15.31
Machinery	11.73	12.12	12.40	12.73	12.94	13.14	13.49	13.94	14.24	14.77	15.22	15.49	15.92	16.30	16.68
Computer and electronic products	10.89	11.35	11.64	11.95	12.19	12.29	12.75	13.24	13.85	14.37	14.73	15.42	16.20	16.69	17.28
Electrical equipment and appliances	10.00	10.30	10.50	10.65	10.94	11.25	11.80	12.24	12.51	12.90	13.23	13.78	13.98	14.36	14.90
Transportation equipment	14.44	15.12	15.59	16.22	16.94	17.21	17.67	18.00	17.92	18.24	18.89	19.48	20.64	21.23	21.49
Furniture and related products	8.52	8.74	9.00	9.24	9.51	9.75	10.08	10.50	10.88	11.27	11.72	12.14	12.61	12.98	13.16
Miscellaneous manufacturing	8.87	9.16	9.44	9.65	9.90	10.23	10.60	10.89	11.18	11.56	11.93	12.46	12.91	13.30	13.85
NONDURABLE GOODS															
Total	9.87	10.18	10.45	10.70	10.96	11.30	11.68	12.04	12.45	12.85	13.31	13.75	14.15	14.63	15.05
Food manufacturing	9.04	9.32	9.59	9.82	10.00	10.27	10.50	10.77	11.09	11.40	11.77	12.18	12.55	12.80	12.98
Beverage and tobacco products	13.24	13.65	14.07	14.30	14.97	15.40	15.73	16.00	16.03	16.54	17.40	17.67	17.73	17.96	19.12
Textile mills	8.17	8.49	8.82	9.12	9.35	9.63	9.88	10.22	10.58	10.90	11.23	11.40	11.73	11.99	12.13
Textile product mills	7.53	7.77	8.03	8.27	8.45	8.76	9.12	9.45	9.75	10.18	10.43	10.60	10.96	11.23	11.39
Apparel	6.22	6.43	6.60	6.74	6.95	7.22	7.45	7.76	8.05	8.35	8.60	8.82	9.10	9.56	9.75
Leather and allied products	7.18	7.43	7.68	7.88	8.23	8.50	8.94	9.31	9.68	9.93	10.35	10.69	11.00	11.66	11.63
Paper and paper products	12.06	12.45	12.78	13.13	13.49	13.94	14.38	14.76	15.20	15.58	15.91	16.38	16.85	17.33	17.90
Printing and related support	11.11	11.32	11.53	11.67	11.89	12.08	12.41	12.78	13.20	13.67	14.09	14.48	14.93	15.37	15.72
Petroleum and coal products	17.00	17.90	18.83	19.43	19.96	20.24	20.18	21.10	21.75	22.22	22.80	22.90	23.04	23.63	24.38
Chemicals	12.85	13.30	13.70	13.97	14.33	14.86	15.37	15.78	16.23	16.40	17.09	17.57	17.97	18.50	19.16
Plastics and rubber products	9.76	10.07	10.35	10.55	10.66	10.86	11.17	11.48	11.79	12.25	12.69	13.21	13.55	14.18	14.58

Table 2-24. Average Hourly Earnings of Production Workers on Manufacturing Payrolls by Industry, SIC Basis, 1947–1989

(Dollars.)

Year	Durable goods												
	Total	Lumber and wood products	Furniture and fixtures	Stone, clay, and glass products	Primary metal industries Total	Blast furnaces and basic steel products	Fabricated metal products	Industrial machinery and equipment	Electronic and other electrical equipment	Transportation equipment Total	Motor vehicles and equipment	Instruments and related products	Miscellaneous manufacturing
1947	1.28	1.09	1.10	1.19	1.39	1.44	1.27	1.34	...	1.44	1.47	...	1.11
1948	1.39	1.19	1.19	1.31	1.52	1.59	1.39	1.46	...	1.57	1.61	...	1.18
1949	1.45	1.23	1.23	1.37	1.59	1.65	1.45	1.52	...	1.64	1.70	...	1.22
1950	1.45	1.30	1.28	1.44	1.65	1.70	1.52	1.60	...	1.72	1.78	...	1.28
1951	1.65	1.41	1.39	1.54	1.81	1.90	1.64	1.75	...	1.84	1.91	...	1.36
1952	1.74	1.49	1.47	1.61	1.90	2.00	1.72	1.85	...	1.95	2.05	...	1.45
1953	1.85	1.56	1.54	1.72	2.06	2.18	1.83	1.95	...	2.05	2.14	...	1.52
1954	1.89	1.57	1.57	1.77	2.10	2.22	1.88	2.00	...	2.11	2.20	...	1.56
1955	1.98	1.62	1.62	1.86	2.24	2.39	1.96	2.08	...	2.21	2.29	...	1.61
1956	2.08	1.69	1.69	1.96	2.37	2.54	2.05	2.20	...	2.29	2.35	...	1.69
1957	2.18	1.74	1.75	2.05	2.50	2.70	2.16	2.29	...	2.39	2.46	...	1.75
1958	2.25	1.80	1.78	2.12	2.64	2.88	2.26	2.37	...	2.51	2.55	...	1.79
1959	2.35	1.87	1.83	2.22	2.77	3.06	2.35	2.48	...	2.64	2.71	...	1.84
1960	2.42	1.90	1.88	2.28	2.81	3.04	2.43	2.55	...	2.74	2.81	...	1.89
1961	2.48	1.95	1.91	2.34	2.90	3.16	2.49	2.62	...	2.80	2.86	...	1.92
1962	2.55	1.99	1.95	2.41	2.98	3.25	2.55	2.71	...	2.91	2.99	...	1.98
1963	2.63	2.05	2.00	2.48	3.04	3.31	2.61	2.78	...	3.01	3.10	...	2.03
1964	2.70	2.12	2.05	2.53	3.11	3.36	2.68	2.87	...	3.09	3.21	...	2.08
1965	2.78	2.18	2.12	2.62	3.18	3.42	2.76	2.95	...	3.21	3.34	...	2.14
1966	2.89	2.26	2.21	2.72	3.28	3.53	2.88	3.08	...	3.33	3.44	...	2.22
1967	2.99	2.38	2.33	2.82	3.34	3.57	2.98	3.19	...	3.44	3.55	...	2.35
1968	3.18	2.58	2.47	2.99	3.55	3.76	3.16	3.36	...	3.69	3.89	...	2.50
1969	3.38	2.75	2.62	3.19	3.79	4.02	3.34	3.58	...	3.89	4.10	...	2.66
1970	3.55	2.97	2.77	3.40	3.93	4.16	3.53	3.77	...	4.06	4.22	...	2.83
1971	3.79	3.18	2.90	3.67	4.23	4.49	3.77	4.02	...	4.45	4.72	...	2.97
1972	4.07	3.34	3.08	3.94	4.66	5.08	4.05	4.32	...	4.81	5.13	...	3.11
1973	4.35	3.62	3.29	4.22	5.04	5.51	4.29	4.60	...	5.15	5.46	...	3.29
1974	4.70	3.90	3.53	4.54	5.60	6.27	4.61	4.94	...	5.54	5.87	...	3.53
1975	5.15	4.28	3.78	4.92	6.18	6.94	5.05	5.37	...	6.07	6.44	...	3.81
1976	5.57	4.74	3.99	5.33	6.77	7.59	5.50	5.79	...	6.62	7.09	...	4.04
1977	6.06	5.11	4.34	5.81	7.40	8.36	5.91	6.26	...	7.29	7.85	...	4.36
1978	6.58	5.62	4.68	6.32	8.20	9.39	6.35	6.78	...	7.91	8.50	...	4.69
1979	7.12	6.08	5.06	6.85	8.98	10.41	6.85	7.32	...	8.53	9.06	...	5.03
1980	7.75	6.57	5.49	7.50	9.77	11.39	7.45	8.00	...	9.35	9.85	...	5.46
1981	8.53	7.02	5.91	8.27	10.81	12.60	8.20	8.81	...	10.39	11.02	...	5.97
1982	9.03	7.46	6.31	8.87	11.33	13.35	8.77	9.26	...	11.11	11.62	...	6.42
1983	9.38	7.82	6.62	9.27	11.35	12.89	9.12	9.56	...	11.67	12.14	...	6.81
1984	9.73	8.05	6.84	9.57	11.47	12.98	9.40	9.97	...	12.20	12.73	...	7.05
1985	10.09	8.25	7.17	9.84	11.67	13.33	9.71	10.30	...	12.71	13.39	...	7.30
1986	10.28	8.37	7.46	10.04	11.86	13.73	9.89	10.58	...	12.81	13.45	...	7.55
1987	10.43	8.43	7.67	10.25	11.94	13.77	10.01	10.73	...	12.94	13.53	...	7.76
1988	10.71	8.59	7.95	10.56	12.16	13.98	10.29	11.08	9.79	13.29	13.99	10.60	8.00
1989	11.01	8.84	8.25	10.82	12.43	14.25	10.57	11.40	10.05	13.67	14.25	10.83	8.29

. . . = Not available.

Table 2-24. Average Hourly Earnings of Production Workers on Manufacturing Payrolls by Industry, SIC Basis, 1947–1989—*Continued*

(Dollars.)

Year	Nondurable goods										
	Total	Food and kindred products	Tobacco products	Textile mill products	Apparel and other textile products	Paper and allied products	Printing and publishing	Chemicals and allied products	Petroleum and coal products	Rubber and miscellaneous plastics products	Leather and leather products
1947	1.15	1.06	0.90	1.04	1.16	1.15	1.48	1.22	1.50	1.29	1.04
1948	1.25	1.15	0.96	1.16	1.22	1.28	1.65	1.34	1.71	1.36	1.11
1949	1.30	1.21	1.00	1.18	1.21	1.33	1.77	1.42	1.80	1.41	1.12
1950	1.30	1.26	1.08	1.23	1.24	1.40	1.83	1.50	1.84	1.47	1.17
1951	1.45	1.35	1.14	1.32	1.31	1.51	1.91	1.62	1.99	1.58	1.25
1952	1.51	1.44	1.18	1.34	1.32	1.59	2.02	1.69	2.10	1.70	1.30
1953	1.58	1.53	1.25	1.36	1.35	1.67	2.11	1.81	2.22	1.79	1.35
1954	1.62	1.59	1.30	1.36	1.37	1.73	2.18	1.89	2.29	1.83	1.36
1955	1.68	1.66	1.34	1.38	1.37	1.81	2.26	1.97	2.37	1.95	1.39
1956	1.77	1.76	1.45	1.44	1.47	1.92	2.33	2.09	2.54	2.02	1.48
1957	1.85	1.85	1.53	1.49	1.51	2.02	2.40	2.20	2.66	2.11	1.52
1958	1.92	1.94	1.59	1.49	1.54	2.10	2.49	2.29	2.73	2.18	1.56
1959	1.98	2.02	1.65	1.56	1.56	2.18	2.59	2.40	2.85	2.27	1.59
1960	2.05	2.11	1.70	1.61	1.59	2.26	2.68	2.50	2.89	2.32	1.64
1961	2.11	2.17	1.78	1.63	1.64	2.34	2.75	2.58	3.01	2.38	1.68
1962	2.17	2.24	1.85	1.68	1.69	2.40	2.82	2.65	3.05	2.44	1.72
1963	2.22	2.30	1.91	1.71	1.73	2.48	2.89	2.72	3.16	2.47	1.76
1964	2.29	2.37	1.95	1.79	1.79	2.56	2.97	2.80	3.20	2.54	1.83
1965	2.36	2.44	2.09	1.87	1.83	2.65	3.06	2.89	3.28	2.61	1.88
1966	2.45	2.52	2.19	1.96	1.89	2.75	3.16	2.98	3.41	2.68	1.94
1967	2.57	2.64	2.27	2.06	2.03	2.87	3.28	3.10	3.58	2.75	2.07
1968	2.74	2.80	2.48	2.21	2.21	3.05	3.48	3.26	3.75	2.93	2.23
1969	2.91	2.96	2.62	2.35	2.31	3.24	3.69	3.47	4.00	3.08	2.36
1970	3.08	3.16	2.91	2.45	2.39	3.44	3.92	3.69	4.28	3.21	2.49
1971	3.27	3.38	3.16	2.57	2.49	3.67	4.20	3.97	4.57	3.41	2.59
1972	3.48	3.60	3.47	2.75	2.60	3.95	4.51	4.26	4.96	3.63	2.68
1973	3.70	3.85	3.76	2.95	2.76	4.20	4.75	4.51	5.28	3.84	2.79
1974	4.01	4.19	4.12	3.20	2.97	4.53	5.03	4.88	5.68	4.09	2.99
1975	4.37	4.61	4.55	3.42	3.17	5.01	5.38	5.39	6.48	4.42	3.21
1976	4.71	4.98	4.98	3.69	3.40	5.47	5.71	5.91	7.21	4.71	3.40
1977	5.11	5.37	5.54	3.99	3.62	5.96	6.12	6.43	7.83	5.21	3.61
1978	5.54	5.80	6.13	4.30	3.94	6.52	6.51	7.02	8.63	5.57	3.89
1979	6.01	6.27	6.67	4.66	4.23	7.13	6.94	7.60	9.36	6.02	4.22
1980	6.56	6.85	7.74	5.07	4.56	7.84	7.53	8.30	10.10	6.58	4.58
1981	7.19	7.44	8.88	5.52	4.97	8.60	8.19	9.12	11.38	7.22	4.99
1982	7.75	7.92	9.79	5.83	5.20	9.32	8.74	9.96	12.46	7.70	5.33
1983	8.09	8.19	10.38	6.18	5.38	9.93	9.11	10.58	13.28	8.06	5.54
1984	8.39	8.39	11.22	6.46	5.55	10.41	9.41	11.07	13.44	8.35	5.71
1985	8.72	8.57	11.96	6.70	5.73	10.83	9.71	11.56	14.06	8.60	5.83
1986	8.95	8.75	12.88	6.93	5.84	11.18	9.99	11.98	14.19	8.79	5.92
1987	9.19	8.93	14.07	7.17	5.94	11.43	10.28	12.37	14.58	8.98	6.08
1988	9.45	9.12	14.67	7.38	6.12	11.69	10.53	12.71	14.97	9.19	6.28
1989	9.75	9.38	15.31	7.67	6.35	11.96	10.88	13.09	15.41	9.46	6.59

Note: Data include Alaska and Hawaii beginning in 1959.

Table 2-25. Average Weekly Earnings of Production or Nonsupervisory Workers on Nonfarm Payrolls by Industry in Current and Constant Dollars, NAICS Basis, 1990–2004

(Dollars.)

Industry	1990	1991	1992	1993	1994	1995	1996	1997	1998	1999	2000	2001	2002	2003	2004
TOTAL PRIVATE															
Current dollars	349.29	358.06	367.83	378.40	390.73	399.53	412.74	431.25	448.04	462.49	480.41	493.20	506.07	517.30	528.56
1982 dollars	262.43	258.34	257.95	258.12	259.97	258.43	259.58	265.22	271.87	274.64	275.62	275.38	278.83	278.72	277.61
Goods–Producing															
Current dollars	459.55	471.32	482.58	498.82	519.58	528.62	546.48	568.43	580.99	599.99	621.86	630.04	651.61	669.13	688.03
1982 dollars	345.27	340.06	338.42	340.26	345.70	341.93	343.70	349.59	352.54	356.29	356.78	351.78	359.01	360.52	361.36
Natural resources and mining															
Current dollars	602.54	625.42	629.02	634.77	653.14	670.32	695.07	720.11	727.28	721.74	734.92	757.92	741.97	765.94	804.03
1982 dollars	452.70	451.24	441.11	432.99	434.56	433.58	437.15	442.87	441.31	428.59	421.64	423.18	408.80	412.68	422.28
Construction															
Current dollars	513.43	520.41	525.13	539.81	558.53	571.57	588.48	609.48	629.75	655.11	685.78	695.89	711.82	726.83	735.70
1982 dollars	385.75	375.48	368.25	368.22	371.61	369.71	370.11	374.83	382.13	389.02	393.45	388.55	392.19	391.61	386.40
Manufacturing															
Current dollars	436.16	449.73	464.43	480.80	502.12	509.26	526.55	548.22	557.12	573.17	590.65	595.19	618.75	635.99	658.53
1982 dollars	327.69	324.48	325.69	327.97	334.08	329.40	331.16	337.16	338.06	340.36	338.87	332.32	340.91	342.67	345.87
Private Service–Providing															
Current dollars	315.49	325.31	335.46	345.03	354.97	364.14	376.72	394.77	412.78	427.30	445.00	460.32	472.88	483.89	493.67
1982 dollars	237.03	234.71	235.25	235.35	236.17	235.54	236.93	242.79	250.47	253.74	255.31	257.02	260.54	260.72	259.28
Trade, transportation, and utilities															
Current dollars	331.55	339.19	348.68	359.33	370.38	378.79	390.64	407.57	423.30	434.31	449.88	459.53	471.27	481.14	488.58
1982 dollars	249.10	244.73	244.52	245.11	246.43	245.01	245.69	250.66	256.86	257.90	258.11	256.58	259.65	259.23	256.61
Wholesale trade															
Current dollars	444.48	459.27	470.51	484.46	501.17	515.14	533.29	559.39	582.21	602.77	631.40	643.45	644.38	657.29	666.93
1982 dollars	333.94	331.36	329.95	330.46	333.45	333.21	335.40	344.03	353.28	357.94	362.25	359.27	355.03	354.14	350.28
Retail trade															
Current dollars	235.62	240.15	249.63	256.89	265.77	272.56	282.76	295.97	310.34	321.63	333.38	346.16	360.81	367.15	371.15
1982 dollars	177.02	173.27	175.06	175.23	176.83	176.30	177.84	182.02	188.31	190.99	191.27	193.28	198.79	197.82	194.93
Transportation and warehousing															
Current dollars	471.72	471.12	478.02	494.36	507.27	513.37	525.60	542.55	546.86	547.97	562.31	562.70	579.75	598.41	614.90
1982 dollars	354.41	339.91	335.22	337.22	337.50	332.06	330.57	333.67	331.83	325.40	322.61	314.18	319.42	322.42	322.95
Utilities															
Current dollars	670.40	693.40	716.36	756.35	789.98	811.52	830.74	865.26	902.94	924.59	955.66	977.18	979.09	1 017.27	1 048.82
1982 dollars	503.68	500.29	502.36	515.93	525.60	524.92	522.48	532.14	547.90	549.04	548.28	545.61	539.44	548.10	550.85
Information															
Current dollars	479.50	495.20	512.01	535.25	551.28	564.98	592.68	622.40	646.52	675.32	700.89	731.11	738.17	760.81	777.42
1982 dollars	360.26	357.29	359.05	365.11	366.79	365.45	372.75	382.78	392.31	401.02	402.12	408.21	406.71	409.92	408.31
Financial activities															
Current dollars	354.65	369.57	386.01	403.02	419.20	436.12	451.49	472.37	500.95	517.57	537.37	558.02	575.51	609.08	622.99
1982 dollars	266.45	266.65	270.69	274.91	278.91	282.10	283.96	290.51	303.97	307.35	308.30	311.57	317.09	328.17	327.20
Professional and business services															
Current dollars	380.61	391.09	400.64	406.20	414.16	426.44	442.81	465.51	490.00	510.99	535.07	557.84	574.66	587.02	596.96
1982 dollars	285.96	282.17	280.95	277.08	275.56	275.83	278.50	286.29	297.33	303.44	306.98	311.47	316.62	316.28	313.53
Education and health services															
Current dollars	319.27	334.55	348.29	359.08	368.14	377.73	388.27	404.65	418.82	431.35	449.29	473.39	492.74	505.69	523.83
1982 dollars	239.87	241.38	244.24	244.94	244.94	244.33	244.19	248.86	254.14	256.15	257.77	264.32	271.48	272.46	275.12
Leisure and hospitality															
Current dollars	152.47	155.16	159.54	163.45	168.00	171.43	176.48	185.81	195.82	202.87	211.79	215.19	221.26	224.30	228.63
1982 dollars	114.55	111.95	111.88	111.49	111.78	110.89	110.99	114.27	118.82	120.47	121.51	120.15	121.91	120.85	120.08
Other services															
Current dollars	297.91	306.91	315.08	322.69	332.44	342.36	352.62	368.63	384.25	398.77	413.41	428.64	439.76	434.41	433.04
1982 dollars	223.82	221.44	220.95	220.12	221.18	221.45	221.77	226.71	233.16	236.80	237.18	239.33	242.29	234.06	227.44

Table 2-26. Average Weekly Earnings of Production or Nonsupervisory Workers on Nonfarm Payrolls by Industry in Current and Constant Dollars, SIC Basis, 1947–1989

(Dollars.)

Year	Total private		Mining		Construction		Manufacturing		Transportation and public utilities	
	Current dollars	1982 dollars	Current dollars	1982 dollars	Current dollars	1982 dollars	Current dollars	1982 dollars	Current dollars	1982 dollars
1947	45.58	196.47	59.89	258.15	58.83	253.58	49.13	211.77	. . .	. . .
1948	49.00	196.00	65.52	262.08	65.23	260.92	53.08	212.32	. . .	. . .
1949	50.24	202.58	62.33	251.33	67.56	272.42	53.80	216.94	. . .	. . .
1950	53.13	212.52	67.16	268.64	69.68	278.72	58.28	233.12	. . .	. . .
1951	57.86	215.09	74.11	275.50	76.96	286.10	63.34	235.46	. . .	. . .
1952	60.65	219.75	77.59	281.12	82.86	300.22	66.75	241.85	. . .	. . .
1953	63.76	229.35	83.03	298.67	86.41	310.83	70.47	253.49	. . .	. . .
1954	64.52	231.25	82.60	296.06	88.54	317.35	70.49	252.65	. . .	. . .
1955	67.72	243.60	89.54	322.09	90.90	326.98	75.30	270.86	. . .	. . .
1956	70.74	250.85	95.06	337.09	96.38	341.77	78.78	279.36	. . .	. . .
1957	73.33	251.13	98.25	336.47	100.27	343.39	81.19	278.05	. . .	. . .
1958	75.08	250.27	96.08	320.27	103.78	345.93	82.32	274.40	. . .	. . .
1959	78.78	260.86	103.68	343.31	108.41	358.97	88.26	292.25	. . .	. . .
1960	80.67	261.92	105.04	341.04	112.67	365.81	89.72	291.30	. . .	. . .
1961	82.60	265.59	106.92	343.79	118.08	379.68	92.34	296.91	. . .	. . .
1962	85.91	273.60	110.70	352.55	122.47	390.03	96.56	307.52	. . .	. . .
1963	88.46	278.18	114.40	359.75	127.19	399.97	99.23	312.04	. . .	. . .
1964	91.33	283.63	117.74	365.65	132.06	410.12	102.97	319.78	118.78	368.88
1965	95.45	291.90	123.52	377.74	138.38	423.18	107.53	328.84	125.14	382.69
1966	98.82	294.11	130.24	387.62	146.26	435.30	112.19	333.90	128.13	381.34
1967	101.84	293.49	135.89	391.61	154.95	446.54	114.49	329.94	130.82	377.00
1968	107.73	298.42	142.71	395.32	164.49	455.65	122.51	339.36	138.85	384.63
1969	114.61	300.81	154.80	406.30	181.54	476.48	129.51	339.92	147.74	387.77
1970	119.83	298.08	164.40	408.96	195.45	486.19	133.33	331.67	155.93	387.89
1971	127.31	303.12	172.14	409.86	211.67	503.98	142.44	339.14	168.82	401.95
1972	136.90	315.44	189.14	435.81	221.19	509.65	154.71	356.47	187.86	432.86
1973	145.39	315.38	201.40	436.88	235.89	511.69	166.46	361.08	203.31	441.02
1974	154.76	302.27	219.14	428.01	249.25	486.82	176.80	345.31	217.48	424.77
1975	163.53	293.06	249.31	446.79	266.08	476.85	190.79	341.92	233.44	418.35
1976	175.45	297.37	273.90	464.24	283.73	480.90	209.32	354.78	256.71	435.10
1977	189.00	300.96	301.20	479.62	295.65	470.78	228.90	364.49	278.90	444.11
1978	203.70	300.89	332.88	491.70	318.69	470.74	249.27	368.20	302.80	447.27
1979	219.91	291.66	365.07	484.18	342.99	454.89	269.34	357.21	325.58	431.80
1980	235.10	274.65	397.06	463.86	367.78	429.65	288.62	337.17	351.25	410.34
1981	255.20	270.63	438.75	465.27	399.26	423.39	318.00	337.22	382.18	405.28
1982	267.26	267.26	459.88	459.88	426.82	426.82	330.26	330.26	402.48	402.48
1983	280.70	272.52	479.40	465.44	442.97	430.07	354.08	343.77	420.81	408.55
1984	292.86	274.73	503.58	472.40	458.51	430.12	374.03	350.87	438.13	411.00
1985	299.09	271.16	519.93	471.38	464.46	421.09	386.37	350.29	450.30	408.25
1986	304.85	271.94	525.81	469.05	466.75	416.37	396.01	353.26	458.64	409.13
1987	312.50	269.16	531.70	457.97	480.44	413.82	406.31	349.97	471.58	406.18
1988	322.02	266.79	541.44	448.58	495.73	410.71	418.81	346.98	467.57	387.38
1989	334.24	264.22	570.18	450.74	513.17	405.67	429.68	339.67	481.43	380.58

. . . = Not available.

Table 2-26. Average Weekly Earnings of Production or Nonsupervisory Workers on Nonfarm Payrolls by Industry in Current and Constant Dollars, SIC Basis, 1947–1989—*Continued*

(Dollars.)

Year	Wholesale trade		Retail trade		Finance, insurance, and real estate		Services	
	Current dollars	1982 dollars	Current dollars	1982 dollars	Current dollars	1982 dollars	Current dollars	1982 dollars
1947	50.06	215.95	33.77	145.56	43.21	186.25	...	...
1948	53.59	214.12	36.22	144.88	45.48	181.92	...	...
1949	55.45	223.59	38.42	154.92	47.63	192.06	...	...
1950	55.31	232.40	39.71	158.84	47.50	202.08	...	...
1951	62.02	230.93	42.82	159.18	54.67	203.20	...	...
1952	65.53	237.17	43.38	157.17	57.08	206.81	...	...
1953	68.61	246.94	45.36	163.17	59.57	214.28	...	...
1954	71.28	255.02	47.04	168.60	62.04	222.37	...	...
1955	74.48	268.02	48.75	175.36	63.92	229.93	...	...
1956	78.17	277.77	50.18	177.94	65.68	232.91	...	...
1957	81.41	278.73	52.20	178.77	67.53	231.27	...	...
1958	84.02	280.47	54.10	180.33	70.12	233.73	...	...
1959	88.51	292.78	56.15	185.93	72.74	240.83	...	...
1960	90.72	293.93	57.76	187.53	75.14	243.96	...	...
1961	93.56	299.87	58.66	188.62	77.12	247.97	...	...
1962	96.22	306.43	60.96	194.14	80.94	257.77	...	...
1963	99.47	312.61	62.66	197.04	84.38	265.35	...	...
1964	102.56	317.89	64.75	201.27	85.79	266.37	70.03	217.55
1965	106.08	324.98	66.61	203.82	88.91	271.71	73.60	225.08
1966	111.11	330.60	68.57	203.87	92.13	274.43	77.04	228.93
1967	115.66	333.86	70.95	204.21	95.72	275.79	80.38	231.41
1968	121.90	337.65	74.95	207.56	101.75	281.72	83.97	232.91
1969	129.85	340.52	78.66	206.48	108.70	284.93	90.57	237.85
1970	136.86	340.57	82.47	204.75	112.67	280.57	96.66	240.10
1971	143.42	342.10	87.62	208.36	117.85	281.00	103.06	245.33
1972	151.69	348.89	91.85	212.05	122.98	283.27	110.85	254.88
1973	159.54	346.51	96.32	209.22	129.20	280.56	117.29	254.86
1974	169.94	332.25	102.68	200.29	137.61	268.91	126.00	246.52
1975	182.19	326.92	108.86	194.68	148.19	265.04	134.67	241.45
1976	194.27	329.07	114.60	194.17	155.43	263.58	143.52	243.27
1977	209.13	332.42	121.66	193.54	165.26	263.41	153.45	244.57
1978	228.14	336.59	130.20	192.23	178.00	262.97	163.67	242.08
1979	247.93	328.45	138.62	184.12	190.77	253.21	175.27	232.57
1980	266.88	312.07	147.38	172.01	209.60	244.95	190.71	223.11
1981	290.68	308.25	158.03	167.58	229.05	242.90	208.97	221.60
1982	309.46	309.46	163.85	163.85	245.44	245.44	225.59	225.59
1983	328.79	319.21	171.05	166.07	263.90	256.21	239.04	232.08
1984	341.88	320.71	174.33	163.54	278.50	261.26	247.43	232.11
1985	351.36	318.55	174.64	158.33	289.02	262.03	256.75	232.77
1986	357.72	319.11	176.08	157.07	304.30	271.45	265.85	237.15
1987	365.38	314.71	178.70	153.92	316.90	272.95	275.93	237.67
1988	380.24	315.03	183.62	152.13	325.25	269.47	289.49	239.84
1989	394.82	312.11	188.72	149.19	341.17	269.70	305.79	241.73

Note: Data include Alaska and Hawaii beginning in 1959.

. . . = Not available.

Table 2-27. Average Weekly Earnings of Production Workers on Manufacturing Payrolls by Industry, NAICS Basis, 1990–2004

(Dollars.)

Industry	1990	1991	1992	1993	1994	1995	1996	1997	1998	1999	2000	2001	2002	2003	2004
TOTAL MANUFACTURING	436.16	449.73	464.43	480.80	502.12	509.26	526.55	548.22	557.12	573.17	590.65	595.19	618.75	635.99	658.53
Total Durable Goods	468.43	483.28	499.59	519.92	544.66	549.49	566.53	589.10	591.68	606.67	624.38	624.54	652.97	671.21	694.16
Wood products	356.38	362.69	377.76	387.38	402.86	406.51	422.32	435.78	449.78	461.61	477.23	481.36	492.00	514.10	529.46
Nonmetallic mineral products	453.98	459.20	474.55	490.54	510.92	517.68	537.81	552.02	572.96	587.53	604.88	618.79	646.91	664.92	688.05
Primary metals	545.22	555.37	581.34	606.37	637.69	639.70	658.68	681.47	681.64	700.76	734.62	723.95	749.32	767.60	799.77
Fabricated metal products	436.12	447.98	459.64	474.21	492.07	498.48	513.57	534.48	543.20	555.86	576.68	576.60	596.38	610.37	628.80
Machinery	493.39	507.96	525.53	549.98	568.12	571.25	584.69	613.49	613.87	625.40	643.92	632.77	645.55	664.79	699.51
Computer and electronic products	450.09	464.25	482.09	499.15	514.92	518.25	534.42	562.69	579.70	596.25	609.70	613.07	642.87	674.72	698.28
Electrical equipment and appliances	412.42	426.96	439.04	451.28	470.21	471.63	496.69	515.73	522.51	538.98	550.56	548.00	560.24	583.23	606.64
Transportation equipment	606.87	633.87	652.95	697.16	750.67	751.74	773.95	795.82	774.82	796.25	817.98	817.08	877.87	889.48	912.97
Furniture and related products	324.08	330.49	348.03	360.63	373.87	375.06	385.68	410.38	428.50	443.38	459.69	464.57	494.01	505.30	519.78
Miscellaneous manufacturing	346.02	358.56	370.75	378.28	389.79	400.85	414.13	431.89	437.99	454.56	465.02	483.44	499.13	510.82	533.47
Total Nondurable Goods	390.65	404.17	417.95	429.15	443.82	452.83	467.88	487.04	503.99	519.91	536.82	548.41	566.84	582.61	602.48
Food manufacturing	355.61	364.90	375.69	386.04	398.54	406.66	414.74	428.58	444.81	458.63	472.09	481.67	496.91	502.92	509.66
Beverage and tobacco products	515.73	530.09	544.25	547.60	588.39	605.00	624.82	639.69	646.26	679.06	730.35	721.68	698.39	702.45	750.51
Textile mills	328.11	345.48	364.45	379.74	391.64	394.17	403.08	425.53	434.15	447.38	464.51	456.64	476.52	469.33	486.69
Textile product mills	293.77	303.81	314.47	329.26	336.96	342.17	356.90	373.95	385.13	401.01	406.24	408.56	429.01	444.70	443.01
Apparel	216.10	227.76	235.20	239.45	248.33	254.85	261.90	275.61	286.07	295.20	307.00	317.15	333.66	340.12	351.28
Leather and allied products	268.32	279.41	291.11	302.85	314.18	319.98	337.86	355.63	361.87	369.80	388.46	388.83	412.99	457.83	446.73
Paper and paper products	525.71	542.26	560.27	575.49	596.19	604.74	625.38	647.55	662.20	679.24	681.34	690.06	705.62	719.73	753.89
Printing and related support	429.93	437.00	450.02	457.91	470.74	472.37	484.99	504.46	518.32	534.15	552.15	560.89	573.05	587.58	604.32
Petroleum and coal products	754.13	786.05	821.72	855.36	883.81	883.68	881.24	908.50	949.28	947.60	973.53	1003.34	990.88	1052.32	1094.83
Chemicals	550.25	573.27	593.17	603.71	622.46	644.30	666.00	685.26	700.53	700.45	721.90	735.54	759.53	783.95	819.59
Plastics and rubber products	396.07	408.22	426.56	436.96	445.87	445.91	458.15	474.87	487.00	505.31	517.74	528.69	549.85	572.26	589.70

Table 2-28. Average Weekly Earnings of Production Workers on Manufacturing Payrolls by Industry, SIC Basis, 1947–1989

(Dollars.)

Year	Total manufac-turing	Durable goods												Instru-ments and related products	Miscel-laneous manufac-turing industries
		Total	Lumber and wood products	Furniture and fixtures	Stone, clay, and glass products	Primary metal industries		Blast furnaces and basic steel products	Fabricated metal products	Industrial machinery and equipment	Electronic and other electrical equipment	Transportation equipment			
						Total	Blast furnaces and basic steel products					Total	Motor vehicles and equipment		
1947	49.13	51.64	43.93	45.53	48.95	55.38	56.51	56.51	51.74	55.78	. . .	56.97	58.63	. . .	44.75
1948	53.08	56.24	47.64	48.83	53.20	61.14	62.84	62.84	56.37	60.38	. . .	61.70	63.15	. . .	48.03
1949	53.80	57.13	48.10	49.36	54.27	60.90	63.34	63.34	57.45	60.27	. . .	65.10	67.33	. . .	48.23
1950	58.28	59.60	51.31	53.55	59.06	67.36	67.95	67.95	63.04	67.04	. . .	71.29	74.85	. . .	52.02
1951	63.34	68.48	55.41	57.13	63.76	75.30	77.71	77.71	68.55	76.13	. . .	75.81	77.16	. . .	55.08
1952	66.75	72.04	59.15	60.86	66.17	77.52	80.00	80.00	71.72	79.55	. . .	81.51	84.87	. . .	59.02
1953	70.47	76.22	61.31	62.99	70.18	84.46	88.29	88.29	76.49	82.68	. . .	85.28	89.88	. . .	61.56
1954	70.49	75.79	61.39	62.80	71.69	81.48	83.92	83.92	76.70	81.40	. . .	86.30	91.30	. . .	61.78
1955	75.30	81.77	63.99	67.07	77.00	92.51	96.80	96.80	81.73	87.15	. . .	93.48	99.84	. . .	64.88
1956	78.78	85.28	65.74	68.78	80.56	97.17	102.87	102.87	84.67	93.06	. . .	94.81	96.82	. . .	67.60
1957	81.19	87.85	66.82	69.83	82.82	99.00	105.57	105.57	88.34	94.12	. . .	97.51	100.61	. . .	69.48
1958	82.32	88.88	69.48	69.95	84.80	101.11	108.00	108.00	90.17	94.33	. . .	100.40	101.24	. . .	70.17
1959	88.26	95.65	74.24	74.48	91.46	112.19	122.71	122.71	96.12	102.92	. . .	107.45	111.38	. . .	73.42
1960	89.72	97.04	74.29	75.20	92.57	109.59	116.13	116.13	98.42	104.55	. . .	111.52	115.21	. . .	74.28
1961	92.34	99.70	77.03	76.40	95.24	114.55	122.92	122.92	100.85	107.16	. . .	113.40	114.69	. . .	75.84
1962	96.56	104.30	79.20	79.37	98.81	119.80	127.40	127.40	104.81	113.01	. . .	122.22	127.67	. . .	78.61
1963	99.23	108.09	82.41	81.80	102.67	124.64	133.06	133.06	107.79	116.20	. . .	126.42	132.68	. . .	80.39
1964	102.97	112.05	85.65	84.46	105.50	129.69	138.43	138.43	111.76	121.69	. . .	130.09	138.03	. . .	82.37
1965	107.53	116.76	89.16	87.98	110.04	133.88	140.90	140.90	116.20	127.15	. . .	137.71	147.63	. . .	85.39
1966	112.19	121.67	92.21	91.72	114.24	138.09	144.73	144.73	122.11	134.90	. . .	141.86	147.23	. . .	88.80
1967	114.49	123.19	95.91	94.13	117.31	137.27	143.51	143.51	123.67	135.58	. . .	142.42	144.84	. . .	92.59
1968	122.51	131.65	104.75	100.28	124.98	147.68	154.16	154.16	131.77	141.12	. . .	155.72	167.66	. . .	98.50
1969	129.51	139.59	110.55	105.85	133.66	158.42	166.03	166.03	138.94	152.15	. . .	161.44	170.97	. . .	103.74
1970	133.33	143.07	117.61	108.58	140.08	158.77	166.40	166.40	143.67	154.95	. . .	163.62	170.07	. . .	109.52
1971	142.44	152.74	126.56	115.42	152.67	169.62	177.80	177.80	152.31	163.21	. . .	181.12	194.46	. . .	115.53
1972	154.71	167.68	134.94	123.82	165.48	192.92	206.25	206.25	166.86	181.87	. . .	200.58	220.59	. . .	122.85
1973	166.46	180.09	144.80	131.60	176.82	213.19	229.77	229.77	178.46	196.88	. . .	216.82	237.51	. . .	128.31
1974	176.80	190.82	152.88	138.02	187.50	232.96	258.95	258.95	188.00	207.97	. . .	224.37	238.32	. . .	136.61
1975	190.79	205.49	166.06	143.64	198.77	247.20	274.13	274.13	202.51	219.10	. . .	245.23	259.53	. . .	146.69
1976	209.32	226.14	189.13	154.81	219.06	276.22	305.88	305.88	224.40	238.55	. . .	276.05	304.16	. . .	156.75
1977	228.90	248.46	203.89	169.26	239.95	305.62	338.58	338.58	242.31	259.79	. . .	309.83	345.40	. . .	169.17
1978	249.27	270.44	223.68	183.92	262.91	342.76	389.69	389.69	260.35	284.76	. . .	333.80	368.05	. . .	181.97
1979	269.34	290.50	240.16	195.82	284.28	371.77	428.89	428.89	278.80	305.24	. . .	350.58	372.37	. . .	195.16
1980	288.62	310.78	253.60	209.17	306.00	391.78	448.77	448.77	300.98	328.00	. . .	379.61	394.00	. . .	211.30
1981	318.00	342.91	271.67	226.94	335.76	437.81	509.04	509.04	330.46	360.33	. . .	424.95	450.72	. . .	231.64
1982	330.26	354.88	284.23	234.73	355.69	437.34	505.97	505.97	343.78	367.62	. . .	449.96	470.61	. . .	246.53
1983	354.08	381.77	313.58	260.83	384.71	459.68	509.16	509.16	370.27	387.18	. . .	491.31	525.66	. . .	266.27
1984	374.03	402.82	321.20	271.55	401.94	478.30	528.29	528.29	389.16	417.74	. . .	520.94	557.57	. . .	277.77
1985	386.37	415.71	329.18	282.50	412.30	484.31	547.86	547.86	401.02	427.45	. . .	541.45	582.47	. . .	287.62
1986	396.01	424.56	338.15	296.91	423.69	496.93	572.54	572.54	408.46	440.13	. . .	541.86	572.97	. . .	298.98
1987	406.31	432.85	342.26	306.80	433.58	514.61	597.62	597.62	416.42	452.81	. . .	543.48	570.97	. . .	305.74
1988	418.81	447.68	344.46	313.23	446.69	528.96	615.12	615.12	431.15	473.12	401.39	567.48	608.57	438.84	313.60
1989	429.68	458.02	354.48	325.88	457.69	534.49	618.45	618.45	439.71	483.36	410.04	579.61	614.18	445.11	326.63

. . . = Not available.

Table 2-28. Average Weekly Earnings of Production Workers on Manufacturing Payrolls by Industry, SIC Basis, 1947–1989—*Continued*

(Dollars.)

Year	Nondurable goods										
	Total	Food and kindred products	Tobacco products	Textile mill products	Apparel and other textile products	Paper and allied products	Printing and publishing	Chemicals and allied products	Petroleum and coal products	Rubber and miscellaneous plastics products	Leather and leather products
1947	46.03	45.92	35.17	40.99	41.80	49.69	59.30	50.26	60.94	51.60	40.07
1948	49.54	48.84	36.58	45.28	43.68	54.70	65.13	55.29	69.30	53.29	41.11
1949	50.41	50.49	37.26	44.52	42.76	55.42	68.60	57.67	72.42	54.13	41.03
1950	51.45	52.88	41.00	48.59	44.60	60.53	71.23	61.64	75.11	60.27	43.95
1951	57.42	56.84	43.89	51.22	46.64	65.08	74.30	66.91	81.19	64.46	46.13
1952	59.95	60.34	45.31	52.39	47.92	68.05	78.58	69.12	85.05	69.53	49.92
1953	62.57	63.50	47.63	53.18	48.74	71.81	82.29	74.21	90.35	72.32	50.90
1954	63.18	65.67	48.88	52.09	48.36	73.18	83.93	77.11	93.20	72.83	50.18
1955	67.03	68.89	51.86	55.34	49.73	78.01	87.91	80.97	96.93	81.32	52.68
1956	70.09	72.69	56.26	57.17	52.92	82.18	90.64	85.90	104.14	81.61	55.65
1957	72.52	75.48	58.75	57.96	53.91	85.45	92.64	89.98	108.53	85.67	56.85
1958	74.50	79.15	62.17	57.51	54.05	87.99	94.62	93.20	111.66	85.67	57.25
1959	78.61	82.82	64.52	63.02	56.63	93.30	99.72	99.36	117.42	93.75	60.26
1960	80.36	86.09	64.94	63.60	56.45	95.15	102.91	103.25	118.78	92.80	60.52
1961	82.92	88.75	69.42	65.04	58.06	99.45	105.05	106.81	124.01	96.15	62.83
1962	86.15	91.84	71.41	68.21	61.18	102.24	108.01	110.24	126.88	100.04	64.67
1963	87.91	94.30	73.92	69.43	62.45	105.90	110.69	113.15	131.77	101.02	66.00
1964	90.91	97.17	75.66	73.39	64.26	109.57	114.35	116.48	133.76	104.90	69.36
1965	94.64	100.28	79.21	77.98	66.61	114.22	118.12	121.09	138.42	109.62	71.82
1966	98.49	103.82	85.19	82.12	68.80	119.35	122.61	125.16	144.58	112.56	74.88
1967	102.03	107.98	87.62	84.25	73.08	122.84	125.95	128.96	152.87	113.85	79.07
1968	109.05	114.24	93.99	91.05	79.78	130.85	133.28	136.27	159.38	121.60	85.41
1969	115.53	120.77	97.99	95.88	82.93	139.32	141.33	145.05	170.40	126.90	87.79
1970	120.43	127.98	110.00	97.76	84.37	144.14	147.78	153.50	183.18	129.36	92.63
1971	128.51	136.21	119.45	104.34	88.64	154.51	157.50	165.15	195.60	137.76	97.64
1972	138.16	145.80	130.47	113.58	93.60	169.06	170.03	177.64	211.79	149.56	102.64
1973	146.52	155.54	145.14	120.66	99.08	180.18	179.08	188.52	223.87	158.21	105.46
1974	156.79	169.28	157.80	126.40	104.54	191.17	188.63	202.52	239.13	166.05	110.33
1975	169.56	185.78	173.81	134.41	111.58	208.42	198.52	220.99	266.98	176.36	119.09
1976	185.57	201.69	186.75	147.97	121.72	232.48	214.13	245.86	303.54	191.70	127.16
1977	201.33	214.80	209.41	161.20	128.87	255.68	230.72	268.13	334.34	214.13	133.21
1978	218.28	230.26	233.55	173.72	140.26	279.71	244.78	294.14	376.27	227.81	144.32
1979	236.19	250.17	253.46	188.26	149.32	303.74	260.25	318.44	409.97	244.41	154.03
1980	255.84	271.95	294.89	203.31	161.42	330.85	279.36	344.45	422.18	263.20	168.09
1981	281.85	295.37	344.54	218.59	177.43	365.50	305.49	379.39	491.62	290.97	183.13
1982	297.60	312.05	370.06	218.63	180.44	389.58	324.25	407.36	546.99	304.92	189.75
1983	318.75	323.51	388.21	249.67	194.76	423.02	342.54	440.13	582.99	332.07	203.87
1984	333.08	333.92	436.46	257.75	202.02	448.67	356.64	463.83	587.33	348.20	210.13
1985	345.31	342.80	444.91	265.99	208.57	466.77	367.04	484.36	604.58	353.46	216.88
1986	357.11	350.00	481.71	284.82	214.33	482.98	379.62	501.96	621.52	363.91	218.45
1987	369.44	358.99	548.73	299.71	219.78	496.06	390.64	523.25	641.52	373.57	232.26
1988	379.89	367.54	583.87	302.58	226.44	506.18	400.14	536.36	664.67	383.22	235.50
1989	391.95	381.77	590.97	313.70	234.32	517.87	412.35	555.02	682.66	391.64	249.76

Note: Data include Alaska and Hawaii beginning in 1959.

Table 2-29. Employees on Total Nonfarm Payrolls by State, 1965–2004

(Thousands of people.)

State	1965	1966	1967	1968	1969	1970	1971	1972	1973	1974	1975	1976	1977	1978
Alabama	886.5	935.6	951.8	970.1	1 000.2	1 010.4	1 021.9	1 072.3	1 135.5	1 169.8	1 155.4	1 207.0	1 269.2	1 336.5
Alaska	70.5	73.1	76.8	79.9	86.8	93.1	97.8	103.5	109.9	127.8	161.9	171.7	163.3	163.5
Arizona	403.7	434.8	445.5	473.4	517.2	547.4	581.3	646.2	714.4	745.9	729.0	758.8	809.4	895.4
Arkansas	458.8	489.8	501.0	514.6	533.8	536.2	551.0	581.5	614.5	640.7	623.8	659.9	695.5	732.7
California	5 800.3	6 145.2	6 367.6	6 642.1	6 931.5	6 946.2	6 917.0	7 209.9	7 621.9	7 834.3	7 847.2	8 154.2	8 599.7	9 199.8
Colorado	599.0	631.3	655.9	686.7	720.8	750.2	787.1	869.4	936.0	959.7	963.5	1 003.4	1 058.1	1 149.9
Connecticut	1 032.9	1 095.4	1 130.1	1 158.0	1 194.1	1 197.5	1 164.3	1 190.4	1 238.7	1 264.0	1 223.4	1 239.7	1 282.3	1 346.1
Delaware	184.1	193.2	197.4	202.9	211.9	216.8	224.9	232.4	239.4	233.1	229.9	236.7	238.8	247.8
District of Columbia	572.5	587.0	594.7	582.8	575.0	566.7	566.6	572.0	573.7	580.1	576.5	575.8	578.7	596.3
Florida	1 619.1	1 726.8	1 816.4	1 932.3	2 069.9	2 152.1	2 276.3	2 513.1	2 778.6	2 863.8	2 746.4	2 784.3	2 933.4	3 180.6
Georgia	1 257.2	1 337.9	1 394.8	1 455.7	1 531.7	1 557.5	1 602.9	1 695.2	1 802.5	1 827.5	1 755.7	1 839.2	1 926.5	2 050.1
Hawaii	219.4	232.1	241.7	255.4	275.8	293.7	301.5	312.7	327.5	335.9	342.8	349.2	359.4	377.3
Idaho	177.6	184.8	187.7	192.9	201.4	207.9	217.2	236.5	251.7	266.8	273.0	291.1	307.4	331.3
Illinois	3 880.4	4 095.4	4 209.7	4 284.9	4 376.1	4 345.6	4 296.4	4 314.8	4 467.0	4 545.7	4 418.9	4 565.0	4 655.5	4 788.8
Indiana	1 631.1	1 737.2	1 777.0	1 817.4	1 880.3	1 849.0	1 841.1	1 921.9	2 028.1	2 031.4	1 941.7	2 023.8	2 114.0	2 205.5
Iowa	752.3	803.9	832.9	852.1	873.4	876.9	882.8	912.3	961.3	999.0	998.7	1 036.9	1 079.2	1 119.2
Kansas	600.4	634.3	652.8	672.1	686.5	678.8	677.9	717.5	763.3	790.0	801.2	834.8	871.0	912.5
Kentucky	758.9	804.0	836.5	868.6	895.5	910.0	931.6	988.3	1 038.6	1 065.9	1 057.6	1 103.1	1 148.2	1 209.9
Louisiana	898.4	957.9	997.2	1 020.5	1 032.8	1 033.6	1 055.9	1 128.6	1 176.1	1 220.8	1 249.5	1 314.4	1 364.6	1 463.5
Maine	295.4	309.3	316.9	323.2	330.1	332.2	332.3	343.7	354.8	361.5	356.9	375.3	387.8	405.5
Maryland	1 057.5	1 132.1	1 178.5	1 223.8	1 272.4	1 349.2	1 371.5	1 415.0	1 471.5	1 493.6	1 479.3	1 498.3	1 545.5	1 625.5
Massachusetts	2 015.8	2 097.4	2 147.9	2 187.9	2 249.4	2 243.5	2 211.4	2 251.7	2 333.4	2 353.8	2 273.1	2 323.5	2 416.1	2 526.3
Michigan	2 685.3	2 861.0	2 900.5	2 959.7	3 081.1	2 999.1	2 995.0	3 118.9	3 284.4	3 277.7	3 136.6	3 283.0	3 442.3	3 609.4
Minnesota	1 080.6	1 148.3	1 199.8	1 243.4	1 299.8	1 315.3	1 310.2	1 357.1	1 436.1	1 481.0	1 474.4	1 520.9	1 597.3	1 689.3
Mississippi	486.6	521.6	535.1	551.9	573.0	583.9	602.2	649.3	693.2	710.8	692.3	727.5	765.9	813.7
Missouri	1 478.3	1 554.2	1 595.6	1 631.3	1 672.2	1 668.1	1 660.9	1 700.1	1 770.8	1 789.3	1 740.6	1 797.8	1 861.9	1 953.2
Montana	179.3	184.7	188.0	192.6	195.6	199.1	204.8	215.4	224.2	234.0	238.2	251.1	264.9	280.4
Nebraska	418.7	434.2	449.3	458.9	474.4	484.3	490.9	517.0	541.3	562.1	557.8	572.1	593.7	610.1
Nevada	157.3	162.0	166.1	177.3	193.5	203.2	210.5	223.5	244.6	256.0	263.1	279.8	308.2	350.2
New Hampshire	220.8	235.2	244.0	251.8	259.2	258.5	259.9	278.5	297.8	300.3	292.8	313.4	337.1	359.7
New Jersey	2 256.5	2 359.1	2 421.5	2 485.2	2 569.6	2 606.2	2 607.6	2 672.5	2 759.7	2 783.0	2 699.9	2 753.7	2 836.9	2 961.9
New Mexico	262.5	271.7	272.6	276.6	287.5	292.6	305.7	327.5	346.0	360.2	370.2	390.0	415.4	444.3
New York	6 518.7	6 709.5	6 858.3	7 001.7	7 182.0	7 156.5	7 011.4	7 038.5	7 132.2	7 077.1	6 829.9	6 789.5	6 857.6	7 044.5
North Carolina	1 431.2	1 534.3	1 600.9	1 678.6	1 747.0	1 782.8	1 813.5	1 912.0	2 018.1	2 048.2	1 979.8	2 082.8	2 170.6	2 277.5
North Dakota	146.1	148.4	151.5	155.7	157.9	163.7	167.1	176.1	183.9	193.8	203.6	215.0	221.1	234.0
Ohio	3 364.3	3 537.3	3 619.8	3 750.8	3 887.3	3 880.7	3 839.6	3 938.3	4 112.9	4 169.4	4 016.2	4 094.6	4 230.1	4 394.9
Oklahoma	642.5	676.0	699.6	720.4	748.2	762.5	774.4	812.0	851.9	886.9	899.7	931.1	971.6	1 035.7
Oregon	608.3	640.4	652.2	679.1	708.7	710.6	728.8	774.7	816.2	838.2	837.3	878.5	936.9	1 009.2
Pennsylvania	3 917.5	4 077.1	4 171.3	4 263.5	4 374.9	4 351.6	4 291.3	4 400.0	4 506.5	4 514.6	4 435.8	4 512.8	4 565.2	4 716.2
Rhode Island	316.3	329.9	338.3	343.0	346.4	344.0	342.8	358.1	365.9	367.0	349.2	366.7	381.7	395.8
South Carolina	686.0	734.9	754.5	782.9	819.8	842.0	862.6	920.3	984.0	1 015.8	982.6	1 038.1	1 081.7	1 137.5
South Dakota	155.6	160.1	163.9	167.9	173.0	175.4	179.0	189.9	199.1	206.6	209.3	218.6	226.6	236.6
Tennessee	1 108.5	1 184.4	1 218.8	1 264.0	1 309.8	1 327.6	1 356.8	1 450.1	1 531.2	1 558.2	1 505.8	1 575.4	1 648.1	1 737.0
Texas	2 932.4	3 108.7	3 259.3	3 424.3	3 597.1	3 625.0	3 683.5	3 884.4	4 141.7	4 360.3	4 462.9	4 683.7	4 906.8	5 271.6
Utah	299.8	317.4	326.6	335.1	348.2	356.9	369.3	393.0	414.8	434.1	440.3	462.8	488.7	525.4
Vermont	121.3	130.8	136.3	140.3	145.5	147.9	148.1	153.6	161.3	162.8	162.0	168.4	178.4	190.6
Virginia	1 218.9	1 285.3	1 330.2	1 385.0	1 436.4	1 518.9	1 567.1	1 655.5	1 753.1	1 804.6	1 778.6	1 848.1	1 930.4	2 033.5
Washington	896.5	988.5	1 045.3	1 099.3	1 120.2	1 079.3	1 064.4	1 100.1	1 152.2	1 199.1	1 225.7	1 282.9	1 366.9	1 485.4
West Virginia	476.6	495.2	503.6	508.4	512.3	516.5	520.0	540.5	561.6	572.4	574.7	596.3	611.5	633.1
Wisconsin	1 331.7	1 394.1	1 430.5	1 472.1	1 525.1	1 530.4	1 525.4	1 580.8	1 660.5	1 703.4	1 676.8	1 725.9	1 798.9	1 887.0
Wyoming	96.7	97.2	99.0	102.9	107.0	108.4	111.1	117.3	126.1	136.5	146.0	156.6	170.6	187.4
Puerto Rico	. . .	. . .	. . .	. . .	. . .	. . .	. . .	. . .	. . .	. . .	. . .	. . .	. . .	. . .
Virgin Islands	. . .	. . .	. . .	. . .	. . .	. . .	. . .	. . .	. . .	. . .	33.1	31.3	32.2	33.8

. . . = Not available.

Table 2-29. Employees on Total Nonfarm Payrolls by State, 1965–2004—*Continued*

(Thousands of people.)

State	1979	1980	1981	1982	1983	1984	1985	1986	1987	1988	1989	1990	1991
Alabama	1 362.0	1 356.1	1 347.6	1 312.5	1 328.8	1 387.7	1 427.1	1 463.3	1 507.7	1 558.7	1 601.2	1 635.8	1 642.0
Alaska	166.9	169.4	186.1	200.4	214.3	225.7	230.7	220.7	210.1	213.7	227.0	238.0	242.7
Arizona	980.0	1 014.0	1 040.8	1 029.8	1 077.8	1 181.9	1 278.6	1 337.8	1 385.8	1 419.3	1 454.5	1 483.0	1 491.2
Arkansas	749.5	742.3	740.1	720.1	741.3	780.2	797.1	813.8	836.6	865.4	893.4	923.4	936.3
California	9 664.6	9 848.8	9 985.3	9 810.3	9 917.8	10 390.0	10 769.8	11 085.5	11 472.6	11 911.5	12 238.5	12 499.8	12 358.9
Colorado	1 218.0	1 251.1	1 295.2	1 316.6	1 327.2	1 402.3	1 418.7	1 408.3	1 412.6	1 436.1	1 482.3	1 520.8	1 544.9
Connecticut	1 398.0	1 426.9	1 438.3	1 428.5	1 444.2	1 517.3	1 558.2	1 598.4	1 638.2	1 667.4	1 665.6	1 623.5	1 555.2
Delaware	256.7	259.2	259.2	259.2	266.1	280.0	293.3	303.2	320.7	334.2	344.5	347.4	341.7
District of Columbia	612.5	616.1	611.0	597.9	596.6	613.8	629.0	640.0	655.6	673.6	680.6	686.0	677.2
Florida	3 381.2	3 576.2	3 736.0	3 761.9	3 905.4	4 204.2	4 410.0	4 599.4	4 848.1	5 066.6	5 260.9	5 387.4	5 294.3
Georgia	2 127.5	2 159.4	2 198.7	2 201.5	2 279.5	2 448.7	2 569.8	2 672.4	2 782.0	2 875.9	2 941.1	2 991.8	2 937.6
Hawaii	394.0	404.1	404.8	399.4	406.2	412.7	425.8	438.6	460.0	478.1	505.5	528.4	539.1
Idaho	338.0	330.0	327.8	312.2	317.9	330.5	336.0	328.2	333.4	348.6	365.8	385.0	398.1
Illinois	4 880.0	4 850.3	4 732.3	4 593.3	4 530.6	4 672.3	4 755.3	4 790.7	4 928.3	5 097.5	5 213.9	5 288.4	5 231.5
Indiana	2 236.3	2 129.5	2 114.5	2 028.1	2 029.5	2 122.3	2 168.6	2 221.8	2 304.9	2 395.6	2 479.3	2 521.9	2 507.3
Iowa	1 131.7	1 109.9	1 088.6	1 041.9	1 040.4	1 074.7	1 074.2	1 073.8	1 109.1	1 156.2	1 200.1	1 226.3	1 238.1
Kansas	946.8	944.7	949.8	921.4	921.5	960.8	967.9	984.8	1 005.1	1 035.4	1 064.2	1 088.4	1 095.3
Kentucky	1 245.3	1 210.0	1 196.4	1 160.7	1 152.3	1 213.8	1 250.4	1 274.1	1 328.2	1 381.9	1 433.0	1 470.5	1 474.7
Louisiana	1 517.4	1 578.9	1 630.5	1 607.0	1 565.2	1 601.5	1 591.2	1 518.5	1 483.6	1 511.6	1 538.5	1 589.8	1 612.9
Maine	415.9	418.3	419.3	415.5	425.1	445.7	458.4	477.4	501.1	527.1	541.9	535.0	513.4
Maryland	1 691.4	1 712.0	1 715.8	1 675.6	1 723.8	1 814.0	1 887.8	1 952.0	2 028.0	2 102.3	2 155.2	2 174.2	2 103.2
Massachusetts	2 603.5	2 654.3	2 671.8	2 642.0	2 696.5	2 855.8	2 930.0	2 988.8	3 065.8	3 130.8	3 108.6	2 984.8	2 821.1
Michigan	3 637.1	3 442.8	3 364.4	3 193.3	3 223.1	3 381.0	3 561.5	3 657.3	3 735.8	3 819.3	3 922.4	3 969.7	3 891.2
Minnesota	1 767.0	1 770.2	1 761.3	1 707.3	1 718.4	1 819.8	1 865.5	1 892.5	1 962.5	2 028.1	2 086.8	2 135.9	2 146.0
Mississippi	838.1	829.3	819.1	790.9	792.8	820.8	838.9	848.2	864.4	896.2	919.3	936.5	937.5
Missouri	2 011.2	1 969.8	1 956.5	1 922.5	1 937.0	2 032.7	2 094.7	2 142.6	2 197.8	2 258.9	2 315.0	2 345.0	2 309.1
Montana	283.9	280.4	281.9	273.7	276.0	281.1	279.1	275.4	274.1	282.9	291.0	297.2	303.6
Nebraska	631.2	627.6	623.2	609.8	610.8	635.4	650.5	652.5	667.2	688.1	708.0	730.1	739.2
Nevada	383.7	399.9	411.1	401.1	402.8	426.0	446.4	468.1	500.2	537.6	581.0	620.9	628.6
New Hampshire	378.5	385.4	394.6	394.4	409.5	441.6	466.1	490.1	512.8	529.0	529.1	508.0	482.0
New Jersey	3 027.2	3 060.4	3 098.9	3 092.7	3 165.1	3 329.2	3 414.1	3 488.1	3 576.3	3 651.0	3 689.8	3 635.1	3 498.6
New Mexico	461.0	465.4	475.5	473.6	479.5	502.7	520.2	525.9	529.3	547.5	562.2	580.4	585.4
New York	7 179.4	7 207.1	7 287.3	7 254.6	7 313.3	7 570.4	7 751.3	7 907.9	8 059.4	8 186.9	8 246.8	8 212.3	7 886.7
North Carolina	2 373.0	2 380.1	2 391.6	2 347.0	2 419.3	2 565.2	2 651.2	2 744.1	2 862.6	2 986.6	3 073.9	3 117.6	3 072.1
North Dakota	244.2	245.2	249.4	249.7	250.7	252.5	252.0	249.9	252.4	256.8	260.4	265.8	270.6
Ohio	4 484.8	4 367.4	4 317.7	4 124.3	4 092.5	4 260.2	4 372.9	4 471.5	4 582.6	4 700.6	4 817.5	4 882.3	4 818.6
Oklahoma	1 088.0	1 138.1	1 201.2	1 216.9	1 170.7	1 180.3	1 165.3	1 124.4	1 108.5	1 131.5	1 163.8	1 195.8	1 210.9
Oregon	1 056.0	1 044.5	1 018.7	961.1	966.7	1 006.9	1 030.0	1 058.5	1 100.1	1 152.8	1 205.8	1 247.0	1 244.6
Pennsylvania	4 806.1	4 753.1	4 728.9	4 580.1	4 524.3	4 654.8	4 730.3	4 790.9	4 915.1	5 041.7	5 138.5	5 170.2	5 083.6
Rhode Island	399.9	398.3	401.4	390.5	396.4	416.4	429.2	442.6	451.9	459.4	461.9	451.2	421.5
South Carolina	1 176.0	1 188.8	1 196.5	1 162.3	1 189.0	1 262.5	1 296.2	1 338.0	1 392.2	1 449.0	1 499.7	1 545.0	1 513.5
South Dakota	241.3	238.0	236.1	230.2	235.3	247.0	249.4	251.9	256.9	266.1	276.0	288.7	296.4
Tennessee	1 777.3	1 746.6	1 755.4	1 703.1	1 719.0	1 812.1	1 867.8	1 929.8	2 011.7	2 092.1	2 167.2	2 193.2	2 183.6
Texas	5 601.8	5 851.3	6 180.0	6 263.4	6 193.6	6 492.3	6 663.1	6 564.2	6 516.9	6 677.8	6 840.0	7 096.8	7 176.5
Utah	548.4	550.8	558.0	560.9	567.0	601.2	624.4	634.1	640.0	660.0	691.1	723.6	745.3
Vermont	197.9	200.1	204.3	202.9	206.4	214.9	224.8	234.4	245.6	256.1	261.8	257.7	249.1
Virginia	2 115.0	2 157.0	2 160.8	2 146.4	2 206.9	2 333.3	2 454.7	2 557.7	2 680.4	2 772.5	2 861.9	2 896.2	2 828.9
Washington	1 581.2	1 608.3	1 612.0	1 568.6	1 586.2	1 659.6	1 710.4	1 769.9	1 851.8	1 941.4	2 046.8	2 143.0	2 177.3
West Virginia	658.6	645.9	628.5	607.8	582.4	596.6	597.2	597.5	599.0	609.8	614.7	630.0	628.8
Wisconsin	1 960.2	1 938.1	1 923.2	1 866.7	1 867.3	1 949.2	1 983.1	2 023.9	2 089.6	2 168.5	2 236.4	2 291.5	2 302.1
Wyoming	200.7	210.2	223.5	217.7	202.5	204.3	206.9	196.3	183.1	189.0	192.8	198.5	203.0
Puerto Rico	. . .	. . .	. . .	. . .	. . .	. . .	. . .	. . .	. . .	. . .	. . .	. . .	. . .
Virgin Islands	36.1	37.3	37.7	36.5	36.4	36.6	36.9	37.7	39.6	41.5	42.0	43.0	43.8

. . . = Not available.

Table 2-29. Employees on Total Nonfarm Payrolls by State, 1965–2004—*Continued*

(Thousands of people.)

State	1992	1993	1994	1995	1996	1997	1998	1999	2000	2001	2002	2003	2004
Alabama	1 674.4	1 716.8	1 758.5	1 803.7	1 828.6	1 866.2	1 898.1	1 919.5	1 931.2	1 908.7	1 883.2	1 875.5	1 901.6
Alaska	247.1	252.8	259.3	261.9	263.5	268.7	274.9	277.8	283.8	289.3	295.0	299.4	304.0
Arizona	1 517.1	1 584.4	1 692.0	1 795.3	1 892.2	1 984.5	2 074.7	2 163.0	2 242.7	2 265.0	2 265.1	2 296.3	2 373.5
Arkansas	963.0	993.9	1 034.0	1 069.3	1 085.9	1 103.9	1 122.1	1 141.7	1 158.5	1 153.7	1 146.3	1 145.1	1 158.7
California	12 153.5	12 045.4	12 159.5	12 422.0	12 743.4	13 129.7	13 596.1	13 991.8	14 488.2	14 601.9	14 457.8	14 392.3	14 538.8
Colorado	1 596.9	1 670.7	1 755.9	1 834.4	1 900.4	1 979.5	2 056.7	2 131.5	2 212.6	2 225.4	2 182.5	2 151.0	2 178.9
Connecticut	1 526.2	1 531.1	1 543.7	1 561.5	1 583.6	1 612.4	1 643.4	1 669.1	1 693.1	1 681.1	1 664.9	1 644.5	1 651.4
Delaware	341.3	348.7	355.8	366.2	376.3	387.9	400.2	412.9	420.0	419.4	414.5	414.5	424.1
District of Columbia	673.6	670.3	658.7	642.6	623.0	618.4	613.5	627.4	650.2	653.7	664.2	665.5	672.4
Florida	5 358.5	5 571.4	5 799.3	5 996.0	6 183.3	6 414.3	6 636.4	6 827.0	7 080.5	7 170.7	7 179.7	7 261.1	7 504.0
Georgia	2 987.2	3 109.2	3 266.0	3 402.3	3 527.3	3 614.4	3 740.8	3 854.6	3 949.3	3 943.2	3 869.5	3 844.9	3 889.9
Hawaii	542.8	538.8	536.1	532.8	530.7	531.6	531.3	535.0	551.4	555.0	556.8	567.6	582.3
Idaho	416.4	436.5	460.9	477.3	491.0	507.5	521.1	538.9	559.6	567.7	568.2	572.0	586.9
Illinois	5 234.8	5 330.4	5 463.0	5 593.2	5 684.6	5 772.1	5 898.6	5 958.5	6 044.8	5 995.2	5 883.9	5 810.8	5 807.1
Indiana	2 554.2	2 626.9	2 712.7	2 786.5	2 814.3	2 858.4	2 917.2	2 969.9	3 000.0	2 933.4	2 900.9	2 895.3	2 929.9
Iowa	1 252.5	1 278.5	1 319.9	1 358.0	1 383.4	1 407.0	1 442.7	1 468.6	1 478.4	1 465.6	1 447.3	1 440.4	1 456.1
Kansas	1 115.0	1 133.3	1 165.8	1 198.0	1 226.6	1 268.4	1 312.3	1 327.1	1 344.9	1 347.7	1 335.0	1 312.2	1 323.2
Kentucky	1 508.5	1 547.8	1 597.1	1 642.8	1 671.7	1 711.2	1 752.7	1 795.4	1 824.6	1 804.0	1 788.8	1 782.7	1 796.1
Louisiana	1 626.9	1 658.6	1 722.1	1 772.3	1 809.6	1 849.9	1 889.4	1 896.2	1 919.9	1 917.5	1 897.8	1 907.7	1 920.2
Maine	511.8	519.3	531.5	538.1	542.4	553.7	569.1	586.3	603.4	608.1	606.5	606.8	613.9
Maryland	2 084.8	2 105.8	2 149.0	2 185.1	2 214.4	2 270.7	2 327.1	2 393.6	2 457.7	2 473.2	2 481.9	2 491.6	2 520.4
Massachusetts	2 795.1	2 840.1	2 903.6	2 976.6	3 035.3	3 109.2	3 178.6	3 236.8	3 322.6	3 327.2	3 246.6	3 185.1	3 180.4
Michigan	3 927.5	4 005.8	4 146.9	4 273.9	4 360.8	4 448.1	4 510.2	4 581.9	4 673.9	4 555.9	4 477.8	4 409.6	4 390.8
Minnesota	2 194.2	2 251.9	2 319.6	2 387.8	2 442.5	2 500.0	2 564.3	2 622.3	2 684.9	2 689.5	2 664.5	2 660.2	2 677.5
Mississippi	960.2	1 002.1	1 055.5	1 074.5	1 088.8	1 107.1	1 133.6	1 153.1	1 153.5	1 129.9	1 123.6	1 114.9	1 125.0
Missouri	2 333.6	2 394.6	2 470.4	2 520.9	2 567.4	2 639.3	2 684.0	2 726.8	2 748.7	2 730.4	2 698.9	2 680.5	2 692.9
Montana	316.5	325.6	340.1	350.7	360.3	364.9	373.0	380.2	387.5	391.7	396.0	400.7	412.0
Nebraska	750.1	767.2	796.3	817.4	836.8	857.1	879.9	897.4	914.0	919.7	911.5	914.3	922.9
Nevada	638.6	671.5	738.0	786.0	842.9	890.7	925.8	983.0	1 026.9	1 051.4	1 052.0	1 088.3	1 152.4
New Hampshire	486.9	502.4	523.1	539.7	553.6	570.2	588.9	605.7	622.0	627.2	618.4	617.9	626.7
New Jersey	3 457.8	3 493.0	3 552.7	3 600.5	3 638.9	3 724.5	3 801.2	3 901.1	3 994.5	3 997.1	3 983.9	3 978.8	4 002.0
New Mexico	601.5	626.1	657.3	682.4	694.5	708.4	719.9	729.7	744.8	757.2	766.1	775.6	790.7
New York	7 730.3	7 759.7	7 831.3	7 892.2	7 938.7	8 067.1	8 236.8	8 455.9	8 635.2	8 591.7	8 459.0	8 407.0	8 446.6
North Carolina	3 125.3	3 244.6	3 358.8	3 459.5	3 546.4	3 663.1	3 773.6	3 870.3	3 933.7	3 898.7	3 837.1	3 789.5	3 829.6
North Dakota	277.1	284.8	294.7	301.7	308.6	314.0	319.4	323.8	327.7	329.7	329.8	332.6	337.2
Ohio	4 847.6	4 918.3	5 075.9	5 221.0	5 296.4	5 392.4	5 482.0	5 563.5	5 624.6	5 542.6	5 445.0	5 397.7	5 407.0
Oklahoma	1 221.6	1 246.9	1 279.4	1 315.6	1 353.4	1 392.5	1 441.1	1 461.9	1 489.4	1 506.8	1 486.5	1 458.2	1 470.4
Oregon	1 267.3	1 308.1	1 362.7	1 418.2	1 474.5	1 526.3	1 551.6	1 574.9	1 606.6	1 593.6	1 572.5	1 562.2	1 593.7
Pennsylvania	5 075.6	5 122.9	5 192.4	5 253.1	5 306.2	5 406.4	5 494.8	5 586.1	5 691.3	5 682.5	5 640.8	5 611.3	5 639.5
Rhode Island	424.7	430.0	434.1	440.1	441.5	449.9	458.0	465.5	476.7	478.4	479.4	484.3	488.4
South Carolina	1 527.7	1 570.0	1 607.3	1 646.1	1 675.1	1 720.2	1 783.3	1 830.6	1 859.4	1 823.4	1 804.7	1 808.0	1 827.7
South Dakota	308.5	318.7	331.9	343.5	348.7	354.9	363.2	373.3	377.7	378.5	377.3	378.2	382.9
Tennessee	2 245.0	2 328.4	2 422.9	2 498.9	2 533.3	2 584.0	2 638.3	2 685.3	2 728.9	2 688.3	2 664.4	2 662.7	2 701.1
Texas	7 270.8	7 483.3	7 752.7	8 024.4	8 257.9	8 608.5	8 938.3	9 155.0	9 426.7	9 513.9	9 416.0	9 370.0	9 478.3
Utah	768.6	809.8	859.7	907.5	954.4	993.5	1 023.2	1 048.5	1 075.4	1 081.3	1 073.4	1 074.1	1 103.2
Vermont	251.2	257.4	263.9	270.2	275.1	279.4	285.0	291.6	298.7	302.1	299.3	299.2	303.2
Virginia	2 848.4	2 918.9	3 003.6	3 069.6	3 135.8	3 231.8	3 319.9	3 412.3	3 516.5	3 516.5	3 494.1	3 497.4	3 584.3
Washington	2 222.4	2 252.9	2 304.2	2 346.9	2 415.5	2 514.2	2 594.9	2 648.6	2 711.2	2 697.0	2 654.1	2 657.8	2 698.2
West Virginia	639.8	652.4	674.4	687.8	698.6	707.8	719.3	726.0	735.8	735.2	733.1	727.6	736.2
Wisconsin	2 357.9	2 412.7	2 490.7	2 558.6	2 600.6	2 655.8	2 718.0	2 784.0	2 833.8	2 813.9	2 782.4	2 775.3	2 803.2
Wyoming	205.6	210.3	216.8	219.3	221.1	224.5	228.3	233.1	239.3	245.4	247.9	250.0	255.4
Puerto Rico	. . .	. . .	. . .	. . .	. . .	. . .	. . .	. . .	. . .	. . .	. . .	1 021.6	1 039.5
Virgin Islands	44.9	48.5	44.4	41.9	41.1	41.7	41.7	40.9	41.6	44.2	43.0	41.9	42.8

. . . = Not available.

Table 2-30. Employees on Manufacturing Payrolls by State, NAICS Basis, 1990–2004

(Thousands of people.)

State	1990	1991	1992	1993	1994	1995	1996	1997	1998	1999	2000	2001	2002	2003	2004
Alabama	363.8	354.2	356.8	359.3	361.8	370.3	362.2	363.8	364.6	357.5	351.4	325.5	307.4	293.8	290.9
Alaska	14.1	15.1	15.8	15.1	14.4	14.7	14.4	13.9	13.0	11.8	11.8	11.7	11.3	11.7	12.2
Arizona	176.5	170.7	166.8	169.6	181.7	191.3	199.1	204.8	210.5	207.4	209.9	201.7	183.5	175.3	175.8
Arkansas	219.3	219.1	223.6	230.6	240.2	246.0	240.7	240.7	241.6	240.7	240.3	226.9	213.7	205.8	204.0
California	1 959.8	1 885.2	1 787.0	1 695.2	1 683.8	1 714.9	1 772.4	1 825.1	1 857.2	1 829.9	1 857.5	1 785.6	1 638.2	1 547.9	1 532.7
Colorado	169.8	164.9	163.6	166.5	172.5	179.5	182.9	189.3	194.4	190.7	191.3	181.9	166.1	156.0	154.6
Connecticut	298.3	285.0	273.6	261.5	253.4	248.5	245.3	245.3	247.8	240.2	235.6	226.7	211.2	200.0	197.5
Delaware	45.8	45.9	44.2	43.8	43.3	43.4	41.4	43.1	44.0	44.0	41.5	39.4	37.1	35.7	34.9
District of Columbia	7.3	6.2	5.4	5.2	5.1	4.9	4.5	4.3	3.9	3.8	3.7	3.4	3.1	2.5	2.5
Florida	485.8	455.5	449.8	455.1	451.1	456.6	462.5	463.3	459.5	455.5	455.0	432.3	405.6	387.5	387.6
Georgia	505.9	482.9	491.0	511.0	526.4	539.6	543.9	547.1	545.2	542.6	530.5	498.3	466.7	452.0	445.2
Hawaii	20.4	19.4	18.8	17.5	16.8	16.2	15.9	15.8	15.6	15.9	16.4	16.4	15.2	15.0	15.4
Idaho	52.6	55.4	57.9	61.0	63.0	63.1	66.1	68.2	69.3	68.9	69.9	68.3	64.9	62.0	61.5
Illinois	914.6	875.7	855.1	860.3	877.8	893.5	898.7	902.2	905.9	882.1	870.5	815.4	753.9	714.1	697.3
Indiana	609.1	589.8	600.5	614.4	625.3	651.3	645.8	650.8	656.7	664.7	663.5	615.4	588.4	572.7	572.2
Iowa	218.9	216.4	216.3	220.7	229.8	236.5	234.7	239.0	250.8	252.7	251.4	240.2	227.3	220.0	222.9
Kansas	177.5	174.5	174.2	172.2	175.9	179.9	185.7	198.1	205.7	204.0	200.6	195.3	183.9	174.6	176.4
Kentucky	272.7	266.7	271.4	278.6	289.4	298.6	297.7	302.4	306.5	309.0	310.4	291.8	275.1	265.4	263.9
Louisiana	176.7	178.5	177.3	176.8	179.0	182.0	183.4	185.6	184.9	181.4	177.4	171.8	160.7	155.8	152.2
Maine	92.9	87.6	84.0	82.5	83.3	83.2	81.2	80.6	81.1	80.5	79.5	74.6	68.0	64.1	63.1
Maryland	198.2	187.4	180.0	176.4	176.7	176.8	174.0	175.2	175.3	173.6	173.9	168.2	156.5	147.0	142.8
Massachusetts	485.7	452.1	436.6	424.8	418.4	417.3	415.9	417.4	417.9	405.2	407.9	388.6	348.8	324.3	313.8
Michigan	837.6	793.0	796.3	805.7	848.4	873.0	866.0	873.4	889.9	898.1	896.7	819.6	760.0	716.3	695.8
Minnesota	341.4	339.2	342.5	351.0	361.2	374.7	380.9	391.1	396.9	395.4	396.5	378.5	355.8	343.3	342.7
Mississippi	229.0	230.4	235.9	239.1	244.3	241.1	230.6	228.4	233.8	232.9	222.5	200.8	187.9	179.0	179.4
Missouri	392.1	373.4	366.4	365.2	366.2	377.1	375.7	376.6	378.6	374.5	364.5	344.9	325.4	314.5	312.2
Montana	19.5	19.1	20.0	20.4	20.7	21.2	21.9	22.2	22.1	22.5	22.5	21.4	20.0	19.0	19.1
Nebraska	97.7	97.2	97.9	100.5	105.6	109.9	111.3	112.7	114.4	113.4	114.3	110.8	106.0	102.3	100.7
Nevada	24.2	24.6	26.1	29.2	32.7	35.7	38.0	39.5	40.5	41.0	42.7	44.0	42.9	43.7	45.9
New Hampshire	98.5	92.1	89.6	91.3	94.2	97.1	98.8	101.5	103.6	101.2	102.5	97.4	85.0	80.4	80.3
New Jersey	529.5	498.3	474.0	462.9	455.9	448.6	437.4	435.4	429.3	422.4	421.5	401.2	367.5	350.4	338.9
New Mexico	38.0	37.6	37.2	39.1	41.7	42.5	42.6	42.7	42.5	41.2	41.7	40.9	38.4	36.5	35.9
New York	983.1	909.9	869.7	836.4	815.7	810.3	796.8	797.1	791.8	772.8	750.8	708.2	652.2	613.4	596.0
North Carolina	823.9	784.7	795.7	813.1	817.3	821.2	807.6	799.9	796.2	776.5	757.9	704.0	643.5	599.3	579.5
North Dakota	15.8	16.3	17.0	18.1	19.7	20.0	20.5	22.1	22.5	22.8	23.9	24.0	23.7	23.5	24.5
Ohio	1 064.6	1 023.1	994.4	980.5	1 003.6	1 037.4	1 030.1	1 027.8	1 030.6	1 027.6	1 021.0	953.0	885.0	843.1	824.5
Oklahoma	156.6	156.6	152.7	156.5	158.8	161.5	162.9	168.9	175.6	177.3	177.5	169.8	152.3	143.2	141.8
Oregon	202.7	195.2	191.7	192.2	199.7	208.1	215.7	225.3	227.0	223.0	223.4	215.7	201.6	194.9	199.5
Pennsylvania	947.1	908.8	887.6	875.4	877.9	878.5	864.8	868.9	871.8	862.5	862.3	820.6	758.9	711.6	691.2
Rhode Island	95.1	87.4	84.8	83.5	82.5	80.3	77.3	76.2	74.8	72.1	71.1	67.8	62.3	58.7	56.9
South Carolina	347.8	333.6	337.5	341.7	345.3	346.8	338.8	338.5	341.2	336.1	336.2	313.6	289.7	275.9	268.5
South Dakota	33.5	34.1	36.0	38.0	40.9	43.5	43.6	44.2	44.0	44.2	43.8	40.9	38.4	37.7	38.9
Tennessee	493.4	480.3	492.8	502.8	513.7	517.9	501.5	498.0	498.6	494.7	488.0	454.2	428.5	413.2	411.5
Texas	947.7	936.3	928.7	942.2	966.2	995.3	1 016.9	1 045.1	1 077.3	1 063.3	1 068.0	1 026.8	948.7	900.0	889.5
Utah	103.5	102.5	102.4	106.4	111.6	116.8	121.5	125.6	126.8	126.0	125.5	122.0	113.9	112.3	114.9
Vermont	42.7	40.1	39.7	39.9	40.4	41.2	42.6	43.8	44.6	45.3	46.3	45.6	40.5	37.5	37.0
Virginia	387.2	375.7	372.7	370.2	370.8	373.1	370.8	374.4	375.5	366.8	363.5	341.2	320.0	304.9	299.2
Washington	336.0	328.8	325.0	312.9	311.6	311.3	324.9	350.3	360.5	343.4	331.8	316.1	285.0	267.1	263.5
West Virginia	82.0	79.0	78.3	78.8	77.2	78.4	77.6	76.9	77.7	76.9	75.9	72.2	68.7	64.5	63.0
Wisconsin	523.0	512.6	516.8	526.2	546.1	566.6	567.6	579.2	593.2	594.8	594.1	560.3	528.3	504.0	501.8
Wyoming	9.1	9.1	9.3	9.6	10.0	10.1	10.0	10.1	10.2	10.2	10.4	10.0	9.5	9.3	9.5
Puerto Rico	. . .	. . .	. . .	. . .	. . .	. . .	. . .	. . .	. . .	. . .	. . .	. . .	. . .	118.2	117.8
Virgin Islands	2.2	2.4	2.5	2.8	2.7	2.3	2.2	2.1	2.2	2.2	2.2	2.1	2.1	2.0	2.1

. . . = Not available.

Table 2-31. Employees on Manufacturing Payrolls by State, SIC Basis, 1964–1989

(Thousands of people.)

State	1964	1965	1966	1967	1968	1969	1970	1971	1972	1973	1974	1975	1976
Alabama	259.2	279.2	296.9	300.6	310.0	327.3	327.2	322.7	333.4	350.9	353.7	321.9	340.2
Alaska	5.6	6.3	6.6	6.6	6.9	7.3	8.6	7.8	8.1	9.5	9.7	9.6	10.3
Arizona	59.5	64.9	77.7	79.1	84.9	94.2	91.2	89.2	98.7	110.2	112.9	99.8	105.6
Arkansas	126.7	135.9	149.7	153.4	159.0	169.1	168.6	172.5	185.2	200.4	203.9	179.2	195.1
California	1 389.4	1 411.2	1 531.3	1 594.0	1 639.7	1 661.3	1 558.0	1 473.2	1 542.7	1 660.7	1 701.3	1 593.7	1 659.8
Colorado	93.5	92.6	102.7	106.1	110.5	118.3	120.8	123.5	131.5	143.3	146.6	137.2	144.5
Connecticut	421.0	436.1	471.4	479.5	474.3	471.7	441.9	399.0	400.1	420.2	430.9	389.8	397.0
Delaware	61.9	67.8	71.0	71.7	72.9	73.6	71.1	68.8	69.4	73.7	70.8	65.7	68.2
Florida	237.9	252.6	276.1	293.8	311.4	329.2	322.5	322.7	351.3	380.6	375.9	339.4	354.0
Georgia	378.9	403.9	431.5	438.9	452.9	477.6	467.1	461.7	476.6	494.5	483.7	439.3	476.3
Hawaii	25.2	24.5	24.2	24.7	23.8	25.2	25.6	25.2	24.9	23.8	22.7	23.7	23.4
Idaho	31.8	33.3	35.6	35.3	37.9	39.9	40.3	41.2	43.6	46.9	48.0	47.8	52.0
Illinois	1 253.3	1 318.4	1 410.5	1 409.6	1 404.0	1 417.4	1 358.6	1 282.4	1 284.2	1 353.5	1 345.1	1 199.8	1 215.2
Indiana	630.9	673.6	719.7	716.0	722.9	752.3	710.2	683.4	709.4	758.2	737.2	647.2	685.1
Iowa	183.5	192.9	212.1	219.3	223.1	225.4	216.0	209.8	222.9	241.3	249.9	230.4	234.0
Kansas	123.1	124.7	142.3	149.3	151.0	150.6	137.2	132.5	145.7	164.5	169.2	164.2	166.6
Kentucky	194.0	207.8	228.6	234.2	242.9	250.4	255.4	253.3	268.3	288.3	290.9	259.7	273.3
Louisiana	155.4	161.1	168.3	176.7	181.9	184.6	179.0	177.7	183.2	190.5	192.5	186.2	195.4
Maine	104.0	108.0	115.0	116.3	118.0	115.7	110.4	102.7	102.4	104.5	105.1	96.3	102.5
Maryland	258.2	264.8	279.8	283.3	280.6	281.7	271.4	252.4	248.8	257.0	254.5	230.0	232.4
Massachusetts	649.9	668.2	699.1	700.8	689.5	681.5	648.2	605.7	610.2	634.7	639.3	577.8	593.6
Michigan	1 032.0	1 112.4	1 179.6	1 148.8	1 172.5	1 203.8	1 081.1	1 059.2	1 097.4	1 178.8	1 114.0	983.7	1 061.7
Minnesota	246.4	261.6	287.4	302.2	314.7	331.4	318.7	298.8	310.2	331.2	340.7	313.0	321.7
Mississippi	140.4	153.0	166.6	167.4	175.5	182.5	182.1	189.5	207.7	221.0	220.0	201.8	218.9
Missouri	405.7	420.1	448.7	457.4	462.7	465.7	449.4	430.3	441.5	459.7	451.6	405.3	424.9
Montana	21.4	22.1	22.9	22.4	23.2	24.1	23.9	23.9	24.5	24.8	24.5	22.1	23.7
Nebraska	67.2	68.7	74.7	79.7	82.8	86.2	84.5	82.6	85.0	90.5	93.4	85.4	87.9
Nevada	6.9	7.1	7.1	6.8	7.1	8.2	8.6	8.8	9.8	11.8	12.3	12.2	13.0
New Hampshire	85.6	89.8	96.0	97.6	99.7	97.9	91.6	86.3	90.8	96.0	94.2	85.1	94.5
New Jersey	806.7	837.5	879.3	882.8	893.7	892.5	860.7	818.3	823.3	842.6	825.9	747.9	756.2
New Mexico	17.9	17.6	18.6	18.3	18.5	20.7	21.4	22.6	26.1	28.9	29.6	28.6	30.3
New York	1 794.8	1 838.1	1 894.5	1 885.7	1 879.0	1 870.8	1 760.6	1 633.5	1 602.2	1 619.1	1 574.6	1 421.9	1 438.9
North Carolina	557.1	590.6	638.1	657.5	686.1	714.0	713.0	716.2	756.8	796.9	789.6	715.5	756.3
North Dakota	8.4	8.7	8.9	8.6	8.9	9.0	9.9	10.2	10.8	12.6	14.7	16.2	16.2
Ohio	1 259.1	1 326.0	1 404.4	1 401.4	1 433.5	1 471.0	1 409.9	1 333.8	1 346.8	1 426.3	1 416.6	1 267.5	1 295.3
Oklahoma	96.6	103.0	113.3	116.4	121.7	129.9	134.1	132.7	141.1	151.9	156.7	150.7	156.1
Oregon	151.7	158.2	167.2	165.4	173.7	180.5	172.3	174.3	184.2	196.9	197.1	182.3	193.7
Pennsylvania	1 434.8	1 494.1	1 565.3	1 562.4	1 570.0	1 588.9	1 528.8	1 438.1	1 444.0	1 480.1	1 464.5	1 334.8	1 335.2
Rhode Island	116.0	121.0	127.6	127.4	127.4	127.9	120.9	115.2	121.0	125.6	126.0	112.7	122.9
South Carolina	277.7	293.0	313.7	319.0	327.3	341.5	340.3	337.2	354.3	374.9	375.9	339.9	371.0
South Dakota	13.3	13.5	14.3	15.4	15.9	15.9	15.8	16.5	18.4	19.8	20.9	19.8	22.2
Tennessee	361.5	386.6	424.2	434.8	454.3	469.0	463.8	459.5	489.2	519.4	513.3	459.0	486.1
Texas	540.5	572.1	622.1	661.9	709.4	750.2	734.3	710.5	738.7	790.2	831.3	815.9	862.3
Utah	52.5	50.0	51.2	50.9	51.9	54.8	56.0	56.5	60.5	65.1	70.4	67.5	70.7
Vermont	34.7	38.6	43.4	44.2	43.7	43.4	40.5	37.9	38.5	41.6	42.8	39.5	41.0
Virginia	308.6	322.5	340.0	346.0	362.7	371.0	366.0	366.2	387.8	401.8	401.9	371.5	387.7
Washington	219.3	227.0	265.2	277.1	286.9	278.5	239.5	214.7	224.1	244.2	253.6	244.0	247.4
West Virginia	126.2	129.2	133.0	133.2	132.4	131.0	126.5	122.9	123.3	129.0	132.1	121.1	124.4
Wisconsin	469.6	491.9	508.6	508.7	510.3	520.9	500.9	479.6	495.4	531.7	546.1	507.0	519.4
Wyoming	7.7	7.1	6.8	7.1	6.8	7.4	7.4	7.5	7.9	8.4	8.4	8.3	8.4
Puerto Rico	...	...	...	...	...	...	...	...	...	...	...	...	...
Virgin Islands	...	...	...	...	...	...	...	...	...	...	...	3.1	3.1

. . . = Not available.

Table 2-31. Employees on Manufacturing Payrolls by State, SIC Basis, 1964–1989—*Continued*

(Thousands of people.)

State	1977	1978	1979	1980	1981	1982	1983	1984	1985	1986	1987	1988	1989
Alabama	259.2	279.2	296.9	300.6	310.0	327.3	327.2	322.7	333.4	350.9	353.7	321.9	340.2
Alaska	5.6	6.3	6.6	6.6	6.9	7.3	8.6	7.8	8.1	9.5	9.7	9.6	10.3
Arizona	59.5	64.9	77.7	79.1	84.9	94.2	91.2	89.2	98.7	110.2	112.9	99.8	105.6
Arkansas	126.7	135.9	149.7	153.4	159.0	169.1	168.6	172.5	185.2	200.4	203.9	179.2	195.1
California	1 389.4	1 411.2	1 531.3	1 594.0	1 639.7	1 661.3	1 558.0	1 473.2	1 542.7	1 660.7	1 701.3	1 593.7	1 659.8
Colorado	93.5	92.6	102.7	106.1	110.5	118.3	120.8	123.5	131.5	143.3	146.6	137.2	144.5
Connecticut	421.0	436.1	471.4	479.5	474.3	471.7	441.9	399.0	400.1	420.2	430.9	389.8	397.0
Delaware	61.9	67.8	71.0	71.7	72.9	73.6	71.1	68.8	69.4	73.7	70.8	65.7	68.2
Florida	237.9	252.6	276.1	293.8	311.4	329.2	322.5	322.7	351.3	380.6	375.9	339.4	354.0
Georgia	378.9	403.9	431.5	438.9	452.9	477.6	467.1	461.7	476.6	494.5	483.7	439.3	476.3
Hawaii	25.2	24.5	24.2	24.7	23.8	25.2	25.6	25.2	24.9	23.8	22.7	23.7	23.4
Idaho	31.8	33.3	35.6	35.3	37.9	39.9	40.3	41.2	43.6	46.9	48.0	47.8	52.0
Illinois	1 253.3	1 318.4	1 410.5	1 409.6	1 404.0	1 417.4	1 358.6	1 282.4	1 284.2	1 353.5	1 345.1	1 199.8	1 215.2
Indiana	630.9	673.6	719.7	716.0	722.9	752.3	710.2	683.4	709.4	758.2	737.2	647.2	685.1
Iowa	183.5	192.9	212.1	219.3	223.1	225.4	216.0	209.8	222.9	241.3	249.9	230.4	234.0
Kansas	123.1	124.7	142.3	149.3	151.0	150.6	137.2	132.5	145.7	164.5	169.2	164.2	166.6
Kentucky	194.0	207.8	228.6	234.2	242.9	250.4	255.4	253.3	268.3	288.3	290.9	259.7	273.3
Louisiana	155.4	161.1	168.3	176.7	181.9	184.6	179.0	177.7	183.2	190.5	192.5	186.2	195.4
Maine	104.0	108.0	115.0	116.3	118.0	115.7	110.4	102.7	102.4	104.5	105.1	96.3	102.5
Maryland	258.2	264.8	279.8	283.3	280.6	281.7	271.4	252.4	248.8	257.0	254.5	230.0	232.4
Massachusetts	649.9	668.2	699.1	700.8	689.5	681.5	648.2	605.7	610.2	634.7	639.3	577.8	593.6
Michigan	1 032.0	1 112.4	1 179.6	1 148.8	1 172.5	1 203.8	1 081.1	1 059.2	1 097.4	1 178.8	1 114.0	983.7	1 061.7
Minnesota	246.4	261.6	287.4	302.2	314.7	331.4	318.7	298.8	310.2	331.2	340.7	313.0	321.7
Mississippi	140.4	153.0	166.6	167.4	175.5	182.5	182.1	189.5	207.7	221.0	220.0	201.8	218.9
Missouri	405.7	420.1	448.7	457.4	462.7	465.7	449.4	430.3	441.5	459.7	451.6	405.3	424.9
Montana	21.4	22.1	22.9	22.4	23.2	24.1	23.9	23.9	24.5	24.8	24.5	22.1	23.7
Nebraska	67.2	68.7	74.7	79.7	82.8	86.2	84.5	82.6	85.0	90.5	93.4	85.4	87.9
Nevada	6.9	7.1	7.1	6.8	7.1	8.2	8.6	8.8	9.8	11.8	12.3	12.2	13.0
New Hampshire	85.6	89.8	96.0	97.6	99.7	97.9	91.6	86.3	90.8	96.0	94.2	85.1	94.5
New Jersey	806.7	837.5	879.3	882.8	893.7	892.5	860.7	818.3	823.3	842.6	825.9	747.9	756.2
New Mexico	17.9	17.6	18.6	18.3	18.5	20.7	21.4	22.6	26.1	28.9	29.6	28.6	30.3
New York	1 794.8	1 838.1	1 894.5	1 885.7	1 879.0	1 870.8	1 760.6	1 633.5	1 602.2	1 619.1	1 574.6	1 421.9	1 438.9
North Carolina	557.1	590.6	638.1	657.5	686.1	714.0	713.0	716.2	756.8	796.9	789.6	715.5	756.3
North Dakota	8.4	8.7	8.9	8.6	8.9	9.0	9.9	10.2	10.8	12.6	14.7	16.2	16.2
Ohio	1 259.1	1 326.0	1 404.4	1 401.4	1 433.5	1 471.0	1 409.9	1 333.8	1 346.8	1 426.3	1 416.6	1 267.5	1 295.3
Oklahoma	96.6	103.0	113.3	116.4	121.7	129.9	134.1	132.7	141.1	151.9	156.7	150.7	156.1
Oregon	151.7	158.2	167.2	165.4	173.7	180.5	172.3	174.3	184.2	196.9	197.1	182.3	193.7
Pennsylvania	1 434.8	1 494.1	1 565.3	1 562.4	1 570.0	1 588.9	1 528.8	1 438.1	1 444.0	1 480.1	1 464.5	1 334.8	1 335.2
Rhode Island	116.0	121.0	127.6	127.4	127.4	127.9	120.9	115.2	121.0	125.6	126.0	112.7	122.9
South Carolina	277.7	293.0	313.7	319.0	327.3	341.5	340.3	337.2	354.3	374.9	375.9	339.9	371.0
South Dakota	13.3	13.5	14.3	15.4	15.9	15.9	15.8	16.5	18.4	19.8	20.9	19.8	22.2
Tennessee	361.5	386.6	424.2	434.8	454.3	469.0	463.8	459.5	489.2	519.4	513.3	459.0	486.1
Texas	540.5	572.1	622.1	661.9	709.4	750.2	734.3	710.5	738.7	790.2	831.3	815.9	862.3
Utah	52.5	50.0	51.2	50.9	51.9	54.8	56.0	56.5	60.5	65.1	70.4	67.5	70.7
Vermont	34.7	38.6	43.4	44.2	43.7	43.4	40.5	37.9	38.5	41.6	42.8	39.5	41.0
Virginia	308.6	322.5	340.0	346.0	362.7	371.0	366.0	366.2	387.8	401.8	401.9	371.5	387.7
Washington	219.3	227.0	265.2	277.1	286.9	278.5	239.5	214.7	224.1	244.2	253.6	244.0	247.4
West Virginia	126.2	129.2	133.0	133.2	132.4	131.0	126.5	122.9	123.3	129.0	132.1	121.1	124.4
Wisconsin	469.6	491.9	508.6	508.7	510.3	520.9	500.9	479.6	495.4	531.7	546.1	507.0	519.4
Wyoming	7.7	7.1	6.8	7.1	6.8	7.4	7.4	7.5	7.9	8.4	8.4	8.3	8.4
Puerto Rico	...	...	...	...	...	...	...	...	...	...	...	...	...
Virgin Islands	...	...	...	...	...	...	...	...	...	...	...	3.1	3.1

. . . = Not available.

Table 2-32. Employees on Government Payrolls by State, NAICS Basis, 1990–2004

(Thousands of people.)

State	1990	1991	1992	1993	1994	1995	1996	1997	1998	1999	2000	2001	2002	2003	2004
Alabama	326.7	332.6	337.9	340.7	346.0	343.2	342.9	346.2	347.1	350.8	351.7	352.0	354.6	358.4	359.9
Alaska	71.0	71.6	73.3	74.6	73.8	72.7	73.0	73.2	73.6	73.6	73.6	74.4	78.9	80.6	81.6	81.2
Arizona	258.9	271.1	276.7	286.6	294.3	310.4	317.8	328.2	341.4	354.1	366.6	377.8	390.4	393.5	400.7
Arkansas	159.2	163.2	167.1	169.7	172.9	177.1	180.2	183.3	185.1	187.4	190.7	193.7	195.4	198.5	200.7
California	2 074.8	2 090.6	2 095.6	2 080.6	2 093.2	2 107.0	2 113.3	2 140.7	2 166.1	2 239.3	2 318.1	2 382.0	2 447.1	2 425.5	2 390.3
Colorado	276.8	283.3	291.0	296.7	299.3	303.7	308.7	315.6	322.3	328.4	337.0	344.1	355.4	356.2	359.2
Connecticut	210.3	207.6	207.3	210.7	217.2	220.8	222.8	225.7	227.7	235.1	241.8	244.4	249.3	246.0	242.4
Delaware	47.9	48.0	48.6	49.6	50.3	50.7	52.4	53.1	54.3	55.1	56.6	56.9	57.1	57.2	58.1
District of Columbia	277.3	281.2	285.8	285.2	270.4	254.8	240.4	233.1	225.8	222.4	223.9	226.1	231.7	230.6	230.6
Florida	846.6	859.3	870.1	881.6	910.5	918.3	928.3	942.1	954.8	965.6	1 001.7	1 023.4	1 039.2	1 053.0	1 069.0
Georgia	531.9	536.6	537.1	548.1	564.0	570.3	569.5	577.3	586.0	589.6	597.2	610.3	624.8	632.4	638.4
Hawaii	105.6	108.9	111.1	111.5	111.8	111.4	110.5	111.7	112.1	112.7	114.6	114.5	117.9	119.1	120.1
Idaho	81.3	84.3	88.1	90.4	92.9	95.7	97.0	100.0	102.6	105.2	108.8	110.1	112.0	113.0	114.2
Illinois	765.9	770.5	773.8	774.4	786.0	798.6	809.3	808.3	816.0	825.5	839.6	850.4	861.0	853.2	843.9
Indiana	378.5	379.9	387.5	391.3	390.6	391.6	391.0	391.9	399.1	402.6	410.3	410.0	417.0	422.6	426.1
Iowa	218.9	220.6	221.0	222.4	226.9	230.2	232.8	234.6	236.1	239.4	243.3	245.2	244.0	244.8	244.3
Kansas	214.4	218.9	225.7	229.5	233.3	236.7	233.5	235.5	239.8	239.6	244.9	248.1	250.8	250.4	252.0
Kentucky	260.2	267.3	273.2	276.5	280.5	286.8	288.8	290.8	294.6	301.1	305.1	310.7	314.8	312.5	309.4
Louisiana	326.1	332.3	339.5	341.9	351.4	358.3	361.8	364.1	367.2	370.3	373.4	373.7	374.9	379.3	382.5
Maine	95.7	95.8	95.7	95.3	94.1	93.2	92.8	92.9	94.6	96.6	99.5	102.0	103.1	103.7	104.9
Maryland	422.6	420.2	418.5	420.6	423.0	424.1	424.1	424.0	434.7	446.1	452.7	458.3	466.2	467.1	465.9
Massachusetts	402.1	389.9	382.5	387.4	389.9	395.0	399.9	404.5	411.5	417.4	423.9	428.2	423.4	412.6	407.6
Michigan	633.9	635.8	639.0	639.4	639.0	640.9	643.8	647.4	656.0	667.6	681.6	686.3	686.6	685.4	682.1
Minnesota	346.9	351.0	355.3	361.3	368.7	387.1	388.7	388.8	390.5	396.6	407.6	409.3	414.0	412.5	411.1
Mississippi	203.3	203.9	207.8	210.1	213.7	214.6	216.8	219.0	223.4	227.0	233.8	237.5	240.1	240.8	242.5
Missouri	369.7	370.6	370.6	376.8	384.9	389.9	400.7	412.8	414.1	421.3	426.2	428.7	431.1	432.2	429.3
Montana	71.3	71.8	74.2	74.1	76.3	76.9	77.0	77.4	78.5	78.8	80.3	84.1	84.9	85.8	87.0
Nebraska	143.4	145.6	147.6	149.0	151.6	150.8	151.4	152.2	150.9	151.4	154.4	156.8	158.9	159.8	160.1
Nevada	75.6	81.2	86.0	88.5	92.2	96.5	101.1	106.5	111.7	117.4	121.7	126.8	130.8	134.9	138.5
New Hampshire	72.6	72.4	73.1	74.3	76.1	76.2	77.9	78.8	79.7	81.5	83.5	85.8	88.3	90.1	89.7
New Jersey	576.7	571.5	571.8	570.6	573.3	573.3	570.6	570.2	571.6	577.5	588.8	602.6	613.5	621.9	634.1
New Mexico	149.7	152.2	156.0	159.1	163.0	166.4	171.4	176.9	178.4	180.2	183.0	185.5	190.9	195.1	198.3
New York	1 473.4	1 445.1	1 428.0	1 433.3	1 436.0	1 416.5	1 400.6	1 406.9	1 424.0	1 445.3	1 467.7	1 467.8	1 492.6	1 487.8	1 483.3
North Carolina	491.9	501.7	502.4	527.0	538.6	550.5	561.3	576.3	593.6	604.2	622.2	636.0	641.5	641.4	650.7
North Dakota	65.4	65.6	66.7	67.1	67.2	71.1	70.8	70.7	71.0	71.8	73.0	73.4	74.2	75.3	74.6
Ohio	722.2	727.9	735.0	735.5	741.0	748.7	752.2	757.8	763.4	772.1	785.0	794.0	800.2	802.6	801.8
Oklahoma	261.8	264.9	270.1	269.7	270.1	269.6	271.4	276.2	278.2	282.6	287.7	296.4	300.9	295.8	301.6
Oregon	223.5	226.4	231.0	232.6	234.7	240.2	246.6	249.5	255.3	261.3	267.3	270.0	272.9	267.7	269.5
Pennsylvania	699.0	694.6	692.6	701.7	706.3	711.9	712.5	714.6	711.5	715.6	725.1	728.3	738.9	745.6	745.1
Rhode Island	62.4	60.9	61.2	61.4	61.6	61.2	61.3	63.2	62.9	63.3	64.3	65.2	66.1	66.2	65.8
South Carolina	282.1	285.6	291.9	295.7	295.3	294.2	294.6	298.8	309.4	315.3	322.8	322.8	325.5	326.1	327.5
South Dakota	62.7	63.4	65.4	66.6	67.1	71.0	70.4	70.5	71.0	71.9	70.3	73.1	74.0	74.3	74.3
Tennessee	351.4	353.1	356.8	361.9	370.7	373.1	381.6	380.3	385.5	390.1	399.0	403.2	410.3	411.1	414.0
Texas	1 263.4	1 287.5	1 334.4	1 376.0	1 413.7	1 445.7	1 457.7	1 483.3	1 504.2	1 534.8	1 561.9	1 586.2	1 626.0	1 646.1	1 655.6
Utah	150.5	153.9	156.8	159.4	161.4	163.5	166.8	172.3	176.7	179.5	185.4	190.1	195.0	196.6	198.7
Vermont	43.5	43.8	43.7	44.0	44.7	45.1	45.4	45.7	46.2	47.6	49.4	50.2	50.8	52.0	52.4
Virginia	578.3	580.5	589.3	597.8	603.1	597.5	596.2	596.6	602.0	611.2	624.7	629.2	634.9	637.5	651.5
Washington	397.5	411.5	423.6	430.0	437.2	444.4	450.5	457.9	465.9	474.2	483.3	505.4	516.1	520.6	523.3
West Virginia	127.4	127.7	132.3	132.8	136.5	136.4	138.7	139.1	140.8	140.9	143.1	141.0	142.8	142.5	143.1
Wisconsin	342.9	346.4	356.9	361.5	367.1	378.5	383.5	386.7	393.2	398.9	405.6	413.7	414.8	412.9	412.1
Wyoming	55.2	55.7	56.8	57.2	58.1	57.7	58.1	58.0	58.4	59.4	60.7	61.5	62.7	63.5	64.6
Puerto Rico	. . .	. . .	. . .	. . .	. . .	. . .	. . .	. . .	. . .	. . .	. . .	. . .	. . .	300.8	307.9
Virgin Islands	13.5	13.4	13.8	13.9	13.8	13.6	14.0	13.7	13.7	13.4	13.0	12.3	12.6	12.6	12.4

. . . = Not available.

Table 2-33. Employees on Government Payrolls by State, SIC Basis, 1964–1989

(Thousands of people.)

State	1964	1965	1966	1967	1968	1969	1970	1971	1972	1973	1974	1975	1976
Alabama	173.3	179.1	191.6	197.7	201.4	204.7	209.5	213.6	220.9	225.7	235.1	247.5	252.9
Alaska	28.1	29.7	30.8	31.8	32.2	33.3	35.6	37.9	40.5	41.5	43.8	47.7	48.2
Arizona	85.3	92.2	98.9	104.7	110.0	113.4	119.5	129.5	139.2	147.6	161.0	169.7	177.3
Arkansas	76.5	84.9	91.6	93.4	97.0	100.9	102.7	104.9	108.5	110.1	115.6	120.9	125.3
California	1 043.5	1 105.4	1 196.7	1 274.3	1 335.8	1 391.7	1 424.7	1 446.3	1 492.7	1 524.8	1 586.0	1 670.6	1 695.6
Colorado	132.0	137.7	148.2	157.7	162.4	166.9	177.2	184.7	190.8	197.2	204.0	216.6	219.5
Connecticut	109.0	115.9	122.5	131.5	140.0	150.9	157.9	160.9	165.2	167.7	171.0	178.7	175.1
Delaware	23.9	25.0	26.3	27.9	29.3	31.9	35.0	36.8	39.0	39.2	39.1	40.3	40.6
Florida	278.7	301.2	326.2	342.3	361.8	377.9	397.8	419.1	437.9	469.9	510.5	546.0	542.8
Georgia	210.8	222.8	243.9	263.0	275.3	286.1	297.5	309.6	320.9	328.2	340.5	354.8	366.1
Hawaii	47.2	50.5	54.9	58.3	60.9	62.5	64.3	68.4	69.3	68.0	68.7	70.8	72.6
Idaho	38.1	39.6	41.9	44.3	45.2	46.8	49.1	51.3	54.5	56.2	59.7	62.3	64.5
Illinois	475.0	502.4	536.5	572.0	593.4	615.6	638.9	648.6	654.3	666.5	680.9	714.5	717.2
Indiana	219.2	232.2	254.1	271.4	285.3	280.9	286.4	296.3	301.4	303.8	308.0	323.3	332.5
Iowa	133.1	138.8	148.8	157.1	163.8	171.7	176.0	178.3	180.2	182.8	186.7	192.0	197.0
Kansas	126.2	130.2	137.0	143.2	146.0	149.6	153.3	155.1	162.8	166.5	164.0	168.7	171.6
Kentucky	128.4	135.2	145.2	155.5	163.3	166.1	172.1	180.5	188.5	194.3	198.5	208.3	213.0
Louisiana	163.4	171.7	185.4	197.4	201.8	208.2	213.2	216.0	227.9	233.2	241.6	248.7	253.0
Maine	52.9	54.3	57.4	59.5	61.6	64.3	66.4	68.7	69.4	70.7	72.9	74.8	75.2
Maryland	174.1	183.8	201.9	218.2	232.3	243.2	301.0	314.9	327.0	338.1	349.1	366.1	372.1
Massachusetts	272.7	278.5	286.2	297.1	302.5	310.7	319.9	330.6	343.1	351.6	354.3	365.1	375.8
Michigan	373.3	395.4	433.0	455.0	471.3	494.5	506.6	509.4	526.8	534.4	562.5	583.1	594.5
Minnesota	179.3	189.9	201.6	214.1	215.4	224.1	234.9	239.7	246.2	256.6	263.8	271.5	276.0
Mississippi	99.5	105.2	114.3	120.6	125.1	128.0	131.2	133.7	139.4	145.0	150.4	153.5	156.2
Missouri	210.6	225.4	244.7	260.3	269.1	276.1	284.1	292.9	297.5	306.9	312.9	316.0	316.5
Montana	44.7	45.9	48.1	51.8	53.3	52.1	52.6	54.3	55.4	55.4	58.2	64.9	65.7
Nebraska	89.1	92.5	93.3	97.6	97.4	100.9	104.7	109.1	114.3	116.9	121.4	124.7	124.3
Nevada	26.4	28.6	30.3	32.3	34.1	35.8	36.9	38.1	39.7	41.4	43.0	45.6	46.8
New Hampshire	29.0	30.1	31.4	33.4	34.4	35.5	37.3	38.8	41.2	43.4	45.6	48.0	49.9
New Jersey	280.0	295.4	312.0	329.2	344.4	360.1	374.8	388.0	405.3	417.1	439.9	470.2	480.5
New Mexico	71.8	75.4	81.0	83.4	85.0	86.3	89.2	92.3	96.0	99.5	102.5	104.8	108.0
New York	924.1	958.6	1 012.4	1 073.1	1 123.8	1 176.0	1 218.1	1 239.8	1 243.9	1 268.6	1 301.9	1 328.7	1 273.6
North Carolina	192.7	201.6	217.4	231.6	244.4	254.3	264.2	268.4	275.3	281.8	303.2	328.3	347.9
North Dakota	38.8	40.3	42.1	44.4	47.2	48.4	49.3	49.3	51.3	52.2	53.3	54.5	56.2
Ohio	440.3	458.6	483.0	509.5	528.3	544.8	565.5	577.2	589.1	597.8	613.1	626.4	632.2
Oklahoma	136.9	145.8	158.8	168.2	171.9	175.5	176.7	179.0	184.9	192.2	199.0	206.3	207.0
Oregon	111.3	118.2	125.3	132.4	136.1	140.8	146.7	152.0	157.5	160.3	168.5	177.1	181.6
Pennsylvania	488.6	508.4	536.1	567.2	588.1	609.4	618.7	629.2	651.9	658.7	682.0	721.4	722.1
Rhode Island	43.4	46.1	48.7	51.2	52.3	52.8	53.6	55.9	56.8	55.5	55.1	56.6	57.0
South Carolina	106.8	111.1	121.0	128.4	134.0	140.8	149.9	156.7	165.6	170.7	182.2	199.8	203.3
South Dakota	44.4	46.6	48.2	49.3	50.3	53.0	53.1	52.6	53.7	53.8	54.9	55.7	55.9
Tennessee	173.3	185.1	195.3	201.8	208.2	214.2	225.9	231.9	240.6	246.2	256.4	271.3	283.1
Texas	500.0	525.6	567.1	607.1	630.1	651.4	662.3	684.2	714.8	745.3	776.0	815.8	847.0
Utah	73.7	79.4	90.7	98.0	98.8	99.6	100.1	103.2	105.5	105.7	108.2	110.3	112.2
Vermont	19.5	20.3	21.2	22.3	23.4	24.4	26.2	27.2	28.2	28.7	29.3	30.5	30.9
Virginia	221.2	232.2	251.2	270.5	283.6	292.4	355.1	371.9	380.0	391.2	405.9	422.8	436.6
Washington	184.6	193.1	206.2	218.5	230.1	237.4	244.5	252.4	258.7	259.0	269.3	280.5	284.8
West Virginia	75.3	81.7	88.5	92.1	94.9	95.0	95.9	98.0	99.4	104.2	106.4	108.1	109.6
Wisconsin	190.4	201.0	215.2	230.3	244.6	255.3	265.5	270.2	275.8	276.3	276.9	285.4	288.6
Wyoming	24.6	25.6	26.9	28.4	28.1	28.1	28.4	29.4	30.5	31.3	32.4	34.5	36.1
Puerto Rico	...	...	...	...	...	...	...	...	...	...	...	...	...
Virgin Islands	...	...	...	...	...	...	...	...	...	...	...	11.7	11.3

. . . = Not available.

Table 2-33. Employees on Government Payrolls by State, SIC Basis, 1964–1989—*Continued*

(Thousands of people.)

State	1977	1978	1979	1980	1981	1982	1983	1984	1985	1986	1987	1988	1989
Alabama	266.3	285.9	291.6	297.4	291.3	290.1	292.7	293.4	295.9	298.0	300.6	309.5	317.9
Alaska	50.1	51.6	54.4	55.0	57.1	59.6	63.0	66.5	68.3	68.0	65.8	66.5	68.7
Arizona	181.9	194.8	196.2	201.8	199.5	199.9	203.1	207.5	218.1	225.0	232.0	237.2	246.4
Arkansas	128.6	135.9	139.1	141.1	138.1	136.0	137.3	139.5	143.0	145.1	146.1	150.0	154.2
California	1 740.7	1 753.1	1 735.0	1 763.9	1 756.4	1 735.2	1 724.3	1 747.4	1 792.8	1 838.8	1 883.7	1 934.1	1 998.7
Colorado	221.1	234.0	238.8	243.6	241.7	238.6	240.7	244.4	248.9	256.0	262.2	266.7	271.4
Connecticut	175.6	179.2	181.3	[1]185.2	182.4	179.6	181.9	185.2	188.8	195.3	201.2	206.3	207.7
Delaware	41.4	42.8	44.4	45.2	44.5	43.8	43.4	43.7	44.8	46.1	46.6	47.5	47.1
Florida	565.7	601.8	600.5	618.8	620.1	632.5	639.3	649.5	674.4	701.9	731.8	773.0	800.1
Georgia	384.0	407.9	418.7	429.2	431.1	434.0	437.6	442.0	448.7	462.2	476.6	494.1	512.2
Hawaii	73.0	73.8	73.4	75.5	75.4	76.5	77.4	77.8	79.0	79.2	80.8	83.5	85.0
Idaho	67.3	69.8	69.6	70.5	69.2	67.8	67.8	68.9	70.2	70.9	73.3	76.0	77.9
Illinois	717.8	728.0	739.8	749.4	734.5	717.9	701.6	687.9	697.8	714.8	724.5	738.8	744.4
Indiana	342.0	349.1	347.6	346.6	339.7	328.7	327.0	328.1	332.9	339.7	347.2	354.5	366.6
Iowa	202.5	208.2	204.5	207.4	203.1	202.0	203.4	204.5	206.8	207.3	210.2	212.1	216.7
Kansas	176.9	180.0	183.3	187.4	185.9	183.8	182.9	185.2	188.7	194.1	199.0	204.4	209.1
Kentucky	212.0	220.3	230.4	230.9	224.3	218.9	216.6	223.0	230.0	236.0	240.2	246.1	253.3
Louisiana	257.4	280.3	289.7	300.8	303.8	307.3	315.0	318.6	322.4	319.3	313.1	312.6	315.7
Maine	77.7	81.5	82.6	83.3	82.6	82.1	83.1	83.9	84.9	86.7	88.4	91.6	94.1
Maryland	378.1	401.9	418.7	434.8	415.9	393.2	379.6	387.9	393.6	391.6	392.9	399.1	411.3
Massachusetts	407.9	429.2	416.7	412.3	394.6	374.7	375.4	375.4	385.3	393.0	401.2	411.3	408.8
Michigan	596.7	611.4	621.0	627.8	598.4	577.8	569.8	567.2	580.7	598.6	611.6	623.5	623.2
Minnesota	286.3	292.8	295.6	300.6	299.0	289.6	286.6	293.7	301.2	307.9	313.8	320.8	328.7
Mississippi	163.9	181.8	192.2	194.5	185.9	180.0	181.1	183.2	188.5	189.5	191.1	196.0	199.8
Missouri	321.5	335.6	338.5	339.2	326.6	328.2	323.2	321.8	334.1	338.5	344.0	351.8	359.3
Montana	70.0	71.7	70.1	70.2	69.3	67.4	68.4	68.7	69.9	70.2	69.4	70.7	70.3
Nebraska	129.2	130.3	130.6	130.8	129.7	129.3	130.2	131.1	133.8	134.9	135.3	137.8	139.7
Nevada	49.2	52.2	54.7	57.0	57.1	58.2	58.0	58.9	60.5	61.6	64.1	67.0	70.8
New Hampshire	[1]53.8	54.3	[1]55.1	57.3	56.7	55.9	56.1	57.5	60.0	62.0	65.4	68.7	71.2
New Jersey	504.0	523.0	517.8	529.7	529.0	528.6	525.9	526.6	536.0	540.8	547.1	556.2	564.2
New Mexico	111.0	116.6	120.5	125.0	125.8	125.6	127.2	129.7	132.8	135.9	137.6	141.6	144.9
New York	1 270.8	1 315.1	1 311.3	1 314.4	1 300.3	1 293.7	1 299.6	1 318.2	1 353.6	1 382.3	1 402.1	1 433.2	1 447.6
North Carolina	367.6	386.4	397.2	409.9	403.7	400.3	407.1	413.7	420.5	430.9	442.3	458.7	477.2
North Dakota	57.5	60.0	60.6	60.9	60.5	60.3	61.3	62.2	63.6	64.4	64.6	64.8	65.6
Ohio	642.3	667.5	674.0	689.9	676.0	659.6	656.1	655.2	665.2	678.9	687.3	693.8	706.4
Oklahoma	212.4	218.4	224.0	228.5	235.7	237.2	245.2	241.4	245.7	246.8	245.4	248.5	257.2
Oregon	186.8	197.1	200.7	203.2	202.6	195.5	192.3	194.1	197.7	200.2	205.6	211.2	215.6
Pennsylvania	710.9	720.7	720.7	723.3	703.4	682.5	673.7	672.9	680.2	679.8	688.7	694.6	697.9
Rhode Island	58.2	59.8	59.3	59.2	58.5	57.8	56.9	57.4	57.7	58.0	58.2	58.9	59.1
South Carolina	213.7	223.8	228.8	236.4	233.0	228.1	230.3	237.3	244.8	251.4	258.0	261.5	273.1
South Dakota	56.6	58.1	58.3	58.6	57.8	56.6	56.9	57.2	57.9	58.8	58.9	60.1	61.6
Tennessee	291.2	305.6	313.9	317.2	311.7	297.5	294.1	296.1	304.2	312.4	321.2	328.4	344.3
Texas	875.5	923.7	953.2	978.1	1 000.8	1 023.6	1 042.0	1 063.5	1 088.9	1 118.8	1 142.7	1 175.5	1 206.6
Utah	115.8	121.0	123.2	125.0	125.1	126.4	128.8	131.5	137.8	141.2	141.5	142.7	146.3
Vermont	[1]34.3	35.1	35.8	37.0	36.2	36.0	36.3	36.5	37.4	38.2	39.0	40.9	42.0
Virginia	453.6	482.7	493.5	511.2	506.6	500.1	500.9	505.0	515.6	519.9	530.3	544.4	562.6
Washington	294.9	308.0	315.5	330.8	326.4	318.5	[1]324.0	334.5	342.8	348.9	357.2	368.8	379.9
West Virginia	111.0	120.3	130.1	133.1	130.2	126.8	127.8	130.7	127.5	128.9	128.2	129.3	125.9
Wisconsin	287.1	298.2	310.1	321.1	318.0	314.1	312.5	314.7	320.6	325.6	325.0	327.8	335.0
Wyoming	38.0	39.1	40.8	43.0	44.5	46.0	48.9	50.9	52.2	53.1	50.5	[1]54.1	54.3
Puerto Rico	. . .	. . .	246.0	254.4	244.6	236.7	240.1	253.2	255.4	267.7	281.2	298.5	298.1
Virgin Islands	11.9	12.8	13.5	13.4	13.9	13.5	14.0	13.8	13.5	13.1	12.8	13.2	13.6

[1]Data not continuous.
. . . = Not available.

Table 2-34. Average Weekly Hours of Production Workers on Manufacturing Payrolls by State, NAICS Basis, 2001–2004

(Hours.)

State	2001	2002	2003	2004
Alabama	41.0	41.4	41.0	40.8
Alaska	43.1	37.4	43.0	40.6
Arizona	40.3	40.0	40.4	40.5
Arkansas	39.9	39.7	39.6	39.9
California	39.6	39.6	39.7	40.0
Colorado	40.7	40.6	40.4	40.4
Connecticut	41.7	41.6	41.4	41.8
Delaware	39.7	40.0	40.3	40.0
District of Columbia	. . .	. . .	. . .	. . .
Florida	40.6	42.1	41.0	41.1
Georgia	40.4	40.9	39.8	39.2
Hawaii	36.0	35.6	37.2	37.9
Idaho	39.1	39.6	41.3	40.5
Illinois	41.0	41.4	40.6	41.0
Indiana	41.0	42.4	42.1	42.1
Iowa	40.9	41.3	41.7	42.2
Kansas	40.7	40.8	40.5	41.0
Kentucky	41.5	42.2	41.7	40.8
Louisiana	43.1	43.9	44.1	43.9
Maine	39.8	39.9	40.0	39.6
Maryland	39.0	40.0	39.5	40.1
Massachusetts	40.3	40.8	40.6	41.1
Michigan	41.9	42.7	42.1	42.4
Minnesota	39.6	39.7	40.2	40.9
Mississippi	39.7	40.6	39.9	40.1
Missouri	40.3	39.3	40.5	40.2
Montana	38.8	38.2	38.4	38.3
Nebraska	41.2	41.9	41.6	41.6
Nevada	38.7	38.8	39.0	40.1
New Hampshire	40.6	39.8	40.0	40.0
New Jersey	40.6	40.9	41.0	42.1
New Mexico	39.0	39.9	39.4	39.6
New York	39.8	40.3	40.0	39.7
North Carolina	39.4	40.2	39.8	40.3
North Dakota	40.9	40.2	40.0	39.3
Ohio	41.2	41.4	41.0	41.7
Oklahoma	39.4	39.2	39.3	40.4
Oregon	39.1	39.1	39.3	39.1
Pennsylvania	40.4	40.3	40.0	40.3
Rhode Island	39.4	38.7	39.3	39.2
South Carolina	41.2	42.1	41.3	39.5
South Dakota	41.7	42.3	42.5	42.0
Tennessee	38.9	40.1	39.8	40.0
Texas	41.6	41.1	41.4	39.8
Utah	38.4	37.8	39.7	38.1
Vermont	39.6	40.0	40.0	40.2
Virginia	40.1	40.8	40.8	41.5
Washington	40.0	40.1	39.5	40.0
West Virginia	41.1	41.4	41.3	41.4
Wisconsin	40.2	40.5	40.3	40.3
Wyoming	38.6	39.3	40.2	39.7
Puerto Rico	. . .	. . .	40.9	41.1
Virgin Islands	43.9	43.7	42.8	46.4

. . . = Not available.

Table 2-35. Average Weekly Hours of Production Workers on Manufacturing Payrolls by State, SIC Basis, 1973–2000

(Thousands of people.)

State	1973	1974	1975	1976	1977	1978	1979	1980	1981	1982	1983	1984	1985	1986
Alabama	41.0	40.5	39.5	40.6	40.5	40.6	40.7	40.1	39.9	38.5	40.7	41.0	40.8	41.1
Alaska	36.6	40.5	36.6	40.5	43.3	42.4	43.9	42.7	40.0	38.6	36.2	39.3	40.7	41.1
Arizona	39.8	39.2	39.0	39.5	40.1	40.3	40.6	40.1	39.6	38.9	40.5	40.8	40.9	41.0
Arkansas	39.9	39.2	38.8	39.6	39.7	39.3	39.6	39.3	39.4	38.6	40.1	40.5	40.2	40.4
California	40.3	39.7	39.4	39.7	40.1	40.1	39.9	39.5	39.6	39.2	40.0	40.3	40.2	40.3
Colorado	. . .	. . .	. . .	. . .	39.4	39.3	39.5	39.8	39.8	39.2	39.9	40.9	40.2	39.9
Connecticut	42.1	41.4	40.5	40.8	41.5	42.0	42.0	41.8	41.6	40.5	41.3	42.5	41.9	41.8
Delaware	40.3	39.4	39.3	40.0	39.6	40.0	39.5	40.5	40.3	39.2	40.6	41.5	41.1	41.3
Florida	41.0	40.2	40.0	40.4	40.7	40.9	40.5	40.8	40.6	39.9	40.7	41.2	41.3	40.8
Georgia	40.5	39.8	39.5	40.1	40.5	40.1	40.4	40.2	40.1	38.6	41.1	41.0	40.6	40.9
Hawaii	39.9	39.4	39.1	39.0	38.0	38.6	38.3	37.8	38.5	37.9	38.6	38.1	37.4	38.9
Idaho	38.8	39.0	38.8	38.7	39.3	38.8	38.3	37.1	37.8	36.7	37.4	37.6	37.8	38.2
Illinois	41.2	40.4	39.7	40.4	40.6	40.1	40.7	39.8	40.0	39.2	40.6	40.6	40.6	40.9
Indiana	0.0	0.0	. . .	. . .	. . .	. . .	. . .	. . .	. . .	. . .	. . .	. . .	. . .	. . .
Iowa	. . .	. . .	. . .	39.9	40.1	40.1	40.5	39.6	39.5	38.7	39.8	40.2	40.2	40.6
Kansas	. . .	. . .	. . .	. . .	. . .	. . .	40.7	40.4	40.4	39.2	39.1	40.1	39.5	40.3
Kentucky	40.3	39.6	38.7	39.4	39.5	39.6	39.4	39.1	39.3	38.4	39.2	39.2	38.9	39.2
Louisiana	41.4	40.1	42.8	41.3	41.8	41.6	41.3	41.2	42.2	41.0	40.0	41.6	41.7	41.8
Maine	40.8	40.3	39.9	39.9	39.8	40.2	40.1	40.0	40.4	40.0	39.9	39.9	40.0	40.6
Maryland	40.5	39.9	39.1	39.6	39.9	39.9	40.0	39.6	39.9	39.2	40.0	41.0	40.3	40.5
Massachusetts	40.5	39.9	39.1	39.7	39.9	40.2	40.1	39.6	40.0	39.2	39.9	40.1	40.7	41.3
Michigan	. . .	. . .	. . .	42.7	43.3	43.0	41.2	40.1	40.5	40.2	42.5	43.2	43.1	42.6
Minnesota	41.0	39.9	39.2	39.8	40.0	40.2	40.0	39.4	39.4	39.1	39.7	40.3	40.3	40.6
Mississippi	40.3	39.3	39.3	40.0	40.1	39.9	39.6	39.3	39.3	38.1	40.1	40.6	40.6	40.2
Missouri	39.8	39.3	39.0	39.8	40.2	40.0	39.5	39.2	39.2	38.6	39.9	40.5	40.2	40.5
Montana	39.3	38.8	38.0	39.8	41.8	42.7	42.9	43.2	41.0	39.3	39.7	39.2	39.1	39.4
Nebraska	41.8	41.2	40.5	41.1	40.8	41.1	41.3	40.6	40.3	39.9	40.3	40.5	40.3	40.4
Nevada	40.0	38.8	38.2	38.9	38.8	38.5	38.5	38.2	38.6	37.3	38.8	39.8	40.4	40.2
New Hampshire	39.8	39.3	39.1	39.6	40.0	40.3	40.1	39.8	39.9	39.6	40.5	41.0	40.7	41.2
New Jersey	41.4	40.7	39.9	40.4	41.1	40.8	41.2	40.7	40.6	39.9	40.6	41.1	40.8	41.2
New Mexico	39.4	38.4	39.0	39.5	38.8	39.2	39.5	39.8	39.5	39.2	39.7	39.9	39.8	39.5
New York	39.9	39.4	38.9	39.4	39.6	39.8	39.6	39.4	39.4	38.8	39.3	39.8	39.8	39.9
North Carolina	40.1	39.1	38.4	39.4	39.6	39.8	39.6	39.6	39.3	39.1	40.0	39.9	39.6	40.7
North Dakota	40.4	40.2	39.9	39.1	38.6	39.7	39.1	37.5	38.1	37.6	38.0	38.4	38.6	38.2
Ohio	42.3	41.2	40.3	41.4	42.0	42.1	41.5	40.6	40.9	40.1	41.4	42.3	42.0	42.1
Oklahoma	40.6	40.5	40.0	40.3	40.4	40.2	40.5	40.1	40.1	39.5	40.5	41.6	41.3	41.3
Oregon	39.3	38.8	38.4	38.9	38.6	39.0	38.5	38.1	37.5	37.9	38.9	39.2	38.7	39.0
Pennsylvania	40.2	39.6	38.8	39.2	39.5	40.0	39.9	38.8	39.2	38.4	39.2	40.2	39.9	40.2
Rhode Island	39.3	39.2	38.9	[1]39.5	39.1	38.9	39.1	39.3	39.3	38.6	39.0	40.9	40.2	40.4
South Carolina	40.5	39.8	39.4	40.4	40.6	40.8	40.8	40.3	40.4	38.2	40.6	40.8	40.4	41.1
South Dakota	42.6	41.7	40.7	39.9	39.3	41.7	41.9	40.9	41.6	41.1	41.6	42.1	41.8	42.1
Tennessee	40.4	39.9	39.8	40.3	40.2	39.6	39.7	39.7	39.9	38.6	40.5	40.9	41.0	41.2
Texas	. . .	. . .	. . .	40.9	41.1	41.3	41.1	41.2	41.3	40.0	40.9	41.7	41.2	41.4
Utah	38.8	38.7	38.1	39.2	40.0	39.5	39.0	39.1	39.7	38.5	39.4	39.9	40.1	40.0
Vermont	41.5	41.1	40.4	41.0	40.8	41.0	40.8	40.6	40.0	39.0	40.0	40.6	40.7	40.7
Virginia	40.6	39.8	39.2	39.9	39.9	39.8	39.7	39.3	39.7	38.4	39.7	40.3	40.1	40.4
Washington	39.2	38.9	38.7	39.1	39.2	39.3	38.6	38.4	38.8	38.5	38.9	38.8	39.0	39.4
West Virginia	40.0	39.6	39.0	39.2	39.5	39.6	39.6	39.2	39.4	38.8	39.6	40.3	39.9	40.3
Wisconsin	41.4	41.1	40.4	40.6	40.6	41.0	40.9	40.2	40.1	39.6	40.7	41.1	41.1	41.3
Wyoming	38.6	38.0	38.6	40.2	39.8	38.6	37.6	38.9	40.0	38.2	36.9	39.5	40.9	39.0
Puerto Rico	. . .	. . .	. . .	. . .	. . .	. . .	. . .	38.0	38.2	37.5	38.7	38.7	38.5	39.0
Virgin Islands	. . .	. . .	. . .	. . .	. . .	40.9	40.9	41.1	42.3	42.3	41.4	42.7	41.7	41.9

[1]Data not continuous.

. . . = Not available.

Table 2-35. Average Weekly Hours of Production Workers on Manufacturing Payrolls by State, SIC Series, 1973–2000—*Continued*

(Thousands of people.)

State	1987	1988	1989	1990	1991	1992	1993	1994	1995	1996	1997	1998	1999	2000
Alabama	41.4	41.4	41.2	41.0	40.8	41.2	41.2	41.9	41.6	41.7	41.9	42.2	42.1	41.9
Alaska	42.7	42.1	44.4	44.9	46.4	45.5	45.0	47.4	47.8	46.5	46.7	49.9	45.3	44.5
Arizona	40.6	41.1	41.2	40.7	40.7	40.8	40.7	42.3	42.5	42.8	41.4	40.4	40.4	40.4
Arkansas	41.0	40.9	40.8	41.0	41.2	41.4	41.4	41.8	41.0	41.5	41.4	41.7	41.7	41.0
California	40.3	40.7	40.7	40.6	40.6	40.6	40.9	41.4	41.2	41.5	41.9	41.8	41.7	41.7
Colorado	40.2	40.4	40.2	41.2	40.4	40.5	41.2	41.3	41.0	41.2	41.8	41.5	41.5	39.8
Connecticut	42.1	42.2	42.2	42.0	41.8	41.7	42.1	42.8	42.8	42.5	42.6	42.7	42.4	42.6
Delaware	40.7	40.0	41.5	41.3	40.8	40.8	42.1	42.8	41.0	40.5	41.9	42.3	43.0	43.3
Florida	40.8	40.7	40.9	40.7	40.7	40.9	41.2	41.4	41.4	41.5	41.8	41.7	41.8	41.9
Georgia	41.6	41.4	41.1	40.9	41.0	41.4	41.7	42.4	42.3	42.3	42.4	41.8	41.9	41.4
Hawaii	39.4	40.0	40.0	40.3	39.8	40.0	39.8	38.3	37.5	38.1	37.9	37.3	39.3	38.3
Idaho	38.1	38.1	38.9	38.9	39.1	39.2	40.1	40.0	39.3	39.5	40.1	38.3	39.4	39.2
Illinois	41.6	42.3	41.9	41.4	41.2	41.0	41.5	41.9	41.7	41.7	42.2	41.8	41.9	41.2
Indiana	. . .	. . .	41.6	41.3	41.2	42.0	42.7	43.3	42.2	42.8	43.2	42.9	42.9	42.1
Iowa	41.3	41.4	40.8	40.5	40.5	41.3	41.6	42.4	41.9	42.0	42.6	41.9	41.4	41.6
Kansas	40.8	40.7	40.2	40.3	40.3	40.9	41.6	41.6	41.1	42.4	42.3	41.9	41.1	40.6
Kentucky	40.5	40.5	40.0	40.1	40.3	40.3	40.5	41.3	41.3	41.1	41.8	41.5	41.7	42.1
Louisiana	41.8	42.5	42.6	42.9	42.7	42.6	42.5	43.4	43.2	44.2	44.1	44.0	43.3	42.8
Maine	41.5	41.0	40.2	40.1	40.0	40.2	40.8	40.6	39.8	39.9	40.6	40.6	40.8	41.3
Maryland	40.8	41.5	41.1	40.8	40.6	40.8	41.1	41.5	41.5	41.0	41.4	41.6	41.4	40.7
Massachusetts	41.0	40.7	40.7	40.7	41.0	41.0	41.3	41.6	41.7	41.8	42.3	42.0	42.0	41.9
Michigan	42.2	43.3	42.9	41.8	41.5	41.8	43.1	44.9	44.3	43.9	44.1	43.3	44.2	43.7
Minnesota	40.9	40.8	40.5	40.3	40.4	40.8	41.1	41.6	41.5	41.4	41.5	41.3	41.2	40.8
Mississippi	40.3	40.3	40.0	39.4	39.7	40.3	41.0	41.7	41.0	41.3	41.5	41.4	41.3	40.7
Missouri	40.6	40.8	40.7	40.7	40.4	40.6	41.4	42.0	41.3	41.5	41.6	41.5	41.5	41.3
Montana	38.6	38.7	39.2	39.0	39.1	38.9	38.6	39.3	39.4	39.1	39.9	39.3	39.0	38.5
Nebraska	40.5	41.1	40.7	40.8	40.4	41.1	41.5	42.1	41.5	41.6	41.3	41.9	41.9	41.4
Nevada	40.3	39.7	40.9	40.7	40.6	40.7	41.4	41.4	41.4	41.6	42.9	42.0	41.3	42.4
New Hampshire	41.2	40.7	41.2	40.8	41.2	41.6	42.1	42.3	41.6	41.8	42.0	41.3	40.6	41.1
New Jersey	41.2	41.0	41.0	41.4	41.4	41.5	41.5	41.8	41.8	41.8	42.0	41.8	41.7	42.0
New Mexico	39.7	40.5	40.0	40.7	40.1	40.0	40.9	40.9	39.9	40.2	39.8	38.6	39.0	38.0
New York	39.9	39.9	40.0	39.6	39.8	40.0	40.4	41.0	40.9	40.8	41.2	41.1	41.2	41.1
North Carolina	41.2	40.5	40.3	39.9	40.1	40.7	40.8	41.1	40.6	40.4	41.2	41.1	41.0	41.4
North Dakota	38.7	38.7	39.8	39.8	39.8	40.4	41.2	42.3	40.7	42.2	40.5	39.9	40.0	40.1
Ohio	42.6	43.0	42.7	42.4	42.2	42.2	43.0	43.9	43.4	43.3	43.6	42.9	42.9	42.9
Oklahoma	41.2	41.1	41.6	41.1	41.0	41.2	41.9	43.1	41.9	42.0	42.4	41.5	41.3	40.9
Oregon	39.2	39.3	39.4	39.3	39.4	39.5	39.5	40.4	40.1	40.2	40.9	40.7	40.4	40.0
Pennsylvania	40.9	41.1	41.0	40.7	40.4	40.8	41.2	41.6	41.3	[1]41.2	42.0	41.9	41.8	42.2
Rhode Island	40.0	39.7	39.3	39.7	40.0	40.1	39.8	40.3	40.5	40.0	40.9	40.6	39.9	40.4
South Carolina	41.7	41.1	41.3	41.0	41.3	41.7	41.6	41.8	41.9	41.8	42.2	42.6	42.6	42.5
South Dakota	41.7	42.5	41.8	40.6	41.2	41.2	41.3	42.0	41.8	41.5	41.9	42.6	42.9	43.1
Tennessee	41.6	41.6	40.8	38.6	39.6	40.3	40.8	40.9	40.4	40.6	41.2	40.5	40.6	40.2
Texas	41.6	41.7	41.8	41.8	42.1	42.5	42.8	43.1	42.8	43.0	43.5	43.7	43.5	43.3
Utah	39.5	40.3	40.0	39.8	39.9	40.3	39.6	40.6	39.8	40.3	40.2	40.4	40.0	39.8
Vermont	40.6	40.4	40.9	40.8	40.8	41.0	41.5	40.9	40.5	40.5	40.7	39.6	39.5	40.3
Virginia	41.1	40.8	40.9	40.4	40.5	41.0	41.0	41.7	41.6	41.5	42.2	42.3	42.4	42.3
Washington	39.9	40.1	39.4	40.6	39.9	40.0	40.2	40.5	40.8	40.8	40.6	40.8	40.9	40.7
West Virginia	40.6	40.6	40.7	40.7	40.6	40.6	40.9	41.3	41.8	41.2	41.7	41.6	41.6	41.3
Wisconsin	41.4	41.8	41.5	41.4	41.4	41.8	42.0	42.7	42.1	42.2	42.4	41.8	41.9	41.5
Wyoming	38.8	[1]38.5	39.8	39.9	38.6	38.6	38.9	40.0	39.4	40.1	40.3	40.4	39.3	38.6
Puerto Rico	38.9	39.1	39.5	39.1	39.0	39.6	39.5	39.9	39.6	38.6	39.6	40.0	41.0	40.6
Virgin Islands	42.2	40.4	41.7	42.4	41.4	42.0	43.5	42.7	41.7	41.5	42.7	40.1	43.8	44.0

[1]Data not continuous.
. . . = Not available.

Table 2-36. Average Hourly Earnings of Production Workers on Manufacturing Payrolls by State, NAICS Basis, 2001–2004

(Dollars.)

State	2001	2002	2003	2004
Alabama	12.76	13.10	13.56	14.33
Alaska	11.70	13.24	12.18	12.01
Arizona	13.80	14.16	14.38	14.20
Arkansas	12.90	13.30	13.55	13.49
California	14.69	14.89	15.04	15.35
Colorado	14.72	15.44	16.89	16.46
Connecticut	16.42	17.24	17.74	18.35
Delaware	16.56	16.60	16.91	17.68
District of Columbia	. . .	. . .	. . .	. . .
Florida	12.68	13.30	14.09	13.84
Georgia	12.50	13.38	14.08	14.53
Hawaii	13.18	13.07	12.90	13.48
Idaho	13.85	13.80	13.72	14.15
Illinois	14.66	14.99	15.20	15.61
Indiana	16.42	17.15	17.84	17.92
Iowa	14.67	15.32	15.70	16.17
Kansas	15.48	15.98	15.83	16.57
Kentucky	15.44	15.73	16.01	16.51
Louisiana	16.18	17.03	16.86	16.40
Maine	14.71	15.55	16.28	16.97
Maryland	14.56	15.21	15.74	16.48
Massachusetts	15.75	16.25	16.53	16.89
Michigan	19.45	20.51	21.20	21.53
Minnesota	14.76	15.06	15.43	16.04
Mississippi	11.93	12.32	12.89	13.12
Missouri	16.11	16.80	18.22	17.92
Montana	14.03	14.43	14.02	14.87
Nebraska	13.64	14.05	14.86	15.19
Nevada	13.79	14.62	14.63	14.60
New Hampshire	13.98	14.21	14.85	15.48
New Jersey	14.74	15.19	15.45	15.67
New Mexico	13.27	13.41	13.19	13.13
New York	16.24	16.75	16.78	17.29
North Carolina	12.81	13.18	13.66	14.25
North Dakota	12.77	13.17	14.04	14.35
Ohio	16.79	17.49	17.99	18.47
Oklahoma	13.66	14.11	14.13	14.25
Oregon	14.74	15.06	15.20	15.34
Pennsylvania	14.37	14.75	14.99	15.15
Rhode Island	12.68	12.75	12.88	13.03
South Carolina	13.79	14.00	14.19	14.73
South Dakota	12.11	12.60	13.13	13.36
Tennessee	12.88	13.15	13.56	13.85
Texas	14.04	13.93	13.94	13.98
Utah	13.76	14.12	14.90	15.38
Vermont	14.18	14.33	14.54	14.60
Virginia	14.50	15.20	15.90	16.10
Washington	17.96	18.15	18.02	18.27
West Virginia	14.80	15.40	16.05	16.57
Wisconsin	15.44	15.86	16.12	16.19
Wyoming	17.26	17.72	16.75	16.58
Puerto Rico	. . .	. . .	10.46	10.80
Virgin Islands	22.57	22.98	23.37	23.34

. . . = Not available.

Table 2-37. Average Hourly Earnings of Production Workers on Manufacturing Payrolls by State, SIC Basis, 1973–2000

(Dollars.)

State	1973	1974	1975	1976	1977	1978	1979	1980	1981	1982	1983	1984	1985	1986
Alabama	3.42	3.73	4.10	4.46	4.89	5.40	5.95	6.49	7.01	7.33	7.58	7.97	8.48	8.64
Alaska	5.97	7.10	8.09	7.82	9.12	8.86	9.14	10.22	11.42	11.74	12.33	12.25	[1]12.19	11.62
Arizona	4.03	4.40	4.85	5.19	5.55	6.03	6.62	7.29	8.02	8.73	8.99	9.09	[1]9.48	9.88
Arkansas	2.99	3.30	3.69	3.91	4.30	4.72	5.19	5.71	6.26	6.69	7.05	7.31	7.57	7.76
California	4.44	4.76	5.22	5.59	6.00	6.43	7.03	7.70	8.56	9.24	9.52	9.77	10.12	10.36
Colorado	...	...	...	...	5.80	6.21	6.93	7.63	8.28	8.63	[1]8.97	9.24	9.52	9.82
Connecticut	4.14	4.42	4.78	5.12	5.56	5.96	6.43	7.08	7.67	8.23	8.76	9.22	9.57	10.07
Delaware	4.29	4.62	5.02	5.51	5.94	6.58	7.04	7.58	8.28	8.64	9.19	9.28	9.86	10.05
Florida	3.45	3.76	4.11	4.36	4.63	5.07	5.48	5.98	6.53	7.02	7.33	7.62	7.86	8.02
Georgia	3.25	3.50	3.80	4.10	4.46	4.88	5.30	5.77	6.37	6.75	7.13	7.58	8.10	8.35
Hawaii	3.93	4.24	4.68	5.14	5.51	5.90	6.38	6.83	7.53	7.97	8.23	8.35	8.65	8.86
Idaho	4.05	4.41	4.77	5.29	5.82	6.53	6.92	7.55	8.23	8.62	8.98	9.34	9.41	9.66
Illinois	4.57	4.97	5.53	5.85	6.28	6.76	7.30	8.02	8.91	9.31	9.70	10.08	10.37	10.67
Indiana	0.00	0.00	...	...	...	...	...	...	...	...	...	...	...	...
Iowa	...	...	...	5.85	6.43	7.02	7.75	8.67	9.60	10.01	10.09	10.24	10.32	10.35
Kansas	...	...	...	...	...	...	6.71	7.37	8.05	8.80	9.23	9.38	9.45	9.76
Kentucky	4.00	4.36	4.77	5.15	5.69	6.26	6.77	7.34	7.86	8.38	8.79	9.28	9.53	9.86
Louisiana	3.98	4.40	4.88	5.33	5.75	6.42	6.97	7.74	8.58	9.38	9.79	10.06	10.43	10.60
Maine	3.23	3.51	3.81	4.16	4.52	4.91	5.42	6.00	6.66	7.22	7.61	8.05	8.40	8.65
Maryland	4.22	4.62	5.04	5.52	6.05	6.46	7.09	7.61	8.39	8.78	9.02	9.45	9.73	9.91
Massachusetts	3.89	4.16	4.48	4.79	5.13	5.54	5.98	6.51	7.01	7.58	8.01	8.50	9.00	9.24
Michigan	...	...	...	6.81	7.54	8.13	8.73	9.52	10.53	11.18	11.62	12.18	12.64	12.80
Minnesota	4.22	4.67	5.10	5.53	5.97	6.44	6.93	7.61	8.40	9.11	9.56	9.75	10.05	10.20
Mississippi	2.95	3.19	3.58	3.83	4.15	4.56	4.95	5.44	6.01	6.41	6.70	6.95	7.22	7.46
Missouri	4.05	4.39	4.80	5.20	5.75	6.21	6.70	7.26	7.90	8.46	8.89	9.31	9.57	9.83
Montana	4.53	5.05	5.53	5.93	6.53	7.81	8.44	8.78	9.09	9.86	10.44	10.76	10.95	10.94
Nebraska	3.75	4.15	4.63	4.93	5.39	5.83	6.53	7.38	8.01	8.47	8.76	8.93	9.02	9.26
Nevada	4.71	4.89	5.26	5.61	6.10	6.54	6.95	7.72	8.42	8.80	9.02	9.12	9.15	9.36
New Hampshire	3.39	3.65	3.97	4.26	4.56	4.94	5.37	[1]5.87	6.41	6.94	7.42	7.86	8.39	8.77
New Jersey	4.26	4.57	4.99	5.33	5.82	6.28	6.71	7.31	8.05	8.66	9.11	9.50	9.86	10.12
New Mexico	3.08	3.31	3.63	4.07	4.43	4.79	5.36	5.79	6.54	7.22	7.60	7.97	8.41	8.75
New York	4.20	4.53	4.91	5.27	5.67	6.08	6.57	7.18	7.84	8.35	8.84	9.22	9.67	9.92
North Carolina	2.99	3.28	3.52	3.79	4.10	4.47	4.87	5.37	5.94	6.35	6.68	7.01	7.29	7.54
North Dakota	3.55	3.83	4.31	4.75	5.19	5.55	5.98	6.56	7.12	7.50	7.73	7.86	8.05	8.19
Ohio	4.76	5.13	5.57	6.10	6.74	7.29	7.84	8.57	9.53	10.07	10.56	10.96	11.38	11.56
Oklahoma	3.69	4.01	4.45	4.83	5.31	5.81	6.53	7.36	8.20	8.69	9.21	9.64	9.86	9.80
Oregon	4.60	5.01	5.53	6.07	6.67	7.23	7.92	8.65	9.47	10.02	10.25	10.44	10.50	10.57
Pennsylvania	4.16	4.57	4.98	5.36	[1]5.85	6.37	6.97	7.59	8.30	8.63	8.95	9.28	9.57	9.74
Rhode Island	3.37	3.62	3.84	4.15	4.39	4.71	5.10	5.59	6.10	6.61	6.92	7.33	7.59	7.90
South Carolina	3.03	3.32	3.59	3.91	4.28	4.66	5.10	5.59	6.18	6.68	7.03	7.28	7.61	7.92
South Dakota	3.37	3.77	4.21	4.51	4.84	5.19	5.70	6.50	7.12	7.36	7.31	7.14	7.43	7.75
Tennessee	3.29	3.62	3.93	4.24	4.68	5.13	5.56	6.08	6.72	7.16	7.49	7.93	8.29	8.58
Texas	5.42	5.88	6.46	7.15	7.95	8.60	8.88	9.04	9.41	9.65	9.85	9.97	10.25	10.47
Utah	3.83	4.19	4.61	4.89	5.18	5.68	6.29	7.02	7.74	8.40	8.69	8.92	9.64	9.98
Vermont	3.50	3.78	4.07	4.40	4.70	5.10	5.53	6.14	6.79	7.35	7.66	8.03	8.41	8.83
Virginia	3.34	3.65	3.99	4.30	4.69	5.11	5.58	6.22	6.84	7.37	7.79	8.10	8.51	8.83
Washington	4.83	5.24	5.82	6.36	6.83	7.56	8.39	9.41	10.44	11.23	11.42	11.57	11.63	11.65
West Virginia	4.14	4.53	4.93	5.42	6.06	6.68	7.41	8.08	8.80	9.40	9.74	9.93	10.24	10.38
Wisconsin	4.45	4.81	5.26	5.69	6.16	6.69	7.27	8.03	8.80	9.37	9.78	10.03	10.26	10.35
Wyoming	4.03	4.52	4.92	5.43	5.70	6.18	6.68	7.01	7.89	8.62	8.73	9.14	9.64	9.68
Puerto Rico	...	...	...	...	...	...	...	4.02	4.39	4.64	4.83	5.02	5.19	5.31
Virgin Islands	...	...	...	...	...	6.12	6.70	7.18	8.50	9.76	10.03	9.51	[1]9.44	9.60

[1]Data not continuous.
. . . = Not available.

Table 2-37. Average Hourly Earnings of Production Workers on Manufacturing Payrolls by State, SIC Basis, 1973–2000—*Continued*

(Dollars.)

State	1987	1988	1989	1990	1991	1992	1993	1994	1995	1996	1997	1998	1999	2000
Alabama	8.76	8.95	9.10	9.39	9.72	9.99	10.35	10.75	11.14	11.55	11.86	12.11	12.54	12.96
Alaska	11.79	11.98	12.01	12.46	11.40	10.75	11.14	10.96	11.00	11.14	11.78	11.09	12.16	12.46
Arizona	9.97	9.85	9.92	10.21	10.70	10.96	11.06	11.17	11.16	11.49	11.67	12.17	12.70	12.78
Arkansas	7.88	8.07	8.26	8.51	8.81	9.05	9.36	9.65	10.05	10.41	10.78	11.12	11.55	11.97
California	10.75	10.80	11.16	11.48	11.87	12.19	12.38	12.44	12.55	12.84	13.24	13.66	13.95	14.26
Colorado	10.05	10.38	10.44	10.94	11.33	11.32	12.01	12.26	12.51	12.83	13.31	13.74	14.19	14.82
Connecticut	10.46	10.78	11.21	11.53	11.99	12.46	13.01	13.53	13.71	14.01	14.46	14.83	15.33	15.70
Delaware	10.67	11.49	12.36	12.39	12.20	12.35	13.29	13.92	14.20	14.02	14.81	15.36	15.91	16.53
Florida	8.16	8.39	8.67	8.98	9.30	9.59	9.76	9.97	10.18	10.55	10.95	11.43	11.83	12.28
Georgia	8.49	8.65	8.87	9.17	9.56	9.86	10.09	10.34	10.71	11.19	11.64	12.03	12.48	12.99
Hawaii	9.30	9.84	10.37	10.99	11.39	11.61	11.98	12.22	12.82	12.79	13.11	13.16	13.49	13.59
Idaho	9.75	10.00	10.21	10.60	11.11	11.42	11.88	11.88	11.46	12.15	12.46	12.80	13.42	14.17
Illinois	10.85	10.98	11.21	11.44	11.68	11.84	12.04	12.25	12.64	13.03	13.35	13.75	14.05	14.36
Indiana	. . .	. . .	11.70	12.03	12.43	12.79	13.17	13.55	13.91	14.33	14.79	14.97	15.26	15.83
Iowa	10.62	10.56	10.82	11.27	11.62	11.92	12.22	12.45	12.73	13.13	13.57	13.91	14.20	14.66
Kansas	9.97	10.24	10.68	10.94	11.24	11.60	11.99	12.15	12.39	12.88	13.45	13.84	14.44	14.98
Kentucky	10.02	10.16	10.37	10.70	11.00	11.28	11.47	11.81	12.22	12.70	13.17	13.82	14.19	14.83
Louisiana	10.90	10.94	11.13	11.61	11.86	12.19	12.66	13.11	13.43	13.65	14.14	14.63	15.18	15.56
Maine	8.77	9.31	9.92	10.59	11.08	11.40	11.63	11.91	12.39	12.71	13.12	13.49	13.94	14.28
Maryland	10.11	10.71	11.19	11.57	11.92	12.50	12.83	13.15	13.49	13.73	14.14	14.31	14.62	14.98
Massachusetts	9.77	10.40	10.87	11.39	11.81	12.15	12.36	12.59	12.79	13.05	13.42	13.80	14.24	14.66
Michigan	12.97	13.31	13.51	13.86	14.52	14.81	15.36	16.13	16.31	16.67	17.18	17.61	18.38	19.26
Minnesota	10.37	10.59	10.95	11.23	11.52	11.92	12.23	12.58	12.79	13.16	13.63	13.92	14.34	14.99
Mississippi	7.59	7.83	8.03	8.37	8.67	8.91	9.16	9.41	9.76	10.18	10.41	10.73	11.17	11.64
Missouri	10.00	10.24	10.49	10.74	10.86	11.24	11.55	11.77	12.17	12.57	12.98	13.38	13.93	14.34
Montana	10.61	10.68	11.15	11.51	11.57	12.18	12.40	12.49	12.94	13.00	13.29	13.76	14.17	14.34
Nebraska	9.33	9.38	9.53	9.66	9.84	10.22	10.46	10.94	11.19	11.51	12.10	12.32	12.77	12.94
Nevada	9.76	10.08	10.33	11.05	11.04	11.55	11.65	11.83	12.62	13.59	14.17	14.42	13.92	13.85
New Hampshire	9.29	9.97	10.37	10.83	10.84	11.22	11.62	11.74	11.94	12.23	12.55	12.79	13.17	13.39
New Jersey	10.40	10.86	11.17	11.76	12.17	12.57	12.98	13.36	13.56	13.85	14.24	14.58	15.11	15.47
New Mexico	8.74	8.87	8.74	9.04	9.40	9.68	9.74	10.13	10.68	10.99	11.74	12.47	12.53	13.26
New York	10.09	10.43	10.67	11.11	11.43	11.72	11.97	12.19	12.50	12.78	13.19	13.47	13.87	14.24
North Carolina	7.84	8.12	8.42	8.79	9.19	9.49	9.81	10.19	10.56	10.97	11.41	11.84	12.32	12.80
North Dakota	8.43	8.36	8.80	9.27	9.25	9.60	9.86	10.19	10.75	10.95	11.29	11.40	11.94	12.64
Ohio	11.73	12.00	12.26	12.64	13.12	13.49	14.05	14.40	14.42	14.70	15.30	15.79	16.26	16.71
Oklahoma	10.14	10.35	10.48	10.73	11.09	11.38	11.42	11.42	11.52	11.78	12.36	12.61	12.70	13.17
Oregon	10.56	10.60	10.81	11.15	11.53	11.97	12.18	12.31	12.75	13.01	13.39	14.07	14.61	15.08
Pennsylvania	9.98	10.33	10.66	11.04	11.46	11.78	12.11	12.49	12.81	[1]13.40	13.78	14.06	14.19	14.60
Rhode Island	8.20	8.64	9.06	9.45	9.73	9.92	10.20	10.35	10.62	10.95	11.31	11.61	11.98	12.17
South Carolina	8.10	8.30	8.54	8.84	9.17	9.48	9.80	10.00	10.16	10.25	10.35	10.52	10.67	10.97
South Dakota	7.92	8.09	8.30	8.48	8.79	8.84	8.89	9.19	9.36	9.59	9.96	10.22	10.58	10.70
Tennessee	8.78	8.96	9.22	9.55	9.92	10.13	10.33	10.50	10.78	11.30	11.71	12.06	12.50	12.92
Texas	10.84	10.92	11.02	11.13	11.47	11.81	12.03	12.14	12.25	12.38	12.57	. . .	. . .	. . .
Utah	9.96	10.11	10.14	10.32	10.77	11.10	11.10	11.28	11.62	12.21	12.85	13.07	13.39	13.68
Vermont	9.12	9.47	9.99	10.52	11.00	11.52	12.09	11.96	12.21	12.42	12.70	13.03	13.65	14.23
Virginia	9.14	9.37	9.69	10.07	10.43	10.62	10.85	11.24	11.72	12.19	12.51	12.90	13.37	13.82
Washington	11.73	11.90	12.12	12.61	13.13	13.59	14.01	14.86	14.73	14.73	15.16	15.76	16.14	16.75
West Virginia	10.55	10.81	11.17	11.53	11.77	12.11	12.27	12.60	12.64	12.96	13.17	13.72	14.09	14.61
Wisconsin	10.55	10.61	10.77	11.11	11.47	11.85	12.17	12.41	12.76	13.14	13.66	14.02	14.50	14.85
Wyoming	9.75	[1]10.27	10.58	10.83	10.98	11.10	11.53	11.79	11.96	13.17	14.54	14.93	15.40	16.18
Puerto Rico	5.43	5.56	5.77	6.04	6.32	6.63	6.98	7.22	7.41	7.70	7.99	8.41	8.93	9.39
Virgin Islands	9.40	9.86	10.87	11.85	12.52	13.68	14.97	15.16	15.82	17.00	18.09	18.60	18.89	21.88

Note: Data include Alaska and Hawaii beginning in 1959.

[1]Data not continuous.

. . . = Not available.

Table 2-38. Average Weekly Earnings of Production Workers on Manufacturing Payrolls by State, NAICS Basis, 2001–2004

(Dollars.)

State	2001	2002	2003	2004
Alabama	523.16	542.34	555.96	584.66
Alaska	504.27	495.18	523.74	487.61
Arizona	556.14	566.40	580.95	575.10
Arkansas	514.71	528.01	536.58	538.25
California	581.72	589.64	597.09	614.00
Colorado	599.10	626.86	682.36	664.98
Connecticut	684.71	717.18	734.44	767.03
Delaware	657.43	664.00	681.47	707.20
District of Columbia	. . .	. . .	. . .	. . .
Florida	514.81	559.93	577.69	568.82
Georgia	505.00	547.24	560.38	569.58
Hawaii	474.48	465.29	479.88	510.89
Idaho	541.54	546.48	566.64	573.08
Illinois	601.06	620.59	617.12	640.01
Indiana	673.22	727.16	751.06	754.43
Iowa	600.00	632.72	654.69	682.37
Kansas	630.04	651.98	641.12	679.37
Kentucky	640.76	663.81	667.62	673.61
Louisiana	697.36	747.62	743.53	719.96
Maine	585.46	620.45	651.20	672.01
Maryland	567.84	608.40	621.73	660.85
Massachusetts	634.73	663.00	671.12	694.18
Michigan	814.96	875.78	892.52	912.87
Minnesota	584.50	597.88	620.29	656.04
Mississippi	473.62	500.19	514.31	526.11
Missouri	649.23	660.24	737.91	720.38
Montana	544.36	551.23	538.37	569.52
Nebraska	561.97	588.70	618.18	631.90
Nevada	533.67	567.26	570.57	585.46
New Hampshire	567.59	565.56	594.00	619.20
New Jersey	598.44	621.27	633.45	659.71
New Mexico	517.53	535.06	519.69	519.95
New York	646.35	675.03	671.20	686.41
North Carolina	504.71	529.84	543.67	574.28
North Dakota	522.29	529.43	561.60	563.96
Ohio	691.75	724.09	737.59	770.20
Oklahoma	538.20	553.11	555.31	575.70
Oregon	576.33	588.85	597.36	599.79
Pennsylvania	580.55	594.43	599.60	610.55
Rhode Island	499.59	493.43	506.18	510.78
South Carolina	568.15	589.40	586.05	581.84
South Dakota	504.99	532.98	558.03	561.12
Tennessee	501.03	527.32	539.69	554.00
Texas	584.06	572.52	577.12	556.40
Utah	528.38	533.74	591.53	585.98
Vermont	561.53	573.20	581.60	586.92
Virginia	581.30	621.30	647.70	668.30
Washington	718.40	727.82	711.79	730.80
West Virginia	608.28	637.56	662.87	686.00
Wisconsin	620.69	642.33	649.64	652.46
Wyoming	666.24	696.40	673.35	658.23
Puerto Rico	. . .	. . .	427.81	443.88
Virgin Islands	990.82	1 004.23	1 000.24	1 082.98

. . . = Not available.

Table 2-39. Average Weekly Earnings of Production Workers on Manufacturing Payrolls by State, SIC Basis, 1973–2000

(Dollars.)

State	1973	1974	1975	1976	1977	1978	1979	1980	1981	1982	1983	1984	1985	1986
Alabama	140.22	151.06	161.95	181.08	198.04	219.24	242.16	260.25	279.70	282.20	308.51	326.77	345.98	355.10
Alaska	239.40	287.55	296.09	316.71	394.90	375.66	401.25	436.49	456.80	453.16	446.35	481.42	¹496.1	477.58
Arizona	160.39	172.48	189.15	205.00	222.56	243.01	268.77	292.33	317.59	339.60	364.10	370.87	¹387.7	405.08
Arkansas	119.30	129.36	143.17	154.84	170.71	185.50	205.52	224.40	246.64	258.23	282.71	296.06	304.31	313.50
California	178.93	188.97	205.67	221.92	240.60	257.84	280.50	304.15	338.98	362.21	380.80	393.73	406.82	417.51
Colorado	. . .	. . .	. . .	. . .	228.52	244.05	273.74	303.67	329.54	338.30	¹357.90	377.92	382.70	391.82
Connecticut	174.29	182.99	193.59	208.90	230.74	250.32	270.06	295.94	319.07	333.32	361.79	391.85	400.98	420.93
Delaware	172.89	182.03	197.29	220.40	235.22	263.20	278.08	306.99	333.68	338.69	373.11	385.12	405.25	415.07
Florida	141.45	151.15	164.40	176.14	188.44	207.36	221.94	243.98	265.12	280.10	298.33	313.94	324.62	327.22
Georgia	131.63	139.30	150.10	164.41	180.63	195.69	214.12	231.95	255.44	260.55	293.04	310.78	328.86	341.52
Hawaii	156.81	167.06	182.99	200.46	209.38	227.74	244.35	258.17	289.90	302.06	317.68	318.14	323.51	344.65
Idaho	157.14	171.99	185.08	204.72	228.73	253.36	265.04	280.11	311.09	316.35	335.85	351.18	355.70	369.01
Illinois	187.85	200.69	219.13	236.11	254.91	271.42	296.66	319.20	356.23	364.86	393.59	409.35	421.02	436.40
Indiana	. . .	. . .	. . .	. . .	. . .	. . .	. . .	. . .	. . .	. . .	. . .	. . .	. . .	. . .
Iowa	. . .	. . .	. . .	233.42	257.84	281.50	313.88	343.33	379.20	387.39	401.58	411.65	414.86	420.21
Kansas	. . .	. . .	. . .	. . .	. . .	. . .	273.10	297.75	325.22	344.96	360.89	376.14	373.28	393.33
Kentucky	161.20	172.66	184.60	202.91	224.75	247.90	266.74	286.99	308.90	321.79	344.57	363.78	370.72	386.51
Louisiana	164.77	176.44	208.86	220.13	240.35	267.07	287.86	318.89	362.08	384.58	391.60	418.50	434.93	443.08
Maine	131.78	141.45	152.02	165.98	179.90	197.38	217.34	240.00	269.06	288.80	303.64	321.20	336.00	351.19
Maryland	170.91	184.34	197.06	218.59	241.40	257.75	283.60	301.36	334.76	344.18	360.80	387.45	392.12	401.36
Massachusetts	157.55	165.98	175.17	190.16	204.69	222.71	239.80	257.80	280.40	297.14	319.60	340.85	366.30	381.61
Michigan	. . .	. . .	. . .	290.97	326.27	349.50	359.72	381.87	426.27	449.33	494.02	526.18	544.78	545.28
Minnesota	173.02	186.33	199.92	220.09	238.80	258.89	277.20	299.83	330.96	356.20	379.53	392.93	405.02	414.12
Mississippi	118.89	125.37	140.69	153.20	166.42	181.94	196.02	213.79	236.19	244.22	268.67	282.17	293.13	299.89
Missouri	161.19	172.53	187.20	206.96	231.15	248.40	264.65	284.59	318.37	326.56	354.71	377.06	384.71	398.12
Montana	178.03	195.94	210.14	236.01	272.95	333.49	362.08	379.30	372.69	387.50	414.47	421.79	428.15	431.04
Nebraska	156.78	170.98	187.66	202.57	219.91	239.61	269.69	299.63	322.80	337.95	353.03	361.67	363.51	374.10
Nevada	188.40	189.73	200.93	218.23	236.68	251.79	267.58	294.90	325.01	328.24	349.98	362.98	369.66	376.27
New Hampshire	134.92	143.44	155.23	168.70	182.40	199.08	215.34	¹233.63	255.76	274.82	300.51	322.26	341.47	361.32
New Jersey	176.41	186.11	199.68	215.71	239.20	256.22	276.45	297.07	327.16	345.53	369.87	390.45	402.29	416.94
New Mexico	121.35	127.10	141.57	160.77	171.88	187.77	211.72	230.44	258.33	283.02	301.72	318.00	334.72	345.63
New York	167.58	178.48	191.00	207.64	224.53	241.98	260.17	282.89	308.90	323.98	347.41	366.96	384.87	395.81
North Carolina	119.90	128.25	135.17	149.33	162.36	177.91	192.85	211.04	232.25	236.86	267.20	279.70	288.68	306.88
North Dakota	143.42	153.97	171.97	185.73	200.33	220.34	233.82	246.00	271.27	282.00	293.74	301.82	310.73	312.86
Ohio	201.35	211.36	224.47	252.54	283.08	306.91	325.36	347.94	389.78	403.81	437.18	463.61	477.96	486.68
Oklahoma	149.81	162.40	178.00	194.65	214.52	233.56	264.46	295.14	328.82	343.26	373.01	401.02	407.22	404.74
Oregon	180.78	194.39	212.35	236.12	257.46	281.97	304.92	329.57	355.13	379.76	398.73	409.25	406.35	412.23
Pennsylvania	167.23	180.97	193.22	210.11	¹231.08	254.80	278.10	294.49	325.36	331.39	350.84	373.06	381.84	391.55
Rhode Island	132.44	141.90	149.04	163.93	171.65	183.22	199.41	219.69	239.73	255.16	269.88	299.80	305.11	319.16
South Carolina	122.72	132.14	141.45	157.96	173.77	190.13	208.08	225.28	249.67	255.18	285.30	297.07	307.44	325.51
South Dakota	143.56	157.21	171.35	179.95	190.21	216.42	238.83	265.85	296.19	302.50	304.10	300.59	310.57	326.28
Tennessee	132.92	144.44	156.41	170.87	188.14	203.15	220.73	241.38	268.13	276.38	303.34	324.34	339.72	353.50
Texas	. . .	. . .	. . .	203.68	222.76	242.84	265.51	294.58	328.34	344.00	363.19	376.97	387.69	399.51
Utah	148.62	162.02	175.77	191.69	207.15	224.36	245.31	274.48	307.28	323.40	342.39	355.91	386.56	399.20
Vermont	145.25	155.36	164.43	180.40	191.76	209.10	225.62	249.28	271.60	286.65	306.40	326.02	342.29	359.38
Virginia	135.60	145.27	156.41	171.57	187.13	203.38	221.53	244.45	271.55	283.01	309.26	326.43	341.25	356.73
Washington	189.34	203.84	225.23	248.68	267.74	297.11	323.85	361.34	405.07	432.36	444.24	448.92	453.57	459.01
West Virginia	165.60	179.39	192.27	212.46	239.37	264.53	293.44	316.74	346.72	364.72	385.70	400.18	408.58	418.31
Wisconsin	183.99	197.43	212.25	230.91	250.06	274.21	297.00	323.10	352.55	370.87	398.05	412.23	421.69	427.46
Wyoming	155.58	171.71	190.36	218.11	226.82	238.55	251.17	272.69	315.60	329.28	322.21	361.03	394.28	377.52
Puerto Rico	. . .	. . .	. . .	. . .	. . .	. . .	. . .	152.76	167.77	174.00	186.92	194.27	199.82	207.09
Virgin Islands	. . .	. . .	. . .	. . .	. . .	250.31	274.03	295.10	359.55	412.85	415.24	405.41	393.65	402.24

¹Data not continuous.
. . . = Not available.

Table 2-39. Average Weekly Earnings of Production Workers on Manufacturing Payrolls by State, SIC Basis, 1973–2000—*Continued*

(Dollars.)

State	1987	1988	1989	1990	1991	1992	1993	1994	1995	1996	1997	1998	1999	2000
Alabama	362.66	370.53	374.92	384.99	396.58	411.59	426.42	450.43	463.42	481.64	496.93	511.04	527.93	543.02
Alaska	503.43	504.36	533.24	559.45	528.96	489.13	501.30	519.50	525.80	518.01	550.13	553.39	[1]550.85	554.47
Arizona	404.78	404.84	408.70	415.55	435.49	447.17	450.14	472.49	474.30	491.77	483.14	491.67	[1]513.08	516.31
Arkansas	323.08	330.06	337.01	348.91	362.97	374.67	387.50	403.37	412.05	432.02	446.29	463.70	481.64	490.77
California	433.23	439.56	454.21	466.09	481.92	494.91	506.34	515.02	517.06	532.86	554.76	570.99	581.72	594.64
Colorado	404.01	419.35	419.69	450.73	457.73	458.46	494.81	506.34	512.91	528.60	[1]556.36	570.21	588.89	589.84
Connecticut	440.37	454.92	473.06	484.26	501.18	519.58	547.72	579.08	586.79	595.43	616.00	633.24	649.99	668.82
Delaware	434.27	459.60	512.94	511.71	497.76	503.88	559.50	595.78	582.20	567.81	620.54	649.73	684.13	715.75
Florida	332.93	341.47	354.60	365.49	378.51	392.23	402.11	412.76	421.45	437.83	457.71	476.63	494.49	514.53
Georgia	353.18	358.11	364.56	375.05	391.96	408.20	420.75	438.42	453.03	473.34	493.54	502.85	522.91	537.79
Hawaii	366.42	393.60	414.80	442.90	453.32	464.40	476.80	468.03	480.75	487.30	496.87	490.87	530.16	520.50
Idaho	371.48	381.00	397.16	412.34	434.40	447.66	476.39	475.20	450.38	479.93	499.65	490.24	528.75	555.46
Illinois	451.36	464.45	469.70	473.62	481.22	485.44	499.66	513.28	527.09	543.35	563.37	574.75	588.70	591.63
Indiana	. . .	. . .	486.72	496.84	512.12	537.18	562.36	586.72	587.00	613.32	638.93	642.21	654.65	666.44
Iowa	438.61	437.18	441.46	456.44	470.61	492.30	508.35	527.88	533.39	551.46	578.08	582.83	587.88	609.86
Kansas	406.78	416.77	429.34	440.88	452.97	474.44	498.78	505.44	509.23	546.11	568.94	579.90	593.48	608.19
Kentucky	405.81	411.48	414.80	429.07	443.30	454.58	464.54	487.75	504.69	521.97	550.51	573.53	595.06	624.34
Louisiana	455.62	464.95	474.14	498.07	506.42	519.29	538.05	568.97	580.18	603.33	623.57	643.72	657.29	665.97
Maine	363.96	381.71	398.78	424.66	443.20	458.28	474.50	483.55	493.12	507.13	532.67	547.69	568.75	589.76
Maryland	412.49	444.47	459.91	472.06	483.95	510.00	527.31	545.73	559.84	562.93	585.40	595.30	605.27	609.69
Massachusetts	400.57	423.28	442.41	463.57	484.21	498.15	510.47	523.74	533.34	545.49	567.67	579.60	598.08	614.25
Michigan	547.33	576.32	579.58	579.35	602.58	619.06	662.02	724.24	722.53	731.81	757.64	762.51	812.40	841.66
Minnesota	424.13	432.07	443.48	452.57	465.41	486.34	502.65	523.33	530.79	544.82	565.65	574.90	590.81	611.59
Mississippi	305.88	315.55	321.20	329.78	344.20	359.07	375.56	392.40	400.16	420.43	432.02	444.22	461.32	473.75
Missouri	406.00	417.79	426.94	437.12	438.74	456.34	478.17	494.34	502.62	521.66	539.97	555.27	578.10	592.24
Montana	409.55	413.32	437.08	448.89	452.39	473.80	478.64	490.86	509.84	508.30	530.27	540.77	552.63	552.09
Nebraska	377.87	385.52	387.87	394.13	397.54	420.04	434.09	460.57	464.39	478.82	499.73	516.21	535.06	535.72
Nevada	393.33	400.18	422.50	449.74	448.22	470.09	482.31	486.21	522.47	565.34	607.89	605.64	574.90	587.24
New Hampshire	382.75	405.78	427.24	441.86	446.61	466.75	489.20	[1]496.60	496.70	511.21	527.10	528.23	534.70	550.33
New Jersey	428.48	445.26	457.97	486.86	503.84	521.66	538.67	558.45	566.81	578.93	598.08	609.44	630.09	649.74
New Mexico	346.98	359.24	349.60	367.93	376.94	387.20	398.37	414.32	426.13	441.80	467.25	481.34	488.67	503.88
New York	402.59	416.16	426.80	439.96	454.91	468.80	483.59	499.79	511.25	521.42	543.43	553.62	571.44	585.26
North Carolina	323.01	328.86	339.33	350.72	368.52	386.24	400.25	418.81	428.74	443.19	470.09	486.62	505.12	529.92
North Dakota	326.24	323.53	350.24	368.95	368.15	387.84	406.23	431.04	437.53	462.09	457.25	454.86	477.60	506.86
Ohio	499.70	516.00	523.50	535.94	553.66	569.28	604.15	632.16	625.83	636.51	667.08	677.39	697.55	716.86
Oklahoma	417.77	425.39	435.97	441.00	454.69	468.86	478.50	492.20	482.69	494.76	524.06	523.32	524.51	538.65
Oregon	413.95	416.58	425.91	438.20	454.28	472.82	481.11	497.32	511.28	523.00	547.65	572.65	590.24	603.20
Pennsylvania	408.18	424.56	437.06	449.33	[1]462.98	480.62	498.93	519.58	529.05	552.08	578.76	589.11	593.14	616.12
Rhode Island	328.00	343.01	356.06	375.17	389.20	397.79	405.96	417.11	430.11	438.00	462.58	471.37	478.00	491.67
South Carolina	337.77	341.13	352.70	362.44	378.72	395.32	407.68	418.00	425.70	428.45	436.77	448.15	454.54	466.23
South Dakota	330.26	343.83	346.94	344.29	362.15	364.21	367.16	385.98	391.25	397.99	417.32	435.37	453.88	461.17
Tennessee	365.25	372.74	376.18	368.63	392.83	408.24	421.46	429.45	435.51	458.78	482.45	488.43	507.50	519.38
Texas	409.76	415.75	428.45	437.65	456.36	464.10	471.66	479.70	490.92	507.83	523.31	530.52	532.88	536.05
Utah	393.42	407.43	405.60	410.74	429.72	446.93	439.56	457.97	462.48	492.06	516.57	528.03	535.60	544.46
Vermont	370.27	382.59	408.59	429.22	448.80	472.32	501.74	489.16	494.51	503.01	516.89	515.99	539.18	573.47
Virginia	375.65	382.30	396.32	406.83	422.42	435.42	444.85	468.71	487.55	505.89	527.92	545.67	566.89	584.59
Washington	468.03	477.19	477.53	511.97	523.89	543.60	563.20	601.83	600.98	600.98	615.50	643.01	660.13	681.73
West Virginia	428.33	438.89	454.62	469.27	477.86	491.67	501.84	520.38	528.35	533.95	549.19	570.75	586.14	603.39
Wisconsin	436.77	443.50	446.96	459.95	474.86	495.33	511.14	529.91	537.20	554.51	579.18	586.04	607.55	616.28
Wyoming	378.30	395.40	421.08	432.12	423.83	428.46	448.52	471.60	471.22	528.12	585.96	603.17	605.22	624.55
Puerto Rico	211.23	217.40	227.92	236.16	246.48	262.55	275.71	288.08	293.44	297.22	316.40	336.40	366.13	381.23
Virgin Islands	396.68	398.34	453.28	502.44	518.33	574.56	651.20	647.33	659.69	705.50	772.44	745.86	827.38	962.72

[1]Data not continuous.
. . . = Not available.

NOTES AND DEFINITIONS

QUARTERLY CENSUS OF EMPLOYMENT AND WAGES

The Quarterly Census of Employment and Wages (QCEW) program, also called the ES-202 program, is a cooperative endeavor of the Bureau of Labor Statistics (BLS) and the employment security agencies of the states. Using quarterly data submitted by the agencies, BLS summarizes the employment and wage data for workers covered by state unemployment insurance laws and for civilian workers covered by the Unemployment Compensation for Federal Employees program.

These tables provide the data that use the 2002 version of the North American Industry Classification System (NAICS) as the basis for the assignment and tabulation of economic data by industry. The NAICS structure is significantly different than that of the 1987 Standard Industrial Classification (SIC) system, which was used for industry classification purposes until this year. This difference results in NAICS-based data that are not comparable with historical SIC-based data. The NAICS classification system was described in the sixth edition of this *Handbook*.

The QCEW data series is the most complete universe of employment and wage information by industry, county, and state. These data serve as the basic source of benchmark information for employment by industry in the Current Employment Statistics (CES) program, which is shown in the first section of Part 2 of this *Handbook*. Therefore, the entire employment series is not presented here. The wage series is presented because the CES provides earnings only for production and non-supervisory employees. The QCEW is more comprehensive.

Total wages

Annual pay data are compiled from reports submitted by employers subject to state and federal unemployment insurance (UI) laws, covering 131.6 million full- and part-time workers. Average annual pay is computed by dividing total annual payrolls of employees covered by UI programs by the average monthly number of these employees. Pay differences among states reflect the varying composition of employment by occupation, industry, hours of work, and other factors. Pay differences among industries are similarly affected. For example, the relatively large share of part-time workers reduces average annual pay levels in retail trade industries. Correspondingly, pay levels in construction industries reflect the prevalence of part-year employment due to weather and seasonal factors. Over-the-year pay changes may reflect shifts in the composition of employment, as well as changes in the average level of pay.

Total wages, for purposes of the quarterly UI reports submitted by private industry employers in private industry in most states, include gross wages and salaries, bonuses, stock options, tips and other gratuities, and the value of meals and lodging (where supplied). In some states, employer contributions to certain deferred compensation plans, such as 401(k) plans, are included in total wages. Total wages, however, do not include employer contributions to Old Age, Survivors', and Disability Insurance (OASDI); health insurance; unemployment insurance; workers' compensation; and private pension and welfare funds.

In most states, firms report the total wages paid during the calendar quarter, regardless of the timing of the services performed. However, under the laws of a few states, the employers report total wages earned during the quarter (payable) rather than actual amounts paid. For federal workers, wages represent the gross amount of all payrolls for all pay periods paid within the quarter. This gross amount includes cash allowances and the cash equivalent of any type of remuneration. It includes all lump-sum payments for terminal leave, withholding taxes, and retirement deductions. Federal employee remuneration generally covers the same types of services as those for workers in private industry.

Sources of Additional Information

Additional information about the QCEW program and NAICS is available from the *Monthly Labor Review*, December 2001, and the BLS Web site.

Table 2-40. Employment and Average Annual Pay for All Covered Workers[1], by State, 2001–2003

(Number, dollars.)

State	2001 Employment	2001 Average annual pay	2002 Employment	2002 Average annual pay	2003 Employment	2003 Average annual pay
United States	129 635 800	36 219	128 233 919	36 764	127 795 827	37 765
Alabama	1 854 462	30 102	1 830 620	31 163	1 823 573	32 236
Alaska	283 033	36 170	287 231	37 134	291 797	37 804
Arizona	2 243 652	33 411	2 240 234	34 036	2 272 393	35 056
Arkansas	1 127 151	27 260	1 119 428	28 074	1 115 891	28 893
California	14 981 757	41 327	14 837 334	41 419	14 807 656	42 592
Colorado	2 201 379	37 952	2 153 857	38 005	2 117 773	38 942
Connecticut	1 665 607	46 993	1 648 547	46 852	1 625 801	48 328
Delaware	406 736	38 427	401 971	39 684	402 166	40 954
District of Columbia	635 749	55 908	650 515	57 914	651 088	60 417
Florida	7 153 589	31 553	7 164 523	32 426	7 248 097	33 544
Georgia	3 871 763	35 136	3 807 915	35 734	3 783 232	36 626
Hawaii	557 146	31 253	558 651	32 671	569 532	33 742
Idaho	571 314	27 768	571 869	28 163	575 889	28 677
Illinois	5 886 248	39 083	5 771 132	39 688	5 698 184	40 540
Indiana	2 871 236	31 779	2 832 553	32 603	2 821 879	33 379
Iowa	1 429 543	28 837	1 412 203	29 668	1 404 377	30 708
Kansas	1 319 667	30 153	1 303 114	30 825	1 284 726	31 489
Kentucky	1 736 575	30 021	1 717 975	30 904	1 714 060	31 855
Louisiana	1 869 966	29 131	1 847 754	30 115	1 855 554	30 782
Maine	593 166	28 815	591 052	29 736	591 372	30 750
Maryland	2 421 899	38 253	2 427 257	39 382	2 434 245	40 686
Massachusetts	3 276 224	44 975	3 202 323	44 954	3 141 089	46 323
Michigan	4 476 659	37 391	4 390 209	38 135	4 321 094	39 433
Minnesota	2 609 669	36 587	2 585 650	37 458	2 576 452	38 610
Mississippi	1 111 255	25 923	1 104 225	26 665	1 096 802	27 591
Missouri	2 652 876	32 421	2 627 082	33 118	2 615 848	33 788
Montana	383 905	25 195	388 161	26 001	393 541	26 907
Nebraska	883 920	28 377	874 063	29 448	875 251	30 382
Nevada	1 043 748	33 121	1 045 012	33 993	1 080 624	35 329
New Hampshire	610 192	35 481	603 234	36 176	604 340	37 321
New Jersey	3 876 194	44 320	3 855 419	45 182	3 850 590	46 351
New Mexico	729 422	28 702	737 418	29 431	745 935	30 202
New York	8 423 312	46 727	8 272 274	46 328	8 224 387	47 247
North Carolina	3 805 498	32 024	3 751 648	32 689	3 719 444	33 532
North Dakota	311 632	25 707	311 800	26 550	314 283	27 628
Ohio	5 434 769	33 283	5 332 891	34 214	5 281 390	35 153
Oklahoma	1 463 622	28 016	1 439 701	28 654	1 411 640	29 699
Oregon	1 596 753	33 204	1 573 057	33 684	1 563 725	34 450
Pennsylvania	5 552 366	34 978	5 504 553	35 808	5 471 255	36 995
Rhode Island	468 952	33 603	468 557	34 810	472 586	36 415
South Carolina	1 786 899	29 255	1 765 717	30 003	1 766 861	30 750
South Dakota	364 715	25 601	363 292	26 360	364 263	27 210
Tennessee	2 625 746	31 520	2 601 518	32 531	2 598 748	33 581
Texas	9 350 770	36 045	9 261 089	36 248	9 208 473	36 968
Utah	1 050 674	30 077	1 041 707	30 585	1 041 938	31 106
Vermont	298 020	30 238	295 443	31 041	294 395	32 086
Virginia	3 436 172	36 733	3 404 760	37 222	3 410 834	38 585
Washington	2 689 507	37 459	2 643 754	38 242	2 653 237	39 021
West Virginia	685 754	27 981	683 183	28 612	677 901	29 284
Wisconsin	2 717 660	31 540	2 690 830	32 464	2 687 919	33 425
Wyoming	237 278	28 043	239 615	28 975	241 699	29 924
Puerto Rico	1 007 919	19 728	992 529	20 662	1 023 102	21 548
Virgin Islands	44 330	29 210	43 070	30 506	41 961	30 994

[1]Includes workers covered by Unemployment Insurance (UI) and Unemployment Compensation for Federal Employees (UCFE) programs.

Table 2-41. NAICS Industry Employment and Average Annual Pay for All Covered Workers, United States, 2001–2003

(Number, dollars.)

Industry	2001		2002		2003	
	Employment	Average annual pay	Employment	Average annual pay	Employment	Average annual pay
Total Private, All Industries	109 304 802	36 157	107 577 281	36 539	107 065 553	37 508
Agriculture, forestry, fishing, and hunting	1 170 570	20 188	1 155 890	20 890	1 156 242	21 366
Mining	535 189	59 686	505 979	60 392	500 103	62 313
Construction	6 773 512	38 412	6 683 553	39 027	6 672 360	39 509
Manufacturing	16 386 001	42 969	15 209 192	44 097	14 459 712	45 916
Wholesale trade	5 730 294	48 791	5 617 456	49 241	5 589 032	50 835
Retail trade	15 179 753	22 667	15 018 588	23 232	14 930 765	23 804
Transportation and warehousing	4 138 146	36 189	3 989 116	36 823	3 946 170	37 436
Utilities	599 899	65 561	592 152	67 374	575 877	68 651
Information	3 591 995	57 288	3 364 485	56 103	3 180 752	58 002
Financial activities	7 678 974	55 515	7 706 265	55 172	7 826 930	57 143
Professional and business services	16 324 890	43 566	15 939 596	43 899	15 858 457	45 052
Education and health services	14 849 666	32 718	15 346 718	33 931	15 738 013	35 071
Leisure and hospitality	11 884 966	15 426	11 995 950	15 777	12 162 238	16 138
Other services	4 206 345	23 220	4 246 011	23 784	4 261 165	24 348
Total Government	20 330 998	36 549	20 656 638	37 935	20 730 273	39 094
Federal	2 752 619	48 940	2 758 627	52 050	2 764 275	54 239
State	4 452 237	37 814	4 485 071	39 212	4 481 845	40 057
Local	13 126 143	33 521	13 412 941	34 605	13 484 153	35 669

Table 2-42. SIC Industry Employment and Average Annual Pay for All Covered Workers[1], United States, Old Series, 1997–2000

(Number, dollars.)

Industry	1997		1998		1999		2000	
	Employment	Average annual pay	Employment	Average annual pay	Employment	Average annual pay	Employment	Average annual pay
Total Private								
Agriculture, forestry, and fishing	1 766 273	17 484	1 813 093	18 611	1 861 280	19 411	1 910 776	20 283
Mining	595 837	49 998	587 912	52 066	535 352	54 636	536 044	58 084
Construction	5 637 876	31 744	5 951 890	33 386	6 341 444	34 812	6 623 902	36 622
Manufacturing	18 654 350	38 306	18 800 265	40 092	18 538 996	41 941	18 420 144	44 776
Transportation and public utilities	6 164 800	37 658	6 366 597	39 345	6 581 586	41 786	6 789 193	43 623
Wholesale trade	6 655 608	39 449	6 817 818	41 831	6 902 441	44 185	7 001 995	46 740
Retail trade	21 927 096	15 878	22 279 033	16 810	22 820 731	17 602	23 298 757	18 430
Finance, insurance, and real estate	6 952 803	44 884	7 224 984	48 641	7 405 144	50 910	7 430 790	56 029
Services	33 679 016	28 466	35 066 554	30 053	36 392 096	31 509	37 666 657	33 678
Public Administration								
Federal	1 408 752	46 835	1 382 158	48 041	1 378 753	48 780	1 477 873	49 840
State	1 787 173	33 741	1 800 690	34 706	1 832 647	35 778	1 840 913	37 792
Local	3 453 703	30 771	3 517 505	32 023	3 573 435	33 184	3 648 745	34 417

[1]Includes workers covered by Unemployment Insurance (UI) and Unemployment Compensation for Federal Employees (UCFE) programs.

BUSINESS EMPLOYMENT DYNAMICS

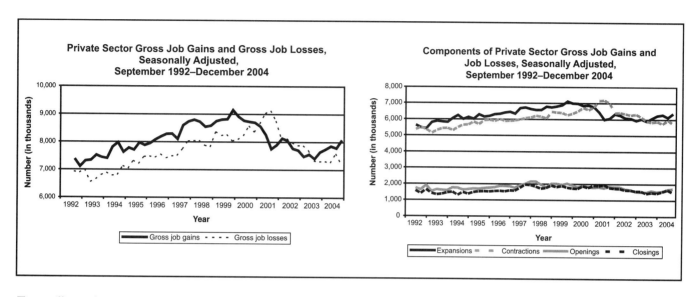

Expanding private sector business establishments gained 8.1 million jobs in the fourth quarter of 2004, an increase of 292,000 jobs from the previous quarter. This was the largest gross job gain since the fourth quarter of 1999. The net change—the difference between total gross job gains and gross job losses—equaled 869,000. (Table 2-43)

OTHER HIGHLIGHTS:

- During the fourth quarter of 2004, expanding establishments added 6.4 million jobs. Opening establishments added another 1.7 million. Gross job losses totaled 7.2 million, the lowest amount since the third quarter of 1995. Contracting establishments accounted for 5.7 million of the decline, while closing establishments lost 1.5 million jobs. (Table 2-43)

- Gross job gains represented 7.4 percent of private sector employment from September to December 2004, the highest percentage since the second quarter of 2002. Meanwhile, gross job losses were at 6.7 percent of private sector employment, down from 7.0 percent the previous quarter. The gross job gain and loss statistics demonstrate that a sizable number of jobs appear and disappear within the short time frame of one quarter. (Table 2-44)

NOTES AND DEFINITIONS

BUSINESS EMPLOYMENT DYNAMICS (BED)

The Business Employment Dynamics (BED) data are a product of a federal-state cooperative program known as Quarterly Census of Employment and Wages (QCEW), or the ES-202 program. The Bureau of Labor Statistics (BLS) compiles the BED data from existing quarterly state unemployment insurance (UI) records. Most employers in the United States are required to file quarterly reports on the employment and wages of workers covered by UI laws and to pay quarterly UI taxes. The quarterly UI reports are sent by the State Workforce Agencies (SWAs) to BLS. These reports form the basis of the BLS establishment universe-sampling frame.

In the BED program, the quarterly UI records are linked across quarters to provide a longitudinal history for each establishment. The linkage process allows the tracking of net employment changes at the establishment level, which in turn allows estimations of jobs gained at opening and expanding establishments and of jobs lost at closing and contracting establishments. The BLS publishes three different establishment-based employment measures for any given quarter. Each of these measures—QCEW, BED, and the Current Employment Statistics (CES) program makes use of the quarterly UI employment reports in producing data. However, each measure has a somewhat different universe coverage, estimation procedure, and publication product. (See notes and tables for QCEW and CES in earlier sections of this part.)

Concepts and Methodology

The BED data measure the net change in employment at the establishment level. These changes can come about in four different ways. A net increase in employment can come from either opening establishments or expanding establishments. A net decrease in employment can come from either closing establishments or contracting establishments.

Gross job gains include the sum of all jobs added at either opening or expanding establishments.

Gross job losses include the sum of all jobs lost in either closing or contracting establishments. The net change in employment is the difference between gross job gains and gross job losses.

Openings. These are either establishments with positive third-month employment for the first time in the current quarter, with no links to the prior quarter, or with positive third-month employment in the current quarter, following zero employment in the previous quarter.

Expansions. These are establishments with positive employment in the third month in both the previous and current quarters, with a net increase in employment over this period.

Closings. These are establishments with positive third-month employment in the previous quarter, with no employment or zero employment reported in the current quarter.

Contractions. These are establishments with positive employment in the third month in both the previous and current quarters, with a net decrease in employment over this period.

Sources of Additional Information

An extensive article appears in the *Monthly Labor Review*, April 2004, and BLS news release 05-1562 contains more information.

Table 2-43. Private Sector Gross Job Gains and Job Losses, Seasonally Adjusted, September 1992– December 2004

(In thousands.)

Year	3 months ended	Net change[1]	Gross job gains			Gross job losses		
			Total	Expanding establishments	Opening establishments	Total	Contracting establishments	Closing establishments
1992	September	455	7 377	5 632	1 745	6 922	5 351	1 571
	December	216	7 101	5 465	1 636	6 885	5 487	1 398
1993	March	313	7 309	5 410	1 899	6 996	5 354	1 642
	June	786	7 330	5 794	1 536	6 544	5 136	1 408
	September	874	7 523	5 881	1 642	6 649	5 316	1 333
	December	641	7 436	5 840	1 596	6 795	5 420	1 375
1994	March	517	7 400	5 807	1 593	6 883	5 435	1 448
	June	1 021	7 807	6 060	1 747	6 786	5 295	1 491
	September	1 175	7 972	6 227	1 745	6 797	5 493	1 304
	December	507	7 630	5 998	1 632	7 123	5 647	1 476
1995	March	746	7 782	6 129	1 653	7 036	5 660	1 376
	June	402	7 714	6 017	1 697	7 312	5 839	1 473
	September	771	7 970	6 291	1 679	7 199	5 680	1 519
	December	407	7 877	6 153	1 724	7 470	5 934	1 536
1996	March	460	7 943	6 190	1 753	7 483	5 957	1 526
	June	642	8 080	6 302	1 778	7 438	5 894	1 544
	September	632	8 189	6 326	1 863	7 557	5 998	1 559
	December	861	8 278	6 409	1 869	7 417	5 889	1 528
1997	March	799	8 292	6 448	1 844	7 493	5 900	1 593
	June	594	8 098	6 342	1 756	7 504	5 925	1 579
	September	854	8 593	6 680	1 913	7 739	5 981	1 758
	December	702	8 731	6 727	2 004	8 029	6 068	1 961
1998	March	747	8 788	6 633	2 155	8 041	6 107	1 934
	June	666	8 722	6 569	2 153	8 056	6 218	1 838
	September	659	8 539	6 574	1 965	7 880	6 161	1 719
	December	759	8 576	6 778	1 798	7 817	6 060	1 757
1999	March	380	8 744	6 733	2 011	8 364	6 466	1 898
	June	569	8 800	6 788	2 012	8 231	6 419	1 812
	September	548	8 817	6 871	1 946	8 269	6 397	1 872
	December	1 105	9 144	7 112	2 032	8 039	6 264	1 775
2000	March	818	8 906	6 988	1 918	8 088	6 361	1 727
	June	541	8 764	6 975	1 789	8 223	6 509	1 714
	September	146	8 724	6 834	1 890	8 578	6 719	1 859
	December	336	8 690	6 862	1 828	8 354	6 582	1 772
2001	March	-101	8 555	6 768	1 787	8 656	6 756	1 900
	June	-771	8 254	6 439	1 815	9 025	7 149	1 876
	September	-1 380	7 749	5 990	1 759	9 129	7 174	1 955
	December	-871	7 893	6 055	1 838	8 764	6 995	1 769
2002	March	-1	8 128	6 324	1 804	8 129	6 400	1 729
	June	-80	8 050	6 246	1 804	8 130	6 411	1 719
	September	-211	7 763	6 083	1 680	7 974	6 345	1 629
	December	-175	7 702	6 059	1 643	7 877	6 267	1 610
2003	March	-404	7 472	5 932	1 540	7 876	6 321	1 555
	June	-142	7 560	6 033	1 527	7 702	6 138	1 564
	September	72	7 396	5 897	1 499	7 324	5 893	1 431
	December	344	7 646	6 063	1 583	7 302	5 816	1 486
2004	March	435	7 745	6 231	1 514	7 310	5 871	1 439
	June	594	7 857	6 292	1 565	7 263	5 726	1 537
	September	191	7 789	6 123	1 666	7 598	5 953	1 645
	December	869	8 081	6 365	1 716	7 212	5 727	1 485

[1]Net change is the difference between total gross job gains and total gross job losses.

Table 2-44. Private Sector Gross Job Gains and Job Losses, as a Percent of Employment[1], Seasonally Adjusted, September 1992–December 2004

(Percent.)

Year	3 months ended	Net change[2]	Gross job gains			Gross job losses		
			Total	Expanding establishments	Opening establishments	Total	Expanding establishments	Closing establishments
1992	September	0.5	8.3	6.3	2.0	7.8	6.0	1.8
	December	0.2	7.9	6.1	1.8	7.7	6.1	1.6
1993	March	0.3	8.1	6.0	2.1	7.8	6.0	1.8
	June	0.8	8.1	6.4	1.7	7.3	5.7	1.6
	September	0.9	8.2	6.4	1.8	7.3	5.8	1.5
	December	0.6	8.0	6.3	1.7	7.4	5.9	1.5
1994	March	0.5	8.0	6.3	1.7	7.5	5.9	1.6
	June	1.1	8.4	6.5	1.9	7.3	5.7	1.6
	September	1.2	8.4	6.6	1.8	7.2	5.8	1.4
	December	0.6	8.0	6.3	1.7	7.4	5.9	1.5
1995	March	0.8	8.1	6.4	1.7	7.3	5.9	1.4
	June	0.5	8.0	6.2	1.8	7.5	6.0	1.5
	September	0.8	8.2	6.5	1.7	7.4	5.8	1.6
	December	0.4	8.1	6.3	1.8	7.7	6.1	1.6
1996	March	0.4	8.1	6.3	1.8	7.7	6.1	1.6
	June	0.6	8.2	6.4	1.8	7.6	6.0	1.6
	September	0.7	8.3	6.4	1.9	7.6	6.0	1.6
	December	0.9	8.3	6.4	1.9	7.4	5.9	1.5
1997	March	0.7	8.2	6.4	1.8	7.5	5.9	1.6
	June	0.5	7.9	6.2	1.7	7.4	5.8	1.6
	September	0.8	8.4	6.5	1.9	7.6	5.9	1.7
	December	0.6	8.4	6.5	1.9	7.8	5.9	1.9
1998	March	0.7	8.5	6.4	2.1	7.8	5.9	1.9
	June	0.6	8.4	6.3	2.1	7.8	6.0	1.8
	September	0.7	8.2	6.3	1.9	7.5	5.9	1.6
	December	0.7	8.1	6.4	1.7	7.4	5.7	1.7
1999	March	0.3	8.2	6.3	1.9	7.9	6.1	1.8
	June	0.6	8.3	6.4	1.9	7.7	6.0	1.7
	September	0.5	8.2	6.4	1.8	7.7	6.0	1.7
	December	1.1	8.5	6.6	1.9	7.4	5.8	1.6
2000	March	0.8	8.2	6.4	1.8	7.4	5.8	1.6
	June	0.4	7.9	6.3	1.6	7.5	5.9	1.6
	September	0.1	7.9	6.2	1.7	7.8	6.1	1.7
	December	0.3	7.9	6.2	1.7	7.6	6.0	1.6
2001	March	-0.1	7.7	6.1	1.6	7.8	6.1	1.7
	June	-0.8	7.4	5.8	1.6	8.2	6.5	1.7
	September	-1.3	7.1	5.5	1.6	8.4	6.6	1.8
	December	-0.8	7.3	5.6	1.7	8.1	6.5	1.6
2002	March	0.1	7.6	5.9	1.7	7.5	5.9	1.6
	June	-0.1	7.5	5.8	1.7	7.6	6.0	1.6
	September	-0.1	7.3	5.7	1.6	7.4	5.9	1.5
	December	-0.2	7.1	5.6	1.5	7.3	5.8	1.5
2003	March	-0.5	6.9	5.5	1.4	7.4	5.9	1.5
	June	-0.2	7.0	5.6	1.4	7.2	5.7	1.5
	September	0.1	6.9	5.5	1.4	6.8	5.5	1.3
	December	0.4	7.2	5.7	1.5	6.8	5.4	1.4
2004	March	0.4	7.2	5.8	1.4	6.8	5.5	1.3
	June	0.5	7.2	5.8	1.4	6.7	5.3	1.4
	September	0.2	7.2	5.7	1.5	7.0	5.5	1.5
	December	0.7	7.4	5.8	1.6	6.7	5.3	1.4

[1]The rates measure gross job gains and job losses as a percentage of the average of the previous and current employment.
[2]Net change is the difference between total gross job gains and total gross job losses.

Table 2-45. Three–Month Private Sector Job Gains and Losses by Industry, Seasonally Adjusted, 2003–2004

(Numbers in thousands.)

Year	Gross job gains (3 months ended)					Gross job losses (3 months ended)				
	December 2003	March 2004	June 2004	September 2004	December 2004	December 2003	March 2004	June 2004	September 2004	December 2004
TOTAL PRIVATE[1]	7 646	7 745	7 857	7 789	8 081	7 302	7 310	7 263	7 598	7 212
Goods-Producing	1 665	1 764	1 696	1 667	1 734	1 697	1 670	1 647	1 691	1 637
Natural resources and mining	286	314	283	271	296	285	282	282	290	275
Construction	793	837	809	799	848	761	759	779	789	747
Manufacturing	586	613	604	597	590	651	629	586	612	615
Service-Providing[1]	5 981	5 981	6 161	6 122	6 347	5 605	5 640	5 616	5 907	5 575
Wholesale trade	317	319	325	329	329	320	314	302	327	294
Retail trade	1 061	1 059	1 058	1 044	1 090	1 016	1 011	974	1 126	992
Transportation and warehousing	227	244	241	244	255	237	228	236	235	217
Utilities	14	15	13	14	11	16	16	14	16	15
Information	172	156	151	163	188	166	169	182	194	169
Financial activities	436	442	461	469	497	462	433	457	452	451
Professional and business services	1 438	1 411	1 509	1 416	1 512	1 302	1 378	1 321	1 366	1 300
Education and health services	744	751	753	757	802	659	672	696	704	647
Leisure and hospitality	1 161	1 138	1 164	1 169	1 204	1 097	1 091	1 090	1 135	1 134
Other services	288	307	301	297	299	293	291	304	308	310

[1]Includes unclassified sector, not shown separately.

PART THREE

OCCUPATIONAL EMPLOYMENT AND WAGES

OCCUPATIONAL EMPLOYMENT AND WAGES

HIGHLIGHTS

This part presents employment and wages for over 400 occupations from the Occupational Employment Statistics (OES) program.

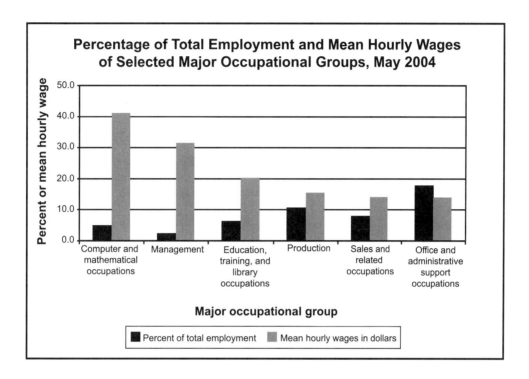

As expected, higher-paying occupations constituted a smaller proportion of total employment than lower paid occupations. In May 2004, 4.8 percent of those employed were in management and earned $41.12 per hour. Comparatively, 17.7 percent of workers were employed in office and administrative support occupations; however, their mean hourly wage was only $13.95 an hour. (Table 3-1)

OTHER HIGHLIGHTS:

• Among the 22 major occupational groups, only life, physical, and social science occupations saw a 5 percent or more increase in annual pay from May 2003 to May 2004. In contrast, wages only increased 0.5 percent in farming, fishing, and forestry. (Table 3-1)

• Management and legal occupations continued to have the highest mean annual wages in 2004, followed by computer and mathematical occupations, architecture and engineering occupations, and health care practitioner and technical occupations. The food preparation and serving related field had the lowest mean annual wages. In fact, five of the six lowest-paying jobs were in food preparation and serving. (Tables 3-1 and 3-3)

• In May 2004, at least 45 percent of workers in personal care and service occupations; in farming, fishing, and forestry occupations; and in food preparation and serving related occupations earned less than $8.50 an hour. (Table 3-2)

• While the mean hourly wage of heath care support workers ranked only 18th out of the 22 groups, 13 of the 15 highest paying jobs were in the health care and technical occupational group. Of the individual occupations, surgeons had the highest mean annual wage in May 2004, earning $181,610. (Tables 3-1 and 3-3)

• The gap between the wages of the highest and the lowest paid major occupations continued to increase. From 2003 to 2004, it grew from 479 percent to 488 percent. (Table 3-1)

NOTES AND DEFINITIONS

Collection and Coverage

The Occupational Employment Statistics (OES) survey is a federal-state cooperative program between the Bureau of Labor Statistics (BLS) and the State Workforce Agencies (SWAs). The OES survey provides estimates of employment and hourly and annual wages for wage and salary workers in 22 major occupational groups and 801 detailed occupations. BLS funds the survey and provides procedural and technical support, while the SWAs collect the data.

Scope of the Survey

In 1999, the OES survey began using the Standard Occupational Classification System (SOC). The SOC system is the first Office of Management and Budget (OMB)-required occupational classification system for federal agencies. The OES survey categorizes workers as being in one of about 770 detailed occupations. Together, these detailed occupations comprise 22 major occupational groups.

Prior to 2002, the OES survey was an annual mail survey measuring occupational employment and occupational wage rates for wage and salary workers in nonfarm establishments by industry. The survey sampled and contacted approximately 400,000 establishments in the fourth quarter of each year. Over the course of a 3-year cycle, approximately 1.2 million establishments were sampled.

Beginning in November 2002, the OES survey converted to a semi-annual survey to sample approximately 200,000 establishments per panel. The reference periods are the second and fourth quarter of each year. For the May 2004 survey, data collected in May 2004 were combined with data collected in November 2003, May 2003, November 2002, November 2001, and a subset of units sampled in 2000 to yield a sample of approximately 1.2 million establishments.

Concepts and Definitions

Employment is the estimate of total wage and salary employment in an occupation across the industries in which it was reported. The OES survey defines employment as the number of workers who can be classified as full-time or part-time employees, including workers on paid vacations or other types of leave; workers on unpaid short-term absences; salaried officers, executives, and staff members of incorporated firms; employees temporarily assigned to other units; and employees for whom the reporting unit is their permanent duty station regardless of whether that unit prepares their paycheck.

The OES survey form sent to an establishment contains between 50 and 225 SOC occupations selected on the basis of the industry classification and size class of the sampled establishments. To reduce paperwork and respondent burden, no survey form contains every SOC occupation. Data for specific occupations are collected primarily from establishments within industries that are the predominant employers of labor in these occupations. However, each survey form is structured to allow a respondent to provide information for each detailed occupation employed at the establishment; unlisted occupations can be added to the survey form.

Wages for the OES survey are straight-time, gross pay, and exclusive of premium pay. Base rate, cost-of-living allowances, guaranteed pay, hazardous-duty pay, incentive pay including commissions and production bonuses, tips, and on-call pay are included. Excluded are back pay, jury duty pay, overtime pay, severance pay, shift differentials, nonproduction bonuses, employer cost of supplementary benefits, and tuition reimbursements.

Mean wage is the estimated total wages for an occupation divided by its weighted survey employment. With the exception of the upper open-ended wage interval (interval L= $70.00 an hour and over in 2000), a mean wage value is calculated for each wage interval based on occupational wage data collected by the BLS Office of Compensation and Working Conditions. The mean wage value for the upper open-ended wage interval is its lower bound (Winsorized mean). These interval mean wage values are then attributed to all workers reported in the interval. For each occupation, total weighted wages in each interval are summed across all intervals and divided by the occupation's weighted survey employment. The median wage is the wage at the midpoint of the distribution of wages.

An *establishment* is defined as an economic unit that processes goods or provides services, such as a factory, store, or mine. The establishment is generally at a single physical location and is primarily engaged in one type of economic activity. The OES survey currently uses the North American Industrial Classification System (NAICS) to classify all establishments.

Additional Information

For additional data, including area data, see BLS news release UDL 05-877 and special reports on the BLS Web site.

Table 3-1. Employment and Wages by Major Occupational Group, May 2003–May 2004

(Number, percent, dollars.)

Occupational group	May 2003				May 2004			
	Employment [1]		Mean hourly wage	Mean annual wage [2]	Employment [1]		Mean hourly wage	Mean annual wage [2]
	Number	Percent			Number	Percent		
All Occupations	127 567 910	100.0	17.41	36 210	128 127 360	100.0	17.80	37 020
Management	6 653 480	5.2	39.80	82 790	6 200 940	4.8	41.12	85 530
Business and financial operations	4 924 210	3.9	26.71	55 550	5 131 840	4.0	27.10	56 380
Computer and mathematical	2 827 010	2.2	30.40	63 240	2 915 300	2.3	31.50	65 510
Architecture and engineering	2 376 650	1.9	28.48	59 230	2 372 770	1.9	29.69	61 750
Life, physical, and social science	1 113 130	0.9	25.58	53 210	1 131 390	0.9	26.89	55 920
Community and social services	1 615 610	1.3	17.03	35 420	1 673 740	1.3	17.52	36 440
Legal	951 510	0.7	37.94	78 910	958 520	0.7	38.42	79 910
Education, training, and library	7 831 630	6.1	19.55	40 660	7 891 810	6.2	20.23	42 080
Arts, design, entertainment, sports, and media	1 538 150	1.2	20.49	42 620	1 595 710	1.2	21.01	43 710
Health care practitioner and technical	6 173 760	4.8	26.62	55 380	6 359 380	5.0	27.55	57 310
Health care support	3 208 770	2.5	10.94	22 750	3 271 350	2.6	11.17	23 220
Protective service	2 999 630	2.4	16.39	34 090	3 006 100	2.3	16.75	34 840
Food preparation and serving related	10 216 620	8.0	8.31	17 290	10 507 390	8.2	8.43	17 530
Building and grounds cleaning and maintenance	4 260 380	3.3	10.12	21 060	4 300 440	3.4	10.33	21 490
Personal care and service	2 988 590	2.3	10.28	21 380	3 099 550	2.4	10.48	21 800
Sales and related	13 534 180	10.6	15.02	31 250	13 507 840	10.5	15.49	32 210
Office and administrative support	22 678 010	17.8	13.59	28 260	22 649 080	17.7	13.95	29 020
Farming, fishing, and forestry	461 630	0.4	9.71	20 200	458 850	0.4	9.76	20 310
Construction and extraction	6 085 510	4.8	17.62	36 650	6 170 410	4.8	18.04	37 520
Installation, maintenance, and repair	5 226 080	4.1	17.41	36 210	5 215 390	4.1	17.89	37 220
Production	10 488 450	8.2	13.80	28 710	10 128 200	7.9	14.08	29 280
Transportation and material moving	9 414 920	7.4	13.27	27 600	9 581 320	7.5	13.41	27 880

[1]Estimates for detailed occupations do not sum to the totals because the totals include occupations not shown separately. Estimates do not include self-employed workers.
[2]Annual wages have been calculated by multiplying the hourly mean wage by a "year-round, full-time" hours figure of 2,080 hours; for those occupations where there is not an hourly mean wage published, the annual wage has been directly calculated from the reported survey data.

Table 3-2. Distribution of Employment by Wage Range and Occupational Group, May 2003–May 2004

(Percent distribution.)

Occupational group	Total	Wage range (May 2003)								
		Under $8.50	$8.50 to $10.74	$10.75 to $13.49	$13.50 to $16.99	$17.00 to $21.49	$21.50 to $27.24	$27.25 to $34.49	$34.50 to $43.74	$43.75 and over
Management	100.0	1.3	1.3	3.0	5.9	9.6	13.7	16.0	16.6	32.4
Business and financial operations	100.0	1.7	2.1	5.7	12.5	19.1	21.4	17.5	10.9	9.1
Computer and mathematical science	100.0	0.9	1.5	3.4	7.3	12.9	18.8	21.7	19.5	14.0
Architecture and engineering	100.0	0.6	1.9	4.4	8.7	14.8	20.9	21.0	17.0	10.7
Life, physical, and social science	100.0	2.2	4.3	8.5	13.7	17.4	18.4	15.3	10.8	9.2
Community and social services	100.0	7.2	11.3	18.5	21.5	18.5	13.3	6.8	2.2	0.8
Legal	100.0	1.5	2.5	5.9	10.7	14.0	13.3	11.4	10.7	30.1
Education, training, and library	100.0	11.9	8.7	10.0	15.0	18.7	16.8	10.8	5.0	3.1
Arts, design, entertainment, sports, and media	100.0	13.3	10.1	12.2	14.9	15.2	13.5	9.3	5.7	5.8
Health care practitioner and technical	100.0	2.8	5.1	8.3	13.2	20.0	20.7	13.0	6.9	10.0
Health care support	100.0	25.5	31.2	23.2	13.4	5.1	1.2	0.3	0.1	. . .
Protective service	100.0	17.1	14.5	15.0	14.5	13.8	13.2	7.8	3.2	0.9
Food preparation and serving related	100.0	67.4	17.4	8.6	4.0	1.8	0.6	0.2	0.1	. . .
Building and grounds cleaning and maintenance	100.0	42.8	24.6	16.0	9.5	5.0	1.6	0.4	0.1	. . .
Personal care and service	100.0	50.3	21.4	11.5	7.1	4.7	2.6	1.2	0.6	0.6
Sales and related	100.0	36.9	16.6	11.3	9.4	8.1	6.3	4.4	3.0	4.0
Office and administrative support	100.0	15.2	19.8	22.6	19.5	14.4	5.7	1.9	0.6	0.3
Farming, fishing, and forestry	100.0	56.8	17.3	11.2	7.2	4.4	2.0	0.7	0.3	0.1
Construction and extraction	100.0	7.3	12.2	16.6	18.8	17.6	14.4	9.0	3.2	0.8
Installation, maintenance, and repair	100.0	7.5	10.6	15.3	19.4	20.7	16.6	7.3	2.0	0.5
Production	100.0	18.0	19.9	20.3	17.4	12.2	8.1	3.1	0.8	0.2
Transportation and material moving	100.0	26.3	19.3	18.0	15.0	11.3	6.2	2.2	0.7	1.0

Occupational group	Total	Wage range (May 2004)								
		Under $8.50	$8.50 to $10.74	$10.75 to $13.49	$13.50 to $16.99	$17.00 to $21.49	$21.50 to $27.24	$27.25 to $34.49	$34.50 to $43.74	$43.75 and over
Management	100.0	1.3	1.0	2.4	5.0	8.6	13.2	15.9	17.4	35.2
Business and financial operations	100.0	1.6	2.0	5.2	11.8	18.9	21.6	17.8	11.6	9.5
Computer and mathematical science	100.0	0.6	1.2	3.1	6.6	12.0	17.8	21.8	20.5	16.4
Architecture and engineering	100.0	0.5	1.5	3.9	7.8	13.7	20.3	21.1	18.2	13.1
Life, physical, and social science	100.0	1.6	3.5	7.5	12.5	17.1	18.5	16.1	12.0	11.3
Community and social services	100.0	6.4	10.4	17.4	21.2	19.3	14.2	7.5	2.7	0.8
Legal	100.0	1.1	2.1	5.1	10.3	14.1	13.8	11.1	11.0	31.3
Education, training, and library	100.0	10.6	8.6	9.7	14.4	18.8	17.0	11.7	5.4	3.7
Arts, design, entertainment, sports, and media	100.0	12.1	9.8	11.8	14.8	15.8	13.8	9.6	6.1	6.2
Health care practitioner and technical	100.0	2.1	4.6	7.7	11.9	18.7	21.1	14.6	8.1	11.1
Health care support	100.0	23.2	31.1	24.2	14.0	5.5	1.5	0.4	0.1	. . .
Protective service	100.0	15.6	14.9	14.6	14.9	13.7	13.1	8.3	3.6	1.2
Food preparation and serving related	100.0	65.6	18.1	9.2	4.3	1.9	0.6	0.2	0.1	. . .
Building and grounds cleaning and maintenance	100.0	40.4	25.2	16.7	9.9	5.4	1.8	0.5	0.1	. . .
Personal care and service	100.0	47.5	22.8	12.2	7.5	4.8	2.7	1.3	0.7	0.6
Sales and related	100.0	34.5	17.1	11.6	9.6	8.3	6.6	4.6	3.2	4.5
Office and administrative support	100.0	13.7	18.9	22.7	20.1	14.6	7.0	2.1	0.7	0.3
Farming, fishing, and forestry	100.0	56.3	18.0	11.0	7.1	4.3	2.1	0.8	0.3	0.1
Construction and extraction	100.0	6.3	11.7	16.5	18.8	17.9	14.8	9.5	3.6	1.0
Installation, maintenance, and repair	100.0	6.5	10.0	14.6	19.4	21.3	17.2	8.1	2.3	0.7
Production	100.0	16.5	19.3	20.3	18.2	12.8	8.5	3.1	0.9	0.2
Transportation and material moving	100.0	25.2	19.3	18.1	15.4	11.6	6.3	2.2	0.8	1.0

. . . = Not available.

Table 3-3. Employment and Wages by Occupation, May 2003–May 2004

(Number of persons, dollars.)

Occupational division and occupation	May 2003				May 2004			
	Employ-ment	Median hourly wages	Mean hourly wages	Mean annual wages[1]	Employ-ment	Median hourly wages	Mean hourly wages	Mean annual wages[1]
Management Occupations								
Chief executives	389 880	64.78	67.58	140 580	346 590	67.47	67.27	139 920
General and operations managers	1 892 060	35.00	42.64	88 700	1 752 910	37.22	44.24	92 010
Legislators	65 280	7.90	15.14	31 490	63 440	(2)	(2)	30 750
Advertising and promotions managers	71 100	29.01	35.18	73 170	57 100	30.58	36.76	76 460
Marketing managers	182 600	40.01	44.32	92 190	177 550	42.13	46.48	96 680
Sales managers	314 180	38.69	44.15	91 840	320 240	40.49	45.68	95 010
Public relations managers	58 490	31.16	35.94	74 750	50 670	33.65	38.26	79 580
Administrative services managers	278 300	27.37	30.67	63 780	254 610	28.99	31.98	66 530
Computer and information systems managers	266 020	43.15	45.78	95 230	267 390	44.51	47.24	98 260
Financial managers	521 750	37.16	41.92	87 190	493 360	39.37	44.04	91 610
Compensation and benefits managers	...	...	...	...	55 040	31.99	35.59	74 020
Training and development managers	...	...	...	...	35 510	32.43	35.45	73 730
Human resources managers, all other	171 530	33.08	36.15	75 190	58 770	39.33	42.11	87 580
Industrial production managers	166 350	33.90	36.88	76 710	155 980	35.09	38.06	79 170
Purchasing managers	91 060	31.22	34.17	71 080	73 480	34.83	37.51	78 020
Transportation, storage, and distribution managers	97 450	30.57	33.50	69 670	88 100	32.02	34.87	72 530
Farm, ranch, and other agricultural managers	5 420	22.83	25.04	52 080	4 810	24.38	26.51	55 140
Farmers and ranchers	...	...	...	...	540	19.44	20.78	43 230
Construction managers	196 110	31.96	35.96	74 790	185 580	33.59	37.83	78 690
Education administrators, preschool and child care center/program	56 030	16.59	19.37	40 290	50 590	17.18	19.74	41 060
Education administrators, elementary and secondary school	206 310	(2)	(2)	76 210	209 630	(2)	(2)	75 640
Education administrators, postsecondary	98 160	32.04	35.60	74 040	101 530	32.86	36.44	75 800
Education administrators, all other	...	...	...	...	22 570	28.96	32.01	66 580
Engineering managers	194 940	45.42	47.94	99 710	186 380	46.94	49.33	102 600
Food service managers	229 960	17.91	20.20	42 010	206 340	19.04	21.13	43 940
Funeral directors	23 080	21.48	25.82	53 710	23 140	22.10	25.82	53 710
Gaming managers	3 560	27.46	30.91	64 300	3 520	28.17	31.77	66 090
Lodging managers	30 760	17.16	19.70	40 980	30 860	18.11	21.18	44 060
Medical and health services managers	226 160	31.04	34.92	72 630	224 070	32.42	36.12	75 140
Natural sciences managers	41 810	41.28	45.19	93 990	40 240	42.63	46.06	95 800
Postmasters and mail superintendents	26 060	24.10	24.51	50 980	26 430	24.32	24.43	50 820
Property, real estate, and community association managers	156 120	18.46	22.86	47 550	159 980	19.22	23.44	48 760
Social and community service managers	116 020	21.85	23.77	49 440	119 280	22.50	24.39	50 740
Managers, all other	...	...	...	...	354 730	37.19	39.28	81 700
Business and Financial Operations								
Agents and business managers of artists, performers, and athletes	12 380	26.27	31.81	66 160	10 860	26.48	33.42	69 520
Purchasing agents and buyers, farm products	15 550	20.60	22.86	47 550	14 300	21.02	24.03	49 980
Wholesale and retail buyers, except farm products	138 630	20.28	23.72	49 350	136 930	20.30	23.29	48 450
Purchasing agents, except wholesale, retail, and farm products	237 210	22.43	24.07	50 060	257 070	22.92	24.60	51 180
Claims adjusters, examiners, and investigators	234 190	21.18	22.58	46 960	234 950	21.26	22.74	47 310
Insurance appraisers, auto damage	11 450	20.99	21.14	43 960	12 520	21.79	22.01	45 780
Compliance officers, except agriculture, construction, health and safety, and transportation	154 600	22.49	24.23	50 390	167 650	22.78	24.64	51 260
Cost estimators	184 620	23.22	25.03	52 050	191 080	24.01	25.90	53 870
Emergency management specialists	9 760	21.68	23.41	48 680	10 070	21.82	23.73	49 350
Employment, recruitment, and placement specialists	164 020	19.60	22.95	47 730	169 750	19.80	22.76	47 330
Compensation, benefits, and job analysis specialists	86 450	22.53	23.86	49 620	92 940	22.83	24.10	50 130
Training and development specialists	199 460	21.23	22.83	47 490	200 440	21.43	22.97	47 780
Human resources, training, and labor relations specialists, all other	...	...	...	...	158 930	22.85	23.67	49 240
Logisticians	...	...	...	...	52 470	27.46	28.99	60 310
Management analysts	423 880	30.09	35.19	73 190	416 340	30.51	34.97	72 730
Meeting and convention planners	32 980	18.78	20.47	42 570	34 640	19.05	20.43	42 490
Business operations specialists, all other	...	...	...	...	847 170	25.70	27.72	57 660
Accountants and auditors	924 640	23.59	26.65	55 430	995 910	24.41	27.35	56 880
Appraisers and assessors of real estate	61 070	20.97	23.99	49 900	62 270	20.86	23.73	49 350
Budget analysts	55 560	26.21	27.56	57 330	53 300	26.94	28.41	59 100
Credit analysts	68 910	21.65	25.25	52 530	67 100	22.72	26.57	55 280
Financial analysts	165 420	28.87	33.67	70 040	177 780	29.76	33.89	70 500
Personal financial advisors	85 670	28.22	38.12	79 290	94 490	30.14	39.70	82 570
Insurance underwriters	96 890	22.75	25.56	53 170	96 110	23.34	26.08	54 240
Financial examiners	22 720	28.36	30.66	63 770	23 400	29.00	31.47	65 450

[1]Annual wages have been calculated by multiplying the hourly mean wage by a "year-round, full-time" hours figure of 2,080 hours; for those occupations where there is not an hourly mean wage published, the annual wage has been directly calculated from the reported survey data.
[2]Hourly wage rates for occupations where workers typically work fewer than 2,080 hours per year are not available.
. . . = Not available.

Table 3-3. Employment and Wages by Occupation, May 2003–May 2004—*Continued*

(Number of persons, dollars.)

Occupational division and occupation	May 2003				May 2004			
	Employ-ment	Median hourly wages	Mean hourly wages	Mean annual wages[1]	Employ-ment	Median hourly wages	Mean hourly wages	Mean annual wages[1]
Loan counselors	30 810	16.09	18.12	37 700	31 160	16.33	18.61	38 710
Loan officers	237 150	22.43	26.73	55 590	278 830	23.48	27.98	58 200
Tax examiners, collectors, and revenue agents	71 060	20.57	22.62	47 060	71 610	20.91	23.18	48 210
Tax preparers	50 410	12.76	15.69	32 630	51 950	13.33	16.50	34 330
Financial specialists, all other	...	...	...	...	119 840	23.82	26.64	55 420
Computer and Mathematical Science Occupations								
Computer and information scientists, research	23 210	39.23	40.64	84 530	24 720	40.96	42.32	88 020
Computer programmers	431 640	29.49	31.01	64 510	412 090	30.24	31.69	65 910
Computer software engineers, applications	392 140	34.87	36.42	75 750	425 890	36.05	37.18	77 330
Computer software engineers, systems software	285 760	36.65	37.69	78 400	318 020	38.34	39.50	82 160
Computer support specialists	482 990	18.96	20.50	42 640	488 540	19.44	20.97	43 620
Computer systems analysts	474 780	30.85	31.82	66 180	489 130	31.95	32.87	68 370
Database administrators	100 890	27.98	29.54	61 440	96 960	29.16	30.51	63 460
Network and computer systems administrators	237 980	26.95	28.43	59 140	259 320	27.98	29.55	61 470
Network systems and data communications analysts	148 030	28.42	29.84	62 060	169 200	29.14	30.49	63 410
Computer specialists, all other	...	...	...	...	130 420	28.60	30.31	63 030
Actuaries	14 680	34.86	41.22	85 730	16 350	36.70	42.05	87 460
Mathematicians	2 470	37.64	37.00	76 960	2 410	39.06	39.18	81 500
Operations research analysts	58 080	28.03	29.66	61 700	55 030	28.94	30.49	63 420
Statisticians	18 370	28.64	29.79	61 970	17 030	28.18	30.42	63 260
Mathematical technicians	2 180	...	19.87	41 320	1 720	18.49	20.99	43 650
Mathematical scientists, all other	...	...	...	...	8 500	29.98	29.67	61 710
Architecture and Engineering Occupations								
Architects, except landscape and naval	91 010	27.86	31.18	64 850	94 280	28.99	31.84	66 230
Landscape architects	18 910	24.27	26.39	54 900	17 960	25.54	27.73	57 680
Cartographers and photogrammetrists	8 940	21.24	22.37	46 520	9 870	22.15	23.48	48 830
Surveyors	51 490	19.64	21.06	43 810	52 680	20.66	22.15	46 080
Aerospace engineers	70 740	35.83	36.54	76 000	73 650	38.03	38.68	80 460
Agricultural engineers	2 270	24.51	27.11	56 380	3 220	27.17	29.04	60 400
Biomedical engineers	6 980	30.61	32.20	66 980	8 650	32.54	34.04	70 800
Chemical engineers	32 490	35.46	36.66	76 250	30 320	36.91	38.49	80 050
Civil engineers	206 350	29.73	31.07	64 620	218 220	30.88	32.18	66 930
Computer hardware engineers	72 550	36.53	38.15	79 350	74 760	39.02	40.39	84 010
Electrical engineers	146 150	33.48	34.66	72 090	148 310	34.43	35.68	74 220
Electronics engineers, except computer	137 320	34.31	35.16	73 140	135 560	36.43	37.24	77 450
Environmental engineers	45 480	30.19	31.16	64 820	47 690	31.96	32.86	68 350
Health and safety engineers, except mining safety engineers and inspectors	29 920	28.68	30.01	62 420	25 860	30.64	31.78	66 110
Industrial engineers	156 780	30.23	30.91	64 290	174 960	31.26	32.05	66 660
Marine engineers and naval architects	4 960	33.89	34.52	71 800	6 620	34.63	35.44	73 720
Materials engineers	23 120	30.25	31.19	64 870	21 130	32.26	33.36	69 390
Mechanical engineers	207 810	30.72	31.75	66 040	217 010	31.88	32.91	68 460
Mining and geological engineers, including mining safety engineers	4 730	30.06	31.78	66 090	5 050	31.10	32.77	68 160
Nuclear engineers	16 010	40.18	41.12	85 520	17 180	40.81	42.67	88 760
Petroleum engineers	11 630	40.34	41.86	87 070	14 690	42.55	44.15	91 820
Engineers, all other	...	...	...	...	159 720	35.78	36.32	75 540
Architectural and civil drafters	97 800	18.12	18.84	39 190	101 060	18.84	19.59	40 750
Electrical and electronics drafters	33 720	20.06	21.56	44 840	34 850	20.76	22.48	46 760
Mechanical drafters	74 010	19.96	20.88	43 430	76 610	20.67	21.70	45 140
Drafters, all other	...	...	...	...	22 620	20.13	21.91	45 560
Aerospace engineering and operations technicians	13 900	25.33	25.91	53 890	9 260	25.24	25.98	54 040
Civil engineering technicians	90 060	18.30	18.89	39 290	90 000	18.50	19.18	39 900
Electrical and electronic engineering technicians	177 940	20.98	21.70	45 150	178 560	22.26	22.66	47 130
Electro-mechanical technicians	25 820	18.88	19.68	40 930	18 770	19.92	20.74	43 130
Environmental engineering technicians	17 630	17.88	19.01	39 530	19 840	18.53	19.55	40 660
Industrial engineering technicians	64 260	20.13	21.68	45 090	68 210	20.96	22.64	47 080
Mechanical engineering technicians	50 510	20.14	20.84	43 340	46 990	20.87	21.66	45 050
Engineering technicians, except drafters, all other	...	...	...	...	88 100	23.77	23.86	49 630
Surveying and mapping technicians	57 740	14.19	15.39	32 000	60 630	14.60	15.76	32 700

[1]Annual wages have been calculated by multiplying the hourly mean wage by a "year-round, full-time" hours figure of 2,080 hours; for those occupations where there is not an hourly mean wage published, the annual wage has been directly calculated from the reported survey data.
. . . = Not available.

Table 3-3. Employment and Wages by Occupation, May 2003–May 2004—*Continued*

(Number of persons, dollars.)

Occupational division and occupation	May 2003				May 2004			
	Employ-ment	Median hourly wages	Mean hourly wages	Mean annual wages[1]	Employ-ment	Median hourly wages	Mean hourly wages	Mean annual wages[1]
Life, Physical, and Social Science Occupations								
Animal scientists	...	...	...	...	1 540	24.00	25.87	53 800
Food scientists and technologists	...	...	...	...	7 210	24.44	26.98	56 110
Soil and plant scientists	...	...	...	...	9 690	24.62	26.67	55 470
Biochemists and biophysicists	14 430	29.95	32.27	67 120	15 200	33.15	34.48	71 730
Microbiologists	14 110	25.21	27.49	57 190	13 880	26.37	29.45	61 250
Zoologists and wildlife biologists	12 880	23.72	24.57	51 100	15 050	24.20	25.54	53 120
Biological scientists, all other	...	...	...	...	26 180	27.05	29.03	60 370
Conservation scientists	13 780	24.63	25.08	52 160	14 290	25.23	25.72	53 500
Foresters	9 840	22.75	23.44	48 760	10 250	23.19	23.91	49 730
Epidemiologists	3 770	26.22	28.30	58 860	4 560	26.35	27.91	58 060
Medical scientists, except epidemiologists	60 830	28.47	32.38	67 360	66 450	29.48	33.04	68 730
Life scientists, all other	...	...	...	...	13 870	26.65	30.63	63 710
Astronomers	770	42.45	40.90	85 070	680	46.79	44.99	93 580
Physicists	12 390	41.17	42.48	88 350	14 150	42.04	42.83	89 090
Atmospheric and space scientists	6 490	31.57	31.65	65 830	7 070	33.70	33.46	69 590
Chemists	82 600	25.79	28.11	58 460	79 650	26.95	29.43	61 220
Materials scientists	7 410	33.15	34.09	70 900	7 330	34.80	35.77	74 390
Environmental scientists and specialists, including health	61 660	23.46	25.23	52 490	66 850	24.56	26.53	55 190
Geoscientists, except hydrologists and geographers	26 090	32.91	37.73	78 480	25 100	33.04	36.96	76 870
Hydrologists	7 060	27.43	28.60	59 490	7 290	29.57	30.82	64 100
Physical scientists, all other	...	...	...	...	25 260	38.53	39.21	81 560
Economists	12 300	33.78	37.41	77 810	12 030	34.99	38.35	79 770
Market research analysts	142 190	26.28	29.65	61 670	170 200	26.99	30.28	62 990
Survey researchers	16 850	11.83	15.76	32 770	19 480	12.74	15.39	32 010
Clinical, counseling, and school psychologists	100 180	25.10	27.80	57 820	96 540	26.42	29.24	60 810
Industrial-organizational psychologists	1 330	30.98	34.26	71 260	1 500	34.33	37.88	78 800
Psychologists, all other	...	...	...	...	6 480	34.57	33.53	69 740
Sociologists	3 060	26.16	28.16	58 570	3 640	27.82	30.46	63 350
Urban and regional planners	30 770	24.73	25.58	53 210	31 140	25.70	26.75	55 640
Anthropologists and archeologists	4 550	19.54	21.28	44 270	4 510	21.10	22.86	47 550
Geographers	700	27.33	27.26	56 690	750	28.35	28.65	59 600
Historians	2 350	20.14	21.78	45 310	2 350	21.39	23.48	48 850
Political scientists	4 840	39.12	38.93	80 980	4 370	41.71	41.24	85 770
Social scientists and related workers, all other	...	...	...	...	31 990	28.12	29.09	60 500
Agricultural and food science technicians	15 990	13.81	14.87	30 920	18 940	14.29	15.37	31 980
Biological technicians	49 550	15.69	16.62	34 570	59 710	15.97	17.04	35 450
Chemical technicians	64 020	17.82	18.51	38 500	61 700	18.35	19.04	39 600
Geological and petroleum technicians	10 150	19.58	20.21	42 040	10 420	19.35	20.85	43 360
Nuclear technicians	6 970	28.47	28.64	59 570	7 210	28.46	28.28	58 830
Social science research assistants	...	...	...	...	15 710	16.52	17.26	35 900
Environmental science and protection technicians, including health	27 800	16.97	17.97	37 380	29 460	16.99	17.90	37 230
Forensic science technicians	8 830	20.18	21.43	44 580	9 230	21.16	22.83	47 490
Forest and conservation technicians	30 140	12.93	14.29	29 730	29 910	13.14	14.79	30 770
Life, physical, and social science technicians, all other	...	...	...	...	72 580	18.19	20.52	42 680
Community and Social Service Occupations								
Substance abuse and behavioral disorder counselors	65 170	14.99	15.95	33 170	68 880	15.45	16.50	34 310
Educational, vocational, and school counselors	214 360	21.46	22.59	46 990	220 690	21.91	22.88	47 590
Marriage and family therapists	22 150	17.71	19.33	40 210	20 710	18.74	20.21	42 040
Mental health counselors	83 450	15.05	16.48	34 280	89 300	15.85	17.31	36 000
Rehabilitation counselors	115 690	12.79	14.06	29 240	115 150	13.40	14.76	30 710
Counselors, all other	...	...	...	...	21 970	16.82	18.21	37 880
Child, family, and school social workers	256 160	16.25	17.64	36 700	250 790	16.74	18.19	37 830
Medical and public health social workers	103 270	18.48	19.10	39 730	103 180	19.27	19.92	41 440
Mental health and substance abuse social workers	96 990	15.88	16.88	35 120	108 950	16.31	17.34	36 060
Social workers, all other	...	...	...	...	60 120	18.96	19.80	41 180
Health educators	42 780	18.00	19.47	40 490	46 490	18.50	20.25	42 120
Probation officers and correctional treatment specialists	86 810	18.64	20.00	41 600	89 170	19.04	20.53	42 690
Social and human service assistants	300 310	11.47	12.24	25 450	331 860	11.67	12.45	25 890
Community and social service specialists, all other	...	...	...	...	89 250	15.64	16.57	34 470
Clergy	38 170	16.25	17.76	36 950	35 790	17.64	19.23	40 000
Directors, religious activities and education	11 840	13.45	15.60	32 460	12 620	14.76	16.14	33 560
Religious workers, all other	...	...	...	...	8 810	9.01	11.41	23 730

[1]Annual wages have been calculated by multiplying the hourly mean wage by a "year-round, full-time" hours figure of 2,080 hours; for those occupations where there is not an hourly mean wage published, the annual wage has been directly calculated from the reported survey data.
... = Not available.

Table 3-3. Employment and Wages by Occupation, May 2003–May 2004—*Continued*

(Number of persons, dollars.)

Occupational division and occupation	May 2003				May 2004			
	Employ-ment	Median hourly wages	Mean hourly wages	Mean annual wages[1]	Employ-ment	Median hourly wages	Mean hourly wages	Mean annual wages[1]
Legal Occupations								
Lawyers	516 220	43.98	51.83	107 800	521 130	45.64	52.30	108 790
Administrative law judges, adjudicators, and hearing officers	16 850	31.81	33.46	69 590	14 830	33.14	35.44	73 710
Arbitrators, mediators, and conciliators	4 640	22.77	26.06	54 210	4 940	26.32	29.08	60 480
Judges, magistrate judges, and magistrates	24 640	46.31	42.09	87 540	25 500	44.75	42.96	89 360
Paralegals and legal assistants	206 700	18.23	19.57	40 710	210 020	18.81	19.95	41 490
Court reporters	15 370	20.31	22.26	46 310	15 520	20.63	22.63	47 070
Law clerks	41 550	15.27	15.88	33 030	43 300	16.34	16.92	35 180
Title examiners, abstractors, and searchers	47 840	16.39	18.69	38 880	53 700	16.77	18.93	39 360
Legal support workers, all other	...	...	...	...	69 590	20.26	21.79	45 330
Education, Training, and Library Occupations								
Business teachers, postsecondary	68 260	(2)	(2)	62 450	68 340	(2)	(2)	65 430
Computer science teachers, postsecondary	34 470	(2)	(2)	56 210	37 260	(2)	(2)	58 140
Mathematical science teachers, postsecondary	41 880	(2)	(2)	55 510	43 760	(2)	(2)	57 240
Architecture teachers, postsecondary	5 270	(2)	(2)	64 300	5 700	(2)	(2)	65 510
Engineering teachers, postsecondary	28 990	(2)	(2)	74 630	33 520	(2)	(2)	77 070
Agricultural sciences teachers, postsecondary	11 260	(2)	(2)	66 780	10 230	(2)	(2)	67 520
Biological science teachers, postsecondary	51 780	(2)	(2)	68 880	60 260	(2)	(2)	73 220
Forestry and conservation science teachers, postsecondary	2 660	(2)	(2)	66 740	2 970	(2)	(2)	67 660
Atmospheric, earth, marine, and space sciences teachers, postsecondary	8 420	(2)	(2)	68 370	8 660	(2)	(2)	70 300
Chemistry teachers, postsecondary	17 100	(2)	(2)	61 820	18 720	(2)	(2)	63 520
Environmental science teachers, postsecondary	3 620	(2)	(2)	62 960	3 860	(2)	(2)	66 790
Physics teachers, postsecondary	11 870	(2)	(2)	67 430	12 590	(2)	(2)	69 210
Anthropology and archeology teachers, postsecondary	4 690	(2)	(2)	64 320	4 990	(2)	(2)	66 060
Area, ethnic, and cultural studies teachers, postsecondary	7 490	(2)	(2)	60 520	7 670	(2)	(2)	62 940
Economics teachers, postsecondary	11 420	(2)	(2)	70 590	12 230	(2)	(2)	73 280
Geography teachers, postsecondary	3 910	(2)	(2)	59 200	4 180	(2)	(2)	61 020
Political science teachers, postsecondary	12 320	(2)	(2)	62 880	13 230	(2)	(2)	64 950
Psychology teachers, postsecondary	27 250	(2)	(2)	59 180	29 400	(2)	(2)	60 800
Sociology teachers, postsecondary	13 990	(2)	(2)	56 830	14 220	(2)	(2)	59 830
Social sciences teachers, postsecondary, all other	...	...	...	...	6 310	(2)	(2)	68 460
Health specialties teachers, postsecondary	88 130	(2)	(2)	73 660	105 610	(2)	(2)	76 720
Nursing instructors and teachers, postsecondary	36 330	(2)	(2)	53 480	34 360	(2)	(2)	55 770
Education teachers, postsecondary	44 880	(2)	(2)	51 830	47 710	(2)	(2)	52 850
Library science teachers, postsecondary	4 110	(2)	(2)	53 660	3 740	(2)	(2)	54 590
Criminal justice and law enforcement teachers, postsecondary	9 610	(2)	(2)	49 180	9 550	(2)	(2)	51 500
Law teachers, postsecondary	11 470	(2)	(2)	91 420	12 580	(2)	(2)	95 300
Social work teachers, postsecondary	6 470	(2)	(2)	55 830	6 670	(2)	(2)	56 620
Art, drama, and music teachers, postsecondary	60 120	(2)	(2)	52 770	63 730	(2)	(2)	52 750
Communications teachers, postsecondary	20 420	(2)	(2)	52 400	20 760	(2)	(2)	53 130
English language and literature teachers, postsecondary	56 540	(2)	(2)	51 780	57 400	(2)	(2)	52 560
Foreign language and literature teachers, postsecondary	19 710	(2)	(2)	50 920	22 460	(2)	(2)	51 620
History teachers, postsecondary	18 110	(2)	(2)	56 550	19 190	(2)	(2)	58 490
Philosophy and religion teachers, postsecondary	15 890	(2)	(2)	53 600	17 170	(2)	(2)	56 630
Graduate teaching assistants	121 760	(2)	(2)	26 440	111 730	(2)	(2)	27 860
Home economics teachers, postsecondary	4 500	(2)	(2)	52 600	3 870	(2)	(2)	50 810
Recreation and fitness studies teachers, postsecondary	14 780	(2)	(2)	47 050	15 470	(2)	(2)	47 360
Vocational education teachers, postsecondary	121 090	19.10	20.80	43 270	112 990	19.59	21.19	44 060
Postsecondary teachers, all other	...	...	...	...	248 330	27.93	30.73	63 920
Preschool teachers, except special education	368 870	9.53	10.67	22 190	354 800	10.09	11.51	23 940
Kindergarten teachers, except special education	162 660	(2)	(2)	42 380	164 530	(2)	(2)	44 000
Elementary school teachers, except special education	1 432 800	(2)	(2)	44 350	1 422 840	(2)	(2)	45 670
Middle school teachers, except special and vocational education	604 370	(2)	(2)	44 830	623 400	(2)	(2)	46 510
Vocational education teachers, middle school	17 430	(2)	(2)	44 930	16 820	(2)	(2)	46 250
Secondary school teachers, except special and vocational education	1 011 240	(2)	(2)	46 790	1 021 180	(2)	(2)	48 420
Vocational education teachers, secondary school	101 190	(2)	(2)	46 100	102 210	(2)	(2)	48 000
Special education teachers, preschool, kindergarten, and elementary school	207 530	(2)	(2)	45 920	205 960	(2)	(2)	46 420
Special education teachers, middle school	93 790	(2)	(2)	44 920	98 840	(2)	(2)	48 910
Special education teachers, secondary school	131 190	(2)	(2)	47 530	138 470	(2)	(2)	49 620
Adult literacy, remedial education, and GED teachers and instructors	62 510	18.10	20.47	42 570	63 200	18.74	20.92	43 520
Self-enrichment education teachers	136 680	14.34	16.15	33 590	141 180	14.85	16.93	35 210
Teachers and instructors, all other	...	...	...	...	505 570	(2)	(2)	33 100
Archivists	...	...	...	...	5 190	17.54	19.05	39 630
Curators	...	...	...	...	8 590	20.97	23.04	47 920
Museum technicians and conservators	...	...	...	...	8 850	15.30	16.96	35 270
Librarians	153 330	21.22	21.89	45 520	149 680	22.07	22.88	47 590

[1]Annual wages have been calculated by multiplying the hourly mean wage by a "year-round, full-time" hours figure of 2,080 hours; for those occupations where there is not an hourly mean wage published, the annual wage has been directly calculated from the reported survey data.
[2]Hourly wage rates for occupations where workers typically work fewer than 2,080 hours per year are not available.
. . . = Not available.

Table 3-3. Employment and Wages by Occupation, May 2003–May 2004—*Continued*

(Number of persons, dollars.)

Occupational division and occupation	May 2003				May 2004			
	Employ-ment	Median hourly wages	Mean hourly wages	Mean annual wages[1]	Employ-ment	Median hourly wages	Mean hourly wages	Mean annual wages[1]
Library technicians	108 940	11.65	12.29	25 570	113 520	11.99	12.63	26 260
Audio-visual collections specialists	8 970	15.67	16.80	34 940	8 420	15.86	17.13	35 630
Farm and home management advisors	12 010	19.20	20.10	41 800	12 620	20.00	21.62	44 960
Instructional coordinators	96 690	22.82	24.09	50 100	106 590	23.46	24.74	51 450
Teacher assistants	1 234 030	(2)	(2)	20 220	1 242 760	(2)	(2)	20 400
Education, training, and library workers, all other	...	...	...	...	65 150	14.29	16.29	33 890
Arts, Design, Entertainment, Sports, and Media Occupations								
Art directors	24 000	29.93	33.70	70 100	26 870	30.69	35.21	73 240
Craft artists	...	...	...	...	3 890	11.31	13.33	27 720
Fine artists, including painters, sculptors, and illustrators	9 690	17.03	20.97	43 610	9 570	18.30	20.98	43 640
Multi-media artists and animators	32 910	22.08	25.42	52 880	30 210	24.21	27.65	57 520
Artists and related workers, all other	...	...	...	...	5 370	14.72	18.02	37 490
Commercial and industrial designers	33 390	25.16	26.41	54 920	33 050	25.15	26.77	55 670
Fashion designers	11 270	25.42	30.12	62 650	12 100	26.85	30.84	64 150
Floral designers	69 730	9.45	10.00	20 810	67 710	9.83	10.51	21 860
Graphic designers	151 950	17.61	19.85	41 300	159 720	18.28	20.25	42 120
Interior designers	46 240	19.29	21.39	44 480	46 360	19.56	21.59	44 900
Merchandise displayers and window trimmers	59 150	10.59	11.99	24 940	62 220	10.89	12.51	26 020
Set and exhibit designers	8 060	16.90	18.78	39 070	8 750	17.21	19.23	40 000
Designers, all other	...	...	...	...	12 650	20.31	22.27	46 320
Actors	51 840	(2)	(2)	48 940	59 000	11.28	22.48	(3)
Producers and directors	54 370	(2)	(2)	64 550	55 260	25.40	34.84	72 470
Athletes and sports competitors	11 840	(2)	(2)	90 410	12 250	(2)	(2)	86 690
Coaches and scouts	105 070	(2)	(2)	33 570	122 930	(2)	(2)	32 780
Umpires, referees, and other sports officials	8 790	(2)	(2)	27 820	11 440	(2)	(2)	27 850
Dancers	15 390	9.45	12.76	26 540	14 880	8.54	12.15	(3)
Choreographers	14 810	14.92	17.16	35 700	15 360	16.19	18.39	38 250
Music directors and composers	9 000	(2)	(2)	41 450	8 870	16.62	21.06	43 810
Musicians and singers	50 600	(2)	(2)	51 580	52 000	17.85	24.96	(3)
Entertainers and performers, sports and related workers, all other	...	...	...	...	54 800	16.73	18.82	(3)
Radio and television announcers	...	...	...	...	41 430	10.64	15.22	31 650
Public address system and other announcers	...	...	...	...	8 180	10.56	14.08	29 290
Broadcast news analysts	...	...	...	...	6 930	17.78	27.28	56 740
Reporters and correspondents	...	...	...	...	52 550	15.06	18.58	38 650
Public relations specialists	...	...	...	...	166 210	21.07	23.80	49 510
Editors	108 990	19.93	22.83	47 490	100 790	21.10	23.65	49 190
Technical writers	44 690	24.80	26.15	54 390	45 100	25.71	27.24	56 650
Writers and authors	43 740	20.35	24.26	50 460	42 780	21.32	25.52	53 080
Interpreters and translators	21 910	16.10	17.22	35 820	25 410	16.28	17.61	36 630
Media and communication workers, all other	...	...	...	...	27 380	19.64	21.66	45 060
Audio and video equipment technicians	37 370	14.81	16.88	35 110	40 050	15.66	17.62	36 650
Broadcast technicians	32 750	13.51	16.62	34 560	29 940	13.47	16.14	33 560
Radio operators	2 060	14.57	15.80	32 870	1 670	15.73	17.06	35 490
Sound engineering technicians	11 840	18.41	22.49	46 780	11 650	18.32	21.91	45 570
Photographers	57 740	12.04	14.23	29 590	54 400	12.54	15.00	31 200
Camera operators, television, video, and motion picture	21 430	16.51	18.34	38 140	21 600	18.08	20.04	41 690
Film and video editors	15 100	19.52	22.32	46 420	15 800	20.96	24.37	50 690
Media and communication equipment workers, all other	...	...	...	...	18 570	19.77	22.36	46 510
Health Care Practitioner and Technical Occupations								
Chiropractors	20 210	31.72	39.72	82 630	21 830	33.61	42.01	87 390
Dentists, general	97 090	57.85	63.08	131 210	84 240	59.16	63.87	132 850
Oral and maxillofacial surgeons	...	...	...	...	4 950	(4)	79.69	165 750
Orthodontists	...	...	...	...	6 190	(4)	72.45	150 700
Prosthodontists	...	...	...	...	730	(4)	70.04	145 670
Dentists, all other specialists	...	...	...	...	2 710	60.64	62.64	130 300
Dietitians and nutritionists	46 190	20.21	20.68	43 020	46 530	20.98	21.46	44 640
Optometrists	22 740	41.07	45.70	95 060	22 780	42.51	46.53	96 780
Pharmacists	215 030	38.72	37.80	78 620	222 960	40.82	40.56	84 370
Anesthesiologists	23 790	(4)	88.89	184 880	25 130	(4)	83.77	174 250
Family and general practitioners	111 990	64.11	67.13	139 640	106 750	65.91	66.58	138 490
Internists, general	50 140	(4)	76.99	160 130	51 180	(4)	76.06	158 200
Obstetricians and gynecologists	19 180	(4)	86.86	180 660	20 850	(4)	84.74	176 270
Pediatricians, general	26 910	64.50	68.90	143 300	26 520	65.26	68.04	141 520
Psychiatrists	19 530	64.41	66.97	139 300	22 440	(4)	72.17	150 110

[1]Annual wages have been calculated by multiplying the hourly mean wage by a "year-round, full-time" hours figure of 2,080 hours; for those occupations where there is not an hourly mean wage published, the annual wage has been directly calculated from the reported survey data.
[2]Hourly wage rates for occupations where workers typically work fewer than 2,080 hours per year are not available.
[3]There is a wide variation in the number of hours worked by those employed as actors, dancers, singers, and musicians. Many jobs are for the duration of 1 day or 1 week, and it is extremely rare for a performer to have guaranteed employment for a period that exceeds 3 to 6 months. Therefore, only hourly wages are available for these occupations.
[4]Median hourly wage is equal to or greater than $70.00 per hour.
... = Not available.

Table 3-3. Employment and Wages by Occupation, May 2003–May 2004—*Continued*

(Number of persons, dollars.)

Occupational division and occupation	May 2003				May 2004			
	Employ-ment	Median hourly wages	Mean hourly wages	Mean annual wages[1]	Employ-ment	Median hourly wages	Mean hourly wages	Mean annual wages[1]
Surgeons	49 730	(4)	91.48	190 280	55 800	(4)	87.31	181 610
Physicians and surgeons, all other	...	...	...	...	162 720	67.44	66.16	137 610
Physician assistants	60 030	31.57	31.15	64 790	59 470	33.37	33.07	68 780
Podiatrists	7 800	45.22	51.17	106 430	7 550	45.38	52.11	108 400
Registered nurses	2 246 430	23.82	24.63	51 230	2 311 970	25.16	26.06	54 210
Audiologists	10 030	23.93	25.23	52 490	9 810	24.74	26.47	55 050
Occupational therapists	81 380	25.27	25.87	53 810	83 560	26.28	27.19	56 550
Physical therapists	134 970	27.75	29.02	60 350	142 940	28.93	30.00	62 390
Radiation therapists	13 990	26.06	30.83	64 130	14 470	27.74	29.05	60 420
Recreational therapists	22 860	15.32	15.82	32 920	23 050	15.82	16.48	34 280
Respiratory therapists	87 180	19.79	20.07	41 750	91 350	20.74	21.24	44 180
Speech-language pathologists	86 640	24.06	25.10	52 210	89 260	25.20	26.71	55 550
Therapists, all other	...	...	...	...	8 090	19.32	21.45	44 620
Veterinarians	43 890	31.13	36.00	74 880	46 090	32.01	36.07	75 030
Health diagnosing and treating practitioners, all other ...	...	...	...	...	56 920	27.87	44.38	92 300
Medical and clinical laboratory technologists	146 900	20.98	21.38	44 480	151 240	21.99	22.41	46 600
Medical and clinical laboratory technicians	146 160	14.24	14.88	30 940	141 720	14.83	15.44	32 120
Dental hygienists	146 360	27.10	28.13	58 520	155 810	28.05	28.58	59 440
Cardiovascular technologists and technicians	43 300	17.99	18.44	38 350	43 540	18.60	19.09	39 710
Diagnostic medical sonographers	37 240	24.02	24.39	50 740	41 280	25.24	25.78	53 620
Nuclear medicine technologists	17 550	24.79	26.57	55 260	17 520	27.14	29.43	61 210
Radiologic technologists and technicians	173 030	19.53	20.03	41 660	177 220	20.84	21.41	44 530
Emergency medical technicians and paramedics	181 750	11.75	12.95	26 930	187 900	12.17	13.30	27 650
Dietetic technicians	26 870	10.78	11.64	24 210	24 630	11.05	11.89	24 730
Pharmacy technicians	211 270	10.94	11.47	23 860	255 290	11.37	11.87	24 700
Psychiatric technicians	56 000	12.39	13.60	28 290	59 010	12.28	13.43	27 940
Respiratory therapy technicians	25 470	16.75	17.11	35 590	24 190	17.67	18.00	37 440
Surgical technologists	73 250	15.45	15.74	32 740	82 280	16.35	16.72	34 770
Veterinary technologists and technicians	53 730	11.22	11.76	24 470	58 570	11.99	12.49	25 990
Licensed practical and licensed vocational nurses	682 590	15.57	15.97	33 210	702 740	16.33	16.75	34 840
Medical records and health information technicians ...	148 380	11.79	12.77	26 550	155 030	12.30	13.30	27 660
Opticians, dispensing	63 780	12.67	13.74	28 570	62 350	13.44	14.37	29 880
Orthotists and prosthetists	4 880	23.90	27.38	56 950	4 930	24.17	27.47	57 130
Health technologists and technicians, all other	...	...	...	...	72 390	16.46	18.10	37 650
Occupational health and safety specialists	42 580	22.88	23.57	49 020	36 360	24.79	25.54	53 110
Occupational health and safety technicians	...	...	...	...	11 190	20.25	21.31	44 320
Athletic trainers	11 750	(2)	(2)	34 860	13 100	(2)	(2)	36 350
Health care practitioners and technical workers, all other ...	...	...	...	...	52 240	16.04	18.20	37 860
Health Care Support Occupations								
Home health aides	583 880	8.77	9.22	19 180	596 330	8.81	9.13	18 980
Nursing aides, orderlies, and attendants	1 341 650	9.85	10.12	21 050	1 384 120	10.09	10.39	21 610
Psychiatric aides	57 770	11.01	11.48	23 880	54 520	11.19	11.70	24 340
Occupational therapist assistants	18 940	17.98	18.04	37 530	20 880	18.48	18.49	38 460
Occupational therapist aides	6 060	10.95	12.21	25 390	5 240	11.13	12.51	26 030
Physical therapist assistants	52 440	17.60	17.67	36 750	57 420	18.22	18.14	37 730
Physical therapist aides	36 870	10.08	10.71	22 270	41 910	10.28	11.14	23 160
Massage therapists	29 940	13.78	16.49	34 310	32 200	15.36	17.63	36 670
Dental assistants	272 030	13.32	13.57	28 230	264 820	13.62	13.97	29 060
Medical assistants	362 670	11.62	11.99	24 940	380 340	11.83	12.21	25 400
Medical equipment preparers	37 140	11.23	11.66	24 260	40 380	11.76	12.14	25 240
Medical transcriptionists	97 810	13.26	13.59	28 270	92 740	13.64	14.01	29 150
Pharmacy aides	61 170	8.84	9.42	19 600	47 720	8.86	9.52	19 810
Veterinary assistants and laboratory animal caretakers	64 490	8.66	9.28	19 310	70 200	8.97	9.44	19 640
Health care support workers, all other	...	...	...	...	182 550	12.01	12.62	26 250
Protective Service Occupations								
First-line supervisors/managers of correctional officers	33 760	21.88	23.00	47 850	35 880	21.50	22.83	47 490
First-line supervisors/managers of police and detectives	101 740	29.98	30.39	63 200	96 080	30.97	31.34	65 180
First-line supervisors/managers of fire fighting and prevention workers	59 000	27.40	28.24	58 750	54 170	28.33	29.26	60 860
First-line supervisors/managers, protective service workers, all other	...	...	...	...	47 280	17.91	20.05	41 690
Firefighters	273 120	17.82	18.41	38 280	273 630	18.43	19.06	39 640
Fire inspectors and investigators	12 320	21.99	22.76	47 340	12 500	22.28	23.03	47 890
Forest fire inspectors and prevention specialists	1 460	18.31	19.72	41 010	1 580	18.77	19.98	41 560
Bailiffs	16 760	16.57	16.81	34 970	17 270	16.28	16.80	34 950
Correctional officers and jailers	417 420	15.94	16.87	35 090	409 580	16.15	17.29	35 970
Detectives and criminal investigators	87 480	25.19	26.17	54 440	86 880	25.96	27.16	56 500

[1]Annual wages have been calculated by multiplying the hourly mean wage by a "year-round, full-time" hours figure of 2,080 hours; for those occupations where there is not an hourly mean wage published, the annual wage has been directly calculated from the reported survey data.
[2]Hourly wage rates for occupations where workers typically work fewer than 2,080 hours per year are not available.
[4]Median hourly wage is equal to or greater than $70.00 per hour.
. . . = Not available.

Table 3-3. Employment and Wages by Occupation, May 2003–May 2004—*Continued*

(Number of persons, dollars.)

Occupational division and occupation	May 2003				May 2004			
	Employ-ment	Median hourly wages	Mean hourly wages	Mean annual wages[1]	Employ-ment	Median hourly wages	Mean hourly wages	Mean annual wages[1]
Fish and game wardens	6 850	19.90	21.41	44 540	7 050	20.57	23.60	49 090
Parking enforcement workers	9 870	13.55	14.22	29 570	9 990	13.64	14.37	29 890
Police and sheriff's patrol officers	609 960	21.16	21.62	44 960	616 340	21.74	22.20	46 180
Transit and railroad police	5 470	21.23	22.09	45 940	4 610	21.84	22.77	47 370
Animal control workers	12 290	12.38	12.93	26 900	13 780	12.60	13.15	27 360
Private detectives and investigators	30 460	14.62	16.87	35 080	31 220	15.44	17.47	36 330
Gaming surveillance officers and gaming investigators	7 560	11.86	12.51	26 030	8 560	12.42	13.69	28 470
Security guards	964 260	9.45	10.34	21 520	978 570	9.77	10.61	22 070
Crossing guards	70 820	9.07	9.86	20 510	70 180	9.28	9.94	20 670
Lifeguards, ski patrol, and other recreational protective service workers	...	...	...	...	108 210	7.95	8.43	17 530
Protective service workers, all other	...	...	...	...	122 740	13.50	14.54	30 240
Food Preparation and Serving Related Occupations								
Chefs and head cooks	118 870	13.82	15.68	32 620	116 930	14.75	16.42	34 160
First-line supervisors/managers of food preparation and serving workers	694 040	11.88	12.90	26 840	733 680	12.22	13.21	27 480
Cooks, fast food	612 960	6.95	7.23	15 030	652 500	7.07	7.33	15 250
Cooks, institution and cafeteria	406 010	8.80	9.31	19 350	401 110	9.10	9.55	19 860
Cooks, private household	...	...	...	...	650	9.42	10.83	22 530
Cooks, restaurant	734 870	9.26	9.62	20 020	765 670	9.39	9.73	20 230
Cooks, short order	227 360	7.90	8.30	17 260	225 740	8.11	8.46	17 590
Cooks, all other	...	...	...	...	10 780	10.09	10.87	22 600
Food preparation workers	852 890	7.92	8.34	17 340	863 700	8.03	8.47	17 620
Bartenders	470 020	7.23	8.14	16 930	463 000	7.42	8.29	17 240
Combined food preparation and serving workers, including fast food	2 047 100	7.00	7.34	15 260	2 140 740	7.06	7.40	15 390
Counter attendants, cafeteria, food concession, and coffee shop	461 700	7.38	7.76	16 140	458 610	7.53	7.78	16 170
Waiters and waitresses	2 125 100	6.78	7.58	15 780	2 219 850	6.75	7.66	15 930
Food servers, nonrestaurant	194 260	7.65	8.28	17 220	186 770	7.95	8.58	17 840
Dining room and cafeteria attendants and bartender helpers	393 500	7.01	7.38	15 350	390 980	7.10	7.44	15 470
Dishwashers	492 620	7.21	7.45	15 490	497 650	7.35	7.50	15 600
Hosts and hostesses, restaurant, lounge, and coffee shop	294 300	7.40	7.77	16 170	316 400	7.52	7.82	16 260
Food preparation and serving related workers, all other	...	...	...	...	62 620	8.26	8.89	18 490
Building and Grounds Cleaning and Maintenance Occupations								
First-line supervisors/managers of housekeeping and janitorial workers	203 770	13.78	14.90	31 000	199 990	14.19	15.32	31 880
First-line supervisors/managers of landscaping, lawn service, and groundskeeping workers	95 450	16.23	17.71	36 840	102 380	16.99	18.38	38 230
Janitors and cleaners, except maids and housekeeping cleaners	2 064 350	8.85	9.77	20 320	2 103 490	9.04	9.91	20 620
Maids and housekeeping cleaners	896 370	7.98	8.42	17 520	880 150	8.13	8.62	17 930
Building cleaning workers, all other	...	...	...	...	13 580	10.17	10.74	22 350
Pest control workers	58 500	12.01	12.75	26 510	59 080	12.61	13.38	27 830
Landscaping and groundskeeping workers	819 780	9.59	10.39	21 610	860 200	9.82	10.62	22 080
Pesticide handlers, sprayers, and applicators, vegetation	23 450	12.25	12.60	26 210	24 200	12.30	12.74	26 500
Tree trimmers and pruners	40 710	12.32	13.11	27 270	39 600	12.57	13.37	27 800
Grounds maintenance workers, all other	...	...	...	...	17 760	9.57	11.18	23 250
Personal Care and Service Occupations								
Gaming supervisors	26 280	19.31	19.64	40 860	25 040	19.64	19.98	41 570
Slot key persons	15 000	11.13	11.98	24 930	16 210	11.06	12.07	25 110
First-line supervisors/managers of personal service workers	110 630	14.18	15.67	32 590	121 250	14.59	16.07	33 430
Animal trainers	6 990	10.75	12.65	26 310	8 060	10.60	12.48	25 950
Nonfarm animal caretakers	85 440	8.26	9.08	18 890	81 110	8.39	9.24	19 220
Gaming dealers	76 120	6.83	7.86	16 350	82 560	6.89	7.89	16 420
Gaming and sports book writers and runners	15 820	9.05	10.04	20 880	18 290	8.84	9.76	20 310
Gaming service workers, all other	...	...	...	...	14 860	10.01	10.85	22 570
Motion picture projectionists	10 450	8.24	9.98	20 750	10 290	8.32	9.55	19 870
Ushers, lobby attendants, and ticket takers	109 290	7.07	7.94	16 520	110 420	7.30	8.07	16 780
Amusement and recreation attendants	236 070	7.23	7.89	16 400	241 110	7.47	8.00	16 630
Costume attendants	3 400	12.22	13.80	28 700	3 460	12.04	13.81	28 720
Locker room, coatroom, and dressing room attendants	21 420	8.25	8.60	17 890	24 320	8.44	8.80	18 310
Entertainment attendants and related workers, all other	...	...	...	...	37 080	8.14	8.57	17 820
Embalmers	7 630	16.51	17.48	36 360	8 660	17.09	17.93	37 300
Funeral attendants	28 120	8.91	9.66	20 090	29 660	9.26	10.05	20 900
Barbers	17 570	9.73	11.16	23 210	15 830	10.19	12.04	25 040
Hairdressers, hairstylists, and cosmetologists	335 860	8.99	10.49	21 810	331 260	9.52	10.95	22 770
Makeup artists, theatrical and performance	720	14.09	16.68	34 700	1 060	11.74	15.28	31 780
Manicurists and pedicurists	32 670	8.52	9.21	19 150	38 030	8.89	9.65	20 080

[1]Annual wages have been calculated by multiplying the hourly mean wage by a "year-round, full-time" hours figure of 2,080 hours; for those occupations where there is not an hourly mean wage published, the annual wage has been directly calculated from the reported survey data.
... = Not available.

Table 3-3. Employment and Wages by Occupation, May 2003–May 2004—*Continued*

(Number of persons, dollars.)

Occupational division and occupation	May 2003				May 2004			
	Employ-ment	Median hourly wages	Mean hourly wages	Mean annual wages[1]	Employ-ment	Median hourly wages	Mean hourly wages	Mean annual wages[1]
Shampooers	15 300	6.90	7.27	15 120	16 180	7.03	7.51	15 610
Skin care specialists	16 820	11.08	12.65	26 310	19 650	11.55	13.20	27 450
Baggage porters and bellhops	55 880	8.51	10.53	21 900	55 910	8.54	10.46	21 760
Concierges	16 710	10.48	11.31	23 520	17 310	11.23	11.93	24 820
Tour guides and escorts	27 390	9.04	9.71	20 190	28 660	9.32	9.92	20 640
Travel guides	5 450	13.24	15.17	31 540	4 140	13.20	14.30	29 750
Flight attendants	107 100	(2)	(2)	47 670	101 980	(2)	(2)	51 160
Transportation attendants, except flight attendants and baggage porters	28 580	9.05	9.99	20 770	27 730	9.17	9.99	20 780
Child care workers	469 150	7.90	8.37	17 400	513 110	8.06	8.57	17 830
Personal and home care aides	487 200	7.91	8.18	17 020	532 490	8.12	8.38	17 430
Fitness trainers and aerobics instructors	177 790	11.78	14.71	30 590	182 280	12.25	14.98	31 170
Recreation workers	265 640	8.94	10.12	21 040	266 520	9.29	10.43	21 690
Residential advisors	49 650	10.06	10.89	22 650	49 960	10.30	11.17	23 240
Personal care and service workers, all other	...	...	...	...	65 070	8.63	9.81	20 410
Sales and Related Occpations								
First-line supervisors/managers of retail sales workers	1 175 310	14.75	17.10	35 560	1 087 830	15.73	18.01	37 470
First-line supervisors/managers of non-retail sales workers	327 180	26.78	32.46	67 520	307 610	28.51	34.33	71 420
Cashiers	3 462 010	7.58	8.14	16 940	3 438 070	7.81	8.29	17 250
Gaming change persons and booth cashiers	30 760	9.63	9.84	20 470	28 830	9.87	10.04	20 890
Counter and rental clerks	442 310	8.48	9.95	20 690	444 850	8.79	10.47	21 770
Parts salespersons	236 090	11.78	13.04	27 120	236 710	12.32	13.58	28 240
Retail salespersons	3 992 930	8.70	10.70	22 260	4 130 470	8.98	11.03	22 930
Advertising sales agents	141 340	18.58	23.26	48 390	144 690	19.37	23.76	49 420
Insurance sales agents	277 120	19.25	25.85	53 770	285 390	20.06	26.77	55 680
Securities, commodities, and financial services sales agents	245 280	29.10	40.94	85 150	240 500	33.27	43.77	91 040
Travel agents	103 840	13.05	14.00	29 110	90 500	13.29	14.25	29 650
Sales representatives, services, all other	390 080	27.46	31.42	65 360	352 050	22.60	25.93	53 940
Sales representatives, wholesale and manufacturing, technical and scientific products	1 421 660	21.09	25.23	52 480	378 080	28.17	32.37	67 330
Sales representatives, wholesale and manufacturing, except technical and scientific products	...	...	...	...	1 385 630	21.83	25.91	53 900
Demonstrators and product promoters	95 300	9.74	12.07	25 110	93 240	9.95	12.00	24 960
Models	1 560	11.67	14.89	30 980	1 410	10.50	13.21	27 480
Real estate brokers	40 590	23.91	33.62	69 920	40 050	28.23	37.43	77 850
Real estate sales agents	123 490	15.68	21.61	44 950	126 470	17.15	23.05	47 950
Sales engineers	73 200	32.59	34.85	72 490	71 690	33.95	36.42	75 740
Telemarketers	404 150	9.55	10.86	22 590	410 360	9.82	11.29	23 490
Door-to-door sales workers, news and street vendors, and related workers	21 600	11.67	13.97	29 050	15 200	10.85	13.36	27 790
Sales and related workers, all other	...	...	...	...	198 230	15.09	18.44	38 350
Office and Adminstrative Support Occupations								
First-line supervisors/managers of office and administrative support workers	1 412 470	18.99	20.46	42 550	1 406 240	19.72	21.15	43 990
Switchboard operators, including answering service	217 700	10.27	10.69	22 230	206 370	10.38	10.81	22 490
Telephone operators	45 310	13.48	14.31	29 770	38 500	13.65	14.53	30 220
Communications equipment operators, all other	...	...	...	...	4 040	15.23	15.98	33 240
Bill and account collectors	417 100	12.98	13.74	28 580	445 180	13.20	13.95	29 010
Billing and posting clerks and machine operators	487 420	12.64	13.13	27 310	490 370	13.00	13.50	28 070
Bookkeeping, accounting, and auditing clerks	1 750 680	13.35	13.93	28 980	1 770 860	13.74	14.34	29 830
Gaming cage workers	18 370	10.61	10.94	22 760	19 710	10.74	11.09	23 070
Payroll and timekeeping clerks	194 330	14.22	14.75	30 670	205 670	14.59	15.02	31 240
Procurement clerks	72 820	14.49	14.79	30 770	71 740	14.85	15.11	31 420
Tellers	538 890	9.94	10.07	20 940	552 860	10.15	10.30	21 420
Brokerage clerks	75 380	16.39	17.46	36 310	73 910	16.94	18.15	37 750
Correspondence clerks	27 460	12.88	13.49	28 050	21 590	13.51	14.19	29 510
Court, municipal, and license clerks	100 310	13.20	14.15	29 430	103 090	13.67	14.63	30 420
Credit authorizers, checkers, and clerks	73 860	13.08	14.22	29 580	66 010	13.97	15.15	31 520
Customer service representatives	1 902 850	12.74	13.73	28 580	2 021 350	12.99	14.01	29 130
Eligibility interviewers, government programs	89 410	15.87	16.23	33 750	93 250	15.92	16.25	33 800
File clerks	249 270	9.84	10.43	21 690	242 640	10.11	10.72	22 310
Hotel, motel, and resort desk clerks	180 410	8.39	8.77	18 240	190 300	8.51	8.93	18 570
Interviewers, except eligibility and loan	190 160	10.86	11.44	23 790	193 780	11.38	11.91	24 770
Library assistants, clerical	109 900	9.58	10.23	21 280	102 310	9.96	10.57	21 990
Loan interviewers and clerks	179 080	13.62	14.34	29 830	209 320	13.94	14.75	30 680
New accounts clerks	105 300	12.47	13.17	27 400	96 560	12.91	13.55	28 180
Order clerks	303 320	12.05	12.77	26 560	289 830	12.07	12.85	26 730

[1]Annual wages have been calculated by multiplying the hourly mean wage by a "year-round, full-time" hours figure of 2,080 hours; for those occupations where there is not an hourly mean wage published, the annual wage has been directly calculated from the reported survey data.
[2]Hourly wage rates for occupations where workers typically work fewer than 2,080 hours per year are not available.
... = Not available.

Table 3-3. Employment and Wages by Occupation, May 2003–May 2004—*Continued*

(Number of persons, dollars.)

Occupational division and occupation	May 2003				May 2004			
	Employment	Median hourly wages	Mean hourly wages	Mean annual wages[1]	Employment	Median hourly wages	Mean hourly wages	Mean annual wages[1]
Human resources assistants, except payroll and timekeeping	165 760	14.93	15.44	32 120	164 940	15.26	15.77	32 810
Receptionists and information clerks	1 058 790	10.25	10.65	22 150	1 071 230	10.50	10.91	22 690
Reservation and transportation ticket agents and travel clerks	165 990	12.60	14.00	29 130	159 910	13.34	14.48	30 120
All other information and record clerks	. . .	. . .	. . .	. . .	269 070	15.44	18.34	38 150
Cargo and freight agents	61 770	15.38	16.29	33 880	70 000	16.47	17.24	35 870
Couriers and messengers	118 210	9.39	10.00	20 790	111 700	9.71	10.26	21 330
Police, fire, and ambulance dispatchers	89 620	13.60	14.27	29 690	90 930	13.91	14.58	30 330
Dispatchers, except police, fire, and ambulance	161 790	14.61	15.80	32 870	165 910	14.87	16.01	33 310
Meter readers, utilities	51 790	13.80	14.67	30 510	48 830	14.15	15.03	31 260
Postal service clerks	78 520	19.13	18.83	39 170	76 870	19.69	19.82	41 230
Postal service mail carriers	344 580	19.05	18.87	39 240	344 050	21.37	20.85	43 370
Postal service mail sorters, processors, and processing machine operators	224 250	18.78	17.79	37 010	214 400	18.96	18.12	37 690
Production, planning, and expediting clerks	277 030	16.74	17.32	36 030	285 940	17.47	18.10	37 650
Shipping, receiving, and traffic clerks	767 470	11.38	12.11	25 200	747 270	11.73	12.43	25 850
Stock clerks and order fillers	1 576 620	9.38	10.33	21 490	1 561 530	9.66	10.52	21 890
Weighers, measurers, checkers, and samplers, recordkeeping	77 770	11.80	13.07	27 180	83 570	11.81	12.92	26 880
Executive secretaries and administrative assistants	1 418 640	16.39	17.22	35 810	1 422 610	16.81	17.69	36 790
Legal secretaries	264 080	17.15	17.87	37 170	264 070	17.65	18.40	38 280
Medical secretaries	349 370	12.50	13.08	27 210	360 850	12.76	13.42	27 900
Secretaries, except legal, medical, and executive	1 845 860	12.22	12.76	26 540	1 743 560	12.55	13.06	27 160
Computer operators	160 170	14.41	15.32	31 870	140 870	14.94	15.79	32 850
Data entry keyers	339 010	10.86	11.34	23 590	313 590	11.18	11.72	24 380
Word processors and typists	191 180	13.05	13.65	28 400	168 430	13.48	14.17	29 480
Desktop publishers	33 590	15.19	16.15	33 590	32 790	15.55	16.40	34 110
Insurance claims and policy processing clerks	239 580	13.71	14.33	29 800	239 250	14.06	14.70	30 580
Mail clerks and mail machine operators, except postal service	152 360	10.47	10.91	22 700	149 700	10.76	11.27	23 440
Office clerks, general	2 926 160	10.80	11.43	23 780	2 970 660	10.95	11.62	24 170
Office machine operators, except computer	90 470	10.68	11.42	23 760	97 140	11.16	11.83	24 610
Proofreaders and copy markers	24 700	11.77	12.76	26 550	20 530	12.18	12.99	27 010
Statistical assistants	20 970	14.37	15.11	31 430	18 560	14.55	15.19	31 600
Office and administrative support workers, all other	. . .	. . .	. . .	. . .	318 430	12.22	13.16	27 380
Farming, Fishing, and Forestry Occupations								
First-line supervisors/managers of farming, fishing, and forestry workers	20 620	16.76	18.14	37 730	19 890	17.06	18.50	38 480
Farm labor contractors	3 340	7.79	10.29	21 390	2 770	8.42	10.84	22 540
Agricultural inspectors	13 670	13.83	15.09	31 390	12 300	14.92	16.05	33 390
Animal breeders	1 750	12.02	14.25	29 640	1 530	13.55	15.74	32 730
Graders and sorters, agricultural products	51 210	7.78	8.53	17 740	50 110	7.90	8.52	17 710
Agricultural equipment operators	21 330	8.59	9.47	19 690	20 960	8.88	9.76	20 300
Farmworkers and laborers, crop, nursery, and greenhouse	233 450	7.43	8.02	16 670	240 000	7.70	8.07	16 780
Farmworkers, farm and ranch animals	42 890	8.12	8.84	18 390	43 250	8.31	9.07	18 870
Agricultural workers, all other	. . .	. . .	. . .	. . .	9 500	10.15	11.06	23 010
Fishers and related fishing workers	. . .	. . .	. . .	. . .	940	11.58	14.04	29 200
Forest and conservation workers	. . .	. . .	. . .	. . .	9 140	9.51	11.34	23 590
Fallers	. . .	. . .	. . .	. . .	10 180	13.23	15.15	31 510
Logging equipment operators	9 620	13.46	15.31	31 850	27 690	13.18	13.75	28 600
Log graders and scalers	28 190	13.00	13.52	28 130	4 870	12.29	13.21	27 480
Logging workers, all other	4 900	13.01	13.94	28 990	5 680	14.29	14.06	29 240
Construction and Extraction Occupations								
First-line supervisors/managers of construction trades and extraction workers	516 540	23.43	25.06	52 130	542 440	24.25	25.95	53 980
Boilermakers	20 270	20.79	20.92	43 510	18 520	21.68	22.29	46 360
Brickmasons and blockmasons	107 900	19.98	20.36	42 350	107 660	20.07	20.42	42 480
Stonemasons	13 710	16.35	17.36	36 110	16 320	16.82	17.75	36 920
Carpenters	852 080	16.47	17.75	36 920	882 490	16.78	18.26	37 970
Carpet installers	37 720	15.82	17.00	35 360	40 170	16.39	17.72	36 860
Floor layers, except carpet, wood, and hard tiles	15 070	16.75	17.19	35 760	15 800	15.68	17.13	35 640
Floor sanders and finishers	6 700	13.08	14.14	29 420	6 430	12.88	13.93	28 980
Tile and marble setters	36 900	17.12	17.95	37 340	42 930	17.02	18.28	38 020
Cement masons and concrete finishers	180 540	14.80	16.23	33 760	191 690	15.10	16.36	34 030
Terrazzo workers and finishers	6 140	13.32	14.64	30 460	6 700	13.45	15.47	32 170
Construction laborers	837 650	11.86	13.64	28 380	854 840	12.10	13.86	28 830
Paving, surfacing, and tamping equipment operators	57 980	14.06	15.86	32 980	61 860	14.42	16.07	33 430
Pile-driver operators	4 390	23.16	22.72	47 260	4 450	21.29	22.46	46 720

[1]Annual wages have been calculated by multiplying the hourly mean wage by a "year-round, full-time" hours figure of 2,080 hours; for those occupations where there is not an hourly mean wage published, the annual wage has been directly calculated from the reported survey data.
. . . = Not available.

Table 3-3. Employment and Wages by Occupation, May 2003–May 2004—*Continued*

(Number of persons, dollars.)

Occupational division and occupation	May 2003				May 2004			
	Employ-ment	Median hourly wages	Mean hourly wages	Mean annual wages[1]	Employ-ment	Median hourly wages	Mean hourly wages	Mean annual wages[1]
Operating engineers and other construction equipment operators	343 640	16.84	18.39	38 260	357 080	17.00	18.62	38 730
Drywall and ceiling tile installers	111 970	16.19	17.56	36 530	113 350	16.36	17.71	36 830
Tapers	33 540	18.81	19.33	40 200	36 370	18.78	19.25	40 040
Electricians	584 010	20.04	21.20	44 090	582 920	20.33	21.58	44 900
Glaziers	46 230	15.53	17.16	35 690	43 140	15.70	17.63	36 680
Insulation workers, floor, ceiling, and wall	52 170	14.04	15.83	32 940	37 000	14.57	16.12	33 530
Insulation workers, mechanical	...	...	...	...	17 110	16.03	17.48	36 350
Painters, construction and maintenance	247 880	14.12	15.36	31 960	249 560	14.55	15.87	33 010
Paperhangers	8 910	15.40	16.45	34 220	7 660	15.73	16.87	35 090
Pipelayers	51 940	13.73	15.38	32 000	54 470	13.68	15.40	32 040
Plumbers, pipefitters, and steamfitters	433 600	19.69	20.89	43 450	424 360	19.85	21.21	44 110
Plasterers and stucco masons	53 530	15.90	17.17	35 720	54 920	15.60	16.96	35 270
Reinforcing iron and rebar workers	30 250	16.80	18.91	39 330	32 660	16.90	19.32	40 190
Roofers	118 390	14.43	15.78	32 820	119 820	14.83	16.17	33 630
Sheet metal workers	189 590	16.83	18.16	37 780	184 740	17.09	18.63	38 760
Structural iron and steel workers	70 420	19.58	20.49	42 610	70 240	20.40	21.30	44 300
Helpers–brickmasons, blockmasons, stonemasons, and tile and marble setters	59 890	11.64	12.99	27 010	61 680	12.00	13.40	27 860
Helpers–carpenters	98 180	10.37	10.93	22 740	106 130	10.38	10.94	22 750
Helpers–electricians	93 520	11.27	12.01	24 980	92 820	11.26	11.97	24 890
Helpers–painters, paperhangers, plasterers, and stucco masons	29 130	9.81	10.97	22 820	26 090	9.87	10.87	22 610
Helpers–pipelayers, plumbers, pipefitters, and steamfitters	77 580	10.77	11.50	23 920	74 820	10.75	11.50	23 930
Helpers–roofers	21 490	9.96	10.64	22 140	21 530	9.93	10.58	22 000
Helpers–construction trades, all other	...	...	...	...	38 310	9.91	10.97	22 820
Construction and building inspectors	79 720	20.50	21.36	44 430	82 690	21.00	21.86	45 460
Elevator installers and repairers	21 470	26.90	26.86	55 860	21 110	28.23	27.98	58 190
Fence erectors	22 550	10.85	12.18	25 340	23 350	11.24	12.27	25 530
Hazardous materials removal workers	36 590	15.72	17.30	35 970	38 550	16.02	17.54	36 480
Highway maintenance workers	140 450	13.77	14.21	29 550	136 550	14.21	14.61	30 390
Rail-track laying and maintenance equipment operators	11 170	17.29	16.91	35 170	10 430	18.35	17.96	37 360
Septic tank servicers and sewer pipe cleaners	16 310	13.45	14.26	29 670	16 670	13.88	14.73	30 640
Segmental pavers	1 710	12.76	14.30	29 740	840	11.74	13.31	27 690
Construction and related workers, all other	...	...	...	...	81 260	11.40	12.71	26 440
Derrick operators, oil and gas	15 080	14.69	15.58	32 400	13 880	16.11	16.74	34 810
Rotary drill operators, oil and gas	14 830	16.78	17.99	37 420	13 860	17.11	18.68	38 860
Service unit operators, oil, gas, and mining	12 640	14.41	15.93	33 140	16 210	14.75	16.05	33 380
Earth drillers, except oil and gas	19 970	15.65	16.46	34 230	19 320	16.07	17.18	35 740
Explosives workers, ordnance handling experts, and blasters	5 140	16.97	17.52	36 450	5 290	17.16	17.85	37 130
Continuous mining machine operators	7 610	17.17	17.18	35 730	8 060	17.87	17.71	36 840
Mine cutting and channeling machine operators	4 460	17.56	17.49	36 370	3 900	17.96	17.95	37 330
Mining machine operators, all other	...	...	...	...	2 710	16.45	17.17	35 710
Rock splitters, quarry	3 240	12.88	13.76	28 620	3 180	12.54	13.43	27 940
Roof bolters, mining	3 980	18.54	18.49	38 460	4 290	18.70	18.54	38 570
Roustabouts, oil and gas	32 720	10.70	11.84	24 640	32 280	11.94	12.74	26 500
Helpers–extraction workers	28 860	12.63	13.21	27 480	26 430	12.66	13.23	27 520
Extraction workers, all other	...	...	...	...	10 450	15.66	16.37	34 050
Installation, Repair, and Maintenance Occupations								
First-line supervisors/managers of mechanics, installers, and repairers	445 520	23.37	24.53	51 020	459 440	24.20	25.34	52 700
Computer, automated teller, and office machine repairers	144 370	16.24	16.98	35 310	141 350	16.90	17.59	36 580
Radio mechanics	6 890	17.82	18.80	39 100	6 340	17.65	18.30	38 070
Telecommunications equipment installers and repairers, except line installers	195 500	23.19	22.31	46 400	202 160	23.96	23.10	48 050
Avionics technicians	21 420	20.73	20.98	43 630	22 310	21.30	21.38	44 460
Electric motor, power tool, and related repairers	26 070	15.53	16.19	33 660	21 910	15.54	16.11	33 520
Electrical and electronics installers and repairers, transportation equipment	17 370	18.89	18.91	39 330	17 390	19.25	19.46	40 470
Electrical and electronics repairers, commercial and industrial equipment	83 820	20.29	19.96	41 520	71 300	20.48	20.63	42 910
Electrical and electronics repairers, powerhouse, substation, and relay	20 700	25.02	24.28	50 500	20 660	25.86	25.51	53 060
Electronic equipment installers and repairers, motor vehicles	14 590	12.64	13.64	28 360	15 490	12.79	14.24	29 610
Electronic home entertainment equipment installers and repairers	33 340	13.14	14.10	29 330	32 210	13.44	14.25	29 640
Security and fire alarm systems installers	46 850	16.00	16.81	34 960	44 710	16.00	16.78	34 900
Aircraft mechanics and service technicians	117 180	20.94	21.37	44 460	112 830	21.77	22.69	47 190
Automotive body and related repairers	173 590	15.93	17.19	35 760	162 820	16.68	18.10	37 650
Automotive glass installers and repairers	18 550	13.06	13.61	28 320	18 150	13.45	13.98	29 080
Automotive service technicians and mechanics	690 780	14.97	16.02	33 320	668 540	15.60	16.61	34 550
Bus and truck mechanics and diesel engine specialists	248 450	16.81	17.27	35 930	251 430	17.20	17.66	36 730
Farm equipment mechanics	33 310	13.21	13.58	28 240	30 770	13.40	13.74	28 580
Mobile heavy equipment mechanics, except engines	115 090	17.69	18.07	37 590	112 000	18.34	18.68	38 860
Rail car repairers	15 810	19.04	18.52	38 530	18 140	19.48	19.01	39 550

[1]Annual wages have been calculated by multiplying the hourly mean wage by a "year-round, full-time" hours figure of 2,080 hours; for those occupations where there is not an hourly mean wage published, the annual wage has been directly calculated from the reported survey data.

... = Not available.

Table 3-3. Employment and Wages by Occupation, May 2003–May 2004—*Continued*

(Number of persons, dollars.)

Occupational division and occupation	May 2003				May 2004			
	Employ-ment	Median hourly wages	Mean hourly wages	Mean annual wages[1]	Employ-ment	Median hourly wages	Mean hourly wages	Mean annual wages[1]
Motorboat mechanics	18 890	14.02	14.63	30 420	17 680	14.74	15.16	31 530
Motorcycle mechanics	13 690	13.29	14.06	29 250	15 920	13.70	14.61	30 380
Outdoor power equipment and other small engine mechanics	24 740	11.93	12.46	25 920	25 170	11.98	12.66	26 340
Bicycle repairers	6 870	9.63	9.99	20 780	7 750	9.71	9.90	20 580
Recreational vehicle service technicians	12 520	13.11	13.83	28 770	12 340	13.93	14.73	30 630
Tire repairers and changers	82 340	10.02	10.72	22 300	87 110	10.01	10.75	22 350
Mechanical door repairers	10 860	14.24	15.75	32 760	10 470	15.38	16.92	35 190
Control and valve installers and repairers, except mechanical door	37 840	20.45	20.34	42 310	37 260	21.01	20.83	43 320
Heating, air conditioning, and refrigeration mechanics and installers	212 200	16.90	17.69	36 790	225 630	17.43	18.30	38 060
Home appliance repairers	37 510	14.37	15.17	31 550	40 300	15.47	16.00	33 280
Industrial machinery mechanics	192 300	18.48	19.06	39 640	212 770	18.78	19.28	40 090
Maintenance and repair workers, general	1 230 880	14.33	15.05	31 300	1 267 390	14.77	15.41	32 060
Maintenance workers, machinery	89 160	15.86	16.41	34 130	84 850	15.79	16.40	34 120
Millwrights	64 910	20.38	20.74	43 150	57 050	21.02	21.63	44 990
Refractory materials repairers, except brickmasons	3 390	17.74	18.29	38 030	3 570	18.09	18.76	39 020
Electrical power-line installers and repairers	95 190	23.54	22.82	47 460	101 760	23.61	22.91	47 640
Telecommunications line installers and repairers	148 060	19.01	19.02	39 560	144 080	19.39	19.55	40 660
Camera and photographic equipment repairers	4 640	15.01	15.81	32 890	3 830	15.54	16.29	33 880
Medical equipment repairers	23 500	18.25	18.91	39 330	23 750	17.90	18.72	38 930
Musical instrument repairers and tuners	5 550	13.89	16.10	33 490	5 290	13.47	14.88	30 950
Watch repairers	3 700	13.16	14.68	30 540	3 450	13.87	15.23	31 670
Precision instrument and equipment repairers, all other	. . .	. . .	. . .	. . .	13 500	21.25	21.64	45 000
Coin, vending, and amusement machine servicers and repairers	35 370	13.36	13.77	28 650	37 230	13.47	13.95	29 020
Commercial divers	2 690	16.48	18.27	38 000	2 230	16.94	18.66	38 820
Fabric menders, except garment	1 720	12.70	14.14	29 410	2 150	15.62	15.60	32 440
Locksmiths and safe repairers	19 340	13.83	14.68	30 540	15 540	14.60	15.30	31 830
Manufactured building and mobile home installers	13 160	11.23	11.65	24 230	12 150	11.23	11.64	24 210
Riggers	12 550	16.25	17.07	35 510	12 480	16.98	17.55	36 500
Signal and track switch repairers	8 680	21.01	21.32	44 350	7 780	21.43	21.73	45 210
Helpers–installation, maintenance, and repair workers	148 890	10.21	11.25	23 400	157 310	10.25	11.18	23 250
Installation, maintenance, and repair workers, all other	. . .	. . .	. . .	. . .	137 650	16.23	17.23	35 830
Production Occupations								
First-line supervisors/managers of production and operating workers	705 270	21.02	22.45	46 690	696 750	21.51	22.96	47 760
Aircraft structure, surfaces, rigging, and systems assemblers	26 150	18.60	18.23	37 920	18 710	17.79	18.02	37 470
Coil winders, tapers, and finishers	33 590	11.48	12.17	25 320	27 360	12.24	12.69	26 400
Electrical and electronic equipment assemblers	245 700	11.28	12.20	25 380	217 360	11.68	12.63	26 270
Electromechanical equipment assemblers	54 690	12.52	13.09	27 230	51 370	12.71	13.29	27 650
Engine and other machine assemblers	50 410	15.58	16.31	33 920	45 730	16.73	17.29	35 960
Structural metal fabricators and fitters	85 330	13.94	14.60	30 380	86 240	14.34	14.94	31 070
Fiberglass laminators and fabricators	31 820	11.87	12.30	25 580	30 250	12.18	12.59	26 190
Team assemblers	1 138 100	11.14	12.10	25 160	1 208 270	11.42	12.36	25 720
Timing device assemblers, adjusters, and calibrators	5 280	12.79	13.55	28 180	3 150	13.76	14.57	30 310
Assemblers and fabricators, all other	. . .	. . .	. . .	. . .	259 830	11.90	14.14	29 410
Bakers	157 110	10.09	10.86	22 600	150 900	10.26	10.97	22 820
Butchers and meat cutters	132 370	12.30	13.07	27 180	131 490	12.45	13.12	27 300
Meat, poultry, and fish cutters and trimmers	150 440	8.69	9.17	19 060	137 370	9.09	9.60	19 970
Slaughterers and meat packers	122 490	9.82	9.94	20 680	134 140	10.03	10.20	21 220
Food and tobacco roasting, baking, and drying machine operators and tenders	17 800	11.89	12.79	26 600	18 110	11.46	12.12	25 210
Food batchmakers	74 650	10.53	11.24	23 390	85 010	10.62	11.34	23 590
Food cooking machine operators and tenders	34 480	10.31	10.99	22 860	41 810	10.02	10.72	22 290
Computer-controlled machine tool operators, metal and plastic	126 150	14.14	14.74	30 650	124 330	14.75	15.22	31 650
Numerical tool and process control programmers	17 820	18.43	19.24	40 020	17 310	19.31	20.27	42 160
Extruding and drawing machine setters, operators, and tenders, metal and plastic	93 600	12.72	13.08	27 210	88 980	13.18	13.54	28 170
Forging machine setters, operators, and tenders, metal and plastic	41 230	13.10	14.28	29 700	37 890	13.22	14.05	29 210
Rolling machine setters, operators, and tenders, metal and plastic	42 090	13.88	14.44	30 040	37 210	14.33	14.81	30 810
Cutting, punching, and press machine setters, operators, and tenders, metal and plastic	260 560	12.12	12.70	26 410	248 800	12.45	13.04	27 120
Drilling and boring machine tool setters, operators, and tenders, metal and plastic	48 730	13.29	14.22	29 570	41 940	13.69	14.72	30 620
Grinding, lapping, polishing, and buffing machine tool setters, operators, and tenders, metal and plastic	97 660	12.80	13.83	28 770	98 770	13.19	14.10	29 330
Lathe and turning machine tool setters, operators, and tenders, metal and plastic	70 300	14.57	15.04	31 290	70 230	15.04	15.47	32 190
Milling and planing machine setters, operators, and tenders, metal and plastic	28 580	14.48	14.91	31 020	30 280	14.91	15.16	31 530
Machinists	368 740	15.91	16.30	33 900	361 280	16.33	16.73	34 790
Metal-refining furnace operators and tenders	17 810	15.24	15.65	32 550	17 150	15.74	16.13	33 560

[1]Annual wages have been calculated by multiplying the hourly mean wage by a "year-round, full-time" hours figure of 2,080 hours; for those occupations where there is not an hourly mean wage published, the annual wage has been directly calculated from the reported survey data.
. . . = Not available.

Table 3-3. Employment and Wages by Occupation, May 2003–May 2004—*Continued*

(Number of persons, dollars.)

Occupational division and occupation	May 2003				May 2004			
	Employ-ment	Median hourly wages	Mean hourly wages	Mean annual wages[1]	Employ-ment	Median hourly wages	Mean hourly wages	Mean annual wages[1]
Pourers and casters, metal	12 770	13.64	14.33	29 810	13 670	13.92	14.68	30 530
Model makers, metal and plastic	7 900	20.90	20.98	43 630	8 030	21.28	21.57	44 870
Patternmakers, metal and plastic	6 090	17.45	18.19	37 830	5 930	17.86	18.19	37 840
Foundry mold and coremakers	20 770	13.05	14.01	29 130	17 320	13.37	14.29	29 720
Molding, coremaking, and casting machine setters, operators, and tenders, metal and plastic	144 140	11.51	12.36	25 720	156 480	11.63	12.47	25 940
Multiple machine tool setters, operators, and tenders, metal and plastic	100 320	13.97	15.20	31 620	97 060	14.06	14.88	30 960
Tool and die makers	104 210	20.67	21.10	43 900	99 390	20.55	21.19	44 070
Welders, cutters, solderers, and brazers	354 300	14.25	15.06	31 330	344 970	14.72	15.41	32 050
Welding, soldering, and brazing machine setters, operators, and tenders	53 750	13.99	15.18	31 580	47 210	14.32	15.39	32 020
Heat treating equipment setters, operators, and tenders, metal and plastic	27 290	13.63	14.39	29 930	25 690	14.26	14.73	30 630
Lay-out workers, metal and plastic	12 540	15.37	16.08	33 450	11 240	15.65	16.23	33 750
Plating and coating machine setters, operators, and tenders, metal and plastic	40 800	12.34	13.00	27 030	38 620	12.96	13.68	28 440
Tool grinders, filers, and sharpeners	22 320	14.22	15.02	31 250	19 750	14.52	15.10	31 410
Metal workers and plastic workers, all other	. . .	. . .	. . .	. . .	53 050	16.15	17.19	35 750
Bindery workers	81 840	10.82	11.81	24 570	73 240	11.31	12.33	25 650
Bookbinders	6 550	13.87	14.74	30 660	7 160	13.71	14.58	30 320
Job printers	54 790	14.83	15.65	32 560	56 770	15.41	16.23	33 750
Prepress technicians and workers	82 970	15.22	15.95	33 170	76 190	15.30	16.08	33 450
Printing machine operators	189 900	14.11	14.93	31 050	184 230	14.38	15.26	31 740
Laundry and dry-cleaning workers	217 820	8.14	8.64	17 960	218 610	8.28	8.74	18 170
Pressers, textile, garment, and related materials	87 500	8.27	8.61	17 900	80 520	8.33	8.62	17 920
Sewing machine operators	265 200	8.51	9.12	18 960	242 500	8.61	9.24	19 230
Shoe and leather workers and repairers	8 090	9.40	9.98	20 750	7 840	9.29	9.68	20 120
Shoe machine operators and tenders	6 020	9.89	10.24	21 300	4 530	9.44	9.85	20 500
Sewers, hand	18 790	8.65	9.57	19 900	12 430	9.13	10.20	21 210
Tailors, dressmakers, and custom sewers	32 150	10.51	11.62	24 170	27 180	10.79	11.76	24 450
Textile bleaching and dyeing machine operators and tenders	24 280	10.30	10.56	21 960	21 480	10.56	10.96	22 790
Textile cutting machine setters, operators, and tenders	32 170	9.87	10.47	21 770	25 320	9.80	10.44	21 700
Textile knitting and weaving machine setters, operators, and tenders	47 720	11.37	11.42	23 740	45 320	11.48	11.47	23 850
Textile winding, twisting, and drawing out machine setters, operators, and tenders	60 550	10.62	11.08	23 040	53 490	10.87	11.41	23 740
Extruding and forming machine setters, operators, and tenders, synthetic and glass fibers	26 700	13.55	13.68	28 460	23 040	13.37	13.71	28 520
Fabric and apparel patternmakers	10 310	13.72	16.30	33 910	9 340	13.85	16.23	33 760
Upholsterers	39 660	12.18	12.97	26 980	38 550	12.35	13.05	27 140
Textile, apparel, and furnishings workers, all other	. . .	. . .	. . .	. . .	21 920	10.34	10.96	22 790
Cabinetmakers and bench carpenters	126 350	11.81	12.56	26 120	121 380	12.16	12.90	26 830
Furniture finishers	28 770	11.13	11.82	24 590	25 770	11.35	12.11	25 190
Model makers, wood	3 820	12.24	14.19	29 520	3 210	12.94	14.82	30 820
Patternmakers, wood	3 470	14.25	14.93	31 060	2 500	14.88	15.74	32 750
Sawing machine setters, operators, and tenders, wood	55 130	10.65	11.12	23 130	56 500	10.91	11.35	23 600
Woodworking machine setters, operators, and tenders, except sawing	89 410	10.76	11.28	23 470	88 870	10.93	11.43	23 780
Woodworkers, all other	. . .	. . .	. . .	. . .	12 190	10.16	10.94	22 760
Nuclear power reactor operators	3 710	29.72	29.99	62 380	4 300	30.81	30.71	63 880
Power distributors and dispatchers	10 270	26.45	26.73	55 590	8 290	27.56	28.03	58 300
Power plant operators	33 250	24.45	24.15	50 220	33 350	25.26	25.02	52 030
Stationary engineers and boiler operators	48 880	20.87	21.32	44 340	46 870	21.22	21.66	45 060
Water and liquid waste treatment plant and system operators	95 870	16.30	16.89	35 130	92 120	16.81	17.32	36 030
Chemical plant and system operators	56 270	21.18	21.10	43 880	59 980	21.55	21.61	44 940
Gas plant operators	11 180	23.45	23.53	48 940	10 670	24.36	24.36	50 660
Petroleum pump system operators, refinery operators, and gaugers	40 980	24.02	22.97	47 780	42 300	24.27	23.44	48 760
Plant and system operators, all other	. . .	. . .	. . .	. . .	14 930	20.10	20.14	41 900
Chemical equipment operators and tenders	59 720	18.62	18.75	39 000	48 450	18.69	18.94	39 390
Separating, filtering, clarifying, precipitating, and still machine setters, operators, and tenders	37 360	15.25	15.99	33 260	38 000	15.98	16.49	34 290
Crushing, grinding, and polishing machine setters, operators, and tenders	43 320	12.96	13.57	28 230	42 600	12.96	13.70	28 490
Grinding and polishing workers, hand	43 910	11.10	12.03	25 030	44 210	11.28	12.03	25 030
Mixing and blending machine setters, operators, and tenders	106 610	13.43	13.94	28 990	119 320	13.51	14.06	29 240
Cutters and trimmers, hand	30 110	10.79	12.01	24 980	28 780	10.59	11.60	24 120
Cutting and slicing machine setters, operators, and tenders	70 960	12.53	13.06	27 170	73 250	12.82	13.46	27 990
Extruding, forming, pressing, and compacting machine setters, operators, and tenders	73 990	13.05	13.84	28 780	73 970	13.20	13.88	28 880
Furnace, kiln, oven, drier, and kettle operators and tenders	30 320	13.95	14.63	30 430	29 750	14.29	15.08	31 360
Inspectors, testers, sorters, samplers, and weighers	497 300	13.34	14.65	30 470	495 430	13.66	15.00	31 210

[1]Annual wages have been calculated by multiplying the hourly mean wage by a "year-round, full-time" hours figure of 2,080 hours; for those occupations where there is not an hourly mean wage published, the annual wage has been directly calculated from the reported survey data.

. . . = Not available.

Table 3-3. Employment and Wages by Occupation, May 2003–May 2004—*Continued*

(Number of persons, dollars.)

Occupational division and occupation	May 2003				May 2004			
	Employ-ment	Median hourly wages	Mean hourly wages	Mean annual wages[1]	Employ-ment	Median hourly wages	Mean hourly wages	Mean annual wages[1]
Jewelers and precious stone and metal workers	30 360	13.06	14.48	30 120	26 360	13.18	14.76	30 700
Dental laboratory technicians	45 480	14.10	15.40	32 030	44 540	14.93	16.21	33 720
Medical appliance technicians	11 270	13.41	14.82	30 820	10 080	13.38	15.19	31 600
Ophthalmic laboratory technicians	30 300	10.67	11.42	23 760	25 170	11.40	12.32	25 620
Packaging and filling machine operators and tenders	400 680	10.45	11.40	23 700	411 660	10.67	11.59	24 110
Coating, painting, and spraying machine setters, operators, and tenders	93 110	12.37	13.06	27 160	96 510	12.64	13.25	27 550
Painters, transportation equipment	46 600	16.39	17.56	36 520	49 810	16.89	18.17	37 800
Painting, coating, and decorating workers	29 590	10.41	11.36	23 640	26 990	10.95	12.01	24 970
Photographic process workers	27 170	9.79	11.19	23 280	31 610	9.63	11.07	23 010
Photographic processing machine operators	54 750	9.11	10.14	21 100	53 350	9.33	10.26	21 340
Semiconductor processors	50 160	13.29	14.14	29 410	44 440	13.85	14.46	30 070
Cementing and gluing machine operators and tenders	25 390	11.24	11.98	24 920	24 630	11.57	12.34	25 660
Cleaning, washing, and metal pickling equipment operators and tenders	17 590	11.07	11.99	24 950	16 860	11.18	12.15	25 270
Cooling and freezing equipment operators and tenders	7 920	10.31	11.46	23 830	8 790	10.96	12.18	25 340
Etchers and engravers	8 800	10.69	11.94	24 840	8 490	11.33	12.59	26 180
Molders, shapers, and casters, except metal and plastic	37 600	11.91	12.70	26 420	37 930	11.58	12.51	26 020
Paper goods machine setters, operators, and tenders	109 600	13.91	14.29	29 720	109 560	14.63	15.01	31 220
Tire builders	14 830	19.01	17.59	36 590	17 960	17.50	17.38	36 150
Helpers–production workers	452 700	9.42	10.09	20 980	480 430	9.70	10.35	21 530
Production workers, all other	...	...	...	...	299 950	11.38	13.47	28 010
Transportation and Material Moving Occupations								
Aircraft cargo handling supervisors	9 440	17.64	19.63	40 830	7 460	16.40	18.90	39 310
First-line supervisors/managers of helpers, laborers, and material movers, hand	154 750	18.16	19.19	39 920	169 860	18.40	19.45	40 460
First-line supervisors/managers of transportation and material-moving machine and vehicle operators	214 030	21.08	22.58	46 960	222 590	21.54	23.23	48 320
Airline pilots, copilots, and flight engineers	79 770	(2)	(2)	129 880	78 490	(2)	(2)	129 620
Commercial pilots	19 980	(2)	(2)	57 950	21 370	(2)	(2)	62 290
Air traffic controllers	23 040	46.28	44.83	93 240	22 260	49.05	47.94	99 710
Airfield operations specialists	5 660	18.79	20.85	43 380	4 810	17.64	20.22	42 050
Ambulance drivers and attendants, except emergency medical technicians	17 650	9.14	9.73	20 230	17 410	9.49	10.17	21 140
Bus drivers, transit and intercity	194 400	14.29	14.98	31 160	183 710	14.30	15.09	31 390
Bus drivers, school	467 840	10.86	11.05	22 990	475 430	11.18	11.33	23 560
Driver/sales workers	380 120	9.79	11.38	23 660	406 910	9.66	11.36	23 620
Truck drivers, heavy and tractor-trailer	1 528 630	16.01	16.51	34 330	1 553 370	16.11	16.63	34 580
Truck drivers, light or delivery services	943 840	11.58	12.76	26 530	938 730	11.80	12.88	26 790
Taxi drivers and chauffeurs	131 570	9.14	10.22	21 260	132 650	9.41	10.34	21 510
Motor vehicle operators, all other	...	...	...	...	85 520	9.45	11.04	22 960
Locomotive engineers	30 450	22.11	24.60	51 160	31 180	24.30	26.29	54 680
Locomotive firers	680	22.75	21.67	45 080	620	21.56	22.23	46 230
Rail yard engineers, dinkey operators, and hostlers	5 680	18.01	19.30	40 140	6 170	17.70	18.41	38 280
Railroad brake, signal, and switch operators	13 850	21.59	23.10	48 040	16 410	21.46	23.03	47 900
Railroad conductors and yardmasters	34 720	21.31	24.36	50 670	35 720	22.28	25.28	52 580
Subway and streetcar operators	9 880	22.97	22.13	46 020	8 900	23.70	22.67	47 150
Rail transportation workers, all other	...	...	...	...	7 680	19.57	19.56	40 680
Sailors and marine oilers	27 570	14.44	15.36	31 950	27 570	14.00	14.98	31 160
Captains, mates, and pilots of water vessels	24 040	24.51	25.50	53 050	25 200	24.20	25.11	52 230
Motorboat operators	3 680	12.51	14.71	30 590	2 830	15.39	16.25	33 790
Ship engineers	8 900	26.01	26.39	54 900	10 330	26.42	27.80	57 830
Bridge and lock tenders	3 270	17.97	16.93	35 220	3 500	17.98	17.05	35 460
Parking lot attendants	113 490	8.00	8.50	17 670	120 080	8.08	8.48	17 650
Service station attendants	96 250	8.11	8.71	18 110	90 640	8.29	8.92	18 560
Traffic technicians	6 460	16.15	16.85	35 040	6 240	16.19	17.11	35 600
Transportation inspectors	27 890	23.84	23.67	49 240	24 140	24.22	24.89	51 780
Transportation workers, all other	...	...	...	...	51 850	15.47	16.11	33 510
Conveyor operators and tenders	58 780	11.87	12.56	26 120	54 380	12.23	12.85	26 720
Crane and tower operators	47 420	17.86	18.73	38 950	43 570	17.99	18.81	39 130

[1]Annual wages have been calculated by multiplying the hourly mean wage by a "year-round, full-time" hours figure of 2,080 hours; for those occupations where there is not an hourly mean wage published, the annual wage has been directly calculated from the reported survey data.
[2]Hourly wage rates for occupations where workers typically work fewer than 2,080 hours per year are not available.
... = Not available.

Table 3-3. Employment and Wages by Occupation, May 2003–May 2004—*Continued*

(Number of persons, dollars.)

Occupational division and occupation	May 2003				May 2004			
	Employ-ment	Median hourly wages	Mean hourly wages	Mean annual wages[1]	Employ-ment	Median hourly wages	Mean hourly wages	Mean annual wages[1]
Dredge operators	3 030	13.37	14.17	29 470	1 730	13.47	14.43	30 010
Excavating and loading machine and dragline operators	68 740	15.46	16.59	34 520	67 080	15.37	16.40	34 120
Loading machine operators, underground mining	3 560	15.46	15.64	32 530	3 330	15.98	16.34	34 000
Hoist and winch operators	8 560	15.40	17.78	36 990	5 550	16.19	18.65	38 790
Industrial truck and tractor operators	604 350	12.68	13.46	27 990	631 530	12.78	13.57	28 230
Cleaners of vehicles and equipment	320 840	8.27	9.15	19 030	330 520	8.41	9.33	19 400
Laborers and freight, stock, and material movers, hand	2 255 780	9.58	10.41	21 650	2 390 910	9.67	10.53	21 910
Machine feeders and offbearers	159 160	10.57	11.27	23 430	149 500	10.68	11.31	23 530
Packers and packagers, hand	901 890	8.14	8.85	18 410	872 260	8.25	8.97	18 660
Gas compressor and gas pumping station operators	6 190	20.97	21.20	44 100	4 680	21.07	21.56	44 850
Pump operators, except wellhead pumpers	12 260	18.00	18.60	38 680	9 810	17.04	17.79	37 000
Wellhead pumpers	8 560	14.89	15.73	32 720	10 040	16.31	16.33	33 960
Refuse and recyclable material collectors	138 480	11.56	12.51	26 030	139 920	12.38	13.37	27 810
Shuttle car operators	3 040	18.79	18.17	37 800	3 000	18.08	17.58	36 570
Tank car, truck, and ship loaders	16 210	15.90	17.13	35 630	16 530	15.59	16.44	34 190
Material moving workers, all other	. . .	. . .	. . .	. . .	57 390	13.87	15.29	31 800

[1]Annual wages have been calculated by multiplying the hourly mean wage by a "year-round, full-time" hours figure of 2,080 hours; for those occupations where there is not an hourly mean wage published, the annual wage has been directly calculated from the reported survey data.
. . . = Not available.

PART FOUR

PROJECTIONS OF LABOR FORCE AND EMPLOYMENT BY INDUSTRY AND OCCUPATION

PROJECTIONS OF LABOR FORCE AND EMPLOYMENT BY INDUSTRY AND OCCUPATION

HIGHLIGHTS

The Bureau of Labor Statistics develops projections for industry output, employment, and occupations every two years. The next publication date is scheduled for 2006. This part presents the employment outlook for 2002–2012. Its projections are based on asset of explicit assumptions and application of a model of economic relationships.

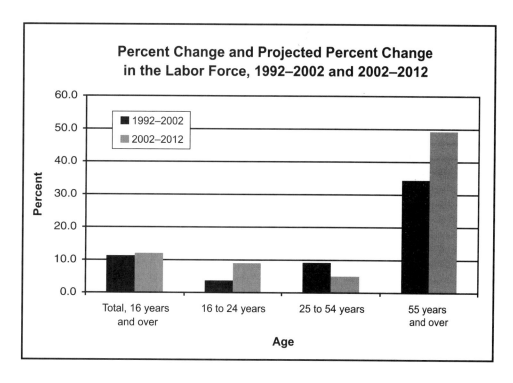

The total labor force is expected to grow slowly from 2002-2012, with a 12 percent (1.2 percent per year) overall gain. A growth of 9 percent, or less than 1 percent per year, is projected for the 16–24 age group. The expectation of a near 50 percent increase (4.1 percent per year) in the 55 and older age group reflects the aging of the baby boomer population. (Table 4-1)

OTHER HIGHLIGHTS:

- Although the Asian labor force is still relatively small, comprising only 4.1 percent of the total labor force in 2000, rapid growth of 50.8 percent is expected between 2002 and 2012. The labor force for Blacks is projected to increase by 19.3 percent; for Whites, the gain is projected at 8.5 percent. (Table 4-1)

- Hispanic labor force growth is expected to be slower than in the previous decade; however, a 32.6 percent growth is still projected. (Table 4-1)

- The labor force of women is projected to continue increasing faster (14.3 percent) than that of men (10.0 percent). (Table 4-1)

NOTES AND DEFINITIONS

Concepts, Definitions, and Procedures

Long-term projections of likely employment conditions in the U.S. economy have been developed by the Bureau of Labor Statistics (BLS) since 1957. These projections cover the future size and composition of the labor force, the aggregate economy, detailed estimates of industrial production, and industrial and occupational employment. The resulting data serve many users who need information on likely patterns of economic growth and their possible effects on employment. Beginning with the projections for 1996–2006, projections have been developed for a 10-year period and published every two years. This is the first set of BLS projections that use the North American Industry Classification System (NAICS).

To carry out the projection process, the BLS makes many underlying assumptions concerning general economic and social conditions. It then sets ranges of acceptability for the key results of the various stages of the projection process.

Projecting employment in industry and occupational detail requires an integrated projection of the total economy and its various sectors. BLS projections are developed in a series of six steps, each of which is based on separate projections procedures and models and various related assumptions. The six steps or analytical phases are: (1) labor force, (2) aggregate economy, (3) final demand (GDP) by sector and product, (4) inter-industry relationships (input-output), (5) industry output and employment, and (6) occupational employment. Each phase is solved separately, with the results of each used as input for the next phase, and with some results feeding back to earlier steps. In each phase, many iterations are made to ensure internal consistency as assumptions and results are reviewed and revised.

Labor force projections are determined by projections of the future age, sex, and racial composition of the population and by trends in labor force participation rates—the percent of the specified group in the population who will be working or seeking work. The population projections, prepared by the U.S. Census Bureau, are based on trends in birth rates, death rates, and net migration. With the population projections in hand, BLS analyzes and projects changes in labor force participation rates for more than 130 age, sex, and race or Hispanic origin groups.

Projections of labor force participation rates for each group are first developed by estimating a trend rate of change based on participation rate behavior during the prior eight-year period. Second, the rate is modified when the time-series projections for the specific group appear inconsistent with the results of cross-sectional and cohort analyses. This second step ensures consistency in the pro-

jections across various groups. Finally, the size of the labor force is derived by applying the participation rates to the population projections. The results are again reviewed for consistency.

Aggregate economic performance—the second phase of the BLS projections process—develops projections of the gross domestic product (GDP) and major categories of demand and income. These results provide control totals that are consistent with each other and with the various assumptions and conditions of the projection scenario. The values generated for each demand sector and subsector are then used in the next phase to develop detailed projections for personal consumption, business investment, foreign trade, and government.

These projections are accomplished using a macroeconomic model. The model consists of sets of equations that intercorrelate various aspects of the economy. It provides internally consistent, moderately detailed projections for each set of given assumptions and goals. The 2002–2012 projections were based upon a long-term macro model developed by DRI-WEFA, Inc. This model has approximately 1,300 equations, which determine factors affecting growth in the U.S. economy. This model is driven by a set of about 300 exogenous variables, which are specified by BLS.

Final demand. The BLS projection then proceeds from the aggregate to the industrial level. For the industry output projections, the economy is disaggregated into about 190 producing sectors that cover the public and private U.S. industrial structure. The framework for this procedure is an input-output model. The initial input-output data used by BLS are prepared by the Bureau of Economic Analysis, U.S. Department of Commerce.

The development of projections of industry output begins with aggregate demand projections from the DRI-WEFA model. In this model, projections are made for 27 major categories of consumption, 15 categories of investment, 19 end-use categories of foreign trade, and 13 categories of government spending. A further disaggregation of the values from the model is then undertaken. (For example, personal consumption expenditures are estimated for 158 detailed categories).

Provision is made to allow for shifts in the commodity makeup of a given demand category. This is accomplished by projecting "bridge tables" relating individual types of demand to the actual industries supplying the goods. The bridge table is a percent distribution for each given demand category—such as the personal consumption or investment category—among each of the sectors in the BLS input-output model. In projecting changes in these bridge tables, expected changes in technology, consumer tastes or buying patterns, the commodity pattern of exports and imports, the future composition of business investment, and other structural factors are considered.

Input-output. The next stage in the projections process is the estimation of the intermediate flow of goods and services required to produce the projected GDP. Only final sales are counted in the GDP to avoid repeated counting of intermediate inputs. However, an industry's total employment depends on its total output, whether sold to another industry or used as a final good. The total output of each industry is projected using an inter-industry or input-output model. This model mathematically solves for all levels of intermediate inputs given industry relationships and final demand.

The BLS input-output model consists of two basic matrices for each year, a "use" and a "make" table. The principal table is the "use" table. This table shows the purchase of commodities by each industry as inputs into its production process. This table's projections must take into account changes in the input pattern, or the way in which goods or services are produced by each industry. In general, two types of changes in these input patterns are made in developing a future input-output table: (a) Those made to the inputs of a specific industry (as, for example, the changes in inputs in the publishing industry); and (b) those made to the inputs of a specific commodity in all or most industries (such as the increased use of business services across a wide spectrum of industries). The "make" table shows the commodity output of each industry. It allocates commodity output to each one's primary industry and to all other industries where the commodity is produced as a secondary product. The "use" table is the basis for the direct requirements table of coefficients showing the inputs required to produce one dollar of that industry's output. The "make" table is used to create a "market shares" table, which shows the values of the "make" table as coefficients. The coefficient tables are used to calculate the total requirements tables, which show the direct and indirect requirements to produce a dollar's worth of final demand. Projection tables are based on historical tables and on studies of specific industries.

Industry Employment. The projected level of industry employment is based on the projected levels of industry output as well as other factors, such as expected technological changes and their impact on labor productivity. After the initial industry output is calculated, employment is derived from a model of the industry-level employment requirements. The employment projections by industry are constrained by the requirement that they sum to the aggregate employment level as determined by the aggregate projections. Employment for wage and salary workers is based on the Current Employment Statistics (payroll) survey, which counts jobs. The self-employed, unpaid family worker, agricultural, and private household data are based on the Current Population Survey (household survey), which counts workers. Therefore, employment

totals for historical periods differ from BLS's official employment estimates.

Employment by Occupation. The model used to develop the occupational employment projections is an industry-occupation matrix showing the distribution of employment for 262 industries and 695 detailed occupations for the years 2002–2012. Occupational staffing patterns for the industries are based on data collected by state employment security agencies. These data are analyzed by the BLS and reflect the 2000 standard occupational classification system. The titles and content of major occupational groups and many detailed occupations are substantially different from those used in previous projections.

Staffing patterns of industries in the base-year industry-occupation matrix are projected to the target year to account for expected advances to occur in technology, shifts in production mix, and other factors. For example, one would expect greater employment of computer specialists as computer technology spreads across industries. In projecting the staffing patterns, the changes introduced into the input-output model for expected change are also analyzed to account for the impact of technological change on future occupational staffing patterns of industries. The projected industry total employment data are applied to the projected industry staffing patterns, yielding employment by occupation for each industry. These data are aggregated across all industries to yield total occupational employment for the projected year.

Final Review. An important element of the projection system is its comprehensive structure. To ensure the internal consistency of this large structure, the BLS procedure encompasses detailed review and analysis of the results at each stage for reasonableness and for consistency with results from other stages of the BLS projections. The final results reflect innumerable interactions among staff members who focus on particular variables in the model. This review enables BLS's projection process to converge to an internally consistent set of employment projections across a substantial number of industries and occupations.

Sources of Additional Information

A complete presentation of the projections including analysis of results and additional tables and a comprehensive description of the methodology is found in the *Monthly Labor Review*, February 2004. A more detailed description of methods is contained in the *BLS Handbook of Methods*, Chapter 13, BLS Bulletin 2490, April 1997, and BLS Bulletin 2572, *Occupational Projections and Training Data*, August 2004. Once the target year is reached, BLS evaluates the projections. An article assessing the year 2000 projections appears in *Occupational Outlook Quarterly*, Spring 2003.

Table 4-1. Civilian Labor Force by Age, Sex, Race, and Hispanic Origin, 1982, 1992, 2002, and Projected 2012

(Number, percent.)

Age, sex, race, and Hispanic origin	Level (thousands)					Change (thousands)			Percent change		
	1982	1992	2002 1990 census weights	2002 2000 census weights	2012	1982–1992	1992–2002	2002–2012	1982–1992	1992–2002	2002–2012
TOTAL, 16 YEARS AND OVER	110 204	128 105	142 534	144 863	162 269	17 901	14 429	17 406	16.2	11.3	12.0
16 to 24 years	24 608	21 617	22 425	22 366	24 377	-2 991	808	2 011	-12.2	3.7	9.0
16 to 19 years	8 526	7 096	7 723	7 586	7 636	-1 430	627	50	-16.8	8.8	0.7
20 to 24 years	16 082	14 521	14 702	14 780	16 740	-1 561	181	1 960	-9.7	1.2	13.3
25 to 54 years	70 506	91 429	99 865	101 720	106 866	20 923	8 436	5 146	29.7	9.2	5.1
25 to 34 years	31 186	35 369	30 831	32 196	35 406	4 183	-4 538	3 210	13.4	-12.8	10.0
35 to 44 years	22 431	33 899	36 998	36 927	34 434	11 468	3 099	-2 493	51.1	9.1	-6.8
45 to 54 years	16 889	22 160	32 036	32 597	37 026	5 271	9 876	4 429	31.2	44.6	13.6
55 years and over	15 092	15 060	20 244	20 777	31 026	-32	5 184	10 249	-0.2	34.4	49.3
55 to 64 years	12 062	11 587	15 863	16 308	24 616	-475	4 276	8 308	-3.9	36.9	50.9
65 years and over	3 030	3 473	4 381	4 469	6 410	443	908	1 941	14.6	26.2	43.4
65 to 74 years	2 566	2 932	3 593	3 665	5 411	366	661	1 746	14.3	22.5	47.6
75 years and over	464	542	789	804	1 000	78	247	196	16.8	45.5	24.3
Men, 16 Years and Over	62 450	69 964	76 052	77 500	85 252	7 514	6 088	7 751	12.0	8.7	10.0
16 to 24 years	13 074	11 521	11 619	11 639	12 461	-1 553	98	822	-11.9	0.8	7.1
16 to 19 years	4 470	3 751	3 926	3 870	3 791	-719	175	-79	-16.1	4.7	-2.0
20 to 24 years	8 604	7 770	7 693	7 769	8 670	-834	-77	901	-9.7	-1.0	11.6
25 to 54 years	40 357	49 882	53 439	54 568	56 435	9 525	3 557	1 866	23.6	7.1	3.4
25 to 34 years	17 793	19 495	16 635	17 596	19 069	1 702	-2 860	1 473	9.6	-14.7	8.4
35 to 44 years	12 781	18 347	19 946	19 829	18 244	5 566	1 599	-1 585	43.5	8.7	-8.0
45 to 54 years	9 784	12 040	16 858	17 143	19 122	2 256	4 818	1 978	23.1	40.0	11.5
55 years and over	9 019	8 561	10 995	11 293	16 356	-458	2 434	5 063	-5.1	28.4	44.8
55 to 64 years	7 174	6 551	8 486	8 750	12 714	-623	1 935	3 964	-8.7	29.5	45.3
65 years and over	1 845	2 010	2 509	2 543	3 641	165	499	1 098	8.9	24.8	43.2
65 to 74 years	1 548	1 681	2 045	2 079	3 077	133	364	998	8.6	21.6	48.0
75 years and over	297	329	464	464	564	32	135	100	10.8	41.1	21.6
Women, 16 Years and Over	47 755	58 141	66 481	67 363	77 017	10 386	8 340	9 654	21.7	14.3	14.3
16 to 24 years	11 533	10 096	10 806	10 727	11 916	-1 437	710	1 189	-12.5	7.0	11.1
16 to 19 years	4 056	3 345	3 797	3 716	3 845	-711	452	129	-17.5	13.5	3.5
20 to 24 years	7 477	6 750	7 009	7 011	8 070	-727	259	1 059	-9.7	3.8	15.1
25 to 54 years	30 149	41 547	46 426	47 152	50 431	11 398	4 879	3 279	37.8	11.7	7.0
25 to 34 years	13 393	15 875	14 196	14 600	16 337	2 482	-1 679	1 737	18.5	-10.6	11.9
35 to 44 years	9 651	15 552	17 052	17 098	16 189	5 901	1 500	-909	61.1	9.6	-5.3
45 to 54 years	7 105	10 120	15 178	15 454	17 905	3 015	5 058	2 451	42.4	50.0	15.9
55 years and over	6 073	6 499	9 250	9 485	14 671	426	2 751	5 186	7.0	42.3	54.7
55 to 64 years	4 888	5 035	7 377	7 558	11 902	147	2 342	4 344	3.0	46.5	57.5
65 years and over	1 185	1 464	1 873	1 927	2 769	279	409	842	23.5	27.9	43.7
65 to 74 years	1 018	1 251	1 548	1 586	2 333	233	297	747	22.9	23.7	47.1
75 years and over	167	213	325	340	436	46	112	96	27.5	52.4	28.1
White, 16 Years and Over	96 143	108 837	118 569	120 150	130 358	12 694	9 732	10 208	13.2	8.9	8.5
Men	55 133	60 168	64 241	65 308	70 592	5 035	5 284	6 291	9.1	6.8	8.1
Women	41 010	48 669	54 328	54 842	59 766	7 659	4 924	5 924	18.7	11.6	9.0
Black, 16 Years and Over	11 331	14 162	16 834	16 564	19 765	2 831	2 672	3 201	25.0	18.9	19.3
Men	5 804	6 997	7 745	7 793	9 318	1 193	748	1 525	20.6	10.7	19.6
Women	5 527	7 166	9 089	8 771	10 447	1 639	1 923	1 676	29.7	26.8	19.1
Asian, 16 Years and Over [1]	2 770	5 109	7 130	5 949	8 971	2 339	2 021	3 022	84.4	39.6	50.8
Men	1 513	2 800	3 839	3 215	4 941	1 287	1 039	1 726	85.1	37.1	53.7
Women	1 257	2 309	3 291	2 734	4 030	1 052	982	1 296	83.7	42.5	47.4
All Other Groups, 16 Years and Over [2]	...	...	...	2 200	3 175	...	...	975	...	...	44.3
Men	...	...	...	1 189	1 732	...	...	543	...	...	45.7
Women	...	...	...	1 011	1 443	...	...	432	...	...	42.7
Hispanic Origin, 16 Years and Over	6 734	16 200	16 200	17 942	23 785	4 604	4 862	5 843	68.4	42.9	32.6
Men	4 148	9 273	9 273	10 609	13 674	2 752	2 373	3 065	66.3	34.4	28.9
Women	2 586	6 927	6 927	7 332	10 111	1 853	2 488	2 779	71.7	56.0	37.9
Other Than Hispanic Origin, 16 Years and Over	103 470	116 767	126 334	126 921	138 484	13 297	9 567	11 562	12.9	8.2	9.1
Men	58 302	63 064	66 779	66 891	71 577	4 762	3 715	4 686	8.2	5.9	7.0
Women	45 169	53 702	59 555	60 031	66 906	8 533	5 853	6 875	18.9	10.9	11.5
White Non-Hispanic, 16 Years and Over	89 630	98 724	103 360	103 348	106 237	9 094	4 636	2 889	10.1	4.7	2.8
Men	51 121	53 984	55 489	55 340	56 849	2 862	1 505	1 509	5.6	2.8	2.7
Women	38 508	44 740	47 871	48 008	49 388	6 232	3 130	1 380	16.2	7.0	2.9

[1]Data for 1982 and 1992 represent the "Asian and other" category with 1990 census weights. Data for 2002 with 1990 census weights represent the "Asian and other" category. Data for 2002 represent the "Asian only" category with 2000 census weights. Data for 2012 represent the "Asian only" category with 2000 census weights.
[2]The "All other groups" category includes those reporting the racial categories of (1a) American Indian and Alaska Native or (1b) Native Hawaiian and Other Pacific Islanders and those reporting two or more races. The category was not defined prior to 2003. Data for 2002 were calculated by BLS.
. . . = Not available.

Table 4-1. Civilian Labor Force by Age, Sex, Race, and Hispanic Origin, 1982, 1992, 2002, and Projected 2012—*Continued*

(Number, percent.)

Age, sex, race, and Hispanic origin	Percent distribution					Annual growth rate (percent)		
	1982	1992	2002		2012	1982–1992	1992–2002	2002–2012
			1990 census weights	2000 census weights				
TOTAL, 16 YEARS AND OVER	100.0	100.0	100.0	100.0	100.0	1.5	1.1	1.1
16 to 24 years	22.3	16.9	15.7	15.4	15.0	-1.3	0.4	0.9
16 to 19 years	7.7	5.5	5.4	5.2	4.7	-1.8	0.9	0.1
20 to 24 years	14.6	11.3	10.3	10.2	10.3	-1.0	0.1	1.3
25 to 54 years	64.0	71.4	70.1	70.2	65.9	2.6	0.9	0.5
25 to 34 years	28.3	27.6	21.6	22.2	21.8	1.3	-1.4	1.0
35 to 44 years	20.4	26.5	26.0	25.5	21.2	4.2	0.9	-0.7
45 to 54 years	15.3	17.3	22.5	22.5	22.8	2.8	3.8	1.3
55 years and over	13.7	11.8	14.2	14.3	19.1	0.0	3.0	4.1
55 to 64 years	10.9	9.0	11.1	11.3	15.2	-0.4	3.2	4.2
65 years and over	2.7	2.7	3.1	3.1	4.0	1.4	2.4	3.7
65 to 74 years	2.3	2.3	2.5	2.5	3.3	1.3	2.1	4.0
75 years and over	0.4	0.4	0.6	0.6	0.6	1.6	3.8	2.2
Men, 16 Years and Over	56.7	54.6	53.4	53.5	52.5	1.1	0.8	1.0
16 to 24 years	11.9	9.0	8.2	8.0	7.7	-1.3	0.1	0.7
16 to 19 years	4.1	2.9	2.8	2.7	2.3	-1.7	0.5	-0.2
20 to 24 years	7.8	6.1	5.4	5.4	5.3	-1.0	-0.1	1.1
25 to 54 years	36.6	38.9	37.5	37.7	34.8	2.1	0.7	0.3
25 to 34 years	16.1	15.2	11.7	12.1	11.8	0.9	-1.6	0.8
35 to 44 years	11.6	14.3	14.0	13.7	11.2	3.7	0.8	-0.8
45 to 54 years	8.9	9.4	11.8	11.8	11.8	2.1	3.4	1.1
55 years and over	8.2	6.7	7.7	7.8	10.1	-0.5	2.5	3.8
55 to 64 years	6.5	5.1	6.0	6.0	7.8	-0.9	2.6	3.8
65 years and over	1.7	1.6	1.8	1.8	2.2	0.9	2.2	3.7
65 to 74 years	1.4	1.3	1.4	1.4	1.9	0.8	2.0	4.0
75 years and over	0.3	0.3	0.3	0.3	0.3	1.0	3.5	2.0
Women, 16 Years and Over	43.3	45.4	46.6	46.5	47.5	2.0	1.3	1.3
16 to 24 years	10.5	7.9	7.6	7.4	7.3	-1.3	0.7	1.1
16 to 19 years	3.7	2.6	2.7	2.6	2.4	-1.9	1.3	0.3
20 to 24 years	6.8	5.3	4.9	4.8	5.0	-1.0	0.4	1.4
25 to 54 years	27.4	32.4	32.6	32.5	31.1	3.3	1.1	0.7
25 to 34 years	12.2	12.4	10.0	10.1	10.1	1.7	-1.1	1.1
35 to 44 years	8.8	12.1	12.0	11.8	10.0	4.9	0.9	-0.5
45 to 54 years	6.4	7.9	10.6	10.7	11.0	3.6	4.1	1.5
55 years and over	5.5	5.1	6.5	6.5	9.0	0.7	3.6	4.5
55 to 64 years	4.4	3.9	5.2	5.2	7.3	0.3	3.9	4.6
65 years and over	1.1	1.1	1.3	1.3	1.7	2.1	2.5	3.7
65 to 74 years	0.9	1.0	1.1	1.1	1.4	2.1	2.2	3.9
75 years and over	0.2	0.2	0.2	0.2	0.3	2.5	4.3	2.5
White, 16 Years and Over	87.2	85.0	83.2	82.9	80.3	1.2	0.9	0.8
Men	50.0	47.0	45.1	45.1	43.5	0.9	0.7	0.8
Women	37.2	38.0	38.1	37.9	36.8	1.7	1.1	0.9
Black, 16 Years and Over	10.3	11.1	11.8	11.4	12.2	2.3	1.7	1.8
Men	5.3	5.5	5.4	5.4	5.7	1.9	1.0	1.8
Women	5.0	5.6	6.4	6.1	6.4	2.6	2.4	1.8
Asian, 16 Years and Over[1]	2.5	4.0	5.0	4.1	5.5	6.3	3.4	4.2
Men	1.4	2.2	2.7	2.2	3.0	6.3	3.2	4.4
Women	1.1	1.8	2.3	1.9	2.5	6.3	3.6	4.0
All Other Groups, 16 Years and Over[2]	. . .	. . .	. . .	1.5	2.0	. . .	. . .	3.7
Men	. . .	. . .	. . .	0.8	1.1	. . .	. . .	3.8
Women	. . .	. . .	. . .	0.7	0.9	. . .	. . .	3.6
Hispanic Origin, 16 Years and Over	6.1	8.9	11.4	12.4	14.7	5.3	3.6	2.9
Men	3.8	5.4	6.5	7.3	8.4	5.2	3.0	2.6
Women	2.3	3.5	4.9	5.1	6.2	5.6	4.5	3.3
Other Than Hispanic Origin, 16 Years and Over	93.9	91.1	88.6	87.6	85.3	1.2	0.8	0.9
Men	52.9	49.2	46.9	46.2	44.1	0.8	0.6	0.7
Women	41.0	41.9	41.8	41.4	41.2	1.7	1.0	1.1
White Non-Hispanic, 16 Years and Over	81.3	77.1	72.5	71.3	65.5	1.0	0.5	0.3
Men	46.4	42.1	38.9	38.2	35.0	0.5	0.3	0.3
Women	34.9	34.9	33.6	33.1	30.4	1.5	0.7	0.3

[1]Data for 1982 and 1992 represent the "Asian and other" category with 1990 census weights. Data for 2002 with 1990 census weights represent the "Asian and other" category. Data for 2002 represent the "Asian only" category with 2000 census weights. Data for 2012 represent the "Asian only" category with 2000 census weights.
[2]The "All other groups" category includes those reporting the racial categories of (1a) American Indian and Alaska Native or (1b) Native Hawaiian and Other Pacific Islanders and those reporting two or more races. The category was not defined prior to 2003. Data for 2002 were calculated by BLS.
. . . = Not available.

PROJECTED EMPLOYMENT

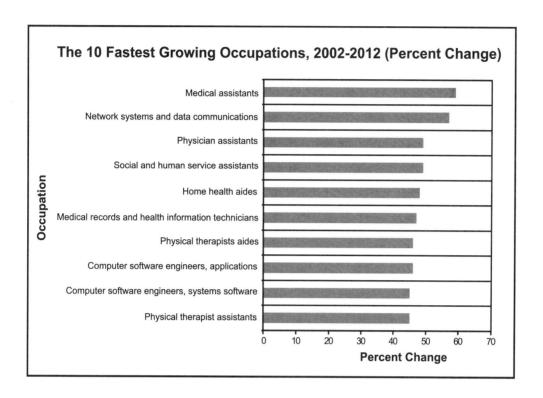

Only 3 of the 10 fastest-growing occupations are directly associated with computers. Six others are related to medical services and one, social and human services assistants, is more general. (Table 4-2)

OTHER HIGHLIGHTS:

• Of the 30 fastest-growing occupations, more than half require an associate's degree or higher. (Table 4-2)

• The fastest-growing occupations are not necessarily the ones projected to supply the largest number of additional jobs. Of the 10 occupations with the greatest job growth, only three (registered nurses, postsecondary teachers and general and operations managers) are in the professional category. None are associated with computers. Most jobs are in lower-level wage occupations such as food preparation and nursing aides. (Table 4-6)

• Three of the industries with the fastest-growing projected wage and salary employment are computer-related. None of the industries projected to provide the largest increase in the number of jobs are computer related. The largest are retail trade, state and local governments, and service providers. (Table 4-5)

• Total job openings result from growth and net replacement. Of the nearly 56 million positions available, almost two-thirds, or 35 million, are projected to be replacements. (Table 4-6)

• Employment in the two largest occupational groups of 2002, professional and related occupations and service occupations, will increase the most quickly and provide the most jobs. These two major groups, the respective highest and lowest in educational requirements and earnings, are expected to provide more than half of the total job growth from 2002 to 2003. (Table 4-6)

Table 4-2. Fastest Growing Occupations, 2002–2012

(Number, percent.)

Occupation	Employment		Change		Quartile rank by 2002 median annual earnings [1]	Most significant source of postsecondary education or training [2]
	2002	2012	Number	Percent		
Medical assistants	365	579	215	59	3	Moderate-term on-the-job training
Network systems and data communications	186	292	106	57	1	Bachelor's degree
Physician assistants	63	94	31	49	1	Bachelor's degree
Social and human service assistants	305	454	149	49	3	Moderate-term on-the-job training
Home health aides	580	859	279	48	4	Short-term on-the-job training
Medical records and health information technicians	147	216	69	47	3	Associate's degree
Physical therapist aides	37	54	17	46	3	Short-term on-the-job training
Computer software engineers, applications	394	573	179	46	1	Bachelor's degree
Computer software engineers, systems software	281	409	128	45	1	Bachelor's degree
Physical therapist assistants	50	73	22	45	2	Associate's degree
Fitness trainers and aerobics instructors	183	264	81	44	3	Postsecondary vocational award
Database administrators	110	159	49	44	1	Bachelor's degree
Veterinary technologists and technicians	53	76	23	44	3	Associate's degree
Hazardous materials removal workers	38	54	16	43	2	Moderate-term on-the-job training
Dental hygienists	148	212	64	43	1	Associate's degree
Occupational therapist aides	8	12	4	43	3	Short-term on-the-job training
Dental assistants	266	379	113	42	3	Moderate-term on-the-job training
Personal and home care aides	608	854	246	40	4	Short-term on-the-job training
Self-enrichment education teachers	200	281	80	40	2	Work experience in a related occupation
Computer systems analysts	468	653	184	39	1	Bachelor's degree
Occupational therapist assistants	18	26	7	39	2	Associate's degree
Environmental engineers	47	65	18	38	1	Bachelor's degree
Postsecondary teachers	1 581	2 184	603	38	1	Doctoral degree
Network and computer systems administrators	251	345	94	37	1	Bachelor's degree
Environmental science and protection technicians, including health	28	38	10	37	2	Associate's degree
Preschool teachers, except special education	424	577	153	36	4	Postsecondary vocational award
Computer and information systems managers	284	387	103	36	1	Bachelor's or higher degree, plus work experience
Physical therapists	137	185	48	35	1	Master's degree
Occupational therapists	82	110	29	35	1	Bachelor's degree
Respiratory therapists	86	116	30	35	2	Associate's degree

[1]The quartile rankings of Occupational Employment Statistics annual earnings data are presented in the following categories: 1 = very high ($41,820 and over), 2 = high ($27,500 to $41,780), 3 = low ($19,710 to $27,380), and 4 = very low (up to $19,600.) The rankings were based on quartiles using one-fourth of total employment to define each quartile. Earnings are for wage and salary workers.
[2]An occupation is placed into one of 11 categories that best describes the education or training needed by most workers to become fully qualified.

Table 4-3. Industries with the Largest Output Growth and Declines, 2000–2012

(Dollars, percent.)

Industry description	Billions of chained 1996 dollars		Change 2000–2012	Average annual rate of change 2000–2012
	2000	2012		
LARGEST GROWTH				
Computer and peripheral equipment manufacturing	262.8	2 292.7	2 029.9	24.2
Wholesale trade	1 025.3	1 622.5	597.2	4.7
Retail trade	1 013.1	1 420.0	406.9	3.4
Credit intermediation and related activities, monetary authorities, and funds, trusts, and other financial vehicles	794.3	1 114.4	320.1	3.4
Telecommunications, except cable and other programming distribution	400.6	644.7	244.0	4.9
Real estate	659.6	873.1	213.5	2.8
Management of companies and enterprises	468.3	668.9	200.6	3.6
Owner-occupied dwellings	710.3	906.9	196.6	2.5
Monetary authorities and depository credit intermediation	408.2	584.5	176.3	3.7
Securities, commodity contracts, and other financial investments and related activities	350.1	525.9	175.8	4.2
Computer systems design and related services	127.1	302.2	175.1	9.0
Communications equipment manufacturing	100.0	268.1	168.1	10.4
Internet services, data processing, and other information services	86.9	232.6	145.7	10.3
Nondepository credit intermediation and related support activities, funds, trusts, and lessors of nonfinancial intangible assets (except copyright works)	386.4	530.4	144.1	3.2
Offices of health practitioners	332.3	468.9	136.6	3.5
Construction	718.7	851.8	133.1	1.7
Software publishers	102.2	228.8	126.6	8.4
Scientific research and development and other professional, scientific, and technical services	166.4	283.7	117.3	5.5
Truck transportation and couriers and messengers	239.5	349.1	109.6	3.8
Hospitals	334.3	424.4	90.1	2.4
LARGEST DECLINES				
Cut and sew apparel manufacturing	39.8	17.1	-22.7	-8.1
Basic chemical manufacturing	97.5	75.6	-21.9	-2.5
Oil and gas extraction	87.4	79.6	-7.8	-0.9
Textile and fabric finishing and fabric coating mills	12.2	6.5	-5.6	-6.0
Apparel knitting mills	6.4	2.3	-4.1	-9.7
Pulp, paper, and paperboard mills	67.7	64.7	-3.0	-0.5
Coal mining	26.2	23.4	-2.8	-1.1
Resin, synthetic rubber, and artificial synthetic fibers and filaments manufacturing	56.4	54.0	-2.4	-0.4
Fiber, yarn, and thread mills	10.5	8.2	-2.4	-0.5
Leather and hide tanning and finishing	2.6	1.2	-1.4	-7.7
Other leather and allied product manufacturing	2.1	1.0	-1.2	-7.7
Tobacco manufacturing	34.2	33.1	-1.0	-0.3
Fabric mills	22.1	21.1	-0.9	-0.4
Nonmetallic mineral mining and quarrying	17.5	16.7	-0.8	-0.5
Nonferrous metal (except aluminum) production and processing	21.8	21.1	-0.6	-0.3
Apparel accessories and other apparel manufacturing	3.8	3.3	-0.6	-1.5

Table 4-4. Percentage of Employees and Projected Net Employment Change in Selected Occupations, by Age Group [1]

(Percent, thousands.)

Occupation	Percent distribution of employees by age group			Employment (thousands)		Change		Total job openings due to growth and net replacements (thousands)
	16-24 years	25-54 years	55 years and older	2002	2012	Number	Percent	
ALL OCCUPATIONS	14.7	71.4	13.9	144 015	165 319	21 305	14.8	56 305
Bus drivers	9.8	45.4	44.8	654	781	106	16.2	249
Ushers, lobby attendants, and ticket takers	7.5	60.1	32.4	105	121	16	15.5	76
Loan counselors and officers	4.8	62.8	32.3	255	302	48	18.7	89
Sales representatives and services, all other	4.7	64.0	31.2	577	717	140	24.3	250
Social workers	3.5	66.4	30.1	477	604	127	26.7	209
Environmental scientists and geoscientists	4.1	67.8	28.1	101	121	20	20.1	38
Network systems and data communications analysts	8.0	64.7	27.3	186	292	106	57.0	128
Aircraft pilots and flight engineers	2.5	70.8	26.7	100	118	18	17.8	45
Transportation, storage, and distribution managers	5.5	68.0	26.5	111	133	22	19.7	44
Clergy	11.2	62.5	26.3	400	463	62	15.5	144
Television, video, and motion picture camera operators and editors	0.3	74.3	25.4	48	56	9	18.7	19
Market and survey researchers	8.4	66.2	25.4	155	193	38	24.7	78
Ambulance drivers and attendants, except emergency medical technicians	5.8	68.9	25.3	17	22	5	26.7	6
Sales engineers	11.7	63.4	24.9	82	98	16	19.9	41
Chief executives	0.6	74.9	24.4	553	645	93	16.7	197
Special education teachers	5.4	70.9	23.7	433	563	130	30.0	233
Chiropractors	2.7	73.8	23.4	49	60	11	23.3	21
Human resources, training, and labor relations specialists	3.7	73.3	23.0	474	606	131	27.7	204
Transit and railroad police	18.0	59.6	22.4	6	7	1	15.9	2
Public relations specialists	5.5	72.8	21.7	158	210	52	32.9	75
Motor vehicle operators, all other	7.9	71.0	21.1	111	139	28	25.2	44
Personal and home care aides	34.8	44.1	21.0	608	854	246	40.5	343
Public relations managers	2.8	76.2	21.0	69	85	16	23.4	28
Food preparation and serving related workers, all other	13.3	66.2	20.5	117	134	18	15.2	54
Human resources assistants, except payroll and timekeeping	9.9	69.8	20.3	174	207	33	19.3	71

[1] Total job openings are given by the sum of net employment increases and net replacements. If employment change is negative, job openings due to growth are zero and total job openings equal net replacements.

Table 4-5. Employment and Output by Industry, 1992, 2002, and Projected 2012

(Number, percent.)

| Industry | Employment | | | | | | | Output | | | | |
| | Thousands of jobs | | | Change | | Average annual rate of change (percent) | | Billions of chained (1996) dollars | | | Average annual rate of change (percent) | |
	1992	2002	2012	1992–2002	2002–2012	1992–2002	2002–2012	1992	2002	2012	1992–2002	2002–2012
TOTAL[1,2]	123 325	144 014	165 319	20 689	21 305	1.6	1.4	12 272	16 822	23 250	3.2	3.3
Nonagriculture Wage and Salary[3]	109 526	131 063	152 690	21 537	21 627	1.8	1.5	11 448	15 818	21 973	3.3	3.3
Mining	610	512	451	-98	-61	-1.7	-1.3	155	166	156	0.7	-0.6
Oil and gas extraction	182	123	88	-60	-34	-3.9	-3.2	94	87	80	-0.7	-0.9
Mining (except oil and gas)	272	212	180	-60	-32	-2.5	-1.6	47	54	52	1.4	-0.5
Coal mining	118	75	52	-43	-23	-4.4	-3.5	22	26	23	1.8	-1.1
Metal ore mining	50	29	18	-21	-11	-5.2	-4.8	11	10	11	-0.6	0.8
Nonmetallic mineral mining and quarrying	104	108	110	3	2	0.3	0.2	14	18	17	2.1	-0.5
Support activities for mining	156	177	183	22	6	1.3	0.3	14	24	26	5.3	0.9
Utilities	726	600	565	-126	-34	-1.9	-0.6	278	267	320	-0.4	1.8
Electric power generation, transmission, and distribution	537	436	405	-101	-31	-2.1	-0.7	207	207	254	0.0	2.0
Natural gas distribution	154	116	90	-38	-26	-2.8	-2.5	66	53	58	-2.1	0.9
Water, sewage, and other systems	35	49	71	13	23	3.2	3.9	5	6	8	2.2	2.7
Construction	4 608	6 732	7 745	2 124	1 014	3.9	1.4	547	719	852	2.8	1.7
Manufacturing	16 799	15 307	15 149	-1 492	-158	-0.9	-0.1	3 067	3 840	5 361	2.3	3.4
Food manufacturing	1 518	1 525	1 597	7	72	0.0	0.5	384	437	517	1.3	1.7
Animal food manufacturing	55	52	52	-4	1	-0.7	0.1	25	30	38	2.1	2.2
Grain and oilseed milling	71	62	61	-9	-1	-1.3	-0.1	49	57	70	1.6	2.0
Sugar and confectionery product manufacturing	103	83	80	-20	-3	-2.1	-0.3	22	26	30	1.7	1.6
Fruit and vegetable preserving and specialty food manufacturing	218	182	180	-36	-2	-1.8	-0.1	44	50	59	1.4	1.7
Dairy product manufacturing	143	137	124	-6	-13	-0.4	-1.0	57	56	58	-0.3	0.4
Animal slaughtering and processing	438	520	601	83	80	1.7	1.4	98	118	144	1.9	2.0
Seafood product preparation and packaging	55	44	40	-11	-4	-2.3	-0.8	8	7	8	-1.2	1.2
Bakeries and tortilla manufacturing	290	295	303	4	9	0.1	0.3	39	43	53	1.1	2.0
Other food manufacturing	146	152	155	5	4	0.4	0.2	44	51	59	1.5	1.5
Beverage and tobacco product manufacturing	209	206	179	-3	-27	-0.1	-1.4	96	98	105	0.3	0.7
Beverage manufacturing	165	172	158	7	-14	0.4	-0.8	59	64	74	0.8	1.3
Tobacco manufacturing	44	33	20	-10	-13	-2.7	-5.0	36	34	33	-0.5	-0.3
Textile mills	479	293	157	-186	-136	-4.8	-6.1	51	45	36	-1.4	-2.2
Fiber, yarn, and thread mills	97	64	37	-33	-27	-4.1	-5.3	12	11	8	-1.0	-2.5
Fabric mills	256	147	80	-109	-67	-5.4	-5.9	26	22	21	-1.7	-0.4
Textile and fabric finishing and fabric coating mills	126	82	40	-44	-42	-4.2	-6.9	13	12	7	-1.0	-6.0
Textile product mills	202	196	181	-6	-16	-0.3	-0.8	26	30	35	1.4	1.3
Textile furnishings mills	120	119	111	-1	-8	-0.1	-0.7	18	21	23	1.8	1.0
Other textile product mills	82	78	70	-5	-8	-0.6	-1.1	9	9	11	0.6	2.1
Apparel manufacturing	905	358	112	-548	-246	-8.9	-11.0	64	50	23	-2.4	-7.6
Apparel knitting mills	110	50	20	-60	-30	-7.7	-8.7	10	6	2	-4.3	-9.7
Cut and sew apparel manufacturing	752	282	77	-470	-205	-9.4	-12.2	50	40	17	-2.2	-8.1
Apparel accessories and other apparel manufacturing	43	26	15	-17	-11	-4.8	-5.4	4	4	3	-1.3	-1.5
Leather and allied product manufacturing	121	50	33	-71	-17	-8.5	-4.0	10	8	6	-2.5	-2.6
Leather and hide tanning and finishing	15	9	5	-7	-4	-5.7	-6.3	3	3	1	-1.5	-7.7
Footwear manufacturing	72	21	18	-51	-4	-11.5	-1.8	5	3	4	-3.6	2.1
Other leather and allied product manufacturing	33	20	11	-13	-9	-5.0	-5.9	3	2	1	-1.6	-7.7
Wood product manufacturing	502	557	634	55	77	1.0	1.3	73	83	112	1.2	3.0
Sawmills and wood preservation	134	121	110	-13	-11	-1.0	-1.0	25	26	34	0.6	2.7
Veneer, plywood, and engineered wood product	88	116	138	28	21	2.8	1.7	17	20	26	1.8	2.6
Other wood product manufacturing	280	320	386	39	67	1.3	1.9	32	37	52	1.5	3.4
Paper manufacturing	640	550	477	-90	-72	-1.5	-1.4	146	141	144	-0.4	0.2
Pulp, paper, and paperboard mills	232	168	126	-63	-42	-3.1	-2.8	73	68	65	-0.8	-0.5
Converted paper product manufacturing	408	382	351	-26	-31	-0.7	-0.8	73	73	79	0.0	0.8
Printing and related support activities	780	710	734	-70	24	-0.9	0.3	92	91	94	-0.1	0.3
Petroleum and coal products manufacturing	152	119	102	-33	-18	-2.4	-1.6	161	181	199	1.2	1.0
Chemical manufacturing	1 029	930	891	-99	-38	-1.0	-0.4	363	401	450	1.0	1.2
Basic chemical manufacturing	246	171	140	-76	-31	-3.6	-2.0	117	98	76	-1.8	-2.5
Resin, synthetic rubber, and artificial synthetic fibers and filaments manufacturing	151	114	89	-37	-26	-2.8	-2.5	54	56	54	0.4	-0.4
Pesticide, fertilizer, and other agricultural chemical manufacturing	54	45	35	-10	-10	-1.9	-2.4	23	19	22	-2.1	1.9
Pharmaceutical and medicine manufacturing	225	293	361	68	68	2.7	2.1	72	112	157	4.5	3.5
Paint, coating, and adhesive manufacturing	81	72	62	-8	-11	-1.1	-1.6	22	24	30	0.8	2.1
Soap, cleaning compound, and toilet preparation manufacturing	127	122	125	-5	3	-0.4	0.3	43	52	64	1.8	2.0
Other chemical product and preparation manufacturing	144	112	79	-32	-33	-2.4	-3.4	34	36	42	0.6	1.3

[1]Wage and salary data are from the Current Employment Statistics survey, which counts jobs, whereas data for the self-employed, for unpaid family workers, and for agriculture, forestry, fishing, and hunting workers are from the Current Population Survey.
[2]Output subcategories do not necessarily add to higher categories as a product of chainweighting.
[3]Includes agriculture, forestry, fishing, and hunting data from the Current Population Survey, except logging, which is from the Current Employment Survey and government wage and salary workers, which are excluded.
. . . = Not available.

Table 4-5. Employment and Output by Industry, 1992, 2002, and Projected 2012—*Continued*

(Number, percent.)

Industry	Employment							Output				
	Thousands of jobs			Change		Average annual rate of change (percent)		Billions of chained (1996) dollars			Average annual rate of change (percent)	
	1992	2002	2012	1992–2002	2002–2012	1992–2002	2002–2012	1992	2002	2012	1992–2002	2002–2012
Plastics and rubber products manufacturing	819	854	991	35	138	0.4	1.5	122	164	245	3.0	4.1
Plastics product manufacturing	620	668	797	48	128	0.8	1.8	95	133	198	3.4	4.1
Rubber product manufacturing	199	185	195	-14	10	-0.7	0.5	27	31	47	1.4	4.0
Nonmetallic mineral product manufacturing	487	519	579	32	60	0.6	1.1	69	85	114	2.1	2.9
Clay product and refractory manufacturing	79	72	80	-7	9	-0.9	1.1	7	8	10	0.2	3.2
Glass and glass product manufacturing	145	126	125	-19	-1	-1.4	-0.1	19	22	33	1.6	3.9
Cement and concrete product manufacturing	178	230	278	52	48	2.6	1.9	27	38	49	3.4	2.5
Lime and gypsum product manufacturing	14	19	21	5	2	3.0	0.9	4	5	6	1.6	2.1
Other nonmetallic mineral product manufacturing	72	72	75	0	3	0.1	0.4	12	13	16	1.0	2.3
Primary metal manufacturing	630	511	494	-119	-17	-2.1	-0.3	140	137	160	-0.2	1.5
Iron and steel mills ferroalloy manufacturing	168	107	76	-61	-31	-4.4	-3.4	47	49	56	0.4	1.4
Steel product manufacturing from purchased steel	66	63	60	-3	-3	-0.4	-0.5	16	15	18	-0.7	1.5
Alumina and aluminum production and processing	100	80	79	-19	-1	-2.1	-0.2	29	25	26	-1.5	0.3
Nonferrous metal (except aluminum) production and processing	102	81	80	-20	-1	-2.2	-0.2	26	22	21	-1.9	-0.3
Foundries	196	180	199	-16	20	-0.9	1.0	21	25	38	2.1	4.2
Fabricated metal product manufacturing	1 497	1 548	1 645	51	97	0.3	0.6	186	226	315	2.0	3.4
Forging and stamping	122	114	132	-9	18	-0.7	1.5	18	23	36	2.6	4.5
Cutlery and handtool manufacturing	73	65	70	-8	6	-1.2	0.8	8	10	15	1.9	3.7
Architectural and structural metals manufacturing	327	400	478	74	77	2.1	1.8	41	55	81	3.1	3.9
Boiler, tank, and shipping container manufacturing	108	95	90	-13	-5	-1.3	-0.5	21	20	26	-0.6	2.6
Hardware manufacturing	54	43	45	-11	3	-2.3	0.6	9	10	14	0.8	3.9
Spring and wire product manufacturing	74	71	59	-4	-12	-0.5	-1.8	6	8	9	2.2	1.2
Machine shops; turned product; and screw, nut, and bolt manufacturing	287	318	333	32	15	1.1	0.5	29	41	62	3.7	4.2
Coating, engraving, heat treating, and allied activities	137	148	151	11	4	0.8	0.2	12	16	25	2.8	4.4
Other fabricated metal product manufacturing	316	296	287	-20	-9	-0.7	-0.3	42	43	49	0.3	1.2
Machinery manufacturing	1 309	1 237	1 357	-72	120	-0.6	0.9	186	230	341	2.1	4.0
Agriculture, construction, and mining machinery manufacturing	201	201	212	1	10	0.0	0.5	33	42	60	2.5	3.5
Industrial machinery manufacturing	142	132	125	-10	-6	-0.7	-0.5	22	31	47	3.3	4.4
Commercial and service industry machinery manufacturing	138	132	141	-6	9	-0.5	0.6	22	19	27	-1.3	3.6
Ventilation, heating, air–conditioning, and commercial refrigeration equipment manufacturing	161	167	189	7	22	0.4	1.2	22	29	40	2.8	3.2
Metalworking machinery manufacturing	241	217	251	-24	34	-1.0	1.5	21	23	38	0.9	4.9
Engine, turbine, and power transmission equipment manufacturing	111	100	100	-11	0	-1.0	0.0	23	34	44	4.1	2.7
Other general purpose machinery manufacturing	317	288	339	-29	51	-0.9	1.6	43	51	84	1.7	5.2
Computer and electronic product manufacturing	1 707	1 521	1 333	-186	-189	-1.1	-1.3	225	557	1 705	9.5	11.8
Computer and peripheral equipment manufacturing	329	250	182	-79	-68	-2.7	-3.1	28	263	2 293	24.9	24.2
Communications equipment manufacturing	210	191	201	-19	10	-0.9	0.5	45	100	268	8.2	10.4
Audio and video equipment manufacturing	58	42	38	. . .	-3	-3.2	-0.8	8	9	10	1.0	1.2
Semiconductor and other electronic component manufacturing	519	531	452	12	-79	0.2	-1.6	67	134	149	7.2	1.1
Navigational, measuring, electromedical, and control instruments manufacturing	549	451	396	. . .	-55	-1.9	-1.3	79	92	126	1.4	3.2
Manufacturing and reproducing magnetic and optical media	44	57	63	13	6	2.7	1.1	8	7	9	-1.4	2.1
Electrical equipment, appliance, and component manufacturing	580	499	486	. . .	-13	-1.5	-0.3	88	103	142	1.6	3.3
Electric lighting equipment manufacturing	74	72	70	. . .	-2	-0.2	-0.3	10	12	14	1.8	1.4
Household appliance manufacturing	106	98	84	. . .	-14	-0.8	-1.5	18	22	29	2.2	2.8
Electrical equipment manufacturing	219	176	180	. . .	4	-2.1	0.2	26	29	46	0.8	4.7
Other electrical equipment and component manufacturing	180	152	151	. . .	-1	-1.7	-0.1	33	41	54	1.9	2.9
Transportation equipment manufacturing	1 977	1 829	1 787	. . .	-41	-0.8	-0.2	462	600	802	2.6	3.0
Motor vehicle manufacturing	260	267	251	7	-16	0.3	-0.6	166	236	319	3.6	3.1
Motor vehicle body and trailer manufacturing	126	154	172	28	18	2.0	1.1	15	22	39	3.7	5.7
Motor vehicle parts manufacturing	661	731	758	70	27	1.0	0.4	115	187	275	5.0	3.9
Aerospace product and parts manufacturing	711	468	386	. . .	-83	-4.1	-1.9	138	116	117	-1.7	0.1
Railroad rolling stock manufacturing	27	23	24	. . .	1	-1.7	0.6	5	8	12	4.0	4.2
Ship and boat building	157	146	157	. . .	11	-0.7	0.7	16	19	27	1.6	3.8
Other transportation equipment manufacturing	36	40	40	4	0	1.0	0.1	7	12	16	5.9	2.4
Furniture and related product manufacturing	563	605	666	42	62	0.7	1.0	51	66	89	2.7	3.0
Household and institutional furniture and kitchen cabinet manufacturing	373	400	450	28	49	0.7	1.2	30	39	53	2.7	3.0
Office furniture (including fixtures) manufacturing	146	151	155	5	5	0.3	0.3	16	20	27	2.2	3.1
Other furniture related product manufacturing	44	54	61	10	7	2.0	1.3	5	7	10	4.1	2.8
Miscellaneous manufacturing	693	692	715	-1	24	0.0	0.3	85	114	151	3.0	2.9

. . . = Not available.

Table 4-5. Employment and Output by Industry, 1992, 2002, and Projected 2012—*Continued*

(Number, percent.)

Industry	Employment							Output				
	Thousands of jobs			Change		Average annual rate of change (percent)		Billions of chained (1996) dollars			Average annual rate of change (percent)	
	1992	2002	2012	1992–2002	2002–2012	1992–2002	2002–2012	1992	2002	2012	1992–2002	2002–2012
Medical equipment and supplies manufacturing	297	309	329	12	20	0.4	0.6	37	55	91	4.1	5.2
Other miscellaneous manufacturing	395	383	387	-12	4	-0.3	0.1	49	59	60	2.0	0.1
Wholesale Trade	5 110	5 641	6 279	531	638	1.0	1.1	600	1 025	1 622	5.5	4.7
Retail Trade	12 828	15 047	17 129	2 219	2 082	1.6	1.3	667	1 013	1 420	4.3	3.4
Transportation and Warehousing	3 462	4 205	5 120	744	914	2.0	2.0	436	576	820	2.8	3.6
Air transportation	520	559	626	40	67	0.7	1.1	100	142	229	3.6	4.9
Rail transportation	248	218	197	-30	-21	-1.3	-1.0	37	44	58	1.8	2.7
Water transportation	57	52	50	-5	-1	-0.9	-0.3	21	21	28	-0.1	2.8
Truck transportation and couriers and messengers	1 496	1 897	2 404	401	507	2.4	2.4	170	240	349	3.5	3.8
Transit and ground passenger transportation	288	372	488	84	116	2.6	2.8	21	26	30	2.2	1.2
Pipeline transportation	60	42	42	-19	0	-3.6	0.0	30	27	29	-1.0	0.7
Scenic and sightseeing transportation and support activities for transportation	388	553	652	165	100	3.6	1.7	36	44	57	2.1	2.6
Warehousing and storage	406	514	660	108	147	2.4	2.5	21	31	42	4.1	3.1
Information	2 641	3 420	4 052	779	632	2.6	1.7	481	891	1 498	6.4	5.3
Publishing industries	854	970	1 133	115	163	1.3	1.6	134	222	334	5.1	4.2
Newspaper, periodical, book and directory publishers	740	714	703	-27	-11	-0.4	-0.1	105	122	132	1.5	0.8
Software publishers	114	256	430	142	174	8.4	5.3	31	102	229	12.6	8.4
Internet services, data processing, and other information services	307	529	773	222	244	5.6	3.9	25	87	233	13.1	10.3
Motion picture and sound recording industries	254	387	503	133	116	4.3	2.7	50	93	178	6.3	6.7
Broadcasting and telecommunications	1 226	1 535	1 643	309	109	2.3	0.7	272	491	745	6.1	4.3
Radio and television broadcasting	226	241	235	15	-6	0.6	-0.2	34	40	46	1.7	1.5
Cable and other subscription programming and program distribution	126	221	300	95	79	5.7	3.1	36	53	64	3.9	1.9
Telecommunications, except cable and other programming distribution	873	1 073	1 108	200	35	2.1	0.3	202	401	645	7.1	4.9
Financial Activities	6 540	7 843	8 806	1 303	964	1.8	1.2	1 525	2 230	3 038	3.9	3.1
Credit intermediation, and related activities, monetary authorities, and funds, trusts, and other financial vehicles	2 414	2 819	3 126	405	308	1.6	1.0	527	794	1 114	4.2	3.4
Monetary authorities and depository credit intermediation	1 793	1 761	1 873	-31	112	-0.2	0.6	281	408	584	3.8	3.7
Nondepository credit intermediation and related support activities, funds, trusts, and lessors of nonfinancial intangible (except copyrighted works)	621	1 058	1 253	436	196	5.5	1.7	246	386	530	4.6	3.2
Securities, commodity, contracts, and other financial investments and related activities	476	801	925	325	124	5.3	1.5	97	350	526	13.6	4.2
Insurance carriers and related activities	2 040	2 223	2 391	184	168	0.9	0.7	313	347	419	1.0	1.9
Insurance carriers	1 367	1 402	1 451	35	49	0.3	0.3	237	237	288	0.0	2.0
Agencies, brokerages, and other insurance related activities	672	821	940	149	119	2.0	1.4	76	112	133	3.9	1.7
Real Estate	1 115	1 348	1 513	233	165	1.9	1.2	542	660	873	2.0	2.8
Rental and leasing services	496	652	852	156	200	2.8	2.7	52	88	127	5.3	3.8
Automotive equipment, rental, and leasing	151	197	225	46	28	2.7	1.3	14	34	51	9.4	4.2
Consumer goods rental and general rental centers	267	353	484	86	131	2.8	3.2	15	20	27	3.2	2.7
Commercial and industrial machinery and equipment, rental, and leasing	78	102	143	24	41	2.7	3.4	24	34	50	3.5	3.9
Professional, Scientific, and Technical Services	4 594	6 715	8 579	2 122	1 864	3.9	2.5	568	881	1 370	4.5	4.5
Legal services	950	1 112	1 330	162	218	1.6	1.8	142	151	171	0.6	1.3
Accounting, tax preparation, bookkeeping, and payroll services	658	867	1 082	209	215	2.8	2.2	58	80	98	3.2	2.1
Architectural, engineering, and related services	902	1 251	1 306	349	54	3.3	0.4	110	157	217	3.7	3.3
Specialized design services	81	123	161	42	38	4.2	2.7	13	21	29	5.0	3.6
Computer systems design and related services	445	1 163	1 798	718	635	10.1	4.5	55	127	302	8.8	9.0
Management, scientific, and technical consulting services ...	358	732	1 137	374	406	7.4	4.5	59	114	169	6.7	4.1
Scientific research and development and other technical services	830	1 026	1 241	196	215	2.1	1.9	90	166	284	6.3	5.5
Advertising and related services	370	442	525	72	84	1.8	1.7	42	67	111	4.8	5.2
Management of companies and enterprises	1 623	1 711	1 906	88	195	0.5	1.1	256	468	669	6.2	3.6

Table 4-5. Employment and Output by Industry, 1992, 2002, and Projected 2012—*Continued*

(Number, percent.)

Industry	Employment							Output				
	Thousands of jobs			Change		Average annual rate of change (percent)		Billions of chained (1996) dollars			Average annual rate of change (percent)	
	1992	2002	2012	1992–2002	2002–2012	1992–2002	2002–2012	1992	2002	2012	1992–2002	2002–2012
Administrative and support and waste management and remediation services	4 753	7 584	10 391	2 831	2 807	4.8	3.2	240	433	638	6.1	4.0
Administrative support services	4 516	7 267	9 987	2 751	2 720	4.9	3.2	206	384	572	6.4	4.1
Office administrative and facilities support services	275	390	508	116	117	3.6	2.7	27	58	87	8.1	4.2
Employment services	1 593	3 249	5 012	1 656	1 764	7.4	4.4	47	104	172	8.3	5.1
Business support and investigation and security services and support services, n.e.c.	1 244	1 772	2 261	528	489	3.6	2.5	64	114	165	6.0	3.7
Travel arrangement and reservation services	245	258	226	13	-32	0.5	-1.3	21	25	36	1.8	3.7
Services to buildings and dwellings	1 160	1 597	1 980	438	383	3.3	2.2	47	81	109	5.5	3.1
Waste management and remediation services	237	317	404	80	87	3.0	2.5	34	49	66	3.7	3.0
Educational services	1 713	2 651	3 410	938	759	4.5	2.6	95	125	149	2.8	1.8
Health care and social assistance	10 178	13 533	17 919	3 355	4 386	2.9	2.8	719	962	1 326	3.0	3.3
Ambulatory health care services	3 200	4 634	6 532	1 434	1 899	3.8	3.5	332	452	656	3.1	3.8
Offices of health practitioners	2 267	3 190	4 419	923	1 229	3.5	3.3	251	332	469	2.9	3.5
Ambulatory health care services except offices of health practitioners	933	1 444	2 113	511	670	4.5	3.9	82	120	. . .	. . .	. . .
Hospitals	3 711	4 153	4 785	442	632	1.1	1.4	256	334	424	2.7	2.4
Nursing and residential care facilities	2 044	2 743	3 685	700	942	3.0	3.0	71	88	114	2.1	2.6
Nursing care and residential and mental health facilities	1 578	2 048	2 607	470	559	2.6	2.4	56	65	82	1.5	2.4
Community care facilities for the elderly and residential care facilities, n.e.c.	465	695	1 078	230	382	4.1	4.5	16	23	33	4.2	3.4
Social assistance	1 223	2 004	2 917	780	913	5.1	3.8	59	88	132	4.1	4.1
Individual, family, community, and vocational rehabilitation services	777	1 269	1 867	493	597	5.0	3.9	34	52	78	4.2	4.1
Child day care services	447	734	1 050	288	316	5.1	3.6	24	37	55	4.3	4.0
Arts, entertainment, and recreation	1 236	1 778	2 275	542	497	3.7	2.5	95	143	200	4.2	3.4
Performing arts, spectator sports, and related industries	290	358	421	68	63	2.1	1.6	41	53	65	2.4	2.2
Performing arts companies, promoters, agents, managers, and independent artists	195	240	277	45	37	2.1	1.4	27	34	43	2.4	2.3
Spectator sports	95	118	144	23	26	2.2	2.0	15	19	22	2.3	1.9
Museums, historical sites, and similar institutions	75	113	136	38	24	4.1	1.9	4	7	9	5.9	2.7
Amusement, gambling, and recreation industries	872	1 308	1 717	436	410	4.1	2.8	49	83	126	5.5	4.2
Accommodation and food services	8 201	10 191	11 829	1 991	1 638	2.2	1.5	347	449	597	2.6	2.9
Accommodation	1 562	1 780	2 080	218	301	1.3	1.6	90	116	173	2.5	4.1
Traveler accommodation	1 517	1 726	2 019	209	293	1.3	1.6	88	113	169	2.5	4.1
RV parks, recreational camps, and rooming and boarding houses	44	53	62	9	8	1.9	1.5	2	3	4	2.1	3.2
Food services and drinking places	6 639	8 412	9 749	1 773	1 337	2.4	1.5	256	333	423	2.7	2.4
Other services	5 120	6 105	7 065	985	960	1.8	1.5	298	382	506	2.5	2.9
Repair and maintenance	964	1 241	1 418	277	177	2.6	1.3	118	158	205	2.9	2.7
Automotive repair and maintenance	636	897	1 046	261	149	3.5	1.6	69	93	124	3.1	2.9
Electronic and precision equipment repair and maintenance	99	105	101	7	-5	0.6	-0.5	17	17	18	0.5	0.2
Commercial and industrial equipment repair and maintenance, except automotive and electric	149	156	185	8	29	0.5	1.7	16	28	42	5.4	4.1
Personal and household goods repair and maintenance	80	82	86	2	3	0.2	0.4	17	20	22	2.0	0.7
Personal and laundry services	1 099	1 247	1 485	148	238	1.3	1.8	76	98	125	2.6	2.4
Personal care servcies	434	523	667	89	144	1.9	2.5	20	27	35	2.8	2.6
Death care services	116	139	155	22	16	1.8	1.1	12	12	13	0.5	0.8
Dry cleaning and laundry services	359	366	393	7	27	0.2	0.7	18	21	25	1.5	1.7
Other personal services	190	219	270	29	51	1.4	2.1	26	38	53	4.0	3.3
Religious, grantmaking, civic, professional, and similar organizations	2 177	2 861	3 460	684	600	2.8	1.9	94	117	166	2.2	3.6
Religious, grantmaking, and giving services and social advocacy organizations	1 403	1 944	2 372	541	428	3.3	2.0	49	66	107	3.1	4.9
Civic, social, business, and similar organizations	774	917	1 088	143	172	1.7	1.7	45	50	59	1.2	1.5
Private households	880	757	703	-123	-54	-1.5	-0.7	10	9	11	-0.8	1.1
Federal Government	3 111	2 767	2 779	-344	12	-1.2	0.0	394	378	443	-0.4	1.6
Postal Service	800	845	807	45	-38	0.5	-0.5	51	61	76	1.7	2.2
Federal electric utilities	28	28	24	1	-4	0.2	-1.7	7	9	11	2.5	2.0
Federal government enterprises	138	52	32	-86	-20	-9.3	-4.6	6	7	11	1.4	4.1
Federal general government	2 145	1 842	1 915	-303	73	-1.5	0.4	252	209	216	-1.9	0.4
Federal government capital services	. . .	. . .	. . .	. . .	. . .	. . .	. . .	78	93	133	1.7	3.7

n.e.c. = not elsewhere classified.

. . . = Not available.

Table 4-5. Employment and Output by Industry, 1992, 2002, and Projected 2012—*Continued*

(Number, percent.)

Industry	Employment							Output				
	Thousands of jobs			Change		Average annual rate of change (percent)		Billions of chained (1996) dollars			Average annual rate of change (percent)	
	1992	2002	2012	1992–2002	2002–2012	1992–2002	2002–2012	1992	2002	2012	1992–2002	2002–2012
Local Government Passenger Transit	210	231	260	21	29	1.0	1.2	7	9	10	2.6	0.4
State and Local Government	15 675	18 722	21 240	3 047	2 518	1.8	1.3	685	839	980	2.0	1.6
State and local electric utilities	85	93	108	9	14	1.0	1.4	18	24	29	2.5	2.2
State and local government enterprises	532	689	734	157	46	2.6	0.6	78	104	131	2.9	2.4
State and local government hospitals	1 083	995	1 024	-89	29	-0.9	0.3	41	48	56	1.5	1.5
State and local government education	7 875	9 876	11 606	2 002	1 730	2.3	1.6	276	321	375	1.5	1.5
State and local government general government, n.e.c.	5 890	6 838	7 508	948	670	1.5	0.9	207	241	260	1.5	0.8
State and local government capital services	...	...	...	...	...	...	...	58	93	122	4.9	2.8
Owner–Occupied Dwellings[3]	...	...	...	...	...	...	...	552	710	907	2.6	2.5
Agriculture	2 639	2 245	1 905	-394	-340	-1.6	-1.6	274	300	352	0.9	1.6
Agricultural products	2 318	1 955	1 632	-362	-324	-1.7	-1.8	221	246	286	1.1	1.5
Forestry, fishing, hunting, and trapping	96	68	50	-28	-17	-3.4	-2.9	12	12	14	-0.4	1.7
Logging	120	98	90	-23	-7	-2.1	-0.8	29	31	36	0.8	1.4
Support activities for agriculture and forestry	105	124	133	19	9	1.6	0.7	11	11	16	-0.3	3.4
Nonagriculture Self-Employed and Unpaid Family Workers[4]	9 009	9 018	9 162	10	144	0.0	0.2	...	...	...	...	...
Secondary Wage and Salary Jobs in Agriculture Production, Forestry, Fishing, and Private Household Industries[5]	178	143	128	-35	-15	-2.2	-1.1	...	...	...	...	...
Secondary Jobs as a Self-Employed or Unpaid Family Worker[6]	1 973	1 545	1 434	-428	-111	-2.4	-0.7	...	...	...	...	...

n.e.c. = not elsewhere classified.

[3]Includes agriculture, forestry, fishing, and hunting data from the Current Population Survey, except logging, which is from the Current Employment Survey and government wage and salary workers, which are excluded.
[4]Comparable estimate of output growth is not available.
[5]Workers who hold a secondary wage and salary job in agricultural production, forestry, fishing, and private household industries.
[6]Wage and salary workers who hold a secondary wage and salary job as a self-employed or unpaid family worker.
... = Not available.

Table 4-6. Employment by Occupation, 2002 and Projected 2012

(Thousands of jobs, percent.)

Occupation	Employment				Change 2002–2012		Total job openings due to growth and replacement 2002–2012 [1]
	Number		Percent distribution		Number	Percent	
	2002	2012	2002	2012			
TOTAL, ALL OCCUPATIONS	144 014	165 319	100.0	100.0	21 305	14.8	56 305
Management, Business, and Financial Occupations	15 501	17 883	10.8	10.8	2 382	15.4	5 319
Management occupations	10 056	11 277	7.0	6.8	1 221	12.1	3 192
Top executives	2 669	3 138	1.9	1.9	469	17.6	969
Chief executives	553	645	0.4	0.4	93	16.7	197
General and operations managers	2 049	2 425	1.4	1.5	376	18.4	762
Legislators	67	68	0.0	0.0	1	1.1	9
Advertising, marketing, promotions, public relations, and sales managers	700	885	0.5	0.5	185	26.5	313
Advertising and promotions managers	85	107	0.1	0.1	21	25.0	37
Marketing and sales managers	546	693	0.4	0.4	148	27.1	249
Marketing managers	203	246	0.1	0.1	43	21.3	81
Sales managers	343	448	0.2	0.3	105	30.5	168
Public relations managers	69	85	0.0	0.1	16	23.4	28
Operations specialties managers	1 807	2 163	1.3	1.3	356	19.7	671
Administrative services managers	321	384	0.2	0.2	63	19.8	126
Computer and information systems managers	284	387	0.2	0.2	103	36.1	154
Financial managers	599	709	0.4	0.4	109	18.3	195
Human resources managers	202	242	0.1	0.1	39	19.4	73
Industrial production managers	182	197	0.1	0.1	14	7.9	50
Purchasing managers	108	113	0.1	0.1	5	4.8	29
Transportation, storage, and distribution managers	111	133	0.1	0.1	22	19.7	44
Other management occupations	4 880	5 090	3.4	3.1	210	4.3	1 240
Agricultural managers	1 376	1 149	1.0	0.7	-227	-16.5	117
Farm, ranch, and other agricultural managers	218	229	0.2	0.1	11	5.1	49
Farmers and ranchers	1 158	920	0.8	0.6	-238	-20.6	68
Construction managers	389	435	0.3	0.3	47	12.0	117
Education administrators	427	527	0.3	0.3	101	23.6	207
Education administrators, preschool and child care center/program	58	77	0.0	0.0	19	32.0	33
Education administrators, elementary and secondary school	217	262	0.2	0.2	45	20.7	99
Education administrators, postsecondary	125	157	0.1	0.1	32	25.9	63
Education administrators, all other	27	32	0.0	0.0	5	19.1	12
Engineering managers	212	231	0.1	0.1	20	9.2	62
Food service managers	386	430	0.3	0.3	44	11.5	107
Funeral directors	24	26	0.0	0.0	2	6.6	9
Gaming managers	6	7	0.0	0.0	1	12.4	2
Lodging managers	69	73	0.0	0.0	5	6.6	16
Medical and health services managers	244	315	0.2	0.2	71	29.3	119
Natural sciences managers	45	51	0.0	0.0	5	11.3	14
Postmasters and mail superintendents	25	25	0.0	0.0	0	-0.5	5
Property, real estate, and community association managers	293	330	0.2	0.2	37	12.8	92
Social and community service managers	129	164	0.1	0.1	36	27.7	60
All other managers	1 256	1 325	0.9	0.8	69	5.5	314
Business and Financial Operations Occupations	5 445	6 606	3.8	4.0	1 162	21.3	2 127
Business operations specialists	3 177	3 910	2.2	2.4	733	23.1	1 295
Agents and business managers of artists, performers, and athletes	15	19	0.0	0.0	4	27.8	7
Buyers and purchasing agents	419	455	0.3	0.3	36	8.6	144
Purchasing agents and buyers, farm products	19	21	0.0	0.0	2	10.2	8
Wholesale and retail buyers, except farm products	155	162	0.1	0.1	7	4.3	47
Purchasing agents, except wholesale, retail, and farm products	245	273	0.2	0.2	27	11.2	88
Claims adjusters, appraisers, examiners, and investigators	241	275	0.2	0.2	34	14.0	64
Claims adjusters, examiners, and investigators	227	260	0.2	0.2	32	14.2	60
Insurance appraisers, auto damage	14	16	0.0	0.0	2	11.7	3
Compliance officers, except agriculture, construction, health and safety, and transportation	158	173	0.1	0.1	15	9.8	52
Cost estimators	188	223	0.1	0.1	35	18.6	77
Emergency management specialists	11	14	0.0	0.0	3	28.2	6
Human resources, training, and labor relations specialists [2]	474	606	0.3	0.4	131	27.7	204
Employment, recruitment, and placement specialists	175	223	0.1	0.1	48	27.3	75
Compensation, benefits, and job analysis specialists	91	116	0.1	0.1	25	28.0	39
Training and development specialists	209	267	0.1	0.2	58	27.9	90
Management analysts	577	753	0.4	0.5	176	30.4	255
Meeting and convention planners	37	45	0.0	0.0	8	21.3	16
All other business operations specialists [3]	1 056	1 346	0.7	0.8	290	27.5	470
Financial specialists	2 268	2 696	1.6	1.6	429	18.9	832
Accountants and auditors	1 055	1 261	0.7	0.8	205	19.5	405
Appraisers and assessors of real estate	88	104	0.1	0.1	16	17.6	34
Budget analysts	62	71	0.0	0.0	9	14.0	19
Credit analysts	66	78	0.0	0.0	12	18.7	23
Financial analysts and advisors	400	486	0.3	0.3	86	21.5	146
Financial analysts	172	204	0.1	0.1	32	18.7	58
Personal financial advisors	126	170	0.1	0.1	44	34.6	60
Insurance underwriters	102	112	0.1	0.1	10	10.0	28
Financial examiners	25	27	0.0	0.0	2	8.9	8
Loan counselors and officers	255	302	0.2	0.2	48	18.7	89
Loan counselors	31	37	0.0	0.0	6	17.8	11
Loan officers	223	266	0.2	0.2	42	18.8	78
Tax examiners, collectors, preparers, and revenue agents	154	176	0.1	0.1	22	14.4	52
Tax examiners, collectors, and revenue agents	75	79	0.1	0.0	4	5.0	21
Tax preparers	79	98	0.1	0.1	18	23.2	32
All other financial specialists	162	190	0.1	0.1	28	17.6	57

[1]Total job openings represent the sum of employment increases and net replacements. If employment change is negative, job openings due to growth are zero and total job openings equal net replacements.
[2]Information about the detailed residual occupation for this broad occupation is not included.
[3]This occupation contains two or more detailed SOC occupations.
0.0 = Quantity equals more than zero but less than 0.05.

Table 4-6. Employment by Occupation, 2002 and Projected 2012—*Continued*

(Thousands of jobs, percent.)

Occupation	Employment				Change 2002–2012		Total job openings due to growth and replacement 2002–2012 [1]
	Number		Percent distribution		Number	Percent	
	2002	2012	2002	2012			
Professional and Related Occupations	27 687	34 147	19.2	20.7	6 459	23.3	11 794
Computer and Mathematical Science Occupations	3 018	4 069	2.1	2.5	1 051	34.8	1 465
Computer specialists	2 911	3 954	2.0	2.4	1 043	35.8	1 429
Computer and information scientists, research	23	30	0.0	0.0	7	29.9	10
Computer programmers	499	571	0.3	0.3	73	14.6	190
Computer software engineers	675	982	0.5	0.6	307	45.5	374
Computer software engineers, applications	394	573	0.3	0.3	179	45.5	218
Computer software engineers, systems software	281	409	0.2	0.2	128	45.5	156
Computer support specialists	507	660	0.4	0.4	153	30.3	216
Computer systems analysts	468	653	0.3	0.4	184	39.4	237
Database administrators	110	159	0.1	0.1	49	44.2	60
Network and computer systems administrators	251	345	0.2	0.2	94	37.4	122
Network systems and data communications analysts	186	292	0.1	0.2	106	57.0	128
All other computer specialists	192	262	0.1	0.2	70	36.5	92
Mathematical science occupations	107	115	0.1	0.1	8	7.4	36
Actuaries	15	18	0.0	0.0	2	14.9	9
Mathematicians	3	3	0.0	0.0	0	-1.0	1
Operations research analysts	62	66	0.0	0.0	4	6.2	17
Statisticians	20	21	0.0	0.0	1	4.8	6
Miscellaneous mathematical science occupations	7	8	0.0	0.0	1	11.8	2
Architecture and Engineering Occupations	2 587	2 809	1.8	1.7	222	8.6	802
Architects, surveyors, and cartographers	204	233	0.1	0.1	29	14.1	67
Architects, except naval	136	161	0.1	0.1	25	18.1	40
Architects, except landscape and naval	113	133	0.1	0.1	20	17.3	32
Landscape architects	23	28	0.0	0.0	5	22.2	8
Surveyors, cartographers, and photogrammetrists	64	68	0.0	0.0	4	5.6	26
Cartographers and photogrammetrists	9	10	0.0	0.0	1	15.1	4
Surveyors	56	58	0.0	0.0	2	4.2	21
All other architects, surveyors, and cartographers [4]	3	4	0.0	0.0	0	10.9	1
Engineers	1 478	1 587	1.0	1.0	109	7.3	431
Aerospace engineers	78	74	0.1	0.0	-4	-5.2	19
Agricultural engineers	3	3	0.0	0.0	0	10.3	1
Biomedical engineers	8	10	0.0	0.0	2	26.1	3
Chemical engineers	33	33	0.0	0.0	0	0.4	10
Civil engineers	228	246	0.2	0.1	18	8.0	55
Computer hardware engineers	74	78	0.1	0.0	5	6.1	17
Electrical and electronics engineers	292	309	0.2	0.2	17	5.7	74
Electrical engineers	156	160	0.1	0.1	4	2.5	34
Electronics engineers, except computer	136	149	0.1	0.1	13	9.4	40
Environmental engineers	47	65	0.0	0.0	18	38.2	26
Industrial engineers, including health and safety	194	213	0.1	0.1	20	10.1	67
Health and safety engineers, except mining safety engineers and inspectors	36	38	0.0	0.0	3	7.9	11
Industrial engineers	158	175	0.1	0.1	17	10.6	55
Marine engineers and naval architects	5	5	0.0	0.0	0	-5.0	2
Materials engineers	24	25	0.0	0.0	1	4.1	7
Mechanical engineers	215	225	0.1	0.1	10	4.8	69
Mining and geological engineers, including mining safety engineers	5	5	0.0	0.0	0	-2.7	2
Nuclear engineers	16	16	0.0	0.0	0	-0.1	5
Petroleum engineers	14	12	0.0	0.0	-1	-9.8	4
All other engineers	243	267	0.2	0.2	24	9.7	70
Drafters, engineering, and mapping technicians	905	990	0.6	0.6	85	9.4	304
Drafters [2]	216	222	0.2	0.1	6	2.8	67
Architectural and civil drafters	106	110	0.1	0.1	4	4.2	34
Electrical and electronics drafters	38	38	0.0	0.0	0	0.7	11
Mechanical drafters	72	74	0.1	0.0	1	1.9	22
Engineering technicians, except drafters [2]	478	526	0.3	0.3	48	10.1	148
Aerospace engineering and operations technicians	15	15	0.0	0.0	0	1.5	3
Civil engineering technicians	92	99	0.1	0.1	7	7.6	26
Electrical and electronic engineering technicians	204	224	0.1	0.1	20	10.0	63
Electro-mechanical technicians	31	35	0.0	0.0	4	11.5	10
Environmental engineering technicians	19	24	0.0	0.0	5	28.4	9
Industrial engineering technicians	62	67	0.0	0.0	5	8.7	18
Mechanical engineering technicians	55	61	0.0	0.0	6	11.0	18
Surveying and mapping technicians	60	74	0.0	0.0	14	23.1	36
All other drafters, engineering, and mapping technicians [4]	150	167	0.1	0.1	17	11.3	53
Life, Physical, and Social Science Occupations	1 237	1 450	0.9	0.9	212	17.2	511
Life scientists	214	253	0.1	0.2	39	18.2	91
Agricultural and food scientists	18	20	0.0	0.0	2	9.1	5
Biological scientists	75	90	0.1	0.1	14	19.0	38
Biochemists and biophysicists	17	21	0.0	0.0	4	22.9	9
Microbiologists	16	20	0.0	0.0	3	20.0	8
Zoologists and wildlife biologists	15	16	0.0	0.0	1	7.7	6
Biological scientists, all other	27	33	0.0	0.0	6	22.3	15
Conservation scientists and foresters	33	34	0.0	0.0	1	4.4	11
Conservation scientists	19	20	0.0	0.0	1	4.1	6
Foresters	14	14	0.0	0.0	1	4.7	5
Medical scientists	62	79	0.0	0.0	17	27.3	28
Epidemiologists	4	5	0.0	0.0	1	32.5	2

[1]Total job openings represent the sum of employment increases and net replacements. If employment change is negative, job openings due to growth are zero and total job openings equal net replacements.
[2]Information about the detailed residual occupation for this broad occupation is not included.
[4]This occupation was created by the OES survey. There is no SIC equivalent.
0.0 = Quantity equals more than zero but less than 0.05.

Table 4-6. Employment by Occupation, 2002 and Projected 2012—*Continued*

(Thousands of jobs, percent.)

Occupation	Employment Number 2002	Employment Number 2012	Percent distribution 2002	Percent distribution 2012	Change 2002–2012 Number	Change 2002–2012 Percent	Total job openings due to growth and replacement 2002–2012 [1]
Medical scientists, except epidemiologists	58	73	0.0	0.0	16	26.9	26
All other life scientists	26	31	0.0	0.0	5	18.3	9
Physical scientists	251	287	0.2	0.2	36	14.4	100
Astronomers and physicists	14	15	0.0	0.0	1	6.8	6
Astronomers	1	1	0.0	0.0	0	4.9	0
Physicists	13	14	0.0	0.0	1	6.9	5
Atmospheric and space scientists	8	9	0.0	0.0	1	16.2	4
Chemists and materials scientists	91	103	0.1	0.1	11	12.4	41
Chemists	84	95	0.1	0.1	11	12.7	38
Materials scientists	7	8	0.0	0.0	1	8.5	3
Environmental scientists and geoscientists	101	121	0.1	0.1	20	20.1	38
Environmental scientists and specialists, including health	65	80	0.0	0.0	15	23.7	27
Geoscientists, except hydrologists and geographers	28	31	0.0	0.0	3	11.5	8
Hydrologists	8	10	0.0	0.0	2	21.0	3
All other physical scientists	37	39	0.0	0.0	2	6.5	11
Social scientists and related occupations	426	512	0.3	0.3	86	20.1	190
Economists	16	18	0.0	0.0	2	13.4	7
Market and survey researchers	155	193	0.1	0.1	38	24.7	78
Market research analysts	134	166	0.1	0.1	31	23.4	66
Survey researchers	20	27	0.0	0.0	7	33.6	12
Psychologists [5]	139	173	0.1	0.1	34	24.3	64
Clinical, counseling, and school psychologists	137	171	0.1	0.1	34	24.4	63
Industrial-organizational psychologists	2	2	0.0	0.0	0	16.0	1
Sociologists	3	3	0.0	0.0	0	13.4	1
Urban and regional planners	32	36	0.0	0.0	3	10.7	14
Miscellaneous social scientists and related workers [5]	14	15	0.0	0.0	1	9.2	4
Anthropologists and archaeologists	5	5	0.0	0.0	1	12.8	2
Geographers	1	1	0.0	0.0	0	19.5	0
Historians	2	2	0.0	0.0	0	6.6	1
Political scientists	6	6	0.0	0.0	0	5.9	2
All other social scientists and related workers [3]	68	74	0.0	0.0	7	9.7	21
Life, physical, and social science technicians	346	397	0.2	0.2	51	14.8	130
Agricultural and food science technicians	20	22	0.0	0.0	2	9.3	6
Biological technicians	48	57	0.0	0.0	9	19.4	17
Chemical technicians	69	72	0.0	0.0	3	4.7	20
Geological and petroleum technicians	11	11	0.0	0.0	0	1.3	3
Nuclear technicians	6	6	0.0	0.0	0	1.5	2
Other life, physical, and social science technicians [5]	55	67	0.0	0.0	12	22.8	25
Environmental science and protection technicians, including health	28	38	0.0	0.0	10	36.8	17
Forensic science technicians	8	10	0.0	0.0	2	18.9	4
Forest and conservation technicians	19	20	0.0	0.0	1	4.0	5
All other life, physical, and social science technicians [3]	137	161	0.1	0.1	24	17.5	56
Community and Social Services Occupations	2 190	2 764	1.5	1.7	574	26.2	992
Counselors, social workers, and other community and social service specialists [2]	1 436	1 853	1.0	1.1	417	29.0	695
Counselors [2]	526	645	0.4	0.4	119	22.6	239
Substance abuse and behavioral disorder counselors	67	83	0.0	0.1	16	23.3	31
Educational, vocational, and school counselors	228	262	0.2	0.2	34	15.0	86
Marriage and family therapists	23	29	0.0	0.0	5	22.4	11
Mental health counselors	85	107	0.1	0.1	23	26.7	42
Rehabilitation counselors	122	164	0.1	0.1	41	33.8	69
Social workers [2]	477	604	0.3	0.4	127	26.7	209
Child, family, and school social workers	274	338	0.2	0.2	64	23.2	111
Medical and public health social workers	107	138	0.1	0.1	31	28.6	49
Mental health and substance abuse social workers	95	128	0.1	0.1	33	34.5	49
Miscellaneous community and social service specialists [2]	434	605	0.3	0.4	171	39.4	247
Health educators	45	54	0.0	0.0	10	21.9	18
Probation officers and correctional treatment specialists	84	97	0.1	0.1	12	14.7	27
Social and human service assistants	305	454	0.2	0.3	149	48.7	202
Religious workers [2]	506	593	0.4	0.4	87	17.3	181
Clergy	400	463	0.3	0.3	62	15.5	144
Directors, religious activities and education	105	131	0.1	0.1	25	24.1	37
All other counselors, social, and religious workers [4]	248	318	0.2	0.2	70	28.3	116
Legal Occupations	1 168	1 357	0.8	0.8	190	16.2	327
Lawyers, judges, and related workers	747	869	0.5	0.5	122	16.4	218
Lawyers	695	813	0.5	0.5	118	17.0	207
Judges, magistrates, and other judicial workers	51	56	0.0	0.0	4	8.3	11
Administrative law judges, adjudicators, and hearing officers	19	20	0.0	0.0	1	5.8	3
Arbitrators, mediators, and conciliators	6	7	0.0	0.0	1	13.7	2
Judges, magistrate judges, and magistrates	27	29	0.0	0.0	2	8.7	6
Legal support workers	320	380	0.2	0.2	60	18.7	91
Paralegals and legal assistants	200	257	0.1	0.2	57	28.7	73
Miscellaneous legal support workers [2]	121	123	0.1	0.1	3	2.1	17
Court reporters	18	20	0.0	0.0	2	12.7	4
Law clerks	48	50	0.0	0.0	2	3.7	7
Title examiners, abstractors, and searchers	55	53	0.0	0.0	-1	-2.7	6
All other legal and related workers [4]	101	109	0.1	0.1	8	7.6	19

[1]Total job openings represent the sum of employment increases and net replacements. If employment change is negative, job openings due to growth are zero and total job openings equal net replacements.
[2]Information about the detailed residual occupation for this broad occupation is not included.
[3]This occupation contains two or more detailed SOC occupations.
[4]This occupation was created by the OES survey. There is no SIC equivalent.
[5]This minor occupation group contains a detailed occupation from another minor occupation group.
0.0 = Quantity equals more than zero but less than 0.05.

Table 4-6. Employment by Occupation, 2002 and Projected 2012—*Continued*

(Thousands of jobs, percent.)

Occupation	Employment				Change 2002–2012		Total job openings due to growth and replacement 2002–2012 [1]
	Number		Percent distribution		Number	Percent	
	2002	2012	2002	2012			
Education, Training, and Library Occupations	8 530	10 639	5.9	6.4	2 109	24.7	3 890
Postsecondary teachers	1 581	2 184	1.1	1.3	603	38.1	960
Primary, secondary, and special education teachers	4 187	4 983	2.9	3.0	795	19.0	1 733
Preschool and kindergarten teachers	592	791	0.4	0.5	199	33.6	270
Preschool teachers, except special education	424	577	0.3	0.3	153	36.2	204
Kindergarten teachers, except special education	168	214	0.1	0.1	46	27.2	66
Elementary and middle school teachers	2 070	2 347	1.4	1.4	277	13.4	734
Elementary school teachers, except special education	1 467	1 690	1.0	1.0	223	15.2	547
Middle school teachers, except special and vocational education	585	637	0.4	0.4	52	9.0	182
Vocational education teachers, middle school	18	19	0.0	0.0	2	9.0	5
Secondary school teachers	1 093	1 282	0.8	0.8	189	17.3	497
Secondary school teachers, except special and vocational education	988	1 167	0.7	0.7	180	18.2	458
Vocational education teachers, secondary school	105	115	0.1	0.1	10	9.0	39
Special education teachers	433	563	0.3	0.3	130	30.0	233
Other teachers and instructors	960	1 285	0.7	0.8	325	33.9	444
Adult literacy, remedial education, and GED teachers and instructors	80	96	0.1	0.1	16	20.4	26
Self-enrichment education teachers	200	281	0.1	0.2	80	40.1	105
All other teachers, primary, secondary, and adult [4]	679	908	0.5	0.5	229	33.7	312
Librarians, curators, and archivists	309	349	0.2	0.2	41	13.2	129
Archivists, curators, and museum technicians	22	26	0.0	0.0	4	17.0	9
Librarians	167	184	0.1	0.1	17	10.1	57
Library technicians	119	139	0.1	0.1	20	16.8	64
Other education, training, and library occupations	1 493	1 838	1.0	1.1	345	23.1	624
Audio-visual collections specialists	10	11	0.0	0.0	2	16.3	3
Farm and home management advisors	16	17	0.0	0.0	1	6.9	3
Instructional coordinators	98	123	0.1	0.1	25	25.4	40
Teacher assistants	1 277	1 571	0.9	1.0	294	23.0	541
All other library, museum, training, and other education workers [4]	93	116	0.1	0.1	23	24.6	37
Arts, Design, Entertainment, Sports, and Media Occupations	2 377	2 769	1.7	1.7	393	16.5	847
Art and design occupations	775	900	0.5	0.5	125	16.1	245
Artists and related workers	149	170	0.1	0.1	21	14.4	54
Art directors	51	56	0.0	0.0	6	11.4	17
Fine artists, including painters, sculptors, and illustrators	23	27	0.0	0.0	4	16.5	9
Multi-media artists and animators	75	87	0.1	0.1	12	15.8	28
Designers	532	625	0.4	0.4	93	17.4	164
Commercial and industrial designers	52	59	0.0	0.0	8	14.7	15
Fashion designers	15	16	0.0	0.0	2	10.6	4
Floral designers	104	117	0.1	0.1	13	12.4	27
Graphic designers	212	258	0.1	0.2	46	21.9	75
Interior designers	60	73	0.0	0.0	13	21.7	21
Merchandise displayers and window trimmers	77	86	0.1	0.1	9	11.3	19
Set and exhibit designers	12	15	0.0	0.0	3	20.9	4
All other art and design workers [3]	95	106	0.1	0.1	11	11.5	28
Entertainers and Performers, Sports and Related Occupations	606	709	0.4	0.4	103	17.0	228
Actors, producers, and directors	139	164	0.1	0.1	25	18.0	44
Actors	63	74	0.0	0.0	11	17.7	19
Producers and directors	76	90	0.1	0.1	14	18.3	25
Athletes, coaches, umpires, and related workers	158	187	0.1	0.1	29	18.3	59
Athletes and sports competitors	15	18	0.0	0.0	3	19.2	6
Coaches and scouts	130	153	0.1	0.1	24	18.3	49
Umpires, referees, and other sports officials	14	16	0.0	0.0	2	16.9	5
Dancers and choreographers	37	42	0.0	0.0	5	13.3	28
Dancers	20	22	0.0	0.0	2	11.1	15
Choreographers	17	20	0.0	0.0	3	15.8	13
Musicians, singers, and related workers	215	250	0.1	0.2	35	16.2	80
Music directors and composers	54	62	0.0	0.0	7	13.5	19
Musicians and singers	161	189	0.1	0.1	27	17.1	61
All other entertainers and performers, sports and related workers	56	65	0.0	0.0	9	16.4	16
Media and communication occupations	700	815	0.5	0.5	115	16.4	260
Announcers	76	68	0.1	0.0	-8	-10.1	19
News analysts, reporters and correspondents	66	70	0.0	0.0	4	6.2	20
Public relations specialists	158	210	0.1	0.1	52	32.9	75
Writers and editors	319	370	0.2	0.2	51	16.0	121
Editors	130	145	0.1	0.1	15	11.8	47
Technical writers	50	63	0.0	0.0	13	27.1	28
Writers and authors	139	161	0.1	0.1	22	16.1	46
Miscellaneous media and communications workers	82	97	0.1	0.1	15	18.6	25
Interpreters and translators	24	29	0.0	0.0	5	22.1	8
All other media and communication workers	58	68	0.0	0.0	10	17.2	17
Media and communication equipment occupations	295	345	0.2	0.2	50	16.9	115
Broadcast and sound engineering technicians and radio operators	93	111	0.1	0.1	18	19.6	41
Audio and video equipment technicians	42	53	0.0	0.0	11	26.7	21
Broadcast technicians	35	39	0.0	0.0	4	11.3	13
Radio operators	3	3	0.0	0.0	0	-6.2	1
Sound engineering technicians	13	16	0.0	0.0	3	25.5	6
Photographers	130	148	0.1	0.1	18	13.6	44
Television, video, and motion picture camera operators and editors	48	56	0.0	0.0	9	18.7	19
Camera operators, television, video, and motion picture	28	32	0.0	0.0	4	13.4	10
Film and video editors	19	25	0.0	0.0	5	26.4	9
All other media and communication equipment workers	24	29	0.0	0.0	5	20.1	10

[1]Total job openings represent the sum of employment increases and net replacements. If employment change is negative, job openings due to growth are zero and total job openings equal net replacements.
[3]This occupation contains two or more detailed SOC occupations.
[4]This occupation was created by the OES survey. There is no SIC equivalent.
0.0 = Quantity equals more than zero but less than 0.05.

Table 4-6. Employment by Occupation, 2002 and Projected 2012—*Continued*

(Thousands of jobs, percent.)

Occupation	Employment				Change 2002–2012		Total job openings due to growth and replacement 2002–2012 [1]
	Number		Percent distribution		Number	Percent	
	2002	2012	2002	2012			
Health Care Practitioners and Technical Occupations	6 580	8 288	4.6	5.0	1 708	26.0	2 959
Health diagnosing and treating practitioners	4 071	5 125	2.8	3.1	1 054	25.9	1 849
Chiropractors	49	60	0.0	0.0	11	23.3	21
Dentists	153	159	0.1	0.1	6	4.1	32
Dietitians and nutritionists	49	58	0.0	0.0	9	17.8	21
Optometrists	32	38	0.0	0.0	5	17.1	14
Pharmacists	230	299	0.2	0.2	69	30.1	114
Physicians and surgeons	583	697	0.4	0.4	114	19.5	191
Physician assistants	63	94	0.0	0.1	31	48.9	40
Podiatrists	13	15	0.0	0.0	2	15.0	5
Registered nurses	2 284	2 908	1.6	1.8	623	27.3	1 101
Therapists [2]	450	592	0.3	0.4	142	31.7	231
Audiologists	11	14	0.0	0.0	3	29.0	6
Occupational therapists	82	110	0.1	0.1	29	35.2	40
Physical therapists	137	185	0.1	0.1	48	35.3	62
Radiation therapists	14	18	0.0	0.0	4	31.6	7
Recreational therapists	27	29	0.0	0.0	2	9.1	9
Respiratory therapists	86	116	0.1	0.1	30	34.8	58
Speech-language pathologists	94	120	0.1	0.1	26	27.2	49
Veterinarians	58	72	0.0	0.0	14	25.1	28
All other health diagnosing and treating practitioners [3]	107	134	0.1	0.1	26	24.5	50
Health technologists and technicians [2]	2 263	2 857	1.6	1.7	593	26.2	1 002
Clinical laboratory technologists and technicians	297	355	0.2	0.2	58	19.4	138
Medical and clinical laboratory technologists	150	179	0.1	0.1	29	19.3	69
Medical and clinical laboratory technicians	147	176	0.1	0.1	29	19.4	68
Dental hygienists	148	212	0.1	0.1	64	43.1	76
Diagnostic related technologists and technicians	271	338	0.2	0.2	67	24.8	118
Cardiovascular technologists and technicians	43	58	0.0	0.0	15	33.5	23
Diagnostic medical sonographers	37	45	0.0	0.0	9	24.0	16
Nuclear medicine technologists	17	21	0.0	0.0	4	23.6	7
Radiologic technologists and technicians	174	214	0.1	0.1	40	22.9	72
Emergency medical technicians and paramedics	179	238	0.1	0.1	59	33.1	80
Health diagnosing and treating practitioner support technicians	451	574	0.3	0.3	123	27.2	181
Dietetic technicians	29	35	0.0	0.0	6	20.2	10
Pharmacy technicians	211	271	0.1	0.2	61	28.8	88
Psychiatric technicians	60	63	0.0	0.0	4	5.9	11
Respiratory therapy technicians	26	35	0.0	0.0	9	34.2	12
Surgical technologists	72	92	0.1	0.1	20	27.9	30
Veterinary technologists and technicians	53	76	0.0	0.0	23	44.1	30
Licensed practical and licensed vocational nurses	702	844	0.5	0.5	142	20.2	295
Medical records and health information technicians	147	216	0.1	0.1	69	46.8	90
Opticians, dispensing	63	75	0.0	0.0	11	18.2	23
Miscellaneous health technologists and technicians [2]	5	6	0.0	0.0	1	18.9	2
Orthotists and prosthetists	5	6	0.0	0.0	1	18.9	2
Other health care practitioners and technical occupations [2]	56	65	0.0	0.0	10	17.4	22
Occupational health and safety specialists and technicians	41	47	0.0	0.0	5	13.2	14
Miscellaneous health practitioners and technical workers [2]	14	19	0.0	0.0	4	29.9	7
Athletic trainers	14	19	0.0	0.0	4	29.9	7
All other health practitioners and technical workers [3]	190	241	0.1	0.1	52	27.2	86
Service Occupations	26 569	31 905	18.4	19.3	5 336	20.1	12 962
Health Care Support Occupations	3 310	4 452	2.3	2.7	1 143	34.5	1 669
Nursing, psychiatric, and home health aides	2 014	2 645	1.4	1.6	630	31.3	894
Home health aides	580	859	0.4	0.5	279	48.1	355
Nursing aides, orderlies, and attendants	1 375	1 718	1.0	1.0	343	24.9	523
Psychiatric aides	59	68	0.0	0.0	9	14.5	16
Occupational and physical therapist assistants and aides	114	164	0.1	0.1	50	44.2	68
Occupational therapist assistants and aides	27	38	0.0	0.0	11	40.2	14
Occupational therapist assistants	18	26	0.0	0.0	7	39.2	10
Occupational therapist aides	8	12	0.0	0.0	4	42.6	5
Physical therapist assistants and aides	87	127	0.1	0.1	40	45.4	54
Physical therapist assistants	50	73	0.0	0.0	22	44.6	31
Physical therapist aides	37	54	0.0	0.0	17	46.4	23
Other health care support occupations	1 182	1 644	0.8	1.0	462	39.1	706
Massage therapists	92	117	0.1	0.1	25	27.1	43
Miscellaneous health care support occupations	1 090	1 527	0.8	0.9	437	40.1	664
Dental assistants	266	379	0.2	0.2	113	42.5	187
Medical assistants	365	579	0.3	0.4	215	58.9	282
Medical equipment preparers	36	43	0.0	0.0	7	18.1	13
Medical transcriptionists	101	124	0.1	0.1	23	22.6	41
Pharmacy aides	60	71	0.0	0.0	11	17.6	22
Veterinary assistants and laboratory animal caretakers	63	79	0.0	0.0	16	26.2	28
All other health care support workers	198	251	0.1	0.2	53	26.6	89

[1]Total job openings represent the sum of employment increases and net replacements. If employment change is negative, job openings due to growth are zero and total job openings equal net replacements.
[2]Information about the detailed residual occupation for this broad occupation is not included.
[3]This occupation contains two or more detailed SOC occupations.
0.0 = Quantity equals more than zero but less than 0.05.

Table 4-6. Employment by Occupation, 2002 and Projected 2012—*Continued*

(Thousands of jobs, percent.)

Occupation	Employment				Change 2002–2012		Total job openings due to growth and replacement 2002–2012 [1]
	Number		Percent distribution		Number	Percent	
	2002	2012	2002	2012			
Protective Service Occupations	3 116	3 885	2.2	2.4	769	24.7	1 649
First-line supervisors/managers, protective service workers	266	315	0.2	0.2	49	18.3	136
First-line supervisors/managers, law enforcement workers	147	171	0.1	0.1	24	16.1	71
First-line supervisors/managers of correctional officers	33	40	0.0	0.0	6	19.0	16
First-line supervisors/managers of police and detectives	114	131	0.1	0.1	17	15.3	55
First-line supervisors/managers of firefighting and prevention workers	63	74	0.0	0.0	12	18.7	37
All other first-line supervisors/managers, protective service workers	56	70	0.0	0.0	13	23.9	28
Firefighting and prevention workers	296	356	0.2	0.2	60	20.3	146
Firefighters	282	340	0.2	0.2	58	20.7	140
Fire inspectors	14	16	0.0	0.0	2	11.6	6
Law enforcement workers	1 179	1 460	0.8	0.9	281	23.9	563
Bailiffs, correctional officers, and jailers	442	547	0.3	0.3	105	23.7	197
Bailiffs	15	16	0.0	0.0	1	9.5	5
Correctional officers and jailers	427	531	0.3	0.3	103	24.2	192
Detectives and criminal investigators	94	115	0.1	0.1	21	22.4	46
Fish and game wardens	8	8	0.0	0.0	1	7.1	2
Parking enforcement workers	11	12	0.0	0.0	1	11.5	3
Police officers	625	779	0.4	0.5	154	24.6	315
Police and sheriff's patrol officers	619	772	0.4	0.5	153	24.7	313
Transit and railroad police	6	7	0.0	0.0	1	15.9	2
Other protective service workers	1 374	1 753	1.0	1.1	379	27.6	804
Animal control workers	11	12	0.0	0.0	1	12.6	9
Private detectives and investigators	48	60	0.0	0.0	12	25.3	22
Security guards and gaming surveillance officers	1 004	1 324	0.7	0.8	319	31.8	538
Gaming surveillance officers and gaming investigators	9	11	0.0	0.0	2	24.6	4
Security guards	995	1 313	0.7	0.8	317	31.9	534
Crossing guards	74	86	0.1	0.1	12	16.5	36
All other protective service workers [3]	237	271	0.2	0.2	34	14.3	199
Food Preparation and Serving Related Occupations	10 200	11 807	7.1	7.1	1 607	15.8	5 659
Supervisors, food preparation and serving workers	824	952	0.6	0.6	128	15.6	332
Chefs and head cooks	132	153	0.1	0.1	21	15.8	60
First-line supervisors/managers of food preparation and serving workers	692	800	0.5	0.5	107	15.5	272
Cooks and food preparation workers [2]	2 836	3 182	2.0	1.9	346	12.2	1 262
Cooks [2]	1 986	2 160	1.4	1.3	174	8.8	789
Cooks, fast food	588	617	0.4	0.4	29	4.9	211
Cooks, institution and cafeteria	436	445	0.3	0.3	9	2.1	144
Cooks, private household	8	8	0.0	0.0	0	-5.4	3
Cooks, restaurant	727	843	0.5	0.5	116	15.9	341
Cooks, short order	227	247	0.2	0.1	20	9.0	91
Food preparation workers	850	1 022	0.6	0.6	172	20.2	473
Food and beverage serving workers	5 211	6 171	3.6	3.7	960	18.4	3 454
Bartenders	463	503	0.3	0.3	40	8.6	223
Fast food and counter workers	2 457	2 989	1.7	1.8	532	21.7	1 699
Combined food preparation and serving workers, including fast food	1 990	2 444	1.4	1.5	454	22.8	1 317
Counter attendants, cafeteria, food concession, and coffee shop	467	545	0.3	0.3	78	16.7	383
Waiters and waitresses	2 097	2 464	1.5	1.5	367	17.5	1 446
Food servers, nonrestaurant	195	215	0.1	0.1	20	10.4	85
Other food preparation and serving related workers [2]	1 328	1 502	0.9	0.9	173	13.0	611
Dining room and cafeteria attendants and bartender helpers	409	470	0.3	0.3	61	14.9	198
Dishwashers	505	551	0.4	0.3	46	9.0	216
Hosts and hostesses, restaurant, lounge, and coffee shop	298	347	0.2	0.2	49	16.4	143
All other food preparation and serving related workers [3]	117	134	0.1	0.1	18	15.2	54
Building and Grounds Cleaning and Maintenance Occupations	5 485	6 386	3.8	3.9	901	16.4	2 000
Supervisors, building and grounds cleaning and maintenance workers	380	449	0.3	0.3	70	18.4	138
First-line supervisors/managers of housekeeping and janitorial workers	230	267	0.2	0.2	37	16.2	92
First-line supervisors/managers of landscaping, lawn service, and groundskeeping workers	150	182	0.1	0.1	32	21.6	46
Building cleaning and pest control workers	3 820	4 381	2.7	2.7	561	14.7	1 314
Building cleaning workers [2]	3 759	4 309	2.6	2.6	550	14.6	1 294
Janitors and cleaners, except maids and housekeeping cleaners	2 267	2 681	1.6	1.6	414	18.3	844
Maids and housekeeping cleaners	1 492	1 629	1.0	1.0	137	9.2	450
Pest control workers	62	72	0.0	0.0	10	17.0	20
Grounds maintenance workers [2]	1 285	1 555	0.9	0.9	270	21.0	548
Grounds maintenance workers	1 160	1 410	0.8	0.9	250	21.5	503
Landscaping and groundskeeping workers	1 074	1 311	0.7	0.8	237	22.0	470
Pesticide handlers, sprayers, and applicators, vegetation	27	30	0.0	0.0	3	9.7	9
Tree trimmers and pruners	59	69	0.0	0.0	11	18.6	24
All other building and grounds cleaning and maintenance workers [3]	125	145	0.1	0.1	20	16.1	46
Personal Care and Service Occupations	4 458	5 375	3.1	3.3	917	20.6	1 985
Supervisors, personal care and service workers	276	305	0.2	0.2	29	10.7	96
First-line supervisors/managers of gaming workers	60	69	0.0	0.0	9	15.4	22
Gaming supervisors	39	45	0.0	0.0	6	15.7	14
Slot key persons	21	24	0.0	0.0	3	14.8	8
First-line supervisors/managers of personal service workers	216	236	0.1	0.1	20	9.4	74
Animal care and service workers	151	183	0.1	0.1	32	20.8	68
Animal trainers	26	30	0.0	0.0	4	14.3	9
Nonfarm animal caretakers	125	153	0.1	0.1	28	22.2	59

[1]Total job openings represent the sum of employment increases and net replacements. If employment change is negative, job openings due to growth are zero and total job openings equal net replacements.
[2]Information about the detailed residual occupation for this broad occupation is not included.
[3]This occupation contains two or more detailed SOC occupations.
0.0 = Quantity equals more than zero but less than 0.05.

Table 4-6. Employment by Occupation, 2002 and Projected 2012—*Continued*

(Thousands of jobs, percent.)

Occupation	Employment				Change 2002–2012		Total job openings due to growth and replacement 2002–2012 [1]
	Number		Percent distribution		Number	Percent	
	2002	2012	2002	2012			
Entertainment attendants and related workers	507	626	0.4	0.4	119	23.6	300
Gaming services workers [2]	92	115	0.1	0.1	23	24.7	52
Gaming dealers	78	97	0.1	0.1	19	24.7	44
Gaming and sports book writers and runners	14	18	0.0	0.0	3	24.4	8
Motion picture projectionists	9	9	0.0	0.0	0	0.4	5
Ushers, lobby attendants, and ticket takers	105	121	0.1	0.1	16	15.5	76
Miscellaneous entertainment attendants and related workers [2]	261	333	0.2	0.2	72	27.6	147
Amusement and recreation attendants	234	299	0.2	0.2	65	27.8	132
Costume attendants	4	5	0.0	0.0	1	25.1	2
Locker room, coatroom, and dressing room attendants	23	29	0.0	0.0	6	26.5	13
All other gaming service workers [4]	40	49	0.0	0.0	9	21.3	21
Funeral service workers	33	38	0.0	0.0	5	16.7	12
Embalmers	7	7	0.0	0.0	1	8.3	2
Funeral attendants	26	31	0.0	0.0	5	18.9	10
Personal appearance workers	754	865	0.5	0.5	111	14.7	262
Barbers and cosmetologists	651	741	0.5	0.4	90	13.8	221
Barbers	66	70	0.0	0.0	4	6.5	23
Hairdressers, hairstylists, and cosmetologists	585	671	0.4	0.4	86	14.7	199
Miscellaneous personal appearance workers	103	124	0.1	0.1	21	20.3	41
Makeup artists, theatrical and performance	2	2	0.0	0.0	0	18.2	1
Manicurists and pedicurists	51	63	0.0	0.0	12	22.7	21
Shampooers	25	29	0.0	0.0	4	16.6	9
Skin care specialists	25	30	0.0	0.0	5	19.4	10
Transportation, tourism, and lodging attendants	248	284	0.2	0.2	36	14.7	84
Baggage porters, bellhops, and concierges	75	86	0.1	0.1	11	14.6	31
Baggage porters and bellhops	58	67	0.0	0.0	8	14.4	24
Concierges	17	20	0.0	0.0	3	15.3	7
Tour and travel guides	43	47	0.0	0.0	4	9.3	15
Tour guides and escorts	36	40	0.0	0.0	4	11.0	14
Travel guides	6	6	0.0	0.0	0	-0.3	2
Transportation attendants	130	152	0.1	0.1	22	16.5	38
Flight attendants	104	121	0.1	0.1	17	15.9	30
Transportation attendants, except flight attendants and baggage porters	26	31	0.0	0.0	5	18.9	8
Other personal care and service workers	2 490	3 073	1.7	1.9	583	23.4	1 161
Child care workers	1 211	1 353	0.8	0.8	142	11.7	471
Personal and home care aides	608	854	0.4	0.5	246	40.5	343
Recreation and fitness workers	485	628	0.3	0.4	143	29.5	254
Fitness trainers and aerobics instructors	183	264	0.1	0.2	81	44.5	123
Recreation workers	302	364	0.2	0.2	62	20.5	131
Residential advisors	53	71	0.0	0.0	18	33.6	29
Personal care and service workers, all other	134	168	0.1	0.1	35	25.9	63
Sales and Related Occupations	15 260	17 231	10.6	10.4	1 971	12.9	6 904
Supervisors, sales workers	2 395	2 599	1.7	1.6	204	8.5	640
First-line supervisors/managers of retail sales workers	1 798	1 962	1.2	1.2	163	9.1	486
First-line supervisors/managers of non-retail sales workers	597	637	0.4	0.4	41	6.8	153
Retail sales workers	8 224	9 392	5.7	5.7	1 167	14.2	4 578
Cashiers	3 465	3 927	2.4	2.4	462	13.3	2 148
Cashiers, except gaming	3 432	3 886	2.4	2.4	454	13.2	2 124
Gaming change persons and booth cashiers	33	41	0.0	0.0	8	24.1	24
Counter and rental clerks and parts salespersons	683	793	0.5	0.5	109	16.0	352
Counter and rental clerks	436	550	0.3	0.3	114	26.3	281
Parts salespersons	248	243	0.2	0.1	-5	-2.0	71
Retail salespersons	4 076	4 672	2.8	2.8	596	14.6	2 077
Sales representatives, services [2]	957	1 033	0.7	0.6	76	7.9	274
Advertising sales agents	157	178	0.1	0.1	21	13.4	52
Insurance sales agents	381	413	0.3	0.3	32	8.4	123
Securities, commodities, and financial services sales agents	300	339	0.2	0.2	39	13.0	73
Travel agents	118	102	0.1	0.1	-16	-13.8	27
Sales representatives, wholesale and manufacturing	1 857	2 213	1.3	1.3	356	19.2	844
Sales representatives, wholesale and manufacturing, technical and scientific products	398	475	0.3	0.3	77	19.3	182
Sales representatives, wholesale and manufacturing, except technical and scientific products	1 459	1 738	1.0	1.1	279	19.1	662
Other sales and related workers	1 827	1 994	1.3	1.2	167	9.2	568
Models, demonstrators, and product promoters	179	210	0.1	0.1	30	16.9	70
Demonstrators and product promoters	175	204	0.1	0.1	30	17.0	68
Models	5	5	0.0	0.0	1	14.5	2
Real estate brokers and sales agents	407	427	0.3	0.3	20	4.9	101
Real estate brokers	99	101	0.1	0.1	2	2.4	22
Real estate sales agents	308	325	0.2	0.2	18	5.7	79
Sales engineers	82	98	0.1	0.1	16	19.9	41
Telemarketers	428	406	0.3	0.2	-21	-4.9	70
Door-to-door sales workers, news and street vendors, and related workers	155	137	0.1	0.1	-18	-11.8	37
All other sales and related workers [3]	577	717	0.4	0.4	140	24.3	250

[1]Total job openings represent the sum of employment increases and net replacements. If employment change is negative, job openings due to growth are zero and total job openings equal net replacements.
[2]Information about the detailed residual occupation for this broad occupation is not included.
[3]This occupation contains two or more detailed SOC occupations.
[4]This occupation was created by the OES survey. There is no SIC equivalent.
0.0 = Quantity equals more than zero but less than 0.05.

Table 4-6. Employment by Occupation, 2002 and Projected 2012—*Continued*

(Thousands of jobs, percent.)

Occupation	Employment				Change 2002–2012		Total job openings due to growth and replacement 2002–2012 [1]
	Number		Percent distribution		Number	Percent	
	2002	2012	2002	2012			
Office and Administrative Support Occupations	23 851	25 464	16.6	15.4	1 613	6.8	7 499
Supervisors, office and administrative support workers	1 459	1 555	1.0	0.9	96	6.6	409
First-line supervisors/managers of office and administrative support workers	1 459	1 555	1.0	0.9	96	6.6	409
Communications equipment operators	304	272	0.2	0.2	-32	-10.5	78
Switchboard operators, including answering service	236	236	0.2	0.1	1	0.3	61
Telephone operators	50	22	0.0	0.0	-28	-56.3	13
All other communications equipment operators	19	14	0.0	0.0	-5	-24.6	4
Financial clerks	3 726	3 987	2.6	2.4	261	7.0	1 143
Bill and account collectors	413	514	0.3	0.3	101	24.5	179
Billing and posting clerks and machine operators	507	547	0.4	0.3	40	7.9	126
Bookkeeping, accounting, and auditing clerks	1 983	2 042	1.4	1.2	59	3.0	431
Gaming cage workers	18	21	0.0	0.0	3	14.5	12
Payroll and timekeeping clerks	198	211	0.1	0.1	13	6.5	65
Procurement clerks	77	72	0.1	0.0	-5	-6.7	20
Tellers	530	580	0.4	0.4	50	9.4	311
Information and record clerks [2]	5 394	6 310	3.7	3.8	916	17.0	2 134
Brokerage clerks	78	67	0.1	0.0	-11	-14.7	10
Correspondence clerks	33	33	0.0	0.0	0	-1.4	10
Court, municipal, and license clerks	106	119	0.1	0.1	13	12.3	36
Credit authorizers, checkers, and clerks	80	74	0.1	0.0	-5	-6.7	15
Customer service representatives	1 894	2 354	1.3	1.4	460	24.3	741
Eligibility interviewers, government programs	94	83	0.1	0.1	-11	-11.6	25
File clerks	265	264	0.2	0.2	-1	-0.3	78
Hotel, motel, and resort desk clerks	178	220	0.1	0.1	42	23.9	122
Interviewers, except eligibility and loan	193	247	0.1	0.1	54	28.0	104
Library assistants, clerical	120	146	0.1	0.1	26	21.5	75
Loan interviewers and clerks	170	146	0.1	0.1	-24	-14.3	23
New accounts clerks	99	110	0.1	0.1	11	11.2	36
Order clerks	330	311	0.2	0.2	-19	-5.7	74
Human resources assistants, except payroll and timekeeping	174	207	0.1	0.1	33	19.3	71
Receptionists and information clerks	1 100	1 425	0.8	0.9	325	29.5	595
Reservation and transportation ticket agents and travel clerks	177	199	0.1	0.1	22	12.2	68
All other financial, information, and record clerks [4]	304	306	0.2	0.2	2	0.5	49
Material recording, scheduling, dispatching, and distributing occupations	4 005	4 025	2.8	2.4	20	0.5	1 306
Cargo and freight agents	59	68	0.0	0.0	9	15.5	22
Couriers and messengers	132	138	0.1	0.1	5	4.0	36
Dispatchers	262	298	0.2	0.2	36	13.8	92
Police, fire, and ambulance dispatchers	92	104	0.1	0.1	12	12.7	32
Dispatchers, except police, fire, and ambulance	170	194	0.1	0.1	24	14.4	61
Meter readers, utilities	54	46	0.0	0.0	-8	-14.1	17
Postal service workers	664	636	0.5	0.4	-28	-4.3	192
Postal service clerks	77	77	0.1	0.0	0	-0.5	20
Postal service mail carriers	334	333	0.2	0.2	-2	-0.5	105
Postal service mail sorters, processors, and processing machine operators	253	226	0.2	0.1	-26	-10.5	67
Production, planning, and expediting clerks	288	328	0.2	0.2	40	14.1	110
Shipping, receiving, and traffic clerks	803	827	0.6	0.5	24	3.0	189
Stock clerks and order fillers	1 628	1 560	1.1	0.9	-68	-4.2	602
Weighers, measurers, checkers, and samplers, recordkeeping	81	93	0.1	0.1	12	14.6	32
All other material recording, scheduling, dispatching, and distributing workers [4]	34	32	0.0	0.0	-2	-6.9	13
Secretaries and administrative assistants	4 104	4 288	2.8	2.6	184	4.5	1 026
Executive secretaries and administrative assistants	1 526	1 658	1.1	1.0	132	8.7	424
Legal secretaries	264	313	0.2	0.2	50	18.8	100
Medical secretaries	339	398	0.2	0.2	58	17.2	123
Secretaries, except legal, medical, and executive	1 975	1 918	1.4	1.2	-57	-2.9	378
Other office and administrative support workers	4 858	5 027	3.4	3.0	169	3.5	1 404
Computer operators	182	151	0.1	0.1	-30	-16.7	39
Data entry and information processing workers [2]	633	519	0.4	0.3	-114	-18.1	146
Data entry keyers	392	371	0.3	0.2	-21	-5.4	93
Word processors and typists	241	148	0.2	0.1	-93	-38.6	53
Desktop publishers	35	45	0.0	0.0	10	29.2	18
Insurance claims and policy processing clerks	266	276	0.2	0.2	10	3.6	53
Mail clerks and mail machine operators, except postal service	170	165	0.1	0.1	-5	-2.9	51
Office clerks, general	2 991	3 301	2.1	2.0	310	10.4	972
Office machine operators, except computer	96	91	0.1	0.1	-4	-4.6	24
Proofreaders and copy markers	27	26	0.0	0.0	-1	-4.8	6
Statistical assistants	23	22	0.0	0.0	-2	-7.2	4
All other secretaries, administrative assistants, and other office workers	435	431	0.3	0.3	-4	-0.9	92
Farming, Fishing, and Forestry Occupations	1 072	1 107	0.7	0.7	35	3.3	335
Supervisors, farming, fishing, and forestry workers	52	58	0.0	0.0	6	11.4	18
Agricultural workers	804	840	0.6	0.5	36	4.5	261
Agricultural inspectors	16	17	0.0	0.0	1	6.7	5
Animal breeders	9	10	0.0	0.0	1	6.1	2
Graders and sorters, agricultural products	49	52	0.0	0.0	3	6.7	16
Miscellaneous agricultural workers [2]	731	762	0.5	0.5	31	4.3	238
Agricultural equipment operators	61	65	0.0	0.0	4	7.3	22
Farmworkers and laborers, crop, nursery, and greenhouse	617	641	0.4	0.4	24	4.0	199
Farmworkers, farm and ranch animals	53	56	0.0	0.0	2	4.4	17
Fishing and hunting workers	38	28	0.0	0.0	-10	-25.5	11
Fishers and related fishing workers	36	27	0.0	0.0	-10	-26.8	10

[1]Total job openings represent the sum of employment increases and net replacements. If employment change is negative, job openings due to growth are zero and total job openings equal net replacements.
[2]Information about the detailed residual occupation for this broad occupation is not included.
[4]This occupation was created by the OES survey. There is no SIC equivalent.
0.0 = Quantity equals more than zero but less than 0.05.

Table 4-6. Employment by Occupation, 2002 and Projected 2012—*Continued*

(Thousands of jobs, percent.)

Occupation	Employment Number 2002	Employment Number 2012	Percent distribution 2002	Percent distribution 2012	Change 2002–2012 Number	Change 2002–2012 Percent	Total job openings due to growth and replacement 2002–2012 [1]
Hunters and trappers	1	2	0.0	0.0	0	6.5	1
Forest, conservation, and logging workers	81	80	0.1	0.0	-2	-1.9	16
Forest and conservation workers	14	15	0.0	0.0	1	4.5	4
Logging workers [2]	67	65	0.0	0.0	-2	-3.2	12
Fallers	14	14	0.0	0.0	0	-3.4	3
Logging equipment operators	43	41	0.0	0.0	-2	-3.7	8
Log graders and scalers	10	10	0.0	0.0	0	-1.2	2
All other farming, fishing, and forestry workers [3]	96	101	0.1	0.1	4	4.5	28
Construction and Extraction Occupations	7 292	8 388	5.1	5.1	1 096	15.0	2 548
Supervisors, construction and extraction workers	633	722	0.4	0.4	89	14.1	197
First-line supervisors/managers of construction trades and extraction workers	633	722	0.4	0.4	89	14.1	197
Construction trades and related workers	5 596	6 452	3.9	3.9	857	15.3	1 887
Boilermakers	25	25	0.0	0.0	0	1.7	9
Brickmasons, blockmasons, and stonemasons	165	188	0.1	0.1	23	14.2	48
Brickmasons and blockmasons	148	169	0.1	0.1	21	14.2	43
Stonemasons	17	19	0.0	0.0	2	14.1	5
Carpenters	1 209	1 331	0.8	0.8	122	10.1	319
Carpet, floor, and tile installers and finishers	164	191	0.1	0.1	27	16.8	53
Carpet installers	82	96	0.1	0.1	14	16.8	27
Floor layers, except carpet, wood, and hard tiles	31	35	0.0	0.0	4	13.4	9
Floor sanders and finishers	17	18	0.0	0.0	1	4.2	3
Tile and marble setters	33	42	0.0	0.0	9	26.5	14
Cement masons, concrete finishers, and terrazzo workers	188	236	0.1	0.1	48	25.7	86
Cement masons and concrete finishers	182	229	0.1	0.1	47	26.1	84
Terrazzo workers and finishers	6	7	0.0	0.0	1	15.2	2
Construction laborers	938	1 070	0.7	0.6	133	14.2	258
Construction equipment operators	416	460	0.3	0.3	45	10.7	144
Paving, surfacing, and tamping equipment operators	58	65	0.0	0.0	7	12.6	16
Pile-driver operators	5	6	0.0	0.0	0	8.2	1
Operating engineers and other construction equipment operators	353	389	0.2	0.2	37	10.4	127
Drywall installers, ceiling tile installers, and tapers	176	214	0.1	0.1	37	21.3	76
Drywall and ceiling tile installers	135	164	0.1	0.1	29	21.4	58
Tapers	41	49	0.0	0.0	8	20.8	17
Electricians	659	814	0.5	0.5	154	23.4	285
Glaziers	49	57	0.0	0.0	8	17.2	19
Insulation workers	53	62	0.0	0.0	8	15.8	25
Painters and paperhangers	468	521	0.3	0.3	53	11.4	124
Painters, construction and maintenance	448	500	0.3	0.3	52	11.6	120
Paperhangers	20	21	0.0	0.0	1	5.9	4
Pipelayers, plumbers, pipefitters, and steamfitters	550	649	0.4	0.4	99	18.0	225
Pipelayers	58	65	0.0	0.0	7	11.8	20
Plumbers, pipefitters, and steamfitters	492	584	0.3	0.4	92	18.7	205
Plasterers and stucco masons	59	67	0.0	0.0	8	13.5	19
Reinforcing iron and rebar workers	29	33	0.0	0.0	5	16.7	10
Roofers	166	197	0.1	0.1	31	18.6	70
Sheet metal workers	205	246	0.1	0.1	41	19.8	90
Structural iron and steel workers	78	90	0.1	0.1	12	15.9	28
Helpers, construction trades	431	490	0.3	0.3	59	13.7	238
Helpers, construction trades	431	490	0.3	0.3	59	13.7	238
Helpers—Brickmasons, blockmasons, stonemasons, and tile and marble setters	59	61	0.0	0.0	1	2.2	26
Helpers—Carpenters	97	111	0.1	0.1	14	14.0	54
Helpers—Electricians	99	117	0.1	0.1	18	17.9	59
Helpers—Painters, paperhangers, plasterers, and stucco masons	31	36	0.0	0.0	5	15.9	18
Helpers—Pipelayers, plumbers, pipefitters, and steamfitters	79	88	0.1	0.1	9	10.9	42
Helpers—Roofers	21	25	0.0	0.0	4	19.3	13
All other helpers, construction trades	44	53	0.0	0.0	9	19.4	27
Other construction and related workers [2]	354	408	0.2	0.2	54	15.2	123
Construction and building inspectors	84	95	0.1	0.1	12	13.8	30
Elevator installers and repairers	21	25	0.0	0.0	4	17.1	9
Fence erectors	27	31	0.0	0.0	4	13.4	8
Hazardous materials removal workers	38	54	0.0	0.0	16	43.1	26
Highway maintenance workers	154	170	0.1	0.1	16	10.4	38
Rail-track laying and maintenance equipment operators	11	9	0.0	0.0	-1	-11.5	2
Septic tank servicers and sewer pipe cleaners	18	22	0.0	0.0	4	21.2	9
Miscellaneous construction and related workers [2]	2	3	0.0	0.0	0	16.5	1
Segmental pavers	2	3	0.0	0.0	0	16.5	1
All other construction trades and related workers [4]	110	146	0.1	0.1	35	32.0	53
Extraction workers	167	169	0.1	0.1	2	1.2	51
Derrick, rotary drill, and service unit operators, oil, gas, and mining	41	41	0.0	0.0	0	0.5	12
Derrick operators, oil and gas	15	15	0.0	0.0	0	0.8	4
Rotary drill operators, oil and gas	14	14	0.0	0.0	0	1.5	4
Service unit operators, oil, gas, and mining	13	13	0.0	0.0	0	-0.8	4
Earth drillers, except oil and gas	23	25	0.0	0.0	2	7.7	7
Explosives workers, ordnance handling experts, and blasters	5	5	0.0	0.0	0	2.0	2
Mining machine operators	18	16	0.0	0.0	-2	-13.3	5
Continuous mining machine operators	8	7	0.0	0.0	-2	-18.5	2
Mine cutting and channeling machine operators	5	5	0.0	0.0	0	-7.1	1
All other mining machine operators	4	4	0.0	0.0	0	-10.8	1
Rock splitters, quarry	3	3	0.0	0.0	0	14.3	1
Roof bolters, mining	4	3	0.0	0.0	-1	-27.7	1
Roustabouts, oil and gas	32	34	0.0	0.0	2	6.4	11
Helpers—Extraction workers	29	30	0.0	0.0	1	3.9	9
Extraction workers, all other	12	12	0.0	0.0	0	-0.8	3

[1]Total job openings represent the sum of employment increases and net replacements. If employment change is negative, job openings due to growth are zero and total job openings equal net replacements.
[2]Information about the detailed residual occupation for this broad occupation is not included.
[3]This occupation contains two or more detailed SOC occupations.
[4]This occupation was created by the OES survey. There is no SIC equivalent.
0.0 = Quantity equals more than zero but less than 0.05.

Table 4-6. Employment by Occupation, 2002 and Projected 2012—*Continued*

(Thousands of jobs, percent.)

Occupation	Employment				Change 2002–2012		Total job openings due to growth and replacement 2002–2012 [1]
	Number		Percent distribution		Number	Percent	
	2002	2012	2002	2012			
Installation, Maintenance, and Repair Occupations	5 696	6 472	4.0	3.9	776	13.6	2 087
Supervisors of installation, maintenance, and repair workers	444	512	0.3	0.3	68	15.4	180
First-line supervisors/managers of mechanics, installers, and repairers	444	512	0.3	0.3	68	15.4	180
Electrical and electronic equipment mechanics, installers, and repairers	689	746	0.5	0.5	57	8.3	193
Computer, automated teller, and office machine repairers	156	180	0.1	0.1	24	15.1	43
Radio and telecommunications equipment installers and repairers	226	222	0.2	0.1	-4	-1.6	47
Radio mechanics	7	5	0.0	0.0	-2	-29.3	2
Telecommunications equipment installers and repairers, except line installers	219	217	0.2	0.1	-1	-0.6	45
Miscellaneous electrical and electronic equipment mechanics, installers, and repairers	284	317	0.2	0.2	33	11.5	95
Avionics technicians	23	24	0.0	0.0	1	3.4	6
Electric motor, power tool, and related repairers	31	33	0.0	0.0	2	5.3	9
Electrical and electronics installers and repairers, transportation equipment	18	19	0.0	0.0	1	7.1	6
Electrical and electronics repairers, commercial and industrial equipment	85	94	0.1	0.1	9	10.3	27
Electrical and electronics repairers, powerhouse, substation, and relay	21	21	0.0	0.0	0	-0.6	5
Electronic equipment installers and repairers, motor vehicles	18	21	0.0	0.0	3	14.8	7
Electronic home entertainment equipment installers and repairers	43	46	0.0	0.0	4	8.6	12
Security and fire alarm systems installers	46	60	0.0	0.0	14	30.2	23
All other electrical and electronic equipment mechanics, installers, and repairers [4]	22	26	0.0	0.0	4	19.6	9
Vehicle and mobile equipment mechanics, installers, and repairers	1 817	2 043	1.3	1.2	226	12.4	695
Aircraft mechanics and service technicians	131	145	0.1	0.1	14	11.0	45
Automotive technicians and repairers	1 038	1 168	0.7	0.7	130	12.5	392
Automotive body and related repairers	198	225	0.1	0.1	26	13.2	67
Automotive glass installers and repairers	22	24	0.0	0.0	2	10.7	6
Automotive service technicians and mechanics	818	919	0.6	0.6	101	12.4	319
Bus and truck mechanics and diesel engine specialists	267	305	0.2	0.2	38	14.2	107
Heavy vehicle and mobile equipment service technicians and mechanics	176	191	0.1	0.1	15	8.8	54
Farm equipment mechanics	35	38	0.0	0.0	3	7.7	10
Mobile heavy equipment mechanics, except engines	126	138	0.1	0.1	12	9.6	39
Rail car repairers	15	15	0.0	0.0	1	4.5	4
Small engine mechanics	67	79	0.0	0.0	12	18.7	29
Motorboat mechanics	22	26	0.0	0.0	4	18.3	9
Motorcycle mechanics	15	18	0.0	0.0	3	18.7	7
Outdoor power equipment and other small engine mechanics	30	36	0.0	0.0	6	18.9	13
Miscellaneous vehicle and mobile equipment mechanics, installers, and repairers	102	113	0.1	0.1	11	10.4	54
Bicycle repairers	7	8	0.0	0.0	1	18.8	4
Recreational vehicle service technicians	13	15	0.0	0.0	3	21.8	8
Tire repairers and changers	83	89	0.1	0.1	7	8.0	42
All other vehicle and mobile equipment mechanics, installers, and repairers [4]	36	41	0.0	0.0	6	15.4	15
Other installation, maintenance, and repair occupations	2 746	3 171	1.9	1.9	424	15.5	1 019
Control and valve installers and repairers	49	55	0.0	0.0	7	14.1	19
Mechanical door repairers	11	13	0.0	0.0	2	21.8	5
Control and valve installers and repairers, except mechanical door	38	42	0.0	0.0	5	12.0	14
Heating, air conditioning, and refrigeration mechanics and installers	249	328	0.2	0.2	79	31.8	112
Home appliance repairers	42	44	0.0	0.0	2	5.5	12
Industrial machinery installation, repair, and maintenance workers	1 628	1 855	1.1	1.1	227	13.9	548
Industrial machinery mechanics	197	208	0.1	0.1	11	5.5	51
Maintenance and repair workers, general	1 266	1 472	0.9	0.9	207	16.3	450
Maintenance workers, machinery	92	97	0.1	0.1	5	5.9	26
Millwrights	69	73	0.0	0.0	4	5.3	21
Refractory materials repairers, except brickmasons	4	4	0.0	0.0	0	5.6	1
Line installers and repairers	268	301	0.2	0.2	33	12.3	111
Electrical power-line installers and repairers	101	103	0.1	0.1	2	1.6	34
Telecommunications line installers and repairers	167	199	0.1	0.1	31	18.8	77
Precision instrument and equipment repairers	64	69	0.0	0.0	6	8.6	24
Camera and photographic equipment repairers	7	6	0.0	0.0	0	-7.1	2
Medical equipment repairers	29	33	0.0	0.0	4	14.8	12
Musical instrument repairers and tuners	6	7	0.0	0.0	0	6.3	2
Watch repairers	5	5	0.0	0.0	0	3.5	2
All other precision instrument and equipment repairers	17	18	0.0	0.0	1	7.0	6
Miscellaneous installation, maintenance, and repair workers	447	518	0.3	0.3	71	15.8	193
Coin, vending, and amusement machine servicers and repairers	43	49	0.0	0.0	6	15.2	17
Commercial divers	4	5	0.0	0.0	0	10.6	1
Fabric menders, except garment	2	2	0.0	0.0	0	-2.2	1
Locksmiths and safe repairers	23	28	0.0	0.0	5	21.0	12
Manufactured building and mobile home installers	18	22	0.0	0.0	4	23.3	9
Riggers	14	16	0.0	0.0	2	14.3	5
Signal and track switch repairers	8	8	0.0	0.0	0	-3.1	3
Helpers—Installation, maintenance, and repair workers	150	181	0.1	0.1	30	20.3	81
Installation, maintenance, and repair workers, all other	185	207	0.1	0.1	23	12.2	65

[1]Total job openings represent the sum of employment increases and net replacements. If employment change is negative, job openings due to growth are zero and total job openings equal net replacements.
[4]This occupation was created by the OES survey. There is no SIC equivalent.
0.0 = Quantity equals more than zero but less than 0.05.

Table 4-6. Employment by Occupation, 2002 and Projected 2012—*Continued*

(Thousands of jobs, percent.)

Occupation	Employment				Change 2002–2012		Total job openings due to growth and replacement 2002–2012 [1]
	Number		Percent distribution		Number	Percent	
	2002	2012	2002	2012			
Production Occupations	11 258	11 612	7.8	7.0	354	3.1	3 361
Supervisors, production workers	733	803	0.5	0.5	70	9.5	224
First-line supervisors/managers of production and operating workers	733	803	0.5	0.5	70	9.5	224
Assemblers and fabricators	2 122	2 044	1.5	1.2	-77	-3.6	547
Aircraft structure, surfaces, rigging, and systems assemblers	27	24	0.0	0.0	-2	-9.4	7
Electrical, electronics, and electromechanical assemblers	377	316	0.3	0.2	-61	-16.3	89
Coil winders, tapers, and finishers	36	31	0.0	0.0	-5	-13.9	9
Electrical and electronic equipment assemblers	281	230	0.2	0.1	-51	-18.3	66
Electromechanical equipment assemblers	60	55	0.0	0.0	-5	-8.3	14
Engine and other machine assemblers	50	49	0.0	0.0	-1	-1.9	14
Structural metal fabricators and fitters	89	94	0.1	0.1	6	6.2	26
Miscellaneous assemblers and fabricators	1 579	1 561	1.1	0.9	-18	-1.1	410
Fiberglass laminators and fabricators	37	39	0.0	0.0	2	5.6	12
Team assemblers	1 174	1 155	0.8	0.7	-19	-1.6	304
Timing device assemblers, adjusters, and calibrators	7	6	0.0	0.0	0	-3.0	2
All other assemblers and fabricators	361	360	0.3	0.2	-1	-0.2	93
Food processing occupations	757	836	0.5	0.5	79	10.5	254
Bakers	173	192	0.1	0.1	19	11.2	59
Butchers and other meat, poultry, and fish processing workers	414	459	0.3	0.3	45	10.9	139
Butchers and meat cutters	132	129	0.1	0.1	-3	-2.5	29
Meat, poultry, and fish cutters and trimmers	154	179	0.1	0.1	25	16.4	59
Slaughterers and meat packers	128	151	0.1	0.1	23	18.1	51
Miscellaneous food processing workers	127	137	0.1	0.1	9	7.2	41
Food and tobacco roasting, baking, and drying machine operators and tenders	19	20	0.0	0.0	1	4.2	6
Food batchmakers	74	79	0.1	0.0	5	7.2	23
Food cooking machine operators and tenders	34	37	0.0	0.0	3	8.8	11
All other food processing workers [4]	42	48	0.0	0.0	6	13.4	15
Metal workers and plastic workers [2]	2 367	2 544	1.6	1.5	177	7.5	754
Computer control programmers and operators	151	166	0.1	0.1	15	9.8	40
Computer-controlled machine tool operators, metal and plastic	132	144	0.1	0.1	12	9.3	34
Numerical tool and process control programmers	19	22	0.0	0.0	3	13.0	6
Forming machine setters, operators, and tenders, metal and plastic	188	198	0.1	0.1	11	5.6	60
Extruding and drawing machine setters, operators, and tenders, metal and plastic	98	105	0.1	0.1	7	7.1	40
Forging machine setters, operators, and tenders, metal and plastic	45	48	0.0	0.0	3	5.9	9
Rolling machine setters, operators, and tenders, metal and plastic	44	45	0.0	0.0	1	2.0	11
Machine tool cutting setters, operators, and tenders, metal and plastic	546	569	0.4	0.3	24	4.3	144
Cutting, punching, and press machine setters, operators, and tenders, metal and plastic	283	302	0.2	0.2	19	6.8	85
Drilling and boring machine tool setters, operators, and tenders, metal and plastic	53	54	0.0	0.0	1	2.1	17
Grinding, lapping, polishing, and buffing machine tool setters, operators, and tenders, metal and plastic	104	106	0.1	0.1	3	2.4	22
Lathe and turning machine tool setters, operators, and tenders, metal and plastic	75	75	0.1	0.0	1	0.8	15
Milling and planing machine setters, operators, and tenders, metal and plastic	31	31	0.0	0.0	0	0.8	6
Machinists	387	419	0.3	0.3	32	8.2	122
Metal furnace and kiln operators and tenders	31	30	0.0	0.0	0	-1.3	7
Metal refining furnace operators and tenders	18	17	0.0	0.0	0	-0.8	4
Pourers and casters, metal	13	13	0.0	0.0	0	-2.0	3
Model makers and patternmakers, metal and plastic	15	16	0.0	0.0	1	9.8	6
Model makers, metal and plastic	9	10	0.0	0.0	1	14.6	4
Patternmakers, metal and plastic	6	7	0.0	0.0	0	3.6	2
Molders and molding machine setters, operators, and tenders, metal and plastic	174	189	0.1	0.1	14	8.2	58
Foundry mold and coremakers	23	24	0.0	0.0	1	3.6	7
Molding, coremaking, and casting machine setters, operators, and tenders, metal and plastic	151	165	0.1	0.1	14	8.9	51
Multiple machine tool setters, operators, and tenders, metal and plastic	99	107	0.1	0.1	8	8.3	35
Tool and die makers	109	110	0.1	0.1	0	0.4	25
Welding, soldering, and brazing workers	452	518	0.3	0.3	67	14.8	194
Welders, cutters, solderers, and brazers	391	457	0.3	0.3	66	17.0	177
Welding, soldering, and brazing machine setters, operators, and tenders	61	62	0.0	0.0	1	0.9	18
Miscellaneous metalworkers and plastic workers	215	221	0.1	0.1	6	2.6	62
Heat treating equipment setters, operators, and tenders, metal and plastic	29	29	0.0	0.0	0	-0.6	9
Lay out workers, metal and plastic	13	15	0.0	0.0	2	15.6	4
Plating and coating machine setters, operators, and tenders, metal and plastic	44	42	0.0	0.0	-1	-2.6	10
Tool grinders, filers, and sharpeners	26	24	0.0	0.0	-2	-7.7	8
All other metal workers and plastic workers	104	111	0.1	0.1	7	6.6	31
Printing occupations	465	466	0.3	0.3	1	0.3	128
Bookbinders and bindery workers	98	93	0.1	0.1	-5	-4.7	26
Bindery workers	91	86	0.1	0.1	-5	-5.2	24
Bookbinders	7	7	0.0	0.0	0	1.3	2
Printers	346	350	0.2	0.2	4	1.2	95
Job printers	56	61	0.0	0.0	5	9.2	18
Prepress technicians and workers	91	81	0.1	0.0	-10	-11.2	21
Printing machine operators	199	208	0.1	0.1	9	4.6	55
All other printing workers [4]	21	23	0.0	0.0	2	9.3	7
Textile, apparel, and furnishings occupations	1 085	932	0.8	0.6	-152	-14.1	240
Laundry and dry-cleaning workers	231	260	0.2	0.2	29	12.3	91
Pressers, textile, garment, and related materials	91	91	0.1	0.1	0	-0.2	14
Sewing machine operators	315	216	0.2	0.1	-99	-31.5	39
Shoe and leather workers	23	18	0.0	0.0	-4	-19.0	6
Shoe and leather workers and repairers	16	14	0.0	0.0	-3	-16.1	5

[1]Total job openings represent the sum of employment increases and net replacements. If employment change is negative, job openings due to growth are zero and total job openings equal net replacements.
[2]Information about the detailed residual occupation for this broad occupation is not included.
[4]This occupation was created by the OES survey. There is no SIC equivalent.
0.0 = Quantity equals more than zero but less than 0.05.

Table 4-6. Employment by Occupation, 2002 and Projected 2012—*Continued*

(Thousands of jobs, percent.)

Occupation	Employment				Change 2002–2012		Total job openings due to growth and replacement 2002–2012 [1]
	Number		Percent distribution		Number	Percent	
	2002	2012	2002	2012			
Shoe machine operators and tenders	7	5	0.0	0.0	-2	-26.1	1
Tailors, dressmakers, and sewers	90	77	0.1	0.0	-13	-14.0	16
Sewers, hand	36	29	0.0	0.0	-8	-21.2	6
Tailors, dressmakers, and custom sewers	53	48	0.0	0.0	-5	-9.1	9
Textile machine setters, operators, and tenders	179	124	0.1	0.1	-56	-31.0	33
Textile bleaching and dyeing machine operators and tenders	27	19	0.0	0.0	-8	-28.7	7
Textile cutting machine setters, operators, and tenders	34	26	0.0	0.0	-8	-22.6	8
Textile knitting and weaving machine setters, operators, and tenders	53	33	0.0	0.0	-20	-38.6	6
Textile winding, twisting, and drawing out machine setters, operators, tenders	66	46	0.0	0.0	-20	-30.3	12
Miscellaneous textile, apparel, and furnishings workers	156	147	0.1	0.1	-9	-5.9	41
Extruding and forming machine setters, operators, and tenders, synthetic and glass fibers	27	24	0.0	0.0	-4	-13.1	5
Fabric and apparel patternmakers	11	8	0.0	0.0	-3	-24.6	5
Upholsterers	56	51	0.0	0.0	-5	-8.7	14
All other textile, apparel, and furnishings workers	61	63	0.0	0.0	2	3.3	16
Woodworkers	374	393	0.3	0.2	19	5.1	115
Cabinetmakers and bench carpenters	147	160	0.1	0.1	14	9.4	50
Furniture finishers	39	41	0.0	0.0	1	3.3	9
Model makers and patternmakers, wood	9	10	0.0	0.0	1	11.1	3
Model makers, wood	4	5	0.0	0.0	0	10.3	2
Patternmakers, wood	4	5	0.0	0.0	0	11.8	2
Woodworking machine setters, operators, and tenders	151	153	0.1	0.1	3	1.8	44
Sawing machine setters, operators, and tenders, wood	56	56	0.0	0.0	0	-0.2	16
Woodworking machine setters, operators, and tenders, except sawing	95	98	0.1	0.1	3	3.0	28
All other woodworkers	29	29	0.0	0.0	0	1.7	9
Plant and system operators	346	353	0.2	0.2	7	2.0	120
Power plant operators, distributors, and dispatchers	51	51	0.0	0.0	0	-0.7	14
Nuclear power reactor operators	3	3	0.0	0.0	0	-3.2	1
Power distributors and dispatchers	12	12	0.0	0.0	0	-3.0	3
Power plant operators	35	36	0.0	0.0	0	0.3	10
Stationary engineers and boiler operators	55	56	0.0	0.0	0	0.3	10
Water and liquid waste treatment plant and system operators	99	115	0.1	0.1	16	16.0	50
Miscellaneous plant and system operators	141	132	0.1	0.1	-9	-6.2	46
Chemical plant and system operators	58	51	0.0	0.0	-7	-12.3	18
Gas plant operators	12	13	0.0	0.0	1	6.7	5
Petroleum pump system operators, refinery operators, and gaugers	39	35	0.0	0.0	-4	-11.0	12
All other plant and system operators	32	33	0.0	0.0	2	5.6	12
Other production occupations	3 010	3 240	2.1	2.0	230	7.7	977
Chemical processing machine setters, operators, and tenders	94	92	0.1	0.1	-2	-2.0	30
Chemical equipment operators and tenders	58	56	0.0	0.0	-2	-3.8	19
Separating, filtering, clarifying, precipitating, and still machine setters, operators, and tenders	36	36	0.0	0.0	0	0.8	12
Crushing, grinding, polishing, mixing, and blending workers	196	192	0.1	0.1	-4	-2.1	55
Crushing, grinding, and polishing machine setters, operators, and tenders	45	44	0.0	0.0	-1	-2.8	12
Grinding and polishing workers, hand	45	49	0.0	0.0	4	9.0	16
Mixing and blending machine setters, operators, and tenders	106	99	0.1	0.1	-7	-6.5	28
Cutting workers	109	116	0.1	0.1	7	6.9	30
Cutters and trimmers, hand	31	33	0.0	0.0	2	7.6	9
Cutting and slicing machine setters, operators, and tenders	77	83	0.1	0.0	5	6.6	21
Extruding, forming, pressing, and compacting machine setters, operators, and tenders	73	73	0.1	0.0	0	-0.1	19
Furnace, kiln, oven, drier, and kettle operators and tenders	31	29	0.0	0.0	-2	-4.9	7
Inspectors, testers, sorters, samplers, and weighers	515	539	0.4	0.3	24	4.7	141
Jewelers and precious stone and metal workers	40	42	0.0	0.0	2	4.5	10
Medical, dental, and ophthalmic laboratory technicians	94	101	0.1	0.1	7	7.4	27
Dental laboratory technicians	47	49	0.0	0.0	2	3.6	12
Medical appliance technicians	14	16	0.0	0.0	2	16.1	5
Ophthalmic laboratory technicians	33	36	0.0	0.0	3	9.2	10
Packaging and filling machine operators and tenders	387	468	0.3	0.3	82	21.1	159
Painting workers	187	211	0.1	0.1	24	13.0	73
Coating, painting, and spraying machine setters, operators, and tenders	103	112	0.1	0.1	10	9.4	36
Painters, transportation equipment	50	59	0.0	0.0	9	17.5	22
Painting, coating, and decorating workers	34	40	0.0	0.0	6	17.6	15
Photographic process workers and processing machine operators	82	89	0.1	0.1	6	7.9	27
Photographic process workers	28	30	0.0	0.0	2	5.4	9
Photographic processing machine operators	54	59	0.0	0.0	5	9.2	18
Semiconductor processors	46	42	0.0	0.0	-5	-10.6	10
Miscellaneous production workers	1 155	1 245	0.8	0.8	90	7.8	388
Cementing and gluing machine operators and tenders	27	28	0.0	0.0	0	1.1	8
Cleaning, washing, and metal pickling equipment operators and tenders	18	19	0.0	0.0	1	6.9	7
Cooling and freezing equipment operators and tenders	7	8	0.0	0.0	1	7.1	3
Etchers and engravers	10	10	0.0	0.0	1	6.1	3
Molders, shapers, and casters, except metal and plastic	46	49	0.0	0.0	3	6.4	14
Paper goods machine setters, operators, and tenders	117	114	0.1	0.1	-3	-2.8	25
Tire builders	14	15	0.0	0.0	1	6.6	4
Helpers—Production workers	467	503	0.3	0.3	36	7.7	167
All other production workers	449	500	0.3	0.3	51	11.3	158

[1]Total job openings represent the sum of employment increases and net replacements. If employment change is negative, job openings due to growth are zero and total job openings equal net replacements.

0.0 = Quantity equals more than zero but less than 0.05.

Table 4-6. Employment by Occupation, 2002 and Projected 2012—*Continued*

(Thousands of jobs, percent.)

Occupation	Employment				Change 2002–2012		Total job openings due to growth and replacement 2002–2012 [1]
	Number		Percent distribution		Number	Percent	
	2002	2012	2002	2012			
Transportation and Material Moving Occupations	9 828	11 111	6.8	6.7	1 282	13.0	3 496
Supervisors, transportation and material moving workers	364	411	0.3	0.2	47	12.9	132
Aircraft cargo handling supervisors	9	10	0.0	0.0	1	15.6	3
First-line supervisors/managers of helpers, laborers, and material movers, hand	147	168	0.1	0.1	21	14.0	55
First-line supervisors/managers of transportation and material-moving machine and vehicle operators	207	232	0.1	0.1	25	12.1	74
Air transportation	144	168	0.1	0.1	24	17.0	62
Aircraft pilots and flight engineers	100	118	0.1	0.1	18	17.8	45
Airline pilots, copilots, and flight engineers	79	94	0.1	0.1	15	18.5	36
Commercial pilots	21	24	0.0	0.0	3	14.9	9
Air traffic controllers and airfield operations specialists	32	36	0.0	0.0	4	13.5	12
Air traffic controllers	26	29	0.0	0.0	3	12.6	10
Airfield operations specialists	6	7	0.0	0.0	1	17.2	3
All other air transportation workers [4]	12	14	0.0	0.0	2	19.4	5
Motor vehicle operators	4 136	4 896	2.9	3.0	760	18.4	1 385
Ambulance drivers and attendants, except emergency medical technicians	17	22	0.0	0.0	5	26.7	6
Bus drivers	654	761	0.5	0.5	106	16.2	249
Bus drivers, transit and intercity	202	233	0.1	0.1	31	15.2	75
Bus drivers, school	453	528	0.3	0.3	76	16.7	174
Driver/sales workers and truck drivers	3 221	3 813	2.2	2.3	592	18.4	1 045
Driver/sales workers	431	450	0.3	0.3	19	4.3	89
Truck drivers, heavy and tractor-trailer	1 767	2 104	1.2	1.3	337	19.0	625
Truck drivers, light or delivery services	1 022	1 259	0.7	0.8	237	23.2	331
Taxi drivers and chauffeurs	132	161	0.1	0.1	29	21.7	41
All other motor vehicle operators	111	139	0.1	0.1	28	25.2	44
Rail transportation occupations	101	96	0.1	0.1	-5	-5.3	28
Locomotive engineers and operators	33	31	0.0	0.0	-2	-7.2	10
Railroad brake, signal, and switch operators	15	12	0.0	0.0	-3	-22.8	2
Railroad conductors and yardmasters	38	36	0.0	0.0	-2	-4.2	10
Subway, streetcar operators and all other rail transportation workers [3]	15	17	0.0	0.0	2	13.2	7
Water transportation occupations	68	70	0.0	0.0	2	3.4	25
Sailors and marine oilers	27	28	0.0	0.0	1	4.0	11
Ship and boat captains and operators	29	30	0.0	0.0	1	2.4	9
Captains, mates, and pilots of water vessels	25	26	0.0	0.0	1	2.4	8
Motorboat operators	4	4	0.0	0.0	0	2.7	1
Ship engineers	8	9	0.0	0.0	0	4.5	4
All other water transportation workers	4	4	0.0	0.0	0	5.6	1
Other transportation workers	294	326	0.2	0.2	32	11.0	135
Bridge and lock tenders	4	3	0.0	0.0	-1	-17.4	1
Parking lot attendants	107	128	0.1	0.1	21	19.2	52
Service station attendants	107	111	0.1	0.1	4	3.3	52
Traffic technicians	6	6	0.0	0.0	1	9.3	2
Transportation inspectors	29	32	0.0	0.0	2	7.7	9
All other related transportation workers [4]	40	47	0.0	0.0	6	15.1	18
Material moving occupations	4 722	5 144	3.3	3.1	422	8.9	1 729
Conveyor operators and tenders	58	65	0.0	0.0	7	-14.1	24
Crane and tower operators	50	55	0.0	0.0	5	13.0	16
Dredge, excavating, and loading machine operators	87	94	0.1	0.1	7	11.1	31
Dredge operators	3	3	0.0	0.0	0	8.4	1
Excavating and loading machine and dragline operators	80	87	0.1	0.1	7	8.7	29
Loading machine operators, underground mining	4	3	0.0	0.0	-1	-14.1	1
Hoist and winch operators	9	10	0.0	0.0	1	13.0	4
Industrial truck and tractor operators	594	659	0.4	0.4	66	11.1	178
Laborers and material movers, hand	3 659	3 967	2.5	2.4	308	8.4	1 376
Cleaners of vehicles and equipment	344	374	0.2	0.2	30	8.7	150
Laborers and freight, stock, and material movers, hand	2 231	2 378	1.5	1.4	147	6.6	876
Machine feeders and offbearers	164	162	0.1	0.1	-2	-1.4	45
Packers and packagers, hand	920	1 052	0.6	0.6	132	14.4	305
Pumping station operators	32	30	0.0	0.0	-2	-6.0	7
Gas compressor and gas pumping station operators	7	7	0.0	0.0	0	1.0	2
Pump operators, except wellhead pumpers	13	13	0.0	0.0	-1	-5.0	3
Wellhead pumpers	11	10	0.0	0.0	-1	-11.7	3
Refuse and recyclable material collectors	134	158	0.1	0.1	24	17.6	58
Shuttle car operators	3	2	0.0	0.0	-1	-31.3	1
Tank car, truck, and ship loaders	17	17	0.0	0.0	0	-2.1	5
Material moving workers, all other	78	86	0.1	0.1	8	10.0	29

Note: Detail may not equal total or 100 percent due to rounding.

[1]Total job openings represent the sum of employment increases and net replacements. If employment change is negative, job openings due to growth are zero and total job openings equal net replacements.
[3]This occupation contains two or more detailed SOC occupations.
[4]This occupation was created by the OES survey. There is no SIC equivalent.
0.0 = Quantity equals more than zero but less than 0.05.

PART FIVE

PRODUCTIVITY AND COSTS

PRODUCTIVITY AND COSTS

HIGHLIGHTS

This part covers the two kinds of productivity measures produced by the BLS: output per hour, or labor productivity, and multifactor productivity. Multifactor productivity is designed to ensure the joint influence of technological change, efficiency improvements, returns to scale, and other factors on economic growth. For some measures, there is a lag in the available data. Industries are presented with the NAICS classification.

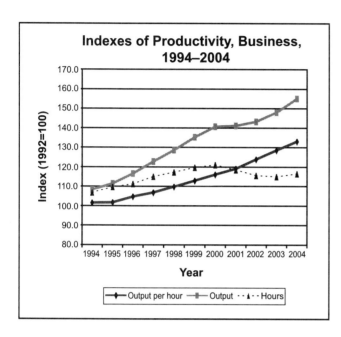

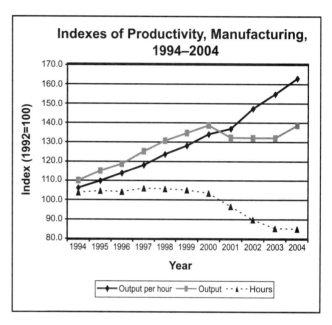

From 2003 to 2004, output in the business sector increased 4.7 percent; however, hours also increased, leading to a smaller increase in output per hour than in previous years. In manufacturing, output increased a significant 4.8 percent, after three years of stagnation, but hours declined at a slower rate than before. Therefore, the rate of increase in output per hours in 2004 was only slightly larger than that in 2003. (Table 5-1)

OTHER HIGHLIGHTS:

• Unit labor costs in business increased slightly in 2004 after three years of virtually no change. In contrast, unit labor costs in manufacturing declined in 2004 after a significant increase the previous year. (Table 5-1)

• Industries producing computers and computer components were among those that had double-digit increases in output per hour in 2004. It was largely a result of high output increases combined with a decline in hours worked. (Table 5-2)

• The non-manufacturing sector also saw increases in output per hour in 2004. Retail electronic and appliance stores had an 18.2 percent increase in output with a 7.4 percent decline in hours. Software publishers in the information sector had only a small increase in output, but had a 10 percent drop in hours. (Table 5-2)

• Most of the remaining industries reported modest drops in hours from 2002 to 2003, but the direction of output was mixed. (Table 5-2)

• Private business multifactor productivity rose 1.9 percent in 2002, the largest rate of increase since 1992. The 2002 gain reflected a 1.9 percent increase in output, while the combined inputs of capital and labor remained virtually unchanged. (Table 5-4)

NOTES AND DEFINITIONS

Concepts and Definitions

Measures of output per hour for the business, nonfarm business, and manufacturing sectors describe the relationship between real output and the labor time involved in its production. The output measures for the business sectors and nonfinancial corporations are based on series prepared by the Bureau of Economic Analysis (BEA) of the U.S. Department of Commerce as part of the national income and product accounts (NIPAs). The BLS derives manufacturing output indexes by combining data from the U.S. Census Bureau, the BEA, and the Federal Reserve Board. All of the output measures are chain-type annual-weighted indexes. This means that the relative prices (weights) used to combine output changes into an aggregate output measure are changed annually, thus minimizing the bias that arises from using fixed weights over long periods of time.

Business sector output is constructed by excluding the following outputs from gross domestic product (GDP): general government, nonprofit institutions, paid employees of private households, and the rental value of owner-occupied dwellings. Corresponding exclusions also are made in labor inputs. These activities are excluded because theoretical or practical difficulties make it impossible to base the computation of meaningful productivity measures on them. Business output accounted for about 77 percent of GDP and nonfinancial corporations about 53 percent of GDP in 1996. Manufacturing indexes are constructed by deflating current-dollar industry value of production data with deflators from the BEA. These deflators are based on data from the BLS producer price program and other sources. To avoid duplication, intrasector transactions are removed when industry shipments are aggregated.

Productivity measures show the changes from period to period in the amount of goods and services produced per hour. Although these measures relate output to hours of persons engaged in a sector, they do not measure the specific contributions of labor, capital, or any other factor of production. Rather, they reflect the joint effects of many influences, including changes in technology, capital, economies of scale, utilization of capacity, the substitution of capital or intermediates for labor, the organization of production, managerial skill, and the characteristics and effort of the work force.

Measures of labor input are based mainly on the monthly BLS survey of nonagricultural establishments. From this survey, measures of employment and average weekly hours paid for employees of these establishments are measured. Weekly hours paid are adjusted to hours at work using information from the National Compensation Survey program for 2000 onward and the annual Hours at Work Survey for years prior to 2000 (the BLS Hours at Work survey was terminated in 2000). Supplementary information for farm workers, the self-employed, and unpaid family workers is obtained from the Current Population Survey, the monthly survey of households.

The *indexes of hourly compensation* are based mainly on the BLS hours data, discussed above, and employee compensation data from the NIPAs. Compensation includes wages and salaries and supplemental payments, such as employer contributions by to Social Security and private health and pension funds. The all persons' compensation data include estimates of proprietors' salaries and contributions for supplementary benefits. Real compensation per hour is derived by adjusting the compensation data with the CPI-U-RS in order to reflect changes in purchasing power.

The *indexes of unit labor costs* are computed by dividing compensation per hour by output per hour.

Nonlabor payments are calculated by subtracting total compensation from current dollar output, and thus include profits, depreciation, interest, and indirect taxes.

The *implicit deflator* reflects changes in all of the costs of production and distribution (unit labor costs plus unit nonlabor payments). To construct the implicit price deflator, the current-dollar measure of output in a sector is divided by the real output series.

Multifactor Productivity

BLS calculates the annual growth of multifactor productivity for the U.S. private business sector. This measure is generally released about 14 months after the end of the measured or target year. The lag occurs because the process of calculating multifactor productivity requires detailed data from many sources. BLS plans to use a simplified methodology to make preliminary estimates of private business sector multifactor productivity changes available within a few months after the end of target year.

Annual measures of output per unit of combined labor and capital input (multifactor productivity) and related measures are produced for the private business and private nonfarm business sectors. The private business and private nonfarm business sectors for which multifactor productivity indexes also are prepared exclude government enterprises, and thus differ from the business and nonfarm business sectors described above.

Multifactor productivity measures refer to the ratio of an output index to an index of combined labor and capital services inputs.

Multifactor productivity growth reflects the amount of output growth that cannot be accounted for by the growth of weighted labor and capital inputs. The weights are associated cost shares. Labor's share is the ratio of compensation to current-dollar output. Capital's share is equal to the ratio of capital cost to current-dollar output. As is the case with the output measures, the weights are updated annually.

Capital services measure the services derived from the stock of physical assets and software. Physical assets included are fixed business equipment, structures, inventories, and land. Structures include nonresidential structures and residential capital that is rented out by profit-making firms or persons. Software includes pre-packaged, custom, and own-account software. Financial assets are excluded, as are owner-occupied residential structures. The aggregate capital measures are obtained by weighting the capital stocks for each asset type within each of 53 industries using capital income shares based on estimated rental prices for each asset type. Data on investments in physical assets and gross product originating by industry, which are used in measuring the rental prices, are obtained from BEA.

Labor input in private business and private nonfarm business is obtained by weighting the hours worked by all persons, classified by education, work experience, and gender, by their shares of labor compensation. Additional information concerning data sources and methods of measuring labor composition can be found in BLS Bulletin 2426 (December 1993), "Labor Composition and U.S. Productivity Growth, 1948-90."

The *manufacturing multifactor productivity index* is derived by dividing an output index by a weighted index of combined hours, capital services, energy, materials and purchased business services. Weights (shares of total costs) are updated annually. The labor hours for the manufacturing measure are directly added and thus do not include the effect of changing labor composition—unlike those used for business multifactor productivity. The manufacturing sector coverage is the same in the multifactor and labor productivity series.

Output per Hour and Related Series in Selected Industries

The BLS industry productivity program produces annual indexes of labor productivity, labor compensation, and unit labor costs for selected 4-, 5- and 6-digit NAICS industries. These data series cover 60 percent of employment in the private, nonfarm business sector, and 100 percent of manufacturing, retail trade, and wholesale trade. The data sources used in the industry measures differ from those used in the productivity and cost measures for the major sectors.

Output per hour and related indexes for manufacturing and nonmanufacturing industries are updated annually and published in a news release and on the BLS Web site at <http://stats.bls.gov>.

Output per hour indexes are obtained by dividing an output index by an index of aggregate hours. Although the measures relate output to one input (labor time) they do not measure the specific contribution of labor or any other factor of production. Rather, they reflect the joint effect of a number of interrelated influences, such as changes in technology, capital investment per worker, and capacity utilization. Caution is necessary when analyzing year-to-year changes in output per hour; the annual changes can be irregular and not necessarily indicative of long-term trends. Conversely, long-term trends are not necessarily applicable to any one year or period in the future.

An *output index* for a particular industry is calculated using a Tornqvist index formula that aggregates the growth rates of the industry products between two periods with weights based on the products' shares in industry value of production. The weight for each product equals its average value share in the two periods. The formula yields the ratio of output in a given period to that in the previous period. The ratios for successive years must be chained together to form a time series. The quantities of products used in the output index are measured either with deflated values of production or with actual quantities. For most industries, output indexes are developed in two stages. First, comprehensive data from the economic censuses conducted by the Census Bureau every five years are used to develop benchmark indexes for the upcoming census years. Second, less comprehensive data are used to prepare annual indexes. The latter indexes are adjusted to the benchmark indexes by means of linear interpolation. Annual indexes are linked to the most recent benchmark index for the period following the last census year.

Indexes of labor input are employee hours indexes or all person hours indexes. In manufacturing industries, employee hours are used. In nonmanufacturing industries where self-employed workers play a significant role, all person hours are used. For most industries, the hours series are based on hours paid. Total hours are calculated by multiplying the number of workers by average weekly hours. Employee hours are treated as homogenous and additive, with no distinction made between hours of different groups. Annual indexes are developed by dividing the aggregate hours for each year by the base period aggregate.

Indexes of unit labor costs are calculated as the ratio of total labor compensation to real output, or equivalently, as the ratio of hourly compensation to labor productivity (output per hour). Unit labor costs measure the cost of labor input required to produce one unit of output.

Indexes of total compensation measure the change in the total costs to the employer of securing labor. Compensation is defined as payroll plus supplemental payments. Payroll includes salaries, wages, commissions, dismissal pay, bonuses, vacation and sick leave pay, and compensation in kind. Supplemental payments are divided into legally required expenditures and payments for voluntary programs. The legally required expenditures include employers' contributions to Social Security, unemployment insurance taxes, and workers' compensation. Payments for voluntary programs include all programs not specifically required by legislation, such as the employer portion of private health insurance and pension plans.

Sources of Additional Information

Productivity concepts and methodology are described in the BLS *Handbook of Methods*, BLS, April 1997. More information on productivity can be found in USDL 05-1820. Additional information on multifactor productivity can be in the *Monthly Labor Review*, June 2005.

Table 5-1. Indexes of Productivity and Related Data, 1947–2004

(1992 = 100.)

Year	Business											
	Output per hour	Output	Hours	Compen-sation per hour	Real compen-sation per hour	Unit labor costs	Unit nonlabor payments	Implicit price deflator	Employ-ment	Output per person	Compen-sation in current dollars	Nonlabor payments in current dollars
1947	32.2	20.4	63.4	7.0	40.7	21.8	18.6	20.6	55.7	36.6	4.4	3.8
1948	33.7	21.5	63.8	7.6	40.9	22.6	20.6	21.8	56.3	38.2	4.9	4.4
1949	34.5	21.3	61.8	7.7	42.0	22.4	20.4	21.6	55.1	38.7	4.8	4.4
1950	37.3	23.4	62.7	8.3	44.4	22.1	21.5	21.9	55.6	42.0	5.2	5.0
1951	38.5	24.9	64.7	9.0	45.0	23.5	23.7	23.6	57.1	43.6	5.8	5.9
1952	39.6	25.7	64.8	9.6	46.9	24.2	23.2	23.8	57.3	44.8	6.2	5.9
1953	41.0	26.9	65.6	10.2	49.5	24.9	22.6	24.0	58.1	46.3	6.7	6.1
1954	41.9	26.6	63.4	10.5	50.7	25.2	22.5	24.2	56.7	46.8	6.7	6.0
1955	43.6	28.7	65.8	10.8	52.2	24.8	24.0	24.5	58.3	49.2	7.1	6.9
1956	43.6	29.1	66.8	11.5	54.8	26.4	23.4	25.3	59.5	48.9	7.7	6.8
1957	45.0	29.6	65.8	12.3	56.5	27.3	24.2	26.1	59.4	49.9	8.1	7.2
1958	46.3	29.1	62.9	12.8	57.4	27.7	24.7	26.6	57.2	50.9	8.1	7.2
1959	48.0	31.4	65.5	13.3	59.4	27.8	25.2	26.8	58.9	53.4	8.7	7.9
1960	48.9	32.0	65.6	13.9	60.8	28.4	24.8	27.1	59.2	54.1	9.1	8.0
1961	50.6	32.7	64.6	14.4	62.5	28.5	25.2	27.3	58.6	55.8	9.3	8.2
1962	52.9	34.8	65.8	15.1	64.6	28.5	26.1	27.6	59.3	58.6	9.9	9.1
1963	54.9	36.4	66.2	15.6	66.1	28.4	26.6	27.7	59.7	61.0	10.3	9.7
1964	56.8	38.7	68.1	16.2	67.7	28.5	27.3	28.1	60.8	63.7	11.0	10.6
1965	58.8	41.4	70.5	16.8	69.1	28.6	28.4	28.5	62.5	66.3	11.8	11.8
1966	61.2	44.2	72.3	17.9	71.7	29.3	29.0	29.2	64.4	68.7	13.0	12.8
1967	62.5	45.1	72.1	19.0	73.5	30.3	29.5	30.0	65.2	69.1	13.7	13.3
1968	64.7	47.3	73.2	20.5	76.2	31.7	30.4	31.2	66.5	71.1	15.0	14.4
1969	65.0	48.8	75.0	21.9	77.3	33.7	30.8	32.6	68.6	71.1	16.4	15.0
1970	66.3	48.7	73.5	23.6	78.8	35.6	31.5	34.1	68.4	71.3	17.4	15.3
1971	69.0	50.6	73.3	25.1	80.2	36.3	34.1	35.5	68.5	73.9	18.4	17.3
1972	71.2	53.9	75.6	26.7	82.6	37.4	35.7	36.8	70.5	76.4	20.2	19.2
1973	73.4	57.6	78.5	28.9	84.3	39.4	37.5	38.7	73.6	78.4	22.7	21.6
1974	72.2	56.8	78.7	31.7	83.3	43.9	39.9	42.4	74.7	76.1	24.9	22.7
1975	74.8	56.3	75.3	34.9	84.1	46.7	46.3	46.6	72.4	77.7	26.3	26.0
1976	77.1	60.0	77.8	38.0	86.4	49.2	48.7	49.0	74.7	80.3	29.5	29.2
1977	78.4	63.3	80.8	41.0	87.6	52.2	51.5	52.0	77.9	81.3	33.1	32.6
1978	79.3	67.3	84.9	44.5	89.1	56.2	54.8	55.6	82.2	81.9	37.8	36.9
1979	79.3	69.6	87.8	48.9	89.3	61.7	58.2	60.4	85.4	81.5	42.9	40.5
1980	79.1	68.8	87.0	54.1	89.1	68.4	61.3	65.8	85.6	80.4	47.1	42.2
1981	80.8	70.7	87.6	59.3	89.3	73.5	69.1	71.8	86.5	81.8	52.0	48.9
1982	80.1	68.6	85.6	63.6	90.4	79.4	70.1	75.9	85.1	80.7	54.5	48.1
1983	83.0	72.3	87.1	66.3	90.3	79.8	76.3	78.5	85.8	84.3	57.7	55.1
1984	85.2	78.6	92.2	69.1	90.7	81.2	80.2	80.8	90.1	87.2	63.8	63.0
1985	87.1	82.2	94.3	72.5	92.0	83.2	82.0	82.7	92.4	89.0	68.4	67.4
1986	89.8	85.3	95.0	76.2	95.0	84.9	82.6	84.1	93.9	90.8	72.4	70.5
1987	90.3	88.3	97.7	79.1	95.3	87.6	83.1	85.9	96.4	91.5	77.3	73.4
1988	91.7	92.1	100.4	83.1	96.6	90.6	85.2	88.6	99.4	92.6	83.4	78.4
1989	92.6	95.4	103.1	85.3	95.1	92.1	91.4	91.9	101.5	94.0	87.9	87.2
1990	94.5	96.9	102.6	90.6	96.3	96.0	93.8	95.1	102.2	94.8	93.0	90.9
1991	95.9	96.1	100.2	95.1	97.4	99.1	96.6	98.2	100.6	95.6	95.3	92.9
1992	100.0	100.0	100.0	100.0	100.0	100.0	100.0	100.0	100.0	100.0	100.0	100.0
1993	100.4	103.1	102.7	102.2	99.7	101.8	102.6	102.1	102.1	101.0	105.0	105.8
1994	101.5	108.2	106.7	103.7	99.1	102.2	106.8	103.9	105.5	102.6	110.6	115.5
1995	101.6	111.4	109.6	105.9	98.8	104.2	108.4	105.7	108.5	102.7	116.0	120.7
1996	104.7	116.5	111.3	109.6	99.6	104.7	112.0	107.4	110.8	105.1	122.0	130.4
1997	106.7	122.7	115.0	113.1	100.6	106.1	113.9	109.0	113.8	107.8	130.1	139.8
1998	109.7	128.6	117.3	120.0	105.3	109.4	110.1	109.7	116.1	110.7	140.7	141.6
1999	112.9	135.2	119.7	125.8	108.1	111.4	109.5	110.7	118.1	114.5	150.6	148.0
2000	116.1	140.5	121.0	134.5	111.9	115.9	107.4	112.7	120.2	116.9	162.8	150.9
2001	119.0	141.0	118.4	140.2	113.4	117.7	110.2	114.9	119.2	118.3	166.0	155.3
2002	123.8	143.1	115.6	145.0	115.4	117.1	114.4	116.1	116.6	122.7	167.6	163.6
2003	128.6	147.9	115.0	150.7	117.3	117.2	118.6	117.7	116.4	127.0	173.3	175.5
2004	133.0	154.9	116.5	157.7	119.5	118.6	123.9	120.6	118.0	131.3	183.7	192.0

Table 5-1. Indexes of Productivity and Related Data, 1947–2004—*Continued*

(1992 = 100.)

| Year | Nonfarm Business | | | | | | | | | | | |
	Output per hour	Output	Hours	Compensation per hour	Real compensation per hour	Unit labor costs	Unit nonlabor payments	Implicit price deflator	Employment	Output per person	Compensation in current dollars	Nonlabor payments in current dollars
1947	37.0	20.1	54.2	7.5	43.3	20.2	17.8	19.3	47.2	42.5	4.0	3.6
1948	38.0	20.9	55.1	8.1	43.6	21.3	19.4	20.6	48.2	43.5	4.5	4.1
1949	39.3	20.8	53.0	8.3	45.4	21.2	20.0	20.8	46.8	44.4	4.4	4.2
1950	41.9	22.9	54.7	8.8	47.5	21.1	20.8	21.0	47.9	47.8	4.8	4.8
1951	43.0	24.6	57.2	9.6	47.8	22.3	22.4	22.4	50.1	49.2	5.5	5.5
1952	43.8	25.3	57.9	10.1	49.5	23.1	22.3	22.8	50.7	50.0	5.9	5.6
1953	44.8	26.6	59.3	10.7	51.9	23.9	22.2	23.3	52.2	50.9	6.3	5.9
1954	45.6	26.1	57.3	11.0	53.1	24.2	22.3	23.5	50.8	51.5	6.3	5.8
1955	47.5	28.3	59.6	11.4	55.3	24.1	23.6	23.9	52.3	54.1	6.8	6.7
1956	47.1	28.8	61.1	12.1	57.8	25.8	23.1	24.8	53.8	53.5	7.4	6.6
1957	48.4	29.4	60.7	12.8	59.2	26.6	23.8	25.6	54.1	54.3	7.8	7.0
1958	49.4	28.7	58.2	13.4	59.9	27.0	24.1	26.0	52.2	55.0	7.8	6.9
1959	51.3	31.2	60.9	13.9	61.8	27.1	25.0	26.3	54.1	57.7	8.5	7.8
1960	51.9	31.8	61.2	14.5	63.3	27.9	24.3	26.6	54.7	58.1	8.9	7.7
1961	53.5	32.4	60.6	15.0	64.8	28.0	24.8	26.8	54.3	59.7	9.1	8.0
1962	55.9	34.6	61.9	15.6	66.7	27.8	25.8	27.1	55.3	62.6	9.6	8.9
1963	57.8	36.2	62.6	16.1	68.1	27.8	26.3	27.3	55.9	64.8	10.1	9.5
1964	59.6	38.7	64.9	16.6	69.3	27.9	27.2	27.6	57.3	67.5	10.8	10.5
1965	61.4	41.4	67.4	17.1	70.5	27.9	28.1	28.0	59.3	69.8	11.6	11.6
1966	63.6	44.4	69.8	18.2	72.6	28.6	28.7	28.6	61.6	72.0	12.7	12.7
1967	64.7	45.1	69.8	19.2	74.5	29.7	29.2	29.5	62.6	72.1	13.4	13.2
1968	66.9	47.5	71.0	20.7	77.1	31.0	30.2	30.7	64.1	74.1	14.7	14.3
1969	67.0	48.9	73.0	22.1	78.1	33.0	30.5	32.1	66.4	73.7	16.2	14.9
1970	68.0	48.9	71.9	23.7	79.2	34.9	31.2	33.5	66.4	73.6	17.0	15.2
1971	70.7	50.7	71.7	25.2	80.7	35.7	33.7	35.0	66.6	76.1	18.1	17.1
1972	73.1	54.1	74.0	26.9	83.2	36.8	34.9	36.1	68.6	78.8	19.9	18.9
1973	75.3	58.0	77.1	29.1	84.8	38.6	35.3	37.4	71.7	81.0	22.4	20.5
1974	74.2	57.3	77.2	31.9	83.8	43.0	38.1	41.2	72.9	78.6	24.6	21.8
1975	76.2	56.3	73.9	35.1	84.5	46.1	44.9	45.6	70.7	79.6	25.9	25.3
1976	78.7	60.2	76.5	38.1	86.6	48.4	47.8	48.1	73.2	82.3	29.1	28.8
1977	80.0	63.6	79.5	41.2	88.0	51.5	50.7	51.2	76.5	83.1	32.7	32.2
1978	81.0	67.8	83.7	44.8	89.6	55.3	53.4	54.6	80.8	83.9	37.5	36.2
1979	80.7	70.0	86.6	49.1	89.7	60.8	56.5	59.2	84.2	83.1	42.5	39.5
1980	80.6	69.2	85.9	54.4	89.5	67.5	60.4	64.9	84.5	82.0	46.8	41.8
1981	81.7	70.7	86.6	59.7	89.8	73.1	67.7	71.1	85.4	82.8	51.7	47.9
1982	80.8	68.4	84.7	64.0	90.8	79.1	69.3	75.5	84.0	81.4	54.1	47.4
1983	84.5	72.9	86.3	66.6	90.9	78.9	76.0	77.9	84.9	85.9	57.5	55.4
1984	86.1	78.9	91.6	69.5	91.1	80.7	79.1	80.1	89.4	88.2	63.6	62.4
1985	87.4	82.2	94.0	72.6	92.2	83.1	81.5	82.5	92.0	89.4	68.3	66.9
1986	90.1	85.4	94.7	76.4	95.2	84.8	82.3	83.9	93.6	91.2	72.4	70.3
1987	90.6	88.4	97.6	79.2	95.4	87.4	82.7	85.7	96.2	91.9	77.3	73.2
1988	92.1	92.4	100.4	83.1	96.6	90.3	85.0	88.3	99.3	93.1	83.4	78.5
1989	92.7	95.7	103.2	85.2	95.0	91.9	90.9	91.5	101.5	94.3	87.9	86.9
1990	94.5	97.1	102.7	90.4	96.0	95.7	93.5	94.9	102.3	94.9	92.9	90.7
1991	96.1	96.3	100.2	95.0	97.4	98.9	96.8	98.1	100.6	95.7	95.2	93.2
1992	100.0	100.0	100.0	100.0	100.0	100.0	100.0	100.0	100.0	100.0	100.0	100.0
1993	100.4	103.4	102.9	102.0	99.5	101.5	103.1	102.1	102.3	101.0	105.0	106.6
1994	101.6	108.3	106.5	103.7	99.1	102.1	107.3	104.0	105.6	102.5	110.5	116.2
1995	102.1	111.8	109.4	106.0	98.9	103.7	109.4	105.8	108.6	102.9	116.0	122.3
1996	104.9	116.8	111.4	109.5	99.5	104.5	112.2	107.3	111.2	105.0	122.0	131.0
1997	106.6	122.8	115.3	112.9	100.4	105.9	114.6	109.1	114.3	107.5	130.1	140.8
1998	109.5	128.9	117.7	119.6	105.0	109.3	111.1	109.9	116.8	110.4	140.9	143.2
1999	112.6	135.6	120.4	125.2	107.5	111.2	111.1	111.1	119.0	113.9	150.7	150.6
2000	115.6	140.8	121.8	134.0	111.4	115.9	108.9	113.3	121.2	116.2	163.1	153.3
2001	118.5	141.3	119.3	139.3	112.6	117.5	111.8	115.4	120.4	117.4	166.1	158.0
2002	123.3	143.4	116.3	144.2	114.8	117.0	116.3	116.7	117.6	121.9	167.7	166.7
2003	128.0	148.2	115.8	149.9	116.7	117.1	120.0	118.2	117.6	126.0	173.6	177.8
2004	132.3	155.3	117.4	156.7	118.7	118.4	124.7	120.7	119.2	130.3	183.9	193.7

Table 5-1. Indexes of Productivity and Related Data, 1947–2004—*Continued*

(1992 = 100.)

Year	Nonfinancial corporations												
	Output per hour	Output	Hours	Compensation per hour	Real compensation per hour	Unit labor costs	Unit nonlabor costs	Unit profits	Implicit price deflator	Employment	Output per person	Compensation in current dollars	Nonlabor payments in current dollars
1947	...	...	...	...	...	...	...	...	...	...	...	...	...
1948	...	...	...	...	...	...	...	...	...	...	...	...	...
1949	...	...	...	...	...	...	...	...	...	...	...	...	...
1950	...	...	...	...	...	...	...	...	...	...	...	...	...
1951	...	...	...	...	...	...	...	...	...	...	...	...	...
1952	...	...	...	...	...	...	...	...	...	...	...	...	...
1953	...	...	...	...	...	...	...	...	...	...	...	...	...
1954	...	...	...	...	...	...	...	...	...	...	...	...	...
1955	...	...	...	...	...	...	...	...	...	...	...	...	...
1956	...	...	...	...	...	...	...	...	...	...	...	...	...
1957	...	...	...	...	...	...	...	...	...	...	...	...	...
1958	52.8	25.4	48.0	15.0	67.2	28.4	23.5	47.2	28.9	43.6	58.2	7.2	7.6
1959	55.3	28.2	50.9	15.6	69.3	28.1	22.3	55.8	29.2	45.6	61.8	7.9	8.8
1960	56.2	29.1	51.8	16.2	70.8	28.8	23.3	50.2	29.4	46.6	62.4	8.4	8.9
1961	57.9	29.7	51.3	16.7	72.4	28.8	23.8	50.3	29.5	46.3	64.2	8.6	9.2
1962	60.4	32.2	53.3	17.4	74.4	28.7	23.4	54.5	29.7	47.8	67.3	9.3	10.2
1963	62.6	34.1	54.5	17.9	75.7	28.6	23.4	57.3	29.9	48.8	69.9	9.8	11.1
1964	63.5	36.5	57.5	18.2	76.2	28.7	23.3	59.7	30.1	50.6	72.1	10.5	12.1
1965	65.1	39.5	60.7	18.8	77.1	28.8	23.1	64.1	30.6	53.3	74.1	11.4	13.5
1966	66.2	42.3	63.9	19.8	79.2	29.9	23.3	63.6	31.3	56.3	75.2	12.7	14.4
1967	67.1	43.4	64.6	20.9	81.1	31.2	24.7	59.9	32.2	57.9	74.9	13.5	14.8
1968	69.5	46.1	66.4	22.5	83.7	32.4	26.2	60.0	33.4	59.9	76.9	14.9	16.3
1969	69.5	47.9	69.0	24.0	84.8	34.6	28.6	54.0	34.8	62.7	76.5	16.6	16.9
1970	69.8	47.4	67.9	25.7	85.9	36.9	32.2	44.4	36.4	62.8	75.5	17.5	16.8
1971	72.7	49.3	67.9	27.3	87.4	37.6	33.6	50.5	37.8	63.0	78.4	18.5	18.8
1972	74.2	53.1	71.6	28.8	89.2	38.8	33.9	54.1	39.0	66.1	80.3	20.6	20.9
1973	74.8	56.3	75.2	31.0	90.4	41.4	35.7	54.9	41.2	69.7	80.7	23.3	23.0
1974	73.3	55.3	75.5	33.9	89.2	46.3	41.1	48.4	45.2	71.1	77.8	25.6	23.8
1975	76.1	54.6	71.7	37.3	89.7	49.0	46.6	63.1	49.6	68.4	79.8	26.7	27.8
1976	78.6	58.9	75.0	40.3	91.8	51.3	46.4	71.4	51.9	71.5	82.4	30.2	31.3
1977	80.6	63.2	78.4	43.5	93.0	54.0	48.4	77.3	54.7	75.1	84.2	34.1	35.5
1978	81.7	67.4	82.5	47.6	95.1	58.2	51.2	79.1	58.4	79.3	84.9	39.2	39.5
1979	81.0	69.5	85.8	51.9	94.9	64.1	55.8	74.0	62.9	83.3	83.4	44.6	42.2
1980	80.8	68.8	85.2	57.2	94.1	70.8	64.9	66.9	69.0	83.6	82.3	48.7	45.0
1981	82.9	71.6	86.4	62.4	93.9	75.3	73.4	81.0	75.4	85.1	84.2	53.9	54.0
1982	83.1	69.9	84.1	66.4	94.4	80.0	81.3	75.2	79.9	83.2	84.0	55.9	55.7
1983	85.7	73.1	85.3	68.9	94.0	80.4	81.6	91.2	81.7	83.5	87.6	58.8	61.6
1984	87.8	79.7	90.8	71.9	94.3	81.9	81.3	107.6	84.1	88.4	90.1	65.3	70.4
1985	89.6	83.2	92.9	75.2	95.4	83.9	83.6	102.3	85.5	90.9	91.5	69.8	73.7
1986	91.4	85.2	93.2	78.9	98.3	86.3	86.3	90.2	86.6	92.3	92.3	73.5	74.4
1987	93.3	89.7	96.1	81.6	98.3	87.4	85.8	100.1	88.1	94.8	94.6	78.4	80.4
1988	95.7	94.9	99.1	84.9	98.7	88.7	86.8	111.6	90.3	97.9	96.8	84.2	88.6
1989	94.6	96.6	102.2	87.0	97.0	92.0	93.3	101.2	93.2	100.4	96.2	88.9	92.2
1990	95.4	97.8	102.5	91.1	96.8	95.5	97.3	96.9	96.1	102.2	95.8	93.4	95.1
1991	97.4	97.0	99.6	95.5	97.9	98.0	102.7	93.2	98.7	100.0	97.0	95.1	97.2
1992	100.0	100.0	100.0	100.0	100.0	100.0	100.0	100.0	100.0	100.0	100.0	100.0	100.0
1993	100.3	102.8	102.4	101.8	99.3	101.4	99.9	114.1	102.2	102.0	100.8	104.2	106.6
1994	102.2	109.2	106.8	103.5	98.9	101.3	100.8	131.7	103.9	105.7	103.3	110.6	119.1
1995	103.3	114.3	110.6	105.3	98.3	101.9	101.2	136.9	104.9	109.5	104.4	116.5	126.6
1996	107.1	120.6	112.6	108.5	98.5	101.3	100.0	150.0	105.3	112.3	107.4	122.1	136.7
1997	109.9	128.4	116.9	111.7	99.4	101.7	99.7	154.3	105.9	115.8	110.9	130.6	146.9
1998	113.5	135.8	119.7	118.1	103.6	104.1	99.5	137.0	105.9	118.8	114.3	141.4	148.8
1999	117.3	144.0	122.8	123.6	106.2	105.3	100.4	129.1	106.2	121.8	118.3	151.7	155.6
2000	121.5	151.5	124.7	132.0	109.7	108.6	104.2	108.7	107.5	124.6	121.6	164.5	159.7
2001	123.5	150.2	121.6	137.3	111.1	111.2	112.6	82.2	108.9	123.3	121.8	166.9	156.9
2002	128.2	151.5	118.1	142.0	113.0	110.7	110.8	98.0	109.6	120.0	126.2	167.7	162.7
2003	133.5	155.6	116.5	147.6	114.8	110.5	110.9	116.7	111.2	118.9	130.8	171.9	174.9
2004	138.7	163.8	118.1	153.5	116.4	110.7	110.5	138.0	113.1	120.5	136.0	181.4	193.1

. . . = Not available.

Table 5-1. Indexes of Productivity and Related Data, 1947–2004—Continued

(1992 = 100.)

Year	Manufacturing											
	Output per hour	Output	Hours	Compen- sation per hour	Real compen- sation per hour	Unit labor costs	Unit nonlabor payments	Implicit price deflator	Employ- ment	Output per person	Compen- sation in current dollars	Nonlabor payments in current dollars
1947	...	...	...	...	...	...	...	...	...	...	...	...
1948	...	...	...	...	...	...	...	...	...	...	...	...
1949	...	...	...	...	...	...	...	...	...	...	...	...
1950	...	...	...	...	...	...	...	...	...	...	...	...
1951	...	...	...	...	...	...	...	...	...	...	...	...
1952	...	...	...	...	...	...	...	...	...	...	...	...
1953	...	...	...	...	...	...	...	...	...	...	...	...
1954	...	...	...	...	...	...	...	...	...	...	...	...
1955	...	...	...	...	...	...	...	...	...	...	...	...
1956	...	...	...	...	...	...	...	...	...	...	...	...
1957	...	...	...	...	...	...	...	...	...	...	...	...
1958	...	...	...	...	...	...	...	...	...	...	...	...
1959	...	...	...	...	...	...	...	...	...	...	...	...
1960	...	...	...	...	...	...	...	...	...	...	...	...
1961	...	...	...	...	...	...	...	...	...	...	...	...
1962	...	...	...	...	...	...	...	...	...	...	...	...
1963	...	...	...	...	...	...	...	...	...	...	...	...
1964	...	...	...	...	...	...	...	...	...	...	...	...
1965	...	...	...	...	...	...	...	...	...	...	...	...
1966	...	...	...	...	...	...	...	...	...	...	...	...
1967	...	...	...	...	...	...	...	...	...	...	...	...
1968	...	...	...	...	...	...	...	...	...	...	...	...
1969	...	...	...	...	...	...	...	...	...	...	...	...
1970	...	...	...	...	...	...	...	...	...	...	...	...
1971	...	...	...	...	...	...	...	...	...	...	...	...
1972	...	...	...	...	...	...	...	...	...	...	...	...
1973	...	...	...	...	...	...	...	...	...	...	...	...
1974	...	...	...	...	...	...	...	...	...	...	...	...
1975	...	...	...	...	...	...	...	...	...	...	...	...
1976	...	...	...	...	...	...	...	...	...	...	...	...
1977	...	...	...	...	...	...	...	...	...	...	...	...
1978	...	...	...	...	...	...	...	...	...	...	...	...
1979	...	...	...	...	...	...	...	...	...	...	...	...
1980	...	...	...	...	...	...	...	...	...	...	...	...
1981	...	...	...	...	...	...	...	...	...	...	...	...
1982	...	...	...	...	...	...	...	...	...	...	...	...
1983	...	...	...	...	...	...	...	...	...	...	...	...
1984	...	...	...	...	...	...	...	...	...	...	...	...
1985	...	...	...	...	...	...	...	...	...	...	...	...
1986	...	...	...	...	...	...	...	...	...	...	...	...
1987	88.4	91.7	103.8	81.3	98.0	92.0	87.6	89.3	104.6	87.7	84.4	80.3
1988	90.0	96.3	107.0	84.1	97.8	93.4	90.9	91.9	106.4	90.5	90.0	87.6
1989	90.3	97.2	107.6	86.6	96.6	95.9	96.1	96.0	107.0	90.9	93.2	93.5
1990	92.9	97.6	105.0	90.5	96.1	97.3	100.8	99.5	105.4	92.6	95.0	98.4
1991	95.4	96.0	100.5	95.6	98.0	100.1	99.4	99.7	101.7	94.3	96.1	95.4
1992	100.0	100.0	100.0	100.0	100.0	100.0	100.0	100.0	100.0	100.0	100.0	100.0
1993	102.7	104.1	101.4	102.0	99.5	99.3	101.4	100.6	100.1	104.0	103.5	105.6
1994	106.1	110.0	103.8	105.3	100.6	99.3	103.3	101.8	101.5	108.5	109.2	113.6
1995	109.9	115.0	104.6	107.3	100.1	97.6	107.7	103.9	102.8	111.9	112.2	123.9
1996	113.9	118.6	104.2	109.3	99.3	96.0	110.7	105.2	102.6	115.6	113.9	131.4
1997	118.0	125.1	106.0	112.2	99.8	95.1	110.4	104.6	103.7	120.6	119.0	138.1
1998	123.6	130.7	105.7	118.7	104.2	96.0	104.2	101.1	104.6	125.0	125.6	136.2
1999	128.1	134.6	105.1	123.4	106.0	96.4	105.1	101.8	103.0	130.7	129.7	141.4
2000	134.1	138.6	103.4	134.7	112.0	100.5	107.1	104.6	102.5	135.3	139.3	148.5
2001	136.9	132.3	96.6	137.8	111.5	100.7	105.9	103.9	97.8	135.3	133.2	140.2
2002	147.3	132.2	89.8	147.9	117.7	100.4	...	...	90.6	145.8	132.7	...
2003	154.8	132.2	85.4	160.1	124.6	103.4	...	...	86.3	153.2	136.7	...
2004	163.0	138.6	85.0	163.6	124.0	100.4	...	...	85.3	162.6	139.1	...

. . . = Not available.

Table 5-2. Average Annual Percent Change in Output per Hour and Related Series, 1987–2003 and 2002–2003

(Number, percent.)

Industry	NAICS Code	2003 Employment (thousands)	Annual percent change 1987–2003			Annual percent change 2002–2003		
			Output per hour	Output	Hours	Output per hour	Output	Hours
Mining								
Mining	21	503	1.9	-0.2	-2.1	2.1	-0.4	-2.4
Oil and gas extraction	211	120	3.1	-0.8	-3.8	5.3	0.0	-5.0
Mining, except oil and gas	212	203	3.1	0.8	-2.2	2.0	-1.3	-3.2
Coal mining	2 121	70	4.2	-0.2	-4.2	0.8	-3.8	-4.5
Metal ore mining	2 122	27	4.4	2.1	-2.2	-1.0	-5.8	-4.9
Nonmetallic mineral mining and quarrying	2 123	106	1.3	0.9	-0.4	4.8	2.9	-1.9
Utilities								
Power generation and supply	2 211	418	3.0	1.2	-1.8	2.1	-1.7	-3.8
Natural gas distribution	2 212	113	3.3	1.6	-1.7	-1.0	-1.6	-0.6
Manufacturing								
Food	311	1 518	1.3	1.7	0.4	0.8	-0.6	-1.4
Animal food	3 111	50	3.3	2.2	-1.1	-1.6	-1.3	0.4
Grain and oilseed milling	3 112	62	2.6	1.6	-0.9	-1.5	-0.7	0.8
Sugar and confectionery products	3 113	85	1.6	1.1	-0.4	3.7	0.2	-3.4
Fruit and vegetable preserving and specialty	3 114	185	1.7	1.8	0.0	-3.9	-2.9	1.0
Dairy products	3 115	135	1.8	1.0	-0.8	4.8	-0.1	-4.7
Animal slaughtering and processing	3 116	516	0.6	2.5	1.9	-0.7	-1.3	-0.6
Seafood product preparation and packaging	3 117	42	2.3	0.9	-1.4	4.6	0.7	-3.7
Bakeries and tortilla manufacturing	3 118	292	0.6	0.5	-0.1	0.2	-3.3	-3.5
Other food products	3 119	152	1.2	2.3	1.0	4.7	3.9	-0.7
Beverages and tobacco products	312	200	0.8	-0.3	-1.1	7.9	2.9	-4.6
Beverages	3 121	169	2.0	1.2	-0.7	5.2	1.6	-3.5
Tobacco and tobacco products	3 122	31	0.5	-2.5	-3.1	17.9	5.2	-10.8
Textile mills	313	261	3.9	-0.8	-4.5	8.1	-5.7	-12.7
Fiber, yarn, and thread mills	3 131	57	5.2	0.3	-4.7	12.5	-2.6	-13.4
Fabric mills	3 132	130	4.4	-0.9	-5.1	8.2	-6.0	-13.2
Textile and fabric finishing mills	3 133	74	2.0	-1.3	-3.3	4.2	-7.6	-11.4
Textile product mills	314	179	1.1	0.4	-0.7	4.9	-1.2	-5.9
Textile furnishings mills	3 141	105	1.3	0.5	-0.7	8.1	-0.2	-7.7
Other textile product mills	3 149	74	0.8	0.1	-0.7	-0.5	-3.6	-3.1
Apparel	315	312	3.1	-4.0	-6.9	8.0	-7.9	-14.8
Apparel knitting mills	3 151	45	2.2	-4.0	-6.1	-6.4	-16.8	-11.1
Cut and sew apparel	3 152	243	3.6	-4.0	-7.3	11.4	-6.6	-16.1
Accessories and other apparel	3 159	24	-1.3	-4.2	-2.9	2.4	-5.0	-7.2
Leather and allied products	316	45	2.3	-4.6	-6.7	-1.4	-6.2	-4.9
Leather and hide tanning and finishing	3 161	8	1.0	-2.7	-3.6	-6.5	-9.5	-3.2
Footwear	3 162	20	1.7	-7.3	-8.9	-1.3	-6.3	-5.1
Other leather products	3 169	17	0.1	-4.3	-4.4	3.4	-2.3	-5.5
Wood products	321	538	1.1	0.8	-0.3	0.1	-0.8	-0.9
Sawmills and wood preservation	3 211	117	2.8	1.1	-1.7	5.4	1.8	-3.4
Plywood and engineered wood products	3 212	114	0.4	1.2	0.8	-3.4	-2.1	1.4
Other wood products	3 219	307	0.6	0.4	-0.1	-1.2	-1.9	-0.7
Paper and paper products	322	516	2.0	0.5	-1.5	3.0	-3.6	-6.4
Pulp, paper, and paperboard mills	3 221	151	3.3	0.1	-3.1	3.7	-5.7	-9.0
Converted paper products	3 222	365	1.3	0.7	-0.6	3.5	-1.8	-5.2
Printing and related support activities	323	680	0.8	0.1	-0.7	0.7	-3.6	-4.2
Petroleum and coal products	324	114	3.2	1.2	-1.9	0.9	1.0	0.2
Chemicals	325	906	1.9	1.5	-0.4	1.8	-0.3	-2.1
Basic chemicals	3 251	162	2.1	-0.2	-2.3	6.5	0.8	-5.3
Resin, rubber, and artificial fibers	3 252	112	2.8	0.9	-1.8	-1.7	-4.0	-2.4
Agricultural chemicals	3 253	42	1.8	0.6	-1.2	8.4	2.5	-5.4
Pharmaceuticals and medicines	3 254	292	0.8	4.3	3.5	2.8	2.9	0.1
Paints, coatings, and adhesives	3 255	69	1.5	0.3	-1.2	4.0	-1.1	-4.9
Soaps, cleaning compounds, and toiletries	3 256	119	1.9	1.7	-0.2	-7.9	-7.0	1.0
Other chemical products and preparations	3 259	111	3.1	0.9	-2.1	3.2	0.7	-2.4
Plastics and rubber products	326	816	2.7	2.9	0.2	3.9	-0.5	-4.2
Plastics products	3 261	639	2.7	3.3	0.6	4.0	-0.6	-4.5
Rubber products	3 262	177	2.5	1.4	-1.1	3.5	0.1	-3.2
Nonmetallic mineral products	327	495	1.5	1.1	-0.3	5.5	0.2	-5.0
Clay products and refractories	3 271	66	1.1	-0.4	-1.5	3.7	-2.8	-6.2
Glass and glass products	3 272	115	2.1	0.8	-1.2	7.2	-1.0	-7.7
Cement and concrete products	3 273	224	0.8	1.8	0.9	4.4	0.5	-3.8
Lime and gypsum products	3 274	19	1.4	0.2	-1.2	9.4	5.0	-4.1
Other nonmetallic mineral products	3 279	71	1.9	1.0	-0.9	5.3	1.6	-3.5
Primary metals	331	478	2.4	0.2	-2.2	1.8	-4.1	-5.9

Table 5-2. Average Annual Percent Change in Output per Hour and Related Series, 1987–2003 and 2002–2003—*Continued*

(Number, percent.)

Industry	NAICS Code	2003 Employment (thousands)	Annual percent change 1987–2003			Annual percent change 2002–2003		
			Output per hour	Output	Hours	Output per hour	Output	Hours
Iron and steel mills and ferroalloy production	3 311	102	4.2	0.7	-3.4	1.7	-5.2	-6.7
Steel products from purchased steel	3 312	61	1.5	0.6	-0.9	-3.4	-10.3	-7.1
Alumina and aluminum production	3 313	75	2.1	-0.3	-2.4	1.6	-1.8	-3.3
Other nonferrous metal production	3 314	74	1.4	-1.0	-2.4	11.0	1.3	-8.7
Foundries	3 315	166	2.3	0.8	-1.5	0.5	-4.3	-4.7
Fabricated metal products	332	1 479	1.7	1.3	-0.4	2.9	-1.5	-4.3
Forging and stamping	3 321	109	2.8	1.5	-1.3	6.1	1.6	-4.2
Cutlery and hand tools	3 322	61	1.5	-0.1	-1.5	1.4	-4.5	-5.9
Architectural and structural metals	3 323	380	1.3	1.8	0.5	2.6	-2.0	-4.5
Boilers, tanks, and shipping containers	3 324	91	1.1	-0.3	-1.3	2.3	-2.7	-4.8
Hardware	3 325	40	2.1	-0.8	-2.8	7.1	-3.0	-9.4
Spring and wire products	3 326	64	3.3	2.1	-1.2	7.5	0.4	-6.5
Machine shops and threaded products	3 327	311	2.6	3.0	0.4	0.2	-1.6	-1.8
Coating, engraving, and heat treating metals	3 328	143	2.8	3.0	0.2	1.5	-3.6	-5.0
Other fabricated metal products	3 329	282	1.3	0.2	-1.0	4.5	-0.2	-4.5
Machinery	333	1 150	2.6	1.3	-1.2	6.8	-0.2	-6.6
Agriculture, construction, and mining machinery	3 331	188	2.8	2.0	-0.8	12.5	6.1	-5.7
Industrial machinery	3 332	123	2.4	1.2	-1.1	2.8	-4.4	-7.0
Commercial and service industry machinery	3 333	118	1.5	-0.2	-1.7	7.6	-3.1	-9.9
HVAC and commercial refrigeration equipment	3 334	157	2.6	2.0	-0.6	8.4	1.0	-6.9
Metalworking machinery	3 335	205	2.0	0.4	-1.6	1.6	-3.4	-5.0
Turbine and power transmission equipment	3 336	94	3.6	2.4	-1.2	6.8	-0.8	-7.1
Other general purpose machinery	3 339	265	2.5	1.1	-1.4	5.9	-1.1	-6.6
Computer and electronic products	334	1 344	13.6	10.8	-2.5	16.0	6.1	-8.6
Computer and peripheral equipment	3 341	224	24.8	20.1	-3.7	27.7	15.2	-9.8
Communications equipment	3 342	155	8.3	5.2	-2.8	11.0	-4.0	-13.5
Audio and video equipment	3 343	37	6.8	3.2	-3.4	15.5	-1.2	-14.4
Semiconductors and electronic components	3 344	461	20.2	18.4	-1.5	21.9	9.8	-10.0
Electronic instruments	3 345	430	3.9	0.9	-2.8	7.8	3.8	-3.7
Magnetic media manufacturing and reproduction	3 346	38	1.5	1.9	0.4	4.2	-4.7	-8.5
Electrical equipment and appliances	335	460	2.9	0.5	-2.3	3.5	-1.9	-5.3
Electric lighting equipment	3 351	67	1.4	0.1	-1.2	0.7	-4.7	-5.4
Household appliances	3 352	92	4.6	2.2	-2.3	11.5	5.7	-5.2
Electrical equipment	3 353	160	2.7	-0.2	-2.8	1.7	-3.2	-4.8
Other electrical equipment and components	3 359	140	2.5	0.3	-2.1	1.1	-4.8	-5.8
Transportation equipment	336	1 775	3.2	1.9	-1.2	7.5	2.6	-4.6
Motor vehicles	3 361	265	3.9	2.9	-0.9	9.8	7.6	-2.0
Motor vehicle bodies and trailers	3 362	153	1.6	2.2	0.6	3.6	4.4	0.8
Motor vehicle parts	3 363	708	3.5	4.1	0.6	4.0	-1.5	-5.3
Aerospace products and parts	3 364	443	2.2	-1.8	-3.9	3.4	-4.1	-7.2
Railroad rolling stock	3 365	23	6.0	4.8	-1.2	-3.1	-6.1	-3.1
Ship and boat building	3 366	146	2.1	0.7	-1.4	2.1	-0.4	-2.4
Other transportation equipment	3 369	39	5.2	5.4	0.2	9.9	4.4	-4.9
Furniture and related products	337	573	2.2	1.7	-0.4	3.9	-1.9	-5.5
Household and institutional furniture	3 371	382	2.1	1.6	-0.5	2.2	-3.4	-5.5
Office furniture and fixtures	3 372	139	2.4	1.6	-0.8	8.8	0.1	-7.9
Other furniture-related products	3 379	52	1.6	2.5	0.9	0.0	0.9	0.9
Miscellaneous manufacturing	339	663	3.3	3.5	0.1	5.8	1.9	-3.7
Medical equipment and supplies	3 391	304	3.7	4.9	1.1	6.6	4.9	-1.6
Other miscellaneous manufacturing	3 399	359	2.9	2.3	-0.6	4.5	-1.1	-5.4
Wholesale Trade								
Wholesale trade	42	5 827	3.6	4.0	0.4	3.4	2.1	-1.3
Durable goods	423	3 054	4.9	5.2	0.3	4.9	2.9	-1.9
Motor vehicles and parts	4 231	358	3.6	3.6	-0.1	5.4	3.8	-1.5
Furniture and furnishings	4 232	118	2.1	2.3	0.1	9.4	2.3	-6.5
Lumber and construction supplies	4 233	235	0.3	1.6	1.3	8.3	10.2	1.8
Commercial equipment	4 234	669	13.5	14.0	0.5	8.2	7.0	-1.1
Metals and minerals	4 235	121	-0.1	-0.2	-0.1	0.2	-5.3	-5.5
Electric goods	4 236	356	9.2	9.2	0.0	6.5	4.0	-2.4
Hardware and plumbing	4 237	237	1.9	2.6	0.7	4.0	-0.4	-4.3
Machinery and supplies	4 238	668	2.1	2.0	-0.1	4.3	1.8	-2.4
Miscellaneous durable goods	4 239	293	2.1	2.6	0.4	-3.3	-3.6	-0.3
Nondurable goods	424	2 109	1.4	1.8	0.3	4.5	1.2	-3.1
Paper and paper products	4 241	160	2.4	2.3	-0.1	2.7	-0.7	-3.3
Druggists' goods	4 242	216	4.1	6.9	2.7	14.0	9.5	-3.9
Apparel and piece goods	4 243	161	1.0	1.2	0.2	-5.3	-5.8	-0.5

Table 5-2. Average Annual Percent Change in Output per Hour and Related Series, 1987–2003 and 2002–2003—*Continued*

(Number, percent.)

Industry	NAICS Code	2003 Employment (thousands)	Annual percent change 1987–2003			Annual percent change 2002–2003		
			Output per hour	Output	Hours	Output per hour	Output	Hours
Grocery and related products	4 244	718	1.4	2.4	1.0	2.8	1.1	-1.7
Farm product raw materials	4 245	80	3.1	0.2	-2.8	-0.1	1.5	1.6
Chemicals	4 246	134	0.3	1.0	0.7	2.9	-2.7	-5.4
Petroleum	4 247	108	1.9	-0.7	-2.6	3.3	0.2	-3.1
Alcoholic beverages	4 248	139	1.1	2.3	1.2	1.3	4.7	3.4
Miscellaneous nondurable goods	4 249	393	0.4	0.3	-0.2	7.7	-1.4	-8.4
Electronic markets and agents and brokers	425	665	4.4	6.2	1.7	-6.2	2.2	8.9
Business to business electronic markets	42 511	69	9.6	8.2	-1.3	32.7	5.0	-20.8
Wholesale trade agents and brokers	42 512	597	2.7	4.8	2.1	-11.5	0.1	13.0
Retail Trade								
Retail trade	44-45	15 872	3.0	3.9	0.8	5.3	4.5	-0.8
Motor vehicle and parts dealers	441	1 974	1.7	3.0	1.2	1.7	3.1	1.5
Automobile dealers	4 411	1 319	1.3	2.7	1.4	-0.8	1.6	2.4
Other motor vehicle dealers	4 412	159	3.7	6.3	2.5	12.0	26.7	13.1
Auto parts, accessories, and tire stores	4 413	497	3.2	3.6	0.4	8.3	4.0	-4.0
Furniture and home furnishings stores	442	601	3.6	4.5	0.9	8.4	7.0	-1.3
Furniture stores	4 421	306	3.5	4.1	0.6	5.7	3.8	-1.8
Home furnishings stores	4 422	295	3.8	5.0	1.1	11.8	10.8	-0.9
Electronics and appliance stores	443	544	14.3	15.5	1.0	28.2	18.7	-7.4
Building material and garden supply stores	444	1 236	3.3	5.1	1.8	7.0	9.3	2.1
Building material and supplies dealers	4 441	1 073	3.2	5.4	2.1	7.2	9.1	1.8
Lawn and garden equipment and supplies stores	4 442	163	3.2	3.5	0.3	5.7	10.8	4.8
Food and beverage stores	445	2 951	0.3	0.6	0.3	4.1	1.7	-2.3
Grocery stores	4 451	2 517	0.2	0.6	0.4	2.9	1.5	-1.4
Specialty food stores	4 452	276	-0.2	0.1	0.2	14.1	6.9	-6.3
Beer, wine, and liquor stores	4 453	157	1.8	0.3	-1.5	12.7	2.1	-9.4
Health and personal care stores	446	976	2.6	3.9	1.2	8.0	4.4	-3.4
Gasoline stations	447	907	2.2	1.6	-0.6	-3.5	-1.7	1.8
Clothing and clothing accessories stores	448	1 398	4.8	4.7	-0.1	6.7	6.8	0.1
Clothing stores	4 481	1 012	4.8	5.0	0.2	4.7	6.6	1.8
Shoe stores	4 482	187	4.5	2.7	-1.7	7.0	3.3	-3.5
Jewelry, luggage, and leather goods stores	4 483	199	4.8	4.9	0.1	14.9	10.6	-3.8
Sporting goods, hobby, book, and music stores	451	729	3.7	5.2	1.4	0.0	0.4	0.4
Sporting goods and musical instrument stores	4 511	491	4.4	5.6	1.2	0.8	2.0	1.2
Book, periodical, and music stores	4 512	238	2.3	4.2	1.9	-1.3	-2.7	-1.4
General merchandise stores	452	2 834	3.9	5.5	1.5	4.9	5.6	0.6
Department stores	4 521	1 623	1.2	2.9	1.7	3.3	-1.3	-4.5
Other general merchandise stores	4 529	1 212	7.9	9.4	1.4	4.6	12.2	7.3
Miscellaneous store retailers	453	1 109	3.9	5.1	1.2	5.5	2.2	-3.2
Florists	4 531	139	3.2	1.9	-1.3	10.3	7.9	-2.1
Office supplies, stationery, and gift stores	4 532	459	6.1	6.8	0.7	7.1	3.4	-3.5
Used merchandise stores	4 533	166	3.3	7.5	4.1	1.5	9.6	7.9
Other miscellaneous store retailers	4 539	346	1.8	3.9	2.1	6.5	-1.4	-7.4
Nonstore retailers	454	612	8.8	9.0	0.2	15.9	9.4	-5.6
Electronic shopping and mail-order houses	4 541	245	11.9	16.6	4.2	18.3	13.8	-3.7
Vending machine operators	4 542	66	1.7	-0.1	-1.8	9.0	-4.8	-12.6
Direct selling establishments	4 543	301	3.4	1.6	-1.8	9.0	3.1	-5.4
Transportation and Warehousing								
Air transportation	481	482	2.0	2.9	0.9	9.9	3.1	-6.2
Line-haul railroads	482 111	176	5.7	2.4	-3.0	7.6	5.3	-2.1
General freight trucking, long-distance	48 412	752	1.4	3.0	1.6	2.1	0.0	-2.0
Used household and office goods moving	48 421	114	-0.9	0.0	0.9	8.5	-1.5	-9.2
Postal service	491	809	1.0	1.3	0.2	1.6	-1.9	-3.4
Couriers and messengers	492	591	-0.6	2.9	3.5	2.2	-1.4	-3.5
Information								
Publishing	511	925	4.1	5.1	0.9	6.7	-1.4	-7.6
Newspaper, book, and directory publishers	5 111	686	0.1	-0.5	-0.6	3.1	-3.9	-6.7
Software publishers	5 112	239	17.7	27.6	8.4	13.0	1.8	-9.9
Motion picture and video exhibition	51 213	139	0.9	3.1	2.2	4.1	1.7	-2.3
Broadcasting, except Internet	515	324	0.6	2.1	1.5	1.8	1.1	-0.7
Radio and television broadcasting	5 151	238	0.1	0.3	0.2	1.9	2.2	0.3
Cable and other subscription programming	5 152	86	1.7	7.9	6.1	1.9	-1.1	-3.0
Wired telecommunications carriers	5 171	579	5.6	4.5	-1.1	4.4	-6.7	-10.6
Wireless telecommunications carriers	5 172	190	7.4	24.7	16.1	13.1	13.6	0.4
Cable and other program distribution	5 175	133	-0.5	5.5	6.0	5.3	7.1	1.7

Table 5-2. Average Annual Percent Change in Output per Hour and Related Series, 1987–2003 and 2002–2003—*Continued*

(Number, percent.)

Industry	NAICS Code	2003 Employment (thousands)	Annual percent change 1987–2003			Annual percent change 2002–2003		
			Output per hour	Output	Hours	Output per hour	Output	Hours
Finance and Insurance								
Commercial banking	52 211	1 280	2.1	1.7	-0.4	3.0	2.6	-0.4
Real Estate and Rental and Leasing								
Passenger car rental	532 111	121	1.8	3.4	1.6	5.4	-1.8	-6.8
Truck, trailer, and RV rental and leasing	53 212	62	3.5	3.7	0.2	0.6	3.0	2.5
Video tape and disc rental	53 223	162	4.9	7.5	2.5	13.4	12.9	-0.4
Professional and Technical Services								
Tax preparation services	541 213	99	1.5	5.6	4.0	-0.9	3.1	4.0
Advertising agencies	54 181	181	2.4	2.0	-0.4	7.9	4.6	-3.1
Photography studios, portrait	541 921	107	0.5	2.7	2.2	9.5	0.5	-8.2
Administrative and Support Services								
Travel agencies	56 151	134	3.2	2.7	-0.5	16.1	5.8	-8.9
Janitorial services	56 172	1 029	3.2	4.7	1.5	11.1	8.5	-2.3
Health Care and Social Assistance [1]								
Medical and diagnostic laboratories	62 151	193	4.4	7.3	2.8	-4.1	-1.2	3.0
Medical laboratories	621 511	133	2.6	5.2	2.5	-7.4	-5.9	1.6
Diagnostic imaging centers	621 512	60	7.1	10.7	3.4	-0.7	5.7	6.4
Accomodation and Food Services								
Traveler accommodations	7 211	1 734	2.0	2.9	0.9	2.2	1.4	-0.7
Food services and drinking places	722	8 816	0.7	2.4	1.7	3.2	4.9	1.7
Full-service restaurants	7 221	4 195	0.9	2.7	1.8	3.0	6.3	3.2
Limited-service eating places	7 222	3 708	0.9	2.6	1.7	3.0	5.3	2.2
Special food services	7 223	522	0.4	1.8	1.3	3.0	-1.6	-4.4
Drinking places, alcoholic beverages	7 224	393	-0.9	-0.7	0.2	11.6	-0.8	-11.1
Other Services								
Automotive repair and maintenance	8 111	1 155	1.2	2.7	1.5	0.8	1.9	1.1
Hair, nail, and skin care services	81 211	819	2.6	3.3	0.7	13.4	5.6	-6.9
Funeral homes and funeral services	81 221	108	-0.3	0.8	1.1	2.6	4.8	2.1
Dry cleaning and laundry services	8 123	391	0.8	0.5	-0.4	-3.4	-6.3	-3.0
Photofinishing	81 292	70	-0.5	-3.1	-2.5	-4.6	-5.4	-0.8

[1]For NAICS industries 62 151, 621 511, and 621 512, annual percent changes are for 1994–2003.

Table 5-3. Annual Percent Change in Output per Hour and Related Series, Retail Trade, Wholesale Trade, and Food Services and Drinking Places Industries, 1987–2004 and 2003–2004

(Number, percent.)

Industry	NAICS code	2004 Employment (thousands)	Annual percent change 1987–2004			Annual percent change 2002–2004		
			Output per hour	Output	Hours	Output per hour	Output	Hours
Wholesale Trade								
Wholesale trade	42	5 832	3.9	4.4	0.4	7.8	7.8	0.0
Durable goods	423	3 042	5.8	6.0	0.2	12.8	12.2	-0.6
Motor vehicles and parts	4 231	354	4.4	4.3	0.0	6.7	7.0	0.3
Furniture and furnishings	4 232	116	2.5	2.5	0.0	10.1	8.6	-1.3
Lumber and construction supplies	4 233	247	1.2	2.7	1.5	16.5	22.5	5.1
Commercial equipment	4 234	653	14.9	15.2	0.3	14.0	10.7	-2.9
Metals and minerals	4 235	123	1.0	0.8	-0.1	15.6	15.1	-0.4
Electric goods	4 236	350	9.8	9.6	-0.2	21.9	17.6	-3.5
Hardware and plumbing	4 237	238	1.8	2.5	0.7	4.7	6.2	1.4
Machinery and supplies	4 238	672	2.8	2.8	0.0	14.9	16.5	1.3
Miscellaneous durable goods	4 239	289	2.1	2.3	0.2	12.9	8.9	-3.5
Nondurable goods	424	2 085	1.9	2.1	0.2	4.4	2.9	-1.5
Paper and paper products	4 241	156	2.6	2.2	-0.3	7.0	3.6	-3.2
Druggists' goods	4 242	224	5.2	7.9	2.5	8.5	8.7	0.2
Apparel and piece goods	4 243	157	2.2	2.4	0.1	4.8	4.6	-0.2
Grocery and related products	4 244	710	1.0	1.8	0.8	0.5	-1.4	-2.0
Farm product raw materials	4 245	75	3.0	-0.1	-3.1	11.3	3.7	-6.9
Chemicals	4 246	135	-0.1	0.7	0.8	-4.9	-1.6	3.4
Petroleum	4 247	103	3.8	0.6	-3.1	14.2	1.5	-11.1
Alcoholic beverages	4 248	143	0.5	1.9	1.5	-3.9	1.8	5.9
Miscellaneous nondurable goods	4 249	384	0.3	0.0	-0.3	8.2	6.0	-2.0
Electronic markets and agents and brokers	425	705	3.3	5.5	2.1	-0.5	7.3	7.9
Retail Trade								
Retail trade	44-45	15 933	3.4	4.3	0.8	6.1	6.5	0.4
Motor vehicle and parts dealers	441	1 989	3.0	4.3	1.3	4.0	6.4	2.3
Automobile dealers	4 411	1 306	2.8	4.2	1.3	6.5	6.5	0.0
Other motor vehicle dealers	4 412	165	3.8	6.5	2.6	5.9	9.7	3.6
Auto parts, accessories, and tire stores	4 413	518	3.2	4.0	0.8	-4.7	2.9	8.0
Furniture and home furnishings stores	442	605	4.6	5.4	0.8	8.4	7.4	-0.9
Furniture stores	4 421	308	4.3	4.9	0.6	9.9	9.6	-0.2
Home furnishings stores	4 422	297	5.0	6.0	1.0	6.6	4.9	-1.6
Electronics and appliance stores	443	549	13.3	14.7	1.2	11.6	16.5	4.4
Building material and garden supply stores	444	1 273	3.7	5.7	1.9	9.9	13.3	3.1
Building material and supplies dealers	4 441	1 113	3.7	5.9	2.2	9.9	14.2	3.9
Lawn and garden equipment and supplies stores	4 442	160	4.0	4.2	0.2	9.3	7.0	-2.2
Food and beverage stores	445	2 918	0.2	0.3	0.0	5.8	1.4	-4.1
Grocery stores	4 451	2 493	0.2	0.3	0.1	5.7	1.1	-4.4
Specialty food stores	4 452	274	-0.3	-0.1	0.1	9.4	7.6	-1.7
Beer, wine, and liquor stores	4 453	152	1.8	0.2	-1.6	6.6	2.7	-3.7
Health and personal care stores	446	968	2.9	4.0	1.0	6.2	3.7	-2.4
Gasoline stations	447	901	2.3	1.8	-0.5	1.4	3.2	1.9
Clothing and clothing accessories stores	448	1 455	4.5	4.8	0.3	-0.1	6.6	6.7
Clothing stores	4 481	1 069	4.6	5.2	0.6	0.0	7.7	7.6
Shoe stores	4 482	192	3.7	2.6	-1.0	-8.5	1.9	11.4
Jewelry, luggage, and leather goods stores	4 483	193	4.7	4.8	0.1	6.3	5.4	-0.9
Sporting goods, hobby, book, and music stores	451	712	4.2	4.9	0.7	15.4	4.1	-9.8
Sporting goods and musical instrument stores	4 511	485	4.9	5.4	0.5	18.1	5.3	-10.9
Book, periodical, and music stores	4 512	227	2.6	3.9	1.3	9.9	1.9	-7.3
General merchandise stores	452	2 864	3.9	5.5	1.6	4.1	6.6	2.4
Department stores	4 521	1 625	1.3	2.9	1.6	1.5	1.3	-0.3
Other general merchandise stores	4 529	1 240	7.6	9.4	1.6	5.3	11.1	5.5
Miscellaneous store retailers	453	1 092	3.8	4.9	1.1	4.1	3.7	-0.4
Florists	4 531	134	1.5	0.2	-1.3	-5.8	-6.6	-0.8
Office supplies, stationery, and gift stores	4 532	440	6.0	6.3	0.3	6.3	0.4	-5.5
Used merchandise stores	4 533	172	2.3	6.4	4.0	0.0	1.3	1.3
Other miscellaneous store retailers	4 539	345	2.0	4.3	2.3	2.7	8.4	5.6
Nonstore retailers	454	607	9.9	10.0	0.1	14.6	14.0	-0.5
Electronic shopping and mail-order houses	4 541	250	12.7	17.2	3.9	17.2	17.4	0.2
Vending machine operators	4 542	62	0.1	-1.8	-1.9	-0.9	-5.4	-4.5
Direct selling establishments	4 543	295	5.0	3.3	-1.7	10.0	9.9	-0.1
Food Services and Drinking Places								
Food services and drinking places	722	9 081	0.7	2.5	1.8	2.4	5.6	3.1
Full-service restaurants	7 221	4 329	0.8	2.7	1.9	2.3	4.8	2.5
Limited-service eating places	7 222	3 830	0.8	2.6	1.8	3.3	7.1	3.7
Special food services	7 223	530	1.2	2.5	1.3	-0.2	1.3	1.5
Drinking places, alcoholic beverages	7 224	392	-0.6	0.0	0.6	0.6	7.9	7.2

Table 5-4. Indexes of Multifactor Productivity and Related Measures, Selected Years, 1960–2002

(2000 = 100, unless otherwise indicated.)

Industry	1960	1965	1970	1975	1980	1985	1986	1987	1988	1989	1990	1991
Private Business												
Productivity												
Output per hour of all persons	40.8	50.0	56.4	63.9	67.8	74.9	77.3	77.7	78.9	79.7	81.4	82.7
Output per unit of capital	113.6	125.1	115.6	107.5	106.6	102.9	102.4	102.4	103.4	103.9	102.6	99.7
Multifactor productivity	61.6	72.1	76.0	80.8	84.1	87.5	88.9	89.1	89.8	90.3	90.9	90.3
Output	22.5	29.1	34.3	39.6	48.5	58.1	60.3	62.5	65.2	67.6	68.6	68.1
Inputs												
Labor input	48.5	52.1	54.8	56.0	64.6	71.8	72.7	75.0	77.7	80.2	80.1	79.1
Capital services	19.8	23.3	29.7	36.9	45.5	56.5	58.9	61.0	63.0	65.0	66.9	68.4
Combined units of labor and capital inputs	36.5	40.4	45.1	49.0	57.7	66.4	67.9	70.1	72.6	74.9	75.5	75.4
Capital services per hour for all persons	35.9	40.0	48.8	59.5	63.6	72.8	75.5	75.9	76.3	76.7	79.3	83.0
Private Nonfarm Business												
Productivity												
Output per hour of all persons	43.6	52.5	58.1	65.4	69.2	75.5	77.9	78.2	79.6	80.1	81.7	83.1
Output per unit of capital	126.0	137.1	124.9	114.3	112.7	106.1	105.2	104.7	105.7	105.9	104.2	101.1
Multifactor productivity	65.8	75.7	78.8	83.3	86.5	88.7	90.0	90.0	90.9	91.1	91.5	91.0
Output	22.2	29.0	34.3	39.5	48.7	58.0	60.3	62.4	65.3	67.6	68.6	68.1
Inputs												
Labor input	45.1	49.8	53.3	54.7	63.5	71.1	72.1	74.5	77.3	79.8	79.8	78.7
Capital services	17.7	21.2	27.5	34.6	43.2	54.7	57.3	59.6	61.8	63.9	65.8	67.4
Combined units of labor and capital inputs	33.8	38.3	43.5	47.4	56.3	65.4	66.9	69.3	71.9	74.3	75.0	74.8
Capital services per hour for all persons	34.6	38.3	46.5	57.2	61.4	71.2	74.0	74.7	75.2	75.7	78.4	82.3
Manufacturing [1]												
Productivity												
Output per hour of all persons	37.0	42.9	48.0	56.8	62.0	72.9	76.1	78.3	79.9	80.0	82.2	84.1
Output per unit of capital	119.7	131.5	112.2	99.9	97.2	96.1	96.3	97.6	100.7	99.2	97.5	93.6
Multifactor productivity	67.9	77.2	78.8	78.5	81.2	89.2	90.7	93.6	95.3	93.5	93.3	92.4
Output	32.8	42.2	48.2	53.3	64.3	73.5	75.6	78.3	82.2	82.6	83.2	81.5
Inputs												
Hours at work of all persons	88.8	98.3	100.6	93.9	103.7	100.8	99.4	100.0	102.8	103.3	101.1	96.9
Capital services	27.4	32.1	43.0	53.4	66.1	76.5	78.5	80.2	81.6	83.2	85.3	87.1
Energy	47.9	62.5	79.7	81.8	86.1	80.7	81.4	86.5	89.9	90.2	93.1	93.2
Non-energy materials	33.0	35.6	38.7	53.1	63.9	72.2	74.2	70.9	71.9	75.0	77.5	78.5
Purchased business services	25.3	33.3	43.6	51.9	65.8	62.1	65.4	70.8	77.4	82.6	84.7	84.6
Combined units of all inputs	48.3	54.7	61.2	67.9	79.2	82.4	83.4	83.7	86.2	88.3	89.1	88.3

[1] 1996 = 100.

Table 5-4. Indexes of Multifactor Productivity and Related Measures, Selected Years, 1960–2002
—Continued

(2000 = 100, unless otherwise indicated.)

Industry	1992	1993	1994	1995	1996	1997	1998	1999	2000	2001	2002
Private Business											
Productivity											
Output per hour of all persons	86.2	86.5	87.5	87.7	90.3	91.9	94.4	97.2	100.0	102.7	107.2
Output per unit of capital	101.7	102.6	104.5	103.6	103.9	104.1	102.6	101.8	100.0	96.3	95.5
Multifactor productivity	92.7	93.1	94.1	93.8	95.5	96.3	97.4	98.7	100.0	100.1	102.0
Output	70.9	73.2	76.9	79.1	82.8	87.2	91.5	96.2	100.0	100.4	102.3
Inputs											
Labor input	80.0	82.4	86.1	88.5	90.4	94.0	96.2	99.0	100.0	98.6	97.4
Capital services	69.7	71.3	73.5	76.4	79.7	83.8	89.2	94.5	100.0	104.2	107.1
Combined units of labor and capital inputs	76.5	78.6	81.7	84.3	86.7	90.5	93.9	97.5	100.0	100.4	100.3
Capital services per hour for all persons	84.8	84.4	83.7	84.6	86.9	88.3	92.0	95.4	100.0	106.6	112.2
Private Nonfarm Business											
Productivity											
Output per hour of all persons	86.5	86.9	87.9	88.4	90.8	92.2	94.7	97.3	100.0	102.6	107.2
Output per unit of capital	102.8	103.8	105.4	104.7	104.7	104.6	103.0	102.1	100.0	96.3	95.4
Multifactor productivity	93.2	93.6	94.5	94.6	96.0	96.6	97.7	98.8	100.0	100.0	102.0
Output	70.8	73.2	76.7	79.3	82.9	87.2	91.5	96.3	100.0	100.5	102.4
Inputs											
Labor input	79.6	82.2	85.6	88.0	90.0	93.7	96.0	99.0	100.0	98.8	97.3
Capital services	68.8	70.6	72.8	75.7	79.2	83.3	88.8	94.3	100.0	104.4	107.3
Combined units of labor and capital inputs	75.9	78.2	81.2	83.8	86.3	90.2	93.7	97.5	100.0	100.5	100.3
Capital services per hour for all persons	84.1	83.7	83.3	84.4	86.7	88.2	91.9	95.3	100.0	106.6	112.4
Manufacturing [1]											
Productivity											
Output per hour of all persons	88.6	90.2	93.0	96.5	100.0	103.8	108.9	114.0	118.3	119.7	. . .
Output per unit of capital	95.9	96.9	99.7	100.6	100.0	101.4	101.7	101.7	101.0	95.1	. . .
Multifactor productivity	94.0	95.1	97.3	99.2	100.0	103.1	105.7	108.7	111.3	110.3	. . .
Output	85.5	88.3	92.9	96.9	100.0	105.6	110.5	114.7	117.4	112.1	. . .
Inputs											
Hours at work of all persons	96.5	97.8	99.9	100.4	100.0	101.7	101.5	100.7	99.2	93.6	. . .
Capital services	89.1	91.1	93.2	96.4	100.0	104.1	108.7	112.8	116.2	117.9	. . .
Energy	93.1	96.6	99.9	102.3	100.0	97.5	100.6	102.9	104.3	98.9	. . .
Non-energy materials	83.5	86.5	90.3	93.1	100.0	101.9	107.5	107.9	106.9	105.5	. . .
Purchased business services	92.0	92.9	96.0	100.4	100.0	103.9	103.1	105.4	106.5	97.7	. . .
Combined units of all inputs	90.9	92.8	95.5	97.7	100.0	102.4	104.6	105.5	105.5	101.6	. . .

[1] 1996 = 100.

. . . = Not available.

Table 5-5. Indexes of Multifactor Productivity and Related Measures, Manufacturing Industries, 1985–2001

(1996 = 100.)

Industry	1985	1986	1987	1988	1989	1990	1991	1992	1993	1994	1995	1996	1997	1998	1999	2000	2001
NONDURABLE GOODS																	
Total Nondurable Goods																	
Output per hour of all persons	79.6	81.9	83.6	84.9	84.5	86.5	88.2	91.9	92.4	94.3	97.1	100.0	103.1	105.8	107.4	110.8	112.1
Output per unit of capital	101.0	101.9	104.3	105.7	104.0	102.9	99.9	101.9	101.3	102.2	101.7	100.0	100.5	98.7	96.5	95.0	90.8
Multifactor productivity	98.8	99.4	101.2	102.4	100.0	99.1	98.1	98.6	99.1	99.6	100.5	100.0	101.0	101.0	101.5	100.4	98.1
Sector output	78.0	80.5	84.0	86.5	87.0	88.6	88.5	92.9	94.5	97.3	99.2	100.0	103.2	104.4	104.9	105.5	101.7
Hours of all persons at work	98.0	98.3	100.4	102.0	103.0	102.5	100.3	101.0	102.3	103.2	102.2	100.0	100.0	98.6	97.7	95.2	90.7
Capital services	77.3	79.0	80.5	81.8	83.6	86.1	88.6	91.1	93.4	95.2	97.6	100.0	102.7	105.8	108.7	111.1	112.1
Energy	76.5	77.6	80.9	83.4	85.3	89.6	90.6	92.6	96.5	98.9	102.4	100.0	95.7	97.1	98.0	97.8	94.8
Non-energy materials	73.9	76.9	77.9	77.3	79.6	82.5	83.5	89.3	91.0	95.2	95.5	100.0	103.8	107.0	106.1	110.2	111.4
Purchased business services	57.4	59.8	65.5	73.2	80.7	87.1	90.3	97.9	96.2	96.6	101.5	100.0	102.7	101.5	102.2	106.8	103.2
Combined units of all inputs	79.0	81.0	83.0	84.5	87.0	89.5	90.2	94.1	95.4	97.7	98.7	100.0	102.1	103.3	103.4	105.1	103.7
Food and Kindred Products																	
Output per hour of all persons	89.0	89.0	89.5	91.9	89.4	90.1	93.2	98.1	98.3	98.8	100.8	100.0	102.2	106.1	104.3	104.7	105.0
Output per unit of capital	102.2	101.2	100.4	102.5	100.7	101.1	100.8	103.6	103.4	103.1	104.2	100.0	101.9	100.2	98.1	95.1	93.6
Multifactor productivity	103.9	102.3	102.9	106.4	102.2	100.9	101.8	101.4	102.7	100.5	104.5	100.0	101.2	100.1	102.9	100.2	97.1
Sector output	81.9	83.1	84.5	87.2	86.9	89.3	90.9	95.8	97.5	98.4	101.8	100.0	103.4	106.6	107.1	106.8	106.6
Hours of all persons at work	92.0	93.4	94.5	94.9	97.2	99.1	97.5	97.6	99.1	99.7	101.0	100.0	101.1	100.4	102.7	102.0	101.4
Capital services	80.1	82.2	84.2	85.1	86.3	88.3	90.2	92.5	94.2	95.5	97.7	100.0	101.5	106.4	109.1	112.3	113.9
Energy	78.9	81.7	84.5	87.1	88.0	88.4	91.3	93.4	96.1	100.1	104.8	100.0	101.3	105.2	105.2	105.6	106.0
Non-energy materials	77.1	79.1	80.6	79.0	81.9	85.6	86.1	92.9	92.5	97.4	95.5	100.0	102.7	109.1	104.2	107.6	112.8
Purchased business services	62.0	69.4	63.9	71.0	79.8	87.3	93.5	102.5	103.9	101.9	101.4	100.0	101.8	103.1	97.2	100.0	102.0
Combined units of all inputs	78.8	81.2	82.2	81.9	85.0	88.4	89.3	94.5	94.9	97.9	97.4	100.0	102.2	106.5	104.1	106.6	109.7
Textile Mill Products																	
Output per hour of all persons	70.1	71.2	72.6	73.6	76.5	78.9	79.7	85.7	88.9	91.2	95.1	100.0	101.0	104.1	109.4	111.2	114.5
Output per unit of capital	84.8	88.4	95.0	94.7	96.5	93.6	93.1	100.3	104.0	105.1	101.8	100.0	98.9	94.3	90.6	89.6	82.4
Multifactor productivity	84.1	85.9	87.1	89.8	90.3	91.0	91.2	95.1	96.5	97.2	98.5	100.0	101.4	100.7	104.7	107.8	110.0
Sector output	77.0	80.4	86.5	86.4	88.3	86.2	85.8	92.9	97.6	101.5	100.5	100.0	100.7	99.6	96.9	95.2	85.3
Hours of all persons at work	109.9	112.8	119.1	117.4	115.5	109.3	107.6	108.5	109.8	111.4	105.7	100.0	99.7	95.7	88.5	85.6	74.5
Capital services	90.8	90.9	91.1	91.2	91.5	92.0	92.1	92.6	93.9	96.5	98.8	100.0	101.8	105.6	106.9	106.2	103.5
Energy	79.5	83.0	91.3	91.3	92.0	88.5	90.5	94.5	98.8	104.7	106.2	100.0	95.9	94.1	91.7	90.3	81.1
Non-energy materials	87.0	88.5	95.1	88.0	90.7	88.2	86.6	91.9	97.4	101.9	99.7	100.0	99.0	101.5	93.7	87.9	76.3
Purchased business services	53.2	55.6	61.2	68.5	77.9	79.2	84.2	95.2	98.3	102.3	102.7	100.0	97.2	92.2	85.2	80.3	68.3
Combined units of all inputs	91.5	93.5	99.4	96.2	97.8	94.7	94.0	97.7	101.1	104.5	102.0	100.0	99.3	98.9	92.5	88.3	77.5
Apparel and Related Products																	
Output per hour of all persons	72.7	75.0	76.0	76.2	72.4	75.1	75.6	81.4	85.2	89.9	95.5	100.0	113.7	117.1	129.1	141.4	144.4
Output per unit of capital	102.9	103.3	105.9	102.6	99.4	97.8	98.1	102.5	101.4	102.9	99.5	100.0	108.0	97.1	95.8	91.8	83.8
Multifactor productivity	94.4	95.4	96.5	96.3	94.9	94.4	92.6	92.1	93.1	95.8	98.2	100.0	102.9	103.6	105.0	108.7	111.5
Sector output	88.6	91.0	93.5	92.3	87.7	87.0	86.2	93.4	96.2	100.8	101.6	100.0	107.0	103.0	104.2	102.1	92.6
Hours of all persons at work	121.9	121.3	123.0	121.1	121.2	115.8	114.1	114.8	112.9	112.1	106.3	100.0	94.1	88.0	80.7	72.2	64.1
Capital services	86.1	88.1	88.3	89.9	88.3	88.9	87.9	91.1	94.9	98.0	102.1	100.0	99.1	106.1	108.8	111.2	110.5
Energy	62.0	66.1	68.7	69.2	60.5	59.8	61.1	95.6	105.9	103.4	110.4	100.0	84.0	81.0	81.7	80.1	73.5
Non-energy materials	98.2	100.9	103.4	98.6	89.3	88.0	87.9	97.4	100.7	103.7	102.0	100.0	110.6	105.8	109.6	106.2	92.5
Purchased business services	31.3	32.5	31.6	39.7	47.5	58.7	70.5	91.8	95.6	99.2	102.1	100.0	108.1	100.9	101.6	93.6	80.6
Combined units of all inputs	93.8	95.4	96.9	95.8	92.5	92.1	93.1	101.3	103.3	105.2	103.4	100.0	104.0	99.4	99.2	93.9	83.1
Paper and Allied Products																	
Output per hour of all persons	81.3	86.6	86.5	88.3	88.1	88.3	90.6	93.0	94.8	98.4	99.1	100.0	101.3	104.8	105.8	108.4	108.2
Output per unit of capital	103.5	105.0	105.6	107.4	104.9	101.0	98.3	100.2	101.3	104.8	103.3	100.0	100.3	99.0	99.0	96.5	91.2
Multifactor productivity	97.9	100.2	99.8	100.8	98.4	97.4	98.2	99.5	103.0	104.1	98.1	100.0	102.7	101.6	101.7	100.0	98.2
Sector output	78.7	82.4	84.5	87.8	89.1	89.5	90.2	94.0	96.3	100.6	100.4	100.0	102.2	103.7	105.1	102.8	97.2
Hours of all persons at work	96.9	95.2	97.8	99.4	101.2	101.4	99.6	101.2	101.6	102.2	101.3	100.0	100.9	98.9	99.3	94.9	89.9
Capital services	76.1	78.5	80.1	81.7	84.9	88.6	91.8	93.9	95.0	96.0	97.2	100.0	102.0	104.7	106.2	106.5	106.6
Energy	77.8	81.2	84.9	86.4	88.8	94.2	94.9	96.8	99.2	101.3	104.5	100.0	98.2	99.5	101.3	99.0	93.8
Non-energy materials	76.8	79.9	81.7	83.3	87.0	87.5	86.9	90.2	87.7	93.5	103.1	100.0	98.3	104.5	106.8	109.0	105.6
Purchased business services	57.1	62.7	69.0	79.2	89.1	89.6	90.1	94.9	90.2	93.9	113.4	100.0	97.0	97.8	97.4	98.1	90.9
Combined units of all inputs	80.4	82.2	84.8	87.1	90.6	91.9	91.8	94.5	93.5	96.6	102.3	100.0	99.6	102.1	103.3	102.8	99.0

Table 5-5. Indexes of Multifactor Productivity and Related Measures, Manufacturing Industries, 1985–2001—*Continued*

(1996 = 100.)

Industry	1985	1986	1987	1988	1989	1990	1991	1992	1993	1994	1995	1996	1997	1998	1999	2000	2001
Printing and Publishing																	
Output per hour of all persons	103.3	104.2	106.6	101.5	99.5	98.0	96.9	100.5	98.4	97.1	97.2	100.0	96.4	97.0	99.0	100.8	97.1
Output per unit of capital	142.9	139.5	138.8	131.6	123.1	117.6	108.4	107.5	105.3	104.3	102.1	100.0	92.4	91.1	86.5	82.3	73.7
Multifactor productivity	114.2	112.8	112.7	110.8	109.5	107.0	104.6	106.0	102.0	102.6	100.9	100.0	95.7	95.7	97.7	98.0	93.1
Sector output	93.4	96.6	101.1	101.4	100.0	99.7	95.3	97.7	98.0	98.5	99.2	100.0	98.4	98.1	99.9	100.4	92.9
Hours of all persons at work	90.3	92.6	94.9	99.9	100.5	101.7	98.3	97.2	99.6	101.4	102.1	100.0	102.2	101.1	100.9	99.6	95.6
Capital services	65.3	69.2	72.8	77.0	81.3	84.8	88.0	90.9	93.0	94.4	97.2	100.0	106.5	107.7	115.5	121.9	126.0
Energy	65.1	70.2	81.9	87.6	87.8	91.6	90.7	91.5	94.4	98.2	102.9	100.0	70.6	70.7	71.2	72.0	66.9
Non-energy materials	82.4	87.0	91.3	88.6	85.3	87.6	85.8	87.5	94.2	91.6	92.4	100.0	104.1	104.7	101.4	99.4	99.6
Purchased business services	74.8	80.9	89.2	88.8	88.3	89.2	84.3	88.1	93.0	92.4	100.4	100.0	101.4	99.8	97.5	100.0	91.6
Combined units of all inputs	81.7	85.6	89.7	91.5	91.3	93.2	91.1	92.2	96.1	96.0	98.4	100.0	102.9	102.5	102.3	102.4	99.7
Chemicals and Allied Products																	
Output per hour of all persons	72.9	78.3	85.1	86.4	86.1	87.5	87.5	89.0	89.2	94.9	97.9	100.0	107.1	106.4	107.4	110.6	108.9
Output per unit of capital	97.0	99.5	107.6	111.3	110.3	109.0	103.5	103.7	101.1	102.4	101.7	100.0	103.0	99.3	97.4	95.9	91.7
Multifactor productivity	92.8	96.7	102.8	101.9	99.7	100.1	97.2	96.9	95.4	98.2	99.1	100.0	102.9	101.8	100.9	97.5	96.4
Sector output	71.2	74.6	82.1	86.2	87.8	90.2	89.5	92.6	93.0	96.6	98.5	100.0	106.5	106.8	107.9	108.8	105.3
Hours of all persons at work	97.7	95.3	96.5	99.7	102.0	103.1	102.3	104.0	104.2	101.8	100.6	100.0	99.4	100.4	100.5	98.4	96.7
Capital services	73.4	75.0	76.3	77.5	79.6	82.8	86.5	89.3	92.0	94.3	96.9	100.0	103.4	107.6	110.7	113.4	114.8
Energy	75.6	73.9	79.6	83.1	85.7	90.7	90.4	91.2	95.7	97.7	99.5	100.0	92.1	93.0	93.1	93.7	91.8
Non-energy materials	72.3	73.6	76.6	82.4	85.7	86.0	88.2	93.0	95.9	99.2	98.3	100.0	108.3	108.4	114.8	131.6	126.0
Purchased business services	55.3	57.6	63.5	75.7	84.7	89.5	93.0	99.4	100.0	99.5	104.5	100.0	105.3	104.2	100.8	103.1	99.0
Combined units of all inputs	76.8	77.1	79.9	84.6	88.1	90.1	92.1	95.6	97.5	98.4	99.4	100.0	103.5	104.9	106.9	111.6	109.3
Petroleum Refining and Related Products																	
Output per hour of all persons	68.2	76.1	78.8	82.7	83.3	83.0	82.3	84.5	90.1	91.6	96.8	100.0	106.2	108.4	112.8	120.2	118.6
Output per unit of capital	92.0	98.6	102.3	105.0	105.6	105.3	102.3	101.3	101.6	99.3	99.0	100.0	103.2	107.2	107.1	110.2	110.6
Multifactor productivity	96.2	98.7	98.7	99.4	99.2	98.5	98.5	99.2	100.1	99.7	99.9	100.0	101.1	104.1	103.3	102.5	102.8
Sector output	83.1	88.3	90.2	92.1	92.1	92.5	91.5	93.3	96.3	96.0	97.4	100.0	103.3	105.7	104.1	105.7	104.7
Hours of all persons at work	121.9	116.1	114.5	111.3	110.5	111.4	111.1	110.4	106.9	104.8	100.6	100.0	97.3	97.5	92.3	87.9	88.2
Capital services	90.4	89.6	88.2	87.7	87.3	87.8	89.4	92.1	94.6	96.7	98.4	100.0	100.0	98.6	97.2	95.9	94.6
Energy	100.9	102.5	90.2	93.9	93.9	106.3	104.5	100.3	103.3	99.6	103.8	100.0	100.5	101.2	104.1	102.1	101.5
Non-energy materials	83.8	89.3	91.9	93.7	93.5	93.4	92.0	93.6	96.8	96.4	97.6	100.0	103.1	105.6	103.6	105.2	104.3
Purchased business services	70.7	53.4	68.4	70.2	79.8	97.4	90.9	84.8	80.5	83.0	88.6	100.0	104.1	75.6	90.1	123.5	114.2
Combined units of all inputs	86.4	89.5	91.4	92.7	92.9	94.0	92.9	94.0	96.3	96.3	97.5	100.0	102.2	101.5	100.7	103.1	101.8
Rubber and Miscellaneous Plastics Products																	
Output per hour of all persons	73.3	74.1	78.3	78.8	79.6	81.9	83.1	90.3	91.7	94.5	95.7	100.0	104.1	106.9	109.6	113.4	113.7
Output per unit of capital	94.8	93.9	99.4	100.6	99.6	97.5	92.1	100.6	103.1	106.7	102.5	100.0	99.4	95.8	93.2	90.5	81.8
Multifactor productivity	88.6	88.6	90.1	90.6	92.4	92.5	93.7	95.7	96.4	97.9	98.1	100.0	102.3	103.4	104.0	105.6	104.5
Sector output	60.4	62.2	67.6	70.1	72.0	73.4	72.0	81.2	86.7	94.3	96.4	100.0	106.1	109.8	114.0	116.7	109.1
Hours of all persons at work	82.3	83.9	86.3	89.0	90.4	89.7	86.6	89.9	94.6	99.8	100.7	100.0	101.9	102.7	104.1	103.0	95.9
Capital services	63.7	66.2	68.0	69.7	72.3	75.3	78.1	80.7	84.1	88.4	94.0	100.0	106.7	114.6	122.4	128.9	133.4
Energy	66.9	70.0	75.4	78.5	81.0	81.4	79.9	83.5	90.3	96.6	101.9	100.0	101.0	104.2	108.6	111.0	104.5
Non-energy materials	64.6	66.8	72.9	74.6	73.7	75.7	72.1	83.0	88.7	95.8	97.1	100.0	104.0	107.0	111.1	112.3	105.7
Purchased business services	46.2	48.0	54.9	61.3	64.7	68.7	69.4	83.1	87.7	95.7	100.6	100.0	106.0	104.3	106.1	106.8	96.8
Combined units of all inputs	68.1	70.2	74.9	77.4	77.9	79.4	76.8	84.8	90.0	96.3	98.3	100.0	103.8	106.2	109.6	110.6	104.4

Table 5-5. Indexes of Multifactor Productivity and Related Measures, Manufacturing Industries, 1985–2001—*Continued*

(1996 = 100.)

Industry	1985	1986	1987	1988	1989	1990	1991	1992	1993	1994	1995	1996	1997	1998	1999	2000	2001
DURABLE GOODS																	
Total Durable Goods																	
Output per hour of all persons	68.1	71.7	74.4	76.1	76.2	78.2	79.4	84.6	87.4	91.4	95.7	100.0	105.2	112.6	120.8	126.0	126.9
Output per unit of capital	92.2	91.7	92.4	96.4	95.0	92.6	87.7	90.9	93.5	98.1	99.9	100.0	102.3	104.2	105.7	105.4	97.5
Multifactor productivity	82.0	84.1	87.5	89.4	88.3	88.9	88.1	90.6	92.2	95.5	98.1	100.0	104.6	109.4	114.4	120.3	121.0
Sector output	70.0	71.8	74.2	78.7	78.9	78.3	75.1	79.0	82.8	89.3	94.9	100.0	108.2	116.6	124.1	128.5	121.4
Hours of all persons at work	102.7	100.1	99.7	103.4	103.5	100.2	94.5	93.3	94.7	97.7	99.1	100.0	102.9	103.5	102.7	102.0	95.7
Capital services	75.9	78.3	80.2	81.7	83.1	84.6	85.6	86.9	88.5	91.0	95.0	100.0	105.8	111.9	117.4	121.9	124.5
Energy	88.1	88.1	95.4	100.2	97.8	98.6	97.3	94.4	97.2	101.7	102.6	100.0	99.4	105.4	110.2	113.6	106.3
Non-energy materials	72.5	73.2	68.4	71.3	73.5	74.0	73.0	77.7	82.5	86.7	92.4	100.0	102.3	109.3	112.2	105.3	98.1
Purchased business services	67.0	71.4	76.5	81.9	84.7	82.3	78.9	86.0	89.5	95.4	99.3	100.0	105.1	104.7	108.6	106.1	91.9
Combined units of all inputs	85.4	85.4	84.7	88.1	89.3	88.1	85.2	87.1	89.8	93.4	96.7	100.0	103.5	106.6	108.5	106.8	100.3
Lumber and Wood Products																	
Output per hour of all persons	101.4	106.4	107.9	105.4	102.5	103.8	105.9	106.2	100.0	99.3	99.5	100.0	98.6	99.5	100.9	100.6	101.5
Output per unit of capital	85.5	93.1	101.9	102.7	101.4	100.1	93.6	98.4	98.6	102.3	102.2	100.0	97.2	99.8	101.4	98.4	93.5
Multifactor productivity	102.0	105.9	110.7	111.7	110.9	111.6	111.3	110.7	101.8	101.1	102.3	100.0	98.5	97.5	96.4	95.6	94.5
Sector output	87.7	94.9	102.1	101.0	97.9	96.2	88.8	92.3	92.1	97.2	99.5	100.0	99.7	103.9	107.6	106.1	100.9
Hours of all persons at work	86.5	89.2	94.6	95.9	95.5	92.8	83.9	86.9	92.2	97.8	100.0	100.0	101.2	104.5	106.7	105.4	99.4
Capital services	102.6	101.9	100.3	98.4	96.5	96.1	94.9	93.7	93.5	95.0	97.4	100.0	102.6	104.2	106.2	107.8	107.9
Energy	69.8	75.8	85.7	90.4	88.5	89.6	89.5	83.1	92.3	97.9	103.3	100.0	88.5	92.5	96.6	94.8	90.6
Non-energy materials	87.7	92.7	94.2	89.1	83.7	80.8	73.6	78.8	85.9	93.8	94.6	100.0	100.8	110.4	119.6	119.8	119.0
Purchased business services	47.4	55.7	59.6	58.0	62.8	63.0	60.4	69.5	100.3	102.6	98.0	100.0	104.5	106.9	112.8	106.8	93.2
Combined units of all inputs	86.0	89.6	92.3	90.4	88.3	86.2	79.8	83.4	90.5	96.1	97.3	100.0	101.3	106.6	111.6	110.9	106.8
Furniture and Fixtures																	
Output per hour of all persons	81.6	84.1	86.8	85.5	85.4	87.6	88.0	91.7	93.5	93.8	98.2	100.0	107.2	111.3	113.0	114.0	116.6
Output per unit of capital	100.4	102.9	104.7	101.0	100.0	96.7	90.5	97.0	99.7	100.5	101.2	100.0	107.0	109.3	108.1	105.5	96.4
Multifactor productivity	95.0	94.5	95.9	95.5	95.4	95.4	95.7	98.7	100.5	99.3	99.9	100.0	103.4	103.2	103.7	103.4	103.0
Sector output	78.6	82.5	87.2	87.1	87.8	86.4	80.9	87.4	92.0	95.0	98.7	100.0	111.0	119.0	123.9	126.1	116.3
Hours of all persons at work	96.3	98.1	100.5	101.9	102.7	98.6	91.9	95.3	98.4	101.3	100.5	100.0	103.5	106.9	109.6	110.6	99.8
Capital services	78.3	80.2	83.3	86.3	87.8	89.4	89.3	90.2	92.3	94.6	97.5	100.0	103.7	108.9	114.5	119.4	120.7
Energy	71.4	76.3	89.6	92.7	97.2	91.3	90.4	91.2	96.3	98.5	103.9	100.0	110.5	118.0	122.7	125.0	117.1
Non-energy materials	74.4	79.8	83.2	82.9	83.9	84.2	78.6	83.5	86.8	92.2	97.5	100.0	109.4	121.2	126.3	129.9	121.6
Purchased business services	90.5	103.0	111.8	108.4	106.1	101.6	90.4	93.4	95.3	97.8	101.3	100.0	112.2	118.1	120.7	120.9	107.4
Combined units of all inputs	82.7	87.3	90.9	91.3	92.0	90.6	84.5	88.6	91.6	95.7	98.8	100.0	107.3	115.3	119.4	122.0	113.0
Stone, Clay, and Glass																	
Output per hour of all persons	85.5	88.9	91.1	90.2	89.9	92.1	90.9	95.7	95.8	96.1	97.3	100.0	103.9	108.4	108.5	107.0	102.3
Output per unit of capital	81.0	84.2	86.4	88.3	87.4	87.0	80.9	86.5	90.1	95.2	96.8	100.0	98.4	97.9	93.7	88.5	80.4
Multifactor productivity	89.6	92.9	94.5	94.7	95.7	96.6	94.4	98.8	97.4	99.2	99.9	100.0	103.9	103.2	102.2	100.1	94.9
Sector output	82.7	86.2	88.4	90.2	89.6	88.7	81.7	85.7	87.6	91.9	94.5	100.0	103.5	108.9	110.4	109.9	104.6
Hours of all persons at work	96.7	97.0	97.0	100.0	99.7	96.4	89.9	89.5	91.4	95.6	97.1	100.0	99.6	100.5	101.8	102.7	102.3
Capital services	102.1	102.4	102.2	102.2	102.5	102.0	101.0	99.1	97.2	96.5	97.6	100.0	105.2	111.3	117.8	124.1	130.1
Energy	95.2	100.4	102.6	104.5	101.7	101.6	97.0	99.6	100.6	98.7	104.3	100.0	101.7	107.1	108.4	108.1	104.5
Non-energy materials	87.2	86.4	86.7	87.6	84.3	83.4	78.3	78.5	84.7	87.8	89.7	100.0	97.3	108.7	111.2	113.1	114.5
Purchased business services	72.6	78.1	85.3	88.0	87.8	86.8	81.6	85.5	87.9	90.3	94.0	100.0	97.4	102.3	102.4	100.2	96.1
Combined units of all inputs	92.3	92.8	93.5	95.3	93.6	91.9	86.6	86.7	89.9	92.7	94.6	100.0	99.6	105.5	108.0	109.8	110.3
Primary Metal Industries																	
Output per hour of all persons	76.0	81.4	85.2	87.8	85.3	85.3	86.0	91.4	95.2	96.1	97.7	100.0	100.9	106.5	105.8	104.0	102.8
Output per unit of capital	74.0	75.3	82.1	90.2	88.6	86.5	82.2	86.1	91.4	97.2	98.5	100.0	101.6	103.9	102.0	100.3	92.1
Multifactor productivity	92.0	98.1	97.0	96.0	94.6	96.2	96.6	99.8	103.4	102.2	99.9	100.0	100.3	102.7	103.4	99.8	101.2
Sector output	81.5	81.0	86.5	93.7	91.1	88.5	83.7	86.6	91.0	96.2	97.7	100.0	102.6	106.3	105.7	104.2	94.4
Hours of all persons at work	107.3	99.6	101.5	106.8	106.8	103.7	97.3	94.8	95.5	100.2	100.0	100.0	101.7	99.8	99.9	100.2	91.9
Capital services	110.1	107.5	105.3	103.9	102.8	102.3	101.8	100.6	99.5	99.0	99.2	100.0	101.0	102.3	103.7	103.9	102.5
Energy	103.5	95.5	98.9	111.5	103.2	105.2	107.0	99.7	99.0	110.2	99.9	100.0	94.6	97.6	97.7	95.9	87.0
Non-energy materials	75.0	69.4	78.6	88.2	86.8	80.9	75.8	78.2	80.2	87.4	94.9	100.0	103.8	107.9	106.4	112.5	98.3
Purchased business services	73.2	70.9	84.0	100.6	101.2	92.9	81.4	83.9	85.0	93.6	101.6	100.0	103.6	100.9	94.1	91.4	76.0
Combined units of all inputs	88.6	82.6	89.1	97.6	96.3	91.9	86.6	86.8	88.0	94.1	97.7	100.0	102.3	103.5	102.3	104.4	93.3

Table 5-5. Indexes of Multifactor Productivity and Related Measures, Manufacturing Industries, 1985–2001—*Continued*

(1996 = 100.)

Industry	1985	1986	1987	1988	1989	1990	1991	1992	1993	1994	1995	1996	1997	1998	1999	2000	2001
Fabricated Metal Products																	
Output per hour of all persons	84.6	87.6	91.4	90.3	87.1	87.8	87.5	92.7	94.5	96.6	98.2	100.0	103.2	106.6	106.3	107.6	106.0
Output per unit of capital	98.0	95.4	95.5	98.4	95.6	92.5	87.3	91.9	94.7	100.0	100.2	100.0	103.5	103.9	101.3	101.4	93.6
Multifactor productivity	94.9	95.7	98.7	99.4	96.6	95.3	93.4	95.1	96.2	99.6	100.3	100.0	101.3	100.7	99.8	101.1	98.0
Sector output	83.3	83.3	85.1	87.7	85.3	83.4	79.1	83.7	86.9	93.5	96.8	100.0	106.4	110.8	111.5	114.0	105.9
Hours of all persons at work	98.4	95.1	93.1	97.2	97.9	95.0	90.3	90.2	92.0	96.8	98.6	100.0	103.1	103.9	104.9	106.0	99.9
Capital services	85.0	87.3	89.1	89.1	89.2	90.1	90.6	91.1	91.9	93.5	96.6	100.0	102.8	106.7	110.1	112.5	113.1
Energy	79.8	80.7	89.6	93.3	93.0	92.3	91.2	88.4	92.8	96.1	102.7	100.0	102.5	106.4	107.3	109.7	102.8
Non-energy materials	82.7	82.6	80.7	81.5	80.9	81.4	79.4	85.2	88.7	91.7	94.3	100.0	106.9	116.1	118.7	119.5	115.1
Purchased business services	79.8	80.3	85.2	89.9	90.7	88.0	83.1	89.5	91.0	94.8	99.2	100.0	106.9	109.5	106.0	105.6	96.0
Combined units of all inputs	87.8	87.0	86.2	88.3	88.2	87.5	84.7	87.9	90.4	93.9	96.5	100.0	105.0	110.0	111.7	112.8	108.1
Industrial and Commercial Machinery																	
Output per hour of all persons	49.7	53.1	55.7	60.1	60.9	62.4	62.3	69.1	74.1	81.2	89.6	100.0	108.5	120.6	132.0	146.4	145.5
Output per unit of capital	75.6	73.5	75.0	81.9	80.9	79.0	73.3	77.2	81.6	88.2	95.1	100.0	104.3	105.8	101.6	103.0	90.5
Multifactor productivity	69.1	71.4	76.2	80.2	80.9	81.7	79.8	84.1	86.3	90.8	95.1	100.0	106.8	118.0	125.2	137.6	139.5
Sector output	50.1	50.4	52.2	59.0	60.5	60.6	57.6	62.3	68.4	77.6	89.0	100.0	113.0	126.2	132.3	143.4	131.8
Hours of all persons at work	100.9	94.9	93.7	98.2	99.3	97.1	92.4	90.2	92.3	95.5	99.4	100.0	104.2	104.6	100.2	98.0	90.6
Capital services	66.2	68.5	69.7	72.0	74.7	76.7	78.5	80.7	83.8	88.0	93.5	100.0	108.3	119.3	130.3	139.3	145.6
Energy	86.1	86.9	92.0	94.9	99.2	99.1	97.7	89.9	92.7	99.5	102.8	100.0	99.9	111.2	117.2	125.6	117.0
Non-energy materials	54.4	53.5	50.1	55.9	56.7	57.0	56.3	60.9	68.4	76.5	88.6	100.0	107.8	108.3	107.9	105.8	92.3
Purchased business services	72.2	74.0	75.2	80.4	80.6	76.1	70.7	73.9	79.8	88.9	95.7	100.0	100.4	96.7	93.2	90.0	77.4
Combined units of all inputs	72.5	70.5	68.6	73.6	74.8	74.2	72.2	74.1	79.2	85.4	93.6	100.0	105.8	106.9	105.7	104.2	94.5
Electrical and Electronic Equipment																	
Output per hour of all persons	38.3	40.7	44.4	46.4	47.9	51.0	54.8	61.9	67.0	75.6	88.8	100.0	113.9	126.3	152.1	184.6	185.0
Output per unit of capital	67.9	65.9	66.0	68.3	67.8	66.8	66.6	71.8	76.2	84.6	94.3	100.0	105.6	110.0	122.1	142.0	123.2
Multifactor productivity	59.8	61.6	65.6	67.6	69.2	70.9	72.7	76.2	79.3	86.6	94.4	100.0	108.7	112.5	126.4	140.0	146.2
Sector output	41.5	42.6	45.2	48.3	49.2	50.0	50.7	55.9	61.5	71.7	86.4	100.0	115.4	128.9	151.2	187.4	172.8
Hours of all persons at work	108.3	104.6	102.0	104.1	102.8	98.2	92.5	90.4	91.7	94.9	97.4	100.0	101.3	102.1	99.4	101.5	93.4
Capital services	61.1	64.6	68.6	70.7	72.7	74.9	76.1	78.0	80.7	84.7	91.7	100.0	109.2	117.3	123.8	131.9	140.3
Energy	75.1	77.7	87.5	88.5	90.8	92.1	90.8	89.8	95.2	97.8	102.6	100.0	107.7	120.8	144.2	178.2	163.7
Non-energy materials	46.2	45.8	44.6	47.1	46.4	47.2	48.7	55.9	62.6	68.7	83.8	100.0	106.9	130.0	139.9	179.6	146.0
Purchased business services	55.7	58.7	62.1	64.5	63.5	60.9	57.9	66.9	70.7	82.1	95.0	100.0	111.8	112.4	132.1	150.1	114.1
Combined units of all inputs	69.3	69.1	68.9	71.4	71.1	70.6	69.7	73.5	77.5	82.8	91.6	100.0	106.1	114.6	119.6	133.8	118.2
Transportation Equipment																	
Output per hour of all persons	72.8	75.9	77.9	78.7	78.6	80.4	80.3	87.8	92.9	97.8	98.0	100.0	106.6	114.7	123.7	119.8	121.4
Output per unit of capital	95.4	94.6	93.2	95.7	94.1	90.9	84.5	90.3	94.2	100.6	100.8	100.0	107.1	110.1	115.1	106.7	101.2
Multifactor productivity	102.3	102.3	103.7	102.8	100.1	99.2	94.0	98.1	100.4	101.8	101.4	100.0	102.5	105.8	108.1	100.8	109.5
Sector output	78.4	81.6	83.2	88.0	88.1	86.4	81.1	86.6	90.5	97.2	98.3	100.0	111.1	120.2	131.2	123.4	116.5
Hours of all persons at work	107.7	107.5	106.7	111.9	112.1	107.5	101.0	98.6	97.4	99.4	100.3	100.0	104.3	104.7	106.1	103.0	96.0
Capital services	82.2	86.2	89.3	92.0	93.6	95.0	95.9	95.9	96.1	96.6	97.5	100.0	103.8	109.1	114.0	115.7	115.2
Energy	75.8	78.1	100.8	97.3	95.2	95.7	92.6	95.9	101.2	101.7	104.9	100.0	103.9	112.6	122.3	114.1	108.5
Non-energy materials	63.7	66.9	66.6	71.8	74.1	74.7	70.0	79.1	83.2	91.2	94.0	100.0	111.6	120.1	131.8	120.9	112.1
Purchased business services	57.1	66.7	71.3	81.3	90.7	91.1	91.3	102.0	100.8	105.5	102.5	100.0	107.6	108.5	118.5	103.9	93.9
Combined units of all inputs	76.7	79.7	80.3	85.6	88.0	87.2	82.7	88.2	90.1	95.4	96.9	100.0	108.4	113.6	121.5	113.9	106.4
Instruments																	
Output per hour of all persons	64.6	68.7	73.5	74.0	74.3	77.4	80.6	87.2	88.3	91.5	95.3	100.0	99.2	103.0	108.3	116.1	113.3
Output per unit of capital	117.1	116.6	125.5	126.1	117.0	112.0	106.3	104.6	100.9	99.1	98.9	100.0	96.7	94.5	91.2	90.8	84.3
Multifactor productivity	90.8	92.1	95.4	99.1	96.6	98.9	98.9	100.0	98.7	99.5	98.9	100.0	98.8	102.6	105.6	112.4	111.4
Sector output	77.4	79.9	84.9	88.3	87.8	89.1	89.3	92.8	92.6	92.5	94.7	100.0	102.1	105.2	108.6	114.1	110.0
Hours of all persons at work	119.9	116.4	115.5	119.3	118.2	115.2	110.7	106.4	104.9	101.1	99.3	100.0	103.0	102.1	100.2	98.3	97.1
Capital services	66.1	68.5	67.7	70.0	75.0	79.6	84.0	88.7	91.8	93.4	95.7	100.0	105.6	111.4	119.0	125.6	130.5
Energy	98.6	102.0	96.3	100.1	99.7	104.2	100.6	99.4	100.5	99.2	104.5	100.0	98.6	100.9	104.3	105.5	107.3
Non-energy materials	60.8	65.0	68.4	65.8	68.7	69.3	72.2	78.7	80.6	82.4	89.7	100.0	104.9	104.3	106.1	104.7	101.3
Purchased business services	80.1	82.3	89.6	89.4	94.8	92.6	92.8	99.8	104.5	103.7	104.3	100.0	99.1	95.3	95.4	94.8	86.5
Combined units of all inputs	85.3	86.7	89.0	89.0	90.9	90.2	90.3	92.8	93.8	93.0	95.7	100.0	103.4	102.6	102.8	101.5	98.8
Miscellaneous Manufacturing																	
Output per hour of all persons	84.2	85.5	89.4	90.4	87.7	90.9	90.0	90.6	92.0	91.1	97.5	100.0	96.9	99.9	104.8	112.5	108.9
Output per unit of capital	87.0	89.9	91.9	96.9	93.6	93.8	91.2	92.3	95.6	96.2	98.5	100.0	100.2	99.9	100.1	102.4	95.7
Multifactor productivity	98.8	97.9	100.0	103.3	101.8	100.9	97.2	95.0	95.4	96.7	99.7	100.0	100.2	99.6	102.7	109.2	105.9
Sector output	77.0	79.7	83.5	88.9	87.0	87.6	84.6	87.6	92.4	94.4	97.1	100.0	102.1	103.9	106.9	111.4	104.7
Hours of all persons at work	91.4	93.2	93.4	98.4	99.2	96.4	94.0	96.7	100.5	103.6	99.6	100.0	105.3	104.0	102.0	99.0	96.1
Capital services	88.5	88.6	90.9	91.7	93.0	93.4	92.7	94.9	96.7	98.1	98.6	100.0	101.9	104.0	106.8	108.8	109.4
Energy	67.8	73.4	90.1	91.9	94.4	95.6	93.3	84.7	95.6	96.2	107.9	100.0	83.8	84.7	87.3	90.4	85.8
Non-energy materials	65.7	69.6	71.0	72.3	71.1	75.9	79.1	87.5	94.0	93.4	94.7	100.0	100.0	107.2	108.2	105.2	101.0
Purchased business services	72.8	83.2	92.1	95.3	91.1	90.3	86.0	92.5	97.6	95.4	97.9	100.0	100.4	98.3	93.7	90.6	84.0
Combined units of all inputs	77.9	81.4	83.6	86.0	85.5	86.9	87.0	92.2	96.9	97.6	97.4	100.0	101.9	104.3	104.1	102.0	98.8

PART SIX

COMPENSATION OF EMPLOYEES

COMPENSATION OF EMPLOYEES

HIGHLIGHTS

This part discusses the Employment Cost Index (ECI), which covers changes in wages and salaries and benefits, Employer Costs for Employee Compensation (ECEC), employee participation in various benefit plans, and mean hourly earnings from the National Compensation Survey (NCS).

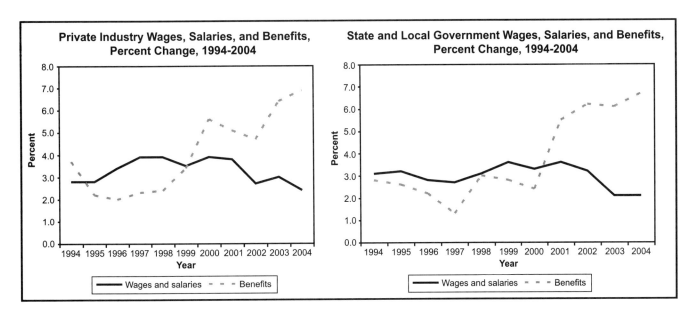

In 2004, as in past years, increases in benefits in both the private and public sectors greatly exceeded increases in wages and salaries. In private industry, wages and salaries rose only 2.4 percent, the smallest gain in at least 14 years. However, benefits increased at a rate of 6.9 percent. Likewise, in government, benefits climbed 6.7 percent, while wages and salaries only rose 2.1 percent. (Tables 6-1, 6-2, and 6-3)

OTHER HIGHLIGHTS:

• Although wages for most industries grew more slowly in 2004, health services, educational services, and transportation and public utilities saw substantially higher pay increases in 2004 than in 2003. (Table 6-1)

• In 2003, banking and other credit agencies experienced the highest wage increase (14.3 percent) of any industry. However, in 2004, this sector experienced one of the lowest wage increases, rising at a rate of only 0.5 percent. No industry had wage increases of more than 3.7 percent in 2004. (Table 6-1)

• A survey of dollar costs per hour between March 2003 and March 2005 shows that wages, as a percent of total compensation, have dropped from 67.7 percent to 65.5 percent in goods-producing industries, from 73.7 percent to 72.6 percent in service-providing industries, and from 70.0 percent to 68.3 percent in state and local governments. (Tables 6-5 and 6-7 in the seventh and ninth editions of the *Handbook*).

NOTES AND DEFINITIONS

The National Compensation Survey (NCS) provides data for the Employment Cost Index (ECI), Employer Costs for Employee Compensation (ECEC), employee benefits, and occupational wages for 400 occupations and local areas.

EMPLOYMENT COST INDEX

Collection and Coverage

The ECI is a quarterly measure of the rate of change in compensation per hour worked and includes wages, salaries, and the employer costs of employee benefits. It uses a fixed market basket of labor—similar in concept to the Consumer Price Index's fixed market basket of goods and services—to measure change over time in employer costs of employing labor.

Statistical series on total compensation costs, on wages and salaries, and on benefit costs are available for private nonfarm workers, excluding proprietors, the self-employed, and household workers. The total compensation costs and wages and salaries series are also available for state and local government workers and for the civilian nonfarm economy, which consists of private industry and state and local government workers combined. Federal workers are excluded.

The ECI probability sample consists of about 9,800 private nonfarm establishments (providing about 44,000 occupational observations) and 1,000 state and local government establishments (providing 6,000 occupational observations) selected to represent total employment in each sector. On average, each reporting unit provides wage and compensation information on five well-specified occupations. The occupations are defined narrowly enough to ensure that all workers in the job carry out the same task at roughly the same level of skill. Data are collected each quarter for the pay period including the 12th days of March, June, September, and December.

From June 1986 to March 1995, fixed employment weights from the 1980 Census of Population were used each quarter to calculate the civilian and private indexes and the index for state and local governments. In March 1995, 1990 employment counts were introduced. Prior to June 1986, the employment weights come from the 1970 Census of Population. These fixed weights, also used to derive all of the industry and occupation series indexes, ensure that changes in these indexes reflect only changes in compensation— not employment shifts among industries or occupations with different levels of wages and compensation. However, for the bargaining status, region, and metropolitan/nonmetropolitan area series, employment data by industry and occupation are not available from the census. Instead, the 1980 employment weights are reallocated

within these series each quarter based on the current sample. Therefore, these indexes are not strictly comparable to those for the aggregate, industry, and occupation series.

Concepts and Definitions

Total compensation costs include wages, salaries, and the employer costs for employee benefits.

Wages and salaries consist of earnings before payroll deductions, including production bonuses, incentive earnings, commissions, and cost-of-living adjustments.

Benefits include the cost to employers for paid leave, supplemental pay (including nonproduction bonuses), insurance, retirement and savings plans, and legally required benefits (such as Social Security, workers' compensation, and unemployment insurance).

Excluded from wages and salaries and employee benefit costs are items such as payment-in-kind, free room and board, and tips.

Bonuses. In June 2000, the BLS expanded the definition of nonproduction bonuses in the ECI to better represent the compensation packages offered to employees. In addition to the traditional types of nonproduction bonuses, such as attendance bonuses and lump sum payments, the ECI will include hiring and referral bonuses. Hiring bonuses are payments made by the employer to induce an individual to accept employment; referral bonuses are made by the employer to an employee for recommending an applicant who is hired by the establishment.

As part of its ongoing research program, the BLS is currently conducting research on stock option plans. This research will be completed in stages. BLS has begun testing the incidence of stock option plans across all industries and occupations. The prevalence of these plans, based on test results and the potential impact on compensation costs, will determine the next stage of research. The results of the pilot incidence survey were published in October 2000.

Costs per hours worked. The ECEC components are based on data from the ECI. Beginning with the March 2004 estimates, industry estimates are based on NAICS 2002 and the occupational categories are classified according to the 2000 Standard Occupational Classification (SOC) system. These systems replace the 1987 Standard Industrial Classification System (SIC) and the Occupational Classification System (OCS).

Current employment weights are used to calculate cost levels. The March 2004 cost levels were calculated using the March 2004 employment counts from the Bureau of

Labor Statistics, Current Employment Statistics (CES) program, benchmarked to the 2003 universe of all private nonfarm establishments.

Sources of Additional Information

Additional information on ECI methodology and data is available in BLS news releases. The quarterly publication, *Compensation and Working Conditions*, contains articles on all aspects of the NCS and is available on the BLS Web site. For more information about ECEC see BLS news release USDL 05-1767. Additional occupation data from the NCS is on the BLS Web site, summary report 05-02 and Bulletin 2568.

Table 6-1. Employment Cost Index, Private Industry Workers [1], Total Compensation and Wages and Salaries by Occupation and Industry, 1990–2004

(June 1989 = 100, not seasonally adjusted.)

Series and year	Total compensation					Wages and salaries				
	Indexes				Percent change for 12 months ended December	Indexes				Percent change for 12 months ended December
	March	June	September	December		March	June	September	December	
WORKERS BY INDUSTRY, TOTAL										
Private Industry Workers										
1990	103.9	105.2	106.2	107.0	4.6	103.2	104.5	105.4	106.1	4.0
1991	108.5	109.8	111.0	111.7	4.4	107.3	108.4	109.3	110.0	3.7
1992	113.1	113.9	114.8	115.6	3.5	110.9	111.6	112.2	112.9	2.6
1993	117.1	118.0	119.1	119.8	3.6	113.9	114.6	115.7	116.4	3.1
1994	121.0	122.0	123.0	123.5	3.1	117.2	118.1	119.1	119.7	2.8
1995	124.5	125.4	126.2	126.7	2.6	120.6	121.5	122.4	123.1	2.8
1996	127.9	129.0	129.8	130.6	3.1	124.4	125.6	126.5	127.3	3.4
1997	131.7	132.8	133.9	135.1	3.4	128.6	129.7	131.0	132.3	3.9
1998	136.3	137.5	139.0	139.8	3.5	133.7	134.9	136.6	137.4	3.9
1999	140.4	142.0	143.3	144.6	3.4	138.1	139.7	141.0	142.2	3.5
2000	146.8	148.5	149.9	150.9	4.4	143.9	145.4	146.8	147.7	3.9
2001	153.0	154.5	155.9	157.2	4.2	149.4	150.9	152.1	153.3	3.8
2002	158.9	160.7	161.6	162.3	3.2	154.7	156.3	157.0	157.5	2.7
2003	165.0	166.4	168.1	168.8	4.0	159.3	160.4	161.7	162.3	3.0
2004	171.4	173.0	174.4	175.2	3.8	163.4	164.5	165.9	166.2	2.4
Private Industry Workers, Excluding Sales Occupations										
1990	103.9	105.1	106.3	107.1	4.9	103.2	104.4	105.4	106.2	4.2
1991	108.6	109.8	111.1	112.0	4.6	107.4	108.4	109.4	110.2	3.8
1992	113.3	114.1	115.1	115.9	3.5	111.1	111.8	112.5	113.2	2.7
1993	117.5	118.5	119.5	120.2	3.7	114.2	115.0	115.9	116.6	3.0
1994	121.4	122.3	123.4	123.9	3.1	117.5	118.3	119.4	120.0	2.9
1995	125.0	125.7	126.5	127.1	2.6	121.0	121.8	122.6	123.4	2.8
1996	128.3	129.2	130.2	130.8	2.9	124.7	125.7	126.8	127.5	3.3
1997	131.9	133.0	134.1	135.2	3.4	128.6	129.9	131.2	132.4	3.8
1998	136.4	137.5	138.8	139.4	3.1	133.7	134.8	136.3	136.9	3.4
1999	140.5	141.9	143.2	144.5	3.7	138.2	139.6	140.8	142.0	3.7
2000	146.5	148.2	149.8	150.9	4.4	143.5	145.1	146.5	147.6	3.9
2001	153.0	154.4	156.0	157.2	4.2	149.5	150.8	152.2	153.3	3.9
2002	159.0	160.5	161.6	162.4	3.3	154.9	156.1	157.0	157.5	2.7
2003	165.1	166.6	168.1	169.0	4.1	159.4	160.5	161.7	162.4	3.1
2004	171.6	173.2	174.6	175.6	3.9	163.5	164.5	165.8	166.5	2.5
WORKERS BY OCCUPATIONAL GROUP										
White-Collar Occupations										
1990	104.1	105.5	106.7	107.4	4.9	103.6	104.9	106.0	106.6	4.1
1991	109.0	110.3	111.4	112.2	4.5	107.9	109.1	110.1	110.7	3.8
1992	113.4	114.2	115.1	115.9	3.3	111.7	112.3	112.9	113.7	2.7
1993	117.4	118.3	119.4	120.2	3.7	114.7	115.5	116.7	117.5	3.3
1994	121.5	122.5	123.5	124.1	3.2	118.3	119.3	120.2	120.8	2.8
1995	125.3	126.2	127.0	127.6	2.8	121.7	122.7	123.6	124.3	2.9
1996	129.0	130.0	131.1	131.7	3.2	125.8	127.0	128.0	128.7	3.5
1997	133.1	134.1	135.2	136.7	3.8	130.2	131.3	132.7	134.2	4.3
1998	138.1	139.4	141.1	142.0	3.9	135.7	137.0	139.0	139.9	4.2
1999	142.4	144.1	145.6	146.9	3.5	140.3	142.1	143.5	144.8	3.5
2000	149.3	151.1	152.6	153.6	4.6	146.6	148.3	149.7	150.6	4.0
2001	155.7	157.4	158.7	160.1	4.2	152.3	153.8	154.8	156.1	3.7
2002	161.9	163.8	164.6	165.2	3.2	157.7	159.4	160.0	160.4	2.8
2003	168.1	169.4	171.2	172.0	4.1	162.6	163.8	165.3	165.9	3.4
2004	174.2	175.7	177.3	178.1	3.5	167.1	168.2	169.7	170.0	2.5
White-Collar Occupations, Excluding Sales Occupations										
1990	104.2	105.4	106.9	107.7	5.4	103.7	104.8	106.2	106.9	4.7
1991	109.2	110.4	111.8	112.7	4.6	108.2	109.2	110.5	111.3	4.1
1992	113.8	114.6	115.8	116.6	3.5	112.1	112.8	113.7	114.4	2.8
1993	118.3	119.2	120.2	121.0	3.8	115.7	116.4	117.4	118.2	3.3
1994	122.4	123.3	124.4	125.1	3.4	119.0	119.9	121.0	121.7	3.0
1995	126.3	127.0	127.8	128.6	2.8	122.8	123.4	124.3	125.2	2.9
1996	129.9	130.7	132.0	132.5	3.0	126.7	127.6	129.0	129.4	3.4
1997	133.7	134.8	135.9	137.4	3.7	130.8	132.0	133.4	134.8	4.2
1998	138.8	139.9	141.3	141.9	3.3	136.3	137.5	139.1	139.7	3.6
1999	143.0	144.5	146.0	147.3	3.8	141.0	142.5	143.9	145.2	3.9
2000	149.4	151.3	152.9	154.1	4.6	146.7	148.5	149.9	151.1	4.1
2001	156.5	158.1	159.6	160.9	4.4	153.0	154.4	155.7	156.9	3.8
2002	162.8	164.3	165.3	165.9	3.1	158.6	160.0	160.8	161.3	2.8
2003	169.1	170.4	172.1	173.0	4.3	163.6	164.8	166.2	167.0	3.5
2004	175.3	176.7	178.3	179.5	3.8	168.1	169.2	170.6	171.4	2.6

[1] Excludes farm and household workers.

Table 6-1. Employment Cost Index, Private Industry Workers[1], Total Compensation and Wages and Salaries by Occupation and Industry, 1990–2004—*Continued*

(June 1989 = 100, not seasonally adjusted.)

Series and year	Total compensation					Wages and salaries				
	Indexes				Percent change for 12 months ended December	Indexes				Percent change for 12 months ended December
	March	June	September	December		March	June	September	December	
Professional Specialty and Technical Occupations										
1990	104.9	105.8	107.5	108.7	5.6	104.1	104.8	106.5	107.5	4.9
1991	110.1	111.1	112.8	113.9	4.8	108.6	109.5	111.1	112.0	4.2
1992	115.3	116.4	118.0	119.0	4.5	113.0	114.0	115.3	116.0	3.6
1993	120.4	121.3	122.2	122.9	3.3	117.1	117.9	118.9	119.5	3.0
1994	124.6	125.3	126.3	126.8	3.2	120.4	121.3	122.2	123.0	2.9
1995	127.7	128.4	129.3	129.9	2.4	123.7	124.4	125.3	126.1	2.5
1996	131.6	132.6	133.3	133.7	2.9	127.8	128.8	129.6	129.9	3.0
1997	134.6	135.9	136.7	137.8	3.1	131.0	132.4	133.7	134.8	3.8
1998	138.8	140.1	141.6	142.6	3.5	135.9	137.1	138.7	139.7	3.6
1999	142.9	144.1	145.2	146.7	2.9	140.7	141.8	142.6	144.1	3.1
2000	148.4	150.7	152.2	153.7	4.8	145.1	147.3	148.6	150.2	4.2
2001	156.3	157.5	159.2	160.3	4.3	152.1	153.2	154.8	155.9	3.8
2002	161.5	162.5	163.6	164.4	2.6	156.7	157.4	158.2	158.5	1.7
2003	166.5	167.7	169.4	170.5	3.7	159.5	160.5	162.1	163.0	2.8
2004	173.4	174.7	176.8	178.1	4.5	164.7	165.5	167.6	168.0	3.1
Executive, Administrative, and Managerial Occupations										
1990	103.7	105.3	106.6	107.2	5.6	103.3	104.9	106.2	106.9	5.3
1991	108.9	110.3	111.5	112.3	4.8	108.2	109.4	110.6	111.4	4.2
1992	112.7	113.1	113.9	114.5	2.0	111.6	112.0	112.5	113.2	1.6
1993	116.5	117.2	118.1	118.9	3.8	114.7	115.3	116.2	117.0	3.4
1994	120.3	121.3	122.6	123.3	3.7	117.8	118.8	120.0	120.5	3.0
1995	124.9	125.4	126.2	126.9	2.9	121.9	122.5	123.4	124.4	3.2
1996	128.0	128.8	130.9	131.3	3.5	125.9	126.8	128.9	129.3	3.9
1997	133.0	133.9	135.2	137.4	4.6	131.0	132.1	133.6	135.8	5.0
1998	139.4	140.0	141.9	141.8	3.2	137.8	138.7	140.9	140.5	3.5
1999	143.7	145.8	147.7	149.1	5.1	141.9	144.3	146.4	147.6	5.1
2000	151.1	152.7	154.4	155.3	4.2	149.2	150.7	152.3	153.0	3.7
2001	157.3	159.4	160.2	161.8	4.2	154.7	156.5	157.2	158.6	3.7
2002	164.4	166.6	167.0	167.2	3.3	161.3	163.6	164.3	164.5	3.7
2003	172.1	173.1	175.0	175.9	5.2	169.1	170.3	171.8	172.5	4.9
2004	176.8	178.1	179.2	180.2	2.4	172.7	173.9	174.9	175.7	1.9
Sales Occupations										
1990	103.6	105.6	105.9	106.0	2.6	103.3	105.3	105.4	105.2	1.4
1991	108.0	109.8	109.8	109.6	3.4	106.8	108.5	108.2	107.9	2.6
1992	111.6	112.2	111.8	112.6	2.7	109.7	110.1	109.7	110.7	2.6
1993	112.9	113.8	115.6	116.5	3.5	110.5	111.6	113.8	114.7	3.6
1994	117.2	118.8	119.2	119.6	2.7	114.8	116.2	116.5	116.7	1.7
1995	120.2	122.4	123.2	123.2	3.0	116.9	119.3	120.5	120.4	3.2
1996	124.8	126.9	126.7	128.1	4.0	122.0	124.4	123.9	125.9	4.6
1997	130.1	130.7	132.2	133.5	4.2	127.8	128.3	129.8	131.4	4.4
1998	135.3	137.3	140.4	142.6	6.8	133.1	135.2	138.8	141.3	7.5
1999	139.6	142.6	144.1	145.3	1.9	137.3	140.5	142.1	143.3	1.4
2000	148.9	150.3	151.2	151.4	4.2	146.7	147.9	149.0	148.7	3.8
2001	152.3	154.5	155.0	156.7	3.5	149.2	151.5	151.2	152.6	2.6
2002	157.7	161.6	161.6	161.9	3.3	153.6	157.0	156.9	156.8	2.8
2003	163.5	165.1	167.2	167.1	3.2	158.1	159.3	161.6	161.1	2.7
2004	169.2	171.2	173.1	171.4	2.6	162.6	163.9	165.9	164.0	1.8
Administrative Support Occupations, Including Clerical Occupations										
1990	104.2	105.3	106.4	107.3	4.9	103.6	104.7	105.7	106.4	4.1
1991	108.6	109.9	111.0	111.9	4.3	107.6	108.6	109.6	110.4	3.8
1992	113.6	114.4	115.5	116.4	4.0	111.6	112.4	113.2	114.0	3.3
1993	118.1	119.2	120.3	121.2	4.1	115.2	116.1	117.1	118.0	3.5
1994	122.5	123.5	124.5	125.1	3.2	119.0	119.9	120.9	121.6	3.1
1995	126.5	127.3	128.1	129.0	3.1	122.9	123.5	124.3	125.3	3.0
1996	130.1	130.8	132.0	132.5	2.7	126.5	127.3	128.5	129.2	3.1
1997	133.7	134.7	135.9	137.0	3.4	130.6	131.7	132.9	133.9	3.6
1998	138.2	139.6	140.6	141.4	3.2	135.3	136.7	137.9	138.9	3.7
1999	142.6	143.7	145.0	146.2	3.4	140.4	141.4	142.7	143.8	3.5
2000	149.0	150.6	152.3	153.4	4.9	146.0	147.5	149.1	150.1	4.4
2001	156.1	157.7	159.5	160.8	4.8	152.3	153.6	155.3	156.5	4.3
2002	162.8	164.2	165.6	166.7	3.7	158.2	159.2	160.3	161.3	3.1
2003	169.0	170.9	172.3	173.1	3.8	162.6	164.0	165.1	165.7	2.7
2004	176.1	178.1	179.4	180.7	4.4	167.2	168.6	169.7	170.8	3.1

[1]Excludes farm and household workers.

Table 6-1. Employment Cost Index, Private Industry Workers[1], Total Compensation and Wages and Salaries by Occupation and Industry, 1990–2004—*Continued*

(June 1989 = 100, not seasonally adjusted.)

Series and year	Total compensation					Wages and salaries				
	Indexes				Percent change for 12 months ended December	Indexes				Percent change for 12 months ended December
	March	June	September	December		March	June	September	December	
Blue-Collar Occupations										
1990	103.5	104.7	105.6	106.4	4.4	102.7	103.8	104.6	105.2	3.5
1991	107.9	109.0	110.2	111.0	4.3	106.4	107.3	108.0	108.8	3.4
1992	112.5	113.4	114.3	115.0	3.6	109.7	110.4	111.1	111.6	2.6
1993	116.6	117.7	118.7	119.3	3.7	112.5	113.2	114.1	114.8	2.9
1994	120.3	121.2	122.3	122.6	2.8	115.6	116.5	117.5	118.0	2.8
1995	123.5	124.4	125.1	125.6	2.4	119.0	120.1	120.8	121.4	2.9
1996	126.6	127.6	128.1	129.0	2.7	122.5	123.7	124.3	125.1	3.0
1997	129.6	130.8	131.7	132.3	2.6	126.0	127.3	128.3	129.1	3.2
1998	133.1	134.3	135.2	135.9	2.7	130.2	131.3	132.4	133.2	3.2
1999	136.9	138.2	139.4	140.5	3.3	134.3	135.6	136.8	137.7	3.4
2000	142.6	144.1	145.5	146.4	4.2	139.1	140.5	141.9	142.8	3.7
2001	148.2	149.3	151.0	151.9	3.8	144.6	145.9	147.5	148.3	3.9
2002	153.6	155.1	156.3	157.3	3.6	149.6	150.9	151.7	152.4	2.8
2003	159.7	161.4	162.8	163.6	4.0	153.6	154.6	155.6	156.1	2.4
2004	166.9	168.8	170.1	170.8	4.4	157.2	158.3	159.5	159.9	2.4
Precision Production, Craft, and Repair Occupations										
1990	103.4	104.7	105.6	106.2	4.1	102.5	103.6	104.4	104.9	3.2
1991	108.0	109.2	110.5	111.0	4.5	106.3	107.0	107.8	108.4	3.3
1992	112.2	113.1	114.3	115.0	3.6	109.3	110.1	111.0	111.5	2.9
1993	116.6	117.6	118.7	118.9	3.4	112.4	113.2	114.2	114.7	2.9
1994	120.2	121.2	122.5	122.5	3.0	115.5	116.5	117.8	117.9	2.8
1995	123.4	124.4	125.4	125.7	2.6	118.8	119.9	121.0	121.4	3.0
1996	126.5	127.7	128.2	129.1	2.7	122.4	123.7	124.2	125.1	3.0
1997	129.6	130.9	131.7	131.9	2.2	125.8	127.4	128.2	128.7	2.9
1998	132.9	134.4	135.4	136.1	3.2	129.8	131.2	132.3	133.0	3.3
1999	137.2	138.4	139.6	140.6	3.3	134.3	135.6	136.7	137.5	3.4
2000	142.3	144.1	145.8	146.7	4.3	138.9	140.6	142.0	142.8	3.9
2001	148.7	149.7	151.8	152.5	4.0	144.6	145.7	147.7	148.4	3.9
2002	153.7	155.7	156.9	157.8	3.5	149.2	151.0	151.8	152.3	2.6
2003	160.0	162.0	163.1	164.2	4.1	153.4	154.7	155.5	156.2	2.6
2004	167.1	169.1	170.2	171.2	4.3	157.1	158.3	159.3	159.7	2.2
Machine Operators, Assemblers, and Inspectors										
1990	103.7	105.0	105.9	106.9	5.0	103.0	104.2	104.9	105.8	4.1
1991	108.3	109.4	110.5	111.6	4.4	107.1	108.0	108.7	109.8	3.8
1992	113.9	114.6	115.0	115.8	3.8	110.9	111.6	111.7	112.4	2.4
1993	117.8	119.0	120.0	120.8	4.3	113.2	113.8	114.7	115.6	2.8
1994	121.3	122.2	122.9	123.4	2.2	116.2	117.2	118.0	118.8	2.8
1995	124.2	124.8	125.1	126.2	2.3	119.6	120.9	121.4	122.3	2.9
1996	127.1	128.1	128.7	129.5	2.6	123.4	124.5	125.4	126.4	3.4
1997	130.0	131.2	132.2	133.0	2.7	127.2	128.5	129.5	130.6	3.3
1998	133.6	134.7	135.7	136.8	2.9	131.6	132.7	133.8	134.9	3.3
1999	137.3	138.4	139.9	141.4	3.4	135.7	136.7	138.3	139.5	3.4
2000	144.0	145.0	146.0	146.8	3.8	140.7	141.6	142.9	143.7	3.0
2001	148.3	149.1	150.4	151.5	3.2	145.6	146.9	148.1	149.0	3.7
2002	153.6	154.7	155.4	156.7	3.4	150.5	151.6	152.0	153.2	2.8
2003	159.9	161.1	162.6	163.2	4.1	154.7	155.3	156.8	156.9	2.4
2004	168.7	170.5	172.2	172.5	5.7	158.6	159.8	161.6	161.6	3.0
Transportation and Material Moving Occupations										
1990	103.1	104.3	104.9	105.5	4.0	102.0	103.1	103.6	104.1	2.9
1991	106.3	107.6	108.3	109.0	3.3	104.5	105.6	106.1	106.7	2.5
1992	110.4	111.4	112.5	113.0	3.7	107.4	108.3	109.3	109.7	2.8
1993	113.9	115.2	115.9	117.0	3.5	110.0	111.2	111.7	112.6	2.6
1994	118.5	119.1	120.3	120.6	3.1	113.5	114.0	115.2	115.6	2.7
1995	121.8	122.4	122.9	123.0	2.0	117.0	117.8	118.5	118.6	2.6
1996	123.9	124.7	124.9	125.2	1.8	120.0	120.6	121.0	121.1	2.1
1997	126.1	126.8	128.0	128.9	3.0	122.3	123.0	124.1	125.1	3.3
1998	129.3	129.9	130.7	130.7	1.4	125.9	126.4	127.6	127.8	2.2
1999	131.6	133.6	134.4	135.2	3.4	129.1	131.0	131.9	132.7	3.8
2000	137.5	138.6	139.9	141.1	4.4	134.1	135.2	136.5	137.6	3.7
2001	142.6	143.9	145.6	146.3	3.7	139.5	140.7	142.1	142.8	3.8
2002	148.7	149.6	151.0	151.8	3.8	144.8	145.2	146.3	146.9	2.9
2003	153.2	155.1	156.7	156.9	3.4	147.8	149.0	149.8	149.8	2.0
2004	158.5	160.6	161.8	162.3	3.4	150.4	151.8	152.9	153.3	2.3

[1]Excludes farm and household workers.

Table 6-1. Employment Cost Index, Private Industry Workers[1], Total Compensation and Wages and Salaries by Occupation and Industry, 1990–2004—*Continued*

(June 1989 = 100, not seasonally adjusted.)

Series and year	Total compensation					Wages and salaries				
	Indexes				Percent change for 12 months ended December	Indexes				Percent change for 12 months ended December
	March	June	September	December		March	June	September	December	
Handlers, Equipment Cleaners, Helpers, and Laborers										
1990	103.6	104.7	105.7	106.7	4.4	103.0	104.4	105.3	106.2	4.1
1991	108.1	109.3	110.4	111.4	4.4	107.3	108.5	109.2	109.9	3.5
1992	112.6	113.4	114.6	115.3	3.5	110.6	111.3	112.1	112.6	2.5
1993	116.8	117.6	118.4	119.1	3.3	113.6	114.3	114.9	115.7	2.8
1994	120.2	121.4	122.7	122.9	3.2	116.6	117.3	117.9	118.9	2.8
1995	124.1	125.3	125.9	126.8	3.2	120.1	121.2	121.5	122.6	3.1
1996	128.5	129.3	130.0	131.3	3.5	124.2	125.1	125.8	127.1	3.7
1997	132.8	133.4	134.2	135.8	3.4	128.4	129.3	130.2	131.8	3.7
1998	137.0	137.6	138.5	139.2	2.5	133.2	133.7	135.1	135.8	3.0
1999	141.0	142.3	143.2	144.4	3.7	137.3	138.3	139.4	140.4	3.4
2000	146.4	148.1	149.4	150.4	4.2	141.8	143.6	145.0	146.2	4.1
2001	152.2	153.4	154.9	156.5	4.1	148.0	149.8	151.0	152.4	4.2
2002	158.7	159.9	161.4	162.9	4.1	154.2	155.1	156.0	157.2	3.1
2003	164.9	166.8	168.6	169.5	4.1	158.4	159.0	159.9	160.6	2.2
2004	171.7	173.2	174.3	175.3	3.4	161.8	162.7	163.6	164.5	2.4
Service Occupations										
1990	103.9	104.9	105.7	107.3	4.7	103.1	104.2	104.9	106.4	4.0
1991	108.3	109.9	111.5	112.4	4.8	106.9	108.3	109.8	110.6	3.9
1992	113.5	114.2	115.4	115.9	3.1	111.2	111.6	112.5	112.9	2.1
1993	117.2	118.0	118.9	119.5	3.1	113.5	114.1	114.9	115.3	2.1
1994	120.6	121.0	121.8	122.9	2.8	116.3	116.8	117.6	118.8	3.0
1995	123.4	124.0	124.7	125.2	1.9	119.4	120.0	120.8	121.4	2.2
1996	125.8	126.5	127.4	128.9	3.0	122.2	123.0	124.1	125.7	3.5
1997	129.8	130.9	133.1	134.1	4.0	126.6	127.6	129.9	131.1	4.3
1998	135.3	136.0	137.3	138.0	2.9	132.1	133.0	134.4	135.3	3.2
1999	139.5	140.6	141.0	142.6	3.3	136.7	137.8	138.0	139.6	3.2
2000	143.9	145.4	146.6	148.1	3.9	141.0	142.5	143.5	144.9	3.8
2001	150.0	151.3	152.6	154.8	4.5	146.4	147.5	148.7	150.6	3.9
2002	156.4	157.4	159.0	159.8	3.2	152.0	152.8	153.9	154.5	2.6
2003	161.7	162.6	163.8	164.9	3.2	155.5	156.1	157.1	157.8	2.1
2004	166.9	168.2	168.9	169.7	2.9	158.4	159.3	159.8	160.6	1.8
Production and Nonsupervisory Occupations										
1990	103.8	105.1	106.0	106.9	4.4	103.2	104.3	105.2	105.9	3.6
1991	108.4	109.6	110.8	111.5	4.3	107.0	108.1	109.0	109.6	3.5
1992	113.0	113.8	114.8	115.5	3.6	110.6	111.3	112.0	112.6	2.7
1993	116.9	117.9	119.0	119.7	3.6	113.4	114.2	115.3	115.9	2.9
1994	120.7	121.6	122.6	123.1	2.8	116.6	117.5	118.5	119.1	2.8
1995	124.1	125.0	125.8	126.3	2.6	119.9	121.0	121.8	122.4	2.8
1996	127.5	128.6	129.2	130.0	2.9	123.7	124.9	125.6	126.5	3.3
1997	131.1	132.1	133.2	134.2	3.2	127.7	128.8	130.1	131.2	3.7
1998	135.3	136.6	138.0	139.0	3.6	132.3	133.6	135.2	136.4	4.0
1999	139.3	140.8	141.9	143.1	2.9	136.8	138.2	139.3	140.4	2.9
2000	145.3	146.9	148.4	149.5	4.5	142.1	143.7	145.0	146.0	4.0
2001	151.4	152.7	154.3	155.5	4.0	147.7	149.0	150.3	151.5	3.8
2002	157.1	158.7	159.7	160.5	3.2	152.7	154.0	154.7	155.2	2.4
2003	162.6	164.1	165.7	166.6	3.8	156.4	157.4	158.8	159.4	2.7
2004	169.3	171.0	172.4	173.0	3.8	160.7	161.7	163.1	163.4	2.5
WORKERS BY INDUSTRY DIVISION										
Goods-Producing Industries[2]										
1990	103.9	105.2	106.2	107.0	4.8	103.1	104.2	105.1	105.8	3.7
1991	108.5	109.8	111.0	111.9	4.6	107.0	108.0	108.7	109.7	3.7
1992	113.5	114.3	115.3	116.1	3.8	110.7	111.4	112.1	112.8	2.8
1993	118.0	119.1	119.9	120.6	3.9	113.8	114.5	115.3	116.1	2.9
1994	121.8	123.0	123.9	124.3	3.1	116.9	118.0	118.9	119.6	3.0
1995	125.3	125.9	126.5	127.3	2.4	120.4	121.4	122.1	122.9	2.8
1996	128.2	129.3	130.1	130.9	2.8	123.9	125.1	126.1	126.8	3.2
1997	131.4	132.7	133.6	134.1	2.4	127.5	128.9	129.9	130.6	3.0
1998	135.1	136.2	137.1	137.8	2.8	132.0	133.2	134.3	135.2	3.5
1999	138.9	139.9	141.1	142.5	3.4	136.3	137.3	138.5	139.7	3.3
2000	144.8	146.6	147.9	148.8	4.4	141.3	143.0	144.3	145.2	3.9
2001	150.7	152.1	153.1	154.4	3.8	147.0	148.6	149.5	150.5	3.7
2002	156.2	157.6	158.6	160.1	3.7	151.7	153.1	153.9	155.0	3.0
2003	163.0	164.5	165.7	166.5	4.0	156.3	157.4	158.3	158.7	2.4
2004	170.3	171.8	173.3	174.3	4.7	159.9	160.9	162.3	162.4	2.3

[1]Excludes farm and household workers.
[2]Includes mining, construction, and manufacturing.

Table 6-1. Employment Cost Index, Private Industry Workers [1], Total Compensation and Wages and Salaries by Occupation and Industry, 1990–2004—*Continued*

(June 1989 = 100, not seasonally adjusted.)

Series and year	Total compensation					Wages and salaries				
	Indexes				Percent change for 12 months ended December	Indexes				Percent change for 12 months ended December
	March	June	September	December		March	June	September	December	
Goods-Producing Industries, Excluding Sales Occupations										
1990	103.9	105.1	106.1	107.0	4.7	103.0	104.2	105.0	105.7	3.6
1991	108.4	109.8	110.9	111.8	4.5	106.9	107.9	108.7	109.7	3.8
1992	113.4	114.1	115.2	115.9	3.7	110.5	111.2	112.0	112.6	2.6
1993	117.8	118.8	119.6	120.1	3.6	113.5	114.2	114.9	115.6	2.7
1994	121.4	122.5	123.5	124.0	3.2	116.4	117.4	118.4	119.1	3.0
1995	124.9	125.6	126.1	127.0	2.4	119.9	120.9	121.6	122.4	2.8
1996	128.0	129.0	129.8	130.5	2.8	123.5	124.6	125.7	126.3	3.2
1997	131.1	132.3	133.1	133.6	2.4	127.0	128.3	129.3	130.0	2.9
1998	134.5	135.6	136.5	137.2	2.7	131.3	132.5	133.6	134.4	3.4
1999	138.3	139.3	140.5	141.8	3.3	135.5	136.6	137.8	138.9	3.3
2000	144.2	145.9	147.2	148.2	4.5	140.5	142.1	143.4	144.6	4.1
2001	150.1	151.5	152.5	153.7	3.7	146.3	147.8	148.7	149.7	3.5
2002	155.5	156.9	157.9	159.2	3.6	150.9	152.2	153.0	154.0	2.9
2003	162.4	163.8	165.0	165.9	4.2	155.4	156.5	157.4	158.0	2.6
2004	169.8	171.2	172.5	173.7	4.7	159.2	160.2	161.2	161.6	2.3
Goods-Producing Industries, White-Collar Occupations										
1990	104.1	105.3	106.7	107.4	5.4	103.5	104.6	105.7	106.3	4.3
1991	108.8	110.1	111.2	112.3	4.6	107.4	108.5	109.5	110.4	3.9
1992	113.6	114.5	115.5	116.7	3.9	111.7	112.5	113.2	114.2	3.4
1993	118.6	119.6	120.5	121.1	3.8	115.4	116.4	117.3	118.2	3.5
1994	123.0	124.3	125.1	125.9	4.0	119.1	120.3	121.1	122.0	3.2
1995	127.2	127.6	128.1	129.0	2.5	123.0	123.8	124.4	125.3	2.7
1996	130.0	131.0	132.2	132.9	3.0	126.2	127.3	128.6	129.1	3.0
1997	133.5	134.8	135.6	136.2	2.5	130.0	131.4	132.3	132.9	2.9
1998	137.7	138.8	139.7	140.2	2.9	135.0	136.3	137.4	138.2	4.0
1999	141.7	142.7	143.9	145.5	3.7	139.4	140.5	141.7	143.0	3.5
2000	148.1	150.1	151.3	151.9	4.4	145.0	146.8	147.9	148.7	4.0
2001	154.5	156.5	156.8	158.1	4.1	150.5	152.3	152.6	153.6	3.3
2002	160.1	161.9	162.9	164.3	3.9	155.0	156.6	157.5	158.6	3.3
2003	167.8	169.2	170.1	170.5	3.8	160.0	161.4	161.9	162.1	2.2
2004	173.5	174.7	176.4	177.8	4.3	163.2	164.5	166.0	165.9	2.3
Goods-Producing Industries, White-Collar Occupations, Excluding Sales Occupations										
1990	103.9	105.2	106.4	107.1	5.0	103.3	104.4	105.6	106.2	4.1
1991	108.5	110.0	111.1	112.2	4.8	107.2	108.5	109.5	110.5	4.0
1992	113.2	113.9	115.1	116.2	3.6	111.3	112.0	112.9	113.7	2.9
1993	118.1	119.0	119.7	119.9	3.2	114.9	115.6	116.4	116.8	2.7
1994	121.9	123.2	124.1	125.0	4.3	117.7	118.8	119.8	120.8	3.4
1995	126.2	126.7	127.2	128.2	2.6	121.8	122.5	123.2	124.2	2.8
1996	129.4	130.2	131.5	132.1	3.0	125.3	126.3	127.7	128.1	3.1
1997	132.6	133.8	134.5	135.0	2.2	128.9	130.0	130.9	131.6	2.7
1998	136.3	137.4	138.3	138.8	2.8	133.3	134.6	135.7	136.4	3.6
1999	140.4	141.3	142.5	143.9	3.7	137.8	138.8	140.1	141.3	3.6
2000	146.5	148.4	149.6	150.5	4.6	143.2	144.9	146.0	147.2	4.2
2001	153.0	155.0	155.3	156.5	4.0	148.9	150.5	150.8	151.7	3.1
2002	158.4	160.2	161.1	162.3	3.7	152.9	154.5	155.4	156.3	3.0
2003	166.3	167.5	168.5	169.2	4.3	158.0	159.2	159.9	160.4	2.6
2004	172.2	173.3	174.5	176.4	4.3	161.5	162.7	163.6	164.1	2.3
Goods-Producing Industries, Blue-Collar Occupations										
1990	103.9	105.1	106.0	106.9	4.5	102.9	104.1	104.7	105.5	3.5
1991	108.4	109.7	110.8	111.6	4.4	106.8	107.6	108.3	109.2	3.5
1992	113.4	114.1	115.1	115.8	3.8	110.1	110.7	111.4	111.9	2.5
1993	117.6	118.7	119.6	120.2	3.8	112.8	113.4	114.1	114.9	2.7
1994	121.1	122.2	123.1	123.4	2.7	115.6	116.6	117.5	118.1	2.8
1995	124.1	124.9	125.5	126.3	2.4	118.8	119.9	120.7	121.4	2.8
1996	127.1	128.3	128.9	129.6	2.6	122.4	123.7	124.5	125.3	3.2
1997	130.2	131.4	132.4	132.8	2.5	126.0	127.3	128.4	129.2	3.1
1998	133.5	134.6	135.5	136.3	2.6	130.1	131.3	132.3	133.3	3.2
1999	137.1	138.3	139.4	140.7	3.2	134.3	135.4	136.6	137.6	3.2
2000	142.8	144.4	145.8	146.8	4.3	139.0	140.5	142.0	143.1	4.0
2001	148.2	149.3	150.8	151.9	3.5	144.7	146.1	147.4	148.4	3.7
2002	153.6	154.8	155.9	157.3	3.6	149.6	150.7	151.5	152.6	2.8
2003	159.9	161.5	162.9	163.9	4.2	153.8	154.8	155.9	156.4	2.5
2004	168.1	169.8	171.3	172.0	4.9	157.7	158.6	159.8	160.1	2.4

[1] Excludes farm and household workers.

Table 6-1. Employment Cost Index, Private Industry Workers [1], Total Compensation and Wages and Salaries by Occupation and Industry, 1990–2004—Continued

(June 1989 = 100, not seasonally adjusted.)

Series and year	Total compensation					Wages and salaries				
	Indexes				Percent change for 12 months ended December	Indexes				Percent change for 12 months ended December
	March	June	September	December		March	June	September	December	
Construction										
1990	103.1	104.3	105.2	105.6	3.1	102.0	102.9	103.5	103.7	2.0
1991	107.4	108.5	109.3	109.9	4.1	105.1	105.9	106.3	106.8	3.0
1992	110.6	111.7	113.1	113.8	3.5	107.2	107.9	108.7	108.9	2.0
1993	114.9	116.0	116.8	116.5	2.4	109.5	110.4	111.3	111.1	2.0
1994	118.6	120.2	121.4	120.8	3.7	112.2	113.6	114.6	114.7	3.2
1995	121.1	122.0	123.1	123.4	2.2	114.8	115.7	116.8	117.4	2.4
1996	124.3	125.3	125.9	126.4	2.4	118.3	119.6	120.4	120.8	2.9
1997	127.2	128.7	129.7	129.7	2.6	122.0	123.6	124.7	124.9	3.4
1998	130.6	132.7	133.4	134.3	3.5	126.0	128.1	128.5	129.3	3.5
1999	135.6	136.9	137.9	138.7	3.3	130.7	131.9	133.0	133.6	3.3
2000	140.8	143.2	145.1	146.7	5.8	136.0	138.0	139.4	140.7	5.3
2001	148.2	150.3	151.7	153.0	4.3	142.1	143.9	145.1	146.3	4.0
2002	154.1	155.2	156.3	157.9	3.2	147.0	148.2	149.0	150.2	2.7
2003	159.1	161.1	162.3	163.3	3.4	150.6	152.4	153.6	154.0	2.5
2004	164.6	165.9	167.0	167.3	2.4	155.1	155.9	157.1	157.0	1.9
Manufacturing										
1990	104.0	105.3	106.4	107.2	5.1	103.3	104.5	105.4	106.2	4.2
1991	108.6	110.0	111.2	112.2	4.7	107.4	108.4	109.3	110.3	3.9
1992	114.0	114.7	115.7	116.5	3.8	111.5	112.2	112.9	113.7	3.1
1993	118.6	119.7	120.6	121.3	4.1	114.7	115.5	116.3	117.3	3.2
1994	122.5	123.5	124.4	125.1	3.1	118.0	119.0	120.0	120.8	3.0
1995	126.2	126.9	127.3	128.3	2.6	121.9	122.9	123.5	124.3	2.9
1996	129.3	130.4	131.3	132.1	3.0	125.4	126.5	127.7	128.4	3.3
1997	132.6	133.8	134.6	135.3	2.4	129.1	130.3	131.3	132.2	3.0
1998	136.4	137.2	138.2	138.9	2.7	133.7	134.6	136.0	136.8	3.5
1999	139.9	140.9	142.1	143.6	3.4	137.9	139.0	140.2	141.5	3.4
2000	146.0	147.5	148.7	149.3	4.0	142.9	144.4	145.7	146.5	3.5
2001	151.3	152.6	153.3	154.6	3.5	148.5	150.0	150.7	151.7	3.5
2002	156.6	158.1	159.1	160.5	3.8	153.1	154.5	155.4	156.5	3.2
2003	164.0	165.4	166.5	167.1	4.1	158.0	159.0	159.7	160.1	2.3
2004	171.7	173.2	174.9	175.4	5.0	161.3	162.4	163.8	164.0	2.4
Manufacturing, White-Collar Occupations										
1990	104.1	105.3	106.8	107.4	5.4	103.7	104.7	105.9	106.4	4.5
1991	108.8	110.2	111.3	112.4	4.7	107.6	108.8	109.8	110.7	4.0
1992	113.6	114.6	115.5	116.6	3.7	111.9	112.9	113.6	114.6	3.5
1993	118.7	119.7	120.5	121.3	4.0	116.0	116.9	117.7	118.8	3.7
1994	122.7	123.9	124.9	126.0	3.9	119.5	120.6	121.7	122.7	3.3
1995	127.4	128.0	128.7	129.5	2.8	123.9	124.7	125.3	126.1	2.8
1996	130.5	131.6	132.8	133.6	3.2	127.1	128.2	129.6	130.1	3.2
1997	133.9	135.2	135.8	136.7	2.3	130.6	131.9	132.8	133.6	2.7
1998	138.2	139.1	140.1	140.5	2.8	135.6	136.8	138.3	139.0	4.0
1999	141.8	143.0	144.3	145.8	3.8	140.1	141.4	142.7	144.0	3.6
2000	148.2	150.2	151.4	151.5	3.9	145.8	147.7	148.7	149.2	3.6
2001	154.2	156.0	156.0	156.9	3.6	151.1	152.7	152.8	153.3	2.7
2002	159.1	161.1	162.2	163.3	4.1	154.9	156.6	157.7	158.6	3.5
2003	167.1	168.7	169.5	169.6	3.9	160.1	161.6	162.0	162.1	2.2
2004	173.2	174.6	176.4	176.7	4.2	163.3	164.7	166.1	166.1	2.5
Manufacturing, White-Collar Occupations, Excluding Sales Occupations										
1990	104.0	105.1	106.4	107.0	5.0	103.4	104.4	105.6	106.2	4.2
1991	108.3	109.9	111.1	112.2	4.9	107.2	108.6	109.7	110.7	4.2
1992	113.0	113.8	115.0	115.9	3.3	111.4	112.2	113.0	114.0	3.0
1993	118.0	118.8	119.5	119.9	3.5	115.3	115.9	116.7	117.2	2.8
1994	121.3	122.5	123.6	124.9	4.2	118.0	119.1	120.2	121.4	3.6
1995	126.1	126.6	127.4	128.3	2.7	122.4	123.2	123.9	124.8	2.8
1996	129.5	130.5	131.8	132.5	3.3	126.0	127.0	128.4	128.9	3.3
1997	132.8	133.8	134.5	135.3	2.1	129.3	130.5	131.3	132.2	2.6
1998	136.5	137.3	138.3	138.7	2.5	133.8	135.0	136.3	137.1	3.7
1999	140.1	141.3	142.5	143.8	3.7	138.3	139.6	140.8	142.0	3.6
2000	146.2	148.2	149.3	149.7	4.1	143.7	145.6	146.6	147.5	3.9
2001	152.2	154.0	153.8	154.7	3.3	149.1	150.5	150.5	151.0	2.4
2002	156.7	158.6	159.6	160.7	3.9	152.3	153.9	155.0	155.9	3.2
2003	165.1	166.4	167.4	167.8	4.4	157.7	158.9	159.5	160.0	2.6
2004	171.3	172.6	174.1	174.7	4.1	161.2	162.5	163.5	163.9	2.4

[1] Excludes farm and household workers.

Table 6-1. Employment Cost Index, Private Industry Workers [1], Total Compensation and Wages and Salaries by Occupation and Industry, 1990–2004—*Continued*

(June 1989 = 100, not seasonally adjusted.)

Series and year	Total compensation					Wages and salaries				
	Indexes				Percent change for 12 months ended December	Indexes				Percent change for 12 months ended December
	March	June	September	December		March	June	September	December	
Manufacturing, Blue-Collar Occupations										
1990	104.0	105.2	106.2	107.2	5.0	103.1	104.4	105.1	106.1	4.0
1991	108.5	109.8	111.1	112.0	4.5	107.3	108.2	109.0	110.0	3.7
1992	114.2	114.8	115.7	116.4	3.9	111.1	111.7	112.4	113.1	2.8
1993	118.5	119.6	120.5	121.3	4.2	113.9	114.5	115.2	116.2	2.7
1994	122.3	123.2	124.0	124.5	2.6	116.9	117.8	118.7	119.5	2.8
1995	125.3	126.0	126.3	127.5	2.4	120.4	121.6	122.2	123.1	3.0
1996	128.4	129.5	130.2	131.1	2.8	124.2	125.4	126.3	127.3	3.4
1997	131.7	132.8	133.7	134.3	2.4	128.0	129.2	130.2	131.2	3.1
1998	135.0	135.9	136.8	137.7	2.5	132.3	133.1	134.3	135.3	3.1
1999	138.5	139.4	140.5	142.1	3.2	136.3	137.2	138.4	139.7	3.3
2000	144.4	145.6	146.7	147.8	4.0	140.8	142.0	143.4	144.6	3.5
2001	149.1	150.0	151.3	152.7	3.3	146.4	147.8	149.1	150.3	3.9
2002	154.6	155.8	156.7	158.3	3.7	151.7	152.8	153.5	154.7	2.9
2003	161.6	162.8	164.1	165.1	4.3	156.3	156.9	157.9	158.5	2.5
2004	170.4	172.0	173.7	174.3	5.6	159.8	160.6	162.1	162.4	2.5
Manufacturing, Durable Goods										
1990	104.0	105.1	106.3	107.2	4.9	103.2	104.3	105.3	106.1	4.1
1991	108.5	109.9	111.2	112.1	4.6	107.3	108.3	109.2	110.2	3.9
1992	114.1	114.8	115.8	116.7	4.1	111.2	111.8	112.7	113.4	2.9
1993	119.0	120.0	121.0	121.9	4.5	114.4	115.1	115.9	117.2	3.4
1994	122.9	123.8	125.1	125.8	3.2	117.8	118.7	119.8	120.8	3.1
1995	127.0	127.7	128.2	129.0	2.5	121.9	122.9	123.6	124.3	2.9
1996	129.7	131.2	131.9	132.6	2.8	125.1	126.5	127.7	128.4	3.3
1997	133.0	134.1	135.0	135.7	2.3	129.0	130.1	131.2	131.9	2.7
1998	136.5	137.4	138.5	139.2	2.6	133.4	134.5	135.9	136.9	3.8
1999	139.9	141.0	142.3	144.0	3.4	137.9	139.1	140.4	141.8	3.6
2000	146.5	148.3	149.4	150.1	4.2	143.0	144.7	146.1	147.3	3.9
2001	151.8	153.1	154.0	155.3	3.5	149.0	150.5	151.5	152.6	3.6
2002	156.9	158.3	158.9	160.6	3.4	153.9	155.3	156.0	157.3	3.1
2003	164.4	165.5	166.6	167.3	4.2	158.8	159.7	160.6	160.9	2.3
2004	172.4	174.0	175.8	176.3	5.4	161.9	162.9	164.5	164.7	2.4
Aircraft Manufacturing (SIC 3721)										
1990	105.4	107.0	108.5	108.6	4.8	103.2	104.9	105.7	107.0	4.7
1991	110.2	111.8	113.1	114.8	5.7	108.4	109.8	110.9	112.6	5.2
1992	116.9	119.0	120.1	122.9	7.1	113.6	115.2	116.0	117.2	4.1
1993	124.1	124.5	126.7	125.2	1.9	117.9	118.8	120.5	121.6	3.8
1994	126.2	127.1	128.7	129.2	3.2	122.4	123.3	124.0	124.8	2.6
1995	130.6	131.0	131.5	133.8	3.6	125.7	126.5	127.4	128.1	2.6
1996	136.9	138.2	138.2	137.4	2.7	129.0	130.3	130.6	130.9	2.2
1997	137.3	138.4	137.8	136.9	-0.4	132.0	133.5	133.3	134.0	2.4
1998	137.2	138.9	139.3	140.6	2.7	135.1	136.9	137.2	138.3	3.2
1999	140.5	142.4	143.7	146.9	4.5	139.4	141.5	142.7	143.6	3.8
2000	151.2	154.3	156.0	155.3	5.7	146.3	148.6	150.0	151.6	5.6
2001	159.8	160.4	160.3	163.4	5.2	154.3	155.1	156.6	158.3	4.4
2002	167.5	168.9	168.8	172.3	5.4	161.4	162.5	162.5	163.1	3.0
2003	183.2	183.7	184.4	182.1	5.7	166.0	166.9	167.4	167.7	2.8
2004	198.9	200.9	201.6	202.0	10.9	170.6	171.9	172.4	172.6	2.9
Aircraft Manufacturing (SIC 3721), White-Collar Occupations										
1990	104.6	105.9	107.2	106.8	3.9	102.3	103.8	104.2	105.0	3.4
1991	108.1	109.7	110.5	112.0	4.9	106.0	107.4	107.9	108.9	3.7
1992	114.2	116.3	117.0	119.0	6.3	110.0	111.6	112.2	113.1	3.9
1993	120.5	121.2	123.2	121.8	2.4	113.9	115.2	116.7	117.3	3.7
1994	122.7	123.8	125.3	125.3	2.9	118.1	119.1	119.8	120.2	2.5
1995	126.7	127.2	127.8	129.0	3.0	121.0	121.6	122.7	123.2	2.5
1996	132.4	133.9	133.8	133.7	3.6	124.1	125.9	126.1	126.5	2.7
1997	133.5	134.9	134.6	134.3	0.4	127.8	129.6	129.3	129.8	2.6
1998	134.7	137.1	137.4	137.4	2.3	131.2	133.7	133.9	134.5	3.6
1999	137.3	139.5	139.8	141.7	3.1	135.5	138.0	138.3	139.1	3.4
2000	146.6	150.7	151.8	151.2	6.7	142.1	145.2	146.0	146.2	5.1
2001	157.3	157.3	156.3	159.0	5.2	149.8	150.1	150.9	152.2	4.1
2002	163.3	164.2	163.7	165.3	4.0	155.9	156.4	155.9	156.2	2.6
2003	177.9	177.3	177.5	177.0	7.1	160.4	160.2	160.3	160.6	2.8
2004	193.9	194.9	195.2	195.3	10.3	164.7	165.5	165.7	165.9	3.3

[1] Excludes farm and household workers.

Table 6-1. Employment Cost Index, Private Industry Workers[1], Total Compensation and Wages and Salaries by Occupation and Industry, 1990–2004—*Continued*

(June 1989 = 100, not seasonally adjusted.)

Series and year	Total compensation					Wages and salaries				
	Indexes				Percent change for 12 months ended December	Indexes				Percent change for 12 months ended December
	March	June	September	December		March	June	September	December	
Aircraft Manufacturing (SIC 3721), Blue-Collar Occupations										
1990	106.6	108.6	110.1	110.9	5.9	104.6	106.7	107.8	110.0	6.5
1991	113.2	114.7	116.7	118.8	7.1	112.0	113.5	115.4	118.0	7.3
1992	120.8	122.8	124.2	128.2	7.9	119.0	120.5	121.5	123.3	4.5
1993	129.2	129.2	131.5	129.8	1.2	123.9	124.1	126.1	127.9	3.7
1994	130.9	131.5	133.2	134.2	3.4	128.7	129.4	130.2	131.7	3.0
1995	135.7	136.1	136.3	140.5	4.7	132.7	133.6	134.1	135.1	2.6
1996	143.3	144.1	144.4	142.3	1.3	136.1	136.4	137.0	137.1	1.5
1997	142.3	142.8	141.8	139.6	-1.9	137.7	138.8	138.4	139.6	1.8
1998	139.6	140.1	140.8	144.4	3.4	140.1	140.5	141.0	143.2	2.6
1999	144.3	145.7	149.0	154.4	6.9	144.5	145.5	148.9	149.9	4.7
2000	157.8	158.5	161.4	160.4	3.9	151.8	152.1	155.1	159.3	6.3
2001	161.9	163.6	165.3	169.1	5.4	160.3	162.1	164.9	167.4	5.1
2002	172.6	174.8	175.4	182.3	7.8	169.0	171.4	172.2	173.2	3.5
2003	189.8	192.3	193.9	188.4	3.3	173.6	176.5	177.8	178.2	2.9
2004	204.5	208.3	210.9	211.8	12.4	178.4	180.7	183.0	183.3	2.9
Manufacturing, Nondurable Goods										
1990	104.1	105.5	106.6	107.4	5.4	103.6	104.8	105.7	106.3	4.4
1991	108.8	110.1	111.2	112.3	4.6	107.6	108.6	109.4	110.6	4.0
1992	113.8	114.7	115.4	116.3	3.6	111.8	112.8	113.2	114.3	3.3
1993	117.9	119.0	119.7	120.3	3.4	115.5	116.3	116.9	117.5	2.8
1994	121.7	122.8	123.2	123.8	2.9	118.3	119.5	120.3	120.8	2.8
1995	124.7	125.4	125.7	127.0	2.6	121.9	122.9	123.3	124.4	3.0
1996	128.3	128.9	130.0	131.0	3.1	125.8	126.5	127.6	128.5	3.3
1997	131.7	133.0	133.7	134.5	2.7	129.3	130.6	131.4	132.6	3.2
1998	135.9	136.7	137.6	138.2	2.8	134.2	134.9	136.0	136.8	3.2
1999	139.6	140.4	141.5	142.8	3.3	138.0	138.7	139.7	140.9	3.0
2000	144.9	146.0	147.5	147.7	3.4	142.7	143.9	145.0	145.4	3.2
2001	150.4	151.6	152.0	153.2	3.7	147.5	149.0	149.3	150.2	3.3
2002	156.0	157.5	159.2	160.3	4.6	151.9	153.1	154.4	155.2	3.3
2003	163.1	164.9	166.0	166.6	3.9	156.6	157.8	158.3	158.7	2.3
2004	170.4	171.7	173.1	173.6	4.2	160.4	161.6	162.8	162.9	2.6
Service-Producing Industries[3]										
1990	103.8	105.2	106.2	107.0	4.6	103.3	104.6	105.7	106.3	4.0
1991	108.5	109.8	111.0	111.6	4.3	107.5	108.7	109.7	110.2	3.7
1992	112.8	113.6	114.4	115.2	3.2	111.1	111.7	112.3	113.0	2.5
1993	116.4	117.3	118.5	119.3	3.6	113.9	114.7	115.9	116.6	3.2
1994	120.4	121.2	122.3	122.8	2.9	117.3	118.2	119.2	119.7	2.7
1995	123.9	124.9	125.8	126.2	2.8	120.7	121.6	122.6	123.2	2.9
1996	127.6	128.6	129.5	130.2	3.2	124.7	125.8	126.7	127.5	3.5
1997	131.6	132.5	133.8	135.3	3.9	129.0	130.1	131.5	133.1	4.4
1998	136.7	137.8	139.6	140.5	3.8	134.4	135.6	137.6	138.4	4.0
1999	140.9	142.8	144.1	145.3	3.4	138.9	140.8	142.1	143.3	3.5
2000	147.4	149.1	150.6	151.7	4.4	145.0	146.5	147.9	148.9	3.9
2001	153.8	155.3	156.9	158.2	4.3	150.5	151.9	153.2	154.5	3.8
2002	159.9	161.8	162.7	163.1	3.1	156.1	157.7	158.4	158.6	2.7
2003	165.6	167.0	168.8	169.7	4.0	160.6	161.7	163.3	163.9	3.3
2004	171.6	173.3	174.7	175.3	3.3	165.0	166.1	167.5	167.9	2.4
Service-Producing Industries, Excluding Sales Occupations										
1990	103.9	105.1	106.4	107.3	5.1	103.4	104.5	105.8	106.6	4.7
1991	108.7	109.9	111.3	112.1	4.5	107.7	108.7	110.0	110.7	3.8
1992	113.2	114.0	115.1	115.9	3.4	111.5	112.2	113.0	113.7	2.7
1993	117.3	118.3	119.3	120.2	3.7	114.8	115.6	116.6	117.4	3.3
1994	121.4	122.1	123.3	123.8	3.0	118.3	119.0	120.2	120.7	2.8
1995	125.0	125.8	126.6	127.2	2.7	121.8	122.5	123.4	124.2	2.9
1996	128.4	129.2	130.3	130.9	2.9	125.6	126.5	127.6	128.3	3.3
1997	132.2	133.3	134.5	136.1	4.0	129.7	130.9	132.3	133.9	4.4
1998	137.4	138.5	140.0	140.6	3.3	135.2	136.2	137.9	138.5	3.4
1999	141.7	143.3	144.6	145.9	3.8	139.8	141.4	142.6	143.8	3.8
2000	147.7	149.4	151.1	152.2	4.3	145.3	146.9	148.3	149.4	3.9
2001	154.6	156.0	157.8	159.0	4.5	151.3	152.6	154.2	155.5	4.1
2002	160.9	162.4	163.5	164.0	3.1	157.2	158.5	159.3	159.6	2.6
2003	166.6	168.0	169.7	170.6	4.0	161.7	162.8	164.2	165.0	3.4
2004	172.5	174.2	175.6	176.5	3.5	166.0	167.1	168.5	169.3	2.6

[1] Excludes farm and household workers.
[3] Includes transportation, communication, and public utilities; wholesale and retail trade; finance, insurance, and real estate; and service industries.

Table 6-1. Employment Cost Index, Private Industry Workers [1], Total Compensation and Wages and Salaries by Occupation and Industry, 1990–2004—*Continued*

(June 1989 = 100, not seasonally adjusted.)

Series and year	Total compensation					Wages and salaries				
	Indexes				Percent change for 12 months ended December	Indexes				Percent change for 12 months ended December
	March	June	September	December		March	June	September	December	
Service-Producing Industries, White-Collar Occupations										
1990	104.2	105.5	106.7	107.4	4.7	103.6	105.0	106.1	106.8	4.2
1991	109.1	110.4	111.5	112.1	4.4	108.1	109.3	110.3	110.7	3.7
1992	113.4	114.1	114.9	115.7	3.2	111.7	112.2	112.8	113.6	2.6
1993	116.9	117.8	119.0	119.8	3.5	114.5	115.2	116.5	117.3	3.3
1994	121.0	121.9	122.9	123.4	3.0	118.0	118.9	119.9	120.4	2.6
1995	124.6	125.6	126.5	127.1	3.0	121.3	122.3	123.2	124.0	3.0
1996	128.5	129.6	130.6	131.1	3.1	125.6	126.8	127.8	128.5	3.6
1997	132.7	133.7	134.9	136.6	4.2	130.1	131.2	132.6	134.3	4.5
1998	138.0	139.3	141.2	142.2	4.1	135.7	137.0	139.2	140.1	4.3
1999	142.3	144.3	145.8	147.0	3.4	140.3	142.3	143.8	145.0	3.5
2000	149.3	151.0	152.6	153.7	4.6	146.9	148.5	150.0	150.9	4.1
2001	155.8	157.4	159.0	160.3	4.3	152.5	154.0	155.2	156.5	3.7
2002	162.1	164.0	164.7	165.1	3.0	158.2	159.9	160.5	160.7	2.7
2003	167.9	169.2	171.2	172.0	4.2	163.0	164.1	166.0	166.6	3.7
2004	174.1	175.7	177.3	177.8	3.4	167.8	168.9	170.4	170.8	2.5
Service-Producing Industries, White-Collar Occupations, Excluding Sales Occupations										
1990	104.4	105.6	107.1	108.0	5.6	103.8	105.0	106.4	107.2	5.0
1991	109.5	110.6	112.1	113.0	4.6	108.5	109.5	110.9	111.6	4.1
1992	114.1	114.9	116.1	116.8	3.4	112.4	113.1	114.0	114.7	2.8
1993	118.4	119.3	120.4	121.4	3.9	116.0	116.8	117.8	118.7	3.5
1994	122.7	123.4	124.6	125.1	3.0	119.6	120.4	121.5	122.1	2.9
1995	126.4	127.1	128.0	128.7	2.9	123.2	123.8	124.7	125.6	2.9
1996	130.0	130.9	132.2	132.6	3.0	127.2	128.1	129.5	129.9	3.4
1997	134.0	135.1	136.3	138.1	4.1	131.5	132.7	134.2	135.9	4.6
1998	139.5	140.6	142.2	142.8	3.4	137.3	138.4	140.2	140.7	3.5
1999	143.8	145.5	147.0	148.3	3.9	142.0	143.7	145.1	146.4	4.1
2000	150.3	152.1	153.9	155.1	4.6	147.8	149.6	151.2	152.3	4.0
2001	157.5	159.1	160.9	162.2	4.6	154.3	155.6	157.2	158.6	4.1
2002	164.1	165.6	166.5	167.0	3.0	160.4	161.6	162.5	162.8	2.6
2003	169.9	171.3	173.1	174.2	4.3	165.3	166.5	168.2	169.0	3.8
2004	176.2	177.8	179.4	180.4	3.6	170.2	171.2	172.8	173.6	2.7
Service-Producing Industries, Blue-Collar Occupations										
1990	102.6	103.9	104.8	105.4	4.3	102.1	103.3	104.2	104.7	3.8
1991	106.6	107.6	108.7	109.4	3.8	105.6	106.5	107.3	107.8	3.0
1992	110.4	111.6	112.4	113.2	3.5	108.7	109.7	110.3	111.0	3.0
1993	114.3	115.5	116.6	117.2	3.5	111.9	112.9	114.1	114.6	3.2
1994	118.4	119.1	120.6	120.7	3.0	115.5	116.2	117.5	117.6	2.6
1995	122.1	123.1	123.9	124.0	2.7	119.2	120.3	121.1	121.4	3.2
1996	125.2	126.0	126.4	127.3	2.7	122.7	123.5	123.8	124.8	2.8
1997	128.2	129.2	130.0	130.9	2.8	126.0	127.2	127.9	128.9	3.3
1998	132.1	133.2	134.3	134.8	3.0	130.2	131.1	132.4	132.9	3.1
1999	136.2	137.8	139.1	139.8	3.7	134.4	135.9	137.0	137.8	3.7
2000	141.8	143.1	144.5	145.3	3.9	139.1	140.3	141.6	142.2	3.2
2001	147.7	148.7	150.9	151.4	4.2	144.3	145.3	147.5	148.1	4.1
2002	153.2	155.2	156.6	156.9	3.6	149.4	151.1	151.8	152.0	2.6
2003	158.7	160.8	162.2	162.6	3.6	153.2	154.3	155.1	155.4	2.2
2004	164.1	166.4	167.4	168.1	3.4	156.2	157.8	158.9	159.4	2.6
Service-Producing Industries, Service Occupations										
1990	103.9	105.0	105.8	107.4	4.8	103.2	104.3	105.0	106.5	4.1
1991	108.4	109.9	111.6	112.5	4.7	107.0	108.4	110.0	110.7	3.9
1992	113.4	114.1	115.2	115.7	2.8	111.3	111.7	112.6	112.9	2.0
1993	116.8	117.7	118.6	119.1	2.9	113.5	114.1	114.9	115.2	2.0
1994	120.2	120.7	121.3	122.5	2.9	116.3	116.7	117.3	118.7	3.0
1995	123.0	123.6	124.2	124.8	1.9	119.3	119.8	120.7	121.3	2.2
1996	125.3	126.1	127.1	128.6	3.0	122.0	122.8	124.0	125.6	3.5
1997	129.5	130.6	132.7	133.9	4.1	126.5	127.5	129.8	131.0	4.3
1998	135.0	135.8	137.0	137.8	2.9	132.1	133.0	134.2	135.2	3.2
1999	139.3	140.5	140.8	142.4	3.3	136.7	137.8	138.0	139.6	3.3
2000	143.6	145.1	146.3	147.9	3.9	141.1	142.5	143.5	144.8	3.7
2001	149.6	150.8	152.2	154.2	4.3	146.1	147.2	148.4	150.2	3.7
2002	155.9	157.0	158.5	159.3	3.3	151.6	152.4	153.5	154.1	2.6
2003	161.1	162.0	163.2	164.3	3.1	155.1	155.6	156.6	157.4	2.1
2004	166.1	167.4	168.1	168.9	2.8	158.0	158.8	159.4	160.2	1.8

[1] Excludes farm and household workers.

Table 6-1. Employment Cost Index, Private Industry Workers [1], Total Compensation and Wages and Salaries by Occupation and Industry, 1990–2004—*Continued*

(June 1989 = 100, not seasonally adjusted.)

Series and year	Total compensation					Wages and salaries				
	Indexes				Percent change for 12 months ended December	Indexes				Percent change for 12 months ended December
	March	June	September	December		March	June	September	December	
Transportation and Public Utilities										
1990	103.0	103.3	104.2	105.1	3.9	102.6	103.2	104.1	104.6	3.4
1991	106.0	107.7	109.0	109.7	4.4	105.4	106.6	107.7	108.4	3.6
1992	111.1	111.9	112.9	113.5	3.5	109.7	110.6	111.2	111.8	3.1
1993	114.8	116.0	116.8	117.5	3.5	112.9	114.0	114.7	115.4	3.2
1994	119.2	119.8	121.4	122.1	3.9	116.4	117.2	118.9	119.6	3.6
1995	124.0	124.7	126.0	126.6	3.7	121.2	122.0	122.9	123.7	3.4
1996	127.9	128.4	129.3	130.4	3.0	124.6	125.0	125.9	127.0	2.7
1997	131.3	131.7	132.9	134.2	2.9	128.2	128.8	130.1	131.3	3.4
1998	135.8	137.1	138.5	139.3	3.8	132.1	132.8	134.3	135.1	2.9
1999	139.7	140.9	141.8	142.3	2.2	135.4	136.8	137.5	137.9	2.1
2000	143.9	145.7	147.4	148.3	4.2	138.5	140.0	141.3	142.3	3.2
2001	150.5	152.4	153.5	155.5	4.9	143.7	145.7	146.7	149.2	4.8
2002	157.3	158.9	160.8	161.7	4.0	150.5	152.1	153.4	154.1	3.3
2003	163.2	165.4	166.5	167.0	3.3	154.8	155.6	156.0	156.5	1.6
2004	169.8	172.5	173.6	173.5	3.9	157.6	159.1	160.4	160.5	2.6
Transportation										
1990	102.8	103.0	103.8	104.6	3.8	102.3	102.3	103.3	103.5	2.8
1991	105.2	106.8	107.8	108.6	3.8	104.3	105.5	106.6	107.0	3.4
1992	109.9	110.5	111.7	111.8	2.9	108.3	109.2	109.8	109.9	2.7
1993	112.8	114.1	114.8	115.7	3.5	110.8	112.0	112.6	113.4	3.2
1994	117.1	117.7	119.7	120.3	4.0	114.2	114.8	116.7	117.5	3.6
1995	122.3	123.0	124.7	125.1	4.0	119.0	119.8	121.0	121.6	3.5
1996	126.9	127.7	128.2	129.2	3.3	122.9	123.2	123.8	124.7	2.5
1997	130.6	130.9	132.1	133.4	3.3	126.5	126.9	128.5	129.5	3.8
1998	134.0	134.9	136.7	137.3	2.9	130.1	130.4	132.4	132.9	2.6
1999	136.8	138.1	138.7	139.5	1.6	132.3	133.7	134.4	134.9	1.5
2000	140.4	141.8	142.8	143.9	3.2	134.9	136.2	137.4	138.6	2.7
2001	145.4	146.9	148.2	151.1	5.0	139.8	141.6	142.6	145.7	5.1
2002	152.5	153.9	155.4	156.1	3.3	147.4	148.6	149.6	150.1	3.0
2003	157.8	158.9	159.4	159.6	2.2	150.5	150.6	150.4	150.8	0.5
2004	162.0	164.7	166.2	166.2	4.1	151.7	153.4	155.0	155.1	2.9
Public Utilities										
1990	103.2	103.8	104.8	105.7	3.9	103.0	104.1	105.0	106.0	4.1
1991	107.0	108.8	110.4	111.2	5.2	106.9	108.0	109.0	110.0	3.8
1992	112.6	113.7	114.4	115.6	4.0	111.4	112.4	113.0	114.1	3.7
1993	117.4	118.3	119.2	119.9	3.7	115.4	116.4	117.2	117.9	3.3
1994	121.7	122.6	123.6	124.4	3.8	119.1	120.1	121.4	122.3	3.7
1995	126.1	126.8	127.5	128.5	3.3	123.9	124.5	125.2	126.1	3.1
1996	128.9	129.1	130.4	131.7	2.5	126.5	127.1	128.4	129.8	2.9
1997	132.0	132.5	133.7	135.1	2.6	130.1	130.9	132.0	133.5	2.9
1998	137.9	139.7	140.7	141.9	5.0	134.5	135.7	136.5	137.8	3.2
1999	143.4	144.6	145.7	146.1	3.0	139.2	140.6	141.5	141.8	2.9
2000	148.6	150.9	153.5	154.1	5.5	143.2	144.9	146.4	147.1	3.7
2001	157.3	159.8	160.7	161.5	4.8	148.7	151.0	152.0	153.6	4.4
2002	163.9	165.5	168.2	169.2	4.8	154.3	156.4	158.2	159.3	3.7
2003	170.5	174.2	176.4	177.0	4.6	160.4	162.1	163.4	164.1	3.0
2004	180.4	183.1	183.6	183.4	3.6	165.3	166.4	167.5	167.5	2.1
Communications										
1990	103.1	103.1	104.2	105.2	3.5	103.1	104.1	105.0	106.1	4.2
1991	106.0	108.0	109.9	110.7	5.2	106.5	107.6	108.5	109.6	3.3
1992	111.8	112.7	113.4	114.7	3.6	110.8	111.7	112.2	113.5	3.6
1993	116.5	117.5	118.5	119.2	3.9	114.7	115.6	116.5	117.1	3.2
1994	121.0	122.1	122.9	124.0	4.0	118.4	119.5	121.0	122.1	4.3
1995	126.3	126.6	127.4	128.3	3.5	124.3	124.6	125.3	126.2	3.4
1996	128.0	127.5	129.1	131.1	2.2	126.1	126.5	128.2	130.3	3.2
1997	130.2	130.5	131.8	134.0	2.2	129.8	130.6	131.8	134.0	2.8
1998	136.6	139.2	140.5	141.7	5.7	134.4	135.8	136.7	138.0	3.0
1999	143.3	144.9	146.1	146.0	3.0	139.4	141.1	141.9	142.2	3.0
2000	148.4	150.9	153.9	154.7	6.0	143.4	145.0	146.7	147.4	3.7
2001	158.3	161.1	162.8	163.4	5.6	149.2	151.8	153.3	155.2	5.3
2002	166.0	166.1	169.0	170.1	4.1	155.3	157.1	159.6	160.7	3.5
2003	171.3	175.5	178.4	179.0	5.2	161.9	163.4	165.4	165.9	3.2
2004	182.2	183.6	183.8	183.5	2.5	167.0	167.5	168.8	168.3	1.4

[1] Excludes farm and household workers.

Table 6-1. Employment Cost Index, Private Industry Workers [1], Total Compensation and Wages and Salaries by Occupation and Industry, 1990–2004—*Continued*

(June 1989 = 100, not seasonally adjusted.)

Series and year	Total compensation					Wages and salaries				
	Indexes				Percent change for 12 months ended December	Indexes				Percent change for 12 months ended December
	March	June	September	December		March	June	September	December	
Electric, Gas, and Sanitary Services										
1990	103.2	104.6	105.5	106.2	4.4	103.0	104.2	105.0	105.7	3.9
1991	108.3	109.8	111.0	111.7	5.2	107.3	108.6	109.5	110.5	4.5
1992	113.7	115.0	115.9	116.7	4.5	112.2	113.3	114.2	114.8	3.9
1993	118.6	119.4	120.2	120.8	3.5	116.3	117.4	118.2	118.8	3.5
1994	122.7	123.2	124.4	124.8	3.3	119.9	120.9	121.9	122.4	3.0
1995	125.9	127.0	127.7	128.7	3.1	123.4	124.4	125.2	125.9	2.9
1996	130.1	131.1	132.0	132.4	2.9	127.0	127.7	128.5	129.0	2.5
1997	134.2	134.9	136.0	136.4	3.0	130.4	131.2	132.2	132.9	3.0
1998	139.6	140.3	141.0	142.1	4.2	134.7	135.6	136.3	137.4	3.4
1999	143.4	144.2	145.1	146.1	2.8	138.9	140.0	140.9	141.3	2.8
2000	148.9	151.0	152.9	153.4	5.0	143.0	144.7	145.9	146.6	3.8
2001	156.0	158.1	158.1	159.1	3.7	148.1	149.9	150.4	151.7	3.5
2002	161.3	164.8	167.2	168.1	5.7	153.0	155.5	156.5	157.4	3.8
2003	169.5	172.6	173.8	174.6	3.9	158.6	160.4	161.0	161.8	2.8
2004	178.2	182.4	183.3	183.3	5.0	163.3	165.1	165.9	166.6	3.0
Wholesale and Retail Trade										
1990	103.5	105.0	105.6	106.2	3.5	103.3	104.6	105.1	105.6	2.8
1991	107.4	109.2	110.3	110.7	4.2	106.6	108.4	109.4	109.6	3.8
1992	111.4	112.5	113.0	113.7	2.7	109.9	111.2	111.5	112.3	2.5
1993	114.7	115.9	116.4	117.1	3.0	113.0	114.2	114.7	115.4	2.8
1994	117.6	119.4	120.5	120.6	3.0	115.5	117.4	118.3	118.4	2.6
1995	121.7	122.8	123.8	124.2	3.0	119.4	120.6	121.6	122.3	3.3
1996	125.5	126.4	127.5	128.6	3.5	123.9	124.8	125.8	127.0	3.8
1997	130.1	131.2	132.4	132.9	3.3	128.5	129.7	130.9	131.6	3.6
1998	134.7	135.8	137.6	138.2	4.0	133.3	134.6	136.6	137.0	4.1
1999	138.9	141.1	142.2	143.5	3.8	137.7	139.6	140.7	142.0	3.6
2000	145.6	147.3	148.3	149.4	4.1	143.8	145.5	146.4	147.4	3.8
2001	151.0	152.6	153.7	155.5	4.1	148.4	150.1	150.6	152.1	3.2
2002	156.5	159.5	159.6	159.7	2.7	153.0	155.7	155.5	155.5	2.2
2003	161.3	162.5	164.3	165.0	3.3	156.7	157.5	159.2	159.5	2.6
2004	166.3	168.1	169.1	169.1	2.5	160.3	161.6	162.5	162.1	1.6
Wholesale and Retail Trade, Excluding Sales Occupations										
1990	103.0	104.5	105.4	106.1	4.0	102.6	104.2	104.9	105.5	3.5
1991	107.7	109.1	110.1	110.8	4.4	106.8	108.3	109.2	109.6	3.9
1992	111.5	112.7	113.5	114.1	3.0	110.1	111.4	112.1	112.6	2.7
1993	115.4	116.2	117.0	118.0	3.4	113.6	114.4	115.2	116.1	3.1
1994	118.6	119.8	120.9	120.9	2.5	116.5	117.8	118.7	118.8	2.3
1995	122.4	123.1	124.1	125.0	3.4	120.2	120.9	121.9	123.2	3.7
1996	125.9	126.4	128.0	129.0	3.2	124.4	124.9	126.5	127.7	3.7
1997	130.4	131.9	133.0	134.0	3.9	129.3	131.1	132.2	133.2	4.3
1998	135.5	136.3	138.1	138.8	3.6	134.7	135.6	137.6	138.2	3.8
1999	139.9	141.9	142.8	144.3	4.0	139.5	141.1	141.8	143.3	3.7
2000	146.4	148.1	149.6	150.6	4.4	145.2	146.8	148.2	149.0	4.0
2001	152.6	153.9	155.4	157.1	4.3	150.7	151.9	153.1	154.6	3.8
2002	157.5	160.0	160.3	160.4	2.1	154.8	157.1	157.1	157.0	1.6
2003	161.8	162.7	165.0	165.9	3.4	157.9	158.7	160.7	161.3	2.7
2004	167.4	168.6	169.6	170.4	2.7	162.3	162.9	163.5	164.1	1.7
Wholesale Trade										
1990	104.8	105.4	105.8	106.5	1.9	104.6	105.2	105.5	106.2	1.0
1991	107.8	109.6	110.7	111.1	4.3	107.3	109.2	110.4	110.3	3.9
1992	112.5	113.5	113.2	114.4	3.0	111.4	112.5	111.9	113.5	2.9
1993	115.3	116.4	116.6	117.8	3.0	113.9	115.1	115.1	116.4	2.6
1994	117.9	119.7	120.6	121.5	3.1	116.2	118.3	118.9	119.9	3.0
1995	123.2	124.8	126.1	127.0	4.5	120.9	122.7	123.9	125.5	4.7
1996	127.5	129.3	129.9	130.9	3.1	126.1	128.0	128.5	129.6	3.3
1997	132.9	133.8	134.6	135.1	3.2	131.4	132.2	133.0	133.6	3.1
1998	137.7	138.6	140.8	142.8	5.7	136.2	137.1	139.3	141.3	5.8
1999	142.7	144.6	146.3	148.5	4.0	140.7	142.3	144.3	146.5	3.7
2000	150.0	151.8	152.1	154.4	4.0	147.4	149.4	149.6	151.6	3.5
2001	155.1	157.8	158.6	159.5	3.3	151.6	154.5	154.1	154.8	2.1
2002	161.9	166.3	165.9	166.7	4.5	157.2	161.3	160.4	161.0	4.0
2003	169.5	171.3	172.0	172.0	3.2	163.4	164.7	164.8	165.3	2.7
2004	173.8	175.9	177.8	176.6	2.7	166.2	167.8	169.7	167.5	1.3

[1] Excludes farm and household workers.

Table 6-1. Employment Cost Index, Private Industry Workers[1], Total Compensation and Wages and Salaries by Occupation and Industry, 1990–2004—*Continued*

(June 1989 = 100, not seasonally adjusted.)

Series and year	Total compensation					Wages and salaries				
	Indexes				Percent change for 12 months ended December	Indexes				Percent change for 12 months ended December
	March	June	September	December		March	June	September	December	
Wholesale Trade, Excluding Sales Occupations										
1990	103.7	105.0	105.4	106.2	3.5	103.2	104.7	105.2	105.9	3.3
1991	108.2	109.6	110.3	111.2	4.7	107.9	109.2	109.8	110.5	4.3
1992	112.5	113.5	114.1	114.9	3.3	111.5	112.7	113.3	114.1	3.3
1993	116.0	116.8	117.6	118.7	3.3	114.7	115.5	116.3	117.5	3.0
1994	119.3	120.3	121.3	122.0	2.8	117.8	118.8	119.6	120.2	2.3
1995	124.4	125.1	126.2	127.1	4.2	122.2	122.9	123.7	125.7	4.6
1996	127.4	128.7	130.0	130.9	3.0	126.3	127.6	128.9	129.8	3.3
1997	132.6	133.7	134.5	135.4	3.4	131.8	132.8	133.9	135.0	4.0
1998	137.0	138.2	140.0	141.2	4.3	136.5	137.8	139.6	140.8	4.3
1999	142.4	144.0	145.8	147.4	4.4	141.9	143.0	144.8	146.4	4.0
2000	149.6	151.1	152.7	154.9	5.1	147.9	149.7	151.3	153.2	4.6
2001	156.9	158.5	160.0	160.6	3.7	154.9	156.5	157.4	157.9	3.1
2002	162.3	164.4	166.1	167.2	4.1	159.4	161.2	162.6	163.7	3.7
2003	168.4	169.9	171.2	171.3	2.5	163.9	165.2	165.7	166.3	1.6
2004	173.7	174.0	175.3	176.3	2.9	167.8	167.6	168.6	168.9	1.6
Retail Trade										
1990	103.0	104.8	105.5	106.0	4.3	102.7	104.4	105.0	105.3	3.6
1991	107.3	109.0	110.1	110.5	4.2	106.2	108.0	109.0	109.2	3.7
1992	110.8	112.1	112.9	113.4	2.6	109.3	110.6	111.3	111.8	2.4
1993	114.5	115.6	116.2	116.8	3.0	112.6	113.8	114.5	115.0	2.9
1994	117.5	119.2	120.4	120.1	2.8	115.2	117.0	118.0	117.8	2.4
1995	120.9	121.8	122.6	122.7	2.2	118.7	119.6	120.5	120.6	2.4
1996	124.5	124.8	126.2	127.4	3.8	122.8	123.1	124.4	125.8	4.3
1997	128.5	129.7	131.1	131.7	3.4	127.1	128.5	129.9	130.6	3.8
1998	133.1	134.4	135.9	135.6	3.0	131.9	133.3	135.2	134.8	3.2
1999	136.8	139.1	140.0	140.7	3.8	136.2	138.3	138.9	139.6	3.6
2000	143.2	144.8	146.2	146.6	4.2	142.1	143.5	144.8	145.2	4.0
2001	148.7	149.7	150.9	153.2	4.5	146.9	147.8	148.8	150.7	3.8
2002	153.5	155.6	156.0	155.8	1.7	150.9	152.7	152.9	152.7	1.3
2003	156.6	157.4	159.9	161.0	3.3	153.1	153.8	156.3	156.5	2.5
2004	162.1	163.7	164.2	164.7	2.3	157.3	158.4	158.7	159.3	1.8
General Merchandise Stores										
1990	102.6	105.7	105.9	106.9	5.3	102.4	105.2	105.6	106.5	5.0
1991	108.3	110.1	111.2	111.1	3.9	107.8	110.0	110.9	110.6	3.8
1992	111.7	112.9	113.3	113.3	2.0	111.1	111.7	111.7	111.8	1.1
1993	114.1	114.7	115.5	116.3	2.6	112.4	113.4	114.5	115.0	2.9
1994	115.3	118.0	118.7	119.3	2.6	114.0	116.4	116.5	117.5	2.2
1995	120.1	120.7	121.0	121.7	2.0	117.9	118.6	119.0	120.1	2.2
1996	122.4	123.6	124.6	126.3	3.8	121.0	121.7	122.6	124.7	3.8
1997	126.4	127.7	128.6	130.0	2.9	125.0	126.2	126.7	128.4	3.0
1998	131.2	133.0	133.2	134.0	3.1	129.4	131.5	132.2	133.0	3.6
1999	135.0	135.6	137.2	138.3	3.2	133.7	134.3	135.6	136.7	2.8
2000	139.7	141.0	142.2	144.4	4.4	137.8	138.5	139.7	142.2	4.0
2001	147.3	149.4	149.7	150.9	4.5	143.8	145.5	145.7	146.5	3.0
2002	152.4	154.2	156.1	155.1	2.8	147.9	148.9	150.1	149.2	1.8
2003	156.4	159.2	161.2	165.6	6.8	149.8	152.0	153.1	153.6	2.9
2004	165.8	166.2	168.8	169.5	2.4	154.1	154.9	157.5	158.1	2.9
Food Stores										
1990	103.2	104.6	105.7	106.4	4.6	102.8	104.3	105.1	105.8	4.0
1991	107.5	109.3	110.3	111.7	5.0	106.9	108.7	109.4	110.4	4.3
1992	112.6	113.6	114.2	115.1	3.0	110.9	112.3	112.9	113.7	3.0
1993	115.9	117.2	117.1	118.3	2.8	114.6	115.4	114.9	115.9	1.9
1994	119.6	120.6	120.3	120.0	1.4	117.0	117.8	117.4	117.3	1.2
1995	120.8	120.7	121.8	122.4	2.0	117.8	117.6	118.6	119.1	1.5
1996	123.6	124.4	127.0	128.4	4.9	120.5	121.2	123.1	124.7	4.7
1997	128.2	128.2	129.8	129.4	0.8	124.8	124.7	126.7	127.0	1.8
1998	131.3	132.9	133.7	132.7	2.6	129.0	130.5	131.7	130.5	2.8
1999	134.3	135.7	137.0	138.1	4.1	131.8	132.8	133.9	134.9	3.4
2000	140.1	142.5	143.4	144.5	4.6	136.7	139.5	140.2	141.6	5.0
2001	146.1	148.2	149.7	151.7	5.0	143.3	144.5	145.7	146.7	3.6
2002	152.9	154.5	156.3	156.3	3.0	148.0	148.9	150.1	150.3	2.5
2003	157.5	158.6	159.3	160.3	2.6	151.0	151.6	152.2	152.8	1.7
2004	162.1	163.5	163.5	164.0	2.3	153.8	154.3	154.5	155.0	1.4

[1] Excludes farm and household workers.

Table 6-1. Employment Cost Index, Private Industry Workers [1], Total Compensation and Wages and Salaries by Occupation and Industry, 1990–2004—*Continued*

(June 1989 = 100, not seasonally adjusted.)

Series and year	Total compensation					Wages and salaries				
	Indexes				Percent change for 12 months ended December	Indexes				Percent change for 12 months ended December
	March	June	September	December		March	June	September	December	
Finance, Insurance, and Real Estate										
1990	102.6	104.4	105.4	105.5	4.0	101.8	103.5	104.9	104.8	3.5
1991	108.3	109.5	109.7	110.0	4.3	107.0	108.1	108.0	108.4	3.4
1992	111.7	110.8	111.1	111.3	1.2	109.5	108.2	108.2	108.3	-0.1
1993	112.6	113.1	115.7	116.4	4.6	109.3	109.3	112.3	112.9	4.2
1994	117.7	117.7	118.5	118.9	2.1	113.7	113.2	113.8	114.2	1.2
1995	120.2	121.8	122.7	123.1	3.5	115.0	117.0	118.0	118.4	3.7
1996	124.5	126.3	126.7	126.0	2.4	119.8	121.9	122.2	122.2	3.2
1997	128.6	129.4	130.5	134.5	6.7	124.5	125.3	126.4	130.6	6.9
1998	136.7	138.4	141.0	142.5	5.9	132.6	134.8	138.1	139.8	7.0
1999	141.5	145.8	147.6	148.3	4.1	137.2	142.4	144.5	145.2	3.9
2000	152.0	153.1	155.2	155.7	5.0	148.7	149.5	151.7	151.7	4.5
2001	157.9	159.5	160.9	161.3	3.6	153.9	154.6	155.8	156.0	2.8
2002	165.2	167.3	168.0	168.5	4.5	160.3	162.0	162.4	162.6	4.2
2003	176.7	178.3	180.2	180.9	7.4	171.1	172.4	174.1	174.5	7.3
2004	182.5	183.6	184.8	186.0	2.8	175.2	175.3	176.5	177.7	1.8
Finance, Insurance and Real Estate, Excluding Sales Occupations										
1990	103.5	104.7	106.3	106.7	5.6	103.0	103.9	105.8	106.1	5.2
1991	108.6	109.5	110.6	111.4	4.4	107.6	108.4	109.5	110.4	4.1
1992	112.5	112.2	112.5	113.0	1.4	110.6	109.9	109.9	110.2	-0.2
1993	114.9	116.4	117.5	118.2	4.6	112.0	113.1	114.0	114.6	4.0
1994	119.7	120.3	121.5	121.8	3.0	115.5	116.0	117.2	117.4	2.4
1995	123.7	124.6	125.4	125.7	3.2	119.3	120.2	121.1	121.3	3.3
1996	127.5	128.5	129.7	129.2	2.8	123.4	124.5	126.0	125.3	3.3
1997	131.5	132.4	133.5	137.6	6.5	127.2	128.1	129.3	133.6	6.6
1998	140.2	141.3	143.2	143.3	4.1	135.9	137.5	139.7	139.6	4.5
1999	145.6	148.8	151.0	151.6	5.8	141.0	144.8	147.5	148.0	6.0
2000	154.2	155.5	157.4	158.4	4.5	150.2	151.5	153.3	154.1	4.1
2001	161.2	163.1	164.7	165.0	4.2	156.6	157.6	159.1	159.1	3.2
2002	169.8	171.3	172.1	173.1	4.9	164.5	165.7	166.1	167.3	5.2
2003	182.0	184.0	185.3	186.1	7.5	176.7	178.5	179.2	179.8	7.5
2004	186.6	188.7	190.0	191.2	2.7	179.2	180.5	181.8	182.9	1.7
Banking, Savings and Loan, and Other Credit Agencies										
1990	102.1	104.1	104.4	105.8	5.1	101.6	103.6	103.9	105.4	4.5
1991	107.4	107.0	107.5	107.4	1.5	106.6	105.9	106.4	106.3	0.9
1992	110.2	110.0	111.0	111.4	3.7	108.2	107.7	108.6	109.0	2.5
1993	114.6	116.0	116.9	117.8	5.7	112.1	112.9	113.7	114.5	5.0
1994	118.7	119.4	120.8	120.5	2.3	114.7	115.0	116.5	116.2	1.5
1995	123.5	124.1	124.8	124.4	3.2	119.2	119.7	120.4	120.1	3.4
1996	126.9	128.2	130.3	128.0	2.9	122.7	124.2	126.8	123.8	3.1
1997	130.6	131.6	133.1	140.6	9.8	125.9	126.8	128.9	138.3	11.7
1998	143.3	145.3	148.4	146.7	4.3	140.9	143.2	147.0	144.4	4.4
1999	148.8	155.4	159.3	159.8	8.9	146.1	154.5	159.2	159.6	10.5
2000	162.7	164.2	165.8	166.5	4.2	162.0	163.3	165.0	165.7	3.8
2001	170.8	172.7	175.4	174.3	4.7	169.4	170.8	173.2	171.7	3.6
2002	182.1	184.2	184.6	185.3	6.3	181.2	182.8	182.7	183.9	7.1
2003	204.3	206.3	207.6	209.0	12.8	206.4	208.7	209.1	210.2	14.3
2004	207.2	208.9	210.5	212.3	1.6	206.7	207.6	209.5	211.3	0.5
Insurance										
1990	103.2	105.2	106.5	106.0	5.0	102.3	104.1	105.8	105.1	4.3
1991	107.4	109.5	109.5	110.7	4.4	105.7	107.8	107.5	108.6	3.3
1992	113.2	114.7	114.9	115.2	4.1	111.2	112.7	112.7	112.7	3.8
1993	114.3	116.1	117.4	119.7	3.9	111.2	112.9	113.9	116.6	3.5
1994	119.9	120.5	121.5	122.3	2.2	116.0	116.8	117.7	118.6	1.7
1995	123.5	124.6	124.9	125.9	2.9	119.8	120.8	121.1	122.2	3.0
1996	127.6	128.2	129.3	129.6	2.9	123.6	124.1	125.4	126.0	3.1
1997	131.9	132.1	133.1	134.8	4.0	127.9	128.0	128.7	130.2	3.3
1998	137.4	138.9	141.9	141.7	5.1	133.1	134.8	138.7	138.5	6.4
1999	141.7	144.0	144.5	145.8	2.9	137.4	139.8	140.2	141.5	2.2
2000	149.9	151.3	154.8	155.2	6.4	145.5	146.6	150.7	150.8	6.6
2001	157.6	159.3	159.9	161.3	3.9	152.4	153.2	153.6	155.0	2.8
2002	164.0	166.1	167.1	167.9	4.1	157.1	158.6	159.6	159.1	2.6
2003	172.1	173.9	175.1	176.2	4.9	161.6	163.0	163.9	164.5	3.4
2004	177.8	180.5	182.1	183.6	4.2	165.1	167.2	168.9	170.4	3.6

[1]Excludes farm and household workers.

Table 6-1. Employment Cost Index, Private Industry Workers [1], Total Compensation and Wages and Salaries by Occupation and Industry, 1990–2004—*Continued*

(June 1989 = 100, not seasonally adjusted.)

Series and year	Total compensation					Wages and salaries				
	Indexes				Percent change for 12 months ended December	Indexes				Percent change for 12 months ended December
	March	June	September	December		March	June	September	December	
Insurance, Excluding Sales Occupations										
1990	104.5	106.1	106.8	107.6	5.7	103.8	105.2	105.9	106.5	4.9
1991	108.7	110.3	111.4	112.5	4.6	107.1	108.7	109.4	110.5	3.8
1992	113.9	115.7	116.1	117.2	4.2	111.7	113.4	113.8	114.9	4.0
1993	118.6	120.6	121.8	122.7	4.7	115.8	117.6	118.3	119.2	3.7
1994	124.4	125.0	126.0	126.5	3.1	120.6	121.4	122.3	122.7	2.9
1995	127.6	129.0	129.6	130.2	2.9	123.8	125.2	125.7	126.3	2.9
1996	132.1	132.7	133.4	133.5	2.5	128.0	128.6	129.3	129.7	2.7
1997	136.0	136.6	137.4	138.6	3.8	131.6	132.2	132.9	133.7	3.1
1998	140.0	140.9	141.6	142.5	2.8	134.7	135.7	136.6	137.9	3.1
1999	144.5	145.4	146.2	147.0	3.2	139.1	139.9	140.9	141.6	2.7
2000	149.4	150.5	152.2	153.1	4.1	143.2	144.1	145.7	146.5	3.5
2001	155.6	157.6	158.0	159.4	4.1	148.3	149.6	149.8	151.2	3.2
2002	163.0	164.3	165.1	165.7	4.0	154.3	155.1	155.9	155.9	3.1
2003	169.6	171.7	172.8	173.7	4.8	157.9	159.6	160.4	160.7	3.1
2004	175.4	178.1	179.1	180.3	3.8	161.7	163.7	164.6	165.5	3.0
Service Industries										
1990	105.0	106.5	108.1	109.3	6.2	104.2	105.7	107.1	108.3	5.7
1991	110.8	111.5	113.1	114.0	4.3	109.5	110.0	111.5	112.2	3.6
1992	115.3	116.4	117.8	118.9	4.3	113.2	114.0	115.2	116.1	3.5
1993	120.1	120.9	122.3	123.1	3.5	117.0	117.6	118.9	119.6	3.0
1994	124.4	124.9	125.9	126.6	2.8	120.8	121.3	122.2	123.0	2.8
1995	127.5	128.2	128.9	129.4	2.2	123.9	124.4	125.3	126.0	2.4
1996	130.7	131.7	132.7	133.4	3.1	127.6	128.7	129.7	130.5	3.6
1997	134.6	135.7	137.0	138.5	3.8	131.8	133.0	134.7	136.2	4.4
1998	139.3	140.3	141.8	142.7	3.0	137.2	138.3	140.0	140.8	3.4
1999	143.5	144.6	146.1	147.6	3.4	142.2	143.2	144.5	146.0	3.7
2000	149.4	151.2	152.9	154.1	4.4	147.4	149.1	150.6	151.8	4.0
2001	156.5	157.8	160.0	161.0	4.5	153.8	155.0	157.1	158.2	4.2
2002	162.6	163.7	164.9	165.4	2.7	159.5	160.3	161.5	161.7	2.2
2003	167.1	168.4	170.4	171.4	3.6	162.8	164.0	165.9	166.7	3.1
2004	173.5	175.1	176.9	177.9	3.8	168.1	169.3	171.1	172.0	3.2
Business Services										
1990	103.6	105.3	106.3	107.4	6.0	103.0	105.1	105.7	107.4	6.1
1991	110.3	110.4	110.0	111.1	3.4	109.6	109.5	108.9	110.0	2.4
1992	112.5	113.6	115.2	115.9	4.3	111.0	111.7	113.3	113.9	3.5
1993	116.5	117.4	118.1	118.6	2.3	114.2	114.6	115.3	115.7	1.6
1994	121.3	122.1	122.4	123.0	3.7	118.8	119.4	119.9	120.4	4.1
1995	124.5	125.3	125.7	126.3	2.7	122.1	122.9	123.6	124.3	3.2
1996	128.9	129.2	130.2	131.8	4.4	126.9	127.7	128.5	130.1	4.7
1997	133.3	134.2	136.3	138.6	5.2	131.4	132.4	134.9	137.3	5.5
1998	139.5	140.7	143.5	145.9	5.3	137.6	139.2	141.8	144.1	5.0
1999	147.5	148.7	150.7	151.9	4.1	145.4	146.3	148.5	149.8	4.0
2000	154.2	156.3	157.5	158.4	4.3	152.0	154.1	155.3	156.0	4.1
2001	160.5	163.0	165.2	166.2	4.9	158.2	160.8	162.8	163.7	4.9
2002	166.3	166.6	167.2	167.5	0.8	164.0	164.0	164.6	164.8	0.7
2003	168.5	169.2	171.9	172.6	3.0	165.6	166.4	169.1	169.8	3.0
2004	174.8	176.9	178.5	179.1	3.8	171.0	172.7	174.3	175.0	3.1
Health Services										
1990	105.8	107.1	109.0	110.8	6.8	105.3	106.3	108.1	109.7	6.0
1991	112.6	113.5	115.3	116.5	5.1	111.1	111.9	113.5	114.6	4.5
1992	117.9	118.9	120.6	121.8	4.5	115.6	116.3	117.9	118.9	3.8
1993	123.0	124.0	125.0	126.0	3.4	119.8	120.7	121.7	122.6	3.1
1994	126.7	127.1	127.9	128.7	2.1	123.1	123.5	124.3	125.4	2.3
1995	129.7	130.3	131.3	132.2	2.7	126.2	126.7	127.5	128.4	2.4
1996	132.6	133.5	134.2	134.5	1.7	129.3	130.1	130.8	131.4	2.3
1997	135.5	135.9	137.0	138.1	2.7	132.5	133.2	134.3	135.4	3.0
1998	138.2	138.7	139.0	139.0	0.7	136.2	136.5	137.5	137.4	1.5
1999	140.5	141.4	142.6	144.2	3.7	138.7	139.6	140.6	142.2	3.5
2000	145.8	147.5	149.0	150.6	4.4	143.5	145.3	146.6	148.1	4.1
2001	152.7	154.7	156.8	158.4	5.2	149.8	151.8	153.6	155.4	4.9
2002	160.6	162.0	163.2	164.4	3.8	157.3	158.4	159.5	160.7	3.4
2003	166.5	167.9	169.4	170.8	3.9	161.9	163.2	164.6	165.8	3.2
2004	173.3	174.8	177.0	178.0	4.2	167.8	168.8	170.9	171.9	3.7

[1] Excludes farm and household workers.

Table 6-1. Employment Cost Index, Private Industry Workers[1], Total Compensation and Wages and Salaries by Occupation and Industry, 1990–2004—*Continued*

(June 1989 = 100, not seasonally adjusted.)

	Total compensation					Wages and salaries				
	Indexes				Percent change for 12 months ended December	Indexes				Percent change for 12 months ended December
Series and year	March	June	September	December		March	June	September	December	
Hospitals										
1990	105.4	106.6	108.9	110.7	7.0	105.0	106.0	108.2	109.8	6.3
1991	112.2	113.2	114.9	116.1	4.9	110.8	111.6	113.2	114.4	4.2
1992	117.7	118.5	120.2	121.6	4.7	115.4	115.9	117.3	118.3	3.4
1993	122.7	123.4	124.5	125.6	3.3	119.3	119.9	121.0	122.0	3.1
1994	126.7	127.1	127.7	128.6	2.4	122.8	123.3	123.9	124.8	2.3
1995	128.9	129.7	130.3	131.3	2.1	125.4	125.9	126.6	127.7	2.3
1996	132.2	132.8	133.4	133.7	1.8	128.5	129.1	129.7	130.3	2.0
1997	134.0	134.4	135.4	136.5	2.1	130.7	131.2	132.2	133.2	2.2
1998	136.7	138.2	139.1	139.9	2.5	133.6	134.7	135.8	136.5	2.5
1999	141.2	142.1	143.0	144.6	3.4	137.6	138.3	139.3	140.9	3.2
2000	145.8	147.5	149.2	151.1	4.5	141.8	143.3	144.9	146.8	4.2
2001	153.5	155.9	158.4	160.3	6.1	148.5	151.0	153.3	155.4	5.9
2002	162.8	164.5	166.2	168.1	4.9	157.1	158.6	160.2	162.1	4.3
2003	170.8	171.9	173.9	175.9	4.6	163.6	164.6	166.5	167.9	3.6
2004	178.1	179.7	181.8	183.2	4.2	169.4	170.5	172.4	173.8	3.5
Nursing Homes										
1993	...	...	...	...	3.9	...	...	...	...	3.7
1994	...	...	...	...	3.3	...	...	...	...	3.6
1995	...	...	...	...	3.4	...	...	...	...	3.3
1996	...	...	...	...	2.6	...	...	...	...	2.8
1997	...	...	...	...	2.6	...	...	...	...	3.1
1998	...	...	...	...	3.2	...	...	...	...	3.7
1999	...	...	...	...	4.2	...	...	...	...	4.4
2000	...	...	...	...	6.1	...	...	...	...	5.8
2001	...	...	...	...	5.1	...	...	...	...	5.1
2002	...	...	...	...	4.0	...	...	...	...	4.1
2003	...	...	...	...	3.4	...	...	...	...	2.8
2004	...	...	...	...	3.0	...	...	...	...	2.5
Educational Services										
1990	105.4	105.9	110.2	111.4	6.9	104.7	105.0	109.2	110.2	6.1
1991	111.9	111.5	114.9	115.7	3.9	110.3	109.7	113.0	113.7	3.2
1992	115.8	116.3	119.3	120.0	3.7	113.4	113.6	116.5	117.1	3.0
1993	120.5	120.6	123.8	124.1	3.4	117.5	117.4	120.7	120.9	3.2
1994	124.5	125.4	128.2	128.4	3.5	121.2	122.2	124.9	125.1	3.5
1995	128.8	130.3	133.2	133.7	4.1	125.4	125.9	128.6	129.4	3.4
1996	134.4	134.8	137.5	138.0	3.2	130.1	130.4	133.3	133.8	3.4
1997	138.5	138.8	141.6	142.6	3.3	134.5	134.8	137.8	138.4	3.4
1998	143.4	143.9	147.0	147.7	3.6	139.1	139.6	142.8	143.5	3.7
1999	148.3	148.7	152.2	153.0	3.6	143.9	144.2	147.5	148.2	3.3
2000	154.0	154.9	158.8	159.9	4.5	148.9	149.6	153.4	154.3	4.1
2001	162.3	162.6	166.4	167.6	4.8	155.4	156.1	159.6	160.6	4.1
2002	168.5	169.0	173.5	175.2	4.5	161.2	161.2	165.2	166.5	3.7
2003	176.3	177.1	180.2	181.3	3.5	167.1	167.7	170.3	171.0	2.7
2004	183.1	184.2	187.0	188.5	4.0	171.9	172.6	175.5	176.8	3.4
Colleges and Universities										
1990	105.2	105.7	109.8	110.6	6.6	104.4	104.8	108.7	109.3	5.4
1991	111.3	112.0	115.5	116.3	5.2	109.6	110.2	113.7	114.2	4.5
1992	116.8	117.4	120.3	120.8	3.9	114.2	114.5	117.3	117.6	3.0
1993	121.5	121.5	125.0	125.3	3.7	118.0	117.7	121.3	121.6	3.4
1994	125.7	126.0	128.5	128.8	2.8	122.0	122.2	124.5	124.9	2.7
1995	129.3	131.3	134.6	135.2	5.0	125.5	125.9	129.0	130.1	4.2
1996	135.9	136.2	138.6	139.1	2.9	130.6	130.9	133.4	133.8	2.8
1997	139.5	139.9	142.5	143.7	3.3	134.6	135.0	137.8	138.7	3.7
1998	144.3	144.8	147.8	148.5	3.3	139.1	139.7	142.8	143.6	3.5
1999	149.2	149.6	152.6	153.3	3.2	144.1	144.4	147.2	147.9	3.0
2000	154.6	155.5	158.6	159.2	3.8	148.9	149.4	152.5	152.9	3.4
2001	162.2	162.6	166.2	167.5	5.2	154.1	155.0	158.4	159.6	4.4
2002	168.1	168.4	172.0	173.7	3.7	159.9	159.9	163.1	164.3	2.9
2003	174.5	175.4	178.4	179.4	3.3	164.4	165.1	167.6	168.4	2.5
2004	181.2	182.5	185.2	186.2	3.8	169.5	170.0	172.9	173.6	3.1

[1]Excludes farm and household workers.
. . . = Not available.

Table 6-1. Employment Cost Index, Private Industry Workers[1], Total Compensation and Wages and Salaries by Occupation and Industry, 1990–2004—*Continued*

(June 1989 = 100, not seasonally adjusted.)

Series and year	Total compensation					Wages and salaries				
	Indexes				Percent change for 12 months ended December	Indexes				Percent change for 12 months ended December
	March	June	September	December		March	June	September	December	
Nonmanufacturing Industries										
1990	103.8	105.1	106.2	106.9	4.5	103.2	104.5	105.4	106.1	3.8
1991	108.5	109.7	110.9	111.5	4.3	107.3	108.4	109.3	109.8	3.5
1992	112.7	113.5	114.4	115.1	3.2	110.7	111.3	111.9	112.6	2.6
1993	116.3	117.2	118.4	119.0	3.4	113.4	114.2	115.4	116.0	3.0
1994	120.3	121.2	122.3	122.6	3.0	116.8	117.7	118.7	119.1	2.7
1995	123.7	124.6	125.5	125.9	2.7	120.0	120.9	121.9	122.5	2.9
1996	127.2	128.2	129.1	129.8	3.1	123.9	125.1	125.9	126.8	3.5
1997	131.1	132.1	133.3	134.7	3.8	128.2	129.3	130.7	132.1	4.2
1998	136.0	137.2	138.9	139.7	3.7	133.4	134.7	136.5	137.4	4.0
1999	140.3	142.0	143.4	144.5	3.4	137.9	139.7	141.0	142.1	3.4
2000	146.7	148.4	150.0	151.1	4.6	143.9	145.5	146.9	147.9	4.1
2001	153.1	154.7	156.3	157.6	4.3	149.5	150.9	152.2	153.5	3.8
2002	159.3	161.1	162.0	162.5	3.1	155.0	156.5	157.2	157.5	2.6
2003	164.9	166.4	168.1	169.0	4.0	159.4	160.5	162.1	162.6	3.2
2004	170.9	172.5	173.9	174.7	3.4	163.7	164.8	166.2	166.6	2.5
Nonmanufacturing, White-Collar Occupations										
1990	104.1	105.5	106.7	107.4	4.7	103.6	105.0	106.1	106.7	4.1
1991	109.1	110.4	111.5	112.1	4.4	108.0	109.2	110.2	110.6	3.7
1992	113.4	114.1	114.9	115.7	3.2	111.6	112.1	112.8	113.5	2.6
1993	117.0	117.9	119.0	119.9	3.6	114.4	115.2	116.4	117.2	3.3
1994	121.1	122.1	123.1	123.5	3.0	117.9	118.9	119.7	120.2	2.6
1995	124.7	125.6	126.5	127.0	2.8	121.1	122.1	123.1	123.8	3.0
1996	128.5	129.5	130.5	131.1	3.2	125.4	126.6	127.6	128.3	3.6
1997	132.7	133.6	134.9	136.5	4.1	129.9	131.0	132.4	134.1	4.5
1998	137.9	139.2	141.1	142.0	4.0	135.5	136.8	138.9	139.8	4.3
1999	142.3	144.1	145.6	146.9	3.5	140.1	142.0	143.5	144.7	3.5
2000	149.2	151.0	152.6	153.7	4.6	146.5	148.2	149.6	150.6	4.1
2001	155.8	157.5	159.0	160.5	4.4	152.3	153.8	155.0	156.4	3.9
2002	162.2	164.1	164.8	165.3	3.0	158.0	159.6	160.2	160.5	2.6
2003	168.0	169.3	171.2	172.1	4.1	162.8	163.9	165.7	166.3	3.6
2004	174.1	175.7	177.2	178.0	3.4	167.5	168.6	170.1	170.5	2.5
Nonmanufacturing, White-Collar Occupations, Excluding Sales Occupations										
1990	104.3	105.6	107.0	108.0	5.6	103.8	105.0	106.3	107.2	5.1
1991	109.5	110.6	112.1	112.9	4.5	108.5	109.4	110.7	111.5	4.0
1992	114.1	114.9	116.0	116.9	3.5	112.3	113.0	113.9	114.6	2.8
1993	118.5	119.4	120.4	121.4	3.8	115.8	116.6	117.6	118.5	3.4
1994	122.8	123.6	124.7	125.1	3.0	119.4	120.2	121.3	121.8	2.8
1995	126.4	127.1	128.0	128.6	2.8	122.9	123.5	124.4	125.4	3.0
1996	130.0	130.8	132.1	132.5	3.0	126.9	127.8	129.2	129.6	3.3
1997	134.0	135.1	136.2	137.9	4.1	131.2	132.4	133.8	135.5	4.6
1998	139.3	140.5	142.0	142.7	3.5	136.9	138.1	139.8	140.3	3.5
1999	143.7	145.3	146.8	148.1	3.8	141.6	143.2	144.6	145.9	4.0
2000	150.2	152.0	153.8	155.1	4.7	147.4	149.1	150.7	151.9	4.1
2001	157.5	159.1	160.9	162.3	4.6	153.9	155.3	156.9	158.3	4.2
2002	164.2	165.7	166.6	167.1	3.0	160.1	161.3	162.1	162.5	2.7
2003	170.0	171.4	173.2	174.2	4.2	164.9	166.1	167.7	168.5	3.7
2004	176.2	177.7	179.3	180.6	3.7	169.7	170.7	172.3	173.1	2.7

[1]Excludes farm and household workers.

Table 6-1. Employment Cost Index, Private Industry Workers [1]**, Total Compensation and Wages and Salaries by Occupation and Industry, 1990–2004**—*Continued*

(June 1989 = 100, not seasonally adjusted.)

Series and year	Total compensation					Wages and salaries				
	Indexes				Percent change for 12 months ended December	Indexes				Percent change for 12 months ended December
	March	June	September	December		March	June	September	December	
Nonmanufacturing, Blue-Collar Occupations										
1990	102.9	104.1	105.0	105.6	3.8	102.2	103.2	104.0	104.3	3.0
1991	107.2	108.2	109.2	109.8	4.0	105.5	106.3	107.1	107.5	3.1
1992	110.7	111.8	112.8	113.4	3.3	108.2	109.1	109.7	110.2	2.5
1993	114.6	115.6	116.6	117.1	3.3	111.1	111.9	113.0	113.4	2.9
1994	118.2	119.1	120.5	120.5	2.9	114.2	115.1	116.4	116.4	2.6
1995	121.5	122.5	123.5	123.7	2.7	117.5	118.5	119.4	119.8	2.9
1996	124.6	125.6	125.9	126.7	2.4	120.9	122.0	122.4	123.1	2.8
1997	127.5	128.6	129.4	130.1	2.7	124.1	125.5	126.4	127.1	3.2
1998	131.0	132.4	133.4	134.0	3.0	128.2	129.5	130.5	131.1	3.1
1999	135.2	136.8	138.0	138.7	3.5	132.4	134.0	135.1	135.8	3.6
2000	140.6	142.3	143.9	144.8	4.4	137.4	138.9	140.3	140.9	3.8
2001	146.9	148.1	150.2	150.6	4.0	142.8	143.9	145.8	146.4	3.9
2002	152.2	154.0	155.4	155.9	3.5	147.5	149.0	149.8	150.2	2.6
2003	157.5	159.7	161.1	161.7	3.7	151.1	152.4	153.4	153.8	2.4
2004	163.4	165.5	166.4	167.3	3.5	154.7	156.1	157.1	157.5	2.4
Nonmanufacturing, Service Occupations										
1990	103.9	105.0	105.8	107.4	4.9	103.2	104.3	105.0	106.5	4.1
1991	108.4	109.9	111.7	112.5	4.7	107.1	108.4	110.0	110.7	3.9
1992	113.4	114.1	115.2	115.7	2.8	111.3	111.7	112.6	112.9	2.0
1993	116.8	117.7	118.6	119.1	2.9	113.4	114.1	114.8	115.1	1.9
1994	120.2	120.7	121.3	122.4	2.8	116.3	116.7	117.3	118.6	3.0
1995	123.0	123.5	124.2	124.7	1.9	119.2	119.8	120.6	121.2	2.2
1996	125.3	126.0	127.0	128.6	3.1	122.0	122.7	123.9	125.5	3.5
1997	129.4	130.5	132.7	133.8	4.0	126.4	127.4	129.7	130.9	4.3
1998	134.9	135.7	136.9	137.7	2.9	132.0	132.9	134.1	135.1	3.2
1999	139.2	140.4	140.7	142.3	3.3	136.5	137.7	137.9	139.5	3.3
2000	143.5	145.1	146.3	147.8	3.9	140.9	142.4	143.4	144.7	3.7
2001	149.5	150.7	152.1	154.1	4.3	146.0	147.1	148.2	150.1	3.7
2002	155.9	156.9	158.4	159.2	3.3	151.4	152.3	153.4	154.0	2.6
2003	161.1	162.0	163.2	164.2	3.1	155.0	155.5	156.5	157.3	2.1
2004	166.0	167.3	168.0	168.9	2.9	157.9	158.7	159.2	160.1	1.8

[1] Excludes farm and household workers.

Table 6-2. Employment Cost Index, State and Local Government Workers, Total Compensation and Wages and Salaries by Occupation and Industry, 1990–2004

(June 1989 = 100, not seasonally adjusted.)

Series and year	Total compensation					Wages and salaries				
	Indexes				Percent change for 12 months ended December	Indexes				Percent change for 12 months ended December
	March	June	September	December		March	June	September	December	
WORKERS BY INDUSTRY, TOTAL										
State and Local Government Workers										
1990	105.8	106.5	109.4	110.4	5.8	105.1	105.7	108.6	109.4	5.3
1991	111.8	112.0	113.9	114.4	3.6	110.6	110.9	112.8	113.2	3.5
1992	115.2	115.7	117.9	118.6	3.7	113.8	114.2	115.9	116.6	3.0
1993	119.3	119.6	121.4	121.9	2.8	117.2	117.4	119.3	119.7	2.7
1994	122.6	123.1	125.0	125.6	3.0	120.4	120.7	122.8	123.4	3.1
1995	126.4	126.9	128.7	129.3	2.9	124.3	124.6	126.6	127.3	3.2
1996	129.9	130.2	131.9	132.7	2.6	127.8	128.1	130.1	130.9	2.8
1997	133.2	133.3	135.0	135.7	2.3	131.4	131.5	133.6	134.4	2.7
1998	136.5	136.9	139.0	139.8	3.0	135.1	135.4	137.6	138.5	3.1
1999	140.5	141.0	143.1	144.6	3.4	139.0	139.6	142.2	143.5	3.6
2000	145.5	145.9	147.8	148.9	3.0	144.3	144.7	147.2	148.3	3.3
2001	150.3	151.2	154.3	155.2	4.2	149.3	150.1	153.0	153.7	3.6
2002	156.1	156.7	160.1	161.5	4.1	154.4	154.9	157.7	158.6	3.2
2003	162.6	163.2	165.9	166.8	3.3	159.2	159.7	161.3	161.9	2.1
2004	168.0	168.7	171.5	172.6	3.5	162.5	162.8	164.5	165.3	2.1
WORKERS BY OCCUPATIONAL GROUP										
White-Collar Occupations										
1990	106.1	106.7	109.9	110.9	6.0	105.5	106.0	109.2	109.9	5.5
1991	112.2	112.3	114.2	114.6	3.3	111.0	111.2	113.1	113.5	3.3
1992	115.4	115.8	118.1	118.9	3.8	114.0	114.3	116.2	116.9	3.0
1993	119.5	119.6	121.5	121.9	2.5	117.5	117.6	119.6	119.9	2.6
1994	122.6	122.9	124.9	125.5	3.0	120.6	120.9	122.9	123.6	3.1
1995	126.2	126.6	128.6	129.1	2.9	124.4	124.6	126.8	127.4	3.1
1996	129.6	129.9	131.8	132.5	2.6	127.9	128.2	130.3	131.1	2.9
1997	132.9	133.0	134.8	135.5	2.3	131.4	131.5	133.7	134.5	2.6
1998	136.1	136.2	138.4	139.3	2.8	135.0	135.2	137.6	138.5	3.0
1999	139.8	140.2	142.6	144.0	3.4	138.9	139.3	142.1	143.4	3.5
2000	144.9	145.3	147.3	148.3	3.0	144.1	144.5	147.1	148.0	3.2
2001	149.5	150.4	153.7	154.4	4.1	149.0	149.8	152.7	153.3	3.6
2002	155.2	155.7	159.3	160.7	4.1	153.9	154.4	157.4	158.4	3.3
2003	161.7	162.2	164.9	165.7	3.1	158.9	159.2	161.0	161.5	2.0
2004	166.8	167.5	170.0	171.2	3.3	162.1	162.4	164.1	164.9	2.1
Professional Specialty and Technical Occupations										
1990	106.4	107.0	110.3	111.2	6.2	105.8	106.3	109.8	110.6	5.9
1991	112.3	112.4	114.5	115.0	3.4	111.5	111.7	113.8	114.2	3.3
1992	115.5	116.0	118.5	119.2	3.7	114.5	114.8	117.0	117.6	3.0
1993	119.6	119.7	121.7	122.0	2.3	118.1	118.2	120.4	120.7	2.6
1994	122.5	122.7	125.0	125.5	2.9	121.1	121.3	123.6	124.2	2.9
1995	126.0	126.3	128.4	128.8	2.6	124.8	125.0	127.4	128.0	3.1
1996	129.1	129.5	131.6	132.3	2.7	128.3	128.6	131.1	131.7	2.9
1997	132.5	132.5	134.6	135.1	2.1	131.9	132.0	134.4	135.1	2.6
1998	135.6	135.6	137.7	138.5	2.5	135.5	135.6	137.9	138.7	2.7
1999	138.8	139.3	142.0	143.2	3.4	138.9	139.4	142.5	143.6	3.5
2000	144.1	144.5	146.6	147.4	2.9	144.3	144.7	147.4	148.2	3.2
2001	148.4	149.2	152.8	153.2	3.9	149.1	149.8	153.0	153.4	3.5
2002	153.6	154.1	158.1	159.4	4.0	153.6	154.1	157.5	158.4	3.3
2003	160.2	160.8	163.4	164.1	2.9	158.8	159.1	161.0	161.4	1.9
2004	165.1	165.6	168.4	169.4	3.2	162.1	162.3	164.4	165.0	2.2
Executive, Administrative, and Managerial Occupations										
1990	105.7	106.4	109.3	110.1	5.8	104.9	105.7	108.4	108.9	5.0
1991	112.2	112.0	113.3	113.7	3.3	110.6	110.7	112.0	112.3	3.1
1992	115.0	115.2	116.8	117.8	3.6	113.3	113.5	114.7	115.5	2.8
1993	119.0	119.2	121.0	121.6	3.2	116.5	116.6	118.2	118.8	2.9
1994	122.8	123.4	124.7	125.3	3.0	119.8	120.3	121.6	122.4	3.0
1995	126.9	127.4	129.1	129.9	3.7	124.1	124.3	126.0	126.9	3.7
1996	130.7	131.0	132.0	132.9	2.3	127.7	128.0	129.3	130.2	2.6
1997	134.1	134.4	135.6	136.4	2.6	131.3	131.7	133.1	134.1	3.0
1998	137.5	137.9	140.4	141.6	3.8	135.1	135.6	138.0	139.3	3.9
1999	142.6	142.8	144.5	146.1	3.2	140.1	140.5	142.7	144.3	3.6
2000	147.0	147.2	149.2	150.7	3.1	144.9	145.1	147.3	148.8	3.1
2001	152.4	153.7	156.4	157.6	4.6	150.1	151.5	153.9	155.1	4.2
2002	159.5	159.8	162.3	163.8	3.9	156.6	156.8	159.0	160.1	3.2
2003	165.3	165.7	168.0	169.1	3.2	160.9	161.0	162.5	163.3	2.0
2004	170.1	171.0	172.1	174.3	3.1	163.5	163.8	164.3	166.1	1.7

Table 6-2. Employment Cost Index, State and Local Government Workers, Total Compensation and Wages and Salaries by Occupation and Industry, 1990–2004—*Continued*

(June 1989 = 100, not seasonally adjusted.)

Series and year	Total compensation					Wages and salaries				
	Indexes				Percent change for 12 months ended December	Indexes				Percent change for 12 months ended December
	March	June	September	December		March	June	September	December	
Administrative Support Occupations, Including Clerical Occupations										
1990	105.4	106.0	108.7	110.2	6.1	104.4	104.8	107.2	107.9	4.8
1991	111.8	111.7	113.5	114.0	3.4	109.4	109.7	111.4	111.8	3.6
1992	115.4	115.7	117.5	118.5	3.9	112.7	112.9	114.1	114.9	2.8
1993	119.2	119.6	121.0	121.6	2.6	115.4	115.9	117.2	117.8	2.5
1994	122.7	123.3	124.9	125.6	3.3	118.9	119.4	120.9	121.7	3.3
1995	126.3	126.9	128.4	129.1	2.8	122.5	122.9	124.4	125.1	2.8
1996	130.0	130.4	131.8	133.0	3.0	125.8	126.1	127.7	129.0	3.1
1997	133.3	133.5	135.3	136.1	2.3	129.2	129.5	131.4	132.3	2.6
1998	136.9	137.2	139.5	140.3	3.1	133.0	133.3	135.4	136.5	3.2
1999	141.4	141.3	143.0	145.0	3.4	137.4	137.5	139.6	141.7	3.8
2000	145.9	146.5	148.3	149.4	3.0	142.4	143.0	145.0	146.2	3.2
2001	150.7	151.6	154.2	155.6	4.1	147.0	147.6	149.8	150.9	3.2
2002	156.9	158.0	161.0	162.4	4.4	151.9	152.8	155.1	156.0	3.4
2003	163.8	164.4	167.9	168.5	3.8	156.9	157.2	159.1	159.5	2.2
2004	170.4	171.8	174.3	175.5	4.2	160.4	160.8	162.6	163.0	2.2
Blue-Collar Occupations										
1990	105.5	106.3	108.2	108.7	4.8	104.3	105.3	107.2	107.7	4.3
1991	110.4	110.9	112.4	112.9	3.9	109.1	110.0	111.1	111.6	3.6
1992	114.2	115.3	116.9	117.8	4.3	112.5	113.7	115.0	115.6	3.6
1993	118.3	118.7	120.5	121.4	3.1	116.2	116.5	118.4	119.0	2.9
1994	122.3	122.7	124.2	124.7	2.7	119.7	120.1	121.8	122.5	2.9
1995	125.4	126.3	127.2	128.0	2.6	123.1	123.8	124.8	125.7	2.6
1996	129.0	129.5	130.3	131.2	2.5	126.6	127.0	127.9	128.8	2.5
1997	132.1	132.3	133.3	134.2	2.3	129.6	129.8	131.2	132.3	2.7
1998	135.0	135.2	136.8	137.8	2.7	133.1	133.5	135.1	136.0	2.8
1999	138.8	139.5	140.9	142.5	3.4	136.9	137.6	139.4	140.7	3.5
2000	143.7	144.2	145.9	147.2	3.3	141.5	142.1	143.9	145.1	3.1
2001	148.6	149.0	151.5	153.2	4.1	146.0	146.5	149.1	150.8	3.9
2002	154.0	154.7	158.4	159.8	4.3	151.6	152.1	154.5	155.1	2.9
2003	161.3	161.7	163.6	165.2	3.4	156.2	156.5	157.6	158.3	2.1
2004	166.7	167.5	169.9	171.0	3.5	158.9	159.2	160.7	161.4	2.0
Service Occupations										
1990	104.8	105.3	108.1	109.2	5.4	103.9	104.2	106.7	107.6	4.6
1991	111.0	111.3	113.4	114.0	4.4	109.3	110.1	112.0	112.7	4.7
1992	115.0	115.6	117.4	118.0	3.5	113.2	113.7	114.9	115.5	2.5
1993	119.1	119.7	121.4	122.1	3.5	116.3	117.1	118.3	118.9	2.9
1994	123.1	123.9	126.0	126.6	3.7	119.7	120.4	122.7	123.3	3.7
1995	127.6	128.8	130.1	131.0	3.5	124.6	125.2	126.6	127.3	3.2
1996	131.9	132.3	133.6	134.5	2.7	128.1	128.6	130.1	131.0	2.9
1997	135.6	135.6	137.0	137.8	2.5	132.4	132.4	134.2	135.2	3.2
1998	139.4	141.0	143.0	143.4	4.1	136.5	137.2	139.2	140.0	3.6
1999	144.3	145.3	146.7	148.6	3.6	141.1	142.1	144.1	145.7	4.1
2000	149.5	149.7	151.5	152.9	2.9	146.4	146.6	149.6	151.2	3.8
2001	155.3	156.5	159.0	160.5	5.0	152.8	153.7	156.1	157.4	4.1
2002	161.5	162.4	165.2	166.3	3.6	158.3	159.2	160.6	161.2	2.4
2003	168.0	168.9	172.0	173.0	4.0	162.7	163.8	164.9	165.8	2.9
2004	174.5	175.3	179.4	180.5	4.3	166.7	167.0	168.5	169.4	2.2
WORKERS BY INDUSTRY DIVISION										
Service Industries										
1990	106.1	106.8	110.2	111.3	6.3	105.5	106.0	109.5	110.3	5.8
1991	112.4	112.6	114.8	115.3	3.6	111.3	111.5	113.7	114.1	3.4
1992	115.8	116.2	118.8	119.6	3.7	114.4	114.7	116.9	117.5	3.0
1993	120.0	120.2	122.2	122.6	2.5	118.1	118.2	120.3	120.6	2.6
1994	123.1	123.4	125.6	126.1	2.9	121.1	121.3	123.6	124.2	3.0
1995	126.7	127.1	129.2	129.6	2.8	124.9	125.1	127.6	128.2	3.2
1996	130.0	130.3	132.4	133.1	2.7	128.6	128.9	131.2	131.9	2.9
1997	133.2	133.3	135.4	136.0	2.2	132.1	132.2	134.7	135.3	2.6
1998	136.5	136.6	139.0	139.7	2.7	135.7	135.9	138.4	139.2	2.9
1999	140.0	140.5	143.2	144.5	3.4	139.5	139.9	142.9	144.0	3.4
2000	145.2	145.5	148.0	148.9	3.0	144.6	144.9	147.9	148.7	3.3
2001	149.9	150.6	154.4	154.9	4.0	149.5	150.2	153.7	154.2	3.7
2002	155.5	155.9	159.7	160.9	3.9	154.6	155.0	158.4	159.2	3.2
2003	161.8	162.3	164.9	165.7	3.0	159.5	159.8	161.6	162.1	1.8
2004	166.5	166.8	169.7	170.8	3.1	162.6	162.7	164.8	165.5	2.1

Table 6-2. Employment Cost Index, State and Local Government Workers, Total Compensation and Wages and Salaries by Occupation and Industry, 1990–2004—*Continued*

(June 1989 = 100, not seasonally adjusted.)

Series and year	Total compensation					Wages and salaries				
	Indexes				Percent change for 12 months ended December	Indexes				Percent change for 12 months ended December
	March	June	September	December		March	June	September	December	
Service Industries, Excluding Schools										
1990	105.4	106.4	108.8	110.2	6.8	105.4	106.4	108.8	109.6	6.4
1991	112.2	111.7	113.7	114.4	3.8	111.4	111.4	113.5	114.2	4.2
1992	115.1	115.6	117.5	118.6	3.7	114.8	115.2	116.4	117.4	2.8
1993	119.6	120.0	121.4	121.9	2.8	118.4	118.7	120.1	120.4	2.6
1994	122.8	123.3	124.9	125.6	3.0	121.3	121.9	123.2	124.0	3.0
1995	126.4	127.7	128.9	129.4	3.0	125.0	125.5	126.9	127.4	2.7
1996	130.3	130.8	131.9	132.0	2.0	128.2	128.7	130.1	130.5	2.4
1997	132.5	132.9	134.4	135.3	2.5	131.2	131.6	133.3	134.4	3.0
1998	136.1	136.2	138.7	138.8	2.6	135.4	135.5	137.8	138.2	2.8
1999	139.6	140.3	142.6	143.8	3.6	139.0	139.6	142.1	143.2	3.6
2000	145.2	145.8	147.6	148.8	3.5	144.3	144.8	146.7	147.9	3.3
2001	150.1	151.9	154.5	156.1	4.9	149.1	150.7	153.2	154.9	4.7
2002	157.9	158.7	161.0	162.8	4.3	156.7	157.3	159.1	160.3	3.5
2003	164.0	164.2	166.8	168.2	3.3	161.4	161.8	163.2	164.5	2.6
2004	169.4	170.1	173.0	173.8	3.3	165.1	165.6	167.5	168.3	2.3
Health Services										
1990	106.2	106.9	109.9	111.1	6.6	105.5	106.1	108.9	109.7	5.8
1991	112.6	112.2	113.9	114.9	3.4	111.1	111.7	113.0	114.0	3.9
1992	115.9	116.8	118.6	119.4	3.9	114.9	115.7	116.7	117.4	3.0
1993	120.2	120.7	122.2	123.1	3.1	118.1	118.8	120.4	121.0	3.1
1994	124.2	125.2	127.2	127.7	3.7	121.9	122.9	124.7	125.3	3.6
1995	128.4	129.8	131.0	131.6	3.1	126.0	126.6	127.9	128.6	2.6
1996	132.5	133.1	134.0	134.1	1.9	129.3	129.9	131.1	131.4	2.2
1997	134.5	134.9	136.0	137.2	2.3	132.1	132.6	133.9	135.3	3.0
1998	137.9	138.0	140.3	140.7	2.6	136.3	136.5	138.7	139.2	2.9
1999	141.2	142.0	144.2	145.8	3.6	139.7	140.4	142.8	144.2	3.6
2000	147.3	147.9	150.0	151.6	4.0	145.3	145.7	147.7	149.3	3.5
2001	152.1	154.4	157.1	158.6	4.6	149.9	151.9	154.2	155.8	4.4
2002	160.4	161.4	163.5	165.5	4.4	157.8	158.8	160.5	162.2	4.1
2003	166.4	166.7	169.5	171.0	3.3	162.9	163.5	165.1	166.7	2.8
2004	172.2	172.9	175.7	176.8	3.4	167.4	167.8	169.6	170.7	2.4
Hospitals										
1990	106.0	107.0	109.8	111.4	6.6	105.0	105.9	108.6	109.8	5.8
1991	112.2	112.1	114.1	115.2	3.4	110.7	111.3	112.9	114.1	3.9
1992	115.9	116.7	118.6	119.4	3.6	114.5	115.2	116.5	117.1	2.6
1993	120.0	120.4	122.0	123.3	3.3	117.6	118.2	119.9	120.7	3.1
1994	123.7	124.5	127.0	127.7	3.6	121.2	122.0	124.2	125.1	3.6
1995	128.4	129.9	131.1	131.7	3.1	125.8	126.3	127.6	128.4	2.6
1996	132.6	133.2	134.2	134.3	2.0	129.1	129.7	130.9	131.3	2.3
1997	134.8	135.2	136.3	137.6	2.5	131.9	132.4	133.7	135.2	3.0
1998	138.4	138.4	140.7	141.2	2.6	136.3	136.5	138.6	139.1	2.9
1999	141.7	142.7	144.8	146.3	3.6	139.7	140.6	142.8	144.1	3.6
2000	147.9	148.4	150.7	152.0	3.9	145.3	145.6	147.7	149.2	3.5
2001	152.2	154.7	157.4	159.1	4.7	149.5	151.8	154.2	155.7	4.4
2002	160.7	161.8	164.1	166.2	4.5	157.7	158.8	160.6	162.5	4.4
2003	167.0	167.3	170.3	171.4	3.1	163.1	163.8	165.5	166.7	2.6
2004	172.4	173.2	176.3	177.4	3.5	167.4	167.9	169.9	171.0	2.6
Educational Services										
1990	106.2	106.8	110.3	111.4	6.2	105.5	106.0	109.7	110.5	5.7
1991	112.4	112.6	114.9	115.3	3.5	111.3	111.5	113.8	114.1	3.3
1992	115.7	116.1	118.9	119.7	3.8	114.3	114.6	116.9	117.6	3.1
1993	120.0	120.1	122.3	122.7	2.5	118.0	118.1	120.3	120.6	2.6
1994	122.9	123.1	125.5	126.0	2.7	120.9	121.1	123.6	124.2	3.0
1995	126.5	126.8	129.0	129.4	2.7	124.8	124.9	127.7	128.3	3.3
1996	129.7	130.0	132.3	133.0	2.8	128.5	128.8	131.3	132.0	2.9
1997	133.1	133.2	135.4	135.9	2.2	132.1	132.2	134.8	135.3	2.5
1998	136.3	136.5	138.8	139.6	2.7	135.7	135.8	138.4	139.3	3.0
1999	139.9	140.3	143.1	144.4	3.4	139.5	139.8	142.9	144.0	3.4
2000	145.0	145.2	147.9	148.7	3.0	144.5	144.8	148.0	148.7	3.3
2001	149.6	150.1	154.1	154.5	3.9	149.5	150.0	153.6	154.0	3.6
2002	154.8	155.1	159.2	160.3	3.8	154.2	154.5	158.1	158.9	3.2
2003	161.1	161.7	164.3	165.0	2.9	159.1	159.3	161.2	161.6	1.7
2004	165.7	165.9	168.8	169.9	3.0	162.0	162.1	164.2	164.9	2.0

Table 6-2. Employment Cost Index, State and Local Government Workers, Total Compensation and Wages and Salaries by Occupation and Industry, 1990–2004—*Continued*

(June 1989 = 100, not seasonally adjusted.)

Series and year	Total compensation					Wages and salaries				
	Indexes				Percent change for 12 months ended December	Indexes				Percent change for 12 months ended December
	March	June	September	December		March	June	September	December	
Schools										
1990	106.4	106.9	110.6	111.6	6.0	105.5	105.9	109.7	110.5	5.5
1991	112.5	112.9	115.2	115.6	3.6	111.2	111.5	113.7	114.0	3.2
1992	116.0	116.4	119.2	119.9	3.7	114.3	114.6	117.0	117.5	3.1
1993	120.2	120.3	122.5	122.9	2.5	117.9	118.0	120.3	120.7	2.7
1994	123.2	123.4	125.9	126.3	2.8	121.0	121.2	123.8	124.3	3.0
1995	126.8	127.1	129.4	129.8	2.8	125.0	125.1	127.8	128.4	3.3
1996	130.0	130.3	132.6	133.4	2.8	128.7	128.9	131.4	132.2	3.0
1997	133.4	133.5	135.7	136.2	2.1	132.2	132.3	134.9	135.5	2.5
1998	136.6	136.7	139.1	139.9	2.7	135.8	136.0	138.5	139.5	3.0
1999	140.2	140.6	143.5	144.7	3.4	139.6	140.0	143.1	144.2	3.4
2000	145.3	145.5	148.2	149.0	3.0	144.7	144.9	148.1	148.9	3.3
2001	149.9	150.5	154.4	154.8	3.9	149.7	150.2	153.8	154.1	3.5
2002	155.1	155.4	159.6	160.7	3.8	154.3	154.6	158.3	159.0	3.2
2003	161.4	162.0	164.7	165.3	2.9	159.2	159.5	161.4	161.8	1.8
2004	166.0	166.3	169.2	170.3	3.0	162.1	162.3	164.3	165.0	2.0
Elementary and Secondary Schools										
1990	106.5	107.1	111.1	112.1	6.3	105.5	105.9	110.1	110.9	5.7
1991	112.9	113.0	115.7	116.2	3.7	111.6	111.7	114.3	114.7	3.4
1992	116.6	117.1	119.9	120.7	3.9	114.9	115.3	117.9	118.5	3.3
1993	120.7	120.8	123.0	123.6	2.4	118.7	118.8	121.1	121.6	2.6
1994	123.7	123.8	126.3	126.5	2.3	121.7	121.8	124.5	124.9	2.7
1995	127.1	127.4	129.8	130.1	2.8	125.5	125.8	128.7	129.2	3.4
1996	130.2	130.5	132.6	133.1	2.3	129.3	129.5	132.0	132.4	2.5
1997	133.1	133.3	135.5	135.8	2.0	132.4	132.6	135.3	135.7	2.5
1998	136.1	136.2	138.8	139.3	2.6	136.0	136.1	138.7	139.3	2.7
1999	139.6	140.0	142.9	144.1	3.4	139.5	139.9	143.1	144.1	3.4
2000	144.5	144.7	147.3	148.1	2.8	144.5	144.6	147.9	148.5	3.1
2001	148.5	149.0	152.8	153.1	3.4	149.0	149.5	152.8	153.1	3.1
2002	153.4	153.6	157.7	158.8	3.7	153.4	153.6	157.4	158.1	3.3
2003	159.4	160.0	163.0	163.7	3.1	158.2	158.5	160.6	160.9	1.8
2004	164.4	164.6	168.0	169.2	3.4	161.3	161.5	163.8	164.5	2.2
Colleges and Universities										
1990	106.1	106.3	109.2	110.2	5.3	105.6	105.9	108.4	109.2	4.9
1991	111.3	112.5	113.4	113.5	3.0	110.2	111.0	112.0	112.0	2.6
1992	114.0	114.1	116.9	117.2	3.3	112.3	112.3	114.1	114.3	2.1
1993	118.4	118.5	120.8	120.7	3.0	115.5	115.6	117.8	117.7	3.0
1994	121.5	122.0	124.5	125.5	4.0	118.6	119.2	121.5	122.5	4.1
1995	126.0	126.1	128.0	128.7	2.5	123.2	122.9	125.0	125.9	2.8
1996	129.4	129.9	132.5	134.0	4.1	126.8	127.1	129.8	131.2	4.2
1997	134.3	134.1	136.3	137.2	2.4	131.5	131.4	133.6	134.6	2.6
1998	137.9	138.1	140.1	141.5	3.1	135.2	135.5	137.7	139.6	3.7
1999	141.7	142.1	144.8	146.5	3.5	139.6	139.8	142.6	144.4	3.4
2000	147.4	147.6	150.5	151.7	3.5	144.9	145.6	148.3	149.5	3.5
2001	153.7	154.3	159.0	159.6	5.2	151.4	151.8	156.5	156.7	4.8
2002	160.0	160.4	164.7	165.8	3.9	156.8	157.3	160.7	161.6	3.1
2003	167.0	167.5	169.2	170.0	2.5	162.1	162.1	163.5	164.0	1.5
2004	170.7	171.0	172.4	173.2	1.9	164.3	164.4	165.4	166.3	1.4
Public Administration [1]										
1990	105.1	105.5	107.8	108.7	5.3	104.3	104.6	106.5	107.3	4.4
1991	110.8	110.9	112.2	112.6	3.6	109.1	109.5	110.6	110.9	3.4
1992	114.0	114.6	115.8	116.3	3.3	111.9	112.4	113.1	113.6	2.4
1993	117.6	118.0	119.3	120.0	3.2	114.4	114.9	115.9	116.6	2.6
1994	121.5	122.2	123.7	124.2	3.5	117.9	118.5	119.9	120.6	3.4
1995	125.4	126.1	127.4	128.3	3.3	121.9	122.3	123.2	124.1	2.9
1996	129.2	129.6	130.7	131.8	2.7	124.9	125.3	126.6	127.7	2.9
1997	133.0	133.0	134.1	135.1	2.5	128.9	129.0	130.3	131.4	2.9
1998	136.4	137.4	138.9	139.9	3.6	132.7	133.2	134.8	135.9	3.4
1999	140.8	141.5	142.4	144.4	3.2	136.9	137.8	139.5	141.5	4.1
2000	145.7	146.1	146.9	148.3	2.7	142.5	142.9	144.6	146.1	3.3
2001	150.6	151.9	153.8	155.2	4.7	147.6	148.7	150.3	151.6	3.8
2002	156.5	157.5	160.2	161.7	4.2	152.5	153.4	154.8	155.8	2.8
2003	163.4	164.3	167.3	168.1	4.0	157.2	158.0	159.4	160.0	2.7
2004	170.1	171.4	174.1	175.4	4.3	161.1	161.4	162.6	163.5	2.2

[1] Includes executive, legislative, judicial, administrative, and regulatory activities of state and local governments, SICs 91 through 96.

Table 6-3. Employment Cost Index, Benefits, by Occupation, Industry, and Bargaining Status, 1990–2004

(June 1989 = 100, not seasonally adjusted.)

Series and year	Indexes				Percent change for 12 months ended December
	March	June	September	December	
Civilian Workers [1]					
1990	105.9	107.2	108.9	110.1	6.7
1991	112.2	113.6	115.4	116.3	5.6
1992	118.6	119.6	121.4	122.5	5.3
1993	125.0	126.2	127.4	128.1	4.6
1994	130.1	131.0	132.3	132.5	3.4
1995	133.8	134.5	135.2	135.5	2.3
1996	136.2	136.9	137.7	138.2	2.0
1997	138.9	139.6	140.3	141.1	2.1
1998	142.0	143.0	144.0	144.7	2.6
1999	145.3	146.6	147.9	149.5	3.3
2000	152.6	154.3	155.8	156.9	4.9
2001	159.7	161.3	163.7	165.1	5.2
2002	167.5	169.4	171.7	173.3	5.0
2003	177.8	180.0	182.8	184.3	6.3
2004	190.0	192.9	195.2	197.0	6.9
State and Local Government					
1990	107.5	108.3	111.3	112.7	7.0
1991	114.6	114.4	116.4	117.1	3.9
1992	118.5	119.3	122.3	123.4	5.4
1993	124.2	124.5	126.2	127.0	2.9
1994	127.9	128.5	130.3	130.5	2.8
1995	131.1	132.2	133.6	133.9	2.6
1996	134.7	135.1	136.1	136.8	2.2
1997	137.4	137.4	138.2	138.6	1.3
1998	139.7	140.3	142.1	142.7	3.0
1999	143.6	144.0	145.0	146.7	2.8
2000	148.2	148.5	149.0	150.2	2.4
2001	152.3	153.5	157.3	158.4	5.5
2002	159.9	160.6	165.8	168.2	6.2
2003	170.5	171.6	176.9	178.5	6.1
2004	181.1	183.0	188.3	190.4	6.7
Private Industry [2]					
1990	105.5	106.9	108.3	109.4	6.6
1991	111.6	113.5	115.2	116.2	6.2
1992	118.6	119.7	121.2	122.2	5.2
1993	125.2	126.7	127.7	128.3	5.0
1994	130.7	131.7	132.8	133.0	3.7
1995	134.5	135.1	135.6	135.9	2.2
1996	136.6	137.4	138.1	138.6	2.0
1997	139.4	140.1	140.8	141.8	2.3
1998	142.6	143.7	144.5	145.2	2.4
1999	145.8	147.3	148.6	150.2	3.4
2000	153.8	155.7	157.5	158.6	5.6
2001	161.5	163.2	165.2	166.7	5.1
2002	169.3	171.6	173.1	174.6	4.7
2003	179.6	182.0	184.3	185.8	6.4
2004	192.2	195.3	196.9	198.7	6.9
White-Collar Occupations					
1990	105.6	107.1	108.6	109.7	6.9
1991	112.1	113.8	115.3	116.4	6.1
1992	118.4	119.4	121.0	122.0	4.8
1993	124.7	125.9	126.8	127.6	4.6
1994	130.5	131.6	132.8	133.3	4.5
1995	135.2	136.0	136.6	136.7	2.6
1996	137.7	138.4	139.5	139.7	2.2
1997	140.8	141.5	142.0	143.4	2.6
1998	144.7	145.6	146.6	147.4	2.8
1999	147.9	149.4	151.0	152.5	3.5
2000	156.3	158.5	160.4	161.5	5.9
2001	165.2	167.4	169.5	171.2	6.0
2002	173.5	176.1	177.2	178.5	4.3
2003	183.6	185.5	187.7	189.2	6.0
2004	194.4	197.4	199.1	201.1	6.3

[1]Includes private industry and state and local government workers and excludes farm, household, and federal government workers.
[2]Excludes farm and household workers.

Table 6-3. Employment Cost Index, Benefits, by Occupation, Industry, and Bargaining Status, 1990–2004—*Continued*

(June 1989 = 100, not seasonally adjusted.)

Series and year	Indexes				Percent change for 12 months ended December
	March	June	September	December	
Blue-Collar Occupations					
1990	105.2	106.6	107.9	109.0	6.2
1991	111.0	112.8	114.9	115.7	6.1
1992	118.7	119.7	121.2	122.2	5.6
1993	125.5	127.3	128.4	128.9	5.5
1994	130.5	131.5	132.7	132.5	2.8
1995	133.3	133.6	134.1	134.7	1.7
1996	135.2	136.1	136.2	137.0	1.7
1997	137.2	138.0	138.8	139.0	1.5
1998	139.1	140.4	141.0	141.6	1.9
1999	142.2	143.6	144.8	146.2	3.2
2000	150.0	151.6	153.1	154.1	5.4
2001	155.7	156.2	158.3	159.2	3.3
2002	162.2	164.0	166.2	167.8	5.4
2003	172.7	176.1	178.4	179.9	7.2
2004	188.3	191.8	193.3	194.9	8.3
Service Occupations					
1990	106.0	107.0	108.1	109.9	6.7
1991	112.3	114.5	116.5	117.8	7.2
1992	120.0	121.6	123.7	124.6	5.8
1993	127.7	129.3	130.5	131.5	5.5
1994	132.9	133.1	134.2	134.7	2.4
1995	135.0	135.6	135.7	136.0	1.0
1996	135.7	136.3	136.2	137.4	1.0
1997	138.3	139.6	141.4	142.0	3.3
1998	143.3	143.7	144.7	144.8	2.0
1999	146.3	147.6	148.4	149.9	3.5
2000	150.8	152.7	154.4	156.4	4.3
2001	159.5	161.1	163.2	166.0	6.1
2002	168.9	170.4	173.4	174.9	5.4
2003	180.2	182.1	184.1	186.4	6.6
2004	193.4	196.1	197.5	198.2	6.3
Goods-Producing Industries [3]					
1990	105.7	107.2	108.7	109.9	7.1
1991	111.9	113.9	115.8	116.7	6.2
1992	119.7	120.6	122.3	123.4	5.7
1993	127.3	129.0	130.0	130.3	5.6
1994	132.7	133.9	134.8	134.8	3.5
1995	135.9	135.9	136.2	137.1	1.7
1996	137.7	138.6	138.8	139.7	1.9
1997	139.9	140.9	141.5	141.5	1.3
1998	141.5	142.5	143.0	143.2	1.2
1999	144.3	145.2	146.3	148.2	3.4
2000	152.3	154.2	155.7	156.2	5.4
2001	158.5	159.6	160.8	162.6	4.1
2002	165.8	167.4	168.8	171.0	5.2
2003	178.0	180.2	182.3	183.8	7.5
2004	193.7	196.2	198.1	201.2	9.5
Manufacturing					
1990	105.5	106.9	108.4	109.5	7.0
1991	111.2	113.3	115.3	116.1	6.0
1992	119.3	120.1	121.5	122.6	5.6
1993	126.8	128.6	129.7	130.0	6.0
1994	132.0	133.0	133.9	134.3	3.3
1995	135.4	135.2	135.5	136.7	1.8
1996	137.5	138.5	138.8	139.8	2.3
1997	139.9	141.0	141.4	141.7	1.4
1998	141.7	142.4	142.6	142.7	0.7
1999	143.6	144.5	145.7	147.8	3.4
2000	152.3	153.9	154.9	154.8	4.7
2001	157.1	157.9	158.5	160.4	3.6
2002	163.7	165.5	166.8	168.9	5.3
2003	176.9	179.0	181.1	182.3	7.9
2004	194.4	196.9	199.2	200.4	9.9

[3]Includes mining, construction, and manufacturing.

Table 6-3. Employment Cost Index, Benefits, by Occupation, Industry, and Bargaining Status, 1990–2004—*Continued*

(June 1989 = 100, not seasonally adjusted.)

Series and year	Indexes				Percent change for 12 months ended December
	March	June	September	December	
Aircraft Manufacturing (SIC 3721)					
1990	110.1	111.4	114.5	111.9	5.1
1991	114.2	116.0	117.7	119.7	7.0
1992	124.1	127.3	128.9	135.1	12.9
1993	137.6	137.0	140.1	133.1	-1.5
1994	134.4	135.3	138.7	138.4	4.0
1995	141.0	140.8	140.5	146.1	5.6
1996	154.2	155.4	154.8	151.6	3.8
1997	148.6	148.8	147.6	143.0	-5.7
1998	141.7	143.1	143.8	145.3	1.6
1999	142.6	144.3	145.6	153.9	5.9
2000	161.9	166.6	168.7	163.1	6.0
2001	171.4	171.7	168.2	174.4	6.9
2002	180.7	182.6	182.6	192.4	10.3
2003	220.4	220.3	221.4	213.4	10.9
2004	260.6	264.0	265.2	266.0	24.6
Aircraft Manufacturing (SIC 3721), White-Collar Occupations					
1990	109.9	110.9	114.3	111.2	5.2
1991	113.1	115.1	116.4	119.2	7.2
1992	124.0	127.5	128.4	133.0	11.6
1993	136.2	135.4	138.7	132.5	-0.4
1994	133.5	134.7	138.0	137.3	3.6
1995	140.1	140.2	139.9	142.5	3.8
1996	152.0	152.9	152.1	150.9	5.9
1997	146.8	147.3	146.8	144.8	-4.0
1998	142.9	145.0	145.5	143.9	-0.6
1999	141.3	142.7	142.9	147.6	2.6
2000	156.8	163.6	165.4	162.8	10.3
2001	175.0	174.2	168.9	175.0	7.5
2002	180.7	182.6	182.2	187.0	6.9
2003	219.7	218.3	218.7	216.3	15.7
2004	264.0	265.3	265.9	265.9	22.9
Aircraft Manufacturing (SIC 3721), Blue-Collar Occupations					
1990	110.5	112.2	114.6	112.8	5.0
1991	115.5	117.1	119.3	120.4	6.7
1992	124.2	127.2	129.5	137.7	14.4
1993	139.3	139.0	141.9	133.5	-3.1
1994	135.0	135.6	139.0	139.2	4.3
1995	141.6	140.9	140.6	150.8	8.3
1996	156.7	158.4	158.4	152.2	0.9
1997	150.9	150.4	148.2	139.6	-8.3
1998	139.0	139.5	140.7	146.6	5.0
1999	144.2	146.3	149.5	163.0	11.2
2000	169.2	170.5	173.3	162.7	-0.2
2001	165.0	166.7	166.1	172.4	6.0
2002	179.5	181.4	181.8	199.3	15.6
2003	220.1	221.8	224.0	207.5	4.1
2004	253.1	259.9	262.9	264.9	27.7
Service-Producing Industries [4]					
1990	105.3	106.6	107.9	109.0	6.2
1991	111.4	113.0	114.6	115.7	6.1
1992	117.7	118.8	120.4	121.2	4.8
1993	123.4	124.6	125.7	126.7	4.5
1994	128.9	129.7	131.2	131.5	3.8
1995	133.2	134.1	134.8	134.7	2.4
1996	135.5	136.2	137.2	137.4	2.0
1997	138.5	139.2	139.8	141.4	2.9
1998	142.7	143.8	144.9	145.7	3.0
1999	146.1	147.9	149.4	150.7	3.4
2000	154.0	156.0	157.9	159.4	5.8
2001	162.6	164.6	167.1	168.4	5.6
2002	170.7	173.3	174.9	175.9	4.5
2003	179.9	182.3	184.7	186.2	5.9
2004	190.6	194.1	195.5	196.5	5.5

[4]Includes transportation, communication, and public utilities; wholesale and retail trade; finance, insurance, and real estate; and service industries.

Table 6-3. Employment Cost Index, Benefits, by Occupation, Industry, and Bargaining Status, 1990–2004—*Continued*

(June 1989 = 100, not seasonally adjusted.)

Series and year	Indexes				Percent change for 12 months ended December
	March	June	September	December	
Nonmanufacturing Industries					
1990	105.4	106.9	108.2	109.3	6.3
1991	111.9	113.5	115.1	116.2	6.3
1992	118.2	119.4	121.0	122.0	5.0
1993	124.2	125.5	126.5	127.4	4.4
1994	129.9	130.8	132.2	132.3	3.8
1995	133.9	134.7	135.4	135.3	2.3
1996	136.0	136.7	137.5	137.9	1.9
1997	138.9	139.5	140.2	141.5	2.6
1998	142.7	143.9	145.0	145.8	3.0
1999	146.3	148.0	149.4	150.7	3.4
2000	154.0	156.1	158.1	159.7	6.0
2001	162.9	164.9	167.4	168.8	5.7
2002	171.1	173.5	175.2	176.3	4.4
2003	180.3	182.8	185.1	186.7	5.9
2004	190.9	194.3	195.7	197.6	5.8
Union Workers					
1990	104.6	105.6	106.7	108.2	6.0
1991	110.1	112.1	113.9	115.2	6.5
1992	119.2	120.0	121.7	122.5	6.3
1993	126.6	128.5	129.7	130.6	6.6
1994	131.9	132.9	133.3	133.7	2.4
1995	134.8	135.5	136.6	138.0	3.2
1996	139.1	140.0	139.9	140.7	2.0
1997	140.2	140.9	142.2	142.0	0.9
1998	142.1	143.8	145.0	145.5	2.5
1999	145.8	146.9	148.3	149.7	2.8
2000	153.7	155.5	157.4	157.5	5.2
2001	158.5	160.1	161.9	163.4	3.7
2002	166.5	168.1	170.8	172.7	5.7
2003	178.7	182.7	185.4	187.1	8.3
2004	198.8	203.3	205.0	206.4	10.3
Nonunion Workers					
1990	105.8	107.4	108.9	109.9	6.8
1991	112.3	114.0	115.7	116.6	6.1
1992	118.4	119.5	121.0	122.1	4.7
1993	124.6	125.9	126.9	127.4	4.3
1994	130.1	131.1	132.6	132.7	4.2
1995	134.2	134.8	135.2	135.1	1.8
1996	135.8	136.5	137.4	137.8	2.0
1997	138.9	139.7	140.2	141.5	2.7
1998	142.5	143.4	144.2	144.9	2.4
1999	145.6	147.1	148.5	150.0	3.5
2000	153.6	155.5	157.3	158.6	5.7
2001	162.0	163.7	165.8	167.2	5.4
2002	169.7	172.1	173.4	174.7	4.5
2003	179.5	181.5	183.7	185.1	6.0
2004	190.2	193.0	194.6	196.5	6.2

Table 6-4. Employment Cost Index, Private Industry Workers [1], Total Compensation and Wages and Salaries by Bargaining Status, Industry, Region [2], and Area Size, 1990–2004

(June 1989 = 100, not seasonally adjusted.)

Series and year	Total compensation					Wages and salaries				
	Indexes				Percent change for 12 months ended December	Indexes				Percent change for 12 months ended December
	March	June	September	December		March	June	September	December	
WORKERS BY BARGAINING STATUS										
Union Workers										
1990	103.3	104.1	105.1	106.2	4.3	102.6	103.3	104.2	105.1	3.4
1991	107.5	108.8	110.1	111.1	4.6	106.2	107.1	108.0	108.9	3.6
1992	113.1	114.0	115.2	115.9	4.3	109.8	110.8	111.7	112.3	3.1
1993	117.8	119.1	120.0	120.9	4.3	113.1	113.9	114.8	115.7	3.0
1994	121.9	123.0	123.8	124.2	2.7	116.5	117.6	118.6	119.1	2.9
1995	125.1	125.8	126.8	127.7	2.8	119.8	120.6	121.5	122.2	2.6
1996	128.5	129.7	130.1	130.8	2.4	122.8	124.2	124.8	125.4	2.6
1997	131.0	131.8	133.2	133.5	2.1	126.0	126.9	128.3	128.9	2.8
1998	134.0	135.3	136.8	137.5	3.0	129.6	130.7	132.4	133.1	3.3
1999	138.0	139.0	140.2	141.2	2.7	133.6	134.7	135.7	136.5	2.6
2000	143.0	144.4	146.1	146.9	4.0	137.2	138.5	140.0	141.2	3.4
2001	147.9	149.5	151.0	153.1	4.2	142.1	143.7	145.1	147.4	4.4
2002	154.8	156.3	158.1	159.5	4.2	148.4	149.8	151.3	152.5	3.5
2003	162.1	164.1	165.7	166.8	4.6	153.3	154.3	155.3	156.2	2.4
2004	171.4	173.9	175.3	176.2	5.6	157.2	158.7	160.0	160.6	2.8
Union Workers, Blue-Collar Occupations										
1990	103.0	104.1	104.8	105.9	4.1	102.2	103.2	103.8	104.8	3.3
1991	107.4	108.6	109.7	110.7	4.5	105.8	106.7	107.3	108.2	3.2
1992	112.9	113.8	114.8	115.5	4.3	109.1	109.9	110.8	111.3	2.9
1993	117.4	118.7	119.7	120.6	4.4	112.0	112.8	113.7	114.5	2.9
1994	121.2	122.4	123.1	123.4	2.3	115.1	116.2	117.3	117.6	2.7
1995	124.0	124.8	125.7	126.3	2.4	118.2	119.1	120.0	120.3	2.3
1996	126.8	128.0	128.3	128.9	2.1	120.9	122.0	122.8	123.4	2.6
1997	128.9	129.9	131.2	131.6	2.1	123.6	124.7	126.0	126.7	2.7
1998	131.8	133.3	134.6	135.3	2.8	127.2	128.5	129.9	130.6	3.1
1999	135.6	136.7	137.8	138.9	2.7	131.2	132.5	133.6	134.5	3.0
2000	141.1	142.5	144.3	145.0	4.4	135.2	136.5	138.2	139.2	3.5
2001	145.9	147.2	148.7	150.0	3.4	140.3	141.8	143.3	144.7	4.0
2002	151.7	153.5	155.2	156.6	4.4	145.6	147.2	148.4	149.6	3.4
2003	159.2	161.4	163.1	164.2	4.9	150.5	151.6	152.8	153.5	2.6
2004	169.0	171.2	172.6	173.5	5.7	154.3	155.5	156.7	157.2	2.4
Union Workers, Goods-Producing Industries [3]										
1990	103.3	104.5	105.1	106.3	4.3	102.3	103.5	104.0	105.0	3.3
1991	107.9	109.2	110.3	111.3	4.7	106.2	107.1	107.7	108.7	3.5
1992	114.0	114.6	115.7	116.4	4.6	109.6	110.2	111.1	111.7	2.8
1993	118.7	120.0	121.0	121.9	4.7	112.2	113.0	113.8	114.8	2.8
1994	122.5	123.8	124.4	124.7	2.3	115.4	116.7	117.5	117.9	2.7
1995	125.2	125.9	126.7	127.5	2.2	118.4	119.3	120.2	120.6	2.3
1996	127.9	129.0	129.2	129.8	1.8	121.3	122.5	123.2	123.6	2.5
1997	130.0	131.2	132.3	132.5	2.1	124.1	125.4	126.6	127.1	2.8
1998	132.7	134.3	135.6	136.5	3.0	127.9	129.4	131.0	131.7	3.6
1999	136.8	138.2	139.2	140.8	3.2	132.3	133.8	134.9	136.1	3.3
2000	143.3	144.8	146.8	147.3	4.6	137.2	138.4	140.2	141.3	3.8
2001	147.9	149.3	150.6	151.8	3.1	142.4	144.2	145.3	146.3	3.5
2002	153.4	154.7	156.2	157.8	4.0	147.2	148.6	150.0	151.2	3.3
2003	161.4	163.4	164.7	165.9	5.1	152.4	153.9	154.8	155.4	2.8
2004	172.3	174.6	176.0	176.7	6.5	156.3	157.5	158.7	158.9	2.3
Union Workers, Service-Producing Industries [4]										
1990	103.2	103.6	104.9	106.0	4.2	102.9	103.1	104.4	105.2	3.4
1991	107.1	108.3	109.8	110.9	4.6	106.1	107.0	108.4	109.2	3.8
1992	111.9	113.2	114.6	115.2	3.9	110.1	111.5	112.5	113.1	3.6
1993	116.7	117.7	118.6	119.6	3.8	114.2	115.1	116.0	116.8	3.3
1994	121.0	121.8	122.9	123.6	3.3	118.0	118.7	120.1	120.6	3.3
1995	124.8	125.6	126.8	127.9	3.5	121.6	122.3	123.2	124.2	3.0
1996	129.0	130.3	131.0	131.7	3.0	124.8	126.2	126.8	127.6	2.7
1997	131.9	132.4	134.0	134.5	2.1	128.2	128.8	130.4	131.2	2.8
1998	135.3	136.2	138.0	138.5	3.0	131.8	132.2	134.1	134.8	2.7
1999	139.2	139.7	141.0	141.4	2.1	135.4	135.8	136.8	137.2	1.8
2000	142.5	143.9	145.2	146.4	3.5	137.6	138.9	140.1	141.5	3.1
2001	147.6	149.5	151.2	154.2	5.3	142.2	143.7	145.4	148.9	5.2
2002	156.0	157.6	159.9	161.1	4.5	150.0	151.4	152.9	154.1	3.5
2003	162.6	164.6	166.5	167.5	4.0	154.6	155.1	156.3	157.3	2.1
2004	170.2	172.9	174.4	175.4	4.7	158.5	160.3	161.7	162.6	3.4

[1] Excludes farm and household workers.
[2] The regional coverage is as follows: Northeast–Connecticut, Maine, Massachusetts, New Hampshire, New Jersey, New York, Pennsylvania, Rhode Island, and Vermont; South–Alabama, Arkansas, Delaware, District of Columbia, Florida, Georgia, Kentucky, Louisiana, Maryland, Mississippi, North Carolina, Oklahoma, South Carolina, Tennessee, Texas, Virginia, and West Virginia; Midwest–Illinois, Indiana, Iowa, Kansas, Michigan, Minnesota, Missouri, Nebraska, North Dakota, Ohio, South Dakota, and Wisconsin; and West–Alaska, Arizona, California, Colorado, Hawaii, Idaho, Montana, Nevada, New Mexico, Oregon, Utah, Washington, and Wyoming.
[3] Includes mining, construction, and manufacturing.
[4] Includes transportation, communication, and public utilities; wholesale and retail trade; finance, insurance, and real estate; and service industries.

Table 6-4. Employment Cost Index, Private Industry Workers[1], Total Compensation and Wages and Salaries by Bargaining Status, Industry, Region[2], and Area Size, 1990–2004—*Continued*

(June 1989 = 100, not seasonally adjusted.)

Series and year	Total compensation					Wages and salaries				
	Indexes				Percent change for 12 months ended December	Indexes				Percent change for 12 months ended December
	March	June	September	December		March	June	September	December	
Union Workers, Manufacturing Industries										
1990	103.6	104.7	105.3	106.6	4.5	102.6	103.8	104.3	105.5	3.7
1991	108.1	109.5	110.6	111.7	4.8	106.7	107.5	108.3	109.4	3.7
1992	114.8	115.2	116.1	116.9	4.7	110.4	110.9	111.7	112.5	2.8
1993	119.8	121.1	121.9	123.0	5.2	113.2	113.9	114.6	115.9	3.0
1994	123.6	124.8	125.3	125.8	2.3	116.6	117.8	118.5	119.2	2.8
1995	126.3	126.6	127.1	128.1	1.8	119.8	120.5	121.3	122.0	2.3
1996	128.8	129.8	129.8	130.6	2.0	122.9	123.9	124.5	125.2	2.6
1997	130.8	131.7	133.0	133.3	2.1	125.6	126.5	127.8	128.6	2.7
1998	133.6	134.6	136.0	136.9	2.7	129.6	130.4	132.2	133.0	3.4
1999	137.0	138.1	139.1	141.0	3.0	133.6	134.7	135.8	137.5	3.4
2000	144.5	145.4	147.1	147.4	4.5	138.8	139.7	141.4	142.6	3.7
2001	147.9	148.8	149.9	151.4	2.7	143.9	145.5	146.7	148.0	3.8
2002	153.4	154.6	155.9	157.9	4.3	149.0	150.2	151.6	153.1	3.4
2003	162.3	163.8	165.0	166.3	5.3	154.6	155.9	156.7	157.1	2.6
2004	175.0	177.0	178.4	178.9	7.6	158.1	159.2	160.5	160.7	2.3
Union Workers, Manufacturing, Blue-Collar Occupations										
1990	103.5	104.6	105.1	106.5	4.5	102.6	103.8	104.2	105.4	3.5
1991	108.1	109.4	110.6	111.6	4.8	106.6	107.5	108.2	109.3	3.7
1992	114.7	115.1	116.0	116.8	4.7	110.3	110.8	111.6	112.4	2.8
1993	119.6	121.0	121.8	122.9	5.2	113.1	113.8	114.4	115.7	2.9
1994	123.5	124.6	125.1	125.6	2.2	116.4	117.6	118.3	118.9	2.8
1995	126.1	126.4	126.8	127.8	1.8	119.5	120.2	121.0	121.6	2.3
1996	128.3	129.4	129.5	130.1	1.8	122.4	123.5	124.2	125.0	2.8
1997	130.5	131.4	132.6	133.0	2.2	125.4	126.2	127.6	128.4	2.7
1998	133.1	134.2	135.5	136.4	2.6	129.0	130.0	131.4	132.4	3.1
1999	136.5	137.5	138.5	140.4	2.9	133.0	134.1	135.1	136.8	3.3
2000	143.9	144.8	146.5	147.0	4.7	137.8	138.7	140.4	141.7	3.6
2001	147.3	148.1	149.4	150.9	2.7	143.0	144.3	145.8	147.0	3.7
2002	152.5	153.7	155.0	157.0	4.0	147.8	149.0	150.3	151.8	3.3
2003	161.1	162.5	163.7	165.1	5.2	153.3	154.4	155.2	155.8	2.6
2004	173.8	175.9	177.3	177.8	7.7	156.7	157.8	159.2	159.2	2.2
Union Workers, Nonmanufacturing Industries										
1990	103.0	103.7	104.9	105.9	4.2	102.5	103.0	104.1	104.8	3.3
1991	107.1	108.3	109.7	110.6	4.4	105.8	106.7	107.9	108.6	3.6
1992	111.8	113.1	114.5	115.1	4.1	109.4	110.7	111.7	112.2	3.3
1993	116.3	117.4	118.5	119.3	3.6	113.0	113.9	114.9	115.5	2.9
1994	120.5	121.5	122.6	123.0	3.1	116.4	117.3	118.6	119.0	3.0
1995	124.0	125.0	126.2	127.1	3.3	119.9	120.6	121.6	122.3	2.8
1996	128.0	129.2	129.9	130.4	2.6	122.8	124.3	124.9	125.5	2.6
1997	130.6	131.5	132.9	133.2	2.1	126.1	127.1	128.6	129.1	2.9
1998	133.9	135.3	136.9	137.4	3.2	129.6	130.8	132.4	133.1	3.1
1999	138.1	139.2	140.3	140.8	2.5	133.7	134.6	135.6	135.9	2.1
2000	141.7	143.4	145.0	146.2	3.8	136.4	137.8	139.2	140.4	3.3
2001	147.3	149.4	151.1	153.5	5.0	141.1	142.7	144.3	147.1	4.8
2002	155.0	156.6	158.8	159.9	4.2	148.1	149.6	151.1	152.1	3.4
2003	161.4	163.7	165.5	166.5	4.1	152.5	153.5	154.6	155.6	2.3
2004	168.8	171.6	173.0	174.1	4.6	156.6	158.4	159.6	160.4	3.1
Nonunion Workers, Total										
1990	104.1	105.5	106.6	107.3	4.8	103.4	104.8	105.8	106.4	4.2
1991	108.8	110.1	111.2	111.9	4.3	107.6	108.7	109.7	110.3	3.7
1992	113.1	113.8	114.7	115.5	3.2	111.2	111.8	112.4	113.1	2.5
1993	116.8	117.7	118.8	119.5	3.5	114.1	114.8	115.9	116.6	3.1
1994	120.7	121.7	122.7	123.2	3.1	117.4	118.3	119.2	119.8	2.7
1995	124.3	125.2	126.0	126.5	2.7	120.8	121.8	122.6	123.3	2.9
1996	127.7	128.7	129.7	130.4	3.1	124.8	125.9	126.9	127.7	3.6
1997	131.8	132.8	133.9	135.3	3.8	129.1	130.3	131.6	133.0	4.2
1998	136.7	137.8	139.3	140.1	3.5	134.5	135.7	137.4	138.3	4.0
1999	140.8	142.5	143.8	145.2	3.6	139.0	140.7	142.0	143.3	3.6
2000	147.4	149.1	150.6	151.6	4.4	145.1	146.7	148.1	149.0	4.0
2001	153.8	155.3	156.7	157.8	4.1	150.8	152.2	153.4	154.4	3.6
2002	159.6	161.4	162.2	162.8	3.2	155.9	157.5	158.1	158.5	2.7
2003	165.4	166.8	168.4	169.1	3.9	160.4	161.5	163.0	163.4	3.1
2004	171.3	172.7	174.2	174.9	3.4	164.6	165.6	167.0	167.3	2.4

[1]Excludes farm and household workers.
[2]The regional coverage is as follows: Northeast–Connecticut, Maine, Massachusetts, New Hampshire, New Jersey, New York, Pennsylvania, Rhode Island, and Vermont; South–Alabama, Arkansas, Delaware, District of Columbia, Florida, Georgia, Kentucky, Louisiana, Maryland, Mississippi, North Carolina, Oklahoma, South Carolina, Tennessee, Texas, Virginia, and West Virginia; Midwest–Illinois, Indiana, Iowa, Kansas, Michigan, Minnesota, Missouri, Nebraska, North Dakota, Ohio, South Dakota, and Wisconsin; and West–Alaska, Arizona, California, Colorado, Hawaii, Idaho, Montana, Nevada, New Mexico, Oregon, Utah, Washington, and Wyoming.

Table 6-4. Employment Cost Index, Private Industry Workers [1], Total Compensation and Wages and Salaries by Bargaining Status, Industry, Region [2], and Area Size, 1990–2004—*Continued*

(June 1989 = 100, not seasonally adjusted.)

Series and year	Total compensation					Wages and salaries				
	Indexes				Percent change for 12 months ended December	Indexes				Percent change for 12 months ended December
	March	June	September	December		March	June	September	December	
Nonunion Workers, Blue-Collar Occupations										
1990	103.9	105.3	106.3	106.8	4.6	103.0	104.3	105.1	105.5	3.7
1991	108.3	109.4	110.6	111.2	4.1	106.8	107.7	108.5	109.2	3.5
1992	112.2	113.0	113.9	114.6	3.1	110.1	110.8	111.3	111.9	2.5
1993	115.9	116.9	117.8	118.2	3.1	112.8	113.6	114.4	115.0	2.8
1994	119.6	120.4	121.7	121.9	3.1	115.9	116.7	117.7	118.3	2.9
1995	123.0	123.9	124.5	125.1	2.6	119.5	120.7	121.4	122.1	3.2
1996	126.3	127.3	127.8	128.9	3.0	123.6	124.7	125.2	126.3	3.4
1997	129.9	131.2	131.8	132.6	2.9	127.5	128.9	129.7	130.6	3.4
1998	133.8	134.7	135.5	136.3	2.8	132.0	132.9	134.0	134.8	3.2
1999	137.6	139.0	140.3	141.4	3.7	136.2	137.5	138.7	139.7	3.6
2000	143.4	144.9	146.1	147.2	4.1	141.4	142.9	144.1	144.9	3.7
2001	149.4	150.3	152.2	152.9	3.9	147.1	148.2	150.0	150.5	3.9
2002	154.7	156.0	156.9	157.7	3.1	151.9	153.1	153.7	154.2	2.5
2003	159.8	161.3	162.6	163.2	3.5	155.5	156.5	157.5	157.8	2.3
2004	165.7	167.4	168.6	169.2	3.7	159.0	160.2	161.4	161.7	2.5
Nonunion Workers, Goods-Producing Industries [3]										
1990	104.2	105.5	106.7	107.4	5.0	103.5	104.5	105.5	106.1	3.9
1991	108.8	110.1	111.3	112.2	4.5	107.3	108.3	109.2	110.1	3.8
1992	113.3	114.1	115.1	116.0	3.4	111.2	111.9	112.6	113.3	2.9
1993	117.7	118.6	119.4	119.9	3.4	114.4	115.2	116.0	116.7	3.0
1994	121.5	122.6	123.6	124.1	3.5	117.6	118.6	119.5	120.3	3.1
1995	125.2	125.9	126.4	127.2	2.5	121.3	122.2	122.9	123.8	2.9
1996	128.3	129.4	130.4	131.3	3.2	124.9	126.1	127.3	128.0	3.4
1997	132.0	133.2	134.0	134.7	2.6	128.9	130.2	131.2	132.0	3.1
1998	135.9	136.9	137.7	138.3	2.7	133.6	134.7	135.7	136.5	3.4
1999	139.7	140.5	141.8	143.1	3.5	137.8	138.8	140.0	141.1	3.4
2000	145.4	147.2	148.4	149.3	4.3	142.9	144.7	145.8	146.8	4.0
2001	151.6	153.1	154.0	155.3	4.0	148.8	150.3	151.1	152.1	3.6
2002	157.2	158.6	159.5	160.8	3.5	153.5	154.8	155.5	156.6	3.0
2003	163.6	164.9	166.1	166.7	3.7	157.8	158.9	159.7	160.1	2.2
2004	169.7	170.9	172.4	173.5	4.1	161.4	162.4	163.8	163.9	2.4
Nonunion Workers, Service-Producing Industries [4]										
1990	103.9	105.5	106.5	107.2	4.7	103.4	104.9	105.9	106.5	4.2
1991	108.8	110.1	111.2	111.8	4.3	107.8	108.9	109.9	110.4	3.7
1992	113.0	113.7	114.4	115.2	3.0	111.2	111.7	112.3	113.0	2.4
1993	116.3	117.2	118.4	119.2	3.5	113.8	114.6	115.9	116.6	3.2
1994	120.3	121.1	122.2	122.7	2.9	117.2	118.1	119.0	119.5	2.5
1995	123.8	124.8	125.6	126.0	2.7	120.5	121.5	122.4	123.0	2.9
1996	127.3	128.3	129.2	129.9	3.1	124.6	125.7	126.6	127.5	3.7
1997	131.5	132.5	133.7	135.3	4.2	129.1	130.2	131.6	133.2	4.5
1998	136.7	138.0	139.7	140.6	3.9	134.6	135.9	137.9	138.8	4.2
1999	141.1	143.0	144.4	145.7	3.6	139.3	141.3	142.6	143.9	3.7
2000	148.0	149.6	151.2	152.3	4.5	145.8	147.3	148.7	149.6	4.0
2001	154.4	155.9	157.5	158.6	4.1	151.4	152.7	154.1	155.1	3.7
2002	160.3	162.2	162.9	163.3	3.0	156.7	158.3	158.9	159.0	2.5
2003	165.9	167.2	169.0	169.8	4.0	161.2	162.3	164.0	164.5	3.5
2004	171.6	173.2	174.6	175.1	3.1	165.6	166.6	168.0	168.4	2.4
Nonunion Workers, Manufacturing Industries										
1990	104.2	105.5	106.9	107.6	5.4	103.6	104.8	105.9	106.5	4.4
1991	108.8	110.2	111.5	112.4	4.5	107.7	108.8	109.7	110.7	3.9
1992	113.6	114.5	115.5	116.4	3.6	111.9	112.7	113.4	114.2	3.2
1993	118.1	119.0	120.0	120.6	3.6	115.4	116.1	117.0	117.9	3.2
1994	122.0	122.9	124.0	124.8	3.5	118.6	119.5	120.5	121.5	3.1
1995	126.1	126.9	127.3	128.3	2.8	122.7	123.8	124.3	125.2	3.0
1996	129.3	130.5	131.7	132.5	3.3	126.3	127.5	128.8	129.6	3.5
1997	133.1	134.4	135.1	135.9	2.6	130.3	131.7	132.6	133.5	3.0
1998	137.2	138.0	138.9	139.4	2.6	135.1	136.2	137.3	138.2	3.5
1999	140.7	141.7	143.0	144.4	3.5	139.4	140.5	141.7	142.9	3.4
2000	146.5	148.2	149.2	149.9	3.8	144.4	146.1	147.2	148.0	3.6
2001	152.4	153.7	154.4	155.5	3.7	150.1	151.6	152.2	153.1	3.4
2002	157.6	159.1	160.1	161.3	3.7	154.7	156.1	156.8	157.8	3.1
2003	164.5	165.8	166.9	167.3	3.7	159.3	160.2	160.9	161.3	2.2
2004	170.6	172.0	173.8	174.3	4.2	162.6	163.7	165.2	165.3	2.5

[1] Excludes farm and household workers.
[2] The regional coverage is as follows: Northeast–Connecticut, Maine, Massachusetts, New Hampshire, New Jersey, New York, Pennsylvania, Rhode Island, and Vermont; South–Alabama, Arkansas, Delaware, District of Columbia, Florida, Georgia, Kentucky, Louisiana, Maryland, Mississippi, North Carolina, Oklahoma, South Carolina, Tennessee, Texas, Virginia, and West Virginia; Midwest–Illinois, Indiana, Iowa, Kansas, Michigan, Minnesota, Missouri, Nebraska, North Dakota, Ohio, South Dakota, and Wisconsin; and West–Alaska, Arizona, California, Colorado, Hawaii, Idaho, Montana, Nevada, New Mexico, Oregon, Utah, Washington, and Wyoming.
[3] Includes mining, construction, and manufacturing.
[4] Includes transportation, communication, and public utilities; wholesale and retail trade; finance, insurance, and real estate; and service industries.

Table 6-4. Employment Cost Index, Private Industry Workers[1], Total Compensation and Wages and Salaries by Bargaining Status, Industry, Region[2], and Area Size, 1990–2004—*Continued*

(June 1989 = 100, not seasonally adjusted.)

Series and year	Total compensation					Wages and salaries				
	Indexes				Percent change for 12 months ended December	Indexes				Percent change for 12 months ended December
	March	June	September	December		March	June	September	December	
Nonunion Workers, Manufacturing, Blue-Collar Occupations										
1990	104.4	105.9	107.2	107.9	5.4	103.6	105.0	106.0	106.7	4.4
1991	109.0	110.3	111.7	112.5	4.3	107.9	108.8	109.7	110.7	3.7
1992	113.8	114.6	115.5	116.2	3.3	111.9	112.5	113.1	113.7	2.7
1993	117.5	118.4	119.4	119.9	3.2	114.6	115.2	116.0	116.7	2.6
1994	121.2	121.9	123.0	123.5	3.0	117.5	118.1	119.1	120.0	2.8
1995	124.5	125.5	125.7	127.0	2.8	121.2	122.6	123.1	124.2	3.5
1996	128.1	129.3	130.3	131.4	3.5	125.4	126.7	127.8	128.8	3.7
1997	132.2	133.5	134.2	134.8	2.6	129.8	131.2	132.0	133.0	3.3
1998	136.0	136.7	137.4	138.3	2.6	134.4	135.1	136.2	137.2	3.2
1999	139.5	140.2	141.6	142.9	3.3	138.5	139.2	140.5	141.6	3.2
2000	144.4	145.8	146.7	148.0	3.6	142.8	144.2	145.4	146.6	3.5
2001	149.9	150.8	152.1	153.5	3.7	148.7	150.1	151.3	152.6	4.1
2002	155.6	156.7	157.5	158.8	3.5	154.3	155.3	155.7	156.8	2.8
2003	161.5	162.6	164.1	164.8	3.8	158.3	158.7	159.8	160.4	2.3
2004	168.1	169.3	171.2	171.9	4.3	161.9	162.6	164.1	164.5	2.6
Nonunion Workers, Nonmanufacturing Industries										
1990	104.0	105.4	106.5	107.2	4.7	103.3	104.8	105.7	106.3	3.9
1991	108.8	110.1	111.2	111.7	4.2	107.6	108.7	109.6	110.1	3.6
1992	112.9	113.5	114.3	115.1	3.0	110.9	111.4	112.0	112.7	2.4
1993	116.3	117.2	118.3	119.0	3.4	113.5	114.3	115.5	116.1	3.0
1994	120.2	121.1	122.2	122.5	2.9	116.9	117.8	118.7	119.1	2.6
1995	123.6	124.5	125.3	125.7	2.6	120.0	121.0	121.9	122.6	2.9
1996	127.0	128.0	128.9	129.6	3.1	124.2	125.2	126.1	127.0	3.6
1997	131.1	132.2	133.4	134.9	4.1	128.5	129.7	131.1	132.6	4.4
1998	136.3	137.5	139.1	140.0	3.8	134.0	135.3	137.1	138.0	4.1
1999	140.6	142.4	143.8	145.1	3.6	138.6	140.5	141.8	143.0	3.6
2000	147.4	149.1	150.7	151.8	4.6	145.0	146.6	148.0	148.9	4.1
2001	153.9	155.4	157.0	158.2	4.2	150.7	152.0	153.3	154.4	3.7
2002	159.9	161.7	162.4	162.9	3.0	155.9	157.5	158.1	158.3	2.5
2003	165.4	166.7	168.5	169.3	3.9	160.4	161.5	163.1	163.7	3.4
2004	171.1	172.6	174.0	174.7	3.2	164.7	165.7	167.1	167.5	2.3
WORKERS BY REGION										
Northeast										
1990	104.4	105.3	106.5	107.6	4.6	104.0	104.8	105.9	106.9	3.9
1991	109.4	110.6	111.7	112.5	4.6	108.3	109.4	110.3	110.9	3.7
1992	113.9	114.5	115.5	116.4	3.5	111.7	112.2	113.0	113.7	2.5
1993	117.8	119.1	120.2	120.7	3.7	114.6	115.7	116.8	117.3	3.2
1994	121.6	122.8	124.0	124.3	3.0	117.8	118.8	120.0	120.2	2.5
1995	125.6	126.6	127.4	127.8	2.8	121.3	122.1	123.1	123.6	2.8
1996	128.9	129.7	130.6	131.1	2.6	124.9	126.0	127.0	127.7	3.3
1997	132.2	133.1	134.0	135.0	3.0	128.8	129.8	130.7	131.6	3.1
1998	136.0	137.0	138.7	139.5	3.3	132.6	133.8	135.4	136.4	3.6
1999	140.5	141.5	143.2	144.3	3.4	137.1	138.2	139.9	140.9	3.3
2000	146.3	147.6	149.3	150.3	4.2	142.3	143.7	145.3	146.0	3.6
2001	151.6	153.7	155.2	156.3	4.0	147.3	149.2	150.6	151.7	3.9
2002	158.3	159.9	160.5	161.3	3.2	153.5	154.9	155.1	155.7	2.6
2003	163.8	165.2	166.9	167.9	4.1	157.3	158.4	160.0	160.9	3.3
2004	170.2	172.3	173.7	174.2	3.8	162.0	163.6	164.9	165.0	2.5
South										
1990	104.0	105.7	106.3	106.9	4.6	103.5	105.2	105.7	106.1	3.9
1991	108.4	109.8	110.7	111.2	4.0	107.4	108.5	109.2	109.6	3.3
1992	112.5	113.3	114.1	114.8	3.2	110.8	111.5	112.0	112.7	2.8
1993	116.2	117.0	118.1	118.8	3.5	113.6	114.3	115.3	116.0	2.9
1994	120.0	120.8	121.8	122.5	3.1	116.6	117.4	118.5	119.1	2.7
1995	123.7	124.3	125.2	125.6	2.5	120.0	120.8	121.8	122.4	2.8
1996	127.0	127.8	128.8	129.7	3.3	124.1	125.1	126.0	127.0	3.8
1997	130.8	131.5	132.5	134.6	3.8	128.5	129.4	130.6	133.0	4.7
1998	135.5	136.4	137.6	138.1	2.6	134.0	134.9	136.5	136.7	2.8
1999	139.1	140.7	141.8	143.0	3.5	137.9	139.4	140.2	141.5	3.5
2000	145.0	146.7	147.6	148.6	3.9	143.0	144.6	145.3	146.3	3.4
2001	151.1	152.3	153.5	154.6	4.0	148.3	149.3	150.2	151.2	3.3
2002	156.2	157.6	158.9	159.0	2.8	152.5	153.6	154.7	154.6	2.2
2003	160.6	161.6	163.2	163.9	3.1	155.3	156.1	157.4	157.9	2.1
2004	166.4	167.9	169.5	170.6	4.1	159.1	160.1	161.6	162.3	2.8

[1] Excludes farm and household workers.
[2] The regional coverage is as follows: Northeast–Connecticut, Maine, Massachusetts, New Hampshire, New Jersey, New York, Pennsylvania, Rhode Island, and Vermont; South–Alabama, Arkansas, Delaware, District of Columbia, Florida, Georgia, Kentucky, Louisiana, Maryland, Mississippi, North Carolina, Oklahoma, South Carolina, Tennessee, Texas, Virginia, and West Virginia; Midwest–Illinois, Indiana, Iowa, Kansas, Michigan, Minnesota, Missouri, Nebraska, North Dakota, Ohio, South Dakota, and Wisconsin; and West–Alaska, Arizona, California, Colorado, Hawaii, Idaho, Montana, Nevada, New Mexico, Oregon, Utah, Washington, and Wyoming.

Table 6-4. Employment Cost Index, Private Industry Workers[1], Total Compensation and Wages and Salaries by Bargaining Status, Industry, Region[2], and Area Size, 1990–2004—*Continued*

(June 1989 = 100, not seasonally adjusted.)

Series and year	Total compensation					Wages and salaries				
	Indexes				Percent change for 12 months ended December	Indexes				Percent change for 12 months ended December
	March	June	September	December		March	June	September	December	
Midwest										
1990	103.5	104.8	106.3	107.1	5.1	102.6	103.7	105.1	105.8	4.1
1991	108.5	109.7	111.2	112.2	4.8	106.9	107.7	108.9	109.9	3.9
1992	113.8	114.6	115.3	116.1	3.5	110.7	111.3	111.8	112.5	2.4
1993	117.9	119.3	120.1	121.2	4.4	113.5	114.6	115.2	116.5	3.6
1994	122.8	123.6	124.6	125.0	3.1	117.5	118.3	119.5	120.1	3.1
1995	125.8	126.9	127.7	128.3	2.6	120.9	122.2	123.0	123.6	2.9
1996	129.5	130.7	131.3	132.1	3.0	125.1	126.2	126.9	127.7	3.3
1997	133.3	134.7	136.2	136.9	3.6	129.0	130.4	132.2	133.0	4.2
1998	138.3	139.6	140.9	141.4	3.3	134.7	136.0	137.5	138.0	3.8
1999	141.7	143.6	145.0	146.3	3.5	138.9	141.0	142.4	143.6	4.1
2000	148.9	150.7	152.2	153.3	4.8	145.3	147.1	148.6	149.6	4.2
2001	154.8	156.0	157.4	158.6	3.5	150.9	152.3	153.6	154.7	3.4
2002	161.1	162.6	163.5	164.6	3.8	157.1	158.5	159.2	160.2	3.6
2003	169.0	170.4	171.7	172.5	4.8	164.1	165.0	166.1	166.5	3.9
2004	174.7	176.2	177.6	177.9	3.1	166.9	167.7	169.2	169.2	1.6
West										
1990	103.3	104.5	105.6	106.3	4.4	102.5	104.0	104.8	105.4	3.9
1991	107.5	108.9	110.0	110.9	4.3	106.4	107.6	108.6	109.4	3.8
1992	111.9	112.9	114.1	114.9	3.6	110.2	111.1	112.2	112.8	3.1
1993	116.2	116.4	117.8	118.1	2.8	113.6	113.7	115.3	115.7	2.6
1994	119.4	120.5	121.3	121.7	3.0	116.6	117.9	118.1	119.0	2.9
1995	122.6	123.4	123.9	125.0	2.7	119.9	120.9	121.4	122.7	3.1
1996	125.9	127.3	128.3	128.9	3.1	123.3	124.8	125.8	126.5	3.1
1997	130.3	131.4	132.5	133.4	3.5	127.7	128.9	130.2	131.2	3.7
1998	135.2	136.6	138.5	140.0	4.9	132.9	134.5	136.7	138.4	5.5
1999	140.3	142.1	143.3	144.7	3.4	138.2	140.2	141.3	142.6	3.0
2000	147.0	148.8	150.8	151.8	4.9	144.7	146.3	148.2	149.2	4.6
2001	154.3	156.0	157.6	159.4	5.0	151.3	152.9	154.3	156.0	4.6
2002	160.4	162.9	163.8	165.0	3.5	156.4	158.7	159.3	160.1	2.6
2003	167.3	169.5	171.4	172.2	4.4	161.3	163.1	164.7	165.2	3.2
2004	175.3	176.8	178.1	179.0	3.9	166.8	167.9	169.1	169.5	2.6
WORKERS BY AREA SIZE										
Metropolitan Areas										
1990	103.9	105.1	106.3	107.1	4.8	103.3	104.4	105.4	106.1	3.9
1991	108.5	109.8	111.0	111.8	4.4	107.3	108.4	109.3	110.1	3.8
1992	113.1	113.9	114.8	115.6	3.4	110.9	111.6	112.3	112.9	2.5
1993	117.1	118.1	119.1	119.8	3.6	113.9	114.7	115.8	116.5	3.2
1994	120.9	121.9	122.9	123.4	3.0	117.2	118.1	119.1	119.7	2.7
1995	124.5	125.4	126.2	126.8	2.8	120.6	121.6	122.4	123.2	2.9
1996	128.0	129.1	130.0	130.6	3.0	124.6	125.8	126.7	127.4	3.4
1997	131.7	132.8	133.9	135.1	3.4	128.7	129.9	131.1	132.3	3.8
1998	136.4	137.5	139.1	139.8	3.5	133.8	135.1	136.9	137.7	4.1
1999	140.4	142.0	143.3	144.7	3.5	138.3	139.9	141.2	142.5	3.5
2000	146.9	148.6	150.1	151.0	4.4	144.1	145.7	147.1	148.0	3.9
2001	153.1	154.6	156.0	157.4	4.2	149.8	151.2	152.4	153.7	3.9
2002	159.1	160.9	161.8	162.5	3.2	155.1	156.7	157.4	157.9	2.7
2003	165.2	166.6	168.3	169.1	4.1	159.6	160.7	162.2	162.7	3.0
2004	171.5	173.1	174.6	175.3	3.7	163.8	164.9	166.3	166.6	2.4
Other Areas										
1990	103.6	105.2	106.0	106.8	4.7	103.0	104.6	105.3	106.0	4.0
1991	108.4	109.9	110.7	111.2	4.1	107.2	108.4	109.0	109.4	3.2
1992	113.1	113.7	114.8	115.6	4.0	110.7	111.2	112.0	112.8	3.1
1993	117.0	117.8	118.7	119.7	3.5	113.5	114.4	115.0	115.8	2.7
1994	121.3	122.5	123.2	123.5	3.2	117.0	118.1	118.6	119.0	2.8
1995	124.8	125.3	126.1	126.5	2.4	120.5	121.3	122.1	122.4	2.9
1996	127.2	128.0	128.7	130.2	2.9	123.4	124.2	125.0	126.5	3.3
1997	131.4	132.4	133.8	135.3	3.9	127.7	128.8	130.4	132.0	4.3
1998	135.9	137.1	138.2	139.4	3.0	132.5	133.4	134.7	136.0	3.0
1999	140.5	141.8	143.1	143.6	3.0	137.1	138.4	139.8	140.2	3.1
2000	146.0	147.7	148.8	150.3	4.7	142.2	143.7	144.7	146.0	4.1
2001	152.1	153.7	154.8	155.6	3.5	147.4	148.8	149.7	150.5	3.1
2002	157.5	158.5	160.0	160.8	3.3	151.7	152.6	153.8	154.8	2.9
2003	163.5	165.0	166.1	166.9	3.8	156.8	158.0	158.9	159.5	3.0
2004	170.2	172.1	173.3	174.3	4.4	160.8	162.1	163.3	163.8	2.7

[1]Excludes farm and household workers.
[2]The regional coverage is as follows: Northeast–Connecticut, Maine, Massachusetts, New Hampshire, New Jersey, New York, Pennsylvania, Rhode Island, and Vermont; South–Alabama, Arkansas, Delaware, District of Columbia, Florida, Georgia, Kentucky, Louisiana, Maryland, Mississippi, North Carolina, Oklahoma, South Carolina, Tennessee, Texas, Virginia, and West Virginia; Midwest–Illinois, Indiana, Iowa, Kansas, Michigan, Minnesota, Missouri, Nebraska, North Dakota, Ohio, South Dakota, and Wisconsin; and West–Alaska, Arizona, California, Colorado, Hawaii, Idaho, Montana, Nevada, New Mexico, Oregon, Utah, Washington, and Wyoming.

Table 6-5. Employer Compensation Costs per Hour Worked for Employee Compensation and Costs as a Percent of Total Compensation: Private Industry Workers, by Major Industry Group, March 2005

(Dollars, percent of total cost.)

Compensation component	Goods-producing [1]						Service-providing [2]					
	All goods-producing [1]		Construction		Manufacturing		All service-providing [2]		Trade, transportation, and utilities		Information	
	Cost	Percent	Cost	Percent	Cost	Percent	Cost	Percent	Cost	Percent	Cost	Percent
TOTAL COMPENSATION	$28.48	100.0	$27.98	100.0	$28.48	100.0	$23.11	100.0	$20.27	100.0	34.60	100.0
WAGES AND SALARIES	18.66	65.5	19.29	68.9	18.26	64.1	16.78	72.6	14.49	71.5	24.19	69.9
TOTAL BENEFITS	9.82	34.5	8.69	31.1	10.21	35.9	6.34	27.4	5.78	28.5	10.41	30.1
Paid Leave	1.72	6.0	0.93	3.3	2.07	7.3	1.50	6.5	1.15	5.7	2.88	8.3
Vacation pay	0.89	3.1	0.52	1.9	1.04	3.7	0.73	3.2	0.57	2.8	1.40	4.1
Holiday pay	0.63	2.2	0.33	1.2	0.76	2.7	0.51	2.2	0.39	1.9	0.93	2.7
Sick leave	0.13	0.5	0.06	0.2	0.16	0.6	0.20	0.9	0.16	0.8	0.32	0.9
Other leave pay	0.07	0.3	0.02	0.1	0.10	0.3	0.06	0.3	0.04	0.2	0.22	0.6
Supplemental Pay	1.24	4.4	1.21	4.3	1.25	4.4	0.54	2.3	0.47	2.3	0.89	2.6
Overtime and premium pay [3]	0.59	2.1	0.52	1.9	0.61	2.1	0.16	0.7	0.21	1.0	0.31	0.9
Shift differentials	0.08	0.3	(4)	(5)	0.12	0.4	0.05	0.2	0.03	0.1	0.05	0.1
Nonproduction bonuses	0.57	2.0	0.68	2.4	0.53	1.8	0.33	1.4	0.23	1.1	0.53	1.5
Insurance	2.45	8.6	1.88	6.7	2.68	9.4	1.59	6.9	1.56	7.7	2.81	8.1
Life insurance	0.06	0.2	0.03	0.1	0.07	0.2	0.04	0.2	0.04	0.2	0.05	0.2
Health insurance	2.28	8.0	1.81	6.5	2.48	8.7	1.48	6.4	1.47	7.2	2.54	7.3
Short-term disability	0.08	0.3	0.03	0.1	0.10	0.3	0.04	0.2	0.04	0.2	0.15	0.4
Long-term disability	0.03	0.1	(4)	(5)	0.04	0.1	0.03	0.1	0.02	0.1	0.07	0.2
Retirement and Savings	1.59	5.6	1.35	4.8	1.64	5.8	0.73	3.1	0.70	3.5	1.24	3.6
Defined benefit plans	1.08	3.8	0.85	3.0	1.13	4.0	0.30	1.3	0.39	1.9	0.61	1.8
Defined contribution plans	0.51	1.8	0.51	1.8	0.51	1.8	0.43	1.9	0.31	1.5	0.63	1.8
Legally Required Benefits	2.73	9.6	3.30	11.8	2.45	8.6	1.95	8.4	1.87	9.2	2.47	7.1
Social Security and Medicare	1.61	5.6	1.61	5.8	1.60	5.6	1.39	6.0	1.20	5.9	2.00	5.8
Social Security [6]	1.29	4.5	1.30	4.6	1.29	4.5	1.12	4.8	0.96	4.8	1.60	4.6
Medicare	0.31	1.1	0.31	1.1	0.31	1.1	0.28	1.2	0.23	1.1	0.40	1.2
Federal unemployment insurance	0.03	0.1	0.03	0.1	0.03	0.1	0.03	0.1	0.04	0.2	0.03	0.1
State unemployment insurance	0.20	0.7	0.25	0.9	0.19	0.7	0.15	0.6	0.14	0.7	0.13	0.4
Workers' compensation	0.89	3.1	1.42	5.1	0.64	2.2	0.37	1.6	0.50	2.5	0.31	0.9
Other Benefits [7]	0.08	0.3	(4)	(5)	0.12	0.4	0.03	0.1	0.02	0.1	0.11	0.3

[1]Includes mining, construction, and manufacturing. The agriculture, forestry, farming and hunting sector is excluded.
[2]Includes utilities; wholesale trade; retail trade; transportation and warehousing; information; finance and insurance; real estate and rental and leasing; professional and technical services; management of companies and enterprises; administrative and waste services; educational services; health care and social assistance; arts, entertainment, and recreation; accommodation and food services; and other services, except public administration.
[3]Includes premium pay for work in addition to the regular work schedule (such as overtime, weekends, and holidays).
[4]Cost per hour worked is $0.01 or less.
[5]Less than .05 percent.
[6]Comprises the Old Age, Survivors, and Disability Insurance (OASDI) program.
[7]Includes severance pay and supplemental unemployment benefits.

Table 6-5. Employer Compensation Costs per Hour Worked for Employee Compensation and Costs as a Percent of Total Compensation: Private Industry Workers, by Major Industry Group, March 2005—*Continued*

(Dollars, percent of total cost.)

Compensation component	Service-providing [2]									
	Financial activities		Professional and business services		Education and health services		Leisure and hospitality		Other services	
	Cost	Percent	Cost	Percent	Cost	Percent	Cost	Percent	Cost	Percent
TOTAL COMPENSATION	33.27	100.0	27.56	100.0	25.77	100.0	10.67	100.0	20.85	100.0
WAGES AND SALARIES	23.13	69.5	20.37	73.9	18.79	72.9	8.43	79.0	15.30	73.4
TOTAL BENEFITS	10.14	30.5	7.19	26.1	6.98	27.1	2.24	21.0	5.55	26.6
Paid Leave	2.35	7.1	1.91	6.9	1.84	7.2	0.34	3.2	1.36	6.5
Vacation pay	1.14	3.4	0.91	3.3	0.91	3.5	0.18	1.7	0.64	3.1
Holiday pay	0.80	2.4	0.68	2.5	0.60	2.3	0.10	0.9	0.49	2.3
Sick leave	0.31	0.9	0.25	0.9	0.26	1.0	0.04	0.4	0.19	0.9
Other leave pay	0.10	0.3	0.07	0.3	0.08	0.3	0.02	0.2	0.04	0.2
Supplemental Pay	1.44	4.3	0.65	2.3	0.44	1.7	0.13	1.2	0.30	1.4
Overtime and premium pay [3]	0.09	0.3	0.17	0.6	0.15	0.6	0.08	0.7	0.09	0.4
Shift differentials	(4)	(5)	0.04	0.1	0.16	0.6	(4)	(5)	0.03	0.1
Nonproduction bonuses	1.34	4.0	0.44	1.6	0.12	0.5	0.05	0.5	0.18	0.8
Insurance	2.53	7.6	1.59	5.8	1.86	7.2	0.44	4.2	1.35	6.5
Life insurance	0.07	0.2	0.05	0.2	0.03	0.1	(4)	(5)	0.03	0.2
Health insurance	2.34	7.0	1.45	5.2	1.75	6.8	0.42	4.0	1.27	6.1
Short-term disability	0.06	0.2	0.05	0.2	0.04	0.1	(4)	(5)	0.02	0.1
Long-term disability	0.06	0.2	0.04	0.2	0.04	0.2	(4)	(5)	0.03	0.1
Retirement and Savings	1.49	4.5	0.77	2.8	0.74	2.9	0.10	0.9	0.63	3.0
Defined benefit plans	0.61	1.8	0.27	1.0	0.21	0.8	0.03	0.3	0.21	1.0
Defined contribution plans	0.88	2.6	0.50	1.8	0.54	2.1	0.07	0.7	0.42	2.0
Legally Required Benefits	2.23	6.7	2.23	8.1	2.08	8.1	1.22	11.5	1.91	9.2
Social Security and Medicare	1.82	5.5	1.66	6.0	1.57	6.1	0.80	7.5	1.27	6.1
Social Security [6]	1.42	4.3	1.33	4.8	1.26	4.9	0.65	6.1	1.02	4.9
Medicare	0.39	1.2	0.33	1.2	0.31	1.2	0.15	1.4	0.25	1.2
Federal unemployment insurance	0.03	0.1	0.03	0.1	0.03	0.1	0.04	0.4	0.03	0.1
State unemployment insurance	0.16	0.5	0.19	0.7	0.13	0.5	0.12	1.1	0.14	0.7
Workers' compensation	0.22	0.7	0.35	1.3	0.35	1.4	0.26	2.4	0.47	2.2
Other Benefits [7]	0.10	0.3	0.04	0.1	(4)	(5)	(4)	(5)	(4)	(5)

Note: The sum of individual items may not equal totals due to rounding.

[2]Includes utilities; wholesale trade; retail trade; transportation and warehousing; information; finance and insurance; real estate and rental and leasing; professional and technical services; management of companies and enterprises; administrative and waste services; educational services; health care and social assistance; arts, entertainment, and recreation; accommodation and food services; and other services, except public administration.
[3]Includes premium pay for work in addition to the regular work schedule (such as overtime, weekends, and holidays).
[4]Cost per hour worked is $0.01 or less.
[5]Less than .05 percent.
[6]Comprises the Old Age, Survivors, and Disability Insurance (OASDI) program.
[7]Includes severance pay and supplemental unemployment benefits.

Table 6-6. Employer Compensation Costs per Hour Worked for Employee Compensation and Costs as a Percent of Total Compensation: Private Industry Workers, by Census Area and Region, March 2005

(Dollars, percent of total cost.)

Compensation component	Northeast		South		Midwest		West		Metropolitan area		Nonmetropolitan area	
	Cost	Percent	Cost	Percent	Cost	Percent	Cost	Percent	Cost	Percent	Cost	Percent
TOTAL COMPENSATION	$27.09	$100.00	$21.36	$100.00	$24.23	$100.00	$25.98	$100.00	$24.80	$100.00	$18.81	$100.00
WAGES AND SALARIES	19.07	70.4	15.41	72.1	16.97	70.1	18.43	70.9	17.62	71.0	13.16	70.0
TOTAL BENEFITS	8.02	29.6	5.95	27.9	7.25	29.9	7.55	29.1	7.18	29.0	5.65	30.0
Paid Leave	1.89	7.0	1.31	6.1	1.51	6.2	1.65	6.3	1.60	6.4	1.08	5.8
Vacation	0.91	3.4	0.65	3.0	0.75	3.1	0.83	3.2	0.79	3.2	0.56	3.0
Holiday	0.66	2.4	0.45	2.1	0.52	2.1	0.56	2.1	0.55	2.2	0.37	2.0
Sick	0.24	0.9	0.16	0.7	0.17	0.7	0.21	0.8	0.20	0.8	0.11	0.6
Other	0.08	0.3	0.05	0.2	0.08	0.3	0.05	0.2	0.07	0.3	0.05	0.2
Supplemental Pay	0.76	2.8	0.55	2.6	0.76	3.1	0.72	2.8	0.69	2.8	0.57	3.0
Overtime and premium pay [1]	0.22	0.8	0.22	1.1	0.29	1.2	0.23	0.9	0.24	0.9	0.29	1.5
Shift differentials	0.06	0.2	0.05	0.2	0.07	0.3	0.05	0.2	0.06	0.2	0.07	0.4
Nonproduction bonuses	0.48	1.8	0.28	1.3	0.40	1.6	0.44	1.7	0.40	1.6	0.21	1.1
Insurance	1.98	7.3	1.53	7.2	1.91	7.9	1.75	6.7	1.78	7.2	1.59	8.5
Life insurance	0.05	0.2	0.04	0.2	0.04	0.2	0.04	0.1	0.04	0.2	0.04	0.2
Health insurance	1.83	6.8	1.42	6.6	1.78	7.3	1.64	6.3	1.65	6.7	1.49	7.9
Short-term disability	0.07	0.2	0.04	0.2	0.05	0.2	0.03	0.1	0.05	0.2	0.04	0.2
Long-term disability	0.04	0.1	0.03	0.2	0.03	0.1	0.03	0.1	0.03	0.1	0.02	0.1
Retirement and Savings	1.04	3.8	0.71	3.3	0.98	4.0	0.96	3.7	0.93	3.7	0.63	3.3
Defined benefit	0.47	1.7	0.32	1.5	0.57	2.4	0.49	1.9	0.47	1.9	0.31	1.7
Defined contribution	0.57	2.1	0.39	1.8	0.41	1.7	0.47	1.8	0.46	1.9	0.32	1.7
Legally Required Benefits	2.30	8.5	1.82	8.5	2.05	8.5	2.46	9.5	2.14	8.6	1.76	9.3
Social Security and Medicare	1.61	5.9	1.29	6.0	1.42	5.8	1.53	5.9	1.47	5.9	1.14	6.1
Social Security [2]	1.29	4.8	1.04	4.9	1.13	4.7	1.23	4.7	1.18	4.7	0.92	4.9
Medicare	0.32	1.2	0.25	1.2	0.28	1.2	0.30	1.2	0.29	1.2	0.22	1.2
Federal unemployment insurance	0.03	0.1	0.03	0.2	0.03	0.1	0.03	0.1	0.03	0.1	0.03	0.2
State unemployment insurance	0.22	0.8	0.11	0.5	0.16	0.7	0.18	0.7	0.16	0.6	0.13	0.7
Workers' compensation	0.44	1.6	0.39	1.8	0.44	1.8	0.71	2.7	0.48	1.9	0.45	2.4
Other Benefits [3]	0.05	0.2	0.03	0.1	0.06	0.2	0.02	0.1	0.04	0.2	(4)	(5)

Note: The sum of individual items may not equal totals due to rounding.

[1] Includes premium pay for work in addition to the regular work schedule (such as overtime, weekends, and holidays).
[2] Comprises the Old Age, Survivors, and Disability Insurance (OASDI) program.
[3] Includes severance pay and supplemental unemployment benefits.
[4] Cost per hour worked is $0.01 or less.
[5] Less than .05 percent.

Table 6-7. Employer Compensation Costs per Hour Worked for Employee Compensation and Costs as a Percent of Total Compensation: State and Local Government, by Major Occupational and Industry Group, March 2005

(Dollars, percent of total cost.)

Compensation component	All workers		Occupational group [1]						Industry group	
			Management, professional, and related		Sales and office		Service		Service-providing [2]	
	Cost	Percent	Cost	Percent	Cost	Percent	Cost	Percent	Cost	Percent
TOTAL COMPENSATION	35.50	100.0	43.18	100.0	24.26	100.0	27.10	100.0	35.66	100.0
WAGES AND SALARIES	24.26	68.3	30.85	71.5	15.31	63.1	16.81	62.0	24.40	68.4
TOTAL BENEFITS	11.24	31.7	12.33	28.5	8.95	36.9	10.29	38.0	11.26	31.6
Paid Leave	2.68	7.6	2.89	6.7	2.29	9.4	2.44	9.0	2.68	7.5
Vacation pay	0.93	2.6	0.84	2.0	0.92	3.8	1.05	3.9	0.93	2.6
Holiday pay	0.89	2.5	0.98	2.3	0.75	3.1	0.79	2.9	0.89	2.5
Sick leave	0.65	1.8	0.81	1.9	0.47	2.0	0.44	1.6	0.66	1.8
Other leave pay	0.21	0.6	0.25	0.6	0.14	0.6	0.17	0.6	0.21	0.6
Supplemental Pay	0.31	0.9	0.19	0.4	0.16	0.7	0.61	2.3	0.31	0.9
Overtime and premium pay [3]	0.14	0.4	0.04	0.1	0.08	0.3	0.33	1.2	0.14	0.4
Shift pay	0.07	0.2	0.05	0.1	0.02	0.1	0.14	0.5	0.07	0.2
Nonproduction bonuses	0.10	0.3	0.10	0.2	0.07	0.3	0.14	0.5	0.10	0.3
Insurance	3.76	10.6	4.11	9.5	3.49	14.4	3.08	11.3	3.76	10.5
Life insurance	0.06	0.2	0.07	0.2	0.05	0.2	0.04	0.2	0.06	0.2
Health insurance	3.63	10.2	3.97	9.2	3.39	14.0	2.94	10.8	3.63	10.2
Short-term disability	0.03	0.1	0.02	0.1	0.02	0.1	0.07	0.2	0.03	0.1
Long-term disability	0.04	0.1	0.05	0.1	0.03	0.1	0.03	0.1	0.04	0.1
Retirement and Savings	2.34	6.6	2.67	6.2	1.43	5.9	2.42	8.9	2.35	6.6
Defined benefit plans	2.08	5.9	2.33	5.4	1.28	5.3	2.30	8.5	2.09	5.9
Defined contribution plans	0.26	0.7	0.34	0.8	0.15	0.6	0.12	0.4	0.26	0.7
Legally Required Benefits	2.10	5.9	2.41	5.6	1.54	6.3	1.69	6.2	2.10	5.9
Social Security and Medicare	1.59	4.5	1.98	4.6	1.17	4.8	1.03	3.8	1.60	4.5
Social Security [4]	1.23	3.5	1.52	3.5	0.92	3.8	0.78	2.9	1.23	3.5
Medicare	0.37	1.0	0.46	1.1	0.25	1.0	0.25	0.9	0.37	1.0
Federal unemployment insurance	(5)	(6)	(5)	(6)	(5)	(6)	(5)	(6)	(5)	(6)
State unemployment insurance	0.07	0.2	0.07	0.2	0.06	0.2	0.07	0.3	0.07	0.2
Workers' compensation	0.44	1.2	0.37	0.8	0.32	1.3	0.59	2.2	0.44	1.2
Other Benefits [7]	0.05	0.2	0.06	0.1	0.04	0.1	0.05	0.2	0.05	0.2

Note: The sum of individual items may not equal totals due to rounding.

[1]This table presents data for the three major occupational groups in state and local government: management, professional, and related occupations, including teachers; sales and office occupations, including clerical workers; and service occupations, including police and firefighters.
[2]Service-providing industries, which include health and educational services, employ a large part of the state and local government workforce.
[3]Includes premium pay for work in addition to the regular work schedule (such as overtime, weekends, and holidays).
[4]Comprises the Old-Age, Survivors, and Disability Insurance (OASDI) program.
[5]Cost per hour worked is $0.01 or less.
[6]Less than .05 percent.
[7]Includes severance pay and supplemental unemployment benefits.

Table 6-8. Employer Compensation Costs Per Hour Worked for Employee Compensation and Costs as a Percent of Total Compensation: State and Local Government Workers, by Occupational and Industry Workers, March 2005

(Dollars, percent of total compensation.)

Series	Total compensation	Wages and Salaries	Cost per hour worked by year						
			Total	Paid Leave	Supplemental pay	Insurance	Retirement and savings	Legally required benefits	Other benefits [1]
COSTS PER HOUR WORKED									
STATE AND LOCAL GOVERNMENT WORKERS	34.21	23.69	10.52	2.60	0.30	3.48	2.07	2.02	0.05
Occupational Group									
Management, professional, and related	41.63	30.05	11.59	2.79	0.18	3.82	2.43	2.31	0.06
Professional and related	41.36	30.17	11.19	2.49	0.18	3.77	2.39	2.29	0.06
Teachers[2]	46.41	34.69	11.73	2.37	0.10	3.87	2.84	2.48	0.07
Primary, secondary, and special education school teachers ...	45.08	33.47	11.61	2.35	0.10	4.08	2.66	2.33	0.09
Sales and office	23.32	14.97	8.35	2.23	0.16	3.18	1.27	1.48	0.03
Office and administrative support	23.31	14.97	8.35	2.22	0.16	3.18	1.27	1.48	0.03
Service	25.94	16.44	9.50	2.38	0.61	2.82	2.00	1.64	0.05
Industry and Health Services									
Education and health services	36.08	25.95	10.13	2.37	0.20	3.46	2.02	2.02	0.05
Educational services	36.76	26.62	10.14	2.27	0.13	3.54	2.12	2.02	0.05
Elementary and secondary schools	35.96	26.13	9.83	2.03	0.11	3.69	2.00	1.94	0.07
Junior colleges, colleges, and universities	39.37	28.27	11.10	2.98	0.17	3.14	2.52	2.28	(3)
Health care and social assistance	31.51	21.45	10.06	3.06	0.68	2.93	1.32	2.04	0.04
Hospitals	28.80	19.19	9.61	2.90	0.70	2.69	1.26	2.01	0.05
Public administration	31.39	20.25	11.15	2.98	0.46	3.47	2.24	1.93	0.06
PERCENT OF TOTAL COMPENSATION									
STATE AND LOCAL GOVERNMENT WORKERS	100.0	69.2	30.8	7.6	0.9	10.2	6.1	5.9	0.2
Occupational Group									
Management, professional, and related	100.0	72.2	27.8	6.7	0.4	9.2	5.8	5.6	0.1
Professional and related	100.0	72.9	27.1	6.0	0.4	9.1	5.8	5.5	0.2
Teachers[2]	100.0	74.7	25.3	5.1	0.2	8.3	6.1	5.3	0.2
Primary, secondary, and special education school teachers ...	100.0	74.2	25.8	5.2	0.2	9.1	5.9	5.2	0.2
Sales and office	100.0	64.2	35.8	9.5	0.7	13.6	5.4	6.4	0.1
Office and administrative support	100.0	64.2	35.8	9.5	0.7	13.6	5.5	6.3	0.1
Service	100.0	63.4	36.6	9.2	2.3	10.9	7.7	6.3	0.2
Industry Group									
Education and health services	100.0	71.9	28.1	6.6	0.5	9.6	5.6	5.6	0.1
Educational services	100.0	72.4	27.6	6.2	0.3	9.6	5.8	5.5	0.1
Elementary and secondary schools	100.0	72.7	27.3	5.6	0.3	10.3	5.5	5.4	0.2
Junior colleges, colleges, and universities	100.0	71.8	28.2	7.6	0.4	8.0	6.4	5.8	(4)
Health care and social assistance	100.0	68.1	31.9	9.7	2.1	9.3	4.2	6.5	0.1
Hospitals	100.0	66.6	33.4	10.1	2.4	9.3	4.4	7.0	0.2
Public administration	100.0	64.5	35.5	9.5	1.5	11.1	7.1	6.1	0.2

Note: The sum of individual items may not equal totals due to rounding.

[1] Includes severance pay and supplemental unemployment benefits.
[2] Includes postsecondary teachers; primary, secondary, and special education teachers; and other teachers and instructors.
[3] Cost per hour worked is $0.01 or less.
[4] Less than .05 percent.

NOTES AND DEFINITIONS

EMPLOYEE BENEFITS SURVEY

Note: The Employee Benefits Survey is now part of the National Compensation Survey (NCS), which also includes the Employment Cost Index.

Collection and Coverage

The statistics in this chapter represent the integration of data on employee benefits into the NCS. Prior to 1999, surveys of different sectors of the economy were conducted in alternating years; medium and large private establishments were studied during odd years, and small private establishments during even years. Since those surveys have been replaced by the new survey, the tables previously presented in this *Handbook* have been discontinued. Data for all private workers are collected annually.

Definition of Survey Terms

Incidence refers to different methods of computing the number or percentage of employees who receive a benefit plan or specific benefit feature. Access to a benefit is determined on an occupational basis within an establishment; either all employees or no employees in a particular occupation in an establishment have the benefit available to them. The benefits published in Table 6-9 refer to employee access.

Participation refers to the proportion of employees covered by a benefit. There will be cases where employees with access to a plan will not participate. For example, some employees may decline to participate in a health insurance plan if there is an employee cost involved. The benefits published in Table 6-9 refer to employee participation. For a listing of selected benefit definitions, see *Glossary of Compensation Terms*, Report 923 (August 1998), Bureau of Labor Statistics, U.S. Department of Labor.

Survey Scope

The 2000 NCS benefits incidence survey obtained data from 1,436 private industry establishments, representing over 107 million workers. Of this number, nearly 86 million were full-time workers and the remainder—nearly 22 million—were part-time workers. The NCS uses the establishment's definition of full- and part-time status. For purposes of this survey, an establishment is an economic unit that produces goods or services, a central administrative office, or an auxiliary unit providing support services to a company. For private industries, the establishment is usually at a single physical location.

Sources of Additional Information

For a listing of selected benefit definitions, see *Glossary of Compensation Terms*, BLS, August 1998, Report 923. Additional data and further information on methodology and sampling are available in BLS Bulletin 2555, January 2003. Also see BLS news release USDL-05-1571. The NCS was described in an article in the fifth edition of this *Handbook*.

Table 6-9. Percent of Workers That are Participating in or with Access to Selected Benefits, March 2005

(Percent.)

Benefit program	Total employees	Worker characteristic[1]							Establishment characteristic			
		White–collar occupations	Blue–collar occupations	Service occupations	Full–time	Part–time	Union	Nonunion	Goods–producing	Service–producing	1–99 workers	100 workers or more
PARTICIPATING IN SELECTED BENEFITS												
Retirement Benefits												
All	50	61	51	22	60	19	85	46	64	47	37	67
Defined benefit	21	24	26	7	25	9	72	15	32	18	9	36
Defined contribution	42	53	38	18	50	14	43	41	50	39	32	53
Health Care Benefits												
Medical care	53	58	61	27	66	12	83	49	70	48	43	65
Dental care	36	42	39	17	45	9	67	33	49	33	24	51
Vision care	22	24	25	12	27	6	51	19	30	20	14	32
Outpatient prescription drug coverage	48	52	56	25	59	11	77	44	66	43	37	61
Insurance and Disability												
Life insurance	49	56	52	24	61	10	63	47	60	46	34	67
Short-term disability	39	43	44	21	47	13	66	36	53	35	27	54
Long-term disability	29	40	21	11	36	5	28	29	30	28	17	43
ACCESS TO SELECTED BENEFITS												
Retirement Benefits												
All	60	70	60	32	69	27	88	56	71	56	44	78
Defined benefit	22	25	26	7	25	10	73	16	33	19	10	37
Defined contribution	53	64	50	28	62	23	49	54	61	51	40	69
Health Care Benefits												
Medical care	70	77	77	44	85	22	92	68	85	66	59	84
Dental care	46	54	47	25	56	14	73	43	56	43	31	65
Vision care	29	33	30	19	35	9	57	26	36	27	19	41
Outpatient prescription drug coverage	64	69	71	41	78	20	87	61	80	59	52	79
Insurance and Disability												
Life insurance	52	59	55	28	64	12	65	50	63	48	37	70
Short-term disability	40	44	46	23	48	14	67	37	55	36	28	55
Long-term disability	30	41	23	12	38	5	30	30	31	30	19	44
Selected Leave Benefits												
Paid holidays	77	85	81	49	89	37	87	75	85	74	68	87
Paid vacations	77	83	80	59	90	36	86	77	86	75	70	87
Paid jury duty	69	80	65	47	77	43	83	68	73	68	57	85
Paid military leave	48	57	43	33	54	30	55	47	54	46	36	64
Employer Assistance for Child Care												
Total	14	19	8	9	16	8	18	14	13	14	5	26
Employer provided funds	3	5	2	2	4	1	3	3	3	3	1	5
On-site and off-site child care	5	7	2	4	6	3	7	5	4	6	2	9
Child care resource and referral	10	14	6	5	11	5	16	9	11	10	3	19
Adoption assistance	9	14	7	2	11	4	13	9	10	9	3	17
Other Benefits												
Long-term care insurance	11	17	6	4	13	6	15	11	10	12	4	21
Flexible work place	4	7	2	1	5	2	2	4	3	4	3	5
Employer-provided home PC	3	4	1	1	3	1	2	3	4	2	1	4
Subsidized commuting	5	7	3	2	6	2	6	5	4	5	2	8

[1]Employees are classified as working either a full-time or part-time schedule based on the definition used by each establishment. Union workers are those whose wages are determined through collective bargaining.

Table 6-10. Medical Care Benefits: Percent of Participants Required to Contribute and Average Employee Contribution, Private Industry, March 2005

(Dollars, percent.)

Benefit program	Total employees	Worker characteristic[1]							Establishment characteristic			
		White-collar occupations	Blue-collar occupations	Service occupations	Full-time	Part-time	Union	Nonunion	Goods-producing	Service-producing	1-99 workers	100 workers or more
SINGLE COVERAGE												
Average monthly employer premium	252.22	251.12	254.98	249.09	252.76	242.43	295.11	243.99	256.05	250.61	245.44	257.80
Employee contributions not required	24	22	29	21	24	20	43	21	27	23	31	18
Employee contributions required	76	78	71	79	76	80	57	79	73	77	69	82
FAMILY COVERAGE												
Average monthly employer premium	575.77	580.17	586.14	515.37	577.24	548.49	645.90	562.48	611.16	560.89	524.54	617.45
Employee contributions not required	12	9	18	11	12	17	35	8	18	10	14	11
Employee contributions required	88	91	82	89	88	83	65	92	82	90	86	89

[1]Employees are classified as working either a full-time or part-time schedule based on the definition used by each establishment. Union workers are those whose wages are determined through collective bargaining.

Table 6-11. Mean Hourly Earnings and Weekly Hours by Selected Characteristics, Private Industry and State and Local Government, National Compensation Survey[1], July 2004

(Dollars, numbers.)

Worker and establishment characteristics and geographic areas	Total		Private		State and local government	
	Mean hourly earnings	Mean weekly hours	Mean hourly earnings	Mean weekly hours	Mean hourly earnings	Mean weekly hours
TOTAL	18.09	35.7	17.25	35.6	22.77	36.8
Worker Characteristics [2]						
White–collar occupations	22.34	36.1	21.53	36.0	25.73	36.5
Professional specialty and technical	29.40	36.3	28.87	36.4	30.50	36.1
Executive, administrative, and managerial	32.43	39.9	32.84	40.2	30.48	38.4
Sales	15.20	32.3	15.21	32.3	14.22	34.1
Administrative support	14.21	36.6	14.13	36.6	14.57	36.5
Blue–collar occupations	15.46	38.0	15.34	38.1	17.59	37.6
Precision production, craft, and repair	19.46	39.5	19.41	39.5	20.05	39.8
Machine operators, assemblers, and inspectors	13.70	39.1	13.69	39.1	16.70	38.4
Transportation and material moving	15.01	37.7	14.83	38.1	16.64	34.4
Handlers, equipment cleaners, helpers, and laborers	11.61	35.0	11.42	34.8	14.45	38.6
Service occupations	10.65	31.8	9.12	30.7	17.06	37.1
Full–time	19.14	39.6	18.36	39.7	23.17	38.8
Part–time	10.01	20.5	9.59	20.6	15.57	19.2
Union	22.18	36.8	20.32	36.9	24.80	36.7
Nonunion	17.21	35.5	16.83	35.4	20.82	36.8
Time	17.86	35.6	16.93	35.4	22.77	36.8
Incentive	22.45	38.3	22.45	38.3	. . .	. . .
Establishment Characteristics						
Goods–producing	(3)	(3)	18.96	39.5	(3)	(3)
Service–producing	(3)	(3)	16.63	34.3	(3)	(3)
1 to 99 workers [4]	15.39	34.5	15.35	34.5	18.23	36.1
100 to 499 workers	17.23	36.3	16.73	36.4	21.18	35.6
500 to 999 workers	19.94	37.0	19.05	37.3	23.00	36.1
1000 to 2499 workers	21.65	36.7	21.27	36.7	22.64	36.6
2500 workers or more	24.72	37.4	25.93	37.3	23.69	37.6
Geographic Areas						
Metropolitan	18.59	35.7	17.76	35.5	23.64	36.7
Nonmetropolitan	14.79	36.2	13.50	35.9	19.15	36.9
New England	20.12	34.5	19.20	34.4	26.10	35.8
Middle Atlantic	20.59	35.0	19.62	35.0	26.15	35.5
East North Central	18.21	35.3	17.38	35.2	23.57	36.0
West North Central	16.84	35.3	16.02	35.0	21.40	37.2
South Atlantic	16.71	36.2	16.05	35.7	19.94	38.4
East South Central	14.49	37.4	13.87	37.4	18.99	37.4
West South Central	16.07	36.6	15.47	36.3	19.10	38.2
Mountain	16.90	35.8	15.80	35.6	23.00	37.2
Pacific	20.70	35.7	19.63	35.8	26.45	35.4

[1]This survey covers all 50 states. Collection was conducted between December 2003 and January 2005. The average reference period was July 2004.
[2]Employees are classified as working either a full-time or part-time schedule based on the definition used by each establishment. Union workers are those whose wages are determined through collective bargaining. Wages of time workers are based solely on hourly rate or salary; incentive workers are those whose wages are at least partly based on productivity payments such as piece rates, commissions, and production bonuses.
[3]Classification of establishments into goods-producing and service-producing industries applies to private industry only.
[4]Estimates include private establishments employing 1 to 99 workers and state and local government establishments employing 50 to 99 workers.
. . . = Not available.

Table 6-12. Mean Hourly Earnings and Weekly Hours for Selected Characteristics, Metropolitan and Nonmetropolitan Areas[1], National Compensation Survey[2], July 2004

(Dollars, numbers.)

Occupation	Total		Metropolitan areas		Nonmetropolitan areas	
	Mean hourly earnings	Mean weekly hours	Mean hourly earnings	Mean weekly hours	Mean hourly earnings	Mean weekly hours
TOTAL	18.09	35.7	18.59	35.7	14.79	36.2
Industry						
Private industry	17.25	35.6	17.76	35.5	13.50	35.9
State and local government	22.77	36.8	23.64	36.7	19.15	36.9
Worker Characteristics[3]						
White–collar occupations	22.34	36.1	22.78	36.1	18.45	36.1
Professional specialty and technical	29.40	36.3	30.13	36.3	23.99	36.1
Executive, administrative, and managerial	32.43	39.9	32.89	39.9	27.39	39.9
Sales	15.20	32.3	15.59	32.3	11.44	32.6
Administrative support	14.21	36.6	14.46	36.6	12.00	36.6
Blue–collar occupations	15.46	38.0	15.66	37.9	14.32	38.6
Precision production, craft, and repair	19.46	39.5	19.73	39.5	17.74	39.8
Machine operators, assemblers, and inspectors	13.70	39.1	13.80	39.0	13.27	39.6
Transportation and material moving	15.01	37.7	15.08	37.7	14.58	37.7
Handlers, equipment cleaners, helpers, and laborers	11.61	35.0	11.78	34.8	10.53	36.3
Service occupations	10.65	31.8	10.92	31.5	9.39	33.3
Full-time	19.14	39.6	19.70	39.5	15.44	39.6
Part-time	10.01	20.5	10.12	20.5	9.23	20.8
Union	22.18	36.8	22.56	36.7	19.11	38.0
Nonunion	17.21	35.5	17.70	35.5	14.03	35.9
Time	17.86	35.6	18.34	35.6	14.70	36.0
Incentive	22.45	38.3	23.11	38.2	16.79	40.0
Establishment Characteristics						
Goods–producing[4]	18.96	39.5	. . .	. . .	. . .	. . .
Service–producing[4]	16.63	34.3	. . .	. . .	. . .	. . .
1 to 99 workers[5]	15.39	34.5	15.69	34.6	12.98	34.0
100 to 499 workers	17.23	36.3	17.66	36.2	15.12	36.9
500 to 999 workers	19.94	37.0	20.46	36.8	17.83	37.8
1000 to 2499 workers	21.65	36.7	22.61	36.4	16.56	38.2
2500 workers or more	24.72	37.4	25.32	37.3	14.19	40.0
Geographic Areas						
New England	20.12	34.5	20.62	34.5	15.85	34.6
Middle Atlantic	20.59	35.0	20.80	35.1	16.59	35.0
East North Central	18.21	35.3	18.60	35.3	15.58	35.6
West North Central	16.84	35.3	17.61	35.5	14.00	35.0
South Atlantic	16.71	36.2	17.06	36.1	14.35	36.8
East South Central	14.49	37.4	15.42	36.6	12.99	38.7
West South Central	16.07	36.6	16.22	36.7	14.94	35.7
Mountain	16.90	35.8	16.97	35.8	16.60	35.5
Pacific	20.70	35.7	20.94	35.7	16.43	34.9

[1]A metropolitan area can be a Metropolitan Statistical Area (MSA) or a Consolidated Metropolitan Statistical Area (CMSA) as defined by the Office of Management and Budget, 1994. Nonmetropolitan areas are counties that do not fit the definitions above.
[2]This survey covers all 50 states. Collection was conducted between December 2003 and January 2005. The average reference period was July 2004.
[3]Employees are classified as working either a full-time or part-time schedule based on the definition used by each establishment. Union workers are those whose wages are determined through collective bargaining. Wages of time workers are based solely on hourly rate or salary; incentive workers are those whose wages are at least partially based on productivity payments such as piece rates, commissions, and production bonuses.
[4]Classification of establishments into goods-producing and service-producing industries applies to private industry only.
[5]Estimates include private establishments employing 1 to 99 workers and state and local government establishments employing 50 to 99 workers.
. . . = Not available.

Table 6-13. Mean Hourly Earnings and Weekly Hours for Selected Occupations, Full-Time and Part-Time Workers, [1] **National Compensation Survey** [2]**, July 2004**

(Dollars, numbers.)

Occupation	Total		Full-time		Part-time	
	Mean hourly earnings	Mean weekly hours	Mean hourly earnings	Mean weekly hours	Mean hourly earnings	Mean weekly hours
ALL OCCUPATIONS	18.09	35.7	19.14	39.6	10.01	20.5
White–Collar Occupations	22.34	36.1	23.40	39.5	12.61	20.3
Professional specialty and technical	29.40	36.3	29.77	38.9	23.92	18.3
Executive, administrative, and managerial	32.43	39.9	32.54	40.4	22.91	18.4
Sales	15.20	32.3	17.74	40.1	7.96	20.8
Administrative support, including clerical	14.21	36.6	14.51	39.3	11.15	21.5
Blue–Collar Occupations	15.46	38.0	15.86	40.0	9.40	21.5
Precision production, craft, and repair	19.46	39.5	19.54	40.0	12.60	20.1
Machine operators, assemblers, and inspectors	13.70	39.1	13.83	39.8	8.98	24.5
Transportation and material moving	15.01	37.7	15.47	40.9	10.35	20.9
Handlers, equipment cleaners, helpers, and laborers	11.61	35.0	12.15	39.7	8.69	21.3
Service	10.65	31.8	11.72	39.0	7.41	20.4

[1]Total includes full-time and part-time workers. Employees are classified as working either a full-time or a part-time schedule based on the definition used by each establishment. Therefore, a worker with a schedule of 35 hours per week might be considered a full-time employee in one establishment, but classified as part-time in another firm with a 40-hour week minimum full-time schedule.
[2]This survey covers all 50 states. Collection was conducted between December 2003 and January 2005. The average reference period was July 2004.

PART SEVEN

PRICES

PRICES

HIGHLIGHTS

This part examines the movement of prices, one of the most important indicators of the state of the economy. It covers three price indexes: prices received by producers (PPI); prices paid by consumers (CPI); and prices involved in foreign trade, export, and import price indexes.

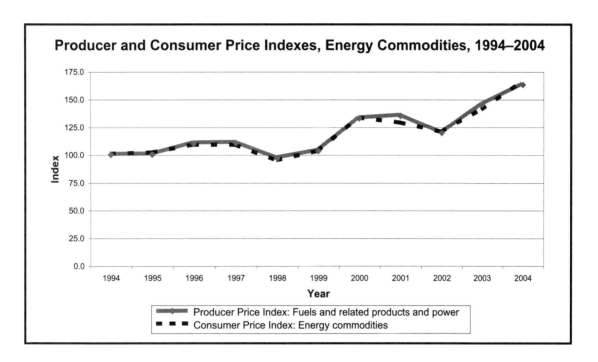

The graph shows that the two indexes have moved virtually identically. There has been a sharp increase in fuel prices since 2002, most notably in gasoline and heating fuel. From 1994 to 2004, energy commodities have increased 65 percent; they have increased 24.5 percent since 2000. (Tables 7-2 and 7-5)

OTHER HIGHLIGHTS:

- The PPI for finished goods continued to rise in 2004. It increased 3.6 percent, largely as a result of the price increase in consumer goods. Capital goods increased much more slowly, having risen at a rate of only 1.4 percent. (Table 7-1)

- The PPI for all commodities rose 6.2 percent from 2003 to 2004. Metal and metal products led the way with a 15.8 percent increase. Additionally, fuels rose 12.4 percent, farm products went up 10.6 percent, and lumber increased 10.2 percent. (Table 7-2)

- The CPI for all items rose 2.7 percent in 2004. Although total commodities increased by only 2.3 percent, the CPI for energy commodities had a significant gain, rising 17.9 percent in just one year. (Table 7-4 and Table 7-5)

- Housing, transportation, and food now constitute 75.8 percent of the total weight in the CPI-W and 74.7 percent of the weight in the CPI-U. (Table 7-9)

- December 2003 to December 2004 saw a 6.7 percent rise in the total import price index with a 43.5 percent increase in the price of gas and a 28 percent increase in petroleum product prices. (Table 7-12) The export price index (XPI) increased 4.0 percent. However, it grew much more rapidly for mineral fuels, lubricants, and related materials, increasing 32.3 percent in just one year. (Table 7-11)

NOTES AND DEFINITIONS

PRODUCER PRICE INDEX

Coverage

The *Producer Price Index* (PPI) measures average changes in prices received by domestic producers of goods and services. Most of the information used in calculating the indexes is obtained through the systematic sampling of nearly every industry in the manufacturing and mining sectors of the economy. The PPI program also includes data from other sectors, including agriculture, fishing, forestry, services, and gas and electricity. As producer price indexes are designed to measure only the change in prices received for the output of domestic industries, imports are not included. The sample currently contains about 100,000 price quotations per month.

Producer price indexes are based on selling prices reported by establishments of all sizes as selected by probability sampling, with the probability of selection proportionate to size. Individual items and transaction terms from these firms are also chosen by probability proportionate to size. BLS strongly encourages cooperating companies to supply actual transaction prices at the time of shipment to minimize the use of list prices. Prices are normally reported monthly by mail questionnaire for the Tuesday of the week containing the 13th of the month.

Price data are always provided on a voluntary and confidential basis; only BLS employees, sworn to secrecy, are allowed access to individual company price reports. BLS publishes price indexes instead of unit dollar prices. All producer price indexes are routinely subject to revision once, four months after original publication, to reflect the availability of late reports and corrections by respondents.

There are three primary systems of indexes within the PPI program: (1) stage-of-processing indexes, (2) indexes for the net output of industries and their products, and (3) commodity indexes. The commodity-based *stage-of-processing* structure organizes products by class of buyer and degree of fabrication. The entire output of various industries is sampled to derive price indexes for the net output of industries and their products. The commodity structure organizes products by similarity of end-use or material composition.

Within the commodity stage-of-processing system, finished goods are commodities that will not undergo further processing and are ready for sale to the final demand user—either an individual consumer or a business firm. Consumer foods include unprocessed foods, such as eggs and fresh vegetables, as well as processed foods, such as bakery products and meats. Other finished consumer goods include durable goods, such as automobiles, household furniture, and appliances; and nondurable goods, such as apparel and home heating oil. Capital equipment includes producer durable goods, such as heavy motor trucks, tractors, and machine tools.

The stage-of-processing category for intermediate materials, supplies, and components consists partly of commodities that have been processed but require further processing. Examples of such semi-finished goods include flour, cotton, yarn, steel mill products, and lumber. The intermediate goods category also encompasses physically complete nondurable goods purchased by business firms as inputs for their operations. Examples include diesel fuel, belts and belting, paper boxes, and fertilizers.

Crude materials for further processing are products entering the market for the first time that have not been manufactured or fabricated and that are not sold directly to consumers. Crude foodstuffs and feedstuffs include items such as grains and livestock. Examples of crude nonfood materials include raw cotton, crude petroleum, coal, hides and skins, and iron and steel scrap.

Producer price indexes for the net output of industries and their products are grouped according to the Standard Industrial Classification (SIC) and the census product code extensions of the SIC. Industry price indexes are compatible with other economic time series organized by SIC codes, such as data on employment, wages, and productivity.

Net output values of shipments are used as weights for industry indexes. Net output values refer to the value of shipments from establishments in one industry shipped to establishments classified in another industry. However, *weights for commodity price indexes* are based on gross shipment values, including shipment values between establishments within the same industry. As a result, commodity aggregate indexes, such as the *all commodities index*, are affected by the multiple counting of price change at successive stages of processing. This can lead to exaggerated or misleading signals about inflation. Stage-of-processing indexes partially correct this defect, but industry indexes consistently correct this weakness at all levels of aggregation. Therefore, industry and stage-of-processing indexes are more appropriate than commodity aggregate indexes for economic analysis of general price trends.

Weights for most traditional commodity groupings of the PPI, as well as all indexes calculated from traditional commodity groupings (such as stage-of-processing indexes), currently reflect 1992 values of shipments as reported in the Census of Manufactures and other sources. Major industry group indexes, which are based on the SIC system, are currently calculated using 1992 net output weights.

With the release of data for January 2004, the Producer Price Index program changed its basis for industry classification from the 1987 Standard Industrial Classification (SIC) system to the North American Industry Classification System (NAICS). The PPI treats the SIC-to-NAICS comparison as continuous if 80 percent or more of the weight of the SIC- based index comprises at least 80 percent of the weight of the NAICS-based index. All index series that have passed this test are published under the NAICS structure using the index base date and price index history established by the SIC-based index.

Sources of Additional Information

Additional information is published monthly by the BLS in the *Producer Price Index Detailed Report*. For information on the underlying concepts and methodology of the Producer Price Index, see Chapter 14 in the *BLS Handbook of Methods* available on the BLS Web site.

Table 7-1. Producer Price Indexes by Stage of Processing, 1947–2004

(1982 = 100.)

Year	Crude materials for further processing				Intermediate materials, supplies, and components						Finished goods		
	Total	Foodstuffs and feedstuffs	Nonfood materials, except fuel	Fuel	Total	Materials and components for construction	Components for manufacturing	Processed fuels and lubricants	Containers	Supplies	Total	Consumer goods	Capital equipment
1947	31.7	45.1	24.0	7.5	23.3	22.5	21.3	14.4	23.4	28.5	26.4	28.6	19.8
1948	34.7	48.8	26.7	8.9	25.2	24.9	23.0	16.4	24.4	29.8	28.5	30.8	21.6
1949	30.1	40.5	24.3	8.8	24.2	24.9	23.4	14.9	24.5	28.0	27.7	29.4	22.7
1950	32.7	43.4	27.8	8.8	25.3	26.2	24.3	15.2	25.2	29.0	28.2	29.9	23.2
1951	37.6	50.2	32.0	9.0	28.4	28.7	27.6	15.9	29.6	32.6	30.8	32.7	25.5
1952	34.5	47.3	27.8	9.0	27.5	28.5	27.6	15.7	28.0	32.6	30.6	32.3	25.9
1953	31.9	42.3	26.6	9.3	27.7	29.0	28.1	15.8	28.0	31.0	30.3	31.7	26.3
1954	31.6	42.3	26.1	8.9	27.9	29.1	28.3	15.8	28.5	31.7	30.4	31.7	26.7
1955	30.4	38.4	27.5	8.9	28.4	30.3	29.5	15.8	28.9	31.2	30.5	31.5	27.4
1956	30.6	37.6	28.6	9.5	29.6	31.8	32.2	16.3	31.0	32.0	31.3	32.0	29.5
1957	31.2	39.2	28.2	10.1	30.3	32.0	33.5	17.2	32.4	32.3	32.5	32.9	31.3
1958	31.9	41.6	27.1	10.2	30.4	32.0	33.8	16.2	33.2	33.1	33.2	33.6	32.1
1959	31.1	38.8	28.1	10.4	30.8	32.9	34.2	16.2	33.0	33.5	33.1	33.3	32.7
1960	30.4	38.4	26.9	10.5	30.8	32.7	34.0	16.6	33.4	33.3	33.4	33.6	32.8
1961	30.2	37.9	27.2	10.5	30.6	32.2	33.7	16.8	33.2	33.7	33.4	33.6	32.9
1962	30.5	38.6	27.1	10.4	30.6	32.1	33.4	16.7	33.6	34.5	33.5	33.7	33.0
1963	29.9	37.5	26.7	10.5	30.7	32.2	33.4	16.6	33.2	35.0	33.4	33.5	33.1
1964	29.6	36.6	27.2	10.5	30.8	32.5	33.7	16.2	32.9	34.7	33.5	33.6	33.4
1965	31.1	39.2	27.7	10.6	31.2	32.8	34.2	16.5	33.5	35.0	34.1	34.2	33.8
1966	33.1	42.7	28.3	10.9	32.0	33.6	35.4	16.8	34.5	36.5	35.2	35.4	34.6
1967	31.3	40.3	26.5	11.3	32.2	34.0	36.5	16.9	35.0	36.8	35.6	35.6	35.8
1968	31.8	40.9	27.1	11.5	33.0	35.7	37.3	16.5	35.9	37.1	36.6	36.5	37.0
1969	33.9	44.1	28.4	12.0	34.1	37.7	38.5	16.6	37.2	37.8	38.0	37.9	38.3
1970	35.2	45.2	29.1	13.8	35.4	38.3	40.6	17.7	39.0	39.7	39.3	39.1	40.1
1971	36.0	46.1	29.4	15.7	36.8	40.8	41.9	19.5	40.8	40.8	40.5	40.2	41.7
1972	39.9	51.5	32.3	16.8	38.2	43.0	42.9	20.1	42.7	42.5	41.8	41.5	42.8
1973	54.5	72.6	42.9	18.6	42.4	46.5	44.3	22.2	45.2	51.7	45.6	46.0	44.2
1974	61.4	76.4	54.5	24.8	52.5	55.0	51.1	33.6	53.3	56.8	52.6	53.1	50.5
1975	61.6	77.4	50.0	30.6	58.0	60.1	57.8	39.4	60.0	61.8	58.2	58.2	58.2
1976	63.4	76.8	54.9	34.5	60.9	64.1	60.8	42.3	63.1	65.8	60.8	60.4	62.1
1977	65.5	77.5	56.3	42.0	64.9	69.3	64.5	47.7	65.9	69.3	64.7	64.3	66.1
1978	73.4	87.3	61.9	48.2	69.5	76.5	69.2	49.9	71.0	72.9	69.8	69.4	71.3
1979	85.9	100.0	75.5	57.3	78.4	84.2	75.8	61.6	79.4	80.2	77.6	77.5	77.5
1980	95.3	104.6	91.8	69.4	90.3	91.3	84.6	85.0	89.1	89.9	88.0	88.6	85.8
1981	103.0	103.9	109.8	84.8	98.6	97.9	94.7	100.6	96.7	96.9	96.1	96.6	94.6
1982	100.0	100.0	100.0	100.0	100.0	100.0	100.0	100.0	100.0	100.0	100.0	100.0	100.0
1983	101.3	101.8	98.8	105.1	100.6	102.8	102.4	95.4	100.4	101.8	101.6	101.3	102.8
1984	103.5	104.7	101.0	105.1	103.1	105.6	105.0	95.7	105.9	104.1	103.7	103.3	105.2
1985	95.8	94.8	94.3	102.7	102.7	107.3	106.4	92.8	109.0	104.4	104.7	103.8	107.5
1986	87.7	93.2	76.0	92.2	99.1	108.1	107.5	72.7	110.3	105.6	103.2	101.4	109.7
1987	93.7	96.2	88.5	84.1	101.5	109.8	108.8	73.3	114.5	107.7	105.4	103.6	111.7
1988	96.0	106.1	85.9	82.1	107.1	116.1	112.3	71.2	120.1	113.7	108.0	106.2	114.3
1989	103.1	111.2	95.8	85.3	112.0	121.3	116.4	76.4	125.4	118.1	113.6	112.1	118.8
1990	108.9	113.1	107.3	84.8	114.5	122.9	119.0	85.9	127.7	119.4	119.2	118.2	122.9
1991	101.2	105.5	97.5	82.9	114.4	124.5	121.0	85.3	128.1	121.4	121.7	120.5	126.7
1992	100.4	105.1	94.2	84.0	114.7	126.5	122.0	84.5	127.7	122.7	123.2	121.7	129.1
1993	102.4	108.4	94.1	87.1	116.2	132.0	123.0	84.7	126.4	125.0	124.7	123.0	131.4
1994	101.8	106.5	97.0	82.4	118.5	136.6	124.3	83.1	129.7	127.0	125.5	123.3	134.1
1995	102.7	105.8	105.8	72.1	124.9	142.1	126.5	84.2	148.8	132.1	127.9	125.6	136.7
1996	113.8	121.5	105.7	92.6	125.7	143.6	126.9	90.0	141.1	135.9	131.3	129.5	138.3
1997	111.1	112.2	103.5	101.3	125.6	146.5	126.4	89.3	136.0	135.9	131.8	130.2	138.2
1998	96.8	103.9	84.5	86.7	123.0	146.8	125.9	81.1	140.8	134.8	130.7	128.9	137.6
1999	98.2	98.7	91.1	91.2	123.2	148.9	125.7	84.6	142.5	134.2	133.0	132.0	137.6
2000	120.6	100.2	118.0	136.9	129.2	150.7	126.2	102.0	151.6	136.9	138.0	138.2	138.8
2001	121.0	106.1	101.5	151.4	129.7	150.6	126.4	104.5	153.1	138.7	140.7	141.5	139.7
2002	108.1	99.5	101.0	117.3	127.8	151.3	126.1	96.3	152.1	138.9	138.9	139.4	139.1
2003	135.3	113.5	116.9	185.7	133.7	153.6	125.9	112.6	153.7	141.5	143.3	145.3	139.5
2004	159.0	127.0	149.2	211.4	142.6	166.4	127.4	124.3	159.3	146.7	148.5	151.7	141.4

Table 7-2. Producer Price Indexes by Commodity Groups, 1913–2004

(1982 = 100.)

| Year | All com-modities | Farm products | Processed foods and feeds | Industrial commodities | | | | | | | | | | | | | |
				Total	Textile products and apparel	Hides, leather, and related products	Fuels and related products and power	Chemic-als and related products	Rubber and plastics products	Lumber and wood products	Pulp, paper, and allied products	Metals and metal products	Machin-ery and equip-ment	Furniture and house-hold durables	Nonme-tallic mineral products	Trans-porta-tion equip-ment	Miscel-laneous products
1913	12.0	18.0	. . .	11.9	. . .	. . .	. . .	. . .	. . .	. . .	. . .	. . .	. . .	. . .	. . .	. . .	. . .
1914	11.8	17.9	. . .	11.3	. . .	. . .	. . .	. . .	. . .	. . .	. . .	. . .	. . .	. . .	. . .	. . .	. . .
1915	12.0	18.0	. . .	11.6	. . .	. . .	. . .	. . .	. . .	. . .	. . .	. . .	. . .	. . .	. . .	. . .	. . .
1916	14.7	21.3	. . .	15.0	. . .	. . .	. . .	. . .	. . .	. . .	. . .	. . .	. . .	. . .	. . .	. . .	. . .
1917	20.2	32.6	. . .	19.5	. . .	. . .	. . .	. . .	. . .	. . .	. . .	. . .	. . .	. . .	. . .	. . .	. . .
1918	22.6	37.4	. . .	21.1	. . .	. . .	. . .	. . .	. . .	. . .	. . .	. . .	. . .	. . .	. . .	. . .	. . .
1919	23.9	39.8	. . .	22.0	. . .	. . .	. . .	. . .	. . .	. . .	. . .	. . .	. . .	. . .	. . .	. . .	. . .
1920	26.6	38.0	. . .	27.4	. . .	. . .	. . .	. . .	. . .	. . .	. . .	. . .	. . .	. . .	. . .	. . .	. . .
1921	16.8	22.3	. . .	17.8	. . .	. . .	. . .	. . .	. . .	. . .	. . .	. . .	. . .	. . .	. . .	. . .	. . .
1922	16.7	23.7	. . .	17.4	. . .	. . .	. . .	. . .	. . .	. . .	. . .	. . .	. . .	. . .	. . .	. . .	. . .
1923	17.3	24.9	. . .	17.8	. . .	. . .	. . .	. . .	. . .	. . .	. . .	. . .	. . .	. . .	. . .	. . .	. . .
1924	16.9	25.2	. . .	17.0	. . .	. . .	. . .	. . .	. . .	. . .	. . .	. . .	. . .	. . .	. . .	. . .	. . .
1925	17.8	27.7	. . .	17.5	. . .	. . .	. . .	. . .	. . .	. . .	. . .	. . .	. . .	. . .	. . .	. . .	. . .
1926	17.2	25.3	. . .	17.0	. . .	17.1	10.3	. . .	47.1	9.3	. . .	. . .	. . .	28.6	16.4	. . .	. . .
1927	16.5	25.1	. . .	16.0	. . .	18.4	9.1	. . .	35.7	8.8	. . .	. . .	. . .	27.9	15.7	. . .	. . .
1928	16.7	26.7	. . .	15.8	. . .	20.7	8.7	. . .	28.3	8.5	. . .	12.9	. . .	27.2	16.2	. . .	. . .
1929	16.4	26.4	. . .	15.6	. . .	18.6	8.6	. . .	24.6	8.8	. . .	13.3	. . .	27.0	16.0	. . .	. . .
1930	14.9	22.4	. . .	14.5	. . .	17.1	8.1	. . .	21.5	8.0	. . .	12.0	. . .	26.5	15.9	. . .	. . .
1931	12.6	16.4	. . .	12.8	. . .	14.7	7.0	. . .	18.3	6.5	. . .	10.8	. . .	24.4	14.9	. . .	. . .
1932	11.2	12.2	. . .	11.9	. . .	12.5	7.3	. . .	15.9	5.6	. . .	9.9	. . .	21.5	13.9	. . .	. . .
1933	11.4	13.0	. . .	12.1	. . .	13.8	6.9	16.2	16.7	6.7	. . .	10.2	. . .	21.6	14.7	. . .	. . .
1934	12.9	16.5	. . .	13.3	. . .	14.8	7.6	17.0	19.5	7.8	. . .	11.2	. . .	23.4	15.7	. . .	. . .
1935	13.8	19.8	. . .	13.3	. . .	15.3	7.6	17.7	19.6	7.5	. . .	11.2	. . .	23.2	15.7	. . .	. . .
1936	13.9	20.4	. . .	13.5	. . .	16.3	7.9	17.8	21.1	7.9	. . .	11.4	. . .	23.6	15.8	. . .	. . .
1937	14.9	21.8	. . .	14.5	. . .	17.9	8.0	18.6	24.9	9.3	. . .	13.1	. . .	26.1	16.1	. . .	. . .
1938	13.5	17.3	. . .	13.9	. . .	15.8	7.9	17.7	24.4	8.5	. . .	12.6	. . .	25.5	15.6	. . .	. . .
1939	13.3	16.5	. . .	13.9	. . .	16.3	7.5	17.6	25.4	8.7	. . .	12.5	14.8	25.4	15.3	. . .	. . .
1940	13.5	17.1	. . .	14.1	. . .	17.2	7.4	17.9	23.7	9.6	. . .	12.5	14.9	26.0	15.3	. . .	. . .
1941	15.1	20.8	. . .	15.1	. . .	18.4	7.9	19.5	25.5	11.5	. . .	12.8	15.1	27.6	15.7	. . .	. . .
1942	17.0	26.7	. . .	16.2	. . .	20.1	8.1	21.7	29.7	12.5	. . .	13.0	15.4	29.9	16.3	. . .	. . .
1943	17.8	30.9	. . .	16.5	. . .	20.1	8.3	21.9	30.5	13.2	. . .	12.9	15.2	29.7	16.4	. . .	. . .
1944	17.9	31.2	. . .	16.7	. . .	19.9	8.6	22.2	30.1	14.3	. . .	12.9	15.1	30.5	16.7	. . .	. . .
1945	18.2	32.4	. . .	17.0	. . .	20.1	8.7	22.3	29.2	14.5	. . .	13.1	15.1	30.5	17.4	. . .	. . .
1946	20.8	37.5	. . .	18.6	. . .	23.3	9.3	24.1	29.3	16.6	. . .	14.7	16.6	32.4	18.5	. . .	. . .
1947	25.6	45.1	33.0	22.7	50.6	31.7	11.1	32.1	29.2	25.8	25.1	18.2	19.3	37.2	20.7	. . .	26.6
1948	27.7	48.5	35.3	24.6	52.8	32.1	13.1	32.8	30.2	29.5	26.2	20.7	20.9	39.4	22.4	. . .	27.7
1949	26.3	41.9	32.1	24.1	48.3	30.4	12.4	30.0	29.2	27.3	25.1	20.9	21.9	40.1	23.0	. . .	28.2
1950	27.3	44.0	33.2	25.0	50.2	32.9	12.6	30.4	35.6	31.4	25.7	22.0	22.6	40.9	23.5	. . .	28.6
1951	30.4	51.2	36.9	27.6	56.0	37.7	13.0	34.8	43.7	34.1	30.5	24.5	25.3	44.4	25.0	. . .	30.3
1952	29.6	48.4	36.4	26.9	50.5	30.5	13.0	33.0	39.6	33.2	29.7	24.5	25.3	43.5	25.0	. . .	30.2
1953	29.2	43.8	34.8	27.2	49.3	31.0	13.4	33.4	36.9	33.1	29.6	25.3	25.9	44.4	26.0	. . .	31.0
1954	29.3	43.2	35.4	27.2	48.2	29.5	13.2	33.8	37.5	32.5	29.6	25.5	26.3	44.9	26.6	. . .	31.3
1955	29.3	40.5	33.8	27.8	48.2	29.4	13.2	33.7	42.4	34.1	30.4	27.2	27.2	45.1	27.3	. . .	31.3
1956	30.3	40.0	33.8	29.1	48.2	31.2	13.6	33.9	43.0	34.6	32.4	29.6	29.3	46.3	28.5	. . .	31.7
1957	31.2	41.1	34.8	29.9	48.3	31.2	14.3	34.6	42.8	32.8	33.0	30.2	31.4	47.5	29.6	. . .	32.6
1958	31.6	42.9	36.5	30.0	47.4	31.6	13.7	34.9	42.8	32.5	33.4	30.0	32.1	47.9	29.9	. . .	33.3
1959	31.7	40.2	35.6	30.5	48.1	35.9	13.7	34.8	42.6	34.7	33.7	30.6	32.8	48.0	30.3	. . .	33.4

. . . = Not available.

Table 7-2. Producer Price Indexes by Commodity Groups, 1913–2004—*Continued*

(1982 = 100.)

Year	All commodities	Farm products	Processed foods and feeds	Industrial commodities													
				Total	Textile products and apparel	Hides, leather, and related products	Fuels and related products and power	Chemicals and related products	Rubber and plastics products	Lumber and wood products	Pulp, paper, and allied products	Metals and metal products	Machinery and equipment	Furniture and household durables	Nonmetallic mineral products	Transportation equipment	Miscellaneous products
1960	31.7	40.1	35.6	30.5	48.6	34.6	13.9	34.8	42.7	33.5	34.0	30.6	33.0	47.8	30.4	. . .	33.6
1961	31.6	39.7	36.2	30.4	47.8	34.9	14.0	34.5	41.1	32.0	33.0	30.5	33.0	47.5	30.5	. . .	33.7
1962	31.7	40.4	36.5	30.4	48.2	35.3	14.0	33.9	39.9	32.2	33.4	30.2	33.0	47.2	30.5	. . .	33.9
1963	31.6	39.6	36.8	30.3	48.2	34.3	13.9	33.5	40.1	32.8	33.1	30.3	33.1	46.9	30.3	. . .	34.2
1964	31.6	39.0	36.7	30.5	48.5	34.4	13.5	33.6	39.6	33.5	33.0	31.1	33.3	47.1	30.4	. . .	34.4
1965	32.3	40.7	38.0	30.9	48.8	35.9	13.8	33.9	39.7	33.7	33.3	32.0	33.7	46.8	30.4	. . .	34.7
1966	33.3	43.7	40.2	31.5	48.9	39.4	14.1	34.0	40.5	35.2	34.2	32.8	34.7	47.4	30.7	. . .	35.3
1967	33.4	41.3	39.8	32.0	48.9	38.1	14.4	34.2	41.4	35.1	34.6	33.2	35.9	48.3	31.2	. . .	36.2
1968	34.2	42.3	40.6	32.8	50.7	39.3	14.3	34.1	42.8	39.8	35.0	34.0	37.0	49.7	32.4	. . .	37.0
1969	35.6	45.0	42.7	33.9	51.8	41.5	14.6	34.2	43.6	44.0	36.0	36.0	38.2	50.7	33.6	40.4	38.1
1970	36.9	45.8	44.6	35.2	52.4	42.0	15.3	35.0	44.9	39.9	37.5	38.7	40.0	51.9	35.3	41.9	39.8
1971	38.1	46.6	45.5	36.5	53.3	43.4	16.6	35.6	45.2	44.7	38.1	39.4	41.4	53.1	38.2	44.2	40.8
1972	39.8	51.6	48.0	37.8	55.5	50.0	17.1	35.6	45.3	50.7	39.3	40.9	42.3	53.8	39.4	45.5	41.5
1973	45.0	72.7	58.9	40.3	60.5	54.5	19.4	37.6	46.6	62.2	42.3	44.0	43.7	55.7	40.7	46.1	43.3
1974	53.5	77.4	68.0	49.2	68.0	55.2	30.1	50.2	56.4	64.5	52.5	57.0	50.0	61.8	47.8	50.3	48.1
1975	58.4	77.0	72.6	54.9	67.4	56.5	35.4	62.0	62.2	62.1	59.0	61.5	57.9	67.5	54.4	56.7	53.4
1976	61.1	78.8	70.8	58.4	72.4	63.9	38.3	64.0	66.0	72.2	62.1	65.0	61.3	70.3	58.2	60.5	55.6
1977	64.9	79.4	74.0	62.5	75.3	68.3	43.6	65.9	69.4	83.0	64.6	69.3	65.2	73.2	62.6	64.6	59.4
1978	69.9	87.7	80.6	67.0	78.1	76.1	46.5	68.0	72.4	96.9	67.7	75.3	70.3	77.5	69.6	69.5	66.7
1979	78.7	99.6	88.5	75.7	82.5	96.1	58.9	76.0	80.5	105.5	75.9	86.0	76.7	82.8	77.6	75.3	75.5
1980	89.8	102.9	95.9	88.0	89.7	94.7	82.8	89.0	90.1	101.5	86.3	95.0	86.0	90.7	88.4	82.9	93.6
1981	98.0	105.2	98.9	97.4	97.6	99.3	100.2	98.4	96.4	102.8	94.8	99.6	94.4	95.9	96.7	94.3	96.1
1982	100.0	100.0	100.0	100.0	100.0	100.0	100.0	100.0	100.0	100.0	100.0	100.0	100.0	100.0	100.0	100.0	100.0
1983	101.3	102.4	101.8	101.1	100.3	103.2	95.9	100.3	100.8	107.9	103.3	101.8	102.7	103.4	101.6	102.8	104.8
1984	103.7	105.5	105.4	103.3	102.7	109.0	94.8	102.9	102.3	108.0	110.3	104.8	105.1	105.7	105.4	105.2	107.0
1985	103.2	95.1	103.5	103.7	102.9	108.9	91.4	103.7	101.9	106.6	113.3	104.4	107.2	107.1	108.6	107.9	109.4
1986	100.2	92.9	105.4	100.0	103.2	113.0	69.8	102.6	101.9	107.2	116.1	103.2	108.8	108.2	110.0	110.5	111.6
1987	102.8	95.5	107.9	102.6	105.1	120.4	70.2	106.4	103.0	112.8	121.8	107.1	110.4	109.9	110.0	112.5	114.9
1988	106.9	104.9	112.7	106.3	109.2	131.4	66.7	116.3	109.3	118.9	130.4	118.7	113.2	113.1	111.2	114.3	120.2
1989	112.2	110.9	117.8	111.6	112.3	136.3	72.9	123.0	112.6	126.7	137.8	124.1	117.4	116.9	112.6	117.7	126.5
1990	116.3	112.2	121.9	115.8	115.0	141.7	82.3	123.6	113.6	129.7	141.2	122.9	120.7	119.2	114.7	121.5	134.2
1991	116.5	105.7	121.9	116.5	116.3	138.9	81.2	125.6	115.1	132.1	142.9	120.2	123.0	121.2	117.2	126.4	140.8
1992	117.2	103.6	122.1	117.4	117.8	140.4	80.4	125.9	115.1	146.6	145.2	119.2	123.4	122.2	117.3	130.4	145.3
1993	118.9	107.1	124.0	119.0	118.0	143.7	80.0	128.2	116.0	174.0	147.3	119.2	124.0	123.7	120.0	133.7	145.4
1994	120.4	106.3	125.5	120.7	118.3	148.5	77.8	132.1	117.6	180.0	152.5	124.8	125.1	126.1	124.2	137.2	141.9
1995	124.7	107.4	127.0	125.5	120.8	153.7	78.0	142.5	124.3	178.1	172.2	134.5	126.6	128.2	129.0	139.7	145.4
1996	127.7	122.4	133.3	127.3	122.4	150.5	85.8	142.1	123.8	176.1	168.7	131.0	126.5	130.4	131.0	141.7	147.7
1997	127.6	112.9	134.0	127.7	122.6	154.2	86.1	143.6	123.2	183.8	167.9	131.8	125.9	130.8	133.2	141.6	150.9
1998	124.4	104.6	131.6	124.8	122.9	148.0	75.3	143.9	122.6	179.1	171.7	127.8	124.9	131.3	135.4	141.2	156.0
1999	125.5	98.4	131.1	126.5	121.1	146.0	80.5	144.2	122.5	183.6	174.1	124.6	124.3	131.7	138.9	141.8	166.6
2000	132.7	99.5	133.1	134.8	121.4	151.5	103.5	151.0	125.5	178.2	183.7	128.1	124.0	132.6	142.5	143.8	170.8
2001	134.2	103.8	137.3	135.7	121.3	158.4	105.3	151.8	127.2	174.4	184.8	125.4	123.7	133.2	144.3	145.2	181.3
2002	131.1	99.0	136.2	132.4	119.9	157.6	93.2	151.9	126.8	173.3	185.9	125.9	122.9	133.5	146.2	144.6	182.4
2003	138.1	111.5	143.4	139.1	119.8	162.3	112.9	161.8	130.1	177.4	190.0	129.2	121.9	133.9	148.2	145.7	179.6
2004	146.7	123.3	151.2	147.6	121.0	164.5	126.9	174.4	133.8	195.6	195.7	149.6	122.1	135.1	153.2	148.6	183.2

. . . = Not available.

Table 7-3. Producer Price Indexes for the Net Output of Selected Industries, 1994–2004

(December 1984 = 100, unless otherwise indicated.)

Industry	1994	1995	1996	1997	1998	1999	2000	2001	2002	2003	2004
Agriculture, Forestry, Fishing, and Hunting											
Logging	192.6	194.3	185.7	191.2	188.1	182.7	177.5	167.5	165.0	168.7	175.2
Mining											
Oil and gas extraction	71.1	66.6	84.8	87.5	68.3	78.5	126.8	127.5	107.0	160.1	192.7
Mining (except oil and gas)	...	...	...	...	...	...	...	...	...	...	109.5
Coal mining	93.2	91.6	91.4	92.2	89.5	87.3	84.8	91.3	93.9	94.4	104.1
Metal ore mining	81.4	101.4	92.1	85.8	73.2	70.3	73.8	70.8	73.6	81.6	111.8
Iron ore mining	82.1	91.0	95.7	95.3	94.5	94.0	93.9	95.2	94.2	95.0	97.2
Gold ore and silver ore mining	75.9	77.1	78.6	67.9	61.1	58.2	57.0	55.2	62.6	72.6	82.6
Copper, nickel, lead, and zinc mining	106.9	157.1	117.0	110.4	76.8	71.3	88.7	81.7	80.1	90.1	147.7
Other metal ore mining	32.9	33.6	31.9	29.9	27.6	25.9	26.4	24.7	28.9	34.9	80.0
Nonmetallic mineral mining and quarrying	120.5	123.8	127.1	128.8	132.2	134.0	137.0	141.0	143.5	146.4	151.2
Stone mining and quarrying	126.3	130.7	133.2	135.4	138.8	142.1	147.3	152.2	156.1	160.2	166.1
Sand, gravel, clay, and refractory minerals mining	...	...	...	...	...	...	...	...	...	...	102.4
Other nonmetallic mineral mining and quarrying	102.1	104.2	108.6	107.6	110.1	108.0	106.8	107.1	107.7	108.4	111.4
Mining support activities	...	...	...	...	...	...	...	...	...	...	104.8
Utilities	...	...	...	...	...	...	...	...	...	...	104.9
Electric power generation, transmission, and distribution	...	...	...	...	...	...	...	...	...	...	103.3
Electric power generation	...	...	...	...	...	...	...	...	...	...	105.2
Electric power transmission, control, and distribution	...	...	...	...	...	...	...	...	...	...	102.5
Natural gas distribution	...	...	...	...	...	...	...	...	...	...	107.3
Manufacturing											
Food	120.1	121.7	127.1	127.9	126.3	126.3	128.5	132.8	132.0	137.4	144.3
Animal food	...	...	...	...	...	...	...	...	...	...	103.3
Grain and oilseed milling	...	...	...	...	...	...	...	...	...	...	103.1
Flour milling and malt	...	...	...	...	...	...	...	...	...	...	102.6
Starch and vegetable fats and oils	...	...	...	...	...	...	...	...	...	...	103.6
Breakfast cereal manufacturing	...	...	...	...	...	...	...	...	...	...	101.7
Sugar and confectionery product	120.4	123.3	127.7	129.3	128.8	129.4	127.5	129.3	133.7	139.5	141.4
Sugar	...	...	...	...	...	...	...	...	...	...	99.7
Chocolate and confectionery from cacao beans	...	...	...	...	...	...	...	...	...	...	100.1
Confectionery from purchased chocolate	...	...	...	...	...	...	...	...	...	...	100.1
Nonchocolate confectionery	...	...	...	...	...	...	...	...	...	...	104.0
Fruit and vegetable preserving and specialty food	123.7	125.5	129.7	129.9	130.1	131.7	132.1	133.3	135.2	136.6	139.2
Fruit and vegetable canning, pickling, and drying	...	...	...	...	...	...	...	...	...	...	100.5
Dairy product	115.6	115.8	125.0	123.9	133.1	133.8	129.9	141.2	133.3	135.8	151.0
Ice cream and frozen dessert	...	...	...	...	...	...	...	...	...	...	103.3
Animal slaughtering and processing	110.7	109.3	114.6	116.1	109.2	108.9	115.0	120.3	114.0	125.8	134.2
Seafood product preparation and packaging	...	...	...	...	...	...	...	...	...	...	102.4
Bakeries and tortilla	...	...	...	...	...	...	...	...	...	...	100.8
Bread and bakery product	...	...	...	...	...	...	...	...	...	...	101.1
Cookie, cracker, and pasta	...	...	...	...	...	...	...	...	...	...	100.5
Tortilla	...	...	...	...	...	...	...	...	...	...	100.4
Other food manufacturing	...	...	...	...	...	...	...	...	...	...	101.1
Snack food	...	...	...	...	...	...	...	...	...	...	101.4
Coffee and tea	...	...	...	...	...	...	...	...	...	...	101.7
Flavoring syrup and concentrate	...	...	...	...	...	...	...	...	...	...	101.0
Seasoning and dressing	...	...	...	...	...	...	...	...	...	...	101.1
All other food	...	...	...	...	...	...	...	...	...	...	100.4
Beverage and tobacco	...	...	...	...	...	...	...	...	...	...	101.0
Beverage	118.8	123.1	125.5	126.3	127.2	129.8	134.4	138.6	140.8	142.7	146.4
Soft drink and ice	...	...	...	...	...	...	...	...	...	...	102.1
Breweries	...	...	...	...	...	...	...	...	...	...	101.3
Wineries	...	...	...	...	...	...	...	...	...	...	100.7
Distilleries	...	...	...	...	...	...	...	...	...	...	100.1
Tobacco	187.8	193.2	199.1	210.8	243.1	325.7	345.8	386.1	401.9	377.9	379.7
Tobacco stemming and redrying	109.4	112.2	109.7	106.5	104.2	104.7	109.0	112.3	114.7	117.5	119.4
Tobacco product	198.9	204.3	210.5	223.3	260.4	356.7	379.3	425.8	442.8	411.7	412.5
Textile mills	...	...	...	...	...	...	...	...	...	...	101.1
Fiber, yarn, and thread mills	107.4	112.1	113.6	114.1	112.1	106.9	105.5	103.0	99.8	100.9	105.6
Fabric mills	...	...	...	...	...	...	...	...	...	...	101.0
Broadwoven fabric mills	...	...	...	...	...	...	...	...	...	...	101.1
Narrow fabric mills and schiffli mach embroidery	116.8	119.7	121.2	122.7	123.8	124.3	125.3	126.2	126.0	125.1	126.2
Nonwoven fabric mills	...	...	...	...	...	...	...	...	...	...	101.5
Knit fabric mills	...	...	...	...	...	...	...	...	...	...	100.4
Textile fabric finishing/fabric coating mills	...	...	...	...	...	...	...	...	...	...	99.9
Textile and fabric finishing mills	...	...	...	...	...	...	...	...	...	...	99.8
Fabric coating mills	...	...	...	...	...	...	...	...	...	...	100.2
Textile product mills	...	...	...	...	...	...	...	...	...	...	101.4
Textile furnishings mills	...	...	...	...	...	...	...	...	...	...	101.1
Carpet and rug mills	110.0	111.6	114.1	115.7	116.3	115.4	117.8	118.9	119.0	121.8	124.6
Curtain and linen mills	...	...	...	...	...	...	...	...	...	...	100.2
Other textile product mills	...	...	...	...	...	...	...	...	...	...	102.0
Textile bag and canvas mills	...	...	...	...	...	...	...	...	...	...	102.7
All other textile product mills	...	...	...	...	...	...	...	...	...	...	101.7
Apparel manufacturing	...	...	...	...	...	...	...	...	...	...	100.0
Apparel knitting mills	113.0	115.7	116.6	117.0	116.6	114.0	113.9	113.7	112.7	111.6	110.3
Hosiery and sock mills	113.0	115.7	116.6	117.0	116.6	114.0	113.9	113.7	112.7	111.6	111.4
Cut and sew apparel	...	...	...	...	...	...	...	...	...	...	100.2
Cut and sew apparel contractors	...	...	...	...	...	...	...	...	...	...	100.2
Men's/boys' cut and sew apparel	...	...	...	...	...	...	...	...	...	...	100.4
Women's/girls' cut and sew apparel	...	...	...	...	...	...	...	...	...	...	100.1
Other cut and sew apparel	...	...	...	...	...	...	...	...	...	...	100.2
Apparel accessories and other apparel	...	...	...	...	...	...	...	...	...	...	100.5
Leather and allied product	130.6	134.1	134.7	137.1	137.1	136.5	137.9	141.3	141.1	142.8	143.6
Leather and hide tanning and finishing	171.9	183.9	172.4	176.9	171.6	168.8	174.6	191.7	191.4	200.5	205.7

. . . = Not available.

Table 7-3. Producer Price Indexes for the Net Output of Selected Industries, 1994–2004—Continued

(December 1984 = 100, unless otherwise indicated.)

Industry	1994	1995	1996	1997	1998	1999	2000	2001	2002	2003	2004
Footwear	...	...	...	...	...	...	...	...	...	...	100.1
Other leather and allied product	...	...	...	...	...	...	...	...	...	...	99.8
Wood products manufacturing	...	...	...	...	...	...	...	...	...	...	106.7
Sawmills and wood preservation	...	...	...	...	...	...	...	...	...	...	110.5
Veneer, plywood, and engineered wood product	...	...	...	...	...	...	...	...	...	...	107.0
Other wood product	...	...	...	...	...	...	...	...	...	...	104.7
Millwork	...	...	...	...	...	...	...	...	...	...	104.8
Wood container and pallet	...	...	...	...	...	...	...	...	...	...	102.8
All other wood product	...	...	...	...	...	...	...	...	...	...	105.0
Paper manufacturing	...	...	...	...	...	...	...	...	...	...	102.6
Pulp, paper, and paperboard mills	116.5	182.4	135.5	131.0	125.1	122.7	143.4	122.9	116.5	120.9	131.3
Pulp mills	128.6	164.8	152.2	143.2	144.5	139.7	148.8	150.5	144.1	145.7	151.1
Paper mills	152.6	203.1	169.7	158.2	165.1	166.9	192.2	187.3	179.5	180.2	189.9
Paperboard mills	...	...	...	...	...	...	...	...	...	...	101.9
Converted paper product	123.7	148.5	140.4	132.9	141.1	144.1	157.1	158.9	157.0	157.3	161.5
Paper container	...	...	...	...	...	...	...	...	...	...	101.7
Paper bag and coated and treated paper	...	...	...	...	...	...	...	...	...	...	101.7
Stationery product	...	...	...	...	...	...	...	...	...	...	97.0
Other converted paper product	...	...	...	...	...	...	...	...	...	...	101.1
Printing and related support activities	...	...	...	...	...	...	...	...	...	...	101.2
Printing	...	...	...	...	...	...	...	...	...	...	100.4
Printing support activities	...	...	...	...	...	...	...	...	...	...	...
Petroleum and coal products	74.8	77.2	87.4	85.6	66.3	76.8	112.8	105.3	98.8	122.0	149.9
Petroleum refineries	72.2	74.5	85.3	83.1	62.3	73.6	111.6	103.1	96.3	121.2	151.5
Asphalt paving, roofing, and saturated materials	94.9	98.1	99.4	102.2	102.8	102.8	113.5	116.9	119.7	125.1	127.1
Other petroleum and coal products	130.6	136.3	140.9	142.0	142.5	142.1	150.3	159.3	160.5	165.3	172.0
Chemical	130.0	143.4	145.8	147.1	148.7	149.7	156.7	158.4	157.3	164.6	172.8
Basic chemical	125.9	158.1	164.0	163.9	160.1	161.4	177.3	173.5	170.6	183.0	197.7
Petrochemical	...	...	...	...	...	...	...	...	...	...	120.7
Industrial gas	...	...	...	...	...	...	...	...	...	...	108.3
Synthetic dye and pigment	...	...	...	...	...	...	...	...	...	...	104.2
Other basic inorganic chemical	...	...	...	...	...	...	...	...	...	...	103.1
Resin, synthetic rubber, and artificial/synthetic fiber/filaments	113.8	127.8	123.1	124.4	115.9	115.4	128.0	126.2	119.7	131.0	145.5
Resin and synthetic rubber	...	...	...	...	...	...	...	...	...	...	115.1
Artificial and synthetic fibers/filaments	...	...	...	...	...	...	...	...	...	...	101.2
Pesticide, fertilizer, and other agricultural chemical	119.6	129.7	133.4	131.9	128.5	123.2	124.9	132.0	127.0	135.3	142.7
Fertilizer	...	...	...	...	...	...	...	...	...	...	107.3
Pesticide and other agricultural chemical	...	...	...	...	...	...	...	...	...	...	100.6
Pharmaceutical and medicine	174.8	178.7	181.2	184.8	203.1	210.1	215.7	220.5	226.3	235.4	244.2
Paint, coating, and adhesive	...	...	...	...	...	...	...	...	...	...	101.9
Adhesive	...	...	...	...	...	...	...	...	...	...	100.5
Soap, cleaners, and toilet preparation	123.0	125.0	126.6	127.3	128.7	130.3	132.5	134.2	134.2	134.9	136.9
Soap and cleaning compound	...	...	...	...	...	...	...	...	...	...	102.0
Toilet preparation	...	...	...	...	...	...	...	...	...	...	100.0
Other chemical product and preparation	...	...	...	...	...	...	...	...	...	...	101.6
Printing ink	...	...	...	...	...	...	...	...	...	...	100.0
All other chemical product and preparation	...	...	...	...	...	...	...	...	...	...	101.8
Plastics and rubber products	117.1	123.3	123.1	122.8	122.1	122.2	124.6	125.9	125.5	128.4	131.7
Plastics product	101.9	108.3	108.0	107.6	106.8	107.1	109.8	111.0	110.2	113.0	116.2
Unsupported plastics film, sheet, and bag	...	...	...	...	...	...	...	...	...	...	104.2
Plastics pipe, fitting, and unsupported shapes	...	...	...	...	...	...	...	...	...	...	108.5
Laminated plastics plate, sheet, and shape	...	...	...	...	...	...	...	...	...	...	101.7
Polystyrene foam product	...	...	...	...	...	...	...	...	...	...	104.6
Foam product (except polystyrene)	...	...	...	...	...	...	...	...	...	...	100.2
Plastics bottle	...	...	...	...	...	...	...	...	...	...	103.1
Other plastics product	...	...	...	...	...	...	...	...	...	...	101.3
Rubber product	...	...	...	...	...	...	...	...	...	...	102.1
Tire	106.4	108.5	105.2	103.4	102.0	100.4	100.4	101.5	102.7	105.6	110.5
Rubber and plastics hose and belting	...	...	...	...	...	...	...	...	...	...	102.3
Other rubber product	111.9	115.6	118.3	119.8	120.2	119.9	120.5	121.3	121.4	121.8	121.9
Nonmetallic mineral product	119.6	124.3	125.8	127.4	129.3	132.6	134.7	136.0	137.1	138.0	142.7
Clay product and refractory	...	...	...	...	...	...	...	...	...	...	101.5
Pottery, ceramics, and plumbing fixture	125.2	129.3	130.0	131.8	133.5	138.1	139.7	150.2	150.1	150.6	152.1
Clay building material and refractories	...	...	...	...	...	...	...	...	...	...	102.2
Glass and glass product	...	...	...	...	...	...	...	...	...	...	100.1
Cement and concrete product	...	...	...	...	...	...	...	...	...	...	104.2
Cement	118.7	127.2	132.9	138.1	144.2	149.1	148.6	148.7	151.1	150.5	155.4
Ready-mix concrete	...	...	...	...	...	...	...	...	...	...	104.5
Concrete pipe, brick, and block	...	...	...	...	...	...	...	...	...	...	102.5
Other concrete products	...	...	...	...	...	...	...	...	...	...	104.7
Lime and gypsum product	...	...	...	...	...	...	...	...	...	...	110.0
Lime	...	...	...	...	...	...	...	...	...	...	103.5
Gypsum product	...	...	...	...	...	...	...	...	...	...	111.9
Other nonmetallic mineral product	119.2	123.6	125.6	126.2	127.4	131.3	130.9	132.0	132.6	133.4	137.2
Abrasive product	...	...	...	...	...	...	...	...	...	...	100.2
All other nonmetallic mineral product	...	...	...	...	...	...	...	...	...	...	103.5
Primary metal	117.0	128.2	123.7	124.7	120.9	115.8	119.8	116.1	116.2	118.4	142.8
Iron and steel mills and ferroalloy	...	...	...	...	...	...	...	...	...	...	127.7
Steel product from purchased steel	...	...	...	...	...	...	...	...	...	...	133.1
Iron/steel pipe and tube from purch steel	...	...	...	...	...	...	...	...	...	...	147.9
Rolling and drawing of purchased steel	...	...	...	...	...	...	...	...	...	...	123.7
Nonferrous (except alum) production and processing	...	...	...	...	...	...	...	...	...	...	113.6
Copper rolling, drawing, extruding, and alloying	...	...	...	...	...	...	...	...	...	...	118.2
Other nonferrous rolling, drawing, extruding, and alloying	...	...	...	...	...	...	...	...	...	...	110.3
Ferrous metal foundries	118.3	124.0	127.6	129.2	129.7	130.4	132.1	132.7	133.0	133.5	140.4
Nonferrous metal foundries	125.7	132.8	131.4	133.8	132.7	131.6	133.5	134.1	134.4	135.6	140.0
Fabricated metal product	120.3	124.8	126.2	127.6	128.7	129.1	130.3	131.0	131.7	132.9	141.3
Forging and stamping	...	...	...	...	...	...	...	...	...	...	107.0
Architectural and structural metals	...	...	...	...	...	...	...	...	...	...	111.2
Plate work and fabricated structural product	...	...	...	...	...	...	...	...	...	...	115.2
Ornamental and architectural metal product	...	...	...	...	...	...	...	...	...	...	108.3
Boiler, tank and shipping container	...	...	...	...	...	...	...	...	...	...	106.8

. . . = Not available.

Table 7-3. Producer Price Indexes for the Net Output of Selected Industries, 1994–2004—*Continued*

(December 1984 = 100, unless otherwise indicated.)

Industry	1994	1995	1996	1997	1998	1999	2000	2001	2002	2003	2004
Light gauge metal container	101.7	109.4	103.9	102.7	102.3	100.7	101.0	100.8	102.7	105.4	110.4
Hardware	...	...	...	...	...	...	...	...	...	...	103.4
Spring and wire product	...	...	...	...	...	...	...	...	...	...	108.9
Mach shops, turn product, screw, nut, and bolt	...	...	...	...	...	...	...	...	...	...	102.8
Machine shops	...	...	...	...	...	...	...	...	...	...	102.4
Turned product and screw, nut and bolt	117.6	120.0	121.6	122.6	122.7	121.8	122.9	122.8	123.4	123.6	128.4
Coating, engrave, heat treating, and other activity	...	...	...	...	...	...	...	...	...	...	102.0
Other fabricated metal product	...	...	...	...	...	...	...	...	...	...	103.8
Metal valve	...	...	...	...	...	...	...	...	...	...	103.0
All other fabricated metal product	...	...	...	...	...	...	...	...	...	...	104.5
Machinery	...	...	...	...	...	...	...	...	...	...	101.9
Agricultural, construction, and mining machinery	...	...	...	...	...	...	...	...	...	...	102.4
Agricultural implement	...	...	...	...	...	...	...	...	...	...	101.8
Construction machinery	...	...	...	...	...	...	...	...	...	...	102.9
Mining and oil and gas field machinery	...	...	...	...	...	...	...	...	...	...	102.7
Industrial machinery	134.2	137.3	140.5	143.0	145.4	147.2	148.7	149.9	149.6	150.1	153.0
Sawmill and woodworking machinery	...	...	...	...	...	...	...	...	...	...	101.5
Plastics and rubber industry machinery	...	...	...	...	...	...	...	...	...	...	102.8
Other industrial machinery	134.2	137.3	140.5	143.0	145.4	147.2	148.7	149.9	149.6	150.1	152.7
Commercial and service industry machinery	...	...	...	...	...	...	...	...	...	...	101.3
HVAC and commercial refrigeration equipment	...	...	...	...	...	...	...	...	...	...	101.9
Metalworking machinery	...	...	...	...	...	...	...	...	...	...	100.8
Engine, turbine, and power transmission equipment	128.3	130.8	132.3	133.6	133.9	135.7	136.6	137.7	138.9	139.1	140.8
Other general purpose machinery	...	...	...	...	...	...	...	...	...	...	103.0
Pump and compressor	...	...	...	...	...	...	...	...	...	...	102.2
Material handling equipment	...	...	...	...	...	...	...	...	...	...	104.6
All other general purpose machinery	...	...	...	...	...	...	...	...	...	...	102.5
Computer and electronic product	...	...	...	...	...	...	...	...	...	...	99.0
Computer and peripheral equipment	...	70.5	63.4	55.9	48.8	44.0	41.3	39.0	35.5	31.6	29.4
Communications equipment	113.3	113.9	115.0	115.7	115.0	113.0	110.4	108.6	105.0	101.7	98.4
Telephone apparatus	...	...	...	...	...	...	...	...	...	...	95.3
Radio/TV broadcast and wireless communication equipment	...	...	...	...	...	...	...	...	...	...	99.4
Other communications equipment	...	...	...	...	...	...	...	...	...	...	99.8
Audio and video equipment	...	...	...	...	...	...	...	...	...	...	98.1
Semiconductor and other electronic component	104.8	102.5	99.3	95.1	91.9	90.1	88.8	86.4	84.9	81.1	78.3
Navigation, measuring, medical, control instruments	...	...	...	...	...	...	...	...	...	...	100.6
Manufacturing and reproducing magnetic and optical media	...	...	...	...	...	...	...	...	...	...	98.0
Electrical equipment, appliance and component	...	...	...	...	...	...	...	...	...	...	103.2
Electric lighting equipment	...	...	...	...	...	...	...	...	...	...	100.8
Electric lamp bulb and part	...	...	...	...	...	...	...	...	...	...	98.1
Lighting fixture	...	...	...	...	...	...	...	...	...	...	101.7
Household appliance	108.7	108.8	109.7	108.3	107.5	107.2	106.2	104.6	104.2	103.1	103.1
Small electrical appliance	...	...	...	...	...	...	...	...	...	...	99.9
Major appliance	...	...	...	...	...	...	...	...	...	...	100.6
Electrical equipment	...	...	...	...	...	...	...	...	...	...	101.9
Other electrical equipment and component	...	...	...	...	...	...	...	...	...	...	106.6
Battery	...	...	...	...	...	...	...	...	...	...	102.2
Communications and energy wire and cable	...	...	...	...	...	...	...	...	...	...	106.8
Wiring device	...	...	...	...	...	...	...	...	...	...	113.6
All other electrical equipment and component	...	...	...	...	...	...	...	...	...	...	101.7
Transportation equipment	...	...	...	...	...	...	...	...	...	...	100.9
Motor vehicle	...	...	...	...	...	...	...	...	...	...	99.4
Automobile and light duty motor vehicle	...	...	...	...	...	...	...	...	...	...	99.2
Heavy duty truck	...	...	...	...	...	...	...	...	...	...	102.2
Motor vehicle body and trailer	...	...	...	...	...	...	...	...	...	...	104.0
Motor vehicle parts	...	...	...	...	...	...	...	...	...	...	101.4
Motor vehicle steering and suspension parts	...	...	...	...	...	...	...	...	...	...	101.8
Aerospace product and parts	134.0	137.3	140.8	142.7	143.4	144.8	149.9	154.7	157.3	162.2	168.0
Railroad rolling stock	122.6	127.6	129.7	127.4	127.6	128.2	128.6	128.3	127.7	129.0	135.8
Ship and boat building	133.0	135.0	138.2	142.0	144.1	145.6	149.0	152.6	156.8	163.0	169.6
Other transportation equipment	...	...	...	...	...	...	...	...	...	...	101.1
Furniture and related product	129.7	133.3	136.2	138.2	139.7	141.3	143.3	145.1	146.3	147.4	151.5
Household and institutional furniture and kitchen cabinet	128.7	132.2	134.7	136.4	138.4	140.3	142.5	144.4	146.2	147.0	148.6
Wood kitchen cabinet and countertop	139.1	144.3	147.3	150.4	153.1	155.7	159.8	162.6	164.5	167.6	170.6
Household and institutional furniture	...	...	...	...	...	...	...	...	...	...	101.1
Office furniture (including fixtures)	...	...	...	...	...	...	...	...	...	...	105.1
Other furniture related product	...	...	...	...	...	...	...	...	...	...	104.0
Mattress	...	...	...	...	...	...	...	...	...	...	105.6
Blind and shade	...	...	...	...	...	...	...	...	...	...	101.3
Miscellaneous	...	...	...	...	...	...	...	...	...	...	101.2
Medical equipment and supplies	...	...	...	...	...	...	...	...	...	...	101.3
Other miscellaneous	123.3	125.9	127.8	129.0	129.7	130.3	130.9	132.4	133.3	133.9	135.2
Jewelry and silverware	124.7	126.3	128.0	128.0	127.1	126.4	127.1	128.0	129.1	131.0	134.6
Sporting and athletic goods	...	...	...	...	...	...	...	...	...	...	101.3
Doll, toy, and game	...	...	...	...	...	...	...	...	...	...	100.3
Office supplies (except paper)	123.2	127.4	130.2	129.8	130.9	132.0	132.0	131.4	132.8	132.9	133.1
Sign	...	...	...	...	...	...	...	...	...	...	100.9
All other miscellaneous manufacturing	...	...	...	...	...	...	...	...	...	...	101.0

. . . = Not available.

Table 7-3. Producer Price Indexes for the Net Output of Selected Industries, 1994–2004—Continued

(December 1984 = 100, unless otherwise indicated.)

Industry	1994	1995	1996	1997	1998	1999	2000	2001	2002	2003	2004
Retail trade											
Motor vehicle and parts dealers											103.5
Automobile dealers											102.9
New car dealers							99.7	103.1	108.7	111.5	113.5
Recreational vehicle dealers									112.2	109.7	121.4
Automotive parts, accessories, and tire stores									100.9	104.2	109.4
Automotive parts and accessories stores											106.8
Tire dealers											102.0
Furniture and home furnishings stores											102.4
Furniture stores											100.8
Floor covering stores											104.6
Electronics and appliance stores											99.0
Appliance, TV, and other electronics stores											101.8
Computer and software stores											95.2
Camera and photographic supplies stores											88.6
Building material and garden equipment and supplies dealers											108.3
Building material and supplies dealers											108.7
Home centers											107.0
Paint and wallpaper stores											99.5
Hardware stores											103.1
Other building material dealers											111.4
Lawn and garden equipment and supplies stores											105.8
Nursery, garden, and farm supply stores											105.8
Food and beverage stores							103.8	109.6	113.4	117.6	123.2
Grocery stores											103.5
Grocery (except convenience) stores											103.5
Specialty food stores											107.1
Beer, wine, and liquor stores								102.9	103.5	106.9	110.7
Health and personal care stores											101.7
Pharmacies and drug stores								102.4	112.4	116.6	119.8
Optical goods stores											99.8
Gasoline stations									66.8	54.1	51.3
Gasoline stations with convenience stores											102.5
Other gasoline stations											132.8
Clothing and clothing accessories stores											100.5
Clothing stores											99.3
Men's clothing stores											100.2
Women's clothing stores											102.9
Family clothing stores											97.8
Shoe stores											103.9
Jewelry, luggage, and leather goods stores											101.8
Jewelry stores											101.8
Luggage and leather goods stores											101.4
Sporting goods, hobby, book, and music stores											96.6
Sporting goods, hobby, and musical instrument stores											97.8
Sporting goods stores											95.0
Hobby, toy, and game stores											100.5
Sewing, needlework, and piece goods stores											103.2
Book, periodical, and music stores											94.7
Bookstores and news dealers											95.0
Prerecorded tape, CD, and record stores											93.9
General merchandise stores											103.1
Department stores											105.4
Other general merchandise stores											97.7
Florists											100.2
Office supplies, stationery, and gift stores											99.7
Office supplies and stationery stores											100.4
Gift, novelty, and souvenir stores											98.7
Manufactured (mobile) home dealers											107.7
Nonstore retailers											107.5
Vending machine operators											101.5
Fuel dealers								120.5	113.8	122.7	129.4
Transportation and Warehousing											
Air transportation	108.5	113.7	121.1	125.3	124.5	130.8	147.7	157.2	157.8	162.1	162.3
Scheduled air transportation	129.1	135.9	145.5	150.8	149.3	157.3	180.1	193.0	193.3	198.5	198.6
Nonscheduled air transportation				97.8	99.2	102.2	107.3	112.7	114.7	117.8	119.9
Rail transportation				100.5	101.7	101.3	102.6	104.5	106.6	108.8	113.4
Water transportation											101.3
Inland water transportation											103.2
Truck transportation											103.1
General freight trucking											103.5
General freight trucking, local											105.2
General freight trucking, long-distance											103.2
Specialized freight trucking											102.3
Used household and office goods moving											102.6
Specialized freight (except used) trucking, local											102.7
Specialized freight (except used) trucking, long-distance											101.7
Pipeline transportation of crude oil											103.9
Other pipeline transportation											101.4
Pipeline transportation of refined petroleum products											101.4
Transportation support activities											101.1
Air transportation support activities				102.5	105.2	108.6	114.2	117.5	121.4	125.1	128.1
Airport operations											101.1
Other air transportation support activities											102.0
Water transportation support activities											101.0
Port and harbor operations											102.4
Marine cargo handling											100.5
Navigational services to shipping											101.5
Freight transportation arrangement				99.4	97.7	97.3	98.3	98.2	97.5	97.9	98.9
Postal service	119.8	132.2	132.3	132.3	132.3	135.3	135.2	143.4	150.2	155.0	155.0

. . . = Not available.

Table 7-3. Producer Price Indexes for the Net Output of Selected Industries, 1994–2004—*Continued*

(December 1984 = 100, unless otherwise indicated.)

Industry	1994	1995	1996	1997	1998	1999	2000	2001	2002	2003	2004
Couriers and messengers	...	...	...	...	...	...	...	...	...	...	106.1
Couriers	...	...	...	...	...	...	...	...	...	...	106.6
Local messengers and local delivery	...	...	...	...	...	...	...	...	...	...	101.1
General warehousing and storage	...	...	...	...	...	...	...	...	...	...	100.3
Refrigerated warehousing and storage	...	...	...	...	...	...	...	...	...	...	100.5
Farm product warehousing and storage	...	...	...	...	...	...	...	...	...	...	100.2
Information											
Publishing industries, except Internet	...	...	...	...	...	...	...	...	...	...	101.5
Newspaper, book, and directory publishers	...	...	...	...	...	...	...	...	...	...	102.1
Newspaper publishers	269.5	286.7	306.9	317.7	328.7	339.3	351.3	367.9	381.9	395.7	409.7
Periodical publishers	239.1	246.3	253.1	263.2	276.9	284.9	292.6	305.9	320.4	332.4	339.1
Book publishers	153.4	162.3	169.4	174.0	178.9	184.7	190.2	195.6	201.5	208.2	215.7
Directory and mailing list publishers	...	...	...	...	...	...	...	...	...	...	101.3
Other publishers	...	...	...	...	...	...	...	...	...	...	100.7
Software publishers	...	...	...	...	...	...	...	...	...	...	99.8
Broadcasting, except Internet	...	...	...	...	...	...	...	...	...	...	101.2
Radio and television broadcasting	...	...	...	...	...	...	...	98.2	97.1	99.8	102.8
Radio broadcasting	...	...	...	...	...	...	...	...	...	...	102.7
Television broadcasting	...	...	...	...	...	...	...	...	...	...	100.5
Cable networks	...	...	...	...	...	...	...	...	...	...	101.4
Telecommunications	...	...	...	...	...	...	...	...	...	...	99.8
Wired telecommunications carriers	...	...	...	...	...	...	96.4	93.6	89.9	88.1	86.3
Wireless telecommunications carriers	...	...	...	...	...	...	...	...	...	...	98.4
Cable and other program distribution	...	...	...	...	...	...	...	...	...	...	102.2
Data processing and related services	...	...	...	...	...	...	...	...	...	...	98.8
Finance and Insurance											
Security, commodity contracts and like activity	...	...	...	...	...	...	...	...	...	...	103.4
Security and commodity contracts, intermediation and brokerage	...	...	...	...	...	...	...	88.1	81.8	82.5	84.2
Investment banking and securities dealing	...	...	...	...	...	...	...	...	...	...	102.6
Securities brokerage	...	...	...	...	...	...	...	...	...	...	100.0
Portfolio management	...	...	...	...	...	...	...	...	...	...	108.1
Investment advice	...	...	...	...	...	...	...	...	...	...	102.0
Other direct insurance carriers	...	...	...	...	...	100.7	101.9	104.3	108.7	115.0	118.7
Insurance agencies and brokerages	...	...	...	...	...	...	...	...	...	...	100.8
Lessors of nonresidential building (except miniwarehouse)	...	...	...	...	...	...	...	...	...	...	102.3
Lessors of miniwarehouse and self-storage units	...	...	...	...	...	...	...	...	...	...	102.0
Offices of real estate agents and brokers	...	...	...	...	...	...	...	...	...	...	101.8
Real estate property managers	...	...	...	...	...	...	...	...	...	...	100.9
Offices of real estate appraisers	...	...	...	...	...	...	...	...	...	...	102.7
Automotive equipment rental and leasing	...	...	...	...	...	...	...	...	103.9	106.6	107.8
Passenger car rental and leasing	...	...	...	...	...	...	...	...	...	...	98.2
Truck, utility trailer, and RV rental and leasing	...	...	...	...	...	...	...	...	...	...	99.9
Legal services	...	...	...	102.5	106.1	108.7	112.5	117.9	121.7	125.6	131.8
Offices of lawyers	...	...	...	102.5	106.1	108.7	112.5	117.9	121.7	125.6	131.8
Architectural, engineering, and related services	...	...	...	102.2	105.1	108.5	111.8	115.9	121.1	124.3	126.8
Architectural services	...	...	...	...	...	...	...	...	...	...	99.7
Engineering services	...	...	...	...	...	...	...	...	...	...	101.5
Advertising agencies	...	...	...	...	...	...	...	...	...	...	100.1
Employment services	...	...	...	101.0	103.2	105.2	107.3	108.2	108.9	111.4	113.9
Employment placement agencies	...	...	...	...	...	...	...	...	...	...	102.2
Temporary help services	...	...	...	...	...	...	...	...	...	...	101.7
Employee leasing services	...	...	...	...	...	...	...	...	...	...	101.3
Travel agencies	...	...	...	...	...	...	...	...	...	...	96.9
Janitorial services	...	...	...	...	...	...	...	...	...	...	100.9
Waste collection	...	...	...	...	...	...	...	...	...	...	101.3
Health Care and Social Assistance											
Offices of physicians	...	...	...	101.0	103.2	105.5	107.3	110.4	110.3	112.1	114.3
Medical and diagnostic laboratories	...	...	...	...	...	...	...	...	...	...	100.0
Home health care services	...	...	...	103.3	106.2	107.1	111.1	114.0	116.6	117.0	119.8
Hospitals	106.2	110.0	112.6	113.6	114.4	116.4	119.4	123.0	127.5	134.9	141.5
General medical and surgical hospitals	...	...	...	...	...	...	...	...	...	...	102.9
Psychiatric and substance abuse hospitals	...	...	...	...	...	...	...	...	...	...	101.1
Other specialty hospitals	...	...	...	...	...	...	...	...	...	...	103.8
Nursing care facilities	...	...	...	...	...	...	...	...	...	...	102.6
Residential mental retardation facilities	...	...	...	...	...	...	...	...	...	...	101.2
Accommodation	...	...	...	104.2	108.1	112.7	116.2	121.3	121.3	122.0	125.2
Hotels (except casino hotels) and motels	...	...	...	...	...	...	...	...	...	...	103.5
Casino hotels	...	...	...	...	...	...	...	...	...	...	105.0

. . . = Not available.

NOTES AND DEFINITIONS

CONSUMER PRICE INDEX

Coverage

The Consumer Price Index (CPI) measures the average change in prices of goods and services purchased by urban consumers for day-to-day living. The weights used in calculating the index, which remain fixed for relatively long periods, are based on actual expenditures reported in the Consumer Expenditure Surveys (CE). The quantities and qualities of the sample items in the "market basket" remain essentially the same between consecutive pricing periods. The index measures only the effect of price change on the cost of living. The index does not measure changes in the total amount families spend for living. Geographic area indexes measure price changes in individual areas over time, not relative differences in prices or living costs between areas.

Periodic Updating

The index for the years 1913–1935 used a study of 1917–1919 spending by households of wage earners and clerical workers as the basis for its weights. Since then, there have been six updates to bring the "market basket" of goods and services up to date, revise the weights, and improve the sampling methods. In the past 20 years, several major changes have been introduced into the CPI.

The 1978 revision of the CPI updated the CPI for Urban Wage Earners and Clerical Workers (CPI-W), and introduced a new index for All Urban Consumers (CPI-U), which includes salaried workers, the self-employed, the retired, the unemployed, and wage earners and clerical workers. The CPI-W now represents the spending patterns of 32 percent of the population; the CPI-U, 87 percent. Before 1978, changes in the CPI-U were based on changes in the CPI-W. The 1978 revision also instituted sampling for all levels of the index down to the selection of items within each retail outlet.

Beginning with the index for January 1983, BLS changed the way the CPI-U measures homeowners' costs; the CPI-W implemented the same change in January 1985. The change converted the homeownership component from an asset approach, including both the investment and consumption aspects of homeownership, to a flow-of-services approach, which only measures the cost of shelter services consumed by homeowners. The new approach uses a rental equivalence method to calculate homeowner shelter costs by estimating the implicit rent owners would have to pay to rent the homes in which they live. The old method calculated homeowner costs as home purchase, mortgage interest costs, property taxes, property insurance, and maintenance and repair.

The 1987 major revision of both the CPI-U and the CPI-W introduced weights based upon data from the 1982, 1983, and 1984 CE. The 1998 CPI revision, which went into effect with the index for January 1998, uses expenditure data from the 1993–1995 Consumer Expenditure Surveys and population data from the 1990 decennial census.

Current Methodology

The CPI selected 87 pricing areas in 38 different index areas from around the United States. BLS revises the outlets and items in its sample on a five-year rotating basis. Before rotating the sample, the Census Bureau conducts a Point of Purchase Survey for BLS. This survey determines the locations of retail outlets where consumers buy goods and services in various categories; it also determines how much they spend on each category in each reported outlet. BLS then draws outlet samples from the Point-of-Purchase Survey information. Field agents visit the selected retail outlets and sample within the item categories with checklists, which exhaustively define these categories of goods and services. A data collector, who uses the checklist in systematic stages, generally does the original selection of the specific items to be priced in a specific retail store. Information provided by the respondent is taken into account at each stage. Outlets may be located outside of the pricing area to represent out-of-town purchases.

After the initial selection, the same item (or a close substitute) is priced from period to period in order that, as far as possible, differences in reported prices are measures of price change only. All taxes directly associated with the purchase, or with the continued use of the items priced, are included in the indexes. Foods, fuels, rents, and other items are priced monthly in all areas. Prices of most other commodities and services are obtained monthly in the three largest areas and every other month in the remaining areas, half in the odd months and half in the even months. Between scheduled survey dates, prices are held at the level of their last pricing. BLS agents also collect data for a sample of rental units drawn from the Decennial Census of Population and Housing. This sample is heavily augmented with renter-occupied housing units in areas where there are many owner-occupied units. This survey is the basis for the Rent and Owners' equivalent rent components of the CPI.

BLS calculates basic indexes (elementary aggregates) for the 211 item strata in each of the 38 index areas. Basic indexes are combined with weights based on the 1993–1995 Consumer Expenditure Surveys and the Census.

BLS publishes CPI indexes for a variety of commodities and services: by region, by size of city, for cross-classifications of regions and population size classes, and for 26 metropolitan areas.

The purchasing power of the consumer dollar for any given date is calculated as the reciprocal of the index for that date, expressed in dollars, with the dollar's value in 1982–1984 equal to $1.00. It shows changes in the value of the dollar resulting from changes in prices of consumer goods and services. Dividing the index for the desired base date by the index for the current date and expressing the result in dollars can calculate the purchasing power of the dollar, with reference to other bases.

The relative importance figures are percentage distributions of the cost or value weights used in the index calculation. The cost weights represent average expenditures by consumers for specific classes of goods and services. However, in the subsequent pricing periods, the value weights and the corresponding relative importance figures change as prices change differentially (i.e., the relative importance increases for an item or group having a greater than average price increase and decreases for one having a less than average price increase). Historically, the weights in the CPI have been updated about once every 10 years. Since 2002, the CPI expenditure weights have been updated every two years to keep the weights more current with consumer spending habits.

Since the CPI traditionally measured price changes for a fixed market basket of goods and services, it was criticized as overstating inflation, as it did not account for the fact that consumers can substitute (buy more or less) as relative prices change. In 1999, the CPI began using a geometric mean formula to average the prices within most item categories. This formula assumes a modest degree of substitution within CPI item categories as relative prices change.

In 2002, BLS created an additional price index using a "superlative" formula to be address consumer substitution across CPI item categories. BLS began publishing this index, called the Chained Consumer Price Index for All Urban Consumers effective with release of July data in August 2002. Designated the C-CPI-U, the index will supplement, not replace, the CPI-U and the CPI-W.

Sources of Additional Information

The C-CPI-U is described in BLS new release 02-480. A press release dated April 1998, "Planned Change In The Consumer Price Index Formula," describes the geometric mean methodology.

The December 1996 issue of the *Monthly Labor Review* was devoted to a description and discussion of issues related to the 1998 CPI Revision. Further changes in methodology are described in BLS press releases. A detailed description of the CPI before 1978 is contained in *The Consumer Price Index: History and Techniques*, BLS Bulletin 1517 (1966). The updated CPI chapter, Chapter 17, is in the BLS *Handbook of Methods* is available on the BLS Web site.

Table 7-4. Consumer Price Indexes, All Urban Consumers (CPI-U): U.S. City Average, Major Groups, 1967–2004

(1982–1984 = 100, unless otherwise indicated.)

Year	All items	Food and beverages	Housing	Apparel	Transportation	Medical care	Recreation [1]	Education and communi- cation [1]	Other goods and services
1967	33.4	35.0	30.8	51.0	33.3	28.2	...	...	35.1
1968	34.8	36.2	32.0	53.7	34.3	29.9	...	...	36.9
1969	36.7	38.1	34.0	56.8	35.7	31.9	...	...	38.7
1970	38.8	40.1	36.4	59.2	37.5	34.0	...	...	40.9
1971	40.5	41.4	38.0	61.1	39.5	36.1	...	...	42.9
1972	41.8	43.1	39.4	62.3	39.9	37.3	...	...	44.7
1973	44.4	48.8	41.2	64.6	41.2	38.8	...	...	46.4
1974	49.3	55.5	45.8	69.4	45.8	42.4	...	...	49.8
1975	53.8	60.2	50.7	72.5	50.1	47.5	...	...	53.9
1976	56.9	62.1	53.8	75.2	55.1	52.0	...	...	57.0
1977	60.6	65.8	57.4	78.6	59.0	57.0	...	...	60.4
1978	65.2	72.2	62.4	81.4	61.7	61.8	...	...	64.3
1979	72.6	79.9	70.1	84.9	70.5	67.5	...	...	68.9
1980	82.4	86.7	81.1	90.9	83.1	74.9	...	...	75.2
1981	90.9	93.5	90.4	95.3	93.2	82.9	...	...	82.6
1982	96.5	97.3	96.9	97.8	97.0	92.5	...	...	91.1
1983	99.6	99.5	99.5	100.2	99.3	100.6	...	...	101.1
1984	103.9	103.2	103.6	102.1	103.7	106.8	...	...	107.9
1985	107.6	105.6	107.7	105.0	106.4	113.5	...	...	114.5
1986	109.6	109.1	110.9	105.9	102.3	122.0	...	...	121.4
1987	113.6	113.5	114.2	110.6	105.4	130.1	...	...	128.5
1988	118.3	118.2	118.5	115.4	108.7	138.6	...	...	137.0
1989	124.0	124.9	123.0	118.6	114.1	149.3	...	...	147.7
1990	130.7	132.1	128.5	124.1	120.5	162.8	...	...	159.0
1991	136.2	136.8	133.6	128.7	123.8	177.0	...	...	171.6
1992	140.3	138.7	137.5	131.9	126.5	190.1	...	...	183.3
1993	144.5	141.6	141.2	133.7	130.4	201.4	90.7	85.5	192.9
1994	148.2	144.9	144.8	133.4	134.3	211.0	92.7	88.8	198.5
1995	152.4	148.9	148.5	132.0	139.1	220.5	94.5	92.2	206.9
1996	156.9	153.7	152.8	131.7	143.0	228.2	97.4	95.3	215.4
1997	160.5	157.7	156.8	132.9	144.3	234.6	99.6	98.4	224.8
1998	163.0	161.1	160.4	133.0	141.6	242.1	101.1	100.3	237.7
1999	166.6	164.6	163.9	131.3	144.4	250.6	102.0	101.2	258.3
2000	172.2	168.4	169.6	129.6	153.3	260.8	103.3	102.5	271.1
2001	177.1	173.6	176.4	127.3	154.3	272.8	104.9	105.2	282.6
2002	179.9	176.8	180.3	124.0	152.9	285.6	106.2	107.9	293.2
2003	184.0	180.5	184.8	120.9	157.6	297.1	107.5	109.8	298.7
2004	188.9	186.6	189.5	120.4	163.1	310.1	108.6	111.6	304.7

[1]December 1997 = 100.
... = Not available.

Table 7-5. Consumer Price Indexes, All Urban Consumers (CPI-U): U.S. City Average, Commodity, Service, and Special Groups, 1967–2004

(1982–1984 = 100, unless otherwise indicated.)

Year	All items less food	All items less shelter	All items less medical care	All items less energy	All items less food and energy	Commodities	Commodities less food and beverages	Energy commodities	Commodities less food and energy	Nondurables	Nondurables less food	Nondurables less food and apparel
1967	33.4	35.2	33.7	34.4	34.7	36.8	38.3	23.9	41.3	35.7	37.6	32.6
1968	34.9	36.7	35.1	35.9	36.3	38.1	39.7	24.4	42.9	37.1	39.1	33.7
1969	36.8	38.4	37.0	38.0	38.4	39.9	41.4	25.2	44.7	38.9	40.9	34.9
1970	39.0	40.3	39.2	40.3	40.8	41.7	43.1	25.6	46.7	40.8	42.5	36.3
1971	40.8	42.0	40.8	42.0	42.7	43.2	44.7	26.1	48.5	42.1	44.0	37.6
1972	42.0	43.3	42.1	43.4	44.0	44.5	45.8	26.4	49.7	43.5	45.0	38.6
1973	43.7	46.2	44.8	46.1	45.6	47.8	47.3	29.1	51.1	47.5	46.9	40.3
1974	48.0	51.4	49.8	50.6	49.4	53.5	52.4	40.4	55.0	54.0	52.9	46.9
1975	52.5	56.0	54.3	55.1	53.9	58.2	57.3	43.4	60.1	58.3	57.0	51.5
1976	56.0	59.3	57.2	58.2	57.4	60.7	60.2	45.4	63.2	60.5	59.5	54.1
1977	59.6	63.1	60.8	61.9	61.0	64.2	63.6	48.7	66.5	64.0	62.5	57.2
1978	63.9	67.4	65.4	66.7	65.5	68.8	67.3	51.0	70.5	68.6	65.5	60.4
1979	71.2	74.2	72.9	73.4	71.9	76.6	75.2	68.7	76.4	77.2	74.6	71.2
1980	81.5	82.9	82.8	81.9	80.8	86.0	85.7	95.2	83.5	87.6	88.4	87.1
1981	90.4	91.0	91.4	90.1	89.2	93.2	93.1	107.6	90.0	95.2	96.7	96.8
1982	96.3	96.2	96.8	96.1	95.8	97.0	96.9	102.9	95.3	97.8	98.3	98.2
1983	99.7	99.8	99.6	99.6	99.6	99.8	100.0	99.0	100.2	99.7	100.0	100.0
1984	104.0	103.9	103.7	104.3	104.6	103.2	103.1	98.1	104.4	102.5	101.7	101.8
1985	108.0	107.0	107.2	108.4	109.1	105.4	105.2	98.2	107.1	104.8	104.1	104.1
1986	109.8	108.0	108.8	112.6	113.5	104.4	101.4	77.2	108.6	103.5	98.5	96.9
1987	113.6	111.6	112.6	117.2	118.2	107.7	104.0	80.2	111.8	107.5	101.8	100.3
1988	118.3	115.9	117.0	122.3	123.4	111.5	107.3	80.8	115.8	111.8	105.8	104.0
1989	123.7	121.6	122.4	128.1	129.0	116.7	111.6	87.9	119.6	118.2	111.7	111.3
1990	130.3	128.2	128.8	134.7	135.5	122.8	117.0	101.2	123.6	126.0	119.9	120.9
1991	136.1	133.5	133.8	140.9	142.1	126.6	120.4	99.1	128.8	130.3	124.5	125.7
1992	140.8	137.3	137.5	145.4	147.3	129.1	123.2	98.3	132.5	132.8	127.6	128.9
1993	145.1	141.4	141.2	150.0	152.2	131.5	125.3	97.3	135.2	135.1	129.3	130.7
1994	149.0	144.8	144.7	154.1	156.5	133.8	126.9	97.6	137.1	136.8	129.7	131.6
1995	153.1	148.6	148.6	158.7	161.2	136.4	128.9	98.8	139.3	139.3	130.9	134.1
1996	157.5	152.8	152.8	163.1	165.6	139.9	131.5	105.7	141.3	143.5	134.5	139.5
1997	161.1	155.9	156.3	167.1	169.5	141.8	132.2	105.7	142.3	146.4	136.3	141.8
1998	163.4	157.2	158.6	170.9	173.4	141.9	130.5	92.1	143.2	146.9	134.6	139.2
1999	167.0	160.2	162.0	174.4	177.0	144.4	132.5	100.0	144.1	151.2	139.4	147.5
2000	173.0	165.7	167.3	178.6	181.3	149.2	137.7	129.5	144.9	158.2	149.1	162.9
2001	177.8	169.7	171.9	183.5	186.1	150.7	137.2	125.2	145.3	160.6	149.1	164.1
2002	180.5	170.8	174.3	187.7	190.5	149.7	134.2	117.1	143.7	161.1	147.4	163.3
2003	184.7	174.6	178.1	190.6	193.2	151.2	134.5	136.7	140.9	165.3	151.9	172.1
2004	189.4	179.3	182.7	194.4	196.6	154.7	136.7	161.2	139.6	172.2	159.3	183.8

Table 7-5. Consumer Price Indexes, All Urban Consumers (CPI-U): U.S. City Average, Commodity, Service, and Special Groups, 1967–2004—*Continued*

(1982–1984 = 100, unless otherwise indicated.)

| Year | Services | | | | | | Services less medical care | Energy | Services less energy |
	Total [1]	Rent of shelter [2]	Gas (piped) and electricity	Transportation services	Medical care services	Other services			
1967	28.8	...	23.7	32.6	26.0	36.0	29.3	23.8	29.3
1968	30.3	...	23.9	33.9	27.9	38.1	30.8	24.2	30.9
1969	32.4	...	24.3	36.3	30.2	40.0	32.9	24.8	33.2
1970	35.0	...	25.4	40.2	32.3	42.2	35.6	25.5	36.0
1971	37.0	...	27.1	43.4	34.7	44.4	37.5	26.5	38.0
1972	38.4	...	28.5	44.4	35.9	45.6	38.9	27.2	39.4
1973	40.1	...	29.9	44.7	37.5	47.7	40.6	29.4	41.1
1974	43.8	...	34.5	46.3	41.4	51.3	44.3	38.1	44.8
1975	48.0	...	40.1	49.8	46.6	55.1	48.3	42.1	48.8
1976	52.0	...	44.7	56.9	51.3	58.4	52.2	45.1	52.7
1977	56.0	...	50.5	61.5	56.4	62.1	55.9	49.4	56.5
1978	60.8	...	55.0	64.4	61.2	66.4	60.7	52.5	61.3
1979	67.5	...	61.0	69.5	67.2	71.9	67.5	65.7	68.2
1980	77.9	...	71.4	79.2	74.8	78.7	78.2	86.0	78.5
1981	88.1	...	81.9	88.6	82.8	86.1	88.7	97.7	88.7
1982	96.0	...	93.2	96.1	92.6	93.5	96.4	99.2	96.3
1983	99.4	102.7	101.5	99.1	100.7	100.0	99.2	99.9	99.2
1984	104.6	107.7	105.4	104.8	106.7	106.5	104.4	100.9	104.5
1985	109.9	113.9	107.1	110.0	113.2	113.0	109.6	101.6	110.2
1986	115.4	120.2	105.7	116.3	121.9	119.4	114.6	88.2	116.5
1987	120.2	125.9	103.8	121.9	130.0	125.7	119.1	88.6	122.0
1988	125.7	132.0	104.6	128.0	138.3	132.6	124.3	89.3	127.9
1989	131.9	138.0	107.5	135.6	148.9	140.9	130.1	94.3	134.4
1990	139.2	145.5	109.3	144.2	162.7	150.2	136.8	102.1	142.3
1991	146.3	152.1	112.6	151.2	177.1	159.8	143.3	102.5	149.8
1992	152.0	157.3	114.8	155.7	190.5	168.5	148.4	103.0	155.9
1993	157.9	162.0	118.5	162.9	202.9	177.0	153.6	104.2	161.9
1994	163.1	167.0	119.2	168.6	213.4	185.4	158.4	104.6	167.6
1995	168.7	172.4	119.2	175.9	224.2	193.3	163.5	105.2	173.7
1996	174.1	178.0	122.1	180.5	232.4	201.4	168.7	110.1	179.4
1997	179.4	183.4	125.1	185.0	239.1	209.6	173.9	111.5	185.0
1998	184.2	189.6	121.2	187.9	246.8	216.9	178.4	102.9	190.6
1999	188.8	195.0	120.9	190.7	255.1	223.1	182.7	106.6	195.7
2000	195.3	201.3	128.0	196.1	266.0	229.9	188.9	124.6	202.1
2001	203.4	208.9	142.4	201.9	278.8	238.0	196.6	129.3	209.6
2002	209.8	216.7	134.4	209.1	292.9	246.4	202.5	121.7	217.5
2003	216.5	221.9	145.0	216.3	306.0	254.4	208.7	136.5	223.8
2004	222.8	227.9	150.6	220.6	321.3	261.3	214.5	151.4	230.2

[1] Includes tenants, household insurance, water, sewer, trash, and household operations services, not shown separately.
[2] December 1982 = 100.
. . . = Not available.

Table 7-6. Consumer Price Indexes, All Urban Consumers (CPI-U): U.S. City Average, Selected Groups, and Purchasing Power of the Consumer Dollar, 1913–2004

(1982–1984 = 100, unless otherwise indicated.)

Year	All items	Food	Rent of primary residence	Owners' equivalent of primary residence [1]	Apparel	Purchasing power of the consumer dollar [2]
1913	9.9	10.0	21.0	. . .	14.9	10.08
1914	10.0	10.2	21.0	. . .	15.0	9.94
1915	10.1	10.0	21.1	. . .	15.3	9.84
1916	10.9	11.3	21.3	. . .	16.8	9.15
1917	12.8	14.5	21.2	. . .	20.2	7.79
1918	15.1	16.7	21.5	. . .	27.3	6.64
1919	17.3	18.6	23.3	. . .	36.2	5.78
1920	20.0	21.0	27.4	. . .	43.1	4.99
1921	17.9	15.9	31.5	. . .	33.2	5.59
1922	16.8	14.9	32.4	. . .	27.0	5.96
1923	17.1	15.4	33.2	. . .	27.1	5.86
1924	17.1	15.2	34.4	. . .	26.8	5.85
1925	17.5	16.5	34.6	. . .	26.3	5.70
1926	17.7	17.0	34.2	. . .	25.9	5.65
1927	17.4	16.4	33.7	. . .	25.3	5.76
1928	17.1	16.3	32.9	. . .	25.0	5.83
1929	17.1	16.5	32.1	. . .	24.7	5.83
1930	16.7	15.6	31.2	. . .	24.2	5.99
1931	15.2	12.9	29.6	. . .	22.0	6.56
1932	13.7	10.7	26.5	. . .	19.5	7.32
1933	13.0	10.4	22.9	. . .	18.8	7.71
1934	13.4	11.6	21.4	. . .	20.6	7.46
1935	13.7	12.4	21.4	. . .	20.8	7.28
1936	13.9	12.6	21.9	. . .	21.0	7.21
1937	14.4	13.1	22.9	. . .	22.0	6.96
1938	14.1	12.1	23.7	. . .	21.9	7.09
1939	13.9	11.8	23.7	. . .	21.6	7.20
1940	14.0	12.0	23.7	. . .	21.8	7.13
1941	14.7	13.1	24.2	. . .	22.8	6.79
1942	16.3	15.4	24.7	. . .	26.7	6.13
1943	17.3	17.1	24.7	. . .	27.8	5.78
1944	17.6	16.9	24.8	. . .	29.8	5.68
1945	18.0	17.3	24.8	. . .	31.4	5.55
1946	19.5	19.8	25.0	. . .	34.4	5.12
1947	22.3	24.1	25.8	. . .	39.9	4.47
1948	24.1	26.1	27.5	. . .	42.5	4.15
1949	23.8	25.0	28.7	. . .	40.8	4.19
1950	24.1	25.4	29.7	. . .	40.3	4.15
1951	26.0	28.2	30.9	. . .	43.9	3.85
1952	26.5	28.7	32.2	. . .	43.5	3.77
1953	26.7	28.3	33.9	. . .	43.1	3.74
1954	26.9	28.2	35.1	. . .	43.1	3.72
1955	26.8	27.8	35.6	. . .	42.9	3.73
1956	27.2	28.0	36.3	. . .	43.7	3.68
1957	28.1	28.9	37.0	. . .	44.5	3.55
1958	28.9	30.2	37.6	. . .	44.6	3.46
1959	29.1	29.7	38.2	. . .	45.0	3.43

[1]December 1982 = 100.
[2]Purchasing power in 1982–1984 = $1.00.
. . . = Not available.

Table 7-6. Consumer Price Indexes, All Urban Consumers (CPI-U): U.S. City Average, Selected Groups, and Purchasing Power of the Consumer Dollar, 1913–2004—_Continued_

(1982–1984 = 100, unless otherwise indicated.)

Year	All items	Food	Rent of primary residence	Owners' equivalent of primary residence [1]	Apparel	Purchasing power of the consumer dollar [2]
1960	29.6	30.0	38.7	...	45.7	3.37
1961	29.9	30.4	39.2	...	46.1	3.34
1962	30.2	30.6	39.7	...	46.3	3.30
1963	30.6	31.1	40.1	...	46.9	3.27
1964	31.0	31.5	40.5	...	47.3	3.22
1965	31.5	32.2	40.9	...	47.8	3.17
1966	32.4	33.8	41.5	...	49.0	3.08
1967	33.4	34.1	42.2	...	51.0	2.99
1968	34.8	35.3	43.3	...	53.7	2.87
1969	36.7	37.1	44.7	...	56.8	2.73
1970	38.8	39.2	46.5	...	59.2	2.57
1971	40.5	40.4	48.7	...	61.1	2.47
1972	41.8	42.1	50.4	...	62.3	2.39
1973	44.4	48.2	52.5	...	64.6	2.25
1974	49.3	55.1	55.2	...	69.4	2.03
1975	53.8	59.8	58.0	...	72.5	1.86
1976	56.9	61.6	61.1	...	75.2	1.76
1977	60.6	65.5	64.8	...	78.6	1.65
1978	65.2	72.0	69.3	...	81.4	1.53
1979	72.6	79.9	74.3	...	84.9	1.38
1980	82.4	86.8	80.9	...	90.9	1.22
1981	90.9	93.6	87.9	...	95.3	1.10
1982	96.5	97.4	94.6	...	97.8	1.04
1983	99.6	99.4	100.1	102.5	100.2	1.00
1984	103.9	103.2	105.3	107.3	102.1	0.96
1985	107.6	105.6	111.8	113.2	105.0	0.93
1986	109.6	109.0	118.3	119.4	105.9	0.91
1987	113.6	113.5	123.1	124.8	110.6	0.88
1988	118.3	118.2	127.8	131.1	115.4	0.85
1989	124.0	125.1	132.8	137.4	118.6	0.81
1990	130.7	132.4	138.4	144.8	124.1	0.77
1991	136.2	136.3	143.3	150.4	128.7	0.73
1992	140.3	137.9	146.9	155.5	131.9	0.71
1993	144.5	140.9	150.3	160.5	133.7	0.69
1994	148.2	144.3	154.0	165.8	133.4	0.68
1995	152.4	148.4	157.8	171.3	132.0	0.66
1996	156.9	153.3	162.0	176.8	131.7	0.64
1997	160.5	157.3	166.7	181.9	132.9	0.62
1998	163.0	160.7	172.1	187.8	133.0	0.61
1999	166.6	164.1	177.5	192.9	131.3	0.60
2000	172.2	167.8	183.9	198.7	129.6	0.58
2001	177.1	173.1	192.1	206.3	127.3	0.57
2002	179.9	176.2	199.7	214.7	124.0	0.56
2003	184.0	180.0	205.5	219.9	120.9	0.54
2004	188.9	186.2	211.0	224.9	120.4	0.53

[1]December 1982 = 100.
[2]Purchasing power in 1982–1984 = $1.00.
. . . = Not available.

Table 7-7. Consumer Price Indexes, Urban Wage Earners and Clerical Workers (CPI-W): U.S. City Average, Major Groups, 1913–2004

(1982–1984 = 100, unless otherwise indicated.)

Year	All items	Food and beverages	Housing	Apparel	Transportation	Medical care	Recreation [1]	Education and communication [1]	Other goods and services
1913	10.0	. . .	. . .	15.0	. . .	. . .	. . .	. . .	. . .
1914	10.1	. . .	. . .	15.1	. . .	. . .	. . .	. . .	. . .
1915	10.2	. . .	. . .	15.4	. . .	. . .	. . .	. . .	. . .
1916	11.0	. . .	. . .	16.9	. . .	. . .	. . .	. . .	. . .
1917	12.9	. . .	. . .	20.3	. . .	. . .	. . .	. . .	. . .
1918	15.1	. . .	. . .	27.5	. . .	. . .	. . .	. . .	. . .
1919	17.4	. . .	. . .	36.4	. . .	. . .	. . .	. . .	. . .
1920	20.1	. . .	. . .	43.3	. . .	. . .	. . .	. . .	. . .
1921	18.0	. . .	. . .	33.4	. . .	. . .	. . .	. . .	. . .
1922	16.9	. . .	. . .	27.2	. . .	. . .	. . .	. . .	. . .
1923	17.2	. . .	. . .	27.2	. . .	. . .	. . .	. . .	. . .
1924	17.2	. . .	. . .	26.9	. . .	. . .	. . .	. . .	. . .
1925	17.6	. . .	. . .	26.4	. . .	. . .	. . .	. . .	. . .
1926	17.8	. . .	. . .	26.0	. . .	. . .	. . .	. . .	. . .
1927	17.5	. . .	. . .	25.5	. . .	. . .	. . .	. . .	. . .
1928	17.2	. . .	. . .	25.1	. . .	. . .	. . .	. . .	. . .
1929	17.2	. . .	. . .	24.8	. . .	. . .	. . .	. . .	. . .
1930	16.8	. . .	. . .	24.3	. . .	. . .	. . .	. . .	. . .
1931	15.3	. . .	. . .	22.1	. . .	. . .	. . .	. . .	. . .
1932	13.7	. . .	. . .	19.6	. . .	. . .	. . .	. . .	. . .
1933	13.0	. . .	. . .	18.9	. . .	. . .	. . .	. . .	. . .
1934	13.5	. . .	. . .	20.7	. . .	. . .	. . .	. . .	. . .
1935	13.8	. . .	. . .	20.9	14.1	10.2	. . .	. . .	. . .
1936	13.9	. . .	. . .	21.1	14.2	10.3	. . .	. . .	. . .
1937	14.4	. . .	. . .	22.1	14.5	10.4	. . .	. . .	. . .
1938	14.2	. . .	. . .	22.0	14.6	10.4	. . .	. . .	. . .
1939	14.0	. . .	. . .	21.7	14.2	10.4	. . .	. . .	. . .
1940	14.1	. . .	. . .	21.9	14.1	10.4	. . .	. . .	. . .
1941	14.8	. . .	. . .	23.0	14.6	10.5	. . .	. . .	. . .
1942	16.4	. . .	. . .	26.8	15.9	10.8	. . .	. . .	. . .
1943	17.4	. . .	. . .	28.0	15.8	11.3	. . .	. . .	. . .
1944	17.7	. . .	. . .	30.0	15.8	11.6	. . .	. . .	. . .
1945	18.1	. . .	. . .	31.5	15.8	11.9	. . .	. . .	. . .
1946	19.6	. . .	. . .	34.6	16.6	12.6	. . .	. . .	. . .
1947	22.5	. . .	. . .	40.1	18.4	13.6	. . .	. . .	. . .
1948	24.2	. . .	. . .	42.7	20.4	14.5	. . .	. . .	. . .
1949	24.0	. . .	. . .	41.0	22.0	14.9	. . .	. . .	. . .
1950	24.2	. . .	. . .	40.5	22.6	15.2	. . .	. . .	. . .
1951	26.1	. . .	. . .	44.1	24.0	15.9	. . .	. . .	. . .
1952	26.7	. . .	. . .	43.7	25.6	16.8	. . .	. . .	. . .
1953	26.9	. . .	. . .	43.3	26.3	17.4	. . .	. . .	. . .
1954	27.0	. . .	. . .	43.3	25.9	17.9	. . .	. . .	. . .

[1]December 1997 = 100.
. . . = Not available.

Table 7-7. Consumer Price Indexes, Urban Wage Earners and Clerical Workers (CPI-W): U.S. City Average, Major Groups, 1913–2004—*Continued*

(1982–1984 = 100, unless otherwise indicated.)

Year	All items	Food and beverages	Housing	Apparel	Transportation	Medical care	Recreation [1]	Education and communication [1]	Other goods and services
1955	26.9	...	...	43.1	25.6	18.3	...	...	...
1956	27.3	...	...	44.0	26.1	19.0	...	...	...
1957	28.3	...	...	44.7	27.6	19.8	...	...	...
1958	29.1	...	...	44.8	28.4	20.7	...	...	...
1959	29.3	...	...	45.2	29.6	21.6	...	...	...
1960	29.8	...	...	45.9	29.6	22.4	...	...	...
1961	30.1	...	...	46.3	30.0	23.0	...	...	...
1962	30.4	...	...	46.6	30.6	23.6	...	...	...
1963	30.8	...	...	47.1	30.8	24.2	...	...	...
1964	31.2	...	...	47.5	31.2	24.7	...	...	...
1965	31.7	...	...	48.0	31.7	25.3	...	...	...
1966	32.6	...	...	49.2	32.2	26.4	...	...	...
1967	33.6	35.0	31.1	51.2	33.1	28.3	...	...	35.4
1968	35.0	36.2	32.3	54.0	34.1	30.0	...	...	37.2
1969	36.9	38.0	34.3	57.1	35.5	32.1	...	...	39.1
1970	39.0	40.1	36.7	59.5	37.3	34.1	...	...	41.3
1971	40.7	41.3	38.3	61.4	39.2	36.3	...	...	43.3
1972	42.1	43.1	39.8	62.7	39.7	37.5	...	...	45.1
1973	44.7	48.8	41.5	65.0	41.0	39.0	...	...	46.9
1974	49.6	55.5	46.2	69.8	45.5	42.6	...	...	50.2
1975	54.1	60.2	51.1	72.9	49.8	47.7	...	...	54.4
1976	57.2	62.0	54.2	75.6	54.7	52.3	...	...	57.6
1977	60.9	65.7	57.9	79.0	58.6	57.3	...	...	60.9
1978	65.6	72.1	62.9	81.7	61.5	62.1	...	...	64.8
1979	73.1	79.9	70.7	85.2	70.4	68.0	...	...	69.4
1980	82.9	86.9	81.7	90.9	82.9	75.6	...	...	75.6
1981	91.4	93.6	91.1	95.6	93.0	83.5	...	...	82.5
1982	96.9	97.3	97.7	97.8	97.0	92.5	...	...	90.9
1983	99.8	99.5	100.0	100.2	99.2	100.5	...	...	101.3
1984	103.3	103.2	102.2	102.0	103.8	106.9	...	...	107.9
1985	106.9	105.5	106.6	105.0	106.4	113.6	...	...	114.2
1986	108.6	108.9	109.7	105.8	101.7	122.0	...	...	120.9
1987	112.5	113.3	112.8	110.4	105.1	130.2	...	...	127.8
1988	117.0	117.9	116.8	114.9	108.3	139.0	...	...	136.5
1989	122.6	124.6	121.2	117.9	113.9	149.6	...	...	147.4
1990	129.0	131.8	126.4	123.1	120.1	162.7	...	...	158.9
1991	134.3	136.5	131.2	127.4	123.1	176.5	...	...	171.7
1992	138.2	138.3	135.0	130.7	125.8	189.6	...	...	183.3
1993	142.1	141.2	138.5	132.4	129.4	200.9	91.2	86.0	192.2
1994	145.6	144.4	142.0	132.2	133.4	210.4	93.0	89.1	196.4
1995	149.8	148.3	145.4	130.9	138.8	219.8	94.7	92.3	204.2
1996	154.1	153.2	149.6	130.9	142.8	227.6	97.5	95.4	212.2
1997	157.6	157.2	153.4	132.1	143.6	234.0	99.7	98.5	221.6
1998	159.7	160.4	156.7	131.6	140.5	241.4	100.9	100.4	236.1
1999	163.2	163.8	160.0	130.1	143.4	249.7	101.3	101.5	261.9
2000	168.9	167.7	165.4	128.3	152.8	259.9	102.4	102.7	276.5
2001	173.5	173.0	172.1	126.1	153.6	271.8	103.6	105.3	289.5
2002	175.9	176.1	175.7	123.1	151.8	284.6	104.6	107.6	302.0
2003	179.8	179.9	180.4	120.0	156.3	296.3	105.5	109.0	307.0
2004	184.5	186.2	185.0	120.0	161.5	309.5	106.3	110.0	312.6

[1]December 1997 = 100.
. . . = Not available.

CONSUMER PRICE INDEX, HEALTH EXPENDITURES

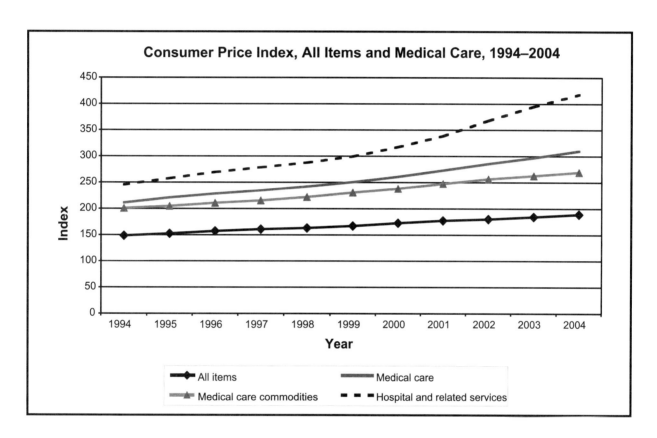

Consumer Price Index, All Items and Medical Care, 1994–2004

The CPI for medical services, with a 5 percent increase, continues to rise more rapidly than both the CPI for medical commodities (2.5 percent) and for medical care professional services (3.9 percent). The CPI for hospital and related services has increased by more than 50 percent since 1997, and it has grown by 31.7 percent since 2000. (Table 7-8)

Table 7-8. Consumer Price Indexes, All Urban Consumers (CPI-U): U.S. City Average, by Expenditure Category, 1990–2004

(1982–1984 = 100, unless otherwise indicated.)

Expenditure category	1990	1991	1992	1993	1994	1995	1996	1997	1998	1999	2000	2001	2002	2003	2004
ALL ITEMS	130.7	136.2	140.3	144.5	148.2	152.4	156.9	160.5	163.0	166.6	172.2	177.1	179.9	184.0	188.9
Food and Beverages	132.1	136.8	138.7	141.6	144.9	148.9	153.7	157.7	161.1	164.6	168.4	173.6	176.8	180.5	186.6
Food	132.4	136.3	137.9	140.9	144.3	148.4	153.3	157.3	160.7	164.1	167.8	173.1	176.2	180.0	186.2
Food at home	132.3	135.8	136.8	140.1	144.1	148.8	154.3	158.1	161.1	164.2	167.9	173.4	175.6	179.4	186.2
Cereals and bakery products	140.0	145.8	151.5	156.6	163.0	167.5	174.0	177.6	181.1	185.0	188.3	193.8	198.0	202.8	206.0
Meats, poultry, fish, and eggs	130.0	132.6	130.9	135.5	137.2	138.8	144.8	148.5	147.3	147.9	154.5	161.3	162.1	169.3	181.7
Dairy and related products	126.5	125.1	128.5	129.4	131.7	132.8	142.1	145.5	150.8	159.6	160.7	167.1	168.1	167.9	180.2
Fruits and vegetables	149.0	155.8	155.4	159.0	165.0	177.7	183.9	187.5	198.2	203.1	204.6	212.2	220.9	225.9	232.7
Nonalcoholic beverages and beverage materials	113.5	114.1	114.3	114.6	123.2	131.7	128.6	133.4	133.0	134.3	137.8	139.2	139.2	139.8	140.4
Other food at home	123.4	127.3	128.8	130.5	135.6	140.8	142.9	147.3	150.8	153.5	155.6	159.6	160.8	162.6	164.9
Sugar and sweets	124.7	129.3	133.1	133.4	135.2	137.5	143.7	147.8	150.2	152.3	154.0	155.7	159.0	162.0	163.2
Fats and oils	126.3	131.7	129.8	130.0	133.5	137.3	140.5	141.7	146.9	148.3	147.4	155.7	155.4	157.4	167.8
Other foods	131.2	137.1	140.1	143.7	147.5	151.1	156.2	161.2	165.5	168.9	172.2	176.0	177.1	178.8	179.7
Other miscellaneous foods [1]	...	...	...	...	...	...	...	...	102.6	104.9	107.5	108.9	109.2	110.3	110.4
Food away from home	133.4	137.9	140.7	143.2	145.7	149.0	152.7	157.0	161.1	165.1	169.0	173.9	178.3	182.1	187.5
Other food away from home [1]	...	...	...	...	...	...	...	...	101.6	105.2	109.0	113.4	117.7	121.3	125.3
Alcoholic beverages	129.3	142.8	147.3	149.6	151.5	153.9	158.5	162.8	165.7	169.7	174.7	179.3	183.6	187.2	192.1
Housing	128.5	133.6	137.5	141.2	144.8	148.5	152.8	156.8	160.4	163.9	169.6	176.4	180.3	184.8	189.5
Shelter	140.0	146.3	151.2	155.7	160.5	165.7	171.0	176.3	182.1	187.3	193.4	200.6	208.1	213.1	218.8
Rent of primary residence	138.4	143.3	146.9	150.3	154.0	157.8	162.0	166.7	172.1	177.5	183.9	192.1	199.7	205.5	211.0
Lodging away from home [1]	...	...	...	...	...	...	...	...	109.0	112.3	117.5	118.6	118.3	119.3	125.9
Owners' equivalent rent of primary residence [2]	144.8	150.4	155.5	160.5	165.8	171.3	176.8	181.9	187.8	192.9	198.7	206.3	214.7	219.9	224.9
Tenants' and household insurance [1]	...	...	...	...	...	...	...	...	99.8	101.3	103.7	106.2	108.7	114.8	116.2
Fuels and utilities	111.6	115.3	117.8	121.3	122.8	123.7	127.5	130.8	128.5	128.8	137.9	150.2	143.6	154.5	161.9
Fuels	104.5	106.7	108.1	111.2	111.7	111.5	115.2	117.9	113.7	113.5	122.8	135.4	127.2	138.2	144.4
Fuel oil and other household fuels	99.3	94.6	90.7	90.3	88.8	88.1	99.2	99.8	90.0	91.4	129.7	129.3	115.5	139.5	160.5
Gas (piped) and electricity	109.3	112.6	114.8	118.5	119.2	119.2	122.1	125.1	121.2	120.9	128.0	142.4	134.4	145.0	150.6
Water, sewer, and trash collection services [1]	...	...	...	...	...	...	...	...	101.6	104.0	106.5	109.6	113.0	117.2	124.0
Household furnishings and operations	113.3	116.0	118.0	119.3	121.0	123.0	124.7	125.4	126.6	126.7	128.2	129.1	128.3	126.1	125.5
Household operations [1]	...	...	...	...	...	...	...	...	101.5	104.5	110.5	115.6	119.0	121.8	125.0
Apparel	124.1	128.7	131.9	133.7	133.4	132.0	131.7	132.9	133.0	131.3	129.6	127.3	124.0	120.9	120.4
Men's and boys' apparel	120.4	124.2	126.5	127.5	126.4	126.2	127.7	130.1	131.8	131.1	131.0	129.7	121.7	118.0	117.5
Women's and girls' apparel	122.6	127.6	130.4	132.6	130.9	126.9	124.7	126.1	126.0	123.3	121.5	119.3	115.8	113.1	113.0
Infants' and toddlers' apparel	125.8	128.9	129.3	127.1	128.1	127.2	129.7	129.0	126.1	129.0	130.6	129.2	126.4	122.1	118.5
Footwear	117.4	120.9	125.0	125.9	126.0	125.4	126.6	127.6	128.0	125.7	123.8	123.0	121.4	119.6	119.3
Transportation	120.5	123.8	126.5	130.4	134.3	139.1	143.0	144.3	141.6	144.4	153.3	154.3	152.9	157.6	163.1
Private transportation	118.8	121.9	124.6	127.5	131.4	136.3	140.0	141.0	137.9	140.5	149.1	150.0	148.8	153.6	159.4
New and used motor vehicles [1]	...	...	...	91.8	95.5	99.4	101.0	100.5	100.1	100.1	100.8	101.3	99.2	96.5	94.2
New vehicles	121.4	126.0	129.2	132.7	137.6	141.0	143.7	144.3	143.4	142.9	142.8	142.1	140.0	137.9	137.1
Used cars and trucks	117.6	118.1	123.2	133.9	141.7	156.5	157.0	151.1	150.6	152.0	155.8	158.7	152.0	142.9	133.3
Motor fuel	101.2	99.4	99.0	98.0	98.5	100.0	106.3	106.2	92.2	100.7	129.3	124.7	116.6	135.8	160.4
Gasoline (all types)	101.0	99.2	99.0	97.7	98.2	99.8	105.9	105.8	91.6	100.1	128.6	124.0	116.0	135.1	159.7
Motor vehicle parts and equipment	100.9	102.2	103.1	101.6	101.4	102.1	102.2	101.9	101.1	100.5	101.5	104.8	106.9	107.8	108.7
Motor vehicle maintenance and repair	130.1	136.0	141.3	145.9	150.2	154.0	158.4	162.7	167.1	171.9	177.3	183.5	190.2	195.6	200.2
Public transportation	142.6	148.9	151.4	167.0	172.0	175.9	181.9	186.7	190.3	197.7	209.6	210.6	207.4	209.3	209.1
Medical Care	162.8	177.0	190.1	201.4	211.0	220.5	228.2	234.6	242.1	250.6	260.8	272.8	285.6	297.1	310.1
Medical care commodities	163.4	176.8	188.1	195.0	200.7	204.5	210.4	215.3	221.8	230.7	238.1	247.6	256.4	262.8	269.3
Medical care services	162.7	177.1	190.5	202.9	213.4	224.2	232.4	239.1	246.8	255.1	266.0	278.8	292.9	306.0	321.3
Professional services	156.1	165.7	175.8	184.7	192.5	201.0	208.3	215.4	222.2	229.2	237.7	246.5	253.9	261.2	271.5
Hospital and related services	178.0	196.1	214.0	231.9	245.6	257.8	269.5	278.4	287.5	299.5	317.3	338.3	367.8	394.8	417.9
Recreation [1]	...	...	...	90.7	92.7	94.5	97.4	99.6	101.1	102.0	103.3	104.9	106.2	107.5	108.6
Video and audio [1]	...	...	...	96.5	95.4	95.1	96.6	99.4	101.1	100.7	101.0	101.5	102.8	103.6	104.2
Education and Communication [1]	...	...	...	85.5	88.8	92.2	95.3	98.4	100.3	101.2	102.5	105.2	107.9	109.8	111.6
Education [1]	...	...	...	78.4	83.3	88.0	92.7	97.3	102.1	107.0	112.5	118.5	126.0	134.4	143.7
Educational books and supplies	171.3	180.3	190.3	197.6	205.5	214.4	226.9	238.4	250.8	261.7	279.9	295.9	317.6	335.4	351.0
Tuition, other school fees, and child care	175.7	191.4	208.5	225.3	239.8	253.8	267.1	280.4	294.2	308.4	324.0	341.1	362.1	386.7	414.3
Communication [1]	...	...	...	96.7	97.6	98.8	99.6	100.3	98.7	96.0	93.6	93.3	92.3	89.7	86.7
Information and information processing [1]	...	...	...	97.7	98.6	98.7	99.5	100.4	98.5	95.5	92.8	92.3	90.8	87.8	84.6
Telephone services [1]	...	...	...	...	...	...	...	...	100.7	100.1	98.5	99.3	99.7	98.3	95.8
Information technology, hardware, and services [3]	93.5	88.6	83.7	78.8	72.0	63.8	57.2	50.1	39.9	30.5	25.9	21.3	18.3	16.1	14.8
Personal computers and peripheral equipment [1]	...	...	...	...	...	...	...	...	78.2	53.5	41.1	29.5	22.2	17.6	15.3
Other Goods and Services	159.0	171.6	183.3	192.9	198.5	206.9	215.4	224.8	237.7	258.3	271.1	282.6	293.2	298.7	304.7
Tobacco and smoking products	181.5	202.7	219.8	228.4	220.0	225.7	232.8	243.7	274.8	355.8	394.9	425.2	461.5	469.0	478.0
Personal care	130.4	134.9	138.3	141.5	144.6	147.1	150.1	152.7	156.7	161.1	165.6	170.5	174.7	178.0	181.7
Personal care products	128.2	132.8	136.5	139.0	141.5	143.1	144.3	144.2	148.3	151.8	153.7	155.1	154.7	153.5	153.9
Personal care services	132.8	137.0	140.0	144.0	147.9	151.5	156.6	162.4	166.0	171.4	178.1	184.3	188.4	193.2	197.6
Miscellaneous personal services	158.4	168.8	177.5	186.1	195.9	205.9	215.6	226.1	234.7	243.0	252.3	263.1	274.4	283.5	293.9

[1] December 1997 = 100.
[2] December 1982 = 100.
[3] December 1988 = 100.
. . . = Not available.

Table 7-9. Relative Importance of Components in the Consumer Price Index: U.S. City Average, December 1997–December 2004

(Percent of all items.)

Index and year	All items	Food and beverages	Housing	Apparel	Transportation	Medical care	Recreation	Education and communication	Other goods and services
All URBAN CONSUMERS (CPI-U)									
December 1997	100.0	16.3	39.6	4.9	17.6	5.6	6.1	5.5	4.3
December 1998	100.0	16.4	39.8	4.8	17.0	5.7	6.1	5.5	4.6
December 1999	100.0	16.3	39.6	4.7	17.5	5.8	6.0	5.4	4.7
December 2000	100.0	16.2	40.0	4.4	17.6	5.8	5.9	5.3	4.8
December 2001 (1993–1995 Weights) ..	100.0	16.4	40.5	4.2	16.6	6.0	5.9	5.4	4.9
December 2001 (1999–2000 Weights) ..	100.0	15.7	40.9	4.4	17.1	5.8	6.0	5.8	4.3
December 2002	100.0	15.6	40.9	4.2	17.3	6.0	5.9	5.8	4.4
December 2003	100.0	15.4	42.1	4.0	16.9	6.1	5.9	5.9	3.8
December 2004	100.0	15.3	42.0	3.8	17.4	6.1	5.7	5.8	3.8
URBAN WAGE EARNERS AND WORKERS (CPI-W)									
December 1997	100.0	17.9	36.5	5.3	19.8	4.6	6.0	5.4	4.5
December 1998	100.0	18.0	36.7	5.2	19.2	4.7	5.9	5.4	5.0
December 1999	100.0	17.9	36.5	5.0	19.7	4.7	5.8	5.3	5.1
December 2000	100.0	17.8	36.8	4.8	19.9	4.7	5.7	5.2	5.2
December 2001 (1993–1995 Weights) ..	100.0	18.0	37.3	4.6	18.8	4.9	5.7	5.3	5.4
December 2001 (1999–2000 Weights) ..	100.0	17.2	38.1	4.8	19.4	4.6	5.6	5.6	4.5
December 2002	100.0	17.1	38.1	4.6	19.7	4.7	5.6	5.6	4.6
December 2003	100.0	17.2	39.1	4.4	19.1	5.0	5.7	5.6	3.9
December 2004	100.0	17.0	39.0	4.2	19.8	5.0	5.5	5.5	3.9

Table 7-10. Consumer Price Indexes, All Urban Consumers, All Items: Selected Areas, Selected Years, 1965–2004

(1982–1984 = 100, unless otherwise indicated.)

Area	1965	1970	1975	1980	1981	1982	1983	1984	1985	1986	1987	1988	1989	1990
NORTHEAST														
New York-Northern New Jersey-Long Island	32.6	41.2	57.6	82.1	90.1	95.3	99.8	104.8	108.7	112.3	118.0	123.7	130.6	138.5
Philadelphia-Wilmington-Atlantic City	32.8	40.8	56.8	83.6	92.1	96.6	99.4	104.1	108.8	111.5	116.8	122.4	128.3	135.8
Boston-Brockton-Nashua	32.5	40.2	55.8	82.6	91.8	95.5	99.8	104.7	109.4	112.2	117.1	124.2	131.3	138.9
Pittsburgh	31.4	38.1	52.4	81.0	89.3	94.4	101.1	104.5	106.9	108.2	111.4	114.9	120.1	126.2
NORTH CENTRAL														
Chicago-Gary-Kenosha	31.7	38.9	52.8	82.2	90.0	96.2	100.0	103.8	107.7	110.0	114.5	119.0	125.0	131.7
Detroit-Ann Arbor-Flint	31.2	39.5	53.9	85.3	93.2	97.0	99.8	103.2	106.8	108.3	111.7	116.1	122.3	128.6
St. Louis	31.7	38.8	52.6	82.5	90.1	96.6	100.1	103.3	107.1	108.6	112.2	115.7	121.8	128.1
Cleveland-Akron	29.6	37.2	50.2	78.9	87.2	94.0	101.2	104.8	107.8	109.4	112.7	116.7	122.7	129.0
Minneapolis-St. Paul	30.1	37.4	51.2	78.9	88.6	97.4	99.5	103.1	107.0	108.4	111.6	117.2	122.0	127.0
Milwaukee-Racine	31.0	37.5	50.8	81.4	90.7	95.9	100.2	103.8	107.0	107.4	111.5	115.9	120.8	126.2
Cincinnati-Hamilton	30.5	37.4	51.8	82.1	87.9	94.9	100.8	104.3	106.6	107.6	111.9	116.1	120.9	126.5
Kansas City	32.2	39.0	53.2	83.6	90.5	95.0	100.5	104.5	107.7	108.7	113.1	117.4	121.6	126.0
SOUTH														
Washington-Baltimore [1]	...	...	...	...	...	...	...	...	...	...	...	...	...	...
Dallas-Fort Worth	29.9	37.6	50.4	81.5	90.8	96.0	99.7	104.3	108.2	109.9	112.9	116.1	119.5	125.1
Houston-Galveston-Brazoria	29.6	36.4	51.4	82.7	91.0	97.3	100.0	102.7	104.9	103.9	106.5	109.5	114.1	120.6
Atlanta	31.2	38.6	53.6	80.3	90.2	96.0	99.9	104.1	108.9	112.2	116.5	120.4	126.1	131.7
Miami-Fort Lauderdale	...	...	...	81.1	90.5	96.7	99.9	103.5	106.5	107.9	111.8	116.8	121.5	128.0
Tampa-St. Petersburg-Clearwater [2]	...	...	...	...	...	...	...	...	...	...	100.0	103.7	107.2	111.7
WEST														
Los Angeles-Riverside-Orange County	32.4	38.7	53.3	83.7	91.9	97.3	99.1	103.6	108.4	111.9	116.7	122.1	128.3	135.9
San Francisco-Oakland-San Jose	30.8	37.7	51.8	80.4	90.8	97.6	98.4	104.0	108.4	111.6	115.4	120.5	126.4	132.1
Seattle-Tacoma-Bremerton	31.0	37.4	51.1	82.7	91.8	97.7	99.3	103.0	105.6	106.7	109.2	112.8	118.1	126.8
San Diego	28.2	34.1	47.6	79.4	90.1	96.2	99.0	104.8	110.4	113.5	117.5	123.4	130.6	138.4
Portland-Salem	32.3	38.7	53.5	87.2	95.0	98.0	99.1	102.8	106.7	108.2	110.9	114.7	120.4	127.4
Honolulu	34.4	41.5	56.3	83.0	91.7	97.2	99.3	103.5	106.8	106.8	109.4	114.9	121.7	138.1
Anchorage	35.3	41.1	57.1	85.5	92.4	97.4	99.2	103.3	105.8	107.8	108.2	108.6	111.7	118.6
Denver-Boulder-Greeley	28.8	34.5	48.4	78.4	87.2	95.1	100.5	104.3	107.1	107.9	110.8	113.7	115.8	120.9

Area	1991	1992	1993	1994	1995	1996	1997	1998	1999	2000	2001	2002	2003	2004
NORTHEAST														
New York-Northern New Jersey-Long Island	144.8	150.0	154.5	158.2	162.2	166.9	170.8	173.6	177.0	182.5	187.1	191.9	197.8	204.8
Philadelphia-Wilmington-Atlantic City	142.2	146.6	150.2	154.6	158.7	162.8	166.5	168.2	171.9	176.5	181.3	184.9	188.8	196.5
Boston-Brockton-Nashua	145.0	148.6	152.9	154.9	158.6	163.3	167.9	171.7	176.0	183.6	191.5	196.5	203.9	209.5
Pittsburgh	131.3	136.0	139.9	144.6	149.2	153.2	157.0	159.2	162.5	168.0	172.5	174.0	177.5	183.0
NORTH CENTRAL														
Chicago-Gary-Kenosha	137.0	141.1	145.4	148.6	153.3	157.4	161.7	165.0	168.4	173.8	178.3	181.2	184.5	188.6
Detroit-Ann Arbor-Flint	133.1	135.9	139.6	144.0	148.6	152.5	156.3	159.8	163.9	169.8	174.4	178.9	182.5	185.4
St. Louis	132.1	134.7	137.5	141.3	145.2	149.6	152.9	154.5	157.6	163.1	167.3	169.1	173.4	180.3
Cleveland-Akron	134.2	136.8	140.3	144.4	147.9	152.0	156.1	159.8	162.5	168.0	172.9	173.3	176.2	181.6
Minneapolis-St. Paul	130.4	135.0	139.2	143.6	147.0	151.9	155.4	158.3	163.3	170.1	176.5	179.6	182.7	187.9
Milwaukee-Racine	132.2	137.1	142.1	147.0	151.0	154.7	157.7	160.3	163.7	168.6	171.7	174.0	177.7	180.2
Cincinnati-Hamilton	131.4	134.1	137.8	142.4	146.2	149.6	152.1	155.1	159.2	164.8	167.9	170.0	173.4	176.5
Kansas City	131.2	134.3	138.1	141.3	145.3	151.6	155.8	157.8	160.1	166.6	172.2	174.0	177.0	180.7
SOUTH														
Washington-Baltimore [1]	...	...	...	...	...	...	100.8	102.1	104.2	107.6	110.4	113.0	116.2	119.5
Dallas-Fort Worth	130.8	133.9	137.3	141.2	144.9	148.8	151.4	153.6	158.0	164.7	170.4	172.7	176.2	178.7
Houston-Galveston-Brazoria	125.1	129.1	133.4	137.9	139.8	142.7	145.4	146.8	148.7	154.2	158.8	159.2	163.7	169.5
Atlanta	135.9	138.5	143.4	146.7	150.9	156.0	158.9	161.2	164.8	170.6	176.2	178.2	180.8	183.2
Miami-Fort Lauderdale	132.3	134.5	139.1	143.6	148.9	153.7	158.4	160.5	162.4	167.8	173.0	175.5	180.6	185.6
Tampa-St. Petersburg-Clearwater [2]	116.4	119.2	124.0	126.5	129.7	131.6	134.0	137.5	140.6	145.7	148.8	153.9	158.1	162.0
WEST														
Los Angeles-Riverside-Orange County	141.4	146.5	150.3	152.3	154.6	157.5	160.0	162.3	166.1	171.6	177.3	182.2	187.0	193.2
San Francisco-Oakland-San Jose	137.9	142.5	146.3	148.7	151.6	155.1	160.4	165.5	172.5	180.2	189.9	193.0	196.4	198.8
Seattle-Tacoma-Bremerton	134.1	139.0	142.9	147.8	152.3	157.5	163.0	167.7	172.8	179.2	185.7	189.3	192.3	194.7
San Diego	143.4	147.4	150.6	154.5	156.8	160.9	164.7	166.9	172.8	182.8	191.2	197.9	205.3	212.8
Portland-Salem	133.9	139.8	144.7	148.9	153.2	158.6	164.0	167.1	172.6	178.0	182.4	183.8	186.3	191.1
Honolulu	148.0	155.1	160.1	164.5	168.1	170.7	171.9	171.5	173.3	176.3	178.4	180.3	184.5	190.6
Anchorage	124.0	128.2	132.2	135.0	138.9	142.7	144.8	146.9	148.4	150.9	155.2	158.2	162.5	166.7
Denver-Boulder-Greeley	125.6	130.3	135.8	141.8	147.9	153.1	158.1	161.9	166.6	173.2	181.3	184.8	186.8	187.0

[1] November 1996 = 100.
[2] 1987 = 100.
. . . = Not available.

NOTES AND DEFINITIONS

EXPORT AND IMPORT PRICE INDEXES

Collection and Coverage

United States export and import price indexes cover non-military goods transactions between the United States and the rest of the world. The export price indexes provide a measure of price change for U.S. products sold to other countries, and the import price indexes provide a measure of price change for goods purchased by U.S. residents from other countries.

BLS field representatives initially collect the prices used in constructing the indexes through personal visits. Thereafter, the prices generally are collected each month by mail questionnaire or telephone. To the extent possible, products are priced at the U.S. border for exports and at both the foreign border and the U.S. border for imports. Only one price basis series is used in constructing the index for each given product. For most products, prices refer to transactions completed during the first week of the month. Indexes published here are based on the Standard Industrial Trade Classification System (SITC), a United Nations product classification system. The SITC is especially useful for international comparisons. Both End Use Category and the Harmonized System nomenclature publish these indexes.

Prices are collected according to the specification method. The specifications for each product include detailed descriptions of the product's physical and functional characteristics. The terms of transaction include information on the number of units bought or sold, discounts, credit terms, packaging, class of buyer or seller, etc. When there are changes in either the specifications or terms of transaction for a product, the dollar value of each change is deleted from the total price change in order to obtain the "pure price change." Once this value is determined, a linking procedure is employed, allowing for continued repricing of the item.

At the elementary level, the price changes for individual items within a given Company/Classification Group cell are generally averaged together using equal weights in order to produce an index at the cell level. These cells are then averaged together using the relative importance of a given company's trade in the product area to produce an index at the Classification Group level. These Classification Group indexes are then averaged together using weights derived from these company weights in order to produce the lowest level publication strata. Successively higher levels of publication strata are then averaged together using their relative importance based on 1995 U.S. trade values.

A limited number of import price indexes based on locality of origin indexes are also produced. BLS also publishes indexes for selected categories of internationally traded services as calculated on an international basis.

Sources of Additional Information

Concepts and methodology are described in Chapter 15 of the BLS *Handbook of Methods* and in monthly press releases.

Table 7-11. U.S. Export Price Indexes for Selected Categories of Goods, by Standard International Trade Classification, 1990–2004

(2000 = 100.)

Categories	Relative import-ance [1]	1990 March	1990 June	1990 September	1990 December	1991 March	1991 June	1991 September	1991 December	1992 March	1992 June	1992 September	1992 December
ALL COMMODITIES	100.00	94.8	95.1	95.8	96.3	96.4	96.1	95.6	95.7	96.2	96.5	96.6	96.3
Food and Live Animals	6.48	101.1	102.4	96.2	93.3	96.4	99.0	98.0	100.3	104.3	101.0	98.8	98.2
Meat and meat preparations	1.20	82.8	81.4	81.8	84.7	85.0	84.2	85.3	82.8	86.6	87.7	86.4	88.2
Fish, crustaceans, aquatic invertebrates, and preparations thereof	0.48	89.9	86.8	88.8	87.2	86.7	83.5	77.6	83.2	90.0	86.5	84.5	80.0
Cereals and cereal preparations	1.66	122.1	126.5	112.4	104.7	107.9	112.7	112.7	119.6	127.4	122.0	115.3	114.2
Vegetables and fruit and nuts, fresh or dried	1.54	92.6	93.2	90.2	89.5	104.0	111.0	103.4	95.6	97.0	91.4	92.0	94.1
Feeding stuff for animals (not including unmilled cereals)	0.59	102.3	99.5	101.0	104.9	105.6	101.9	107.2	108.0	103.9	104.1	107.0	105.8
Miscellaneous edible products and preparations	0.49	93.4	94.0	93.8	95.0	93.9	94.5	93.8	94.0	93.4	94.2	94.9	95.1
Beverages and Tobacco	0.68	83.4	84.9	85.6	88.0	89.9	90.4	90.9	92.6	93.1	93.8	94.7	95.5
Tobacco and tobacco manufactures	0.42	83.4	85.0	85.7	87.9	89.9	90.3	90.7	92.4	92.9	93.7	94.5	95.4
Crude Materials, Inedible, Except Fuels	5.50	96.4	96.7	97.1	94.7	94.6	91.8	88.2	86.2	87.6	89.9	90.4	90.0
Oil seeds and oleaginous fruits	1.17	115.2	116.1	123.5	123.3	124.1	118.7	116.8	111.8	113.8	117.6	110.1	110.2
Cork and wood	0.52	77.1	76.5	74.2	71.9	72.2	73.4	74.3	74.2	78.9	82.5	89.8	93.7
Textile fibers and their waste	0.62	111.2	118.2	116.0	115.3	120.3	123.2	112.5	102.6	97.9	99.1	94.7	94.1
Metalliferous ores and metal scrap	1.43	102.8	105.9	111.9	103.5	102.2	94.5	92.3	87.2	91.0	90.2	91.0	87.0
Mineral Fuels, Lubricants, and Related Materials	2.95	68.9	67.2	78.3	80.7	69.1	66.3	66.3	67.0	61.3	63.8	64.7	63.6
Petroleum, petroleum products, and related materials	2.27	60.1	57.5	77.2	79.2	59.3	54.9	54.9	56.1	47.4	52.9	54.6	52.2
Chemicals and Related Products, n.e.s.	14.94	90.4	90.4	93.3	97.1	96.1	92.5	91.0	90.3	90.2	90.4	90.1	89.0
Organic chemicals	3.60	97.4	93.9	99.5	105.1	100.7	93.6	88.6	88.6	88.5	90.5	91.9	89.7
Inorganic chemicals	0.96	...	...	...	...	...	...	...	...	...	...	...	87.9
Medicinal and pharmaceutical products	2.71	91.4	91.7	92.0	92.5	92.2	92.4	94.0	94.0	95.1	95.7	95.6	95.8
Essential oils, polishing, and cleansing preparations	1.05	86.2	87.4	87.6	87.9	88.1	88.2	88.8	88.5	90.0	90.5	89.6	89.5
Fertilizers	0.42	...	...	...	...	...	...	...	...	...	...	...	...
Plastics in primary forms	2.74	...	...	...	...	...	...	...	...	...	...	...	78.8
Plastics in nonprimary forms	0.94	...	...	...	...	...	...	...	...	...	...	...	92.9
Chemical materials and products, n.e.s.	1.89	85.8	86.4	88.0	90.0	91.7	90.5	89.6	89.5	90.1	90.1	90.5	90.6
Manufactured Goods Classified Chiefly by Material	10.50	86.7	86.8	87.2	87.1	87.3	87.0	86.7	86.7	87.2	87.5	87.8	87.7
Rubber manufactures, n.e.s.	0.70	81.3	81.4	82.2	84.2	85.7	86.4	86.6	87.0	86.8	86.9	87.5	87.7
Uncoated paper, paperboard, linerboard	1.47	91.1	90.8	91.3	91.5	91.1	90.7	90.0	90.2	89.9	89.7	89.2	88.8
Textile yarn, fabrics, and made-up articles, n.e.s.	1.58	91.7	91.2	91.2	92.1	94.1	95.3	94.8	95.1	96.5	96.7	97.0	97.3
Nonmetallic mineral manufactures, n.e.s.	1.56	86.3	85.8	85.8	86.6	87.2	87.2	87.2	88.0	88.2	89.2	89.3	89.4
Iron and steel	1.42	...	...	...	...	...	...	...	...	...	...	...	...
Nonferrous metals	1.20	86.1	87.1	89.2	85.0	81.0	76.5	76.0	73.9	75.4	76.3	76.4	73.9
Manufactures of metals, n.e.s.	2.17	80.9	81.2	81.3	82.0	83.1	83.5	83.7	84.0	84.2	84.2	84.8	85.6
Machinery and Transport Equipment	46.83	97.4	97.9	98.3	98.8	100.3	101.0	101.4	101.7	102.1	102.4	102.6	102.6
Power generating machinery and equipment	4.59	76.3	77.0	77.2	77.8	79.8	80.7	81.4	81.8	82.9	84.5	84.4	84.6
Machinery specialized for particular industries	3.59	82.6	82.7	83.4	84.5	85.3	86.1	86.2	86.6	87.3	88.0	88.4	89.0
Metalworking machinery	0.60	81.1	82.1	82.2	84.2	85.9	87.7	87.9	88.3	89.4	89.9	89.9	89.8
General industrial machinery, equipment, and parts, n.e.s.	4.66	81.8	82.5	83.0	83.4	85.3	85.8	86.4	86.4	87.6	87.8	88.1	88.6
Computer equipment and office machines	5.21	193.4	193.2	192.9	190.5	190.9	189.4	187.2	185.0	183.8	182.2	180.9	176.9
Telecommunications and sound recording and reproducing apparatus and equipment	3.13	95.5	97.3	97.8	98.3	100.7	103.4	104.9	105.8	104.5	105.3	105.7	105.8
Electrical machinery and equipment	11.41	113.1	112.7	112.4	112.7	112.8	113.4	115.5	116.3	117.6	116.8	117.4	117.2
Road vehicles	8.67	88.2	88.7	89.1	90.1	90.9	91.2	91.4	92.1	92.2	92.6	92.8	93.2
Miscellaneous Manufactured Articles	11.06	89.7	90.5	91.8	93.2	94.4	95.1	95.4	95.9	96.6	97.0	97.2	97.3
Furniture and parts thereof	0.60	92.3	93.6	93.4	95.2	96.9	97.6	97.7	97.5	98.4	98.2	97.8	98.1
Articles of apparel and clothing accessories	0.76	...	...	...	...	...	...	...	...	...	...	...	...
Professional, scientific and controlling instruments, and apparatus, n.e.s.	4.27	80.5	81.9	83.8	85.6	86.6	87.8	88.0	88.8	89.7	90.1	90.0	90.1
Photographic apparatus, equipment and supplies, and optical goods, n.e.s.	0.90	95.0	94.6	96.0	98.4	98.8	98.6	98.4	99.4	99.3	98.2	99.1	99.7
Miscellaneous manufactured articles, n.e.s.	4.16	97.6	98.1	98.7	99.4	101.1	101.2	101.9	101.7	102.1	103.0	103.6	103.3

n.e.s. = not elsewhere specified.

[1]Percent of total, relative importance in December 1999, based on 1995 trade values.
. . . = Not available.

Table 7-11. U.S. Export Price Indexes for Selected Categories of Goods, by Standard International Trade Classification, 1990–2004—*Continued*

(2000 = 100.)

Categories	1993 March	1993 June	1993 September	1993 December	1994 March	1994 June	1994 September	1994 December	1995 March	1995 June	1995 September	1995 December
ALL COMMODITIES	96.6	96.9	96.9	97.3	98.2	98.5	99.1	101.1	103.0	104.5	104.4	104.4
Food and Live Animals	97.7	96.1	100.4	105.9	106.7	102.0	100.6	104.9	106.3	112.1	121.6	126.5
Meat and meat preparations	89.8	92.2	88.4	88.5	91.3	88.7	89.0	90.1	92.9	95.7	99.4	101.4
Fish, crustaceans, aquatic invertebrates, and preparations thereof	81.5	85.1	79.8	77.8	83.1	86.5	93.4	97.8	106.8	107.1	105.6	96.3
Cereals and cereal preparations	112.7	105.8	111.8	129.4	130.4	118.5	111.9	121.0	120.1	133.2	149.6	167.9
Vegetables and fruit and nuts, fresh or dried	94.7	94.1	107.8	104.5	102.5	100.1	100.1	103.5	106.8	107.2	122.7	111.2
Feeding stuff for animals (not including unmilled cereals)	101.9	102.7	109.6	112.0	108.8	108.2	105.9	101.0	99.1	104.9	107.1	122.4
Miscellaneous edible products and preparations	93.9	94.4	94.0	90.6	91.9	92.0	93.1	93.1	92.9	94.8	94.0	95.3
Beverages and Tobacco	96.4	96.7	97.5	96.5	96.9	97.0	96.8	96.9	97.9	98.2	98.7	98.5
Tobacco and tobacco manufactures	96.3	96.4	97.2	96.1	96.6	96.7	96.4	96.5	97.5	98.1	98.6	98.3
Crude Materials, Inedible, Except Fuels	93.4	95.8	94.3	95.0	100.7	104.0	104.8	112.4	122.6	125.4	119.0	116.0
Oil seeds and oleaginous fruits	114.4	117.0	130.0	133.9	134.2	134.9	115.0	109.8	112.0	115.6	123.1	136.0
Cork and wood	110.0	121.0	111.4	110.0	114.7	112.0	111.8	113.6	117.9	117.5	111.4	112.0
Textile fibers and their waste	97.8	96.1	93.3	95.6	113.3	120.9	117.3	127.3	152.6	154.3	141.2	142.2
Metalliferous ores and metal scrap	87.8	89.0	89.0	90.3	96.0	96.7	106.2	123.5	132.4	132.2	125.0	116.4
Mineral Fuels, Lubricants, and Related Materials	64.5	64.9	63.2	60.4	61.8	64.5	64.6	65.9	65.6	68.5	67.5	68.5
Petroleum, petroleum products, and related materials	53.5	55.3	52.6	48.2	50.1	55.0	55.6	56.7	56.1	59.6	57.4	59.2
Chemicals and Related Products, n.e.s.	89.1	89.2	88.5	88.6	89.5	91.9	96.4	101.3	107.1	108.4	104.3	102.1
Organic chemicals	89.2	89.5	87.8	86.7	87.7	91.8	97.9	107.4	117.0	122.8	112.6	105.8
Inorganic chemicals	86.0	85.1	82.5	82.5	79.7	82.8	88.2	90.4	102.4	100.9	101.7	100.2
Medicinal and pharmaceutical products	97.2	98.3	98.7	99.5	100.0	99.6	99.2	98.7	99.5	100.4	100.5	99.9
Essential oils, polishing, and cleansing preparations	90.6	90.5	91.0	91.6	92.9	95.3	95.8	95.5	96.4	96.4	96.8	97.7
Fertilizers	...	...	...	...	...	...	...	...	...	...	...	...
Plastics in primary forms	78.7	80.5	79.9	79.2	80.1	83.9	95.8	105.6	111.8	110.6	99.7	94.4
Plastics in nonprimary forms	92.6	90.0	90.7	90.6	91.3	92.5	94.2	97.4	99.0	101.8	102.0	101.3
Chemical materials and products, n.e.s.	91.9	92.5	92.6	92.6	94.7	95.2	95.4	97.1	99.2	100.7	101.4	101.3
Manufactured Goods Classified Chiefly by Material	88.4	87.6	88.1	87.6	89.5	90.8	92.6	96.4	99.0	100.6	100.6	99.4
Rubber manufactures, n.e.s.	88.7	89.3	89.6	89.5	89.7	89.9	90.7	90.9	95.3	95.7	97.1	98.3
Uncoated paper, paperboard, linerboard	87.5	85.6	84.7	84.9	85.5	87.7	92.9	101.2	108.0	115.6	114.0	109.0
Textile yarn, fabrics, and made-up articles, n.e.s.	97.3	97.8	97.8	97.0	97.7	97.7	97.0	97.2	99.0	102.8	102.6	103.7
Nonmetallic mineral manufactures, n.e.s.	89.6	90.8	91.9	91.2	92.1	92.4	92.7	93.5	94.1	94.3	94.4	95.2
Iron and steel	...	...	...	93.4	95.3	96.4	97.2	99.0	101.7	104.0	104.0	104.7
Nonferrous metals	74.3	70.6	72.3	68.6	76.3	80.3	85.7	96.7	100.1	98.2	98.9	93.7
Manufactures of metals, n.e.s.	86.1	85.5	86.2	86.8	87.5	87.3	87.7	89.4	91.6	92.3	92.7	93.2
Machinery and Transport Equipment	102.3	102.5	102.2	102.4	102.4	102.1	101.7	101.7	102.2	102.8	103.0	103.2
Power generating machinery and equipment	85.2	85.3	85.7	86.2	86.8	86.9	87.6	88.4	88.3	88.5	88.7	90.3
Machinery specialized for particular industries	89.6	90.0	90.5	91.0	91.1	91.5	91.6	91.6	93.0	94.0	94.8	95.2
Metalworking machinery	91.3	91.4	91.2	91.3	91.1	91.2	90.5	91.1	92.0	92.3	92.8	92.8
General industrial machinery, equipment, and parts, n.e.s.	89.2	89.6	90.1	90.6	90.9	91.0	91.3	91.3	90.9	91.0	91.3	91.3
Computer equipment and office machines	171.0	168.9	165.3	162.9	158.9	156.0	151.8	150.4	148.1	147.5	144.7	142.9
Telecommunications and sound recording and reproducing apparatus and equipment	105.0	106.4	105.7	105.6	104.6	104.4	103.8	103.4	103.4	103.8	103.2	102.4
Electrical machinery and equipment	116.1	116.7	115.9	116.6	116.8	116.3	114.8	114.4	115.2	117.2	117.5	116.8
Road vehicles	93.6	93.7	93.7	94.0	94.5	94.7	94.9	95.5	96.0	96.1	96.2	97.1
Miscellaneous Manufactured Articles	97.5	97.6	97.6	97.6	97.5	97.8	98.1	98.1	98.3	98.6	98.6	98.8
Furniture and parts thereof	95.9	94.3	94.2	94.4	94.6	94.9	95.4	94.1	94.0	94.7	94.8	95.1
Articles of apparel and clothing accessories	...	...	...	102.4	102.5	103.3	103.2	103.6	103.4	102.5	104.4	102.6
Professional, scientific, and controlling instruments and apparatus, n.e.s.	90.8	91.3	92.0	91.9	92.4	92.6	93.3	93.4	93.9	94.3	94.4	94.5
Photographic apparatus, equipment and supplies, and optical goods, n.e.s.	98.8	101.0	101.2	101.4	101.8	102.0	103.4	102.8	103.3	103.5	102.3	102.1
Miscellaneous manufactured articles, n.e.s.	102.8	102.5	101.7	101.5	100.6	100.9	100.6	100.7	100.9	101.0	100.9	101.9

n.e.s. = not elsewhere specified.

. . . = Not available.

Table 7-11. U.S. Export Price Indexes for Selected Categories of Goods, by Standard International Trade Classification, 1990–2004—*Continued*

(2000 = 100.)

Categories	1996				1997				1998			
	March	June	September	December	March	June	September	December	March	June	September	December
ALL COMMODITIES	104.6	105.4	103.9	103.2	103.6	103.2	102.9	102.0	100.7	99.9	98.5	98.5
Food and Live Animals	131.8	140.4	123.4	117.3	119.0	113.3	114.4	111.3	106.4	104.6	99.8	103.0
Meat and meat preparations	94.0	97.4	94.4	93.7	92.4	91.3	91.3	90.7	88.3	93.7	92.3	86.2
Fish, crustaceans, aquatic invertebrates, and preparations thereof	91.2	92.8	96.9	100.5	92.5	88.5	102.9	96.6	86.0	83.8	99.5	99.3
Cereals and cereal preparations	183.0	203.3	152.6	140.4	146.4	128.9	132.7	131.9	126.3	115.4	98.0	110.2
Vegetables and fruit and nuts, fresh or dried	114.9	117.8	119.0	112.6	112.8	113.3	108.8	102.6	102.3	109.8	110.6	111.1
Feeding stuff for animals (not including unmilled cereals)	129.5	130.7	135.5	128.0	133.7	135.7	128.9	121.1	107.8	101.3	94.4	98.4
Miscellaneous edible products and preparations	96.0	96.6	96.2	97.1	96.7	96.9	98.3	98.2	98.1	98.3	99.5	100.0
Beverages and Tobacco	98.7	98.8	98.8	98.7	98.4	99.1	99.3	98.8	98.4	98.2	98.0	99.0
Tobacco and tobacco manufactures	98.5	98.6	98.6	98.5	98.1	98.9	99.1	98.4	98.2	97.8	97.5	98.4
Crude Materials, Inedible, Except Fuels	109.6	108.7	109.3	106.8	112.2	112.4	110.3	105.6	101.4	98.7	93.8	91.8
Oil seeds and oleaginous fruits	143.0	152.0	157.6	137.5	159.3	161.1	143.8	139.4	129.7	122.8	109.8	114.4
Cork and wood	113.0	109.0	110.9	112.3	110.5	107.3	104.7	98.6	96.8	94.5	94.7	93.7
Textile fibers and their waste	133.4	131.6	125.1	120.5	122.9	120.3	121.2	115.5	112.5	114.4	110.2	101.9
Metalliferous ores and metal scrap	114.8	113.4	108.6	108.7	113.8	116.4	119.8	106.5	101.2	97.2	88.4	86.1
Mineral Fuels, Lubricants, and Related Materials	71.8	73.3	75.6	78.4	74.8	74.5	75.1	75.8	71.3	69.3	62.8	63.0
Petroleum, petroleum products, and related materials	64.1	65.4	69.6	73.9	68.7	68.7	70.1	68.5	63.6	61.4	52.3	53.0
Chemicals and Related Products, n.e.s.	102.5	102.6	101.8	101.5	102.3	102.0	100.9	100.3	99.0	97.9	97.0	96.2
Organic chemicals	103.9	100.9	97.6	97.6	99.0	97.6	96.2	96.0	91.2	88.7	86.4	85.3
Inorganic chemicals	105.6	106.1	103.3	103.5	100.9	101.1	100.3	100.9	103.7	105.2	104.9	105.1
Medicinal and pharmaceutical products	101.9	101.6	101.7	101.7	100.8	101.4	101.0	100.7	102.2	101.4	101.5	100.4
Essential oils, polishing, and cleansing preparations	96.8	97.6	98.5	98.3	99.0	99.7	100.4	98.7	98.4	98.2	99.4	98.5
Fertilizers	. . .	. . .	. . .	133.3	128.2	128.1	126.6	125.6	122.7	128.0	130.5	127.8
Plastics in primary forms	96.4	100.7	101.3	99.0	103.1	102.4	98.8	98.2	96.7	93.7	92.4	90.2
Plastics in nonprimary forms	101.5	100.8	98.9	98.3	99.6	100.0	99.8	99.6	100.6	98.7	98.1	96.3
Chemical materials and products, n.e.s.	101.5	102.6	103.5	103.8	104.2	104.6	104.2	102.6	101.2	101.2	100.6	101.8
Manufactured Goods Classified Chiefly by Material	98.5	97.7	97.0	96.8	97.4	98.1	98.5	98.4	98.2	97.7	96.7	96.3
Rubber manufactures, n.e.s.	98.0	98.6	98.5	98.7	98.5	99.0	97.7	97.9	97.9	97.7	98.2	101.6
Uncoated paper, paperboard, linerboard	103.6	97.7	97.9	95.0	93.0	93.4	95.1	95.2	94.7	93.7	91.0	91.0
Textile yarn, fabrics, and made-up articles, n.e.s.	104.8	105.5	104.8	104.1	103.4	105.0	105.0	104.8	105.3	104.9	103.0	102.7
Nonmetallic mineral manufactures, n.e.s.	96.1	95.4	96.3	97.9	98.0	98.3	100.0	100.9	100.8	100.6	100.7	101.1
Iron and steel	104.7	106.0	104.8	104.9	106.7	106.0	106.2	106.3	103.9	103.7	102.9	100.0
Nonferrous metals	91.6	91.9	87.3	86.9	90.3	92.0	91.8	89.6	89.8	86.7	84.1	82.6
Manufactures of metals, n.e.s.	94.4	93.6	93.6	93.7	95.1	96.3	96.2	96.3	96.8	98.6	98.4	98.1
Machinery and Transport Equipment	103.3	103.6	103.3	103.2	103.3	103.3	102.9	102.5	102.0	101.4	100.9	100.9
Power generating machinery and equipment	91.9	92.9	92.8	93.1	94.0	94.4	94.5	94.6	95.1	95.3	95.2	96.6
Machinery specialized for particular industries	95.9	96.5	97.0	96.8	97.6	98.0	98.3	98.7	98.8	99.0	99.2	98.9
Metalworking machinery	93.7	94.4	94.6	94.5	96.7	96.3	96.4	97.5	99.5	100.0	100.1	100.5
General industrial machinery, equipment, and parts, n.e.s.	94.0	94.8	95.0	95.4	96.3	97.3	97.3	97.5	97.9	98.1	98.4	98.5
Computer equipment and office machines	139.7	137.2	132.3	128.7	126.9	123.9	122.5	119.5	116.9	112.0	109.4	108.9
Telecommunications and sound recording and reproducing apparatus and equipment	104.6	104.6	103.7	104.2	103.4	103.0	102.6	102.1	102.0	102.1	101.6	100.9
Electrical machinery and equipment	116.2	115.3	113.9	113.5	112.5	112.3	110.7	109.9	108.3	107.2	106.1	105.4
Road vehicles	97.1	97.2	97.2	97.6	98.0	98.0	97.9	98.2	98.0	98.1	98.2	98.3
Miscellaneous Manufactured Articles	99.4	99.4	99.5	99.9	100.2	100.3	100.4	100.4	100.0	99.4	99.2	99.2
Furniture and parts thereof	96.7	96.0	96.4	96.4	97.0	97.9	97.9	98.1	98.7	98.4	98.5	98.5
Articles of apparel and clothing accessories	103.0	103.8	104.2	104.4	105.0	104.9	107.1	107.2	107.4	107.4	106.2	104.4
Professional, scientific, and controlling instruments and apparatus, n.e.s.	95.4	95.8	96.1	96.7	97.8	97.5	97.4	97.6	97.7	97.8	97.8	98.1
Photographic apparatus, equipment and supplies, and optical goods, n.e.s.	102.2	101.4	101.7	102.2	101.4	102.0	101.6	101.0	98.4	96.5	95.2	97.3
Miscellaneous manufactured articles, n.e.s.	102.0	101.9	101.7	101.9	101.4	101.8	101.6	101.5	100.6	99.3	99.5	99.3

n.e.s. = not elsewhere specified.

. . . = Not available.

Table 7-11. U.S. Export Price Indexes for Selected Categories of Goods, by Standard International Trade Classification, 1990–2004—*Continued*

(2000 = 100.)

Categories	1999				2000				2001			
	March	June	September	December	March	June	September	December	March	June	September	December
ALL COMMODITIES	97.9	98.2	98.5	99.0	100.0	100.1	100.4	100.1	100.0	99.4	99.0	97.6
Food and Live Animals	101.1	102.6	99.6	98.5	99.9	100.6	98.8	102.1	102.5	101.1	103.3	101.2
Meat and meat preparations	86.2	87.6	93.4	96.7	95.3	104.8	100.8	101.5	102.6	106.1	107.8	97.8
Fish, crustaceans, aquatic invertebrates, and preparations thereof	109.8	123.0	100.8	102.6	98.9	100.6	100.1	98.4	99.0	90.8	90.4	88.6
Cereals and cereal preparations	105.9	106.0	101.5	95.7	103.9	100.0	94.7	105.8	107.9	102.6	106.4	107.2
Vegetables and fruit and nuts, fresh or dried	105.8	109.9	105.1	101.7	98.8	97.9	102.5	99.1	97.9	98.6	100.8	100.6
Feeding stuff for animals (not including unmilled cereals)	96.8	92.5	93.6	97.4	98.2	100.4	99.2	104.6	100.7	101.1	103.6	102.4
Miscellaneous edible products and preparations	100.0	100.1	100.6	100.7	99.8	100.0	100.0	100.2	100.1	100.1	100.1	100.1
Beverages and Tobacco	99.5	99.4	99.8	100.1	100.2	100.0	99.9	99.8	98.9	98.4	98.4	98.3
Tobacco and tobacco manufactures	99.3	99.2	99.7	100.1	100.1	99.9	99.9	99.9	98.9	98.2	98.2	98.1
Crude Materials, Inedible, Except Fuels	89.1	90.2	93.5	94.9	100.2	101.6	100.7	99.4	96.0	92.6	89.5	87.1
Oil seeds and oleaginous fruits	93.7	94.8	101.7	95.2	102.9	103.3	100.3	101.8	94.5	95.6	99.0	90.9
Cork and wood	93.8	94.4	95.4	97.9	100.4	99.8	100.1	98.9	96.1	92.8	90.2	88.0
Textile fibers and their waste	100.7	99.1	92.9	90.2	99.1	100.5	104.3	105.7	97.6	90.9	87.7	84.0
Metalliferous ores and metal scrap	88.6	89.7	93.3	99.5	102.6	99.2	99.9	94.8	92.0	91.0	85.1	81.9
Mineral Fuels, Lubricants, and Related Materials	62.5	68.5	77.5	85.0	102.2	97.4	111.7	105.8	102.4	103.2	103.3	82.4
Petroleum, petroleum products, and related materials	52.3	61.9	74.0	80.6	103.1	96.8	117.0	105.6	99.2	101.8	103.6	74.6
Chemicals and Related Products, n.e.s.	95.7	96.4	97.6	98.9	99.7	100.9	99.8	98.3	98.7	96.2	93.8	92.8
Organic chemicals	84.7	86.4	90.6	96.3	98.8	102.1	99.9	96.0	95.9	90.6	84.9	83.9
Inorganic chemicals	104.7	102.7	100.4	99.7	99.6	101.2	99.8	101.4	104.1	103.3	103.2	102.8
Medicinal and pharmaceutical products	100.3	100.4	99.6	100.1	100.0	99.5	100.0	100.0	99.2	99.5	101.1	100.9
Essential oils, polishing, and cleansing preparations	98.3	98.7	98.9	100.1	99.8	99.6	100.1	100.0	100.2	99.7	99.1	98.8
Fertilizers	125.2	119.4	113.2	97.8	96.5	96.1	105.3	102.0	105.3	94.9	91.8	94.0
Plastics in primary forms	89.0	93.2	97.2	100.2	100.8	103.4	97.8	94.9	97.8	93.9	88.6	86.5
Plastics in nonprimary forms	97.3	98.1	98.4	98.9	101.0	100.2	100.2	99.2	97.6	97.4	97.2	95.8
Chemical materials and products, n.e.s.	101.1	100.3	99.9	99.7	100.3	99.7	99.8	100.5	99.1	99.1	99.0	97.6
Manufactured Goods Classified Chiefly by Material	96.3	96.7	97.3	98.1	99.6	100.2	100.9	100.3	100.2	99.5	98.2	96.7
Rubber manufactures, n.e.s.	102.4	101.2	102.5	104.0	99.4	100.1	100.4	99.5	100.4	99.8	101.0	100.9
Uncoated paper, paperboard, linerboard	90.5	93.3	96.6	97.6	98.9	100.5	100.7	99.7	98.4	97.4	95.6	95.1
Textile yarn, fabrics, and made-up articles, n.e.s.	101.3	100.8	100.3	100.3	100.0	100.2	100.1	98.4	98.8	98.5	98.8	97.5
Nonmetallic mineral manufactures, n.e.s.	100.3	100.2	99.9	99.7	100.1	100.4	100.0	99.5	99.8	100.8	101.1	102.1
Iron and steel	98.7	97.5	97.6	97.7	99.9	101.2	100.0	99.5	96.8	97.8	98.3	95.7
Nonferrous metals	82.7	83.7	86.6	90.9	100.3	98.5	103.4	103.3	104.9	98.0	90.2	83.1
Manufactures of metals, n.e.s.	99.8	100.2	99.0	98.8	98.6	100.9	101.5	101.1	100.9	101.5	101.8	101.7
Machinery and Transport Equipment	100.6	100.3	99.9	99.9	99.9	100.0	100.1	100.1	100.6	100.3	100.0	99.6
Power generating machinery and equipment	97.4	97.6	98.0	98.8	99.5	99.7	100.0	101.2	102.0	102.3	103.0	103.9
Machinery specialized for particular industries	99.4	99.8	99.5	98.4	99.8	100.2	100.0	100.3	100.5	100.3	99.5	100.5
Metalworking machinery	100.6	100.4	100.4	100.1	100.1	99.3	100.1	99.8	101.1	101.0	101.2	100.7
General industrial machinery, equipment, and parts, n.e.s.	99.1	99.2	99.5	99.8	99.9	100.1	100.0	100.3	101.0	101.3	101.1	101.7
Computer equipment and office machines	106.9	104.8	102.8	102.7	100.5	99.9	99.3	99.0	97.8	95.9	94.8	92.9
Telecommunications and sound recording and reproducing apparatus and equipment	100.9	100.2	100.2	100.0	99.9	100.3	100.1	99.6	99.8	99.8	98.5	97.7
Electrical machinery and equipment	104.0	103.1	102.0	100.9	100.5	99.8	99.9	99.3	99.2	98.3	97.6	95.9
Road vehicles	98.4	98.6	98.6	99.3	100.1	100.0	100.2	100.1	100.2	100.2	100.2	100.3
Miscellaneous Manufactured Articles	99.6	99.6	99.8	99.9	99.6	99.7	100.2	100.2	100.0	100.1	100.4	100.4
Furniture and parts thereof	98.5	99.0	99.7	99.5	99.4	100.1	99.8	101.1	101.0	101.0	101.8	101.6
Articles of apparel and clothing accessories	104.7	103.8	103.9	103.7	100.1	99.8	99.0	99.5	96.9	96.6	98.1	98.2
Professional, scientific, and controlling instruments and apparatus, n.e.s.	99.0	99.2	99.4	99.3	99.6	99.7	100.4	100.4	100.8	100.9	100.9	100.9
Photographic apparatus, equipment and supplies, and optical goods, n.e.s.	97.9	97.2	98.6	100.3	97.9	98.0	101.6	101.3	99.1	98.2	98.7	97.6
Miscellaneous manufactured articles, n.e.s.	99.2	99.5	99.4	99.5	99.7	99.9	100.0	99.9	100.3	100.5	100.6	101.0

n.e.s. = not elsewhere specified.

Table 7-11. U.S. Export Price Indexes for Selected Categories of Goods, by Standard International Trade Classification, 1990–2004—*Continued*

(2000 = 100.)

Categories	2002				2003				2004			
	March	June	September	December	March	June	September	December	March	June	September	December
ALL COMMODITIES	97.6	98.0	98.8	98.6	99.7	99.5	99.8	100.8	103.0	103.4	103.8	104.8
Food and Live Animals	100.3	99.8	107.7	105.8	105.9	107.5	112.1	116.5	122.7	123.9	117.6	118.1
Meat and meat preparations	93.2	90.0	89.8	90.3	96.4	102.9	117.2	123.0	127.1	127.3	124.8	124.6
Fish, crustaceans, aquatic invertebrates, and preparations thereof	94.3	97.9	98.6	101.7	108.2	108.2	103.3	103.1	107.2	108.6	108.8	110.3
Cereals and cereal preparations	105.4	106.5	133.4	126.3	122.2	118.5	124.2	130.8	139.6	141.2	122.0	116.4
Vegetables and fruit and nuts, fresh or dried	102.5	99.0	98.9	98.3	95.1	99.6	101.4	103.2	110.1	111.1	119.8	129.9
Feeding stuff for animals (not including unmilled cereals)	99.6	101.2	106.8	103.5	105.5	108.8	112.7	123.2	133.6	131.9	109.8	107.5
Miscellaneous edible products and preparations	100.7	100.7	100.7	100.5	101.0	101.5	101.0	100.3	102.0	101.6	102.1	102.6
Beverages and Tobacco	97.4	98.2	98.8	98.7	97.4	98.2	97.8	100.6	102.1	101.6	101.7	101.5
Tobacco and tobacco manufactures	96.8	97.6	98.0	97.8	95.9	96.6	96.2	99.7	100.5	100.0	100.3	100.6
Crude Materials, Inedible, Except Fuels	87.7	95.3	97.3	98.5	102.3	103.9	106.2	116.9	129.0	125.7	119.4	119.4
Oil seeds and oleaginous fruits	92.0	102.9	114.1	116.2	116.6	122.7	121.1	152.5	181.6	168.5	125.1	111.1
Cork and wood	87.2	87.1	90.0	90.3	91.2	90.4	91.6	93.7	96.5	98.3	99.1	98.8
Textile fibers and their waste	86.2	88.6	93.1	98.3	105.0	103.2	109.6	121.2	121.9	108.7	102.1	96.4
Metalliferous ores and metal scrap	87.3	99.8	93.9	96.3	105.8	109.0	119.9	136.6	171.4	167.5	178.5	195.0
Mineral Fuels, Lubricants, and Related Materials	89.8	93.9	102.8	99.5	130.1	107.6	108.7	110.7	123.0	131.8	141.2	146.5
Petroleum, petroleum products, and related materials	83.6	87.9	98.0	92.2	130.2	102.7	104.2	106.2	120.1	129.7	138.0	144.6
Chemicals and Related Products, n.e.s.	93.2	95.3	96.8	96.6	100.6	100.8	100.3	101.4	104.9	105.8	109.7	114.0
Organic chemicals	84.9	90.8	95.3	94.9	103.4	103.1	100.4	103.3	110.8	114.6	120.5	128.4
Inorganic chemicals	101.6	102.1	101.0	96.9	98.1	98.6	99.1	99.1	99.5	98.7	107.6	113.7
Medicinal and pharmaceutical products	100.5	100.4	101.4	101.2	104.1	104.8	105.4	105.8	105.5	105.8	108.0	107.2
Essential oils, polishing, and cleansing preparations	97.6	97.3	97.4	97.3	96.2	97.3	98.2	100.1	104.3	104.3	105.6	109.1
Fertilizers	98.1	95.5	100.9	104.3	108.2	117.2	122.8	123.1	138.1	137.4	143.9	148.3
Plastics in primary forms	87.6	92.5	92.9	92.9	99.5	96.6	95.4	96.5	102.1	103.2	109.9	118.9
Plastics in nonprimary forms	95.8	96.0	96.9	95.9	97.2	98.8	98.2	97.2	97.4	96.5	97.4	99.9
Chemical materials and products, n.e.s.	98.0	97.5	98.3	98.8	100.7	101.6	101.9	102.6	104.8	104.9	105.5	105.8
Manufactured Goods Classified Chiefly by Material	96.7	98.1	99.1	99.0	99.4	100.0	100.2	100.8	104.1	107.0	110.5	112.2
Rubber manufactures, n.e.s.	100.8	102.7	105.6	105.6	108.4	110.1	109.2	109.9	110.4	111.2	111.4	112.9
Uncoated paper, paperboard, linerboard	92.5	94.8	96.3	96.8	96.7	98.3	98.3	97.6	97.9	99.2	102.7	104.2
Textile yarn, fabrics, and made-up articles, n.e.s.	97.8	100.0	100.6	101.1	102.0	102.7	102.1	102.5	104.1	105.4	105.7	107.2
Nonmetallic mineral manufactures, n.e.s.	102.1	102.2	102.2	101.3	100.2	100.4	99.5	99.8	99.7	99.9	100.4	101.6
Iron and steel	96.6	101.0	103.6	104.3	104.5	106.8	106.1	109.6	124.9	145.4	166.8	170.6
Nonferrous metals	85.1	85.3	84.4	83.5	84.3	80.3	81.6	84.5	94.1	95.4	99.0	101.5
Manufactures of metals, n.e.s.	101.9	102.5	103.4	103.3	103.5	104.8	104.4	104.4	105.5	108.4	111.6	113.5
Machinery and Transport Equipment	99.5	98.9	98.7	98.5	98.5	97.8	97.9	97.8	98.2	98.2	98.2	98.5
Power generating machinery and equipment	104.6	104.5	104.4	105.1	106.9	107.2	107.5	108.7	109.4	108.7	109.0	110.4
Machinery specialized for particular industries	101.1	101.8	101.8	101.7	102.2	102.6	103.1	103.4	104.2	105.4	106.1	108.0
Metalworking machinery	100.0	99.9	100.2	100.5	101.7	101.0	100.8	100.7	100.9	100.0	101.0	101.9
General industrial machinery, equipment, and parts, n.e.s.	102.2	102.3	102.3	101.6	102.1	102.4	102.6	102.8	104.0	104.9	105.3	106.6
Computer equipment and office machines	93.1	90.4	89.4	88.6	88.6	88.1	87.8	88.6	88.4	87.2	86.0	83.8
Telecommunications and sound recording and reproducing apparatus and equipment	97.5	97.7	96.4	95.8	95.0	93.8	93.3	92.0	92.4	91.8	90.7	90.4
Electrical machinery and equipment	94.7	93.9	93.5	92.9	92.2	89.7	89.4	88.1	88.6	88.2	88.1	87.9
Road vehicles	100.3	100.3	100.6	101.0	100.9	101.1	101.4	101.5	101.9	102.4	102.4	103.0
Miscellaneous Manufactured Articles	100.5	100.4	100.4	100.6	100.5	101.2	100.7	101.1	100.9	100.9	101.2	102.3
Furniture and parts thereof	101.7	101.6	101.5	101.4	101.1	101.4	102.6	102.5	102.4	102.3	102.8	104.4
Articles of apparel and clothing accessories	98.3	98.8	97.8	97.2	97.5	97.0	96.8	97.1	96.8	96.9	96.9	97.1
Professional, scientific, and controlling instruments and apparatus, n.e.s.	101.2	101.3	101.4	101.7	101.5	102.2	102.2	102.3	102.3	102.0	101.8	102.6
Photographic apparatus, equipment and supplies, and optical goods, n.e.s.	96.6	97.5	97.3	97.4	97.1	98.9	94.4	95.6	95.0	94.5	95.7	97.0
Miscellaneous manufactured articles, n.e.s.	100.9	100.4	100.5	101.1	100.9	101.6	101.2	101.6	101.4	101.6	102.3	104.0

n.e.s. = not elsewhere specified.

Table 7-12. U.S. Import Price Indexes for Selected Categories of Goods, by Standard International Trade Classification, 1990–2004

(2000 = 100.)

Categories	Relative import- ance [1]	1990 March	1990 June	1990 Septem- ber	1990 Decem- ber	1991 March	1991 June	1991 Septem- ber	1991 Decem- ber	1992 March	1992 June	1992 Septem- ber	1992 Decem- ber
ALL COMMODITIES	100.00	92.4	90.8	96.5	98.4	95.0	93.4	93.3	94.3	93.9	94.8	95.9	94.4
Food and Live Animals	3.76	91.9	92.1	93.9	95.7	95.7	95.6	94.6	95.6	97.4	91.4	92.1	93.2
Meat and meat preparations	0.41	113.1	118.4	121.7	120.5	120.9	125.0	119.5	115.9	114.8	112.3	111.5	109.5
Fish, crustaceans, aquatic invertebrates, and preparations thereof	0.89	70.7	70.9	74.5	77.1	79.7	78.9	78.2	78.3	79.1	79.1	80.3	78.3
Vegetables and fruit and nuts, fresh or dried	0.98	90.7	87.0	83.1	90.6	88.3	91.4	91.9	95.6	107.7	89.9	89.6	91.7
Coffee, tea, cocoa, spices, and manufactures thereof	0.53	103.7	105.4	110.6	104.5	104.7	98.8	98.2	98.5	90.0	82.0	81.6	96.1
Beverages and Tobacco	0.93	74.7	76.5	77.6	79.6	84.2	85.4	85.3	86.3	87.1	87.5	88.3	87.2
Beverages	0.84	77.3	78.9	80.0	81.5	86.6	87.6	87.2	88.2	89.0	89.4	90.5	89.1
Crude Materials, Inedible, Except Fuels	1.98	91.3	90.4	88.0	85.0	84.4	85.0	81.8	81.5	84.6	85.0	86.3	85.9
Cork and wood	0.75	66.0	66.7	66.2	61.6	62.9	70.1	66.6	68.0	75.3	76.1	77.1	79.1
Woodpulp and recovered paper	0.24	118.9	116.6	112.5	105.6	97.1	89.8	80.7	78.6	81.2	84.4	88.2	83.9
Metalliferous ores and metal scrap	0.39	97.5	93.2	90.2	89.1	89.1	86.6	86.8	86.2	86.0	84.3	85.4	83.7
Crude animal and vegetable materials, n.e.s.	0.22	...	...	...	...	...	...	...	...	...	...	...	...
Mineral Fuels, Lubricants, and Related Materials	17.70	64.3	54.7	87.3	93.0	65.8	62.3	63.6	63.3	56.8	64.9	65.3	60.0
Petroleum, petroleum products, and related materials	15.79	64.6	54.8	89.8	95.1	66.3	63.0	64.5	63.9	57.4	66.0	66.2	60.2
Gas, natural and manufactured	1.91	63.7	54.9	57.7	69.2	61.5	54.1	53.4	57.8	49.7	51.4	55.4	58.1
Chemicals and Related Products, n.e.s.	8.48	94.3	93.7	94.9	97.6	97.4	95.8	95.4	95.6	96.2	96.8	97.5	97.1
Organic chemicals	2.82	98.7	98.1	100.0	104.7	101.8	98.6	96.1	97.1	97.0	96.8	96.5	94.4
Inorganic chemicals	0.67	95.4	95.8	97.0	100.7	101.5	100.2	98.1	94.9	95.5	94.1	93.7	99.0
Dyeing, tanning, and coloring materials	0.19	...	...	...	...	...	...	...	...	...	...	...	...
Medicinal and pharmaceutical products	2.57	80.5	80.6	81.5	83.6	83.2	81.7	83.2	86.4	87.3	87.6	90.1	89.8
Essential oils, polishing, and cleansing preps	0.42	90.5	91.6	92.1	94.6	93.4	93.2	96.0	95.2	97.5	98.6	98.8	98.8
Plastics in primary forms	0.68	...	...	...	...	...	...	...	...	...	...	...	96.8
Plastics in nonprimary forms	0.38	...	...	...	...	...	...	...	...	...	...	...	109.9
Chemical materials and products, n.e.s.	0.54	97.2	92.9	91.6	90.2	89.6	88.1	88.3	90.1	94.0	97.1	101.0	100.1
Manufactured Goods Classified Chiefly by Material	11.82	90.5	91.3	93.2	92.3	92.7	91.1	90.3	90.6	91.0	91.3	92.0	90.4
Rubber manufactures, n.e.s.	0.67	102.9	103.3	103.3	104.6	104.3	104.1	103.7	104.8	105.7	105.6	107.0	106.8
Cork and wood manufactures other than furniture	0.87	84.7	86.4	87.8	85.3	84.1	84.8	85.9	86.3	90.0	93.0	95.1	92.4
Paper and paperboard, cut to size	1.20	86.5	89.3	89.8	90.2	92.2	89.9	88.2	87.8	85.1	83.7	84.3	84.3
Textile yarn, fabrics, made-up articles, and related products, n.e.s.	1.36	90.6	91.4	93.4	94.8	96.3	95.4	96.8	98.4	98.9	98.1	100.9	99.3
Nonmetallic mineral manufactures, n.e.s.	2.11	87.7	88.9	89.4	90.3	91.9	92.1	92.2	93.0	93.3	94.0	94.9	94.6
Iron and steel	1.58	100.4	98.2	97.1	98.4	98.1	97.8	96.9	97.2	96.6	96.1	94.8	94.8
Nonferrous metals	1.85	80.9	84.2	92.6	83.6	82.1	75.9	72.9	70.8	73.7	75.6	75.6	70.0
Manufactures of metals, n.e.s.	2.10	94.6	93.9	95.2	96.0	96.8	96.1	95.5	96.9	97.6	97.8	99.6	97.9
Machinery and Transport Equipment	38.70	101.6	100.8	101.8	104.2	105.4	103.7	103.8	105.4	105.6	105.6	106.9	106.1
Power generating machinery and equipment	2.51	...	...	...	...	...	...	...	...	...	...	...	...
Machinery specialized for particular industries	1.68	86.3	87.1	90.4	94.1	95.6	91.0	90.7	93.4	94.2	94.3	99.0	95.4
Metalworking machinery	0.43	86.9	87.8	89.2	92.1	92.8	89.6	89.6	92.1	92.3	92.5	94.8	93.7
General industrial machinery, equipment, and machine parts, n.e.s.	3.08	86.5	87.6	90.9	93.6	94.5	91.0	91.1	93.7	94.0	94.0	96.8	95.0
Computer equipment and office machines	5.31	200.8	198.5	196.8	199.2	197.3	193.4	191.2	191.7	192.2	190.2	190.9	189.0
Telecommunications and sound recording and reproducing apparatus and equipment	4.97	122.5	120.9	119.3	120.1	118.7	118.0	117.3	117.8	117.4	117.3	117.3	117.6
Electrical machinery and equipment	6.12	113.1	111.3	112.7	114.0	115.5	113.4	112.8	114.5	114.3	115.1	116.3	114.6
Road vehicles	13.27	83.2	82.0	82.9	85.4	87.1	86.3	86.8	88.1	88.2	88.0	88.6	88.8
Miscellaneous Manufactured Articles	16.20	94.5	94.7	96.2	97.5	97.7	96.3	96.5	98.0	99.1	99.3	101.0	99.9
Prefabricated buildings; plumbing and heat and lighting fixtures, n.e.s.	0.46	102.7	102.0	104.2	105.6	101.9	101.6	101.4	102.8	103.8	105.2	106.8	105.5
Furniture and parts thereof	1.94	95.1	96.0	97.2	99.1	99.6	98.0	98.4	99.0	99.8	100.1	102.6	100.7
Travel goods, handbags, and similar containers	0.38	89.7	89.8	88.8	90.6	90.7	91.1	91.0	91.8	92.9	96.2	96.6	94.5
Articles of apparel and clothing accessories	5.10	95.7	96.5	96.4	95.5	95.5	94.8	95.4	95.9	96.9	97.7	97.5	97.9
Footwear	1.17	95.2	96.5	98.2	100.0	100.2	98.4	98.1	98.8	99.4	100.0	101.5	98.7
Professional, scientific, and controlling instruments and apparatus, n.e.s.	1.80	87.7	89.1	92.0	96.9	98.0	93.4	93.0	95.6	95.7	95.4	101.2	98.4
Photographic apparatus, equipment and supplies, and optical goods, n.e.s.	0.87	93.7	94.0	97.0	98.8	99.1	96.0	96.3	98.6	99.3	98.6	102.1	100.5
Miscellaneous manufactured articles, n.e.s.	4.48	95.6	94.3	96.6	98.6	98.5	98.0	98.3	100.8	102.6	102.0	104.1	103.1

n.e.s. = not elsewhere specified.

[1]Percent of total, relative importance in December 1999, based on 1995 trade values.
. . . = Not available.

Table 7-12. U.S. Import Price Indexes for Selected Categories of Goods, by Standard International Trade Classification, 1990–2004—*Continued*

(2000 = 100.)

Categories	1993				1994				1995			
	March	June	September	December	March	June	September	December	March	June	September	December
ALL COMMODITIES	94.7	95.0	94.5	93.5	94.0	96.3	97.2	98.4	99.9	101.4	100.8	101.0
Food and Live Animals	91.2	94.4	95.6	95.3	96.3	101.8	110.9	110.8	112.6	108.6	106.7	104.7
Meat and meat preparations	113.4	117.6	115.9	111.3	114.3	107.8	108.8	108.5	104.9	100.8	97.3	99.6
Fish, crustaceans, aquatic invertebrates, and preparations thereof	78.9	79.1	79.9	83.6	85.5	88.9	90.6	93.8	93.6	92.5	89.2	86.5
Vegetables and fruit and nuts, fresh or dried	85.4	96.6	93.6	89.3	88.0	90.1	88.0	99.0	100.5	97.6	101.0	106.4
Coffee, tea, cocoa, spices, and manufactures thereof	89.8	86.1	104.2	107.8	109.3	145.4	214.4	182.7	194.8	176.3	165.7	141.9
Beverages and Tobacco	86.8	86.8	86.2	86.9	86.6	87.3	87.5	87.5	88.2	88.6	89.4	90.6
Beverages	89.1	89.6	89.0	89.3	89.2	89.6	90.1	90.2	91.0	91.2	91.7	92.0
Crude Materials, Inedible, Except Fuels	92.2	84.5	85.9	90.7	93.4	94.7	96.2	101.6	107.6	109.5	113.6	111.0
Cork and wood	105.9	84.9	92.4	110.9	108.7	104.1	101.3	97.4	93.4	85.3	94.7	88.5
Woodpulp and recovered paper	74.3	72.2	68.5	66.2	69.8	79.5	90.8	102.9	118.8	131.6	134.8	138.4
Metalliferous ores and metal scrap	82.8	81.7	80.6	77.0	83.5	82.9	85.4	90.0	98.6	98.4	101.5	100.2
Crude animal and vegetable materials, n.e.s.	...	...	...	...	...	...	...	...	...	...	...	...
Mineral Fuels, Lubricants, and Related Materials	61.5	59.8	55.0	47.7	48.2	57.1	55.0	56.4	59.2	61.9	57.6	59.2
Petroleum, petroleum products, and related materials	62.1	60.3	55.4	47.0	47.7	57.6	55.2	56.7	60.1	63.0	58.5	60.2
Gas, natural and manufactured	54.9	55.4	56.3	57.7	55.6	51.4	53.6	54.2	48.8	49.3	47.1	49.1
Chemicals And Related Products, n.e.s.	97.1	97.8	97.1	96.4	96.3	97.6	100.5	103.5	105.4	106.8	106.6	106.4
Organic chemicals	94.0	94.6	94.3	92.8	92.6	95.2	100.0	104.5	102.5	100.6	101.0	100.3
Inorganic chemicals	99.1	97.9	97.7	97.5	96.9	97.9	99.9	104.6	110.0	111.1	110.9	110.2
Dyeing, tanning, and coloring materials	104.8	106.7	105.6	105.5	106.7	107.2	108.2	108.7	112.3	114.7	114.7	115.9
Medicinal and pharmaceutical products	91.0	95.9	94.4	95.1	95.8	95.9	97.6	98.3	99.2	104.4	104.1	105.6
Essential oils, polishing, and cleansing preps	100.9	102.2	100.2	101.4	99.6	99.9	101.9	104.6	107.7	113.8	114.7	115.5
Plastics in primary forms	97.7	95.8	96.5	96.5	97.6	97.9	98.4	99.6	103.4	106.1	105.1	107.9
Plastics in nonprimary forms	109.0	109.3	108.5	107.1	104.7	108.0	112.9	117.7	126.9	129.6	124.5	117.4
Chemical materials and products, n.e.s.	98.7	98.0	96.1	94.5	95.4	94.5	97.8	96.4	96.5	98.7	101.6	104.2
Manufactured Goods Classified Chiefly by Material	90.8	91.2	90.7	89.8	91.2	92.8	94.6	97.7	100.2	102.7	105.0	104.3
Rubber manufactures, n.e.s.	107.6	107.5	106.8	106.9	105.2	106.0	105.0	105.9	106.4	108.7	110.0	110.4
Cork and wood manufactures other than furniture	100.5	103.8	104.8	103.9	106.1	108.8	101.7	99.4	101.4	102.7	100.1	100.9
Paper and paperboard, cut to size	85.6	86.0	84.9	83.8	83.6	85.1	88.4	93.6	101.8	111.3	120.5	121.6
Textile yarn, fabrics, made-up articles, and related products, n.e.s.	99.4	100.0	98.9	98.2	98.8	100.8	101.8	102.0	103.2	106.3	106.4	106.1
Nonmetallic mineral manufactures, n.e.s.	95.1	96.2	96.0	96.2	96.1	96.7	97.8	98.4	98.7	99.2	99.6	99.9
Iron and steel	95.1	96.7	96.6	96.4	97.3	97.6	99.7	101.6	104.0	106.9	110.7	108.1
Nonferrous metals	68.3	65.4	64.8	61.7	68.5	72.7	77.6	88.0	90.3	88.5	90.5	87.2
Manufactures of metals, n.e.s.	98.1	99.2	99.0	98.7	98.6	99.3	100.7	101.0	102.9	105.1	105.2	105.9
Machinery and Transport Equipment	106.1	107.2	107.7	108.4	108.6	109.1	109.7	110.3	110.8	112.4	112.1	112.0
Machinery specialized for particular industries	94.9	96.2	95.8	96.0	96.9	98.1	99.8	100.6	102.0	104.7	103.8	105.6
Metalworking machinery	93.5	95.9	96.4	96.9	97.1	98.0	100.3	101.4	103.1	108.9	108.3	108.9
General industrial machinery, equipment, and machine parts, n.e.s.	94.4	95.9	95.9	96.7	97.2	97.7	98.9	100.0	101.3	104.5	104.7	105.5
Computer equipment and office machines	186.2	182.8	180.1	178.0	175.5	173.2	171.1	168.5	167.0	167.2	165.9	163.4
Telecommunications and sound recording and reproducing apparatus and equipment	117.3	118.3	119.5	118.5	117.5	117.6	117.7	118.0	117.8	119.1	119.0	118.0
Electrical machinery and equipment	115.2	117.2	119.4	118.9	119.1	119.6	120.2	120.1	120.5	122.9	120.7	119.7
Road vehicles	89.1	90.4	90.9	92.9	93.3	94.0	94.7	96.0	96.6	97.3	97.9	98.2
Miscellaneous Manufactured Articles	99.7	100.7	100.7	100.5	100.6	100.9	101.3	101.5	102.2	103.2	103.1	103.7
Prefabricated buildings; plumbing, and heat and lighting fixtures, n.e.s.	104.4	105.7	105.9	105.6	104.9	103.2	104.4	103.3	107.2	107.4	108.3	109.7
Furniture and parts thereof	100.2	100.8	100.2	99.7	100.2	100.6	100.9	101.2	101.7	103.1	102.9	103.5
Travel goods, handbags, and similar containers	94.8	95.5	95.8	94.9	94.8	94.5	95.7	96.0	96.4	98.5	100.5	99.3
Articles of apparel and clothing accessories	97.5	98.1	98.2	97.8	97.7	98.1	97.9	98.2	98.8	99.0	99.0	99.5
Footwear	98.0	98.7	97.8	97.6	97.1	97.7	98.4	98.5	98.5	99.3	99.6	100.1
Professional, scientific, and controlling instruments and apparatus, n.e.s.	98.9	101.0	100.2	100.9	102.0	103.3	104.2	105.1	105.1	107.2	107.5	107.1
Photographic apparatus, equipment and supplies, and optical goods, n.e.s.	100.5	102.5	103.5	104.2	104.0	104.6	106.2	106.0	106.4	110.6	109.9	109.9
Miscellaneous manufactured articles, n.e.s.	103.1	104.2	104.4	104.3	104.4	104.4	104.7	104.8	106.1	106.5	106.1	107.2

n.e.s. = not elsewhere specified.

. . . = Not available.

Table 7-12. U.S. Import Price Indexes for Selected Categories of Goods, by Standard International Trade Classification, 1990–2004—*Continued*

(2000 = 100.)

Categories	1996				1997				1998			
	March	June	September	December	March	June	September	December	March	June	September	December
ALL COMMODITIES	101.6	100.7	101.8	102.5	100.0	98.8	98.4	97.2	94.1	93.1	92.2	91.0
Food and Live Animals	103.2	102.7	104.8	102.6	110.4	112.5	109.8	108.0	106.1	106.3	103.5	103.2
Meat and meat preparations	93.7	92.0	102.6	100.7	105.3	103.6	105.7	106.0	103.0	100.0	98.9	93.4
Fish, crustaceans, aquatic invertebrates, and preparations thereof	86.8	88.8	88.3	89.4	90.7	94.3	95.2	96.1	97.4	99.6	94.4	91.2
Vegetables and fruit and nuts, fresh or dried	102.4	98.8	107.1	102.4	111.8	102.2	104.0	103.1	96.2	104.0	107.3	111.2
Coffee, tea, cocoa, spices, and manufactures thereof	144.3	143.7	135.8	129.0	169.7	203.7	172.1	158.5	161.8	141.3	133.1	129.2
Beverages and Tobacco	91.2	92.1	93.2	93.4	95.0	95.5	95.8	96.5	97.0	97.4	97.5	97.6
Beverages	92.1	92.5	93.5	93.9	94.3	94.9	95.2	96.1	96.6	97.0	97.1	97.3
Crude Materials, Inedible, Except Fuels	105.8	103.4	106.4	105.6	108.5	106.8	106.0	102.6	99.9	96.2	94.0	92.2
Cork and wood	91.3	104.5	115.9	110.9	116.2	112.7	111.5	104.1	101.8	93.1	98.7	98.4
Woodpulp and recovered paper	100.2	79.2	84.9	84.4	82.7	83.9	86.9	87.6	81.8	84.2	77.5	73.7
Metalliferous ores and metal scrap	100.3	100.1	95.9	96.0	101.4	104.1	102.9	100.7	98.8	97.0	91.5	91.3
Crude animal and vegetable materials, n.e.s.	. . .	. . .	. . .	94.2	99.1	91.7	97.1	100.8	103.7	106.6	99.2	93.6
Mineral Fuels, Lubricants, and Related Materials	66.3	65.1	72.6	79.8	67.1	61.6	63.0	60.8	47.3	45.7	45.6	38.0
Petroleum, petroleum products, and related materials	67.4	66.3	74.3	80.0	67.6	62.2	63.0	59.8	45.5	43.9	44.2	35.1
Gas, natural and manufactured	54.7	52.7	56.3	76.7	61.3	55.1	60.2	65.0	55.9	54.5	51.8	53.9
Chemicals and Related Products, n.e.s.	106.5	104.9	105.1	105.1	103.7	102.3	102.1	101.1	99.2	99.3	97.4	96.7
Organic chemicals	100.7	99.9	100.4	100.9	101.3	97.3	98.5	96.7	93.5	93.6	92.7	91.1
Inorganic chemicals	111.5	109.2	109.9	113.3	111.0	108.4	109.0	106.4	103.7	107.0	102.8	99.5
Dyeing, tanning, and coloring materials	117.6	116.4	116.9	114.4	110.5	111.5	107.1	110.5	108.1	108.1	108.1	110.0
Medicinal and pharmaceutical products	103.9	102.7	104.4	102.0	98.9	99.3	98.7	99.8	98.8	98.3	97.5	98.7
Essential oils, polishing, and cleansing preps	116.8	112.8	112.8	112.6	110.5	109.2	109.1	109.7	106.2	106.7	105.6	107.1
Plastics in primary forms	108.2	102.6	98.8	100.3	96.7	96.7	97.8	97.1	99.6	99.2	96.8	96.4
Plastics in nonprimary forms	110.8	108.6	108.1	108.2	107.4	110.6	108.5	103.3	101.7	98.7	92.4	92.0
Chemical materials and products, n.e.s.	107.4	107.1	107.5	105.3	104.1	103.0	102.7	102.6	101.2	100.9	100.1	99.0
Manufactured Goods Classified Chiefly by Material	103.3	102.0	99.8	98.2	98.7	99.5	99.6	98.7	97.3	96.7	95.4	94.3
Rubber manufactures, n.e.s.	108.7	108.8	108.2	107.0	105.7	106.0	103.2	103.7	102.8	103.1	102.4	102.5
Cork and wood manufactures other than furniture	101.4	104.4	103.7	101.7	102.2	102.0	102.4	102.1	95.7	95.6	98.6	98.0
Paper and paperboard, cut to size	118.9	112.7	104.0	96.3	95.0	97.7	99.2	98.9	98.2	97.8	97.2	96.2
Textile yarn, fabrics, made-up articles, and related products, n.e.s.	105.9	105.4	105.5	105.8	105.8	105.8	105.2	104.5	103.1	102.3	101.8	101.4
Nonmetallic mineral manufactures, n.e.s.	100.9	100.8	101.6	102.3	102.5	101.9	101.4	101.0	100.0	99.9	99.4	100.0
Iron and steel	105.7	104.8	104.8	104.1	103.2	103.3	103.3	103.3	101.9	99.7	96.7	93.5
Nonferrous metals	85.4	84.2	77.8	76.0	81.8	85.4	87.1	82.7	81.9	81.6	77.5	74.5
Manufactures of metals, n.e.s.	106.0	105.0	105.8	105.7	104.0	103.6	102.6	103.1	101.8	101.0	101.0	101.1
Machinery and Transport Equipment	111.2	110.1	110.2	109.6	107.8	106.9	105.9	105.0	103.8	102.6	101.6	102.0
Power generating machinery and equipment	. . .	. . .	. . .	100.2	99.7	99.4	99.0	99.2	100.1	98.1	97.4	98.1
Machinery specialized for particular industries	106.3	104.7	104.9	105.1	103.2	102.8	102.0	102.6	101.6	101.1	100.2	102.0
Metalworking machinery	108.3	108.1	108.4	108.0	104.4	104.9	103.8	105.3	104.1	103.4	103.0	104.2
General industrial machinery, equipment, and machine parts, n.e.s.	104.9	104.4	105.2	104.6	102.2	102.1	101.0	101.0	100.3	100.3	100.3	102.1
Computer equipment and office machines	158.5	152.8	149.7	146.9	140.6	135.3	130.2	128.0	121.5	117.2	114.5	111.1
Telecommunications and sound recording and reproducing apparatus and equipment	116.5	115.3	114.3	113.5	111.9	110.6	109.8	108.7	107.5	105.9	105.3	104.6
Electrical machinery and equipment	118.0	115.6	114.8	112.1	109.9	109.1	107.9	104.7	103.4	102.2	100.6	101.8
Road vehicles	97.9	97.8	98.3	98.1	98.1	98.1	98.6	98.8	98.8	98.4	98.1	98.8
Miscellaneous Manufactured Articles	103.7	103.5	103.5	103.2	102.9	103.0	102.7	102.5	102.0	101.4	101.0	101.0
Prefabricated buildings; plumbing, and heat and lighting fixtures, n.e.s.	108.6	106.5	108.7	106.2	102.7	103.0	101.9	103.1	103.5	102.7	102.2	100.9
Furniture and parts thereof	103.2	103.3	103.3	104.3	104.9	105.4	104.9	105.6	105.4	102.6	102.6	102.8
Travel goods, handbags and similar containers	99.6	99.6	99.6	99.2	99.9	99.7	99.5	98.9	98.0	99.6	98.7	99.5
Articles of apparel and clothing accessories	99.9	100.4	100.1	99.9	100.6	101.5	101.7	101.7	101.5	101.5	101.7	100.9
Footwear	100.7	100.6	100.3	100.2	100.3	100.3	100.0	100.5	100.0	100.0	100.2	100.1
Professional, scientific, and controlling instruments and apparatus, n.e.s.	107.4	105.9	107.0	106.5	103.9	103.6	103.4	102.8	101.4	101.3	100.8	101.4
Photographic apparatus, equipment and supplies, and optical goods, n.e.s.	108.4	106.3	106.7	105.7	104.0	103.0	102.1	101.6	100.1	99.3	98.3	99.4
Miscellaneous manufactured articles, n.e.s.	107.1	107.2	107.2	106.5	105.9	105.6	104.7	104.2	103.5	102.2	101.1	101.4

n.e.s. = not elsewhere specified.

. . . = Not available.

Table 7-12. U.S. Import Price Indexes for Selected Categories of Goods, by Standard International Trade Classification, 1990–2004—Continued

(2000 = 100.)

Categories	1999				2000				2001			
	March	June	September	December	March	June	September	December	March	June	September	December
ALL COMMODITIES	91.5	92.9	95.8	97.4	99.9	100.2	101.6	100.5	98.3	97.6	95.9	91.4
Food and Live Animals	101.1	101.2	99.3	102.7	101.0	99.0	99.0	100.2	100.9	96.0	95.1	94.8
Meat and meat preparations	95.7	96.1	101.2	100.1	100.9	100.8	100.7	99.1	102.2	106.2	113.5	109.8
Fish, crustaceans, aquatic invertebrates, and preparations thereof	94.0	94.9	93.9	97.2	98.3	99.3	102.5	99.3	93.0	90.0	86.3	82.9
Vegetables and fruit and nuts, fresh or dried	102.3	103.7	102.2	104.2	101.8	96.2	98.4	105.1	110.1	97.6	98.5	99.3
Coffee, tea, cocoa, spices and manufactures thereof	122.1	119.4	105.7	121.4	105.0	102.3	93.9	87.4	88.7	85.8	80.1	78.5
Beverages and Tobacco	98.1	98.1	99.7	99.5	99.2	100.4	100.9	100.5	100.4	101.7	102.0	103.0
Beverages	97.6	97.9	99.6	99.3	99.1	100.5	101.0	100.9	100.8	102.4	102.4	103.1
Crude Materials, Inedible, Except Fuels	94.7	99.1	100.5	101.1	103.5	99.4	97.5	97.0	94.5	102.8	96.6	89.9
Cork and wood	104.2	112.5	112.0	109.3	109.2	101.3	91.8	93.6	89.8	122.1	112.2	91.7
Woodpulp and recovered paper	73.5	77.3	84.1	86.9	92.3	102.0	104.5	106.3	102.5	87.1	77.3	77.7
Metalliferous ores and metal scrap	88.5	90.4	92.8	97.4	102.3	99.1	100.0	97.3	96.6	93.9	92.8	91.2
Crude animal and vegetable materials, n.e.s.	103.1	95.8	104.7	105.5	105.5	87.4	97.0	91.5	92.0	92.9	83.8	96.0
Mineral Fuels, Lubricants, and Related Materials	43.1	54.6	74.5	83.2	97.4	101.3	111.3	106.1	90.8	90.4	85.8	61.2
Petroleum, petroleum products, and related materials	41.9	54.6	75.1	84.5	99.5	102.2	112.1	97.9	86.5	89.3	86.8	59.8
Gas, natural and manufactured	47.5	51.8	69.2	73.1	83.1	95.2	106.2	161.6	119.1	97.4	77.8	68.6
Chemicals and Related Products, n.e.s.	96.4	96.2	96.9	97.6	98.5	99.8	101.2	100.7	102.4	100.5	98.3	97.4
Organic chemicals	91.7	91.6	93.2	94.3	95.9	100.4	102.5	102.1	101.5	102.1	99.3	96.1
Inorganic chemicals	97.0	94.9	94.8	96.3	97.2	100.1	101.2	103.0	107.2	100.1	98.1	97.6
Dyeing, tanning, and coloring materials	107.4	104.7	102.8	102.3	100.7	98.1	100.1	99.1	101.4	98.1	96.3	97.1
Medicinal and pharmaceutical products	99.7	99.1	100.0	100.3	100.3	99.8	99.7	98.6	97.5	96.7	97.0	97.0
Essential oils, polishing, and cleansing preps	105.3	104.1	103.9	101.6	101.0	100.8	100.0	96.2	99.7	98.4	99.7	100.1
Plastics in primary forms	97.1	98.8	99.1	99.2	99.2	99.6	100.6	101.2	101.1	102.1	99.7	99.8
Plastics in nonprimary forms	91.3	94.4	97.2	99.5	100.3	100.8	100.8	98.0	105.3	102.4	99.3	100.9
Chemical materials and products, n.e.s.	97.4	97.0	97.6	99.1	100.2	99.2	100.7	100.1	101.4	99.9	99.0	98.0
Manufactured Goods Classified Chiefly by Material	94.5	94.6	95.2	96.6	100.8	100.4	100.6	100.0	100.0	98.0	94.8	92.0
Rubber manufactures, n.e.s.	102.6	102.4	103.1	102.5	100.2	99.7	99.6	99.7	99.7	99.0	98.7	97.9
Cork and wood manufactures other than furniture	103.5	107.7	106.8	102.8	106.3	99.2	95.8	94.1	92.0	96.2	90.4	88.3
Paper and paperboard, cut to size	95.8	93.6	93.5	96.3	97.3	99.6	102.1	103.0	103.6	102.7	99.3	96.2
Textile yarn, fabrics, made-up articles, and related products, n.e.s.	100.6	99.7	99.9	99.8	100.7	99.7	99.8	99.5	99.1	98.8	98.1	97.1
Nonmetallic mineral manufactures, n.e.s.	100.6	100.2	100.4	100.5	100.1	99.8	100.1	99.5	99.9	99.4	99.3	97.4
Iron and steel	91.2	92.0	92.5	95.5	100.4	103.9	100.7	97.9	95.5	93.5	94.0	92.5
Nonferrous metals	77.1	78.8	81.8	85.9	103.4	99.4	102.7	102.7	104.6	95.3	82.2	73.8
Manufactures of metals, n.e.s.	100.3	100.6	100.2	100.3	100.6	100.1	99.8	99.4	99.3	100.1	99.3	99.0
Machinery and Transport Equipment	101.6	100.9	100.5	100.3	100.2	100.1	99.8	99.4	99.2	98.5	98.0	97.7
Power generating machinery and equipment	98.8	98.5	98.6	99.3	99.5	100.4	99.9	100.1	99.2	98.8	98.6	98.5
Machinery specialized for particular industries	101.8	101.1	101.1	101.3	100.7	99.5	99.3	98.7	99.7	99.1	99.1	98.7
Metalworking machinery	102.6	100.9	100.6	101.5	100.2	98.8	100.3	99.8	100.6	99.4	100.1	99.7
General industrial machinery, equipment, and machine parts, n.e.s.	102.1	101.3	101.1	100.7	100.7	99.9	99.7	99.0	99.3	98.2	98.0	97.8
Computer equipment and office machines	107.3	105.1	102.7	102.7	101.6	99.9	99.5	97.8	95.7	93.6	90.0	88.8
Telecommunications and sound recording and reproducing apparatus and equipment	104.8	103.8	103.2	101.4	100.6	100.2	99.6	99.0	98.1	97.2	96.8	96.3
Electrical machinery and equipment	101.3	100.1	99.8	99.3	99.4	100.7	99.9	99.4	99.9	98.8	98.6	97.8
Road vehicles	99.2	99.6	99.5	99.6	99.9	100.1	99.9	100.1	100.1	99.8	100.0	100.3
Miscellaneous Manufactured Articles	101.1	100.5	100.7	100.7	100.3	99.7	99.7	99.7	100.2	99.8	99.6	99.1
Prefabricated buildings; plumbing, and heat and lighting fixtures, n.e.s.	99.9	99.5	97.6	99.4	100.9	99.2	99.5	99.2	98.8	99.2	98.3	98.4
Furniture and parts thereof	102.6	101.1	100.8	100.1	100.5	99.6	100.3	99.7	99.8	98.5	98.9	98.9
Travel goods, handbags, and similar containers	99.2	100.3	100.9	100.1	100.5	99.8	99.9	99.8	100.1	99.0	99.3	98.7
Articles of apparel and clothing accessories	101.1	100.6	101.1	100.8	100.4	99.6	99.7	99.9	101.1	100.6	100.1	100.2
Footwear	100.4	100.0	100.1	100.1	100.0	99.6	100.2	99.8	100.8	100.1	100.4	100.3
Professional, scientific, and controlling instruments and apparatus, n.e.s.	101.0	100.4	100.8	101.3	100.1	99.8	99.8	99.2	99.1	98.7	98.5	98.5
Photographic apparatus, equipment and supplies, and optical goods, n.e.s.	100.1	99.6	99.7	100.9	100.1	99.9	99.7	98.9	99.7	98.5	98.2	98.4
Miscellaneous manufactured articles, n.e.s.	101.5	100.9	100.9	100.8	100.3	99.8	99.5	99.7	99.7	99.7	99.6	97.8

n.e.s. = not elsewhere specified.

Table 7-12. U.S. Import Price Indexes for Selected Categories of Goods, by Standard International Trade Classification, 1989–2003—*Continued*

(2000 = 100.)

Categories	2002				2003				2004			
	March	June	September	December	March	June	September	December	March	June	September	December
ALL COMMODITIES	92.8	94.1	95.5	95.2	99.1	96.2	96.2	97.5	100.2	101.7	104.1	104.0
Food and Live Animals	96.4	94.5	98.8	98.8	101.2	99.4	100.0	101.0	105.4	106.9	109.2	111.9
Meat and meat preparations	109.8	104.0	103.4	106.8	108.5	102.9	112.8	120.4	120.4	128.9	134.9	133.0
Fish, crustaceans, aquatic invertebrates, and preparations thereof	80.4	79.8	84.9	82.5	81.4	81.3	82.2	79.2	83.3	84.1	86.0	85.0
Vegetables and fruit and nuts, fresh or dried	104.0	102.2	106.7	105.6	110.7	108.9	105.0	109.4	111.3	105.9	109.2	112.2
Coffee, tea, cocoa, spices and manufactures thereof	83.3	84.6	93.5	99.9	100.2	94.8	98.6	96.0	101.7	107.0	105.6	114.4
Beverages and Tobacco	102.1	103.0	102.6	102.7	104.0	103.9	104.0	104.4	105.3	105.3	106.2	107.1
Beverages	102.5	102.8	102.2	102.4	103.0	103.7	103.9	104.3	105.5	105.6	106.7	107.6
Crude Materials, Inedible, Except Fuels	95.8	96.4	96.4	94.5	98.5	99.5	106.1	107.9	120.0	125.8	135.1	125.5
Cork and wood	106.6	103.1	98.3	94.0	95.0	94.4	113.0	108.0	123.3	136.1	151.1	124.7
Woodpulp and recovered paper	74.9	77.1	82.3	78.9	86.5	95.3	90.4	92.8	95.4	106.5	105.5	100.3
Metalliferous ores and metal scrap	93.7	95.9	93.3	94.7	99.9	99.7	103.7	115.3	148.0	140.4	162.6	167.3
Crude animal and vegetable materials, n.e.s.	92.3	92.8	104.0	101.4	102.6	104.9	95.7	99.6	99.7	98.0	98.7	98.3
Mineral Fuels, Lubricants, and Related Materials	76.4	86.1	96.3	94.9	126.0	101.7	101.5	108.2	120.8	131.5	146.8	140.6
Petroleum, petroleum products, and related materials	77.4	85.9	97.8	94.2	118.1	97.6	99.4	106.9	120.0	130.0	149.5	137.0
Gas, natural and manufactured	64.8	83.6	81.1	97.0	185.9	130.1	114.4	113.9	122.9	140.0	121.9	163.5
Chemicals and Related Products, n.e.s.	96.3	97.0	98.7	98.2	101.1	100.1	99.2	101.1	103.8	103.8	106.7	109.6
Organic chemicals	96.6	97.2	99.7	98.5	99.4	97.0	97.0	97.5	98.7	99.8	106.1	109.3
Inorganic chemicals	97.8	98.6	100.1	102.5	110.8	106.4	105.4	114.0	120.5	119.8	124.1	126.7
Dyeing, tanning, and coloring materials	97.2	96.2	96.6	96.7	97.6	98.0	97.7	99.6	99.5	100.3	98.4	98.7
Medicinal and pharmaceutical products	96.0	98.0	99.6	99.2	101.3	102.5	101.9	103.4	108.1	107.1	106.6	108.9
Essential oils, polishing, and cleansing preps	99.8	99.9	98.4	99.2	98.4	99.4	91.6	91.6	93.7	93.5	93.4	94.4
Plastics in primary forms	91.5	91.8	97.9	94.8	99.3	106.1	102.7	105.5	106.9	104.6	109.6	116.1
Plastics in nonprimary forms	100.6	100.3	99.4	99.6	100.4	100.8	101.4	101.8	102.9	102.3	103.8	105.7
Chemical materials and products, n.e.s.	93.6	93.6	92.4	91.6	97.6	92.3	91.8	93.3	95.8	95.2	94.4	96.1
Manufactured Goods Classified Chiefly by Material	92.2	92.8	93.5	93.7	94.1	94.4	95.7	97.8	103.6	106.1	108.9	110.4
Rubber manufactures, n.e.s.	97.6	98.2	99.3	99.3	99.0	99.2	98.5	98.8	99.7	100.5	100.8	101.9
Cork and wood manufactures other than furniture	96.2	93.2	93.9	89.8	94.4	95.8	113.7	112.0	127.8	118.7	116.6	113.0
Paper and paperboard, cut to size	93.4	91.7	93.7	93.0	93.0	93.5	94.5	93.7	95.0	95.5	97.9	99.0
Textile yarn, fabrics, made-up articles, and related products, n.e.s.	97.3	96.9	97.0	97.8	100.3	100.8	100.6	101.8	103.7	103.8	104.0	104.1
Nonmetallic mineral manufactures, n.e.s.	96.9	96.9	97.5	97.7	97.6	97.9	97.8	98.1	99.0	99.4	100.4	100.7
Iron and steel	90.9	94.6	99.9	101.9	99.0	101.2	99.9	105.1	119.2	144.6	157.4	160.1
Nonferrous metals	76.9	79.7	76.4	77.3	80.0	78.1	80.7	87.7	102.6	101.6	106.3	111.0
Manufactures of metals, n.e.s.	98.5	98.3	98.6	98.3	97.9	98.3	98.5	99.5	101.1	102.4	103.9	106.7
Machinery and Transport Equipment	97.1	97.1	96.7	96.1	95.8	95.8	95.5	95.3	95.5	95.1	95.0	95.2
Power generating machinery and equipment	98.0	98.2	99.4	98.7	99.1	99.9	99.7	100.4	101.3	101.5	101.4	102.5
Machinery specialized for particular industries	98.5	99.0	98.3	99.2	100.7	101.4	102.2	103.6	106.7	106.6	107.4	109.5
Metalworking machinery	98.4	100.8	102.4	101.4	104.0	105.2	103.6	105.0	107.4	106.2	108.0	112.5
General industrial machinery, equipment, and machine parts, n.e.s.	97.5	97.8	98.4	98.6	99.8	100.8	100.2	101.2	103.3	103.5	104.3	105.3
Computer equipment and office machines	88.1	87.8	86.4	84.2	82.7	81.8	80.5	78.2	77.7	75.5	73.9	72.8
Telecommunications and sound recording and reproducing apparatus and equipment	94.8	94.4	92.8	92.0	90.0	89.3	88.6	86.7	85.1	84.7	83.8	83.1
Electrical machinery and equipment	96.8	97.1	96.5	95.6	95.3	95.4	96.0	95.3	95.6	94.7	94.6	94.6
Road vehicles	100.1	100.2	100.3	100.5	100.6	100.7	100.6	101.6	102.0	102.4	103.1	103.7
Miscellaneous Manufactured Articles	98.8	98.6	98.7	99.0	99.5	99.7	99.6	99.9	100.1	99.9	100.1	100.5
Prefabricated buildings; plumbing, and heat and lighting fixtures, n.e.s.	98.9	98.5	96.5	95.6	95.8	94.8	95.1	93.2	93.2	93.5	93.5	94.8
Furniture and parts thereof	99.1	98.8	98.8	99.4	99.5	100.2	100.4	100.1	100.8	102.3	103.1	104.7
Travel goods, handbags, and similar containers	99.3	99.0	100.5	99.2	101.5	101.6	102.9	103.8	103.6	103.4	103.6	105.2
Articles of apparel and clothing accessories	100.1	99.7	99.5	100.5	100.8	100.6	100.5	100.7	100.6	100.7	100.8	100.7
Footwear	99.5	99.2	99.4	99.6	99.8	100.0	99.9	100.1	100.6	100.4	100.5	100.5
Professional, scientific, and controlling instruments and apparatus, n.e.s.	97.9	97.8	98.2	98.2	98.5	99.5	99.3	100.0	99.6	99.6	99.9	100.2
Photographic apparatus, equipment and supplies, and optical goods, n.e.s.	97.2	97.8	98.4	98.5	99.4	100.0	99.2	99.9	100.0	99.0	98.2	98.6
Miscellaneous manufactured articles, n.e.s.	97.3	97.1	97.6	97.5	98.1	98.3	98.3	98.8	99.4	98.5	98.6	99.1

n.e.s. = not elsewhere specified.

Table 7-13. U.S. Import Price Indexes for Selected Categories of Goods, by Locality of Origin, 1994–2004

(2000 = 100.)

Category and year	Percent of U.S. imports 2000	Months			
		March	June	September	December
INDUSTRIALIZED COUNTRIES	48.0				
1994		92.3	93.4	94.8	96.1
1995		97.4	99.8	100.0	100.0
1996		99.7	98.8	99.3	99.4
1997		97.4	96.5	96.4	96.1
1998		94.6	94.0	93.3	93.8
1999		94.1	94.8	96.4	97.5
2000		99.5	100.1	100.9	101.4
2001		100.2	99.0	96.5	93.7
2002		94.3	95.7	96.9	96.7
2003		100.0	98.4	98.6	100.0
2004		103.4	104.7	106.3	107.5
Manufactured Goods	43.7				
1994		95.1	95.9	97.4	98.8
1995		100.0	102.6	102.9	102.9
1996		102.1	101.1	101.4	100.7
1997		99.5	98.9	98.8	98.6
1998		97.8	97.5	96.7	97.3
1999		97.6	97.7	98.1	98.9
2000		100.2	99.9	100.2	99.8
2001		99.9	99.2	97.6	96.0
2002		95.6	96.3	96.9	96.7
2003		97.8	97.7	98.2	99.4
2004		102.1	102.8	104.0	104.6
Nonmanufactured Goods	4.0				
1994		58.2	64.3	64.3	64.1
1995		66.3	67.6	65.2	66.0
1996		71.6	72.3	76.0	84.3
1997		73.3	68.9	69.4	68.5
1998		59.3	56.8	57.2	55.7
1999		56.9	65.1	78.7	83.2
2000		92.7	102.2	107.5	118.2
2001		103.9	97.2	85.2	69.9
2002		82.9	93.8	102.4	102.7
2003		134.3	113.7	108.9	112.4
2004		122.9	133.1	138.7	147.1
OTHER COUNTRIES	52.0				
1994		90.1	94.2	95.0	95.7
1995		97.5	98.7	97.4	97.6
1996		99.8	99.0	101.3	102.7
1997		100.6	99.4	98.7	96.6
1998		92.4	90.7	89.5	86.8
1999		87.7	90.3	94.5	96.9
2000		99.8	100.4	102.5	99.5
2001		97.0	96.6	95.0	88.6
2002		90.9	92.2	94.3	93.4
2003		96.7	93.1	93.3	94.1
2004		96.3	97.9	101.5	99.7
Manufactured Goods	43.3				
1994		104.2	105.1	105.8	106.5
1995		107.3	108.8	108.6	108.4
1996		108.9	108.4	107.9	108.6
1997		108.4	107.8	107.0	105.3
1998		103.5	102.2	100.6	99.6
1999		98.8	98.9	99.0	99.3
2000		99.8	99.7	100.3	100.2
2001		99.6	98.8	97.9	96.0
2002		95.6	95.9	96.2	95.8
2003		96.5	95.1	95.1	94.5
2004		95.2	96.2	97.2	97.1
Nonmanufactured Goods	8.6				
1994		52.0	63.8	64.8	65.5
1995		69.5	70.3	66.1	67.3
1996		73.7	72.1	80.9	84.5
1997		75.8	72.6	72.2	68.8
1998		57.1	54.9	54.5	46.8
1999		53.0	63.6	80.3	89.2
2000		99.9	102.4	109.2	97.4
2001		88.9	89.7	86.1	65.3
2002		81.3	88.2	99.6	96.4
2003		113.3	98.0	98.8	106.5
2004		118.1	123.2	141.5	130.3

Table 7-13. U.S. Import Price Indexes for Selected Categories of Goods, by Locality of Origin, 1994–2004
—Continued

(2000 = 100.)

Category and year	Percent of U.S. imports 2000	Months			
		March	June	September	December
CANADA	17.2				
1994		85.5	87.2	88.1	90.2
1995		92.1	93.8	94.8	94.7
1996		94.3	93.5	93.8	95.1
1997		93.2	92.6	93.2	92.0
1998		90.1	89.7	89.3	88.7
1999		88.8	90.6	93.5	94.7
2000		97.2	99.8	102.4	105.6
2001		102.6	101.8	97.0	93.2
2002		96.1	97.8	99.6	99.2
2003		106.6	103.1	103.9	104.4
2004		110.0	112.3	114.4	116.6
Manufactured Goods	13.9				
1994		91.4	92.3	93.6	95.9
1995		98.0	99.4	100.7	100.5
1996		99.0	98.0	97.7	97.4
1997		98.0	98.0	98.3	97.3
1998		96.7	96.6	96.3	95.5
1999		95.5	96.1	96.9	97.7
2000		98.8	98.9	101.3	101.8
2001		101.6	102.8	99.9	98.1
2002		99.1	98.7	99.5	98.9
2003		100.9	101.1	103.2	103.3
2004		107.4	108.2	110.3	110.7
Nonmanufactured Goods	3.1				
1994		54.7	61.1	60.1	60.3
1995		61.7	64.4	63.9	64.8
1996		70.3	70.7	74.4	84.3
1997		69.9	66.6	68.1	66.4
1998		58.4	56.6	56.5	56.3
1999		56.5	64.2	76.8	79.9
2000		89.3	103.6	107.6	124.4
2001		108.1	97.9	83.1	69.8
2002		83.8	96.8	104.1	104.9
2003		143.1	119.0	111.5	114.0
2004		126.1	138.0	138.9	150.5
EUROPEAN UNION	19.6				
1994		91.9	93.1	94.9	96.2
1995		97.7	99.5	99.7	100.4
1996		101.3	101.0	101.7	101.9
1997		100.5	100.0	99.1	100.1
1998		98.9	98.8	98.7	99.4
1999		98.8	99.1	99.9	100.3
2000		100.8	100.1	100.0	98.9
2001		99.0	98.8	98.2	97.4
2002		97.4	99.2	101.0	100.9
2003		103.2	102.8	102.8	104.3
2004		107.4	108.5	110.0	111.6
Manufactured Goods	19.0				
1994		92.9	93.9	95.8	97.1
1995		98.6	100.4	100.9	101.5
1996		102.3	101.8	102.4	102.3
1997		101.0	100.8	100.1	101.0
1998		100.4	100.6	100.5	101.5
1999		100.9	100.6	100.8	100.8
2000		100.8	99.9	99.6	98.6
2001		99.2	98.8	98.7	98.4
2002		98.1	99.9	101.5	101.4
2003		103.3	103.2	103.2	104.5
2004		107.4	108.4	109.3	110.9
Nonmanufactured Goods	0.5				
1994		67.6	73.5	71.9	72.0
1995		72.8	74.5	71.2	73.0
1996		78.8	80.6	85.7	91.7
1997		89.3	82.2	76.5	78.4
1998		65.6	58.7	58.8	53.4
1999		53.6	66.6	81.3	88.7
2000		100.4	102.9	107.9	106.2
2001		96.0	99.5	89.1	75.7
2002		86.6	88.7	99.6	104.1
2003		118.8	106.7	111.5	118.8
2004		128.4	135.1	157.9	163.1

Table 7-13. U.S. Import Price Indexes for Selected Categories of Goods, by Locality of Origin, 1994–2004
—*Continued*

(2000 = 100.)

Category and year	Percent of U.S. imports 2000	Months			
		March	June	September	December
LATIN AMERICA	17.3				
1997		. . .	. . .	. . .	89.0
1998		84.3	83.9	83.0	80.4
1999		81.7	85.3	90.7	94.2
2000		98.9	100.9	103.5	99.5
2001		99.5	98.9	97.2	90.6
2002		94.0	96.2	100.0	98.9
2003		104.8	99.6	99.8	102.6
2004		106.3	108.6	114.7	113.1
Manufactured Goods	13.4				
1997		. . .	. . .	. . .	97.2
1998		94.8	95.0	93.8	93.5
1999		92.0	93.6	94.6	96.0
2000		98.3	99.6	101.6	102.3
2001		104.2	103.5	102.5	101.4
2002		101.5	102.4	104.2	103.8
2003		108.2	103.6	104.4	105.8
2004		107.5	109.1	112.0	113.9
Nonmanufactured Goods	3.9				
1997		. . .	. . .	. . .	70.8
1998		60.8	59.7	59.4	51.9
1999		59.3	67.2	82.1	90.2
2000		100.2	103.5	107.8	93.6
2001		89.3	89.0	86.0	67.3
2002		83.5	90.7	103.0	99.3
2003		111.7	103.5	100.9	109.8
2004		121.1	125.9	144.6	130.1
JAPAN	9.5				
1994		105.2	105.8	107.0	108.0
1995		108.6	112.5	112.0	111.0
1996		110.1	108.4	107.8	106.5
1997		104.6	103.2	102.7	101.0
1998		99.8	98.2	96.8	98.0
1999		98.2	98.2	98.6	99.6
2000		99.6	100.0	99.9	99.9
2001		99.4	98.6	97.8	97.0
2002		95.6	95.4	95.0	94.6
2003		94.4	94.2	93.8	94.7
2004		95.2	95.1	95.3	95.9
ASIAN NEWLY INDUSTRALIZED COUNTRIES	7.4				
1994		120.7	120.4	120.2	120.2
1995		120.9	121.3	121.5	120.8
1996		120.6	119.6	118.1	117.3
1997		116.6	115.3	113.8	111.3
1998		108.7	105.2	103.0	102.0
1999		101.3	100.8	100.7	100.8
2000		100.6	99.9	100.0	99.3
2001		97.3	96.4	95.2	93.8
2002		93.3	92.6	92.5	91.3
2003		91.2	91.5	91.7	90.9
2004		90.3	90.6	91.0	90.6

. . . = Not available.

Table 7-14. U.S. Import and Export Price Indexes and Percent Changes for Selected Categories of Services, December 2003–December 2004

(2000 = 100.)

Category	Trade (millions of dollars)	Index		Percent change				
				Annual	Quarterly			
		September 2004	December 2004	December 2003 to December 2004	December 2003 to March 2004	March 2004 to June 2004	June 2004 to September 2004	September 2004 to December 2004
IMPORTS								
Air Freight	4 168	120.0	126.8	10.4	1.9	0.3	2.1	5.7
Asia	2 329	109.3	113.0	2.4	-0.4	-1.3	0.6	3.4
Air Passenger Fares	18 253	121.0	111.7	4.4	-3.2	18.8	-1.7	-7.7
Europe	11 250	118.1	101.3	5.6	0.7	24.1	-1.5	-14.2
Asia	2 626	111.1	120.8	1.7	-15.2	20.8	-8.8	8.7
Latin American/Caribbean	1 916	112.9	114.8	6.0	1.2	4.5	-1.4	1.7
EXPORTS								
Air Freight	2 836	100.3	106.1	11.2	1.8	2.1	1.2	5.8
Air Passenger Fares	20 319	130.1	134.0	13.2	4.1	0.5	5.1	3.0
Europe	5 394	151.3	158.9	13.6	7.9	-0.2	0.4	5.0
Asia	8 936	120.4	117.5	13.5	3.5	-0.1	12.5	-2.4
Japan	5 473	118.8	115.7	14.3	6.2	-1.7	12.4	-2.6
Latin American/Caribbean	3 413	130.1	135.9	6.9	1.4	1.2	-0.3	4.5

PART EIGHT

CONSUMER EXPENDITURES

CONSUMER EXPENDITURES

HIGHLIGHTS

The principal objective of the Consumer Expenditure Survey is to collect information about the buying habits of American households. This survey uniquely breaks down expenditures for different demographic categories, such as income, age, family size, and geographic location. These data are use in a variety of government, business, and academic research projects. The survey also provides important weights for the periodic revisions of the Consumer Price Index.

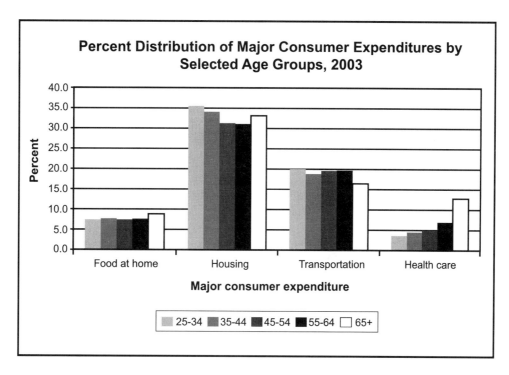

The most significant difference in expenditures between the age groups occurred in health care. The percentage of health spending predictably increased with age. 25-34 year olds only spent 3.6 percent of their earnings on health care in 2003, while 45-54 year olds spent 4.9 percent. Lower income and higher spending levels led Americans aged 65 years and older to spend 12.7 percent on health care during that same year. (Table 8-6)

OTHER HIGHLIGHTS:

- The past 10 years have seen the percentage of homeowner households increase from 63 percent to 67 percent. Of these households, 26 percent had no mortgage in 2003, down from 41 percent in 1963. This may be a reflection of how low mortgage interest rates, when combined with high housing prices, can lead homeowners to capture some of their property's equity by refinancing. (Table 8-1)

- In 2003, persons earnings $100,000 or more constituted 11.8 percent of the total; however, this group consumed 25.9 percent of total aggregate expenditures. Expenditures for this group included: 25 percent of total housing, 23 percent of total transportation, and 28 percent of total entertainment. Households with income of over $150,000 accounted for only 4 percent of the population, but consumed 11.4 percent of the total aggregate expenditures. (Table 8-4)

- Hispanic and Latino households spent a higher proportion of income on housing (35.6 percent) than non-Hispanic households (32.7 percent). Latino and Hispanic households also had higher proportional expenditures for food (16.5 percent versus 12.7 percent) and transportation (19.6 versus 19.0 percent) than non-Hispanic households. However, non-Hispanic households spent more on health care (6.1 percent) than did Hispanic and Latino households (4.2 percent). (Table 8-15)

- Single women (8.1 percent) continued to spend a significantly higher proportion on health care than did single men (4.6 percent). Much of this difference is due to fact that the average age of single women is more than 11 years higher than that of single men. Single men, however, spent more than single women on food, transportation, and entertainment. (Tables 8-23 and 8-24)

407

NOTES AND DEFINITIONS

Purpose, Collection, and Coverage

The buying habits of American consumers change over time due to changes in relative prices, real income, family size and composition, and other determinants of people's tastes and preferences. The introduction of new products into the marketplace and the emergence of new concepts in retailing also have influence on consumer buying habits. Data from the Consumer Expenditure Survey (CE), the only national survey that can relate family expenditures to demographic characteristics, are of great importance to researchers. The survey data are also used to revise the Consumer Price Index market baskets and item samples.

The Bureau of Labor Statistics (BLS) historically conducted surveys of consumer expenditures at about 10-year intervals. The last such survey was conducted in 1972–1973. In late 1979, in a significant departure from previous methodology, BLS initiated a survey to be conducted on a continuous basis with rotating panels of respondents. The regular flow of data resulting from this design substantially enhances the usefulness of the survey by providing more timely information on consumption patterns within different kinds of consumer units.

The current CE is similar to its 1972–1973 predecessor in that it consists of two separate components. Each component has its own questionnaire and sample: (1) an interview panel survey, in which an interviewer visits each consumer unit every three months for a 12-month period, and (2) a diary, or record-keeping survey, completed by other consumer units for two consecutive one-week periods. The Census Bureau, under contract to BLS, collects the data for both components of the survey. Beginning in 1999, the sample was increased from 5,000 to 7,500 households.

In 2003, the survey modified the questions on race and Hispanic origin to comply with new standards for maintaining, collecting, and presenting federal data on race and ethnicity for federal statistical agencies. Beginning with the 2003 data, the CE tables have used data collected from the new race and ethnicity questions.

In addition to these changes, a more comprehensive review was undertaken to evaluate the classifications of published CE data. The purpose of this review was to provide data users with additional information while maintaining data reliability and continuity with previously published data. As a result of both this review and the new race and ethnicity changes, a number of new classifications of CE data are being made available with the publication of the 2003 data.

The *Interview Survey* is designed to collect data on the types of expenditures that respondents can be expected to recall after a period of three months or longer. These include relatively large expenditures (such as those for property, travel, automobiles, and major appliances) and expenditures that occur on a regular basis (such as rent, utilities, insurance premiums, and clothing) The interview also obtains "global estimates" of food expenditures for both food at home and food away from home. For food-at-home expenditures, respondents are asked to estimate their typical weekly spending at the grocery store and to determine how much of the expenditure was for nonfood items. Nonfood items are then subtracted from the total. Convenience and specialty stores are included in the food-at-home estimates. The survey also collects data for approximately 95 percent of total expenditures. Excluded from the interview survey are nonprescription drugs, household supplies, and personal care products.

The *Diary Survey* is designed to collect data on expenditures for frequently purchased items that are more difficult to recall over longer periods of time. Respondents keep detailed records of expenses for food and beverages at home and meals in eating places away from home. Expenditures for tobacco, drugs—including nonprescription drugs—and personal care supplies and services are also collected in the diary.

Participants in both surveys record dollar amounts for goods and services purchased during the reporting period, regardless of whether payment was made at the time of purchase. Excluded from both surveys are business-related expenditures as well as expenditures for which the family is reimbursed. At the initial interview for each survey, information is collected on demographic and family characteristics.

The tables present integrated data from the Diary and Interview Surveys, providing a complete accounting of consumer expenditures and income, which neither survey component is designed to do alone. Data on some expenditure items are collected in either the Diary or Interview survey only. For example, the Diary does not collect data for expenditures on overnight travel or information on reimbursements as the Interview does. Examples of expenditures for which any reimbursements are netted out include those for medical care; auto repair; and construction, repairs, alterations, and maintenance of property.

For items unique to one survey or the other, the choice of which survey to use as the source of data is obvious. However, there is considerable overlap in coverage between the surveys. Integrating the data thus presents the problem of determining the appropriate survey component. When data are available from both survey sources, the more reliable of the two is selected as determined by statistical methods. As a result, some items are selected from the Interview Survey and others from the Diary Survey.

Research is underway to evaluate survey methodology and is described in *Consumer Expenditure Survey Anthology, 2003,* on the BLS Web site.

Data Included in this Book

The data in this edition for a single characteristic are for the calendar year 2003 and for two cross-classified characteristics are for an average of calendar years 2002–2003. Income values from the survey are derived from "complete income reporters" only. Complete income reporters are defined as consumer units that provide values for at least one of the major sources of their income: wages and salaries, self-employment income, retirement income, dividends and interest, and welfare benefits. Some consumer units are defined as complete income reporters even though they may not have provided a full accounting of all income from all sources.

Consumer units are classified by quintiles of income before taxes, age of reference person, size of consumer unit, region, composition of consumer unit, number of earners in consumer unit, housing tenure, race, type of area (urban or rural), and occupation.

Concepts and Definitions

A consumer unit comprises either (1) all members of a particular household related by blood, marriage, adoption, or other legal arrangements; (2) a person living alone, sharing a household with others, living as a roomer in a private home or lodging house or in permanent living quarters in a hotel or motel, but who is financially independent; or (3) two or more persons living together who pool their income to make joint expenditure decisions. Financial independence is determined by the three major expense categories: housing, food, and other living expenses. To be considered financially independent, at least two of the three major expense categories have to be provided by the respondent. The terms "family," "household," and "consumer unit" are used interchangeably in descriptions of the CE.

The *"householder"* or *"reference person"* is the first member of the consumer unit mentioned by the respondent as owner or renter of the premises at the time of the initial interview.

Expenditures are averages for consumer units with the specified characteristics, regardless of whether a particular unit incurred an expense for that specific item or service during the record-keeping period. An individual consumer unit may have spent substantially more or substantially less than the average. The less frequently an item or service is purchased, the greater the difference between the average for all consumer units and the average of those purchasing the item or service. Income, age of family members, taste, personal preferences, and geographic location are among the factors that influence expenditures and should be considered when relating averages to individual circumstances.

Expenditures reported are the direct out-of-pocket expenditures of consumer units. Indirect expenditures may be significant for some expenditure categories, such as utilities. Rental contracts may include some or all utilities, and renters with such contracts would record little or no direct expense for utilities. Therefore, caution should be exercised in making comparisons of expenditures for utilities by consumers of various income classes and types of housing.

Earner is a consumer unit member who reported having worked at least one week during the 12 months prior to the interview date.

Sources of Additional Information

For additional information on changes in 2003, see the special note on the subject on the BLS Web site. More extensive descriptions and tables are contained in Report 986. Report 981 is an anthology of articles. An updated chapter of the BLS *Handbook of Methods*, Chapter 16, is available on the BLS Web site.

Table 8-1. Consumer Expenditures, Average Annual of All Consumer Units, 1993–2003

(Number, dollar, percent.)

Item	All consumer units										
	1993	1994	1995	1996	1997	1998	1999	2000	2001	2002	2003
NUMBER OF CONSUMER UNITS (THOUSANDS)	100 049	102 210	103 123	104 212	105 576	107 182	108 465	109 367	110 339	112 108	115 356
CONSUMER UNIT CHARACTERISTICS											
Average Income Before Taxes[1]	34 868	36 181	36 918	38 014	39 926	41 622	43 951	44 649	47 507	49 430	51 128
Age of Reference Person	47.8	47.6	48.0	47.7	47.7	47.6	47.9	48.2	48.1	48.1	48.4
Average Number in Consumer Unit											
Persons	2.5	2.5	2.5	2.5	2.5	2.5	2.5	2.5	2.5	2.5	2.5
Children under 18	0.7	0.7	0.7	0.7	0.7	0.7	0.7	0.7	0.7	0.7	0.6
Persons 65 and over	0.3	0.3	0.3	0.3	0.3	0.3	0.3	0.3	0.3	0.3	0.3
Earners	1.3	1.3	1.3	1.3	1.3	1.3	1.3	1.4	1.4	1.4	1.3
Vehicles	1.9	1.9	1.9	1.9	2.0	2.0	1.9	1.9	1.9	2.0	1.9
Percent Homeowner	63.0	63.0	64.0	64.0	64.0	64.0	65.0	66.0	66.0	66.0	67.0
With mortgage	37.0	37.0	38.0	38.0	38.0	39.0	38.0	39.0	40.0	41.0	41.0
Without mortgage	26.0	26.0	26.0	26.0	26.0	26.0	27.0	27.0	26.0	26.0	26.0
AVERAGE ANNUAL EXPENDITURES	30 692	31 731	32 264	33 797	34 819	35 535	36 995	38 045	39 518	40 677	40 817
Food	4 399	4 411	4 505	4 698	4 801	4 810	5 031	5 158	5 321	5 375	5 340
Food at home	2 735	2 712	2 803	2 876	2 880	2 780	2 915	3 021	3 086	3 099	3 129
Cereals and bakery products	434	429	441	447	453	425	448	453	452	450	442
Meats, poultry, fish, and eggs	434	429	441	447	453	425	448	453	452	798	825
Dairy products	295	289	297	312	314	301	322	325	332	328	328
Fruits and vegetables	444	437	457	490	476	472	500	521	522	552	535
Other food at home	827	825	856	889	895	858	896	927	952	970	999
Food away from home	1 664	1 698	1 702	1 823	1 921	2 030	2 116	2 137	2 235	2 276	2 211
Alcoholic Beverages	268	278	277	309	309	309	318	372	349	376	391
Housing	9 636	10 106	10 458	10 747	11 272	11 713	12 057	12 319	13 011	13 283	13 432
Shelter	5 415	5 686	5 928	6 064	6 344	6 680	7 016	7 114	7 602	7 829	7 887
Owned dwellings	3 331	3 492	3 749	3 783	3 935	4 245	4 525	4 602	4 979	5 165	5 263
Rented dwellings	1 714	1 799	1 788	1 864	1 983	1 978	2 027	2 034	2 134	2 160	2 179
Other lodging	370	395	391	417	426	458	465	478	489	505	445
Utilities, fuels, and public services	2 112	2 189	2 191	2 347	2 412	2 405	2 377	2 489	2 767	2 684	2 811
Household operations	469	490	509	522	548	546	666	684	676	706	707
Housekeeping supplies	410	393	430	464	455	482	498	482	509	545	529
Household furnishings and equipment	1 230	1 348	1 401	1 350	1 512	1 601	1 499	1 549	1 458	1 518	1 497
Apparel and Services	1 676	1 644	1 704	1 752	1 729	1 674	1 743	1 856	1 743	1 749	1 640
Transportation	5 453	6 044	6 014	6 382	6 457	6 616	7 011	7 417	7 633	7 759	7 781
Vehicle purchases (net outlay)	2 319	2 725	2 638	2 815	2 736	2 964	3 305	3 418	3 579	3 665	3 732
Gasoline and motor oil	977	986	1 006	1 082	1 098	1 017	1 055	1 291	1 279	1 235	1 333
Other vehicle expenses	1 843	1 953	2 015	2 058	2 230	2 206	2 254	2 281	2 375	2 471	2 331
Public transportation	314	381	355	427	393	429	397	427	400	389	385
Health Care	1 776	1 755	1 732	1 770	1 841	1 903	1 959	2 066	2 182	2 350	2 416
Entertainment	1 626	1 567	1 612	1 834	1 813	1 746	1 891	1 863	1 953	2 079	2 060
Personal Care Products and Services	385	397	403	513	528	401	408	564	465	526	527
Reading	166	165	162	159	164	161	159	146	141	139	127
Education	455	460	471	524	571	580	635	632	648	752	783
Tobacco Products and Smoking Supplies	268	259	269	255	264	273	300	319	308	320	290
Miscellaneous	715	749	766	855	847	860	867	776	750	792	606
Cash Contributions	961	960	925	940	1 001	1 109	1 181	1 192	1 258	1 277	1 370
Personal Insurance and Pensions	2 908	2 938	2 964	3 060	3 223	3 381	3 436	3 365	3 737	3 899	4 055
Life and other personal insurance	399	398	373	353	379	398	394	399	410	406	397
Pensions and Social Security	2 509	2 540	2 591	2 707	2 844	2 982	3 042	2 966	3 326	3 493	3 658

[1]Components of income and taxes are derived from "complete income reporters" only.

Table 8-2. Shares of Average Annual Expenditures and Characteristics of All Consumer Units, 1993–2003

(Number, dollar, percent.)

Item	1993	1994	1995	1996	1997	1998	1999	2000	2001	2002	2003
NUMBER OF CONSUMER UNITS (THOUSANDS)	100 049	102 210	103 123	104 212	105 576	107 182	108 465	109 367	110 339	112 108	115 356
CONSUMER UNIT CHARACTERISTICS											
Average Income Before Taxes[1]	34 868	36 181	36 918	38 014	39 926	41 622	43 951	44 649	47 507	49 430	51 128
Age of Reference Person	47.8	47.6	48.0	47.7	47.7	47.6	47.9	48.2	48.1	48.1	48.4
Average Number in Consumer Unit											
Persons	2.5	2.5	2.5	2.5	2.5	2.5	2.5	2.5	2.5	2.5	2.5
Children under 18	0.7	0.7	0.7	0.7	0.7	0.7	0.7	0.7	0.7	0.7	0.6
Persons 65 and over	0.3	0.3	0.3	0.3	0.3	0.3	0.3	0.3	0.3	0.3	0.3
Earners	1.3	1.3	1.3	1.3	1.3	1.3	1.3	1.4	1.4	1.4	1.3
Vehicles	1.9	1.9	1.9	1.9	2.0	2.0	1.9	1.9	1.9	2.0	1.9
Percent Homeowner	63.0	63.0	64.0	64.0	64.0	64.0	65.0	66.0	66.0	66.0	67.0
With mortgage	37.0	37.0	38.0	38.0	38.0	39.0	38.0	39.0	40.0	41.0	41.0
Without mortgage	26.0	26.0	26.0	26.0	26.0	26.0	27.0	27.0	26.0	26.0	26.0
AVERAGE ANNUAL EXPENDITURES	30 692	31 731	32 264	33 797	34 819	35 535	36 995	38 045	39 518	40 677	40 817
Food	14.3	13.9	14.0	13.9	13.8	13.5	13.6	13.6	13.5	13.2	13.1
Food at home	8.9	8.5	8.7	8.5	8.3	7.8	7.9	7.9	7.8	7.6	7.7
Cereals and bakery products	1.4	1.4	1.4	1.3	1.3	1.2	1.2	1.2	1.1	1.1	1.1
Meats, poultry, fish, and eggs	2.4	2.3	2.3	2.2	2.1	2.0	2.0	2.1	2.1	2.0	2.0
Dairy products	1.0	0.9	0.9	0.9	0.9	0.8	0.9	0.9	0.8	0.8	0.8
Fruits and vegetables	1.4	1.4	1.4	1.4	1.4	1.3	1.4	1.4	1.3	1.4	1.3
Other food at home	2.7	2.6	2.7	2.6	2.6	2.4	2.4	2.4	2.4	2.4	2.4
Food away from home	5.4	5.4	5.3	5.4	5.5	5.7	5.7	5.6	5.7	5.6	5.4
Alcoholic Beverages	0.9	0.9	0.9	0.9	0.9	0.9	0.9	1.0	0.9	0.9	1.0
Housing	31.4	31.8	32.4	31.8	32.4	33.0	32.6	32.4	32.9	32.7	32.9
Shelter	17.6	17.9	18.4	17.9	18.2	18.8	19.0	18.7	19.2	19.2	19.3
Owned dwellings	10.9	11.0	11.6	11.2	11.3	11.9	12.2	12.1	12.6	12.7	12.9
Rented dwellings	5.6	5.7	5.5	5.5	5.7	5.6	5.5	5.3	5.4	5.3	5.3
Other lodging	1.2	1.2	1.2	1.2	1.2	1.3	1.3	1.3	1.2	1.2	1.1
Utilities, fuels, and public services	6.9	6.9	6.8	6.9	6.9	6.8	6.4	6.5	7.0	6.6	6.9
Household operations	1.5	1.5	1.6	1.5	1.6	1.5	1.8	1.8	1.7	1.7	1.7
Housekeeping supplies	1.3	1.2	1.3	1.4	1.3	1.4	1.3	1.3	1.3	1.3	1.3
Household furnishings and equipment	4.0	4.2	4.3	4.0	4.3	4.5	4.1	4.1	3.7	3.7	3.7
Apparel and Services	5.5	5.2	5.3	5.2	5.0	4.7	4.7	4.9	4.4	4.3	4.0
Transportation	17.8	19.0	18.6	18.9	18.5	18.6	19.0	19.5	19.3	19.1	19.1
Vehicle purchases (net outlay)	7.6	8.6	8.2	8.3	7.9	8.3	8.9	9.0	9.1	9.0	9.1
Gasoline and motor oil	3.2	3.1	3.1	3.2	3.2	2.9	2.9	3.4	3.2	3.0	3.3
Other vehicle expenses	6.0	6.2	6.2	6.1	6.4	6.2	6.1	6.0	6.0	6.1	5.7
Public transportation	1.0	1.2	1.1	1.3	1.1	1.2	1.1	1.1	1.0	1.0	0.9
Health Care	5.8	5.5	5.4	5.2	5.3	5.4	5.3	5.4	5.5	5.8	5.9
Health insurance	2.6	2.6	2.7	2.4	2.5	2.6	2.5	2.6	2.7	2.9	3.1
Medical services	1.9	1.8	1.6	1.6	1.5	1.5	1.5	1.5	1.4	1.5	1.4
Drugs	1.0	0.9	0.9	0.9	0.9	1.0	1.0	1.1	1.1	1.2	1.1
Medical supplies	0.3	0.3	0.2	0.3	0.3	0.3	0.3	0.3	0.3	0.3	0.3
Entertainment	5.3	4.9	5.0	5.4	5.2	4.9	5.1	4.9	4.9	5.1	5.0
Personal Care Products and Services	1.3	1.3	1.2	1.5	1.5	1.1	1.1	1.5	1.2	1.3	1.3
Reading	0.5	0.5	0.5	0.5	0.5	0.5	0.4	0.4	0.4	0.3	0.3
Education	1.5	1.4	1.5	1.6	1.6	1.6	1.7	1.7	1.6	1.8	1.9
Tobacco Products and Smoking Supplies	0.9	0.8	0.8	0.8	0.8	0.8	0.8	0.8	0.8	0.8	0.7
Miscellaneous	2.3	2.4	2.4	2.5	2.4	2.4	2.3	2.0	1.9	1.9	1.5
Cash Contributions	3.1	3.0	2.9	2.8	2.9	3.1	3.2	3.1	3.2	3.1	3.4
Personal Insurance and Pensions	9.5	9.3	9.2	9.1	9.3	9.5	9.3	8.8	9.5	9.6	9.9
Life and other personal insurance	1.3	1.3	1.2	1.0	1.1	1.1	1.1	1.0	1.0	1.0	1.0
Pensions and Social Security	8.2	8.0	8.0	8.0	8.2	8.4	8.2	7.8	8.4	8.6	9.0

[1]Components of income and taxes are derived from "complete income reporters" only.

Table 8-3. Consumer Expenditures, Averages by Income Before Taxes, 2003

(Number, dollar, percent.)

Item	Complete reporting of income, total	Complete reporting of income								
		Less than $5,000	$5,000 to $9,999	$10,000 to $14,999	$15,000 to $19,999	$20,000 to $29,999	$30,000 to $39,999	$40,000 to $49,999	$50,000 to $69,999	$70,000 and over
NUMBER OF CONSUMER UNITS (THOUSANDS)	97 391	4 398	7 155	8 145	7 402	13 182	10 759	8 891	13 890	23 567
CONSUMER UNIT CHARACTERISTICS										
Average Income Before Taxes[1]	51 128	1 200	7 799	12 455	17 410	24 655	34 485	44 294	58 900	117 960
Average Income After Taxes[1]	48 596	1 218	7 866	12 549	17 456	23 197	33 370	42 842	56 428	110 756
Age of Reference Person	48.4	41.2	52.6	55.9	52.9	50.1	47.4	46.7	45.6	46.1
Average Number in Consumer Unit										
Persons	2.5	1.7	1.6	1.9	2.1	2.3	2.5	2.6	2.8	3.0
Children under 18	0.6	0.4	0.4	0.4	0.5	0.6	0.6	0.7	0.8	0.8
Persons 65 and over	0.3	0.2	0.4	0.5	0.5	0.4	0.3	0.2	0.2	0.1
Earners	1.3	0.8	0.5	0.6	0.8	1.1	1.3	1.5	1.7	2.0
Vehicles	2.0	0.9	0.8	1.1	1.4	1.6	2.0	2.2	2.5	2.8
Percent Distribution										
Male	51.0	42.0	35.0	36.0	44.0	47.0	51.0	56.0	57.0	60.0
Female	49.0	58.0	65.0	64.0	56.0	53.0	49.0	44.0	43.0	40.0
Percent Homeowner	66.0	32.0	38.0	48.0	54.0	57.0	63.0	71.0	78.0	89.0
With mortgage	41.0	13.0	9.0	11.0	18.0	26.0	36.0	47.0	58.0	71.0
Without mortgage	25.0	19.0	29.0	37.0	35.0	31.0	27.0	23.0	20.0	18.0
AVERAGE ANNUAL EXPENDITURES	42 742	19 272	16 013	20 061	23 715	29 034	34 931	39 757	49 789	77 521
Food	5 593	3 433	2 760	3 422	3 721	4 338	4 993	5 486	6 511	8 794
Food at home	3 236	2 081	1 825	2 425	2 479	2 856	3 048	3 234	3 700	4 472
Cereals and bakery products	456	314	272	365	364	403	415	468	511	617
Meats, poultry, fish, and eggs	837	496	481	633	632	800	784	821	1 011	1 100
Dairy products	343	218	181	252	272	302	321	367	384	475
Fruits and vegetables	556	353	323	428	448	498	550	524	585	783
Other food at home	1 044	699	567	746	762	852	978	1 053	1 209	1 497
Food away from home	2 358	1 352	936	997	1 242	1 483	1 945	2 252	2 811	4 323
Alcoholic Beverages	442	263	153	200	210	247	309	407	556	858
Housing	13 653	6 929	6 145	7 457	8 571	9 828	11 259	12 728	15 106	23 693
Shelter	7 921	4 317	3 690	4 268	4 955	5 635	6 510	7 269	8 679	13 795
Owned dwellings	5 247	1 761	1 244	1 553	2 170	2 702	3 511	4 578	6 253	11 230
Rented dwellings	2 220	2 350	2 327	2 591	2 642	2 780	2 794	2 389	1 986	1 400
Other lodging	455	206	119	123	143	154	204	303	439	1 165
Utilities, fuels, and public services	2 820	1 499	1 605	1 945	2 191	2 394	2 666	2 906	3 217	3 976
Household operations	730	211	162	337	397	414	449	560	749	1 597
Housekeeping supplies	582	260	257	348	410	426	494	542	628	1 010
Household furnishings and equipment	1 600	643	432	558	618	958	1 142	1 450	1 834	3 315
Apparel and Services	1 744	1 056	769	912	1 069	1 112	1 503	1 515	1 967	3 139
Transportation	8 041	3 041	2 329	3 130	4 033	5 615	6 973	7 949	10 656	14 006
Vehicle purchases (net outlay)	3 871	1 284	946	1 397	1 589	2 607	3 264	3 686	5 407	6 964
Gasoline and motor oil	1 353	648	532	652	906	1 053	1 309	1 494	1 712	2 041
Other vehicle expenses	2 416	921	699	952	1 349	1 686	2 145	2 486	3 104	4 161
Public transportation	400	187	152	129	190	269	256	284	433	839
Health Care	2 495	1 010	1 249	1 834	2 015	2 286	2 460	2 629	2 811	3 429
Health insurance	1 267	495	644	975	1 046	1 190	1 270	1 355	1 461	1 666
Medical services	612	232	187	340	345	451	591	660	717	1 008
Drugs	501	236	365	456	543	535	490	516	508	574
Medical supplies	115	48	53	64	81	111	110	99	125	182
Entertainment	2 155	787	616	716	946	1 517	1 742	1 925	2 363	4 270
Personal Care Products and Services	559	270	256	335	362	384	452	533	637	966
Reading	133	54	47	72	77	95	105	129	144	243
Education	792	1 023	540	361	332	251	320	400	600	1 902
Tobacco Products and Smoking Supplies	307	179	238	257	305	324	323	415	345	290
Miscellaneous	658	336	267	292	418	510	545	693	919	1 008
Cash Contributions	1 458	548	305	519	602	904	1 138	1 070	1 383	3 217
Personal Insurance and Pensions	4 710	345	337	554	1 054	1 622	2 810	3 878	5 792	11 705
Life and other personal insurance	414	110	112	142	255	217	281	347	429	894
Pensions and Social Security	4 296	235	225	412	799	1 405	2 529	3 532	5 363	10 811

[1]Components of income and taxes are derived from "complete income reporters" only.

Table 8-4. Consumer Expenditures, Averages by Higher Income Before Taxes, 2003

(Number, dollar, percent.)

Item	Complete reporting of income							
	Total complete reporting	Less than $70,000	$70,000 to $79,000	$80,000 to $99,999	$100,000 and over	$100,000 to $119,000	$120,000 to $149,999	$150,000 and over
NUMBER OF CONSUMER UNITS (THOUSANDS)	97 391	73 824	5 121	6 909	11 537	4 384	3 151	4 002
CONSUMER UNIT CHARACTERISTICS								
Average Income Before Taxes[1]	51 128	29 793	74 560	88 832	154 665	108 087	131 885	223 634
Average Income After Taxes[1]	48 596	28 752	71 388	84 176	144 146	101 871	121 640	208 186
Age of Reference Person	48.4	49.1	45.1	45.9	46.7	45.8	46.4	47.8
Average Number in Consumer Unit								
Persons	2.5	2.3	3.0	3.0	3.1	3.1	3.1	3.1
Children under 18	0.6	0.6	0.8	0.8	0.8	0.8	0.8	0.9
Persons 65 and over	0.3	0.4	0.1	0.1	0.1	0.1	0.1	0.1
Earners	1.3	1.1	1.8	2.0	2.0	2.0	2.1	1.9
Vehicles	2.0	1.7	2.7	3.0	2.8	2.8	3.0	2.8
Percent Distribution								
Male	51.0	48.0	60.0	60.0	59.0	57.0	63.0	59.0
Female	49.0	52.0	40.0	40.0	41.0	43.0	37.0	41.0
Percent Homeowner	66.0	59.0	83.0	88.0	92.0	91.0	91.0	94.0
With mortgage	41.0	31.0	66.0	69.0	74.0	76.0	74.0	73.0
Without mortgage	25.0	28.0	17.0	19.0	18.0	15.0	17.0	21.0
AVERAGE ANNUAL EXPENDITURES	42 742	31 737	57 128	65 957	93 515	75 601	86 451	118 674
Food	5 593	4 619	7 548	7 840	9 926	8 714	9 689	11 435
Food at home	3 236	2 862	4 354	4 136	4 726	4 304	4 934	5 023
Cereals and bakery products	456	408	617	591	632	606	619	670
Meats, poultry, fish, and eggs	837	757	1 094	967	1 183	1 042	1 264	1 274
Dairy products	343	304	455	457	494	437	530	528
Fruits and vegetables	556	488	780	704	830	741	916	861
Other food at home	1 044	906	1 407	1 417	1 586	1 478	1 605	1 690
Food away from home	2 358	1 757	3 195	3 703	5 201	4 410	4 755	6 411
Alcoholic Beverages	442	316	618	589	1 127	785	865	1 703
Housing	13 653	10 464	17 081	19 841	28 941	23 204	26 719	36 971
Shelter	7 921	6 046	9 912	10 899	17 253	13 623	16 128	22 117
Owned dwellings	5 247	3 336	7 643	8 858	14 242	11 269	13 211	18 310
Rented dwellings	2 220	2 481	1 713	1 357	1 288	1 272	1 562	1 090
Other lodging	455	228	557	684	1 723	1 081	1 355	2 717
Utilities, fuels, and public services	2 820	2 450	3 433	3 779	4 336	3 895	4 146	4 969
Household operations	730	453	912	1 168	2 158	1 438	1 848	3 191
Housekeeping supplies	582	453	769	897	1 186	1 072	1 083	1 390
Household furnishings and equipment	1 600	1 062	2 055	3 098	4 008	3 177	3 514	5 304
Apparel and Services	1 744	1 314	2 549	2 546	3 756	2 695	3 541	5 083
Transportation	8 041	6 138	11 540	13 295	15 526	14 178	15 785	16 799
Vehicle purchases (net outlay)	3 871	2 884	5 698	6 834	7 604	7 295	7 932	7 683
Gasoline and motor oil	1 353	1 134	1 861	2 038	2 123	2 063	2 195	2 133
Other vehicle expenses	2 416	1 860	3 531	3 842	4 632	4 191	4 612	5 130
Public transportation	400	260	449	582	1 167	629	1 046	1 853
Health Care	2 495	2 199	2 700	3 335	3 809	3 465	3 478	4 447
Health insurance	1 267	1 140	1 400	1 577	1 837	1 669	1 718	2 115
Medical services	612	485	716	1 032	1 122	972	890	1 470
Drugs	501	479	446	555	642	622	678	636
Medical supplies	115	94	138	171	208	203	192	226
Entertainment	2 155	1 484	3 243	3 607	5 124	3 810	4 382	7 147
Personal Care Products and Services	559	433	722	871	1 131	874	1 139	1 405
Reading	133	98	180	202	296	228	293	372
Education	792	439	855	1 082	2 858	2 093	2 165	4 243
Tobacco Products and Smoking Supplies	307	313	325	358	234	243	259	204
Miscellaneous	658	547	750	843	1 221	1 267	965	1 373
Cash Contributions	1 458	896	1 627	2 173	4 547	2 238	2 698	8 534
Personal Insurance and Pensions	4 710	2 476	7 390	9 375	15 016	11 808	14 474	18 958
Life and other personal insurance	414	261	490	659	1 214	729	944	1 958
Pensions and Social Security	4 296	2 215	6 901	8 715	13 802	11 079	13 530	17 001

[1]Components of income and taxes are derived from "complete income reporters" only.

Table 8-5. Consumer Expenditures, Averages by Quintiles of Income Before Taxes, 2003

(Number, dollar, percent.)

Item	Complete reporting of income						Incomplete reporting of income
	Complete reporting of income, total	Lowest 20 percent	Second 20 percent	Third 20 percent	Fourth 20 percent	Highest 20 percent	
NUMBER OF CONSUMER UNITS (THOUSANDS)	97 391	19 455	19 482	19 472	19 481	19 501	17 965
CONSUMER UNIT CHARACTERISTICS							
Average Income Before Taxes[1]	51 128	8 201	21 478	37 542	61 132	127 146	(1)
Average Income After Taxes[1]	48 596	8 260	20 543	36 363	58 593	119 091	(1)
Age of Reference Person	48.4	51.2	51.4	47.2	45.7	46.3	48.5
Average Number in Consumer Unit							
Persons	2.5	1.8	2.3	2.5	2.8	3.1	2.5
Children under 18	0.6	0.4	0.6	0.7	0.7	0.8	0.6
Persons 65 and over	0.3	0.4	0.5	0.3	0.2	0.1	0.3
Earners	1.3	0.6	1.0	1.4	1.7	2.0	1.3
Vehicles	2.0	0.9	1.5	2.0	2.5	2.9	1.8
Percent Distribution							
Male	51.0	37.0	45.0	53.0	58.0	59.0	49.0
Female	49.0	63.0	55.0	47.0	42.0	41.0	51.0
Percent Homeowner	66.0	41.0	55.0	65.0	79.0	90.0	71.0
With mortgage	41.0	11.0	22.0	40.0	59.0	72.0	41.0
Without mortgage	25.0	30.0	33.0	25.0	20.0	18.0	31.0
AVERAGE ANNUAL EXPENDITURES	42 742	18 492	26 729	36 213	50 468	81 731	32 054
Food	5 593	3 178	4 102	5 098	6 544	9 039	4 593
Food at home	3 236	2 119	2 713	3 114	3 726	4 503	2 837
Cereals and bakery products	456	318	390	429	528	616	403
Meats, poultry, fish, and eggs	837	550	727	814	982	1 111	792
Dairy products	343	219	289	337	392	480	287
Fruits and vegetables	556	369	484	538	601	788	480
Other food at home	1 044	664	823	996	1 224	1 509	875
Food away from home	2 358	1 059	1 389	1 983	2 818	4 535	1 756
Alcoholic Beverages	442	198	230	329	552	902	248
Housing	13 653	6 858	9 285	11 709	15 357	25 033	12 550
Shelter	7 921	4 071	5 329	6 770	8 838	14 585	7 704
Owned dwellings	5 247	1 488	2 466	3 841	6 460	11 964	5 352
Rented dwellings	2 220	2 442	2 714	2 689	1 924	1 332	1 961
Other lodging	455	140	149	240	454	1 290	391
Utilities, fuels, and public services	2 820	1 719	2 309	2 731	3 238	4 098	2 767
Household operations	730	241	406	500	762	1 739	583
Housekeeping supplies	582	299	417	481	660	1 051	387
Household furnishings and equipment	1 600	528	824	1 226	1 859	3 559	1 110
Apparel and Services	1 744	913	1 073	1 458	2 018	3 255	1 330
Transportation	8 041	2 859	4 920	7 210	10 677	14 525	6 404
Vehicle purchases (net outlay)	3 871	1 240	2 164	3 367	5 351	7 229	2 975
Gasoline and motor oil	1 353	614	981	1 352	1 736	2 083	1 221
Other vehicle expenses	2 416	852	1 539	2 233	3 159	4 292	1 897
Public transportation	400	154	235	258	432	922	311
Health Care	2 495	1 439	2 132	2 553	2 745	3 606	2 055
Health insurance	1 267	742	1 124	1 306	1 440	1 723	1 167
Medical services	612	262	378	636	695	1 087	480
Drugs	501	378	531	504	486	607	332
Medical supplies	115	57	100	107	124	189	77
Entertainment	2 155	703	1 307	1 776	2 471	4 516	1 634
Personal Care Products and Services	559	295	368	484	638	1 011	436
Reading	133	58	88	114	151	254	95
Education	792	576	287	351	623	2 121	752
Tobacco Products and Smoking Supplies	307	237	315	347	356	281	195
Miscellaneous	658	298	461	591	888	1 054	359
Cash Contributions	1 458	449	789	1 071	1 458	3 517	894
Personal Insurance and Pensions	4 710	433	1 373	3 123	5 990	12 615	508
Life and other personal insurance	414	125	226	305	435	979	306
Pensions and Social Security	4 296	308	1 147	2 818	5 555	11 637	201

[1]Components of income and taxes are derived from "complete income reporters" only.

Table 8-6. Consumer Expenditures, Averages by Age of Reference Person, 2003

(Number, dollar, percent.)

Item	Under 25 years	25 to 34 years	35 to 44 years	45 to 54 years	55 to 64 years	65 years and over	65 to 74 years	75 years and over
NUMBER OF CONSUMER UNITS (THOUSANDS)	8 584	19 737	24 413	23 131	16 580	22 912	11 495	11 417
CONSUMER UNIT CHARACTERISTICS								
Average Income Before Taxes[1]	20 680	50 389	61 091	68 028	58 672	30 437	35 314	25 492
Average Income After Taxes[1]	20 259	48 410	58 275	64 080	55 844	28 559	33 859	23 185
Age of Reference Person	21	30	40	49	59	75	69	81
Average Number in Consumer Unit								
Persons	1.8	2.9	3.2	2.6	2.1	1.7	1.9	1.5
Children under 18	0.4	1.1	1.3	0.6	0.2	0.1	0.1	(2)
Persons 65 and over	(2)	(2)	(2)	(2)	0.1	1.4	1.4	1.3
Earners	1.2	1.5	1.6	1.8	1.4	0.4	0.6	0.2
Vehicles	1.1	1.8	2.1	2.4	2.3	1.5	1.8	1.2
Percent Distribution								
Male	49.0	51.0	52.0	51.0	53.0	45.0	50.0	41.0
Female	51.0	49.0	48.0	49.0	47.0	55.0	50.0	59.0
Percent Homeowner	15.0	48.0	69.0	76.0	82.0	80.0	83.0	78.0
With mortgage	9.0	42.0	57.0	56.0	44.0	17.0	27.0	8.0
Without mortgage	7.0	7.0	12.0	20.0	38.0	63.0	56.0	70.0
AVERAGE ANNUAL EXPENDITURES	22 396	40 525	47 175	50 101	44 191	29 376	33 629	25 016
Food	3 401	5 318	6 272	6 381	5 530	3 896	4 544	3 208
Food at home	1 766	2 976	3 600	3 693	3 315	2 575	2 888	2 241
Cereals and bakery products	256	421	523	509	427	387	414	358
Meats, poultry, fish, and eggs	438	769	933	1 002	914	661	758	558
Dairy products	193	317	388	378	326	277	308	243
Fruits and vegetables	272	495	593	621	593	484	537	428
Other food at home	607	974	1 164	1 184	1 054	767	872	654
Food away from home	1 636	2 342	2 672	2 688	2 215	1 321	1 656	968
Alcoholic Beverages	509	446	424	477	372	184	237	128
Housing	7 095	14 392	16 098	15 624	13 714	9 729	10 761	8 678
Shelter	4 574	8 915	9 678	9 237	7 571	5 201	5 764	4 635
Owned dwellings	765	4 837	6 940	6 893	5 769	3 515	4 300	2 725
Rented dwellings	3 593	3 835	2 315	1 656	1 179	1 331	1 045	1 619
Other lodging	216	243	423	688	623	355	419	291
Utilities, fuels, and public services	1 329	2 580	3 142	3 335	3 089	2 484	2 723	2 244
Household operations	230	872	949	633	604	635	504	768
Housekeeping supplies	225	455	597	618	618	485	590	373
Household furnishings and equipment	737	1 571	1 731	1 801	1 831	923	1 180	657
Apparel and Services	1 117	1 849	2 091	1 953	1 562	908	1 190	611
Transportation	4 674	8 106	8 892	9 766	8 680	4 824	6 015	3 622
Vehicle purchases (net outlay)	2 241	3 932	4 255	4 632	4 289	2 247	2 770	1 721
Gasoline and motor oil	947	1 388	1 582	1 644	1 411	792	1 019	563
Other vehicle expenses	1 299	2 446	2 643	3 013	2 484	1 487	1 857	1 112
Public transportation	187	340	411	476	495	298	370	226
Health Care	546	1 468	2 105	2 479	3 059	3 741	3 626	3 856
Health insurance	281	810	1 109	1 166	1 572	2 002	1 974	2 031
Medical services	129	394	598	718	742	688	681	695
Drugs	100	202	301	459	627	905	838	971
Medical supplies	37	62	97	137	118	146	133	159
Entertainment	950	1 958	2 519	2 407	2 414	1 469	2 016	909
Personal Care Products and Services	326	498	602	616	549	440	491	387
Reading	53	99	114	150	168	141	149	134
Education	1 490	684	694	1 377	743	129	176	81
Tobacco Products and Smoking Supplies	230	285	312	385	337	162	219	105
Miscellaneous	251	532	601	830	675	533	547	519
Cash Contributions	371	754	1 256	1 651	1 568	1 969	1 811	2 127
Personal Insurance and Pensions	1 382	4 137	5 196	6 003	4 819	1 251	1 847	651
Life and other personal insurance	40	200	382	600	570	388	504	270
Pensions and Social Security	1 342	3 937	4 814	5 403	4 249	864	1 342	382

[1]Components of income and taxes are derived from "complete income reporters" only.
[2]Value less than 0.05.

Table 8-7. Consumer Expenditures, Averages by Size of Consumer Unit, 2003

(Number, dollar, percent.)

Item	One person	Two or more persons	Two persons	Three persons	Four persons	Five or more persons
NUMBER OF CONSUMER UNITS (THOUSANDS)	33 929	81 427	36 830	17 701	15 464	11 432
CONSUMER UNIT CHARACTERISTICS						
Average Income Before Taxes[1]	27 131	61 165	55 980	62 780	70 136	63 106
Average Income After Taxes[1]	25 539	58 240	52 279	60 448	67 298	61 662
Age of Reference Person	51.4	47.1	53.2	43.9	40.9	40.9
Average Number in Consumer Unit						
Persons	1.0	3.1	2.0	3.0	4.0	5.6
Children under 18	X	0.9	0.1	0.8	1.6	2.7
Persons 65 and over	0.3	0.3	0.5	0.2	0.1	0.1
Earners	0.6	1.6	1.3	1.7	1.9	2.2
Vehicles	1.0	2.3	2.2	2.3	2.5	2.5
Percent Distribution						
Males	45.0	52.0	56.0	47.0	51.0	51.0
Females	55.0	48.0	44.0	53.0	49.0	49.0
Percent Homeowner	49.0	74.0	76.0	70.0	76.0	73.0
With mortgage	21.0	49.0	40.0	51.0	64.0	58.0
Without mortgage	29.0	25.0	36.0	19.0	12.0	15.0
AVERAGE ANNUAL EXPENDITURES	23 657	47 921	43 693	47 406	55 201	52 565
Food	2 831	6 357	5 432	6 173	7 472	8 178
Food at home	1 525	3 778	3 128	3 664	4 472	5 157
Cereals and bakery products	217	532	425	508	644	772
Meats, poultry, fish, and eggs	359	1 013	824	976	1 213	1 422
Dairy products	161	396	324	383	467	555
Fruits and vegetables	280	639	552	609	740	832
Other food at home	507	1 198	1 003	1 188	1 407	1 577
Food away from home	1 306	2 579	2 304	2 509	3 000	3 020
Alcoholic Beverages	280	436	468	419	436	358
Housing	8 768	15 369	13 536	15 596	18 322	16 930
Shelter	5 614	8 835	7 730	8 949	10 622	9 801
Owned dwellings	2 692	6 334	5 263	6 220	8 299	7 304
Rented dwellings	2 679	1 971	1 869	2 229	1 818	2 109
Other lodging	242	529	597	501	505	388
Utilities, fuels, and public services	1 758	3 250	2 905	3 320	3 615	3 762
Household operations	343	859	565	1 026	1 337	899
Housekeeping supplies	284	628	582	636	685	690
Household furnishings and equipment	769	1 798	1 754	1 666	2 064	1 778
Apparel and Services	837	1 968	1 547	1 916	2 503	2 698
Transportation	3 839	9 422	8 683	9 562	10 459	10 185
Vehicle purchases (net outlay)	1 692	4 582	4 363	4 644	4 929	4 720
Gasoline and motor oil	674	1 607	1 388	1 619	1 859	1 956
Other vehicle expenses	1 217	2 795	2 458	2 910	3 220	3 122
Public transportation	256	439	473	389	452	387
Health Care	1 558	2 774	3 093	2 532	2 581	2 379
Health insurance	779	1 449	1 597	1 326	1 402	1 224
Medical services	360	687	700	642	694	705
Drugs	356	512	653	450	365	355
Medical supplies	63	125	142	114	120	95
Entertainment	1 041	2 482	2 421	2 263	2 821	2 554
Personal Care Products and Services	316	614	563	603	693	689
Reading	93	142	159	130	135	110
Education	498	902	597	938	1 426	1 119
Tobacco Products and Smoking Supplies	193	330	310	351	329	364
Miscellaneous	423	682	650	658	801	661
Cash Contributions	1 032	1 511	1 810	1 179	1 270	1 385
Personal Insurance and Pensions	1 948	4 933	4 424	5 087	5 952	4 956
Life and other personal insurance	159	497	496	488	498	511
Pensions and Social Security	1 790	4 436	3 928	4 599	5 454	4 446

[1]Components of income and taxes are derived from "complete income reporters" only.
X = Not applicable.

Table 8-8. Consumer Expenditures, Averages by Composition of Consumer Unit, 2003

(Number, dollar, percent.)

Item	Husband and wife consumer units						Other husband and wife consumer units	One parent, at least one child under 18 years	Single person and other consumer units
	Total	Husband and wife only	Husband and wife with children						
			Total	Oldest child under 6 years	Oldest child 6 to 17 years	Oldest child 18 years or over			
NUMBER OF CONSUMER UNITS (THOUSANDS)	58 448	25 132	28 584	5 496	15 047	8 041	4 732	6 999	49 909
CONSUMER UNIT CHARACTERISTICS									
Average Income Before Taxes[1]	69 472	62 930	75 557	66 317	77 508	78 307	66 597	29 154	32 970
Average Income After Taxes[1]	65 839	58 260	72 564	64 106	74 270	75 236	64 547	28 846	31 399
Age of Reference Person	48.6	56.8	41.6	32.1	40.0	51.2	47.3	37.4	49.6
Average Number in Consumer Unit									
Persons	3.2	2.0	3.9	3.5	4.1	4.0	4.9	2.9	1.6
Children under 18	0.9	X	1.6	1.5	2.1	0.7	1.4	1.8	0.2
Persons 65 and over	0.3	0.6	0.1	(2)	(2)	0.2	0.4	(2)	0.3
Earners	1.7	1.2	2.0	1.7	1.8	2.6	2.3	1.0	1.0
Vehicles	2.6	2.4	2.7	2.1	2.6	3.3	2.8	1.2	1.3
Percent Distribution									
Males	61.0	64.0	57.0	58.0	55.0	60.0	61.0	16.0	43.0
Females	39.0	36.0	43.0	42.0	45.0	40.0	39.0	84.0	57.0
Percent Homeowner	83.0	85.0	82.0	72.0	81.0	90.0	78.0	40.0	52.0
With mortgage	56.0	43.0	68.0	64.0	70.0	66.0	55.0	30.0	24.0
Without mortgage	27.0	42.0	14.0	8.0	12.0	24.0	23.0	10.0	27.0
AVERAGE ANNUAL EXPENDITURES	53 030	47 896	57 702	51 503	59 183	59 180	52 110	30 535	27 867
Food	6 864	5 927	7 553	6 224	7 844	7 937	7 732	4 804	3 577
Food at home	4 047	3 402	4 476	3 952	4 551	4 710	4 993	2 979	2 039
Cereals and bakery products	571	458	652	547	691	650	692	445	285
Meats, poultry, fish, and eggs	1 077	912	1 169	890	1 213	1 283	1 461	787	525
Dairy products	427	352	485	444	497	491	468	307	211
Fruits and vegetables	688	606	735	672	723	808	858	455	363
Other food at home	1 285	1 074	1 435	1 399	1 428	1 479	1 515	985	656
Food away from home	2 817	2 525	3 077	2 272	3 293	3 226	2 739	1 826	1 538
Alcoholic Beverages	447	478	440	445	429	459	288	220	348
Housing	16 648	14 352	18 679	19 303	19 235	17 215	16 533	11 772	9 885
Shelter	9 480	8 001	10 812	10 963	11 292	9 812	9 289	7 152	6 125
Owned dwellings	7 433	5 973	8 773	8 440	9 213	8 175	7 100	3 234	3 006
Rented dwellings	1 405	1 280	1 455	2 204	1 488	883	1 764	3 724	2 870
Other lodging	642	748	584	319	591	753	425	195	249
Utilities, fuels, and public services	3 444	3 075	3 695	3 030	3 745	4 055	3 882	2 595	2 101
Household operations	970	596	1 316	2 365	1 286	656	865	725	397
Housekeeping supplies	699	659	734	645	728	813	683	349	348
Household furnishings and equipment	2 055	2 021	2 122	2 300	2 183	1 880	1 814	951	914
Apparel and Services	2 085	1 632	2 431	2 232	2 614	2 219	2 441	1 799	1 085
Transportation	10 627	9 580	11 546	9 832	11 526	12 755	10 658	4 592	4 893
Vehicle purchases (net outlay)	5 308	4 933	5 713	4 953	5 849	5 977	4 858	1 734	2 166
Gasoline and motor oil	1 740	1 463	1 949	1 613	1 927	2 220	1 956	993	903
Other vehicle expenses	3 078	2 638	3 418	2 925	3 261	4 049	3 381	1 632	1 553
Public transportation	501	547	466	342	489	509	463	234	271
Health Care	3 202	3 713	2 760	2 177	2 764	3 151	3 157	1 201	1 666
Health insurance	1 663	1 906	1 455	1 253	1 429	1 642	1 623	644	855
Medical services	809	847	783	536	844	838	767	330	372
Drugs	584	792	391	296	361	514	644	164	371
Medical supplies	146	167	131	92	130	157	123	63	68
Entertainment	2 793	2 699	2 958	2 401	3 414	2 478	2 295	1 453	1 281
Personal Care Products and Services	668	617	713	559	713	821	670	459	369
Reading	163	186	149	121	151	167	118	64	95
Education	1 053	610	1 510	413	1 438	2 393	639	493	508
Tobacco Products and Smoking Supplies	300	275	298	220	291	365	447	230	286
Miscellaneous	712	638	778	626	696	1 035	702	510	494
Cash Contributions	1 762	2 174	1 441	1 060	1 430	1 723	1 507	622	1 016
Personal Insurance and Pensions	5 707	5 015	6 445	5 891	6 638	6 462	4 923	2 315	2 365
Life and other personal insurance	599	625	585	378	618	665	550	181	191
Pensions and Social Security	5 108	4 390	5 860	5 513	6 021	5 798	4 374	2 134	2 174

[1]Components of income and taxes are derived from "complete income reporters" only.
[2]Value less than 0.05.
X = Not applicable.

Table 8-9. Consumer Expenditures, Averages by Number of Earners, 2003

(Number, dollar, percent.)

Item	Single consumer		Consumer units of two or more persons			
	No earner	One earner	No earner	One earner	Two earners	Three or more earners
NUMBER OF CONSUMER UNITS (THOUSANDS)	12 482	21 447	10 056	23 586	38 486	9 299
CONSUMER UNIT CHARACTERISTICS						
Average Income Before Taxes[1]	14 696	33 732	27 491	47 408	73 689	80 310
Average Income After Taxes[1]	14 581	31 356	25 216	45 835	69 932	76 640
Age of Reference Person	68.6	41.4	65.0	46.5	43.0	46.2
Average Number in Consumer Unit						
Persons	1.0	1.0	2.4	3.0	3.0	4.4
Children under 18	X	X	0.4	1.1	0.9	1.0
Persons 65 and over	0.7	0.1	1.2	0.3	0.1	0.1
Earners	X	1.0	X	1.0	2.0	3.4
Vehicles	0.8	1.1	1.7	1.9	2.5	3.2
Percent Distribution						
Males	31.0	54.0	54.0	45.0	56.0	54.0
Females	69.0	46.0	46.0	55.0	44.0	46.0
Percent Homeowner	59.0	44.0	77.0	67.0	76.0	81.0
With mortgage	9.0	27.0	19.0	41.0	59.0	62.0
Without mortgage	50.0	16.0	58.0	26.0	18.0	18.0
AVERAGE ANNUAL EXPENDITURES	17 431	27 277	29 730	41 737	53 621	59 832
Food	2 330	3 120	4 483	5 652	6 824	8 300
Food at home	1 567	1 501	3 047	3 590	3 830	4 835
Cereals and bakery products	244	202	443	515	530	684
Meats, poultry, fish, and eggs	369	353	819	957	1 028	1 302
Dairy products	163	160	323	385	396	501
Fruits and vegetables	310	263	546	621	631	811
Other food at home	481	522	915	1 113	1 245	1 536
Food away from home	763	1 620	1 436	2 063	2 995	3 466
Alcoholic Beverages	123	370	211	347	534	518
Housing	7 140	9 714	10 116	14 285	16 866	17 632
Shelter	4 097	6 496	5 173	8 302	9 787	10 206
Owned dwellings	1 955	3 121	3 287	5 572	7 261	7 725
Rented dwellings	1 984	3 084	1 419	2 306	1 952	1 799
Other lodging	157	292	468	423	574	681
Utilities, fuels, and public services	1 720	1 781	2 712	3 077	3 310	4 023
Household operations	493	256	567	747	1 038	713
Housekeeping supplies	293	279	506	566	673	738
Household furnishings and equipment	538	902	1 157	1 594	2 056	1 953
Apparel and Services	590	980	965	1 878	2 159	2 507
Transportation	2 229	4 776	5 108	7 569	10 882	12 747
Vehicle purchases (net outlay)	912	2 145	2 227	3 569	5 541	5 728
Gasoline and motor oil	398	835	933	1 353	1 768	2 317
Other vehicle expenses	746	1 491	1 600	2 287	3 087	4 163
Public transportation	172	305	348	360	487	539
Health Care	2 192	1 189	3 790	2 573	2 626	2 796
Health insurance	1 158	558	2 091	1 301	1 359	1 500
Medical services	384	346	673	630	720	711
Drugs	580	226	862	530	427	446
Medical supplies	70	58	164	113	120	140
Entertainment	741	1 216	1 719	2 113	2 887	2 581
Personal Care Products and Services	265	345	429	533	664	813
Reading	85	98	139	123	150	155
Education	213	664	289	673	947	1 957
Tobacco Products and Smoking Supplies	156	215	196	321	340	456
Miscellaneous	308	490	533	608	721	872
Cash Contributions	872	1 124	1 330	1 506	1 508	1 728
Personal Insurance and Pensions	186	2 974	422	3 556	6 512	6 770
Life and other personal insurance	165	155	368	461	519	633
Pensions and Social Security	[2]21	2 819	53	3 094	5 993	6 138

[1]Components of income and taxes are derived from "complete income reporters" only.
[2]Data are likely to have large sampling errors.
X = Not applicable.

Table 8-10. Consumer Expenditures, Averages by Occupation of Reference Person, 2003

(Number, dollar, percent.)

Item	Self-employed workers	Wage and salary earners						Retired	All others, including not reporting
		Total wage and salary earners	Managers and professionals	Technical sales and clerical workers	Service workers	Construction workers and mechanics	Operators, fabricators, and laborers		
NUMBER OF CONSUMER UNITS (THOUSANDS)	4 987	76 802	28 105	21 533	11 621	4 780	10 764	19 592	13 976
CONSUMER UNIT CHARACTERISTICS									
Average Income Before Taxes[1]	58 302	58 773	83 126	50 321	35 496	50 805	41 020	27 695	37 616
Average Income After Taxes[1]	55 982	55 691	77 733	48 018	34 529	48 388	39 811	26 157	36 823
Age of Reference Person	52.0	42.2	43.5	41.2	41.8	39.5	42.0	73.8	45.6
Average Number in Consumer Unit									
Persons	2.4	2.6	2.6	2.5	2.7	2.9	2.8	1.7	2.8
Children under 18	0.5	0.7	0.7	0.7	0.8	0.9	0.9	0.1	0.9
Persons 65 and over	0.4	0.1	0.1	0.1	0.1	0.1	0.1	1.2	0.2
Earners	1.6	1.7	1.7	1.7	1.7	1.8	1.7	0.2	0.7
Vehicles	2.3	2.1	2.2	2.0	1.7	2.4	2.1	1.6	1.6
Percent Distribution									
Male	64	54	53	44	45	93	72	45	29
Female	36	46	47	56	55	7	28	55	71
Percent Homeowner	81	65	75	62	49	65	59	81	56
With mortgage	44	48	59	46	34	51	39	19	30
Without mortgage	37	16	16	16	15	14	19	62	26
AVERAGE ANNUAL EXPENDITURES	51 006	44 934	58 236	40 564	32 066	40 620	34 603	28 418	32 042
Food	6 563	5 743	6 743	5 317	4 531	5 924	5 125	3 937	4 698
Food at home	3 617	3 229	3 521	2 972	2 764	3 590	3 267	2 594	3 162
Cereals and bakery products	493	451	487	418	383	490	471	389	447
Meats, poultry, fish, and eggs	1 049	840	852	771	768	1 050	914	662	885
Dairy products	344	339	379	312	275	367	335	278	338
Fruits and vegetables	636	542	618	490	462	551	522	490	522
Other food at home	1 095	1 058	1 185	981	875	1 132	1 025	775	971
Food away from home	2 946	2 514	3 222	2 345	1 766	2 333	1 857	1 343	1 535
Alcoholic Beverages	557	455	597	415	358	373	300	208	248
Housing	14 996	14 652	18 940	13 567	10 888	12 520	10 614	9 813	11 251
Shelter	8 650	8 788	11 375	8 193	6 658	7 346	6 162	5 204	6 430
Owned dwellings	6 422	5 897	8 331	5 290	3 493	5 002	3 747	3 538	3 783
Rented dwellings	1 457	2 427	2 257	2 535	2 935	2 116	2 244	1 281	2 337
Other lodging	772	464	787	367	231	228	171	385	309
Utilities, fuels, and public services	3 122	2 911	3 313	2 773	2 494	2 813	2 630	2 493	2 600
Household operations	869	757	1 161	648	394	628	368	623	494
Housekeeping supplies	593	546	713	494	426	456	375	489	471
Household furnishings and equipment	1 761	1 651	2 378	1 459	916	1 277	1 079	1 005	1 256
Apparel And Services	1 691	1 854	2 343	1 778	1 348	1 414	1 454	911	1 509
Transportation	9 325	8 758	10 469	7 907	6 626	9 576	7 931	4 805	6 028
Vehicle purchases (net outlay)	4 512	4 215	4 927	3 689	3 169	5 170	4 113	2 157	3 006
Gasoline and motor oil	1 510	1 495	1 622	1 423	1 271	1 715	1 452	825	1 089
Other vehicle expenses	2 643	2 637	3 254	2 465	1 936	2 521	2 173	1 511	1 687
Public transportation	659	411	666	329	249	170	192	312	246
Health Care	3 794	2 098	2 708	1 972	1 554	1 697	1 521	3 623	1 981
Health insurance	1 849	1 082	1 360	1 027	841	908	805	1 996	926
Medical services	1 051	557	782	490	350	442	380	655	522
Drugs	759	357	434	361	296	253	261	836	444
Medical supplies	135	101	132	93	67	95	75	137	89
Entertainment	2 866	2 231	3 096	1 993	1 371	1 801	1 564	1 560	1 515
Personal Care Products and Services	580	571	724	541	446	459	415	420	423
Reading	174	128	197	108	72	77	72	143	83
Education	813	963	1 554	759	622	513	395	164	654
Tobacco Products and Smoking Supplies	297	309	210	292	338	596	440	168	353
Miscellaneous	1 124	641	815	589	397	543	593	513	359
Cash Contributions	2 661	1 380	2 221	1 004	716	1 036	803	1 355	875
Personal Insurance and Pensions	5 565	5 151	7 617	4 323	2 798	4 090	3 376	797	2 065
Life and other personal insurance	593	421	609	357	245	322	290	335	285
Pensions and Social Security	4 972	4 730	7 008	3 966	2 553	3 767	3 086	462	1 780

[1]Components of income and taxes are derived from "complete income reporters" only.

Table 8-11. Consumer Expenditures, Averages by Housing Tenure and Type of Area, 2003

(Number, dollar, percent.)

Item	Housing tenure				Type of area			
	Homeowner			Renter	Urban			Rural
	Total	Homeowner with mortgage	Homeowner without mortgage		Total	Central city	Other urban	
NUMBER OF CONSUMER UNITS (THOUSANDS)	77 194	47 104	30 090	38 163	101 047	34 423	66 625	14 309
CONSUMER UNIT CHARACTERISTICS								
Average Income Before Taxes[1]	62 053	72 831	44 609	29 827	52 728	43 768	57 352	40 140
Average Income After Taxes[1]	58 739	69 112	41 951	28 822	50 075	41 234	54 638	38 439
Age of Reference Person	52	46	62	41	48	47	49	51
Average Number In Consumer Unit								
Persons	2.6	3.0	2.1	2.2	2.5	2.4	2.6	2.4
Children under 18	0.7	0.9	0.3	0.6	0.6	0.6	0.7	0.6
Persons 65 and over	0.4	0.2	0.7	0.1	0.3	0.3	0.3	0.4
Earners	1.4	1.7	1.0	1.2	1.3	1.2	1.4	1.3
Vehicles	2.3	2.5	2.0	1.1	1.9	1.5	2.1	2.5
Percent Distribution								
Males	52	54	50	46	50	47	52	50
Females	48	46	50	54	50	53	48	50
Percent Homeowner	100	100	100	X	65	52	72	80
With mortgage	61	100	X	X	41	32	46	39
Without mortgage	39	X	100	X	24	21	26	41
AVERAGE ANNUAL EXPENDITURES	47 396	55 419	34 467	27 522	41 619	36 444	44 297	35 157
Food	5 917	6 473	4 851	4 177	5 413	4 962	5 648	4 821
Food at home	3 447	3 667	3 015	2 489	3 142	2 892	3 272	3 035
Cereals and bakery products	491	515	442	344	446	403	468	414
Meats, poultry, fish, and eggs	894	956	772	685	819	768	845	863
Dairy products	365	388	318	254	329	298	345	322
Fruits and vegetables	588	611	543	430	547	512	566	452
Other food at home	1 110	1 196	940	777	1 001	909	1 049	985
Food away from home	2 470	2 806	1 837	1 688	2 271	2 070	2 375	1 786
Alcoholic Beverages	418	487	284	337	405	378	420	292
Housing	15 186	18 960	9 221	9 886	13 971	12 501	14 732	9 623
Shelter	8 471	11 488	3 749	6 706	8 325	7 637	8 681	4 797
Owned dwellings	7 832	10 792	3 197	67	5 491	4 098	6 210	3 653
Rented dwellings	64	55	78	6 459	2 369	3 175	1 953	840
Other lodging	576	640	474	181	465	363	518	303
Utilities, fuels, and public services	3 321	3 616	2 860	1 780	2 834	2 524	2 994	2 652
Household operations	882	1 015	673	354	748	652	798	416
Housekeeping supplies	631	673	549	323	528	452	567	538
Household furnishings and equipment	1 880	2 168	1 390	723	1 536	1 235	1 692	1 220
Apparel and Services	1 809	2 116	1 253	1 300	1 700	1 597	1 754	1 215
Transportation	9 199	10 788	6 708	4 912	7 659	6 609	8 202	8 639
Vehicle purchases (net outlay)	4 505	5 300	3 261	2 167	3 578	3 145	3 802	4 814
Gasoline and motor oil	1 529	1 753	1 179	936	1 297	1 055	1 422	1 587
Other vehicle expenses	2 727	3 250	1 906	1 529	2 367	1 990	2 562	2 078
Public transportation	437	485	362	279	417	419	416	160
Health Care	3 009	2 773	3 386	1 218	2 390	2 045	2 568	2 600
Health insurance	1 564	1 439	1 760	619	1 236	993	1 361	1 365
Medical services	739	747	727	292	594	530	627	569
Drugs	575	458	765	248	454	421	471	560
Medical supplies	131	129	135	58	107	102	110	107
Entertainment	2 525	2 921	1 901	1 119	2 076	1 629	2 307	1 942
Personal Care Products and Services	599	658	492	382	544	500	567	408
Reading	155	158	149	72	133	119	141	86
Education	843	1 071	480	662	845	718	911	348
Tobacco Products and Smoking Supplies	283	310	242	302	278	261	287	372
Miscellaneous	720	780	626	376	615	509	670	541
Cash Contributions	1 742	1 650	1 887	616	1 428	1 207	1 543	956
Personal Insurance and Pensions	4 992	6 273	2 986	2 161	4 161	3 410	4 548	3 312
Life and other personal insurance	527	626	373	134	400	308	448	375
Pensions and Social Security	4 464	5 647	2 612	2 027	3 760	3 102	4 100	2 937

[1]Components of income and taxes are derived from "complete income reporters" only.
X = Not applicable.

Table 8-12. Consumer Expenditures, Averages by Region of Residence, 2003

(Number, dollar, percent.)

Item	Northeast	Midwest	South	West
NUMBER OF CONSUMER UNITS (THOUSANDS)	22 182	26 438	41 325	25 412
CONSUMER UNIT CHARACTERISTICS				
Average Income Before Taxes[1]	56 513	52 445	46 729	52 506
Average Income After Taxes[1]	54 219	49 591	44 461	49 667
Age of Reference Person	49.8	48.8	48.2	47.1
Average Number in Consumer Unit				
Persons	2.4	2.5	2.5	2.6
Children under 18	0.6	0.6	0.6	0.7
Persons 65 and over	0.3	0.3	0.3	0.3
Earners	1.3	1.4	1.3	1.4
Vehicles	1.7	2.1	1.9	2.0
Percent Distribution				
Males	52.0	51.0	49.0	51.0
Females	48.0	49.0	51.0	49.0
Percent Homeowner	64.0	70.0	69.0	63.0
With mortgage	37.0	42.0	40.0	43.0
Without mortgage	27.0	28.0	28.0	20.0
AVERAGE ANNUAL EXPENDITURES	42 162	40 280	37 625	45 381
Food	5 730	5 088	4 960	5 876
Food at home	3 306	2 904	2 996	3 428
Cereals and bakery products	485	411	413	482
Meats, poultry, fish, and eggs	889	734	835	849
Dairy products	353	323	298	359
Fruits and vegetables	586	472	489	633
Other food at home	994	962	961	1 104
Food away from home	2 424	2 184	1 964	2 449
Alcoholic Beverages	427	403	345	421
Housing	14 811	12 634	12 006	15 371
Shelter	9 134	7 086	6 660	9 630
Owned dwellings	5 932	4 908	4 528	6 244
Rented dwellings	2 664	1 720	1 802	2 848
Other lodging	537	458	330	538
Utilities, fuels, and public services	2 889	2 855	2 891	2 569
Household operations	813	614	666	778
Housekeeping supplies	523	575	496	537
Household furnishings and equipment	1 452	1 504	1 294	1 858
Apparel and Services	1 859	1 563	1 451	1 834
Transportation	7 043	7 817	7 621	8 645
Vehicle purchases (net outlay)	3 040	3 775	3 893	4 028
Gasoline and motor oil	1 157	1 357	1 321	1 479
Other vehicle expenses	2 307	2 314	2 154	2 659
Public transportation	539	371	253	479
Health Care	2 127	2 586	2 396	2 525
Health insurance	1 237	1 332	1 223	1 227
Medical services	448	621	563	729
Drugs	358	513	520	426
Medical supplies	84	119	90	143
Entertainment	2 117	1 978	1 812	2 494
Personal Care Products and Services	532	499	494	606
Reading	153	141	93	146
Education	1 040	796	581	875
Tobacco Products and Smoking Supplies	306	363	275	224
Miscellaneous	548	647	556	695
Cash Contributions	1 161	1 469	1 344	1 491
Personal Insurance and Pensions	4 308	4 295	3 690	4 179
Life and other personal insurance	454	423	381	347
Pensions and Social Security	3 855	3 872	3 309	3 832

[1]Components of income and taxes are derived from "complete income reporters" only.

Table 8-13. Consumer Expenditures, Averages by Population Size of Area of Residence, 2003

(Number, dollar, percent.)

Item	Outside urbanized area	All urbanized area consumer units	Urbanized area consumer units					
			Less than 100,000	100,000 to 249,000	250,000 to 999,999	1,000,000 to 2,499,000	2,500,000 to 4,999,999	5,000,000 and over
NUMBER OF CONSUMER UNITS (THOUSANDS)	44 208	71 149	9 148	12 114	10 528	16 547	10 340	12 472
CONSUMER UNIT CHARACTERISTICS								
Average Income Before Taxes[1]	46 893	53 785	40 234	44 131	52 325	55 281	64 595	63 343
Average Income After Taxes[1]	44 358	51 255	39 258	41 812	49 242	52 484	60 885	61 280
Age of Reference Person	49.5	47.7	47.7	45.7	48.4	48.4	46.5	48.9
Average Number in Consumer Unit								
Persons	2.5	2.5	2.3	2.4	2.4	2.5	2.6	2.7
Children under 18	0.6	0.7	0.6	0.7	0.6	0.6	0.7	0.7
Persons 65 and over	0.3	0.3	0.3	0.3	0.3	0.3	0.2	0.3
Earners	1.3	1.3	1.2	1.3	1.3	1.3	1.4	1.4
Vehicles	2.3	1.7	1.8	1.7	1.8	1.8	1.7	1.5
Percent Distribution								
Males	51	49	47	49	49	49	52	51
Females	49	51	53	51	51	51	48	49
Percent Homeowner	76	61	61	60	63	65	63	56
With mortgage	42	40	34	38	41	46	41	37
Without mortgage	34	21	26	22	22	19	22	19
AVERAGE ANNUAL EXPENDITURES	38 340	42 342	33 376	38 866	39 103	44 006	46 751	49 118
Food	4 961	5 565	4 600	5 059	5 030	5 731	5 769	6 807
Food at home	2 980	3 218	2 898	3 049	2 891	3 379	3 149	3 747
Cereals and bakery products	421	454	416	447	423	460	420	538
Meats, poultry, fish, and eggs	785	848	780	733	756	899	855	1 018
Dairy products	319	334	298	328	299	357	307	387
Fruits and vegetables	470	574	468	522	478	616	568	737
Other food at home	985	1 008	936	1 019	935	1 047	999	1 067
Food away from home	1 981	2 348	1 701	2 010	2 139	2 352	2 620	3 061
Alcoholic Beverages	345	419	281	378	339	458	503	498
Housing	11 606	14 566	10 467	12 517	12 856	15 180	16 460	18 625
Shelter	6 299	8 874	5 698	7 265	7 490	9 146	10 552	12 185
Owned dwellings	4 735	5 591	3 586	4 574	4 674	5 918	6 723	7 450
Rented dwellings	1 151	2 819	1 771	2 354	2 381	2 717	3 319	4 129
Other lodging	413	465	341	336	435	512	511	605
Utilities, fuels, and public services	2 782	2 830	2 583	2 537	2 890	2 938	3 029	2 936
Household operations	543	809	558	723	712	828	895	1 063
Housekeeping supplies	541	522	466	529	445	542	530	588
Household furnishings and equipment	1 442	1 531	1 161	1 462	1 320	1 726	1 454	1 853
Apparel and Services	1 351	1 815	1 217	1 675	1 501	1 742	2 153	2 444
Transportation	8 180	7 532	6 615	7 571	7 101	7 970	8 179	7 412
Vehicle purchases (net outlay)	4 192	3 446	3 216	3 940	3 259	3 637	3 837	2 715
Gasoline and motor oil	1 497	1 231	1 147	1 161	1 268	1 268	1 291	1 230
Other vehicle expenses	2 240	2 387	1 970	2 135	2 202	2 635	2 510	2 664
Public transportation	252	467	282	335	372	429	541	804
Health Care	2 583	2 313	2 216	2 429	2 278	2 427	2 253	2 199
Health insurance	1 384	1 170	1 079	1 125	1 121	1 256	1 213	1 169
Medical services	587	594	549	688	611	585	540	577
Drugs	511	439	483	466	454	477	394	357
Medical supplies	102	111	105	151	93	109	106	95
Entertainment	2 146	2 009	1 786	1 957	2 020	2 112	1 879	2 188
Personal Care Products and Services	461	567	477	492	527	581	593	702
Reading	116	134	123	135	135	132	134	145
Education	646	869	609	852	681	786	959	1 269
Tobacco Products and Smoking Supplies	330	265	292	240	331	264	247	227
Miscellaneous	607	605	442	582	719	614	649	601
Cash Contributions	1 274	1 429	1 120	1 443	1 411	1 544	1 632	1 339
Personal Insurance and Pensions	3 735	4 254	3 131	3 536	4 172	4 467	5 343	4 661
Life and other personal insurance	403	394	313	330	424	438	381	440
Pensions and Social Security	3 332	3 861	2 818	3 206	3 748	4 029	4 961	4 221

[1]Components of income and taxes are derived from "complete income reporters" only.

Table 8-14. Consumer Expenditures, Averages by Race of Reference Person, 2003

(Number, dollar, percent.)

Item	White, Asian, and Other races			Black
	Total	White and Other races	Asian	
NUMBER OF CONSUMER UNITS (THOUSANDS)	101 614	98 041	3 573	13 743
CONSUMER UNIT CHARACTERISTICS				
Average Income Before Taxes[1]	53 292	53 039	60 393	34 485
Average Income After Taxes[1]	50 557	50 309	57 511	33 519
Age of Reference Person	48.6	48.8	42.4	46.7
Average Number in Consumer Unit				
Persons	2.5	2.5	2.8	2.6
Children under 18	0.6	0.6	0.7	0.9
Persons 65 and over	0.3	0.3	0.2	0.2
Earners	1.3	1.3	1.5	1.2
Vehicles	2.0	2.1	1.6	1.3
Percent Distribution				
Males	52.0	52.0	62.0	36.0
Females	48.0	48.0	38.0	64.0
Percent Homeowner	69.0	70.0	57.0	49.0
With mortgage	42.0	42.0	42.0	30.0
Without mortgage	27.0	28.0	15.0	19.0
AVERAGE ANNUAL EXPENDITURES	42 451	42 360	44 923	28 708
Food	5 518	5 488	6 285	4 007
Food at home	3 191	3 186	3 302	2 664
Cereals and bakery products	451	452	437	370
Meats, poultry, fish, and eggs	817	811	978	882
Dairy products	342	345	247	227
Fruits and vegetables	548	539	788	438
Other food at home	1 033	1 040	852	747
Food away from home	2 327	2 302	2 983	1 343
Alcoholic Beverages	421	425	308	169
Housing	13 811	13 719	16 326	10 622
Shelter	8 127	8 026	10 902	6 117
Owned dwellings	5 563	5 517	6 835	3 042
Rented dwellings	2 076	2 018	3 661	2 946
Other lodging	488	491	406	129
Utilities, fuels, and public services	2 798	2 808	2 536	2 910
Household operations	742	740	783	453
Housekeeping supplies	552	555	471	357
Household furnishings and equipment	1 593	1 591	1 634	785
Apparel and Services	1 645	1 642	1 736	1 601
Transportation	8 147	8 172	7 454	5 074
Vehicle purchases (net outlay)	3 953	3 988	2 992	2 097
Gasoline and motor oil	1 376	1 378	1 313	1 016
Other vehicle expenses	2 412	2 414	2 383	1 728
Public transportation	406	393	766	233
Health Care	2 566	2 588	1 955	1 309
Health insurance	1 316	1 325	1 071	774
Medical services	640	646	476	229
Drugs	494	500	340	263
Medical supplies	116	117	69	43
Entertainment	2 202	2 220	1 713	1 007
Personal Care Products and Services	536	536	520	461
Reading	137	138	111	52
Education	829	791	1 890	442
Tobacco Products and Smoking Supplies	305	311	119	180
Miscellaneous	627	635	432	447
Cash Contributions	1 443	1 447	1 311	832
Personal Insurance and Pensions	4 265	4 247	4 762	2 504
Life and other personal insurance	411	411	414	295
Pensions and Social Security	3 854	3 836	4 348	2 209

[1]Components of income and taxes are derived from "complete income reporters" only.

Table 8-15. Consumer Expenditures, Averages by Hispanic or Latino Origin of Reference Person, 2003

(Number, dollar, percent.)

Item	Hispanic or Latino	Not Hispanic or Latino		
		Total	White, Asian, and Other races	Black
NUMBER OF CONSUMER UNITS (THOUSANDS)	11 727	103 629	90 019	13 610
CONSUMER UNIT CHARACTERISTICS				
Average Income Before Taxes[1]	37 150	52 797	55 463	34 537
Average Income After Taxes[1]	36 469	50 044	52 450	33 564
Age of Reference Person	41.6	49.2	49.5	46.7
Average Number in Consumer Unit				
Persons	3.3	2.4	2.4	2.6
Children under 18	1.1	0.6	0.5	0.9
Persons 65 and over	0.2	0.3	0.3	0.2
Earners	1.6	1.3	1.3	1.2
Vehicles	1.6	2.0	2.1	1.3
Percent Distribution				
Males	52.0	50.0	52.0	36.0
Females	48.0	50.0	48.0	64.0
Percent Homeowner	48.0	69.0	72.0	49.0
With mortgage	34.0	42.0	43.0	30.0
Without mortgage	14.0	27.0	29.0	19.0
AVERAGE ANNUAL EXPENDITURES	34 575	41 521	43 459	28 667
Food	5 717	5 291	5 486	3 977
Food at home	3 597	3 070	3 134	2 639
Cereals and bakery products	486	436	447	366
Meats, poultry, fish, and eggs	1 059	795	783	876
Dairy products	374	322	337	223
Fruits and vegetables	686	516	529	432
Other food at home	992	1 000	1 038	742
Food away from home	2 120	2 221	2 353	1 338
Alcoholic Beverages	315	401	437	158
Housing	12 300	13 562	14 005	10 621
Shelter	7 672	7 912	8 185	6 105
Owned dwellings	3 889	5 418	5 775	3 063
Rented dwellings	3 560	2 023	1 889	2 912
Other lodging	224	470	521	130
Utilities, fuels, and public services	2 490	2 848	2 837	2 920
Household operations	454	736	779	453
Housekeeping supplies	476	536	563	353
Household furnishings and equipment	1 208	1 531	1 642	789
Apparel and Services	1 756	1 626	1 631	1 590
Transportation	6 780	7 894	8 317	5 094
Vehicle purchases (net outlay)	3 063	3 807	4 063	2 117
Gasoline and motor oil	1 328	1 333	1 381	1 017
Other vehicle expenses	2 057	2 362	2 458	1 729
Public transportation	331	391	416	230
Health Care	1 439	2 527	2 711	1 311
Health insurance	747	1 309	1 389	775
Medical services	365	616	675	229
Drugs	263	490	524	264
Medical supplies	65	112	122	43
Entertainment	1 245	2 153	2 326	1 009
Personal Care Products and Services	490	531	541	460
Reading	48	136	149	53
Education	477	818	877	425
Tobacco Products and Smoking Supplies	171	303	322	179
Miscellaneous	419	627	655	447
Cash Contributions	594	1 458	1 552	835
Personal Insurance and Pensions	2 824	4 195	4 450	2 507
Life and other personal insurance	160	424	444	296
Pensions and Social Security	2 664	3 770	4 006	2 211

[1]Components of income and taxes are derived from "complete income reporters" only.

Table 8-16. Consumer Expenditures, Averages by Education of Reference Person, 2002–2003

(Number, dollar, percent.)

Item	Less than college graduate					College graduate		
	Total	Less than high school graduate	High school graduate	High school graduate with some college	Associate degree	Total	Bachelor's degree	Master's, professional, doctorate degree
NUMBER OF CONSUMER UNITS (THOUSANDS)	84 768	17 721	31 552	24 514	10 981	30 589	19 557	11 032
CONSUMER UNIT CHARACTERISTICS								
Average Income Before Taxes[1]	40 164	25 028	40 113	45 113	54 087	81 842	74 921	93 948
Average Income After Taxes[1]	38 558	24 716	38 258	43 304	51 525	76 716	70 375	87 806
Age of Reference Person	49.0	55.6	50.2	44.4	45.4	46.6	44.7	49.9
Average Number in Consumer Unit								
Persons	2.5	2.6	2.5	2.3	2.6	2.5	2.5	2.4
Children under 18	0.7	0.7	0.6	0.6	0.7	0.6	0.6	0.6
Persons 65 and over	0.3	0.5	0.3	0.2	0.2	0.2	0.2	0.3
Earners	1.3	1.0	1.3	1.3	1.5	1.5	1.5	1.5
Vehicles	1.9	1.4	2.0	1.9	2.2	2.1	2.1	2.2
Percent Distribution								
Males	48	45	49	48	47	57	56	60
Females	52	55	51	52	53	43	44	40
Percent Homeowner	64	57	68	59	72	76	73	82
With mortgage	36	22	37	37	50	55	53	58
Without mortgage	28	35	31	22	22	21	20	24
AVERAGE ANNUAL EXPENDITURES	34 372	23 901	33 956	37 912	44 547	58 480	54 726	65 203
Food	4 838	4 086	4 701	5 136	5 783	6 641	6 381	7 127
Food at home	2 987	2 913	2 986	2 907	3 298	3 491	3 414	3 637
Cereals and bakery products	425	408	424	423	456	485	482	493
Meats, poultry, fish, and eggs	832	860	839	758	941	805	794	825
Dairy products	307	290	307	302	344	382	374	397
Fruits and vegetables	488	502	479	479	519	655	621	720
Other food at home	935	853	937	945	1 037	1 164	1 143	1 202
Food away from home	1 850	1 173	1 715	2 229	2 486	3 150	2 967	3 490
Alcoholic Beverages	302	161	255	401	453	620	565	725
Housing	11 181	8 351	10 923	12 260	14 060	19 631	18 357	21 908
Shelter	6 417	4 865	6 178	7 121	8 032	11 963	11 233	13 258
Owned dwellings	4 001	2 427	4 040	4 365	5 618	8 760	7 995	10 117
Rented dwellings	2 158	2 346	1 917	2 373	2 071	2 238	2 406	1 939
Other lodging	257	92	222	383	344	966	832	1 203
Utilities, fuels, and public services	2 647	2 311	2 740	2 610	3 000	3 268	3 159	3 461
Household operations	498	237	447	652	718	1 288	1 177	1 484
Housekeeping supplies	468	323	477	481	639	683	639	768
Household furnishings and equipment	1 152	615	1 080	1 396	1 670	2 429	2 149	2 937
Apparel and Services	1 406	1 017	1 260	1 713	1 779	2 260	2 197	2 377
Transportation	6 954	4 412	7 296	7 265	9 380	10 068	9 717	10 694
Vehicle purchases (net outlay)	3 396	2 059	3 659	3 382	4 833	4 661	4 577	4 810
Gasoline and motor oil	1 266	942	1 306	1 331	1 530	1 517	1 502	1 545
Other vehicle expenses	2 053	1 263	2 131	2 243	2 683	3 097	2 967	3 330
Public transportation	238	148	200	308	334	793	671	1 009
Health Care	2 193	1 797	2 287	2 249	2 439	3 031	2 812	3 420
Health insurance	1 160	976	1 246	1 129	1 280	1 506	1 425	1 650
Medical services	490	317	499	568	572	869	782	1 024
Drugs	450	445	447	444	482	510	474	575
Medical supplies	93	59	95	108	105	145	131	171
Entertainment	1 678	882	1 607	2 023	2 384	3 110	2 893	3 498
Personal Care Products and Services	453	305	436	518	592	725	694	781
Reading	90	42	83	118	125	230	194	294
Education	492	102	328	859	776	1 587	1 339	2 029
Tobacco Products and Smoking Supplies	342	342	380	305	318	144	158	119
Miscellaneous	521	312	515	633	619	840	791	928
Cash Contributions	952	574	990	1 043	1 248	2 529	2 307	2 922
Personal Insurance and Pensions	2 970	1 519	2 895	3 388	4 590	7 064	6 321	8 381
Life and other personal insurance	304	180	334	303	417	657	587	781
Pensions and Social Security	2 666	1 339	2 561	3 085	4 174	6 407	5 734	7 600

[1]Components of income and taxes are derived from "complete income reporters" only.

Table 8-17. Consumer Expenditures, Averages for Age Groups by Income Before Taxes, 2002–2003: Reference Person Under Age 25

(Number, dollar, percent.)

Item	Complete reporting of income, total	Complete reporting of income						
		Less than $5,000	$5,000 to $9,999	$10,000 to $14,999	$15,000 to $19,999	$20,000 to $29,999	$30,000 to $39,999	$40,000 and over
NUMBER OF CONSUMER UNITS (THOUSANDS)	7 239	1 555	1 333	911	702	1 010	674	1 052
CONSUMER UNIT CHARACTERISTICS								
Average Income Before Taxes [1]	20 726	2 518	7 227	12 108	17 266	24 224	33 837	62 756
Average Income After Taxes [1]	20 233	2 524	7 211	12 303	17 257	23 797	32 821	60 273
Age of Reference Person	21.3	20.2	20.8	21.5	21.7	21.8	22.3	22.4
Average Number in Consumer Unit								
Persons	1.9	1.2	1.4	1.7	2.1	2.3	2.4	2.6
Children under 18	0.4	0.1	0.2	0.4	0.5	0.6	0.5	0.5
Persons 65 and over	(2)	(2)	(2)	(2)	(2)	(2)	(2)	(2)
Earners	1.3	1.0	1.0	1.2	1.3	1.4	1.6	2.0
Vehicles	1.2	0.5	0.7	1.0	1.3	1.5	1.6	2.1
Percent Distribution								
Male	48.0	48.0	47.0	46.0	45.0	47.0	49.0	53.0
Female	52.0	52.0	53.0	54.0	55.0	53.0	51.0	47.0
Percent Homeowner	14.0	5.0	8.0	7.0	15.0	16.0	23.0	36.0
With mortgage	8.0	1.0	2.0	2.0	8.0	9.0	15.0	29.0
Without mortgage	6.0	4.0	5.0	6.0	7.0	7.0	8.0	7.0
AVERAGE ANNUAL EXPENDITURES	24 327	12 343	15 866	19 625	24 311	26 990	32 605	47 049
Food	3 581	2 262	2 619	2 586	3 477	3 819	4 216	6 104
Food at home	1 825	940	1 220	1 478	1 974	2 132	2 031	3 126
Cereals and bakery products	266	142	186	200	288	316	274	463
Meats, poultry, fish, and eggs	419	180	240	318	445	478	512	796
Dairy products	197	95	148	151	213	223	224	338
Fruits and vegetables	304	157	185	227	290	355	366	559
Other food at home	639	366	461	583	738	760	655	970
Food away from home	1 756	1 321	1 399	1 108	1 502	1 687	2 185	2 979
Alcoholic Beverages	481	233	242	381	453	480	600	1 006
Housing	7 445	3 670	4 976	6 146	8 083	8 621	10 150	13 714
Shelter	4 787	2 591	3 465	4 004	5 278	5 387	6 487	8 395
Owned dwellings	789	150	248	201	612	636	1 329	2 845
Rented dwellings	3 680	1 994	2 789	3 473	4 408	4 598	5 042	5 242
Other lodging	318	447	429	330	258	153	116	308
Utilities, fuels, and public services	1 370	537	875	1 235	1 491	1 687	2 057	2 517
Household operations	220	54	81	198	202	329	325	497
Housekeeping supplies	238	105	134	180	361	266	238	429
Household furnishings and equipment	830	382	422	529	751	951	1 043	1 875
Apparel and Services	1 310	554	792	1 349	1 217	1 118	1 773	2 656
Transportation	5 161	1 695	2 668	3 975	5 597	6 619	7 775	11 084
Vehicle purchases (net outlay)	2 608	556	1 172	2 016	3 219	3 518	4 150	5 702
Gasoline and motor oil	958	493	662	857	985	1 170	1 285	1 678
Other vehicle expenses	1 381	475	625	978	1 235	1 776	2 057	3 292
Public transportation	214	171	209	123	158	156	282	412
Health Care	619	173	204	438	571	895	800	1 586
Health insurance	289	70	49	224	264	410	443	772
Medical services	170	37	60	103	93	251	214	507
Drugs	125	51	65	85	174	192	117	230
Medical supplies	35	[3]14	31	25	[3]40	42	26	77
Entertainment	1 150	600	929	884	1 039	1 264	1 541	2 114
Personal Care Products and Services	337	174	239	457	262	329	367	585
Reading	57	43	48	54	44	66	65	89
Education	1 637	2 428	2 122	1 969	1 524	923	957	765
Tobacco Products and Smoking Supplies	270	122	189	247	359	352	423	373
Miscellaneous	345	123	253	163	302	375	684	691
Cash Contributions	333	108	167	210	206	348	530	928
Personal Insurance and Pensions	1 602	158	418	767	1 177	1 781	2 722	5 352
Life and other personal insurance	48	[3]5	[3]19	[3]34	35	62	75	141
Pensions and Social Security	1 554	154	399	733	1 142	1 719	2 647	5 211

[1]Components of income and taxes are derived from "complete income reporters" only.
[2]Value less than 0.05.
[3]Data are likely to have large sampling errors.

Table 8-18. Consumer Expenditures, Averages for Age Groups by Income Before Taxes, 2002–2003: Reference Person Age 25–34

(Number, dollar, percent.)

Item	Complete reporting of income, total	Complete reporting of income								
		Less than $5,000	$5,000 to $9,999	$10,000 to $14,999	$15,000 to $19,999	$20,000 to $29,999	$30,000 to $39,999	$40,000 to $49,999	$50,000 to $69,999	$70,000 and over
NUMBER OF CONSUMER UNITS (THOUSANDS)	16 373	475	742	984	1 138	2 419	2 156	1 836	2 870	3 751
CONSUMER UNIT CHARACTERISTICS										
Average Income Before Taxes[1]	49 779	1 547	7 671	12 430	17 293	24 784	34 270	44 165	58 653	104 878
Average Income After Taxes[1]	47 665	1 826	8 020	12 771	17 642	24 596	33 202	42 547	56 235	98 723
Age of Reference Person	29.7	29.3	28.9	29.1	29.1	29.4	29.5	29.8	29.9	30.5
Average Number in Consumer Unit										
Persons	2.9	2.3	2.7	2.7	2.8	2.7	2.7	2.9	3.0	3.0
Children under 18	1.1	1.0	1.3	1.3	1.3	1.2	1.1	1.0	1.1	0.9
Persons 65 and over	(2)	(2)	(2)	(2)	(2)	(2)	(2)	(2)	(2)	(2)
Earners	1.5	0.9	0.9	1.0	1.3	1.3	1.4	1.6	1.8	1.9
Vehicles	1.8	1.0	1.0	1.0	1.3	1.4	1.7	1.9	2.3	2.3
Percent Distribution										
Male	52.0	39.0	31.0	37.0	43.0	48.0	50.0	61.0	59.0	61.0
Female	48.0	61.0	69.0	63.0	57.0	52.0	50.0	39.0	41.0	39.0
Percent Homeowner	48.0	18.0	19.0	19.0	18.0	30.0	43.0	51.0	64.0	76.0
With mortgage	41.0	12.0	10.0	7.0	10.0	21.0	35.0	44.0	57.0	72.0
Without mortgage	7.0	6.0	8.0	12.0	7.0	9.0	8.0	6.0	6.0	5.0
AVERAGE ANNUAL EXPENDITURES	42 239	21 926	21 114	20 665	24 580	28 160	33 986	41 218	49 124	69 031
Food	5 610	4 516	3 791	4 187	4 237	4 330	4 964	5 534	5 783	7 982
Food at home	3 126	2 913	2 450	2 854	2 657	2 715	3 082	3 213	2 915	3 914
Cereals and bakery products	439	383	330	470	381	379	421	458	422	533
Meats, poultry, fish, and eggs	804	819	735	769	687	765	813	798	690	974
Dairy products	332	330	242	284	296	275	327	387	309	404
Fruits and vegetables	524	486	355	490	452	489	492	502	480	678
Other food at home	1 027	894	789	841	841	806	1 029	1 068	1 014	1 325
Food away from home	2 484	1 603	1 341	1 333	1 580	1 616	1 882	2 322	2 869	4 068
Alcoholic Beverages	476	184	279	226	208	243	383	507	578	804
Housing	14 261	7 581	7 329	7 139	8 827	10 354	11 430	13 585	15 718	23 334
Shelter	8 689	4 740	4 226	4 365	5 281	6 247	7 095	8 177	9 469	14 388
Owned dwellings	4 729	1 058	782	654	751	1 826	2 985	4 060	5 805	10 631
Rented dwellings	3 680	3 631	3 355	3 660	4 429	4 337	3 979	3 921	3 407	3 025
Other lodging	280	[3]51	[3]89	[3]51	101	84	130	196	258	732
Utilities, fuels, and public services	2 540	1 661	1 738	1 750	2 002	2 127	2 290	2 523	2 887	3 335
Household operations	936	172	410	287	310	631	566	763	1 132	1 840
Housekeeping supplies	457	436	296	242	466	312	354	400	507	684
Household furnishings and equipment	1 638	572	660	496	769	1 036	1 126	1 722	1 722	3 087
Apparel and Services	2 035	1 894	884	1 323	1 266	1 250	1 885	1 990	2 185	3 219
Transportation	8 536	3 430	4 777	3 833	4 316	5 529	6 727	8 788	11 025	13 394
Vehicle purchases (net outlay)	4 254	[3]1 143	2 606	1 908	1 808	2 588	3 062	4 365	5 859	6 807
Gasoline and motor oil	1 351	796	757	723	968	1 087	1 280	1 417	1 606	1 802
Other vehicle expenses	2 559	1 254	1 160	1 043	1 330	1 604	2 153	2 688	3 169	4 091
Public transportation	373	237	254	158	211	250	231	318	390	694
Health Care	1 487	479	650	506	762	911	1 360	1 733	2 083	2 127
Health insurance	799	218	279	196	372	453	783	935	1 081	1 213
Medical services	410	81	175	146	244	287	318	463	660	534
Drugs	218	146	144	134	111	138	213	269	269	286
Medical supplies	60	[3]34	53	30	35	34	46	66	72	94
Entertainment	2 090	904	838	835	1 124	1 243	1 600	1 900	2 528	3 688
Personal Care Products and Services	521	435	233	305	413	408	446	493	533	800
Reading	106	46	51	58	55	70	91	92	115	184
Education	619	1 248	877	400	780	352	428	530	566	862
Tobacco Products and Smoking Supplies	317	184	277	347	424	340	334	428	305	232
Miscellaneous	667	289	300	384	357	492	535	701	949	912
Cash Contributions	796	551	358	322	392	595	685	875	939	1 207
Personal Insurance and Pensions	4 717	184	469	800	1 418	2 042	3 118	4 060	5 816	10 288
Life and other personal insurance	220	[3]33	86	54	112	107	136	202	275	437
Pensions and Social Security	4 497	151	383	745	1 306	1 936	2 982	3 858	5 541	9 851

[1]Components of income and taxes are derived from "complete income reporters" only.
[2]Value less than 0.05.
[3]Data are likely to have large sampling errors.

Table 8-19. Consumer Expenditures, Averages for Age Groups by Income Before Taxes, 2002–2003: Reference Person Age 35–44

(Number, dollar, percent.)

Item	Complete reporting of income, total	Less than $5,000	$5,000 to $9,999	$10,000 to $14,999	$15,000 to $19,999	$20,000 to $29,999	$30,000 to $39,999	$40,000 to $49,999	$50,000 to $69,999	$70,000 and over
NUMBER OF CONSUMER UNITS (THOUSANDS)	20 356	605	768	872	961	2 216	2 353	2 141	3 800	6 639
CONSUMER UNIT CHARACTERISTICS										
Average Income Before Taxes[1]	61 309	-17	7 859	12 508	17 479	24 681	34 355	44 539	59 222	114 217
Average Income After Taxes[1]	58 365	282	8 136	12 888	17 792	24 600	33 429	43 047	56 941	107 178
Age of Reference Person	39.7	39.8	39.9	40.1	39.9	39.7	39.5	39.5	39.7	39.7
Average Number in Consumer Unit										
Persons	3.2	2.7	2.5	2.7	3.1	2.8	3.0	3.2	3.3	3.6
Children under 18	1.3	1.2	1.1	1.2	1.4	1.2	1.2	1.3	1.3	1.4
Persons 65 and over	(2)	(2)	(2)	(2)	(2)	(2)	(2)	(2)	(2)	(2)
Earners	1.7	1.1	0.7	1.1	1.2	1.4	1.6	1.7	1.9	2.0
Vehicles	2.2	1.2	1.0	1.2	1.4	1.5	1.9	2.2	2.5	2.8
Percent Distribution										
Males	52.0	38.0	40.0	36.0	43.0	46.0	49.0	53.0	57.0	58.0
Females	48.0	62.0	60.0	64.0	57.0	54.0	51.0	47.0	43.0	42.0
Percent Homeowner	68.0	39.0	33.0	34.0	36.0	45.0	59.0	68.0	79.0	88.0
With mortgage	57.0	25.0	14.0	16.0	23.0	32.0	47.0	57.0	68.0	80.0
Without mortgage	11.0	13.0	19.0	17.0	13.0	12.0	12.0	11.0	10.0	8.0
AVERAGE ANNUAL EXPENDITURES	50 141	25 937	18 639	23 217	25 099	28 832	34 183	42 678	52 508	76 970
Food	6 687	4 591	3 572	4 882	4 218	4 781	4 989	5 991	7 040	9 091
Food at home	3 787	3 107	2 073	3 650	2 952	3 118	2 986	3 534	3 803	4 748
Cereals and bakery products	565	481	286	513	416	450	427	517	575	727
Meats, poultry, fish, and eggs	959	813	585	1 244	814	888	785	873	1 007	1 081
Dairy products	415	336	215	356	323	330	319	399	413	532
Fruits and vegetables	621	520	325	523	519	512	519	590	569	798
Other food at home	1 228	957	662	1 013	880	938	937	1 155	1 239	1 609
Food away from home	2 900	1 484	1 498	1 232	1 266	1 662	2 003	2 458	3 237	4 344
Alcoholic Beverages	454	375	164	183	223	290	279	430	481	672
Housing	16 507	9 297	7 015	7 971	9 208	10 275	11 462	14 002	16 254	25 261
Shelter	9 857	5 906	4 038	4 653	5 766	6 401	6 964	8 469	9 518	14 986
Owned dwellings	7 045	2 842	1 171	1 264	2 072	2 621	3 816	5 551	7 126	12 644
Rented dwellings	2 365	2 884	2 815	3 325	3 579	3 662	3 038	2 622	1 996	1 422
Other lodging	446	[3]180	52	[3]64	115	119	110	296	396	920
Utilities, fuels, and public services	3 088	2 035	1 904	2 082	2 120	2 375	2 642	2 972	3 308	3 902
Household operations	1 006	185	209	274	319	323	490	547	806	2 041
Housekeeping supplies	669	391	325	420	348	379	430	576	754	980
Household furnishings and equipment	1 886	781	540	542	656	796	936	1 438	1 868	3 351
Apparel and Services	2 223	2 122	1 273	1 523	1 694	1 266	1 593	1 594	2 005	3 384
Transportation	9 385	5 202	2 973	4 158	4 822	5 345	6 776	8 804	11 358	13 185
Vehicle purchases (net outlay)	4 536	[3]2 920	1 307	2 084	2 471	2 404	3 139	4 371	5 932	6 138
Gasoline and motor oil	1 547	802	653	895	918	1 081	1 328	1 513	1 720	2 040
Other vehicle expenses	2 884	1 336	863	1 041	1 277	1 622	2 071	2 648	3 308	4 274
Public transportation	419	145	151	138	156	238	238	271	398	733
Health Care	2 117	812	782	1 036	836	1 256	1 723	2 021	2 473	2 972
Health insurance	1 085	318	280	446	409	655	902	1 048	1 327	1 511
Medical services	601	274	258	264	234	336	456	521	666	895
Drugs	327	194	212	216	164	218	278	338	367	417
Medical supplies	104	[3]26	[3]32	111	28	46	87	115	112	148
Entertainment	2 708	933	780	1 025	1 037	1 256	1 432	2 171	2 609	4 719
Personal Care Products and Services	660	308	345	429	331	371	470	584	666	993
Reading	131	46	45	53	42	60	70	100	140	221
Education	730	300	272	331	220	295	297	505	623	1 382
Tobacco Products and Smoking Supplies	363	320	435	404	360	444	389	436	406	270
Miscellaneous	782	611	251	230	353	469	653	702	899	1 103
Cash Contributions	1 318	481	282	222	414	647	808	989	1 438	2 232
Personal Insurance and Pensions	6 076	539	451	771	1 342	2 079	3 240	4 349	6 117	11 485
Life and other personal insurance	396	146	91	69	136	158	240	339	415	678
Pensions and Social Security	5 679	393	359	703	1 206	1 921	3 000	4 010	5 702	10 807

[1]Components of income and taxes are derived from "complete income reporters" only.
[2]Value less than 0.05.
[3]Data are likely to have large sampling errors.

Table 8-20. Consumer Expenditures, Averages for Age Groups by Income Before Taxes, 2002–2003: Reference Person Age 45–54

(Number, dollar, percent.)

Item	Complete reporting of income, total	Complete reporting of income								
		Less than $5,000	$5,000 to $9,999	$10,000 to $14,999	$15,000 to $19,999	$20,000 to $29,999	$30,000 to $39,999	$40,000 to $49,999	$50,00^ to $69,999	$70,000 and over
NUMBER OF CONSUMER UNITS (THOUSANDS)	18 793	452	782	862	925	1 950	1 989	1 898	3 146	6 790
CONSUMER UNIT CHARACTERISTICS										
Average Income Before Taxes [1]	66 549	-794	7 817	12 521	17 350	24 608	34 680	44 139	59 217	122 395
Average Income After Taxes [1]	62 551	-1 164	7 831	12 460	17 320	23 997	33 539	41 956	56 275	113 847
Age of Reference Person	49.3	49.7	49.5	49.3	49.5	49.4	49.4	49.4	49.3	49.2
Average Number in Consumer Unit										
Persons	2.6	1.9	1.8	2.2	2.3	2.4	2.4	2.3	2.7	3.1
Children under 18	0.6	0.4	0.4	0.6	0.5	0.5	0.4	0.5	0.6	0.7
Persons 65 and over	(2)	(2)	(2)	(2)	0.1	(2)	0.1	(2)	(2)	(2)
Earners	1.8	1.0	0.6	1.0	1.2	1.4	1.6	1.6	1.9	2.3
Vehicles	2.4	1.5	0.8	1.2	1.6	1.7	2.1	2.3	2.6	3.3
Percent Distribution										
Males	53.0	49.0	38.0	37.0	43.0	45.0	52.0	47.0	56.0	60.0
Females	47.0	51.0	62.0	63.0	57.0	55.0	48.0	53.0	44.0	40.0
Percent Homeowner	75.0	52.0	37.0	42.0	52.0	59.0	65.0	75.0	82.0	93.0
With mortgage	56.0	32.0	16.0	18.0	30.0	37.0	46.0	53.0	63.0	76.0
Without mortgage	19.0	20.0	21.0	24.0	23.0	22.0	19.0	21.0	19.0	17.0
AVERAGE ANNUAL EXPENDITURES	52 136	29 006	15 955	22 857	25 052	28 348	35 887	39 303	49 772	81 792
Food	6 595	4 596	2 719	3 712	3 891	4 389	5 095	5 212	6 971	9 316
Food at home	3 740	3 136	2 010	2 611	2 703	3 096	3 181	3 076	4 081	4 693
Cereals and bakery products	526	409	271	418	407	427	456	441	564	656
Meats, poultry, fish, and eggs	988	942	475	684	705	966	868	770	1 108	1 184
Dairy products	390	320	242	257	304	303	314	336	424	493
Fruits and vegetables	637	506	382	433	438	488	552	495	686	825
Other food at home	1 199	960	638	820	850	912	990	1 034	1 300	1 535
Food away from home	2 854	1 460	710	1 100	1 188	1 292	1 915	2 136	2 890	4 623
Alcoholic Beverages	515	275	122	214	203	221	291	310	471	909
Housing	15 885	10 854	6 402	8 517	8 873	9 489	11 680	12 230	14 465	24 003
Shelter	9 339	6 563	3 797	5 123	5 191	5 538	6 908	7 308	8 122	14 199
Owned dwellings	6 884	4 123	1 447	2 017	2 542	2 883	4 045	4 819	6 093	11 826
Rented dwellings	1 758	2 037	2 286	3 021	2 559	2 506	2 678	2 168	1 620	874
Other lodging	698	402	[3]63	[3]85	90	149	185	321	408	1 498
Utilities, fuels, and public services	3 243	2 441	1 731	2 198	2 290	2 512	2 708	2 850	3 208	4 188
Household operations	648	261	131	168	227	226	318	424	486	1 207
Housekeeping supplies	673	588	231	432	376	413	573	416	683	995
Household furnishings and equipment	1 982	1 002	512	596	790	799	1 174	1 232	1 887	3 415
Apparel and Services	2 143	2 259	861	1 135	1 492	1 266	1 275	1 490	2 123	3 240
Transportation	9 820	4 558	2 246	4 782	4 433	5 814	7 648	7 959	9 615	14 821
Vehicle purchases (net outlay)	4 572	[3]2 110	[3]809	2 639	1 788	2 648	3 693	3 762	4 162	7 020
Gasoline and motor oil	1 600	839	568	759	987	1 107	1 390	1 386	1 721	2 165
Other vehicle expenses	3 171	1 389	726	1 203	1 466	1 856	2 356	2 570	3 327	4 769
Public transportation	477	219	143	182	191	203	209	240	405	867
Health Care	2 598	1 728	1 133	1 158	1 442	1 704	2 163	2 337	2 650	3 603
Health insurance	1 207	852	420	548	716	720	1 020	1 197	1 311	1 621
Medical services	758	355	316	311	323	428	584	625	725	1 149
Drugs	501	444	296	266	326	499	447	426	484	631
Medical supplies	132	75	102	33	77	57	113	90	130	202
Entertainment	2 580	1 541	580	807	1 142	1 135	1 403	1 811	2 299	4 415
Personal Care Products and Services	648	415	290	348	352	362	446	516	646	970
Reading	169	85	44	61	82	69	85	135	165	280
Education	1 301	485	149	277	429	244	344	465	868	2 758
Tobacco Products and Smoking Supplies	417	269	422	394	407	464	507	450	485	350
Miscellaneous	974	539	256	451	470	504	707	847	1 144	1 387
Cash Contributions	1 741	740	323	266	367	635	881	1 068	1 442	3 243
Personal Insurance and Pensions	6 751	664	407	735	1 470	2 054	3 361	4 472	6 427	12 499
Life and other personal insurance	621	384	112	128	327	231	345	399	504	1 108
Pensions and Social Security	6 130	280	296	607	1 143	1 823	3 016	4 073	5 923	11 391

[1]Components of income and taxes are derived from "complete income reporters" only.
[2]Value less than 0.05.
[3]Data are likely to have large sampling errors.

Table 8-21. Consumer Expenditures, Averages for Age Groups by Income Before Taxes, 2002–2003: Reference Person Age 55–64

(Number, dollar, percent.)

Item	Complete reporting of income, total	Less than $5,000	$5,000 to $9,999	$10,000 to $14,999	$15,000 to $19,999	$20,000 to $29,999	$30,000 to $39,999	$40,000 to $49,999	$50,000 to $69,999	$70,000 and over
NUMBER OF CONSUMER UNITS (THOUSANDS)	13 209	370	959	905	870	1 597	1 550	1 372	2 135	3 451
CONSUMER UNIT CHARACTERISTICS										
Average Income Before Taxes[1]	56 036	1 229	7 813	12 440	17 306	24 944	34 616	44 319	58 627	123 573
Average Income After Taxes[1]	53 195	1 341	7 733	12 395	17 085	24 489	33 409	42 461	55 998	115 894
Age of Reference Person	59.1	59.4	60.0	59.8	59.6	59.7	59.5	59.1	58.8	58.4
Average Number in Consumer Unit										
Persons	2.1	1.8	1.5	1.8	1.9	1.9	2.1	2.2	2.3	2.5
Children under 18	0.2	[2]0.2	0.2	0.2	0.2	0.2	0.2	0.2	0.2	0.2
Persons 65 and over	0.1	[2]0.1	(3)	0.1	0.1	0.1	0.1	0.1	0.1	0.1
Earners	1.3	0.7	0.4	0.6	0.9	1.1	1.3	1.5	1.5	1.9
Vehicles	2.3	1.5	1.0	1.6	1.6	1.8	2.3	2.3	2.6	3.0
Percent Distribution										
Males	52.0	31.0	34.0	40.0	43.0	40.0	50.0	55.0	59.0	66.0
Females	48.0	69.0	66.0	60.0	57.0	60.0	50.0	45.0	41.0	34.0
Percent Homeowner	80.0	62.0	49.0	62.0	67.0	78.0	81.0	83.0	88.0	94.0
With mortgage	43.0	29.0	20.0	20.0	27.0	36.0	40.0	48.0	52.0	60.0
Without mortgage	37.0	33.0	29.0	42.0	40.0	43.0	41.0	35.0	36.0	34.0
AVERAGE ANNUAL EXPENDITURES	46 353	24 768	17 619	22 569	24 644	29 610	37 414	41 306	50 088	79 670
Food	5 776	3 677	2 914	3 481	3 735	4 153	5 310	5 250	6 309	8 721
Food at home	3 334	2 682	1 954	2 315	2 479	2 645	3 351	3 101	3 840	4 361
Cereals and bakery products	442	408	276	306	353	357	454	383	485	577
Meats, poultry, fish, and eggs	874	627	555	611	622	666	864	914	1 140	1 061
Dairy products	343	268	207	227	269	307	325	319	377	449
Fruits and vegetables	615	526	340	421	463	484	645	577	649	831
Other food at home	1 059	853	577	750	772	831	1 063	908	1 188	1 443
Food away from home	2 442	995	960	1 166	1 256	1 508	1 960	2 149	2 469	4 360
Alcoholic Beverages	445	211	167	200	148	259	290	333	373	910
Housing	13 974	10 162	6 934	8 023	8 678	9 393	11 073	12 359	15 271	22 487
Shelter	7 603	5 212	3 855	4 444	4 994	4 765	5 926	6 657	7 756	12 733
Owned dwellings	5 641	3 334	1 907	2 139	2 880	3 151	4 087	4 609	6 094	10 521
Rented dwellings	1 283	1 561	1 789	2 137	1 921	1 393	1 427	1 678	1 018	618
Other lodging	679	317	159	169	193	222	412	371	643	1 594
Utilities, fuels, and public services	3 033	2 484	1 908	2 180	2 248	2 589	2 847	3 037	3 255	3 975
Household operations	606	758	176	222	178	300	320	495	553	1 267
Housekeeping supplies	847	399	356	436	415	544	573	660	1 853	987
Household furnishings and equipment	1 886	1 309	639	741	844	1 195	1 407	1 510	1 854	3 525
Apparel and Services	1 802	697	542	799	926	1 165	1 262	1 506	1 699	3 420
Transportation	8 778	3 707	3 226	4 370	4 642	5 381	8 054	8 785	10 124	14 115
Vehicle purchases (net outlay)	4 223	[2]1 396	1 637	2 253	2 101	2 238	4 070	4 321	4 983	6 776
Gasoline and motor oil	1 375	702	500	731	889	991	1 409	1 394	1 629	1 978
Other vehicle expenses	2 650	1 436	935	1 269	1 454	1 935	2 310	2 573	2 907	4 266
Public transportation	530	173	154	117	198	217	264	497	605	1 096
Health Care	3 071	2 390	1 404	2 066	2 255	2 639	3 314	3 480	3 134	3 967
Health insurance	1 452	1 009	749	992	1 051	1 390	1 608	1 505	1 452	1 854
Medical services	804	896	174	453	578	436	799	1 070	829	1 168
Drugs	678	387	437	532	552	713	752	787	691	747
Medical supplies	137	[2]97	44	88	73	100	154	118	162	198
Entertainment	2 495	988	758	857	920	1 456	1 642	1 786	2 759	4 929
Personal Care Products and Services	597	306	244	290	343	416	426	564	711	968
Reading	179	96	62	96	82	103	145	191	186	308
Education	706	[2]177	[2]30	[2]103	101	129	288	287	430	2 050
Tobacco Products and Smoking Supplies	366	244	309	390	351	429	337	430	428	312
Miscellaneous	875	742	269	460	649	604	872	748	971	1 344
Cash Contributions	1 619	1 022	337	352	622	964	1 064	1 023	1 753	3 329
Personal Insurance and Pensions	5 670	349	423	1 082	1 191	2 518	3 338	4 564	5 939	12 810
Life and other personal insurance	611	244	232	331	289	373	463	507	597	1 138
Pensions and Social Security	5 059	105	190	751	902	2 145	2 875	4 057	5 342	11 672

[1]Components of income and taxes are derived from "complete income reporters" only.
[2]Data are likely to have large sampling errors.
[3]Value less than 0.05.

Table 8-22. Consumer Expenditures, Averages for Age Groups by Income Before Taxes, 2002–2003: Reference Person Age 65 and Over

(Number, dollar, percent.)

Item	Complete reporting of income, total	Complete reporting of income								
		Less than $5,000	$5,000 to $9,999	$10,000 to $14,999	$15,000 to $19,999	$20,000 to $29,999	$30,000 to $39,999	$40,000 to $49,999	$50,000 to $69,999	$70,000 and over
NUMBER OF CONSUMER UNITS (THOUSANDS)	18 920	682	2 518	3 542	2 639	3 554	2 022	1 232	1 335	1 396
CONSUMER UNIT CHARACTERISTICS										
Average Income Before Taxes [1]	30 085	1 514	8 007	12 493	17 418	24 293	34 625	44 708	58 741	120 302
Average Income After Taxes [1]	28 615	1 293	7 945	12 393	17 243	21 606	34 055	43 547	56 346	112 172
Age of Reference Person	75.0	76.5	76.4	76.6	75.3	75.3	73.7	73.5	72.1	71.6
Average Number in Consumer Unit										
Persons	1.7	1.3	1.2	1.3	1.6	1.8	2.0	2.0	2.2	2.3
Children under 18	0.1	(2)	0.1	(2)	(2)	(2)	0.1	0.1	0.1	0.1
Persons 65 and over	1.4	1.2	1.1	1.1	1.4	1.5	1.5	1.5	1.6	1.6
Earners	0.5	0.3	0.1	0.2	0.3	0.4	0.6	0.8	1.0	1.3
Vehicles	1.6	0.9	0.7	1.1	1.4	1.7	2.0	2.1	2.4	2.5
Percent Distribution										
Male	46.0	36.0	25.0	30.0	41.0	53.0	61.0	60.0	66.0	73.0
Female	54.0	64.0	75.0	70.0	59.0	47.0	39.0	40.0	34.0	27.0
Percent Homeowner	80.0	63.0	58.0	71.0	83.0	85.0	88.0	92.0	93.0	93.0
With mortgage	18.0	9.0	8.0	10.0	13.0	20.0	20.0	29.0	34.0	40.0
Without mortgage	62.0	54.0	51.0	61.0	69.0	66.0	68.0	63.0	59.0	53.0
AVERAGE ANNUAL EXPENDITURES	29 894	18 263	13 825	18 884	23 659	30 136	35 231	38 874	47 614	72 451
Food	4 047	3 243	2 355	2 780	3 357	4 290	4 722	5 319	6 150	7 961
Food at home	2 647	2 224	1 768	2 102	2 288	2 817	3 047	3 265	3 495	4 435
Cereals and bakery products	400	382	292	324	373	425	428	487	483	624
Meats, poultry, fish, and eggs	661	577	465	523	548	711	718	808	799	1 257
Dairy products	286	219	182	226	253	309	346	379	376	425
Fruits and vegetables	520	410	341	428	458	560	601	576	690	891
Other food at home	779	636	488	602	657	812	954	1 015	1 146	1 238
Food away from home	1 400	1 019	588	677	1 069	1 473	1 675	2 054	2 655	3 526
Alcoholic Beverages	239	79	98	100	143	207	274	317	584	880
Housing	9 581	6 853	5 659	6 942	8 179	9 524	10 933	12 157	13 737	19 397
Shelter	5 022	4 023	3 233	3 733	4 337	4 793	5 265	5 748	7 235	10 776
Owned dwellings	3 322	1 818	1 503	1 999	2 860	3 304	3 572	4 498	5 489	8 141
Rented dwellings	1 298	1 951	1 673	1 574	1 248	1 185	1 146	683	905	1 118
Other lodging	402	254	56	159	228	304	547	566	840	1 518
Utilities, fuels, and public services	2 424	1 810	1 641	1 963	2 268	2 501	2 746	2 924	3 178	3 781
Household operations	633	224	177	435	536	611	881	1 014	828	1 519
Housekeeping supplies	523	351	296	295	428	554	689	777	862	1 002
Household furnishings and equipment	978	446	313	516	610	1 065	1 352	1 693	1 634	2 319
Apparel and Services	997	658	552	610	719	927	1 237	1 107	1 691	2 863
Transportation	4 850	2 366	1 281	2 674	3 834	4 967	5 886	6 696	10 116	11 489
Vehicle purchases (net outlay)	2 140	[3]897	[3]297	1 147	1 609	2 141	2 498	2 834	5 118	5 621
Gasoline and motor oil	793	482	314	470	683	862	1 043	1 135	1 377	1 433
Other vehicle expenses	1 600	781	568	906	1 363	1 636	1 989	2 279	3 011	3 467
Public transportation	317	206	103	150	178	328	356	447	610	968
Health Care	3 784	2 378	1 952	2 884	3 632	4 432	4 482	4 722	4 928	5 782
Health insurance	1 972	1 293	1 163	1 560	1 991	2 275	2 242	2 542	2 460	2 643
Medical services	671	312	187	417	461	718	1 008	951	988	1 594
Drugs	975	618	549	775	1 041	1 208	1 050	1 055	1 276	1 268
Medical supplies	166	154	53	132	138	232	183	173	204	277
Entertainment	1 370	588	440	662	835	1 604	2 262	1 913	2 252	3 030
Personal Care Products and Services	458	303	233	315	417	474	519	595	762	866
Reading	150	69	58	98	113	170	171	209	255	328
Education	188	[3]170	[3]19	48	59	126	200	336	369	958
Tobacco Products and Smoking Supplies	167	116	117	122	158	177	189	226	187	280
Miscellaneous	633	403	339	366	516	840	660	687	937	1 293
Cash Contributions	1 991	662	537	818	1 208	1 686	2 397	2 140	2 517	9 278
Personal Insurance and Pensions	1 440	377	185	466	490	712	1 299	2 450	3 130	8 046
Life and other personal insurance	423	162	160	248	324	368	464	529	650	1 418
Pensions and Social Security	1 018	215	25	218	167	344	835	1 920	2 480	6 628

[1]Components of income and taxes are derived from "complete income reporters" only.
[2]Value less than 0.05.
[3]Data are likely to have large sampling errors.

Table 8-23. Consumer Expenditures, Averages for Single Men by Income Before Taxes, 2002–2003

(Number, dollar, percent.)

Item		Complete reporting of income							
	All single men	Complete reporting of income, total	Less than $5,000	$5,000 to $9,999	$10,000 to $14,999	$15,000 to $19,999	$20,000 to $29,999	$30,000 to $39,999	$40,000 and over
NUMBER OF CONSUMER UNITS (THOUSANDS)	15 055	12 792	1 199	1 720	1 492	1 204	1 942	1 678	3 557
CONSUMER UNIT CHARACTERISTICS									
Average Income Before Taxes[1]	31 591	31 591	1 524	7 482	12 327	17 058	24 505	34 089	69 076
Average Income After Taxes[1]	29 221	29 221	1 533	7 408	12 136	16 628	23 439	32 222	62 275
Age of Reference Person	45.1	45.2	33.0	47.6	51.5	49.5	45.6	43.7	44.4
Average Number in Consumer Unit									
Persons	1.0	1.0	1.0	1.0	1.0	1.0	1.0	1.0	1.0
Children under 18	X	X	X	X	X	X	X	X	X
Persons 65 and over	0.2	0.2	0.1	0.3	0.4	0.3	0.2	0.1	0.1
Earners	0.7	0.8	0.7	0.5	0.5	0.7	0.8	0.9	1.0
Vehicles	1.2	1.2	0.7	0.8	1.0	1.2	1.2	1.5	1.7
Percent Distribution									
Male	100.0	100.0	100.0	100.0	100.0	100.0	100.0	100.0	100.0
Percent Homeowner	45.0	44.0	17.0	28.0	38.0	43.0	41.0	49.0	63.0
With mortgage	22.0	22.0	5.0	5.0	7.0	14.0	15.0	30.0	47.0
Without mortgage	22.0	22.0	12.0	23.0	31.0	29.0	27.0	19.0	16.0
AVERAGE ANNUAL EXPENDITURES	25 883	27 178	14 129	13 696	16 459	20 150	23 216	29 923	45 545
Food	3 239	3 420	2 350	2 221	2 714	2 663	2 989	3 489	4 962
Food at home	1 477	1 509	985	1 063	1 570	1 406	1 462	1 577	1 838
Cereals and bakery products	205	210	147	161	246	205	193	211	244
Meats, poultry, fish, and eggs	371	368	207	258	405	346	363	409	430
Dairy products	151	158	117	118	164	151	152	159	189
Fruits and vegetables	254	259	171	163	256	238	252	273	328
Other food at home	496	514	343	364	500	466	503	525	647
Food away from home	1 762	1 911	1 365	1 158	1 144	1 257	1 527	1 912	3 124
Alcoholic Beverages	420	464	190	216	298	359	388	452	794
Housing	8 877	9 051	4 417	4 840	5 906	7 467	7 751	10 723	14 389
Shelter	5 937	6 000	3 081	3 245	3 768	4 982	4 932	6 815	9 797
Owned dwellings	2 674	2 681	636	758	1 143	1 668	1 608	3 024	5 714
Rented dwellings	2 943	2 984	2 108	2 317	2 462	3 213	3 203	3 590	3 338
Other lodging	321	335	337	171	164	101	122	201	745
Utilities, fuels, and public services	1 642	1 645	787	1 050	1 329	1 567	1 662	1 941	2 232
Household operations	321	343	91	113	289	182	370	698	435
Housekeeping supplies	217	247	126	145	171	234	205	297	357
Household furnishings and equipment	759	816	332	287	349	501	583	972	1 568
Apparel and Services	717	764	496	403	360	409	540	874	1 363
Transportation	4 600	4 792	2 343	2 253	2 795	3 345	4 543	5 884	7 787
Vehicle purchases (net outlay)	2 041	2 151	[2]875	1 007	1 314	1 194	2 114	2 732	3 555
Gasoline and motor oil	818	822	520	456	594	757	849	1 049	1 098
Other vehicle expenses	1 460	1 526	815	638	760	1 221	1 389	1 904	2 509
Public transportation	280	294	134	153	127	172	190	199	625
Health Care	1 202	1 233	457	753	1 107	1 308	1 157	1 510	1 664
Health insurance	602	603	180	390	624	639	595	743	765
Medical services	339	357	122	166	189	294	223	482	637
Drugs	219	226	111	138	273	334	307	232	204
Medical supplies	42	46	[2]43	60	21	41	32	53	58
Entertainment	1 341	1 395	658	638	671	913	1 399	1 317	2 491
Personal Care Products and Services	193	203	141	109	209	167	159	228	286
Reading	93	99	48	48	84	67	93	99	159
Education	685	699	2 052	1 043	523	581	364	447	491
Tobacco Products and Smoking Supplies	270	284	191	286	282	336	323	267	285
Miscellaneous	557	595	230	266	297	432	686	571	1 008
Cash Contributions	1 224	1 306	302	320	499	1 002	1 081	1 167	2 752
Personal Insurance and Pensions	2 465	2 874	254	300	714	1 103	1 745	2 895	7 113
Life and other personal insurance	163	175	41	51	135	157	144	158	330
Pensions and Social Security	2 302	2 698	213	249	580	945	1 601	2 737	6 783

[1]Components of income and taxes are derived from "complete income reporters" only.
[2]Data are likely to have large sampling errors.
X = Not applicable.

Table 8-24. Consumer Expenditures, Averages for Single Women by Income Before Taxes, 2002–2003

(Number, dollar, percent.)

Item	All single women	Complete reporting of income, total	Less than $5,000	$5,000 to $9,999	$10,000 to $14,999	$15,000 to $19,999	$20,000 to $29,999	$30,000 to $39,999	$40,000 and over
					Complete reporting of income				
NUMBER OF CONSUMER UNITS (THOUSANDS)	18 437	15 422	1 456	3 048	2 969	1 724	2 357	1 381	2 487
CONSUMER UNIT CHARACTERISTICS									
Average Income Before Taxes [1]	23 352	23 352	2 332	7 809	12 308	17 315	24 354	34 203	65 098
Average Income After Taxes [1]	22 204	22 204	2 300	7 757	12 231	16 987	23 399	32 494	60 236
Age of Reference Person	56.4	56.6	42.6	59.4	66.2	61.2	55.4	51.8	50.4
Average Number in Consumer Unit									
Persons	1.0	1.0	1.0	1.0	1.0	1.0	1.0	1.0	1.0
Children under 18	X	X	X	X	X	X	X	X	X
Persons 65 and over	0.4	0.4	0.2	0.5	0.7	0.6	0.4	0.2	0.1
Earners	0.5	0.6	0.6	0.3	0.3	0.5	0.7	0.8	0.9
Vehicles	0.9	0.9	0.5	0.6	0.8	1.0	1.0	1.1	1.2
Percent Distribution									
Female	100.0	100.0	100.0	100.0	100.0	100.0	100.0	100.0	100.0
Percent Homeowner	55.0	54.0	24.0	39.0	58.0	61.0	59.0	63.0	71.0
With mortgage	20.0	20.0	7.0	8.0	10.0	12.0	24.0	37.0	49.0
Without mortgage	35.0	34.0	18.0	31.0	48.0	49.0	35.0	26.0	22.0
AVERAGE ANNUAL EXPENDITURES	22 321	23 504	13 289	13 197	17 876	21 641	25 513	30 867	43 323
Food	2 585	2 757	1 995	2 060	2 274	2 687	2 824	3 241	4 010
Food at home	1 590	1 699	1 200	1 470	1 623	1 709	1 705	1 862	2 127
Cereals and bakery products	234	250	185	243	256	280	254	246	259
Meats, poultry, fish, and eggs	350	369	286	340	350	358	360	390	453
Dairy products	173	185	126	168	181	203	177	199	223
Fruits and vegetables	311	333	203	275	336	330	343	355	426
Other food at home	522	563	401	444	500	538	571	671	767
Food away from home	995	1 058	796	590	651	978	1 119	1 379	1 883
Alcoholic Beverages	175	197	94	87	127	162	142	316	427
Housing	8 540	8 662	5 106	5 314	6 642	8 401	9 329	10 762	15 486
Shelter	5 217	5 216	3 252	3 190	3 739	4 873	5 591	6 619	9 713
Owned dwellings	2 629	2 591	878	960	1 554	2 257	2 736	3 597	6 366
Rented dwellings	2 338	2 363	2 109	2 088	2 042	2 324	2 667	2 784	2 736
Other lodging	250	262	265	142	143	293	187	238	611
Utilities, fuels, and public services	1 812	1 823	1 026	1 336	1 708	1 937	1 968	2 239	2 575
Household operations	412	410	81	168	362	481	489	440	816
Housekeeping supplies	323	368	261	268	296	435	359	405	535
Household furnishings and equipment	777	845	485	352	536	674	923	1 058	1 846
Apparel and Services	1 002	1 087	892	659	707	989	1 141	1 297	1 940
Transportation	3 264	3 407	1 410	1 448	2 526	2 788	4 351	4 885	6 721
Vehicle purchases (net outlay)	1 380	1 444	[2]463	529	1 161	[2]914	1 962	1 916	3 088
Gasoline and motor oil	531	534	366	304	392	563	638	770	837
Other vehicle expenses	1 099	1 159	403	471	821	1 110	1 500	1 808	2 184
Public transportation	254	270	178	144	152	201	251	391	611
Health Care	1 815	1 895	911	1 349	2 390	2 286	2 100	1 896	2 077
Health insurance	905	922	450	729	1 183	1 208	1 024	834	878
Medical services	350	368	183	133	400	323	427	456	655
Drugs	476	511	237	443	668	653	559	479	434
Medical supplies	85	94	42	45	138	103	90	127	109
Entertainment	934	991	578	520	665	954	1 070	1 308	1 927
Personal Care Products and Services	409	448	254	259	369	487	446	515	781
Reading	107	112	54	54	95	101	147	128	205
Education	403	431	1 125	437	277	360	202	278	550
Tobacco Products and Smoking Supplies	146	155	99	163	118	158	205	156	173
Miscellaneous	475	516	358	230	350	556	595	852	869
Cash Contributions	845	934	254	344	724	930	1 072	1 913	1 632
Personal Insurance and Pensions	1 622	1 912	158	271	612	780	1 888	3 321	6 528
Life and other personal insurance	177	196	40	142	180	200	200	277	320
Pensions and Social Security	1 445	1 716	118	129	432	580	1 688	3 043	6 208

[1]Components of income and taxes are derived from "complete income reporters" only.
[2]Data are likely to have large sampling errors.
X = Not applicable.

Table 8-25. Consumer Expenditures, Averages by Selected Metropolitan Statistical Areas, 2002–2003: Northeast Region

(Number, dollar, percent.)

Item	All consumer units in the Northeast	New York	Philadelphia	Boston	Pittsburgh
NUMBER OF CONSUMER UNITS (THOUSANDS)	21 748	7 446	2 404	2 605	1 038
CONSUMER UNIT CHARACTERISTICS					
Average Income Before Taxes[1]	55 278	66 643	59 006	59 648	52 988
Age of Reference Person	49.4	49.2	49.9	47.8	52.6
Average Number in Consumer Unit					
Persons	2.4	2.7	2.6	2.3	2.3
Children under 18	0.6	0.7	0.7	0.6	0.5
Persons 65 and over	0.3	0.3	0.3	0.3	0.4
Earners	1.3	1.4	1.3	1.3	1.3
Vehicles	1.7	1.4	1.7	1.6	2.0
Percent Homeowner	64	56	74	62	73
AVERAGE ANNUAL EXPENDITURES	42 274	50 319	40 986	41 814	42 102
Food	5 771	7 005	4 862	5 627	5 295
Food at home	3 301	3 808	2 630	3 303	3 102
Cereals and bakery products	491	570	411	495	473
Meats, poultry, fish, and eggs	883	1 079	711	897	821
Dairy products	350	396	280	356	322
Fruits and vegetables	595	732	470	562	515
Other food at home	981	1 031	758	994	972
Food away from home	2 470	3 197	2 232	2 324	2 192
Alcoholic Beverages	442	469	448	504	403
Housing	14 687	18 919	14 780	15 211	12 310
Shelter	9 049	12 402	8 843	10 145	6 528
Owned dwellings	5 864	7 640	6 522	6 318	4 562
Rented dwellings	2 617	4 066	1 867	3 203	1 481
Other lodging	569	696	454	623	485
Utilities, fuels, and public services	2 821	3 055	3 105	2 676	2 902
Household operations	809	1 113	789	772	639
Housekeeping supplies	511	553	517	407	532
Household furnishings and equipment	1 497	1 796	1 527	1 212	1 708
Apparel and Services	1 911	2 638	2 106	1 610	1 630
Transportation	7 113	7 729	6 510	7 175	6 972
Vehicle purchases (net outlay)	3 038	2 928	2 399	3 518	2 769
Gasoline and motor oil	1 120	1 101	1 142	1 159	1 164
Other vehicle expenses	2 380	2 658	2 596	2 074	2 639
Public transportation	575	1 042	374	424	399
Health Care	2 166	2 235	2 138	2 007	2 459
Entertainment	2 200	2 350	2 031	2 019	2 550
Personal Care Products and Services	525	643	567	496	533
Reading	159	166	132	163	169
Education	1 051	1 260	834	1 118	1 139
Tobacco Products and Smoking Supplies	311	266	289	273	492
Miscellaneous	639	771	682	473	705
Cash Contributions	1 180	949	1 050	1 016	3 570
Personal Insurance and Pensions	4 120	4 918	4 556	4 121	3 875
Life and other personal insurance	456	531	461	235	485
Pensions and Social Security	3 664	4 388	4 095	3 886	3 390

[1]Components of income and taxes are derived from "complete income reporters" only.

Table 8-26. Consumer Expenditures, Averages by Selected Metropolitan Statistical Areas, 2002–2003: South Region

(Number, dollar, percent.)

Item	All consumer units in the South	Washington, D.C.	Baltimore	Atlanta	Miami	Tampa	Dallas-Fort Worth	Houston
NUMBER OF CONSUMER UNITS (THOUSANDS)	40 664	2 090	1 083	1 804	1 681	937	2 159	1 756
CONSUMER UNIT CHARACTERISTICS								
Average Income Before Taxes[1]	46 201	73 732	58 371	60 529	48 411	49 794	63 972	57 114
Age of Reference Person	48.2	45.9	51.8	45.8	48.4	50.3	46.1	45.0
Average Number in Consumer Unit								
Persons	2.5	2.6	2.5	2.6	2.7	2.4	2.6	2.8
Children under 18	0.6	0.7	0.7	0.7	0.7	0.6	0.7	0.9
Persons 65 and over	0.3	0.2	0.4	0.2	0.4	0.4	0.2	0.2
Earners	1.3	1.6	1.2	1.4	1.4	1.3	1.6	1.5
Vehicles	1.9	1.8	1.6	1.8	1.6	1.9	2.0	1.9
Percent Homeowner	69	71	69	73	63	73	66	60
AVERAGE ANNUAL EXPENDITURES	37 456	50 985	39 909	39 549	42 656	35 776	49 899	47 434
Food	5 030	6 288	5 411	5 085	5 704	4 074	6 537	5 822
Food at home	2 978	3 180	3 148	2 811	3 757	2 429	3 697	3 026
Cereals and bakery products	417	446	436	375	520	330	492	401
Meats, poultry, fish, and eggs	822	806	911	841	1 058	681	1 007	809
Dairy products	299	320	287	279	425	263	368	328
Fruits and vegetables	500	633	550	539	732	464	604	512
Other food at home	940	974	965	778	1 022	691	1 226	977
Food away from home	2 051	3 109	2 263	2 274	1 947	1 645	2 840	2 795
Alcoholic Beverages	314	641	465	279	432	425	405	346
Housing	11 888	18 863	13 801	14 548	16 178	13 355	15 726	15 121
Shelter	6 571	12 189	8 648	8 783	10 161	7 800	9 209	8 515
Owned dwellings	4 427	8 641	6 102	6 383	6 685	5 561	6 065	5 417
Rented dwellings	1 773	2 958	2 036	2 024	3 155	1 889	2 528	2 719
Other lodging	371	589	510	376	321	350	616	379
Utilities, fuels, and public services	2 834	3 067	2 767	3 421	3 068	3 021	3 538	3 284
Household operations	678	932	598	699	991	848	794	1 030
Housekeeping supplies	493	648	588	401	524	398	559	585
Household furnishings and equipment	1 313	2 028	1 199	1 243	1 434	1 288	1 627	1 707
Apparel and Services	1 520	2 240	1 920	1 567	1 545	994	2 055	2 078
Transportation	7 509	7 853	5 605	7 400	8 348	7 291	9 815	9 891
Vehicle purchases (net outlay)	3 744	3 374	1 852	3 610	3 709	3 546	4 939	5 243
Gasoline and motor oil	1 281	1 318	1 139	1 222	1 324	1 142	1 510	1 467
Other vehicle expenses	2 225	2 454	2 215	2 289	2 868	2 407	3 018	2 794
Public transportation	259	707	400	280	447	196	348	386
Health Care	2 413	2 289	2 108	1 903	2 059	2 167	2 833	2 494
Entertainment	1 759	2 340	1 756	1 463	1 549	1 684	2 135	2 515
Personal Care Products and Services	502	651	643	422	589	383	624	648
Reading	98	164	101	59	65	88	125	115
Education	535	1 219	717	596	690	388	558	728
Tobacco Products and Smoking Supplies	297	184	295	145	256	308	253	316
Miscellaneous	658	732	539	626	1 334	564	594	721
Cash Contributions	1 270	1 474	1 092	1 016	595	773	2 150	1 823
Personal Insurance and Pensions	3 662	6 046	5 456	4 438	3 313	3 283	6 089	4 816
Life and other personal insurance	385	537	405	494	231	372	430	403
Pensions and Social Security	3 277	5 509	5 051	3 945	3 082	2 911	5 659	4 413

[1]Components of income and taxes are derived from "complete income reporters" only.

Table 8-27. Consumer Expenditures, Averages by Selected Metropolitan Statistical Areas, 2002–2003: Midwest Region

(Number, dollar, percent.)

Item	All consumer units in the Midwest	Chicago	Detroit	Milwaukee	Minneapolis-St. Paul	Cleveland	Cincinnati	St. Louis	Kansas City
NUMBER OF CONSUMER UNITS (THOUSANDS)	26 161	3 097	2 019	746	1 254	1 267	956	1 011	804
CONSUMER UNIT CHARACTERISTICS									
Average Income Before Taxes[1]	50 861	64 670	57 541	48 531	69 758	50 391	52 271	55 698	57 460
Age of Reference Person	48.6	47.7	48.8	49.9	47.4	49.2	48.6	49.6	47.2
Average Number in Consumer Unit									
Persons	2.5	2.8	2.6	2.5	2.4	2.4	2.3	2.4	2.7
Children under 18	0.6	0.8	0.7	0.7	0.6	0.6	0.6	0.6	0.8
Persons 65 and over	0.3	0.2	0.3	0.3	0.2	0.3	0.3	0.3	0.2
Earners	1.4	1.5	1.3	1.3	1.4	1.4	1.3	1.3	1.5
Vehicles	2.2	1.7	2.0	2.0	2.6	1.8	1.9	1.9	2.1
Percent Homeowner	70	69	74	61	71	73	58	70	69
AVERAGE ANNUAL EXPENDITURES	40 435	47 016	44 039	40 890	54 088	37 487	39 030	44 654	43 450
Food	5 133	6 001	5 511	5 234	6 235	4 574	5 303	5 662	5 672
Food at home	2 918	3 418	3 073	2 882	3 444	2 761	3 052	3 363	3 421
Cereals and bakery products	423	472	466	424	501	395	448	478	496
Meats, poultry, fish, and eggs	721	875	781	717	738	844	776	902	876
Dairy products	322	354	329	286	409	291	320	326	388
Fruits and vegetables	481	624	545	475	592	448	457	562	545
Other food at home	971	1 093	950	980	1 203	784	1 051	1 095	1 115
Food away from home	2 215	2 583	2 439	2 352	2 791	1 813	2 250	2 299	2 250
Alcoholic Beverages	406	486	430	536	634	306	363	330	313
Housing	12 636	17 059	14 429	14 364	17 451	12 335	13 072	13 961	14 022
Shelter	7 091	10 290	8 814	8 786	10 575	7 262	7 715	7 980	7 848
Owned dwellings	4 926	7 333	6 504	5 594	7 365	5 349	4 246	5 303	5 463
Rented dwellings	1 689	2 344	1 717	2 596	2 377	1 565	3 084	1 977	2 007
Other lodging	477	612	593	596	833	348	385	699	378
Utilities, fuels, and public services	2 769	3 190	2 911	2 558	2 766	3 079	2 520	3 083	3 329
Household operations	592	876	732	622	849	472	586	877	718
Housekeeping supplies	640	624	530	601	730	432	510	434	560
Household furnishings and equipment	1 543	2 080	1 442	1 796	2 531	1 089	1 741	1 587	1 567
Apparel And Services	1 643	2 017	2 473	1 880	2 056	1 378	1 435	1 874	1 490
Transportation	7 973	7 961	9 024	6 797	9 280	7 702	7 803	8 359	8 794
Vehicle purchases (net outlay)	3 904	3 570	3 955	3 002	4 209	3 716	3 917	4 231	4 255
Gasoline and motor oil	1 314	1 325	1 354	1 284	1 400	1 107	1 152	1 261	1 559
Other vehicle expenses	2 399	2 410	3 229	2 142	3 007	2 531	2 466	2 545	2 655
Public transportation	357	657	486	368	664	349	269	322	324
Health Care	2 486	2 462	1 999	2 429	2 576	2 035	2 126	2 588	2 533
Entertainment	2 060	2 326	1 950	2 114	3 596	1 794	2 047	2 218	2 047
Personal Care Products and Services	507	588	630	521	650	397	502	558	555
Reading	145	138	145	147	202	125	166	159	166
Education	757	1 224	767	634	1 044	789	629	956	647
Tobacco Products and Smoking Supplies	379	300	383	368	309	347	323	358	301
Miscellaneous	710	945	805	537	1 126	616	554	677	640
Cash Contributions	1 417	1 431	1 158	1 342	1 937	863	1 229	2 182	1 625
Personal Insurance and Pensions	4 181	4 077	4 335	3 988	6 993	4 227	3 478	4 771	4 643
Life and other personal insurance	435	324	304	414	641	469	331	746	397
Pensions and Social Security	3 746	3 754	4 031	3 575	6 352	3 758	3 147	4 025	4 246

[1]Components of income and taxes are derived from "complete income reporters" only.

Table 8-28. Consumer Expenditures, Averages by Selected Metropolitan Statistical Areas, 2002–2003: West Region

(Number, dollar, percent.)

Item	All consumer units in the West	Los Angeles	San Francisco	San Diego	Portland	Seattle	Honolulu	Anchorage	Phoenix	Denver
NUMBER OF CONSUMER UNITS (THOUSANDS)	25 159	5 169	2 770	871	1 071	1 578	275	91	1 297	1 234
CONSUMER UNIT CHARACTERISTICS										
Average Income Before Taxes[1]	52 267	56 275	74 377	55 169	53 706	56 590	59 114	64 301	49 640	62 567
Age of Reference Person	47.0	47.4	48.0	48.8	46.5	47.7	53.7	43.6	46.7	44.0
Average Number in Consumer Unit										
Persons	2.6	2.8	2.6	2.7	2.5	2.3	2.8	2.8	2.5	2.6
Children under 18	0.7	0.8	0.7	0.7	0.7	0.5	0.6	0.9	0.7	0.7
Persons 65 and over	0.3	0.3	0.2	0.3	0.3	0.3	0.5	0.1	0.3	0.2
Earners	1.4	1.5	1.4	1.4	1.4	1.4	1.4	1.5	1.3	1.5
Vehicles	2.0	1.9	1.9	2.0	2.2	2.3	1.6	2.7	1.8	2.2
Percent Homeowner	62.0	56.0	63.0	58.0	63.0	65.0	57.0	67.0	63.0	66.0
AVERAGE ANNUAL EXPENDITURES	45 058	49 765	53 135	47 137	45 172	49 114	44 505	54 229	44 078	50 208
Food	5 755	6 402	6 551	5 929	5 423	6 465	5 819	6 898	5 615	6 489
Food at home	3 373	3 506	3 628	3 175	3 239	4 176	3 269	4 096	3 244	3 903
Cereals and bakery products	476	481	492	423	454	586	462	530	488	552
Meats, poultry, fish, and eggs	828	875	887	810	712	1 029	866	1 015	833	930
Dairy products	362	375	359	323	384	433	287	478	355	438
Fruits and vegetables	634	737	780	635	542	714	630	700	585	709
Other food at home	1 073	1 039	1 109	985	1 148	1 414	1 024	1 373	983	1 274
Food away from home	2 382	2 895	2 923	2 754	2 184	2 289	2 549	2 802	2 372	2 586
Alcoholic Beverages	420	467	607	382	472	369	357	419	436	680
Housing	15 335	17 986	20 349	17 797	15 590	16 619	15 156	17 178	14 515	16 584
Shelter	9 710	11 852	14 552	11 553	9 457	10 850	10 067	10 591	8 411	10 272
Owned dwellings	6 227	7 218	9 322	6 407	6 102	7 531	5 367	7 081	5 427	6 616
Rented dwellings	2 925	4 089	4 580	4 520	2 702	2 646	3 971	2 946	2 514	3 228
Other lodging	558	544	649	627	653	674	728	563	470	428
Utilities, fuels, and public services	2 527	2 568	2 566	2 608	2 778	2 687	2 492	2 703	2 773	2 660
Household operations	783	947	1 208	930	898	745	707	896	821	955
Housekeeping supplies	522	585	514	582	453	542	480	665	489	638
Household furnishings and equipment	1 793	2 035	1 510	2 123	2 003	1 795	1 410	2 323	2 021	2 059
Apparel and Services	1 835	2 246	2 196	1 897	1 831	1 994	1 467	1 822	1 539	1 659
Transportation	8 548	9 162	8 802	8 652	6 807	9 347	8 023	10 765	8 659	9 652
Vehicle purchases (net outlay)	3 983	4 019	3 776	3 600	2 417	4 592	3 724	5 487	3 947	4 301
Gasoline and motor oil	1 403	1 580	1 455	1 513	1 253	1 342	1 142	1 450	1 266	1 327
Other vehicle expenses	2 700	3 070	2 870	3 109	2 639	2 844	2 208	3 043	3 017	3 484
Public transportation	462	493	701	429	497	568	948	784	430	540
Health Care	2 418	2 196	2 580	2 275	2 751	2 730	2 617	2 595	2 551	2 652
Entertainment	2 465	2 386	2 273	2 122	2 803	2 936	2 276	3 604	2 318	2 667
Personal Care Products and Services	587	755	595	683	571	581	542	715	584	643
Reading	154	152	207	137	205	182	170	253	148	142
Education	911	899	933	901	855	761	1 040	714	505	748
Tobacco Products and Smoking Supplies	235	194	223	209	275	329	300	405	325	302
Miscellaneous	799	911	774	848	1 028	652	831	1 332	980	1 085
Cash Contributions	1 440	1 426	1 218	1 003	1 690	1 432	1 226	1 545	1 397	1 589
Personal Insurance and Pensions	4 156	4 582	5 825	4 302	4 872	4 716	4 684	5 985	4 506	5 316
Life and other personal insurance	346	340	470	369	492	417	607	585	395	413
Pensions and Social Security	3 810	4 243	5 355	3 933	4 380	4 300	4 076	5 400	4 112	4 903

[1]Components of income and taxes are derived from "complete income reporters" only.

PART NINE

OCCUPATIONAL SAFETY AND HEALTH

OCCUPATIONAL SAFETY AND HEALTH

HIGHLIGHTS

This part includes data on work-related illnesses and fatal work injuries based on the Annual Survey of Occupational Injuries and Illnesses and the Census of Fatal Occupations. Data are classified by industry and selected worker characteristics.

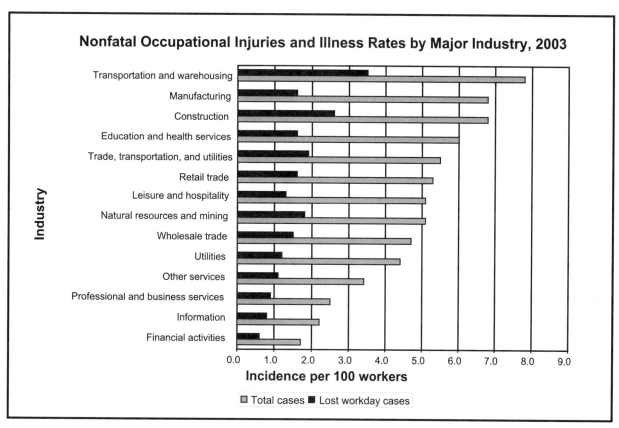

Among the major industries, transportation and warehousing had the highest incidence rate of injuries in 2003, followed by manufacturing. The incidence rate of injuries that required days away from work was much lower. It ranged from 0.6 percent for financial activities to 3.5 percent for transportation and warehousing. Education and health services had the highest injury incidence rate, 6.0 percent, within the service-providing sector. (Table 9-1)

OTHER HIGHLIGHTS:

• In 2003, the service-providing sector accounted for 69 percent of all nonfatal occupational injuries and illnesses. The goods-producing sector was responsible for 31 percent of all incidents, but a greater proportion of its workers suffered injuries or became ill. (Table 9-2)

• Within the goods-producing sector, manufacturing was responsible for more than half of all injuries and illnesses, with construction accounting for 38.1 percent of incidents. Only 6.5 percent of nonfatal injuries and illnesses occurred in natural resources and mining. (Table 9-2)

• Laborers and material movers, with 89,510 cases, had the highest number of nonfatal injuries and illnesses involving days away from work. Truck drivers and nursing aides and orderlies followed with 71,900 and 56,820, respectively. (Table 9-3)

• Men suffered approximately 93 percent of all fatal injuries and 65 percent of all nonfatal injuries in 2003. (Tables 9-2 and 9-4)

• While the number of fatal injuries declined for workers ages 16–24 between 2003 and 2004, the number rose for workers 55 years and over. (Table 9-4 in the eighth and ninth editions of this *Handbook*)

NOTES AND DEFINITIONS

Collection and Coverage

Nonfatal Occupational Injuries and Illnesses

The Survey of Occupational Injuries and Illnesses is a federal/state program that collected employer reports from about 182,800 private industry establishments in 2003. The reports were then processed by state agencies cooperating with the Bureau of Labor Statistics (BLS). The survey measures nonfatal injuries and illnesses only. It excludes the self-employed, farms with fewer than 11 employees, private households, federal government agencies, and, for national estimates, employees in state and local government agencies

BLS has reported annually on the number and rate of days-away-from-work injuries and illnesses in private industry since the early 1970s. The 2002 national survey marks the 11th year that BLS has collected additional detailed information concerning worker and case characteristics data, including lost work time. On January 19, 2001, OSHA promulgated revisions to its requirements for recording occupational injuries and illnesses. These revisions became effective January 1, 2002, and are reflected in the 2002 survey.

Due to the revised requirements, the estimates from the 2002 survey are not comparable with those from previous years. The survey was not designed to determine the impact of the revision on the estimates of nonfatal occupational injuries and illnesses.

The term "lost workdays" is eliminated and the revision requires recording of days-away-from-work and days of restricted work or transfer to another job. In addition, the new rules for counting rely on calendar days instead of workdays. Employers are no longer required to count days away from work or days of job transfer or restriction beyond 180 days. These changes affect the calculation of median days away from work, making it non-comparable to previous years.

The number and frequency (incidence rates) of days away from work cases are based on logs and other records kept by private industry employers throughout the year. These records reflect the year's injury and illness experience in addition to the employers' understanding of which cases are work related under the current record keeping guidelines of the U. S. Department of Labor. The number of injuries and illnesses reported in a given year can be influenced by changes in the level of economic activity, working conditions and work practices, worker experience and training, and the number of hours worked.

The Mine Safety and Health Administration and the Federal Railroad Administration furnish mining and railroad data to BLS. They are therefore not comparable to other industries.

Industry data are classified according to the Standard Industrial Classification (SIC).

Concepts and Definitions

Recordable occupational injuries and illnesses are: (1) nonfatal occupational illnesses; or (2) nonfatal occupational injuries that involve one or more of the following: loss of consciousness, restriction of work or motion, transfer to another job, or medical treatment (other than first aid). The annual survey measures only nonfatal injuries and illnesses. To better address fatalities, BLS implemented the Census of Fatal Occupational Injuries (see below).

Occupational injury is any injury—such as a cut, fracture, sprain, amputation, and so forth—that results from a work accident or from exposure involving an incident in the work environment.

Occupational illness is an abnormal condition or disorder (other than one resulting from an occupational injury) caused by exposure to environmental factors associated with employment. It includes acute and chronic illness or disease that may be caused by inhalation, absorption, ingestion, or direct contact. Long-term latent illnesses can be difficult to relate to the workplace and are believed to be understated in this survey.

Days-away-from-work are cases that involve days away from work, days of restricted work activity, or both.

The data are presented in the form of incidence rates, defined as the number of injuries and illnesses or cases of days away from work per 100 full-time employees. The formula is (N/EH) x 200,000, where N=number of injuries and illnesses or days away from work, EH=total hours worked by all employees during the calendar year, and 200,000 represents the base for 100 full-time equivalent workers (working 40 hours per week, 50 weeks per year).

Comparable data for individual states are available from the BLS Office of Safety, Health, and Working Conditions.

Fatal Occupational Injuries

Since 1992, BLS has collected a comprehensive count of work-related deaths in the Census of Fatal Occupational Injuries (CFOI). The BLS fatality census covers not only private wage and salary workers, but also workers on small farms, the self-employed, family workers, and public sector workers.

The CFOI program is a cooperative venture between the state and federal governments. The program collects and cross checks fatality information from multiple sources, including death certificates, state and federal workers' compensation reports, OSHA and Mine Safety and Health Administration records, medical examiner and autopsy reports, media accounts, state motor vehicle fatality records, and follow-up questionnaires to employers.

Fatality counts from the BLS Census are combined with annual average employment from the Current Population Survey to produce a fatal work injury rate.

For a fatality to be included in the CFOI, the decedent must have been employed at the time of the event and present at the site of the incident as a job requirement. Due to the latency period of many occupational illnesses and the resulting difficulty associated with linking illnesses to work, it is difficult to compile a complete count of all fatal illnesses in a given year. Thus, information on illness-related deaths are excluded from the basic fatality count.

Industries are classified according to the North American Industry Classification system (NAICS) and occupations according to the Standard Occupational System (SOC).

Sources of Additional Information

For more extensive definitions and description of collection methods see BLS news release USDL 05-521 for illnesses, USDL 05-1598 for fatalities, occasional articles in *Compensation and Working Conditions*, and BLS Report 954.

Table 9-1. Incidence Rates of Nonfatal Occupational Injuries and Illnesses by Selected Industries and Case Types, 2003

(Number, rate.)

Industry [1]	NAICS code [2]	2003 average annual employment [3]	Total recordable cases	Cases with days away from work, job transfer, or restriction			Other recordable cases
				Total	Cases with days away from work [4]	Cases with job transfer or restriction	
PRIVATE INDUSTRY [5]		106 183.1	5.0	2.6	1.5	1.1	2.4
Goods-Producing [5]		22 788.4	6.7	3.7	1.9	1.8	3.0
Natural resources and mining [5, 6]		1 465.1	5.1	2.8	1.8	1.0	2.3
Agriculture, forestry, fishing, and hunting	11	1 156.2	6.2	3.3	2.1	1.2	2.9
Crop production	111	555.9	6.1	3.3	2.1	1.2	2.8
Animal production	112	205.5	8.2	3.8	2.3	1.5	. . .
Forestry and logging	113	72.8	6.2	4.2	4.0	0.3	2.0
Fishing, hunting, and trapping	114	10.1	1.5	1.2	0.9	0.2	0.4
Support activities for agriculture and forestry		311.9	5.5	2.9	1.6	1.3	2.6
Mining [6]	21	500.1	3.3	2.0	1.4	0.6	1.2
Oil and gas extraction	211	120.3	1.8	0.8	0.6	0.2	1.0
Mining, except oil and gas [7]	212	200.3	4.6	3.1	2.4	0.8	1.4
Support activities for mining	213	179.5	2.7	1.5	0.9	0.6	. . .
Construction	23	6 672.4	6.8	3.6	2.6	1.0	3.2
Construction of buildings	236	1 565.4	5.7	3.0	2.2	0.8	2.7
Heavy and civil engineering construction	237	891.5	6.5	3.5	2.4	1.2	3.0
Specialty trade contractors	238	4 215.5	7.3	3.9	2.8	1.1	3.4
Manufacturing	31-33	14 459.7	6.8	3.8	1.6	2.2	3.1
Food manufacturing	311	1 513.4	8.6	5.5	1.9	3.7	3.1
Beverage and tobacco product manufacturing	312	199.4	10.7	7.1	3.2	3.9	3.6
Textile mills	313	261.3	5.0	2.8	0.8	1.9	2.2
Textile product mills	314	182.6	5.5	3.2	1.3	1.9	2.3
Apparel manufacturing	315	309.0	3.6	1.9	0.9	1.0	1.7
Leather and allied product manufacturing	316	45.6	7.8	4.8	2.1	2.7	3.0
Wood product manufacturing	321	534.3	10.0	5.4	2.8	2.6	4.6
Paper manufacturing	322	514.1	4.8	2.9	1.5	1.4	1.9
Printing and related support activities	323	672.3	4.5	2.7	1.2	1.5	1.9
Petroleum and coal products manufacturing	324	115.5	2.8	1.6	0.9	0.7	1.2
Chemical manufacturing	325	905.5	3.4	2.0	0.9	1.0	1.4
Plastics and rubber products manufacturing		814.6	7.4	4.4	1.7	2.8	2.9
Nonmetallic mineral product manufacturing	327	496.0	7.9	4.6	2.2	2.4	3.3
Primary metal manufacturing	331	474.5	9.6	4.8	2.1	2.7	4.8
Fabricated metal product manufacturing	332	1 476.2	8.5	4.2	2.0	2.2	4.3
Machinery manufacturing	333	1 145.8	6.9	3.1	1.5	1.6	3.8
Computer and electronic product manufacturing	334	1 354.0	2.4	1.2	0.6	0.6	1.1
Electrical equipment, appliance, and component manufacturing	335	457.8	6.1	3.1	1.2	1.9	2.9
Transportation equipment manufacturing	336	1 753.7	9.3	5.1	1.8	3.3	4.1
Furniture and related product manufacturing	337	570.3	8.7	4.7	1.9	2.8	4.1
Miscellaneous manufacturing	339	663.6	5.0	2.7	1.2	1.5	2.3
Service-Providing		83 394.6	4.4	2.3	1.4	0.9	2.1
Trade, transportation, and utilities [8]		25 041.8	5.5	3.2	1.9	1.3	2.4
Wholesale trade	42	5 589.0	4.7	2.8	1.5	1.3	1.9
Merchant wholesalers, durable goods	423	2 929.2	4.3	2.4	1.3	1.0	2.0
Merchant wholesalers, nondurable goods	424	1 998.4	5.7	3.7	1.9	1.8	2.0
Wholesale electronic markets and agents and brokers	425	661.4	2.9	1.5	. . .	0.5	1.4

[1] Totals include data for industries not shown separately.
[2] North American Industry Classification System-United States, 2002.
[3] Employment is expressed as an annual average and is derived primarily from the Bureau of Labor Statistics (BLS)-Quarterly Census of Employment and Wages (QCEW) program.
[4] Days-away-from-work cases include those which result in days away from work with or without job transfer or restriction.
[5] Excludes farms with fewer than 11 employees.
[6] Data for mining include establishments not governed by the Mine Safety and Health Administration (MSHA) rules and reporting, such as those in oil and gas extraction and related support activities. Data for mining operators in coal, metal, and nonmetal mining are provided to BLS by MSHA, U.S. Department of Labor. Independent mining contractors are excluded from the coal, metal, and nonmetal mining industries.
[7] Data for mining operators in this industry are provided to BLS by MSHA, U.S. Department of Labor. Independent mining contractors are excluded. These data do not reflect the changes the Occupational Safety and Health Administration made to its recordkeeping requirements effective January 1, 2002; therefore, estimates for these industries are not comparable to estimates in other industries.
[8] Data for employers in railroad transportation are provided to BLS by the Federal Railroad Administration (FRA), U.S. Department of Transportation. These data do not reflect the changes the Occupational Safety and Health Administration made to its recordkeeping requirements effective January 1, 2002; therefore, estimates for these industries are not comparable to estimates for other industries.
. . . = Not available.

Table 9-1. Incidence Rates of Nonfatal Occupational Injuries and Illnesses by Selected Industries and Case Types, 2003—*Continued*

(Number, rate.)

Industry [1]	NAICS code [2]	2003 average annual employment [3]	Total recordable cases	Cases with days away from work, job transfer, or restriction			Other recordable cases
				Total	Cases with days away from work [4]	Cases with job transfer or restriction	
Retail trade	44	14 930.8	5.3	2.7	1.6	1.2	2.6
Motor vehicle and parts dealers	441	1 878.8	5.1	2.2	1.5	0.7	2.9
Furniture and home furnishings stores	442	547.7	5.2	2.7	1.6	1.1	2.6
Electronics and appliance stores	443	517.6	3.3	1.3	0.7	0.6	2.0
Building material and garden equipment and							
supplies dealers	444	1 190.6	6.4	3.4	2.0	1.4	3.0
Food and beverage stores	445	2 842.4	6.8	3.6	2.1	1.5	3.2
Health and personal care stores	446	935.8	2.6	1.2	0.8	0.4	1.4
Gasoline stations	447	879.2	3.7	1.7	1.2	0.5	1.9
Clothing and clothing accessories stores	448	1 309.2	2.8	1.0	0.7	0.3	1.8
Sporting goods, hobby, book, and music stores		655.3	3.6	1.3	0.7	0.6	2.3
General merchandise stores	452	2 813.4	7.2	4.3	1.9	2.3	2.9
Miscellaneous store retailers	453	937.5	3.6	1.9	1.3	0.7	1.7
Nonstore retailers	454	423.4	5.6	3.5	1.7	1.8	2.1
Transportation and warehousing [8]	48	3 946.2	7.8	5.4	3.5	1.8	2.4
Air transportation	481	527.0	11.0	8.0	5.8	2.2	3.0
Rail transportation [8]	482	...	2.9	2.2	2.0	0.2	0.7
Water transportation	483	53.1	...	2.3	1.8	0.4	1.1
Truck transportation	484	1 322.4	6.8	4.5	3.4	1.1	2.3
Transit and ground passenger transportation		375.4	6.4	3.8	2.8	1.0	2.6
Pipeline transportation	486	40.3	2.1	1.0	0.5	0.5	1.1
Scenic and sightseeing transportation	487	26.7	3.9	2.3	1.9	0.4	1.6
Support activities for transportation	488	513.2	5.6	3.5	2.4	1.1	2.1
Couriers and messengers	492	565.1	12.1	8.8	5.5	3.3	3.3
Warehousing and storage	493	519.6	10.1	7.3	3.0	4.4	2.7
Utilities	22	575.9	4.4	2.2	1.2	1.0	2.2
Information	51	3 180.8	2.2	1.1	0.8	0.3	1.1
Publishing industries, except Internet		929.5	2.3	1.1	0.7	0.4	1.2
Motion picture and sound recording industries	512	368.5	...	...	0.5	0.2	...
Broadcasting, except Internet	515	323.9	2.0	1.0	0.6	0.4	1.0
Telecommunications	517	1 079.1	...	...	1.1	...	...
Internet service providers, Web search portals,							
and services	518	402.2	1.4	0.5	0.3	0.2	...
Other information services	519	48.1	2.1	1.5	1.3	...	0.6
Financial activities		7 826.9	1.7	0.8	0.6	0.2	0.9
Finance and insurance	52	5 782.1	1.1	0.4	0.3	0.1	0.7
Monetary authorities-central bank	521	22.8	3.1	1.4	0.7	0.7	1.7
Credit intermediation and related activities	522	2 780.4	1.1	0.4	0.3	0.1	0.7
Securities, commodity contracts, and other							
financial investments and related activities	523	757.0	0.5	0.2	0.1	0.1	0.3
Insurance carriers and related activities	524	2 137.9	1.2	0.5	0.4	0.1	0.7
Funds, trusts, and other financial vehicles	525	83.9	1.0	0.5	0.3	0.2	0.5
Real estate and rental and leasing	53	2 044.9	3.9	2.1	1.5	0.6	1.8
Real estate	531	1 381.3	3.6	1.9	1.4	0.5	1.7
Rental and leasing services	532	637.2	4.7	2.5	1.6	1.0	2.2
Lessors of nonfinancial intangible assets,							
except copyrighted works	533	26.4	1.2	0.9	0.7	...	...
Professional and business services		15 858.5	2.5	1.4	0.9	0.5	1.1
Professional, scientific, and technical services	54	6 638.7	1.3	0.6	0.4	0.2	0.7
Management of companies and enterprises	55	1 660.1	3.0	1.6	0.9	0.7	1.3
Administrative and support and waste							
management and remediation services	56	7 559.6	4.0	2.4	1.6	0.8	1.6
Administrative and support services	561	7 241.4	3.7	2.1	1.4	0.6	1.6
Waste management and remediation services ..	562	318.2	8.3	5.7	3.5	2.2	2.6
Education and health services	...	15 738.0	6.0	2.9	1.6	1.3	3.1
Educational services	61	2 016.2	2.7	1.2	0.8	...	1.5
Health care and social assistance	62	13 721.9	6.5	3.1	1.7	1.4	3.3
Ambulatory health care services	621	4 783.4	3.3	1.2	0.8	0.4	2.1
Hospitals	622	4 201.3	8.7	3.6	2.0	1.6	5.1
Nursing and residential care facilities	623	2 776.5	10.1	6.3	3.2	3.1	3.9
Social assistance	624	1 960.7	4.1	2.3	1.4	0.9	1.8

[1]Totals include data for industries not shown separately.
[2]North American Industry Classification System-United States, 2002.
[3]Employment is expressed as an annual average and is derived primarily from the Bureau of Labor Statistics (BLS)-Quarterly Census of Employment and Wages (QCEW) program.
[4]Days-away-from-work cases include those which result in days away from work with or without job transfer or restriction.
[8]Data for employers in railroad transportation are provided to BLS by the Federal Railroad Administration (FRA), U.S. Department of Transportation. These data do not reflect the changes the Occupational Safety and Health Administration made to its recordkeeping requirements effective January 1, 2002; therefore, estimates for these industries are not comparable to estimates for other industries.
... = Not available.

Table 9-1. Incidence Rates of Nonfatal Occupational Injuries and Illnesses by Selected Industries and Case Types, 2003—*Continued*

(Number, rate.)

| Industry [1] | NAICS code [2] | 2003 average annual employment [3] | Total recordable cases | Cases with days away from work, job transfer, or restriction | | | Other recordable cases |
				Total	Cases with days away from work [4]	Cases with job transfer or restriction	
Leisure and hospitality		12 162.2	5.1	2.1	1.3	0.8	3.0
Arts, entertainment, and recreation	71	1 816.9	5.9	2.9	1.6	1.4	3.0
Performing arts, spectator sports, and related industries	711	383.3	6.7	2.6	1.6	1.0	4.1
Museums, historical sites, and similar institutions	712	115.4	4.2	2.2	1.6	0.6	2.0
Amusement, gambling, and recreation industries	713	1 318.2	5.8	3.1	1.5	1.6	2.7
Accommodation and food services	72	10 345.3	5.0	2.0	1.3	0.7	3.0
Accommodation	721	1 768.0	6.7	3.6	1.9	1.6	3.2
Food services and drinking places	722	8 577.3	4.6	1.6	1.1	0.5	3.0
Other services		3 777.7	3.4	1.7	1.1	0.6	1.7
Other services, except public administration	81	3 777.7	3.4	1.7	1.1	0.6	1.7
Repair and maintenance	811	1 224.3	4.2	2.1	1.4	0.7	2.1
Personal and laundry services	812	1 258.9	2.8	1.7	0.9	0.7	1.2
Religious, grantmaking, civic, professional, and similar organizations	813	1 294.5	2.9	1.3	0.9	0.4	1.6

Note: Due to rounding, components may not add to totals.

[1]Totals include data for industries not shown separately.
[2]North American Industry Classification System-United States, 2002.
[3]Employment is expressed as an annual average and is derived primarily from the Bureau of Labor Statistics (BLS)-Quarterly Census of Employment and Wages (QCEW) program.
[4]Days-away-from-work cases include those which result in days away from work with or without job transfer or restriction.

Table 9-2. Number of Nonfatal Occupational Injuries and Illnesses Involving Days Away from Work[1] by Selected Worker Characteristics and Industry Division, Private Industry, 2003

(Numbers in thousands.)

Characteristic	Total cases	Goods-producing			
		Total goods-producing [2]	Natural resources and mining [3]	Construction	Manufacturing
TOTAL CASES	13 159.2	4 076.1	263.9	1 554.2	2 258.0
Sex					
Men	8 517.9	3 465.2	230.0	1 522.6	1 712.6
Women	4 590.9	609.3	33.7	31.5	544.1
Age [4]					
14 to 15 years	2.1	. . .	. . .	. . .	. . .
16 to 19 years	422.1	78.8	8.3	31.6	39.0
20 to 24 years	1 438.0	429.1	33.0	208.0	188.1
25 to 34 years	3 134.3	1 037.4	69.5	470.2	497.7
35 to 44 years	3 570.5	1 165.9	59.1	446.4	660.4
45 to 54 years	2 846.9	908.2	62.6	285.4	560.1
55 to 64 years	1 321.3	377.4	24.1	90.1	263.3
65 and over	243.8	42.0	5.0	8.6	28.4
Length of Service With Employer					
Less than 3 months	1 584.5	554.2	59.7	287.6	206.9
3 to 11 months	2 636.2	741.6	47.5	366.5	327.6
1 to 5 years	4 812.5	1 368.5	88.0	546.8	733.7
More than 5 years	4 027.6	1 396.6	64.2	350.2	982.2
Race or Ethnic Origin					
White only	6 171.6	2 185.9	73.3	885.3	1 227.3
Black only	1 084.7	244.1	5.1	66.5	172.5
Hispanic or Latino only	1 600.8	689.1	98.4	267.5	323.2
Asian only	154.1	44.3	0.9	9.1	34.3
Native Hawaiian or Pacific Islander only	49.9	12.2	0.4	6.7	5.1
American Indian or Alaskan Native only	69.1	24.6	0.8	12.0	11.7
Hispanic or Latino and other race	12.5	3.5	. . .	1.7	1.7
Multi-race	13.1	3.3	. . .	0.7	2.5
Not reported	4 004.6	869.2	84.8	304.6	479.8

[1]Days-away-from-work cases include those which result in days away from work with or without restricted work activity.
[2]Exclude farms with fewer than 11 employees.
[3]Data for Mining (Sector 21 in the North American Industry Classification System–United States, 2002) include establishments not governed by the Mine Safety and Health Administration (MSHA) rules and reporting, such as those in oil and gas extraction and related support activities. Data for mining operators in coal, metal, and nonmetal mining are provided to the Bureau of Labor Statistics (BLS) by MSHA, U.S. Department of Labor. Independent mining contractors are excluded from the coal, metal, and nonmetal mining industries. These data do not reflect the changes the Occupational Safety and Health Administration (OSHA) made to its recordkeeping requirements effective January 1, 2002; therefore, estimates for these industries are not comparable to estimates in other industries.
[4]Information is not shown separately for injured workers under age 14; they accounted for fewer than 50 cases.
. . . = Not available.

Table 9-2. Number of Nonfatal Occupational Injuries and Illnesses Involving Days Away from Work [1] by Selected Worker Characteristics and Industry Division, Private Industry, 2003—*Continued*

(Numbers in thousands.)

Characteristic	Total service-providing	Service-providing						
		Trade, transportation, and utilities [5]	Information	Financial activities	Professional and business services	Educational and health services	Leisure and hospitality	Other services
TOTAL CASES	9 083.1	4 053.0	215.5	403.7	1 025.0	1 997.7	1 057.3	331.0
Sex								
Men	5 052.7	2 869.8	144.1	225.9	683.6	402.3	494.0	233.1
Women	3 981.6	1 135.7	71.4	177.8	340.8	1 595.0	563.1	97.8
Age [4]								
14 to 15 years	2.0	0.6	. . .	. . .	. . .	. . .	0.7	. . .
16 to 19 years	343.3	141.9	2.6	7.0	25.6	39.5	115.4	11.2
20 to 24 years	1 008.8	444.2	14.6	37.1	121.3	182.0	171.4	38.1
25 to 34 years	2 096.9	919.1	55.4	86.3	265.5	457.3	241.7	71.6
35 to 44 years	2 404.6	1 101.9	57.4	105.9	279.6	520.6	243.7	95.6
45 to 54 years	1 938.8	880.0	51.2	92.6	205.5	472.7	172.4	64.4
55 to 64 years	943.9	415.9	24.8	55.0	91.8	240.5	81.7	34.2
65 and over	201.7	87.5	2.0	16.1	18.8	46.4	22.5	8.4
Length of Service With Employer								
Less than 3 months	1 030.3	442.0	8.0	33.5	136.5	175.7	186.5	48.0
3 to 11 months	1 894.6	780.7	17.7	89.7	230.1	439.0	265.9	71.6
1 to 5 years	3 444.1	1 459.9	90.5	162.2	396.2	800.8	411.5	123.0
More than 5 years	2 631.0	1 307.2	98.9	117.9	254.8	575.1	189.6	87.6
Race or Ethnic Origin								
White only	3 985.7	1 735.8	80.0	178.4	486.5	920.7	419.7	164.5
Black only	840.5	278.5	13.3	42.1	99.1	285.9	93.4	28.1
Hispanic or Latino only	911.7	339.1	11.9	44.2	153.2	143.7	174.8	44.7
Asian only	109.7	34.3	1.3	4.3	14.3	30.8	21.3	3.4
Native Hawaiian or Pacific Islander only	37.7	11.1	0.8	2.3	3.0	9.9	9.2	1.6
American Indian or Alaskan Native only	44.5	21.8	0.6	3.5	5.4	8.8	2.8	1.6
Hispanic or Latino and other race	9.0	4.8	. . .	. . .	0.8	1.6	1.5	. . .
Multi-race	9.9	4.7	. . .	. . .	0.9	2.0	1.7	. . .
Not reported	3 135.4	1 622.7	107.4	128.5	262.2	594.3	333.5	86.7

Note: Because of rounding and nonclassifiable responses, components may not add to totals.

[1]Days-away-from-work cases include those which result in days away from work with or without restricted work activity.
[4]Information is not shown separately for injured workers under age 14; they accounted for fewer than 50 cases.
[5]Data for employers in railroad transportation are provided to BLS by the Federal Railroad Administration (FRA), U.S. Department of Transportation. These data do not reflect the changes OSHA made to its recordkeeping requirements effective January 1, 2002; therefore, estimates for these industries are not comparable with estimates for other industries.
. . . = Not available.

Table 9-3. Number and Percent Distribution of Nonfatal Occupational Injuries and Illnesses Involving Days Away from Work[1] by Selected Occupation and Number of Days Away from Work, Private Industry, 2003

(Number, percent.)

Occupation	Total cases	Total percent of cases	Percent of days-away-from-work-cases involving							Median days away from work
			1 day	2 days	3 to 5 days	6 to 10 days	11 to 20 days	21 to 30 days	31 days and over	
Total	1 315 920	100.0	14.3	11.1	18.0	12.4	11.3	6.8	26.2	8
Labor and freight, stock, and material movers, hand	89 510	100.0	13.8	11.2	17.7	13.3	10.9	7.2	25.9	8
Truck drivers, heavy and tractor trailer	71 900	100.0	8.6	8.3	17.3	11.0	12.1	8.7	34.1	14
Nursing aides, orderlies, and attendants	56 820	100.0	14.9	15.2	21.2	14.9	11.0	5.1	17.7	5
Construction laborers	41 620	100.0	12.5	11.3	17.4	11.1	10.5	7.9	29.5	9
Janitors and cleaners, except maids and housekeeping cleaners	35 660	100.0	15.0	11.4	19.3	11.2	10.5	7.5	25.0	7
Retail salespersons	35 420	100.0	14.2	11.4	21.4	13.0	10.2	5.7	24.1	7
Truck drivers, light or delivery services	33 280	100.0	11.1	7.9	15.5	13.1	13.9	7.2	31.3	11
Carpenters	29 480	100.0	13.1	11.0	18.5	11.7	8.5	6.1	31.1	8
Stock clerks and order fillers	26 520	100.0	15.5	11.1	20.7	12.3	12.6	6.6	21.3	7
Registered nurses	20 650	100.0	15.0	12.5	20.1	14.7	10.8	6.7	20.1	6
Maids and housekeeping cleaners	20 410	100.0	11.4	13.5	19.9	14.1	9.8	8.2	23.2	7
Maintenance and repair workers, general	20 350	100.0	14.8	10.0	18.3	11.8	11.0	5.9	28.1	8
Automotive service technicians and mechanics	17 240	100.0	17.9	9.8	18.2	10.4	11.8	8.7	23.1	7
Cashiers	16 990	100.0	12.0	15.4	16.7	11.9	13.1	8.8	22.2	7
First line supervisors/managers of retail sales work	16 900	100.0	13.2	14.4	18.6	14.5	8.5	5.0	25.8	6
Combined food preparation and service workers, including fast food	15 970	100.0	20.7	12.0	20.8	15.3	7.1	5.4	18.7	5
Customer service representatives	12 930	100.0	14.0	10.4	18.1	13.7	13.0	5.6	25.2	8
Waiters and waitresses	11 930	100.0	14.8	9.1	20.3	12.5	8.1	6.8	28.5	7
Cooks, restaurant	11 920	100.0	15.9	15.9	19.0	12.4	13.9	5.1	17.8	5
Landscaping and groundskeeping workers	11 890	100.0	13.6	8.8	22.2	14.6	13.0	6.6	21.1	7
Welders, cutters, solderers, and brazers	11 680	100.0	21.5	11.1	15.3	12.5	10.2	5.1	24.2	6
Industrial machinery mechanics	10 730	100.0	12.1	9.2	15.4	10.7	14.0	8.7	29.7	12
Shipping, receiving, and traffic clerks	10 660	100.0	15.9	12.2	16.7	10.6	13.7	7.7	23.3	7
Electricians	10 650	100.0	15.3	11.9	15.5	9.8	13.2	7.0	27.2	10
Plumbers, pipefitters, and steamfitters	10 570	100.0	19.1	6.5	17.4	9.8	10.3	8.2	28.6	8

Note: Due to rounding and nonclassifiable responses, percentages may not add to 100.

[1]Days-away-from-work cases include those which result in days away from work with or without restricted work activity.

Table 9-4. Fatal Occupational Injuries by Selected Worker Characteristics and Selected Event or Exposure, 2004

(Number, percent.)

Characteristics	Fatalities		Selected event or exposure [1] (percent of total for characteristic category)			
	Number	Percent	Highway [2]	Homicides	Falls	Struck by object
TOTAL	5 703	100	24	10	14	10
Employee Status						
Wage and salary workers [3]	4 537	80	27	8	14	10
Self-employed [4]	1 166	20	14	14	14	13
Sex And Age						
Men	5 292	93	24	9	15	11
Women	411	7	30	24	9	2
Both Sexes, by Age [5]						
Under 16 years	12	(6)	. . .	. . .	. . .	. . .
16 to 17 years	25	(6)	28	. . .	. . .	. . .
18 to 19 years	102	2	24	8	13	8
20 to 24 years	415	7	23	10	11	10
25 to 34 years	988	17	25	12	10	10
35 to 44 years	1 325	23	25	10	14	10
45 to 54 years	1 370	24	24	9	14	11
55 to 64 years	899	16	25	9	18	10
65 and over	563	10	18	8	21	15
Race or Ethnic Origin [7]						
White	4 030	71	25	7	14	11
Black	542	10	26	22	12	8
Hispanic	883	15	21	9	19	13
American Indian or Alaskan Native	26	(6)	31	. . .	19	12
Asian	165	3	12	36	6	3
Native Hawaiian or Pacific Islander	12	(6)	. . .	33	. . .	. . .
Multiple races	4	(6)	. . .	. . .	. . .	. . .
Other or not reported	41	1	17	15	22	10

Note: Totals for 2004 are preliminary. Totals for major categories may include subcategories not shown separately. Percentages may not add to totals because of rounding.

[1]The figure shown is the percent of the total fatalities for that demographic group.
[2]"Highway" includes deaths to vehicle occupants resulting from traffic incidents that occur on the public roadway, shoulder, or surrounding area. It excludes incidents occurring entirely off the roadway, such as in parking lots and on farms. "Nonhighway" includes transport related deaths of vehicle occupants that occur or originate entirely off the road. Incidents involving trains, and deaths to pedestrians or other non-passengers, are excluded from both categories.
[3]May include volunteers and other workers receiving compensation.
[4]Includes paid and unpaid family workers, and may include owners of incorporated businesses or members of partnerships.
[5]There were three fatalities for which there was insufficient information to determine the age of the decedent.
[6]Less than or equal to 0.5 percent.
[7]Persons identified as Hispanic may be of any race. The individual racial categories shown exclude data for Hispanics.
. . . = Not available.

Table 9-5. Fatal Occupational Injuries by Occupation and Selected Event or Exposure, 2004

(Number, percent.)

Occupation [1]	Fatalities		Selected event or exposure [2] (percent of total for characteristic category)			
	Number	Percent	Highway [3]	Homicide	Falls	Struck by object
Total	5 703	100	24	10	14	10
Management occupations	629	11	17	9	10	12
Top executives	27	(4)	30	. . .	11	. . .
Advertising, marketing, promotions, public relations, and sales managers	19	(4)	47	16	. . .	. . .
Operations specialties managers	43	1	30	23	16	. . .
Other management occupations	540	9	14	8	10	14
Business and financial operations occupations	27	(4)	48	15	. . .	. . .
Business operations specialists	18	(4)	61	17	. . .	. . .
Financial specialists	9	(4)	. . .	. . .	. . .	. . .
Computer and mathematical occupations	7	(4)	57	. . .	. . .	. . .
Computer specialists	7	(4)	57	. . .	. . .	. . .
Architecture and engineering occupations	68	1	28	. . .	7	. . .
Architects, surveyors, and cartographers	6	(4)	. . .	. . .	. . .	. . .
Engineers	36	1	31	. . .	. . .	. . .
Drafters, engineering, and mapping technicians	26	(4)	23	. . .	12	. . .
Life, physical, and social science occupations	25	(4)	32	. . .	. . .	. . .
Life scientists	11	(4)	27	. . .	. . .	. . .
Physical scientists	4	(4)	. . .	. . .	. . .	. . .
Life, physical, and social science technicians	8	(4)	38	. . .	. . .	. . .
Community and social services occupations	44	1	36	25	14	. . .
Counselors, social workers, and other community and social service specialists	21	(4)	52	33	. . .	. . .
Religious workers	23	(4)	22	17	22	. . .
Legal occupations	3	(4)	. . .	. . .	. . .	. . .
Lawyers, judges, and related workers	3	(4)	. . .	. . .	. . .	. . .
Education, training, and library occupations	27	(4)	30	. . .	19	. . .
Postsecondary teachers	7	(4)	. . .	. . .	. . .	. . .
Primary, secondary, and special education school teachers	12	(4)	42	. . .	. . .	. . .
Other teachers and instructors	3	(4)	. . .	. . .	. . .	. . .
Other education, training, and library occupations	4	(4)	. . .	. . .	. . .	. . .
Arts, design, entertainment, sports, and media occupations	51	1	20	16	14	6
Art and design workers	8	(4)	. . .	. . .	. . .	. . .
Entertainers and performers, sports and related workers	32	1	16	12	19	9
Media and communication workers	9	(4)	. . .	33	. . .	. . .
Health care practitioners and technical occupations	72	1	26	12	7	. . .
Health diagnosing and treating practitioners	40	1	30	12	8	. . .
Health technologists and technicians	31	1	23	13	. . .	. . .
Health care support occupations	11	(4)	. . .	27	. . .	. . .
Nursing, psychiatric, and home health aides	8	(4)	. . .	. . .	. . .	. . .
Other healthcare support occupations	3	(4)	. . .	. . .	. . .	. . .
Protective service occupations	271	5	31	31	4	3
First-line supervisors, managers, and protective service workers	24	(4)	50	21	. . .	. . .
Firefighting and prevention workers	30	1	37	. . .	. . .	. . .
Law enforcement workers	136	2	41	33	3	. . .
Other protective service workers	81	1	6	38	7	4
Food preparation and serving related occupations	52	1	. . .	65	10	. . .
Supervisors, food preparation and serving workers	10	(4)	. . .	90	. . .	. . .
Cooks and food preparation workers	10	(4)	. . .	40	. . .	. . .
Food and beverage serving workers	27	(4)	. . .	63	15	. . .
Other food preparation and serving related workers	5	(4)	. . .	80	. . .	. . .
Building and grounds cleaning and maintenance occupations	277	5	13	6	25	15
Supervisors, building and grounds cleaning and maintenance workers	43	1	19	. . .	19	30
Building cleaning and pest control workers	66	1	11	18	27	5
Grounds maintenance workers	168	3	12	. . .	25	15
Personal care and service occupations	55	1	15	25	. . .	. . .
Supervisors, personal care and service workers	6	(4)	. . .	67	. . .	. . .
Animal care and service workers	11	(4)	. . .	. . .	. . .	. . .
Entertainment attendants and related workers	7	(4)	. . .	. . .	. . .	. . .
Personal appearance workers	7	(4)	. . .	86	. . .	. . .
Transportation, tourism, and lodging attendants	7	(4)	. . .	. . .	. . .	. . .
Other personal care and service workers	16	(4)	25	19	. . .	. . .
Sales and related occupations	352	6	21	47	8	2
Supervisors, sales workers	156	3	6	58	10	4
Retail sales workers	101	2	10	63	8	. . .

[1]Based on the 2000 Standard Occupational Classification System.
[2]The figure shown is the percentage of the total fatalities for that occupation group.
[3]"Highway" includes deaths to vehicle occupants resulting from traffic incidents that occur on the public roadway, shoulder, or surrounding area. It excludes incidents occurring entirely off the roadway, such as in parking lots and on farms; incidents involving trains; and deaths to pedestrians or other nonpassengers.
[4]Less than or equal to 0.5 percent.
. . . = Not available.

Table 9-5. Fatal Occupational Injuries by Occupation and Selected Event or Exposure, 2004—*Continued*

(Number, percent.)

Occupation [1]	Fatalities		Selected event or exposure [2] (percent of total for characteristic category)			
	Number	Percent	Highway [3]	Homicide	Falls	Struck by object
Supervisors, sales workers	156	3	6	58	10	4
Retail sales workers	101	2	10	63	8	. . .
Sales representatives, services	21	(4)	57	. . .	. . .	. . .
Sales representatives, wholesale and manufacturing	34	1	74	. . .	. . .	. . .
Other sales and related workers	40	1	45	20	. . .	. . .
Office and administrative support occupations	91	2	40	21	9	4
Supervisors, office and administrative support	4	(4)	. . .	75	. . .	. . .
Financial clerks	8	(4)	. . .	50	. . .	. . .
Information and record clerks	9	(4)	33	44	. . .	. . .
Material recording, scheduling, dispatching, and distributing workers ...	50	1	52	6	10	6
Secretaries and administrative assistants	6	(4)	. . .	67	. . .	. . .
Other office and administrative support workers	14	(4)	29	. . .	. . .	. . .
Farming, fishing, and forestry occupations	281	5	17	1	4	26
Supervisors, farming, fishing, and forestry workers	11	(4)	36	. . .	. . .	. . .
Agricultural workers	143	3	22	2	6	8
Fishing and hunting workers	38	1	. . .	. . .	. . .	. . .
Forest, conservation, and logging workers	89	2	13	. . .	. . .	66
Construction and extraction occupations	1 129	20	10	2	36	12
Supervisors, construction and extraction workers	116	2	17	. . .	28	12
Construction trades workers	870	15	8	2	41	11
Helpers, construction trades	21	(4)	. . .	. . .	19	. . .
Other construction and related workers	45	1	13	. . .	18	. . .
Extraction workers	77	1	13	. . .	12	22
Installation, maintenance, and repair occupations	382	7	10	5	18	17
Supervisors of installation, maintenance and repair	43	1	7	14	19	21
Electrical and electronic equipment mechanics, installers, and repairers ...	13	(4)	. . .	. . .	23	. . .
Vehicle and mobile equipment mechanics, installers, and repairers ...	120	2	9	8	5	31
Other installation, maintenance, and repair occupations	206	4	12	. . .	25	9
Production occupations	288	5	7	5	11	15
Supervisors, production workers	37	1	11	8	11	14
Assemblers and fabricators	19	(4)	. . .	. . .	21	21
Food processing workers	13	(4)	. . .	. . .	. . .	. . .
Metal workers and plastic workers	84	1	5	4	11	26
Printing workers	4	. . .	. . .	. . .	. . .	. . .
Textile, apparel, and furnishings workers	7	(4)	. . .	. . .	. . .	. . .
Woodworkers	15	(4)	. . .	. . .	. . .	27
Plant and system operators	14	(4)	. . .	. . .	. . .	. . .
Other production occupations	95	2	8	4	12	9
Transportation and material moving occupations	1 490	26	47	5	5	9
Supervisors, transportation and material moving occupations	24	(4)	17	. . .	12	. . .
Air transportation workers	109	2	. . .	. . .	. . .	. . .
Motor vehicle operators	1 005	18	65	6	4	8
Rail transportation workers	21	(4)	. . .	. . .	. . .	. . .
Water transportation workers	45	1	. . .	. . .	. . .	. . .
Other transportation workers	15	(4)	. . .	33	. . .	. . .
Material moving workers	271	5	11	3	11	17
Military occupations	64	1	19	. . .	. . .	5

Note: Totals for major categories may include subcategories not shown separately. Percentages may not add to totals because of rounding.

[1] Based on the 2000 Standard Occupational Classification System.
[2] The figure shown is the percentage of the total fatalities for that occupation group.
[3] "Highway" includes deaths to vehicle occupants resulting from traffic incidents that occur on the public roadway, shoulder, or surrounding area. It excludes incidents occurring entirely off the roadway, such as in parking lots and on farms; incidents involving trains; and deaths to pedestrians or other nonpassengers.
[4] Less than or equal to 0.5 percent.
. . . = Not available.

PART TEN

LABOR MANAGEMENT RELATIONS

LABOR MANAGEMENT RELATIONS

HIGHLIGHTS

This part contains information on historical trends in union membership and earnings and work stoppages.

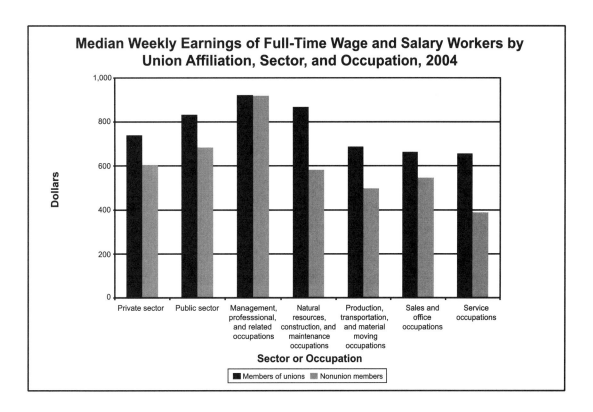

In both the public and private sector, the median weekly earnings of workers represented by unions were approximately 22 percent higher than those of non-union workers. In service occupations, the gap was significantly larger at 66 percent. However, in management, professional, and related occupations, the median weekly earnings were virtually the same, regardless of union status. (Table 10-4)

OTHER HIGHLIGHTS:

• The percentage of employed workers who were union members continued to decline, falling from 12.9 percent in 2003 to 12.5 percent in 2004. (Table 10-2)

• Unions represented 40.7 percent of public service workers in 2004, the highest percentage of representation in any industry. Within the public sector, unions represented 35 percent of federal workers, 34.3 percent of state employees, and 45.8 percent of local government workers. (Table 10-3)

• In 2004, education, training, and library occupations had the highest proportion of employees represented by unions with 42.4 percent. Protective service occupations followed with 39.4 percent. These occupations account for the high union representation in local government. (Table 10-3)

• Six states had at least 20 percent of their workers represented by unions in 2004. New York had the highest with 26.4 percent, followed by Hawaii (24.8 percent), Alaska (22.4 percent), Michigan (22.4 percent), New Jersey (21.6 percent), and Washington (20.3 percent). (Table 10-6)

NOTES AND DEFINITIONS

WORK STOPPAGES

Collection and Coverage

Data on work stoppages measure the number and duration of major strikes or lockouts (involving 1,000 workers or more) during the year, the number of workers involved, and the amount of work time lost due to stoppages.

Data are largely from newspaper accounts and cover only those establishments directly involved in a stoppage. They do not measure the indirect or secondary effect of stoppages on other establishments whose employees are idle from material shortages or lack of service.

The current series is not comparable with the one terminated in 1981, which covered strikes involving six workers or more.

Concepts and Definitions

Stoppages are strikes and lockouts involving 1,000 workers or more and lasting a full shift or longer.

Workers involved are workers directly involved in the stoppage.

Number of days idle is the aggregate number of workdays lost by workers involved in the stoppages.

Days of idleness as a percent of estimated working time are the aggregate workdays lost as a percent of the aggregate number of standard workdays during the period multiplied by total employment (excluding forestry, fisheries, and private household workers) during the period.

Sources of Additional Information

Additional information is available in BLS news release USDL 05-598.

UNION MEMBERSHIP

Collection, Coverage, and Definitions

The estimates of union membership are obtained from the Current Population Survey (CPS). The union membership and earnings data are tabulated from one-quarter of the CPS monthly sample and are limited to wage and salary workers. Excluded are all self-employed workers.

Union members are members of a labor union or an employee association similar to a union.

Represented by unions refers to union members, as well as workers who have no union affiliation but whose jobs are covered by a union contract.

Sources of Additional Information

Additional information is available in BLS news release USDL 05-112, *Union Membership (Annual)*.

Table 10-1. Work Stoppages Involving 1,000 Workers or More, 1947–2004

(Number, percent.)

Year	Stoppages beginning in the year [1]		Days idle during the year [2]	
	Number	Workers involved (thousands)	Number (thousands)	Percent of estimated total working time [3]
1947	270	1 629	25 720	. . .
1948	245	1 435	26 127	0.22
1949	262	2 537	43 420	0.38
1950	424	1 698	30 390	0.26
1951	415	1 462	15 070	0.12
1952	470	2 746	48 820	0.38
1953	437	1 623	18 130	0.14
1954	265	1 075	16 630	0.13
1955	363	2 055	21 180	0.16
1956	287	1 370	26 840	0.20
1957	279	887	10 340	0.07
1958	332	1 587	17 900	0.13
1959	245	1 381	60 850	0.43
1960	222	896	13 260	0.09
1961	195	1 031	10 140	0.07
1962	211	793	11 760	0.08
1963	181	512	10 020	0.07
1964	246	1 183	16 220	0.11
1965	268	999	15 140	0.10
1966	321	1 300	16 000	0.10
1967	381	2 192	31 320	0.18
1968	392	1 855	35 367	0.20
1969	412	1 576	29 397	0.16
1970	381	2 468	52 761	0.29
1971	298	2 516	35 538	0.19
1972	250	975	16 764	0.09
1973	317	1 400	16 260	0.08
1974	424	1 796	31 809	0.16
1975	235	965	17 563	0.09
1976	231	1 519	23 962	0.12
1977	298	1 212	21 258	0.10
1978	219	1 006	23 774	0.11
1979	235	1 021	20 409	0.09
1980	187	795	20 844	0.09
1981	145	729	16 908	0.07
1982	96	656	9 061	0.04
1983	81	909	17 461	0.08
1984	62	376	8 499	0.04
1985	54	324	7 079	0.03
1986	69	533	11 861	0.05
1987	46	174	4 481	0.02
1988	40	118	4 381	0.02
1989	51	452	16 996	0.07
1990	44	185	5 926	0.02
1991	40	392	4 584	0.02
1992	35	364	3 989	0.01
1993	35	182	3 981	0.01
1994	45	322	5 021	0.02
1995	31	192	5 771	0.02
1996	37	273	4 889	0.02
1997	29	339	4 497	0.01
1998	34	387	5 116	0.02
1999	17	73	1 996	0.01
2000	39	394	20 419	0.06
2001	29	99	1 151	(4)
2002	19	46	660	(4)
2003	14	129	4 091	0.01
2004	17	171	3 344	0.01

[1]Workers are counted more than once if they are involved in more than one stoppage during the reference period.
[2]Days idle include all stoppages in effect during the reference period. For work stoppages that are still ongoing at the end of the calendar year, only those days of idleness in the calendar year are counted.
[3]Agricultural and government workers are included in the calculation of estimated working time; private households, forestry, and fishery employees are excluded.
[4]Less than .005 percent.
. . . = Not available.

Table 10-2. Union Affiliation of Employed Wage and Salary Workers by Selected Characteristics, 1999–2004

(Numbers in thousands, percent.)

Characteristics	1999					2000					2001				
	Total em-ployed	Members of unions [1]		Represented by unions [2]		Total em-ployed	Members of unions [1]		Represented by unions [2]		Total em-ployed	Members of unions [1]		Represented by unions [2]	
		Total	Percent em-ployed	Total	Percent em-ployed		Total	Percent em-ployed	Total	Percent em-ployed		Total	Percent em-ployed	Total	Percent em-ployed
SEX AND AGE															
Total, 16 Years and Over	118 963	16 477	13.9	18 182	15.3	120 786	16 258	13.5	17 944	14.9	122 482	16 387	13.4	18 114	14.8
16 to 24 years	19 606	1 110	5.7	1 239	6.3	20 166	1 010	5.0	1 152	5.7	19 698	1 015	5.2	1 184	6.0
25 years and over	99 358	15 367	15.5	16 943	17.1	100 620	15 248	15.2	16 792	16.7	102 784	15 372	15.0	16 930	16.5
25 to 34 years	28 657	3 415	11.9	3 785	13.2	28 406	3 369	11.9	3 720	13.1	28 809	3 264	11.3	3 659	12.7
35 to 44 years	32 438	4 918	15.2	5 428	16.7	32 470	4 822	14.9	5 293	16.3	31 962	4 733	14.8	5 191	16.2
45 to 54 years	24 665	4 881	19.8	5 377	21.8	25 651	4 815	18.8	5 305	20.7	26 909	5 068	18.8	5 543	20.6
55 to 64 years	10 880	1 932	17.8	2 107	19.4	11 204	1 998	17.8	2 193	19.6	12 032	2 063	17.1	2 265	18.8
65 years and over	2 718	221	8.1	247	9.1	2 889	243	8.4	281	9.7	3 072	243	7.9	272	8.9
Men, 16 Years and Over	61 914	9 949	16.1	10 758	17.4	62 853	9 578	15.2	10 355	16.5	63 756	9 578	15.0	10 410	16.3
16 to 24 years	10 116	716	7.1	781	7.7	10 440	618	5.9	697	6.7	10 137	607	6.0	704	6.9
25 years and over	51 797	9 232	17.8	9 977	19.3	52 412	8 960	17.1	9 657	18.4	53 619	8 971	16.7	9 706	18.1
25 to 34 years	15 330	2 142	14.0	2 325	15.2	15 197	2 030	13.4	2 207	14.5	15 627	1 983	12.7	2 169	13.9
35 to 44 years	17 020	2 993	17.6	3 241	19.0	17 028	2 871	16.9	3 077	18.1	16 657	2 821	16.9	3 028	18.2
45 to 54 years	12 395	2 800	22.6	3 026	24.4	12 898	2 739	21.2	2 956	22.9	13 561	2 840	20.9	3 070	22.6
55 to 64 years	5 622	1 186	21.1	1 267	22.5	5 770	1 191	20.6	1 268	22.0	6 168	1 195	19.4	1 292	20.9
65 years and over	1 431	111	7.7	118	8.2	1 519	129	8.5	148	9.8	1 605	131	8.1	148	9.2
Women, 16 Years and Over	57 050	6 528	11.4	7 425	13.0	57 933	6 680	11.5	7 590	13.1	58 726	6 809	11.6	7 704	13.1
16 to 24 years	9 489	393	4.1	458	4.8	9 726	392	4.0	455	4.7	9 561	409	4.3	480	5.0
25 years and over	47 560	6 135	12.9	6 966	14.6	48 207	6 288	13.0	7 135	14.8	49 166	6 400	13.0	7 224	14.7
25 to 34 years	13 327	1 273	9.6	1 460	11.0	13 209	1 340	10.1	1 513	11.5	13 181	1 281	9.7	1 490	11.3
35 to 44 years	15 418	1 924	12.5	2 187	14.2	15 441	1 951	12.6	2 215	14.3	15 305	1 912	12.5	2 163	14.1
45 to 54 years	12 270	2 081	17.0	2 351	19.2	12 752	2 077	16.3	2 348	18.4	13 349	2 227	16.7	2 474	18.5
55 to 64 years	5 258	746	14.2	839	16.0	5 434	807	14.9	925	17.0	5 864	868	14.8	973	16.6
65 years and over	1 287	110	8.5	129	10.0	1 370	114	8.3	133	9.7	1 467	113	7.7	124	8.5
RACE, HISPANIC ORIGIN, AND SEX															
White, 16 Years and Over [3]	99 147	13 349	13.5	14 668	14.8	100 455	13 094	13.0	14 453	14.4	101 546	13 209	13.0	14 574	14.4
Men	52 492	8 246	15.7	8 896	16.9	53 105	7 911	14.9	8 541	16.1	53 731	7 909	14.7	8 585	16.0
Women	46 655	5 103	10.9	5 771	12.4	47 350	5 183	10.9	5 912	12.5	47 815	5 300	11.1	5 989	12.5
Black, 16 Years and Over [3]	14 346	2 463	17.2	2 757	19.2	14 544	2 489	17.1	2 744	18.9	14 261	2 409	16.9	2 668	18.7
Men	6 585	1 348	20.5	1 464	22.2	6 701	1 282	19.1	1 388	20.7	6 488	1 221	18.8	1 330	20.5
Women	7 760	1 116	14.4	1 293	16.7	7 843	1 208	15.4	1 356	17.3	7 773	1 188	15.3	1 338	17.2
Asian, 16 Years and Over [3]	...	...	...	...	...	...	...	...	...	...	...	...	...	...	...
Men	...	...	...	...	...	...	...	...	...	...	...	...	...	...	...
Women	...	...	...	...	...	...	...	...	...	...	...	...	...	...	...
Hispanic, 16 Years and Over	12 810	1 525	11.9	1 684	13.1	13 609	1 554	11.4	1 740	12.8	15 174	1 679	11.1	1 876	12.4
Men	7 457	966	13.0	1 052	14.1	7 884	972	12.3	1 063	13.5	8 997	1 032	11.5	1 136	12.6
Women	5 353	559	10.4	632	11.8	5 725	582	10.2	677	11.8	6 177	647	10.5	740	12.0
FULL- OR PART-TIME STATUS [4]															
Full-Time Workers	97 626	14 974	15.3	16 501	16.9	99 917	14 822	14.8	16 306	16.3	101 187	14 921	14.7	16 445	16.3
Part-Time Workers	21 065	1 459	6.9	1 634	7.8	20 619	1 395	6.8	1 593	7.7	21 057	1 437	6.8	1 637	7.8

[1]Data refer to members of a labor union or to an employee association similar to a union.
[2]Data refer to members of a labor union or to an employee association similar to a union, as well as to workers who report no union affiliation but whose jobs are covered by a union or an employee association contract.
[3]Beginning in 2003, persons who selected this race group only; persons who selected more than one race group are not included. Prior to 2003, persons who reported more than one race group were included in the group they identified as their main race.
[4]The distinction between full- and part-time workers is based on hours usually worked. Data will not sum to totals because full- or part-time status on the principal job is not identifiable for a small number of multiple jobholders.
. . . = Not available.

Table 10-2. Union Affiliation of Employed Wage and Salary Workers by Selected Characteristics, 1999–2004—*Continued*

(Numbers in thousands, percent.)

Characteristics	2002					2003					2004				
	Total em-ployed	Members of unions [1]		Represented by unions [2]		Total em-ployed	Members of unions [1]		Represented by unions [2]		Total em-ployed	Members of unions [1]		Represented by unions [2]	
		Total	Percent em-ployed	Total	Percent em-ployed		Total	Percent em-ployed	Total	Percent em-ployed		Total	Percent em-ployed	Total	Percent em-ployed
SEX AND AGE															
Total, 16 Years and Over	121 826	16 145	13.3	17 695	14.5	122 358	15 776	12.9	17 448	14.3	123 554	15 472	12.5	17 087	13.8
16 to 24 years	19 216	995	5.2	1 126	5.9	18 904	966	5.1	1 124	5.9	19 109	890	4.7	1 019	5.3
25 years and over	102 610	15 151	14.8	16 569	16.1	103 454	14 810	14.3	16 324	15.8	104 444	14 581	14.0	16 069	15.4
25 to 34 years	28 232	3 172	11.2	3 522	12.5	28 179	3 097	11.0	3 455	12.3	28 202	2 982	10.6	3 316	11.8
35 to 44 years	31 253	4 455	14.3	4 859	15.5	30 714	4 308	14.0	4 717	15.4	30 470	4 173	13.7	4 590	15.1
45 to 54 years	27 040	5 016	18.6	5 446	20.1	27 567	4 848	17.6	5 307	19.3	28 039	4 771	17.0	5 233	18.7
55 to 64 years	12 952	2 256	17.4	2 456	19.0	13 633	2 300	16.9	2 547	18.7	14 239	2 390	16.8	2 617	18.4
65 years and over	3 133	251	8.0	285	9.1	3 361	258	7.7	297	8.8	3 495	264	7.5	314	9.0
Men, 16 Years and Over	63 272	9 325	14.7	10 066	15.9	63 236	9 044	14.3	9 848	15.6	64 145	8 878	13.8	9 638	15.0
16 to 24 years	9 857	616	6.3	687	7.0	9 683	595	6.1	685	7.1	9 835	557	5.7	627	6.4
25 years and over	53 415	8 709	16.3	9 379	17.6	53 553	8 450	15.8	9 163	17.1	54 310	8 321	15.3	9 010	16.6
25 to 34 years	15 284	1 877	12.3	2 061	13.5	15 263	1 826	12.0	2 005	13.1	15 391	1 722	11.2	1 873	12.2
35 to 44 years	16 355	2 631	16.1	2 805	17.1	16 080	2 535	15.8	2 735	17.0	16 035	2 449	15.3	2 658	16.6
45 to 54 years	13 578	2 784	20.5	2 982	22.0	13 723	2 684	19.6	2 891	21.1	14 026	2 699	19.2	2 903	20.7
55 to 64 years	6 570	1 281	19.5	1 376	21.0	6 776	1 271	18.8	1 377	20.3	7 117	1 309	18.4	1 414	19.9
65 years and over	1 627	136	8.4	155	9.5	1 710	133	7.8	155	9.0	1 741	142	8.2	163	9.4
Women, 16 Years and Over	58 555	6 820	11.6	7 629	13.0	59 122	6 732	11.4	7 601	12.9	59 408	6 593	11.1	7 450	12.5
16 to 24 years	9 359	378	4.0	439	4.7	9 221	371	4.0	439	4.8	9 274	333	3.6	391	4.2
25 years and over	49 196	6 441	13.1	7 190	14.6	49 901	6 360	12.7	7 161	14.4	50 134	6 260	12.5	7 058	14.1
25 to 34 years	12 948	1 295	10.0	1 461	11.3	12 916	1 270	9.8	1 451	11.2	12 811	1 261	9.8	1 443	11.3
35 to 44 years	14 898	1 825	12.2	2 055	13.8	14 634	1 773	12.1	1 982	13.5	14 435	1 725	11.9	1 931	13.4
45 to 54 years	13 462	2 232	16.6	2 464	18.3	13 844	2 163	15.6	2 416	17.5	14 014	2 072	14.8	2 330	16.6
55 to 64 years	6 383	975	15.3	1 080	16.9	6 857	1 029	15.0	1 170	17.1	7 122	1 081	15.2	1 203	16.9
65 years and over	1 506	115	7.6	130	8.6	1 651	125	7.6	142	8.6	1 753	121	6.9	151	8.6
RACE, HISPANIC ORIGIN, AND SEX															
White, 16 Years and Over [3]	100 923	12 958	12.8	14 178	14.0	100 589	12 535	12.5	13 849	13.8	101 340	12 381	12.2	13 657	13.5
Men	53 198	7 689	14.5	8 284	15.6	52 827	7 378	14.0	8 016	15.2	53 432	7 260	13.6	7 854	14.7
Women	47 725	5 269	11.0	5 894	12.3	47 762	5 157	10.8	5 834	12.2	47 908	5 121	10.7	5 803	12.1
Black, 16 Years and Over [3]	14 108	2 386	16.9	2 624	18.6	13 928	2 298	16.5	2 540	18.2	14 090	2 130	15.1	2 355	16.7
Men	6 493	1 183	18.2	1 281	19.7	6 302	1 153	18.3	1 249	19.8	6 409	1 085	16.9	1 185	18.5
Women	7 615	1 204	15.8	1 343	17.6	7 626	1 145	15.0	1 291	16.9	7 681	1 045	13.6	1 170	15.2
Asian, 16 Years and Over [3]	...	...	...	...	...	5 096	581	11.4	659	12.9	5 280	603	11.4	670	12.7
Men	...	...	...	...	...	2 699	296	11.0	346	12.8	2 815	328	11.7	371	13.2
Women	...	...	...	...	...	2 397	285	11.9	313	13.1	2 465	275	11.1	299	12.1
Hispanic, 16 Years and Over	15 486	1 639	10.6	1 810	11.7	16 068	1 712	10.7	1 913	11.9	16 533	1 676	10.1	1 888	11.4
Men	9 098	1 006	11.1	1 100	12.1	9 567	1 050	11.0	1 160	12.1	9 857	1 016	10.3	1 130	11.5
Women	6 387	633	9.9	710	11.1	6 501	662	10.2	753	11.6	6 676	661	9.9	758	11.4
FULL- OR PART-TIME STATUS [4]															
Full-Time Workers	100 081	14 622	14.6	16 005	16.0	100 302	14 263	14.2	15 732	15.7	101 224	14 029	13.9	15 463	15.3
Part-Time Workers	21 513	1 492	6.9	1 654	7.7	21 809	1 479	6.8	1 679	7.7	22 047	1 406	6.4	1 587	7.2

Note: Data for 2003 have been revised to incorporate changes to the class of worker status associated with the introduction of the 2002 Census industry and occupational classication systems into the Current Population Survey. Beginning in January 2003, data reflect revised population controls used in the household survey. Estimates for the above race groups (White and Black) do not sum to totals because data are not presented for all races. In addition, persons whose ethnicity is identified as "Hispanic or Latino" may be of any race and therefore are classified by ethnicity as well as race. Data refer to the sole or principal job of full and part-time workers. Excluded are all self-employed workers, regardless of whether or not their businesses are incorporated.

[1]Data refer to members of a labor union or to an employee association similar to a union.
[2]Data refer to members of a labor union or to an employee association similar to a union, as well as to workers who report no union affiliation but whose jobs are covered by a union or an employee association contract.
[3]Beginning in 2003, persons who selected this race group only; persons who selected more than one race group are not included. Prior to 2003, persons who reported more than one race group were included in the group they identified as their main race.
[4]The distinction between full- and part-time workers is based on hours usually worked. Data will not sum to totals because full- or part-time status on the principal job is not identifiable for a small number of multiple jobholders.
. . . = Not available.

Table 10-3. Union Affiliation of Wage and Salary Workers by Occupation and Industry, 2003–2004

(Thousands of people, percent.)

Characteristics	2003					2004				
	Total employed	Members of unions [1]		Represented by unions [2]		Total employed	Members of unions [1]		Represented by unions [2]	
		Total	Percent of employed	Total	Percent of employed		Total	Percent of employed	Total	Percent of employed
OCCUPATION										
Management, professional, and related occupations	40 883	5 331	13.0	6 130	15.0	41 451	5 418	13.1	6 256	15.1
Management, business, and financial operations	15 465	727	4.7	882	5.7	15 758	732	4.6	895	5.7
Management	10 713	436	4.1	546	5.1	10 796	441	4.1	553	5.1
Business and financial operations	4 753	291	6.1	336	7.1	4 962	291	5.9	342	6.9
Professional and related	25 418	4 604	18.1	5 248	20.6	25 693	4 686	18.2	5 361	20.9
Computer and mathematical	2 947	154	5.2	197	6.7	2 962	128	4.3	171	5.8
Architecture and engineering	2 592	202	7.8	240	9.2	2 597	209	8.0	246	9.5
Life, physical, and social science	1 203	108	9.0	136	11.3	1 204	106	8.8	129	10.7
Community and social services	2 118	351	16.6	395	18.6	2 132	370	17.4	422	19.8
Legal	1 134	54	4.8	65	5.7	1 216	75	6.2	92	7.6
Education, training, and library	7 584	2 861	37.7	3 207	42.3	7 636	2 874	37.6	3 235	42.4
Arts, design, entertainment, sports, and media	1 879	140	7.5	157	8.4	1 894	162	8.6	184	9.7
Healthcare practitioner and technical	5 961	733	12.3	853	14.3	6 052	762	12.6	882	14.6
Service occupations	20 183	2 318	11.5	2 562	12.7	20 724	2 371	11.4	2 552	12.3
Healthcare support	2 824	312	11.0	341	12.1	2 791	290	10.4	315	11.3
Protective service	2 699	974	36.1	1 038	38.5	2 840	1 059	37.3	1 118	39.4
Food preparation and serving related	7 150	292	4.1	347	4.9	7 164	294	4.1	337	4.7
Building and grounds cleaning and maintenance	4 426	490	11.1	550	12.4	4 597	490	10.7	529	11.5
Personal care and service	3 084	251	8.1	286	9.3	3 331	238	7.1	254	7.6
Sales and office	32 323	2 642	8.2	2 974	9.2	32 322	2 493	7.7	2 780	8.6
Sales and related	13 378	533	4.0	599	4.5	13 527	488	3.6	548	4.1
Office and administrative support	18 945	2 109	11.1	2 375	12.5	18 795	2 005	10.7	2 232	11.9
Natural resources, construction, and maintenance	11 894	2 288	19.2	2 409	20.3	12 081	2 222	18.4	2 343	19.4
Farming, fishing, and forestry	921	33	3.5	38	4.1	862	27	3.1	34	3.9
Construction and extraction	6 412	1 394	21.7	1 457	22.7	6 680	1 312	19.6	1 370	20.5
Installation, maintenance, and repair	4 560	862	18.9	913	20.0	4 540	883	19.4	939	20.7
Production, transportation, and material moving	17 074	3 196	18.7	3 374	19.8	16 976	2 968	17.5	3 156	18.6
Production	9 261	1 624	17.5	1 710	18.5	9 085	1 485	16.3	1 582	17.4
Transportation and material moving	7 814	1 572	20.1	1 664	21.3	7 891	1 483	18.8	1 574	20.0
INDUSTRY										
Private sector	102 648	8 452	8.2	9 264	9.0	103 584	8 205	7.9	8 956	8.6
Agriculture and related industries	1 089	17	1.6	23	2.1	1 023	23	2.2	30	2.9
Nonagricultural industries	101 559	8 435	8.3	9 241	9.1	102 560	8 182	8.0	8 926	8.7
Mining	504	46	9.1	53	10.5	496	57	11.4	58	11.7
Construction	7 126	1 139	16.0	1 188	16.7	7 550	1 110	14.7	1 162	15.4
Manufacturing	16 130	2 173	13.5	2 314	14.3	15 754	2 036	12.9	2 183	13.9
Durable goods	10 049	1 411	14.0	1 497	14.9	9 885	1 316	13.3	1 407	14.2
Nondurable goods	6 081	762	12.5	817	13.4	5 869	720	12.3	776	13.2
Wholesale and retail trade	18 343	1 130	6.2	1 210	6.6	18 754	1 028	5.5	1 107	5.9
Wholesale trade	3 878	197	5.1	213	5.5	4 083	189	4.6	214	5.2
Retail trade	14 466	933	6.4	997	6.9	14 671	839	5.7	893	6.1
Transportation and utilities	4 942	1 294	26.2	1 350	27.3	4 893	1 218	24.9	1 287	26.3
Transportation and warehousing	4 081	1 051	25.8	1 094	26.8	4 043	976	24.2	1 031	25.5
Utilities	861	243	28.2	256	29.8	850	241	28.4	256	30.1
Information [3]	3 297	448	13.6	481	14.6	3 058	433	14.2	470	15.4
Publishing, except Internet	781	58	7.4	60	7.7	778	52	6.7	59	7.6
Motion pictures and sound recording	333	40	12.0	46	13.8	329	52	15.7	54	16.4
Broadcasting, except Internet	489	45	9.2	48	9.7	502	47	9.3	53	10.5
Telecommunications	1 414	296	21.0	316	22.3	1 218	273	22.4	292	24.0
Financial activities	8 360	176	2.1	237	2.8	8 490	171	2.0	209	2.5
Finance and insurance	6 246	98	1.6	142	2.3	6 301	96	1.5	124	2.0
Finance	4 079	63	1.5	96	2.3	4 111	56	1.4	73	1.8
Insurance	2 167	35	1.6	47	2.1	2 191	40	1.8	51	2.3
Real estate and rental and leasing	2 114	77	3.7	95	4.5	2 188	76	3.5	85	3.9

[1]Data refer to members of a labor union or an employee association similar to a union.
[2]Data refer to members of a labor union or to an employee association similar to a union, as well as to workers who report no union affiliation but whose jobs are covered by a union or an employee association contract.
[3]Includes other industries, not shown separately.

Table 10-3. Union Affiliation of Wage and Salary Workers by Occupation and Industry, 2003–2004
—Continued

(Thousands of people, percent.)

Characteristics	2003					2004				
	Total employed	Members of unions [1]		Represented by unions [2]		Total employed	Members of unions [1]		Represented by unions [2]	
		Total	Percent of employed	Total	Percent of employed		Total	Percent of employed	Total	Percent of employed
Professional and business services	10 588	243	2.3	312	2.9	10 815	246	2.3	306	2.8
Professional and technical services	6 146	88	1.4	125	2.0	6 263	70	1.1	102	1.6
Management, administrative, and waste services	4 443	155	3.5	187	4.2	4 552	177	3.9	204	4.5
Education and health services	16 635	1 324	8.0	1 560	9.4	16 870	1 405	8.3	1 593	9.4
Educational services	3 062	371	12.1	452	14.8	3 243	421	13.0	475	14.6
Health care and social assistance	13 573	953	7.0	1 108	8.2	13 627	984	7.2	1 119	8.2
Leisure and hospitality	10 207	281	2.8	333	3.3	10 326	319	3.1	368	3.6
Arts, entertainment, and recreation	1 764	95	5.4	111	6.3	1 777	114	6.4	123	6.9
Accommodation and food services	8 443	187	2.2	222	2.6	8 548	205	2.4	245	2.9
Accommodation	1 396	116	8.3	126	9.0	1 431	117	8.2	132	9.2
Food services and drinking places	7 046	70	1.0	96	1.4	7 117	88	1.2	112	1.6
Other services [3]	5 425	181	3.3	203	3.7	5 556	158	2.8	183	3.3
Other services, except private households	4 645	174	3.8	196	4.2	4 782	148	3.1	172	3.6
Public sector	19 710	7 324	37.2	8 185	41.5	19 970	7 267	36.4	8 131	40.7
Federal government	3 247	1 004	30.9	1 196	36.8	3 298	985	29.9	1 153	35.0
State government	5 636	1 706	30.3	1 929	34.2	5 712	1 751	30.7	1 961	34.3
Local government	10 827	4 614	42.6	5 060	46.7	10 961	4 532	41.3	5 017	45.8

Note: Beginning in January 2004, data reflect revised population controls used in the household survey. Data refer to the sole or principal job of full- and part-time workers. Excluded are all self-employed workers regardless of whether or not their businesses are incorporated.

[1] Data refer to members of a labor union or an employee association similar to a union.
[2] Data refer to members of a labor union or to an employee association similar to a union, as well as to workers who report no union affiliation but whose jobs are covered by a union or an employee association contract.
[3] Includes other industries, not shown separately.

Table 10-4. Median Weekly Earnings of Full-Time Wage and Salary Workers by Union Affiliation, Occupation, and Industry, 2003–2004

(Dollars.)

Characteristics	2003				2004			
	Total	Members of unions [1]	Represented by unions [2]	Non-union	Total	Members of unions [1]	Represented by unions [2]	Non-union
OCCUPATION								
Management, professional, and related occupations	887	896	892	886	918	921	916	918
Management, business, and financial operations	961	985	994	959	965	963	972	965
Management	1 023	1 102	1 109	1 019	1 052	1 065	1 074	1 050
Business and financial operations	842	864	873	839	847	880	881	844
Professional and related	845	885	879	833	883	915	907	875
Computer and mathematical	1 049	963	979	1 057	1 114	1 000	983	1 124
Architecture and engineering	1 053	1 037	1 028	1 058	1 098	1 080	1 090	1 100
Life, physical, and social science	891	944	945	876	957	949	977	955
Community and social services	686	848	832	650	707	827	817	666
Legal	1 051	1 362	1 317	1 032	1 070	1 174	1 155	1 058
Education, training, and library	754	864	854	644	781	899	886	687
Arts, design, entertainment, sports, and media	745	947	933	734	768	953	972	754
Health care practitioner and technical	816	877	876	801	852	938	933	841
Service occupations	403	606	596	382	411	655	647	389
Health care support	400	452	452	394	407	458	462	401
Protective service	630	857	850	510	700	907	897	567
Food preparation and serving related	349	415	410	344	360	445	435	355
Building and grounds cleaning and maintenance	390	503	498	372	385	515	513	368
Personal care and service	391	532	520	381	402	522	518	394
Sales and office	545	629	624	530	558	662	658	545
Sales and related	598	597	601	598	604	576	577	606
Office and administrative support	523	639	632	510	535	676	671	519
Natural resources, construction, and maintenance	608	851	843	558	621	867	858	581
Farming, fishing, and forestry	369	(3)	(3)	365	356	(3)	(3)	352
Construction and extraction	599	851	840	531	604	861	852	555
Installation, maintenance, and repair	673	858	856	622	704	886	880	662
Production, transportation, and material moving	519	688	684	493	523	687	681	498
Production	519	670	665	495	526	681	674	503
Transportation and material moving	520	710	704	490	520	695	689	491
INDUSTRY								
Private sector	603	717	713	592	615	739	734	604
Agriculture and related industries	397	(3)	(3)	396	403	(3)	(3)	402
Nonagricultural industries	605	718	713	595	617	740	735	606
Mining	797	(3)	783	799	874	905	911	865
Construction	615	884	873	580	618	893	884	588
Manufacturing	637	689	689	626	662	694	692	654
Durable goods	668	714	712	655	691	707	706	687
Nondurable goods	597	635	637	590	611	670	662	602
Wholesale and retail trade	533	590	586	528	550	596	590	547
Wholesale trade	670	694	689	668	677	722	709	674
Retail trade	497	562	554	494	509	567	560	507
Transportation and utilities	704	817	816	653	711	854	850	662
Transportation and warehousing	668	782	780	620	668	819	814	619
Utilities	899	965	979	857	957	979	978	948
Information [4]	776	868	862	758	828	893	887	808
Publishing, except Internet	690	740	747	684	720	844	829	710
Motion pictures and sound recording	704	(3)	(3)	669	805	(3)	(3)	762
Broadcasting, except Internet	724	(3)	(3)	703	763	(3)	(3)	749
Telecommunications	857	877	875	848	918	910	897	929
Financial activities	691	618	625	694	706	657	649	708
Finance and insurance	728	607	623	732	738	636	629	740
Finance	726	614	640	730	735	606	616	737
Insurance	731	(3)	(3)	734	743	(3)	(3)	744
Real estate and rental and leasing	604	642	630	603	615	677	670	613

[1]Data refer to members of a labor union or to an employee association similar to a union.
[2]Data refer to members of a labor union or to an employee association similar to a union, as well as to workers who report no union affiliation but whose jobs are covered by a union or an employee association contract.
[3]Data not shown where base is less than 50,000.
[4]Includes other industries, not shown separately.

Table 10-4. Median Weekly Earnings of Full-Time Wage and Salary Workers by Union Affiliation, Occupation, and Industry, 2003–2004—*Continued*

(Dollars.)

Characteristics	2003				2004			
	Total	Members of unions [1]	Represented by unions [2]	Non-union	Total	Members of unions [1]	Represented by unions [2]	Non-union
Professional and business services	692	699	691	692	709	679	694	710
Professional and technical services	885	897	911	884	927	940	937	927
Management, administrative, and waste services	486	640	617	482	478	607	606	470
Education and health services	598	670	684	590	613	717	728	603
Educational services	681	756	760	659	716	828	831	679
Health care and social assistance	582	627	639	577	595	656	671	588
Leisure and hospitality	400	497	485	395	407	518	508	402
Arts, entertainment, and recreation	492	546	529	489	523	677	662	513
Accommodation and food services	385	478	470	381	391	477	473	387
Accommodation	435	485	482	423	432	481	490	422
Food services and drinking places	371	467	456	369	378	467	422	377
Other services [4]	515	726	709	510	528	749	750	521
Other services, except private households	544	730	720	533	560	764	764	551
Public sector	728	801	795	656	751	832	827	683
Federal government	818	809	816	821	856	840	848	869
State government	702	764	759	652	725	788	781	681
Local government	709	814	803	606	731	844	834	627

Note: Beginning in January 2004, data reflect revised population controls used in the household survey. Data refer to the sole or principal job of full- and part-time workers. Excluded are all self-employed workers, regardless of whether or not their businesses are incorporated.

[1] Data refer to members of a labor union or to an employee association similar to a union.
[2] Data refer to members of a labor union or to an employee association similar to a union, as well as to workers who report no union affiliation but whose jobs are covered by a union or an employee association contract.
[4] Includes other industries, not shown separately.

Table 10-5. Union or Employee Association Members Among Wage and Salary Employees, 1977–2004

(Numbers in thousands, percent.)

Year	Total wage and salary employment	Union or employee association members	Union or association members as a percent of wage and salary employment
1977	81 334	19 335	23.8
1978	84 968	19 548	23.0
1979	87 117	20 986	24.1
1980	87 480	20 095	23.0
1981	...	...	...
1982	...	...	...
1983 [1]	88 290	17 717	20.1
1984	92 194	17 340	18.8
1985	94 521	16 996	18.0
1986	96 903	16 975	17.5
1987	99 303	16 913	17.0
1988	101 407	17 002	16.8
1989	103 480	16 980	16.4
1990	103 905	16 740	16.1
1991	102 786	16 568	16.1
1992	103 688	16 390	15.8
1993	105 087	16 598	15.8
1994 [2]	107 989	16 748	15.5
1995	110 038	16 360	14.9
1996	111 960	16 269	14.5
1997	114 533	16 110	14.1
1998	116 730	16 211	13.9
1999	118 963	16 477	13.9
2000	120 786	16 258	13.5
2001	122 482	16 387	13.4
2002	121 826	16 145	13.3
2003	122 358	15 776	12.9
2004	123 554	15 472	12.5

[1]Annual average data beginning in 1983 are not directly comparable with the May data for 1977–1980.
[2]Data beginning in 1994 are not strictly comparable with data for 1993 and earlier years because of the introduction of a major redesign of the Current Population Survey questionnaire and collection methodology and the introduction of 1990 census-based population controls.
. . . = Not available.

Table 10-6. Union Affiliation of Employed Wage and Salary Workers by State, 2003–2004

(Numbers in thousands, percent.)

| State | 2003 | | | | | 2004 | | | | |
| | Total employed | Members of unions [1] | | Represented by unions [2] | | Total employed | Members of unions [1] | | Represented by unions [2] | |
		Total	Percent of employed	Total	Percent of employed		Total	Percent of employed	Total	Percent of employed
U.S. TOTAL	122 358	15 776	12.9	17 448	14.3	123 554	15 472	12.5	17 087	13.8
Alabama	1 822	147	8.1	172	9.5	1 861	181	9.7	213	11.5
Alaska	265	59	22.3	65	24.6	268	54	20.1	60	22.4
Arizona	2 191	113	5.2	140	6.4	2 323	145	6.3	183	7.9
Arkansas	1 035	50	4.8	61	5.9	1 058	51	4.8	65	6.2
California	14 350	2 414	16.8	2 647	18.4	14 414	2 385	16.5	2 588	18.0
Colorado	2 007	156	7.8	180	9.0	2 050	172	8.4	191	9.3
Connecticut	1 489	229	15.4	244	16.4	1 539	235	15.3	256	16.6
Delaware	366	42	11.4	46	12.5	373	46	12.4	49	13.2
District of Columbia	268	39	14.6	46	17.2	258	33	12.7	38	14.5
Florida	6 652	407	6.1	557	8.4	6 943	414	6.0	533	7.7
Georgia	3 703	249	6.7	298	8.0	3 773	242	6.4	282	7.5
Hawaii	511	122	23.8	127	24.8	533	126	23.7	132	24.8
Idaho	548	39	7.0	47	8.6	561	33	5.8	44	7.9
Illinois	5 399	967	17.9	1 003	18.6	5 410	908	16.8	971	17.9
Indiana	2 768	327	11.8	352	12.7	2 717	311	11.4	338	12.4
Iowa	1 365	157	11.5	196	14.4	1 345	141	10.5	171	12.7
Kansas	1 204	96	7.9	124	10.3	1 223	103	8.4	132	10.8
Kentucky	1 681	175	10.4	216	12.8	1 699	164	9.6	197	11.6
Louisiana	1 685	109	6.5	132	7.9	1 697	129	7.6	157	9.3
Maine	567	73	12.8	81	14.3	564	64	11.3	74	13.2
Maryland	2 481	354	14.3	410	16.5	2 502	272	10.9	313	12.5
Massachusetts	2 925	416	14.2	454	15.5	2 920	393	13.5	430	14.7
Michigan	4 188	919	21.9	968	23.1	4 305	930	21.6	966	22.4
Minnesota	2 435	414	17.0	441	18.1	2 429	424	17.5	443	18.3
Mississippi	1 117	55	5.0	73	6.6	1 108	53	4.8	70	6.3
Missouri	2 546	336	13.2	363	14.2	2 546	315	12.4	357	14.0
Montana	360	50	14.0	54	14.9	366	43	11.7	46	12.6
Nebraska	819	64	7.9	87	10.6	831	69	8.3	83	10.0
Nevada	943	136	14.4	149	15.8	1 006	126	12.5	144	14.3
New Hampshire	607	56	9.3	69	11.3	618	61	9.9	68	11.0
New Jersey	3 777	737	19.5	801	21.2	3 769	745	19.8	813	21.6
New Mexico	741	57	7.6	70	9.5	734	49	6.7	65	8.9
New York	7 874	1 936	24.6	2 017	25.6	7 901	1 996	25.3	2 085	26.4
North Carolina	3 576	111	3.1	135	3.8	3 549	97	2.7	127	3.6
North Dakota	284	21	7.3	26	9.0	292	22	7.7	26	9.0
Ohio	5 100	850	16.7	923	18.1	4 998	759	15.2	820	16.4
Oklahoma	1 406	96	6.8	111	7.9	1 402	86	6.1	100	7.1
Oregon	1 466	230	15.7	240	16.4	1 471	224	15.2	243	16.5
Pennsylvania	5 261	794	15.1	847	16.1	5 298	793	15.0	842	15.9
Rhode Island	494	84	17.0	86	17.5	487	79	16.3	83	17.0
South Carolina	1 689	71	4.2	90	5.3	1 765	54	3.0	74	4.2
South Dakota	353	19	5.4	23	6.4	347	21	6.0	27	7.7
Tennessee	2 384	179	7.5	218	9.2	2 465	164	6.7	191	7.7
Texas	9 072	508	5.6	621	6.8	9 072	457	5.0	573	6.3
Utah	1 015	53	5.2	69	6.8	1 001	58	5.8	67	6.7
Vermont	281	27	9.7	33	11.7	291	29	9.8	33	11.4
Virginia	3 243	210	6.5	251	7.7	3 308	176	5.3	218	6.6
Washington	2 539	502	19.7	531	20.9	2 645	510	19.3	536	20.3
West Virginia	671	88	13.1	95	14.2	700	99	14.2	110	15.7
Wisconsin	2 613	414	15.9	438	16.8	2 597	414	16.0	439	16.9
Wyoming	224	18	8.0	22	9.8	222	18	8.0	22	9.8

Note: Beginning in January 2004, data reflect revised population controls used in the household survey. Data refer to the sole or principal job of full and part-time workers. Excluded are all self-employed workers, regardless of whether or not their businesses are incorporated.

[1] Data refer to members of a labor union or an employee association similar to a union.
[2] Data refer to members of a labor union or to an employee association similar to a union, as well as to workers who report no union affiliation but whose jobs are covered by a union or an employee association contract.

PART ELEVEN

FOREIGN LABOR AND PRICE STATISTICS

FOREIGN LABOR AND PRICE STATISTICS

HIGHLIGHTS

This part compares several summary statistics of labor force status, manufacturing productivity, and consumer prices from the United States with those from other countries. Different concepts and methodologies make inter-country comparison difficult. BLS makes such adjustments as it can to reconcile some of the data. There are lags in the receipt of data from other countries; thus, comparisons here are based on the latest data available.

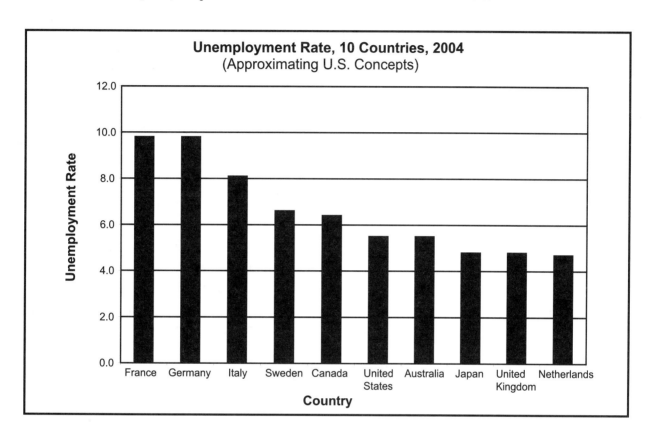

Unemployment Rate, 10 Countries, 2004
(Approximating U.S. Concepts)

In 2004, the unemployment rate in the United States was 5.5 percent. This was somewhat higher than the unemployment rate in Japan and the United Kingdom, but considerably lower than those of France, Germany, and Italy. (Table 11-1)

OTHER HIGHLIGHTS:

- In 2004, Canada had the highest labor force participation at 67.3 percent, followed by the United States with 66.0 percent. In contrast, Italy had a labor force participation rate of only 49.1 percent. (Table 11-1)

- Inflation in 2004 continued to be moderate in all countries. Spain and the United Kingdom had the highest rate at 3.0 percent. Japan had zero inflation while prices in both Norway and Sweden went up by only 0.4 percent. (Table 11-5)

- In 2004, manufacturing productivity grew at a much faster rate in Korea than in the United States (12.1 percent compared to 4.7 percent). While total hours declined for both countries, output rose 11.4 percent in Korea while only increasing 4.3 percent in the United States. (Table 11-2)

- Gross Domestic Product (GDP) per capita grew the fastest in Korea in 2004, but Sweden had the highest rate of increase in GDP per employed person. (Table 11-9)

- The United States had the highest amount of real GDP per capita in 2004 (as adjusted for purchasing power parity, or price differences) at $38,392. Korea had the lowest at $19,715. (Table 11-6)

469

NOTES AND DEFINITIONS

Collection and Coverage

From its inception, the Bureau of Labor Statistics (BLS) has conducted a program of research and statistical analysis to compare labor conditions in the United States and selected foreign countries. The principal comparative measures cover the labor force, employment, and unemployment; trends in labor productivity and unit labor costs in manufacturing; and hourly compensation costs for manufacturing production workers. All of the measures are based upon statistical data and other source materials from (a) the statistical agencies of the foreign countries studied; (b) international and supranational bodies such as the United Nations, the International Labour Office (ILO), the Organization for Economic Cooperation and Development (OECD), and the Statistical Office of the European Communities (EUROSTAT), which attempt to obtain comparable country data; and (c) other secondary sources.

International statistical comparisons should be used cautiously, as the statistical concepts and methods in each country are primarily fashioned to meet domestic (rather than international) needs. Wherever possible, BLS adjusts the data to improve comparability.

The first table provides BLS comparative measures of the civilian labor force participation rate, employment, and unemployment, approximating U.S. concepts. The second table provides trend indexes of manufacturing labor productivity (output per hour), hourly compensation, unit labor costs (labor compensation per unit of output), and related measures for the United States and 14 other countries. The next table is limited to production workers in manufacturing. It shows hourly compensation costs in U.S. dollars for the United States and 29 other countries.

The fourth and fifth tables provide consumer price indexes for selected countries. No adjustments for comparability are made in the total indexes except to convert them to a uniform base year (1982–1984=100). The final tables present comparative levels and trends in real gross domestic product (GDP) per capita and per employed person for 15 countries. All GDP series are converted to U.S. dollars through the use of purchasing power parities.

United States and Canada

U.S. data in this chapter have been revised from 1998 forward and are based on the North American Industry Classification System (NAICS). Output, a value-added measure, is based on a new methodology that balances and reconciles industry production with commodity usage. Canadian data are also on a NAICS basis for 1997 onward.

Labor productivity is defined as real output per hour worked. Although the labor productivity measure presented in this part relates output to the hours worked of persons employed in manufacturing, it does not measure the specific contributions of labor as a single factor of production. Rather, it reflects the joint effects of many influences, including new technology, capital investment, capacity utilization, energy use, managerial skills, and the skills and efforts of the workforce. Unit labor costs are defined as the cost of labor input required to produce one unit of output. They are computed as compensation in nominal terms divided by real output.

Sources of Additional Information

An extensive description of the methodology can be found in the *BLS Handbook of Methods*, April 1997, and in special reports on the BLS Web site.

Table 11-1. Employment Status of the Working-Age Population, Approximating U.S. Concepts, 10 Countries, 1970–2004

(Numbers in thousands, percent.)

Year and category	United States	Canada	Australia	Japan	France	Germany [1]	Italy	Nether-lands	Sweden	United Kingdom
Employed										
1970	78 678	7 919	5 388	50 140	20 270	26 100	19 080	. . .	3 850	24 330
1971	79 367	8 104	5 517	50 470	20 420	26 220	19 020	. . .	3 854	[2]24 323
1972	[2]82 153	8 344	5 601	50 590	20 540	26 280	18 710	. . .	3 856	24 394
1973	85 064	8 761	5 765	51 920	20 840	26 590	18 870	5 050	3 873	24 785
1974	86 794	9 125	5 891	51 710	21 030	26 240	19 280	5 100	3 956	24 857
1975	85 846	9 284	5 866	51 530	20 860	25 540	19 400	5 070	4 056	24 765
1976	88 752	[2]9 652	5 946	52 030	21 030	25 400	19 500	5 100	4 082	24 618
1977	92 017	9 825	6 000	52 720	21 220	25 430	19 670	5 210	4 093	24 646
1978	[2]96 048	10 124	6 038	53 370	21 320	25 650	19 720	5 260	4 109	24 781
1979	98 824	10 561	6 111	54 040	21 390	26 080	19 930	5 350	4 174	25 038
1980	99 303	10 872	6 284	54 600	21 440	26 490	20 200	5 520	4 226	24 925
1981	100 397	11 192	6 416	55 060	21 330	26 450	20 280	5 550	4 219	24 263
1982	99 526	10 847	6 415	55 620	[2]21 390	26 150	20 250	5 520	4 213	23 789
1983	100 834	10 936	6 300	56 550	21 380	[2]25 770	20 320	[2]5 420	4 218	23 614
1984	105 005	11 211	6 494	56 870	21 200	25 830	20 390	5 490	4 249	24 122
1985	107 150	11 526	6 697	57 260	21 150	26 010	20 490	5 650	4 293	24 430
1986	[2]109 597	11 873	[2]6 984	57 740	21 240	26 380	[2]20 610	5 740	4 326	24 585
1987	112 440	12 222	7 142	58 320	21 320	26 590	20 590	5 850	[2]4 340	25 079
1988	114 968	12 590	7 413	59 310	21 520	26 800	20 870	[2]5 884	4 410	25 912
1989	117 342	12 865	7 734	60 500	21 850	27 200	20 770	5 989	4 480	26 595
1990	[2]118 793	12 956	7 877	61 700	[2]22 081	27 950	21 080	6 267	4 513	26 720
1991	117 718	12 748	7 698	62 920	22 120	[2]36 871	[2]21 360	6 383	4 447	26 014
1992	118 492	12 632	7 660	63 620	22 002	36 390	21 230	6 549	4 265	25 391
1993	120 259	12 694	7 699	63 820	21 714	35 989	[2]20 543	6 572	4 028	25 165
1994	[2]123 060	12 960	7 942	63 860	21 750	35 756	20 171	6 664	3 992	25 691
1995	124 900	13 185	8 256	63 900	21 956	35 780	20 030	6 730	4 056	25 696
1996	126 708	13 309	8 364	64 200	22 039	35 637	20 120	6 858	4 019	25 945
1997	[2]129 558	13 607	8 444	64 900	22 169	35 508	20 165	7 163	3 973	26 418
1998	[2]131 463	13 946	8 618	64 450	22 597	36 061	20 366	7 321	4 034	26 691
1999	[2]133 488	14 314	8 762	63 920	23 053	[2]36 042	20 613	7 595	4 117	27 056
2000	[2]136 891	14 676	8 989	63 790	23 693	36 236	20 969	7 912	4 229	27 373
2001	136 933	14 866	9 091	63 460	24 128	36 346	21 356	8 130	4 303	27 604
2002	136 485	15 221	9 271	62 650	24 293	36 061	21 665	8 059	4 310	27 817
2003	[2]137 736	15 579	9 481	62 510	24 293	35 754	21 973	8 035	4 303	28 079
2004	[2]139 252	15 864	9 677	62 630	. . .	35 796	22 105	8 061	4 276	28 334
Unemployed										
1970	4 093	476	91	590	530	140	640	. . .	59	770
1971	5 016	535	107	640	580	160	640	. . .	101	[2]1 059
1972	4 882	553	150	730	610	190	740	. . .	107	1 116
1973	4 365	515	136	680	590	190	720	160	98	946
1974	5 156	514	162	730	630	420	620	190	80	949
1975	7 929	690	302	1 000	910	890	690	270	67	1 174
1976	7 406	[2]716	298	1 080	1 020	890	790	290	66	1 414
1977	6 991	836	358	1 100	1 160	900	840	270	75	1 470
1978	6 202	898	405	1 240	1 220	870	850	280	94	1 453
1979	6 137	831	408	1 170	1 390	780	920	290	88	1 432
1980	7 637	854	409	1 140	1 490	770	920	350	86	1 833
1981	8 273	887	394	1 260	1 760	1 090	1 040	540	108	2 609
1982	10 678	1 298	495	1 360	[2]1 930	1 560	1 160	630	137	2 875
1983	10 717	1 437	697	1 560	2 020	[2]1 900	1 270	[2]700	151	3 081
1984	8 539	1 377	641	1 610	2 360	1 970	1 280	710	136	3 241
1985	8 312	1 309	603	1 560	2 470	2 010	1 310	600	125	3 151
1986	8 237	1 216	[2]601	1 670	2 520	1 860	[2]1 680	640	117	3 161
1987	7 425	1 123	612	1 730	2 570	1 800	1 760	650	[2]97	2 940
1988	6 701	1 000	558	1 550	2 460	1 810	1 790	[2]458	84	2 445
1989	6 528	986	490	1 420	2 320	1 640	1 760	427	72	2 082
1990	[2]7 047	1 087	563	1 340	[2]2 084	1 460	1 590	390	81	2 053
1991	8 628	1 388	788	1 360	2 210	[2]2 204	[2]1 580	373	144	2 530
1992	9 613	1 511	897	1 420	2 443	2 615	1 680	373	255	2 823
1993	8 940	1 538	914	1 660	2 776	3 113	[2]2 227	442	416	2 930
1994	[2]7 996	1 376	829	1 920	2 926	3 318	2 421	489	426	2 433
1995	7 404	1 254	739	2 100	2 787	3 200	2 544	478	404	2 439
1996	7 236	1 295	751	2 250	2 946	3 505	2 555	443	440	2 298
1997	[2]6 739	1 256	759	2 300	2 940	3 907	2 584	374	445	1 987
1998	[2]6 210	1 169	721	2 790	2 837	3 693	2 634	296	368	1 788
1999	[2]5 880	1 075	652	3 170	2 711	[2]3 333	2 559	253	313	1 726
2000	[2]5 692	956	602	3 200	2 385	3 065	2 388	237	260	1 584
2001	6 801	1 026	[2]661	3 400	2 226	3 109	2 164	208	227	1 486
2002	8 378	1 146	636	3 590	2 393	3 438	2 062	227	234	1 524
2003	[2]8 774	1 150	611	3 500	2 577	3 838	2 048	318	264	1 484
2004	[2]8 149	1 092	567	3 130	2 630	3 899	1 960	396	300	1 414

[1]Unified Germany for 1991 onward. Prior to 1991, data relate to the former West Germany.
[2]Break in series.
. . . = Not available.

Table 11-1. Employment Status of the Working-Age Population, Approximating U.S. Concepts, 10 Countries, 1970–2004—*Continued*

(Numbers in thousands, percent.)

Year and category	United States	Canada	Australia	Japan	France	Germany [1]	Italy	Nether- lands	Sweden	United Kingdom
Civilian Labor Force Participation Rate										
1970	60.4	57.8	62.1	64.5	57.5	56.9	49.0	...	64.0	61.1
1971	60.2	58.1	62.2	64.3	57.4	56.5	48.7	...	64.2	[2]62.8
1972	60.4	58.6	62.3	63.8	57.2	56.2	47.7	...	64.1	62.9
1973	60.8	59.7	62.6	64.0	57.3	56.3	47.6	53.4	64.1	63.1
1974	61.2	60.5	63.0	63.1	57.4	55.7	47.7	53.5	64.8	63.1
1975	61.2	61.1	63.2	62.4	57.2	55.0	47.7	54.5	65.9	63.1
1976	61.6	[2]62.5	62.7	62.4	57.5	54.6	48.0	54.1	66.0	63.0
1977	62.3	62.8	62.7	62.5	57.8	54.4	48.2	54.2	65.9	62.8
1978	63.2	63.7	61.9	62.8	57.7	54.4	47.8	54.0	66.1	62.6
1979	63.7	64.5	61.6	62.7	57.8	54.5	48.0	54.2	66.6	62.7
1980	63.8	65.0	62.1	62.6	57.5	54.7	48.2	55.4	66.9	62.8
1981	63.9	65.6	61.9	62.6	57.5	54.7	48.3	56.7	66.8	62.7
1982	64.0	64.9	61.7	62.7	[2]57.5	54.6	47.7	56.6	66.8	61.9
1983	64.0	65.2	61.4	63.1	57.2	[2]54.3	47.5	[2]55.7	66.7	61.6
1984	64.4	65.5	61.5	62.7	57.2	54.4	47.3	55.7	66.6	62.8
1985	64.8	65.9	61.7	62.3	56.8	54.7	47.2	55.5	66.9	62.9
1986	65.3	66.4	[2]62.8	62.1	56.7	54.9	[2]47.8	56.0	67.0	62.9
1987	65.6	66.7	62.9	61.9	56.5	55.0	47.6	56.3	[2]66.4	63.2
1988	65.9	67.1	63.3	61.9	56.2	55.1	47.4	[2]54.4	66.9	63.8
1989	66.5	67.4	64.1	62.2	56.1	55.2	47.3	54.6	67.3	64.3
1990	[2]66.5	67.3	64.7	62.6	[2]55.7	55.3	47.2	56.2	67.3	64.4
1991	66.2	66.7	64.2	63.2	55.7	[2]58.8	[2]47.7	56.6	67.0	63.7
1992	66.4	65.9	63.9	63.4	55.7	58.1	47.5	57.5	65.7	62.9
1993	66.3	65.5	63.5	63.3	55.4	57.8	[2]48.3	57.9	64.5	62.6
1994	[2]66.6	65.1	63.9	63.1	55.6	57.4	47.6	58.6	63.7	62.4
1995	66.6	64.8	64.5	62.9	55.4	57.1	47.3	58.8	64.1	62.4
1996	66.8	64.6	64.6	63.0	55.7	57.1	47.3	59.2	64.0	62.4
1997	67.1	64.9	64.3	63.2	55.6	57.3	47.3	60.8	63.3	62.5
1998	67.1	65.3	64.3	62.8	55.9	57.7	47.6	61.1	62.8	62.5
1999	67.1	65.7	64.0	62.4	56.3	[2]56.9	47.9	62.6	62.8	62.8
2000	67.1	65.8	64.4	62.0	56.6	56.7	48.1	64.5	63.8	62.9
2001	66.8	65.9	64.4	61.6	56.9	56.7	48.2	65.6	63.7	62.7
2002	66.6	66.7	64.4	60.8	57.2	56.5	48.5	64.7	64.0	62.9
2003	66.2	67.3	64.6	60.3	57.4	56.4	49.1	64.9	64.0	63.0
2004	66.0	67.3	64.7	60.0	...	...	49.1	65.5	63.7	63.0
Unemployment Rate										
1970	4.9	5.7	1.6	1.2	2.5	0.5	3.2	...	1.5	3.1
1971	5.9	6.2	1.9	1.3	2.8	0.6	3.3	...	2.6	[2]4.2
1972	5.6	6.2	2.6	1.4	2.9	0.7	3.8	...	2.7	4.4
1973	4.9	5.5	2.3	1.3	2.8	0.7	3.7	3.1	2.5	3.7
1974	5.6	5.3	2.7	1.4	2.9	1.6	3.1	3.6	2.0	3.7
1975	8.5	6.9	4.9	1.9	4.2	3.4	3.4	5.1	1.6	4.5
1976	7.7	[2]6.9	4.8	2.0	4.6	3.4	3.9	5.4	1.6	5.4
1977	7.1	7.8	5.6	2.0	5.2	3.4	4.1	4.9	1.8	5.6
1978	6.1	8.1	6.3	2.3	5.4	3.3	4.1	5.1	2.2	5.5
1979	5.8	7.3	6.3	2.1	6.1	2.9	4.4	5.1	2.1	5.4
1980	7.1	7.3	6.1	2.0	6.5	2.8	4.4	6.0	2.0	6.9
1981	7.6	7.3	5.8	2.2	7.6	4.0	4.9	8.9	2.5	9.7
1982	9.7	10.7	7.2	2.4	[2]8.3	5.6	5.4	10.2	3.1	10.8
1983	9.6	11.6	10.0	2.7	8.6	[2]6.9	5.9	[2]11.4	3.5	11.5
1984	7.5	10.9	9.0	2.8	10.0	7.1	5.9	11.5	3.1	11.8
1985	7.2	10.2	8.3	2.7	10.5	7.2	6.0	9.6	2.8	11.4
1986	7.0	9.3	[2]7.9	2.8	10.6	6.6	[2]7.5	10.0	2.6	11.4
1987	6.2	8.4	7.9	2.9	10.8	6.3	7.9	10.0	[2]2.2	10.5
1988	5.5	7.4	7.0	2.5	10.3	6.3	7.9	[2]7.2	1.9	8.6
1989	5.3	7.1	6.0	2.3	9.6	5.7	7.8	6.7	1.6	7.3
1990	[2]5.6	7.7	6.7	2.1	[2]8.6	5.0	7.0	5.9	1.8	7.1
1991	6.8	9.8	9.3	2.1	9.1	[2]5.6	[2]6.9	5.5	3.1	8.9
1992	7.5	10.7	10.5	2.2	10.0	6.7	7.3	5.4	5.6	10.0
1993	6.9	10.8	10.6	2.5	11.3	8.0	[2]9.8	6.3	9.4	10.4
1994	[2]6.1	9.6	9.4	2.9	11.9	8.5	10.7	6.8	9.6	8.7
1995	5.6	8.7	8.2	3.2	11.3	8.2	11.3	6.6	9.1	8.7
1996	5.4	8.9	8.2	3.4	11.8	9.0	11.3	6.1	9.9	8.1
1997	4.9	8.4	8.3	3.4	11.7	9.9	11.4	5.0	10.1	7.0
1998	4.5	7.7	7.7	4.1	11.2	9.3	11.5	3.9	8.4	6.3
1999	4.2	7.0	6.9	4.7	10.5	[2]8.5	11.0	3.2	7.1	6.0
2000	4.0	6.1	6.3	4.8	9.1	7.8	10.2	2.9	5.8	5.5
2001	4.7	6.5	[2]6.8	5.1	8.4	7.9	9.2	2.5	5.0	5.1
2002	5.8	7.0	6.4	5.4	9.0	8.7	8.7	2.7	5.1	5.2
2003	6.0	6.9	6.1	5.3	9.6	9.7	8.5	3.8	5.8	5.0
2004	5.5	6.4	5.5	4.8	9.8	9.8	8.1	4.7	6.6	4.8

[1]Unified Germany for 1991 onward. Prior to 1991, data relate to the former West Germany.
[2]Break in series.
... = Not available.

Table 11-2. Indexes of Manufacturing Productivity and Related Measures, 15 Countries, 1970 and 1990–2004

(1992=100.)

Item and year	United States[1]	Canada[2]	Japan	Korea	Taiwan	Belgium	Den-mark	France	Ger-many[3]	Italy	Nether-lands	Norway	Sweden	United King-dom	Austra-lia
Output per Hour [4]															
1970	. . .	55.9	37.7	. . .	. . .	32.9	46.3	38.5	52.0	46.2	38.5	59.1	52.2	47.0	. . .
1990	93.5	93.4	94.4	81.5	89.0	96.8	98.5	92.7	99.0	96.6	98.7	98.1	94.6	90.2	91.6
1991	96.3	95.3	99.0	91.7	96.6	99.1	99.7	96.4	98.3	96.1	99.0	98.2	95.5	94.3	96.4
1992	100.0	100.0	100.0	100.0	100.0	100.0	100.0	100.0	100.0	100.0	100.0	100.0	100.0	100.0	100.0
1993	102.7	105.8	101.7	108.5	102.7	102.5	100.3	101.2	101.0	101.2	102.0	99.6	107.3	103.9	106.1
1994	108.1	110.8	103.3	117.7	106.3	108.4	112.7	109.4	108.5	104.8	113.1	99.6	117.8	108.0	104.9
1995	112.1	112.4	111.0	128.8	114.6	113.2	112.7	116.0	110.2	107.9	117.3	100.7	124.5	106.3	105.8
1996	116.8	109.7	116.1	141.6	122.3	116.3	109.0	116.7	113.3	108.3	119.3	102.5	129.5	105.5	113.6
1997	121.7	113.5	121.0	159.7	127.9	125.5	117.7	125.8	120.0	110.3	121.4	102.0	141.0	106.8	115.2
1998	130.2	117.7	121.2	178.0	134.3	126.9	117.1	132.7	120.4	110.8	124.1	99.9	149.5	108.4	118.5
1999	136.7	124.2	126.7	198.0	141.5	125.5	119.0	138.8	123.4	110.5	127.0	103.6	162.7	113.6	119.9
2000	147.7	131.4	135.9	214.9	149.5	130.8	123.2	148.7	132.0	113.5	132.7	106.6	175.5	120.9	128.1
2001	149.2	129.2	135.9	213.4	158.1	132.1	123.4	151.0	135.7	114.0	132.5	109.8	171.4	124.9	132.2
2002	164.3	134.1	139.2	234.2	170.0	137.6	125.7	158.4	137.4	112.2	139.8	112.8	189.2	127.8	136.7
2003	180.5	137.2	154.5	250.5	176.1	144.0	132.1	158.8	140.9	111.2	146.7	114.4	201.5	134.1	142.0
2004	189.0	141.2	165.1	280.7	184.3	148.7	133.2	164.4	147.4	110.6	. . .	116.8	220.3	140.8	141.2
Output															
1970	. . .	59.9	39.4	7.0	12.7	57.6	72.7	56.9	70.9	48.1	59.8	91.0	80.7	90.2	. . .
1990	98.2	106.0	97.1	86.7	90.2	101.0	101.7	97.7	99.1	99.4	99.0	101.4	110.1	105.4	104.1
1991	96.8	99.0	102.0	95.0	96.2	100.7	100.3	99.2	102.4	99.3	99.8	99.0	104.1	100.1	100.7
1992	100.0	100.0	100.0	100.0	100.0	100.0	100.0	100.0	100.0	100.0	100.0	100.0	100.0	100.0	100.0
1993	104.2	105.9	96.3	105.4	102.3	97.0	97.0	95.9	92.0	96.5	97.7	101.7	101.9	101.4	103.8
1994	112.2	114.1	94.9	116.8	108.1	101.4	107.5	100.6	94.9	102.4	104.5	104.6	117.0	106.2	109.1
1995	117.3	119.6	98.9	129.9	114.4	104.2	112.7	106.2	94.0	107.2	108.2	107.3	131.9	107.8	108.7
1996	121.6	119.6	103.0	138.3	119.5	105.9	107.5	106.3	92.0	105.4	108.9	110.3	136.4	108.7	112.6
1997	129.0	127.7	106.5	145.0	126.9	112.7	116.3	113.3	96.1	108.8	111.6	114.2	146.5	110.7	115.1
1998	137.7	134.0	100.2	133.5	131.1	114.4	117.2	119.0	97.2	110.7	114.9	113.7	158.3	111.3	118.6
1999	143.7	145.0	101.9	162.6	139.6	114.4	118.2	123.1	98.2	110.3	117.6	113.6	172.5	112.2	118.3
2000	152.7	159.3	109.2	190.2	150.3	119.9	122.5	128.8	104.8	113.6	122.8	112.8	188.3	114.9	123.8
2001	144.2	152.7	105.5	194.3	140.8	119.9	122.5	130.1	106.8	113.0	121.9	112.3	184.3	113.4	123.7
2002	147.5	155.9	102.8	209.1	151.2	120.0	120.8	129.9	104.9	111.7	122.0	112.2	194.8	109.9	129.1
2003	154.1	156.5	112.6	220.6	159.9	121.0	120.4	129.2	104.7	110.2	120.0	107.6	199.9	110.0	131.4
2004	160.7	162.4	118.8	245.8	174.9	123.8	117.0	130.5	109.5	110.2	121.4	109.5	218.7	112.0	131.3
Total Hours															
1970	104.3	107.1	104.3	. . .	. . .	174.7	157.0	147.5	. . .	104.0	155.5	153.9	154.7	191.9	. . .
1990	105.0	113.5	102.9	106.4	101.4	104.3	103.3	105.5	100.1	102.9	100.3	103.4	116.4	116.9	113.6
1991	100.5	103.9	103.1	103.6	99.6	101.5	100.6	102.9	104.1	103.3	100.8	100.8	109.0	106.1	104.4
1992	100.0	100.0	100.0	100.0	100.0	100.0	100.0	100.0	100.0	100.0	100.0	100.0	100.0	100.0	100.0
1993	101.4	100.1	94.7	97.1	99.6	94.7	96.8	94.8	91.1	95.4	95.8	102.1	94.9	97.7	97.8
1994	103.8	103.0	91.9	99.2	101.7	93.6	95.4	91.9	87.5	97.7	92.4	105.0	99.4	98.3	103.9
1995	104.6	106.4	89.1	100.9	99.8	92.0	100.0	91.6	85.3	99.4	92.3	106.6	105.9	101.4	102.8
1996	104.2	109.0	88.7	97.6	97.7	91.0	98.6	91.1	81.2	97.3	91.2	107.6	105.3	103.0	99.1
1997	106.0	112.4	88.0	90.8	99.2	89.8	98.8	90.0	80.1	98.6	91.9	112.0	103.9	103.6	100.0
1998	105.7	113.8	82.7	75.0	97.6	90.2	100.1	89.7	80.7	99.9	92.6	113.7	105.9	102.7	100.1
1999	105.1	116.8	80.4	82.1	98.7	91.2	99.4	88.7	79.6	99.8	92.6	109.6	106.0	98.8	98.7
2000	103.4	121.3	80.3	88.5	100.5	91.7	99.4	86.6	79.4	100.1	92.5	105.9	107.3	95.1	96.7
2001	96.6	118.2	77.7	91.1	89.0	90.8	99.3	86.1	78.7	99.1	92.0	102.3	107.5	90.8	93.5
2002	89.8	116.2	73.9	89.3	89.0	87.2	96.1	82.0	76.4	99.6	87.3	99.4	103.0	86.0	94.5
2003	85.4	114.1	72.9	88.1	90.8	84.0	91.1	81.3	74.3	99.1	81.8	94.0	99.2	82.0	92.5
2004	85.0	115.0	72.0	87.6	94.9	83.3	87.8	79.4	74.3	99.6	. . .	93.8	99.3	79.5	93.0
Compensation per Hour— National Currency Basis [4, 5]															
1970	23.9	17.2	16.4	. . .	. . .	13.7	11.1	10.5	. . .	5.3	19.4	11.8	10.7	6.6	. . .
1990	90.5	88.5	90.6	68.0	85.2	90.1	93.6	91.0	89.4	87.6	89.8	92.3	87.8	83.8	86.3
1991	95.6	95.0	96.5	85.5	93.5	97.3	97.8	96.4	91.4	94.2	94.8	97.5	95.5	94.3	94.0
1992	100.0	100.0	100.0	100.0	100.0	100.0	100.0	100.0	100.0	100.0	100.0	100.0	100.0	100.0	100.0
1993	102.0	102.0	102.7	115.9	105.9	104.8	102.4	102.9	106.2	105.7	104.5	101.5	97.4	104.6	105.9
1994	105.3	103.9	104.7	133.1	111.1	106.1	106.0	106.8	111.0	106.8	109.0	104.4	99.8	107.4	104.3
1995	107.3	106.5	108.3	161.6	120.2	109.2	108.2	110.6	117.0	111.3	112.1	109.2	106.8	108.9	113.3
1996	109.3	107.4	109.1	188.1	128.2	111.1	112.6	112.3	122.5	119.0	114.4	113.6	115.2	109.7	122.9
1997	112.2	108.4	112.6	204.5	132.1	115.2	116.5	112.0	124.9	123.0	117.2	118.7	121.0	113.4	124.6
1998	118.7	112.9	115.4	222.7	137.1	117.0	119.6	113.0	126.7	122.2	122.0	125.7	125.6	122.2	128.3
1999	123.4	116.7	114.8	223.9	139.6	118.5	122.6	117.2	129.6	124.1	126.0	133.0	130.3	129.6	133.0
2000	134.7	120.5	113.7	239.1	142.3	120.6	125.0	123.3	136.3	127.8	132.0	140.5	136.8	137.1	140.2
2001	137.8	124.8	114.6	246.7	151.4	127.2	130.9	126.7	140.6	132.5	138.2	148.9	143.8	142.8	149.3
2002	147.9	128.8	114.7	271.6	145.0	131.8	136.8	134.0	144.0	135.8	149.7	156.7	151.7	151.3	154.2
2003	160.1	133.2	115.5	285.0	147.3	137.2	143.7	139.3	147.1	140.1	160.6	163.4	157.0	159.0	162.4
2004	163.6	133.1	116.1	316.6	149.3	. . .	149.9	142.7	148.0	143.8	. . .	166.4	160.6	164.5	. . .

[1]U.S. data have been revised from 1998 forward and are based on the 1997 North American Industry Classification System (NAICS).
[2]Canadian data have been revised and are based on NAICS data for 1997 onward.
[3]Unified Germany for 1991 onward. Prior to 1991, data relate to the former West Germany.
[4]The data relate to employees (wage and salary earners) in Belgium, Denmark, and Italy, and to all employed persons (employees and self-employed workers) in the other countries.
[5]Compensation adjusted to include changes in employment taxes that are not compensation to employees, but are labor costs to employers.
. . . = Not available.

Table 11-2. Indexes of Manufacturing Productivity and Related Measures, 15 Countries, 1970 and 1990–2004—*Continued*

(1992=100.)

Item and year	United States[1]	Canada[2]	Japan	Korea	Taiwan	Belgium	Denmark	France	Germany[3]	Italy	Netherlands	Norway	Sweden	United Kingdom	Australia
Compensation per Hour–U.S. Currency Basis [4,5]															
1970	23.9	19.9	5.8	...	...	8.9	11.1	10.0	8.9	10.3	9.4	10.3	12.0	9.0	...
1990	90.5	91.6	79.2	75.0	79.6	86.6	91.2	88.4	86.4	90.1	86.7	91.7	86.4	84.6	91.7
1991	95.6	100.2	90.9	91.1	87.9	91.5	92.2	90.4	86.0	93.5	89.1	93.3	91.9	94.4	99.6
1992	100.0	100.0	100.0	100.0	100.0	100.0	100.0	100.0	100.0	100.0	100.0	100.0	100.0	100.0	100.0
1993	102.0	95.6	117.2	112.9	100.9	97.4	95.3	96.2	100.3	82.8	98.9	88.8	72.8	88.9	97.9
1994	105.3	91.9	129.9	129.5	105.6	102.1	100.7	101.9	107.0	81.7	105.4	91.9	75.3	93.2	103.8
1995	107.3	93.7	146.1	164.1	114.2	119.1	116.6	117.4	127.6	84.2	122.8	107.1	87.1	97.4	114.1
1996	109.3	95.2	127.2	183.4	117.4	115.3	117.2	116.2	127.2	95.0	119.3	109.3	100.1	96.9	130.8
1997	112.2	94.6	117.9	169.3	115.5	103.4	106.4	101.5	112.5	88.9	105.6	104.1	92.2	105.1	126.1
1998	118.7	91.9	111.7	124.8	102.8	103.6	107.7	101.4	112.5	86.7	108.2	103.4	92.0	114.7	109.8
1999	123.4	94.9	128.0	147.6	108.7	100.6	105.9	100.8	110.3	84.1	107.1	105.9	91.7	118.7	116.8
2000	134.7	98.0	133.7	165.9	114.6	88.7	93.2	91.9	100.5	75.1	97.3	99.1	86.9	117.7	110.8
2001	137.8	97.4	119.5	149.8	112.6	90.8	94.9	91.5	100.5	75.5	98.8	102.9	81.0	116.4	105.0
2002	147.9	99.2	116.2	170.4	105.6	99.3	104.7	102.2	108.7	81.7	112.9	121.9	90.9	128.7	114.1
2003	160.1	114.9	126.3	187.6	107.7	123.8	131.9	127.2	132.9	101.0	145.1	143.4	113.2	147.1	144.1
2004	163.6	123.5	136.0	216.9	112.5	...	151.1	143.2	147.0	113.8	...	153.5	127.4	170.7	...
Unit Labor Costs–National Currency Basis [4,5]															
1970	...	30.8	43.6	7.8	23.7	41.7	23.9	27.2	39.8	11.4	50.4	20.0	20.6	14.1	...
1990	96.8	94.8	95.9	83.4	95.7	93.0	95.0	98.2	90.3	90.7	91.1	94.1	92.9	92.9	94.2
1991	99.2	99.7	97.5	93.3	96.7	98.1	98.1	100.0	93.0	98.0	95.7	99.2	100.0	100.0	97.5
1992	100.0	100.0	100.0	100.0	100.0	100.0	100.0	100.0	100.0	100.0	100.0	100.0	100.0	100.0	100.0
1993	99.3	96.5	101.0	106.8	103.2	102.3	102.2	101.7	105.2	104.5	102.4	101.9	90.8	100.7	99.8
1994	97.4	93.8	101.4	113.1	104.5	97.9	94.1	97.6	102.4	101.9	96.4	104.8	84.7	99.4	99.4
1995	95.7	94.7	97.5	125.5	104.9	96.4	96.0	95.3	106.2	103.2	95.6	108.4	85.8	102.5	107.1
1996	93.6	97.9	94.0	132.8	104.8	95.5	103.3	96.2	108.2	109.8	95.9	110.8	89.0	104.0	108.2
1997	92.2	95.5	93.0	128.0	103.3	91.8	98.9	89.0	104.1	111.4	96.5	116.4	85.8	106.1	108.2
1998	91.2	95.9	95.2	125.1	102.1	92.2	102.1	85.2	105.2	110.3	98.3	125.7	84.0	112.8	108.3
1999	90.3	94.0	90.6	113.1	98.7	94.4	103.0	84.5	105.1	112.3	99.1	128.3	80.1	114.1	110.9
2000	91.2	91.7	83.6	111.2	95.2	92.2	101.4	83.0	103.3	112.6	99.5	131.9	77.9	113.4	109.4
2001	92.4	96.6	84.4	115.6	95.7	96.3	106.1	83.9	103.6	116.2	104.3	135.6	83.9	114.3	112.9
2002	90.0	96.1	82.4	116.0	85.3	95.7	108.8	84.6	104.8	121.1	107.1	138.8	80.1	118.4	112.8
2003	88.7	97.1	74.8	113.8	83.7	95.3	108.8	87.7	104.4	126.0	109.5	142.8	77.9	118.5	114.4
2004	86.6	94.2	70.3	112.8	81.0	...	112.5	86.8	100.4	130.1	108.0	142.5	72.9	116.8	...
Unit Labor Costs–U.S. Currency Basis [4,5]															
1970	...	35.7	15.4	19.6	14.9	27.0	19.3	26.0	17.1	22.3	24.5	17.4	23.1	19.1	...
1990	96.8	98.1	83.9	92.1	89.4	89.5	92.7	95.4	87.3	93.3	87.9	93.5	91.3	93.9	100.1
1991	99.2	105.2	91.8	99.3	91.0	92.3	92.5	93.8	87.5	97.3	90.0	95.0	96.3	100.0	103.3
1992	100.0	100.0	100.0	100.0	100.0	100.0	100.0	100.0	100.0	100.0	100.0	100.0	100.0	100.0	100.0
1993	99.3	90.4	115.3	104.0	98.3	95.1	95.1	95.0	99.3	81.8	96.9	89.1	67.8	85.6	92.3
1994	97.4	83.0	125.8	110.0	99.3	94.2	89.4	93.2	98.6	77.9	93.2	92.3	64.0	86.2	98.9
1995	95.7	83.4	131.6	127.4	99.7	105.2	103.5	101.2	115.8	78.0	104.8	106.4	70.0	91.6	107.9
1996	93.6	86.7	109.5	129.5	96.0	99.1	107.6	99.6	112.2	87.7	100.0	106.6	77.3	91.9	115.2
1997	92.2	83.3	97.4	106.0	90.3	82.4	90.4	80.7	93.8	80.6	87.0	102.1	65.4	98.4	109.5
1998	91.2	78.1	92.2	70.1	76.6	81.6	92.0	76.4	93.4	78.2	87.2	103.5	61.5	105.8	92.6
1999	90.3	76.5	101.0	74.6	76.8	80.2	89.0	72.6	89.4	76.2	84.3	102.5	56.4	104.5	97.4
2000	91.2	74.6	98.4	77.2	76.6	67.8	75.6	61.8	76.2	66.2	73.3	93.0	49.5	97.3	86.5
2001	92.4	75.4	88.0	70.2	71.2	68.7	76.9	60.6	74.1	66.2	74.5	93.7	47.3	93.2	79.4
2002	90.0	74.0	83.5	72.8	62.1	72.1	83.3	64.5	79.1	72.8	80.8	108.1	48.0	100.7	83.4
2003	88.7	83.8	81.7	74.9	61.2	86.0	99.9	80.1	94.4	90.8	98.9	125.3	56.2	109.7	101.5
2004	86.6	87.5	82.4	77.3	61.1	...	113.4	87.1	99.7	103.0	107.2	131.4	57.8	121.2	...
Exchange Rate [6]															
1970	100.0	115.8	35.4	252.7	62.9	64.7	80.5	95.7	42.8	196.5	48.6	86.9	112.3	135.6	152.3
1990	100.0	103.6	87.4	110.4	93.5	96.2	97.5	97.2	96.6	102.8	96.6	99.4	98.4	101.0	106.3
1991	100.0	105.5	94.2	106.5	94.0	94.0	94.3	93.7	94.0	99.3	93.9	95.7	96.3	100.1	106.0
1992	100.0	100.0	100.0	100.0	100.0	100.0	100.0	100.0	100.0	100.0	100.0	100.0	100.0	100.0	100.0
1993	100.0	93.7	114.1	97.4	95.2	93.0	93.1	93.4	94.4	78.3	94.6	87.5	74.7	85.0	92.5
1994	100.0	88.4	124.1	97.2	95.1	96.2	95.0	95.4	96.3	76.5	96.7	88.1	75.5	86.7	99.5
1995	100.0	88.1	134.9	101.5	95.0	109.1	107.8	106.2	109.1	75.6	109.6	98.1	81.6	89.4	100.7
1996	100.0	88.6	116.5	97.5	91.6	103.8	104.1	103.5	103.8	79.9	104.3	96.2	86.8	88.4	106.5
1997	100.0	87.3	104.7	82.8	87.4	89.8	91.3	90.7	90.0	72.3	90.1	87.7	76.2	92.7	101.1
1998	100.0	81.5	96.8	56.0	75.0	88.5	90.1	89.7	88.8	70.9	88.7	82.3	73.3	93.8	85.6
1999	100.0	81.3	111.5	65.9	77.8	84.9	86.4	86.0	85.1	67.8	85.0	79.6	70.4	91.6	87.8
2000	100.0	81.4	117.6	69.4	80.5	73.6	74.6	74.5	73.7	58.7	73.7	70.5	63.5	85.8	79.1
2001	100.0	78.0	104.3	60.7	74.4	71.3	72.5	72.2	71.5	57.0	71.4	69.1	56.3	81.5	70.3
2002	100.0	77.0	101.2	62.8	72.9	75.3	76.6	76.3	75.5	60.2	75.4	77.8	59.9	85.1	73.9
2003	100.0	86.3	109.3	65.8	73.1	90.2	91.8	91.4	90.4	72.0	90.3	87.8	72.1	92.5	88.7
2004	100.0	92.8	117.2	68.5	75.4	99.1	100.8	100.4	99.3	79.2	99.3	92.2	79.3	103.8	100.2

[1]U.S. data have been revised from 1998 forward and are based on the 1997 North American Industry Classification System (NAICS).
[2]Canadian data have been revised and are based on NAICS data for 1997 onward.
[3]Unified Germany for 1991 onward. Prior to 1991, data relate to the former West Germany.
[4]The data relate to employees (wage and salary earners) in Belgium, Denmark, and Italy, and to all employed persons (employees and self-employed workers) in the other countries.
[5]Compensation adjusted to include changes in employment taxes that are not compensation to employees, but are labor costs to employers.
[6]Index of value of foreign currency relative to the U.S. dollar.
. . . = Not available.

Table 11-3. Hourly Compensation Costs in U.S. Dollars for Production Workers in Manufacturing, 30 Countries and Selected Areas, Selected Years, 1975–2003

(Dollars.)

Country or area	1975	1980	1985	1990	1995	2000	2001	2002	2003
Americas									
United States	6.16	9.63	12.71	14.72	17.02	19.46	20.29	21.11	21.97
Brazil	. . .	. . .	. . .	. . .	. . .	3.50	2.94	2.53	2.67
Canada	6.11	8.87	11.20	16.33	16.50	16.48	16.24	16.68	19.28
Mexico	1.47	2.21	1.59	1.58	1.46	2.19	2.51	2.60	2.48
Asia and Oceania									
Australia	5.62	8.47	8.21	13.14	15.42	14.48	13.31	15.50	20.05
Hong Kong SAR [1]	0.75	1.50	1.73	3.22	4.80	5.45	5.74	5.66	5.54
Israel	2.03	3.41	3.66	7.71	9.50	11.49	12.26	11.01	11.73
Japan	2.97	5.46	6.27	12.54	23.55	21.89	19.25	18.49	20.09
Korea	0.32	0.95	1.23	3.69	7.26	8.23	7.69	9.00	10.28
New Zealand	3.10	5.14	4.30	8.01	9.78	7.91	7.53	8.63	11.13
Singapore	0.84	1.48	2.45	3.73	7.23	7.36	7.28	6.90	7.41
Sri Lanka	0.28	0.22	0.28	0.35	0.48	0.48	0.45	0.49	. . .
Taiwan	0.38	1.02	1.50	3.89	5.88	6.18	6.03	5.73	5.84
Europe									
Austria	4.50	8.87	7.57	17.91	25.26	19.17	19.08	20.69	25.38
Belgium	6.39	13.07	8.94	19.10	27.53	21.53	20.98	22.74	27.73
Czech Republic	. . .	. . .	. . .	. . .	2.53	2.83	3.13	3.83	4.71
Denmark	6.24	10.77	8.10	18.35	25.43	22.76	23.26	25.62	32.18
Finland	4.63	8.30	8.20	21.15	24.31	19.44	19.85	21.78	27.17
France	4.50	8.90	7.48	15.36	19.26	15.46	15.65	17.12	21.13
Germany, Former West	6.26	12.16	9.46	21.71	31.40	23.66	23.55	25.44	31.25
Germany, Unified	. . .	. . .	. . .	. . .	30.08	22.65	22.54	24.34	29.91
Greece	1.69	3.72	3.65	6.69	8.94	. . .	. . .	. . .	. . .
Ireland	3.06	6.03	6.00	11.78	13.77	12.76	13.64	15.31	19.14
Italy	4.64	8.09	7.56	17.28	15.91	14.05	13.81	14.97	18.35
Luxembourg	6.22	11.51	7.48	16.00	23.36	17.51	17.21	18.71	23.11
Netherlands	6.58	12.05	8.73	17.98	24.03	19.33	19.65	21.62	26.84
Norway	6.90	11.80	10.47	21.76	24.84	22.66	23.29	27.29	31.55
Portugal	1.52	1.98	1.46	3.59	5.09	4.49	4.59	5.07	6.23
Spain	2.52	5.86	4.64	11.30	12.70	10.66	10.76	11.93	14.96
Sweden	7.14	12.44	9.61	20.82	21.46	20.18	18.39	20.23	25.18
Switzerland	6.03	10.96	9.55	20.63	28.99	21.02	21.60	23.84	27.87
United Kingdom	3.39	7.52	6.23	12.62	13.79	16.82	16.50	17.89	20.37
Trade-Weighted Measures [2,3]									
All 30 foreign economies	. . .	. . .	. . .	. . .	. . .	14.16	13.70	14.22	16.42
All 30 foreign economies less Brazil and the Czech Republic	3.86	6.54	6.73	11.99	15.35	14.37	13.92	14.45	16.69
OECD [4,5]	4.21	7.11	7.26	12.88	16.35	15.20	14.69	15.32	17.79
Europe [5]	5.01	9.75	7.88	17.10	21.66	18.42	18.34	20.00	24.22
European Union-15 [6]	4.94	9.67	7.77	16.88	21.33	18.31	18.19	19.80	24.05
Asian NIEs [7]	0.51	1.16	1.64	3.70	6.46	6.99	6.79	7.02	7.57

[1]Hong Kong Special Administrative Region of China.
[2]Since data for Germany are not available before 1993, data for the former West Germany are only included in the trade-weighted measures.
[3]The trade weights used to compute the average compensation cost measures for selected country or economic groups are relative importances derived from the sum of the U.S. imports of manufactured products for consumption (customs value) and the U.S. exports of domestic manufactured products (free alongside ship value) in 1992 for each country or area and each economic group.
[4]Organization for Economic Cooperation and Development.
[5]Data for the Czech Republic are not included for 1975–1994.
[6]European Union-15 refers to European Union member countries prior to the European Union's expansion to 25 countries on May 1, 2004.
[7]The Asian NIEs are Hong Kong, Korea, Singapore, and Taiwan.
. . . = Not available.

Table 11-4. Consumer Price Indexes, 16 Countries, 1950–2004

(1982–1984=100.)

Year	Consumer price index [1]															
	United States [2]	Canada [3]	Japan	Australia [4]	Austria	Belgium [5]	Denmark [6]	France [7]	Germany [8]	Italy	Netherlands	Norway [9]	Spain	Sweden	Switzerland [10]	United Kingdom
1950	24.1	21.6	14.8	12.6	...	24.0	12.3	11.1	...	...	...	13.6	5.5	13.4	33.2	9.8
1951	26.0	23.9	17.2	15.1	...	26.3	13.5	13.0	...	...	...	15.7	6.0	15.5	34.8	10.7
1952	26.5	24.5	18.0	17.7	...	26.5	14.0	14.6	...	...	...	17.1	5.9	16.7	35.7	11.7
1953	26.7	24.2	19.2	18.4	...	26.4	14.1	14.4	...	10.3	...	17.5	6.0	16.9	35.4	12.1
1954	26.9	24.4	20.5	18.5	...	26.9	14.2	14.3	...	10.6	...	18.2	6.1	17.1	35.7	12.3
1955	26.8	24.4	20.2	18.9	...	26.8	15.0	14.5	...	10.9	...	18.4	6.3	17.5	36.0	12.9
1956	27.2	24.8	20.3	20.1	...	27.4	15.8	14.8	...	11.2	...	19.1	6.7	18.4	36.5	13.5
1957	28.1	25.6	20.9	20.6	...	28.2	16.1	15.3	...	11.4	...	19.6	7.4	19.2	37.3	14.0
1958	28.9	26.3	20.8	20.9	31.6	28.6	16.3	17.6	...	11.7	...	20.6	8.4	20.0	37.9	14.4
1959	29.1	26.6	21.1	21.3	32.0	29.0	16.5	18.7	...	11.7	...	21.0	9.0	20.2	37.7	14.5
1960	29.6	26.9	21.8	22.1	32.6	29.1	16.7	19.4	...	11.9	...	21.1	9.1	21.0	38.2	14.6
1961	29.9	27.1	23.0	22.6	33.8	29.3	17.4	20.0	...	12.2	...	21.6	9.2	21.5	38.9	15.1
1962	30.2	27.4	24.6	22.6	35.3	29.8	18.8	21.0	43.1	12.7	...	22.8	9.7	22.5	40.6	15.8
1963	30.6	27.9	26.4	22.7	36.2	30.4	19.8	22.0	44.4	13.7	...	23.4	10.6	23.2	42.0	16.1
1964	31.0	28.4	27.4	23.2	37.6	31.7	20.5	22.7	45.4	14.5	...	24.7	11.3	23.9	43.3	16.6
1965	31.5	29.1	29.5	24.1	39.5	32.9	21.8	23.3	46.9	15.2	...	25.7	12.8	25.1	44.8	17.4
1966	32.4	30.2	31.0	24.9	40.3	34.3	23.3	23.9	48.6	15.5	...	26.6	13.6	26.8	46.9	18.1
1967	33.4	31.3	32.3	25.7	41.9	35.3	25.0	24.6	49.4	16.1	...	27.8	14.5	27.9	48.8	18.5
1968	34.8	32.5	34.0	26.3	43.1	36.3	27.0	25.7	50.2	16.3	...	28.7	15.2	28.4	50.0	19.4
1969	36.7	34.0	35.8	27.1	44.4	37.6	27.9	27.3	51.1	16.7	40.6	29.6	15.5	29.2	51.3	20.5
1970	38.8	35.1	38.5	28.2	46.4	39.1	29.8	28.8	52.8	17.5	42.1	32.8	16.4	31.3	53.1	21.8
1971	40.5	36.2	40.9	29.9	48.5	40.8	31.5	30.3	55.6	18.4	45.3	34.8	17.7	33.6	56.6	23.8
1972	41.8	37.9	42.9	31.6	51.6	43.0	33.6	32.2	58.7	19.4	48.9	37.3	19.2	35.6	60.4	25.5
1973	44.4	40.7	47.9	34.6	55.5	46.0	36.7	34.6	62.8	21.6	52.9	40.1	21.4	38.0	65.7	27.9
1974	49.3	45.2	59.1	39.9	60.8	51.9	42.3	39.3	67.2	25.7	58.1	43.8	24.8	41.7	72.1	32.3
1975	53.8	50.1	66.0	45.9	65.9	58.5	46.4	43.9	71.2	30.0	63.8	49.0	29.0	45.8	76.9	40.1
1976	56.9	53.8	72.2	52.1	70.8	63.8	50.5	48.2	74.2	35.1	69.6	53.5	34.1	50.5	78.2	46.8
1977	60.6	58.1	78.1	58.5	74.6	68.4	56.1	52.7	77.0	41.0	74.1	58.3	42.4	56.3	79.2	54.2
1978	65.2	63.3	81.4	63.1	77.3	71.4	61.8	57.5	79.0	46.0	77.2	63.1	50.8	61.9	80.1	58.7
1979	72.6	69.1	84.4	68.8	80.2	74.6	67.7	63.6	82.3	52.8	80.5	66.1	58.8	66.4	83.0	66.6
1980	82.4	76.1	90.9	75.8	85.3	79.6	76.1	72.3	86.7	64.0	86.1	73.3	67.9	75.5	86.3	78.5
1981	90.9	85.6	95.4	83.2	91.1	85.6	85.0	82.0	92.2	75.4	91.9	83.3	77.8	84.6	91.9	87.9
1982	96.5	94.9	98.0	92.4	96.0	93.1	93.6	91.6	97.1	87.8	97.2	92.7	89.0	91.9	97.1	95.4
1983	99.6	100.4	99.8	101.8	99.2	100.3	100.0	100.5	100.3	100.7	100.7	100.5	99.9	100.0	100.0	99.8
1984	103.9	104.7	102.1	105.8	104.8	106.6	106.4	107.9	102.7	111.5	103.0	106.8	111.1	108.1	102.9	104.8
1985	107.6	108.9	104.2	112.9	108.2	111.8	111.4	114.2	104.8	121.8	105.3	112.9	120.9	116.0	106.4	111.1
1986	109.6	113.4	104.8	123.2	110.0	113.3	115.4	117.2	104.7	129.0	105.6	121.0	131.5	121.0	107.2	114.9
1987	113.6	118.4	104.9	133.7	111.6	115.0	120.0	120.9	104.9	135.1	105.1	131.6	138.5	126.1	108.8	119.7
1988	118.3	123.2	105.7	142.9	113.8	116.4	125.5	124.2	106.3	141.9	106.1	140.4	145.1	133.4	110.8	125.6
1989	124.0	129.3	108.1	154.1	116.6	120.0	131.5	128.6	109.2	150.8	107.1	146.8	155.0	142.0	114.3	135.4
1990	130.7	135.5	111.4	165.3	120.5	124.1	135.0	133.0	112.1	160.5	109.9	152.8	165.4	156.7	120.5	148.2
1991	136.2	143.1	115.1	170.7	124.4	128.1	138.2	137.2	81.9	170.6	113.3	158.0	175.2	171.5	127.5	156.9
1992	140.3	145.3	117.0	172.4	129.5	131.2	141.1	140.6	86.1	179.4	116.9	161.7	185.6	175.6	132.7	162.7
1993	144.5	147.9	118.5	175.5	134.1	134.8	142.9	143.5	89.9	187.5	120.0	165.4	194.1	183.9	137.0	165.3
1994	148.2	148.2	119.3	178.8	138.2	138.0	145.8	145.9	92.3	195.0	123.3	167.7	203.3	187.8	138.3	169.3
1995	152.4	151.4	119.2	187.1	141.3	140.1	148.8	148.4	93.9	205.1	125.7	171.8	212.8	192.4	140.8	175.2
1996	156.9	153.8	119.3	192.0	143.9	142.9	151.9	151.3	95.3	213.4	128.2	174.0	220.3	193.5	141.9	179.4
1997	160.5	156.2	121.5	192.5	145.8	145.3	155.3	153.2	97.1	217.7	131.0	178.5	224.8	194.8	142.5	185.1
1998	163.0	157.7	122.2	194.1	147.1	146.7	158.2	154.3	98.0	222.0	133.6	182.5	228.8	194.2	142.7	191.4
1999	166.6	160.5	121.8	197.0	147.9	148.3	162.0	155.0	98.6	225.7	136.5	186.7	234.2	195.1	143.8	194.3
2000	172.2	164.8	121.0	205.8	151.4	152.1	166.8	157.7	100.0	231.4	140.0	192.5	242.1	196.9	146.0	200.1
2001	177.1	169.0	120.1	214.8	155.5	155.8	170.8	160.3	102.0	237.8	145.9	198.4	250.8	201.6	147.4	203.6
2002	179.9	172.8	119.1	221.2	158.2	158.4	174.8	163.4	103.4	243.7	150.7	200.9	259.6	206.0	148.4	207.0
2003	184.0	177.6	118.7	227.4	160.3	160.9	178.5	166.8	104.5	250.3	153.9	205.9	267.6	209.9	149.3	213.0
2004	188.9	180.9	118.7	232.7	163.7	164.3	180.7	170.3	106.2	255.8	155.7	206.8	275.7	210.7	150.5	219.4

[1]The indexes are calculated by rebasing the official indexes of each country to the official U.S. base year. Because of the rebasing to 1982–1984, the indexes may differ from official indexes published by national statistical agencies.
[2]Urban worker households prior to 1978.
[3]All households from January 1995, all urban households from September 1978 to December 1994, and middle-income urban households prior to September 1978. In February 1994, excise and duty taxes on cigarettes were reduced by the federal government and three provinces.
[4]Urban worker households prior to September 1998.
[5]Excluding rent and several other services prior to 1976.
[6]Excluding rent prior to 1964.
[7]Paris only prior to 1962. Urban worker households prior to 1991.
[8]Unified Germany from 1991 onward. Prior to 1991, data relate to the former West Germany.
[9]Urban worker households prior to 1960.
[10]Urban worker households prior to May 1993.
. . . = Not available.

Table 11-5. Consumer Price Indexes, 16 Countries, Percent Change from Previous Year, 1956–2004

(1982–1984=100.)

Year		Percent change in consumer price index [1]														
	United States [2]	Canada [3]	Japan	Australia [4]	Austria	Bel-gium [5]	Den-mark [6]	France [7]	Ger-many [8]	Italy	Nether-lands	Norway [9]	Spain	Sweden	Switzer-land [10]	United Kingdom
1956	1.5	1.5	0.4	6.3	. . .	2.9	5.3	1.9	. . .	3.4	. . .	3.7	5.9	5.0	1.5	4.9
1957	3.3	3.2	3.1	2.7	. . .	3.1	2.2	3.5	. . .	1.3	. . .	2.7	10.8	4.3	1.9	3.7
1958	2.8	2.6	-0.5	1.1	. . .	1.3	0.7	15.1	. . .	2.8	. . .	4.8	13.4	4.4	1.8	3.0
1959	0.7	1.1	1.1	1.9	. . .	1.2	1.8	6.1	. . .	-0.4	. . .	2.2	7.3	0.8	-0.7	0.6
1960	1.7	1.2	3.7	4.0	. . .	0.3	1.2	3.6	. . .	2.3	. . .	0.3	1.2	4.1	1.4	1.0
1961	1.0	0.9	5.3	2.6	3.6	1.0	4.2	3.3	. . .	2.1	. . .	2.6	1.1	2.1	1.9	3.4
1962	1.0	1.2	6.8	-0.3	4.4	1.4	7.5	4.8	. . .	4.7	. . .	5.3	5.7	4.8	4.3	4.3
1963	1.3	1.8	7.6	0.5	2.7	2.1	5.3	4.8	2.9	7.5	. . .	2.5	8.8	2.9	3.4	2.0
1964	1.3	1.8	3.8	2.4	3.8	4.2	3.6	3.4	2.4	5.9	. . .	5.7	7.0	3.4	3.1	3.3
1965	1.6	2.4	7.6	4.0	5.0	4.1	6.5	2.5	3.1	4.6	. . .	4.3	13.2	5.0	3.4	4.8
1966	2.9	3.7	5.1	3.0	2.2	4.2	6.7	2.7	3.7	2.3	. . .	3.2	6.2	6.4	4.7	3.9
1967	3.1	3.5	4.0	3.2	4.0	2.9	7.5	2.7	1.7	3.7	. . .	4.4	6.4	4.2	4.0	2.5
1968	4.2	4.1	5.3	2.7	2.8	2.8	8.0	4.5	1.5	1.4	. . .	3.5	4.9	1.9	2.4	4.7
1969	5.5	4.5	5.2	2.9	3.1	3.7	3.5	6.4	1.9	2.7	. . .	3.1	2.2	2.7	2.5	5.4
1970	5.7	3.3	7.7	3.9	4.4	3.9	6.5	5.2	3.4	4.9	3.7	10.6	5.7	7.0	3.6	6.4
1971	4.4	2.9	6.3	6.1	4.7	4.3	5.8	5.5	5.3	4.8	7.6	6.2	8.2	7.4	6.6	9.4
1972	3.2	4.8	4.9	5.9	6.3	5.5	6.6	6.2	5.5	5.7	8.0	7.2	8.3	6.0	6.7	7.1
1973	6.2	7.5	11.7	9.5	7.6	7.0	9.3	7.3	6.9	10.8	8.1	7.5	11.5	6.8	8.7	9.2
1974	11.0	10.9	23.2	15.1	9.5	12.7	15.2	13.7	7.0	19.1	9.8	9.4	15.7	9.9	9.8	16.0
1975	9.1	10.8	11.7	15.1	8.4	12.8	9.6	11.8	6.0	17.0	9.9	11.7	17.0	9.8	6.7	24.2
1976	5.8	7.5	9.4	13.5	7.3	9.2	9.0	9.6	4.3	16.8	9.0	9.1	17.6	10.3	1.7	16.5
1977	6.5	8.0	8.1	12.3	5.5	7.1	11.1	9.4	3.7	17.0	6.4	9.1	24.5	11.4	1.3	15.8
1978	7.6	9.0	4.2	7.9	3.6	4.4	10.1	9.1	2.7	12.1	4.2	8.1	19.8	10.0	1.1	8.3
1979	11.3	9.1	3.7	9.1	3.7	4.5	9.6	10.8	4.1	14.8	4.3	4.8	15.7	7.2	3.6	13.4
1980	13.5	10.1	7.7	10.2	6.4	6.6	12.3	13.6	5.4	21.2	7.0	10.9	15.5	13.7	4.0	18.0
1981	10.3	12.5	4.9	9.7	6.8	7.6	11.7	13.4	6.3	17.8	6.7	13.6	14.6	12.1	6.5	11.9
1982	6.2	10.8	2.8	11.2	5.4	8.7	10.1	11.8	5.3	16.5	5.7	11.3	14.5	8.6	5.6	8.6
1983	3.2	5.8	1.9	10.1	3.3	7.7	6.9	9.6	3.3	14.7	2.7	8.4	12.2	8.9	2.9	4.6
1984	4.3	4.4	2.3	4.0	5.6	6.3	6.3	7.4	2.4	10.8	3.2	6.2	11.3	8.1	3.0	5.0
1985	3.6	4.0	2.0	6.7	3.2	4.9	4.7	5.8	2.1	9.2	2.3	5.7	8.8	7.3	3.4	6.1
1986	1.9	4.1	0.6	9.1	1.7	1.3	3.6	2.7	-0.1	5.9	0.2	7.2	8.8	4.3	0.7	3.4
1987	3.6	4.4	0.1	8.5	1.4	1.6	4.0	3.1	0.2	4.7	-0.4	8.7	5.3	4.2	1.5	4.2
1988	4.1	4.1	0.7	6.9	2.0	1.2	4.6	2.7	1.3	5.0	0.9	6.7	4.8	5.8	1.8	4.9
1989	4.8	5.0	2.3	7.9	2.5	3.1	4.8	3.6	2.8	6.3	1.0	4.6	6.8	6.5	3.2	7.8
1990	5.4	4.8	3.1	7.3	3.3	3.5	2.6	3.4	2.7	6.5	2.6	4.1	6.7	10.4	5.4	9.5
1991	4.2	5.6	3.3	3.2	3.3	3.2	2.4	3.2	3.7	6.3	3.1	3.4	6.0	9.4	5.8	5.9
1992	3.0	1.5	1.6	1.0	4.1	2.4	2.1	2.4	5.1	5.2	3.2	2.3	5.9	2.4	4.0	3.7
1993	3.0	1.8	1.3	1.8	3.6	2.8	1.2	2.1	4.4	4.5	2.6	2.3	4.6	4.7	3.3	1.6
1994	2.6	0.2	0.7	1.9	3.0	2.4	2.0	1.7	2.7	4.0	2.7	1.4	4.8	2.1	0.9	2.4
1995	2.8	2.1	-0.1	4.6	2.2	1.5	2.1	1.7	1.7	5.2	2.0	2.4	4.6	2.5	1.8	3.5
1996	3.0	1.6	0.1	2.6	1.9	2.1	2.1	2.0	1.5	4.0	2.0	1.3	3.6	0.5	0.8	2.4
1997	2.3	1.6	1.8	0.3	1.3	1.6	2.2	1.2	1.9	2.0	2.2	2.6	2.0	0.7	0.5	3.1
1998	1.6	0.9	0.6	0.9	0.9	1.0	1.9	0.7	0.9	2.0	2.0	2.3	1.8	-0.3	0.1	3.4
1999	2.2	1.7	-0.3	1.5	0.6	1.1	2.5	0.5	0.6	1.7	2.2	2.3	2.3	0.5	0.8	1.5
2000	3.4	2.7	-0.7	4.5	2.3	2.5	3.0	1.7	1.4	2.5	2.6	3.1	3.4	0.9	1.5	3.0
2001	2.8	2.6	-0.7	4.4	2.7	2.5	2.4	1.7	2.0	2.7	4.5	3.0	3.6	2.4	1.0	1.8
2002	1.6	2.2	-0.9	3.0	1.8	1.6	2.3	1.9	1.4	2.5	3.5	1.3	3.5	2.2	0.7	1.7
2003	2.3	2.8	-0.3	2.8	1.3	1.6	2.1	2.1	1.1	2.7	2.1	2.5	3.1	1.9	0.6	2.9
2004	2.7	1.9	0.0	2.3	2.1	2.1	1.2	2.1	1.6	2.2	1.2	0.4	3.0	0.4	0.8	3.0

[1]The figures may differ from official percent changes published by national statistical agencies due to rounding. In the case of Sweden, the official percent changes are not calculated from the published index.
[2]Urban worker households prior to 1978.
[3]All households from January 1995, all urban households from September 1978 to December 1994, and middle-income urban households prior to September 1978. In February 1994, excise and duty taxes on cigarettes were reduced by the federal government and three provinces. In 1994, the consumer price index excluding tobacco increased 1.5 percent.
[4]Urban worker households prior to September 1998.
[5]Excluding rent and several other services prior to 1976.
[6]Excluding rent prior to 1964.
[7]Paris only prior to 1962. Urban worker households prior to 1991.
[8]Unified Germany for 1991 onward. Prior to 1991, data relate to the former West Germany.
[9]Urban worker households prior to 1960.
[10]Urban worker households prior to May 1993.
. . . = Not available.

Table 11-6. Real GDP Per Capita, 15 Countries, 1960–2004

(2002 U.S. dollars.)

Year	United States	Canada	Australia	Japan	Korea	Austria	Bel-gium	Den-mark	France	Ger-many [1]	Italy	Nether-lands	Norway	Sweden	United Kingdom
1960	14 407	11 448	11 474	5 329	1 684	9 290	9 570	11 259	9 427	11 361	8 187	11 195	10 473	11 345	11 716
1961	14 503	11 573	11 501	5 961	1 730	9 730	10 012	11 841	9 843	11 730	8 800	11 367	11 023	11 926	11 904
1962	15 147	12 136	11 403	6 413	1 718	9 902	10 492	12 400	10 313	12 134	9 283	11 691	11 229	12 366	11 935
1963	15 583	12 520	11 889	6 906	1 823	10 240	10 867	12 358	10 670	12 355	9 732	11 912	11 566	12 951	12 468
1964	16 263	13 090	12 497	7 597	1 948	10 787	11 514	13 360	11 249	13 046	9 922	12 765	12 054	13 732	13 072
1965	17 091	13 686	12 997	7 864	2 008	11 023	11 816	13 892	11 688	13 593	10 161	13 258	12 593	14 123	13 288
1966	17 997	14 314	13 046	8 685	2 196	11 564	12 108	14 101	12 196	13 847	10 685	13 452	12 966	14 282	13 475
1967	18 250	14 479	13 651	9 536	2 272	11 823	12 507	14 547	12 668	13 772	11 370	14 005	13 663	14 650	13 730
1968	18 940	15 020	14 095	2 472	12 287	12 823	12 981	15 061	13 111	14 471	12 038	14 792	13 854	15 098	14 243
1969	19 333	15 595	14 789	11 675	2 751	13 014	13 804	15 964	13 915	15 404	12 700	15 617	14 361	15 743	14 480
1970	19 144	15 782	15 533	12 613	2 928	13 892	14 675	16 194	14 581	16 024	13 304	16 314	14 542	16 606	14 762
1971	19 539	16 123	15 624	12 989	3 107	14 537	15 179	16 579	15 135	16 343	13 498	16 831	15 181	16 648	14 984
1972	20 355	16 789	15 748	13 886	3 186	15 350	15 921	17 227	15 669	16 931	13 845	17 176	15 826	16 979	15 478
1973	21 323	17 778	15 952	14 794	3 506	16 012	16 810	17 854	16 389	17 651	14 652	17 898	16 405	17 621	16 544
1974	21 021	18 258	16 387	14 419	3 694	16 615	17 446	17 689	16 788	17 663	15 324	18 479	16 985	18 132	16 316
1975	20 778	18 392	16 317	14 683	3 849	16 598	17 139	17 342	16 665	17 505	14 921	18 349	17 877	18 522	16 231
1976	21 673	19 148	16 590	15 111	4 188	17 389	18 065	18 354	17 304	18 526	15 816	19 065	18 835	18 650	16 670
1977	22 447	19 580	16 980	15 626	4 536	18 218	18 130	18 693	17 781	19 094	16 120	19 394	19 547	18 287	17 085
1978	23 448	20 177	16 951	16 303	4 882	18 208	18 611	18 995	18 297	19 690	16 649	19 757	20 126	18 553	17 652
1979	23 922	20 818	17 476	17 055	5 135	19 237	18 995	19 628	18 862	20 511	17 519	19 984	20 940	19 224	18 109
1980	23 594	20 836	17 832	17 400	4 980	19 580	19 794	19 602	19 112	20 643	18 091	20 157	21 907	19 506	17 707
1981	23 948	21 212	18 161	17 782	5 206	19 501	19 533	19 429	19 305	20 624	18 211	19 914	22 042	19 449	17 444
1982	23 261	20 362	18 421	18 147	5 501	19 867	19 805	20 067	19 757	20 445	18 312	19 569	21 999	19 666	17 798
1983	24 093	20 709	17 711	18 314	6 005	20 509	19 808	20 543	20 045	20 877	18 532	19 835	22 703	20 027	18 420
1984	25 599	21 707	18 320	18 765	6 412	20 506	20 299	21 418	20 283	21 552	19 039	20 376	23 969	20 869	18 863
1985	26 420	22 538	19 046	19 597	6 781	21 020	20 493	22 280	20 574	22 044	19 599	20 823	25 144	21 288	19 485
1986	27 089	22 856	19 589	20 076	7 427	21 470	20 790	23 306	20 946	22 545	20 093	21 358	25 951	21 822	20 208
1987	27 755	23 514	19 754	20 739	8 170	21 787	21 266	23 309	21 275	22 874	20 691	21 609	26 354	22 476	21 084
1988	28 640	24 365	20 487	22 051	9 461	22 510	22 153	23 215	22 065	23 582	21 498	22 108	26 184	22 952	22 087
1989	29 375	24 557	20 964	23 131	9 461	23 200	22 911	23 390	22 774	24 195	22 098	23 032	26 316	23 412	22 503
1990	29 593	24 235	21 406	24 254	10 226	24 084	23 519	23 824	23 261	25 094	22 516	23 806	26 743	23 486	22 610
1991	29 152	23 446	21 088	24 968	11 077	24 703	23 892	24 096	23 425	23 606	22 813	24 183	27 445	23 068	22 223
1992	29 724	23 371	20 881	25 116	11 606	25 010	24 175	24 469	23 762	23 949	22 971	24 359	28 244	22 533	22 218
1993	30 125	23 655	21 407	25 104	12 194	24 887	23 849	24 477	23 429	23 586	22 754	24 344	28 798	21 991	22 693
1994	30 958	24 520	22 016	25 315	13 102	25 451	24 542	25 866	23 832	24 140	23 251	24 893	30 133	22 745	23 646
1995	31 360	24 948	22 684	25 742	14 160	25 897	25 075	26 610	24 308	24 525	23 930	25 517	31 353	23 543	24 266
1996	32 144	25 088	23 356	26 565	15 008	26 540	25 321	27 114	24 489	24 697	24 185	26 181	32 880	23 809	24 900
1997	33 190	25 889	23 947	26 998	15 559	26 998	26 135	27 790	24 991	25 095	24 661	27 045	34 363	24 376	25 661
1998	34 176	26 726	24 746	26 633	14 388	27 928	26 608	28 343	25 789	25 612	25 096	28 049	34 993	25 250	26 392
1999	35 291	27 976	25 778	26 616	15 642	28 800	27 394	28 965	26 532	26 108	25 509	28 974	35 513	26 386	27 065
2000	36 181	29 166	26 436	27 323	16 828	29 695	28 388	29 619	27 453	26 913	26 269	29 766	36 130	27 483	28 032
2001	36 078	29 369	26 639	27 365	17 346	29 791	28 494	29 819	27 843	27 183	26 717	29 963	36 467	27 696	28 479
2002	36 386	29 937	27 327	27 196	18 453	29 986	28 623	29 825	28 009	27 179	26 737	29 939	36 615	28 152	28 894
2003	37 125	30 263	27 876	27 823	18 931	30 087	28 864	29 905	28 062	27 167	26 596	29 535	36 537	28 459	29 438
2004	38 392	30 872	28 588	28 337	19 715	30 620	29 637	30 473	28 538	27 600	26 658	29 786	37 379	29 333	30 273

[1]Unified Germany for 1991 onward. Prior to 1991, data relate to the former West Germany.

Table 11-7. Real GDP per Employed Person, 15 Countries, 1960–2004

(2002 U.S. dollars.)

Year	United States	Canada	Australia	Japan	Korea	Austria	Bel-gium	Den-mark	France	Ger-many [1]	Italy	Nether-lands	Norway	Sweden	United Kingdom
1960	38 133	32 583	. . .	10 671	. . .	17 607	24 884	23 948	22 162	24 163	19 640	27 909	24 779	23 359	25 441
1961	39 005	33 089	. . .	11 779	. . .	18 441	25 929	24 992	23 385	24 935	21 118	28 306	25 882	24 487	25 791
1962	40 649	34 409	. . .	12 646	. . .	18 972	26 865	25 971	24 951	26 007	22 494	28 943	26 430	25 392	25 968
1963	41 844	35 346	. . .	13 641	6 571	19 882	27 838	25 774	26 076	26 675	24 156	29 496	27 309	26 612	27 238
1964	43 325	36 388	. . .	14 945	7 080	21 118	29 356	27 511	27 472	28 428	24 918	31 480	28 586	28 025	28 375
1965	45 003	37 372	. . .	15 551	7 105	21 868	30 284	28 314	28 697	29 781	26 376	32 869	29 848	28 897	28 747
1966	46 544	38 240	. . .	16 783	7 766	23 296	31 131	28 494	29 970	30 706	28 419	33 529	30 841	29 459	29 246
1967	46 611	38 293	. . .	18 266	7 939	24 394	32 479	29 642	31 294	31 642	30 084	35 415	32 546	30 779	30 320
1968	47 853	39 628	. . .	20 060	8 413	25 824	33 882	30 658	32 724	33 339	32 070	37 440	33 239	31 565	31 750
1969	48 146	40 497	. . .	22 242	9 347	27 496	35 525	32 084	34 486	35 278	34 271	39 331	34 436	32 533	32 421
1970	47 959	41 132	. . .	24 251	9 815	29 395	37 754	32 383	35 974	36 591	35 924	41 106	34 566	33 974	33 247
1971	49 379	42 446	. . .	25 138	10 272	30 562	38 867	33 449	37 526	37 558	36 607	42 682	36 024	34 362	33 941
1972	50 507	43 465	. . .	27 112	10 283	32 222	41 007	34 318	38 958	38 999	37 860	44 392	37 408	35 034	35 059
1973	51 712	44 404	. . .	28 643	10 928	33 331	43 049	35 368	40 517	40 416	39 776	46 612	38 752	36 288	36 991
1974	50 508	44 421	. . .	28 411	11 222	34 200	44 149	35 503	41 417	40 992	41 234	48 035	39 831	36 720	36 409
1975	50 980	44 639	. . .	29 362	11 615	34 330	44 131	35 369	41 664	41 596	40 358	48 481	41 459	36 929	36 358
1976	52 001	46 167	. . .	30 281	12 097	35 781	46 840	36 924	43 093	44 044	42 562	50 497	42 459	37 191	37 553
1977	52 521	46 930	. . .	31 236	12 890	37 049	47 253	37 808	44 113	45 232	43 433	50 606	43 044	36 524	38 442
1978	53 178	47 408	. . .	32 565	13 458	36 811	48 506	38 264	45 367	46 212	44 870	51 380	43 709	37 025	39 511
1979	53 364	47 376	41 200	34 001	14 170	38 659	49 092	39 278	46 732	47 367	46 831	51 365	44 995	37 895	40 172
1980	52 984	46 671	41 578	34 722	13 877	38 988	51 278	39 573	47 474	47 104	47 770	50 653	46 077	38 104	39 507
1981	53 718	46 732	41 810	35 470	14 375	39 082	51 582	39 854	48 408	47 202	48 181	50 125	45 917	37 979	39 968
1982	53 111	46 826	42 591	36 155	15 046	40 393	53 008	41 040	49 770	47 321	48 386	49 746	45 993	38 497	41 550
1983	54 795	47 706	42 311	36 190	16 522	41 909	53 557	41 955	50 919	48 849	48 828	51 629	47 746	39 131	43 339
1984	56 438	49 253	43 930	37 192	17 955	41 933	54 993	43 082	51 889	50 144	50 178	52 535	50 181	40 476	43 522
1985	57 608	50 198	44 928	38 872	18 483	42 880	55 228	43 831	53 301	50 783	51 186	52 449	51 398	40 936	44 512
1986	58 296	49 921	44 940	39 818	19 740	43 698	55 679	44 862	54 327	51 264	52 120	53 246	51 561	41 802	45 991
1987	58 764	50 559	44 750	41 166	20 794	44 392	56 703	44 796	55 059	51 648	53 554	53 337	51 550	42 858	47 156
1988	59 890	51 536	45 776	43 446	22 304	45 527	58 524	44 943	56 935	53 157	55 078	54 550	51 716	43 371	47 929
1989	60 787	51 759	45 801	45 081	22 872	46 606	59 695	45 601	58 138	54 293	56 274	56 248	53 708	43 895	47 741
1990	61 206	51 497	45 805	46 647	24 241	47 883	60 575	46 856	59 224	55 733	56 484	55 992	55 219	43 970	47 889
1991	61 676	51 241	46 010	47 249	25 716	48 971	61 697	47 796	59 877	48 889	56 218	56 398	57 462	44 146	48 514
1992	63 398	52 169	46 990	47 176	26 711	49 860	62 968	49 146	61 398	50 715	56 924	55 796	59 607	45 395	49 801
1993	64 230	53 134	48 753	47 115	28 018	50 261	62 834	50 095	61 584	50 983	57 865	55 990	60 835	47 021	51 453
1994	65 366	54 559	49 726	47 582	29 469	51 581	65 108	53 318	62 774	52 392	60 031	56 935	63 153	49 425	52 685
1995	66 079	55 151	49 868	48 437	31 279	52 690	66 212	54 197	63 687	53 262	61 855	58 194	64 672	50 650	54 219
1996	67 593	55 550	50 693	49 893	32 763	53 883	66 782	55 223	64 143	53 939	62 142	58 894	66 805	51 742	55 233
1997	69 120	56 647	52 116	50 306	33 704	54 399	68 472	56 128	65 397	54 964	63 160	58 567	68 202	53 702	56 055
1998	70 987	57 546	53 716	50 080	33 403	55 613	68 626	56 423	66 715	55 417	63 625	59 868	68 138	54 811	57 203
1999	73 050	59 175	55 479	50 553	35 935	56 420	69 845	56 640	67 596	55 777	63 974	59 993	69 065	56 138	58 052
2000	73 875	60 753	56 422	52 065	37 391	57 712	71 186	57 801	68 529	56 508	64 681	59 621	70 431	57 180	59 604
2001	74 403	61 066	56 407	52 601	38 077	57 785	70 661	58 175	68 747	56 930	64 557	58 829	71 256	56 706	60 476
2002	76 021	61 484	57 888	53 074	39 634	58 528	71 506	58 495	69 090	57 341	63 652	59 711	71 859	57 737	61 077
2003	77 619	61 286	58 313	54 552	40 917	58 916	72 372	59 250	69 700	57 895	63 090	59 363	72 570	58 684	61 833
2004	80 187	61 954	59 475	55 474	42 023	59 539	73 927	60 472	71 341	58 595	63 310	60 023	74 539	61 044	63 205

[1]Unified Germany for 1991 onward. Prior to 1991, data relate to the former West Germany.
. . . = Not available.

Table 11-8. Employment–Population Ratios, 15 Countries, 1960–2004

(Percent.)

Year	United States	Canada	Australia	Japan	Korea	Austria	Bel-gium	Den-mark	France	Ger-many [1]	Italy	Nether-lands	Norway	Sweden	United Kingdom
1960	37.8	35.1	...	49.9	...	52.8	38.5	47.0	42.5	47.0	41.7	40.1	42.3	48.6	46.1
1961	37.2	35.0	...	50.6	...	52.8	38.6	47.4	42.1	47.0	41.7	40.2	42.6	48.7	46.2
1962	37.3	35.3	...	50.7	...	52.2	39.1	47.7	41.3	46.7	41.3	40.4	42.5	48.7	46.0
1963	37.2	35.4	...	50.6	27.7	51.5	39.0	47.9	40.9	46.3	40.3	40.4	42.4	48.7	45.8
1964	37.5	36.0	...	50.8	27.5	51.1	39.2	48.6	40.9	45.9	39.8	40.5	42.2	49.0	46.1
1965	38.0	36.6	...	50.6	28.3	50.4	39.0	49.1	40.7	45.6	38.5	40.3	42.2	48.9	46.2
1966	38.7	37.4	...	51.7	28.3	49.6	38.9	49.5	40.7	45.1	37.6	40.1	42.0	48.5	46.1
1967	39.2	37.8	...	52.2	28.6	48.5	38.5	49.1	40.5	43.5	37.8	39.5	42.0	47.6	45.3
1968	39.6	37.9	...	52.6	29.4	47.6	38.3	49.1	40.1	43.4	37.5	39.5	41.7	47.8	44.9
1969	40.2	38.5	...	52.5	29.4	47.3	38.9	49.8	40.3	43.7	37.1	39.7	41.7	48.4	44.7
1970	39.9	38.4	...	52.0	29.8	47.3	38.9	50.0	40.5	43.8	37.0	39.7	42.1	48.9	44.4
1971	39.6	38.0	...	51.7	30.2	47.6	39.1	49.6	40.3	43.5	36.9	39.4	42.1	48.4	44.1
1972	40.3	38.6	...	51.2	31.0	47.6	38.8	50.2	40.2	43.4	36.6	38.7	42.3	48.5	44.1
1973	41.2	40.0	...	51.6	32.1	48.0	39.0	50.5	40.4	43.7	36.8	38.4	42.3	49.4	44.7
1974	41.6	41.1	...	50.7	32.9	48.6	39.5	49.8	40.5	43.1	37.2	38.5	42.6	49.4	44.8
1975	40.8	41.2	...	50.0	33.1	48.3	38.8	49.0	40.0	42.1	37.0	37.8	43.1	50.2	44.6
1976	41.7	41.5	...	49.9	34.6	48.6	38.6	49.7	40.2	42.1	37.2	37.8	44.4	50.1	44.4
1977	42.7	41.7	...	50.0	35.2	49.2	38.4	49.4	40.3	42.2	37.1	38.3	45.4	50.1	44.4
1978	44.1	42.6	...	50.1	36.3	49.5	38.4	49.6	40.3	42.6	37.1	38.5	46.0	50.1	44.7
1979	44.8	43.9	42.4	50.2	36.2	49.8	38.7	50.0	40.4	43.3	37.4	38.9	46.5	50.7	45.1
1980	44.5	44.6	42.9	50.1	35.9	50.2	38.6	49.5	40.3	43.8	37.9	39.8	47.5	51.2	44.8
1981	44.6	45.4	43.4	50.1	36.2	49.9	37.9	48.8	39.9	43.7	37.8	39.7	48.0	51.2	43.6
1982	43.8	43.5	43.3	50.2	36.6	49.2	37.4	48.9	39.7	43.2	37.8	39.3	47.8	51.1	42.8
1983	44.0	43.4	41.9	50.6	36.3	48.9	37.0	49.0	39.4	42.7	38.0	38.4	47.6	51.2	42.5
1984	45.4	44.1	41.7	50.5	35.7	48.9	36.9	49.7	39.1	43.0	37.9	38.8	47.8	51.6	43.3
1985	45.9	44.9	42.4	50.4	36.7	49.0	37.1	50.8	38.6	43.4	38.3	39.7	48.9	52.0	43.8
1986	46.5	45.8	43.6	50.4	37.6	49.1	37.3	52.0	38.6	44.0	38.6	40.1	50.3	52.2	43.9
1987	47.2	46.5	44.1	50.4	39.3	49.1	37.5	52.0	38.6	44.3	38.6	40.5	51.1	52.4	44.7
1988	47.8	47.3	44.8	50.8	40.1	49.4	37.9	51.7	38.8	44.4	39.0	40.5	50.6	52.9	46.1
1989	48.3	47.4	45.8	51.3	41.4	49.8	38.4	51.3	39.2	44.6	39.3	40.9	49.0	53.3	47.1
1990	48.3	47.1	46.7	52.0	42.2	50.3	38.8	50.8	39.3	45.0	39.9	42.5	48.4	53.4	47.2
1991	47.3	45.8	45.8	52.8	43.1	50.4	38.7	50.4	39.1	48.3	40.6	42.9	47.8	52.3	45.8
1992	46.9	44.8	44.4	53.2	43.5	50.2	38.4	49.8	38.7	47.2	40.4	43.7	47.4	49.6	44.6
1993	46.9	44.5	43.9	53.3	43.5	49.5	38.0	48.9	38.0	46.3	39.3	43.5	47.3	46.8	44.1
1994	47.4	44.9	44.3	53.2	44.5	49.3	37.7	48.5	38.0	46.1	38.7	43.7	47.7	46.0	44.9
1995	47.5	45.2	45.5	53.1	45.3	49.2	37.9	49.1	38.2	46.0	38.7	43.8	48.5	46.5	44.8
1996	47.6	45.2	46.1	53.2	45.8	49.3	37.9	49.1	38.2	45.8	38.9	44.5	49.2	46.0	45.1
1997	48.0	45.7	46.0	53.7	46.2	49.6	38.2	49.5	38.2	45.7	39.0	46.2	50.4	45.4	45.8
1998	48.1	46.4	46.1	53.2	43.1	50.2	38.8	50.2	38.7	46.2	39.4	46.9	51.4	46.1	46.1
1999	48.3	47.3	46.5	52.6	43.5	51.0	39.2	51.1	39.3	46.8	39.9	48.3	51.4	47.0	46.6
2000	49.0	48.0	46.9	52.5	45.0	51.5	39.9	51.2	40.1	47.6	40.6	49.9	51.3	48.1	47.0
2001	48.5	48.1	47.2	52.0	45.6	51.6	40.3	51.3	40.5	47.7	41.4	50.9	51.2	48.8	47.1
2002	47.9	48.7	47.2	51.2	46.6	51.2	40.0	51.0	40.5	47.4	42.0	50.1	51.0	48.5	47.3
2003	47.8	49.4	47.8	51.0	46.3	51.1	39.9	50.5	40.3	46.9	42.2	49.8	50.3	48.5	47.6
2004	47.9	49.8	48.1	51.1	46.9	51.4	40.1	50.4	40.0	47.1	42.1	49.6	50.1	48.1	47.9

[1]Unified Germany for 1991 onward. Prior to 1991, data relate to the former West Germany.
. . . = Not available.

Table 11-9. Real GDP per Capita and per Employed Person, 15 Countries, 1980–2004

(Average annual percent changes.)

Country	1980–2004	1980–1990	1990–1995	1995–2000	2000	2001	2002	2003	2004
Real Gross Domestic Product per Capita									
United States	2.0	2.3	1.2	2.9	2.5	-0.3	0.9	2.0	3.4
Canada	1.7	1.5	0.6	3.2	4.3	0.7	1.9	1.1	2.0
Australia	2.0	1.8	1.2	3.1	2.6	0.8	2.6	2.0	2.6
Japan	2.1	3.4	1.2	1.2	2.7	0.2	-0.6	2.3	1.8
Korea	5.9	7.5	6.7	3.5	7.6	3.1	6.4	2.6	4.1
Austria	1.9	2.1	1.5	2.8	3.1	0.3	0.7	0.3	1.8
Belgium	1.7	1.7	1.3	2.5	3.6	0.4	0.5	0.8	2.7
Denmark	1.9	2.0	2.2	2.2	2.3	0.7	0.0	0.3	1.9
France	1.7	2.0	0.9	2.5	3.5	1.4	0.6	0.2	1.7
Germany [1]	1.6	2.0	1.5	1.9	3.1	1.0	0.0	0.0	1.6
Italy	1.6	2.2	1.2	1.9	3.0	1.7	0.1	-0.5	0.2
Netherlands	1.6	1.7	1.4	3.1	2.7	0.7	-0.1	-1.3	0.8
Norway	2.3	2.0	3.2	2.9	1.7	0.9	0.4	-0.2	2.3
Sweden	1.7	1.9	0.0	3.1	4.2	0.8	1.6	1.1	3.1
United Kingdom	2.3	2.5	1.4	2.9	3.6	1.6	1.5	1.9	2.8
Real Gross Domestic Product per Employed Person									
United States	1.7	1.5	1.5	2.3	1.1	0.7	2.2	2.1	3.3
Canada	1.2	1.0	1.4	2.0	2.7	0.5	0.7	-0.3	1.1
Australia	1.5	1.0	1.7	2.5	1.7	0.0	2.6	0.7	2.0
Japan	2.0	3.0	0.8	1.5	3.0	1.0	0.9	2.8	1.7
Korea	4.7	5.7	5.2	3.6	4.1	1.8	4.1	3.2	2.7
Austria	1.8	2.1	1.9	1.8	2.3	0.1	1.3	0.7	1.1
Belgium	1.5	1.7	1.8	1.5	1.9	-0.7	1.2	1.2	2.1
Denmark	1.8	1.7	3.0	1.3	2.1	0.6	0.5	1.3	2.1
France	1.7	2.2	1.5	1.5	1.4	0.3	0.5	0.9	2.4
Germany [1]	1.6	1.7	2.2	1.2	1.3	0.7	0.7	1.0	1.2
Italy	1.2	1.7	1.8	0.9	1.1	-0.2	-1.4	-0.9	0.3
Netherlands	0.7	1.0	0.8	0.5	-0.6	-1.3	1.5	-0.6	1.1
Norway	2.0	1.8	3.2	1.7	2.0	1.2	0.8	1.0	2.7
Sweden	2.0	1.4	2.9	2.5	1.9	-0.8	1.8	1.6	4.0
United Kingdom	2.0	1.9	2.5	1.9	2.7	1.5	1.0	1.2	2.2

[1] Unified Germany for 1995–2000 onward. Prior to that, the data relate to the former West Germany.

PART TWELVE

AMERICAN TIME USE SURVEY (ATUS)

AMERICAN TIME USE SURVEY (ATUS)

HIGHLIGHTS

This part presents the first data from the new American Time Use Survey (ATUS). The survey was introduced in the sixth edition of this *Handbook*. Its purpose is to collect data on the activities people do during the day and the amount of time spent on each one.

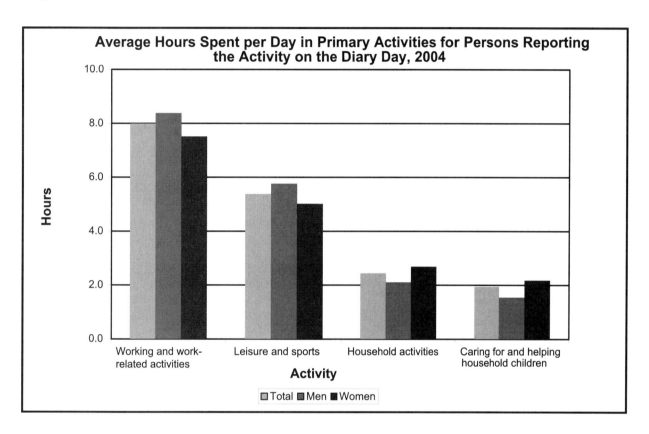

Among those reporting having worked on the diary day, men worked 8.4 hours while women worked 7.5 hours. One reason why women averaged fewer hours is that they are more likely than men to hold part-time jobs. Meanwhile, women spent 2.17 hours per day caring for and helping household children, compared to 1.54 hours for men. (Table 12-1)

OTHER HIGHLIGHTS:

- On an average day in 2004, 84 percent of women and 63 percent of men spent some time doing household activities. Women spent 2.7 hours on such activities, while men spent 2.1 hours. (Table 12-1)

- Approximately 76 percent of persons employed in management, business and financial operations occupations reported working on an average day, a higher percentage than in any other occupation. (Table 12-4)

- Women living with children under 6 years of age provided them with 1.2 hours of physical care per day. Men provided 0.4 hours, or 24 minutes. (Table 12-7)

- Persons 65 years and over spent the most time on an average day (7.3 hours) participating in leisure activities, while 35–44 year olds spent the least time per day (4.2 hours). (Table 12-2)

NOTES AND DEFINITIONS

Survey Methodology

While the Bureau of Labor Statistics (BLS) has long produced statistics about the labor market, such as employment, hours, and earnings, the American Time Use Survey (ATUS) marks the first time that a federal statistical agency has produced estimates on how Americans spend another critical resource—their time. Data collection for the ATUS began in January 2003. Sample cases for the survey are selected monthly, and interviews are conducted continuously throughout the year. In 2004, approximately 14,000 individuals were interviewed.

ATUS sample households are chosen from the households that have completed their eighth (final) interview for the Current Population Survey (CPS), the nation's monthly household labor force survey. (See Part 1 of this *Handbook* for a description of the CPS.) ATUS sample households are selected to ensure that estimates will be representative of the nation.

One individual age 15 or older is randomly chosen from each sample household. This "designated person" takes part in a one-time telephone interview about his or her activities on the previous day—the "diary day."

Concepts and Definitions

Average hours per day. The average number of hours spent in a 24-hour day (between 4 a.m. on the diary day and 4 a.m. on the interview day) doing a specified activity.

Average hours per day, population. The average number of hours per day is computed using all responses from a given population, including respondents who did not do a particular activity on their diary day. These estimates reflect how many population members engaged in an activity and the amount of time they spent engaged in it.

Average hours per day, persons reporting the activity on the diary day. The average number of hours per day is computed using responses only from those who engaged in a particular activity on their diary day.

Diary day. The diary day is the day about which the designated person reports. For example, the diary day of a designated person interviewed on Tuesday is Monday.

Employment status:

Employed. All persons who, at any time during the seven days prior to the interview: 1) did any work at all as paid employees, worked in their own business profession, or on their own farm; usually worked 15 hours or more as unpaid workers in a family-operated enterprise; and 2) all those who were not working but had jobs or businesses from which they were temporarily absent due to illness, bad weather, vacation, childcare problems, labor-management dispute, maternity or paternity leave, job training, or other family or personal reasons, whether or not they were paid for the time off or were seeking other jobs.

Employed full time. Full-time workers are those who usually work 35 hours or more per week at all jobs combined.

Employed part time. Part-time workers are those who usually work fewer than 35 hours per week at all jobs combined.

Not employed. Persons are not employed if they do not meet the conditions for employment. Not employed workers include those classified as unemployed as well as those classified as not in the labor force (using CPS definitions).

The numbers of employed and not employed persons in this report do not correspond to published totals from the CPS. While the information on employment from the ATUS is useful for assessing work in the context of other daily activities, the employment data are not intended for analysis of current employment trends. Compared to the CPS and other estimates of employment, the ATUS estimates are based on a much smaller sample and are only available with a substantial lag.

Household children. Household children are children under 18 years old residing in the household of the ATUS respondent. The children may be related to the respondent (such as their own children, grandchildren, nieces, nephews, brothers, or sisters) or not related (such as foster children or children of roommates). For secondary childcare calculations, respondents are asked about care for household children under 13 years old.

Primary activity. A primary activity is the main activity of a respondent at a specified time.

Major Activity Category Definitions

Personal care activities. Personal care activities include sleeping, bathing, dressing, health-related self-care, and personal or private activities. Receiving unpaid personal care from others (for example, "my sister put polish on my nails") is also captured in this category.

Eating and drinking. All time spent eating or drinking (except when identified by the respondent as part of a work or volunteer activity), whether alone, with others, at home, at a place of purchase, in transit, or somewhere else, is classified here.

Household activities. Household activities are those done by respondents to maintain their households. These include housework; cooking; yard care; pet care; vehicle maintenance and repair; and home maintenance, repair, decoration, and renovation. Food preparation is always classified as a household activity. Household management and organizational activities—such as filling out paperwork, balancing a checkbook, or planning a party—are also included in this category.

Purchasing goods and services. This category includes the purchase of consumer goods as well as the purchase or use of professional and personal care services, household services, and government services. Most purchases and rentals of consumer goods, regardless of mode or place of purchase or rental (in person, via telephone, over the Internet, at home, or in a store) are classified in this category. Time spent obtaining, receiving, and purchasing professional and personal care services provided by someone else also is classified in this category. Time spent arranging for and purchasing household services provided by someone else also is classified here.

Caring for and helping household members. Time spent doing activities to care for or help any child or adult in the respondent's household, regardless of the relationship to the respondent or the physical or mental health status of the person being helped, are classified here. Household members are considered children if they are under 18 years old. Caring for and helping household members also includes a range of activities done to benefit adult members of households, such as providing physical and medical care or obtaining medical services.

Caring for and helping non-household members. Time spent caring for and helping any child or adult who is not part of the respondent's household, regardless of the relationship to the respondent or the physical or mental health status of the person being helped, is classified here.

Working and work-related activities. This category includes time spent working, doing activities as part of one's job, engaging in income-generating activities (not as part of one's job), and job search activities. "Working" includes hours spent doing the specific tasks required of one's main or other job, regardless of location or time of day. Travel time related to working and work-related activities includes time spent commuting to and from one's job, as well as time spent traveling for work-related, income generating, and job search activities.

Educational activities. Educational activities include taking classes (including Internet and other distance-learning courses); doing research and homework; and taking care of administrative tasks, such as registering for classes or obtaining a school ID. For high school students, before and after-school extracurricular activities (except sports) also are classified as educational activities.

Organizational, civic, and religious activities. This category captures time spent volunteering for or through an organization, performing civic obligations, and participating in religious and spiritual activities.

Leisure and sports. The leisure and sports category includes sports, exercise, and recreation; socializing and communicating; and other leisure activities such as watching television, reading, or attending entertainment events.

Telephone calls, mail, and email. This category captures telephone communication and handling household or personal mail and email. Telephone and Internet purchases are classified in purchasing goods and services.

Other activities, not elsewhere classified. This residual category includes security procedures related to traveling, traveling not associated with a specific activity category, ambiguous activities that could not be coded, or missing activities that were considered too private to report.

Sources of Additional Information

Additional information, including expanded definitions and estimation methodology, is available from BLS news release USDL 05-1766; the *Monthly Labor Review*, June 2005; and the ATUS User's Guide, August 2005, on the BLS Web site.

Table 12-1. Average Hours per Day Spent in Primary Activities [1] for the Total Population and for Persons Reporting the Activity on the Diary Day by Activity Category and Sex, 2004 Annual Averages

(Number, percent.)

Activity	Hours per day, total population			Percent of population reporting the activity on the diary day			Hours per day, persons reporting the activity on the diary day		
	Total	Men	Women	Total	Men	Women	Total	Men	Women
Total, All Activities [2]	24.00	24.00	24.00	X	X	X	X	X	X
Personal care activities	9.34	9.16	9.51	100.0	100.0	100.0	9.34	9.16	9.52
Sleeping	8.56	8.51	8.61	99.9	99.9	100.0	8.56	8.51	8.61
Eating and drinking	1.24	1.31	1.18	97.0	97.0	97.0	1.28	1.35	1.22
Household activities	1.80	1.32	2.25	74.0	63.2	84.1	2.44	2.10	2.68
Housework	0.59	0.22	0.93	37.4	19.2	54.3	1.58	1.16	1.72
Food preparation and cleanup	0.51	0.25	0.75	51.2	35.0	66.3	1.00	0.73	1.14
Lawn and garden care	0.19	0.25	0.14	9.9	11.4	8.6	1.96	2.22	1.64
Household management	0.14	0.11	0.17	16.6	13.6	19.5	0.84	0.82	0.85
Purchasing goods and services	0.81	0.65	0.96	45.7	40.6	50.5	1.78	1.61	1.90
Consumer goods purchases	0.41	0.30	0.50	41.2	37.1	45.1	0.98	0.82	1.11
Professional and personal care services	0.09	0.07	0.11	9.4	7.0	11.6	0.96	0.99	0.95
Caring for and helping household members	0.56	0.35	0.76	26.6	21.0	31.9	2.10	1.67	2.37
Caring for and helping household children	0.43	0.25	0.59	22.0	16.2	27.4	1.94	1.54	2.17
Caring for and helping non-household members	0.27	0.24	0.30	15.3	13.1	17.3	1.79	1.86	1.73
Caring for and helping non-household adults	0.10	0.11	0.10	10.0	9.3	10.7	1.05	1.19	0.93
Working and work-related activities	3.65	4.37	2.98	45.7	52.1	39.7	7.99	8.38	7.50
Working	3.31	3.96	2.71	43.6	49.5	38.1	7.60	7.99	7.13
Educational activities	0.50	0.49	0.50	9.1	8.5	9.7	5.46	5.84	5.15
Attending class	0.31	0.33	0.29	6.6	6.3	6.8	4.71	5.20	4.29
Homework and research	0.14	0.12	0.16	5.6	4.7	6.3	2.56	2.53	2.58
Organizational, civic, and religious activities	0.32	0.28	0.35	13.6	11.7	15.3	2.33	2.40	2.27
Religious and spiritual activities	0.12	0.12	0.13	7.6	6.8	8.4	1.63	1.73	1.55
Volunteering (organizational and civic activities)	0.15	0.13	0.17	7.1	5.9	8.2	2.09	2.12	2.07
Leisure and sports	5.18	5.56	4.82	96.3	96.6	96.1	5.37	5.76	5.01
Socializing and communicating	0.75	0.71	0.78	40.1	37.0	43.0	1.87	1.92	1.83
Watching television	2.64	2.85	2.44	80.5	82.5	78.6	3.28	3.46	3.10
Participating in sports, exercise, and recreation	0.30	0.40	0.20	17.7	20.2	15.3	1.67	1.98	1.28
Telephone calls, mail, and email	0.18	0.11	0.25	24.9	18.6	30.7	0.74	0.62	0.81
Other activities, not elsewhere classified	0.14	0.13	0.15	10.8	9.4	12.2	1.30	1.41	1.22

Note: Data refer to respondents 15 years and over.

[1]Primary activities are those respondents identify as their main activity. Other activities done simultaneously are not included.
[2]All major activity categories include related travel time.
X = Not applicable.

Table 12-2. Average Hours per Day Spent in Primary Activities [1] for the Total Population by Age, Sex, Race, Hispanic or Latino Ethnicity and Educational Attainment, 2004 Annual Averages

(Number.)

Characteristic	Personal care activities	Eating and drinking	Household activities	Purchasing goods and services	Caring for and helping household members	Caring for and helping non-household members	Working and work-related activities	Educational activities	Organizational, civic, and religious activities	Leisure activities	Telephone calls	Other activities not elsewhere classified
Total, 15 Years and Over	9.34	1.24	1.80	0.81	0.56	0.27	3.65	0.50	0.32	5.18	0.18	0.14
15 to 24 years	10.00	1.03	0.83	0.60	0.30	0.24	2.43	2.19	0.28	5.68	0.27	0.15
25 to 34 years	9.25	1.18	1.53	0.85	1.15	0.25	4.71	0.28	0.20	4.40	0.12	0.09
35 to 44 years	9.03	1.17	1.90	0.82	1.05	0.22	4.98	0.15	0.31	4.15	0.13	0.10
45 to 54 years	9.01	1.25	2.05	0.87	0.40	0.30	4.87	0.10	0.34	4.51	0.17	0.14
55 to 64 years	9.09	1.37	2.16	0.89	0.18	0.39	3.75	(5)	0.33	5.45	0.18	0.15
65 years and over	9.65	1.53	2.55	0.89	0.11	0.28	0.70	0.03	0.46	7.31	0.25	0.23
Men, 15 Years and Over	9.16	1.31	1.32	0.65	0.35	0.24	4.37	0.49	0.28	5.56	0.11	0.13
15 to 24 years	9.78	1.02	0.60	0.48	0.11	0.22	2.71	2.16	0.25	6.31	0.19	0.16
25 to 34 years	9.09	1.27	1.02	0.68	0.52	0.25	5.74	0.26	0.20	4.80	0.08	0.08
35 to 44 years	8.93	1.23	1.32	0.63	0.74	0.25	5.89	(5)	0.30	4.45	0.08	0.08
45 to 54 years	8.77	1.39	1.59	0.63	0.33	0.21	5.59	(5)	0.30	4.86	0.08	0.13
55 to 64 years	8.94	1.43	1.66	0.68	0.14	0.28	4.44	(5)	0.27	5.89	0.10	0.13
65 years and over	9.43	1.67	2.06	0.90	0.12	0.27	0.96	(5)	0.40	7.77	0.16	0.24
Women, 15 Years and Over	9.51	1.18	2.25	0.96	0.76	0.30	2.98	0.50	0.35	4.82	0.25	0.15
15 to 24 years	10.22	1.05	1.07	0.72	0.49	0.26	2.14	2.22	0.32	5.03	0.35	0.13
25 to 34 years	9.41	1.09	2.05	1.01	1.76	0.24	3.69	0.30	0.20	3.99	0.15	0.10
35 to 44 years	9.14	1.11	2.46	1.00	1.35	0.18	4.08	0.21	0.31	3.86	0.17	0.12
45 to 54 years	9.24	1.13	2.47	1.08	0.46	0.38	4.20	0.10	0.37	4.18	0.24	0.14
55 to 64 years	9.23	1.31	2.61	1.08	0.23	0.50	3.12	(5)	0.38	5.05	0.25	0.17
65 years and over	9.82	1.43	2.91	0.89	0.10	0.28	0.51	(5)	0.50	6.96	0.32	0.23
White, 15 Years and Over	9.27	1.29	1.87	0.81	0.55	0.28	3.73	0.45	0.30	5.14	0.18	0.14
Men	9.09	1.37	1.36	0.65	0.34	0.24	4.52	0.46	0.26	5.47	0.11	0.13
Women	9.44	1.22	2.35	0.96	0.74	0.31	2.98	0.44	0.34	4.83	0.24	0.15
Black or African American, 15 Years and Over	9.87	0.88	1.39	0.79	0.54	0.26	3.14	0.71	0.42	5.65	0.23	0.13
Men	9.68	0.86	1.13	0.62	0.33	0.28	3.21	(5)	0.45	6.52	0.18	0.12
Women	10.02	0.89	1.60	0.92	0.71	0.24	3.08	0.77	0.40	4.96	0.26	0.14
Hispanic or Latino Ethnicity, 15 Years and Over	9.82	1.15	1.86	0.89	0.61	0.24	3.50	0.61	0.29	4.81	0.11	0.11
Men	9.63	1.21	1.10	0.74	0.29	0.29	4.24	(5)	0.26	5.34	0.10	0.11
Women	10.02	1.09	2.64	1.04	0.94	0.19	2.73	0.52	0.32	4.26	0.13	0.11
Marital Status and Sex												
Married, Spouse Present	9.07	1.32	2.14	0.87	0.77	0.27	4.05	0.11	0.35	4.77	0.13	0.14
Men	8.85	1.40	1.56	0.69	0.54	0.24	5.00	0.08	0.34	5.09	0.07	0.13
Women	9.29	1.25	2.71	1.04	1.01	0.31	3.10	0.15	0.36	4.45	0.19	0.15
Other Marital Status	9.68	1.14	1.39	0.75	0.30	0.27	3.16	0.97	0.27	5.68	0.25	0.14
Men	9.57	1.19	1.00	0.61	0.10	0.25	3.52	1.05	0.21	6.19	0.17	0.14
Women	9.77	1.10	1.72	0.86	0.47	0.29	2.85	0.91	0.33	5.24	0.31	0.14
Educational Attainment, 25 Years and Over												
Less than a high school diploma	9.93	1.14	2.20	0.75	0.42	0.26	2.59	(5)	0.31	6.13	0.08	0.15
High school graduates, no college [3]	9.30	1.26	2.10	0.83	0.52	0.33	3.56	0.08	0.28	5.45	0.15	0.14
Less than a bachelor's degree	9.12	1.25	1.98	0.90	0.65	0.27	4.14	0.17	0.32	4.89	0.18	0.13
Bachelor's degree or higher [4]	8.83	1.41	1.87	0.91	0.78	0.24	4.71	0.20	0.38	4.33	0.21	0.15

Note: Hispanics or Latinos may be of any race.

[1] Primary activities are those respondents identify as their main activity. Other activities done simultaneously are not included.
[2] All major activity categories include related travel time.
[3] Includes persons with a high school diploma or equivalent.
[4] Includes persons with bachelor's, master's, professional, and doctoral degrees.
[5] Data not shown where base is less than 800,000.

Table 12-3. Average Hours Worked per Day by Employed Persons on Weekdays and Weekends by Selected Characteristics, 2004 Annual Averages

(Number.)

Characteristic	Total employed	Worked on an average day			Worked on an average weekday			Worked on an average Saturday, Sunday, or holiday [1]		
		Number	Percent	Hours per day [2]	Number [3]	Percent	Hours per day [2]	Number [4]	Percent	Hours per day [2]
Total, 15 Years and Over [5]	145 279	98 665	67.9	7.63	120 437	82.9	7.93	47 732	32.9	5.82
Full-time workers	112 274	80 678	71.9	8.08	99 865	88.9	8.45	37 271	33.2	5.87
Part-time workers	33 005	17 987	54.5	5.58	20 863	63.2	5.58	10 418	31.6	5.60
Men [5]	76 709	54 106	70.5	8.02	66 282	86.4	8.38	26 788	34.9	6.06
Full-time workers	66 283	47 978	72.4	8.28	59 414	89.6	8.67	22 812	34.4	6.02
Part-time workers	10 426	6 128	58.8	6.02	6 959	66.7	5.95	4 012	38.5	6.31
Women [5]	68 570	44 560	65.0	7.15	54 226	79.1	7.41	20 841	30.4	5.49
Full-time workers	45 991	32 701	71.1	7.80	40 461	88.0	8.13	14 419	31.4	5.64
Part-time workers	22 579	11 859	52.5	5.35	13 909	61.6	5.39	6 381	28.3	5.13
Multiple Job Holding Status										
Single jobholders	131 273	87 166	66.4	7.58	107 771	82.1	7.85	39 226	29.9	5.84
Multiple jobholders	14 005	11 499	82.1	8.02	12 648	90.3	8.66	8 667	61.9	5.73
Educational Attainment, 25 Years and Over										
Less than high school	10 212	6 936	67.9	8.03	8 959	87.7	8.09	3 350	32.8	7.79
High school graduates, no college [6]	37 091	25 716	69.3	7.86	31 399	84.7	8.03	12 231	33.0	6.79
Less than a bachelor's degree	32 455	22 203	68.4	7.70	27 391	84.4	8.04	9 705	29.9	5.36
Bachelor's degree or higher [7]	43 193	31 290	72.4	7.60	37 936	87.8	8.08	14 704	34.0	4.54

Note: Unless otherwise specified, data refer to persons 15 years and over.

[1] Holidays are New Year's Day, Easter, Memorial Day, the Fourth of July, Labor Day, Thanksgiving Day, and Christmas Day. In 2003, data were not collected for Thanksgiving Day or Christmas Day.
[2] Includes work at main and other job(s), and excludes travel related to work.
[3] Number was derived by multiplying the "total employed" by the percent of employed persons who worked on an average weekday.
[4] Number was derived by multiplying the "total employed" by the percent of employed persons who worked on an average Saturday, Sunday, and holiday.
[5] Includes workers whose hours vary.
[6] Includes persons with a high school diploma or equivalent.
[7] Includes persons with bachelor's, master's, professional, and doctoral degrees.

Table 12-4. Average Hours Worked per Day at Main Job Only by Employed Persons on Weekdays and Weekend Days by Selected Characteristics, 2004 Annual Averages

(Number.)

Characteristic	Total employed	Worked on an average day			Worked on an average weekday			Worked on an average Saturday, Sunday, or holiday [1]		
		Number	Percent	Hours per day [2]	Number [3]	Percent	Hours per day [2]	Number [4]	Percent	Hours per day [2]
Class of Worker										
Wage and salary workers	134 445	89 336	66.4	7.61	110 710	82.3	7.87	39 605	29.5	5.91
Self-employed workers	10 664	7 914	74.2	6.75	9 024	84.6	7.16	5 086	47.7	4.91
Occupation										
Management, business, and financial operations	21 538	16 266	75.5	7.72	19 745	91.7	8.15	7 182	33.3	4.64
Professional and related	31 739	21 408	67.5	7.53	26 352	83.0	7.90	9 096	28.7	4.83
Services	24 295	14 693	60.5	7.04	16 648	68.5	7.10	9 904	40.8	6.82
Sales and related	14 967	10 000	66.8	7.04	11 582	77.4	7.36	6 326	42.3	5.70
Office and administrative support	19 816	12 784	64.5	7.23	16 947	85.5	7.40	3 634	18.3	5.50
Farming, fishing, and forestry	1 296	(6)	(6)	(6)	(6)	(6)	(6)	(6)	(6)	(6)
Construction and extraction	8 606	5 814	67.6	8.10	7 769	90.3	8.32	1 664	19.3	5.95
Installation, maintenance, and repair	5 383	3 711	68.9	7.83	4 778	88.8	8.00	(6)	(6)	(6)
Production	9 826	6 536	66.5	8.28	8 317	84.6	8.45	2 561	26.1	7.01
Transportation and material moving	7 812	5 164	66.1	8.17	6 641	85.0	8.42	2 628	33.6	7.09
Earnings of Full-time Wage and Salary Earners [5]										
0 - $450	26 711	17 976	67.3	7.85	22 481	84.2	7.97	8 045	30.1	7.14
$451 - $675	24 596	17 159	69.8	8.04	22 193	90.2	8.33	6 140	25.0	5.70
$676 - $1,050	24 857	17 643	71.0	8.04	22 216	89.4	8.34	7 142	28.7	5.92
$1,051 and higher	25 313	18 207	71.9	8.06	22 577	89.2	8.51	7 803	30.8	4.97

Note: Unless otherwise specified, data refer to persons 15 years and over.

[1]Holidays are New Year's Day, Easter, Memorial Day, the Fourth of July, Labor Day, Thanksgiving Day, and Christmas Day. In 2003, data were not collected for Thanksgiving Day or Christmas Day.
[2]Includes work at main job only, and excludes travel related to work.
[3]Number was derived by multiplying the "total employed" by the percent of employed persons who worked on an average weekday.
[4]Number was derived by multiplying the "total employed" by the percent of employed persons who worked on an average Saturday, Sunday, and holiday.
[5]These values are based on usual weekly earnings. Each earnings range represents approximately 25 percent of full-time wage and salary workers.
[6]Data not shown where base is less than 800,000.

Table 12-5. Average Hours Worked per Day at All Jobs by Employed Persons at Workplace or Home by Selected Characteristics, 2004 Annual Averages

(Number.)

Characteristic	Total employed	Employed persons who reported working on the diary day [1]								
		Number	Percent	Hours of work	Location of work [2]					
					Persons who reported working at the workplace on the diary day			Persons who reported working at home on the diary day [3]		
					Number	Percent	Hours of work at workplace	Number	Percent	Hours of work at home
Full and Part-time Status and Sex										
Total, 15 years and over [4]	145 279	98 665	67.9	7.63	85 822	87.0	7.86	19 155	19.4	2.83
Full-time workers	112 274	80 678	71.9	8.08	71 472	88.6	8.22	15 296	19.0	2.99
Part-time workers	33 005	17 987	54.5	5.58	14 350	79.8	6.06	3 858	21.5	2.20
Men [4]	76 709	54 106	70.5	8.02	47 478	87.7	8.16	10 373	19.2	3.17
Full-time workers	66 283	47 978	72.4	8.28	42 498	88.6	8.38	9 277	19.3	3.20
Part-time workers	10 426	6 128	58.8	6.02	4 979	81.3	6.30	1 096	17.9	2.92
Women [4]	68 570	44 560	65.0	7.15	38 344	86.1	7.49	8 781	19.7	2.43
Full-time workers	45 991	32 701	71.1	7.80	28 974	88.6	7.99	6 019	18.4	2.68
Part-time workers	22 579	11 859	52.5	5.35	9 370	79.0	5.94	2 762	23.3	1.91
Multiple Jobholding Status										
Single jobholders	131 273	87 166	66.4	7.58	76 245	87.5	7.82	15 576	17.9	2.86
Multiple jobholders	14 005	11 499	82.1	8.02	9 577	83.3	8.17	3 579	31.1	2.69
Educational Attainment, 25 Years and Over										
Less than a high school diploma	10 212	6 936	67.9	8.03	6 571	94.7	8.11	(7)	(7)	(7)
High school graduates, no college [5]	37 091	25 716	69.3	7.86	23 442	91.2	7.97	3 241	12.6	2.81
Some college or associate degree	32 455	22 203	68.4	7.70	19 470	87.7	7.99	4 249	19.1	2.85
Bachelor's degree or higher [6]	43 193	31 290	72.4	7.60	24 694	78.9	7.98	10 378	33.2	2.86

Note: Unless otherwise specified, data refer to persons 15 years and over.

[1] Includes work at main and other job(s) and at locations other than home or workplace. Excludes travel related to work.
[2] Respondents can report working at more than one location during the diary day.
[3] "Working at home" includes any time the respondent reported doing activities that were identified as "part of one's job," and is not restricted to persons whose usual workplace is their home.
[4] Includes workers whose hours vary.
[5] Includes persons with a high school diploma or equivalent.
[6] Includes persons with bachelor's, master's, professional, and doctoral degrees.
[7] Data not shown where base is less than 800,000.

Table 12-6. Average Hours Worked per Day at Main Job Only by Employed Persons at Workplace or Home by Selected Characteristics, 2004 Annual Averages

(Number.)

Characteristic	Total employed	Employed persons who reported working on the diary day [1]								
		Number	Percent	Hours of work	Location of work [2]					
					Persons who reported working at the workplace on the diary day			Persons who reported working at home on the diary day [3]		
					Number	Percent	Hours of work at workplace	Number	Percent	Hours of work at home
Class of Worker										
Wage and salary workers	134 445	89 336	66.4	7.61	80 041	89.6	7.82	13 795	15.4	2.57
Self-employed workers	10 664	7 914	74.2	6.75	4 735	59.8	7.37	3 829	48.4	3.90
Occupation										
Management, business, and financial operations	21 538	16 266	75.5	7.72	13 003	79.9	8.26	4 302	26.4	3.23
Professional and related	31 739	21 408	67.5	7.53	17 510	81.8	7.84	6 067	28.3	2.81
Services	24 295	14 693	60.5	7.04	13 573	92.4	7.23	1 437	9.8	2.49
Sales and related	14 967	10 000	66.8	7.04	8 406	84.1	7.36	2 391	23.9	2.56
Office and administrative support	19 816	12 784	64.5	7.23	11 625	90.9	7.44	1 345	10.5	3.15
Farming, fishing, and forestry	1 296	(5)	(5)	(5)	(5)	(5)	(5)	(5)	(5)	(5)
Construction and extraction	8 606	5 814	67.6	8.10	5 327	91.6	8.27	(5)	(5)	(5)
Installation, maintenance, and repair	5 383	3 711	68.9	7.83	3 483	93.9	7.99	(5)	(5)	(5)
Production	9 826	6 536	66.5	8.28	6 252	95.7	8.35	(5)	(5)	(5)
Transportation and material moving	7 812	5 164	66.1	8.17	4 928	95.4	8.11	(5)	(5)	(5)
Earnings of Full-time Wage and Salary Earners [4]										
0 - $450	26 711	17 976	67.3	7.85	17 151	95.4	7.90	1 065	5.9	2.65
$451 - $675	24 596	17 159	69.8	8.04	16 048	93.5	8.19	1 730	10.1	2.34
$676 - $1,050	24 857	17 643	71.0	8.04	16 249	92.1	8.18	2 614	14.8	2.11
$1,051 and higher	25 313	18 207	71.9	8.06	15 199	83.5	8.42	4 933	27.1	2.69

Note: Unless otherwise specified, data refer to persons 15 years and over.

[1]Includes work at main and other job(s) and at locations other than home or workplace. Excludes travel related to work.
[2]Respondents can report working at more than one location during the diary day.
[3]"Working at home" includes any time the respondent reported doing activities that were identified as "part of one's job," and is not restricted to persons whose usual workplace is their home.
[4]These values are based on usual weekly earnings. Each earnings range represents approximately 25 percent of full-time wage and salary workers.
[5]Data not shown where base is less than 800,000.

Table 12-7. Average Hours per Day Spent by Persons 18 Years and Over, Caring for Household Children Under 18 Years, by Sex of Respondent and Age of Youngest Household Child, 2004 Annual Averages

(Number.)

Characteristic	Hours per day caring for household children		
	Total	Men	Women
Persons in Households with Children Under 18 Years, Total			
Caring for household children as a primary activity	1.34	0.84	1.76
Physical care	0.47	0.22	0.67
Education-related activities	0.10	0.06	0.13
Reading to/with children	0.04	0.02	0.05
Talking to/with children	0.05	0.02	0.07
Playing/doing hobbies with children	0.26	0.23	0.29
Looking after children	0.08	0.06	0.11
Attending children's events	0.06	0.05	0.06
Travel related to care of household children	0.17	0.10	0.23
Other childcare activities	0.12	0.06	0.17
Persons in Households with Youngest Child 6 to 17 Years			
Caring for household children as a primary activity	0.79	0.52	1.00
Physical care	0.15	0.06	0.23
Education-related activities	0.12	0.07	0.16
Reading to/with children	0.02	(1)	0.03
Talking to/with children	0.06	0.03	0.09
Playing/doing hobbies with children	0.06	0.08	0.04
Looking after children	0.05	(1)	0.06
Attending children's events	0.08	0.07	0.08
Travel related to care of household children	0.15	0.11	0.19
Other childcare activities	0.10	0.06	0.12
Persons in Households with Youngest Child Under 6 Years			
Caring for household children as a primary activity	2.02	1.21	2.73
Physical care	0.85	0.41	1.22
Education-related activities	0.07	(1)	0.10
Reading to/with children	0.06	0.04	0.08
Talking to/with children	0.03	(1)	0.04
Playing/doing hobbies with children	0.51	0.41	0.60
Looking after children	0.13	0.09	0.16
Attending children's events	0.04	(1)	0.04
Travel related to care of household children	0.19	0.09	0.27
Other childcare activities	0.15	0.07	0.22

Note: Universe includes respondents 18 years and over living in households with children under 18 years, even if they did not report doing childcare on the diary day.

[1]Data not shown where base is less than 800,000.

Table 12-8. Average Hours per Day Spent in Primary Activities[1] for the Total Population Age 18 Years and Older by Activity Category, Employment Status, Presence and Age of Household Children, and Sex, 2004 Annual Averages

(Number.)

Characteristic	Hours spent per day in primary activities								
	Household with children under 6 years			Household with children 6–17 years old			Household with no children under 18 years		
	Total	Men	Women	Total	Men	Women	Total	Men	Women
TOTAL									
Total, All Activities[2]	24.00	24.00	24.00	24.00	24.00	24.00	24.00	24.00	24.00
Personal care activities	9.13	8.86	9.36	9.11	8.97	9.23	9.37	9.17	9.56
Sleeping	8.45	8.24	8.64	8.30	8.24	8.36	8.57	8.54	8.60
Eating and drinking	1.14	1.23	1.06	1.15	1.27	1.05	1.34	1.39	1.29
Household activities	1.94	1.24	2.54	1.94	1.36	2.41	1.86	1.45	2.27
Housework	0.72	0.22	1.15	0.67	0.22	1.03	0.57	0.24	0.90
Food preparation and cleanup	0.67	0.29	0.99	0.60	0.27	0.86	0.48	0.26	0.70
Lawn and garden care	0.16	0.24	0.09	0.15	0.19	0.12	0.24	0.30	0.18
Household management	0.11	0.09	0.14	0.12	0.10	0.14	0.16	0.13	0.19
Purchasing goods and services	0.85	0.72	0.96	0.86	0.59	1.06	0.82	0.69	0.95
Consumer goods purchases	0.47	0.38	0.56	0.44	0.29	0.57	0.39	0.30	0.48
Professional and personal care services	0.07	0.06	0.08	0.07	0.04	0.10	0.11	0.09	0.13
Caring for and helping household members	2.11	1.28	2.82	0.84	0.57	1.05	0.08	0.07	0.08
Caring for and helping household children	1.84	1.11	2.46	0.63	0.41	0.81	. . .	. . .	. . .
Caring for and helping non-household members	0.18	0.19	0.17	0.23	0.22	0.23	0.33	0.28	0.37
Caring for and helping non-household adults	0.09	0.10	0.08	0.10	0.09	0.11	0.12	0.13	0.11
Working and work-related activities	3.99	5.63	2.59	4.60	5.52	3.87	3.55	4.11	3.01
Working	3.62	5.11	2.34	4.19	5.02	3.53	3.23	3.73	2.75
Educational activities	0.20	(3)	0.23	0.34	0.26	0.40	0.26	0.25	0.28
Attending class	0.10	(3)	(3)	0.18	(3)	0.22	0.12	0.12	0.13
Homework and research	0.08	(3)	(3)	0.11	(3)	0.13	0.11	0.10	0.12
Organizational, civic, and religious activities	0.26	0.28	0.24	0.40	0.46	0.35	0.30	0.23	0.37
Religious and spiritual activities	0.13	0.15	0.12	0.14	0.18	0.11	0.12	0.10	0.14
Volunteering (organizational and civic activities)	0.09	0.09	0.09	0.21	0.22	0.19	0.14	0.10	0.18
Leisure and sports	4.01	4.28	3.77	4.30	4.58	4.08	5.72	6.09	5.37
Socializing and communicating	0.75	0.73	0.76	0.71	0.70	0.72	0.74	0.68	0.79
Watching television	2.09	2.18	2.02	2.17	2.32	2.05	2.99	3.26	2.73
Participating in sports, exercise, and recreation	0.25	0.37	0.14	0.27	0.35	0.20	0.27	0.36	0.19
Telephone calls, mail, and email	0.10	0.06	0.14	0.12	0.08	0.15	0.21	0.12	0.30
Other activities, not elsewhere classified	0.11	0.07	0.13	0.12	0.12	0.11	0.15	0.14	0.16
EMPLOYED									
Total, All Activities[2]	24.00	24.00	24.00	24.00	24.00	24.00	24.00	24.00	24.00
Personal care activities	8.86	8.65	9.14	8.94	8.83	9.04	9.02	8.92	9.15
Sleeping	8.18	8.05	8.35	8.12	8.09	8.15	8.23	8.27	8.19
Eating and drinking	1.15	1.23	1.04	1.17	1.27	1.06	1.29	1.34	1.24
Household activities	1.53	1.14	2.03	1.66	1.30	2.01	1.43	1.15	1.74
Housework	0.51	0.22	0.89	0.51	0.18	0.83	0.41	0.20	0.66
Food preparation and cleanup	0.49	0.27	0.77	0.48	0.25	0.72	0.36	0.20	0.54
Lawn and garden care	0.17	0.24	0.08	0.15	0.18	0.12	0.17	0.20	0.13
Household management	0.10	0.07	0.14	0.12	0.11	0.14	0.12	0.11	0.14
Purchasing goods and services	0.84	0.75	0.96	0.76	0.57	0.95	0.76	0.61	0.95
Consumer goods purchases	0.46	0.40	0.54	0.39	0.28	0.50	0.37	0.28	0.48
Professional and personal care services	0.07	0.05	0.08	0.06	0.03	0.09	0.07	0.04	0.11
Caring for and helping household members	1.82	1.25	2.55	0.73	0.53	0.92	0.06	0.06	0.07
Caring for and helping household children	1.58	1.10	2.19	0.53	0.37	0.69	. . .	. . .	. . .
Caring for and helping non-household members	0.15	0.16	0.13	0.18	0.17	0.19	0.31	0.28	0.35
Caring for and helping non-household adults	0.07	0.09	0.05	0.08	0.09	0.08	0.12	0.14	0.11
Working and work-related activities	5.37	6.29	4.19	5.83	6.34	5.33	5.85	6.25	5.40
Working	4.91	5.73	3.87	5.37	5.82	4.93	5.38	5.74	4.97
Educational activities	0.17	(3)	(3)	0.25	(3)	0.32	0.24	0.20	0.29
Attending class	(3)	(3)	(3)	0.14	(3)	(3)	0.13	0.11	0.15
Homework and research	(3)	(3)	(3)	0.08	(3)	(3)	0.09	(3)	0.11
Organizational, civic, and religious activities	0.22	0.22	0.21	0.36	0.42	0.31	0.21	0.16	0.27
Religious and spiritual activities	0.11	0.11	0.10	0.12	0.14	0.10	0.09	0.08	0.11
Volunteering (organizational and civic activities)	0.08	0.09	0.08	0.19	0.22	0.17	0.09	0.06	0.12
Leisure and sports	3.70	4.08	3.22	3.90	4.19	3.62	4.52	4.83	4.18
Socializing and communicating	0.68	0.70	0.66	0.65	0.65	0.65	0.67	0.60	0.74
Watching television	1.89	2.07	1.66	1.94	2.08	1.81	2.29	2.57	1.96
Participating in sports, exercise, and recreation	0.27	0.38	0.13	0.27	0.34	0.19	0.26	0.32	0.19
Telephone calls, mail, and email	0.09	0.05	0.13	0.10	0.07	0.14	0.17	0.10	0.25
Other activities, not elsewhere classified	0.10	0.08	0.13	0.11	0.13	0.10	0.11	0.10	0.12

[1]Primary activities are those respondents identify as their main activity. Other activities done simultaneously are not included.
[2]All major activity categories include related travel time.
[3]Data not shown where base is less than 800,000.
. . . = Not available.

Table 12-8. Average Hours per Day Spent in Primary Activities [1] for the Total Population Age 18 Years and Older by Activity Category, Employment Status, Presence and Age of Household Children, and Sex, 2004 Annual Averages—*Continued*

(Number.)

Characteristic	Hours spent per day in primary activities								
	Household with children under 6 years			Household with children 6–17 years old			Household with no children under 18 years		
	Total	Men	Women	Total	Men	Women	Total	Men	Women
NOT EMPLOYED									
Total, All Activities [2]	24.00	24.00	24.00	24.00	24.00	24.00	24.00	24.00	24.00
Personal care activities	9.85	10.57	9.68	9.74	9.86	9.70	9.89	9.66	10.07
Sleeping	9.20	9.79	9.07	8.95	9.15	8.88	9.07	9.04	9.09
Eating and drinking	1.10	1.17	1.08	1.07	1.22	1.02	1.41	1.47	1.36
Household activities	3.07	2.09	3.29	2.92	1.72	3.38	2.52	2.00	2.92
Housework	1.29	(3)	1.52	1.23	(3)	1.53	0.82	0.32	1.20
Food preparation and cleanup	1.15	0.47	1.30	1.01	0.45	1.22	0.68	0.38	0.90
Lawn and garden care	0.14	(3)	(3)	0.15	(3)	(3)	0.35	0.49	0.24
Household management	0.15	(3)	0.13	0.11	(3)	0.13	0.21	0.16	0.26
Purchasing goods and services	0.87	(3)	0.97	1.18	0.75	1.34	0.92	0.86	0.96
Consumer goods purchases	0.51	(3)	0.58	0.62	0.35	0.73	0.42	0.35	0.47
Professional and personal care services	0.08	(3)	(3)	0.12	(3)	0.13	0.16	0.16	0.16
Caring for and helping household members	2.90	1.55	3.21	1.23	0.84	1.38	0.09	0.08	0.10
Caring for and helping household children	2.56	1.21	2.87	0.97	0.66	1.10	. . .	. . .	. . .
Caring for and helping non-household members	0.25	(3)	0.22	0.39	(3)	0.33	0.35	0.29	0.40
Caring for and helping non-household adults	0.12	(3)	0.12	0.17	(3)	(3)	0.12	0.12	0.11
Working and work-related activities	(3)	(3)	(3)	(3)	(3)	(3)	0.08	(3)	(3)
Working	(3)	(3)	(3)	(3)	(3)	(3)	(3)	(3)	(3)
Educational activities	(3)	(3)	(3)	0.64	(3)	(3)	0.29	0.33	0.25
Attending class	(3)	(3)	(3)	(3)	(3)	(3)	0.12	(3)	0.09
Homework and research	(3)	(3)	(3)	(3)	(3)	(3)	0.14	(3)	(3)
Organizational, civic, and religious activities	0.38	(3)	0.30	0.52	(3)	0.44	0.43	0.36	0.48
Religious and spiritual activities	0.20	(3)	0.14	0.21	(3)	0.14	0.16	0.13	0.18
Volunteering (organizational and civic activities)	0.12	(3)	(3)	0.24	(3)	0.25	0.22	0.18	0.25
Leisure and sports	4.84	5.96	4.59	5.72	6.98	5.23	7.53	8.43	6.84
Socializing and communicating	0.92	(3)	0.91	0.92	0.98	0.90	0.85	0.84	0.86
Watching television	2.64	3.04	2.54	2.97	3.84	2.64	4.06	4.54	3.69
Participating in sports, exercise, and recreation	0.18	(3)	0.14	0.27	(3)	0.22	0.29	0.44	0.18
Telephone calls, mail, and email	0.14	(3)	0.14	0.17	(3)	0.18	0.28	0.17	0.36
Other activities, not elsewhere classified	0.12	(3)	0.14	0.13	(3)	0.14	0.21	0.23	0.21

[1] Primary activities are those respondents identify as their main activity. Other activities done simultaneously are not included.
[2] All major activity categories include related travel time.
[3] Data not shown where base is less than 800,000.
. . . = Not available.

Table 12-9. Average Hours per Day Spent in Leisure and Sports Activities for the Total Population by Selected Characteristics, 2004 Annual Averages

(Number.)

Characteristic	Total, all leisure and sports activities			Participating in sports, exercise, and recreation		Socializing and communicating		Watching TV	
	Total, all days	Weekdays	Weekends and holidays [1]	Weekdays	Weekends and holidays [1]	Weekdays	Weekends and holidays [1]	Weekdays	Weekends and holidays [1]
Sex									
Men	5.56	5.00	6.86	0.35	0.52	0.56	1.04	2.61	3.43
Women	4.82	4.45	5.71	0.20	0.19	0.61	1.21	2.36	2.62
Age									
Total, 15 years and over	5.18	4.71	6.28	0.27	0.35	0.59	1.13	2.48	3.02
15 to 24 years	5.68	5.26	6.62	0.50	0.57	0.81	1.27	2.36	2.77
25 to 34 years	4.40	3.63	5.93	0.18	0.46	0.55	1.27	2.02	2.78
35 to 44 years	4.15	3.59	5.55	0.25	0.28	0.46	1.14	1.94	2.67
45 to 54 years	4.51	3.99	5.77	0.21	0.28	0.48	1.00	2.18	2.89
55 to 64 years	5.45	5.04	6.56	0.21	0.28	0.59	0.99	2.79	3.32
65 years and over	7.31	7.17	7.68	0.27	0.17	0.65	1.00	3.82	4.04
Race and Hispanic or Latino Ethnicity									
White	5.14	4.67	6.30	0.28	0.37	0.59	1.15	2.40	2.94
Black or African American	5.65	5.35	6.23	0.23	0.16	0.58	0.95	3.15	3.62
Hispanic or Latino ethnicity	4.81	4.24	5.85	0.25	0.41	0.57	1.24	2.41	2.95
Employment Status									
Employed	4.24	3.61	5.73	0.23	0.37	0.50	1.09	1.87	2.71
Full-time workers	4.07	3.33	5.74	0.22	0.37	0.43	1.07	1.79	2.78
Part-time workers	4.83	4.52	5.67	0.27	0.38	0.72	1.17	2.16	2.42
Not employed	6.82	6.64	7.29	0.34	0.32	0.74	1.19	3.53	3.59
Earnings of Full-time Wage and Salary Earners [2]									
0 to $450	4.21	3.56	5.64	0.21	0.32	0.45	1.09	2.04	2.80
$451 to $675	4.21	3.42	5.96	0.11	0.37	0.44	1.00	1.95	3.13
$676 to $1,050	4.17	3.45	5.82	0.23	0.31	0.47	1.14	1.80	2.98
$1,051 and higher	3.84	3.05	5.70	0.32	0.45	0.40	1.15	1.40	2.30
Presence and Age of Children									
No household children under 18 years	5.74	5.32	6.75	0.27	0.33	0.59	1.13	2.84	3.27
Household children under 18 years	4.35	3.79	5.62	0.28	0.38	0.59	1.12	1.93	2.67
Children 13 to 17 years, none younger	4.62	4.03	6.24	0.32	0.41	0.60	1.10	1.91	2.78
Children 6 to 12 years, none younger	4.50	3.91	5.81	0.34	0.40	0.58	1.15	1.97	2.77
Youngest child under 6 years	4.06	3.54	5.17	0.21	0.36	0.59	1.11	1.91	2.54
Marital Status and Sex									
Married, spouse present	4.77	4.30	5.92	0.24	0.31	0.55	1.12	2.28	2.88
Men	5.09	4.50	6.47	0.29	0.43	0.50	1.08	2.46	3.32
Women	4.45	4.11	5.33	0.19	0.18	0.60	1.16	2.12	2.40
Other marital statuses	5.68	5.24	6.70	0.31	0.40	0.64	1.14	2.72	3.18
Men	6.19	5.68	7.37	0.43	0.64	0.65	0.99	2.80	3.56
Women	5.24	4.86	6.12	0.21	0.20	0.62	1.27	2.66	2.86
Educational Attainment, 25 Years and Over									
Less than a high school diploma	6.13	5.91	6.57	0.15	0.21	0.59	1.11	3.72	3.85
High school graduates, no college [3]	5.45	5.07	6.38	0.18	0.29	0.56	1.09	2.95	3.37
Some college or associate degree	4.89	4.37	6.16	0.20	0.30	0.52	1.03	2.32	3.03
Bachelor's degree or higher [4]	4.33	3.73	5.85	0.32	0.37	0.51	1.16	1.67	2.39

[1]Holidays are New Year's Day, Easter, Memorial Day, the Fourth of July, Labor Day, Thanksgiving Day, and Christmas Day. In 2004, data were not collected about Thanksgiving Day.
[2]These values are based on usual weekly earnings. Each earnings range represents approximately 25 percent of full-time wage and salary workers.
[3]Includes persons with a high school diploma or equivalent.
[4]Includes persons with bachelor's, master's, professional, and doctoral degrees.

Table 12-9. Average Hours per Day Spent in Leisure and Sports Activities for the Total Population by Selected Characteristics, 2004 Annual Averages—*Continued*

(Number.)

Characteristic	Reading		Relaxing/thinking		Playing games and computer use for leisure		Other leisure and sports activities including travel [5]	
	Weekdays	Weekends and holidays [1]	Weekdays	Weekends and holidays [1]	Weekdays	Weekends and holidays [1]	Weekdays	Weekends and holidays [1]
Sex								
Men	0.30	0.37	0.31	0.29	0.43	0.46	0.44	0.75
Women	0.42	0.49	0.28	0.26	0.25	0.29	0.34	0.65
Age								
Total, 15 years and over	0.36	0.43	0.29	0.28	0.34	0.37	0.38	0.70
15 to 24 years	0.12	0.13	0.20	0.21	0.71	0.70	0.56	0.97
25 to 34 years	0.16	0.17	0.17	0.20	0.23	0.38	0.32	0.67
35 to 44 years	0.22	0.30	0.23	0.23	0.22	0.28	0.27	0.63
45 to 54 years	0.30	0.47	0.24	0.27	0.24	0.22	0.34	0.63
55 to 64 years	0.53	0.66	0.31	0.29	0.23	0.32	0.37	0.70
65 years and over	0.95	1.11	0.64	0.53	0.38	0.27	0.46	0.56
Race and Hispanic or Latino Ethnicity								
White	0.39	0.47	0.27	0.26	0.35	0.38	0.40	0.73
Black or African American	0.26	0.24	0.52	0.39	0.27	0.30	0.35	0.56
Hispanic or Latino ethnicity	0.21	0.15	0.27	0.19	0.22	0.22	0.32	0.67
Employment Status								
Employed	0.23	0.33	0.20	0.22	0.23	0.32	0.34	0.69
Full-time workers	0.21	0.32	0.20	0.23	0.18	0.31	0.31	0.66
Part-time workers	0.30	0.35	0.21	0.19	0.39	0.35	0.46	0.80
Not employed	0.59	0.62	0.45	0.38	0.52	0.47	0.46	0.71
Earnings of Full-time Wage and Salary Earners [2]								
0 to $450	0.13	0.21	0.26	0.28	0.22	0.25	0.25	0.69
$451 to $675	0.19	0.25	0.21	0.20	0.18	0.41	0.35	0.61
$676 to $1,050	0.28	0.32	0.21	0.23	0.17	0.23	0.29	0.61
$1,051 and higher	0.26	0.49	0.14	0.23	0.18	0.30	0.35	0.79
Presence and Age of Children								
No household children under 18 years	0.47	0.57	0.36	0.32	0.39	0.39	0.41	0.74
Household children under 18 years	0.20	0.23	0.20	0.22	0.25	0.35	0.35	0.65
Children 13 to 17 years, none younger	0.21	0.32	0.21	0.30	0.38	0.54	0.41	0.78
Children 6 to 12 years, none younger	0.23	0.25	0.21	0.21	0.22	0.37	0.37	0.67
Youngest child under 6 years	0.16	0.16	0.18	0.19	0.21	0.24	0.29	0.57
Marital Status and Sex								
Married, spouse present	0.38	0.48	0.29	0.27	0.24	0.26	0.32	0.60
Men	0.34	0.43	0.31	0.30	0.26	0.28	0.34	0.63
Women	0.43	0.53	0.27	0.24	0.22	0.24	0.29	0.58
Other marital statuses	0.34	0.38	0.30	0.28	0.46	0.50	0.47	0.81
Men	0.25	0.29	0.30	0.29	0.67	0.69	0.57	0.91
Women	0.41	0.45	0.29	0.28	0.28	0.34	0.39	0.73
Educational Attainment, 25 Years and Over								
Less than a high school diploma	0.34	0.32	0.63	0.51	0.19	0.10	0.30	0.47
High school graduates, no college [3]	0.39	0.39	0.38	0.35	0.29	0.31	0.33	0.59
Some college or associate degree	0.42	0.51	0.24	0.22	0.30	0.37	0.37	0.69
Bachelor's degree or higher [4]	0.46	0.70	0.17	0.18	0.22	0.32	0.37	0.72

Note: Unless otherwise specified, data refer to respondents 15 years and over. Hispanics and Latinos may be of any race.

[1] Holidays are New Year's Day, Easter, Memorial Day, the Fourth of July, Labor Day, Thanksgiving Day, and Christmas Day. In 2004, data were not collected about Thanksgiving Day.
[2] These values are based on usual weekly earnings. Each earnings range represents approximately 25 percent of full-time wage and salary workers.
[3] Includes persons with a high school diploma or equivalent.
[4] Includes persons with bachelor's, master's, professional, and doctoral degrees.
[5] Includes other leisure and sports activities, not elsewhere classified, and travel related to leisure and sports activities.

INDEX

INDEX